CULINOLOGY®

THE INTERSECTION OF CULINARY ART AND FOOD SCIENCE

RESEARCH CHEFS ASSOCIATION

EDITOR: J. JEFFREY COUSMINER

WILEY

Library of Congress Cataloging-in-Publication Data:

Names: Cousminer, J. Jeffrey, editor.
Title: Culinology : blending culinary arts and food science / editor, J. Jeffrey Cousminer.
Description: Hoboken : Wiley, 2016. | Includes index. |
   Includes bibliographical references and index.
Identifiers: LCCN 2015043962 (print) | LCCN 2015046487 (ebook) |
   ISBN 9780470481349 (hardback) | ISBN 9781119034254 (Adobe PDF) |
   ISBN 9781119193609 (ePub)
Subjects: LCSH: Food—Analysis. | Food—Research. | Processed foods. | Cooking. |
   BISAC: COOKING / Reference.
Classification: LCC TX541 .C854 2016 (print) | LCC TX541 (ebook) |
   DDC 664/.07—dc23
LC record available at http://lccn.loc.gov/2015043962

ISBN: 978-0-470-48134-9

Printed in the United States of America

10 9 8 7 6 5 4 3 2 1

"The mediocre teacher tells. The good teacher explains. The superior teacher demonstrates.
The great teacher inspires.*"*
— WILLIAM ARTHUR WARD

We dedicate this book in memory of our inspirational predecessors:

GARY HOLLEMAN

WILLIAM "POPS" HAHNE

MICHELE BLOCK

JOHN MATCHUK, CRC

CRAIG "SKIP" JULIUS, CRC, CCS, CEC, CCP, CFE

for their passion and dedication to education in the field of food research and development, and their legacy of commitment to ensuring that Culinology® will continue to grow and thrive.

Foreword to *Culinology®*: The Intersection of Culinary Art and Food Science

When I started my career in the food and beverage industry in the 70s, I could not have imagined life as a research chef, food scientist, or manufacturer. Those options just did not exist in my world. And the term Culinology® would not be coined for several decades.

I backed into the field of Culinology® with a phone call from Chef Gary Barnette of the newly opened Casino Magic Hotel and Gaming Resort on the Gulf Coast of Mississippi. Gary was faced with a flood of hungry gamers all looking for regional favorites such as gumbo, jambalaya, and crawfish etouffée. With a cadre of chefs on the team, I was perplexed as to what Gary might need from me. He explained that his talented chefs hailed from Vegas and Atlantic City; none were familiar with Gulf Coast cuisine. That's where I came in. Gary needed Cajun and Creole food, and he wanted it yesterday. Being a businessman and needing a little extra money, I told him I would cook whatever he needed. Only then did I learn that he needed 600 gallons of each every four days.

I was a restaurateur and a fine dining chef, not a product development specialist. Everything I cooked came out of a sauté pan. My largest piece of cooking equipment was a five-gallon Groen kettle. But he wanted 1,800 pounds of multiple products every few days! And that's when I learned about food manufacturing as I was thrust into the emerging field of Culinology®.

I was quickly introduced to local packers, and as things rolled along I began to develop 1,000-pound capacity, auger-driven kettles of cast iron. With direct heat to the metal, I could create authentic and traditional dark-and light-brown rouxs, which set us apart from other manufacturers. Before long, word spread about my little food manufacturing plant, and that's when Chef Tim Soufan of TGI Friday's called to see if I might consider working with him to create a special barbecue glaze for a Friday's menu promotion. I simply could not say no, and, with Chef Soufan's guidance, Jack Daniel's Glaze was born. That product ultimately built and solidified Chef John Folse & Company Manufacturing.

Realizing that I was now in product development, it was time to visit the chef oracle for advice and guidance. It was on the apron strings of world-renowned culinarian Warren Leruth, owner of LeRuth's fine dining in Gretna, that I first learned the terms *food science, R & D Chef, modified food starch,* and *flavor bases.* Chef Leruth had created many of the foods and flavors for Popeyes, including their famous biscuits. He had worked with the L.J. Minor Corporation, Nestlé, and Outback Steakhouse among numerous others. At this time, most food products for volume feeding were created by food scientists. For the most part, chefs had not yet thrown their toques into the arena. I was mesmerized by Chef Leruth, who was a genius and a phenomenal storyteller.

He talked about Nicolas Appert, who answered Napoleon Bonaparte's challenge to create transportable, quality food for troops on the move. Chef Leruth talked about Louis Pasteur, the chemist and microbiologist, who developed the principles of pasteurization during the mid-1800s. He talked about John Mason, the Philadelphia tinsmith who invented and patented the Mason jar; Henri Nestlé, a pharmacist who helped develop condensed milk; Henry Heinz, founder of H. J. Heinz Company; and Clarence Birdseye, founder of the modern frozen food industry. We discussed names like J.L. Kraft, who revolutionized cheese production, and John Dorrance, who devised a method to condense soup and eventually bought out the Campbell's Soup Company. We even discovered we had a mutual friend, Louis Szathmary, who in just 10 years went from immigrant short-order cook to developer of frozen food products for Stouffer's and, later, NASA. As a lover of history, I was enthralled and found his document about stocks and coagulation by Marie-Antoine Carême fascinating.

As I got up to leave, Chef Leruth jotted a quick note, then sealed it in an envelope inscribed with my name. It was a gift that I was not to open until he was gone. Many years later, after eulogizing Chef Leruth at his funeral in November 2001, I opened the envelope to discover his secret recipe for his magnificent golden vanilla ice cream, which he had created as the base for his Chelsey's Frozen Custard company. It is one of the greatest gifts I have ever received. When I left Chef Leruth's company, my brain was spinning with thoughts and possibilities. That is how I spent my first day of school in volume food manufacturing.

In 1995, I acquired a small USDA food manufacturing plant in New Orleans. As I became more involved in food manufacturing, I met icons such as Ferdinand Metz of H. J. Heinz; Juerg Aeschbach, product developer for Albertsons and Wolfgang Puck Food Company; and John and Betsy Lattanza, who were also mentors. At that time, chefs really had few resources to learn about the science of cooking. Thank goodness we did have Harold McGee's *On Food and Cooking*, which was published in 1984.

In 1994, I became president of the American Culinary Federation, the largest organization of professional chefs in the United States. It was a great time for chefs in America, and my goal as president was to better understand the diversity within the organization and the need for specialization in culinary education. I was proud to lead the movement to establish the African American Chefs Association within our ranks and the Women Chefs of America. At our annual convention in 1995, a small group of chefs involved in product development met to discuss the concept of their own association to meet the needs of the research chef community that was slowly growing.

Among the leaders of this group were Winston Riley (who headed the group and coined the word "Culinology"), Walter Zuromski, Jeff Cousminer, and our late colleagues Skip Julius, Bill "Pops" Hahne, and others who wanted their own organization. By 1996, the Research Chefs Association (RCA) hosted its first annual conference in Cleveland, Ohio. Finally, there was an organization representing that group of men and women who were filling a much-needed niche: culinary research and development for food manufacturing.

At one time, chefs and food scientists existed in two different worlds, knowing nothing of each other. Now, both were playing a role in the emerging American food movement. For chefs wanting to push their creative boundaries, the science behind the mystique of food was calling.

RCA focused on the scientific and technical curiosities of food products and was quickly and successfully generating tremendous interest on the culinary landscape. By 1999, the RCA touted a 500-chef membership, including me. In 2000, the RCA conference was held in New Orleans, and I was elected to the board of directors. I remember the excitement as Dan Sortwell, Skip Julius, Greg Grisanti, and Joe O'Connor were awarded the very first Certified Research Chef certificates. It was a great day!

Research chefs, or those desiring to become research and development chefs, found a home within this emerging association. Culinology®, the marriage of culinary arts and food science, was born, and the first Culinology® class for chefs was held at Rutgers University in 2001. Jeff Cousminer and his education committee were working feverishly to expand Culinology® curricula, first in continuing education programs and then in undergraduate degree programs throughout the country. How could one possibly forget the roar of applause at our conference in 2003 when Donald Moss earned the first bachelor's degree in Culinology® from the University of Nebraska-Lincoln?

Soon, four-year degrees in Culinology® were available at colleges across the country, including Clemson University, Rutgers University/Mercer County Community College, the University of Massachusetts-Amherst, Louisiana State University/Nicholls State University, Southwest Minnesota State, and more. And then Culinology® education went global, when in 2011 the first international bachelor's degree program in Culinology® was launched at Taylor's University in Kuala Lumpur, Malaysia.

Imagine how proud I was to become national president of the RCA in 2005. Our marketing campaigns created a buzz throughout the industry, and RCA members were taking the stage at annual conferences from the National Restaurant Association to the International Hotel/Motel Show. Our membership growth was constant, and our strategic partnerships were strong. Our educational programs and certifications continued to become the reason for belonging to RCA. I am so proud to have been in a position to see Culinology® become a sought-after industry standard with more and more national and international food companies seeking Culinologists in their kitchens, thereby growing the value of this unique brand. Our national headquarters was set up in Atlanta, and alliances with the Institute of Food Technologists were established.

Now, within the ranks of RCA, *the* book on the subject has been written! And what better way to mark the 20th anniversary of the Association than with the publication of *Culinology®: The Intersection of Culinary Art and Food Science*. I am ecstatic to see it become a reality under Jeff Cousminer's vision. Congratulations to everyone who has made this long anticipated book a reality, and to Jeff for inspiring others to achieve culinary research greatness as well.

—Chef John Folse

Contents

Foreword to *Culinology*®:
The Intersection of Culinary Art and Food Science   iv

Preface So What the Heck *Is* Culinology®,
Anyway?   viii
J. Jeffrey Cousminer
Jim (J.D.) Pintner, CRC®

Acknowledgments   xiii
Research Chefs Association

● Chapter 1: The Business of New Product
Development and the Role of the Culinology®
Professional   1
Mark Crowell, CRC®
Barb Stuckey

● Chapter 2: The Principles of Food Science   19
Lisa J. Mauer, Ph.D.
M. Fernanda San Martin-Gonzalez, Ph.D.

● Chapter 3: Review of Cooking Techniques   46
Charlie Baggs
Herbert A. Stockschlaeder II, CRC®, DTR

● Chapter 4: Protein-Based Foods:
Introduction and Red Meats   57
James W. Lamkey, Ph.D.

● Chapter 5: Protein-Based Foods: Poultry   77
L. Cain Cavitt, Ph.D., CCS®
Contributor: Jason M. Behrends, Ph.D., CCS®

● Chapter 6: Protein-Based Foods: Seafood   85
Lucina E. Lampila, Ph.D., R.D., C.F.S.
Contributor: Jeff Cowles, CCS®

● Chapter 7: Protein-Based Foods: Vegetable
Sources of Protein and Protein Complementation   106
Natalie Pitchford Levy, CCS®
Contributor: Hinnerk von Bargen, CHE

● Chapter 8: Carbohydrate-Based Foods   128
Allen J. Freed
Dan Putnam
Contributors: Hinnerk von Bargen, CHE
Jason R. Gronlund

● Chapter 9: Lipid-Based Foods   166
Marilynn Schnepf, Ph.D., R.D.
Lynne Morehart
Brian K. Yager

● Chapter 10: Egg- and Milk-Based Foods   180
John U. McGregor, Ph.D.
Julie K. Northcutt, Ph.D.
Michelle Parisi, Ph.D.
Tonya C. Schoenfuss, Ph.D.
Christian Thormose

● Chapter 11: Fermentation   196
James R. Adams, CCS®, CFS
Charles Hayes, CRC®, CEC

● Chapter 12: Food Additives   220
Andres V. Ardisson Korat, MS, CCS®
Melissa Haupt, CRC®, CEC
Jerome Lombardo

● Chapter 13: Food Safety and Spoilage   245
O. Peter Snyder, Jr., Ph.D.
Rachel B. Zemser, MS, CCS®

● Chapter 14: **Shelf-Life Extension**   286

Klaus Tenbergen, Ed.D., CMB, ASBPB, MCFE
Priscila D. Santiago-Mora
Dennis Ferris, Ph.D.
Contributors: Dominic Man. BSc, MSc, FIFST,
Shirley VanGarde, Ph.D.

● Chapter 15: **Food Packaging**   305

Dr. Aaron L. Brody
Mark Thomas
Contributors: Thomas Trimarco, Jr.

● Chapter 16: **Developing Nutritious
Food Products**   321

Darryl L. Holliday, Ph.D., CRC®
Margaret D. Condrasky, Ed.D, R.D., CCE
Marie Hegler
Contributor: John W. Finley

● Chapter 17: **Sensory Evaluation**   352

Witoon Prinyawiwatkul, Ph.D.
Robert Delaney
M. Michele Foley
Dustin Hilinski
Howard R. Moskowitz, Ph.D.

● Chapter 18: **Culinology® Applications
in Food Processing—From the Chef's
and Food Scientist's Perspective**   365

Mark A. Uebersax, Ph.D.
Muhammad Siddiq, Ph.D.
Carl P. Borchgrevink, Ph.D.

● Chapter 19: **Commercializing the Culinary
Gold Standard**   396

Marilyn Carlson, CFS
Robert Danhi
Craig "Skip" Julius, CRC®, CCS®, CEC, CCP

Index   414

Preface: So What the Heck *Is* Culinology®, Anyway?

J. Jeffrey Cousminer, Past President, Research Chefs Association; R&D Manager, Stonewall Kitchen
Jim (J.D.) Pintner, CRC; Consulting Chef, Sandridge Food Corporation

As chefs, the foods we handle every day have deep scientific underpinnings. But approaching the whole subject of food science can be scary to people who equate it with long-forgotten and even intimidating high-school chemistry.

Yet once a chef gains the kitchen skills necessary to work through the most challenging meal service periods and create awesome signature dishes, what's next? For successful chefs who really want to push their creative boundaries, the science behind the mystique of food is calling. The next challenge is exploring the origins, the make-up, and the scientific and technical curiosities of the foods we devote ourselves to every day. Enter Culinology®.

Simply put, Culinology® helps us understand how and why things happen to food during the preparation and cooking process, and once learned, how we can manipulate them to our advantage. Have you ever picked up a jar of commercial mayonnaise, looked at the ingredient statement on the label, and wondered why it was different from the mayonnaise you might make in your kitchen? Well, each ingredient in the jar is necessary for a commercial product to enter and survive in the mass marketplace. And this is true for more than mayonnaise. Today's supermarket shelves are lined with products carefully developed to satisfy the savvy tastes of our food-obsessed nation while maintaining high standards of quality, safety, stability, and affordability.

Today, the public wants and expects their favorite foods to be available everywhere, from the finest restaurants to supermarket shelves. But how does this happen? How does a chef who has mastered the most creative restaurant menu items take one of them and reproduce it to meet the demands of a mass-market launch? How is restaurant food transformed into a mass-produced item while maintaining quality and authenticity but without incurring staggering costs? How do the culinary skills of the chef and the food science experimentations of the product developer work together to create delicious food that won't perish before it reaches the consumer? **The answers are found in the study of Culinology®.**

Culinology® blends the underlying principles of food science and technology with the chef's skilled art of culinary creativity and originality to satisfy public tastes in the marketplace.

Culinology®: The Intersection of Culinary Art and Food Science, by the Research Chefs Association, is designed to help professional chefs (as well as culinary students and product developers) approach the science behind the foods they are developing in their labs and test kitchens, and learn how to apply Culinology® to the challenging and rewarding career of new product development (NPD).

The trained Culinology® professional plays an important role in the development of a food item from concept to mass-market launch. Let's return to the example of mayonnaise.

Chefs find it fairly easy to make mayonnaise in a restaurant setting: Blend together egg yolks, vinegar or lemon juice, sugar, salt, and a touch of mustard, and then slowly drizzle in a generous measure of vegetable oil while whisking rapidly; very soon, the mixture starts turning lighter and thicker and shinier and . . . *voilà:* mayonnaise! In comparison, look again at the ingredient statement on the label of a jar of commercial mayonnaise. Why is there a difference between the two?

The difference is that in the much larger scale of the new product development world, additional considerations must be taken into account, such as safety, shelf life, nutritional value, and ingredient and production costs. A lot is riding on these decisions. The Culinology® professional understands the full cost of developing a product from start to finish and the risks entailed if the product fails.

For example, let's say you want to develop a better version of commercial mayonnaise. This book will help you identify and explore questions such as these *before* you begin:

- What is different about this better mayonnaise that will make it competitive (and successful) in the marketplace?
- Will it be a standard mayonnaise (containing eggs, full fat, etc.), or will it be a specialty product that may not

meet the government's *standard of identity* for mayonnaise (and will therefore require special labeling)?

- Will any of the ingredients require call-outs on the label for allergens (eggs or soy), vegan (egg-free), or other label claims (low fat, reduced sodium, good source of omega-3 fatty acids, organic, GMO-free)?
- Will it be packaged in glass or plastic? pails? jars? pouches? tubes?
- Will it be available in multiple sizes: large bulk packages, gallons, quarts, pints, single-serve squeeze packs?
- Will it be marketed to industrial accounts to be used as an ingredient in another manufacturer's products, or to foodservice—that is, the restaurant trade—or to retail supermarkets or specialty stores? Or all of the above?
- How will you ensure shelf stability and safety?
- Will the new product run on standard machinery, or will it require capital investment in new equipment?
- How will you tell when you've achieved your objectives (sensory, health or other benefits, preference over market leaders, profitability, and so on), and how can you predict success in the marketplace?

- Once the product is launched, how will you measure its success, and how can you ensure continuing success?

And that is only the beginning!

Through the study and application of Culinology®, more food scientists are exploring culinary arts and more chefs are studying food science with the common goal of giving consumers the best possible foods while ensuring product profitability. This book will help you begin thinking like a Culinology® professional by explaining what it takes to bring a product to market.

Culinology® is a shift in how we think about food and food production. No longer must food science and culinary arts work in isolation; they have formed a symbiotic marriage, mutually dependent and interactive, mutually strengthening and reinforcing. By studying the science behind the food, you can become a Culinology® professional: a leader in the development of a new wave of exciting, crave-worthy, nutritious, safe, and profitable food products. Welcome to your future!

Welcome to Culinology®!

Contributors

James R. Adams, CCS®, CFS
Director, Process Optimization,
Tyson Prepared Foods Operations

Charlie Baggs
President and Executive Chef, Charlie Baggs, Inc.

Jason M. Behrends, Ph.D., CCS®
Project Leader, Tyson Foods, Inc.

Carl P. Borchgrevink, Ph.D.
Associate Professor, The School of Hospitality Business,
The Eli Broad Graduate School of Management,
Michigan State University

Aaron L. Brody, Ph.D.
Adjunct Professor, University of Georgia Department
of Food Science and Technology, and President/CEO,
Packaging/Brody

Marilyn Carlson, CFS
Owner/Principal, Dogwood Solutions

L. Cain Cavitt, Ph.D., CCS®
Project Leader, Research & Development,
Tyson Foods, Inc.

Margaret D. Condrasky, Ed.D, R.D., CCE
Associate Professor, Food, Nutrition, and Packaging
Sciences Department, Clemson University

J. Jeffrey Cousminer
Past President, the Research Chefs Association;
R&D Manager, Stonewall Kitchen

Jeff Cowles, CCS®
Research Chef, Kerry Americas

Mark Crowell, CRC®
Principal Culinologist, CuliNex, LLC

Robert Danhi, CCE, CEC, CHE, CCP
Curator of Culture, Chef Danhi & Co.,
Global Flavor Shakers

Robert Delaney
Manager of Product Innovation, Smithfield

Dennis Ferris, Ph.D.
Professor, Department of Food Science and Nutrition,
California State University, Fresno

John W. Finley
Professor and Department Head of Food Science,
Louisiana State University

M. Michele Foley
Director, Sensory and Consumer Insights, Nestlé

Allen J. Freed
President, AJ Freed, LLC

Jason R. Gronlund
VP Culinary, Smokey Bones Bar & Fire Grill,
Johnson & Wales Alumnus

Melissa Haupt, CRC®, CEC
Executive Research Chef, Applebee's

Charles Hayes, CRC®, CEC
Director of R&D, National Accounts, JMH Premium

Marie Hegler
Food Safety and Nutrition Agent, Cooperative Extension
Service, Clemson University

Dustin Hilinski
Director of Culinary Development, Red Lobster

Darryl L. Holliday, Ph.D., CRC®
Assistant Professor, Our Lady of Holy Cross College

Craig "Skip" Julius, CRC®, CCS®, CEC, CCP
Manager of Culinary Solutions, Sensient Flavors

Andres V. Ardisson Korat, MS, CCS®
Doctoral Student, Harvard, T. H. Chan
School of Public Health

James W. Lamkey, Ph.D.
Director of Technical Services, Spicetec Flavors
and Seasonings

Lucina E. Lampila, Ph.D., R.D., C.F.S.
Food Safety Institute

Natalie Pitchford Levy, CCS®
Quality Control Manager, Bedemco, Inc.

Jerome Lombardo
Certified Flavor Chemist

Dominic Man, BSc, MSc, FIFST
Principal Lecturer, Department of Applied Science,
Faculty of Engineering, Science, and the Built
Environment, London South Bank University

M. Fernanda San Martin-Gonzalez, Ph.D.
Associate Professor, Department of Food Science,
Purdue University

Lisa J. Mauer, Ph.D.
Professor, Department of Food Science, Purdue University

John U. McGregor, Ph.D.
Professor, Food, Nutrition, and Packaging Sciences
Department, Clemson University

Lynne Morehart
Technical Service Manager, Cargill Oils and Shortenings

Howard R. Moskowitz, Ph.D.
Chairman, iNovum LLC Chairman, Mind Genomics
Associates

Julie K. Northcutt, Ph.D.
Professor, Food, Nutrition, and Packaging Sciences
Department, Clemson University

Michelle Parisi, Ph.D.
Food, Nutrition, and Packaging Sciences Department,
Clemson University

Jim (J.D.) Pintner
CRC®, Consulting Chef, Sandridge Food Corporation

Witoon Prinyawiwatkul, Ph.D.
School of Nutrition and Food Sciences, Louisiana State
University Agricultural Center

Dan Putnam
Technical Manager, Grain Processing Corporation

Priscila D. Santiago-Mora
Food Industry Engineer, Instituto Tecnológico y de Estudios
Superiores de Monterrey, Campus Querétaro, México

Marilynn Schnepf, Ph.D., R.D.
Professor, Nutrition and Health Sciences,
University of Nebraska

Tonya C. Schoenfuss, Ph.D.
Associate Professor, Department of Food Science
and Nutrition, University of Minnesota

Muhammad Siddiq, Ph.D.
Associate Professor, Department of Food Science
and Human Nutrition, Michigan State University

O. Peter Snyder, Jr., Ph.D.
President, SnyderHACCP

Herbert A. Stockschlaeder II, CRC®, DTR
Director of Technical Services,
Rosina Food Products, Inc.

Barb Stuckey
Executive Vice President, Mattson

Klaus Tenbergen, Ed.D., CMB, CEPC, ASBPB, MCFE
Dean of Career Technical Education and Economic
Development, Columbia College, Sonora, CA.

Mark Thomas
President, MDT, Ltd.

Christian Thormose
Chef/Food Production Manager, ARAMARK

Thomas Trimarco, Jr.
Operations/Production Manager,
Greencore Rhode Island

Mark A. Uebersax, Ph.D.
Professor Emeritus, Department of Food Science
and Human Nutrition, Michigan State University

Shirley VanGarde, Ph.D.
VanGarde Consulting

Hinnerk von Bargen, CHE
Associate Professor in Culinary Arts,
Culinary Institute of America

Brian K. Yager
Chef/Owner, Cuisine 256, LLC

Rachel B. Zemser, M.S., CCS®
Owner, A La Carte Connections, LLC

About the Author

RESEARCH CHEFS ASSOCIATION:
Defining the Future of Food®

Headquartered in Atlanta, Georgia, the Research Chefs Association (RCA) is a not-for-profit organization dedicated to the education and professional growth of individuals engaged in food product development. RCA was founded in 1995 (and incorporated in 1996) by a small group of research chefs hoping to learn from and share with other like-minded professionals facing common challenges in the development of new food products at the commercial level.

Today, the organization boasts 2000+ members including chefs, food scientists, food technologists, writers, nutritionists, academicians, researchers, consultants, sales and marketing professionals, suppliers, co-packers, distributors, and students. Its mission: Empower the food community to enhance food experiences through Culinology®, a fast-growing approach to food product development that requires a deep understanding of culinary arts as well as food science.

Having pioneered the discipline, RCA is the premier authority on the practice of Culinology® and owns the registered trademark. Today, more than a dozen RCA-approved undergraduate Culinology® degree programs in the United States and Malaysia offer well-rounded, interdisciplinary curricula that focus on culinary arts and food science but also incorporate other aspects of food product development, including business management, nutrition, processing technology, and government regulations, to name a few.

The Research Chefs Association also offers a robust certification program that certifies qualified candidates as Certified Research Chefs (CRC®) or Certified Culinary Scientists (CCS®), which, together with the Culinology® degree programs, provides the food industry with today's most valued product developers in the world. Culinology® graduates and RCA-certified professionals are sought by employers because they guide innovation in this dynamic industry, offering unique credentials and powerful, value-added skills that are truly Defining the Future of Food®.

Acknowledgments

Countless individuals have played a role in bringing this body of work to fruition. None were more pivotal in its production than Jeffrey Cousminer and the 56 authors and contributors responsible for its content. No doubt most of them would say their individual contributions rest on the shoulders of those that came before them and those that work beside them. We'd also like to thank Allison Rittman, CRC®, for pulling together a small band of educators to create the teaching tools that support this book in the classroom setting. A few other hard-working professionals also played an important role in the completion of this book. Not chefs, not food scientists, but professionals from other fields who believed passionately in this project and did their level best to move it forward. Special thanks to Jim Fowler, Tim Kline, and Annaliese Doyle Klainbaum as well as our taskmaster and fearless editor at Wiley, Andrea Brescia.

Lastly, we are all indebted to Winston Riley, the man who laid the foundation for the Research Chefs Association, brought together the early adopters, set forth its goals, created its infrastructure, and set in motion the groundswell of support and recognition that brought us to where we are today. Oh, and by the way, he invented the term *Culinology*®. Thank you, Winston!

1 The Business of New Product Development and the Role of the Culinology® Professional

Mark Crowell, CRC®, Principal Culinologist, CuliNex, LLC

Barb Stuckey, Executive Vice President, Mattson

●Introduction: Why Is New Product Development Important?

New product development is fraught with difficulty, cost, and high rates of failure. Why do companies pursue it? Would it not be simpler to do the minimal amount of development necessary to stay in business? Or simpler still, wouldn't it be easier to coast along with existing products?

Both options would certainly be simpler, but the company would not be profitable for long. Food companies must grow to make money and survive. As John Maynard Keynes put it so succinctly in *A Treatise on Money,* "The engine which drives Enterprise is not Thrift, but Profit."[1]

Developing new food products is one of the major ways a food company can build profits. It is estimated that only one new product idea in 58 actually makes it through the development process and yields a successful new product.[2] Yet some companies realize a whopping 50 percent of their sales and 40 percent of their profits from products on the market five years or less, according to Robert Cooper, professor of marketing and technology management at McMaster University in Ontario.[3]

Five dominant forces drive the need for new food product development:

1. Life Cycle
   - Nearly all products have life cycles. They enter the marketplace, flourish for a time, then die and must be replaced. A very few defy the odds and seem to stay in the market indefinitely: Kellogg's Corn Flakes®, Spam®, Kool-Aid®. But they are the exceptions.

2. Stakeholders' Expectation of Growth and Profit
   - A company's management may adopt a policy of aggressive growth to satisfy long-range business goals and repay investors or stakeholders. New products are seen as a way to achieve these growth goals.

3. Changing Consumers
   - Consumer populations may change due to immigration, demographic shifts, and a host of other means of social evolution. These changes may require the development of new products more suited to the makeup of the new marketplace.

4. Technology Advancement
   - New technology may enable development of new food products more suited to the lifestyles of current consumers. It may also offer increased assurances of food safety, higher food quality, or greater efficiency in production.

5. Evolution in Regulations or Public Health
   - Changes in government legislation, health programs, agricultural policy, or agricultural support programs may dictate (or support) the development of new food products.

●Sources of Growth

Most companies exist to generate profit. Senior management, under the direction of the owners or the shareholders, follows a corporate business plan that sets out specific financial and growth objectives.

Food companies can achieve growth in a limited number of ways:

1. *Expanding into New Markets*

   Many companies that launch a product in California decide they next want to tackle the New York market because coastal consumers tend to be similar in attitudes, behavior, and product preference. This can be expensive for products with short shelf lives due to the need for distribution in refrigerated or freezer trucks. Extremely perishable fresh products may last only a few days, making cross-country distribution impossible under any conditions. A distribution system and its cost may limit expansion. Export markets present their own unique risks.

2. *Growing Market Share*

   One of the most logical places to find customers for a new product is to grab them from a competitor. This means of growth is about trying to achieve market penetration and share within existing markets by slugging it out with competitors. Large sums of money are required for advertising and promotion, buying shelf space (slotting allowances), and funding sampling programs.

3. *Developing Targeted New Products*

   New products can contribute to growth and profitability. For example, as the baby boomer population ages, a food company may decide to develop new products that offer benefits that appeal to aging seniors.

   At the same time, another company may decide that aging baby boomers moving into retirement (and, hence, fixed incomes) may no longer be able to afford their products (or services—for example, dining in expensive restaurants). Their new approach may focus on developing products to target the younger generation of consumers—for example, the Millennials (those who came of age in 2000 and are at the beginning of their prime earning years).

   Either of these new consumer targets could provide a huge profit opportunity. There are, however, associated costs with each, to be explained later in this chapter.

   New products can also help a company differentiate its offerings, reducing the need to compete on price, which often occurs when competitors enter an existing market and drive profit margins down.

4. *Cost Containment*

   Reducing expenses and overhead costs is also a common practice during a company's growth phase. Methods of reducing expenses include reducing staff, implementing an energy conservation program, improving process efficiency, adopting a waste management program, streamlining procurement, negotiating better prices, and adopting a process and quality control program (to reduce losses through overfill, waste, and product returns). These thrift measures may help companies' profitability but are of limited value to growth. Companies may own food or beverage manufacturing plants that cost hundreds of thousands—if not millions—of dollars to build, purchase, or lease. These plants often carry mortgages or rental payments. As a result, it behooves companies to make sure these fixed assets operate at full capacity. An underutilized plant is a drain on resources because it costs money to maintain whether it is producing a low or high volume of goods. The more goods it cranks out (maximizing throughput), the more income the company can make to pay for its operation and maintenance.

So companies usually decide to develop new products that can be manufactured in their existing plants. If these products can be produced during the off (or slow) season, this makes new product development even more attractive, as there is incentive to spread production evenly throughout the year. This keeps trained workers continuously employed, reduces plant overhead, provides a steadier cash flow, and benefits the community (provides jobs, raises the standard of living, increases discretionary spending, and improves the tax base). A plant operating year-round is more profitable than one that is idle part of the year, and a plant operating at full capacity is usually more profitable than one operating at reduced capacity.

●The Food Industry

The U.S. food processing industry is often taken for granted. Except in times of crisis, such as a national food poisoning outbreak (like the salmonella-contaminated peanut case in 2009), it has become a feature of the economic landscape so unremarkable as to be nearly invisible.

The food industry may appear unremarkable for many reasons. Many processed food products that were wildly innovative when originally developed many years ago (canned foods, frozen foods, etc.) are now so familiar in this high-tech age that they are viewed as humdrum. Another reason may be that the food industry runs so incredibly efficiently. In fact, in the latter part of the late twentieth and early twenty-first centuries, the food production, distribution, and retailing systems were optimized to the point where cereal seemed to sprout from the shelves of Safeway, Kroger, and Wal-Mart, meat and poultry came from the deli or fresh meats counter, and produce grew itself into plastic trays in the produce section. We became completely separated from where our food actually came from.

Food processing used to be closely linked to agriculture or domestic household activities. Many processing industries were originally part of farm operations (such as butter- and cheese-making) or were based on domestic kitchen skills (pickling, canning, baking). Modern food processing is more like that of other mass-manufactured products (such as cell phones, clothing, and cars) than the local crafts of the recent past. The chasm between farming and processing is widening.

Some operations employed by food processors, such as flour milling, are indeed ancient in their origins, but the methods and equipment in use today bear little resemblance to ancient gristmills. Most of today's food processing technologies are the result of modern scientific discoveries and decades, if not centuries, of technological refinement.

Food Development Today

The food marketplace is a constantly changing organism; it is never static. Several factors contribute to this dynamism. Today's consumers are bombarded with food media. With round-the-clock cable network food programs, splashy food magazines and cookbooks, morning and evening news programs showcasing cooking, and the celebrity status of big-name chefs, the average U.S. consumer is now savvier about food than ever. For many people, food preparation has gone from daily drudgery to a medium for creative expression, relaxation, and entertainment.

As a reaction to the evolving food culture, consumers now have more choices than ever. With the ability to buy food via warehouse stores, mail-order catalogs, convenience stores, ethnic groceries, specialty food stores, farmer's markets, the telephone, the Internet, and increasingly, directly from farmers, consumer buying habits are changing. Because of this, the traditional supermarket has had to adapt. For example, some grocery stores, such as Whole Foods, have become a collection of food boutiques surrounding the traditional center-store aisles of staples. An abundance of restaurants, cafés, fast food outlets, service delis, gourmet bakeries, smoothie bars, fresh juice stands, and store-made sushi and pizza are all available at a wide range of supermarkets (or "hypermarkets" as some of the larger stores like to call themselves). These operations give consumers many ready-to-eat, prepared food options where they used to just purchase food for cooking or reheating at home.

The consumer has a strong influence on the food and beverage marketplaces. But who *is* the consumer?

The profile of consumers in any marketplace, particularly the retail marketplace, is constantly changing. The result is a change in buying habits. Many factors cause this. Population movement brings changes in the ethnic background of neighborhoods, and with these shifts come consumers with different food needs. Populations, and thus neighborhoods, age. Formerly vibrant city neighborhoods may decline due to economic downturns. Empty downtown city neighborhoods may enjoy a rebirth as a fashionable area for young professionals. Most geographic market areas are in a constant state of flux with respect to the ethnic makeup, incomes, education, and lifestyles of their consumers. As both consumers and marketplaces change, food manufacturers serving those market sectors must respond to those changes quickly.

This fluidity in the marketplace must be accepted by the food processor as a challenge (and a never-ending source of work for Culinology® professionals!). No single product can answer all the demands of consumers all of the time. New products are needed to satisfy emerging market niches, new lifestyle trends, and changing demographics. The subtle and not-so-subtle changes in the marketplace can be a great motivator for product development.

Another major factor driving the marketplace is competition. A competitor can launch a new and improved product into the marketplace at any time. This can instigate a reaction from any company whose sales might suffer from the new product. This retaliatory action may involve new pricing strategies, promotional activities, or the development of new products to combat the competitor's intrusions.

Product Life Cycles

Every product has a life cycle. When first introduced, new product volumes are low. It takes time to build a business. Volume grows as consumers buy, are satisfied, and make repeat purchases. In time, competitors enter the market, which eventually becomes saturated; sales volume levels off and gradually declines as consumers grow bored with or switch to other products.

A product life cycle has five phases:[4]

The Stages of a Typical New Product Life Cycle

1. New product development
   - very expensive
   - no sales revenue
   - research and development costs

2. Market introduction
   - high cost (retail slotting fees)
   - low sales volume
   - no known competition; competitive manufacturers watch for acceptance/segment growth
   - continued research and development costs
   - demand must be created
   - customers must be prompted to try the product

3. Growth
   - significant increase in sales volume
   - costs reduced due to economies of scale
   - growth of profitability
   - increased public awareness
   - increased competition, with a few new players entering the market
   - margins sacrificed to allow lower pricing to maximize market share (for trade deals, trial coupons, etc.)

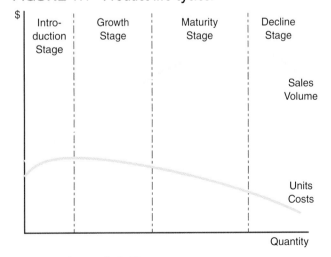

FIGURE 1.1 **Product life cycles.**

Source: Mark Crowell, CRC®.

4. Maturity
  - lower costs in an established market (less need for publicity)
  - sales volume peaks
  - increase in competitive offerings
  - prices tend to drop due to the proliferation of competing products
  - brand differentiation, feature diversification as each player seeks to differentiate from competition
  - still very profitable

5. Decline or Stability
  - costs become suboptimal
  - sales volumes plateau or decline
  - prices, profitability diminish
  - more profit comes from efficiencies in production/distribution rather than increased sales

Profit is always a better indicator of new product success than sales.

The introductory phase (2) shows minimal net profit. This period bears the cost of research and development as well as the additional heavy costs of promotion and market penetration. Business (and profit) continues to improve throughout the growth phase (3) but eventually drops off as costs for market expansion take their toll. During the maturation phase (4), costs to support the product match profits as sales rapidly drop off. The company eventually sees the product as an unprofitable item that cannot be maintained. Manufacture of the product ceases (5).

To maintain the viability of the company, replacement products must be launched. The company should not wait for profit to dip as its product loses ground in the marketplace. It must keep a series of new products in various stages of development at all times. A good rule of thumb is that for every one product on the national market, two should be in test markets, and several others should be in the last stages of consumer testing. The cumulative profitability of these new food products, if they are successful, assures a good long-term return on investment.

Some products, of course, defy the odds and become long-term successes, finding a permanent home on supermarket shelves. But they are the exception. These successful products serve another function: As proven winners, they become the base for new variations. Products launched as variations of a successful product require less risk and upfront investment than truly new and unique products.

⬤Technological Influences on New Product Development

Scientific discoveries provide insights into the physical world, human health, the environment, and materials. This knowledge can then be applied to processing technologies that lead to innovative new products and services.

Using today's Internet, any company can access vast quantities of business and technical information that previously were accessible only in specialized libraries in major urban centers. Expert technical information to assist in product development programs is available to even the smallest food processing company in remote regions of the country.

One can find many examples of technical advances in food packaging. A multitude of materials are now available, where at one time the packaging industry relied primarily on tin-coated steel, glass, and aluminum. The three-piece can, with its lead-soldered side seam, was once the mainstay of ambient long-shelf-life product packaging. This gave way to the two-piece seamless can. Nowadays, plastic-coated paperboard, composites of aluminum, plastic, and paper, and even edible food cartons can preserve and protect the high quality and shelf life of foods. Containers are also now available in microwavable, dual ovenable, biodegradable, recyclable, and compostable forms.

Greater knowledge of food spoilage mechanisms and preservation technologies has given rise to new products with better safety, stability, quality, taste, and nutrition. For example, improvements in retort technology and equipment have elevated canning, historically the blue-collar workhorse of food preservation, to a contemporary processing method that improves texture, color, flavor, and convenience without the need for a can—a relatively heavy and expensive package that isn't microwavable and produces a lot of solid waste. New ingredient technologies can enhance flavor, texture, and other product attributes while protecting them during severe processing procedures.

Advances in nutrition science have produced a growing awareness of the role food plays in our health—specifically, the relationship of certain foods to disease prevention. The food industry now has an entirely new class of foods called *nutraceuticals* (nutrition + pharmaceutical = nutraceutical, meaning foods with health benefits beyond basic nutrition) purporting to help prevent cancer, heart disease, aging, and other ailments. This topic is discussed in later chapters.

Food products are now recognized as much for the absence of harmful ingredients (sodium, cholesterol, saturated and trans fats, and refined sugars) as for the presence of beneficial ones (calcium, dietary fiber, mono- or polyunsaturated fats, antioxidants, vitamins).

Food processors and brand owners cannot afford to be unaware of developments in science and technology and the impact of these advances on consumers and food retailers, particularly given the growing role of social media and the public-relations savvy of watchdog groups such as the Center for Science in the Public Interest.

⬤Food Industry Segments

When consumers make food choices, they have an incredible number of places where they can satisfy their hunger. Millions of meals are eaten every day, and they are eaten in almost as many different locations. The industry is segmented in many ways. The U.S. Department of Agriculture's (USDA) Economic Research Service (ERS) and most food businesses categorize the industry into two segments: food eaten at home versus food eaten away from home.

Food-at-home refers to foods and beverages purchased at traditional food retailers like supermarkets. However, the term may be a bit misleading. Food-at-home may in fact be consumed *outside* the home in the form of lunchboxes carried to school or work. It also may include prepared foods purchased at a food-at-home retailer and eaten somewhere other than home. For example, a sandwich purchased at a grocery store and eaten in the car ("dashboard dining") might still fall under the heading of food-at-home because it was purchased at a grocery store, which is classified as a food-at-home retailer by the ERS. Recently the growth in prepared foods within traditional retailers, such as convenience stores and grocery stores, is changing how companies classify prepared foods within the traditional food-at-home category.

An outgrowth of this changing mindset was the 2008 inaugural Foodservice at Retail Expo, a conference focused on prepared foods sold in traditionally food-at-home retail environments. The Foodservice at Retail Expo also explored non-food retail environments such as bookstores, airports, and drugstores, many of which offer food and drink and are now becoming much more sophisticated in their food and beverage offerings.

Food-away-from-home refers mainly to purchases at restaurants but also to "food purchased at such outlets as hotels and motels, recreational places, vending machines, and schools and colleges and food provided to domestic military personnel."[5]

Using the human stomach as a metaphor for a pie chart, consider that a human being can eat only a finite amount of food. This entire amount constitutes 100 percent "share of stomach," a term used to indicate what percent of the food dollar is spent on a particular type of food or in a particular channel of food distribution. A highly influential 2005 study by the consulting firm McKinsey Co. predicted that foodservice would continue to gain on and eventually overtake sales in retail stores (then almost evenly divided between the two channels). Contrary to their predictions, U.S. consumers have steadily increased purchases at retail while cutting spending at foodservice.[6] The global recession of 2008 and 2009 further hurt food-away-from-home sales as consumers cut back on dining out. Retail sales data through the first half of 2013 indicate that retail remains ahead of foodservice 52 percent to 48 percent (see Figure 1.2).

Food-at-Home

The largest food-at-home segment is traditional grocery stores—the stores we think of as supermarkets. U.S. shoppers made an average of 1.9 trips to the grocery store per week in 2007. That year, a typical grocery store averaged about 47,000 square feet and carried an average of 45,000 items.

There was a flurry of consolidation in the supermarket industry in the late 1990s and early 2000s. As a result, the largest supermarket companies operate a number of store chains under many different brand names, a carryover from the days

FIGURE 1.2 Monthly retail sales for food-at-home and food-away-from home.

	Annual						2013			Year-to-Date Cumulative			
	2009		2010		2011		Mar	Apr	May	Mar	Apr	May	
							$ billion						
Sales													
At home	600.4	52.6%	617.5	52.4%	654.4	52.6%	63.1	58.8	58.8	177.9	236.7	295.5	52.0%
Away from home	541.4	47.4%	561.8	47.6%	588.9	47.4%	58.1	56.1	56.2	160.3	216.4	272.6	48.0%
Total	1,141.8	100.0%	1,179.3	100.0%	1,243.3	100.0%						568.1	
							Percent change from year earlier						
Sales													
At home	−1.4		2.8		6.0		4.9	1.2	-3.9	2.8	2.4	1.1	
Away from home	−1.4		3.8		4.8		2.3	7.2	2.5	9.5	11.2	11.6	

Source: USDA.
Notes: Food sales exclude alcoholic beverages as well as home production, donations, and supplied and donated foods.
Annual food sales data in Table 36 are from Table 1; monthly food sales in Table 36 may not add to the annual food
sales in Table 1 due to differences in Census sampling.
http://www.ers.usda.gov/data-products/food-expenditures.aspx#26634
As of January 2011, Table 36 uses revised 2007 Census data.
Source: Based on food sales from monthly and annual data in Census Retail Trade, available at:http://www.census.gov/retail/ Historical
data are available to 2003 in archived agricultural outlook files at:http://www.ers.usda.gov/data-products/food-expenditures.aspx
Information contact: Annette Clauson
aclauson@ers.usda.gov

when each brand (also known as a banner) was a separate chain of stores.

In 1988 Wal-Mart opened its first Supercenter, and the grocery industry changed forever. Ten years later, Wal-Mart accounted for 21 percent of every dollar spent on groceries in the United States, an incredible feat considering how recently it entered the grocery retailing business.[7] In contrast, Safeway has been in business since 1915 and Kroger since 1883, and they both account for smaller percentages than Wal-Mart.

Other food-at-home chain retailers include mass merchants such as Target, club stores such as Costco and B.J's, drugstores such as Walgreen's and CVS, dollar stores such as Dollar General, and convenience stores such as 7-Eleven and Wawa. Other non-traditional chain retailers include natural food stores such as Whole Foods, which carry a mix of merchandise similar to traditional grocery stores. Their point of differentiation is that their products are held to strict ingredient and ethical standards that offer consumers more natural, organic, locally sourced, and supposedly healthier alternatives. In addition, there are also upscale supermarket chains such as Wegmans and Dean & Deluca that offer its customers a large selection of premium-quality products (at premium prices!).

Trader Joe's is an example of a non-traditional retailer that almost defies categorization. The typical Trader Joe's store is about 2700 square feet, 10 times smaller than a typical grocery store, and it sells far more store-brand products (as a percentage of all products sold) than its competitors. Trader Joe's sells an average of 80 percent store-brand products. Yet Trader Joe's has a loyal fan base that shops at their stores more frequently than consumers in general shop at their primary traditional grocer. This helped Trader Joe's rack up an estimated $8.5 billion in sales in 2011. As of 2013 there are 400 Trader Joe's stores in 39 states and the District of Columbia.[8]

In the past few decades, these non-traditional food retailers have taken "share of stomach" away from grocery stores. According to the ERS, consumers purchased food from non-traditional outlets 13.8 percent of the time in 1988. In 2006, this number had increased to almost 33 percent of at-home food purchases.

Food-Away-From-Home

Food-away-from-home goes by many different names: food-service, on-premise, and, most familiarly, restaurants. In the 1970s, food-away-from-home represented about 18 percent of U.S. daily caloric intake and about one-third of the dollars. In 2004 (the latest USDA numbers available), U.S. consumers spent half their food dollars on food-away-from home (ERS).

The restaurant industry is generally categorized into segments that refer to service style. At the less expensive end of the industry are Quick-Serve Restaurants (QSRs). These are relatively inexpensive places with a walk-up counter and/or drive-through window, and they do primarily take-out business. In years past they were identified by the term *fast food*, which has developed a derogatory connotation.

The largest, most widely known (and geographically widespread) QSRs are mostly large multi-unit (and multinational) chains. McDonald's and Subway are the largest, each with 30,000+ restaurants worldwide. Smaller, independent QSRs like the 260-unit chain In-N-Out Burger in California, Nevada, Arizona, and Utah, and the single-unit operation Box Car Burgers in Ellensburg, Washington, exist in almost every market, but there are fewer independent QSRs every year as the cost of doing business for independents makes it difficult to survive.

QSRs traditionally serve burgers, fries, tacos, and fried chicken. Today you can get almost any type of food in a QSR format. For example, Panda Express offers quick-serve Chinese food, Fazoli's offers quick-serve Italian, and Jamba Juice offers quick-serve fruit smoothies and juices.

Fast casual restaurants are similar to fast food restaurants in that they feature walk-up counter service but have more upscale interiors, a higher proportion of diners eat their meals

FIGURE 1.3 The ten largest U.S. retailers of food and beverage.

	Company Name	Top Banners
1	Wal-Mart Stores Inc.[1]	Walmart Supercenter, Walmart Neighborhood Market, Walmart Express
2	The Kroger Co.	Harris Teeter, Ralphs, Kroger Southwest
3	AB Acquisition LLC	Safeway, Albertsons, Vons
4	Publix Super Markets Inc.	Publix, Publix Sabor, Publix GreenWise
5	Ahold USA Inc.	Stop & Shop, Giant-Landover, Giant-Carlisle
6	H-E-B Grocery Co.	H-E-B, H-E-B Plus, H-E-B Central Market
7	Delhaize America Inc.	Food Lion, Hannaford
8	Meijer Inc.	Meijer
9	Wakefern Food Corp.	ShopRite, Price Rite, The Fresh Grocer
10	Whole Foods Market	Whole Foods

[1]Sales figure represents total annual sales; retailer does not break out segmented sales by category.
Source: "The Super 50 Food Retailers," *Progressive Grocer*, May 2012.

FIGURE 1.4 Share of stomach.

1988	% Share of Stomach
Traditional Retailers	86.20%
Nontraditional Retailers	13.80%
2006	**% Share of Stomach**
Traditional Retailers	66.67%
Nontraditional Retailers	33.33%
	100.00%

Source: Mark Crowell, CRC®.

FIGURE 1.5 Supermarket sales by format.

	Number of Stores	Percent of Total	Sales ($ Millions)	Percent of Total
Total Supermarkets ($2 million or more)	37,716	100.0%	$638,338	100.0%
Supermarket-Conventional	26,487	70.2	414,794	65.0
Supercenter (Grocery and Mass Merch.)*	4,150	11.0	159,824	25.0
Supermarket Limited Assortment	3,242	8.6	16,106	2.5
Supermarket Natural/Gourmet Foods	3,144	8.3	38,372	6.0
Warehouse Grocery	523	1.4	4,367	0.7
Military Commissary	170	0.5	4,876	0.8
Other Food Retail Formats				
Conventional Convenience**	152,120	n/a	$412,703	n/a
Gas Station/Kiosk	22,303	n/a	n/a	n/a
Superette	13,070	n/a	19,974	n/a
Conventional Club	1,320	n/a	136,339	n/a
Military Convenience Store	674	n/a	4,067	n/a

*Supermarket-type items only
**Excluding gas
Source: *Progressive Grocer Magazine.*

in the restaurant, and average checks are higher. The best-known fast casual companies are Chipotle Mexican Grill and Panera Bread. Food offerings at fast casual restaurants are typically perceived as healthier and fresher, part of the reason they command higher prices. Chipotle, for instance, promotes "Food with Integrity," which includes pasture-raised pork and beef and foods free from genetically modified organisms (GMOs). Panera Bread bakes many of their products fresh each day in their stores and promotes a food policy of "Clean Ingredients." They have committed to removing all artificial colors, preservatives, sweeteners, and flavors from their menu by the end of 2016.

At a price premium to QSRs is the next segment of the restaurant industry: Family Dining. This segment usually offers table service, otherwise known as *full service*. The acronym FSR is often used to denote full-service restaurants, which are differentiated from QSRs. Examples include Denny's, Coco's, and Sizzler.

Casual Dining is the next segment in terms of increasing average guest check. Casual Dining offers full table service and usually serves alcoholic beverages. Examples include Chili's, Olive Garden, and Red Lobster.

These days it is highly likely that you will find chefs, food technologists, and/or Culinology® professionals on the menu development teams or research and development (R&D) staffs of all three types of chain dining operations. Culinology® professionals fulfill many roles at QSR, Family, and Casual Dining restaurant chains but are most typically responsible for menu planning and product development. Identifying menu concepts is something that normally revolves around consumer research.

FIGURE 1.6 Largest restaurant chains ranked by 2013 U.S. systemwide sales.

1	McDonald's	$35,856.30
2	Subway	$12,221.00
3	Starbucks Coffee	$11,864.00
4	Burger King	$8,501.00
5	Wendy's	$8,354.00
6	Taco Bell	$7,800.00
7	Dunkin' Donuts	$6,742.50
8	Pizza Hut	$5,700.00
9	Chick-fil-A	$4,988.50
10	Applebee's Neighborhood Grill & Bar	$4,517.00

Sales and revenue figures are in U.S. millions.
Source: *Nation's Restaurant News.* Copyrighted 2015. Penton Media. 11786:0615BN.

The most important consumer research a chain restaurant Culinology® professional can do is to understand their company's core customer. Many times (especially in the QSR segment) this is referred to as the "heavy user." Heavy users are restaurant patrons who frequent the chain more often than the general population. Once a chain identifies its core customers, the job of creating new menu items that appeal to them becomes much easier.

Trend-tracking is another responsibility of chain restaurant Culinology® professionals. Because most consumers eat more experimentally in restaurants than at home, the job of

FIGURE 1.7 Largest family dining restaurant chains ranked by 2013 U.S. systemwide sales.

1	International House of Pancakes	$2,650.00
2	Denny's	$2,379.00
3	Cracker Barrel Old Country Store	$2,012.00
4	Waffle House	$1,007.00
5	Bob Evans Restaurants	$980.00
6	Perkins Restaurant & Bakery	$657.70
7	Friendly's Ice Cream	$451.20
8	Big Boy/Frisch's Big Boy	$395.00

Sales and revenue figures are in U.S. millions.
Source: *Nation's Restaurant News.* Copyrighted 2015. Penton Media. 117896:0615BN

the Culinology® professional is to identify exciting foods and beverages that will appeal to the core customer as well as attract the non-core visitor (this is known as *building traffic*).

The last and, some would say top restaurant segment is called *white tablecloth*. This term comes from the days when upscale restaurants always covered their tabletops with linen. Another term that denotes this segment is *Fine Dining*.

Most fine dining restaurants are independently owned and operated. However, multiple-unit operators like Ruth's Chris Steak House and Morton's have existed for years, and recent successful chef-owned restaurant groups like those of Jean-Georges Vongerichten, Pano Karatassos's Buckhead Life Group, and Emeril's New Orleans are also finding success beyond their home markets.

Formally trained food technologists are rare in the fine dining segment, where culinary arts rule and science is relegated to cooking techniques. The exceptions to this rule are singular restaurants focused on molecular gastronomy, such as the Fat Duck in Bray, England; Alinea and Moto in Chicago; Minibar in D.C.; and Noma in Copenhagen, which tap into food technology to create new menu items.

●The Supply Side of the Business

Culinology® professionals must work with suppliers whether they are developing products for the food-at-home or food-away-from-home segments. Suppliers offer opportunity for employment for Culinology® professionals as well.

Suppliers can range from small, local farmers who raise a few dozen fowl for fine dining restaurants, to divisions of the world's largest food companies, such as Kraft, Unilever, Nestle, and ConAgra, which supply numerous raw materials and finished products to the largest chain restaurant and supermarket operations. All of the larger suppliers employ culinary professionals to help develop new value-added products using their ingredients and to help develop strong relationships with their culinary (and Culinology®) colleagues at the chain client's headquarters.

Food Ingredient Suppliers

The food industry segment that once was called *industrial supplier* today goes more frequently by the name *ingredient supplier*. Rather than providing complete finished products (entrées, side dishes, sauces, etc.), they tend to specialize in specific ingredients such as starches, gums, flavors, colors, preservatives, and the like. They often sell their ingredients to the large food manufacturers mentioned above rather than directly to restaurants or supermarket chains (the "end-users"). As such, they are typically referred to as *secondary suppliers*, while the large companies that use these ingredients to manufacture finished products for the end-users are called *primary suppliers*.

A burgeoning part of today's ingredient sector is companies marketing ingredients that can be added to food to increase its nutritional content. Examples of these so-called "functional ingredients" include omega-3 fatty acids (which, according to the U.S. Food and Drug Administration [FDA], may reduce the risk of heart disease), probiotic cultures (which may aid digestion and nutrient absorption in the small intestine), and dietary fiber (which may inhibit colon cancer).

Before they can be used in foods, all food ingredients must first be classified by the FDA as GRAS (generally recognized as safe). A GRAS ingredient is "generally recognized, among qualified experts, as having been adequately shown to be safe under the conditions of its intended use."[9] There are strict rules about how the FDA arrives at that conclusion, and it is the responsibility of food companies to prove that new ingredients meet those requirements. In addition, there are strict labeling laws that regulate the claims that can be made for foods using these ingredients.

All Other

It is impossible to list all of the other parts of the food industry that a Culinology® professional might come into contact with. However, packaging suppliers are critical for ensuring that food remains fresh, stable, and safe. Packaging is also critical for displaying a food in an appetizing way. For example, consider how the appearance of packaging affects your opinion of frozen entrées in the freezer case.

Food equipment manufacturers, agricultural co-operatives, and agri-business companies are just a few of the other types of companies that can benefit from the services of Culinology® professionals.

●Governmental Influences on New Product Development

The objectives of government with regard to food legislation are:

1. To ensure that the food supply is safe and free from contamination within the limits of available knowledge and at a cost affordable by the consumer.

2. To develop, with food manufacturers, standards of composition for foods as well as labeling standards.

3. To conduct research, and influence and educate consumers regarding diet and nutrition.

4. To maintain fair trade and competition both domestically and internationally among retailers and manufacturers in such a way as to benefit consumers and businesses.

5. To maintain U.S. competitiveness in, and access to, international export markets.

The first three objectives certainly affect the technical development of food products and influence marketing and product development personnel as they create new products and marketing campaigns.

Government legislation operates at the federal level, the state or provincial level, and the municipal, local, or county level. Government at all levels strongly influences the business activities of food companies—but in truth, it often lacks the political will or the muscle to enforce many of its most critical protections. Examples include major safety inspection lapses in the case of salmonella-contaminated peanuts at Peanut Corporation of America,[10] the inability to pinpoint the cause of a major outbreak of Salmonella Saintpaul in 2007, originally linked to tomatoes,[11] and the failure to enforce inspections in the case of an outbreak of *E. coli* in spinach in 2008.[12] The Food Safety and Modernization Act of 2010 gave major new powers to the FDA to regulate industry by shifting its focus from responding to contamination to preventing it. It is considered the first major piece of federal legislation addressing food safety since 1938.

●The Food and Drug Administration and the U.S. Department of Agriculture

FDA

The Food and Drug Administration (FDA) is an agency of the U.S. government, within the Department of Health and Human Services (DHHS). Its charter is to "safeguard the nation's food supply by making sure all ingredients used in foods are safe and that food is free of contaminants."[13]

The FDA approves new food additives, monitors dietary supplements, infant formula, and medical foods, and publishes them in the Code of Federal Regulations (CFR) annually under Title 21, Chapter 1, Section 100, which is the portion that covers food and is the food safety reference for foodservice operators. The FDA is also responsible for food labeling (not including meats and poultry, which are the responsibility of the USDA) and conducts site inspections of food processing facilities.

USDA

Many areas within the USDA are of interest to Culinology® professionals. The two most important are the areas of (1) nutrition and health and (2) food safety.

From the USDA's website under Food, Nutrition, and Consumer Services:

> [T]he USDA works to harness the Nation's agricultural abundance to end hunger and improve health in the United States. Its agencies administer federal domestic nutrition assistance programs and the Center for Nutrition Policy and Promotion, which links scientific research to the nutrition needs of consumers through science-based dietary guidance, nutrition policy coordination, and nutrition education. Food Safety ensures that the Nation's commercial supply of meat, poultry, and egg products is safe, wholesome, and properly labeled and packaged.[14]

Note that the FDA governs most of the food supply, with these few exceptions: meat, poultry, and eggs, which are generally within the purview of the USDA within the Food Safety and Inspection Service. The USDA does not, however, govern seafood or (non-egg) dairy products—which fall under the FDA.

Compounding the influence of these official levels of government are international bodies and quasi-governmental agencies like the World Trade Organization (WTO), Food and Agriculture Organization/World Health Organization (FAO/WHO), and the International Organization for Standardization (ISO). These organizations can also impose regulations on manufactured food for international trade and, indirectly, on new food product development.

- The World Trade Organization (WTO) provides a forum for negotiating agreements aimed at reducing obstacles to international trade and ensuring a level playing field for all, thus contributing to economic growth and development. The WTO also provides a legal and institutional framework for the implementation and monitoring of these agreements as well as for settling disputes arising from their interpretation and application. As an example, the WTO acted on a number of disputes between countries regarding bovine spongiform encephalopathy (BSE, also known as *mad cow disease*), most recently in September 2009 between South Korea and Canada.

- The European Union (EU) is a unique economic and political partnership of 28 European countries. EU legislation is made up of Directives and Regulations that must be implemented by each member state. Directives define the result that must be achieved but leave to each member state the choice of form and methods to transpose the directive into national laws. Regulations are binding in their entirety and automatically enter into force on a set date in all member states. The EU regulates food safety within member countries through Regulation (EC) No 178/2002. The EU follows a dual approach in harmonizing food laws: horizontal legislation, which covers aspects common to all foodstuffs (such as additives, labeling, hygiene, etc.), and vertical legislation on specific products (cocoa and chocolate products, sugars, honey, fruit juices, fruit jams, etc.). Still under discussion are legislative initiatives for issues such as maximum acceptable levels for vitamins and minerals and certain pesticide residues, among others.

- The International Organization for Standardization (ISO) and the ISO 22000 Standard specifies requirements for a food safety management system whereby an organization in the food chain must demonstrate its ability to control food safety hazards in order to ensure that food is safe at the time of human consumption. The standard incorporates the principles of HAACP (Hazard Analysis, Critical Control Points). ISO accreditation is voluntary, but many larger companies like the Kraft Heinz Company and Costco either give preference to suppliers that have achieved ISO accreditation or require it of their suppliers before they will do business with them.

- The Codex Alimentarius Commission, under the joint direction of the FAO/WHO Food Standards Program, generates internationally recognized standards, codes of practice, guidelines, and other recommendations relating to foods, food production, and food safety. The Codex is broad in scope and covers everything from setting limits on pesticide residues in food to determining how countries operate their import and export inspection services. The standards are voluntary and there is no enforcement mechanism, nor is there an obligation for member countries to adopt Codex standards; however, the WTO treats the Codex as an international reference standard for the resolution of disputes concerning food safety and consumer protection.

- Regional trade agreements such as the North American Free Trade Agreement (NAFTA) and many others can indirectly affect national food regulation, causing unintended consequences. One example involves the U.S. ban on transportation of food (and other products) from Mexico into the United States using unapproved vehicles. Rather than resulting in reduced prices on these products ("Free Trade"), the ban resulted in $2.4 billion in retaliatory tariffs on U.S. goods, including food products, imposed by the Mexican government when Congress canceled a Bush-era pilot project that gave a select group of Mexican carriers access to U.S. highways beyond the border commercial zone.

- The Food and Agriculture Organization (FAO) of the United Nations leads international efforts to defeat worldwide hunger. It helps developing countries and countries in transition to modernize and improve agriculture, forestry, and fisheries practices and to ensure good nutrition for all.

- Quasi-governmental bodies do not have the same legislative powers as the various tiers of government, but they do have the support of government or the effect of law, as when the USDA sets the price processors pay for raw milk when it issues "milk marketing orders." These bodies can establish regulations that participating parties must adhere to. Other examples are the various marketing boards that exist in many countries to regulate the local supply, importation,

and price of many food commodities and ingredients derived from them.

- Influence can also come from professional and trade associations. These may establish rules of conduct and wage scales for their members as well as influence government rule-making through lobbying efforts—as, for example, when the Organic Trade Association lobbies the National Organic Standards Board (NOSB), which makes policy recommendations on the USDA's National Organic Program (NOP).

● Societal Influences on New Product Development

Organic and natural foods have seen tremendous growth. This growth was spawned by a desire for products grown free of chemicals, focusing on local agriculture and sustainable crop and animal husbandry. Many underlying societal forces have supported this trend, including the aging of the baby boomer generation, an increasing scientific understanding of the link between health and diet, and a growing foreboding about the consequences of dwindling natural resources and humanity's impact on the earth's delicate environmental balance.

Science and technology have also played a large role in spurring this growth. The development of transgenic genetic modification, scientific advances in nutrition research, and studies on global warming and sustainable fishing practices are just a few of the ways science serves to educate and motivate (either positively or negatively) the public to change their eating habits. For some consumers, shopping is as much a political act as a commercial one.

The media play a large role in both informing and shaping the public's perception of current food issues. The International Food Information Council tracks media coverage of food issues, reporting that in 2000 there were 4000 news articles on obesity.[15] That number climbed to 14,000 in 2006 and rose to 16,000 during 2007 as various cities and states debated laws on restaurant nutrition labeling, high-profile lawsuits were brought against several quick-service restaurant chains by obese patrons, and movies such as *Fast Food Nation* debuted.

● Classification and Characterization of New Food Products

What defines a new product? No single definition works across all facets of the industry. This may explain some of the disparity in the estimates of introductions and failures. Simply repackaging an old product may justify its classification as a new product.

Likewise, an old, established product may be marketed in a new segment of the industry—for example, introducing an existing domestic product to the export market. A new package size of an old product may also be considered a new product, and a so-called "improved" product may be simply marketing hype or a new package, or may be an actual reformulation of an existing product.

The never-before-seen product is the only *truly* new product. It is far less common than the other types simply because it is the most difficult, risky, and costly to develop and launch.

Each of these new product classifications presents different challenges to the food company, whether seen through the eyes of marketing, manufacturing, finance, or R&D.

Whether new products are introduced into the foodservice, retail, or ingredient segments, they fall into one of the following classifications:

- Line extensions
- Repositioning of existing products
- New forms of existing products
- Reformulation of existing products
- New packaging or brand labeling of existing products
- New-to-the-company product lines
- New-to-the-world creative products

Not all of these product classifications are truly the result of product development efforts; some are simply marketing or procurement exercises. However, all can be important in extending the product life cycle by generating news for the product.

Line Extensions

A line extension can best be described as a variation on an established product—a new flavor of ice cream or a new seasoning on a potato chip. Line extensions represent a logical extension of a family of similar products. They are food products that generally require:

FIGURE 1.8 Newness to market.

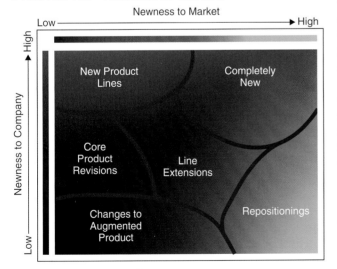

Source: Mark Crowell, CRC®.

- Less time or effort for development than wholly new products
- No major manufacturing changes in processing lines or major equipment purchases
- Relatively little change in marketing strategy
- No new purchasing skills (commodity trading) or raw material sources
- No new storage or handling techniques for either the raw ingredients or the final product, meaning that regular distribution systems can be used

There are gray areas in classifying each type of new product. For instance, a ready-to-eat (RTE) soup and a condensed soup are very different products in their marketing and in marketplace competition, but there are minimal differences in their manufacture. Even so, they are best not considered as line extensions of each other. Rather, the condensed soup and the RTE soup should be classified as very different products marketed to entirely different customers in both the retail and foodservice channels.

Development of a line extension is normally (but not always) expected to involve less development time and, consequently, less development money. The type of product dictates the amount of effort required for line extensions. For example, a new flavor of bottled water simply requires the addition of the new flavor (at an appropriate level) to the existing base (water). The packaging remains the same, but a new label will have to be created. On the other hand, something more complex, such as a new addition to a line of retorted entrées, will require extensive testing, new ingredient sourcing, modifications to the label (ingredient listings and nutritional facts panels will change), and submission to the USDA for label approval. The new products also must undergo shelf life testing, including microbial analysis.

Manufacturing is generally not disturbed by such a line extension, except for the impact on production scheduling (including additional wash-down of the line and training for the line workers) and procurement. Nor are production systems such as quality control, plant maintenance, sanitation, and hygiene unduly affected. Minor impact on storage and warehousing may be felt due to different case sizes and pallet configurations, but only if the line extension requires a different-size package.

On the other hand, unexpected difficulties may arise. For example, extending a line of canned beans to make them more convenient by putting them in flexible pouch packaging may present developmental problems plus manufacturing and manufacturing-support systems changes. Retort times, processing and packaging requirements, filling equipment, shelf life, and warehouse storage of the finished product may change. Similarly, changes in ingredients may necessitate extensive changes in processing parameters because of how the new ingredients react to various steps in the manufacturing process.

By contrast, if a snack manufacturer extends its product offerings from potato chips to corn chips to corn puffs to peanuts to popcorn, these are not simple line extensions. Such products have in common only the snack food positioning. They may be distributed through the same channels and displayed in the same section of a retail store, but they should not be considered line extensions. Purchasing strategies, storage facilities, and manufacturing technologies—to name just three areas of concern—are completely different for each of these snack forms.

Marketing programs are usually not affected by line extensions, but surprises do occur. If adult flavors are introduced into a family of snack products originally positioned for children, these flavors may not be successful for either adults or children. Therefore, different promotions, advertisements, and store placements for the adult products must be considered. Similar problems might be caused by animal shapes of pasta in a sauce or children's bite-size pieces for cookies and crackers if the products are to be extended to the adult market.

Repositioned Existing Products

A company can be startled to discover, either through consumers' letters or product usage surveys, that their consumers have come up with a new use for an existing product, giving it unexpected new life. The use of baking soda as a refrigerator deodorizer is an example of such repositioning. The promotion of soft drinks from leisure-time beverages to meal accompaniments, especially in the breakfast market, is another repositioning that has proved worthwhile, as younger consumers do not take to coffee the way prior generations did. According to The NPD Group (formerly known as the National Purchase Diary), a market research company that monitors consumer purchase data from over 165,000 stores, consumers eating breakfast outside the home order soda pop with 15.1 percent of their breakfasts, compared with 7.9 percent in 1990. Of meals eaten at home, 2.4 percent now include carbonated soft drinks, compared with only 0.5 percent in 1985.[16]

Oatmeal became perceived as a health food on the basis of the FDA's approval of fiber claims as a dietary factor in reducing cholesterol. Oatmeal and products containing oatmeal or oatmeal fiber were repositioned as healthy food, not just warm breakfast options. Cheerios' soluble fiber heart health claim has been FDA-approved since 1997. As another example, in older women with minimal calcium intake, osteoporosis was identified as a major health problem. A popular antacid that contains a high amount of calcium was repositioned as a good source of this mineral.

The product development time required for repositioning existing products is minimal. Often, all that is necessary is for the marketing department to design and print new labels, to design a new package, or to prepare a new advertising strategy with promotional material. Manufacturing is unaffected. The responsibility is with the marketing department to capitalize on the new niche.

New Forms of Existing Products

Creating a new product form represents a radical departure from the type of new product development classifications previously discussed. It is also the downfall of many new product ventures. An instantized, solubilized, granulated, tableted, powdered, solidified, foamed, concentrated, spreadable, frozen, or otherwise modified version of an existing food product can involve extensive development time. It may also require major equipment purchases, both for manufacturing and for packaging. In addition, processing and the support systems for processing may diverge considerably from the original product. The company may face vastly different warehousing and distribution system problems.

For this type of product to succeed, it is critical that the consumer recognizes and appreciates the claimed improvement in the modified product. There must be a perceived advantage of the new form over the old if the new product form is to take hold in the marketplace. For example, the advantage of a dried, sprinkle-on version of a condiment, such as mustard or ketchup, may not be appreciated or preferred over the traditional liquid form because it does not provide the moisture that consumers associate with and enjoy from the condiment. However, whipped cream cheese has been successful. This is because it offers consumers the clear benefit of being easier to spread on breads without needing time to soften at room temperature. For the company, it offers the added benefit of a much higher sales price per pound.

The phenomenal successes of instant coffee, foam-dispensed whipped dairy toppings, and spreadable margarines continue to tempt many food manufacturers into this class of development. Miniaturization, that is, bite-size pieces, has proven very popular for snack items such as cookies and crackers, as are 100-calorie packs of popular snacks. The new subcategory called *calorie-controlled snacks* is currently worth more than $200 million per year.[17] Ninety-two different 100-calorie products were on the market as of July 2007, according to Tom Vierhile, director of Datamonitor's Productscan Online Datamonitor. That's up from 51 in 2006, 33 in 2005, and only 13 in 2004. Today, thousands of 100-calorie products are on the market.

Reformulation of Existing Products

The "new, improved" product is typical of this category; the product is altered in some way but retains its essential characteristics. Reformulation of a product to make some improvement (for example, better color, better flavor, more fiber, less fat, greater stability) has a high probability of technical success. Usually, but not always, reformulation for improvement can be accomplished comparatively inexpensively and in a relatively short development time.

Reformulation may be necessary for any number of reasons. For example, an ingredient may have become unavailable, or new sources of an ingredient must be located. Reformulation may be needed to lower costs to meet the challenge of cheaper competitors. It can also allow a company to take advantage of ingredients with improved characteristics and properties, such as the line of resistant starches introduced by National Starch in 2007 that allowed the formulation of products with fewer calories and a lower glycemic index.

Reformulation may also be necessary to satisfy consumer demand for healthier products, such as one with fewer calories. This can also create a new market niche for existing products. High-fiber bread, low-fat ice cream, lactose-free milk products, and baked goods free of partially hydrogenated vegetable oils (a primary source of trans fat) are good examples of such products. In fact, starting in 2006, the FDA mandated that trans fats be labeled on all food nutrition facts panels. This was based on the scientific discovery that trans fats contribute to the risk of heart disease and prompted the entire food industry to reformulate products to remove or replace all but trace amount of trans fats. Similar events over the past decade have centered on removal of monosodium glutamate (MSG), replacement of GMO (genetically modified organism) - containing ingredients, and the phenomenal recent growth in the demand for gluten-free, dairy-free, organic, and all-natural foods. And don't overlook the size of the Kosher and Halal markets as possible targets for reformulated foods.

New Packaging or Brand Labeling of Existing Products

In its simplest form, the packaging of bulk product into smaller (sometimes individual) packages typifies this category. The reverse is also true, as many manufacturers make special bulk packages of their most popular branded products for club store and foodservice channels. New technologies such as modified atmosphere packaging (MAP) and controlled atmosphere packaging (CAP) have permitted the creation of a number of new products such as prepackaged sliced luncheon meats and bagged cut-up salad greens, providing existing products with an extended shelf life to create new market niches in existing markets and allow access to new geographical markets.

The packaging and brand labeling of commodity items such as produce and meats are other examples of existing products being reborn as a new product. As a classic example, chickens were simply chickens until a man named Frank Purdue (with a remarkably bird-like face) became famous through a series of 1970s television ads, asserting that "It takes a tough man to make a tender chicken." Angus beef is another good example.

Here, of course, product development is minimal. Getting this type of product to market requires purchasing, inspection, grading, cleaning, trimming, storage, weighing, packaging, and distribution—that is, the same requirements for bringing an unbranded commodity to market. However, the responsibility for making the product a success rests mainly in convincing consumers that the branded item is somehow better or more trustworthy than the commodity (less expensive) item, and hence more appealing and worthy of commanding a higher price.

On the other hand, using new packaging for an existing product may require the purchase of expensive packaging equipment. Major changes, such as from metal to glass containers, require a redesign of the entire packaging line. Even the change from steel cans to aluminum cans to save weight, and hence shipping costs, requires an extensive overhaul of the packaging operation. Similarly, the use of plastic squeeze bottles with snap-cap lids for dispensing mustard, ketchup, or other sauces is a major packaging change from glass and screw-top containers. However, these are one-time capital investments that should be recouped over time, assuming that the material and shipping cost savings are realized and the consumer continues to purchase the product in its new package. Ketchup, mustard, salad dressings, jams, jellies, and syrups have all undergone this process successfully.

The use of re-sealable pouches or trays (both thin-profile containers) for thinly sliced meats and non-thermally processed foods (using high-pressure pasteurization [HPP]) provides value-added features such as resealability, improved convenience, and superior shelf life. However, switching to such a new style of packaging may require significant equipment investments and product reformulation, such as using different hydrocolloid systems to maintain meat texture during high-pressure processing.

New-to-the-Company Product Lines

New and innovative products are difficult to categorize. Generally, the more innovation (change) in a product, the longer the development time and the higher the research and development costs will be. Marketing the uniqueness of a product may be costly because the consumer may need to be educated as to its benefits. In short, the development of innovative products can be both costlier and riskier than any other path of new product development.

On the other hand, relatively little research and development in terms of costs and time were required for Birdseye to put individually quick frozen vegetables together with sauce pellets into a bag 25 years ago. Likewise, putting a can of tomato sauce, a package of spaghetti sauce spices, and a package of dry pasta together to make a dinner kit requires little research and development effort. Over time, both scenarios have been extensively copied by many food companies.

New ingredients can also form the basis for innovative products. Simulated crab legs, lobster chunks, shrimp, and scallops based on surimi technology have led to the development of many new seafood dishes.

New-to-the-World Creative Products

Creative, never-before-seen products are harder to define and still more difficult to execute. The relatively recent transformation of surimi, a fish gel invented several hundred years ago in Japan, into texturized shellfish analogs was considered a creative product when it first came out. So were tofu (bean curd) and puffed cereals in their day. Today, one might consider reformed meat products, steamer technology packaging, and zero-calorie bottled salad dressings as creative developments.

Creative development products are characterized by the following:

- Extensive development time
- High research and development costs
- Costly marketing to educate consumers about something new
- High capital costs for equipment, as machinery frequently must be built from scratch if novel processing steps are involved
- Risky introduction, because consumer reaction is difficult to predict
- If successful, a flood of imitators who will take advantage of the time and effort developers of the original product took to create a market for it

In general, the more creative a product is, the greater the development costs, and development time may be many months or even years.

⬤Sales and Marketing Influences on New Product Development
Brand Management

In the retail food world, companies are organized into divisions by brand or category. There is usually a Brand Manager who holds responsibility for everything that has to do with the brand, including managing the brand's product portfolio, profit and loss, establishing and maintaining brand equity (the economic value of the brand name itself), marketing, promotion, and spearheading the product strategy. Product strategy may include working on any or all of the types of new product classifications discussed previously in this chapter.

Brand Managers are, in essence, "caretakers of the brand." They establish new product development parameters; for example, a brand manager for Ben & Jerry's might push culinary boundaries with innovative flavor combinations and unusual ingredients, and encourage marketing the products with tongue-in-cheek names like Chubby Hubby or Chunky Monkey. At the same time, consumer knowledge of what the Ben & Jerry's brand "stands for" communicates that the milk used to make the product is free of recombinant bovine growth hormone (rBGH), which would also affect product development (and cost) if the availability of hormone-free milk was limited.

It is absolutely critical to understand brand parameters before beginning any creative or product development project. This is true for retail foods as well as restaurant foods.

Restaurant Foods

It is critical to understand what a restaurant brand stands for. Chipotle Grill, for example, uses the phrase "food with integrity" to stand for how they source, serve, and stand behind their food. Unlike most other QSR chains, Chipotle indicates on their menu the name of the ranch from which they buy their pork because they are proud to serve meat from a responsible rancher who treats his animals well. In addition to polishing Chipotle's reputation, this also helps create and build the brand equity of the rancher's meat, elevating it from a commodity to a recognized (and highly desired) branded item. At the retail level, Whole Foods is the best-known pioneer of this kind of social responsibility.

Equally important in developing new items for restaurants is a clear understanding of the core customer (discussed earlier in this chapter). A spicy dish at Chipotle Grill may appeal to their core customers, but this same level of spice may be too strong for a McDonald's or Subway customer, for example. These subtleties can drive new concept and product decisions.

An additional factor when developing restaurant foods is in-depth knowledge of the equipment, kitchen layout, and capabilities of the kitchen personnel. Is the kitchen fully or only minimally equipped? Are food prep times measured in minutes, or does time allow preparation of more sophisticated dishes? Are kitchen employees trained culinary professionals or hourly workers? It is of no value to develop a new seasoning for deep-fried applications if your foodservice client doesn't use fryers!

Retail Grocery

Large chain retail operations can also strongly influence the product development process. Most retailers these days practice "category management," where managers are given complete responsibility for everything sold in their "category" in the same way the brand managers of food products manage everything related to their brand. For example, a Beverage Category Manager is responsible for managing the retailer's entire business with regard to carbonated beverages, energy drinks, sports drinks, enhanced waters, and the like.

Wal-Mart category managers wield enormous power in the area of product development. They understand their customers well and will often ask suppliers to revise their product offering to meet Wal-Mart's particular needs in the category they manage. Due to their enormous purchasing clout, they usually get what they ask for.

Other retailers set criteria for the products they will accept on their shelves. Whole Foods Market is the largest chain in the natural foods industry, with 420 stores as of January 2015. They make public the list of ingredients they do not accept in their stores. Thus, a product development project for Whole Foods should start with a thorough knowledge of this list.

When developing new products, it is important to know what retailer you are designing your product for because each has its own idiosyncrasies. In this case, one size definitely does

FIGURE 1.9 **A representative selection of the many ingredients banned from foods sold at organic grocery stores.**

acesulfame-K (acesulfame potassium)	BHT (butylated hydroxytoluene)	caprocaprylobehenin
acetylated esters of mono- and diglycerides	bleached flour	certified colors
ammonium chloride	bromated flour	cyclamates
artificial colors	brominated vegetable oil (BVO)	cysteine (l-cysteine), as an additive for bread products
artificial flavors	calcium bromate	dimethylpolysiloxane
aspartame	calcium disodium EDTA	dioctyl sodium sulfosuccinate (DSS)
azodicarbonamide	calcium peroxide	dimethylpolysiloxane

Source: http://www.wholefoodsmarket.com/products/unacceptable-ingredients.php

not fit all. It is much better to know retailers' individual restrictions up front than to have to reformulate a product after it has been developed, tested, and commercialized.

Strategies for Global Product Development

The world has become much smaller. The Internet makes it easy to do business with people all over the world, and relatively low-cost travel makes it easy for people as well as products to get there—or here, as well as to get products to and from there.

Many companies source ingredients from afar, whether they are marketed as such or not. Starbucks has long touted the unique flavors of coffee beans imported from Ethiopia, Costa Rica, and Guatemala. Other imported ingredients may be buried deep in a recipe or formula and can be completely unknown to the consumer of the product. For example, China produces most of the world's garlic, and the United States is the largest importer of this crop. There is a good chance that at least some of the garlic in just about anything you're eating came from China. The same can be said for most of the B vitamins and ascorbic acid consumed in this country: They are mostly manufactured in China.

International trade in food and beverage is big business. It is highly complex as well. Tariffs and quotas attempt to control the amount of products that flow from one country to another. This can put foreign products at a disadvantage to local options. With the current interest in eating locally grown food, this is bound to get even more attention.

Trade in food and beverage is also influenced by fluctuating currencies, which can render foreign goods cheaper or more expensive depending on the exchange rate on any given day. The cost of products that must travel great distances, such as the garlic imported from China, is also affected by the cost of oil, which fuels transportation, whether by sea, air, or ground.

Food safety is another huge concern. The 2000s saw several food safety problems with food and feed ingredients imported from China. While China is not the only country to export tainted products, their rapid economic development seems to come at the expense of safety controls. As a result, many companies stopped using ingredients imported from developing nations.

The risks fall into several categories: insufficient quality control at the point of manufacture, willful contamination due to fraud, weak or corrupt government oversight, poor sanitation practices, opaque distribution chains, and poor documentation.

On the export side, when a company decides to start marketing products in other countries, it can do so in a number of ways. The easiest is to simply sell the same product abroad as at home. This requires no product development or reformulation, unless local restrictions ban the use of certain ingredients outright due to religious, cultural, or governmental regulations, but these products will likely require new labels that meet the language and regulatory requirements of the new market.

Another option is to adapt an existing product for a foreign market. Along with the labeling changes referenced above, the name may need to be changed and the product may need to be reformulated. This requires knowledge of the receiving country's language, culture, ingredient restrictions, and taste preferences.

Irish Mist® introduced its drink brand in Germany without knowing that "mist" is German slang for excrement. A Spanish potato chip brand called Bum did not sell well in the United States due to the negative connotations of the name. On the other hand, a recent Japanese import into the United States is the ion-replacement beverage Pocari Sweat®. Despite its somewhat off-putting name (at least to many Americans), the beverage is already available at Amazon.com and is selling well, at least to its target market of young athletic hipsters.

Cultural differences can also affect product decisions. A product such as Nestlé's Beso de Negra ("Kiss of the Black Woman"), with a scantily clad, buxom woman on the front, is unacceptable in many Middle Eastern countries, where the norms are much more conservative when it comes to showing skin. If Nestlé ever decided to market the product in the Middle East, they would no doubt have to re-brand and re-label it.

Taste and texture preferences vary widely by geography as well. Many Asian snacks come in flavors that U.S. consumers consider too "fishy." If these companies plan to expand their U.S. presence, they would be wise to develop more U.S.-acceptable flavors. Yogurt is another product that varies widely. In Greece, the product is thick and very tangy. In Europe, it is thin and tangy. In the United States, many yogurts are thickened with gums or starches and sweetened at a much higher level than in Europe. That said, Greek-style yogurt has become a huge business in the United States in the past 5 years.

The best way to ensure success in a new market is to develop the product from the ground up based on the specific characteristics of the market. This means starting with consumer research to identify concept opportunities, flavor preferences, and market positioning. It is also smart to hire at least some of your R&D and Marketing staff (or consultants) from the target countries you wish to do business in. A lot of research and investigation must be done long before the first product prototypes are developed. The key takeaway is that exporting products is one way to grow a food business, but it is not as easy as it may look from the shores of the home country.

●The Role of the Culinology® Professional
Why Consider a Career as a Culinology® Professional?

A career in food product development can be both challenging and rewarding. Every sector of the food industry employs people who perform new product development (NPD) and NPD-related tasks. Large industrial concerns such as Kraft Heinz and General Mills employ hundreds of highly skilled scientists, many with graduate degrees in general food science or in specific areas such as cereal or meat science. Small concerns might employ one or two part-time food scientists.

Chefs working in R&D for retail or foodservice manufacturers tend to have culinary rather than scientific backgrounds. Culinology® program graduates can enjoy the best of both worlds with integrated training that gives them the flexibility to practice culinary arts, food science, or, ideally, both.

The scientific/technical side of product development requires both theoretical and applied knowledge of chemistry, nutrition, government regulations, food safety, sensory science, food processing, the use of functional food additives, packaging, and knowledge of the physical properties and interactions of food ingredients. The culinary side requires both theoretical and applied knowledge of the principles of cooking, the culinary use and application of ingredients, production systems, recipe and formula development, food

trends, equipment operation, and of course, the creativity and refined sensory skills that come from years of practical kitchen experience.

Over time, all areas of the food industry will come to value and benefit from the breadth of knowledge Culinology® professionals bring to the workplace. It is too soon to measure the salary premium they might earn over one discipline or the other, but Culinology® professionals are both highly sought after and well compensated.

The work of Culinology® professionals is never dull. Each day brings new challenges and important decisions that can affect their employer's bottom line for years to come. To truly succeed as a Culinology® professional, one must combine the creativity, ability to be calm under fire, and passion for excellence of the chef with the organizational skills, analytical ability, and attention to detail of the scientist. In addition, Culinology® professionals are organizationally valuable for their unique ability to understand the worlds and languages of chefs and food scientists on large cross-functional development teams. Their experience in both camps can help them build bridges between the two disciplines.

There's nothing quite like walking into a national restaurant chain or major grocery store and seeing consumers purchasing a product you had a hand in developing. It is truly rewarding to know that hundreds of thousands, perhaps millions, of people are experiencing your creation.

The discipline of product development is the true challenge for Culinology® professionals. It is the real world, where theories are put to the test and honed into practical experience. This is the world where business makes, and sometimes loses, millions of dollars introducing and marketing new food products—and Culinology® professionals are at center stage.

Considering how large and seemingly sophisticated many food companies are, you might assume that they would have product development down cold and turn out one winning product after another. Nothing could be further from the truth. The results of the Booz Allen Global Innovation 1000 in 2005 found little correlation between R&D spending at the world's largest 1000 companies and the company's gross margins.[18] Why?

One reason is that very few companies actually employ the correct product development and marketing methodologies necessary to succeed in today's highly segmented and hyper-competitive marketplace. Few companies are patient enough or invest enough, and they do not reward intelligent risk taking—a key to developing breakthrough products. Development budgets within food companies are typically

FIGURE 1.10 Culinology® Venn diagram.

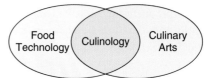

Source: Mark Crowell, CRC®.

dwarfed by advertising, promotion, and other marketing expenditures. R&D spending in the food industry typically represents only 1 to 2 percent of revenues, compared to 8 to 15 percent of revenues in the high-tech sector. However, while an aggressive advertising and promotional campaign can invigorate even poorly developed products, the results are typically short-lived, with little positive impact on company growth and long-term profitability.

Most food companies have a marketing focus that also puts them at a disadvantage. They view product development as a reactive process rather than a cross-functional management process, where the need to closely link engineering, operations, procurement, marketing, and R&D activities to customer requirements is more obvious. As a result, many food companies have never optimized their product development capabilities in a concerted, cross-functional fashion.

Examples of famous product and food company failures include Anheuser-Busch's Eagle Snacks, Campbell's Souper Combos, and New Coke.

Creating and Managing Product Development Teams

The most successful product development project includes members from all disciplines within a company. Culinology® professionals play a key role in integrating the culinary and food science disciplines to accomplish project objectives. In addition, it is important to have a strong Project Manager to pull all members of the project team together. The following list of disciplines includes those most directly involved in a product development team.

Project Manager

The Project Manager's responsibilities are to communicate and uphold the project's objectives and to keep the team members on strategy and on time. Perhaps more important, though, the Project Manager provides leadership.

Successful Project Managers will encourage the team to work together in a cooperative, mutually beneficial manner by creating a culture of openness. They ensure that the team members share a common understanding of the project goals and a common language. This is where a Culinology® professional can be especially valuable.

Culinology® professionals should possess the ability to speak the language of culinary arts as well as the language of the scientist. The ability to bridge this gap in everyday language makes Culinology® professionals extremely valuable as well as appropriate for overall project management responsibility.

Product Developer

There should be one person on the team who has primary responsibility for the development of the actual food prototypes. If the project is highly technical in nature, this person may be a Food Technologist; if it is largely culinary, it may be a Chef. However, it is always a good idea to have a number of Culinology® professionals working together on the project. After one person develops a prototype, he or she should have other team members evaluate it and then make revisions, again and again, until it is ready to show to the Project Manager and any other project stakeholders. Early handmade prototype development is usually referred to as *bench-top development* because much of it occurs at the lab bench of a developer.

Consumer Insights

The discipline of consumer research, more recently called *consumer insights*, is imperative to the process. Many small companies forgo spending any of their small budget on consumer insights, but this is often a mistake. It is much more costly to develop and launch a product that fails than to spend money on gaining consumer insights up front. A frugal manager with consumer insights responsibility may learn things in unconventional ways—for example, through polling friends and family, doing online research, and secondary research from sources such as newspapers, books, the Internet, and so on—all of which can be less expensive than traditional research. Regardless of the approach or budget, any consumer insight is better than none at all.

Packaging

Regardless of whether the project is for retail packaged food or a restaurant menu item, there is a packaging component that must be considered during product development. The packaging person may be a designer, engineer, or a supply or sourcing specialist. The key responsibilities of this person are to assure that the chosen package supports the requirements of the processing parameters, shelf life, safety, distribution, and marketing of the product.

Commercialization

At least one member of a product development team should be responsible for making sure that the concept is feasible from a food safety, sensory quality, economic, and manufacturability perspective. This person should also be heavily involved in the development of the product during the early phases of the project to save the development team from pursuing unrealistic ideas while at the same time gaining familiarity with the "Gold Standard": the target product to be commercialized. It is critical that this person be able to minimize the differences in product quality that inevitably occur during scale-up and production.

The commercialization team is also responsible for identifying appropriate manufacturing processes and then finding the facilities and equipment required to produce the product. This may be in a company-owned facility or in one outside the company under a contract manufacturing (co-packing) arrangement.

Regulatory

As the product is being developed, a number of regulatory issues must be addressed, including restrictions on what the product can be called. For example, the USDA specifies what qualifies to be labeled as "Beef Chili" versus what needs to be labeled "Chili with Beef." The FDA mandates an entire list of food "Standards of Identity" that define a food's composition by the specific ingredients (and amounts of ingredients) it must contain in order to be labeled as that food.

The regulatory role on a food product development team also includes overseeing the development of the nutrition facts panel and ingredient declaration, both required by law. Depending on the product, other regulatory issues may pertain, such as getting process approval from the FDA on low-acid, shelf-stable products, and label review will have to be conducted by the USDA in most cases if the product contains meat or poultry.

● Conclusion

The business of new product development offers challenging, technically demanding careers for Culinology® professionals that feature opportunities in almost every food business segment. Culinology® professionals may find themselves creating organic frozen meals from ethically sourced ingredients, designing the next hit snack food, or developing new QSR sandwiches that will be consumed by millions of people. The opportunities are enormous in this ever-evolving landscape of food technology, trends, and consumer tastes, and the Culinology® professional is uniquely positioned to take advantage of them

[1] J. M. Keynes, *A Treatise on Money* (New York: AMS Pr. Inc. , 1976).

[2] B. Jaruzelski, "The Booz Allen Hamilton Global Innovation 1000: Money Isn't Everything," *Strategy+Business* 7, no. 41 (2005), retrieved November 15, 2009, from http://www.ausicom.com/filelib/PDF/Research Library/Booz%20Allen%20Hamilton%20Innovation-1000.pdf.

[3] R. G. Cooper, *Winning at New Products: Accelerating the Process from Idea to Launch*, 3rd ed. (New York: Perseus Books Group, 2001).

[4] R. Vernon, "International Investment and International Trade in the Product Cycle," in *The Quarterly Journal of Economics* (Cambridge: MIT Press, 1966).

[5] ERS/USDA, "Briefing Room: Food CPI and Expenditures," Measuring the ERS Food Expenditure Series, retrieved November 16, 2009, from http://www.ers.usda.gov/Briefing.

[6] "U.S. Monthly Advanced Retail Sales Survey, August 2009," *U.S. Census Bureau News*, retrieved from http://www2.census.gov/retail/releases/historical/marts/adv0908.pdf.

[7] Food Marketing Institute, "Facts and Figures," *Supermarket Facts* (May 1, 2008), retrieved November 15, 2009, from http://www.fmi.org/facts_figs/?fuseaction=superfact.

[8] Trader Joe's, http://traderjoes.com/our-story/timeline, 2013.

[9] Food and Drug Administration, "Guidance for Industry: Frequently Asked Questions about GRAS," December 2004, retrieved from http://www.fda.gov/Food/GuidanceRegulation/GuidanceDocumentsRegulatoryInformation/ucm061846.htm.

[10] M. Moss, "Peanut Case Shows Holes in Food Safety Net," *New York Times: Breaking News, World News, and Multimedia*, February 9, 2009, retrieved November 15, 2009, from http://www.nytimes.com/2009/02.

[11] "Politics of the Plate," *Food Safety Lapses: Food Politics*, July 8, 2008, retrieved November 15, 2009, from http://www.gourmet.com/foodpolitics.

[12] C. Lee, "FDA Safety Lapses: The Food Times," *All-Consuming News*, March 18, 2008, retrieved November 15, 2009, from http://www.thefoodtimes.com/2008.

[13] M. Neumann and N. Fortin, eds., *Food and Drug Regulation: A Web Book of Student Papers*, on file with the Institute for Food Laws and Regulations at Michigan State University.

[14] "About FSIS," *USDA Food Safety and Inspection Service Home*, n.d., retrieved November 15, 2009, from http://www.fsis.usda.gov/about_fsis.

[15] "Food for Thought VI," *Diet, Nutrition, and Food Safety News*, December 2005.

[16] NPD, National Eating Trends® (NET®).

[17] Jeremy W. Peters, "In Small Packages, Fewer Calories and More Profit," *New York Times*, July 7, 2007.

[18] http://www.boozallen.com/media/file/Global_Innovation_1000_2006.pdf.

2 The Principles of Food Science

Lead Author: Lisa J. Mauer, Ph.D., Professor, Department of Food Science, Purdue University

M. Fernanda San Martin-Gonzalez, Ph.D., Associate Professor, Department of Food Science, Purdue University

● Introduction

To create high-quality foods, it is important to understand the basic structures and functions of food ingredients, including both macro and micro nutrients, their interactions, how cooking techniques influence these, and ultimately their physical and chemical stability in foods. This chapter introduces the structures of water, proteins, lipids, and carbohydrates, otherwise known as the "building blocks" of foods. Emphasis will be on the types of solids, liquids, and gases; water-solid interactions; phase transitions; and chemical reactions in foods. Because most cooking techniques involve heat interacting with foods, understanding the effects of temperature on food component structures and reactions is essential. The types of heat, thermal properties, and heat transfer will be described before addressing culinary cooking techniques from the chef's viewpoint in the following chapter.

● The Nature of Matter

Food matrix, intermediate-moisture food, amorphous food components—sometimes it sounds as if food scientists cannot possibly be talking about the foods everyone eats. Why use these terms instead of more simply describing a soft food? The reason is that food scientists seek to understand the fundamental nature of food so that they can control and predict what will happen to food when it is formulated, cooked, packaged, and stored. Because prediction is useful only when it is precise, the study of food requires the precise language of science.

The first challenge is simply to describe the way foods occupy space. Matter exists as solid, liquid, or gas, but many foods are combinations of two different phases of matter, which is why it is hard to say whether jelly is a solid or a liquid, or beer foam a liquid or a gas. In other words, foods are complex physical structures that are best described as *dispersions*. Dispersions are systems of discrete particles of one phase of matter suspended or dispersed within a second continuous phase of matter. Dispersions are characterized by having both continuous phases (usually the majority ingredient that serves as a matrix) and discontinuous or "dispersed" phases (the discontinuous phase is incorporated within the continuous phase). The amounts and types of solids, liquids, and gases, and their location within these two phases, influence the ultimate texture, stability, and acceptability of food products. For example, a dispersion with water as the continuous phase and fat as the discontinuous phase dispersed within it (such as cream) has much different properties than a dispersion with a solid fat as the continuous phase and water as the discontinuous phase (such as refrigerated butter). Creating dispersions from the macro- and micronutrients that comprise foods is much like constructing a building in which the walls, floors, and ceilings form the continuous phase and everything within the "rooms" is the dispersed phase. The combinations are endless.

The ways that the basic functional ("reactive") groups of atoms in food dispersions interact with each other determines the structure, texture, and stability of foods as well as how they react to cooking. For example, both gelatin and egg white proteins can create *gels*—structures with a continuous solid phase (the protein gel matrix) and a dispersed liquid phase (the water trapped within the protein matrix)—but each responds differently to heat. An initial dispersion of gelatin proteins in water (called a sol, a solid dispersed in a liquid) will become a gel (like Jell-O®) with a continuous protein matrix containing a discontinuous water phase after heating and cooling. This type of gel is thermo-reversible—that is, it will liquefy when heated and reforms as a gel when chilled. Egg whites, on the other hand, form irreversible gel structures when heated that are unaffected by cooling and actually toughen with reheating. Therefore, the strength of the

FIGURE 2.1 Classification of food dispersions by types of continuous and dispersed phases. Most foods are dispersions, and examples of each type of dispersion are provided.

Continuous Phase	Dispersed Phase	Descriptive Words for Each Type of Dispersion	Food Examples
Liquid	Gas	Foam, froth, bubble, air, carbonated liquid	Whipped egg white, whipped cream, champagne, soda
Liquid	Liquid	Emulsion	Milk, cream, salad dressing, mayonnaise, cream soup, many sauces (béchamel, hollandaise)
Liquid	Solid	Suspension, sol, colloidal dispersion	Eggnog, chocolate milk, coffee, herbs suspended in sauces and dressings
Solid	Gas	Foam, suspension	Marshmallow, leavened bread, nougat, ice cream, angel cake, meringue
Solid	Liquid	Gel	Gelatin gels (Jello®), custard, cooked egg, tofu
Solid	Solid	Solid	Toffee, chocolate, noodles, herbs in cheeses and butters

Source: L. Mauer and F. San Martin-Gonzalez.

FIGURE 2.2 Common interactions in foods responsible for structure, function, stability, and resistance to external forces applied during food production (such as mixing and cooking), organized in order of increasing strength.

Common Molecular Interactions in Food					
Van der Waals	Hydrophobic	Hydrogen Bond	Dipole-dipole	Ionic and Ion-dipole	Covalent
Weak attractive and repulsive forces between neutral molecules.	Attractive forces between "water-fearing" molecules, such as fatty acid hydrocarbon chains, that lead to self-aggregation in aqueous environments.	The relatively weak attraction between a partial-positive charge on a hydrogen atom and a partial-negative charge on another atom, typically N or O in foods.	Electronic attractive or repulsive interactions between functional groups of opposite charge; electronic opposites always attract.	Ionic bonds are strong electronic bonds between charged atoms or molecules. Solid ionic compounds form stable crystal structures (salts). Water easily dissolves ionic compounds.	Extremely strong interaction between atoms caused by a shared pair of electrons. Covalent bonds break at temperatures above that of boiling water.
Van der Waals attractive forces between fatty acids are responsible for the crystallization of lipids. When fats are heated, the heat energy can disrupt the Van der Waals attractions, at which point the lipids melt (e.g., melting of butter and chocolate).	Hydrophobic interactions are a driving force for the separation of mixtures of hydrophilic and hydrophobic ingredients (emulsions), such as salad dressings and mayonnaise, in the absence of an emulsifier.	Water interacts with itself and other compounds via hydrogen bonds. The solubility of many ingredients and the crystallization of sugar are governed by hydrogen bonding.	The structural changes of proteins in response to changing pH are a result of changing dipole-dipole interactions between amino acids, as is seen when milk curdles upon acidification.	Ionic interactions are responsible for the crystallization of salt and the gelation of ion-setting gels (such as sodium alginate in the presence of calcium ions).	Covalent interactions (such as glycosidic linkages and amide bonds) are responsible for the formation of polymer structures (carbohydrates and proteins, respectively). Covalent crosslinks between polymers form very strong gels, such as those established with transglutaminase or disulfide linkages.

Source: J. Sanchez and L. Mauer.

FIGURE 2.3 Common functional groups (sequences of atoms) found in the building blocks of foods (carbohydrates, proteins, and lipids). The types, locations, and sequences of these functional groups in the building blocks of foods govern the structure, function, texture, and reactivity of foods. The use of "R" is an abbreviation for carbon-containing molecules attached to the identified structure.

Functional Group	Definition	Structure	Presence in the Building Blocks of Food
Methyl	A methyl group is a carbon atom bound to three hydrogen atoms. It is hydrophobic.	CH₃ / R	Carbohydrates, lipids, and proteins
Hydroxyl	A hydroxyl group is an oxygen atom bound to a hydrogen atom. It is hydrophilic.	OH / R	Carbohydrates and proteins
Sulfhydryl (Thiol)	A sulfhydryl or thiol group is a sulfur atom bound to a hydrogen atom. It is somewhat hydrophilic.	SH / R	Proteins
Carbonyl	A carbonyl group is a carbon atom double bonded to an oxygen atom. Additional bonds to the carbon determine the nature and name of groups that contain the carbonyl functional group.	O ‖ C	Carbohydrates, lipids, and proteins
Aldehyde	An aldehyde group is a carbonyl group with one bond to carbon and one bond to hydrogen.	O ‖ R—C—H	Carbohydrates
Ketone	A ketone group is a carbonyl group with two bonds to carbon.	O ‖ R₁—C—R₂	Carbohydrates
Carboxyl (Carboxylic acid)	A carboxyl, or carboxylic acid group, is a carbonyl group with one bond to carbon and one bond to a hydroxyl group.	O ‖ R—C—OH	Proteins
Ester	An ester group is a carboxylic acid group where the oxygen-hydrogen bond is replaced with an oxygen-carbon bond.	O ‖ R₁—C—O—R₂	Lipids
Amide	An amide group is a carbonyl group with one bond to carbon and one bond to nitrogen.	O ‖ R₁—C—N—R₂ | H	Proteins
Disulfide	A disulfide group is a pair of sulfur atoms with two bonds: one to each other and one to a carbon atom.	R₁—S—S—R₂	Proteins

Source: J. Sanchez and L. Mauer.

intermolecular bonds holding the egg protein gel together must be stronger, or at the very least different, from the bonds creating the gelatin gel. In fact, gelatin gels are stabilized by a combination of *hydrogen bonding* and *hydrophobic interactions* that are about 10 times weaker than the combined bond strengths of the hydrogen and *disulfide bonding* that stabilize egg protein gels. Understanding the structures of food components, including the types of elements and bonds of which they are built, is an important first step in understanding and creating food texture.

●Types of Solids

The previous section discussed how the physical structures of foods are dispersed systems composed of different states of matter. Dispersions describe the large-scale properties of foods but not the microscopic and molecular level composition of foods. This section dives down to the atomic level to explain the chemical, not physical, composition of food. Ultimately, the chemical forces and attractions at the molecular level influence how all matter behaves at the visible physical scale.

The solid building blocks of foods are carbohydrates, fats (fats are lipids that are solid at room temperature, while oils are lipids that are liquid at room temperature), and proteins. At the molecular level, these compounds are composed mainly of atoms of carbon, oxygen, and hydrogen. The atoms are *covalently bound*, which means that they share electron pairs to form *chemical bonds* between each other in characteristic sequences. These sequences form functional groups of atoms, and the nature of these functional groups gives each of the three building blocks their unique set of appearances, structures, functions, and reactivity.

Bond or interaction energies (the strength with which a chemical bond or interaction holds two atoms together) are important in determining the effects of cooking on the food structure. The type and amount of energy (from heating or physical work such as beating, whipping, shaking, etc.) determines which, if any, bonds are disrupted. Weaker bonds, such as *hydrogen bonds*, are more easily disrupted than stronger bonds, such as *covalent bonds* or *ionic bonds*. Egg whites are a good example. Egg whites beaten to stiff peaks have had their proteins gently unfolded by physical shear. Their exposed hydrophobic centers trap air and form small bubbles to create a foam. On the other hand, egg whites cooked on the stove have had their proteins highly disrupted by heat. The disrupted hydrogen bonds denature the proteins and cause them to bind together in a continuous phase, stabilized by disulfide covalent bonds, to form a gel. The types of bonds present in the food ingredients, as well as those developed during food preparation and cooking, in turn influence the structure, reactivity, and texture of each of the components in the food. They also affect the *sensory qualities* (appearance, taste, aroma, texture) of the finished product.

FIGURE 2.4 Functions of water, proteins, carbohydrates, and lipids in foods.

Food Component	Functions
Water	Hydration, solvent or dispersion medium, reaction medium, heat transfer medium, mobility, hygroscopicity, softness, basic part of the structure ("bound" water) and/or main constituent of the food, polar phase, surface or interfacial tension, vapor pressure or water activity
Protein	Structure, texture, viscosity, water binding or water retention, heat denaturation, coagulation, gelation, cohesion, adhesion, elasticity, emulsification, foaming, fat and flavor binding, nonenzymatic Maillard browning for color and flavor development, nutritional source of essential amino acids
Sugars (mono- and disaccharides)	Sweeteners, structure, texture, solubility, crystallization controllers, control of a_w, Maillard (nonenzymatic) browning, caramelization, humectants, bulk, viscosity, fermentation source
Polysaccharides (starches, gums)	Thicken, improve texture, form gels, inhibit crystallization, whipping agents, stabilize foams, stabilize emulsions, binders, stabilize proteins, encapsulate, flocculate/clarify, processing aids, provide specific rheology, inhibit syneresis, stabilize suspensions, dispersing agents, to bind/hold water, to form films and coatings
Lipids	Texture, structure, mouthfeel, flavor, satiety, medium of heat transfer, tenderizing agent, carrier of fat-soluble vitamins ADEK, nutritional source of essential fatty acids (linoleic, linolenic), development of rancidity (hydrolytic or oxidative), emulsion formation and stabilization, delivery agent of lipophilic flavors, nutrients, and colors

Source: L. Mauer and F. San Martin-Gonzalez.

Carbohydrates

Carbohydrates are composed of carbon, hydrogen, and oxygen in the following ratio: $(C \cdot H_2O)_n$, where n is ≥ 3. The chemical formula gives sense to the name: With one molecule of water for each atom of carbon, carbohydrates are essentially hydrates of carbon. Each carbon atom in a carbohydrate is bound to an oxygen atom, typically as a *hydroxyl* group but sometimes as a carbonyl. If fully digestible, carbohydrates contribute 4 kcal/g to foods. Monosaccharides, the basic building blocks of carbohydrates, are by definition the simplest (and smallest) carbohydrates. They are classified by the location of the carbonyl group, which makes them either aldehydes or ketones. A carbonyl group is composed of a carbon atom double-bonded to an oxygen atom: $C=O$. When this group is found at the end of a molecule's carbon backbone, the molecule is an aldehyde. When this group is found in the middle of a molecule's carbon backbone, the molecule is a ketone. Most of the major monosaccharides used as food ingredients are aldehydes. The only major monosaccharide used as a food ingredient that is a ketone is fructose.

Common monosaccharides used or found in foods, such as *glucose* and *fructose*, have a $C_6H_{12}O_6$ structure and are called hexoses because they both contain 6 carbon atoms. The difference in the carbonyl location between glucose (aldehyde group) and fructose (ketone group) contributes to the greater hygroscopicity (affinity for binding water) and lower melting point of fructose. Because they both have a $C_6H_{12}O_6$ composition but a different location of the carbonyl group, glucose and fructose are isomers of each other—that is, they have the same chemical formula but different arrangement of the atoms. Isomerization reactions, such as those driven by the enzyme glucose isomerase, can be used to convert glucose into fructose, which is widely used in the later stages of the production of high-fructose corn syrup from *starch* (a polymer or long chain of glucose subunits). In addition, all monosaccharides can participate in non-enzymatic browning reactions (Maillard browning and caramelization), and they are called reducing sugars because their ring structures are able to open while in solution to expose the reactive carbonyl group. The many –OH (*hydroxyl*) groups present in the monosaccharide structure enable hydrogen bonding with water, making them highly water soluble.

In nature, carbohydrates are rarely found in their simple monosaccharide form. Simple sugars are sweet and scarce, which is why animals and humans alike treasure their common sources: the fruits of plants and the nectar of flowers. The carbonyl functional group allows monosaccharides to act as building blocks that can join together via *glycosidic linkages* (covalent bonds). For the most part, monosaccharides in nature combine (*polymerize*) to form *disaccharides* (2 monosaccharide units), *oligosaccharides* (2 to 10 units), and *polysaccharides* (more than 10 units; some contain as many as 15,000). Polysaccharides are by far the most abundant carbohydrate structures in nature—they will be discussed later on.

Disaccharides, like monosaccharides, are rare in nature and also tend to be sweet. Common disaccharides include *sucrose* or table sugar (glucose+fructose), *maltose* (glucose+glucose), and *lactose* (glucose+galactose). Disaccharides vary in sweetness, hygroscopicity, solubility, crystallization tendency, and reactivity, depending on how their monosaccharides are bound together. For example, sucrose is not a *reducing sugar* and cannot participate in Maillard browning because of its inability to expose a carbonyl group while in solution, while maltose and

FIGURE 2.5 **The basic structures of common carbohydrates: the monosaccharide glucose and the polysaccharide components of starch (amylose and amylopectin).**

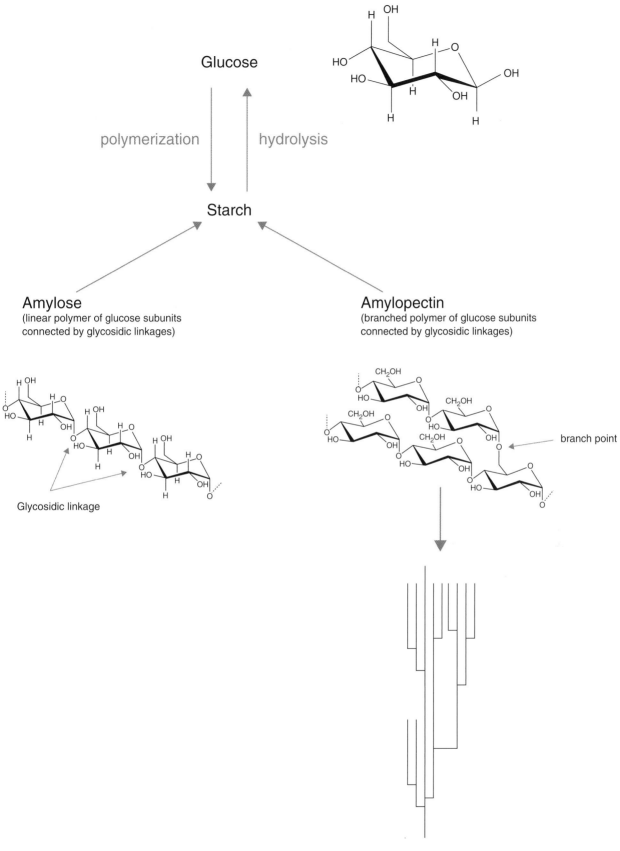

Source: L. Mauer.

lactose are reducing sugars and can participate in Maillard browning. Enzymes can be used to hydrolyze (break apart with water) complex carbohydrates into their monosaccharide components to alter sweetness, viscosity, and other properties in a food product. One example is the use of the *invertase enzyme* in chocolate-covered cherries to hydrolyze the disaccharide sucrose (a crystalline solid) into glucose and fructose. The enzyme hydrolysis creates a sugar syrup inside the chocolate coating after the candies are formed because glucose and fructose have weaker crystallization tendencies (and a lower mutual deliquescence point) than sucrose.

Polysaccharides constitute more than 90 percent of the carbohydrate *biomass* found in nature; they form the rigid polymer structures that give plants their shape. Uncooked, they are tough, bland, and hard to digest. In purified form, they are added as ingredients to most processed food products. Examples of polysaccharides include starch, cellulose, hemicellulose, pectin, glycogen, chitin, inulin, gums (guar, locust bean, alginate, agar, carrageenan, etc.), and other classes of *dietary fiber*. The functions of polysaccharides reflect the diversity of their many sizes and structures.

At the molecular level, the many hydroxyl groups along polysaccharide polymer structures facilitate hydrogen bonding with water molecules. Most polysaccharides have the ability to thicken solutions due to their long polymer structures, which entangle as a solution is stirred; their long structures entrap large volumes of water within their sweeping volume (radius of gyration). In addition to thickening, some polysaccharides are able to form gels if the conditions are right for intermolecular interactions between them, leading to a polysaccharide continuous phase in the dispersion. For example, the gel formation ability of the polysaccharide sodium alginate in the presence of calcium ions is the basis for many spherification applications.

Starch is found in discrete particles (starch granules) in nature and is the major form of energy stored in higher plants (seeds, roots, fruits, leaves, etc.). Starch is used in foods for multiple purposes, including thickening, gel formation, stabilizing suspensions, etc. Starch is made of amylose (a linear *polysaccharide* of repeating glucose subunits) and amylopectin (a branched *polysaccharide* of glucose subunits). In general, amylose makes up about 30 percent of the starch structure and amylopectin makes up 70 percent, but the ratio is strongly dependent on the plant source. These linear and branched structures exhibit different physical and functional properties. In starch granules, the amylopectin structures orient out radially from the core (hilum) and create rings of crystalline and amorphous regions. The branched areas of amylopectin molecules create the amorphous regions in the starch granule. The hard outer crystalline structure of native starch granules results in their insolubility in cold water. To obtain improved functionality from native (unmodified) starch (beyond dusting on surfaces to prevent sticking or using as an anticaking agent), its granular structure must be disrupted by processing (adding moisture, heat, enzymes, etc.) to alter its structure, chemical, and/or physical properties. To enhance or alter native starch functionality, modified

starches were developed to reduce the energy required to cook them or to modify their cooking characteristics; impart cold water swelling or increased solubility; increase or decrease paste viscosity or gel formation and strength; enhance clarity; increase resistance to shear; increase freeze-thaw and pH stability; enhance interactions with other ingredients (for example, lipids); and reduce gel *syneresis* or breakdown. Frequently, starch is heated above the melting temperature of its crystalline structures to enhance its water solubility and functionality in foods, either by the chef when using a native starch or starch-containing ingredient (such as wheat flour) or by the modified starch manufacturer during the ingredient production process.

Many types of non-starch polysaccharides are used as food ingredients to take advantage of their thickening, stabilizing, and/or gelling abilities. Examples of non-starch polysaccharides include pectins, plant seed gums (guar gum, locust bean gum), plant exudate gums (gum Arabic, gum tragacanth), seaweed gums (agar, carrageenans, and alginates), bacterial gums (xanthan gums, gellan), and cellulose gums (methylcellulose, carboxymethyl cellulose, microcrystalline cellulose). Unlike starch, many of these polysaccharides contain more monosaccharide types than simply glucose. Whole books are dedicated to the structure-function relationships of these polysaccharides, encompassing their unique properties, textures, typical use conditions, synergies, promoters, inhibitors, viscosities, and so on. This breadth of functional traits enables a chef to create unique formulations targeted to specific applications, whether they be a spherified sodium alginate–based gel, a thermo-reversible soft elastic methylcellulose gel that uniquely thickens as it is heated and thins as it is cooled, or a stable quick-acting guar gum used as a thickener in cold and hot water applications.

Lipids

Lipids, like carbohydrates, are composed of carbon, oxygen, and hydrogen, but most of the carbon atoms in lipids are bound only to other carbon atoms and to hydrogen. Without many oxygen atoms or hydroxyl groups, lipids are unable to hydrogen-bond with water. This makes them mostly insoluble in water but soluble in organic solvents like other oils. Lipids provide the most concentrated source of energy (9 kcal/g) of the food solids, essential dietary fatty acids (*linoleic* and *alpha-linolenic acids*), and are thought to contribute to the feeling of satiety (fullness) after eating.

Food lipids are classified as either oils or fats depending on their physical form at 68°F (20°C): Oils are liquid, and fats are solid. Oils typically come from plant sources (except for fish oils), and fats typically come from animal sources (except for coconut and palm kernel oils). Fats form crystal (physical) structures, and their melting points govern their stability and texture in foods.

Lipids in foods are most often triglyceride structures comprised of a glycerol backbone with three fatty acids bound to it via ester bonds. Factors that influence the functionality of lipids include the types, ratios, and locations of

FIGURE 2.6 **The structure of a native starch granule.**

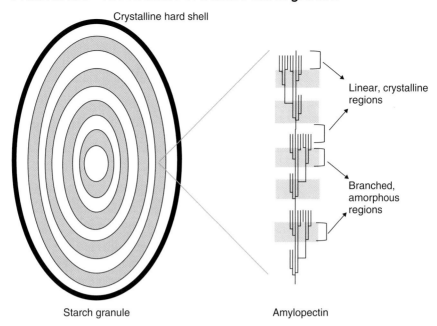

Crystalline hard shell

Linear, crystalline regions

Branched, amorphous regions

Starch granule

Amylopectin

Source: L. Mauer.

FIGURE 2.7 **Lipids: triglyceride structure. The** *R* **groups on the triglyceride structure represent individual fatty acids.**

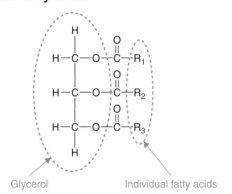

Glycerol   Individual fatty acids

Source: L. Mauer.

the fatty acids on the triglyceride backbone (including fatty acid chain length [number of carbons], level of saturation, number and location of double bonds, and whether they have a straight "*trans*" or kinked "*cis*" structure); the sources of the lipids (soybean, olive, lard, cocoa, etc.); the ratio of solid to liquid fractions at a given temperature; treatment of the lipids by *hydrogenation* or *interesterification*; the conditions used during chilling and tempering; the type and quantity of *emulsifiers* (if any); the degree of *oxidative* or *hydrolytic rancidity*; the smoke point; and the shipping and storage conditions.

The fatty acids that make up lipids are classified by the number of carbons (chain length between 4 and 24 carbons) and the presence and location of double bonds along this chain. Double bonds are areas of *unsaturation* because the carbon atom is not fully saturated with hydrogen atoms.

Saturated fatty acids contain no carbon-carbon double bonds (C=C), and *unsaturated fatty acids* contain at least one carbon-carbon double bond. Monounsaturated fatty acids, such as oleic acid, contain one carbon-carbon double bond, while polyunsaturated fatty acids, such as linolenic acid, contain more than one carbon-carbon double bond.

The linear structure of saturated fatty acids allows for closer chain packing in the triglyceride structure, which results in higher melting temperatures and greater likelihood that lipids containing more saturated fatty acids will be solid at room temperature than lipids containing more unsaturated fatty acids. The closer packing of straight fatty acids increases the van der Waals attractive forces between the fatty acids and provides greater resistance to melting—that is, more heat energy is required to destabilize them. Fats used for baking must have high melting points to impart the desired functionality to bakery products, such as laminating the dough and entrapping steam to leaven croissants or puff pastries. Therefore, baking fats contain a high concentration of saturated fats and/or trans fats. Solid products such as chocolates also contain saturated fats. Saturated fats (and *cholesterol*, a waxy substance found only in animals, including seafood) have been linked to negative health effects, including heart disease, obesity, and other illnesses, and must be declared on the *nutrition facts panel* on food labels. While all fats and oils are in reality made up of mixtures of saturated and unsaturated fatty acids distributed among the triglyceride "backbones," animal fats (except for fish oils) consist predominantly of saturated fatty acids, while vegetable oils are predominantly made up of unsaturated fatty acids (except for tropical oils such as coconut and palm kernel oil).

Unsaturated fatty acids can be classified as *cis* or *trans* based on the location of the hydrogen atoms attached to each

FIGURE 2.8 Common saturated and unsaturated fatty acids containing 18 carbons. The hydrogenation process can be used to convert fatty acids containing the same number of carbons from lower to higher degrees of saturation (for example, linolenic acid to linoleic acid, linoleic acid to oleic acid, and so on).

Fatty Acid Common Name	Number of Carbon Atoms	Number of Double Bonds	Typical Fat Source	Structure
Stearic	18	0 (saturated)	In most fats and oils, although it is more prevalent in animal fats than most plant fats (excluding cocoa butter and shea butter)	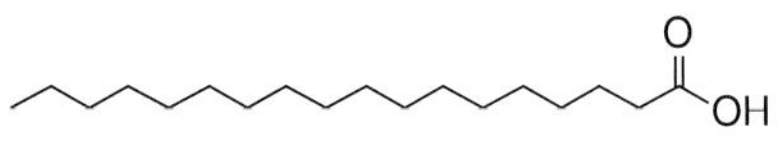
Oleic	18	1 (monounsaturated)	Although present in many animal and vegetable lipids, oleic acid is most commonly associated with olive oil.	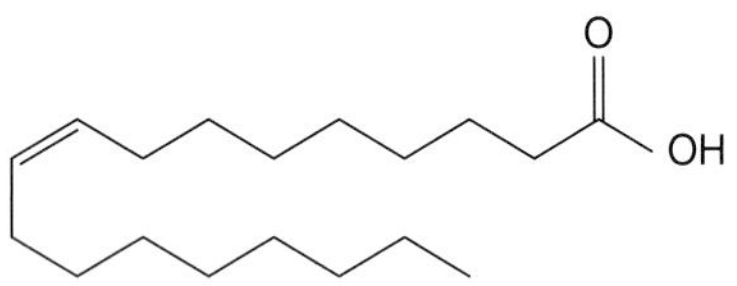
Linoleic	18	2 (polyunsaturated)	An essential omega-6 fatty acid found in nuts, seeds, and vegetable oils.	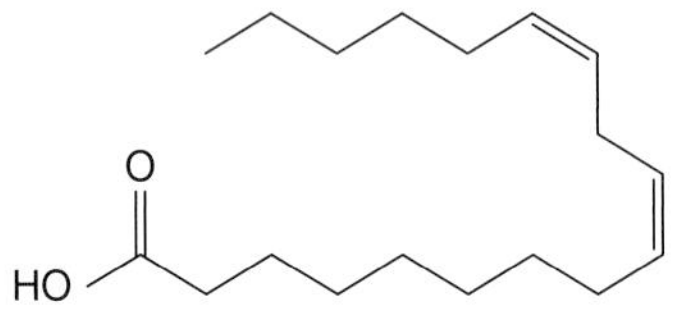
Alpha-Linolenic	18	3 (polyunsaturated)	An essential omega-3 fatty acid found in seeds, nuts, and notably soybean and canola oils.	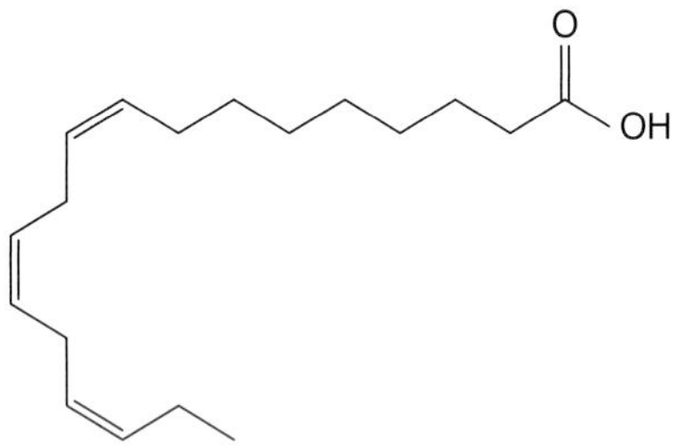

Source: L. Mauer.

of the paired carbons bound together by a double bond. Most natural sources of lipids contain cis unsaturated fatty acids that have the hydrogens on the same side of the C=C double bond, creating kinks in the linear structure. These kinks limit the closeness of fatty acid chain packing, thus reducing the melting point of the lipid (that is, less heat energy is required to destabilize them because there are fewer van der Waals attractive forces between the fatty acids). As the number of double bonds in a fatty acid increases, the structure becomes more kinked and the melting point decreases. That is why polyunsaturated fatty acids (containing more than one double bond) have very low melting temperatures (below room temperature) and are therefore liquid at room temperature. On the other hand, most trans fatty acids are created synthetically via *hydrogenation* and have hydrogens on opposite sides of the C=C double bond, creating a more linear structure that is similar to saturated fatty acids. The more linear trans structure allows *partially hydrogenated* vegetable shortenings to mimic the functionality and melting points of saturated fats

such as lard, but without the presence of cholesterol. Concerns have been raised about the negative health effects associated with consuming trans fats, and since 2006 trans fats must be declared on the nutrition facts panel of all packaged foods.

Hydrogenation is a reaction between hydrogen gas and unsaturated fatty acids in the presence of catalysts that ultimately results in a more saturated fatty acid. This is how unsaturated liquid oils are transformed into saturated (or partially saturated) solid fats and shortenings. Important uses of hydrogenation include control of physical and chemical properties, increasing the melting temperature of a lipid, enabling a cheaper oil to mimic more expensive fats, creating unique functional characteristics, and increasing the shelf life or stability of a liquid oil by saturating most of its highly reactive C=C double bonds, thereby reducing its tendency to undergo oxidative rancidity. As an intermediate of the hydrogenation reaction, trans fatty acids are produced, and partially hydrogenated lipids often contain trans fats. These trans fats have straighter structures than the initial cis structures and therefore have increased melting temperatures. A fully hydrogenated lipid does not contain trans fats; when the hydrogenation reaction is taken to completion, all fatty acids are converted into saturated structures.

Interesterification is used as an alternative to hydrogenation in order to solidify oils without trans fat formation. Interesterification is the process by which fatty acids are rearranged on the glycerol backbone to achieve desired performance characteristics. Because lipid function is determined by the types of fatty acids and their distribution on the glycerol backbone, interesterification can be used to modify or create new triglycerides to improve consistency and usefulness of the fats or oils for targeted applications by replacing unsaturated fatty acids with more saturated ones on the glycerol backbone, or rearranging the fatty acid locations on the glycerol backbone to change triglyceride packing structures. The process can be conducted enzymatically or with chemical catalysts. However, even though it is now possible to create vegetable oil-based shortenings without trans fats, these methods are more expensive than hydrogenation.

Rancidity, or off-flavor development in lipids, is caused by hydrolytic or oxidative reactions. Hydrolytic rancidity involves the cleavage of the ester bond of one or more fatty acids in the triglyceride structure, resulting in free fatty acids as they are cut from the glycerol backbone. Chemicals, high heat (such as deep frying), or lipase enzymes in the presence of water can cause hydrolytic rancidity. The reaction can be either desirable (as in the flavor development in mold-ripened cheeses) or undesirable (rancid, "painty" or varnish-like flavor development in oils or fried products). The reaction cannot be reversed; once the rancid flavor has developed, it is permanent. And any foods prepared with rancid oil will taste rancid as well; it will not be diminished by cooking.

Oxidative rancidity results most often from a complex series of reactions between oxygen in the environment and unsaturated fatty acids, causing the formation of a *free radical* due to the abstraction (removal) of a hydrogen atom from the fatty acid molecule. The most reactive hydrogen atoms (those requiring the least energy for their removal from the fatty acid molecule) are attached to carbon atoms adjacent to the C=C double bonds. When the hydrogen is removed from the carbon, the carbon is left with an unpaired electron, and the resulting fatty acid radical is known as the *alkyl radical*. A series of structural shifts occur in the fatty acid once the alkyl radical is formed; then, during the propagation phase of lipid oxidation, the free radical covalently binds with oxygen. The reaction terminates when this oxygen then covalently binds to an additional hydrogen (which might have been abstracted from another fatty acid, thereby cascading and perpetuating the oxidation process), and the structure becomes a *hydroperoxide*.

As the number of double bonds on a fatty acid molecule increases (i.e., the molecule is more unsaturated), the susceptibility of the fatty acid to oxidative reactions increases.

Polyunsaturated fatty acids (typically found in vegetable and fish oils) are more likely to be involved in oxidative rancidity reactions than monounsaturated or saturated fatty acids. This is evident when comparing the oxidative rancidity reaction rates in polyunsaturated fish oils, which develop off flavors extremely rapidly, to more saturated butter or palm oil products. Increased oxidative rancidity occurs when the degree of unsaturation in the fatty acids increases, oxygen or metal catalysts (iron, copper, tin, nickel) are present, pro-oxidants such as lipoxygenase or singlet oxygen are present, and/or there is prolonged exposure to high temperatures or ionizing radiation. Oxidative rancidity can be delayed by removing as much oxygen as possible from the packaged product (using vacuum packaging or *gas flushing* with an inert gas such as nitrogen, or adding an oxygen-scavenging sachet to the package), storing products at low temperatures, and/or adding *antioxidants* (ascorbic acid, tocopherols, BHA, BHT, TBHQ) or *metal chelating agents* (such as EDTA) to the product.

Proteins

Food proteins are composed of carbon, oxygen, hydrogen, and nitrogen. Proteins, like carbohydrates, exist as small building blocks that polymerize via unique covalent bonds to form large molecules. The building blocks of proteins are 20 unique *amino acids* that contain *amine* ($-NH_2$) and *carboxylic acid* ($-COOH$) functional groups. These allow amino acids to link together via strong covalent bonds known as *peptide bonds*. Amino acids can only link together in a linear sequence. Sequences of up to about 10 amino acids are known as *peptides*, and sequences of many amino acids (typically from 100 to 500) are known as *proteins*.

The varieties of structure and texture that proteins give to many foods surpass those of carbohydrates and lipids. Proteins accomplish this diversity thanks to the different *polarities* and unique side groups of the 20 standard amino acids found in nature. *Polarity* is a measure of the orientation of electronic charge in a molecule. Charged, partially charged, or unbalanced molecules are *polar* and *hydrophilic* (water-loving) because water molecules themselves are polar. Neutral molecules are *non-polar*, unlike water, so they are *hydrophobic* (water-fearing). The polymer chain length and sequence of amino acids determine the physico-chemical, structural, biological, and functional properties of a protein.

The 20 amino acids, with their unique polarities, form the basis for a kind of code. In the same way that a binary sequence of only 1's and 0's can represent any number, the amino acid sequence of a protein can create countless varieties of structures. A protein's amino acid sequence is known as its *primary structure*. The primary structure describes the amino acid sequence but not the shape of the protein.

Protein shape and structure are so complex that proteins are described by their *secondary*, *tertiary*, and *quaternary* structures in addition to the amino acid sequence. The amino acids of a protein chain attract and repel one another because of their different polarities and their tendency to hydrogen bond with each other. These interactions cause sections of the protein to bend and fold into characteristic structures.

FIGURE 2.9 The primary, secondary, tertiary, and quaternary structure of proteins.

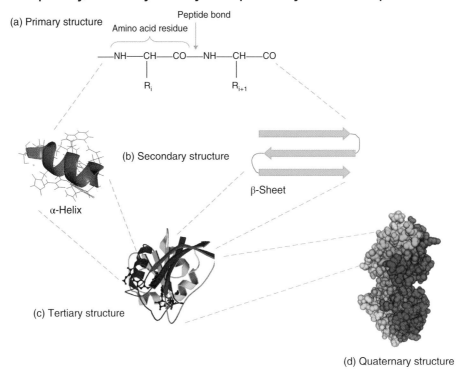

(a) Primary structure

Peptide bond

Amino acid residue

$-NH-CH-CO-NH-CH-CO$

R_i R_{i+1}

(b) Secondary structure

β-Sheet

α-Helix

(c) Tertiary structure

(d) Quaternary structure

Source: L. Mauer.

Common structures include helices, sheets, turns, and random coils. These structural configurations define a protein's *secondary structure*.

The tertiary structure of proteins is the three-dimensional organization of the complete ("folded" or "unfolded") protein chain as determined by the primary and secondary structures, the environment, and any processing treatments the protein has undergone. Proteins in foods are generally divided into two main classes of tertiary structures: fibrous proteins (common in structural proteins, such as meat proteins) and globular proteins (compact, spherical, or elliptical molecules, such as enzymes, egg proteins, myoglobin, and the whey proteins in milk).

In an aqueous (water-based) environment, globular proteins will fold into tertiary structures that minimize the exposure of hydrophobic amino acids to the water, orienting these amino acids in the interior of the folded structure. Heating a globular protein above its denaturation temperature causes an unfolding of the tertiary structure and exposure of these hydrophobic amino acids to the environment. This unfolded, denatured structure has different properties (including reduced solubility and potential for precipitation, increased viscosity, and gel formation) than the native, unheated protein. The shear forces created in mixing (such as whipping an egg white) or alterations in pH can also denature the tertiary structure of globular proteins. In general, globular proteins are more sensitive to heat or shear than are fibrous proteins and have lower denaturation temperatures.

Quaternary protein structures are created by the merging of two or more proteins. Important examples of quaternary structures are casein micelles in milk, which further aggregate to form cheese; *myoglobin*, responsible for the color of meat muscle tissues; and wheat gluten complexes (between gliadin and glutenin wheat proteins). Wheat gluten is formed from glutenin and gliadin when water and mechanical energy (kneading) are added to make bread dough. Gluten complexes form a viscous, elastic, and extensible mesh that traps steam and carbon dioxide and allows breads to rise during baking.

●Physical Structures (Amorphous and Crystalline) of Solids

Foods are typically very complex mixtures of carbohydrates, lipids, and proteins. On their own as pure ingredients, most of these building blocks exist as solids at room temperature, and often remain solid even during cooking. Oils are the only significant exception. Because the solid state is the norm for the majority of the building blocks of food, its properties must be well understood.

Solid compounds can be classified into two groups of relevance to foods: *crystalline* solids and *amorphous* solids. Common *crystalline ingredients* include sugar and table salt. To the naked eye, particles of granulated sugar and table salt seem to have well-defined geometric shapes. This is because at the molecular level, each individual atom or molecule in a crystal arranges itself in a consistent, repeating pattern. The orderly geometry of a crystal observed by the naked eye reflects the orderly geometry of its atoms or molecules at the atomic scale.

Crystalline structure is not limited to individual crystalline ingredients. Many foods also contain crystalline solids. Milk fat in cold butter exists as a crystalline solid, as do the cocoa butter in chocolate and the amylopectin regions of starch in native starch granules.

Common *amorphous ingredients* include powdered milk and instant coffee granules. To the naked eye, these particles seem to have no uniform shape of any kind. The same logic applies to amorphous ingredients as to crystalline ones. Their visible structures have no well-defined geometric shapes because their atoms or molecules arrange themselves in random jumbles that lack a consistent, repeating pattern. The random shape of an amorphous particle observed by the naked eye reflects the disorderly geometry of its atoms or molecules at the atomic scale. Amorphous structures are typical of most foods containing complex mixtures of ingredients.

The amorphous or crystalline structures of the assorted solid components in a complex food dictate molecular mobility, water-solid interactions, and the ultimate texture and stability of the food. Food properties related to changes in crystalline and amorphous structures include annealing (heat treatment used in modification of starches), starch retrogradation (a reaction in which the amylose and amylopectin chains realign themselves into crystalline formations, causing staling in baked goods and *syneresis* in starch-thickened puddings), film formation and properties, physical aging, chemical and physical stability, encapsulation and controlled release, stickiness, agglomeration (a process for adhering smaller, finer particles together into larger clusters or "agglomerates" used to enhance solubility of powdered ingredients), and caking (unwanted clumping of free-flowing powders).

For all practical food purposes, solid fats (for example, refrigerated butter), salt, and ice are crystalline structures. Crystalline solids are characterized by having long-range or three-dimensional atomic order and defined melting temperatures. Table salt (sodium chloride) is an *ionically bonded* crystalline structure; ice is a *hydrogen-bonded* crystal; and the relatively weak *van der Waals forces* between fatty acids in lipids contribute to the crystalline structure of fats. Because fatty acid and triglyceride structures vary in food fats, the melting temperature range of fats is much broader than the melting temperature range of the more uniform ice crystal structure. A "plastic fat" (spreadable fat, such as room-temperature butter) has both solid crystalline fat structures and liquid oil regions in combination such that the plastic fat behaves as a solid at rest but deforms (spreads) easily once a force is applied.

Polymorphism describes a solid, such as cocoa butter in chocolate, which can exist in more than one crystalline form. Changes in the fat crystal structure can lead to unwanted fat bloom and related texture and melting point changes in chocolates, resulting in a product that does not melt in the mouth but instead has a grainy or brittle mouthfeel. Crystal structure changes during storage always shift to a more stable, lower-energy polymorph. In the case of chocolates, however, the most desirable polymorph is not the most stable

form but can exist in a metastable state. The tempering of chocolates is used to control the fat crystal structure by controlled heating, cooling, and crystal seeding processes designed to stabilize the desirable metastable crystal structure. However, improper tempering or storage in fluctuating temperatures enables the metastable crystals to reorient themselves into the most stable polymorph, which has a larger crystal packing habit and higher melting temperature. Because this melting temperature is higher than the temperature in our mouths, the bloomed chocolate has a very different texture than the desirable "melt-in-your-mouth," creamy characteristics of well-tempered chocolate. Control of temperature, formulation, mixing, and storage conditions can ensure desired crystal structures in foods (such as confectioneries). Challenges can arise in foods with different lipid systems in different components, such as a cookie with a chocolate coating, wherein lipid migration or bloom can result from interactions between the lipid systems, resulting in unwanted sensory defects.

●Water

Depending on your point of view, the preceding sections may have been misleading: *water* is the true building block of food. To the food scientist, water is H_2O—a small, polar, ubiquitous molecule that interacts with all foods and controls the way foods change temperature (exchange heat with their environment), texture (lose crispiness or chewiness), shape (dissolve in water), and even how likely they are to support the growth of spoilage organisms or pathogens. The following sections will explore water's relationship to food in great detail because of its central importance to all foods.

A water molecule is comprised of one oxygen atom and two hydrogen atoms bound by strong O-H covalent ("shared electron") bonds into an H-O-H structure. The electrons are more attracted to the oxygen atom, which causes the oxygen atom to have a slight negative charge and the hydrogen atoms to have a slight positive charge, creating a large dipole moment (separation of positive and negative charges) in the water molecule. As a result, water is a polar molecule—that is, one with a positive end (South pole) and a negative end (North pole). This distribution of charges and polar traits contributes to the ability of microwaves to heat foods. In a microwave, the oscillating electric field causes the charged water molecules within the food to spin, creating friction, and this internal friction creates heat.

Water molecules interact with each other via hydrogen bonds, attractive interactions between a hydrogen atom from one water molecule and a lone pair of electrons on the oxygen atom from another water molecule (the hydrogen-bond acceptor). As such, each water molecule can hydrogen-bond with up to four other water molecules via two hydrogen-bond donor and two hydrogen-bond acceptor interactions. The physical state of water (ice, water, steam) depends on the extent of hydrogen bonding—ice has the most, steam has the least. The network created between water molecules results in large values for *heat capacity*, melting point, boiling point,

FIGURE 2.10 **Arrangement of atoms in crystalline and amorphous structures, and resulting appearance under a polarized light microscope.**

Ordered crystalline structure

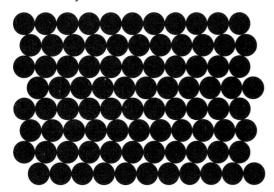

Random amorphous structure

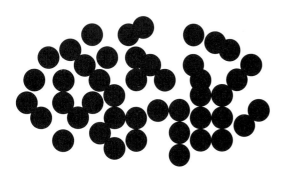

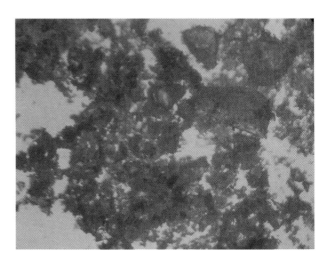

Source: M. Allan and L. Mauer.

and enthalpies (energy needed to break the hydrogen bonds) of phase transitions between ice, water, and steam. Water has a high *surface tension*, evident by the formation of water droplets, due to the strong attraction of the water molecules to each other.

Water is a common heat-transfer medium used in traditional food preparation (boiling, steaming, simmering, poaching, parboiling, blanching, stewing, braising, etc.). There are numerous reasons why water must be controlled in food preparation and processing: to prevent microbial growth from causing spoilage or disease, to extend shelf life and allow for distribution and storage by reducing the rates of biochemical, chemical, physical, and microbiological reactions; to minimize textural, quality, functional, and nutritional changes during distribution; and to improve convenience with new products. The amount of water in foods can be controlled by dehydration or evaporation (using dry-heat methods such as baking, deep frying, extrusion, air tunnel, spray, drum, or freeze drying), crystallization of solids, the addition of *humectants* (compounds such as salts,

sugars, and glycols that promote the retention of water), or freezing. While *dehydration* and *evaporation* both involve physical removal of water, dehydration typically results in a solid product such as dried fruits and vegetables, or powders, whereas evaporation or concentration results in a viscous liquid product such as sweetened condensed milk or juice concentrates.

A food emulsion is a liquid system containing two phases (continuous and dispersed) comprised of two immiscible liquids (typically, oil and water) that is often stabilized by *emulsifiers*. The creation and stabilization of emulsions is important because water is polar and is a major component of most foods, while lipids are non-polar and are largely insoluble (immiscible) in water. Without an emulsifier present, the density and solubility differences between the oil and the water will promote separation, although increasing the viscosity of the continuous phase (for example, by using gums or starches to thicken water) or decreasing the droplet size of the dispersed phase (for example, by homogenization of the fat globules present in milk, or by high-shear mixing in the

FIGURE 2.11   Water: single molecule and multiple hydrogen-bound molecules.

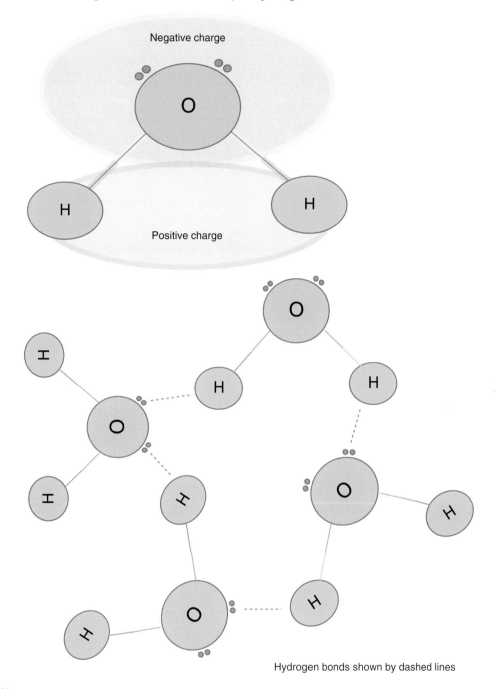

Hydrogen bonds shown by dashed lines

Source: L. Mauer.

preparation of "creamy" salad dressings or mayonnaise) can slow the separation. Of course, in the case of mayonnaise, it is not just high-shear mixing that holds the emulsion together. One of the key ingredients in mayonnaise is egg yolk, which is rich in *lecithin*, a powerful emulsifier.

An emulsifier is an ingredient (sometimes called a surfactant, or surface active agent) that stabilizes an emulsion by reducing interfacial tension (the tension that occurs in the contact area between a hydrophilic and hydrophobic substance that creates a drive for separation) between the oil and water. Different emulsifiers function in different ways: by creating repulsive forces between the dispersed droplets that prevent them from *coalescing*; by creating steric hindrance, in which the size of the emulsifier coating the dispersed droplets prevents interactions between them; or by physically separating the dispersed droplets from the continuous phase via a solid adsorbed coating (such as paprika or mustard solids in mayonnaise).

Some emulsifiers employ several of these mechanisms. For example, amphiphilic proteins (compounds having both hydrophilic and lipophilic groups) and phospholipids (like the lecithin in egg yolks) orient themselves between the dispersed and continuous phases in an emulsion and provide a coating that separates the phases and reduces interfacial tension while also creating electrostatic repulsive forces to keep the dispersed droplets apart. In theory, the selection of an emulsifier is based on HLB values (the ratio between hydrophilic and lipophilic groups in the emulsifier) and the type of product the emulsifier will be added to. HLB values for food emulsifiers range between 1 and 20; values of 1 to 8 indicate a more lipophilic emulsifier, and values of 9 to 20 correspond to hydrophilic emulsifiers. Acetylated monoglycerides have an HLB of 1.5, soy lecithin has an HLB near 8, and polysorbates generally have HLB values greater than 10. Emulsion stability is favored by the solubility of a given emulsifier in the continuous phase; therefore, lipophilic emulsifiers work better in water-in-oil emulsions (such as oil-based salad dressings, sauces, and butters), while hydrophilic emulsifiers work better in oil-in-water emulsions (such as beverages). In practice, most stable food emulsions contain more than one type of emulsifier.

Water-Solid Interactions

Because combinations of solid food ingredients (fats, carbohydrates, and proteins) and water are common in most foods, understanding and controlling water-solid interactions is important for creating and stabilizing foods. Special characteristics enable the water molecule to interact with solids by various modes. These include its small size (which makes it a good penetrant and space filler) and its ability to form extensive hydrogen bond networks as a direct result of its ability to act as both a hydrogen-bond donor and acceptor. Understanding how water interacts with solids is important for ensuring shelf stability of food products.

Water interacts with solids through several mechanisms, but deliquescence (adsorption and condensation of moisture from the air leading to dissolution) by crystalline ingredients, and absorption of moisture into the internal structure of amorphous (non-crystalline) materials are likely to have the greatest impact on food product quality when solid products are stored in environments containing high relative humidity.

Deliquescent, crystalline food ingredients such as sugars (glucose, fructose, sucrose, lactose), inorganic salts (sodium and potassium chlorides), organic acids (citric and acetic acids), and vitamins (ascorbic acid, sodium ascorbate, some of the B vitamins) are highly water soluble. Deliquescence is a *first-order phase transformation* in which certain crystalline solids dissolve when the relative humidity (RH) of the surroundings exceeds the critical relative humidity (RH_0) of the solid ingredient. A familiar example of deliquescence is the caking of sodium chloride in saltshakers during the humid summer months, when the RH exceeds 75 percent, which is the RH_0 of NaCl. Deliquescence affects both the chemical and physical stability of food products and is particularly important in dry powder products, ingredient blends, and products like candies and pralines in which crystallization is important to control. Vitamin C is much more stable below its deliquescence point than above it. Individual ingredients are

FIGURE 2.12 An oil-in-water emulsion depicting a continuous water phase, a dispersed oil phase, and an amphiphilic emulsifier oriented between the two phases.

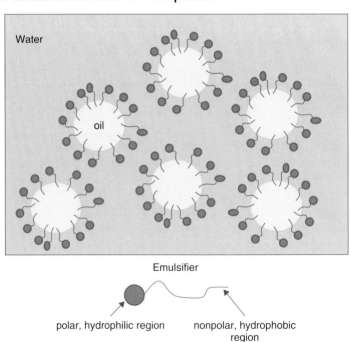

Source: L. Mauer.

FIGURE 2.13 **Water-solid interactions.**

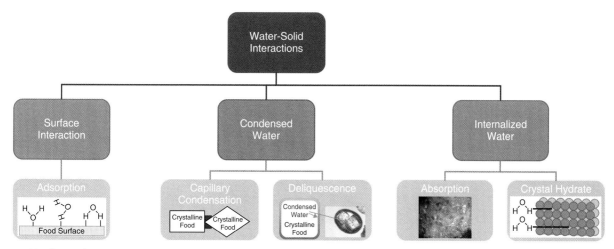

Source: M. Allan and L. Mauer.

more stable than ingredient blends in which interactions between the ingredients lower the deliquescence RH and the product becomes more susceptible to lower RHs. To avoid deliquescence in ingredients, premixes, and products, it is important to maintain storage conditions below the deliquescence RH of these products, both outside and inside the package, by using packaging materials with appropriate barrier properties or *desiccants*.

To promote the deliquescence of an ingredient or ingredient blend, the product can be stored at RHs above the deliquescence RH, or the deliquescence RH can be lowered to below that of the surroundings. For example, sucrose can be hydrolyzed by an invertase enzyme or acidic ingredient to produce glucose and fructose, and the blend of ingredients has a lower deliquescence point than the starting sugar. In RH and temperature conditions in which the sucrose is stable as a crystalline solid, the hydrolyzed blend of monosaccharides deliquesces (dissolves) to form a sweet, viscous syrup.

An amorphous material is a non-crystalline solid in which the atoms have a less ordered arrangement than a crystal; therefore, amorphous solids are not as compact in structure as crystalline materials, and thus water can be absorbed into their inner structure (much like a sponge absorbs water). Absorbed water acts as a plasticizer and has numerous effects on the structure and functionality of the material. Some of these changes include decreases in mechanical strength and viscosity and increases in chemical reactivity and the tendency to crystallize. Amorphous solids can exist in a brittle, glassy form or a viscous, rubbery form, depending on the conditions (most notably temperature or RH). Think of the difference in structure and texture of a fresh, crisp cracker (glassy) and a stale cracker that has been exposed to environmental RHs high enough to soften the texture (rubbery), or a soft candy at room temperature (rubbery) and that same candy hardened at refrigerated temperature (glassy).

The temperature at which an amorphous solid transitions between the glassy and the rubbery state is defined as the glass transition temperature (T_g), the temperature at which the amorphous solid becomes soft upon heating or brittle upon cooling. Increasing the amount of absorbed moisture decreases the temperature at which the glass transition occurs because water has a very low T_g itself and acts as a plasticizer. In temperatures at and above T_g or RH conditions that lower the T_g below the environmental temperature, the molecular mobility increases and the viscosity decreases, resulting in structural changes such as loss of crispness, collapse, and increased stickiness. Cotton candy is an example of an amorphous product that is initially below its T_g when formed but becomes quite sticky after absorbing moisture from a humid environment that drops the T_g to below room temperature, at which point the spun sugar threads collapse into a sticky, viscous mass.

Understanding how water interacts with solids when they are directly combined is important in preparing batters, doughs, sauces, and beverages. To be functional in a product, the ingredients must be soluble in water to some extent. *Solubility* is the ability of a substance to dissolve; the substance that is dissolving is called a *solute*, and the substance in which the solute is dissolved is called a *solvent*. A mixture of solute and solvent is called a *solution*. A solid dissolves best in a solvent with similar polarity: "like dissolves like." Water is polar and therefore readily dissolves polar solids; lipids are non-polar and do not dissolve in water. As a solid dissolves, bonds that hold it together are broken, and molecules of the solid are inserted into the structure of the solvent and surrounded by its molecules. The hydrogen bonds in water readily break and reform (which enables it to be poured) and will readily form hydrogen bonds with polar solids (such as sugars). Solids with charges (such as ionic charges in salts) also readily dissolve in water, and salt forms of ingredients (such as the sodium salt of ascorbic acid, known as sodium ascorbate, or sodium caseinate, compared to casein) tend to be more soluble than the parent compound.

Beverages and sauces are obvious examples of foods requiring high solubility of ingredients. If ingredients are insoluble, they will precipitate out or float to the surface of

FIGURE 2.14 A glass transition phase diagram for amorphous solids, showing the effects of moisture content and temperature on the glass transition temperature and state of the solid during storage and during product preparation.

Glass transition phase diagram for products during storage

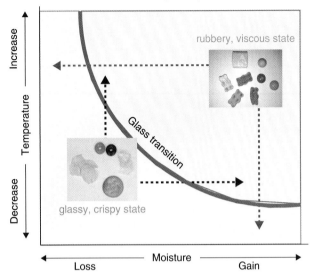

Glass transition phase diagram for a pasta product from production through preparation

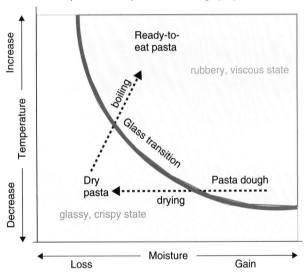

Source: M. Allan and L. Mauer.

the solution unless formulation strategies for stabilization are employed (such as adding gums to chocolate milk to suspend the insoluble chocolate solids, or adding an emulsifier to keep the oil in a salad dressing in suspension). Proteins may contain both hydrophilic and hydrophobic (polar and non-polar) amino acids and therefore have varying degrees of solubility. Interestingly, the protein complex of wheat gluten, once formed in dough, becomes insoluble in water. This allows wheat bread doughs to expand and trap steam pockets during baking, and *durum wheat* pastas to remain intact during boiling. Wheat doughs can be washed in water, rinsing away the starch fraction and leaving behind the water-insoluble mass of gluten. Although likely not appetizing, this gluten mass can be baked to visualize the viscoelastic expansion of the protein and entrapment of steam during baking.

The State of Water When Solids Are Present

Water is a small and mobile molecule. In fact, water is continuously moving within food products, although the rate of movement differs significantly depending on the location and type of solids present, and the temperature. Water can be classified into categories based on differences in mobility and interactions with solids. In Zone I (low *water activity* and *moisture content*), water is strongly attracted (sorbed) to the surface of a solid. This is the least mobile form of water, and the water acts as if it is part of the solid. Sometimes this water is referred to as "tightly bound"; however, it is important to keep in mind that water does not covalently bond to anything and interacts only via weak hydrogen bonding networks that are constantly breaking and reforming. The term "tightly bound" refers most closely to the difficulty in removing this type of water from a food system. It is nearly impossible to remove all water from foods.

Additional water beyond Zone I can influence chemical reactivity by acting as a reactant, product, medium, or a plasticizer. In Zone II (intermediate moisture and water activity), additional layers of water build up on the surface of the solid. The attraction of this water to the solid is reduced compared with Zone I water, but the water is still close enough to be attracted to the solid surface. Due to this decreased (but still present) attraction, Zone II water is more mobile than Zone I water. This mobility enables reactions (such as *Maillard browning*) that could not occur if only Zone I water was present. As water activity and moisture content increase in Zone II, water mobility increases and food texture softens. Small increases in moisture content will lead to large increases in water activity, which can have drastic effects on the texture of dry or crispy food products (crackers, potato chips, etc.).

When enough water is present to no longer be attracted to the solid surface, the additional water is classified as bulk phase or free water (Zone III). This water is highly mobile, reactive (for example, in *hydrolysis reactions*), can act as a solvent, and supports the growth and toxin production of pathogens and the proliferation of spoilage microorganisms. Many preservation processes attempt to eliminate spoilage by lowering the availability of water to microorganisms. Reducing the amount of free water also minimizes other undesirable chemical changes that occur during storage. The processes used to reduce the amount of free water in consumer products include techniques such as evaporation and concentration, dehydration, and freeze drying. Freezing is another common approach to controlling spoilage. Water in frozen foods is in the form of ice crystals and therefore unavailable to microorganisms and for reactions with other food components.

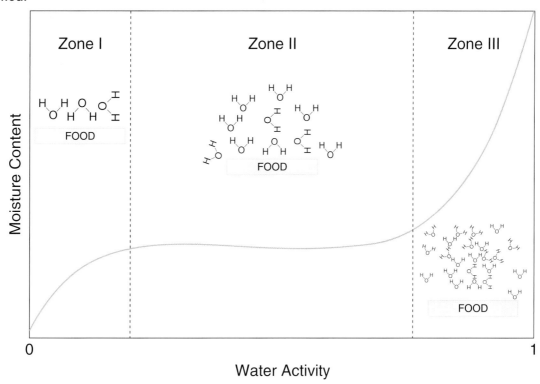

Source: L. Mauer.

Water Activity

Water activity (a_w), is a measure of the relative escaping tendency (also known as "fugacity" or tendency for evaporation) of water from a food compared to the behavior of pure water. Water activity has been loosely described as the availability of water present in a food to act as a solvent and participate in chemical or biochemical reactions, but it is important to note here that the "a" in "a_w" stands for *activity*, not availability or amount. By definition, water activity is the ratio of the *equilibrium partial vapor pressure of water in a system* (p_w) to the *equilibrium partial vapor pressure of pure liquid water* (p^o_w) at the same temperature. The water activity can be measured as the relative humidity (RH) directly above the sample at a constant temperature (T) and pressure when in equilibrium. Water activity is used as a measure of risk to understand what microorganisms can grow in a food product (keeping in mind that lower water activities do not necessarily kill the microorganisms; they may remain dormant at a_ws below their threshold for growth) and what types of chemical reactions might occur. The higher the water activity (up to a maximum of 1: the a_w of pure water), the more likely that food will spoil. In addition to influencing microbial spoilage, water activity can play a significant role in determining the activity of enzymes in foods and can have a major impact on their color, texture, taste, and aroma.

As stated, the a_w of pure water is 1, the a_w of oil (or solids in the complete absence of water) is 0, and most foods have an intermediate a_w between 0 and 1. As a rule of thumb, the higher the a_w, the more mobile the water and the faster it can diffuse within a food or escape from it entirely.

It is important to note that the water activity of a food is not the same thing as its moisture content. Water activity, unlike moisture content, expresses how water behaves in food instead of how much water is in the food. In a comparison of equal mixtures of sugar, salt, and sand (50 g) in water (200 mL), the water activity of the sugar and salt solutions was much lower than that of the sand mixture, even though the water-solid ratio was constant. Because there was little interaction between the sand and water, the water activity of this mixture (>0.998) was close to that of water (1). The hydrogen bonding between the sugar and water slowed the water's escaping tendency, resulting in a water activity of 0.977. The a_w of the salt solution was even lower, 0.851, because salt dissociates into two ions (sodium and chloride) in solution (compared to the single sugar molecule), and the molecular weight of salt is less than that of sugar, resulting in more molecules per gram (therefore more opportunities for binding more water molecules), and ionic interactions of water with salt are stronger than simple hydrogen bonding with sugar. All of these factors decrease the ability of water to escape from the salt solution, thereby lowering its a_w.

When we try to expand the concept of a_w and moisture content relationships to food reformulations, such as reducing sodium or creating sugar-free products, it becomes a challenge to keep the water-solid ratio constant. For example, a sugar-sweetened strawberry jam has a lower a_w than an artificially sweetened one. In both jams, water binds to every molecule of sweetener in order to dissolve it. But the sugar-sweetened jam contains far more molecules of sugar to bind far more molecules of water than the artificially sweetened one. This lowers the a_w of the naturally sweetened jam to 0.87, compared to the a_w of the artificially sweetened jam, which is closer to 0.95. When food products are reformulated to reduce or remove sugar and salt, two ingredients that are capable of lowering the a_w of solutions, the reformulated product usually has a higher a_w.

Many foods have similar moisture contents but drastically different a_ws. Examples include honey and condensed milk, with a_ws of 0.56 and 0.84, respectively. Some foods with higher moisture content have a lower a_w than foods with lower moisture content. Examples include sliced bread (with a_w of 0.94) and soy sauce (with a_w of 0.86), even though the soy sauce has more than twice the moisture content of the bread.

Moisture migration within a multi-component food product (for example, a filled pastry) or between a food product and the environment is driven by differences in water activity, *not* differences in moisture content. Water moves from a region of high a_w to a region of low a_w until an equilibrium a_w is reached. If the environmental RH is higher than the a_w of a food product (that is, high relative humidity in the air), moisture will migrate into the product if a barrier package does not separate the product from the environment. Potato chips often lose their crispness after the package has been opened because the environmental RH on a humid summer day exceeds the a_w of the product. In the case of a pastry with a fruit filling, it is important to formulate the crust and the filling to the same a_w to avoid moisture migration from the filling into the crust, making it soggy, or to provide an edible moisture barrier between the crust and filling.

Adding deliquescent ingredients (soluble solids such as salt or sugar) to food products can lower the water activity of a product by interacting with the water and slowing down its escaping tendency; however, the a_w cannot easily be lowered below the deliquescence RH of the added ingredient(s) without removing water. Salt can be added to processed cheese spread to lower the a_w and enable a longer shelf life for cheese-and-cracker snack products, although the deliquescence point of salt (75 percent RH) is higher than the a_w of the cracker (often near 0.3 a_w, which is equivalent to 30 percent RH), so an additional hurdle for moisture migration is needed. Spray oil coating applied to crackers is one mechanism to hinder moisture migration into the cracker. Modifying the cheese filling formulations to blend a cheese powder with lipids and flavors is another approach for lowering the a_w of the cheese filling to that of the cracker. Replacing water with glycerol or oil can also lower the a_w while maintaining a soft texture in a product. Glycerol is commonly added to raisins to maintain a soft texture in the presence of crisp cereal flakes and is also added to tortillas to maintain a soft texture for extended shelf life applications (including space travel!).

Water activity affects chemical and physical degradation reactions (for example, lipid oxidation, *non-enzymatic browning*, loss of crispness) and microbial growth in food products. In fact, it is a_w, and not moisture content, that has been linked to the growth of microorganisms, and there are upper and lower critical a_ws for a given reaction or microorganism. At an

FIGURE 2.16 **The relationship between moisture content and water activity for a range of foods.**

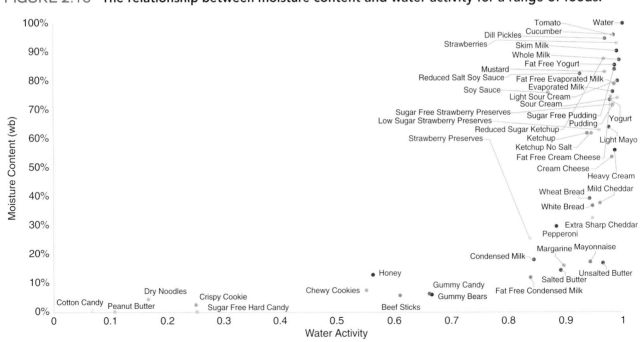

Source: Y. Ismail, Y. Shao, J. Sanchez, M. Allan, and L. Mauer.

a_w of 0.85 and higher, pathogenic microorganisms can grow and produce toxins in foods, while below a_w 0.85 the growth and toxin production of pathogens is prevented. Therefore, a potentially hazardous food (PHF) has an a_w ≥0.85 (and pH greater than 4.6). *Intermediate moisture foods* (such as raisins, jams, and jellies) have water activities in the range of 0.6 to 0.8, below the cutoff for pathogen growth. In this intermediate a_w range, products can have soft, deformable textures, and even though they won't promote the growth of pathogens, may still support the growth of molds. The critical a_w lower limit for any microbial growth is 0.6.

The *Maillard reaction* (non-enzymatic browning) occurs rapidly in this intermediate a_w range; this reaction requires an aqueous phase for the reactants (reducing sugars and proteins) to interact; therefore, if the a_w is too low, the reaction will be inhibited due to the lack of molecular mobility, while at an a_w above 0.8, the reaction will be inhibited due to too much water diluting the reactants. Enzyme activity increases as a_w rises above the minimum threshold because many enzymes require mobility to interact with substrates (either the enzyme or the substrate must have mobility).

Moisture Sorption Isotherms

Comparing water activity and moisture content enables the product developer to determine which reactions might be of concern for a given food product as well as the optimum range for the desired texture and stability. Formulation strategies, storage conditions, and packaging technologies can then be developed to address the reactions that might limit the quality of the product.

A moisture sorption isotherm (or *water vapor sorption isotherm*) shows the relationship between the moisture content and water activity of a food (at a constant temperature and pressure). The shape of an isotherm is governed by the

FIGURE 2.17 Water activity. Stability of foods as a function of water activity. Note the relative reaction rates across different water activities. Also note that foods formulated above water activity 0.85 must be temperature controlled or further processed for safety.

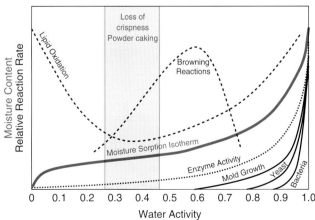

Source: Decagon Devices, Inc.

FIGURE 2.18 The moisture sorption profile of two different amorphous foods: cotton candy and wheat cracker. Different formulations and food types will exhibit different moisture sorption profiles as environmental relative humidity (equivalent to water activity) is increased.

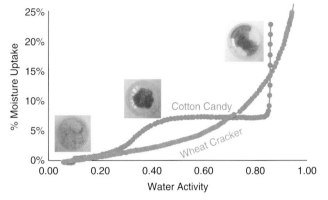

Source: M. Allan and L. Mauer.

chemical components and physical structure of the food product. When the moisture content is 0, the a_w of the product is also 0 (although this rarely, if ever, happens). As moisture content increases, a_w increases, although the relationship is not linear. Given enough time, food products equilibrate with the humidity of the environment (an open package of crackers on a humid day eventually results in a loss of texture when the moisture content and a_w exceed the crispy range). A moisture sorption isotherm illustrates how the moisture content of a food will respond to an increase or decrease in humidity because the a_w will equilibrate with the environmental RH. Understanding these responses is important for the analysis and design of various food transformation processes (e.g., drying, mixing, and storage), to predict changes in the chemical and physical stability of foods, and for the selection of suitable packaging materials. This in turn will influence the chemical stability and physical properties of the product. Comparing the moisture sorption isotherm of a product to the food stability map helps the product developer determine what reactions might be a concern in a food product with different moisture contents and water activities.

⬤Molecular Mobility

Another important contributor to food texture and stability is molecular mobility (Mm)—a term used to describe the movement and motion of food components. Chemical reactions depend on the molecular reactants coming into contact with each other with the proper orientation. To do this, the molecules must be mobile, and the rate of the reactions will depend on the amount of time it takes the molecules to "meet" each other in the food. Small molecules (water, oxygen) move more quickly than larger molecules (fats, proteins, carbohydrates). Liquids have more mobility than solids, and gases are the most mobile. An amorphous solid in the glassy state (such as a crisp potato chip or spun sugar in cotton candy) has less mobility than an amorphous solid in the rubbery state (the same potato chip after exposure to humidity loses its crispness, and cotton candy becomes a sticky mass). The molecular mobility in crystalline solids is the most restricted.

If molecular movement is slowed or inhibited, then the stability of the food product will be enhanced because molecular reactivity will be reduced. Water can act as a plasticizer (a structure softener) and thus influence the molecular mobility of the material. This is seen in a cracker when it loses crispness as humidity or moisture content increases, the glass transition temperature is exceeded, and the structure enters the rubbery amorphous state. Mobility in dispersions depends on the state of the continuous phase. There is more mobility in a viscous solution in which water is the continuous phase than in a gel that has a protein or carbohydrate as the continuous phase. A product containing a filling (for example, fruit or cream) in contact with a pastry crust maintains crust quality longer if the continuous phase of the filling is in the form of a gel where water is the dispersed phase rather than a viscous solution where water is the continuous phase. This is because the water is less mobile when it is trapped in the dispersed phase rather than free to move around as the continuous phase. Therefore, it takes longer for the water to migrate from the filling into the crust.

⬤Heat-Driven Chemical Reactions in Foods
Gelatinization of Starches

Native starch has both crystalline and amorphous regions, which influences the important functionalities related to granule swelling: *gelatinization*, *pasting*, and *retrogradation*. Native undamaged starch is insoluble in cold water but reversibly absorbs small amounts of water and swells slightly, returning to its original size on drying. When starch is heated in water, the starch granules begin to swell as the heat and water disrupt the molecular order in the granules. As the temperature rises, the molecular mobility in the granule increases, more water enters the granule structure, and the granule irreversibly swells. As temperature further increases, hydrogen bonds are broken, and the crystalline regions in the granule structure begin to melt and further disrupt the granule structure. This loss of molecular order is called starch gelatinization. Amylose leaches out of gelatinized starch granules into the surrounding aqueous environment and thickens the solution, forming a starch paste or viscous solution with continued heating and stirring. During cooking, the starch granules continue to rupture, leaching more amylose and amylopectin into the solution and leaving starch granule fragments or "ghosts." For most food applications, starch gelatinization is a prerequisite for obtaining the desired functionality—that is, thickening, freeze-thaw stabilization,

FIGURE 2.19 **The effects of heat on wheat starch in water, as observed under a polarized light microscope. Gelatinization occurs when birefringence is lost.**

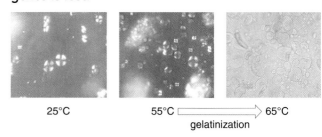

25°C   55°C ⬜➡ 65°C

gelatinization

Source: M. Allan and L. Mauer.

emulsification, and so on. *Note:* Pregelatinized or instantized starches have had their molecular structure disrupted by precooking to induce gelatinization and then have been dried down for later use in instant products or foods where the desirable functions of a cooked starch are wanted without the need to cook the product.

Upon cooling of the cooked starch paste or solution, the amylose and amylopectin that leached out of the starch granules will begin to interact with other starch molecules, forming small helical crystalline regions (junction zones) and possibly forming a gel. This process is called *starch retrogradation*. Amylose tends to retrograde faster than amylopectin (the branched structure of amylopectin slows down its retrogradation). Starch retrogradation is desirable for the formation of starch-based gels; however, it can also lead to undesirable quality changes such as *syneresis* (the contraction of a gel accompanied by the separating out of liquid) in puddings and custards, decreased viscosity and precipitation out of solution in soups and sauces, and bread staling. Staling is a slower process that involves the retrogradation of amylopectin; it can be reversed temporarily by reheating the product above the melting temperature of the starch crystalline structure (as in toasting). To slow the staling process, additives such as polar lipids and/or emulsifiers (e.g., lecithin, mono- and diglycerides) can be added to baked products; these interact with the starch and delay retrogradation.

Denaturation of Proteins

Heat denaturation of proteins involves conformational changes in the thermodynamically stable native structure of the protein via unfolding or alteration of the quaternary, tertiary, and/or secondary structure as a response to heat exposure. Denaturation can disrupt hydrogen and disulfide bonds, hydrophobic interactions, and salt bridges, but peptide bonds remain intact. The primary structure, or amino acid sequence, of the protein remains unchanged, as does the molecular weight. Functional properties affected by denaturation include changes in solubility, emulsifying capacity, *gelation* capacity, foaming properties, and enzyme or biological activity. In addition to heat, denaturation can be caused by changes in pH, salt

FIGURE 2.20   **Properties of denatured proteins.**

- Increased viscosity:
  - Unfolded proteins take up more space

Favorable in products like soups and gravies where consistency is important for consumer acceptance.

- Aggregation to form a gel

As in coagulated egg white or whey cheese due to denatured ovalbumin in egg white and whey proteins of milk.

- Decreased solubility

Affects the capacity of a protein to form emulsions, foams, or gels.

- Loss of biological activity or altered reactivity

Favorable in the prevention of enzymatic browning by inactivation of enzymes such as polyphenoloxidase, which cause browning in apples, avocados, and many other fruits and vegetables.

- More digestible

After they are unfolded, exposing more of their polymer structure to the environment, certain proteins such as egg white become more susceptible to the action of proteases—enzymes that break down proteins—thus improving the digestibility of the denatured protein versus the raw one.

Source: L. Mauer.

concentration, enzymes, addition of energy (shear, pressure), or freezing. Some ingredients can delay denaturation or protect the protein, including sugars, some salts, and some starches.

Gelation (Gel Formation)

Gelation occurs when a network of solids interacts in junction zones and entraps water (or other fluid). Although gels are mostly liquid, they behave like solids due to their continuous solid network. Many of the polymeric structures in foods (proteins and polysaccharides) are able to form the continuous networks characteristic of gels. A variety of junction zone types are formed in the polymer matrices of different types of polymers, including hydrophobic interactions, hydrogen bonds, electrostatic interactions, covalent interactions, crystallization, helix formation, and complexation. Stronger gels are formed by more numerous junction zones, and junction zones are formed by higher-energy interactions (such as covalent interactions).

To create a protein-based gel, the proteins dispersed in water are often heated beyond their denaturation temperature, and the unfolded proteins interact or cross-link to form the continuous solid structure of the gel. The junction zones formed between proteins and entrapment of water during gelation may be either reversible or irreversible, depending on the protein and type of junction zone. The polymeric networks formed by hydrogen bonding of *gelatin* molecules (a fibrous protein) are thermo-reversible. On cooling, the gelatin molecules begin to interact in helical segments that form junction zones leading to the formation of a gel; on reheating, the hydrogen bonds break and gelatin returns to the dispersed phase in the solution. Conversely, denatured globular proteins often form thermo-irreversible gels. When exposed to heat, whey and egg white proteins first denature and then interact via disulfide, hydrogen, and hydrophobic interactions to form gels. These gels are heat-set and stiffen,

instead of liquefy, when exposed to additional heat. The term coagulation is often applied to irreversible heat-setting of proteins. Soy protein gels, such as tofu, are formed by electrostatic bridges with divalent cations (calcium) between the proteins. Treating proteins with the enzyme transglutaminase can result in stable covalently cross-linked gels. This is how the ingredient popularly known as "meat glue" works.

Other polymers, such as starches and gums (for example, agar and sodium alginate), can also form the continuous phase in a gel structure. Starch gels are often formed by heating starch granules above the gelatinization temperature, which enables the amylose to leach out of the granule structure, and then cooling down the paste. During the cooling process, the amylose polymers realign themselves, form helical regions, and begin to crystallize in junction zones. When enough junction zones are formed between the amylose molecules, the viscous solution or paste (in which water is the continuous phase) converts to a gel structure in which the amylose is the continuous phase. Many gums used in foods are also able to form gels, and different gums form junction zones by different mechanisms and bonds, resulting in a variety of textures (tender, elastic, firm, brittle, malleable, etc.) and appearances (clear, shiny, opaque, cloudy, etc.). Unlike starch, some gums are able to form gels without heating, and a variety of cold gel structures are possible. Sodium alginate, iota carrageenan, and low-methoxyl pectins form gels in the presence of calcium ions, known as *ion-coagulated gels*, wherein calcium ions form the junction zones between these polymers. The alginate-calcium gel system is used extensively in the creation of an assortment of novel "caviars" (usually fruit-based) often seen where molecular gastronomy is practiced. Synergistic interactions between locust bean gum and xanthan gum lead to the formation of a firm thermo-reversible gel that is quite different from the hyperentangled solution structures of locust bean gum and xanthan gum when in solution by themselves.

Non-Enzymatic Browning Reactions

What makes many foods so appealing are the new flavors, aromas, and colors produced during cooking with *dry-heat methods*. Two main *non-enzymatic browning* reactions, caramelization and the Maillard reaction, produce these beneficial profiles. The result of these reactions is the reason bones are roasted and vegetables are caramelized for use in stocks and soups. Browned foods can have great-tasting roasted flavors, distinctive aromas, and rich dark amber colors.

Note: Certain foods, typically fresh fruits and vegetables, can undergo *enzymatic browning* that is not dependent on heating. Instead, these reactions typically take place at ambient temperatures, and are the result of cutting or bruising of the fruit or vegetable whereby cells are torn open, releasing enzymes (typically polyphenol oxidase), and the protective peel is breached, allowing exposure to oxygen, which is essential for this enzyme's activity. The enzyme acts on naturally occurring phenolic compounds found in fruits and vegetables, converting them to melanins (brown pigments). This is commonly seen in cut apples, bananas, avocados, potatoes, mushrooms, and many others. This type of browning can be inhibited by limiting exposure to oxygen (modified atmosphere or vacuum packaging), refrigeration, and acid dips to reduce the pH below the range where the enzyme is most active. Cooking will also eliminate this type of browning by irreversibly denaturing the enzyme.

Caramelization

Caramelization is the non-enzymatic browning of sugars when they are heated for prolonged times in concentrated solutions or dry forms, in the absence of proteins, particularly if the temperature exceeds the melting temperature of the sugar. During heating, sugar molecules expel water and undergo a series of thermal decomposition reactions that result in the production of brown-colored compounds. The familiar result of caramelization is the sweet brown flavor associated with caramelized sugar made from the pyrolysis of sucrose, but *not* caramel candies; these get their color from the *Maillard reaction* between the milk proteins and sugars in the formula. Other sugars such as maltose, fructose, and glucose also undergo pyrolysis, though the caramelization point varies for each. These reactions are mainly responsible for the rich colors and flavors that develop in crème brûlée and in caramelized vegetables (onions, mirepoix, roasted potatoes, etc.) through sautéing, roasting, grilling, and frying—but not through any moist-heat cooking techniques (the water prevents the temperature from rising high enough). That is why recipes calling for "sweating" vegetables (cooking without any added liquid) require a lid to be placed on the pan—to capture any moisture that exudes from the vegetables in order to provide a humid environment to prevent browning. Caramelization is also responsible for making brittle-type candies and caramel color, commonly used to provide brown coloring to an assortment of foods and beverages. Caramelization, if overdone, can also lead to undesirable flavors and colors, including a burnt-sugar smell.

FIGURE 2.21 Caramelization temperatures of mono- and disaccharides. Response of crystalline and amorphous sugars to heating. After 10 minutes at 320°F (160°C), crystalline sucrose and galactose did not melt, crystalline maltose and glucose melted but did not caramelize, crystalline fructose melted and caramelized, and amorphous sucrose caramelized. After 10 minutes at 392°F (200°C), all sugars melted and caramelized. Brown pigment differences are evident between the different types of sugars as well as between the crystalline and amorphous sucrose.

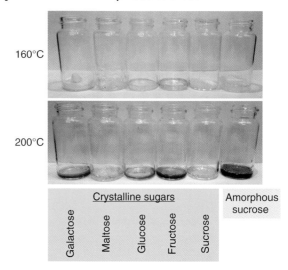

Source: Y. Ismail, Y. Shao, M. Allan, and L. Mauer.

Maillard Reaction

The *Maillard ("my-yard") reaction*, named after Louis-Camille Maillard, who investigated these reactions in the early 1800s, produces the roasted flavors and colors of products such as baked goods, toasted bread, French fries, roasted coffee, malted barley (for making beer and spirits), and seared meats. It is also responsible for the off colors produced as a result of extended dry storage of many foods, including powdered or condensed milk and cereal. The reaction occurs between the *carbonyl group* of a *reducing sugar* and the *amino group* of a protein, and is another type of non-enzymatic browning. (*Note:* Sucrose is not a reducing sugar and therefore cannot participate in Maillard browning without first being hydrolyzed into its component glucose and fructose monosaccharides.) The product then undergoes subsequent rearrangements, fragmentations, and polymerizations to form brown pigments called melanoidins. This reaction can happen at room temperature after lengthy storage but is accelerated by high heat, especially at intermediate water activities. The lowering of the water activity on the surface of bread during baking facilitates Maillard browning of the bread crust while the interior of the bread remains unbrowned.

During the Maillard reaction it is possible to create hundreds of new flavor components that would not have otherwise been present in the food. The amino groups most commonly involved in the Maillard reaction are those in the side chains of lysine and histidine. Alpha amino groups of other free amino acids can

FIGURE 2.22 Simplified Maillard reaction. This reaction mechanism follows the general sequence of the Maillard reaction. The free amine on lysine attacks the open form of fructose to form a glucosamine; the attack releases one molecule of water. Further dehydration can produce hydroxymethylfurfural, a common Maillard product. Reactions with amino acids can generate nitrogen-containing polymers known as melanoidins, which contribute to the brown color formation.

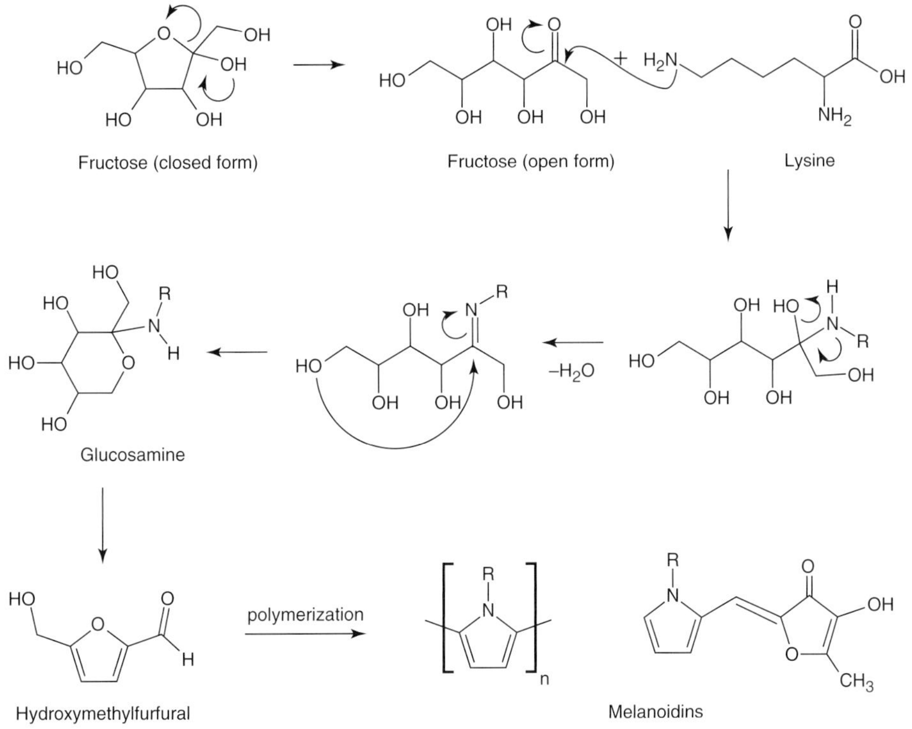

Fructose (closed form) Fructose (open form) Lysine

Glucosamine

Hydroxymethylfurfural polymerization Melanoidins

Source: J. Sanchez and L. Mauer.

also participate. The type of amino acid reacting drives the development of aroma more than the type of reducing sugar. Each type of food, because of its unique combination of amino acids, sugars, and the cooking technique used, can therefore develop almost an infinite array of flavor possibilities. For example, baked bread, grilled steak, and roasted peanuts all have unique aromas and flavors that develop during heating.

That said, *moist-heat cooking techniques* (boiling, poaching, steaming, etc.) do not support Maillard browning or the flavors, aromas, and colors that are produced through these reactions because the environment is too moist and the temperature is not high enough. This is the main reason why meats are seared before braising or stewing.

It is interesting to note that flavor chemists have taken advantage of the Maillard reaction for many years to develop a wide range of "process flavors" in the laboratory. These are often characterized as roasted, toasted, sautéed, fried, or seared notes.

Heat as Individual Processes

During cooking and many food processing operations, foods are changed by added heat. The specific type of change depends on the composition and thermophysical properties of the food product, the heating temperature, and the heat transfer medium (air, aqueous liquid, oil, etc.), as well as on the rate and mechanism by which heat is transferred. To understand heat transfer, the term *heat* must first be defined.

Heat is one of the ways in which systems, in this case food, exchange energy with their surroundings. In many cases, the exchange of heat between a food and its surroundings is easily recognized due to the close relationship between heat and temperature. However, there are instances in which the transfer of heat does not produce a change in temperature but rather a change in phase. Consider a container with liquid water that is heated from a low temperature (77°F [25°C]) to the point where water begins to boil (212°F [100°C] at sea level). During the heating process, energy is continuously transferred from the heating source into the water. At the beginning of the process, the temperature of the water increases continuously. Heat transferred during this stage is known as sensible heat. As more energy is transferred into the system, the water molecules eventually contain enough energy to overcome the attractive forces that keep them in a liquid state and begin to vaporize. This is called *the boiling point*, and at this point in the process, although energy continues to be transferred into the water as long as the heat source is maintained, the water temperature remains constant at 212°F (100°C), with more water molecules changing from the liquid into the vapor state (steam). Heat transferred during this stage is known as latent heat. In summary, the transfer of sensible

FIGURE 2.23 Phase diagram of water.

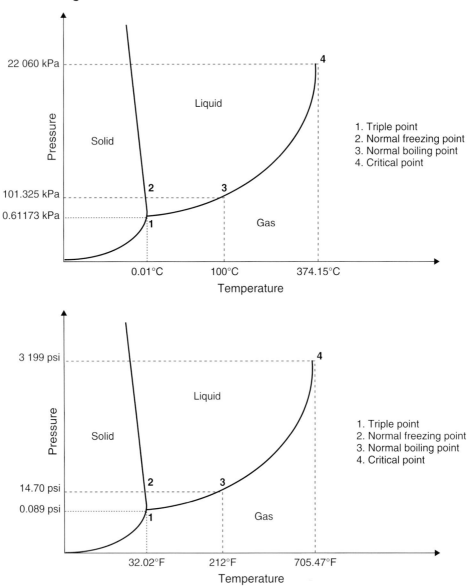

Source: F. San Martin-Gonzalez.

heat results in a change in temperature, whereas the transfer of latent heat results in a change in phase (liquid water into steam). A similar approach describes the freezing process, where sensible heat is removed to the point where water begins to freeze. Once the water molecules begin to crystallize, the temperature remains constant during the phase change as latent heat is removed from the crystallizing water.

The amount of energy required to change a given amount of liquid water into vapor is different from the amount of energy required to change that same amount of liquid water into ice. Therefore, the type of phase transition must be specified within the latent heat. Thus, water has a latent heat of vaporization (liquid water to water vapor), a latent heat of fusion (ice to liquid water), and a latent heat of sublimation (ice directly to water vapor under vacuum conditions), depending on the spe-~ change in phase. As seen in Figure 2.23, the pressure at ~ change in phase occurs is a function of the temperature.

Thus, the boiling point of water is lower or greater than 212°F (100°C) for pressures below or above 1 atmosphere, respectively. The pressure-temperature dependence of the boiling point can be observed by boiling water at different altitudes. The higher you go, the lower the atmospheric pressure and the lower the temperature required for water to boil. Therefore, it takes longer to cook food if you live on a mountain; for example, it takes longer to cook anything by boiling (eggs, pasta, rice, vegetables) because the water boils at a lower temperature. Recipes for certain bakery products must be adjusted for altitude because decreased atmospheric pressure may result in excessive rising, which stretches the cell structure of cakes, making the texture coarse, or breaks the cells, causing the cake to fall. This usually is corrected by decreasing the amount of leavening agent. Increasing the baking temperature 15–25°F (10–15°C) can also help "set" the batter before the cells formed by the leavening gas expand too much.

Another example of the relevance of the pressure-temperature dependence during cooking is in the use of pressure cookers. A pressure cooker is a closed container in which foods and an appropriate amount of water are exposed to high pressures. Under pressure, the boiling point of water rises, thus allowing foods to reach temperatures higher than 212°F (100°C) and requiring shorter cooking times. In industrially processed ("retorted") canned foods, these high pressure–high temperature combinations are also used to inactivate bacterial spores, which are resistant, latent forms of certain microorganisms (in particular, *Clostridium botulinum*) that are not effectively destroyed by normal boiling temperatures. Foods processed by these more severe heat treatments are considered commercially sterile and can be stored safely at normal room temperature for extended periods, provided that they are packed in a *hermetically sealed* (airtight) container such as a can.

Phase Transitions

Phase transitions are useful in understanding why ingredients behave the way they do. In pure systems, such as liquid water, phase transitions are easily illustrated. The transition from liquid to solid state results in ice, whereas liquid to vapor transition produces steam. While the chemical structure of the water (H_2O) remains the same through the phase transitions, its *density*, *specific heat*, and *thermal conductivity* are examples of properties that change with each phase. Changes in density explain why ice, which has a lower density than liquid water, floats in water. For pure substances such as water, phase transitions (such as melting point or freezing point) can be predicted relatively easily, while in the case of blended, multi-ingredient food systems, the presence of many different components results in a more complex behavior. In more complex systems, phase transitions tend to occur over a range of temperatures rather than at a single point. Nevertheless, understanding the behavior of each single component is a prerequisite to understanding the behavior of more complex food systems. For example, lipids in foods are called fats or oils depending on whether they exist in solid or liquid state at room temperature. However, common fats such as tallow, lard, or shortening are rather complex mixtures containing both liquid and solid phases of microscopic triglyceride crystals. The proportion of solid triglycerides in any given fat is known as its solid fat index (SFI), which, along with the number, size, and kind of fat crystals, temperature, and mechanical history (whether the fat has been agitated or mixed) determines its consistency at any given temperature.

Thermal Properties

Thermal properties are important in cooking and processing operations because they influence the rate at which heat is transferred into or out of a food product. The thermal property that specifies the amount of energy required to cause a change in temperature of a given substance is called specific heat (C_p). Think of specific heat as the amount of energy required to increase the temperature of a given unit mass of product by 1 degree. (Heat is usually expressed in calories, kilocalories, or joules, and the degree is in Kelvin or Celsius.)

This property is important when designing food processes and processing equipment to calculate the amount of energy required to increase the temperature of a product from an initial temperature to a required final value. For example, the specific heat of water is 4.18 joule/gram °C (that is, it takes 4.18 joules of energy to raise the temperature of 1 gram of water 1°C), whereas the specific heat of butter is 2.04 joule/gram °C. Therefore, if identical amounts of water and butter were to be heated at the same starting temperature using identical electric ranges, which one would you expect to increase its temperature faster, water or butter? (*Answer:* Butter heats faster because it has a lower specific heat.)

Another important thermal property that influences heat transfer is thermal conductivity (k). Simply stated, this is a measure of how easily a material conducts heat. In cooking, the thermal properties of the cooking utensils are very important. For example, copper has a very high thermal conductivity—it heats up very quickly—and this property is used to improve the heating efficiency and uniformity in pots constructed with copper bases.

The thermal properties of pure substances are known. For foods that contain considerable amounts of water (such as stocks and broths), the values of thermal properties are similar to those of water. However, for more complex systems (most other foods), the numerical values of thermal properties are a function of the composition of the product and the temperature at which they are measured.

FIGURE 2.24 Thermal properties of liquid water, ice, butter, and air.

Property	Liquid water @ 20°C	Ice @ −18°C	Butter @ 4.4°C	Air @ 20°C
Specific heat (kJ/kg °C)	4.185	1.955	2.043	1.012
Thermal conductivity (W/m °C)	0.602	2.370	0.197	0.0251
Density (kg/m³)	997.0	919.4	—	1.164

Adapted from Singh and Heldman (2009) and Geankoplis (1993).
Source: F. San Martin-Gonzalez.

FIGURE 2.25 Modes of heat transfer: conduction, convection, radiation. Inside an oven, the fire emits radiant heat, which in turns heats the air in the oven. The air transfers heat by convection to the surface of the turkey, the pan, and the walls of the oven. When the heat reaches the surface of solids (the turkey, the pan, the walls), it is transferred by conduction. For all practical purposes, solid foods are considered to behave as solids.

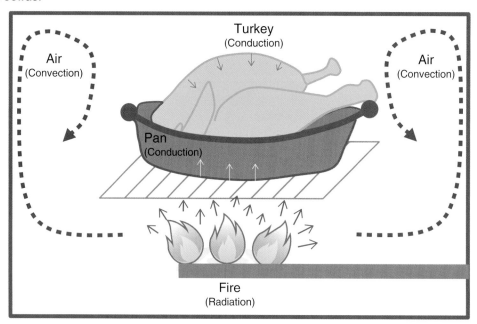

Source: F. San Martin-Gonzalez.

In food processing and cooking, the thermal properties of the heating medium are key factors in determining the rate of heat transfer. The thermal properties of air, water, and oil for operations involving baking, boiling, or frying are all different. It is possible to heat fats and oils to very high temperatures (350°F [177°C] to more than 400°F [204°C]), whereas water in an open container can only reach its boiling temperature (212°F [100°C]). On the other hand, air can be heated to high temperatures, but it has a very low thermal conductivity; therefore, air is not as efficient as fats, oils, or water in transferring heat. This explains why fried products cook faster than boiled or baked products. This is also why you can place your hand inside a 350°F (177°C) oven (at least for a short time) but not in water boiling at "only" 212°F (100°C).

Heat Transfer

Heat transfer occurs when energy from a heat source is transferred directly or indirectly to the food. The heat source can be a simple gas flame, an electric element, a microwave generator, an infrared appliance, or a magnetic element. Heat is transferred to food in one of three basic ways: conduction, convection, and radiation.

Conduction

Heat transfer by *conduction* refers to two things. First, it is the mechanism by which solid food products are heated internally, with heat being transferred from hotter outer surfaces to cooler interiors until the food is considered cooked and is removed from the heat source. The rate at which a solid product heats depends on the heat source and the product's thermal conductivity.

Second, *conduction* refers to a method of heating involving direct heat transfer, where the food is heated due to direct contact with a heat source. Conduction can happen between any two solid objects as long as they touch, as in the transfer of heat from a hot pan to a piece of food being sautéed. Heat always flows from the hot areas to the cold areas, with the rate of transfer being faster or slower depending on the size of contacted surface area and the difference in temperature between the hotter and colder surfaces.

Convection

Convection is the transfer of heat through moving fluids, such as air, water, or oil. Heat transfer by convection is the result of molecules physically moving from one location to another and exchanging energy with molecules at the other location. It occurs at the interface between heated liquids or gases and solids. The physical movement of molecules is caused by changes in density and viscosity within the heating medium due to differences in temperature. If the heated molecules move freely as a consequence of gravity, the process is known as natural convection. Due to the natural tendency of hot liquids and gases to rise and colder ones to fall, natural convection occurs in any oven or fryer. Inside a fryer, the oil that has been cooled by the submersion of colder food naturally falls and the hot oil rises, creating a current of oil inside the fryer. On the other hand, if the fluid is moved by mechanical action, such as fans or agitators, the process is known as forced convection. In a convection oven, the movement of the hot air from hotter to colder areas is assisted by the addition of a mechanical blower or fan inside the oven. It must be noted, however, that heat transfer by convection occurs only at the food's surface. Once the energy is transferred from the heated liquid or gas to the surface of the solid food, the food keeps transferring the heat to its interior by conduction.

Thermal Radiation

Heating by *radiation* (or "radiant energy") is the result of *electromagnetic radiation* (in the form of light photons) being absorbed by a given food's surface. (*Note:* This is a form of non-ionizing radiation. It has nothing to do with radiation caused by nuclear reactions or radioactive materials, which is ionizing radiation.) No medium (hot air, hot oil, a hot pan) is needed between the food and the radiant heat source for heat transfer to take place (unlike with conduction and convection). Like convection, heat transfer by radiation is also a surface phenomenon. One example of heating by radiation is the use of infrared heat lamps to keep foods hot. Another is broiling, where the heat source is hot enough and close enough to cook the food without direct contact. Recently a radiant fryer was launched, where partially fried products are exposed to radiant energy, thereby increasing the temperature on the surface of the food and developing the appropriate texture without using large volumes of oil.

Microwave Heating

Microwave heating deserves special consideration due to the extensive use of microwave ovens in many households. It is also used in commercial food manufacturing as an aid to thawing and in heat processing. Microwave energy is a form of electromagnetic radiation that uses microwave radiation rather than light as the generator of heat. In addition, unlike other forms of heating, which are primarily surface heat transfer phenomena, microwave heating takes place at the molecular level of the food product. When a food product is exposed to microwave energy, heating occurs internally by the friction created by water molecules (and other charged

atoms or molecules) trying to align themselves under the rapidly oscillating energy field. This results in foods heating volumetrically—that is, the food heats simultaneously at various depths, as opposed to other forms of heating, where the surface is heated first and then the heat is conducted to the interior of the solid. The volumetric heating effect is a consequence of the ability of microwaves to penetrate the food below the surface level. Penetration depth of microwaves is dependent on food composition and the frequency of the microwave generator, with lower microwave frequencies (longer wavelengths) penetrating further. That said, maximum penetration depth is only a few centimeters; microwave ovens do not cook foods "from the inside out."

Induction Heating

Induction heating is a method of instantaneously raising the temperature of a pan made of *ferromagnetic* material by applying a magnetic field generated by a powerful, high-frequency electromagnet. This in turn heats whatever is inside the pan by conventional conduction or convection mechanisms. Unlike other forms of cooking, heat is generated directly in the pan rather than generated in the stovetop by electrical coils or burning gas. The amount of heat generated can be moderated by controlling the strength of the electromagnetic field (just like raising or lowering the gas flame or electric coil on a standard stove). The material of which induction cookware is made is very important for induction heating to work: it must be magnetic. Cast iron and stainless steel are suitable, whereas aluminum (unless it has a steel bottom), copper, and Pyrex are not. An induction cooker is faster and more energy efficient than a traditional gas or electric stove. It allows rapid control of cooking energy similar to gas burners. Because induction heats the cooking vessel itself, the possibility of a burn injury is significantly less than with other methods; the surface of the cooktop is heated only from contact with the pot or pan. There are no flames or red-hot electric heating elements, as in traditional cooking equipment. Also, because energy is not wasted heating the air around the cooking vessel, induction cooking is much more energy efficient than gas or electric.

3 | Review of Cooking Techniques

Lead Authors: **Charlie Baggs,** President and Executive Chef, Charlie Baggs, Inc.
Herbert A. Stockschlaeder II, CRC®, DTR, Director, Technical Services, Rosina Food Products, Inc.

Understanding Cooking Techniques from a Chef's Viewpoint

Cooking has long been used as a means to alter raw food materials into a more palatable and nutritious form, render them safer for eating and storing, and provide a broader range of flavors than their raw form. Over centuries of experimentation and documentation, chefs have created a universal set of cooking methods that are the foundation for all modern cooking techniques. Heat and other forms of energy applied to food alters its structure, nutrition, sensory attributes, and chemical makeup in a wide variety of ways.

Modern cooking techniques typically involve some or all of the heat transfer methods mentioned in the preceding chapter, and they can all be classified into two main categories: dry-heat and moist-heat cooking.

Dry-heat cooking methods do not involve the use of water in the cooking process. These methods include baking, roasting, grilling, broiling, barbecue, sautéing, stir-frying, pan-frying, and deep frying. Foods are cooked with heat transferred directly through exposure to an open flame, hot air, hot surface, radiant heat, or hot fat or oil.

Moist-heat cooking methods use water or steam to transmit heat to foods. These include blanching, simmering, boiling, steaming, poaching, stewing, and braising. Braising and stewing also usually incorporate an initial searing step (a dry-heat method) for flavor and color development prior to completion of the cooking in a moist-heat environment. As a result, these are sometimes referred to as combination cooking methods.

Dry- and moist-heat cooking are drastically different in the ways they act on the food to produce a broad and varied array of tastes, textures, aromas, and appearance. These two types of cooking methods also have greatly different effects on the development, concentration, and evaporation of flavor components.

Dry-Heat Cooking Methods

During dry-heat cooking, the outer surface of a food is subjected to elevated temperatures in a water-free environment. This develops flavors and browning by a combination of caramelization and the Maillard reaction. It is commonly used as a preliminary step to develop color and flavor in meats and vegetables before finishing cooking using other methods. Contrary to popular belief, however, searing does not "seal in" juices in preparation for follow-up cooking. It has been shown scientifically that meat loses the same amount of moisture whether or not it is seared before final cooking.

Baking

Baking uses heat transmitted by the convection and conduction of hot air to cook foods inside an oven or other heatproof cooker. Any source of heat—gas, charcoal, wood, or electric element—can be used. Heat transmission can occur via conduction alone or be enhanced by the use of a convection oven (via air flow created by a fan inside the oven). The forced hot air provides a more even temperature throughout the oven and speeds the transfer of heat, allowing for lower cooking temperatures, shorter cooking times, and less expenditure of energy. Baking is typically used for "baked goods," that is, breads and pastries, pies and cakes, cookies and crackers. But many other foods are also baked: ham and meatloaf, casseroles and quiches, flans and soufflés, pizza and lasagna, potatoes, apples, baked beans, and winter squash. There is a fine line between baking and roasting, which are virtually the

FIGURE 3.1 **Baked goods.**

Source: Charlie Baggs, Inc.

same cooking process. Whether a food is said to be baked or roasted is pretty much the result of historical terminology rather than clear-cut identifiable differences in the cooking process. Regardless of what you call it, dry-heat cooking in heated air causes a change to the structure of sugars, resulting in caramelization, and an interaction of proteins and reducing sugars through the Maillard browning reaction. Both of these contribute to the development of colors, aromas, and flavors made possible only with dry-heat cooking methods.

Roasting

Like baking, roasting uses hot air as the heating medium in an oven or above an open flame, as in rotisserie cooking, wood-fired oven cooking, and "spit-roasting." Heat is transferred by convection from the air to the surface of the food and by conduction from the surface of the food to its interior. The heating medium is dry, and the process is designed to prevent the foods from simmering in their own juices as they are exuded, either by suspending the food above the flame or by placing it on a raised rack inside the roasting pan.

Figure 3.2 **Pistachio-crusted roasted meat.**

Source: Charlie Baggs, Inc.

Roasting is usually used to cook large, tender cuts of meat, but it can also be used for coffee beans, vegetables, or peanuts. Vegetables such as potatoes, shallots, cauliflower, squash, onions, and others with high sugar concentrations are very flavorful when prepared this way because of the caramelization of the sugars. A perfectly roasted item should be a rich amber or golden brown color and have an evenly crisped surface.

Roasting meat should be placed fat side up; in this manner it bastes itself. Added fat, meat juices expelled during roasting, or sauces can be used to baste meats during cooking to provide additional flavor. The goal is an evenly crisp and well-browned surface.

Interior portions of roasting foods cook slowly by conduction alone. The larger the piece of meat, the longer it takes to roast because of the greater distance the heat must travel to reach the center. When cooking a large piece of meat, it is a good idea to start with an oven temperature of 450 to 500°F (204 to 260°C) to quickly brown the outside of the meat. Once good color is achieved, the oven temperature is reduced to 225 to 350°F (107 to 177°C) for the rest of the cooking period. The objective is to cook to the proper temperature throughout the meat without overcooking the exterior. Shielding the food's surface with aluminum foil can slow the browning process while the interior continues to cook. It is important to balance browning the outside of the product evenly with cooking the center of the product to the exact desired doneness.

Keep in mind that for nearly every cooking method, the larger the food, the longer the residual or carryover cooking that will occur. Cooking doesn't stop immediately when the heat is turned off. When food is removed from the heat source, initially the outside of the food is much hotter than the center. However, heat continues to move into the food's interior (by conduction) until the entire food reaches equilibrium. Therefore, it is important that larger foods be removed from the heat when the core temperature is *lower* than the final desired temperature, as it can rise as much as 10 to 20°F (5 to 10°C) before the product begins to cool.

Establishments producing cooked meat and poultry products are required by the Food Safety and Inspection Service (FSIS) of the United States Department of Agriculture (USDA) to meet specific lethality standards for the reduction of salmonella. To assist establishments in meeting the lethality requirements, FSIS has issued compliance guidelines, which are based on established time/temperature thermal processing requirements to achieve the required level of lethality.

FIGURE 3.3 **Internal beef doneness temperatures.**

130°F = rare
140°F = medium rare
150°F = medium
155°F = medium well
160°F+ = well

Source: Charlie Baggs, Inc

FIGURE 3.4 Safe minimum cooking temperatures.

Category	Food	Temperature (°F)	Rest Time
Ground Meat & Meat Mixtures	Beef, pork, veal, lamb	160	None
	Turkey, chicken	165	None
Fresh Beef, Veal, Lamb	Steaks, roasts, chops	145	3 minutes
Poultry	Chicken & turkey, whole	165	None
	Poultry breasts, roasts	165	None
	Poultry thighs, legs, wings	165	None
	Duck & goose	165	None
	Stuffing (cooked alone or in bird)	165	None
Pork and Ham	Fresh pork	145	3 minutes
	Fresh ham (raw)	145	3 minutes
	Precooked ham (to reheat)	140	None
Eggs & Egg Dishes	Eggs	Cook until yolk and white are firm	None
	Egg dishes	160	None
Leftovers & Casseroles	Leftovers	165	None
	Casseroles	165	None
Seafood	Fin Fish	145 or cook until flesh is opaque and separates easily with a fork.	None
	Shrimp, lobster, and crabs	Cook until flesh is pearly and opaque.	None
	Clams, oysters, and mussels	Cook until shells open during cooking.	None
	Scallops	Cook until flesh is milky white or opaque and firm.	

Source: Foodsafety.gov.

These guidelines (in table form) provide the acceptable amount of time that various types of meat and poultry products must be held at different internal temperatures in order to achieve a 6.5-log or 7-log reduction in living Salmonella organisms. Log reduction is a mathematical term used to show the reduction in the number of live germs logarithmically. It denotes the relative number of live microbes eliminated from a food due to thermal processing (or other microbial control treatments). A 1-log reduction means the number of germs is 10 times smaller than before heating. A 2-log reduction means the number is 100 times smaller, a 3-log reduction is 1,000 times smaller and so on up to 7-log reduction (10,000,000 times smaller). FSIS requires a 7-log reduction for poultry and 6.5-log reduction for red meat. A 7-log reduction is included in the red meat chart for those processors wanting an extra safety net.

In addition to time/temperature heating tables, the FSIS also provides cooling tables. Both sets of tables can be found at: Compliance Guidelines for Meeting Lethality Performance Standards for Certain Meat and Poultry Products (http://www.fsis.usda.gov/OPPDE/rdad/FRPubs/95-033F/95-033F_Appendix%20A.htm).

Safe Minimum Cooking Temperatures

Use the chart in Figure 3.4 and a food thermometer to ensure that meat, poultry, seafood, and other cooked foods reach a safe minimum internal temperature. Remember, you can't tell whether meat is safely cooked by looking at it. Any cooked, uncured red meats, including pork, can be pink even when the meat has reached a safe internal temperature.

Why Resting Time After Cooking Is Important

After removing meat from a grill, oven, or other heat source, allow it to rest for the specified amount of time (usually 10–20 minutes depending on the size of the roast). During the rest time, its internal temperature will continue to rise until the entire piece of meat reaches equilibrium. This allows internal juices, which have been pushed toward the surface as the interior temperature rises, to redistribute throughout the muscle, reducing drip loss when the meat is cut or sliced.

Grilling

Grilling is one of the oldest and most dynamic cooking methods. Grilling often implies the use of hardwood or coals, which impart a distinctive taste and additional complexity from the smoke in addition to the "char" flavors that develop from the intense heat. Charcoal provides a strong heat source with minimal flavor impact of its own. The smoke coming off the grill is normally the fat melting and burning off the hot embers. Grilled flavors are usually much more pronounced than those created during roasting. When grilling, it is especially critical to control the amount of browning, as charred flavors have a bitter component that must be carefully balanced. That said,

FIGURE 3.5 **Grilled chicken with mushroom sauce.**

Source: Charlie Baggs, Inc.

the charred flavor provides a mouthwatering savory building block that can be used to create wonderful, deep flavor experiences.

Grilling is not to be confused with *barbecuing* (cooking "low and slow" in an enclosed heated box). Grilling is more like broiling—cooking one side at a time, in this case from the bottom up, with intense radiant heat. In commercial manufacturing, the traditional use of wood or charcoal has largely been replaced with gas-fired burners. While this has eliminated the wait for wood or charcoal to generate the right heat level and provides a greater level of control, efficiency, and consistency to the process, there is less depth of flavor development due to the absence of the complexities that wood smoke imparts. Using smoke, roast, and grill flavors can compensate for this to some degree.

Items that are grilled are usually seasoned via marinating or dry rubs before they are cooked. Meats can also be seasoned while on the grill. Remember, though, if the food item is to be exposed to high temperatures for extended periods, high-sugar sauces (barbecue sauces or glazes) and seasonings should be applied late in the cooking process so as not to burn.

Typically, tender, thinner cuts of meat and vegetables are grilled or broiled because they do not need extended periods of moist cooking to break down connective tissues. They must be turned partway through the cooking process. Because fruits and vegetables have high concentrations of sugar, they tend to caramelize (and scorch) faster than meats, so care should be taken not to burn them. The best way to cook on the grill is to set up high and low heat "zones." Caramelize the exterior of the food quickly over the high heat zone, then move the food to a cooler area of the grill to allow the heat to penetrate the product without further charring.

Broiling

Broiling is closely related to grilling, but the radiant heat source is above the food, and wood is never used as a fuel. Modern broilers are designed to use both convection and radiant heat, and are typically either gas-fired or electric.

Often, delicate items such as fish are broiled on an oiled metal heat-safe platter (sizzle platter) that can withstand the high temperatures in a commercial broiler (700+°F [370+°C]). This eliminates the potential for the fish to stick to the broiler grate. Broiling is also used to "finish" a product by quickly adding a golden brown surface or melting a topping, or doing both, such as browning cheese on French onion soup or the sugar on a crème brûlée. These products can be browned quickly on the surface while the interior temperature of the rest of the food remains largely unaffected. In the restaurant kitchen, the *salamander* broiler is specifically designed for this purpose.

In commercial settings, broiling temperatures can reach up to 1000°F (538°C), depending on the type of heat source used. This high heat facilitates the Maillard browning and caramelization reactions on the outside of the food by immediately lowering the surface water concentration and cooking the outside by direct radiant heat. Depending on the thickness and delicacy of the product, the radiant heat may be enough to completely cook it. If it is not, the interiors of thicker products cook by conduction. To perfectly cook a thicker piece of food, it must be located in exactly the proper location relative to the heat source so the outside doesn't overcook while the inside remains underdone. One benefit of using a top-mounted broiler instead of a grill is that juices dripping from the cooking food do not drop onto the heat source (hot coals, gas burners, etc.), causing smoke and undesirable flavors to rise back onto the food.

Barbecue

Unlike grilling, which is hot and fast, barbecue is a process of cooking meats in an enclosed chamber at a relatively low temperature (usually 225 to 350°F [107 to 177°C]) for an extended period, usually in conjunction with smoking. In fact, because barbecue is carried out in an enclosed chamber where the humidity is higher than in typical dry-heat methods, it can be considered a combination cooking method (moist and dry heat together). Popularized in the southern United States, "low and slow" is barbecue's motto. Larger cuts

FIGURE 3.6 **Broiled pork chop.**

Source: Charlie Baggs, Inc.

FIGURE 3.7   Barbecued ribs.

Source: Charlie Baggs, Inc.

of meat from the shoulder or leg that have plenty of fat marbling and lots of *collagenous connective tissue* are perfect for this method.

Collagen is the main component of *connective tissue* and the most abundant protein in mammals, making up 25 to 35 percent of the whole-body protein content. Collagen is mostly found in fibrous tissues such as tendon, ligament, and skin, and is responsible for the tough and chewy cuts of meat found primarily in the leg and shoulder muscles of meat animals. When exposed to heat and moisture, the collagen hydrolyzes into *gelatin*, a protein with "melt-in-the-mouth" texture and exceptional flavor release.

The lower temperature, longer cooking time, and higher humidity in the enclosed barbecue cook chamber break down the fat and collagen, while the smoke adds exceptional flavor. The meats are seasoned, placed indirectly above or next to the heat source, and allowed to cook slowly for hours until the fat and connective tissues melt and create a moist, tender, succulent product. When properly prepared, slow-cooked barbecue falls off the bone and melts in the mouth.

Beef, pork, whole turkeys, chicken, lamb, bison, duck, and mutton can all be cooked successfully using this method.

The characteristic flavor of barbecued meats is often due to the creative use of wood types. Hardwoods such as hickory, oak, apple, and mesquite, as well as wood from other fruit and nut trees, make excellent additions to the barbecue fire. Saplings and soft woods are not generally used because their resins and sap contain *phenols* and other undesirable components, which create acrid, bitter flavors and may form unsafe chemical compounds on the food. Successful smoking is evidenced by the presence of a pink "smoke ring" that can be seen near the surface of meat when it is sliced; the wider the ring, the more smoke the meat has absorbed. This happens when nitrogen dioxide from the burning wood combines with *myoglobin* in the muscle tissues to form nitrites and nitrates. These cure the meat, similarly to the way hams and bacon are cured, and also the way they get their pink coloration.

Hot-Oil Cooking Methods

Considered a type of dry-heat cooking because it does not rely on moisture for heat transfer (in fact, this technique removes moisture from food during cooking), frying, when properly executed, is an excellent way to keep foods succulent and evenly browned on the outside. The foods that benefit most are small or thin cuts of tender meats or vegetables (although in recent years, even full-size turkeys are being deep fried). Potatoes, doughnuts, and many other carbohydrate-based products are also fried. The sugars and small amounts of proteins within these foods react to form Maillard browning compounds, resulting in tasty, golden-crisp coatings and flavors. Meat tenderness can be affected because frying is a high-temperature, rapid method of cooking, so muscle fibers shorten more severely than with slower methods of cooking. Therefore, only thin or tender cuts with little to no connective tissue should be fried. Fish, shrimp, scallops, chicken, pork, and tender cuts of beef are the best choices.

Sautéing

Sautéing (from the French for "to jump") is rapidly cooking foods in small amounts of oil over high heat. This method is used for quickly searing and browning foods with a limited amount of hot oil. Before sautéing, meats are usually lightly dusted with flour to enhance browning and reduce sticking to the pan, shaken to remove excess flour, and then placed presentation side down into the *sauteuse*—a wide, shallow pan that is curved outward where the sides meet the bottom. This aids in flipping or making the foods "jump" without the need for utensils.

Sautéing is the cooking method of choice for "*à la minute*" ("in a minute") cooking. Because the foods cooked in this manner are usually small and tender, they cook very quickly. When a larger food, such as a whole chicken breast, is sautéed, a two-stage approach is used. First, the presentation side (skin side) of the breast is seared on the stovetop, then it

FIGURE 3.8   Breaded, stuffed banana peppers.

Source: Rosina Food Products, Inc.

is flipped over and the pan is placed in a hot oven to finish the cooking. It takes practice and experience to judge how long it takes to finish cooking each product perfectly with this method, but in a busy restaurant, this approach frees up stovetop space, which is often in short supply.

Sometimes the best sauce for a dish is one made from the caramelized juices, protein, and carbohydrates, or fond, left behind in the sauté pan after the meat is removed after cooking. During cooking, flavorful meat juices (including fats, proteins, sugars, and water) seep onto the hot pan's surface, where they cook and harden as the water evaporates, forming "crisps" of concentrated flavor. It is a shame to let this flavor wash away with the dishwater! Instead, excess fat, if any, is poured out, the pan is deglazed with wine, stock, or water, rehydrating and (with some judicious scraping) solubilizing the caramelized fond. The liquid is briefly simmered, seasoned, and used as-is for an au jus preparation, or else it can be thickened for a more sauce-like consistency before serving.

The pan sauce can be thickened by reduction via continued simmering (as water evaporates, the sauce thickens and flavors become concentrated), cornstarch slurry (for a more translucent sauce; is added after the slurry reaches 180–190ºF), small amounts of *roux* (a combination of cooked fat and flour used for thickening opaque soups, gravies, and sauces), *beurre manié* (a blend of softened butter and uncooked flour used to thicken sauces), or even by whisking in small amounts of chilled whole butter (which thickens and emulsifies via the presence of small amounts of protein and *lecithin* in the butter). The result is a rich sauce bursting with flavor.

Additional commercial thickening methods include numerous gums (*hydrocolloids*), starches, and blends of both that have been developed to provide viscosity to all types of liquids in all types of systems and processing conditions (low pH, high shear, freeze-thaw, retort stable, etc.). These can easily be added to commercial products during processing. Raw flour needs to "cook out" when used in a sauce, which requires extra processing time. On the other hand, food starches and gums thicken quickly and (usually) don't leave an aftertaste. That said, one is often forced to sacrifice a certain amount of sensory quality for functionality when developing products for mass production.

Stir-Frying

Asian cuisine incorporates a quick cooking technique similar to sautéing. Using slightly more oil and a higher heat than is traditional with sautéing, small and tender cuts of meats and vegetables (commonly dredged in cornstarch rather than flour) are quickly cooked by stir-frying—typically associated with the use of a wok. Unlike the flat-bottomed sauté pan, the wok is round-bottomed and bowl-shaped to facilitate constant stirring. The concept of keeping the food moving when placed in the hot oil is consistent with sautéing, albeit often with greater velocity due to the higher heat.

Stir-frying is a great way to build complex flavors, and the high temperature and quick-cooking technique is a great way to retain natural juices. Once the oil is hot, it is commonly seasoned with aromatics such as ginger, garlic, scallions, and chilies. After the oil is seasoned, these ingredients may be removed or left in as desired. Adding the meat at this stage continues flavor development and starts the cooking process. Once the meat is almost cooked, it can either be removed while the vegetables are cooking and added back at the end (typically done with meats normally served more rare), or the vegetables can be added to the meat in the wok while continuously moving the mixture (best used when the meats are to be cooked well done, such as poultry or shrimp). A splash of liquid (broth, sherry, soy sauce, etc.) at the end deglazes the pan, creates a light sauce, and can add another flavor. A cornstarch slurry may be added if additional thickening is desired.

Pan-Frying and Deep Frying

Unlike sautéing and stir-frying, which minimize oil use, pan-frying uses enough oil to reach one-half to two-thirds the height of the food being fried. The food is generally larger, like a pounded pork cutlet or even whole bone-in chicken parts. Deep frying and pan-frying differ mainly in the amount of oil used. When deep frying, enough oil is used to completely cover the item being fried. Also, deep frying is more commonly used to cook smaller foods—nuggets, strips, fingers, and the like. A related frying system called *broasting* involves deep frying under pressure, and is the "secret" to Colonel Sander's Kentucky Fried Chicken. This method is excellent for preparing crispy but juicy chicken.

In either case, the food is usually coated with some sort of breading. This can be as simple as seasoned flour or bread crumbs or can incorporate nuts, cereals, or grains. These coatings help retain moisture, leading to crisp exteriors with golden colors and tender and juicy interiors. The standard commercial breading procedure follows a wet, dry, wet, dry system. Chicken, for example, which is wet by nature, is dredged in a dry, often seasoned flour mixture (called the *predust*), then dipped in a wet egg-based mixture to promote adhesion of the final surface breading (panko, cracker crumbs, seasoned bread crumbs, and the like). This treatment can be carried out multiple times to build a thick crust and interesting craggy surface features, but care must be taken not to overwhelm the product with the breading. *Seeding* is a process of adding a liquid or water to a flour for breading. The flour will turn into small seed-like shapes; when these are adhered to the fried item, they provide seeds of crunchy fried flour, a great way to add texture to a breading system.

A common alternative to breading, especially for deep-fried applications, is a *batter coating*, a semiliquid mixture of flour, eggs, milk, and sometimes seltzer to provide lightness, used to coat individual pieces of meat, cheese, seafood, or vegetables. Unlike breaded foods, which can be stored after breading without frying for some time, battered foods are fried immediately in order to set the coating quickly and reduce drip loss. *Tempura* batter is an especially thin and light batter used in Japanese cooking. Baking powder is added to the tempura mixture to add chemical leavening. The tempura batter should be cold to prevent the batter from reacting before frying.

Flavors can be added to fried products at several points in the process: meats can be marinated and seasoned before coating, and seasonings can be added to the pre-dust, the egg wash, the batter, or the crumb coating. As the flavors or spices tend to flash off the exterior of the food quickly, they are best applied directly to the product itself before coating or else in one of the interior coating steps (the pre-dust or egg wash) where they will be better protected.

The type of oil chosen also alters the final flavor profile. Plain shortening, peanut oil, vegetable oil, clarified butter oil, and rendered meat fats such as lard, tallow, and bacon drippings each add distinctive flavor characteristics to the fried food. Likewise, old oil that has darkened and is littered with burnt crumbs, and oil in which strongly flavored items such as fish have been fried contribute off notes to the fried food.

The lifespan of fryer oil depends on many factors: the type of oil, how high it is heated, its *smoke point,* how long it is used, the volume of food cooked in it, the amount of moisture present in the foods, the type of coatings and the amount of salt used, how well the oil is cleaned and filtered between uses, and how it is stored. Fats in the presence of oxygen and high heat (and water, metals, and salt) break down (oxidize), becoming rancid and bad-tasting. This is known as *fatty acid oxidation.* Therefore, oil should be strained, cooled, and covered after each use to lengthen its lifespan, or properly discarded when it is too old. Old oil does not transfer heat as efficiently, and besides tasting bad and looking dark and unappetizing, foods fried in old oil absorb more fat because they take longer to cook.

The smoke point is another consideration when choosing oil for deep frying. The higher the smoke point, the better the oil is for deep frying. Typical frying temperatures are from 350 to 400°F (177 to 204°C); therefore, a fat with a smoke point well above these works best. Fats with lower smoke points break down more rapidly when exposed to higher temperatures for extended times, and may ignite as well (not to mention spoil the food). In general, refined oils that have had impurities removed have higher smoke points than unrefined oils.

Fats with emulsifiers (such as shortenings intended for baking), unrefined vegetable oils, and used oil all have lower smoke points and should not be used for deep frying. Likewise, unrefined animal fats (lard, tallow) and whole butter decompose quickly under high-heat conditions and are better suited to shallow frying and sautéing. Even then, they should be blended first with oils having a higher smoke point (and butter should be clarified to remove milk solids that would otherwise burn). With all of these concerns in mind, oil manufacturers are able to custom-blend specially designed fats specifically for deep frying.

When oils begin to smoke, they also begin to break down, forming free fatty acids. As these acids build up, they reduce the oil's heat transfer efficiency and stability and generate off flavors. When the triglycerides break down, the oil smokes, and more of it is absorbed into the product. Other factors that affect fat absorption are quality of fat, age of the oil, amount of exposed food surface, type of food, amount of coating, frying temperature, and length of cook time.

French fries are probably the most popular deep fried food in the world. In commercial production, the potato strips are first blanched in water, dried, then dipped in a light batter coating, par-fried, and frozen. They are fully cooked later by deep frying and then held for service. The coating adds extra crispness and extends shelf life.

⬤ Moist-Heat Cooking Methods

Moist-heat cooking methods work by conduction and convection from hot water or other aqueous liquids such as water, stock, milk, or wine (or steam) to the surface of the food and then by conduction to the interior of the food. These methods include boiling, blanching, simmering, poaching, parboiling, steaming, braising, stewing, combi-oven cooking, *sous vide* (cooking by submersion in a vacuum-sealed pouch), and *en papillote* (cooked in an envelope, usually of parchment paper). Because water transmits heat better than air does, moist-heat methods cook foods faster than most dry-heat methods (other than frying, which is faster than any moist-heat method because oil conducts heat better than water and can be raised to much higher temperatures than water can). Moist-heat cooking methods are essential to *gelatinize* (tenderize) connective tissue. For this reason, moist-heat cookery is usually reserved for less tender cuts of meat. The trade-off is dilution of flavor and nutrients and the inability to develop any browning reaction flavors, colors, or aromas, not to mention crisp textures. Because the moist heat does not brown the meat while cooking, a combination cooking technique is used: searing the exterior of a seasoned meat before beginning the braising or stewing process. The exception is when your final product needs to remain white, such as a *veal de blanc.*

Boiling, Blanching, and Simmering

Cooking in water is the least complicated of all the cooking techniques. Foods are simply immersed in heated water and are cooked to the desired doneness.

Boiling is very effective in cooking many food products, yet it is inappropriate for delicate items that may fall apart. One limitation of boiling is that no matter how high the heat under the pot of water, the temperature of water never exceeds 212°F (100°C) (at sea level). Boiling is ideal for starches that must be hydrated and tenderized by the absorption of water (for example, pasta and potatoes).

Blanching involves completely submerging foods in boiling water for a very short time, then shocking them in ice water to immediately halt any further cooking. Blanching is used for quickly setting the color of green vegetables, inactivating enzymes that produce off flavors and degrade color, and reducing the number of microorganisms. In addition, blanching forces out dissolved gases in plant tissues, thereby reducing their volume for easier packaging into containers for subsequent freezing or canning. Blanching is also used as a peeling aid for foods like almonds and tomatoes, and as a delivery system for functional ingredients (flavors, antioxidants, whiteners, and so on), as in the processing of potatoes for frozen French fries.

Simmering (slow cooking in barely bubbling liquid) allows very tough cuts of meat or vegetables to be slowly tenderized by breaking down (hydrolyzing) complex proteins and carbohydrates, making these foods more tender and palatable. Simmering is also useful for stock-making, where slow extraction of flavor from bones and vegetables without cloudiness is desired. It is also commonly used for preparing rice and other grains.

Poaching (Shallow and Deep)

Poaching is a versatile cooking technique, suitable for boneless chicken breasts, fish, eggs, and fruit. It is often considered a healthy method of cooking because it does not use fat to cook the food. There are two types of poaching: shallow and deep. Both include the cooking of the food in some type of liquid, and the basic difference lies in the fact that in shallow poaching the liquid covers roughly one-third of the height of the food, while in deep poaching the food is almost entirely covered by the liquid.

This poaching liquid (called court bouillon) is usually a mixture of stock or water; an acidic element, such as lemon juice, vinegar, or wine; aromatic vegetables; herbs; and spices. The liquid can be strained or not during poaching.

Shallow poaching is a popular method of cooking that is usually used with tender fish and poultry breasts. The food is placed on a bed of aromatic ingredients, then combined with a few ounces of flavorful liquid, covered loosely, and gently simmered until done. The poaching liquid is often used as a sauce— for example, *sauce vin blanc*. After the food item is cooked and removed from the poacher, the poaching liquid is strained and reduced and can be finished with cold whole butter to add viscosity, flavor, and mouthfeel. The butter also rounds out the flavors of the wine or citrus in the poaching liquid.

Deep poaching is completely submerging the food in the concentrated poaching liquid at a temperature between 160 and 185°F (71 and 85°C). Proteins and vegetables prepared by this method can be very appetizing; without Maillard browning, poached foods are paler and have more delicate flavor profiles, depending on the flavor impact of the poaching liquid. The poaching liquid is usually a highly acidulated medium with herbs and spices. A fish fumé or fish stock can be used to poach fish, thus building on the fish flavor. Poaching can be done either on the stovetop or in the oven as long as the water temperature is closely monitored not to exceed 185°F (85°C). Otherwise the protein will overcook and become tough and dry, in spite of being cooked in an aqueous environment.

Poaching eggs is a deep-poaching technique. The poaching liquid is on the acidic side, typically from the addition of a small amount of vinegar, which helps to set the protein in the egg white. The amount of acid should not be enough to affect the flavor of the egg.

Individual portions are typical for deep poaching. Cook times are relatively short; therefore, the cooking liquid must be flavored quite aggressively to achieve a high level of flavor transfer to the finished product. Aromatic herbs, flavorful broth, and wine are used to add flavor. Court bouillon is a cooking liquid specially designed for poaching fish. It is strongly acidic (vinegar, white wine, lemon juice) to help set the fish proteins at lower temperatures (similar to ceviche) so as to keep the texture extremely tender and prevent overcooking. It is also highly flavored, as there is less time for the cooking food to absorb flavors. Because it is so acidic and strongly flavored, court bouillon is not reserved after poaching for turning into a sauce.

Par-boiling and Steaming

Par-boiling is partially cooking food items in boiling water. Like blanching, it is a preparatory treatment before a second, final cook step, but the foods are more fully cooked. In restaurants, vegetables, rice dishes, risotto, and pasta are often par-boiled as part of the *mise en place*. This reduces the final cooking period at the time of service and assures proper cooking and flavor development. A parboiled product is often sautéed to order. Seasonings are also adjusted to taste at the time of final cooking.

Steaming is cooking food in superheated water vapor—a highly efficient method. Properly steamed foods retain more of their initial volume and many of their water-soluble nutrients. Many meat processors choose steaming to cook their products to maximize yield. This is often done in heatproof bags placed on large rolling racks that fit into walk-in steam ovens. Steaming can also be done under pressure. Pressure increases the attainable temperature of the steam, resulting in a higher cook temperature and faster cook times than with atmospheric steam. Steaming is a great benefit when avoiding added calories from fat. When the temperature and time relationship of steaming are carefully controlled, high-quality products are attainable. While it is possible to overcook foods using steam, the consequences are primarily loss of color and texture; steamed foods (like all moist-heat cooked foods) never burn. Because steaming uses water in its vapor phase, there is less transfer of beneficial nutrients, pigments, and flavor compounds into the water during cooking. This results in a more flavorful, colorful, and healthful cooked food.

Steaming is also an excellent process to use in reheating previously cooked food items, even those prepared using dry-heat methods. Steaming previously cooked foods brings them back up to serving temperature quickly, maintaining the maximum amount of moisture while reheating evenly in a short period.

While commercial kitchens typically use a steam oven for steaming, age-old steaming techniques using stovetop bamboo steamers may be used to produce well-known classic food items such as tamales (steamed in a cornhusk wrapper), Greek dolmades (wrapped in grape leaves), fish cooked in banana leaves, and steamed Asian dumplings.

En Papillote

En papillote (French for "in paper") steaming is achieved inside a man-made wrapper such as parchment paper or aluminum foil. The food is enveloped in a pouch completely sealed along the edges; the pouch usually contains flavor-building ingredients such as herbs, wine, spices, and julienne vegetables. These additional items, along with the main food, give off steam when heated. This steam is contained by the pouch and gently cooks the food within. Delicate foods such as fish are best cooked this way. One benefit of this method is that volatile flavor and aroma compounds are trapped inside the pouch until the pouch is cut open for consumption.

Pressure-Cooking

Pressure-cooking (retorting) is a high-temperature thermal process that allows water to achieve a higher-than-usual boiling point—around 250°F (121°C) at 15 psi. Because the temperature is higher, this process can quickly cook foods that normally take a long time to cook. This process is also widely used in the canned food industry to ensure that *botulism spores* are killed. The time and temperature are determined by the type of product and package being processed. Some foods, such as broths, have rapid heat transfer and require shorter processing times. Products that are denser, or contain particulates that can stick together (such as thick soups or stews) require a longer cook time to ensure the product is heated to the appropriate safe temperature all the way through. Container size and material (metal, glass, plastic) have a critical impact on process time, as does the acidity of the product; process time to control microbial growth is shorter for acidic foods with a pH below 4.6 (the pH below which pathogens do not survive) and much longer for foods above pH 4.6. Low-pH foods create a less favorable growth environment for bacteria and hence require less thermal processing.

Braising and Stewing

Braising encompasses two cooking methods and is generally reserved for tougher cuts of meat with plenty of connective tissue. First the item is seared (dry heat) in a bit of oil to create a dark brown color and to develop the complex flavors and colors produced by the Maillard reaction. After the meat is seared, *mirepoix* and a tomato product (if used) are also seared to develop additional flavor compounds.

FIGURE 3.9 Braised meat.

Source: Charlie Baggs, Inc.

The meat is then submerged two-thirds in a liquid, the cooking vessel is covered, and the product is simmered (moist heat) until fork tender. The juices from the meat provide some of the moisture, but most is added separately in the form of water, stock, wine, or juices. The complex flavors created by the dry-heat browning step solubilize in the cooking liquid and add a depth of flavor and color that otherwise would be absent. Typical braised items are lamb or veal shank (osso buco), short ribs, pot roast, and oxtail.

Because meat cuts best for braising are tough and full of connective tissue, they are slowly cooked in a low to moderate oven (300 to 325°F [149 to 163°C]) for an extended period. Smaller items are braised for a shorter time (2 to 3 hours, or until fork tender). Larger items are braised for 4 to 5 hours (for example, large, tough pieces of meat from the shoulder, shank, and leg quarters).

During the moist cooking phase, the tough connective tissue, collagen, is converted to gelatin, the meat becomes succulent and tender, and the sauce begins to thicken both from evaporation and also from the gelatin that is produced.

Stewing differs from braising mainly in the size of the item cooked. In general, stews are made from bite-size pieces of meat that are completely submerged in the stewing liquid. Also, cook times are shorter due to the smaller size of the items being cooked. Examples of stewing are chili, beef stroganoff, beef stew, and beef bourguignon. Note that stews and braises containing "white" meats (chicken, veal) are not typically seared before simmering as browning is not desired in these cases.

Immersion Cooking (Sous Vide)

Immersion cooking or *sous vide* cooking is the process of cooking food, sealed under vacuum (usually in a heat-proof plastic bag), in a temperature-controlled water bath. *Sous vide* literally translates as "under vacuum," which is the key to this cooking method. This moist-heat cooking method brings distinct advantages because the vacuum bag prevents escape of volatile flavors and aromas, and allows the food to gently cook in its own juices. The method also eliminates the possibility of overcooking because food is cooked in water maintained at the exact same temperature as the desired finished product's final temperature. Take for example, a vacuum-packed seasoned piece of meat immersed in a bath of water maintained at 145°F (63°C) and circulated to ensure even temperature. Regardless of how long the meat is kept in this heated water, it will never be cooked beyond medium doneness, and the entire piece of meat will be cooked to the same degree. Understandably, because the temperature variance between the food being heated and the heating medium is low, the heating times can be very long. However, the longer cooking times enable virtually the complete breakdown of connective tissues, producing a very tender, perfectly cooked end product. In addition, flavors and nutrients are trapped inside the bag and can easily be turned into a delicious and nutritious sauce. Of course, because this is a moist-heat process, caramelization and Maillard browning do not occur. If those flavors and colors are desired, the meats must be seared before being placed in the vacuum bag. Likewise, if a surface crust is desired (for a steak, for instance), searing can also take place after removal from the bag at the conclusion of *sous vide* cooking. In this case, the meat should be blotted dry before searing. With *sous vide* cooking, it is essential to use proper procedures and well-maintained equipment because the food product spends a large amount of time in the microbial growth danger zone (40 to 140°F [4.5 to 60°C]), and anaerobic bacterial spores from *Clostridium botulinum* can germinate if proper temperature control is not maintained. Therefore, *sous vide* foods must be refrigerated or frozen for storage if not immediately consumed. As a result of this concern for safety, the USDA and many local health departments require restaurants and food processors who wish to use this process to be fully trained and certified.

●Thickeners

In addition to cooking method and flavor development, sauce texture is next in importance to delivering a rewarding eating experience. A variety of thickeners are used as important tools in the creation of a great dish, and it is important to understand them and why and how they work. Commonly used thickening methods include roux, reductions, starches, gelatin, purees, and emulsions. Each of these provides distinctive characteristics and mouthfeel.

Roux

A roux is a combination of equal parts by weight of fat and flour that are cooked to remove the raw cereal taste of the flour. The cooked roux is then added to sauces to thicken them. Typically, all-purpose flour is used for roux because its starch content is higher than that of durum flour or bread flour. The fat portion of the roux can come from any source; oil or clarified butter are most commonly used in the restaurant kitchen. However, many chefs choose a fat whose distinctive flavor enhances the dish, for example, duck fat or bacon grease. Roux is cooked in a sauté pan or skillet for varying lengths of time, depending on the color and flavor desired. White, blond, brown, and black roux are the traditional descriptions. Each is cooked a little longer, further caramelizing the starches in the flour while rendering them less able to swell and hydrate. The darker the roux, the more is needed to thicken the same volume of liquid.

Thickening with roux is simply adding and hydrating the starch molecules contained in the flour. The fat serves as a medium to cook the flour, but it also separates each small granule of starch so it can be incorporated into the sauce without clumping. Starch swelling of roux made with all-purpose flour begins when the liquid reaches about 155°F (68°C).

Reductions

A reduction is the simplest and oldest form of concentrating and thickening sauces or broths; it also captures more of the flavor and clarity of the original ingredients without added flavors from the addition of other thickeners. The process of evaporating the water from a sauce or gravy results in an increase in the concentration of solids. This results in a thickening effect by increasing the level of solids in suspension; it also concentrates the flavor compounds and salts that are in the solution. Because of this, it is better to season to taste once the sauce or broth is reduced. Examples of reductions include demi-glace, tomato sauce and ketchup, maple syrup, cream reductions, and fruit jellies.

Starches

Starch *slurries* (starch suspended in a liquid, usually water) are used in a wide variety of applications to provide rapid thickening. Starches can be extracted from a wide variety of source materials, including corn, wheat, potato, rice, and tapioca. Each type has its own functional benefits and brings different character to the sauce. For instance, wheat starches develop much more opacity in a sauce than does cornstarch, which yields a translucent sauce.

Modified food starches are manufactured with functional qualities that are custom-designed for nearly any application. Starch manufacturers can custom-craft starches to tolerate different levels of shear, freeze-thaw stability, high or low pH, and hydration temperatures. For example, native "cook-up" starches require being transformed into a slurry before being added to a hot liquid to prevent the starches from clumping up. The liquid then needs to be heated so that the starch granules can begin taking up water (gelatinize) and provide thickening. Modified "cold set" ("instantized" or pre-gelatinized starches) do not require being made into a slurry or heating to work. They have already gone through the gelatinization process by the starch processor, then have been dried for shelf stability and ease of use.

Gelatin

Gelatin is a thickening agent that is virtually odorless, colorless, and tasteless. Formed from the *hydrolysis* of collagen, this protein, when dissolved in water and heated, forms a matrix that entraps water. Gelatin forms a reversible gel (discussed in Chapter 2). It is unique in that it creates more viscosity the colder the product becomes. This is particularly useful when a food must be solid at room temperature but pourable when hot. Gelatins are commonly used in cold dessert applications. That said, small amounts of gelatin added to a sauce will also provide viscosity and mouthfeel.

Pureeing

Using the process of pureeing to thicken is accomplished by the mechanical breakdown of cooked solids along with some or all of the liquid in which they were cooked. Purees can be chunky or silky smooth, depending on the desired texture, and pureeing is accomplished through the use of high-speed blenders, commercial food processors, homogenizers, or mills of various types. Examples of commercial purees include applesauce, mashed potatoes, pesto, hummus, and all types of baby foods.

Conclusion

In summary, it is critical that today's research chef and food product developer understand the fundamentals of cooking techniques, how to choose the right methods to achieve the desired results, and how each method impacts the product. This combined expertise is what we know today as Culinology®. It leads to greater food development efficiency, quality, speed to market, and profitability for the processor, and better-tasting, more nutritious, and affordable foods for consumers. This collaboration of chefs and scientists, of art and science, is fundamental to the future of food product development.

4

Protein-Based Foods: Introduction and Red Meats

James W. Lamkey, Ph.D., Technical Services, Spicetec Flavors and Seasonings

Introduction to Protein Chemistry

High-quality protein is a key nutrient in a healthy diet. It is a major part of the skin, muscles, organs, and glands, where it provides structure, support, and cellular repair and helps regulate many functions of the body. Immunity, digestion, muscle contraction, wound healing, and reproduction all rely on proteins for proper function.

Nutritional Properties of Proteins

Amino acids are the basic building blocks of proteins and the nutrients necessary for normal bodily functions. Twenty amino acids are found in proteins, but only nine are considered essential to adult humans: phenylalanine, valine, threonine, tryptophan, isoleucine, methionine, leucine, histidine, and lysine. Cysteine (or sulfur-containing amino acids), tyrosine (or aromatic amino acids), and arginine are additionally required by infants and growing children.[1] Essential amino acids are so called because the body cannot synthesize them, which makes it necessary to include them in one's diet.

The quality of a protein is measured by its amino acid content. Proteins that do not contain all the essential amino acids are considered incomplete proteins. All animal-derived proteins (except for gelatin), including eggs and milk, are complete proteins. Most vegetable-derived proteins (with few exceptions) are incomplete, usually lacking in either lysine (grains) or methionine (legumes). In each case, the missing essential amino acid is called the limiting amino acid. A well-balanced diet is essential to meet dietary requirements, particularly when following a vegetarian diet. Failure to include even one of the limiting amino acids in the diet can result in serious health consequences.

Animal-derived proteins are often considered nutritionally superior to plant proteins. That said, abundant controversy regarding the harvesting of meat is based on personal preference, religious beliefs, ethical issues, and environmental concerns. However, meat protein continues to play a major role in the American diet.

Although most plant proteins do not contain all of the essential amino acids, through careful planning and selection the consumption of complementary vegetables can provide a highly nutritious diet. Complementary vegetables, when eaten over the course of a day, can provide all the essential amino acids needed to maintain a nutritionally balanced diet.

The body requires a high degree of net protein utilization (NPU), which is the ratio of amino acids converted into protein versus the amount of amino acids actually consumed. When consuming complete proteins, the body is able to use the amino acids to synthesize all of the critical structural and functional proteins required for the maintenance of good health. When consuming incomplete proteins, the body converts the amino acids into energy (calories) rather than using them for protein building. Thus, they are unavailable for all of the critical protein-dependent life functions the body depends on.

If, however, a variety of incomplete proteins is consumed within the same day (e.g., beans and rice), they become complementary (beans lack methionine but supply lysine; rice lacks lysine but supplies methionine), and the body is able to recognize the entire meal as a complete protein. Called protein complementation, this strategy is essential for the maintenance of good health in individuals who eat a predominantly vegetarian diet.

Once consumed, proteins are broken down (hydrolyzed) by acids and enzymes (other proteins) in the stomach. First, hydrochloric acid hydrolyzes proteins into long-chain peptides, and then stomach enzymes reduce these peptides to di- and tripeptides. One of the more commonly recognized protease enzymes (enzymes that break down proteins only) in the stomach is pepsin. Finally, enzymes located in the small intestine (such as trypsin) hydrolyze the di- and tripeptides to individual amino acids, which are then absorbed by the small intestine.

FIGURE 4.1 Protein quality comparison chart.

Protein Type	PDCAAS	AAS	PER	BV	% Digestibility
Whey Protein	1.00	1.14	3.2	100	99
Whole Egg	1.00	1.21	3.8	88–100	98
Casein	1.00	1.00	2.5	80	99
Soy Protein Concentrate	1.00	0.99	2.2	74	95
Beef Protein	0.92	0.94	2.9	80	98
Wheat Gluten	0.25	0.47	NA	54	91

Source: Whey Protein Institute (http://wheyoflife.com/consumer/requirements).

The nutritive value of a protein is not only related to its amino acid content but also its overall digestibility. This is measured by comparing the total amount of protein consumed with that excreted in feces. Eggs, for example, are 98 percent digestible, while wheat protein (gluten) is 91 percent digestible.

There are five current methods for assessing protein quality. The Amino Acid Score (AAS) is a basic measure of protein quality, but it is not adjusted for the digestibility of the protein, which depends on the type of protein (animal proteins are more digestible than plant proteins) as well as on the method of food preparation. If digestibility is factored in, the AAS will be somewhat lower than stated. An updated version of AAS, and the one most widely used, is the Protein Digestibility Corrected Amino Acid Score (PDCAAS). As the name implies, a digestibility factor based on fecal protein is added to the AAS, giving truer results. The next three methods, Protein Efficiency Ratio (PER), Biological Value (BV), and Net Protein Utilization (NPU), are all based on feeding studies with rats. There is some concern among researchers as to how well rat studies reflect the needs of growing human infants and the maintenance of human adults.

Although soybeans are typically limited in the amino acid methionine, soy protein is commonly touted as a complete plant protein. According to the PDCAAS system, soybeans have a score of 0.91 while soy protein isolate has the maximum score of 1.0 (the same as egg whites), followed by milk and meat proteins.[2] Other plant-based sources of complete protein receiving growing recognition and achieving growing popularity include quinoa and amaranth, grains common in Latin America.

Protein Structure

Proteins are differentiated by their primary, secondary, tertiary, and sometimes quaternary structures, which influence functionality in the body and in foods. The primary structure is defined as the unbranched sequence of amino acids that comprises the backbone of proteins. This sequence is unique to each type of protein, within species as well as between species. The secondary structure is defined by patterns of hydrogen bonds between the backbone amino acids. The most common secondary structures are alpha helix (coiled arrangement), which is the format typically shown when illustrating DNA structures, and beta sheets (uncoiled arrangement). Examples of beta sheet proteins are collagen and connective tissue.

The tertiary structure, the further folding of the protein, is greatly influenced by the primary structure. Depending on the tertiary structure, proteins can be classified as globular or fibrous. Globular proteins (spheroproteins) are generally water soluble and folded. Globular proteins do not provide structure. They are primarily enzymes, transporters, and regulators of everyday functions. In aqueous environments, hydrophobic (water-fearing) groups are located on the inside of the fold while the hydrophilic (water-loving) groups are extended into the aqueous environment. In a hydrophobic environment, one that is dominated by oil or fat, these proteins refold so the hydrophobic groups are exposed while the hydrophilic groups are protected.

The second type of tertiary structure is identified as fibrous; it is found in animals only. Fibrous proteins (scleroproteins) are rod-like in shape and have the primary function of providing support and locomotion. They are usually water insoluble but can be solubilized with weak salt solutions (such as brines or marinades) under certain process conditions. They can then be used as water binders and texture builders.

The quaternary structure is how proteins interact with other proteins. Not all proteins have quaternary structures. One that does is hemoglobin, which has four identical but individual protein units grouped together with the ultimate goal of transporting oxygen to the muscles and organs of the body (hemoglobin is responsible for the color of blood). Each subgroup has an affinity for oxygen that diminishes as another subgroup entraps oxygen within its matrix. This diminished affinity for oxygen allows the fully saturated

FIGURE 4.2 Basic chemical structure of amino acids, with *R* representing various side groups.

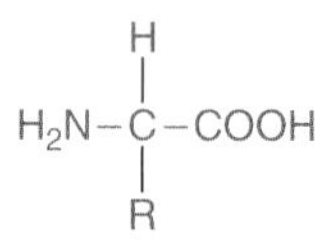

$$H_2N-\underset{\underset{R}{|}}{\overset{\overset{H}{|}}{C}}-COOH$$

hemoglobin to release its entrapped oxygen molecules to myoglobin, which in turn delivers the oxygen to the muscles and organs of the body. Myoglobin is responsible for the color of meat.

Functional Properties of Proteins

Having both hydrophobic and hydrophilic regions makes proteins excellent stabilizers of high-fat emulsions (mayonnaise) and foams (whipped cream) and as binders (bread dough). Proper processing procedures, such as optimal temperature and agitation, assist with the unfolding of the proteins to expose the hydrophobic groups, allowing them to interact with oil, fat, air, or other denatured proteins in the emulsion while the hydrophilic side chains interact with the aqueous component in the emulsion. It is the association of these proteins in stable networks that provides the desired functionality.

The protein's environment also has a significant impact on its functionality in foods. This environmental influence is primarily related to how the protein hydrates (absorbs water) and retains (or loses) water throughout the manufacturing and/or cooking process. In many cases, we want to retain as much of the moisture as possible, as in the case of roasts, steaks, or chops. In other cases, as with salamis and pepperoni, we want to reduce the moisture level under controlled conditions to improve color, texture, and shelf life. The simple task of cooking a steak is in reality a chemical process that changes the protein structure to improve tenderness, palatability, and digestibility, and that causes chemical reactions between proteins and sugars to create a more desirable color and flavor. Product developers can provide the right kind of environment to get the optimal value from any protein.

Keep in mind that any change in protein structure is considered denaturation because the protein is being taken out of its natural state. This may be temporary if the environment reverts to its original state or the processing is gentle. On the other hand, if the environmental change is permanent or the processing is severe, the structural change may become permanent. At this point, denaturation turns into coagulation, which in terms of cooking is irreversible and evidenced by curdling.

The most influential environmental characteristics affecting the structure and function of protein are pH and heat. The acidity of a substance is measured in terms of pH. As pH drops, the overall environment becomes more acidic. As pH increases, the environment becomes more basic.

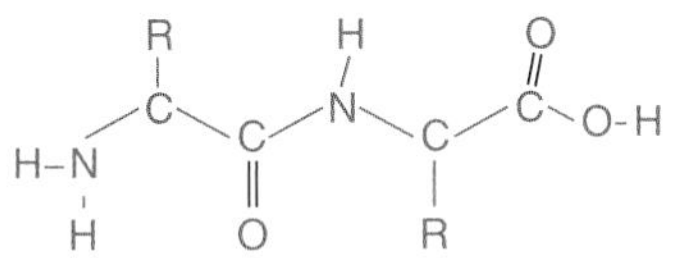

Amino acids, the building blocks of proteins, are amphoteric compounds that contain both basic (amine) groups and acidic (carboxyl) groups. This makes proteins good buffers that help aqueous systems resist sudden changes in pH.

Because of its unique combination of amino acids, each protein has both positive and negative charges that change as pH changes. When an amino acid loses a proton (a positively charged particle), the protein becomes more negatively charged. When an amino acid gains a proton, the protein becomes more positively charged. The point where the number of positive charges equals the number of negative charges is called the isoelectric point. Each type of protein has its own isoelectric point; this can be used as an analytical tool to separate and identify proteins.

In a solution with a pH below (more acidic than) the isoelectric point, the protein carries a net positive charge. Conversely, as the pH rises above (becomes more basic than) the isoelectric point, the net charge on the protein becomes negative. The impact of this change in net charge becomes apparent when we take into account one of the laws of nature: Like charges repel, while opposite charges attract. At the isoelectric point, attraction between the charges is strongest. This means the protein molecule is closed and very tightly folded. As pH moves higher than the isoelectric point, the number of negative charges increases, resulting in greater repulsion between the amino acids. This repulsion along the backbone of the protein opens up the structure, allowing for more moisture retention, which in turn improves solubility. Therefore, the solubility of a protein is lowest at its isoelectric point. *Note:* Very rarely does meat go below the isoelectric point. At some point the acid starts to hydrolyze the protein and functionality is lost.

Knowing these characteristics of proteins helps processors manipulate the functionality as well as the texture of a protein through pH modification. A marinade containing alkaline phosphates, for example, increases the pH of the meat above the isoelectric point, causing greater repulsion between the amino acids and resulting in greater moisture retention. Alternatively, fermentation of meat creates sausages (such as pepperoni) by increasing the level of acid in the meat, thus moving the pH closer to the isoelectric point, causing greater attraction between the amino acids and thereby reducing the protein's ability to retain moisture. This reduces water activity (a_w) and extends shelf life without the need for refrigeration.

Three types of protein are found in muscle foods: myofibrillar, which makes up the bulk of muscle tissue (what we characterize as meat); sarcoplasmic; and connective tissue. In the processing of meats, each protein type plays a role in the overall desirability of the finished product.

Sarcoplasmic proteins are soluble in water or very low ionic strength salt solutions (weak brines). This group contains a variety of proteins, some related to color, some to tenderness, and others to the overall function of the muscle tissue. Of these proteins, those responsible for color and

FIGURE 4.3 A dipeptide comprised of two amino acids.

FIGURE 4.4 Basic structure of proteins.

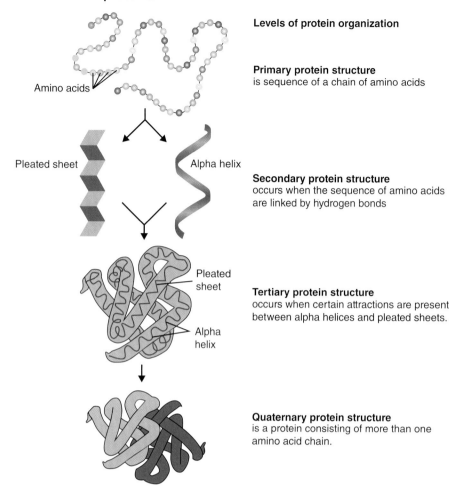

Levels of protein organization

Amino acids

Primary protein structure
is sequence of a chain of amino acids

Pleated sheet

Alpha helix

Secondary protein structure
occurs when the sequence of amino acids
are linked by hydrogen bonds

Pleated sheet

Alpha helix

Tertiary protein structure
occurs when certain attractions are present
between alpha helices and pleated sheets.

Quaternary protein structure
is a protein consisting of more than one
amino acid chain.

Source: National Institutes of Health. National Human Genome Research Institute, "Talking Glossary of Genetic Terms," accessed April 23, 2015, http://www.genome.gov/glossary/y/?id=169.

tenderness are most important. Myoglobin is a sarcoplasmic protein and, as the major pigment in red meat, is responsible for changes in color. Enzymes also belong to this category and help break down other proteins for improved tenderness.

The second group of functional proteins in meat are the stromal proteins. They include collagen, elastin, and reticulin, collectively referred to as connective tissue. Collagen is the most abundant protein in the body, as it is present in muscle, skin, and bone. In many meat cuts, the collagen is trimmed and discarded to make the meat more palatable. However, in certain cuts of meat, primarily meat from muscles used for locomotion, the collagen cannot be trimmed without losing too much of the meat to be economically feasible (yield loss). It is therefore up to the cooking conditions to improve the tenderness of these cuts. These types of meats may be cooked with moist heat to break down the collagen, which turns into gelatin, thereby tenderizing the cut. This is the basis for braising and stewing.

Myofibrillar proteins are the third type of functional protein. With the highest level of functionality in meat,

these proteins are primarily responsible for moisture retention and texture (to maximize yield and enhance eating quality). These are also known as the salt-soluble proteins; as the name implies, these proteins can be extracted from meat using salt. The addition of salt allows the meat filaments to absorb water and thus increase meat weight, volume, and flexibility. Salt dramatically enhances the water-holding capacity and the stickiness of the meat. The salt-soluble proteins combine with water through both direct molecular interactions (adsorption) and physical entrainment (absorption). The sticky marinated meat forms a binding glue-like layer of extracted proteins on its surface; this denatures or coagulates upon heating and forms a rigid, firm mass. This is the principle used in preparation of many formed meat products such as chicken nuggets or meat loaves. The three proteins of primary interest are actin, myosin, and actomyosin, the proteins responsible for muscular contraction and relaxation. Myosin has the best water-holding capacity and emulsifying properties, followed by actomyosin and finally actin.

Muscle Structure

Skeletal, smooth, and cardiac muscles are the three types of structural muscles found in food animals, with skeletal muscle comprising the majority of meat. Cardiac muscle is found only in the heart. Smooth muscle comprises the organs and membranes of the body.

Skeletal muscle, the primary functional component of meat, is also referred to as striated muscle because of its appearance, which is banded when viewed under a microscope. The striations in skeletal muscle are caused by sarcomeres, the individual contractile units of muscle. The appearance is the result of alternating dark and light areas caused by the various proteins responsible for contraction. The primary proteins involved in contraction are actin and myosin, the combination of which forms actomyosin. Contraction occurs when myosin, stimulated by a nerve impulse, pulls the actin filament into the center of the sarcomere, resulting in a shortening of the sarcomere.

Myofibrils are composed of multiple sarcomeres, the length of which are determined by the size and function of the muscle with which they are associated. The sarcomeres contract unilaterally, resulting in the contraction of the myofibril. Muscle fibers, which are the cellular structures of muscle, are composed of multiple myofibrils. Muscle fibers in turn form muscle bundles and, ultimately, whole muscles. All of the muscle fibers within a muscle work in unison when stimulated by nerve signals to perform the work requested.

● Meat

Meat is commonly recognized as the flesh of animals used for food. Usually the term refers to skeletal muscle, but it also includes other edible tissues such as the organs—liver, brains, tongue, kidneys, tripe (stomach), chitterlings (intestines), sweetbreads (pancreas and thymus), and skin (pork rinds). Offal is the general term for edible internal organs. Although generally we think of meat as referring to mammalian species (cows, pigs, sheep, and goats), technically speaking, fish and poultry provide "meat" as well.

Whatever its source, meat has been a substantial part of the human diet from earliest times. Initially, humans resorted exclusively to hunting to acquire meat. Then, approximately 7500 years ago, at the time of the earliest civilizations, domestication of meat animals began. This included sheep in Egypt and Mesopotamia from 3500 to 3000 BC, pigs in Hungary as early as 2500 BC, and cattle, also in Mesopotamia, from as early as 5000 BC. Selective cattle breeding that resulted in certain animals bred for meat production and others for milk production did not occur until the mid-1700s.

Meat consists of approximately 75 percent water, 19 percent protein, 2.5 percent fat, 1.2 percent carbohydrates, and 2.3 percent non-protein substances (minerals and free amino acids). All muscle tissue is very high in complete protein, containing all of the essential amino acids, and is also a good source of zinc, vitamin B_{12}, selenium, phosphorous, niacin, vitamin B_6, iron, and riboflavin. Meat is low in carbohydrates and does not contain any dietary fiber. While each kind of meat has about the same content of protein and carbohydrates, fat content varies widely depending on the species and breed of animal, the way in which the animal was raised (including what it was fed), the anatomical part of the body, and the methods of butchering and cooking. Fat contributes most of the calorie content of meat and is relevant to concerns about dietary health, particularly because mammalian animal fat is saturated and contains cholesterol.

Overconsuming large quantities of food, including meat, can have adverse effects on health, including obesity, heart disease, hypertension and diabetes. In recent years, health concerns have been raised about the consumption of meat increasing the risk of cancer. In particular, red meat and processed meat were found to be associated with higher risk of cancer, particularly cancer of the colon. The complexity of cancer limits our ability to be absolutely sure about cause and effect for any behavior in which a person participates. The consumption of meat is one way to achieve the nutritional requirements a body needs. Maintaining a healthy weight

FIGURE 4.5 **The contractile proteins of muscle.**

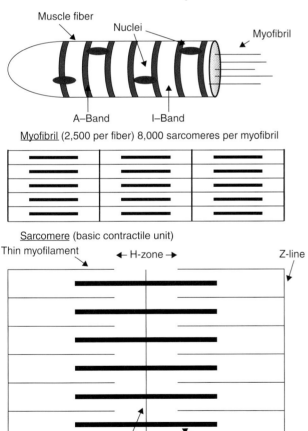

Myofibril (2,500 per fiber) 8,000 sarcomeres per myofibril

Sarcomere (basic contractile unit)

Source: Texas A & M University, accessed September 24, 2015, http://meat.tamu.edu/ansc-307-honors/structure-muscle.

and a healthy lifestyle are the key ingredients to reduce the risk of chronic diseases, including cancer.

Meat Production

Meat is produced by killing livestock animals and harvesting their edible parts. The age at the time of slaughter varies depending on the animal as well as the target market for the meat. As a general rule, beef destined for retail and foodservice markets is harvested from cattle that are 24 to 30 months of age. Veal, on the other hand, is from cattle harvested at 6 to 8 months of age, which is similar for pigs and lambs. Many processors vary this time depending on the cost of feed and other environmental conditions, taking a risk that they will not get the full value of the carcass.

A calf increases in size tenfold from a birthweight of 100 pounds to 1000 pounds at the time of harvest. The first six months after birth, calves live on mother's milk and grass. Then the calf is weaned from the cow and dines mostly on grass with some grain supplementation. For grass-fed animals, this scenario plays out until the day of harvest. Alternatively, at 18 months of age, grain-fed cattle are started on a highly concentrated, nutrient-balanced diet consisting of corn and soybeans for 180 days, at which time they are harvested.

The fat from grass-fed cattle may have a yellow tinge that comes from the large quantities of carotene in grass. The fat from grain-fed cattle is almost white in color. Whether the fat from grass-fed beef provides significant nutritional benefits over grain-fed is still a controversial subject, especially as most consumers trim the majority of fat from their beef before eating it.

Because of the higher calorie content of grain, grain-fed cattle generally lay down more marbling (intramuscular fat deposits) than the same animal on a grass diet. More marbling means the animal can receive a higher quality grade (prime, choice, select, etc.). The higher the quality grade, the higher the price paid for the carcass. Although some breeds of animals can become sufficiently marbled while eating grass, a grain diet allows more fat to be deposited. This means cattle that are genetically unable to become highly marbled on a grass diet achieve more marbling and a higher quality grade on a grain diet.

One of the main differences between cattle and pigs is their ability to digest cellulose. Pigs have simple stomachs, much like humans, and cannot digest cellulose. Cattle, on the other hand, are ruminants and have very complex digestive systems. For that reason, cattle can use grass as a source of nutrients while pigs cannot. Other animals that are ruminants include sheep, goats, and deer (venison).

Harvesting Muscle Proteins

Each step in the harvesting of meat is designed to assure high quality, worker safety, and, ultimately, safe and healthy food for consumers. Time, temperature, good sanitation practices, and condition of the animal are all important to maximizing the quality of the protein being harvested.

Immobilization, or stunning, is the first step of the harvest process. This renders the animal unconscious so it does not feel pain or become a safety hazard to individuals during the rest of the slaughter process. Immobilization is accomplished by one of three methods: physical, electrical, or modified atmosphere.

Physical immobilization is normally used for large animals such as cattle, while electrical and modified atmosphere methods are used for smaller animals. The physical method is a high-impact force delivered to a targeted spot on the head, usually delivered by a mechanical device such as captive bolt or plastic bullet. This renders the animal unconscious.

Electricity, when applied to an animal's body, sends electrical currents through the muscles, causing violent contractions. These can cause bones or blood vessels to break, resulting in blood spotting. It is important for proper settings to be used so these defects are minimized.

Use of modified atmosphere techniques, such as vacuum chambers or carbon monoxide, can reduce the defects that occur with electrical stunning. Oxygen is removed until the animal is unconscious. As a result, there are no violent contractions that could damage the meat.

The process of converting muscle to meat begins when the supply of oxygen to the muscles and major organs is lost. For terrestrial animals, this begins with the removal of blood, known as exsanguination. When blood is removed, not only the supply of oxygen but also the ability to remove cellular waste products is lost. Without oxygen, anaerobic fermentation becomes the primary source of energy for the muscles, which are still trying to maintain homeostasis (the body's physiologic status quo). As a result, lactic acid, a major byproduct of anaerobic fermentation, begins to accumulate in the muscles. Without blood to remove it, the buildup of lactic acid causes the overall pH of the meat to decline and become more acidic. Muscle pH is normally close to neutral (6.2 to 7.2), while meat, under normal conditions, has a pH in the range of 5.7 to 6.2, depending on the species, the muscle within the animal, and the ultimate concentration of lactic acid. Extenuating circumstances could make the ultimate pH higher or lower. This could have a tremendous impact on the appearance and functionality of the protein.

If an animal is overly excited for a short period (1 to 2 hours) before slaughter, large quantities of lactic acid will be produced in the muscle. This also occurs under times of heavy exercise. (The pain or burn you feel in your muscles after lengthy exercise or running is the result of high levels of lactic acid.) If lactic acid is still present at the time of exsanguination, circulating blood is no longer available to remove it, and the pH of the meat drops rapidly to a point lower than it would be normally. A rapid drop in pH when the temperature of the muscle is still above 90°F (32°C) results in a breakdown of the protein and loss of functionality. The meat will look very pale, be soft to the touch, and release moisture easily (be exudative). Pork and turkey are more prone to this condition, which is called PSE, for pale, soft, and exudative. In hogs, this is a genetic condition that was inadvertently selected when pigs were bred for leanness. As pigs became leaner, they also

Food quality issues are more commonly associated with whole muscle products, but food safety issues are the greater concern with ground meat products. With whole muscle products, the interior is not contaminated unless the surface of the meat is penetrated; therefore, it is easy to destroy surface bacteria through the cooking process. With ground products, however, the very act of grinding has the potential to mix bacteria throughout the product. Without reaching proper internal temperatures, bacteria can survive the cooking process. To be completely sure proper temperatures are attained, thermometers should be used to check the internal temperature.

Channels of Distribution

Meat packers are businesses that harvest animals grown for meat. *Purveyors* are businesses that buy primal cuts from packers and cut the meat into wholesale and retail cuts for the retail and foodservice industries. *Processors* take raw materials from the packers and further process them into products such as hams, frankfurters, roast beef, and sausages. Some retail supermarket and big-box chains buy primals directly from the packer and cut the meat themselves.

In the late 1970s and early 1980s, the industry shifted from shipping animal carcasses to shipping boxed meat, an innovation started by a company then known as IBP (now known as Tyson). Where purveyors and retail outlets once had to deal with marketing the entire carcass and disposing of waste fat and bone, the advent of boxed meat allowed them to buy only the wholesale cut needed, usually boneless, trimmed to specification, and vacuum packaged. More than 90 percent of the beef in this country is merchandized as boxed beef. Consolidation in the meat industry has also streamlined meat channels so that many packers are also purveyors and processors, selling product directly to foodservice and retail outlets. In some cases, the processor prepares retail cuts at a central location and ships to stores to save time and labor.

Boxed beef and veal is usually based on the primal cuts of the carcass: chuck, rib, loin, round, plate, brisket, and flank. Currently, retailers and foodservice companies can buy subprimals (smaller cuts of meat obtained from the larger primal cuts of an animal) based on specifications outlined by International Meat Product Specifications (IMPS).

Pork processors quickly followed suit, offering pork subprimals vacuum packaged and shipped in boxes. Pork loin, ham, belly, and shoulder are the four primals offered to retailers and processors. The ham and belly are often further processed into cured ham and bacon, respectively. Loins are used to create pork chops and roasts. Shoulders are often separated into the shoulder picnic and shoulder butt. The picnic can be cured to provide a smoked picnic. The shoulder butt is often offered as a pork roast. Both can be used for trimming to make sausage products. *Note:* Only cured meat from the ham (the back leg and buttock) can legally be called *ham*. Even though meat from the shoulder (picnic and butt) can be cured to look and taste exactly like ham, it cannot be labeled as such. It can only be labeled *picnic ham, smoked shoulder,* or *smoked butt.*

Lamb primals—leg, loin, rack, and shoulder—are also offered boxed. The most popular retail lamb cuts are shoulder blade chops, loin chops, rack of lamb, shoulder chops, lamb leg, and lamb rib chops.

Meat that has been recently harvested and has been maintained at a temperature below 40°F (4.4°C) and above 28°F (2.2°C) is considered fresh. One exception to this is poultry, which is normally cooled to 26°F (–3.3°C) for distribution, putting a slight ice crust on the surface.

Wholesale red meat is usually distributed in plastic bags under vacuum (generally known as Cryovac®, although this is actually a trade name of the Sealed Air Corporation). Storing meat under vacuum removes the oxygen required for the growth of spoilage microorganisms, resulting in extended shelf life. In most cases, vacuum-packaged wholesale cuts have a shelf life of 120 days or more. However, the removal of oxygen results in the meat becoming purple as myoglobin reverts to the deoxymyoglobin state.

Meat can also be stored and distributed under modified atmosphere packaging (MAP). This system begins in much the same way as vacuum packaging, as all the air is removed. However, a special mixture of gases (combinations of carbon dioxide, nitrogen, and oxygen) is put back into the bag (via gas flushing), thus modifying the atmosphere inside the bag. MAP helps optimize shelf life, flavor, and appearance by reducing oxidation and the growth of spoilage bacteria. In some cases, the modified-atmosphere package is referred to as a *pillow pack* when the package appears to have excessive air inside. Pillow packs are more often used for processed meat and consumer packaged meat rather than wholesale meat cuts to maintain the integrity of the slices and keep them from sticking together.

One recent addition to MAP is carbon monoxide (CO), which has long been used in Europe as part of MAP packaging. Although carbon monoxide is toxic to breathe at high levels, it is considered safe at the levels used in packaging. Flushing packaged raw meats with carbon monoxide allows for the retention of the characteristic cherry-red color of fresh meat beyond what would be normal because CO binds more tightly to myoglobin than does oxygen while still providing the color effects of oxygenation. The downside is that meat can retain a fresh appearance well beyond the stage where it is no longer wholesome for consumption. In this case, strict attention must be paid by both the packer and the consumer to package dating.

Aging of Beef

It is well known that aging beef creates a product that is superior in both texture and flavor to unaged beef. This is not true for other protein-based products (seafood, poultry, pork). What makes beef so different?

Most domestically raised meat animals are slaughtered when less than 1 year of age; many are less than 6 months of age. Beef, on the other hand, comes from animals more than 1 year old and more typically approaching 24 months of age. As an animal ages, connective tissue increases and becomes less soluble, causing a reduction in tenderness of the meat.

Enzymes are inherent in meat and become active a short time after harvest, usually due to the release of calcium as the cells start to die. These enzymes, collectively identified as proteases (enzymes that break down proteins), begin to break down the protein, resulting in more tender meat. This is the initiation of the aging process. The longer the aging time, the more tender the meat. However, during the aging process, microorganisms actively grow on the surface of the meat if it is not handled properly. While certain microorganisms are desirable for flavor development, those responsible for spoilage or safety issues must be controlled.

There are two methods for aging meat. The older method is dry aging, where the meat is aged unwrapped and exposed to the air, while wet aging is relatively new (being associated with the development of boxed beef) and takes place while the meat is enclosed in its vacuum package.

Temperature, relative humidity, air movement, and general sanitation of the area where the meat is dry aged are essential considerations in successfully aging beef. Temperature of the aging room should be maintained at 34 to 36°F (1 to 2°C), relative humidity at 85 to 90 percent, and an air flow of 15 to 20 linear feet per minute at the surface of the product.

The area where the aging takes place should be cleaned and sanitized before and during the process. Beef cuts are perishable, and many factors can contribute toward spoilage. Aside from poor sanitation in the area causing bad odors to occur, storing any other strongly scented product in the room can cause off-flavor development. Excessive aging results in an accumulation of microorganisms. Their presence in large numbers results in a slimy-appearing surface, as the most likely places for microorganisms to grow are on the moist surfaces. If these contaminated areas are not completely trimmed off and discarded during processing, the end products of microbial growth will produce undesirable flavors and odors in the finished product.

Shrinkage occurs during dry aging because the meat is unwrapped and exposed to moving air. In fact, shrinkage (due to dehydration) is necessary in order to concentrate flavor components in the beef, increasing its desirability. The longer the aging period, the greater the total loss in weight due to dehydration and the need for trimming of surfaces that have dried excessively or have detectable microbial growth. As a result, dry-aged beef is much more expensive than wet-aged beef due to the large amount of dehydration and trim loss.

Wet aging is accomplished by leaving vacuum-packaged cuts of meat under refrigeration for an extended period before sale. As in dry aging, the primary objective is to tenderize the meat. However, the meat resulting from this type of aging has a different flavor and texture than dry-aged beef because it does not get dehydrated, and the organisms that grow under vacuum are different from those that grow in air. The microbes that grow on the surface of dry-aged meats are aerobic organisms (including bacteria and molds), whereas anaerobic bacteria, which produce lactic acid, primarily grow in vacuum-packaged meats. This lactic acid production helps with the tenderizing process and contributes to overall flavor.

Because there is no moisture loss, yields are higher and therefore cost to both the processor and the consumer is lower.

● Common Concerns in the Meat Industry
Bovine Spongiform Encephalopathy

Bovine spongiform encephalopathy (BSE), also known as *mad cow disease*, belongs to the family of transmissible spongiform encephalopathies (TSE)—rare progressive neurodegenerative disorders that affect both humans and animals. TSEs are distinguished by long incubation periods, characteristic spongiform (sponge-like) appearance of the brain associated with neuronal loss, and a failure to induce inflammatory response. BSE is a chronic, degenerative disease that affects the brain and central nervous system in adult cattle after a long incubation period; it is progressive and always fatal. The disease is not caused by a virus or bacterium but is thought to be the result of a pathological change in the structure of a naturally occurring brain protein, the prion protein. A prion is a transmissible agent that is able to induce abnormal folding of cellular proteins in the brain, leading to brain damage and the characteristic signs and symptoms of the disease. The change makes the prion proteins very resistant to degradation and extremely infectious, thus enabling transmission of the disease.[4]

Other TSEs include scrapie (affecting sheep and goats), chronic wasting disease (CWD, affecting deer and elk), transmissible mink encephalopathy (TME), and feline spongiform encephalopathy (FSE). However, BSE is the only one found in an animal raised for human consumption where transmission of the disease to humans has been seen (known as a "zoonose").

The spread of the disease has been exacerbated by the practice of feeding cattle (which are herbivores) with feed containing mammalian nervous systems (typically from other infected cattle).

BSE has been detected only in the brain, spinal cord, bone marrow, and retina of affected cattle. No BSE agents have been detected in muscle tissue/meat, milk, or blood. Although widespread in Europe, to date the United States has seen only three documented cases of BSE-infected cows, the last one in 2006.[5]

There are human forms of these diseases (Creutzfeldt-Jakob Disease [CJD]; Gerstmann-Straussler-Scheinker syndrome [GSS]; fatal familial insomnia [FFI]; and kuru, which is seen in certain cannibalistic tribes), but variant CJD (vCJD) is the only one caused by ingestion of BSE-diseased cattle. The pathologies of all of these diseases are the same, with extensive irreversible degenerative changes to the brain leading to death. Among humans, as of October 2009,[6] the total worldwide number of confirmed vCJD deaths is 213, including 167 in the United Kingdom, 25 in France, 5 in Spain, 4 in Ireland, 3 each in the United States and the Netherlands, 2 in Portugal, and 1 each in Italy, Canada, Saudi Arabia, and Japan. There has never been a case of vCJD that did not have a history of exposure within a country where the cattle disease BSE was occurring. There is no known treatment for vCJD, and it is invariably fatal.[7]

U.S. agencies have acted quickly with precautionary steps to prevent BSE in cattle and vCJD in humans from spreading. These steps include:

- Prohibiting importation of live ruminant animals and most ruminant products from all of Europe (USDA)
- Examining U.S. cattle exhibiting abnormal neurological behavior to test for BSE (USDA)
- Prohibiting the use of most mammalian protein in the manufacture of animal feeds given to ruminant animals (FDA)
- Recommending that animal tissues used in drug products not come from a country with BSE (FDA)
- Issuing guidelines asking blood centers to exclude potential donors who have spent six or more cumulative months in the United Kingdom between 1980 and 1996 from donating blood (FDA)
- Conducting regular surveillance for cases of vCJD among humans (Centers for Disease Control [CDC])
- Conducting research on BSE, CJD, vCJD, and related neurological diseases (National Institute of Health [NIH])

Parasites: *Trichina spiralis*

Trichina spiralis is a roundworm (nematode) parasite that can live in the muscles of animals such as pigs and rats, and when ingested by humans can cause the disease trichinosis. Poor management practices were one of the main reasons for high incidences of *Trichina spiralis* in pigs raised in the United States. Many years ago, pigs were primarily fed garbage and other scraps, which were the primary source of the parasite. Modern methods use corn and soybeans as the primary feed for commercial hog operations, with tight controls on vermin (mice and rats) infestation. Until recently, consumers were instructed to only eat pork products that were cooked well done to assure the parasite was killed. Now, chefs and other food preparers can cook pork to a lower degree of doneness, resulting in a juicier and more tender product.

Note: Besides cooking, freezing is also an acceptable method for eliminating *Trichina* in pork. The USDA's Code of Federal Regulations requires that pork intended for use in processed products be frozen at 0°F (−17.8°C) or below for a minimum of 106 hours. Curing (application of salt, nitrites, smoking, and/or drying) and irradiation are also effective ways to render *Trichina* noninfective.

Bacterial Concerns

The CDC has reported that about 48 million people—one in six Americans—get sick, 128,000 are hospitalized, and 3000 die annually from foodborne diseases.[8] Meat products, which are an excellent source of nutrients for bacterial pathogens, can be a major source of foodborne illnesses. These, however, can be prevented with proper handling, processing, and storage. Proper handling of meat begins with the live animal and must not end until the product is consumed. Each step must set up hurdles so that microorganisms of concern do not cause illness.

Antibiotics are used in the livestock industry to prevent disease, which is important for both animal and human health. Farmers and ranchers believe that not treating cattle that become sick is inhumane. The use of antibiotics in the meat industry is controversial because of their effects on microbial resistance. Antibiotics used in beef cattle production must go through a rigorous testing process before being approved by the Food and Drug Administration (FDA). The Center for Veterinary Medicine (CVM), a branch of the FDA, is responsible for ensuring that animal drugs are safe, effective, and manufactured to the highest quality standards. While there are many aspects that go into the animal antibiotic approval process, human safety is a key component. Withdrawal times are established as part of the approval process to specify the number of days that must pass between the last antibiotic treatment and before the animal can enter the food supply. This ensures that an antibiotic has sufficiently cleared an animal's system. By law, any person administering antibiotics to livestock must follow withdrawal periods. Additionally, the FDA and U.S. Department of Agriculture (USDA) have a coordinated surveillance program to monitor for antibiotic residues.[9]

Four organisms are of primary concern to the meat industry: *Campylobacter jejuni*, *Salmonella* (various subspecies), *Escherichia coli* (especially E. coli O157:H7), and *Listeria monocytogenes*. The following information is taken from the Centers for Disease Control and Prevention.[10]

Campylobacter jejuni

- *Campylobacter jejuni* is the most commonly reported bacterial cause of foodborne illness (FBI) in the United States. The CDC estimates (2011) that *C. jejuni* causes approximately 845,000 illnesses, 8400 hospitalizations, and 76 deaths in the United States each year. Most cases of *Campylobacter* infection occur as isolated, sporadic events, and are not usually a part of large outbreaks.
- *C. jejuni* is a curved gram-negative rod that grows best at 107°F (41.67°C) and low oxygen concentrations. These characteristics are ideal for growth in its normal habitat—the intestines of warm-blooded birds and mammals.
- It can be found in retail poultry. Produce may also become contaminated with *Campylobacter* if it is exposed to raw meat or poultry products or juices in the kitchen, or if it is contaminated by animal feces in the fields where it is grown. *Campylobacter* is also commonly found in raw milk and dairy products. However, the source is unknown for more than 50 percent of campylobacteriosis infections.

- *Campylobacter* causes gastroenteritis with fever, bloody diarrhea, abdominal pain, malaise, nausea, and vomiting two to five days after ingestion; symptoms last a week. In a small number of cases, *Campylobacter* infection can also cause a rare disease called *Guillain-Barré syndrome*, which occurs several weeks after the acute diarrheal illness and may result in permanent paralysis.[11]
- *Campylobacter* readily develops antibiotic resistance from continuous exposure to antibiotic-treated chicken feed.
- *Campylobacter* is easily destroyed by cooking; the primary modes of transmission are through consumption of unwashed raw or undercooked foods and cross-contamination whereby uncooked foods come into contact with contaminated surfaces. Ingestion of as few as 500 organisms—an amount that can be found in one drop of chicken juice—has been proven to cause human illness.[12]

Salmonella Species

- *Salmonella* is the second most commonly reported cause of bacterial FBI, with approximately 30,000 confirmed cases yearly in the United States. (The CDC estimates (2011) that over 1 million cases occur annually in the United States, but the majority go unreported). Of these cases, approximately 20,000 result in hospitalization, and 378 result in death. This means that *Salmonella* accounts for almost 30 percent of foodborne illness–related deaths each year.
- *Salmonella* can cause three kinds of illness: gastroenteritis, typhoid fever, and bacteremia (infection of the blood). Symptoms of salmonella gastroenteritis include diarrhea, abdominal cramps, fever, nausea, and/or vomiting. In mild cases, the diarrhea may be non-bloody, occur several times per day, and not be very voluminous; in severe cases, it may be frequent, bloody and/or mucoidal, and of high volume. Fever generally occurs in the 100–102°F (37.8–38.9°C) range. Whereas the diarrhea typically lasts 24 to 72 hours, patients often report fatigue and other nonspecific symptoms lasting seven days or longer.
- An infectious dose of *Salmonella* is incredibly small, between 15 and 20 cells.
- *Salmonella* is found in meats, poultry, eggs (even inside the shell!), milk and dairy, seafood, sauces and salad dressings, cake mixes, cream-filled desserts, and so on.

Escherichia coli (E. coli)

- *E. coli* is a normal inhabitant of the intestinal tract of humans and other warm-blooded animals and birds. It is the dominant bacterial species found in feces. Newborns have a sterile alimentary tract, which within two days becomes colonized with *E. coli*.

- Most kinds of *E. coli* bacteria do not cause disease in humans. Normally, *E. coli* serves a useful function in the body by competitively suppressing the growth of harmful bacterial species in the gut and by synthesizing appreciable amounts of vitamins.
- The CDC estimates that every year at least 75,000 Americans are sickened, 2000 are hospitalized, and about 60 die as a direct result of *E. coli* infections and its complications.
- More than 700 serotypes of *E. coli* have been identified. Those that are responsible for the numerous reports of outbreaks traced to the consumption of contaminated foods and beverages produce Shiga toxin (Stx), so called because it is virtually identical to that produced by another bacterium known as *Shigella dysenteriae* type 1 (which also causes bloody diarrhea and hemolytic uremic syndrome [HUS]). Shiga toxin is one of the most potent toxins known to man, so much so that the CDC lists it as a potential bioterrorism agent.
- The best-known and most notorious Stx-producing *E. coli* is *E. coli* O157:H7. Stx-producing *E. coli* do not sicken the animals that carry it. The animals are merely the reservoir for the bacteria.
- Although *E. coli* O157:H7 is responsible for the majority of human illnesses attributed to *E. coli*, additional Stx-producing *E. coli* can also cause hemorrhagic colitis and post-diarrheal hemolytic uremic syndrome (D+HUS). HUS is a syndrome that is defined by the trilogy of hemolytic anemia (destruction of red blood cells), thrombocytopenia (low platelet count), and acute kidney failure. It can lead to permanent kidney failure and death (it is the number-one cause of kidney failure in children). In about 10 percent of *E. coli* cases, the Shiga toxin results in HUS.
- Stx-producing *E. coli* organisms are hardy and can survive several weeks on surfaces such as countertops and up to a year in some materials like compost. They have a very low infectious dose, meaning that a relatively small number of bacteria (fewer than 50) are needed to cause infection.
- The CDC estimates that 85 percent of *E. coli* O157:H7 infections are foodborne in origin.[13] In fact, consumption of any food or beverage that becomes contaminated by animal (especially cattle) manure can result in contracting the disease. Foods identified as sources of contamination include ground beef, venison, sausages, dried (noncooked) salami, unpasteurized milk and cheese, unpasteurized apple juice and cider, orange juice, alfalfa and radish sprouts, lettuce, spinach, and water. Pizza and cookie dough have also been identified as sources of *E. coli* outbreaks.
- It is important to note that only about 10 percent of infections occur in outbreaks; the rest are sporadic.

E. coli in Ground Beef

At one time, before the widespread dissemination of *E. coli* throughout the food chain, HUS secondary to *E. coli* O157:H7 infection was known as *hamburger disease*. The ground beef connection has not gone away. Numerous outbreaks and massive recalls of contaminated ground beef continue to plague both the industry and the public.

Meat can become contaminated at any point along the supply chain and even during preparation. With ground meat, unlike steak and chops where the contamination stays on the surface, processing and preparation can result in the contamination being carried into the center of the meat. It is recommended that ground beef be cooked to an internal temperature of 165°F (74°C).

Irradiation offers the most practical and effective way of sterilizing foods and protecting the consumer. It is already being used for poultry and ground beef and is approved for many other foods. Even though the word *irradiation* conjures up fears of radiation exposure, irradiated food does not become radioactive; it is safe, and if properly applied does not change the taste or texture of food.

Listeria monocytogenes

- *Listeria monocytogenes* is an extremely serious illness; although there are only 2500 confirmed cases a year, the fatality rate is high (25–75 percent) and depends on the health condition of the person affected. Although healthy adults and children may consume contaminated foods without becoming ill, those at increased risk for infection (especially immuno-compromised, elderly, or children) can get listeriosis after eating food contaminated with even a few bacteria. It is especially dangerous for babies, both in utero and newborn. Immuno-compromised persons have the highest listeriosis fatality rates.
- *Listeria* has the unique ability to enter white blood cells, thereby avoiding recognition by the immune system, and from there it can invade the bloodstream and every organ in the body, including the brain and, in pregnant women, the fetus. In addition to gastroenteritis, fever, vomiting, and diarrhea, illness can progress to meningitis, septicemia, encephalitis, spontaneous abortion, and death. The incubation period (time between ingestion and the onset

of symptoms) can be as many as 70 days. This makes identification and elimination of the contaminated food very difficult and can lead to many more individuals becoming infected before the contaminated food is identified, resulting in many more resulting illnesses and deaths.

- Unique to pathogens, *Listeria* can grow and multiply *under refrigerated temperatures* (37°F [2.78°C]), which makes this organism of particular concern to food plants where uncooked, chilled foods (deli salads, deli meats, sandwiches, etc.) are manufactured.
- *Listeria* is found in raw or improperly pasteurized milk, raw milk cheeses, ice cream, raw vegetables, fermented raw-meat sausages, raw and cooked poultry, raw meats (all types), deli meats, and raw and smoked fish. *Listeria* is killed by pasteurization and cooking; however, in certain ready-to-eat foods, like hot dogs and cold cuts, contamination may occur after cooking but before packaging.

●Meat Cookery

Meat is the most expensive part of any meal; extra attention must be paid to preparing it properly to maximize taste, texture, juiciness, color, and aroma. Selecting the right cut of meat for each preparation method is critical to a successful meal; even the highest-quality cut of meat can be ruined by selecting the wrong cooking method. However, the least tender cut of meat can be made flavorful and tender with the right cooking method.

Choosing the correct cooking method (dry heat/moist heat) based on knowledge of the different meat cut characteristics, along with appropriate seasoning, timing, and saucing, is critical to culinary success.

Applying heat to meat not only changes the flavor and nutritional availability but also can have a big impact on tenderness. The two components of meat most responsible for tenderness, or lack thereof, are muscle fibers and connective tissue (collagen). With excessive heat, muscle fibers shrink

FIGURE 4.11 **Beef carcass wholesale cuts.**

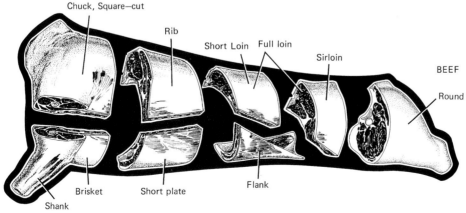

Source: National Cattlemen's Beef Association.

FIGURE 4.12 Pork carcass wholesale cuts.

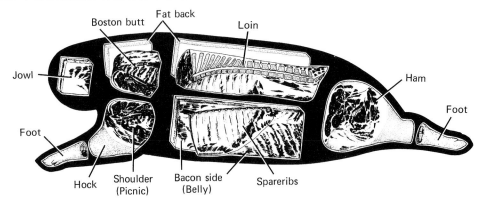

Source: National Cattlemen's Beef Association.

FIGURE 4.13 Veal carcass wholesale cuts.

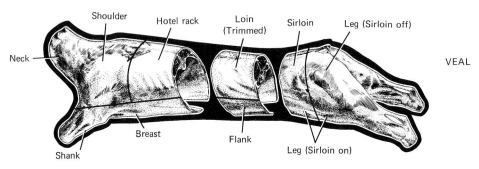

Source: National Cattlemen's Beef Association.

FIGURE 4.14 Lamb carcass wholesale cuts.

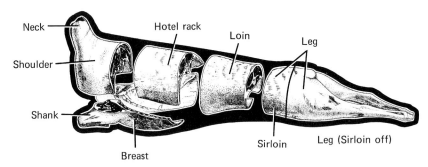

Source: National Cattlemen's Beef Association.

and squeeze out moisture, becoming dry and tough. This can be minimized by low and slow moist-heat cooking methods, but then flavor can be compromised. Low heat and high moisture inhibit the chemical processes of caramelization and the Maillard reaction, both responsible for much of the roasted and browned flavor development in meat cooked by dry-heat methods. On the other hand, collagen, a normally tough and chewy connective tissue, gelatinizes and softens when subjected to slow heating with high moisture. In general, muscles with lesser amounts of connective tissue (tender cuts such as tenderloin, rib eye, etc.) should be cooked via dry-heat methods; muscles with higher amounts of connective tissue (tough cuts such as chuck, shoulder, shank, etc.) do better with moist-heat cooking methods.

Changes During Cooking

Dry-heat cooking methods bring about the following flavor and textural events due to chemical and physical changes:

- Proteins coagulate, meat fibers shorten.
- Fats melt and break down.
- Organic acids, which enhance flavor and texture, are released.
- Nitrogen-containing compounds react to form meaty flavors.
- Water evaporates, causing flavors to concentrate.
- Maillard browning occurs (dry-heat cooking only), providing brown, roasted flavors and colors.

Obviously, moist-heat cooking methods do not provide an environment that supports most of these changes, so most flavor generation must take place outside the meat—that is, by means of flavorful marinades, highly seasoned cooking liquids, and tantalizing sauces.

● Meat Processing Ingredients

As you read ingredient statements, you will find differences in the types of ingredients as well as the amounts used. These become even more obvious as you begin to compare similar products from different regions of the world. Economics play a major role; in poorer countries, many people cannot afford to buy products with high levels of protein, so protein is replaced with larger amounts of carbohydrates, fats, and even water.

Availability also plays a major role in the types of ingredients used in the formulation. For example, corn or potato starch is likely to be used in the United States, while wheat starch may be the ingredient of choice in Russia.

Food safety is always a concern, with new methods and ingredients constantly being developed to enhance the safety of food. Some of these methods affect the proteins, causing a loss of moisture or a change in texture. Addition of other ingredients that help retain these components may be required to preserve the original palatability.

As market size increases and processors expand the areas where their products are offered, regional regulations, religious prohibitions, and ethnic preferences may also require changes in ingredients to fit the prevailing culture. These changes may affect both texture and flavor. Other ingredients may be required to increase shelf life or allow meat products to survive long distance, even international, distribution.

Consumer trends also play a big role. Sodium reduction is a health trend that requires the replacement of sodium with other ingredients that perform a similar function, whether it is for flavor, longer shelf life, or texture modification. Salt is a basic ingredient for most protein-based foods; it provides

both functionality and flavor. The salt used for manufacturing is primarily sodium chloride (NaCl), which comes in many forms. Table salt, the most common type, is finely ground, while kosher salt is coarser. Because sodium is implicated in high blood pressure and other heath disorders, salt has been targeted for reduction in many foods. As an alternative, potassium chloride has been used. Unfortunately, potassium has a bitter, metallic taste when used at high levels, with some people having greater sensitivity to its flavor than others. A rule of thumb is to keep the potassium chloride level at less than 50 percent of the sodium chloride—but even at that level some people can detect the off flavor.

Another alternative is sea salt. Today a variety of sea salts are available from different regions, with different flavors, different mineral makeup (including different levels of sodium), and different appearances. Sea salt is not all sodium chloride; it contains varying quantities of potassium chloride, magnesium chloride, and other impurities—minerals that impart different taste sensations, one of which may be enhancement of flavor. These impurities can also impart bitter off notes that may be detected by some consumers.

Before the advent of refrigeration, salting meat was a way to extend shelf life and minimize the growth of both spoilage and pathogenic organisms. Adding salt essentially decreases water activity (free water) and creates an environment less suitable for microbial growth. Reducing the level of salt can reduce the shelf life of the product, so alternative preservatives may need to be added.

The chlorine in salt aids in the extraction of salt-soluble proteins from the muscle, allowing the retention of higher amounts of water and creating a sticky surface following a period of mixing or tumbling. This sticky surface gels upon cooking and acts as glue to hold pieces of meat together. This methodology is used in the manufacture of sausages, restructured hams, hot dogs, and other comminuted (minced) or re-formed meat products. Even though many smaller pieces of meat are used in the formation of these products, after heating they can be sliced and remain intact.

The use of alkaline phosphates in commercial marinades can optimize moisture retention and maximize yield in meats as well as enhance emulsification and texture. Sodium tripolyphosphate (STPP) is the one most common in the meat processing industry. Adding STPP to meat raises the pH to a more alkaline level, resulting in more negative charges on the protein molecule, which allows for more moisture to be trapped. But higher pH in meat may also have detrimental effects. Meat pigments become more heat stable at a higher pH. As discussed earlier, this means that the red or pink color associated with undercooked meat products is retained even when the product is fully cooked. This can be off-putting, especially in poultry.

Phosphates with high pH can also result in off flavors that are described as metallic or soapy. Moving away from using a phosphate with a high pH to one that is closer to a pH of 7 can reduce or eliminate some of these detrimental effects. To achieve a pH of 7, combinations of alkaline phosphates and acid phosphates have been created. Although there may be some reduction of moisture retention as it relates to yield, modern processing systems help minimize this effect.

Antioxidants are often used in protein foods to protect flavor and shelf life, particularly to prevent those off flavors (such as warmed-over flavor) that are the result of the oxidation of fats. Butylated hydroxyanisole (BHA) and butylated hydroxytoluene (BHT) are common synthetic antioxidants used together or individually in many food products. Use levels are regulated and cannot exceed 0.01 percent of the fat (oil) component if used individually or 0.02 percent of the fat (oil) component if used together. Propyl gallate is another ingredient commonly used to reduce oxidation.

These antioxidants are not considered natural. Rosemary extract (carnosic acid and carnosol) has antioxidant properties and is often substituted for BHA and BHT where a natural claim is desired. The antioxidant properties of rosemary can be as effective as BHA and BHT at the same use levels, but unlike the synthetics, which have no taste, rosemary extract does add an herbal flavor to the food.

A variety of sweeteners are used in the food industry. Especially in meat processing, sugars are added to reduce the harshness of salt. Sucrose, or table sugar, is the most common and provides the anchor for the sweetness scale, having a value of 100. Sucrose is often derived from sugar cane or sugar beets. Being a non-reducing sugar, it does not promote Maillard reactions and therefore is considered non-browning. Dextrose is another sweetener used in meat preparations, but it is not as sweet as sucrose, having a sweetness index of 75. However, being a reducing sugar, dextrose is involved in Maillard reactions and can cause browning in food products, which may or may not be an advantage.

Fermentation of meats is a common and inexpensive way to preserve them while creating a range of sensory enhancements (flavor, texture, aroma). Salami, pepperoni, and chorizo are all examples of fermented meats. Meat does not contain sufficient intrinsic levels of carbohydrate to support fermentation, so some amount of fermentable carbohydrate must be added. Dextrose is a simple sugar (monosaccharide) composed solely of glucose, therefore it is easily metabolized by microorganisms and is the carbohydrate of choice for fermentation. Corn syrup and corn syrup solids are also used. *Note:* These ingredients have a sweetness and browning potential measured as dextrose equivalents (D.E.). As the D.E. increases, sweetness and browning potential increases.

A number of other natural and artificial sweeteners are available to the food industry, but none have been approved for use in meat applications.

A number of microbial inhibitors are available; the two most often seen on the ingredient statement of a cooked meat product, such as turkey deli meat or bologna, are sodium lactate and sodium diacetate. These are derivatives of lactic acid and acetic acid, respectively. Used in combination, these ingredients have been found most effective against *Listeria monocytogenes* in ready-to-eat (RTE) meat products. Their use is required to achieve the highest-level processing for RTE meat products as established by the USDA.

Mold growth on meat products is usually seen only on products with lower water activity that won't support the growth of bacteria. These products include salami, jerky, and, in some cases, hams. For some salamis, the white coating on the outside is a *Penicillium* sp. that is desirable and provides preservative qualities. For other products, mold growth is detrimental, as it reduces yield and is aesthetically displeasing. Propylparaben and potassium sorbate are two products that minimize mold growth. They are normally used as a spray or dip application to the surface of the product to help prevent mold from growing. Casings on meat products are sometimes dipped in a solution of one of these mold inhibitors to eliminate growth.

Flavor enhancers are sometimes added to give a more savory note (known as umami). Monosodium glutamate (MSG) is one of the more widely used and most controversial enhancers used in foods. As the name implies, MSG is a derivative of glutamic acid, one of the amino acid building blocks of protein. MSG has a binding site on the taste buds that enhances flavors when it is present. Other sources of glutamates (flavor-enhancing salts of glutamic acid) include hydrolyzed vegetable protein (HVP) and autolyzed yeast extract (AYE). Hydrolysis and autolysis break down a protein into its amino-acid building blocks, releasing glutamic acid and providing a taste response similar to MSG without having to put MSG on the ingredient label.

Ribotides such as inosinate and guanylate (I + G) are also highly effective flavor modifiers in many foods. However, they are phosphorylated molecules and consequently susceptible to phosphatase enzyme activity. Food ingredients that possess phosphatase activity, such as raw meats or untreated wheat flour, must be heat-treated to inactivate these enzymes before ribotide is added to the product.

By definition, products with added sodium nitrate or sodium nitrite are considered cured. Nitrites, when combined with meat pigments, result in the characteristic pink color consumers expect in hams, frankfurters, bacon, and other cured products. (In the United States, nitrate is not allowed in cured meat products other than dried sausages.) In addition to color fixing, nitrite also provides antioxidant activity, imparts some of the flavor associated with cured meat products, and has antimicrobial activity, in particular against *Clostridium botulinum*. The latter is extremely important in light of the controversy surrounding the use of nitrite.

Under certain conditions not yet fully understood, the natural breakdown products of proteins, known as amines, can combine with nitrites to form compounds known as nitrosamines. There are many different types of nitrosamines, most of which are known carcinogens in test animals. Many variables influence nitrosamine levels: amount of nitrite added during processing, concentrations of amines in meat, types and amounts of other ingredients used in processing, actual processing conditions, length of storage, storage temperatures, method of cooking, and degree of doneness. For example, well-done bacon is potentially more hazardous than less well-done bacon. Bacon cooked by microwave has less nitrosamine than fried bacon. Drippings usually contain more nitrosamines than the cooked bacon. That said, no link has been proven between eating bacon or other cured meats and cancer in humans, only in laboratory animals.

Nitrite is the only known compound added at 200 ppm or less that has the ability to restrict the growth of *Clostridium botulinum*. This is a major reason why it has not been removed from cured meat products. Clostridia are anaerobic microorganisms. Cured meats are normally vacuum packed. If this organism were inadvertently introduced to the interior of the meat during processing, the oxygen-less environment would encourage its growth. Although current sanitation procedures virtually eliminate this possibility, nitrite is a tool that guards against its occurrence. In addition, consumers also look for the characteristic color associated with cured meats. Without nitrite, these meats (bacon, ham, sausage, etc.) would look gray rather than pink. In fact, in some parts of the country, corned beef is available in both standard cure (pink) as well as "gray cure" for consumers accustomed to (and preferring) that appearance.

The processes followed for curing meat products have changed throughout the years, with processing times getting shorter due to improved technology. Where hams were once brined for up to 10 days before cooking, they are now injected, tumbled, and cooked within 24 hours. Processors discovered, however, that the color developed with these shorter processing methods is not as stable as with the longer curing times. It was found that reductants (antioxidants), in the form of sodium erythorbate or sodium ascorbate, could be added to commercial meat cures to promote more stable color formation. These reductants assist in the transformation of nitrite to nitric oxide, which is the form that reacts with the meat pigment for color formation. As a bonus, use of these compounds not only allows for less nitrite to be added but also inhibits the formation of nitrosamines. In fact, in commercially mass-produced ("pumped") bacon, addition of ascorbate or erythorbate is required by the USDA.

For the manufacture of dry products such as salami and pepperoni, the goal is to reduce the amount of moisture in the meat to enhance shelf stability, texture, and flavor. Reducing pH assists in accomplishing that goal by decreasing the protein's ability to bind water. However, adding acid directly to proteins hydrolyzes the protein and destroys meat texture. Instead, using fermentative lactic acid bacteria to form lactic acid in the meat more gradually allows for dehydration without degrading the texture. Today, modern processors purchase specific bacterial starter cultures selected for their ability to grow and produce acid in meat mixtures under established conditions. Dextrose must always be added, as not enough carbohydrate is normally present in meat to support fermentation.

To enhance texture or improve the product's ability to retain moisture, some processors add starches and gums, collectively referred to as *binders*, to meat. Starches come from a variety of sources, most often corn, potato, or rice. Rice starch is usually the starch of choice because it has the smallest granules and can squeeze into tight spaces in the muscle more easily than potato or corn can.

Carrageenan is a hydrocolloid gum derived from seaweed; it is used by meat processors to help retain moisture, firm texture, and improve slicing. Having characteristics similar to starch, carrageenan swells and eventually solubilizes when heated and then, depending on the type used, can form a gel upon cooling. The specific characteristics of the gel are dependent on the type of carrageenan used. Kappa carrageenan forms a very firm but brittle gel, whereas iota carrageenan is less firm and more elastic. Lambda carrageenan does not gel. Kappa and iota carrageenans are most often used in meat processing where gelling helps lock moisture in the meat, while lambda carrageenan is used in sauces and dressings where gelling is not desired.

Not all of the meat harvested from an animal can be cut into roasts, steaks, or chops. The trimmings are commonly used for the manufacture of ground meat products. Restructured meat, also known as *chopped and formed* meat (as opposed to whole muscle), uses meat trimmings and binding agents (such as egg albumin, gelatin, soy or milk proteins, or enzymes) to produce re-formed meat items that can be very similar in appearance, taste, and texture to the real thing. The ability to manufacture these items with uniform shape and consistent weight makes them ideal for foodservice operations to eliminate waste and maximize profit.

Alginate is another carbohydrate extracted from seaweed. It has the unique ability to gel in the presence of calcium and thus can be used to bind together smaller pieces of meat. Combining the meat chunks with alginate and a calcium source and pressing them into a mold yields a product with the characteristics and appearance of whole muscle.

Transglutaminase is an enzyme that promotes binding between proteins and assists in the formation of a whole muscle–type product from meat trimmings.

Fibrimex® is a system composed of thrombin and fibrinogen. These products are normal components of blood and are responsible for the clotting mechanism of blood when the body is cut or injured. This clotting mechanism has been adapted to meat products to help hold pieces together for a whole muscle characteristic. One of the primary uses of Fibrimex® is binding two whole beef tenderloins butt to tail to achieve a higher yield of tenderloin steaks. Using current market conditions, this process could improve the return on 100 pounds of tenderloins by $300. *Note:* These ingredients work equally well with any protein source: meat, poultry, or seafood. *A word of caution:* Any restructured meat product may allow pathogenic organisms that were on the outside surface to wind up on the internal portion of the meat. The resulting product should be cooked to an internal temperature sufficient to kill those microorganisms.

● Conclusion

An understanding of protein chemistry is essential for the practicing Culinology® professional. Regardless of the source—red meat, poultry, seafood, or vegetable—protein is an essential component of the human diet; we cannot live without it! As such, it is very likely that at some point in your career you will be involved in developing protein-based foods. The information presented in this and the following three chapters provides a solid overview of this subject.

[1] K. Imura and A. Okada, "Amino Acid Metabolism in Pediatric Patients." *Nutrition* 14:1(1998): 143–148.

[2] G. Sarwar and F. E. McDonough, "Evalution of Protein Digestibility: Corrected Amino Acid Score Method for Assessing Protein Quality of Foods." *Journal of the Association of Analytical Chemists* 731(1990): 347–356.

[3] M. C. Hunt, O. Sorheim, and E. Slinde, "Color and Heat Denaturation of Myoglobin Forms in Ground Beef." *Journal of Food Science* 64(1999): 847–851.

[4] Center for Disease Control. www.cdc.gov/ncidod/dvrd/prions/ Accessed March 17, 2011.

[5] Center for Disease Control. www.cdc.gov/ncidod/dvrd/bse Accessed March 17, 2011.

[6] Creutzfeldt-Jakob Disease International Surveillance Network www .eurocjd.ed.ac.uk/surveillance%20data%201.html#vcjd-cases Accessed November 15, 2015.

[7] E. D. Belay and L. B. Schonberger, *Annual Review Public Health* 26(2005): 191–212.

[8] E. Scallan, R. M. Hoekstra, F. J. Angulo, R. V. Tauxe, M. A. Widdowson, S. L. Roy, J. L. Jones, P. M. Griffin, "Foodborne Illness Acquired in the United States—Major Pathogens." *Emerging Infectious Diseases* 17:1(2011): 7–15.

[9] Explore Beef. www.explorebeef.org/cmdocs/explorebeef/factsheet_ antibioticuseincattleproduction.pdf Accessed November 15, 2015.

[10] Centers for Disease Control and Prevention. http://www.cdc.gov.

[11] C. W. Ang, M. A. De Klerk, H. P. Endtz, B. C. Jacobs, J. D. Laman, F. G. van der Meche, P. A. van Doorn. "Guillain-Barre Syndrome and Miller Fisher Syndrome-associated Campylobacter jejuni Lipopolysaccharides Induce anti-GM1 and anti-GQ1b Antibodies in Rabbits." *Infection and Immunity* Apr;69(2001)(4): 2462–2469.

[12] R. V. Tauxe, "Epidemiology of Campylobacter jejuni Infections in the United States and Other Industrial Nations." In: I. Nachamkin, M. J. Blaser, and L. S. Tompkins (eds.). *Campylobacter jejuni: Current and Future Trends* (Washington: American Society for Microbiology, 1992, pp. 9–12).

[13] P. S. Mead, L. Slutsker, V. Dietz, L. F. McCraig, J. S. Bresee, C. Shapiro, P. M. Griffin, and R. V. Tauxe, "Food Related Illness and Death in the United States." *Emerging Infectious Diseases* 1999 Sep-Oct; 5(5): 607–625..

5 Protein-Based Foods: Poultry

Lead Author: L. Cain Cavitt, Ph.D., CCS®, Project Leader, Research & Development, Tyson Foods, Inc.
Contributor: Jason M. Behrends, Ph.D., CCS®, Project Leader, Tyson Foods, Inc.

●Introduction

The United States may be the land of the hamburger, but Americans eat more poultry than any other protein. According to the American Meat Institute, poultry consumption continues to grow and remains a large percentage of the food market—some 48.2 percent of all meat consumed in the United States.[1]

In 2012, U.S. poultry production totaled 43.5 billion pounds.[2] Of that, chicken accounted for 37.6 billion pounds, and turkey totaled nearly 6 billion pounds.[3]

Over the past several decades, poultry production has become highly vertically integrated from production to harvest. This vertical integration has allowed the industry to streamline and reduce production costs, making poultry a very affordable food for the consumer. Advancements are enormous in the areas of raising, harvesting, fabrication, packaging, and transportation. In addition, the poultry industry continues to lead the way in new products and innovation.

In the last few decades, the marketing of poultry has increasingly changed from whole birds to bone-in parts to skinless and boneless products. Consumers now focus on convenience and health, and as their needs have changed, so has the way poultry is processed and marketed. In addition, the industry continues to find ways to add value to lower-cost cuts, such as thigh and leg meat.

The processing of live birds remains similar to the past, though novel approaches to improve food safety continue to emerge. Improvements in handling and animal welfare, along with key improvements in processing efficiency and yield enhancement, are a major priority for the industry as profit margins shrink due to rising feed, transportation, and processing costs.

●Pre-Harvest Handling

It is important to handle poultry, like other livestock, carefully to avoid bruises, abrasions, and broken limbs. Typically, poultry used for meat production are raised on wood shavings in large commercial houses that contain approximately 25,000 broilers (chickens under 13 weeks old, which constitute virtually all commercial chicken production) or 13,000 turkeys. Through advancements in poultry genetics and feed formulations, commercial broilers are typically ready for processing 6 to 7 weeks from hatch, turkeys in 15 to 20 weeks.

Before catching, loading, and transporting commercial poultry to the processing plant, feed is removed from the birds for 8 to 12 hours in order to help empty their intestinal contents. This process is commonly known as *feed withdrawal*. During feed withdrawal, the birds are allowed unrestricted access to water until they are caught and loaded for processing. Once the birds arrive at the processing plant, they are processed according to standard ethical processing procedures. If birds are not allowed adequate time for feed withdrawal at the time of processing, there is an increased risk of intestinal breakage during slaughter, leading to fecal contamination inside or on the surface of the bird. The USDA has a zero tolerance for visible fecal contamination, so any carcasses that are contaminated must then be segregated, thoroughly cleaned, and re-inspected before entering the chiller.

Most poultry is loaded into catch modules or coops for transportation by either manned mechanical loaders or catch-crews. During the loading and unloading process, special care must be taken in order to minimize any additional stress or injuries to the birds. Some of the most common injuries include broken wings, lower leg injuries, bruises, and scratches, all of which can potentially lead to carcass downgrades during processing and compromise ethical treatment. Once the birds reach the plant, the modules or coops are removed from the truck to a conveyor belt where the birds are disgorged. The birds are then transported by conveyor belt into the plant, and enter the hanging room where they are hung upside down on shackles before they are stunned. Often the hanging room is lit only with ultraviolet lights in order to calm the birds and minimize additional stress during this process.

Stunning

The majority of all commercially processed birds are stunned (by either electricity or modified atmosphere gases) before slaughter. In addition to immobilizing the birds, electrical stunning helps facilitate the removal of their feathers by paralyzing the muscles in which their feather follicles are embedded. Typically, stunning is done by electrical shock in a charged 1% salt-water bath. Salt water is used because it is a better conductor of electricity than water alone. This type of stun is called a "reversible stun," which means that the birds are not actually killed during the stunning process. The stun only renders the birds unconscious for 1–2 minutes and, if left alone, they will completely recover within about 5 minutes. A reversible stun allows for the birds' heart rate to slow down and become more uniform before slaughter. A traditional electric stun is applied for approximately 10–12 seconds at 10–20 mA per chicken and 20–40 mA for turkeys.[4]

With electrical stunning, certain processing issues can occur, resulting in potential carcass downgrades. Oftentimes if the amperage is too high the result can lead to broken bones in the wing and clavicle due to an involuntary super-contraction of the skeletal muscles. It can also result in *petechial hemorrhaging* of residual blood in the capillaries of the breast muscle, resulting in small visible blood spots just under the surface of the muscle membrane. If too low an amperage is used, it is possible that the birds will not be rendered unconscious and could be miscut entering the kill machine. This might result in poor bleed-out, or in increased broken wing bones due to excess flapping as the disoriented chicken passes through the stunning cabinet and kill machine. Of course, a primary objective of stunning is to eliminate as much as possible any suffering that the animal might experience as it continues through the slaughter process.

Alternative methods have been tested including *modified atmosphere stunning*, which has gained popularity in Europe and is beginning to be used here. Modified atmosphere stunning typically either uses a mixture of carbon dioxide (10–40%) and air (60–90%) or carbon dioxide (30%), argon (55–70%), and nitrogen (0–15%).[5] Both of these methods render the birds near death before bleed-out, which reduces the frequency of broken bones and blood spotting. This type of stunning is referred to as an "irreversible stun," which means that the birds cannot recover from the stunning process.

Note: Certain religious food rituals, such as halal (Islamic) or kosher (Jewish), do not allow stunning before processing: They feel that the stunning process itself is inhumane. Instead, the birds are blessed by an Islamic imam or Jewish rabbi before entering the kill step and are then quickly dispatched by a cleric trained in ritual slaughter.

Killing and Bleeding

Immediately after stunning, the birds enter the kill machine where a rotating circular blade severs the carotid artery and jugular vein, allowing for a quick and uniform bleed-out. Potential carcass downgrades can result if the blade cuts too deeply, thereby cutting the esophagus and spinal cord. If the spinal cord or head is completely severed, the carcass can begin to twitch and jerk uncontrollably, leading to broken wings and blood splash in the breast muscle due to involuntary muscular contractions. On the other hand, if the cut is too shallow, the result could be a poor bleed-out, which could discolor the muscle tissue because of elevated amounts of blood remaining in the bird when entering the scalding phase. Normally birds are allowed to bleed-out for a period of 90–120 seconds before entering the scalder.

Scalding and Feather Removal

Scalding entails submerging the carcass in hot water to loosen the feathers from the follicles. There are two types of scalding methods most commonly used: hard and soft scalding. *Hard or hot scalding* water (145–148°F) for 45 seconds is a method that removes the "waxy" pigmented *cuticle layer* (outer, epidermal layer) from the skin, leaving it with a washed-out white appearance.[6] Removing the waxy cuticle allows for better batter-breading adhesion when making fried products.

The temperature for *soft-scalding* ranges from 125–132°F for 20–30 seconds for broilers, and up to 60 seconds for older birds.[7] Soft scalding, due to the lower water temperature, does not remove the pigmented waxy cuticle layer of the skin. A soft scald is most often employed when the processor wants to keep the yellow skin color. This type of appearance is highly desired in certain parts of the United States and other countries. Because the cuticle has not been removed in soft-scalded birds, trying to batter-bread and fry them is more difficult as the breading doesn't properly adhere to the skin.

After scalding, all birds then pass through the feather picker. Most commercial feather pickers consist of a series of rotating rubber fingers that gently remove the feathers from the birds as they pass through picker tunnels that are pre-set for each size of bird. If the rotating fingers are set too close to the bird, skin tears and broken bones may result. Alternatively, if the rotating rubber fingers are set too far away from the birds, the result could be a poorly picked bird with numerous feathers left on the carcass.

Evisceration

Evisceration is the process in which the *viscera*—internal organs, both edible and inedible—are removed from the carcass. Edible viscera (the "giblets") include the liver, heart, and gizzard while the inedible viscera include the crop, intestines, kidneys, lungs, and reproductive tract. In the past, this part of the process tended to be the most labor-intensive as it was performed by hand. Today, in most commercial processing plants, this phase of processing has become almost completely automated. The *visceral package* (intestines, heart, lungs, liver, gizzard, and reproductive organs) is removed from the carcass, presented to USDA inspectors, and then separated into edible and inedible components. The edible viscera is commonly packaged and placed in the cavity of carcasses being sold "whole." Additionally, the neck is often (especially in turkeys) included in the edible viscera. In addition to the edible viscera, the feet (commonly referred to as "paws") are harvested shortly after evisceration, cleaned, and sold to countries that use them for human consumption.

Chilling and Carcass Aging

As with all livestock carcasses, it is important to remove body heat as quickly as possible to reduce microbial spoilage and potential pathogen growth. U.S. regulations require that all commercially processed poultry reach 39.2°F (4°C) or less within 4 hours of death for chickens and 8 hours for turkeys.[8] Two types of commercially available chilling methods are normally used today: immersion (water chilling) and air chilling. Immersion is most commonly used by the commercial broiler industry in the United States.

Immersion chilling consists of a two-step system: the pre-chill stage followed by the chill stage. In the first step, fresh carcasses enter a large tank filled with cold water (45–55°F [7.2–10°C]) and are pushed along by either a screw-type auger or large paddles. The carcasses remain here for approximately 15 minutes and then transition to the chill stage, during which they remain in 33–35°F (0.6–1.7°C) water for 45–55 minutes.

As the carcasses enter the chiller, they typically have an internal body temperature of 100.4°F (38°C). By gradually reducing the temperature of the water from 55°F (10°C) to 33°F (0.6°C) over the course of the chilling time, the core body temperature of the bird is slowly reduced. A warm carcass immediately subjected to the colder chiller water has an increased chance of undergoing cold shortening. Cold shortening is a quality issue that dramatically reduces the amount of tender meat by causing a supercontraction of the actin and myosin filaments of muscle fibers, which become locked in place due to the sudden exposure to extreme cold. The outcome is a carcass or parts that are both extremely tough and have reduced water absorption and holding capacity during marination.

Air chilling is more commonly used in Europe. It requires substantially more room than immersion chilling (air is a less efficient temperature transfer medium than water). The fresh carcasses pass through a large room where temperature and wind velocity are controlled; the cold air flow reduces the core body temperature of the bird over 1 to 2 hours. Upon completion of this stage, air-chilled carcasses are at the same temperature as those that pass through the immersion chilling process. The major difference between the two processes is that the immersion chilling system allows for some water uptake in the carcass, thereby slightly increasing yield, while

birds sent through the air-chilling system typically dry out more and have a greater yield loss.

Carcasses exiting the chiller (approximately 2 hours postmortem) often are cut in half around the middle. The back half is typically sold as leg quarters, whole legs, or drumsticks and thighs rather than boneless items, so no additional aging is required. The front half contains the breast fillet, tenderloin, and wings attached to the back and rib cage. (The so-called "football" contains just the breast fillet and tenderloin still attached to the back and rib cage.) Because a large majority of products use either the boneless breast fillet or tenderloin, it is essential that these two sets of muscles, left on the bone, be aged on ice or in a cooler 6 to 8 hours before harvesting in order to ensure a tender product.

Rigor mortis (Latin for "stiffness of death") is classified as one of the most dramatic postmortem changes that occur during the conversion of muscle to meat. The rate of rigor mortis development and resolution varies with the species and body size. It typically takes 6–8 hours for commercial broilers and 8–10 hours for commercial turkeys to complete the rigor process. Harvesting or deboning breast fillets or tenderloins before the completion of rigor mortis results in a toughening of the meat due to residual energy as adenosine triphosphate (ATP) is still present within the muscle cell. If too much ATP is left in the muscle at deboning, the muscle fibers contract, creating a denser piece of meat that in turn is tough when cooked. Tenderness is one of the most important factors in overall consumer acceptability of broiler breast,[9] and commercial processors take special care when harvesting breast meat and tenderloins to ensure it.

Dressing Percentage

The breed and species of poultry play a huge role in the value and variety of meat produced. Poultry varieties may be thinly muscled to heavily muscled, and many species are used for food, including chicken, turkey, ostrich, duck, and so on. These factors dramatically change the dressing percentage (amount of salable carcass after harvest and removal of head, feet, feathers, blood, and viscera) that can be achieved. For the most part, the chicken and turkey industries produce birds that are thick and heavily muscled to optimize meat production; these have an average dressing percentage of 70–80 percent.

Breed, species, ability to convert feed to muscle efficiently (feed is 70 percent of the production cost of raising poultry), and condition of the birds all affect dressing percentage. For example, chickens weighing less than 5 pounds versus those weighing more than 5 pounds can lose an average of 11 percent versus 9 percent, respectively, in blood and feathers, and when completely dressed can lose a total of 27 percent versus 25 percent, respectively.[10] These differences give the industry an economic incentive to produce chickens over 5 pounds to reduce cost per pound.

Whichever breed, species, or size of bird the industry targets, the goal is to improve dressing yields and lower the cost per pound of meat produced.

Poultry Types

The Meat Buyer's Guide, published by the North American Meat Institute (formerly NAMP, the North American Meat Processors Association), is a recognized reference for cutting and grading meat. The *Guide* provides a standard numbering system for all classes and cuts of meat and poultry sold commercially, and assigns each one a code number. For poultry, the code numbers all contain the prefix "P" followed by a four-digit number.

Here are the sizes of chicken along with their NAMP codes, from largest to smallest:

- Roasters (P1100; NAMP, 2007) are typically 12–16 weeks old and weigh 3.5–5 pounds once processed.
- Broiler/fryers (P1000; NAMP, 2007) are typically processed at 6–8 weeks and weigh 3.5 pounds or less once processed.
- Rock Cornish game hens or Cornish game hens are young, immature birds (P1500; NAMP, 2007) typically processed at 4–5 weeks. They weigh 2 pounds or less once processed.
- Poussin (P1400; NAMP, 2007) are very small, immature birds, typically processed at 3–4 weeks and weighing approximately 1–1.5 pounds once processed.

Roasters are similar in size to capons (P1200; NAMP, 2007), which are castrated males that typically weigh 5 pounds or greater at processing. Fowl (P1300; NAMP, 2007), known as *stewing* or *baking hens*, are generally egg layers processed for meat once they are no longer able to regularly produce eggs (spent hens). Spent hens or fowl are processed between 10 and 12 months of age and generally weigh 2.5 pounds or greater once processed. Meat from fowl is generally tougher than meat from other chickens, so it is used in products such as diced meat for soups. Additionally, fowl meat is often exported to Canada, Mexico, and other countries.

The only breed of turkey raised commercially in the United States is the broad-breasted white. Turkeys are available as hens (P2201; NAMP, 2007) or toms (P2101; NAMP, 2007) and in sizes ranging from 9 to 30 pounds. They are typically processed between 16 and 18 weeks of age. Turkeys are most often sold whole (with giblets) during the Thanksgiving and Christmas season. Parts that are further processed, such as drumsticks, boneless, skinless breast, and ground turkey have gained popularity due to the lean nature of turkey meat. Fully cooked refrigerated and frozen turkey entrées are also popular. The primary uses for turkey meat throughout the year are as deli meat, hot dogs, and fresh ground.

Ducks are classified as duckling (broiler/fryer), roaster duckling, and mature duck (P3000; NAMP, 2007). The most common farm-raised breeds are the Pekin and the Rouen. Geese are classified as young goose or mature goose (P4010; NAMP, 2007). The most common farm-raised breeds are the Emden and the Toulouse. Game birds now routinely farmed and commonly available include guinea fowl, pheasant, quail, common or gray partridge, and Chukar partridge. Ostrich is also readily available.

Basic Cuts of Poultry

Commercially processed poultry is generally sold raw as whole birds or cut-up parts, or processed into boneless, skinless meat. A cut-up bird consists of whole leg (drumstick and thigh), split breast with tenderloin, wing with tip, wing flat (mid-joint), and drummette. Whole birds are sold with or without giblets ("WOG"). The usual arrangement of cut birds is called an *eight-piece cut*, including two breast halves with the ribs and back portion attached, two wings, two thighs with back portion and tail attached, and two drumsticks. The most common cuts of boneless, skinless poultry items sold raw are breast, tenderloins, and thighs. These cuts are often sold marinated as well. Marinated items can include just about any flavor profile, from basic saltwater brine to a highly seasoned and complex flavor such as a teriyaki or buffalo. Today, boneless, skinless processed poultry has the highest sales volume due to its unmatched convenience.

Poultry Meat Functionality

The functionality of poultry meat refers to any inherent physicochemical and/or rheological property intrinsic to poultry protein that influences final product quality. (*Note:* Many of the textural properties human beings perceive when they consume foods are largely rheological in nature—for example, creaminess, juiciness, smoothness, brittleness, tenderness, hardness.) The three most important functional properties for the poultry industry are gelation, emulsification, and water binding/holding.

Gelation is the process whereby a protein unfolds, followed by orderly cross-linking, to form viscoelastic (gel-like) three-dimensional networks or matrices. Gelation provides

FIGURE 5.1   Cut pieces of poultry.

Source: YinYang/Getty Images, Inc.

structure and texture to such products as hot dogs, meat binding in restructured meats, fat stabilization, and water holding. Myofibrillar proteins, the salt-soluble proteins, provide the most gelation. These include actin, myosin, and actomysosin, the proteins responsible for muscular contraction and relaxation—and therefore the texture of processed meat products.

Meat emulsification is normally achieved by homogenizing a mixture of meat (protein) and fat, using pressure or high shear energy to disperse the fat (the *discontinuous phase*) as droplets evenly throughout the protein (the *continuous phase*). A typical meat emulsion consists of fat globules (usually ground poultry skin) coated with salt-soluble proteins and imbedded in a protein matrix. Examples include bologna and hot dogs. The coating of salt-soluble proteins around the tiny fat globules lowers the surface tension of the fat droplets, preventing them from coalescing (reuniting) and thus stabilizing the emulsion system.

Factors affecting emulsion stability include the type and amount of protein available to form the film coating for the fat droplets as well as processing parameters such as chopping time, meat mixture temperature, and fat-to-protein ratios. These depend on the type of product being produced.

If the product contains too much fat or is overworked, the meat matrix can collapse and cause the emulsion to break down, leading to a quality defect known as *fatting out* or *fat caps*. This occurs during the cooking process when fat globules expand while the proteins coagulate and shrink slightly, thus rupturing the protein matrix and allowing the fat to rise to the surface of the product.[11]

Traditionally, the meat used for emulsified products is made in part with ground breast meat or mechanically separated chicken or turkey (MSC or MST). MSC or MST is generated by taking trimmed carcass parts such as frames (denuded carcasses) and backs and separating the remaining scraps of meat from the skeletal structure by grinding the starting material and then passing it under high pressure through a sieve, which removes bones and cartilage. Once the mechanically separated meat is harvested from the frames, it is ground or emulsified, then bulk packed and shipped out either refrigerated or frozen. This inexpensive product is used as filler for hot dogs and other emulsified products.

Water-holding capacity is also an important factor in poultry processing. Hydrating poultry products can improve or sustain palatability, tenderness, and juiciness. Product yield may also be improved, which has economic significance. Typical methods used to increase water binding include the use of sodium chloride (NaCl) and phosphates, both of which help attract and bind water molecules to protein. Phosphates help dissociate actomyosin and weaken electrostatic interactions between peptide chains, reducing the muscle's resistance to water absorption. NaCl shifts the protein's isoelectric point to a lower pH. The result is the swelling of muscle fibers, which increases hydration or water-holding capacity. The net result is improved yield and better eating quality (texture, mouthfeel, moistness, tenderness, flavor release).

Further-Processed or Value-Added Poultry

Through advancements in technology, the growing influence of Culinology® professionals, and the expanding taste buds of the American consumer, the poultry industry is a leader in the muscle foods area in developing value-added products. This can be seen in the multitude of value-added poultry products in the market, including marinated raw or frozen chicken, fully cooked grilled strips, fully cooked and ready-to-eat breaded tenders and strips, pizza toppings, deli meats, turkey bacon, popcorn chicken, and pre-seasoned products of all types with flavors from every corner of the globe. Understanding technical capabilities, market demands, and economics is important in developing new products. Improved technical capabilities have led to new technologies in shaping and forming products ("chopped and formed" products), emulsifying, marinating (injection and vacuum tumbling), coating, a multitude of cooking and smoking methods, chilling and freezing systems, and packaging.

Poultry is one of the most adaptable of meat products and provides a blank canvas for professionals in research and development. Poultry meat can be converted to fit just about any flavor profile and has been the source of much advancement in new protein products over the past several years. The basic steps to producing further-processed poultry include piece-size reduction or portioning, formulation/ingredient incorporation, forming, and cooking.

Portioning

Controlling piece or portion size of the raw starting material is a critical key to developing a new product. Over the last several years, the majority of broiler processors are moving to larger birds (from about 6 pounds to 8 pounds) in order to maximize carcass and processing yields. With the increase in weight comes an increase in muscle size. Portioning equipment has been developed that can cut horizontally or

FIGURE 5.2 **Grilled chicken breast.**

Source: Barcin/Getty Images, Inc.

vertically, slice, or dice boneless, skinless breast meat to fit any portion size desired by the customer. In addition to horizontal and vertical slicers, other common types of portioning equipment include high-pressure water-knives, industrial patty-formers, and portioners that can turn out millions of identically shaped and sized breast fillets and patties for fast food restaurants. Portion control in foodservice is critical to maintaining profitability.

Ingredient Functionality and Flavor Enhancement

Today a large percentage of all further processed poultry products is marinated. Cooked poultry meat, especially white meat, is inherently bland and dry; therefore, it is often marinated to enhance its overall palatability. A typical marinade consists of water, salt, sodium phosphates, and other seasonings and is applied at 10–20 percent of the raw product weight. Each of the ingredients in a marinade has a specific function. Salt (sodium chloride; NaCl) is the most common ingredient used to season any type of food product. In addition to flavor enhancement, salt causes protein extraction, which allows for the marinade to be absorbed into the product. Typical salt usage in poultry products ranges from 0.25–1.0 percent.

Phosphates are traditionally used in conjunction with salt to help increase the overall moisture-binding ability of the meat muscle, which enhances the juiciness, tenderness, flavor, and palatability of the product. Sodium phosphates, such as sodium tripolyphosphate (STPP), are the type most commonly used in meat applications. Phosphate usage is regulated by the U.S. Department of Agriculture (USDA) and is allowed up to 0.50 percent in the finished product.

Other functional ingredients such as starches, gums, and soy proteins are often added to commercial marinades as a means of retaining moisture, both from the marinade and from free moisture within the muscle tissue. In addition, these functional ingredients aid in the enhancement of overall juiciness and flavor impact of the marinated product.

FIGURE 5.3 **Whole roasted chicken.**

Source: Robert Linton/Getty Images, Inc.

Starches generally come in two types: native or modified, and are derived from corn, potato, tapioca, or rice. They are used at a concentration of 0.75–1.25 percent in the finished product. Starches are further broken down into two subgroups: cold swelling and hot swelling, depending on their ability to hydrate and absorb moisture at different temperatures. Cold swelling, pregelatinized starches are used in items that will not be exposed to extensive heating, while hot swelling, cook-up starches are commonly used in items that will be fully cooked. At lower use levels, starches are neutral in flavor impact, but at higher levels, they can leave an off-white starchy appearance on the product.

Gums such as xanthan and carrageenan are also used as a means of retaining moisture and enhancing juiciness. Xanthan is produced through bacterial fermentation, while carrageenan is derived from a specific seaweed family. Gums traditionally have very little to no flavor impact on the finished product and are used at 0.1–0.3 percent in the finished product. They are often used to suspend ingredients in marinades that have a lot of visible solids. Like starches, gums thicken or gel at different strengths and temperatures depending on their functionality and use. (See Chapter 8 for a more complete discussion on gums and starches.)

Soy proteins are another set of functional ingredients often used in commercial marinades to enhance juiciness and flavor development. Unlike starches and gums, soy proteins often impart a slight beany or soy note when used in savory commercial marinades, and they must be declared as a soy allergen on the ingredient statement. Soy proteins are broken down into three groups: soy flour (50 percent protein), soy protein concentrate (SPC) (70 percent protein), and soy protein isolate (SPI) (90 percent protein) and are typically used at 0.75–1.25 percent in the finished product. Like gums, soy proteins immediately begin to hydrate in the presence of water, whereas cook-up starches don't begin to hydrate until a certain temperature is achieved. Soy flour and soy protein concentrate are most often used in marinades applied to whole-muscle items; soy protein isolates are most often used in chopped and formed or emulsified products due to their ability to bind together lipids and proteins.

Whey proteins (derived from milk) are another functional ingredient used in further processed meats such as hot dogs and bologna. They must be declared as a dairy allergen on the ingredient statement.

Sodium Reduction

Over the past several years, responding to pressure from consumers, the medical community, government, and the media, the poultry industry has pushed to reduce overall sodium content in further-processed meat products. Salt traditionally is used as a means of extracting protein and enhancing overall flavor. However, it contains approximately 39 percent sodium, which is a major contributor to overall sodium content. Salt substitutes such as potassium chloride (KCl) are gaining popularity as a way to reduce overall sodium content while maintaining similar functionality. Potassium chloride by itself has a bitter and metallic taste, so is usually used in a blended form with sodium chloride at a ratio of 2:1 sodium chloride to potassium chloride.

Another way to reduce overall sodium content and enhance flavor is to add onion powder and garlic powder to marinades. These two items add to the overall savory taste of the product, thereby tricking the taste buds into perceiving a salty or savory note.

Reducing sodium content also affects ingredient cost. Sodium chloride and sodium phosphates are two of the most commonly used and cheapest ingredients in further-processed meats and poultry; replacing or reducing their use with more expensive lower-sodium options increases the overall cost of the product.

Effect of pH on Marination Effectiveness

When developing a marinade for a particular meat product, the overall pH is very important. Typically, poultry meat has a slightly acidic muscle pH of 5.6–5.8. Alkaline or basic pH marinades (pH of 8–9) containing water, salt, phosphate, and spice extractives tend to absorb into the meat readily and do not purge or weep out much over time or through the cooking process. On the other hand, acidic marinades such as buffalo, tequila-lime, and lemon-pepper often have a pH of 5–6 and have a hard time binding with and absorbing into the muscle tissue. The primary reason is that the more acidic the marinade, the closer the muscle shifts to its isoelectric point (pI), typically at a pH of approximately 5.1. At the isoelectric point, the muscle proteins have no net charge due to the equal number of positive and negative charges on the muscle molecule, resulting in poor moisture uptake and retention. This is why acidic flavors are more successfully added as glazes, dry rubs, or topical seasonings to chicken that has previously been marinated in a more effective alkaline marinade.

Marination Methods

The process of marination can be conducted in a number of ways. The most common commercial methods are needle injection and vacuum tumbling. Vacuum tumbling is a widely used technique for infusing marinades into poultry. The process is commonly used in boneless, skinless meat items such as breast fillets or tenderloins, and in bone-in wing sections.

Vacuum tumbling involves placing meat and marinade in a cylindrical container, pulling a vacuum (20–25 Hg), and allowing the meat and marinade to tumble for 15–20 minutes. As the vacuum is pulled, the muscle tissue begins to swell, allowing the marinade to penetrate the meat. Vacuum tumbling can result in a pick-up of 10–15 percent marinade in only a few minutes, while static marination (submerging meat in a marinade at ambient pressure, without tumbling) rarely produces more than 5 percent pick-up even after many hours, as marinades penetrate only 2–3 millimeters into the muscle without a vacuum.

Needle injection marination is most commonly used in bone-in poultry items as well as larger items (even whole birds). It works by inserting a series of needles into the prod-

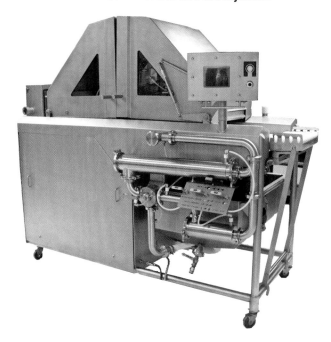

FIGURE 5.4 Commercial needle injector.

Source: Courtesy of Marel Stork Poultry Processing.

uct to directly inject the marinade deep into the muscle. Needle injection allows greater and much faster penetration of the marinade throughout the piece of meat. Some processors use needle injection followed by vacuum tumbling to assure complete and uniform marinade dispersion throughout the muscle.

Forming Strategies

Forming is used in the poultry industry to make consistently uniform products such as nuggets, fingers, and patties. This process, often referred to as *chopped and formed*, involves grinding whole muscle pieces such as boneless, skinless breast or thigh meat, mixing the ground meat with a seasoning, and then placing it into a forming machine (with different shaped plates, dies or molds) that uses pressure to stamp out the formed product. Chopped and formed products are usually either batter-breaded and fried, or glazed and sold fully cooked or ready to cook.

Salt-soluble proteins play a major role in the development of formed poultry products. The major salt-soluble proteins are myosin and actin, the proteins responsible for muscular contraction and relaxation. Salt is added to brines or marinades for meat to be made into formed products in order to extract the salt-soluble proteins. Through this extraction process, the solubilized proteins coat all of the meat's surfaces and serve as an adhesive to help glue individual chunks of meat back together. This helps the re-formed muscles to appear whole, especially after they have been shaped and sized to natural proportions, coated, and fried. This is particularly important for the mass production of products for the fast food industry (chicken patties, nuggets, etc.), where cost and consistent portion size are critical factors.

⬤ Conclusion

Poultry is a major source of protein in the human diet. Of all of the animal-based proteins, poultry is the most versatile, the most economical, the most heavily propagated, and also one of the most efficiently produced proteins on a pounds-per-acre basis. Unlike other meats and certain seafoods, there are no religious proscriptions against eating poultry anywhere in the world (except for strictly vegetarian cultures). Poultry protein is easily transformed into foods as upscale as chicken cordon bleu and as commonplace as chicken nuggets. As such, the ability to manipulate and be creative with poultry, particularly chicken and turkey, is of major importance to Culinology® professionals, who will almost certainly deal with both of these proteins at some stage in their career.

[1] American Meat Institute (AMI), "U.S. Meat and Poultry Production and Consumption: An Overview," AMI Fact Sheet, 2009.

[2] Ibid.

[3] Ibid.

[4] A. R. Sams, *Poultry Meat Processing* (Boca Raton, FL: CRC Press, 2001).

[5] Ibid.

[6] Ibid.

[7] J. R. Romans, W. J. Costello, C. W. Carlson, M. L. Greaser, and K. W. Jones, *The Meat We Eat* (Danville, IL: Interstate Publishers, 1994).

[8] Sams, *Poultry Meat Processing*.

[9] M. W. Schilling, J. K. Schilling, J. R. Claus, N. G. Marriott, S. E. Duncan, and H. Wang, "Instrumental Texture Assessment and Consumer Acceptability of Cooked Broiler Breasts Evaluated Using a Geometrically Uniform-Shaped Sample," *Journal of Muscle Foods* 14 (2003), 11–23.

[10] Romans, et al. *The Meat We Eat*.

[11] Sams, *Poultry Meat Processing*.

6 Protein-Based Foods: Seafood

Lead Author: Lucina E. Lampila, Ph.D., R.D., C.F.S., Senior Food Scientist, Evergreen Packaging
Contributor: Jeff Cowles, CCS®, Research Chef, Kerry Americas

●Introduction

Seafood is the only major source of protein in the mainstream U.S. diet that is still harvested from the wild, despite the farming of shrimp, catfish, tilapia, and salmon that surpasses the wild catches in some regions of the world. Major terrestrial protein sources (cattle, sheep, pigs, poultry, etc.) have been almost exclusively farm raised for hundreds of years. Globally, due to farming, seafood production now exceeds that of beef.

Seafood differs from chicken, beef, and pork in that migratory species are never guaranteed to be in a given location, or else are seasonal. In either case, the product developer, food manufacturer, or multi-unit foodservice operator must determine the amount of product needed before beginning a project. Limitations to the available amount, size, or quality of selected seafood will ruin any chance for success. Seafood is a true global resource, and the impact of worldwide demand on the availability of stocks must be taken into account. In many cases, the most coveted sizes of fillets and shrimp are relatively expensive, and large users, such as chain and club stores, may have existing supply contracts. Begin each project with an assessment of what is available in the required size and price range. This sounds rudimentary but reinforces the observation that seafood is unlike any other protein used by the product developer.

●Seafood Classifications

Tens of thousands of species of edible sea life are known, but only about 1500 are harvested globally, with approximately 400 species of finfish and 80 species of shellfish commercially harvested in the United States.[1] Millions of tons of seafood are served annually. The most popular seafoods in the United States are shrimp, canned tuna, salmon, pollock, and tilapia.[2]

Seafood can be generally classified along three criteria:

1. *Vertebrate or invertebrate*: Vertebrates include those species with internal skeletons (sharks have cartilage rather than bone), and these species may or may not have scales. Examples of vertebrates with fins are halibut, cod, salmon, flounder, tuna, eels, and swordfish. Turtles, alligators, and frogs are also considered seafood (21CFR123.3) and are vertebrates with neither fins nor scales. Invertebrates, commonly referred to as shellfish, are divided into two groups: crustaceans (crab, lobster, crawfish, and shrimp), which all have an exoskeleton; and mollusks, which are further divided into three subgroups: bivalves (clams, oysters, scallops, and mussels), gastropods (abalone, snails, whelk, and conch), and cephalopods (squid, cuttlefish, and octopi). Other invertebrates used for food include jellyfish (*Scyphozoa*), the sea cucumber (*Holothuridea*), and the sea urchin (*Echinoidea*).

2. *Saltwater (and brackish water) or freshwater*: These species may spend their lives in the ocean (cod); may be born in fresh water, live their lives at sea, and return to the fresh water to spawn (salmon); or may live their entire lives in fresh water, such as large-mouth bass, trout, walleye, pike, and catfish.

3. *Lean or fatty*: Lean species contain 2 percent or less total lipid (cod, flounder, lobster). Fatty species, such as wild salmonids, sablefish, mackerel, herring, and anchovy, can vary greatly in total lipid content depending on the season and whether or not they have been feeding heavily. Lipid content ranges from 5 percent (cultured salmon) to 22 percent (sablefish, also known as black cod or butterfish).

●Market Forms of Finfish

Finfish are available fresh or frozen in several forms: *whole fish* (entirely intact), *drawn fish* (whole with entrails removed), *dressed fish* (entrails, head, tail, fins and scales removed), *steaks* (crosscut slices of varying thickness from dressed fish; contains a piece of backbone in the center of each slice), *fillets* (boneless flesh of the fish sliced front to back by cutting lengthwise along each side of the fish parallel to the backbone; may or may not be skinless).

Muscle Structure of Finfish

Proteins derived from seafood have biochemical characteristics different from those of their terrestrial counterparts (poultry, pork, and beef). In most cases, their structure is far more delicate and must be treated with greater care.

Finfish have one long lateral muscle, unlike land animals, which have muscles of varying length and strength, depending on their function. Finfish muscle fibers run parallel to the backbone of the fish. Unlike the bundles of muscle fibers in meat (up to 3 feet in length) and poultry, fish muscles are made up of layers of short fibers (less than an inch in length, or a bit longer) called myotomes. These layers contribute to the characteristic flakiness of fish as it cooks. The number of myotomes corresponds to the number of vertebrae in the fish's backbone,[3] with the average fillet containing 50 myotomes. Myotomes are separated from each other by thin connective tissue, or myocommata, analogous to the connective tissue collagen in terrestrial animals. Myocommata is more densely concentrated at the tail of the fish, where strength is required for locomotion. Therefore, the eating quality of finfish is least desirable close to the tail. Seafood connective tissue does not become as highly cross-linked as that of beef, so toughness is rarely an issue. With the exception of the pedal sole (the inedible bottom of the foot) of the abalone, the content of connective tissue is 0.2 to 2.2 percent in most seafood,[4] as opposed to about 15 percent in mature beef.[5] The amount of cross-linking increases with age, which leads to increased toughness in meat.

Identifying Freshness in Seafood

One commonality of finfish of marine (saltwater) and freshwater origin is the fundamental characteristics of post-harvest quality determination. Some species may be more resilient than others; however, patterns of deterioration are typically indicative of eating quality.

The most obvious sign of freshness is aroma: as fish ages it rapidly develops an objectionable odor that is immediately apparent. In addition, fresh fish should have tightly fitting scales, firm yet resilient flesh that "bounces back" when depressed, protuberant and translucent corneas free from any cloudiness, and bright red gills.

Rigor and pH

As a rule, living finfish have a pH of 6.2 to 7.2 and an ultimate pH of 5.8 to 6.2 within hours of death. If fish are caught while heavily feeding or post-spawning, high glycogen reserves result in large drops in pH (due to the postmortem formation of lactic acid via anaerobic glycolysis) that lead in turn to protein damage and moisture loss. As pH departs from neutrality and approaches the isoelectric point of the protein (the point

---

FIGURE 6.1 **Recognizing finfish quality.**

Select for	Fresh Whole Fish	Avoid
Clear, bright, full, often protruding	EYES	Cloudy, pink, sunken
Red, free from mucous or slime	GILLS	With age fades to pink to gray and eventually brown or green; strong odor
Fresh, mild, slight seaweed	ODOR	Strong odor, ammonia-like, putrid
Shiny with vibrant color	SKIN	Dull, faded color
Firm and elastic to the touch	FLESH	Soft, separating from the bone
Clean cut, free of viscera; lining intact, clean aroma (if gutted)	BELLY CAVITY	Belly burst (rupture of cut through the flesh if not eviscerated); bones projecting through the cavity lining; yellow, orange, brown or green discoloration; objectionable odor
Fresh Fillets and Steaks		
Appearance should be freshly cut, texture should be firm and elastic	FLESH	Gaping (a separation between) of muscle bundles; protruding bones; soft or mushy texture or desiccated (dried out) appearance
Fresh, mild, seaweed-like	ODOR	Ammonia-like, putrid, strongly fruit-like
Bright, shiny, consistent	COLOR	Dull and grey to tan, which is indicative of desiccation; reddish-brown discolorations, which are indicative of blood spots; yellow to orange to brown edges, which are indicative of rancidity of the fish oils

Source: Sea Grant College Program.

at which the protein has no net charge, or the least functionality), it can no longer bind water.

If fish are caught during spawning (e.g., wild salmon), lipid content (due to gonad development), moisture content (as unbound water), and free amino acids are elevated, with a concomitant reduction in both myofibrillar protein (the muscle protein fraction, including actin and myosin, that are functional proteins—that is, that binds water and is extractable by strong salt solutions) and sarcoplasmic protein (the muscle protein fraction, including enzymes and myoglobin, that is soluble in water or dilute salt solutions).[6] The ultimate pH in these fish does not drop as low as usual, and the higher pH leads to more rapid onset of bacterial spoilage. The increased moisture in the presence of reduced myofibrillar protein tends to allow for migration of sarcoplasmic protein to the surface, where it coagulates upon heating. This coagulum resembles a dry curd that may be visually unappealing. A similar curd results when salmonids are frozen and subsequently canned.[7] It is important to note that salmon are graded for quality, and those that appear spent (show signs of deterioration) are diverted to fish meal or other by-product uses.

Finfish proceed through rigor mortis similarly to terrestrial animals; the key difference is the speed of each phase. In typical finfish, onset of rigor occurs in 1 to 2 hours, and resolution is complete within several hours. Very large species, such as bluefin tuna, take longer to undergo rigor; whales take up to 50 hours. Most animal proteins are prepared for consumption after rigor is resolved and the muscle tissues have relaxed. The exception is in Asia, where it is not uncommon for a seafood species to be selected live from a tank, slaughtered, and consumed pre-rigor. The texture then is very tender and delectable.

Immediately after death, finfish are limp and pliable, and the flesh is elastic. Most finfish species begin stiffening at the head and progress to the tail. As this occurs, actin binds to myosin, with a shortening of the myotomes, which ranges from 5 to 15 percent but may be significantly higher in deepwater species.[8] When the fish is in full rigor, it is contracted to the greatest extent; it stiffens to the point where it may appear concave when laid on its side on a flat surface.

During full rigor, tension may be sufficient to rupture the myocommata and cause gaping, a noticeable void between myotomes (separations or gaps in the cut surface of a fillet). Gaping may also be caused by attempts to straighten a fish in full rigor, by rough handling, after filleting a fish in rigor, or by inadequate chilling. Fish should not be frozen before or during rigor because this leads to thaw rigor: Upon thawing, rigor continues with an exaggerated muscle contraction that causes excessive drip loss and dryness of the flesh. The two exceptions to this rule are long line–caught fish of high value that can be frozen pre-rigor (such as swordfish and tuna), and aquacultured finfish that may be processed immediately. These two types are well nourished and not exhausted (no stress resulting from struggling at catch and consequential depletion of glycogen reserves); they pass through rigor later without excessive muscle damage.[9]

After the resolution of rigor, the pH of the fish rises to 5.8 to 6.2, although those fish entering rigor at a higher pH usually show a final pH above this range. As with all seafoods, there are exceptions, and some values may be higher than usual but typically not above pH 6.7. The higher pH leads to more rapid onset of bacterial spoilage.

Fresh Finfish Protein Quality

The functional quality of the salt-soluble protein of finfish is extremely high immediately after catch. With time, even on ice where the temperature is maintained at 33°F (<0.5°C), the extractability of the salt-soluble protein (the myofibrillar proteins composed of actin and myosin) decreases. By six days after catch, fresh West Coast rockfish (*Sebastes* species) held at 39°F (4°C) show a 73 percent reduction in salt-soluble protein.[10] This is significant because the protein responsible for keeping the flesh moist is compromised. This becomes evident by increased drip loss and toughening of the flesh, accompanied by dryness or loss of succulence. Fishermen and processors are frequently accused of not meeting net stated weight (the Food and Drug Administration [FDA] terms this *economic fraud*) when in reality the increased drip loss is a natural phenomenon. Attempts to overpack in order to compensate for drip loss are difficult because of the large variation in stability of myofibrillar protein among finfish families.

Protein Measurement

Total protein varies widely in wild species, ranging from 7 to 24 percent. Mollusks, such as oysters and clams, tend to contain lower protein, while albacore, halibut, and skipjack tuna tend to contain higher protein. Digestibility of seafood protein typically exceeds 90 percent, with a high PER (protein efficiency ratio). Unlike terrestrial animals, most fish species contain appreciable levels of non-protein nitrogen compounds, which may include trimethylamine oxide and its downstream products, urea (especially in sharks and rays), taurine, peptides, free amino acids, nucleotides, purines (adenosine triphosphate [ATP], the energy storage compound), and products of decomposition. For this reason, total protein cannot be determined directly by either of the two analytical methods used most widely for protein determination, Kjeldahl Digestion[11] or the more rapid Combustion Method. Both measure total nitrogen present in a sample, but because non-protein nitrogen is measured along with nitrogen from proteins, the results must be corrected for non-protein nitrogen to be accurate. The Combustion Method uses a conversion factor of $5.8 \times N$ (N = nitrogen) for seafood, compared to $6.25 \times N$ for terrestrial meats.[12] The product developer must keep this in mind when designing a nutrition panel. Failure to do so leads to a falsely high apparent protein content.

Trimethylamine Oxide and Ammonia

Gadoids (finfish of the family Gadidae, which includes pollock, cod, whiting, hake, cusk, and turbot) contain extremely high levels of trimethylamine oxide (TMAO, an osmoregulatory compound that works to balance osmotic pressure and to regulate buoyancy of the fish). Gadoids also have the enzyme trimethlyamine oxidase (TMAOase), which accelerates the breakdown of TMAO to trimethylamine (TMA), the highly aromatic compound most commonly associated with fish decomposition (fishy smell). TMA is hydrolyzed to DMA (dimethylamine) to MMA (monomethylamine) to FA (formaldehyde). Formaldehyde (not at levels harmful to humans) denatures the protein and results in excessive cook loss, toughening of the flesh, and decreased succulence. TMAOase is also active at frozen temperatures, and this hydrolysis cascade occurs with rapid toughening of the flesh (within six weeks at high, 14°F [–10°C] frozen storage temperatures).[13] Gadoid species naturally have a short shelf life if stored raw, but this can be extended by par-cooking in order to denature the enzymes. The breakdown of TMAO also occurs in nongadoids by the action of spoilage bacteria of the genera Alteromonas, Photobacterium, and Vibrio.

Elasmobranchs (sharks, dogfish, skates, and rays) contain high levels of urea as an osmoregulator. Shark flesh has some desirable eating qualities; however, if not bled after catch, urease-positive microorganisms convert the urea to ammonia, which has a highly objectionable odor.[14] Ammonia is also a decomposition product in other seafood species (shrimp, crab, and finfish).

A simple but effective way to determine the decomposition (freshness) of seafood is:

1. Place a small amount (about 1 ounce) into a plastic sealable bag and seal.
2. Place the sample in a microwave oven and cook for 30 to 60 seconds on high, or until the bag begins to puff and is full of steam.
3. Immediately remove the bag, open it, and carefully sniff the steam coming from the seafood. If ammonia, muddiness, algae, or other off aromas are present, the smell will be obvious.
4. If any unpleasant odors are detected, discard the seafood.

Fat Content

In finfish, fat content can vary significantly within species depending on spawning, feeding, and migration patterns. Albacore tuna in the far Pacific tend to be lean or very low (1 percent) in fat content, while the same species feeding in coastal waters tends to deposit lipids in significant quantities (16 percent). Those tuna that are fattier and caught close to shore are superior for preparing smoked and pickled products, or for consumption as sashimi or ceviche. The elevated fat content is ideal for absorption of flavor compounds (such as smoke and spice), and it allows for a tender pickled product without toughening due to the reduced pH caused by vinegar. Belly flaps tend to harbor fatty tissue and are the most delectable part of smoked and pickled fish.

Note: The omega-3, -6, and -9 fatty acid levels in fish are dependent on the composition of the fish's dietary intake.

It is incorrect to assume that all marine species are good sources of the heart-healthy omega-3 fatty acids. Fish such as the sablefish (*Anopoploma fimbria*) and spiny dogfish (*Squalus acanthias*) instead may contain as much as 70 percent omega-9 fatty acids (oleic acid, present at high levels in olive oil and part of the Mediterranean diet).[15] Sablefish, also known as butterfish or black cod, have, when smoked, a consistency that is almost buttery or pâté-like, and, when pickled, a texture that defies a description other than marvelous.

Marine fish chilled in refrigerated sea water (RSW) or seawater-based ice slush, or frozen in a concentrated (23 percent) brine, absorb sodium chloride (NaCl). The quantity of NaCl is greatest in fish frozen and held in concentrated brine (wet holding), next-highest in fish frozen in concentrated brine and drained after freezing (dry holding), next-highest in fish held for a day or two in RSW, and least in fish that are briefly chilled in slush. This is significant because NaCl is a pro-oxidant of the polyunsaturated fatty acids present in fish oils.[16] Phospholipids, especially phosphatidylcholine (lecithin), are the most susceptible and the first to undergo oxidation. Breakdown products of lipid oxidation (aldehydes) combine with proteins and render them hydrophobic[17]—that is, causing them to repel water and toughen the fish flesh. The product developer is probably best served by specifying that frozen tuna for product development never be held wet for long periods after freezing, as that flesh is fit only for canning.

Dark and Light Flesh

Dark fish flesh is readily distinguishable and usually concentrated adjacent to the backbone or along the sides in either narrow bands or in wide zones. The dark flesh is used for continuous motion, while the light flesh is used for sudden bursts of speed.[18] Similarly, poultry muscle contains more dark tissue in those areas (legs and thighs) used for continuous locomotion. Dark meat in fish is due primarily to the presence of myoglobin (the iron-containing pigment that stores oxygen in the muscles for respiration) and hemoglobin.[19] The dark flesh not only contains myoglobin that can oxidize to metmyoglobin and form a brown discoloration, but it also tends to carry higher levels of lipid in the form of polyunsaturated oils that can quickly oxidize in the presence of the iron (an oxidation catalyst). This results in a strong, often objectionable flavor, which is the reason domestic consumers often remove the dark flesh before cooking or scrape it off after cooking.

Tuna species have this dark flesh immediately under the skin, at the center of the loin, and along the backbone.[20] In canneries, tuna is precooked so this dark flesh can more easily be separated from the light meat and sent for pet food processing. In Asia, however, properly handled dark flesh is prized for sashimi. In the United States, it is now common practice to treat tuna and mahi loins and portions with carbon monoxide or tasteless purified smoke to form carboxymyoglobin, providing a vibrant red color.

Adenosine Triphosphatase (ATPase) Test for Freshness

Adenosine triphosphatase (ATPase) is the enzyme that hydrolyzes ATP, the energy storage compound in muscle that allows dissociation of actin from myosin in the actomyosin complex (causing the muscle to relax). Postmortem, ATPase is not regenerated, and its loss is directly correlated with loss of protein functionality. The higher the content of residual ATPase, the greater the ability of the actomyosin complex to dissociate. The presence of residual ATPase is also positively correlated with water-holding capacity and, in re-formed products (such as surimi), the strength of the gel formed on heating. ATPase breakdown slows at colder holding temperatures: $32°F/0°C > -0.4°F/-20°C > -40°F/-40°C > -112°F/-80°C$. That said, while holding seafood at ultralow temperatures is common practice for laboratory samples, it is not realistic for commercial settings.

The Japanese are connoisseurs of sashimi and have conducted some of the best and most detailed studies to determine finfish quality. ATP is hydrolyzed postmortem to adenosine triphosphate (ADP) to adenosine monophosphate (AMP) to inosine monophosphate (IMP) to inosine (INO) to hypoxanthine (Hx) to uric acid (U). A complex equation has been developed involving ATP and its downstream products to determine the K-value, which is used to predict the quality of fish sold for sashimi.[21] The K-value is species-specific because it increases dramatically depending on the species. For example, Fraser et al. determined that IMP was depleted in iced cod in 9 days.[22] Spinelli demonstrated the presence of IMP in iced halibut at 41 days.[23] For optimal-quality sashimi, the K-value should be 3.5 percent immediately after catch, less than 20 percent for good quality, and about 50 percent for medium quality.[24] This is one of the means used by the Japanese to determine the quality (and price) of sashimi.

● Preserving Seafood

The supplier of fresh, never-frozen seafood should be able to state where it was caught or aquacultured and the methods used to ship the product. Seafood sold at retail must be labeled to indicate if it was wild caught or aquacultured (7CFR60.200). An abundance of ice surrounding the seafood within the pack should keep the temperature close to 32°F (0°C) to retard spoilage. There should be no question that the seafood was treated with respect and urgency for its delivery. Seafood destined for raw consumption (i.e., for sashimi, ceviche, or crudo) requires special handling, discussed further in the Fish- and Shellfish-Derived Foodborne Illnesses section below.

Fresh seafood offers a distinctive eating experience that elevates the consumers' experience and produces a greater respect for the product, which results in a higher selling price than most previously frozen product (sashimi notwithstanding). That said, a variety of shelf life extenders, including freezing, canning, salting, and packaging strategies, are used to extend seafood shelf life.

FIGURE 6.2 **Freeze temperatures: percentage of water frozen in finfish as a function of temperature.**

Temperature of Flesh °F (°C)	Water Frozen (%)
30.4 (–0.9)	0
30 (–1.1)	32
28 (–2.2)	61
26 (–3.3)	76
24 (–4.4)	83
22 (–5.6)	86
18 (–7.8)	89

Source: Lucina Lampila.

Freezing

Most commercial processors of raw seafood do an excellent job of freezing fish. Rapid freezing produces a superior product when thawed and eaten. In many cases, commercially processed seafood that is frozen at sea has better sensory attributes than its fresh, unfrozen counterpart. Most wild or aquacultured fish are frozen within minutes of being caught or harvested. Therefore, it is possible to catch high-quality seafood in remote locations, freeze it quickly, and ship it rapidly to the distributor, retailer, and finally, the consumer.

Once-frozen seafood is the primary process used in the industry. In this technique, wild-caught or aquacultured seafood is trimmed or portioned shortly after harvest and immediately frozen. Many times this occurs at sea on the harvesting vessel or within a few hours' drive of the aquaculture ponds. The seafood is not thawed until use.

Twice-frozen seafood refers to wild finfish that are caught, headed and gutted (H&G), and frozen at sea. The H&G frozen finfish are shipped to a processing plant where they are carefully thawed, filleted, portion-cut, and then refrozen. This process is safe and can produce uniform hand-cut portions available for breading, further processing, or cooking. The care taken in thawing, trimming, and refreezing determines the quality of the finished product. It is possible to source twice-frozen products of the highest quality. Some of these may contain added ingredients (typically, phosphates) to protect protein and to maintain moisture during freezing and cooking.

Freezing temperature affects ice crystal formation. The higher the freezer storage temperature, the longer it takes products to freeze, and the larger the ice crystals that are formed. As water freezes, it expands and can rupture cell membranes, resulting in increased drip loss on thawing. Temperature rise during frozen storage results in changes to the size of the ice crystals. For example, if a fillet is frozen to –40°F (–40°C) and later moved to a 0°F (–17.8°C) freezer, the ice crystals will grow or accrete.[25] This can also occur in frost-free freezers, where warming and cooling cycles occur multiple times each day to prevent accumulation of excessive

FIGURE 6.3 Freezing curve. This figure shows the rate of freezing of whole bonito *(Sarda chiliensis)* in either a eutectic (NaCl) brine or potable water.

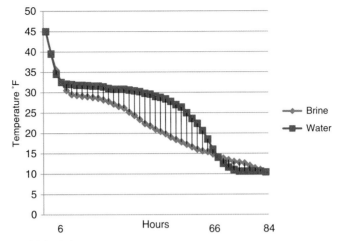

Source: Lampila and Rittmanic, unpublished data.

FIGURE 6.4 Micrograph: ice crystals. This micrograph shows the sites of presumed ice crystals and the damage mediated as they accrete or grow after the rockfish *(Bocaccio, Sebastus paucispinis)* fillet is moved from –4°F (–20°C) to 23°F (–5°C). The sharp edges of the ice crystals presumably rupture the cell and exacerbate the loss of natural fluids observed as thaw-drip loss.

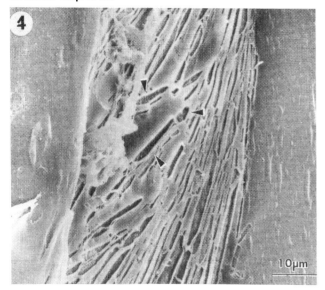

Source: Lampila et al., 1985.

FIGURE 6.5 Micrograph: crushed muscle. This piece of rockfish *(Bocaccio, Sebastus paucispinis)* fillet was frozen at –4°F (–20°C). After 10 days in frozen storage, the crushing of the muscle structure can be observed in this cross section. These two micrographs (Figures 6.4 and 6.5) were taken of rockfish flesh preserved by isothermal freeze fixation, a process whereby the flesh was chemically fixed at the frozen storage temperature to the size and shape of ice crystals.

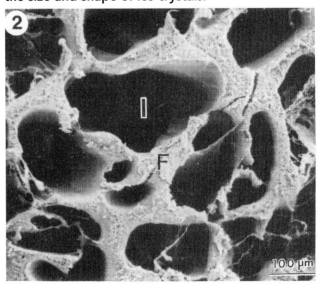

Source: Lampila et al., 1985.

ice deposits inside the chamber. Packaged seafood subjected to excessive freeze-thaw cycles accumulates large ice crystals between the frozen flesh and the packaging material. This is moisture from the flesh that has sublimated (passed from a solid to a vapor and back to a solid state) into the headspace between the fillet and the packaging material. The result is freezer burn, featuring significant surface dehydration and loss of overall eating quality. If frost-free storage is the only option, it is best to vacuum package the seafood to eliminate, as much as possible, any headspace, or to overwrap frozen packages with several layers of paper for insulation against the freeze-thaw cycling.

During the freezing process, water slowly migrates out of the cells, causing salts normally present in the interior of the cells to become more concentrated. This concentration may result in the salting out of proteins, which can accelerate denaturation. Salting out precipitates proteins from solution as ionic strength increases. Over time, this can cause the proteins to irreversibly denature. A denatured protein has an unfolded structure, and many of its functional properties are compromised or eliminated—in particular, its ability to bind water, leading to excessive drip loss and dry texture upon thawing.

Several other problems are indicated by thawed fish fillets that drip excessively or have flesh that becomes chalky or rubbery, or pulls into ridges. Chalky flesh is usually freezer burned; rubbery flesh was frozen too long for its species type, and flesh pulling into ridges is indicative of thaw rigor (due to fish being frozen before going through rigor mortis). Cod and pollock are among the species with a very short frozen shelf life.

It is important to note that some enzymes, such as TMAOase (the enzyme responsible for the formation of trimethylamine—one odorant responsible for the fishy smell in spoiling seafood), are still active at normal frozen temperatures (i.e., between 0 and 32°F [−18 and 0°C]). This is why commercial freezers are maintained at −20°F (−28.9°C) or colder.

This is not to say that finfish should not be frozen. On the contrary, freezing finfish quickly and to a low temperature maintains the quality of the flesh closer to the point of freshness. That said, it is critical to package the product so oxygen is excluded or under vacuum, and that the packaging material has low oxygen permeability. The polyunsaturated fatty acids in fish oils are highly subject to autoxidation (the oxygen-mediated breakdown of lipids resulting in free radical formation and rancidity) even when frozen. And as mentioned previously, breakdown products of lipid oxidation (aldehydes) combine with proteins and render them hydrophobic, causing them to repel water and toughen the fish flesh.[26] Exclusion of oxygen slows this reaction.

Seafood can be packaged so each individual piece or portion is separated while frozen. Layers of plastic can separate each fillet (cello-pack, vacuum pack, or shatter-pack), or seafood pieces can be individually quick-frozen (IQF). Fillets can also be frozen into blocks that facilitate cutting the fish into portions for breading, par-frying, and freezing.

Thawing Vacuum-Packaged Seafood

Vacuum packaging introduces an anaerobic (oxygen-free) environment. *Clostridium botulinum* Type E and non-proteolytic Types B and F are anaerobic, spore-forming bacterial pathogens most often associated with raw seafood. This type of *C. botulinum* is unusual in that it tolerates lower temperatures than others. Vacuum-packaged raw fish must be stored at less than 37.9°F (3.3°C), according to the FDA's recommended handling practices, as this prevents the germination of spores (which results in toxin production) and growth of the organism. Some states have regulations that require any vacuum-packaged raw seafood to be kept frozen. With all types of frozen, vacuum-packaged seafoods, it is recommended that the packaging be pierced (or removed entirely) to release the vacuum and to introduce oxygen before thawing. The FDA (2011) recommends that all frozen, reduced-oxygen-packaged seafood bear the warning "*Important:* Keep frozen until use. Thaw under refrigeration immediately before use."

Canned Fish

Per-capita consumption of canned fish in the United States was 3.9 pounds in 2010.[27] Nearly 70 percent of all canned fish consumed in the United States is tuna. Shellfish and other fishery products (mackerel, anchovies, clam juice, etc.) account for 10 percent each of canned products, with salmon and sardines accounting for about 5 percent each. True canning (retort sterilization) makes fish shelf stable at room temperature, and the shelf life is in years. Pasteurized canned crab is not shelf stable and must be refrigerated. Pasteurization extends the refrigerated shelf life of crab to approximately six months.

Several species are permitted by the FDA's Standard of Identity (complete information can be found at: 21CFR161.190) for canned tuna to be labeled as light-meat tuna, including bluefin, yellowfin, blackfin, bigeye, and skipjack, but only one, *Thunnus alalunga* (Bonnaterre, 1788), or albacore, is permitted for use as white-meat canned tuna.

Albacore tuna feed near the top of the predatory chain and as a consequence bioaccumulate higher levels of methyl mercury than other species of tuna; this sort should be eaten sparingly by pregnant women and young children. Skipjack, on the other hand, neither live long enough nor grow sufficiently large (average size is less than 10 pounds) to bioaccumulate dangerous levels of methyl mercury, so, generally speaking, light tuna is a much safer option for children and pregnant women. Skipjack comprises approximately 70 percent of all light-meat canned tuna.

Chinook *Oncorhynchus tshawytscha* (king) salmon is the most expensive variety of salmon. It is primarily used for fresh, frozen, and hot- or cold-smoked products (including "lox"). Less expensive varieties are sockeye or red salmon (*Oncorhynchus nerka*), coho (*Oncorhynchus kisutch*), pink salmon (*Oncorhynchus gorbuscha*), and chum (*Oncorhynchus keta*), which are more often canned—with or without the bones. If salmon is packed with the bones, they are softened in the retort (commercial pressure cooker) to the point where they become edible and contribute calcium and phosphorus as nutrients.

Other seafoods commonly available in canned form include sardines, mackerel, oysters, mussels, octopus, kippers (smoked herring), and anchovies.

Restructured Fish

One means of restructuring fish is to transform fish fillets into uniformly portioned products, such as fish sticks or nuggets. Cleaned fish fillets are frozen at sea into 40-pound blocks. Once landed, the blocks are tempered and sawed into standard portions. They can then be breaded and fried or par-fried, then refrozen for retail or foodservice sale.

A second means of restructuring fish involves the production of *surimi*. Surimi, originally of Japanese origin, is a gelled paste made from fish used to mimic the appearance, texture, and color of more expensive lobster, crab, and other shellfish. The most common surimi product in the Western market is imitation crab meat (also known as "crab stick"). Surimi is made from lean, light-fleshed fish that are mechanically deboned and minced. The minced flesh is typically washed two to three times in chilled potable water. Because the flesh absorbs water during washing, it is dewatered and then screen-refined to remove small pieces of skin, connective tissue, and bone. The washed, refined fish mince is then mixed with cryoprotectants (4 percent each of sucrose and sorbitol, plus 0.5 percent of a blend of phosphates) and frozen into 44-pound blocks for later restructuring. Low-cost species (pollock or Pacific whiting) must be used because the yield is less than 30 percent of the whole fish. Later, the frozen block is tempered and blended with potato starch, dried egg white, flavorings, salt, and phosphate to prepare the analog. The blended fish paste is extruded onto a belt, steam cooked, and cut into fibers. The fibers are then cut and rolled with more of the paste as a binder, and steam cooked again. A food-grade red color is typically sprayed onto the product to provide pigmentation characteristic of the intended end species. In addition to use as low-cost crabmeat replacements (so-called krab or sea legs), surimi is also available as shrimp and lobster analogs used in salad bars.

Salting: Caviar and Preserved Roe

Caviar is the processed roe of any species of sturgeon or paddlefish (order *Acipenseriformes*, 50CFR23.71). The most expensive (hundreds to thousands of dollars *per pound*) is Russian or Iranian black Beluga caviar, which comes from the black sturgeon (also caught in the United States, but not commercially for the roe). Other fish eggs are also harvested and sold as caviar, but the species (salmon, lumpfish, flying fish, etc.) must be named on the label. Sea urchin roe, extremely popular in Japan for many years (where it is called *uni*), became trendy in the United States with the exploding growth of sushi restaurants.

In finfish, the roe is contained in skeins or sacs. It is not uncommon for the Japanese to fly in workers to harvest the skeins from salmon (for example) before the fish are filleted at the processing facilities. The skeins are carefully placed in sturdy packaging and flown to Japan. In the United States, depending on the species, the skeins may be broken by hand and the eggs removed, or the skeins may be rubbed against a screen to loosen the eggs. The eggs are then hand culled to remove bits of membrane, blood, intestine, or black skin. The roe is held in a salt solution for 1 to 5 hours (depending on the species), rinsed, drained, and packed into a container and refrigerated.[28] Alternatively, the roe may have salt added directly with mild agitation until it is dissolved. If the intent is to hold the roe for any length of time, it is critical to assure that water activity is reduced to $a_w \leq 0.97$ and/or that the water phase salt is sufficiently high (5 percent) to inhibit growth of *C. botulinum* by the reduced-oxygen environment. Roe can also be salted and dried, as is commonly done in Italy in the preparation of bottarga, salted and pressed roe of gray mullet, bluefin tuna, and other fish species.

Treating Seafood with Phosphate

As with all proteins, when used properly, phosphates allow seafood to stay moist and succulent after cooking. When seafood is breaded or battered and fried, phosphates help retain moisture as well as the shape and size of the original uncooked protein. This improves the moistness of the cooked product, keeps the seafood from pulling away from the breading (creating a shell effect), and enhances the holding quality of the cooked product. With the increasing volume of twice-frozen products into the marketplace, phosphate plays an important role in keeping these products moist when held cooked or eaten. Maintaining protein hydration also helps maintain natural color and flavor. Alkaline phosphates also raise the temperature for denaturation to occur.[29] Thus, phosphate-treated seafood products are more forgiving to overcooking.

As previously indicated, the level of salt-soluble protein (the myofibrillar or functional protein) is an indicator of eating quality. This is the same protein that binds water to form a sol (protein hydration, dispersion, and swelling) and, after heating, a gel. Water binding is positively correlated with juiciness and tenderness of the cooked protein. Salt-soluble protein also interacts with fats and oils in the development of emulsions and contributes to emulsifying capacity. The food developer must keep in mind that myofibrillar protein is best solubilized by low levels of sodium chloride together with sodium tripolyphosphate to entrap moisture and lipids in a stable protein matrix upon heating, thus ensuring maximum eating quality.

The optimal concentration of sodium chloride for extracting the salt-soluble proteins is 3.5 percent (0.6M) salt.[30] However, this level of salinity is unpalatable to many individuals, and the public has been encouraged to consume less sodium. Commercially, salt-soluble protein is extracted with a combination of 1.4 to 1.8 percent salt[31] plus 0.4 to 0.5 percent alkaline phosphate (typically sodium tripolyphosphate [STPP] or combinations of STPP plus tetrasodium pyrophosphate [TSPP],[32] with lesser quantities of sodium acid pyrophosphate [SAPP]). Salt and the alkaline phosphates work synergistically (less salt is required with a low level of phosphate, and the impact of the two ingredients is greater than the sum of the two ingredients added alone). Each ingredient extracts different regions of the sarcomere (individual subunit of myofibril) and results in enhanced salt-soluble protein solubility. In addition, salt is a pro-oxidant (it promotes oxidation); STPP negates this oxidative effect, thereby prolonging product shelf life.[33]

Condensed (long-chain) alkaline phosphates alone are also used as cryoprotectants in finfish. The fillets are conveyed through a solution of STPP, with a flex in the belt to expedite penetration between myotomes on the upper and lower sides. This creates a surface coating of protein that acts as a glue to allow adhesion of fillets to each other when block-freezing. This process eliminates voids that could harbor air pockets during freezing and, if destined for standard portion cutting, holes in the portion. Similar protocols are also used on fillets to be sold as fresh to better predict and control the amount of overpack needed to meet net stated weight.[34]

Phosphates may be present in purchased commercial marinades or added to those prepared on site. It is important never to use copper or aluminum ware to either prepare solutions or hold product while marinating. Copper interacts with the phosphate and forms a green color on the fish, and although not harmful, the result is visually unappealing. Aluminum vessels can pit and in severe cases develop pinhole leaks. It is also important to know the water quality used in food preparation. Hard water containing appreciable levels of minerals, especially copper, iron, and manganese, used in phosphate-based marinades may result in discolorations to the finished food products. Hard water containing 200 ppm or more of calcium and magnesium may also form precipitates with condensed phosphates, which can clog injector needles or leave surface residue.

Similar to its use in meat and poultry, phosphate use in seafood products is limited by the FDA to 0.5 percent in the finished food. However, even though long-chain potassium phosphates provide excellent water-binding properties, at levels greater than 0.3 percent, potassium phosphates may contribute a bitter flavor (similar to when potassium chloride is used as a substitute for table salt). Sodium phosphates used in excess may contribute a slightly soapy note to the flavor. Further, fillets overtreated with alkaline phosphates feel slippery or slimy. Phosphate added in excess to seafood tends to cause the protein to absorb and hold an unnatural amount of water. Shrimp and finfish overtreated with solutions of salt

and alkaline phosphate look glassy and have a rubbery texture, and the flesh resists becoming opaque despite extended heating. Phosphate producers have long encouraged the responsible and appropriate use of their products for maintaining the quality of seafood products.

Economic Fraud and Species Substitution

Species substitution is considered economic fraud. This is a criminal act, and the FDA encourages prosecution of vendors taking part in species substitution. Figure 6.6 shows some of the most commonly substituted species, as identified by the FDA. A good working relationship with a seafood supplier can be the best defense against species substitution. Testing methods (genetic and electrophoretic) can accurately identify some species, but these tests are best conducted by contract laboratories.

A second area of economic fraud is the substitution of imported product for domestic species. The Tariff Act of 1930 mandates that imported seafood be labeled in English with the country of origin (19CFR134). This is not an FDA requirement but one of Customs and Border Protection for identification of the country of origin at the port of entry. The Country of Origin Labeling ("COOL") law requiring retailers to identify the origin of seafood at the point of sale became effective in 2005 (7CFR60). A third area of economic fraud involves overglazing of seafood. A glaze is a coating of ice to prevent desiccation. During extended periods of frozen storage—for example, six months—it is normal to place a maximum of 18 percent glaze on the seafood immediately after processing because it sublimates over time.

Fish- and Shellfish-Derived Foodborne Illnesses

Ciguatera fish poisoning (CFP) is caused by the consumption of certain predatory fish (grouper, snapper, barracuda, amberjack, wrasse, surgeon fish, parrot fish, and others) harvested from coral reefs in tropical and subtropical waters.[35] Smaller species in the reefs consume microscopic marine algae that contain ciguatoxin, which, through predation, bioaccumulates up the food chain and becomes concentrated in the larger fish, which are commonly eaten by humans. CFP symptoms begin with tingling and numbness of the lips and tongue, sometimes spreading to the extremities, and also include nausea, vomiting, diarrhea, headache, reversal of sensitivity of hot and cold, acute sensitivity to temperature extremes, vertigo, muscular weakness, irregular heartbeat, and reduced blood pressure.[36] Gastrointestinal symptoms usually begin within two hours of ingestion, and cardiovascular and neurologic symptoms begin about four hours later. Symptoms can last

FIGURE 6.6 Economic fraud: examples of species substitution.

Products in Column A have been known to be substituted for those in Column B, which in most cases are more expensive (FDA, 2014).	
Column A	Column B
Various Snappers (*Lutjanus spp.*)	Red Snapper (*Lutjanus campechanus*)
Rockfish (*Sebastes* spp.)	Red Snapper (*Lutjanus campechanus*)
Yellowtail	Mahi Mahi
Mako Shark	Swordfish
Oreo Dory or John Dory	Orange Roughy
Alaska Pollock	Cod
Sea Bass	Halibut
Arrowtooth Flounder	Dover Sole
Black Drum	Red Drum (Red Fish; Southern or Gulf)
White Perch	Lake or Yellow Perch (Great Lakes)
Zander	Lake or Yellow Perch (Great Lakes)
Paddlefish and other fish roe	Caviar (Sturgeon species)
Sauger	Walleye
Pink Salmon	Chum Salmon
Skate Wings	Scallops
Alaskan Pollock	Walleye
Steelhead Trout	Salmon
Imported Crabmeat	Blue Crabmeat
Farm Raised Salmon	Wild Caught Salmon
Top Shell	Abalone

Source: U.S. Food and Drug Administration, www.fda.gov (2014).

from weeks to months. Ciguatoxin is odorless and tasteless, heat stable,[37] and extremely potent: 0.01 ppb (parts per billion) for Pacific ciguatoxin equivalents and 0.1 ppb ciguatoxin equivalent for the Caribbean.[38]

The five types of shellfish poisoning are paralytic (PSP); diarrhetic (DSP), caused by saxitoxin; neurotoxic (NSP), caused by brevetoxin; amnesic (ASP), caused by domoic acid; and azaspiracid (AZP), attributed to azaspiracids. All are caused by the consumption of molluscan shellfish (clams, oysters, mussels, scallops), but exceptions exist. Whelk are also associated with NSP; the viscera of Dungeness and red rock crabs and roe from scallops are associated with ASP; and conch, snails, whelk, abalone from South Africa, and the viscera of crab and lobster are associated with PSP intoxication.[39] Shellfish poisoning is widespread, with outbreaks occurring mainly in warm waters but also in colder areas during the summer months. Gastrointestinal effects (nausea, vomiting, and abdominal pain) are reported with DSP, ASP, and AZP intoxication, while neurological effects are reported as a result of NSP, PSP, and ASP intoxication. Onset of symptoms is minutes to hours with NSP, DSP, AZP, and PSP, while ASP onset is 24 to 48 hours. Resolution of symptoms is several days. Action levels for each toxin are PSP, 0.8 ppm saxitoxin equivalents; NSP, 0.8 ppm brevitoxin-2 equivalents; DSP, 0.16 ppm as okadaic acid; ASP, 20 ppm domoic acid, except in the viscera of Dungeness crab, where the action level is 30 ppm; and AZP, 0.16 ppm azaspiracid equivalents.[40] Like ciguatoxin, the causative agents of shellfish poisoning are heat stable and cannot be destroyed by cooking.

Scombroid poisoning is caused by consumption of certain species of fish that naturally contain high levels of the amino acid histidine. Typical species include tuna, mackerel, bluefish, bonito, amberjack, bluefish, alewife, escolar, herring, jack, marlin, sailfish, shad, mahi-mahi, sardines, and anchovies. If the fish is not kept adequately chilled after capture or during storage, bacteria multiply and secrete histidine decarboxylase, an enzyme that breaks down the histidine to histamine. This is the same histamine that causes allergic reactions. Symptoms begin within minutes to hours and may last from 12 hours to several days and include tingling around the mouth or throat; rash or hives on the upper body; dizziness; itching; nausea, vomiting, diarrhea; asthmatic-like constriction of the air passage; heart palpitations; and respiratory distress.[41] Histamine is not destroyed by normal cooking temperatures, so even properly cooked fish can be affected. Freezing, cooking, smoking, curing, and canning are also ineffective in eliminating the toxin.

Escolar (*Lepidocybium flavobrunneum*) and oilfish (*Ruvettus pretiosus*) are two species associated with gempylid fish poisoning. These fish produce gempylotoxin, which is a strong purgative. This is actually an indigestible wax ester that causes sudden diarrhea. The FDA warns against consumption of these species. Orange roughy (*Hoplostethus atlanticus*) is another species that contains high levels of wax esters capable of causing sudden diarrhea in susceptible individuals. Food formulators must be wary of consumer complaints of foodborne illness after consumption of orange roughy.

Tetrodotoxin is associated with *pufferfish* (fugu, swellfish, bok, blowfish, globefish, balloonfish, and sea squab) poisoning. The United States restricts importation of pufferfish and products that contain it. The gonads, liver, intestines, and skin of the pufferfish can contain enough toxin to produce rapid and violent death. The lethal potency is 5000 to 6000 MU/mg (1 MU, or mouse unit, is defined as the amount of toxin required to kill a 20-gram male mouse within 30 minutes of intraperitoneal injection), and the minimum lethal dose (MLD) for humans is estimated to be approximately 10,000 MU ($\approx$2 mg).[42] Tetrodotoxin is of major public health concern primarily in Japan and the Far East, where pufferfish liver (and other parts) were a traditional delicacy until banned in restaurants and markets. Pufferfish is prepared and sold in special restaurants where trained and licensed chefs carefully remove the viscera to reduce the danger of poisoning. More recent research shows that the pufferfish's diet and enteric bacteria cause the formation of tetrodotoxin. Mortality from pufferfish poisoning in Japan was 57.9 percent in 1965 but reduced to 5.3 percent by 2007. Symptoms of tetrodotoxin poisoning begin between one-half and three hours after ingestion and include headache and numbness that gradually progresses to paralysis, irregular heartbeat, respiratory failure, and death within four to six hours.[43] Depending on the dose, death may occur due to respiratory arrest within two hours of consumption. There is no antidote. Treatment typically includes intravenous fluids and respiratory support for approximately a week in a hospital intensive care unit.

Fresh fish is not always better than frozen fish. For fish preparations that are normally consumed uncooked, such as ceviche (which is acid marinated) and sashimi, freezing is strongly recommended for destruction of parasites. These are present in some percentage of any catch.

The anasakid roundworm (a nematode) is associated with saltwater finfish species of the West Coast such as cod, flounder, halibut, herring, plaice, pollock, and sea bass. These parasites can cause gastrointestinal discomfort but do not typically remain viable for more than three weeks in healthy humans.

Diphyllobothrium tapeworms (cestodes) are associated with freshwater fish (perch and pike) and anadromous species (those that migrate from fresh to salt water, such as salmon).[44] Tapeworms can grow to several yards long inside the human digestive tract if not diagnosed and treated but can live for months or longer without causing acute illness. They can successfully be treated with antihelminthic medications.

Clonorchis sinensis, the Chinese liver fluke, is transmitted from snails to freshwater fish to humans. This parasite lives in the liver of humans and is isolated mainly to the common bile duct and gallbladder, feeding on bile. These organisms, among the most prevalent worm parasites in the world, are endemic to Japan, China, Taiwan, and Southeast Asia, where they infect millions of people. While normally asymptomatic, most pathological manifestations result from inflammation and intermittent obstruction of the biliary ducts. The acute phase consists of abdominal pain with associated nausea and diarrhea. Recent studies have shown that *Clonorchis* can cause cancer of the liver and bile duct. These liver flukes are extremely rare in the United States.

The traditional way to control for parasites is *candling*, or holding thin slices of fish flesh over a bright light to look for the presence of parasites, followed by their excision. Candling is estimated to be 70 percent effective (dark tissue or thick slices are difficult to illuminate from behind), but freezing is 100 percent effective. As a result, the FDA recommends that seafood to be consumed raw be frozen first. The recommendation is usually freezing solid for 15 hours in a blast freezer

($-31°F$ [$-35°C$]) or for one week in a freezer at $-20°F$ ($-29°C$). The texture may be somewhat compromised depending on the freezing temperature, efficiency of the freezer, and the means of thawing; however, the fish can be served without fear of harming anyone.

The thawed flesh can then be served raw as sashimi or as ceviche, where fish is pickled in an acidic fruit juice marinade that denatures the proteins, firming the flesh and causing its cooked appearance. Some ceviche restaurants, to be safe, gently steam the seafood first (until barely cooked), then mix it with fresh vegetables and citrus juices. Heating to an internal temperature of $140°F$ ($60°C$) or greater—i.e., *cooking*—also destroys parasites.

Shellfish
Shellfish Certification

The U.S. Department of Commerce maintains a list of approved shippers of oysters, clams, mussels, and scallops (the *Interstate Certified Shellfish Shippers List*). Only shellfish from these shippers (whose shellfish come from certified pathogen-tested waters) can be sold for consumption. Wholesale containers must be labeled with the harvester's name, address, certification number, date and location of harvest, and type and quantity of shellfish. *Shucked* shellfish (removed from their shells) must also be tagged with a *sell-by date* or a *date shucked*, and these tags must be kept by foodservice operators for a minimum of 90 days after receipt. Any violations are reported to the FDA, which has jurisdiction over shellfish commerce.

Mollusks
Gastropods (Univalves): Abalone, Whelk, and Conch

The abalone is a gastropod (or univalve). The adductor muscle, or foot, is the predominant protein structure of the abalone. It has a unique muscle structure (Figure 6.8) that allows the animal to adhere to its habitat, usually a rock, at pressures up to 200 psi. This structure allows for great strength but requires the muscle to be physically tenderized before preparation, typically by gently pounding with a mallet.

Abalone was overfished in California by World War II and hence became only a recreational (sport) fishery. Abalone fishing in Alaska was closed to commercial fishing in the early 1980s. Abalone is now aquacultured in California, Japan, China, Korea, Taiwan, Thailand, Australia, New Zealand, and, to a lesser extent, in Europe, Iceland, and other Pacific Rim countries.

The bottom of the foot is the *pedal sole*, which is not typically consumed, as it contains up to 22 percent collagen and is extremely tough.[45] Domestically, this part is removed and discarded in the butchering process. For the export market, it may be salted and dried for later addition to soups and stews.

FIGURE 6.7 Evaluating live and fresh shellfish.

Select for	Live Shellfish	Avoid
Firmly closed shells or gaping shells that close firmly when tapped	Oysters and clams	Gaping or open shells that do not close when tapped; the animal is dead and inedible.
Animals that seem heavy for their size and have leg movement	Hard and soft shell crabs and lobster	Sluggish or inanimate animals are either dying or dead and are inedible. Note: Animals should never be shipped in dry ice.
A tail that curves under the animal when picked up	Lobster	A tail that hangs limply when the animal is picked up
	Fresh Shellfish	
Shucked meats should be plump with no more than 10% liquor that is creamy in color and clear.	Oysters	Meats that appear to be misshapen and dispersed in turbid liquor and/or an overabundance of liquor
Shucked meats will be yellow to pink in a clear liquor.	Clams	Orange to brown meats in turbid liquor
Scallops are firm with a slightly sweet aroma and have very little liquor; sea scallops are white to pink to orange; bay scallops are smaller with white, tan, or pink coloration. (Note: Color is primarily due to dietary carotenoids.)	Scallops	Soft or mushy meats; strong, putrid, or ammonia-like odors; excessive fluid in the package
- Slightly softer than other species of shrimp; easier to peel - Natural sweet flavor; seaweed-like aroma - White to grayish-pink - Cooked flesh has pink color	White shrimp	Pitted or bleached shells (over-sulfited); intense pink raw flesh indicates temperature abuse; strong or chemical odors; frozen, clumped shrimp indicate previously frozen product.
- Slightly firmer than white U.S. Gulf shrimp - Larger sizes (10/15) may have a stronger iodine flavor and more intense brown coloration - Tend to be rounder than white shrimp so counts may appear skewed - Have a groove in the last tail segment	Brown shrimp	Soft or mushy tails; strong or ammonia-like odors; black spot (melanosis) caused by a natural enzymatic process post-harvest (which can be inhibited by brief dips in sodium metabisulfite or Everfresh [4-hexylresorcinol on a NaCl carrier])

Source: Sea Grant College Program.

Some abalone flesh is canned. Due to the presence of hemocyanin, some blue discoloration may occur over time. This can be prevented by adding sodium acid pyrophosphate (SAPP) to the pack before the thermal process.

Abalone is one of the most expensive seafoods in the marketplace. Fresh abalone steaks are available on Amazon.com for $125.00/pound (plus shipping). Not surprisingly, the FDA has observed illegal species substitution with gastropods from the Trochidae family (whelks).

Both the conch and the whelk are univalves, like abalone, and must be similarly tenderized because the meat is rather tough in its native state. The flavor is clam-like. Preparation time is short, and overcooking causes toughening. Whelk is commonly used in Italian cooking, where it is known as *scungilli*. Conch (pronounced "konk") is famous in the Caribbean for use in fritters. Due to overharvesting, the United States has neither a commercial nor a recreational fishery for queen conch. There is a controlled fishery for queen conch in the Caribbean.

Whelk of the *Neptunia* species have a toxin, teramine, in their salivary glands. Symptoms of teramine poisoning include double vision, temporary blindness, difficulty focusing, tingling of the fingers, vomiting, diarrhea, and loss of muscle control. Symptoms develop within one hour of consumption.[46]

FIGURE 6.8 Abalone structure. The microstructure of abalone *(Haliotis rufescens)* is shown. The transverse fibrils show the strength of the adductor and the need for mechanical tenderization before consumption.

Source: Lampila, unpublished data.

Bivalves: Clams

Clams are mollusks with two shells (bivalves). Clams can be eaten raw, steamed, boiled, baked, or fried. The method of preparation depends partly on the size and species of the clam. They can also be made into clam chowder (a popular soup in the United States and Canada), or they can be cooked using hot rocks and seaweed in a New England clambake.

The two general categories of clams are hard shell and soft shell. The hard-shell clam (*Mercenaria mercenaria*) is also known as the Northern quahog, cherrystone clam, and little-neck clam. It is harvested either wild or farmed from the Gulf of St. Lawrence to the Gulf coast of Texas. The ocean (or deep-water) quahog or mahogany clam (*Artica islandica*) is dredged from deeper waters of the North Atlantic and brought to shore in large metal cages.[47] Once ashore, they are offloaded to refrigerated areas. Typically, they are conveyed through a flame or steam or water bath to open the shell. The meats may then be hand shucked (or mechanically eviscerated by shakers); the viscera, or sandbag, is then removed and discarded. The cleaned meat is washed and cut or diced and then packed for refrigerated distribution, freezing, or canning (retorting). Clams may also be sold live for cooking or for raw consumption. Other hard-shell clams of economic importance include the surf or bar clam (*Spisula solidissima*) from the Gulf of St. Lawrence to Hatteras, North Carolina, and the Pacific razor clam (*Siliqua patula*), with shells shaped like an old-fashioned straight razor; these are harvested from southern California to the Aleutian Islands of Alaska. *Protothaca*

tapes, the littleneck clam, and *Saxidomus giganeus* or *S. nuttalli*, the butter clam, are two other hard-shell clams harvested off the Pacific coast.

The other major category of clam is the soft-shell or steamer clam. Soft-shell (long-neck) clams or steamers (*Mya arenaria*) occur naturally from Labrador, Canada, to North Carolina and were introduced on the West Coast. They are dug and sold live for the traditional clambake or steaming, or they may be shucked and preserved for stews and chowders. They are characterized by an elongated and flattened shell that is much thinner and more brittle than hard-shell clamshells and more easily broken, hence the term soft-shell clams. They are also characterized by a long siphon from which they eject seawater, which has given them the colorful nickname "piss clam."

The largest edible clam is the geoduck (*Panopea generosa*), pronounced "gooey-duck." This West Coast clam has a large shell (7 to 9 inches [17 to 23 cm]) and an unusually long siphon (typically 2 to 3 feet [0.6 to 0.9 m]), as it buries itself to the depth of the siphon below the surface of the beach.[48] Typical harvest weights are in the 2-pound (0.9 kg) range. It is also one of the longest-living animals on Earth, with a known lifespan in excess of 100 years. The market for these clams is primarily in Asia, where they are highly valued. As such, these clams are actively farmed, especially in Washington State's Puget Sound. Geoduck is often seen at the Pike Street Market in Seattle and sold live to specialty restaurants.

A note on color: Green gills on clams and oysters may result from diet. The single-cell alga *Haslea ostrearia* (a *diatom*) produces the water-soluble blue pigment marennine. Marennine deposits in the gills after filter feeding and as it concentrates imparts a green color to the natural yellowish color of the organs. This diatom tends to flourish in colder weather but varies from one body of water to another. Marennine is not toxic to humans but in the United States is considered a sensory defect. In France, however, oysters that have bioaccumulated marennine are considered a delicacy. There, the diatoms are actually cultivated to be released into oyster "finishing beds" (*clairs*) to encourage the development of green gills.

Yellow to orange colors are imparted by dietary carotenoids from phytoplankton, which are estimated to produce several hundred tons of carotenoid each year. Clams, like humans, must derive carotenoids from the diet, as they cannot be synthesized. Carotenoids are normally considered fat soluble. When bound to hydrophobic sites on proteins, they can become soluble in an aqueous medium and are termed *carotenoproteins*. Carotenoproteins primarily occur in invertebrates.

The forms of carotenoid seen most often in clams include β-carotene (yellow to orange in color and most bioactive precursor to vitamin A), zeaxanthin (yellow), and lutein (yellow). The functions of the carotenoids in mollusks are not known but may include strengthening the protein structure; as antioxidants to quench singlet oxygen (free radicals); imparting resistance to bacterial or fungal diseases; enhancing immune function; promoting wound healing; and providing protection from light. They are known to take part in the development of reproductive organs.[49]

Pink to red colorations can be caused by the reduction of nitrate deposited by certain strains of sulfur-oxidizing bacteria living within the gills of the host clam. Elevated levels of nitrite postmortem can lead to pinking of the natural meat color. Residual nitrate (NO_3^-) can also be reduced to nitrite (NO_2^- and nitric oxide (NO) by microbial decomposition. This is analogous to the reactions that create the permanent pink color in cured meats.

myoglobin + nitric oxide → nitric oxide myoglobin → Δ → nitrosyl hemochrome (pink color)

Black discolorations (spots to streaks) can be imparted by hydrogen sulfide binding to essential iron-containing compounds such as hemoglobin (which carries oxygen) and cytochromes (the compounds responsible for aerobic respiration). Some sulfur-oxidizing bacteria can concentrate sulfur and form filaments; this is a mechanism of energy storage, and more prevalent in cultured than in wild-caught clams. While not harmful, it is probably best to not use clams with blackening, as the consumer would probably deem these spoiled.

Bivalves: Mussels

Blue mussels (*Mytilus edulis*) are harvested from the waters of the North Atlantic. They are sold live, and normally the whole animal in the shell is steamed before serving. Mussels may be commercially steam cooked and the meats removed and frozen for later addition to soups, stews, and chowders. At −4°F (−20°C), storage time is estimated to be nine months without flavor deterioration; however, shelf life is reduced to approximately three months at 19°F (−7°C). The New Zealand green-lipped mussel (*Perna canaliculus*) has recently received a great deal of attention due to reports that it possesses anti-inflammatory (anti-arthritic) compounds. For the formulator, the flavor of mussels is the most intense of the bivalves; they can be used in highly seasoned tomato or other sauces, where the flavor of oysters and clams would be masked.

Bivalves: Oysters

Three primary oyster species are harvested in the United States: *Crassostrea gigas*, or the West Coast oyster, transplanted from Japan and maricultured (a type of aquaculture where the farming takes place in sea water); *Crassostrea virginica*, or Eastern variety, native to the waters of the mid-Atlantic; and the Olympia oyster (*Ostrea lurida*), indigenous to the Pacific Northwest. There is also a limited fishery of the European oyster (*Ostrea edulis*) off the Maine and Gulf coasts.[50]

C. gigas was imported to the Northwest from Japan after the indigenous species (*Ostrea lurida*) was overfished, compromised by other environmental factors, and subsequently failed to thrive. This is a large, meaty oyster whose slightly salty flavor is distinctive to its growing waters. *C. virginica*, a smaller cousin, is said to have a sweeter flavor reflective of Eastern growing waters. The Olympia oyster is the smallest (about the size of a half-dollar), and its culture is limited to a modest area (700 acres) in Washington State.

All three primary oyster types can be consumed raw, directly out of the shell. The two larger species may be shucked and sold in that form in their liquor or juices. The FDA standard of identity for fresh shucked oysters allows not more than 5 percent weight loss when a representative gallon of oysters is drained for 2 minutes in a sieve within 15 minutes of packing. Furthermore, no added food ingredients are permitted.

Shucked oysters have a unique pH profile during spoilage because pH continues to decrease with time. This is directly related to the naturally high glycogen (stored carbohydrate) content of the oyster, which continues to degrade to lactic acid postmortem. Glycogen content is highest in May and lowest in August. After shucking, the pH ranges from 5.9 to 6.2; at pH 5.8, the odor is considered off; at pH 5.7 to 5.5, it is characterized as musty, and at pH 5.2 or less, it is putrid or sour.[51]

Pathogens can be of concern with the consumption of raw oysters. Waters are routinely monitored for viruses and fecal indicators and, when present, the relevant government entity closes the harvesting beds. The bacterium of greatest concern is *Vibrio vulnificus*, which is seen only in warm waters; consumption of it can be fatal to susceptible populations. Those most susceptible are individuals with hemochromatosis (a condition where excess iron is carried in the blood); hypochlorohydria (low stomach acid) as a result of genetics or partial gastrectomy (partial stomach loss due to accident or disease); cirrhosis of the liver (especially middle-aged men) or immunocompromised individuals (people who have AIDS, who are receiving cancer treatments, etc.). *Vibrio vulnificus* is closely related to *Vibrio cholerae*, the microbe responsible for cholera.

Regulation of oysters is voluntary (with essentially 100 percent compliance), sponsored by the Interstate Shellfish Sanitation Conference; its protocol is called the National Shellfish Sanitation Program (NSSP). The NSSP has an initiative to prevent foodborne infection via *V. vulnificus*. The state of California mandated that beginning in 2003, during the warmer summer months, states bordering the Gulf of Mexico could sell in-shell oysters only if they are processed through a post-harvest *V. vulnificus* destruction step. This may be high-pressure processing (HPP), low-temperature pasteurization, cryogenic freezing, or irradiation. Each of these processes is currently in commercial application. The only process that results in a live oyster is irradiation; however, the animal lives just seven to nine days after exposure.

Bivalves: Scallops

Scallops are harvested and shucked on board the fishing vessel for the adductor muscle that holds the two shells together. The body of the scallop is not normally eaten. The color of the scallop varies with its diet and may be ivory, tan, light yellow, pink, or a light coral. The two major types are ocean and bay scallops (large and small, respectively). Occasionally, a third type of intermediate size, the calico scallop, is seen.[52] For the most part, scallops are hand shucked on smaller vessels; however, on larger factory vessels, the scallops may be steam shucked. This steaming process often causes a case hardening (surface denaturation due to heat), and the scallops may have a slightly different appearance. To flavor steam-shucked scallops with a marinade, vacuum tumbling is recommended to encourage absorption of the marinade.

Scallops can be vacuum tumbled to promote penetration and distribution of the marinade. All massaging or tumbling should be conducted under refrigeration <41°F (5°C). Never tumble in an excess of marinade containing salt or alkaline phosphate, which causes extraction of functional (water-binding) protein because any liquid that is not absorbed will be discarded when the tumbler is drained. This will result in tough, dry scallops. Under 50 percent vacuum, smaller pieces must be tumbled for 30 to 45 minutes. Phosphate-containing blends accelerate uptake of marinades so tumbling time can be reduced. Larger pieces may require longer tumbling. Rotation of the tumbler should be gentle—6 to 8 rpm—to keep the scallops intact. The seafood may be immediately cooked, vacuum packaged and frozen, or atmospherically packaged and stored at refrigerated temperature for wholesale or retail use.

Other species similar to scallops that have a hearty or robust structure (firm, dense flesh; dense myocommata; resistance to gaping), such as catfish and shrimp, can also be vacuum tumbled. The structure of tuna and salmon does not lend itself to tumbling (but can withstand spice rubs or 10- to 15-minute dips in marinades).

Scallops are prone to economic fraud due to species substitution. The muscle bundles should run longitudinally in a scallop. Skate or ray wings are sometimes substituted and can be identified by the horizontal orientation of muscle bundles and a difference in aroma, as the substituted species is an elasmobranch (shark family) that contains abundant urea that hydrolyzes to ammonia. This entrepreneurial effort is illegal; it arises approximately every 15 years and is quickly responded to by the FDA.

Cephalopods: Squid, Octopus, and Cuttlefish

Squid, cuttlefish, and octopus are members of the molluscan class Cephalopoda (from the Greek for "head-footed"). Cephalopods are among the smallest classes of seafood harvested (together with mollusks, about 3 percent of the total seafood harvest).

Squid is prized for its mantle (body) and tentacles. A popular means of preparing squid is by slicing, battering, breading, and deep-frying these parts as *calamari*. The muscle structure is similar to abalone in that the layers of horizontal fibers overlay shorter perpendicular fibers. Squid salt-soluble (functional) protein has an isoelectric point lower than that of finfish and swells in dilute salt solutions to a greater extent. Squid also has an unusual water-soluble actomyosin (contractile protein).[53] Fresh meat should be white; with age, freezing, and alkaline treatments, it reddens. Purple colorations result from pigment in the chromatophores: tiny sacs of pigment in the skin that allow the squid to change color at will. These provide the squid with instantaneous camouflage that in life act as a defense mechanism.

Cuttlefish (*Sepia officinalis* and *S. orientalis*) are widely used in Asian and Italian cooking as an inexpensive replacement for squid, which has similar flavor and texture profiles. Cuttlefish, squid, and octopus are also preserved by drying and are consumed that way as a snack.

Octopus (*Octopus vulgaris*) is commonly harvested off the East and West coasts of the United States. It has been fished for many years to be used as bait for halibut. Octopus is popular in many Spanish, Italian, French, Latin American, and Asian cuisines, where the tentacles and body sac are stewed or braised and occasionally grilled. It has become more commonly consumed in the United States as ethnic cooking has become mainstream. It is also eaten raw as sashimi. Large octopi must be tenderized in a manner similar to abalone. Octopus contains a high level of moisture

(76 to 82 percent) and between 0.25 to 0.50 percent lipid. The lipids are composed of about 55 percent polyunsaturated fatty acids, 30 percent saturated fatty acids, and 10 percent monounsaturated fatty acids.[54] Due to the high percentage of polyunsaturates, octopus must be kept iced and, once cleaned, packaged to exclude oxygen to prevent rancidity.

Crustaceans

The pH of crustaceans (lobsters, crabs, shrimp, crawfish, etc.) tends to run higher than finfish and mollusks—between 6.8 and 8.2, with the higher end of the scale occurring at or near the time of molting (shedding the shell and growing a new and larger shell). This is a direct cause of excess calcium carbonate (an alkaline substance) that is briefly free-circulating in the animal in preparation for formation of the new shell.

Crabs

Unlike other animals, most other crustaceans, and mollusks (but similar to abalone), crabs have a blood protein called *hemocyanin* in which copper is the oxygen acceptor rather than the iron in the hemoglobin contained in red blood cells. Postmortem, especially in pasteurized flesh, the copper may bind with phenolic groups present in the structure of the amino acid tyrosine and cause a blue discoloration. The bluing can be prevented by adding a sequestrant (typically sodium acid pyropyhosphate at 0.25 to 0.5 percent of the meat), which binds the copper to prevent this reaction.

Note: Sequestrants are food additives, also known as chelating agents, used to bind to and literally sequester metals—keeping them away from other compounds found naturally occurring in seafoods (and other foods) that the metals can react with and cause assorted problems during processing and storage. In addition to preventing bluing in canned shellfish and crustacea, sequestrants can prevent the formation of "black spot" in shrimp stored on ice, and struvite crystal formation in various canned seafood products. (Struvite crystals are harmless crystals of magnesium ammonium phosphate resembling glass, which can form following retorting and continue to "grow" during storage.) Sequestrants are also effective in preventing rancidity in oily fish such as salmon fillets.

Blue crabs (*Callinectes sapidus*) are harvested from waters on the East Coast of the United States and the Gulf states. Live crabs are typically steam cooked under 12 to 15 pounds of pressure (in some states of the mid-Atlantic) or boiled, cooled, and picked (Gulf region). The yield is 10 to 12 percent for the typical blue crab and up to 14 percent for a large crab. As these crabs are cooked live, their form of blood protein, hemocyanin, remains within the edible flesh. *Soft-shell crab* is a culinary term for blue crabs that have recently molted their old exoskeleton; they are consumed while the new shell is still soft. The shell is left intact when soft-shell crabs are prepared for cooking and eating, as it is entirely edible. They are most typically prepared by lightly dredging in seasoned flour and sautéing.

Stone crabs (*Menippe* spp.) are similar to blue crabs, but their front claws grow larger and are the only part that is consumed. These claws can regenerate several times, and while it is legal to remove both claws before releasing the crab, mortality rates are twice as high for doubly amputated crabs as for single amputees. Claws must be at least 2¾ inches (7 cm) long from the tips of the immovable finger to the first joint, and it is illegal to harvest the whole animal. Although they exist along the coast of the Gulf of Mexico, most are harvested for commerce from Florida waters.[55]

Dungeness crab (*Cancer magister*) is harvested off the West Coast from California to Alaska. They may be cooked and picked immediately or "backed" (butchered with viscera removed but legs remaining attached to each half of the frame) and brine-frozen raw for later cooking and picking. Unlike blue crab, Dungeness is either steamed or immersion boiled without pressure. The shells of Dungeness crab are extremely hard and must be broken for picking with the aid of a small mallet or nutcracker. Yield of Dungeness crab may be as high as 55 percent.

Alaska king crab (*Paralithoides* spp.) is the largest domestic crab, with an average weight of 12 pounds (5.5 kg). The carapace (shell covering the back) is small (7 to 9 inches [17 to 23 cm]) relative to the legs (easily 3 to 4 feet [0.9 to 1.2 m]), where the edible flesh is located. After cooking, the meat falls easily from the shell, making this one of the easier crabs to pick. The yield of the legs averages 55 to 60 percent cooked meat.[56] Snow or tanner crab (Chionecetes spp.) is a smaller, 2½- to 3-pound (1.13 to 1.36 kg) version of the Alaska king crab. The yield of cooked meat from the legs is similar as well.

Lobsters

Three types of lobsters are commercially fished in the United States. The Northern or cold-water lobster (*Homerus americanus*) is fished from Newfoundland, Canada, to Maine; the Southern or warm-water lobster (also known as the spiny or rock lobster, *Panulirus argus*); and the California spiny lobster (*Panulirus interruptus*). The Northern lobster has the distinguishing large front claws and substantial tail from which edible flesh is removed, while the *Panulirus* spp have no claws and yield meat only from the tail. Legal size of harvest for the Southern lobster is a 3-inch (7.6 cm) carapace; for the California, a 3¼-inch (8.3 cm) carapace; and for the Northern, a carapace between 3¼ and 5 inches (8.3 to 12.7 cm) in length.

Langostinos are similar to lobsters, although they are actually related to hermit and porcelain crabs. Lobsters have larger tails than langostinos (*Pleuroncodes monodon, Cervimunida jolni, Pleuroncodes planipes, Munida gregaria*), whose short tail is perfect for bites, or restructured lobster products and mixtures containing meat pieces.[57] The flavors of lobster and langostinos are similarly sweet and delicate, but the texture of the langostino is closer to shrimp than to lobster. The FDA requires that langostino not be marketed as lobster; if lobster is in the name of the product, the word *langostino* must precede the word *lobster*. (Due to its firm texture and somewhat similar flavor, monkfish is also sometimes substituted; it is referred to as *poor man's lobster*.)

Lobsters are immersion cooked in either plain water or salt water (containing 3 to 5 percent salt), cooled, and hand picked in commercial plants. Struvite crystals (magnesium ammonium phosphate) resembling shards of glass may form in lobster flesh cooked in seawater (due to the presence of magnesium) if not consumed immediately. Lobsters are also shipped live but should never be shipped with dry ice as the carbon dioxide gas causes asphyxiation. Soft-shelled Northern lobsters (similar to soft-shelled crabs) exist but do not generally survive being shipped long distances.

Shrimp

Several species of shrimp are harvested from domestic waters, but these constitute only about 10 percent of all shrimp consumed in the United States, most of which is aquacultured product imported from Thailand, Indonesia, Ecuador, China, India, the Philippines, Mexico, and other countries. The edible flesh of shrimp is located in the tail. The yield of edible flesh from domestic shrimp is just over 60 percent. In the southern United States, it is common to cook and serve whole shrimp, head-on and unpeeled, to enhance flavor.

FIGURE 6.9   Shrimp counts. Count range per pound of shrimp.

Count per Pound Size Name	Green Headless	Number of Shrimp per Pound (over)	Number of Shrimp per Pound (not over)
Extra Colossal	Under 10	0	9.9
Colossal	10/15	9.9	15.0
Extra Jumbo	16/20	15.0	20.0
Jumbo	21/25	20.0	25.0
Extra Large	26/30	25.0	30.0
Large	31/35	30.0	35.0
Medium Large	36/42	35.0	42.0
Medium	43/50	42.0	50.0
Small	51/60	50.0	60.0
Extra Small	61/70	60.0	70.0
Tiny	>70	70	—

Source: Idyll, 1976.[58]

Warm-water shrimp from the Gulf of Mexico—white (*Penaeus setiferus*), brown (*Penaeus aztecus*), and pink (*Penaeus duorarum*)—are among those wild caught.[59] Cold-water shrimp on the West Coast include *Pandalus jordani* (high counts per pound), and off the Northeast coast, *Pandalus borealis*.[60] White shrimp are also caught off the Southeast coast. *P. vannemei* is aquacultured in North Carolina and Texas.

Warm-water shrimp can be wild caught to large sizes: *P. aztecus* in 2009 was reaching counts of 13 per pound. This is significant because the larger a brown shrimp is, the more iodine flavor it exhibits. The preferred wild Gulf shrimp flavor (sweet with a hint of iodine) has been analyzed and compared with that of the aquacultured imported product. The flavor differs with bromophenol content[61] (bromophenols are natural chemicals that occur in small amounts in the muscle tissue of wild shrimp), which reflects the specific diet of the wild shrimp. Efforts to simulate the wild diet in aquacultured shrimp have been thus far unsuccessful. Despite the significant difference in the flavor of wild Gulf shrimp, geographic source indicators on packaging to identify better-tasting shrimp have not yet been used to generate premium pricing. A strong education effort is needed.

Market forms of shrimp are: cooked and peeled (especially *P. jordani*); in the round (whole, head on); green headless (*green* indicates unprocessed shrimp, not its color); peeled and deveined (P&D); and peeled and undeveined (PUD). Products may be sold in individual quick-frozen (IQF) forms in poly bags or in blocks ranging from 1 to 5 pounds (0.45 to 2.3 kg) each in 20-pound (9.1 kg) master cartons. One pound (0.45 kg) head-on shrimp yields 0.65 pounds (0.3 kg) of white shrimp meat and slightly less of pink and brown shrimp meat. Well-handled and chilled, fresh, headless shrimp have a shelf life of 10 to 12 days; head-on product has significantly shorter shelf life due to the presence of the *hepatopancreas* in the head, which contains an extremely high concentration of digestive enzymes and bacteria. (The hepatopancreas is the primary digestive organ of shrimp. It has the dual role of secreting digestive enzymes and absorbing nutrients.)

Shrimp are sold by count per pound, typically green and headless. Historically, the ratios run around 21/30, 31/40, 41/50, etc. Increasingly, imported shrimp are sold within narrower ranges such as 31/35, 36/40, or similar. This is in response to wholesalers desiring greater size consistency and uniformity, especially in volume feeding outlets.

All shrimp (and lobster) are susceptible to *melanosis*, or black spot. This is caused by the enzyme polyphenoloxidase (also called phenolase, oxidase, or tyrosinase), the same enzyme that causes browning in cut fruits and vegetables such as bananas, avocados, apples, and potatoes. It causes harmless but unappetizing black spots to form along the tail of the shrimp. This visual defect can be inhibited by dipping the shrimp in a solution of either sodium metabisulfite or Everfresh® (4-hexylresorcinol on a salt carrier). Some individuals, especially asthmatics, are sensitive to the presence of sulfite; therefore, if metabisulfite is used, the FDA requires labeling when levels exceed 10 ppm.

Crawfish

Crawfish (*Procambarus clarkii* [red swamp crawfish] and *P. zongangulus* [white river crawfish]) are also referred to as crayfish, mud bugs, and crawdads. A blue crawfish also exists, but this is prized in private aquariums. Domestic production of these crustaceans is in the Atchafalaya Basin of Louisiana. Availability of fresh product is greatest in March, April, and May. Crawfish are also wild caught in Louisiana and southern Mississippi. Annual production is subject to boom and bust years. Crawfish are boiled, the tail peeled, frozen, and sold in 1-pound (0.45 kg) blocks in poly bags.

Yield is greatest (to 20 percent) among medium-size animals and lowest (8 percent) among larger animals, as development of the tail is sacrificed as the head and claws grow. For crawfish boils (with seasoning, corn, potatoes, and other desired ingredients), larger animals are preferred.

Historically, it was thought that the tails of crawfish must curl when cooked. A straight tail was thought to indicate an animal that was dead when boiled. Research shows that the straight tail is caused by overcrowding in the boiling vessel, allowing inadequate room for the tail to curl.

Other Seafood

Alligator (*Alligator mississippiensis*) is a reptile that spends much of its life in the water. The primary source of meat is from farmed animals. Contrary to popular belief, alligator is not an endangered species. In fact, meat from wild animals is legally marketed in September, the official alligator-hunting season.

The flesh is white to light red, and the texture is chewy. The flavor is mild if the meat is fresh and well handled, but it can vary according to diet. Protein content is around 22 percent, and total lipid ranges from 1 to 3 percent depending on location in the body.[62] Fatty acid content is highly unsaturated if the diet is high in fish of marine origin but more saturated if beef is a staple. The diet depends on the grower.

Nutritional Value of Seafood
Protein Quantity and Quality

Total protein can vary widely in wild species from 7 to 24 percent. Mollusks, such as oysters and clams, tend to contain less protein, while albacore, halibut, and skipjack tuna tend to contain more. Digestibility of seafood protein typically exceeds 90 percent, with a high PER and Amino Acid Score (the ratio of 1 gram of the limiting amino acid in a test diet to the same amount of the corresponding amino acid in a reference diet).[63] All seafood protein has a full complement of the essential amino acids and is therefore considered complete protein.

As early as the first quarter of the twentieth century, digestibility of seafood protein was under evaluation. Boiled fish was shown to be more readily used than beef.[64] Katsch, using human stomachs, reported greater gastric secretion to fish than to beef, leading to speedier digestion. Some processing, smoking in particular, was shown to slow the digestion of fish to nearly the level of beef.[65]

Digestibility (the relative ease of digesting a food compared to one with a perfect value of 1.00) of fish typically ranges between 0.78 and 0.89,[66] and Acton and Rudd estimated digestibility to range between 0.90 and 0.99, while beef and chicken range from 0.87 to 0.90.[67] Egg white, casein (milk protein), whey protein, and soy protein have scores of 1.00. White bread is reported to be 0.87 and whole wheat bread 0.68.[68]

Terrestrial animals tend to contain higher concentrations of saturated fat, which digests more slowly than the polyunsaturated oils of seafood, and this extends the feeling of fullness or satiety. Second, as animals age, especially cattle and sheep, collagen becomes more highly cross-linked, and it takes longer to hydrolyze during the digestive processes. Historically, it was thought that myocommata did not cross-link, but this was disproved by Bremner, who demonstrated cross-linking in some fish species (for example, blue grenadier).[69] Cross-linking slows digestibility of the protein. The third factor that may allow for high and rapid digestibility of seafood is the shortness of the muscle fiber in fish as compared with terrestrial animals.

Fat Content

In general, many seafood species (halibut, offshore tuna, lobster, shrimp, crab, crawfish, clams, and oysters) are low in total fat, certainly lower than in equivalent amounts of terrestrial proteins, including chicken.

Unlike terrestrial animal fats, up to 30 percent of the fatty acids contained in some seafood are the highly unsaturated omega-3 fatty acids. This includes docosohexaenoic acid (DHA) and eicosapentenoic acid (EPA). Some fish (wild-caught salmon, mackerel, herring, locally caught tuna, and anchovy) are excellent sources of omega-3 fatty acids, which are important in decreasing the risk of heart disease and inflammatory diseases such as rheumatoid arthritis, and are a building block of brain and retinal tissues. It is recommended that two to three meals each week have wild-caught seafood as the center of the plate. Saturated fatty acids commonly isolated from terrestrial animals are replaced in most seafood by monounsaturated fatty acids such as oleic acid, which is common in avocados and olives. The highest levels of monounsaturated fatty acids are observed in wild black cod (sablefish) and spiny dogfish. The fatty acid content of aquacultured seafood depends on its diet.

With the exception of the fattier species (mackerel, herring, salmon), most fish contain <120 calories per 3-ounce (85 g) cooked serving. The fattier fish are closer to

175 calories per 3-ounce serving. A 3-ounce (85 g) serving of steamed or boiled wild-caught Louisiana shrimp is less than 100 calories.

Although relatively low in fat, some shellfish, especially shrimp, contain levels of cholesterol nearing 150 mg per standard 3-ounce (85 g) serving. The cholesterol content is outweighed by the other health benefits (high polyunsaturated fatty acids [PUFAs] and lean protein) that eating seafood provides.

When calculating the caloric content, multiply grams of protein and carbohydrate each by 4 (4 kilocalories per gram) and the grams of fat by 9 (9 kilocalories per gram). When calculating the macronutrient content, it is important to consider proximate composition. This is: the content of total moisture (water) + protein + lipid (fat or oil) + ash (the inorganic residue after incinerating biologic material)[70] + carbohydrate = 100 percent. For muscle foods, the equation is usually [100 − (moisture + protein + fat + ash)] = carbohydrate, as total carbohydrate is typically negligible and the most difficult component to assay.

Mineral Content

Saltwater fish contribute iodine, which prevents goiter (extreme swelling of the thyroid gland due to iodine deficiency), and selenium, which is associated with reducing toxicity of organic mercury (methyl mercury or MeHg).[71] The bones in canned salmon, mackerel, and sardine provide a measurable source of calcium and phosphorus.

Mercury

Inorganic mercury occurs naturally in the environment. However, a great deal makes its way into the waterways from smelting, the combustion of fossil fuels, and the manufacture of electronics and amalgam (used for dental fillings). Once consumed, it is methylated by bacteria in the gut of fish. Methylmercury bioaccumulates in fish as smaller species are consumed by larger predators. Human exposure to methylmercury occurs when the larger predators, such as tuna and swordfish, are consumed. Methylmercury leads to neural defects in children, expressed as impaired behavioral and cognitive development. The fetus and young children are at greatest risk for developmental delay through exposure to methylmercury, as it can cross both the placenta and the blood-brain barrier. Elevated prenatal exposure to methylmercury is associated with mental retardation, limb deformity, poor growth, and sensory impairment.[72] The FDA recommends that women of childbearing age and young children avoid consuming shark, swordfish, tilefish, and king mackerel. In order to partake of the health benefits of seafood, the FDA recommends eating two meals or 12 ounces each week of shrimp, canned light-meat tuna (not albacore or white-meat tuna), salmon, pollock, and catfish.

● Conclusion

As the public becomes more aware of the myriad healthful benefits of increasing the amount of seafood in the diet, Culinology® professionals are expected not just to identify the various species but also to become more proficient in using them creatively to develop restaurant-quality applications that are safe, delicious, and economical to produce.

Acknowledgments

The senior author wishes to acknowledge Tony's Seafood and Louisiana Fish Fry of Baton Rouge, Louisiana, for their generosity in permitting free access to their facility to photograph seafood species and their products. Also acknowledged for her professional photography and artistic ability is Paula Ouder, photographer for the Louisiana Sea Grant College Program.

[1] K. A. Lellis-Dibble, K. E. McGlynn, and T. E. Bigford, "Estuarine Fish and Shellfish Species in U.S. Commercial and Recreational Fisheries: Economic Value as an Incentive to Protect and Restore Estuarine Habitat," NOAA Technical Memorandum NMFS-F/SPO-90 (2008), Silver Spring, MD, 102.

[2] About Seafood.com, accessed August 27, 2013, http://www.aboutseafood.com/about/about-seafood/top-10-consumed-seafoods.

[3] M. V. Lebour, "The Larval and Post-Larval Stages of the Pilchard, Sprat and Herring from Plymouth District," Journal of the Marine Biological Association of the United Kingdom (New Series), 12, no. 3 (1921): 427–457.

[4] Z. E. Sikorski, A. Kolakowska, and B. S. Pan, "The Nutritive Composition of the Major Groups of Marine Food Organisms," in Seafood: Resources, Nutritional Composition, and Preservation, ed. Z. E. Sikorski (Boca Raton, FL: CRC Press, 1990).

[5] A. Brown, "Composition of Fish: Collagen," in Understanding Food (Belmont, CA: Thomson Wadsworth, 2008), 166–167.

[6] S. Ando, M. Hatano, and K. Zama, "Protein Degradation and Protease Activity of Chum Salmon (Onchorhychus keta) Muscle During Spawning Migration," Fish Physiology and Biochemistry 1 (1986a), 17–26; S. Ando, F. Yamazaki, M. Hatano, and K. Zama, "Deterioration of Chum Salmon (Onchorhychus keta) Muscle During Spawning Migration: Changes in Protein Composition and Protease Activity of Juvenile Chum Salmon Muscle upon Treatment with Sex Steroids, Comparative Biochemistry and Physiology, Part B: Biochemistry and Molecular Biology 2 (1986b): 325–330.

[7] J. Wekell and F. Teeny, "Canned Salmon Curd Reduced by Use of Polyphosphates," Journal of Food Science 53 (1988): 1009–1013.

[8] Sikorski, Kolakowska, and Pan, "Nutritive Composition."

[9] P. O. Skjervold, A. M. B. Rora, S. O. Fjaera, A. Vegusdal, A. Vorre, and O. Einen, "Effects of Pre-, In-, or Post-Rigor Filleting of Live Chilled Atlantic Salmon," Aquaculture 194 (2001): 315–326.

[10] K. S. Morey, L. D. Satterlee, and W. D. Brown, "Protein Quality of Fish in Modified Atmospheres as Predicted by the C-PER Assay," Journal of Food Science 47 (1982): 1399–1400.

[11] E. Gnaiger and G. Bitterlich, "Proximate Biochemical Composition and Caloric Content Calculated from Elemental CHN Analysis: A Stoichiometric Concept," Oecologia 62 (1984): 289–298.

[12]J. Spinelli and J. A. Dassow, "Fish Proteins: Their Modification and Potential Uses in the Food Industry," in *Chemistry and Biochemistry of Marine Food Products*, eds. R. E. Martin, G. J. Flick, C. E. Hebard, and D. R. Ward (Westport, CT: AVI Publishing Co., 1982).

[13]F. Badii and N. K. Howell, "Changes in the Texture and Structure of Cod and Haddock Fillets During Frozen Storage," *Food Hydrocolloids* 16 (2002): 313–319.

[14]W. L. Cheuk and G. Finne, "Enzymatic Determination of Urea and Ammonia in Refrigerated Seafood Products," *Journal of Agricultural and Food Chemistry* 32 (1984): 14–18.

[15]L. E. Lampila, "Seafood Lipids: Analysis and Health Benefits," in *Seafood Quality Determination*, eds. D. E. Kramer and J. Liston (Amsterdam: Elsevier Science Publishers, 1987), 497–515.

[16]J. E. Osinchak, H. O. Hultin, O. T. Zajichek, S. D. Kelleher, and C.-H. Huang, "Effect of NaCl on Catalysis of Lipid Oxidation by the Soluble Fraction of Fish Muscle." *Free Radical Biology and Medicine* 12 (1992): 35–41.

[17]Z. E. Sikorski, "Protein Changes in Muscle Foods Due to Freezing and Frozen Storage," *International Journal of Refrigeration* 1 (1978): 173–180.

[18]H. H. Huss, "Fresh Fish: Quality and Quality Changes," training manual (Rome: FAO/DANIDA Training Program on Fish Technology and Quality Control, 1998), 5–14.

[19]W. D. Brown, "The Concentration of Myoglobin and Hemoglobin in Tuna Flesh," *Journal of Food Science* 27 (1962): 26–28.

[20]Love, *Chemical Biology of Fishes*.

[21]S. Ehira and H. Uchiyama, "Determination of Fish Freshness Using the K-value and Comments on Some Other Biochemical Changes in Relation to Freshness," in *Seafood Quality Determination*, ed. D. E. Kramer and J. Liston (Amsterdam: Elsevier Science Publishers, 1987), 185–207.

[22]D. J. Fraser, J. R. Dingle, J. A. Hines, S. C. Nowlan, and W. J. Dyer, "Nucleotide Degradation, Monitored by Thin-Layer Chromatography and Associated Postmortem Changes in Relaxed Cod Muscle," *Journal of the Fisheries Research Board of Canada* 24 (1967): 1837–1843.

[23]J. Spinelli, "Degradation of Nucleotides in Ice-Stored Halibut," *Journal of Food Science* 32 (1967): 38–41.

[24]Ehira and Uchiyama, "Determination of Fish Freshness," 185–207.

[25]L. E. Lampila, V. Mohr, and D. S. Reid, "Scanning Electron Microscopic Study of Rockfish Preserved at Either Ambient Temperature or by Isothermal Freeze-Fixation," *Food Microstructure* 4 (1985): 11–16.

[26]Sikorski, "Protein Changes in Muscle Foods," 173–180.

[27]National Marine Fisheries Service (NMFS), 2011, accessed August 25, 2013, http://www.st.nmfs.noaa.gov/st1/fus/fus10/08_perita2010.pdf.

[28]R. J. Price, "Fish Eggs for Caviar and Bait," in Leaflet 21114, California Sea Grant Marine Advisory Publication, Division of Agricultural Sciences, University of California, 1979.

[29]G. S. Trout and G. R. Schmidt, "The Effect of Cooking Temperature on the Functional Properties of Beef Proteins: The Role of Ionic Strength, pH, and Pyrophosphate," *Meat Science* 20 (1987): 129–136.

[30]J. C. Acton, "Effect of Heat Processing on Extractability of Salt-Soluble Protein, Tissue Binding Strength, and Cooking Losses in Poultry Loaves," *Journal of Food Science* 37 (1972): 244–246.

[31]R. Hamm and R. Grau, "The Effect of Phosphates on the Bound Water of Meat," *Deutsch Lebensmittel Rdsch* 51 (1955): 106–113.

[32]G. W. Schults, D. R. Russel, and E. Wierbicki, "Effect of Condensed Phosphates on pH, Swelling, and Water-Holding Capacity of Beef," *Journal of Food Science* 37 (1972): 860–864.

[33]R. G. Matlock, R. N. Terrell, J. W. Savell, et al., "Factors Affecting Properties of Raw-Frozen Pork Sausage Patties Made with Various NaCl/Phosphate Combinations," *Journal of Food Science* 49 (1984): 1363–1366.

[34]L. E. Lampila and J. P. Godber, "Food Phosphates," in *Food Additives*, eds. A. L. Branen, P. M. Davidson, S. Salminen, and J. H. Thorngate III (New York: Marcel Dekker, 2001), 809–896.

[35]Food and Drug Administration, *Fish and Fisheries Products Hazards and Controls Guidance*, 4th ed. (Washington, DC: Department of Health and Human Services, 2011), 31–61.

[36]FDA, *Fish and Fisheries Products Hazards and Controls Guidance*, p. 101.

[37]M. A. Friedman, L. E. Fleming, M. Fernandez, P. Bienfang, K. Schrank, R. Dickey, M.-Y. Bottein, et al., "Ciguatera Fish Poisoning: Treatment, Prevention and Management," *Marine Drugs* 6 (2008): 456–479.

[38]FDA, *Fish and Fisheries Products Hazards and Controls Guidance*, p. 102.

[39]Ibid., p. 99.

[40]Ibid., p. 102.

[41]Ibid., p. 113.

[42]T. Noguchi and O. Arakawa, "Tetrodotoxin Distribution and Accumulation in Aquatic Organisms, and Cases of Human Intoxication," *Marine Drugs* 6 (2008): 220–242.

[43]FDA, *Fish and Fisheries Products Hazards and Controls Guidance*, p. 103.

[44]Ibid., pp. 91–92.

[45]J. Olley and S. J. Thrower, "Abalone: An Esoteric Food," *Advances in Food Research* 23 (1977): 143–186.

[46]FDA, *Fish and Fisheries Products Hazards and Controls Guidance*, p. 103.

[47]M. Castagna, "Shellfish: Mollusks," in *The Seafood Industry*, eds. R. E. Martin and G. J. Flick (New York: Van Nostrand Reinhold, 1990), 77–87.

[48]Ibid.

[49]F. Shahidi and J. A. Brown, "Carotenoid Pigments in Seafoods and Aquaculture," *Critical Reviews in Food Science* 38 (1998): 1–67.

[50]Castagna, "Shellfish: Mollusks," 77–87.

[51]A. C. Hunter and B. A. Linden, "An Investigation of Oyster Spoilage," *American Food Journal* 18 (1923): 538.

[52]Castagna, "Shellfish: Mollusks," 77–87.

[53]Z. Sikorski and I. Kolodziejska, "The Composition and Properties of Squid Meat," *Food Chemistry* 20 (1986): 213–224.

[54]M. P. Sieiro, S. P. Aubourg, and F. Rocha, "Seasonal Study of the Lipid Composition in Different Tissues of the Common Octopus (*Octopus vulgaris*)," *European Journal of Lipid Science and Technology* 108 (2006): 479–487.

[55]W. J. Lindberg and M. J. Marshall, Species Profiles: Life Histories and Environmental Requirements of Coastal Fishes and Invertebrates (South Florida)–Stone Crab. U.S. Fish and Wildlife Service. (1984). FWS/OBS-82 /11.21. U.S. Army Corps of Engineers, TR EL-82-4. 17 p.

[56]C. Crapo, B. Paust, and J. Babbitt, "Recoveries and Yields from Pacific Fish and Shellfish," *Marine Advisory Bulletin* 37 (Fairbanks, AK: Alaska Sea Grant College Program, 1993).

[57]S. Hedlund, "Langostino versus Lobster: What's the Difference?" *Seafood Business* 25 (2006): 32.

[58]C. P. Idyll, "The Shrimp Fishery: A Survey of Methods for Domestic Harvesting, Preservation, and Processing of Fish Used for Food and Industrial Products," in *Industrial Fishery Technology*, ed. M. E. Stansby (Huntington, NY: Robert E. Krieger Publishing Company, 1976), 150–170.

[59]Louisiana Seafood Promotion and Marketing Board, *Louisiana Seafood Products Handbook: A Guide to Species, Availability, Product Forms, and Fisheries Facts*, 3rd ed. (New Orleans: Louisiana Seafood Promotion and Marketing Board, 1998).

[60]M. J. Oesterling, "Shellfish: Crustaceans," in *The Seafood Industry*, eds. R. E. Martin and G. J. Flick (New York: Van Nostrand Reinhold, 1990), 88–102.

[61]R. J. Miget and M. G. Haby, "*Naturally Occurring Compounds Which Create Unique Flavors in Wild-Harvested Shrimp*" (College Station, TX: Texas Cooperative Extension and Sea Grant College Program, 2007).

[62]M. W. Moody, "Other Aquatic Life of Economic Significance: Alligators," in *Marine and Freshwater Products Handbook*, eds. R. E. Martin, E. P. Carter, G. J. Flick, and L. M. Davis (Lancaster, PA: Technomic, 2000), 273–278.

[63]S. J. Bell, B. R. Bistrian, L. B. M. Ainsley, N. Manji, E. J. Lewis, C. Joyce, and G. L. Blackburn, "A Chemical Score to Evaluate the Protein Quality of Commercial Parenteral and Enteral Formulas: Emphasis on Formulas for Patients with Liver Failure," *Journal of the American Dietetic Association* 91 (1991): 586–589.

[64]B. Slowtzoff, "Die Ausnutzung des Fischfleisches im Vergleich mit der des Rindfleisches und die Wirkung des Fischfleisches auf die Zusammensetzung des Harns," *Z. Physik. Diatet. Therap* 14 (1910): 22–29.

[65]G. Katsch, "Normale und Veranderte Tatigkeit des Magens," in *Handbuch der Inneren Medizin* Vol. 3, Part 1, eds. G. von Bergmann and R. Staehelin, (Berlin: Springer, 1926).

[66]K. H. Lee and H. S. Ryu, "Evaluation of Seafood Protein Quality as Predicted by C-PER Assays," in *Seafood Quality Determination*, eds. D. E. Kramer and J. Liston (Amsterdam: Elsevier Science Publishers, 1987), 473–485.

[67]J. C. Acton and C. L. Rudd, "Protein Quality Methods for Seafoods," in *Seafood Quality Determination*, eds. D. E. Kramer and J. Liston (Amsterdam: Elsevier Science Publishers, 1987), 453–472.

[68]E. Geiger, and G. Borgstrom, "Fish Protein: Nutritive Aspects," in *Fish as Food* Vol. 2, ed. G. Borgstrom, (New York: Academic Press, 1962).

[69]H. A. Bremner, *Post Mortem Breakdown of the Myotendinosus Junction in Fish*, doctoral dissertation, University of Tasmania, 1993.

[70]A. D. Woyewoda, S. J. Shaw, P. J. Ke, and B. G. Burns, "Recommended Laboratory Methods for Assessment of Fish Quality," *Canadian Technical Report of Fisheries and Aquatic Sciences No. 1448* (Canada Department of Fisheries and Oceans, 1986).

[71]N. V. Ralston, C. R. Ralston, J. L. Blackwell, and L. J. Raymond, "Dietary and Tissue Selenium in Relation to Methylmercury Toxicity," *Neurotoxicology* 29 (2008): 802–811.

[72]National Research Council, *Toxicological Effects of Methylmercury* (Washington, DC: National Academy Press, 2000).

7 Protein-Based Foods: Vegetable Sources of Protein and Protein Complementation

Lead Author: Natalie Pitchford Levy, CCS®, Quality Control Manager, Bedemco, Inc.

Contributor: Hinnerk von Bargen, CHE, Associate Professor in Culinary Arts, Culinary Institute of America

⦿ Introduction: The Culture of Vegetarian Diets

Animals are defined by where they get their protein. The terms herbivore, carnivore, and omnivore are used to describe animals whose diets are exclusively vegetarian, meat-eating, or a combination of the two. The success of the human species is largely because they are omnivores (eaters of everything). Early humans were opportunistic eaters, able to derive nutrition from virtually any food source, making survival much more likely. Today, in developed countries, where starvation is less of a threat, choice is the number-one factor in what humans eat. While we are still an omnivorous species by nature, humans can survive quite well on an exclusively vegetarian diet, if managed properly.

In the United States, consumption of large quantities of meat protein is relatively common, while most other cultures consume much smaller portions of meat (or none at all). As Americans become more health conscious and more aware of the widely reported links between diet and disease, however, various degrees of vegetarian diet have become more common.

There are many types of vegetarian diet. Vegans are so-called strict vegetarians who choose to eat no animal products, not even eggs or milk-derived products such as cheese, yogurt, or ice cream, and some even exclude honey as the product of an exploited species. Another common type of vegetarian diet is lacto-ovo or ovo-lacto, which allows eggs and dairy in the diet in addition to plant-based foods. *Pescatarians* eat seafood. Flexitarians practice varying degrees of vegetarianism but do occasionally eat animal-derived foods.

The results of a Harris poll conducted in 2008 (on behalf of the *Vegetarian Times*) indicate as many as 1 million practicing vegans in the United States, nearly 7½ million vegetarians, and nearly 23 million who follow a "vegetarian-inclined" diet. And the market for vegetarian foods is growing. According to a study done by Mintel, the value of vegetarian food sales at retail only (no foodservice figures are included) was $815 million in 2001 and $1.4 billion in 2008; it is expected to grow to $1.6 billion in 2015.

The rationale of people who follow a vegetarian diet may be moral, ethical, religious, and/or political as well as health-based. Vegetarians are often concerned with animal welfare, the environmental impact of the diet (such as recyclable packaging and local, sustainable farming), and its socioeconomic impact (such as the Fair Trade movement).

When formulating vegetarian foods, it is important to create products that appeal to this spectrum of beliefs and values as well as provide an adequate source of vegetable protein—and of course, something that tastes good. It is also important to be aware that many of the functional ingredients in the product developer's toolbox may themselves be animal-derived. It is easy for the vegetarian consumer to identify the difference between a hamburger and a veggie burger but much more difficult to know whether any of the multitude of ingredients in a snack seasoning have an animal source. For example, in 2002 McDonald's was forced to pay $10 million to settle a lawsuit brought on behalf of members of the American Hindu vegetarian community who ate McDonald's French fries because the giant restaurant chain claimed they were cooked in pure vegetable oil. Unfortunately, the vegetarians were unaware that this oil contained a natural flavor that was partially derived from beef fat.

Other hidden animal-derived ingredients include gelatin (used to make marshmallows and gummy candies and as a thickener in some yogurts), lard (traditional in pie crusts), milk products (in many candies and chocolate), casein (ironically, used in the manufacture of margarine and creamy salad dressings), whey protein (used to bulk up the protein in boxed cereals and provide structure in cake mixes), rennet (an enzyme derived from calf stomachs used in the manufacture of cheese), and bone char (used in the refining of sugar to remove color impurities in the syrup prior to crystallization into table sugar).

It is generally recognized that a vegetarian diet is not only healthy but may be even healthier than the typical meat-centric diet followed by most Americans. The 2010 version of *Dietary Guidelines for Americans*, a report issued by the U.S. Department of Agriculture (USDA) and the U.S. Department of Health and Human Services (DHHS) every five years, states:

> In prospective studies of adults, compared to non-vegetarian eating patterns, vegetarian-style eating patterns have been associated with improved health outcomes—lower levels of obesity, a reduced risk of cardiovascular disease, and lower total mortality. Several clinical trials have documented that vegetarian eating patterns lower blood pressure.
>
> On average, vegetarians consume a lower proportion of calories from fat (particularly saturated fatty acids), fewer overall calories, and more fiber, potassium, and vitamin C than do non-vegetarians. Vegetarians generally have a lower body mass index. These characteristics and other lifestyle factors associated with a vegetarian diet may contribute to the positive health outcomes that have been identified among vegetarians.

Nutritionally speaking, vegetarian diets tend to be lacking in those nutrients found mainly (or even exclusively) in non-vegetarian diets. These include vitamin B_{12} (found only in foods derived from animals) and the essential omega-3 fatty acids DHA and EPA (primarily from fish). These nutrients must be taken as supplements if individuals are unwilling to consume meat from any source (aquatic or terrestrial). Other essential vitamins and minerals can be found in certain vegetables: calcium in collards, bok choy, kale, and turnip greens; iron in legumes, raisins, nuts and seeds, and in fortified foods such as breakfast cereals; vitamin D in fortified soymilk. Lysine, threonine, methionine, and tryptophan are the essential amino acids typically lacking in the vegetarian diet. As such, they are known as the limiting amino acids, and are found in the shortest supply in incomplete proteins (those found in most plant sources). They can, however, be successfully provided via the practice of protein complementation.

Protein complementation occurs when two vegetable proteins (legumes and grains, for example), each containing the amino acid that the other lacks, are combined so the body gets both. In this way, all of the limiting amino acids can be acquired, as long as the diet contains enough of the vegetable varieties that provide the lacking amino acids in sufficient concentrations to have a significant effect in the body. For instance, legumes are low in methionine and high in lysine; grains are low in lysine and high in methionine. So if rice (grain) and beans (legume) are eaten together, both of the limiting amino acids are consumed. Contrary to earlier belief, protein complementation need not be done at the same meal. As long as the two foods are consumed within a few hours of each other (or even the same day), the body treats them as a complete protein.

⬤Vegetable Sources of Protein
Legumes

Legumes are among the simplest and oldest sources of vegetable protein, and their cultivation and culinary use is well developed. They are fruits or seeds of plants from the legume family, with characteristic pods that split along the center into two sides with a single row of seeds. Legume plant roots contain nodules with nitrogen-fixing bacteria that capture nitrogen in the soil, improving soil fertility. In addition, the seeds (peas and beans) contain significant amounts of protein compared to other plants.

Types of Legumes

Legumes include fresh beans and peas with edible pods that are picked while immature, such as green beans, wax beans, haricots verts, snow peas, and sugar snap peas. The category also includes fresh shelling beans and peas whose pod is removed to reveal an edible seed—for example, sweet peas, fava beans, edamame (soybeans), flageolets, and lima beans. Lentils and peanuts are also in the legume family.

Large legume varieties are allowed to mature and dry on the vine and then are harvested, shelled, and further dried before storage and sale. Dried legumes that are not raised for fresh use or for oil extraction are known as "pulses." Dried beans include black, kidney, pinto, Great Northern, cannellini, garbanzo (chickpeas), black-eyed peas, lentils, and split peas (green and yellow). When selecting dried beans, look for uniform color, few chipped or broken beans, and an absence of shriveled skins.

Although they are technically a legume, peanuts are discussed in the section on nuts and seeds, as they are most commonly sold and processed like nut products.

Fresh, frozen, and dried beans do not typically contain additives or processing aids. Canned beans typically contain beans, water, and salt (or kombu seaweed, in more natural versions), and may contain firming agents such as calcium chloride or color preservatives such as disodium EDTA.

Storage and Shelf Life

The varying moisture content of different forms of beans contributes to differences in handling and shelf life. Fresh beans are chosen for bright color and firm texture, with no brown or soft areas. Fresh beans (such as raw green beans) contain 80 to 90 percent moisture and should be washed just prior to use, as additional water can compromise shelf life in storage. If properly stored in a sealed container under refrigeration, fresh beans can last several days.

Uncooked dried beans typically have moisture below 14 percent and are best if used within one year of drying. Beyond this time, color may begin to fade and they may get even drier, causing cracks, dull flavor, and longer cook times. Dried beans are sold and may be stored in polyethylene bags; however, for long-term storage, bulk dried beans should be stored in airtight containers in a cool, dry location to prevent infestation. Rehydration through cooking in boiling water typically increases moisture content to between 50 and 70 percent. This greatly reduces shelf life, and cooked beans may begin to exhibit off odors indicative of microbial growth after several days. However, commercially canned beans are cooked and effectively sterilized in the can through a retort process; they can last over two years in their original sealed can.

A food processor must be aware of the shelf-life limitations of fresh beans and non-retort cooked dried beans when using them in fresh or refrigerated products. Cooked beans are rich in protein and vitamins and minerals and provide an ample growth medium for bacteria, yeasts, and molds. Improper canning can lead to growth of anaerobic bacteria such as *Clostridium botulinum*, so strict HACCP (Hazard Analysis Critical Control Points) guidelines with time, temperature, and pressure controls must be followed when canning beans for storage, particularly because they are a low-acid (above pH 4.6) food.

Cooked dried beans may be frozen to extend shelf life for several months. Frozen cooked dried beans should be thawed slowly to maintain their shape and reduce splitting. For commercial usage (soups, chili, etc.), thaw cooked beans under refrigeration overnight prior to usage, or they may be added frozen to the kettle toward the end of heating as long as the cook time and temperature of the product in the kettle is adjusted to compensate for the sudden drop in temperature, and to provide the required kill step. Some mild grittiness in texture may occur when freezing cooked beans; however, bean-based soups and stews freeze quite well because the liquid medium and other ingredients can mask off-textures.

Preparation and Cooking Methods

Fresh beans with edible pods are best cooked quickly in large volumes of salted water to avoid loss of color and flavor. Commercially sourced beans typically have the stem-end and strings along the spine of the pods removed by the supplier. The beans can be steamed, boiled, sautéed, or added to a composed dish at the end of cooking to maintain crisp-tender texture and vibrant color.

The chlorophyll in freshly cooked green-colored beans reacts with acidic foods to turn from bright green to a dull olive color. It can also be degraded by overcooking. This also occurs at a very slow rate in frozen raw beans during long storage. The only way to prevent this color change is to cook green vegetables in large volumes of water, uncovered (to allow vaporized acids from the beans to escape), and to shock or chill them rapidly as soon as they reach the appropriate doneness. The addition of an alkalizing agent (such as sodium bicarbonate) to cooking liquid can inhibit, but not eliminate, this dulling of chlorophyll in the cooking of fresh beans. That said, this is not recommended since bicarbonate can also

FIGURE 7.1 Protein in beans (cooked).

Bean (1 cup)	Protein (grams)
Adzuki (Aduki)	17
Anasazi	15
Black beans	15
Black-eyed peas	14
Cannellini (white beans)	17
Cranberry beans	17
Fava beans	13
Garbanzos (chickpeas)	15
Great Northern beans	15
Green peas, whole	9
Kidney beans	15
Lentils	18
Lima beans	15
Mung beans	14
Navy beans	16
Pink beans	15
Pinto beans	14
Soybeans	29
Split peas	16

Source: USDA National Nutrient Database for Standard Reference, http://www.nal.usda.gov/fnic/foodcomp/search.

destroy the water-soluble vitamins (especially vitamin C) and can degrade the structural components in vegetables, leading to limp, mushy texture.

Blanching can act as a par-cooking step for fresh beans in frozen meals and must be taken into account when determining the overall cook time of a prepared bean-containing meal. The different components of a mixed dish may need to be combined at various levels of doneness to ensure a brief reheating by the consumer properly heats the entire product without overcooking or undercooking individual ingredients.

It is important to note that unlike the green color in raw vegetables, which is unaffected by exposure to fluorescent light, the green color in refrigerated blanched vegetables is sensitive to extended fluorescent light exposure (as typical of a refrigerated supermarket shelf, where the light is always on); it starts to turn khaki-colored in only a few hours. Therefore, it is critical for the product developer to know where and how a finished product containing blanched green vegetables will be merchandised in order to determine not just the best processing methods but also the best packaging. In the above example, the best solution might be to place the vegetables in an opaque package to block exposure to light.

Dried beans require intensive measures to rehydrate them. The protein and starch are stored in the cotyledons (two inner halves) of the legume, covered by an outer seed coat made of hemicellulose structures. A small pore called the hilum (which previously attached the bean to the plant) is the only break in the outer seed coat that allows water to penetrate into the bean. As the water infuses the bean through the hilum, the starches inside absorb water, causing the bean to expand. The expansion breaks down the cell walls, softens the hemicellulose, and dissolves the pectin. The bean can then swell proportionately. As the starches and proteins inside the bean cook, the flavors are developed.

Dried beans should be soaked prior to cooking to speed the cooking process and to remove indigestible compounds. In addition, dried beans often contain agricultural contaminants and should be rinsed with water and checked for stones. Beans may be presoaked using either the overnight cold-soak or the hot quick-soak method. To quick soak, bring rinsed beans to boil in surplus water to cover, then simmer for 2 minutes, remove from heat, cover, and allow to soak for 1 hour. The quick-soak method typically results in more split beans than the gentler overnight method.

After either presoak method, the soak water is discarded and the beans are cooked in fresh water that is brought to a boil and then simmered for the specified time (typically from 15 minutes to 1 hour, depending on size and variety). Lentils and split peas are small and delicate enough to not require presoaking; they may be cooked just after rinsing.

It is important to note how other cooking ingredients can affect the cook time and characteristics of beans. Several factors can slow the cooking of beans:

- Minerals (such as calcium or magnesium) in hard water strengthen cell wall pectin by cross-linking.
- Acids (lemon juice, tomato juice, wine) stabilize hemicellulose walls.
- Molasses and sugar strengthen cell walls, cross-link pectin, stabilize hemicellulose, and slow starch granule swelling.

Any of these cause slower cooking and the potential for toughening of the outer skin if added early in the normal cooking process. However, they are useful in slow-cooked applications such as chili or baked beans because they protect the bean from cooking too quickly, and inhibit splitting. Molasses is particularly useful, as its acidity, sugar, and mineral content all contribute to longer cooking times.

Adding salt to bean cooking water sparks debate among chefs and food scientists. If added early, salt begins to slow the rate of water absorption; however, after a time it adds flavor to the beans and speeds the cooking process. The U.S. Dry Bean council recommends adding 0.5 percent salt to bean cooking liquid.

One pound of dried beans yields about 6 cups cooked, depending on the variety. Rehydration typically causes a doubling in volume, so ½ cup dry equals approximately 1 cup cooked.

For some preparations, cooked legumes are pureed (as for refried beans and hummus). Their high starch content also makes legumes perfect candidates for dry heat preparations with a crunchy, crisp texture profile. Middle Eastern cuisine is famous for falafel, which are deep-fried fritters made from soaked chickpeas coarsely ground with spices, herbs, and aromatics.

Nutritional Profile

Dried beans and other pulses are a good source of protein (17 to 25 percent), with significantly less fat than meat. Beans (other than soybeans) are not a complete protein, as they are limiting in the essential amino acid methionine. They are, however, rich in other essential amino acids, such as lysine and cysteine, which are limiting in other non-meat proteins such as grains and corn. Combining beans with whole grains (protein complementation) such as wheat, rice, or corn (typically 2 parts grain to 1 part bean) can complete the amino acid profile. The nutritional value of dried beans, peas, lentils and chickpeas is so great, especially in parts of the world where hunger and starvation is common, that the United Nations has declared 2016 the "International Year of Pulses" to heighten public awareness of the nutritional benefits of pulses as part of sustainable food production aimed toward food security and nutrition. In addition, pulses, like other leguminous plants, have nitrogen-fixing properties that can contribute to increasing soil fertility and have a positive impact on the environment.

Beans are slow to metabolize and can provide a carbohydrate source that does not dramatically increase blood sugar levels, and they contribute potassium, zinc, iron, calcium, and several B vitamins to the diet.[1] It is important to soak beans not only to speed cook time but also to soften them and remove phytic acid (an antinutritional compound that binds to minerals, inhibiting their absorption in the body) and to assist in leaching out some of the indigestible and flatulence-causing carbohydrates (oligosaccharides) stachyose and raffinose. Humans do not possess the enzyme required to break down these compounds to simple sugars, but bacteria in the lower intestine are able to digest them, producing copious amounts of methane, carbon dioxide, and hydrogen as a result. Interestingly, these oligosaccharides (now known as prebiotics) provide a food source for these beneficial gut bacteria (known as probiotics, or live microorganisms that confer a health benefit to the host). The soaking does not eliminate the oligosaccharides but does reduce the level. Some cuisines add the herbs epazote and summer savory to cooking beans for the same purpose.

Traditional cultures have long appreciated the value of beans in the diet and intuitively combined beans with their complementary grains in both farming and cuisine. Beans, corn, and squash crops were grown as the "three sisters" in Native American agriculture, and traditional complementary pairings such as rice and beans, barley and lentils, and cornbread and black-eyed peas sustained humanity for many years.

Dried beans may also be sprouted or soaked in water until they begin to germinate. Sprouting is accompanied by the enzymatic hydrolysis of protein; large proteins are broken down into amino acids. Likewise, large carbohydrates are broken down into smaller, more easily digestible sugars. Thiamin increases fivefold, and niacin content doubles. Carotene and vitamins C and E increase. In fact, the vitamin C content of many sprouts is as rich as that of tomatoes. Overall digestibility is vastly improved. Some common sprouting beans include mung and adzuki. Sprouting can take from three to five days, during which the bean opens up and releases a small shoot that can be eaten raw; however, it is best to lightly cook all sprouted beans if large quantities will be eaten. Although a favorite of raw foodists, sprouts are notorious for harboring bacteria such as salmonella, so sprouting must be undertaken with care and HACCP principles in mind (such as attention to water quality, container, frequency of changing sprouting water) to prevent foodborne illness.

Soybeans and Soy Foods

The soybean (*Glycine max*) is a legume that can produce at least twice as much protein per acre as any other major vegetable or grain crop, 5 to 10 times more than land set aside for dairy cattle, and up to 15 times more protein per acre than meat production.

Soy-based foods have increased in visibility and consumption in the U.S. market over the past several years, partly due to greater acceptance of vegetarian diets and partly because of health claims of soy as a miracle food. Soybeans and soy products remain controversial and may pose health risks as well as benefits (especially if consumed in large quantities). However, in October 1999 the U.S. Food and Drug Administration (FDA) authorized the following claims for soy protein:

1. 25 grams of soy protein a day, as part of a diet low in saturated fat and cholesterol, may reduce the risk of heart disease. A serving of [name of food] supplies __ grams of soy protein.
2. Diets low in saturated fat and cholesterol that include 25 grams of soy protein a day may reduce the risk of heart disease. One serving of [name of food] provides __ grams of soy protein.

It should also be noted that the FDA declared soy as one of the "major eight" allergens in the Food Allergen Labeling and Consumer Protection Act (FALCPA) of 2004. (In fact, it is the second most allergenic food, after peanuts.) Therefore, any product that contains soybeans or soy derivatives must be clearly labeled with soy or soybeans in the ingredient statement and/or in a comprehensive statement after the ingredient list that includes any of the major eight allergens in the food (for example, "Contains soy").

Fresh soybeans (edamame) can be eaten as a whole-food source of protein. Mature dried soybeans can be hydrated and then fermented into tempeh, miso, or soy sauce, further processed into soy milk and then tofu, or manufactured into soy protein isolates and concentrates and textured vegetable protein (TVP). Soy isolates and TVP can then be used to create a new generation of processed soy food analogs such as soy cheese, soy sausage, and other meat replacements.

The nutritional value of soy, as well as its texture, flavor, culinary use, and food manufacturing applications, vary widely as the bean is processed into these forms.

General Nutrition of Soy

Although soy is typically limiting in the sulfur-containing amino acids methionine and cysteine, it is commonly touted as the only complete plant protein equivalent to animal protein, as all nine essential amino acids are present (and accessible) in comparable ratios to those needed for human growth and health. The Protein Digestibility Corrected Amino Acids Score (PDCAAS) is used by the USDA to determine protein quality. According to the PDCAAS system, soybeans have a score of 0.91, while soy protein isolate has the maximum score of 1.0 (the same as egg whites), followed by milk and meat proteins.[2]

However, studies have shown that more soy protein might be needed than egg-white protein to maintain healthy nitrogen balance in the body. Consuming soy protein sources along with protein foods high in methionine (whole wheat, rice, corn, eggs) can supplement this amino acid to create a more complete protein source, according to the USDA National Nutrient Database for Standard Reference.

Soybeans are rich in isoflavones (a class of phytoestrogens, or plant hormones, chemically similar to estrogen).[3] These may contribute to the functionality of soy in alleviating some of the symptoms of menopause (North American Menopause Society, 2000) and in preventing certain cancers and osteoporosis (Messina, 2003). However, they are also controversial and contribute to cautionary consumption of soy foods, especially among males.[4] That said, a recent article summarizing the findings of dozens of clinical trials and epidemiological reviews found that neither soy protein nor isoflavones had any effect on reproductive hormones in men.[5]

Due to the apparent significant health functionality of soy (for better or for worse), it seems wise to consume soy products in moderation as part of a varied and healthy diet.

Soy Milk

Soy milk is the liquid extracted from ground, hydrated, and cooked soybeans. Plain soy milk is bright white to tan; its flavor varies depending on the type of soy milk and processing but can include beany, grassy, milky, nutty, metallic, earthy, and doughy notes.

Soybeans or soy flour are soaked in water for a minimum of several hours or overnight, ground with added water to create a paste, and then boiled. Then the liquid is filtered to remove the insoluble soy pulp; therefore, soy milk is not technically a whole-food form of soy.

The boiling step is important in inactivating protease (trypsin) inhibitors, naturally found in raw soybeans, which prevent the pancreas from generating the necessary enzymes to digest proteins.[6] Heating also inactivates lipoxygenase present in the beans, which can create free radicals, rancidity, and off flavors. Most varieties of soy milk sold in the United States are certified organic and made from non-GMO (genetically modified organism) soybeans, both factors of importance to the majority of soy milk purchasers.

Traditionally, soy milk was available mainly in shelf-stable, ultra-high temperature (UHT) aseptic packages, typically laminated "juice-box"-style cartons. These shelf-stable containers are sterile and hermetically sealed, like cans, and can be stored unopened without refrigeration. Once opened, however, they must be kept refrigerated. Brands such as Edensoy and Vitasoy are examples.

Refrigerated soy milks are also available, competing directly with cow's milk and claiming cow's milk-like flavor and texture. Brands such as Silk (White Wave), 8th Continent, Organic Valley, and even private-label store brands are widely available.

Refrigerated soy milks have similar formulations to shelf-stable soy milks; however, they are not packaged in sterile aseptic boxes but rather traditional gable-top milk containers. Refrigerated soy milk was created to have the appearance, flavor, and mouthfeel that appeals to the mainstream milk consumer. It is similarly pasteurized (typically UHT) and sometimes contains carrageenan (seaweed extract), which contributes to mouthfeel. It is also commonly available in sweetened and unsweetened versions, as well vanilla and chocolate flavored. Refrigerated soy milk manufacturers also produce soy creamers, soy yogurt, soy ice cream, dips, and spreads.

Ingredients

Traditional, organic, minimally processed commercial soy milk typically contains some variation of the following ingredients: purified or filtered water, organic soybeans, sweetener (dried organic cane juice and/or malted organic wheat extract and/or organic barley extract), calcium carbonate (for dietary calcium), kombu seaweed (for minerals [optional]), salt or sea salt, and carrageenan (for texture and mouthfeel [optional]).

Soy milk may also contain natural flavors (such as cocoa powder or vanilla) and may also be enriched, like cow's milk, with zinc oxide, riboflavin (vitamin B_2), vitamin A acetate (or palmitate), vitamin D_2, and vitamin B_{12}. Soy milks are also being fortified with fiber, extra calcium, and omega-3 oils.[7] Fortification of soy milk makes it an excellent source of nutrients, such as vitamin B_{12} and omega-3 oils, that are difficult to attain in a strict vegetarian diet.

New, more highly processed fat-free and light versions of soy milks can be found with added fillers, emulsifiers, flavorings, and sweeteners. The ingredient lists of these soy milks may include soybean oil (for mouthfeel), calcium phosphate (for dietary calcium and pH), potassium citrate (for dietary potassium and pH), magnesium phosphate (for dietary magnesium), sodium phosphate (to stabilize flavor), dipotassium phosphate (for dietary potassium), soy lecithin (to emulsify), xanthan gum (for texture and to emulsify), natural and artificial flavors, and sucralose (to sweeten without added sugar).[8]

Storage and Shelf Life

Shelf-stable soy milk typically can be stored unopened at room temperature for one year from production. Once the package is opened, shelf life is reduced to 5 to 10 days with refrigeration. Spoiled soy milk tends to exhibit a sour smell, sour beany flavor, and watery, clumped texture.

The soy protein in shelf-stable soy milk without stabilizers may coagulate into small lumps, which usually break apart upon shaking. These are safe to consume if not accompanied by signs of spoilage, such as a sour smell or taste.

Unopened refrigerated soy milk keeps fresh under refrigeration until the best-by date stamped on the carton. Once opened, it lasts 7 to 10 days if refrigerated.

Although both forms of soy milk can be frozen, freezing is not recommended. Frozen and thawed soy milk is safe to consume; however, texture deteriorates markedly. The soy protein and soybean oil separate from the liquid on thawing, causing unattractive flocculation that cannot be reintegrated through blending.

Preparation and Cooking Methods

For manufacturers of vegetarian prepared foods, it is essential to know how to use soy products as ingredients. Both shelf-stable and refrigerated soy milks can be substituted 1:1 for dairy milk in recipes. However, soy milk (especially shelf stable) should not be brought to a rolling boil when used in gravies or sauces, as it may curdle as the stabilizers lose effectiveness. It should be heated to a simmer only, then reduced in heat.[9]

Soy milk cannot typically be whipped into a stable cream due to low fat content.[10] However, oil and stabilizers may be added to create soy whipped cream.

Soy milk can be coagulated to make tofu, soy cheese, or custards such as flan and crème caramel.

Nutritional Profile

Calcium naturally occurs in soybeans; however, in order to compete with cow's milk, soy milks must be fortified with additional calcium, some claiming up to 20 percent of the daily value per 8-ounce (89 mL) serving, depending on the level of fortification.[11] Soy milk can also provide naturally occurring omega-3 essential fatty acids. Soy milk is a vegetable product and contains no cholesterol, and it is very low in saturated fat yet high in protein.[12]

Tofu

Tofu is a soft, cheese-like soy product made from coagulated and pressed soy milk. Known also as bean curd, it is a traditional part of Asian cuisine.[13]

To make tofu, soybeans are prepared as for soy milk. As in cheese-making, coagulants are dissolved in water and then stirred into the boiled soy milk until it curdles into a gel or curd.[14] The curd is separated from the soy whey, pressed into blocks, and packaged.

Typical coagulants include acids and various mineral salts, such as calcium sulfate, seawater, nigari (magnesium chloride), and glucono delta lactone (GDL).[15] The coagulants used determine the final texture of the tofu, as they create curds with different-sized pores. Tofu products can be divided into fresh tofu, which is produced directly from soy milk, and processed tofu, made from fresh tofu.

Fresh Tofu

Fresh tofu is usually sold in water to maintain its moisture content. Pasteurized versions sold in the U.S. market can be eaten raw. The excess liquid should be drained before cooking.

Fresh tofu is typically white to light beige in color. It is classified by the density of the curd, which varies depending on the amount of water removed from it. Varieties include silken/soft, firm, extra firm, and dried. All fresh tofu has a raw, beany, grassy, green flavor. Fresh tofu is typically sold as organic and non-GMO in U.S. supermarkets. Softer styles work well in soups, sauces, desserts, and shakes. Generally, firmer tofu can act as meat replacements in many recipes.

Silken or Soft

Silken tofu has the highest moisture content, as the soy milk is curdled directly in the package and the product is undrained.[16] It has the texture of flan or fine custard. Silken tofu can simulate the thick, custardy mouthfeel of dairy ingredients for vegan menu items such as cream-style dips and spreads. Vegan versions of sour cream, mayonnaise dips, cream soups, lasagna filling, milk shakes/smoothies, cheesecake, pudding, and custards can be prepared using silken tofu.

Soft tofu is very similar to silken, with a slightly thicker texture. It can be used in similar ways and works well gently sliced or crumbled into soups, salads, and sauces. Soft tofu can also be mashed and mixed with chopped vegetables or meat before being cooked. The mixture can be bound with starch and deep fried like a dumpling, or steamed to make a meat loaf or meatballs. It is also commonly used as a filling in dumplings.

Silken and soft tofu cannot typically withstand harsh cooking methods such as deep frying and stir-frying. These products work well in blending and whipping and in gentler cooking such as steaming, baking, or simmering in soup broth.

Firm and Extra-Firm

In firm and extra-firm tofu, the soy curd is cut, the liquid is strained through muslin or cheesecloth, and the curd is pressed into a cake. One can often see the fine-grained pattern of the straining cloth on the surface of the tofu. Firm and extra-firm tofu can be used in recipes that require more vigorous cooking methods.

Firm tofu is still very moist, with a more resilient, bouncy outer skin and inner custardy texture. Firm tofu can be cut into distinct shapes such as slices or diced bits, which can be stir-fried, pan-fried, or deep fried. These cooking methods yield a crisp exterior and soft interior. Firm tofu can also be crumbled or cut into small cubes to replace eggs in vegan egg salads.

Extra-firm tofu is created with a coagulant that creates a drier, more brittle texture and stronger cake. It has a firmer texture throughout and is easily cut into shapes that can hold up to the most intense cooking methods such as pan-frying, stir-frying, deep frying, grilling, broiling, and even simmering in stews and casseroles.

As firm and extra-firm tofu are generally served in intact pieces, it is beneficial to remove as much of the water from the product as possible, followed by marination to infuse flavor into the interior. Marinating works best if the tofu is cut into pieces or gently pricked with a fork along the surface. Tofu can be pressed for several hours between two plates or flat pans, with the top pan weighted down, to further firm the texture and reduce residual water that might splatter when frying.

Draining excess liquid, slicing, and freezing firm and extra-firm tofu increases pore size, creates a yellower color, and develops a tougher, chewier texture. The water in the tofu expands as it freezes, creating larger openings to absorb liquid once thawed. This allows the tofu to absorb additional marinade. The chewy texture of frozen and thawed tofu makes it a suitable meat substitute when grilling and barbecuing.

Dried Tofu

Dried tofu, made from extra-firm tofu, has a rubbery texture that can be crumbled, sliced, or pressed and cut or shredded into long, noodle-type strings. Dried tofu is usually not eaten raw but stewed in a mixture of soy sauce and spices. The noodle form can be served cold or stir-fried.[17]

Processed Tofu

Fried Tofu

Firmer forms of tofu are sometimes sold cut into bite-size pieces and fried in oil to create a golden crisp exterior and airy interior. Tofu may be lightly dredged in cornstarch before frying to absorb excess surface moisture and impart a crisp texture. These pieces may be eaten alone, with a dipping sauce, or added to recipes such as hotpots and stews.

Frozen Tofu

In Asia (and some Asian markets), thawed and sliced frozen tofu called *thousand-layer tofu* can be found. Made from frozen soft tofu, the ice crystals create large layered cavities, a tougher texture, and a yellowish color. Thousand-layer tofu may be squeezed of excess moisture and eaten as is with a dip or dressing, or it can be grilled, fried, or roasted and used as a meat replacer in a variety of Asian-inspired vegetarian entrées.

Freeze-Dried Tofu

Tofu is also available in freeze-dried blocks and cubes from Asian food suppliers. These must be soaked in water before eating. This product is commonly simmered in broth, rice wine, and/or soy sauce. It has a spongy texture and absorbs the soaking liquid flavor. This type of tofu is also added in smaller pieces, along with other freeze-dried toppings, to instant soups such as miso soup.

Flavored Tofu

Sweeteners and flavorings can be mixed into soy milk before curdling. Fresh tofu marinated in sauces and spices is also becoming more common in Western markets.

Sweet: Most sweet tofu is silken and served cold. Common flavors include peanut, almond, mango, and coconut.

Savory: Varieties include egg tofu (with added eggs), chili-peppered egg tofu, and tofu marinated with garlic, spices, or soy sauce.

Fermented Tofu and Tofu By-Products

Asian suppliers also offer versions of fermented tofu such as pickled or "stinky" tofu, as well as by-products such as tofu skin and okara.

Pickled or preserved tofu are cubes of air-dried tofu fermented under hay and then soaked in various flavored acidic liquids.[18] Due to its strong flavor, pickled tofu is often used in small amounts as a condiment or to flavor stir-fries or braised dishes.

Stinky tofu is a soft tofu fermented in vegetable and fish brine.[19] The blocks have a soft texture and a strong, pungent, almost cheese-like aroma, rotten to some but appreciated by aficionados. When fried, it develops a crisp rind that can be topped with Asian sauces.

Tofu skin, or soy milk skin, is produced by boiling down soy milk in a shallow pan to produce a soy protein–lipid film that is collected and dried into yellowish sheets. It has a pliable, rubbery texture. The skin can be used as a wonton wrapper, folded or shaped to mimic meat, or formed into sticks and dried into tofu bamboo.

Okara is the soy pulp (press cake) remaining after soy milk is filtered. It is quite flavorless and has a sawdust-like mouthfeel, although it maintains some nutrient value, primarily as dietary fiber. Okara may be used to make porridge, stew, or patties but is more commonly used as animal feed. It can even be further processed into soy yarn!

Storage and Shelf Life

Typical fresh tofu has a shelf life of 70 days from the date of manufacture, if the package is unopened and refrigerated. This type of tofu is pasteurized to prevent spoilage.

Once the package is opened, any leftover tofu should be transferred to an airtight container and submerged under fresh water, changed daily or every other day, and refrigerated. Following this procedure, tofu lasts 3 to 5 days.

If the unopened fresh tofu is spoiled, the package may become bloated and puffy. If the water is cloudy and the tofu has a sour smell or taste, it should not be consumed. Cloudy or murky water alone is not a sign of spoilage.

Tofu can be frozen for up to 3 months; however, freezing result in darker, spongier tofu. Dried tofu is typically shelf stable, and freeze-dried tofu has a significantly longer shelf life than fresh, typically around 1 year.

Nutritional Profile

Tofu contains over 30 percent of the USDA recommended daily value for calcium and iron and contains nearly twice as much protein (8 g protein per 3½-ounce [100 g] serving) as it does fat.[20] Tofu also contains over 20 mg soy isoflavones per 3½-ounce (100 g) serving.[21]

Tempeh and Other Fermented Soy Products

Tempeh is a mold-fermented soybean cake or loaf made from dehulled and cooked soybeans (traditionally soybeans only; modern varieties may include brown rice, other grains such as barley or millet, and even flaxseeds or bits of vegetables) fermented with a *Rhizopus* mold. Tempeh originated in Indonesia but has gained more widespread recognition in the West as soy and fermented foods have gained in popularity. Tempeh has a grainy, nutty, almost mushroom flavor and patty-like texture, with visible beans and grains joined together by a web of edible mold. Tempeh is considered a whole-food form of soy, as it contains the entire soybean, and it is acclaimed for the bioavailability of nutrients released in the fermentation process.

Traditionally, the fresh soybeans are soaked overnight, par-cooked, cooled, mixed with a portion of previously made tempeh to serve as starter, and then wrapped in a large banana leaf to maintain humidity and provide exposure to oxygen. Indonesia's climate provides the appropriate temperature and humidity for the molds to grow and transform the soybeans into tempeh within 24 hours.

In the commercial process, dehulled soybeans are soaked overnight, cooked for about 30 minutes, cooled, and mixed with a tempeh starter such as *Rhizopus oligosporus* or *Rhizopus oryzae*. Other mixed cultures containing both *Rhizopus* and bacterial components such as *Klebsiella* species may be used in order to generate higher levels of vitamin B_{12}, which is normally not found in vegetables.[22] After 24 hours of incubation (temperature should be in the 90s °F [33 or so °C] with high humidity), the starter culture creates a web-like mycelium that binds the beans into a patty of fresh tempeh.

Storage and Shelf Life

Tempeh has a shelf life of 80 days in sealed packaging under refrigeration.[23] Due to the fermentation process, tempeh has a high content of live bacteria, mold, and yeast, but under proper fermentation these microorganisms are not harmful. That said, tempeh is never eaten raw. After opening, tempeh should be used in 3 to 4 days to avoid spoilage as the microorganisms continue to grow. Tempeh may exhibit a blackened or white fuzzy color and texture, which is normal to the product and not indicative of spoilage. High levels of mold growth, slimy texture, or off odors, however, may indicate spoilage.[24] Tempeh freezes well in sealed containers for up to one year with no apparent change in texture or flavor.

Preparation and Cooking Methods

Tempeh maintains its dense, beany texture and distinct flavor if sliced raw and dry-cooked (pan-seared, fried, grilled, etc.). This texture and flavor is somewhat polarizing, appreciated by some but off-putting to others. To counteract this, marinate tempeh overnight or simmer in a flavorful sauce for an hour or so prior to cooking to loosen texture and infuse flavor. Common marinades include light stock, soy sauce, herbs, spices, wine, garlic, dried mushrooms, and smoke flavoring, among others. Tempeh can be baked in a casserole, and cubed tempeh is an excellent addition to stews because it absorbs the flavors of the cooking liquid.

Dry or marinated tempeh can be pan-fried or deep fried for crisp texture and golden color. Chunks of tempeh can be pan- or deep fried into croutons or sliced into sticks and deep fried to resemble French fries. Tempeh's patty-like shape can be used in place of meat cutlets, and it works well marinated and flour-coated or traditionally breaded and then pan-fried (as a chicken cutlet). This style of tempeh can be made into vegetarian marsala, française, bordelaise, and other classic dishes by sautéing mushrooms or other ingredients and deglazing the pan with the appropriate wine.

A very useful application is to grate tempeh on a coarse cheese grater to mimic chopped meat. One can marinate, season, and pan-fry grated tempeh to make taco-style meat, vegetarian Bolognese sauce, and chili. The resulting crumbled texture is like that of the commercial frozen vegetarian chopped meat analog typically made of TVP.

Nutritional Profile

Tempeh is considered less refined than other soy products, such as tofu, as the whole soybean is retained. The fermentation process leads to significant nutritional changes to the soybean. Tempeh is limiting in the amino acids methionine and cysteine and is best served with rice to make a complete protein. However, the mold in tempeh partially digests the soybean proteins, liberating numerous amino acids, and breaks down the trypsin inhibitors, making them more easily digestible. This results in a higher protein efficiency ratio (PER) than other soy foods. The fermentation process also breaks down the oligosaccharide carbohydrates to make the tempeh more digestible. The bacterial cultures used in tempeh also result in increased vitamin B_{12} content compared with other vegetarian foods.[25]

Other Forms of Fermented Soy

Additional fermented forms of soybeans include miso, soy sauce, and natto.

Miso is a paste of finely ground soybeans that often includes barley and/or rice, salt, and a starter culture composed primarily of the mold *Aspergillus oryzae*. This mixture is allowed to ferment from 6 to 36 months, resulting in a savory paste ranging in color from golden to reddish-brown to dark brown to black. Miso paste is rich in mouth-filling free glutamates, which give foods the meaty taste enhancement known as umami. Commonly used to give depth and flavor to soups, miso is also used to make sauces, marinades, and salad dressings. High in salt, it is also rich in B vitamins and protein.

Soy sauce is the most popular Asian condiment in the world, including the United States. It is an ancient condiment; its origin dates back to China, 200 BC. It is used in countless commercially manufactured foods, even non-Asian ones, for its salty tang and flavor enhancement of soups, sauces, dressings, marinades, and so on. It is made primarily

from soybeans, but traditional recipes use roasted wheat as well. Soy sauce undergoes a similar fermentation to miso, with *Aspergillus oryzae* as the primary organism involved, although lactic acid bacteria and alcohol-producing yeasts get involved over time as well to provide their important flavor characteristics to the sauce. The process takes several months. At the end of the fermentation period the paste, unlike miso, is filtered to separate the liquid soy sauce from the press cake, which is used as animal feed. The sauce is then pasteurized and bottled. Typically, soy sauce contains 14 to 18 percent salt, although reduced-salt varieties are available. In addition, a reduced-color soy sauce can be used in applications requiring a lighter finished product.

Note: In addition to the traditional fermented soy sauce, there are also some brands of soy sauce that are made from acid-hydrolyzed soy protein instead of brewed with a traditional culture. This takes about three days. Although they have a different flavor, aroma, and texture when compared to brewed soy sauces, they have a longer shelf life and are usually made for this reason. The clear plastic packets of dark sauce common with Chinese-style take-out food typically use a hydrolyzed vegetable protein formula.

Natto is the term for whole cooked soybeans fermented with *Bacillus subtilis*, resulting in a slimy, ammoniac, and pungent product that is often served with rice as a breakfast food in Japan. It is not very popular in the United States (outside of Asian communities) due to its extreme sensory qualities.

Other Forms of Unfermented Soy

Soy protein isolate (SPI) is a highly refined or purified form of soy protein with a minimum protein content of 90 percent on a dry basis. It is made from defatted soy flour from which most of the non-protein components, fats, and carbohydrates are removed. Soy isolates are mainly used to improve the texture of meat products but are also used to increase protein content, enhance moisture retention, and as an emulsifier. Flavor can be affected, but overall impact depends on usage level. Food uses include protein supplementation and emulsification in beverage powders, infant formulas, liquid nutritional meals, and some varieties of liquid soymilk; enhanced moisture retention in meat and poultry marinades; nutritional enhancement in cereals and baked goods; and the primary protein source in power bars. It is the most expensive (and most concentrated) form of soy protein.

Soy protein concentrate (SPC) is about 70 percent soy protein and is basically defatted soy flour without the water-soluble carbohydrates. Unlike SPI, it is made by removing part, but not all, of the carbohydrates (soluble sugars) from dehulled and defatted soybeans. SPC retains most of the fiber of the original soybean. It is widely used as a functional or nutritional ingredient in a wide variety of food products, mainly baked foods, breakfast cereals, and some meat products. SPC is used in meat and poultry products to increase water and fat retention and to improve nutritional values (more protein, less fat). Soy protein concentrates are available as granules, flour, and spray-dried powders.

Soy flour is made by grinding soybeans into a fine powder. It comes in several forms: full-fat; defatted (oils removed); with 50 percent protein content and with either high water solubility or low water solubility; and lecithinated (lecithin added for additional emulsifying properties). Soy flour is gluten-free and can be used in gluten-free baked goods, but gluten-free breads made exclusively with soy flour are very dense in texture. In addition, soy flour is the basic ingredient used in the manufacture of textured vegetable protein.

Soy grits are made from soybeans that have been toasted and cracked into coarse pieces. They may be stirred into soups, stews, or casseroles, toasted with granola, or mixed into ground beef or other proteins to make meatballs and meatloaves. They can also be added to baked goods to provide texture and enhanced nutrition, and can be eaten like cereal with milk and fruit.

Textured Vegetable Protein (TVP®)

Textured vegetable protein (TVP) is a refined soy food made from soy concentrate or defatted soy flour and water. TVP is a trademarked name of Archer Daniels Midland Co. (ADM), which invented it. It is a spongy product that can be extruded into various shapes and textures to mimic meat, thereby providing a vegetarian and low-cost substitute for many meat products. It may also be called *textured soy protein* (TSP).

Soy flour is defatted to remove oils and mixed with varying ratios of water to create a pliable vegetable protein dough. This dough can be extruded in the presence of steam and cut into shapes such as flakes, nuggets, patties, ground bits, and slices. These can then be flavored with natural or artificial, vegetable-derived beef or chicken flavors and combined with water or other liquid and further cooked to yield meat-like analogs. TVP is also made as a byproduct of the soybean oil industry.[26]

Ingredients

Plain TVP typically has just one ingredient: soy flour. However, it may also contain natural and artificial flavorings (such as chicken, beef, turkey, bacon, sausage, pepperoni, or ham flavor) when processed and sold to resemble a particular meat product. More highly processed versions of TVP may include added soy protein isolate or other proteins, such as wheat gluten.

Storage and Shelf Life

Dry (non-rehydrated) TVP has a minimum shelf life of one year if stored in a sealed bag or container at room temperature. Some products claim a shelf life of two years from manufacture. As TVP is made from defatted flour, rancidity is not a major concern in storage. Moisture absorption can be controlled by ensuring the product is hermetically sealed. Once rehydrated in a recipe, TVP shelf life is greatly reduced to less than one week under refrigeration, depending on the other ingredients, unless further processed (canned, for example) or frozen.

Preparation and Cooking Methods

TVP is available in various sizes, including basic flakes, crumbles, and larger cubed chunks and strips. It must be rehydrated prior to or during cooking, most efficiently in boiling water or flavored liquid (stock, broth, or other sauce). The specific ratio of hot liquid to TVP depends on the particle size; it varies from 1:1 for softer textured product to 0.75:1 or 0.5:1 for a tougher, denser texture. TVP typically rehydrates within 2 to 10 minutes of soaking in boiling liquid, depending on particle size.

Some small-flake bacon-flavored TVP (Bac-Os®) can be sprinkled on salads without rehydration. The smallest granulated TVP can be added without rehydrating directly into liquid stocks, broths, soups, and stews to cook along with other ingredients. Larger chunks of TVP should be partially rehydrated with water and then cooked further (typically 5 to 10 minutes or more) directly in a liquid-containing recipe. If not pre-hydrated, these larger chunk-type products must be cooked for longer periods in soups and stews.

The texture of the cooked TVP is a good indicator of doneness. Adding acid to TVP loosens texture and speeds up rehydration.[27] TVP in crumble or small-flake form can make vegetarian versions of taco filling, chili, sloppy joes, and Bolognese sauce, and may be blended with bread crumbs and eggs to form burgers, meatballs, or meat loaf. Chunk-style TVP can make vegetarian stews, kebabs, satays, and stir-fries.

Nutritional Profile

TVP is an excellent source of protein, with 50 g protein per 3½-ounce (100 g) serving before rehydration. It also provides 18 percent of the RDV of dietary fiber and is low in fat due to the oil removal from the soy flour.[28]

New-Generation Soy Foods

Vegetarian diets have grown in popularity throughout the United States, and the functionality of soy foods has been well advertised in recent years. In addition, awareness of food allergies or intolerances to dairy products has risen in the mainstream marketplace. This combination of trends has led to a new generation of soy foods that mimic meat and dairy products. These analogs fill a void in the vegetarian diet and can provide a cholesterol-free and lower-fat option even to non-vegetarians who simply want to eat healthier. However, unlike the soy foods previously described, this new generation of soy foods is often highly processed and refined with many ingredients, additives, and processing aids to mimic the flavor and texture of the meat and dairy items they replace.

Types and Styles of New-Generation Soy Foods

Soy versions of sliced and grated cheese, soy-based versions of ice cream and yogurt, breakfast sausage, cold cuts, Thanksgiving turkey, buffalo wings, chicken nuggets, pepperoni, chopped meat, ribs, hot dogs, bacon, and burgers can be found in most major supermarkets and health food stores. Combination items such as frozen pizza with soy cheese and soy pepperoni can be found in the freezer section. Soy-based

FIGURE 7.2 Protein in soy products.

Product	Serving Size	Protein (grams)
Tofu—medium to extra firm	3 oz.	7 to 12
Tofu—soft or silken	3 oz.	4 to 6
Tempeh	4 oz.	12 to 20
Textured vegetable protein (TVP)	¼ cup	10 to 12

Source: USDA National Nutrient Database for Standard Reference, http://www.nal.usda.gov/fnic/foodcomp/search.

sports and snack bars have gained in popularity due to their ability to pack a high serving of protein in a small package. Major U.S. brands include Lightlife, Morningstar Farms, Boca, Dr. Praeger, Amy's Organics, Vegan Gourmet, and Tofutti.

Production methods often involve blending soy flour, other vegetable proteins, flavorings, texturizing agents, and colors, and molding, forming, or extruding the finished product under heat and pressure to resemble meat or cheese.

Ingredients

A look at the ingredient panel of many new-generation soy foods tells the trained food scientist or nutritionist that these are not necessarily health foods. The multitude of ingredients and processing aids in some of these products can resemble the list commonly found on a snack or junk food item. Many of these foods not only contain a soy protein base but also wheat gluten (also an allergen under FALCPA) as well as many other starches, fillers, and flavorings.

New soy foods can have higher protein contents than traditional soy foods due to the addition of more concentrated protein isolates as well as added wheat proteins. However, these refined ingredients may present greater challenges for digestion. It is important to note that some new soy foods also contain wheat and even dairy-derived ingredients (non-vegan) as well as potentially sensitizing ingredients such as monosodium glutamate (MSG), and these must be noted on all labels for manufactured products.

Grains

Cereal grains make up half of the top 18 crops grown around the world, with wheat, maize (corn), rice, and barley taking the top four spots, responsible for nearly three times the annual volume of all the other crops combined.

Grains have been part of the traditional diets of both ancient and modern cultures for thousands of years, and especially important in cultures where the availability of animal proteins is limited. Their limiting lysine content can be complemented by legumes to make a complete protein. Although rice and beans come to mind as an example of such a complementary pairing, several grains (quinoa, buckwheat, amaranth) have a very high protein and lysine content. It is important to note that whole grains (with the germ, bran, and endosperm intact) have significantly higher protein, fiber, and vitamin content than refined grains (which are proportionately higher in starch). For example, wheat processed into white flour has 10 g protein and 2.7 g dietary fiber per 3½-ounce (100 g) serving, while whole wheat flour contains 13.7 g protein and 12.2 g dietary fiber per 3½-ounce (100 g) serving.[29]

The preference of the U.S. public for refined white flour products (white bread, crackers, pasta) and resulting nutritional deficiencies (especially in infants and children) by the 1920s led to research on nutrient losses in processing. Thus, the idea of enrichment, or adding back the most essential nutrients lost in processing, was born. Thiamin, riboflavin, niacin, folic acid, iron, and even calcium have been commercially

FIGURE 7.3 The most commonly grown crops in the world.

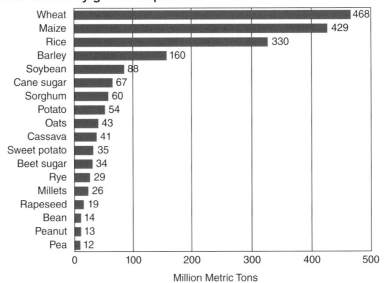

Source: Adapted from University of Wisconsin Alternative Field Crops Manual, 2000, and USDA Standard Reference.

FIGURE 7.4 Protein in grains (cooked).

Grain (1 cup)	Protein (grams)
Amaranth	7
Barley, pearled	4 to 5
Barley, flakes	4
Buckwheat groats	5 to 6
Cornmeal (fine grind)	3
Cornmeal (polenta, coarse)	3
Millet, hulled	8.4
Oat groats	6
Oat, bran	7
Quinoa	5
Rice, brown	3 to 5
Rice, white	4
Rice, wild	7
Rye, berries	7
Rye, flakes	6
Spelt, berries	5
Teff	6
Triticale	25
Wheat, whole berries	6 to 9
Couscous, whole wheat	6
Wheat, bulgur	5 to 6

Source: USDA National Nutrient Database for Standard Reference, http://www.nal.usda.gov/fnic/foodcomp/search.

added to white flour since the 1940s. Interestingly, there was no widespread effort to return proteins and amino acids lost in processing of grains because grains were never seen as primary sources of protein in the U.S. diet.

Whole Grain–Enhanced Products

Over the years, the comparative health benefits of whole versus refined or processed grains has been the subject of significant research, which has led to an enormous increase in product development, marketing, and sales of whole-grain products. The focus on whole foods and whole grains has gained enormous awareness and popularity along with vegetarian diets. The use of the claim "contains whole grains" is a powerful marketing tool for virtually every grain-based food on the supermarket shelf: breads and rolls, waffles, pasta, crackers, cereals, pizza dough, muffins, sports bars and granola bars, rice dishes, baking mixes and flours, snack chips, cookies, and cakes. Even beverages, soups, and dairy products can contain soluble fiber extracted from grains.

An industry association, the Whole Grains Council, helps consumers identify foods that are good sources of whole grains by awarding special stamps that can be placed on the packaging of qualifying products. Of course, the presence of a Whole Grain Stamp on a food package doesn't guarantee the healthfulness of the food inside; even foods high in fat, sodium, and sugar (such as highly sweetened breakfast cereals) can carry the stamp as long as they are made from whole grains. In addition, the Council provides a list of restaurants that offer at least one whole-grain offering at every meal, a list of bulk vendors of whole-grain products for food manufacturers and chain restaurants, and a list of private-label manufacturers specializing in the development and manufacturing of whole-grain foods.

The USDA's *Dietary Guidelines for Americans* recommends eating at least 3 ounces (85 g) of whole-grain products per day, with the rest of the recommended daily intake (if not from additional whole grains) coming from refined grain products (breads, pasta, cereals, etc.) that have been enriched with B vitamins and iron. Further, individuals should "[c]onsume at least half of all grains as whole grains [and] increase whole-grain intake by replacing refined grains with whole grains."[30]

U.S. consumers have begun embracing whole grains for health; however, the taste and texture of whole-grain products can differ significantly from the highly processed white-flour counterparts to which they are accustomed. Thus, blended, or "made with whole grains" products have come to the forefront of the market, combining traditional white flour with whole wheat flour or a combination of wheat germ, wheat gluten, wheat bran, or other grain components. In the past, the cardboard color, texture, and taste of whole wheat pastas, cereals, and baked goods frightened away all but the healthiest-minded eater, and much formulation and marketing has gone into improving the palatability and image of whole-grain and whole grain–enhanced products. One might think of them as "gateway foods" that prepare the consumer palate for the texture and flavor of 100 percent whole-grain products.

The FDA has reinforced the message of whole grains and health, and many companies have jumped on the bandwagon. The largest breakfast cereal manufacturers now proudly tout that their cereals are made with whole grains. Even many traditional white breads now have added wheat protein and fiber. Hybrid pastas are made of white flour with added protein, fiber, and even omega-3 oils in varying ratios. Supermarket shelves teem with 100 percent whole wheat pastas, including many private-label versions. Some well-known crackers and snack crisps are now available with some amount of whole wheat flour or added protein or fiber. Many commercial ground-meat products contain oat fiber or oatmeal to reduce calories and increase dietary fiber.

Initially, the key to making whole grain–enhanced products a success in the mainstream marketplace was to hide the flavor, color, and texture of the whole grain. Finely milled flours, innovative fiber extracts, and various forms of grain proteins were formulated to blend seamlessly with white-flour products.

FIGURE 7.5 **Grain characteristics.**

Name of Grain	Grain Characteristics
Amaranth	Ancient Aztec grain. Nutty, slightly spicy and sticky, gelatinous texture. High in fiber and protein. A superfood with superior protein quality.
Barley	Pearled barley is lightly milled or refined and is mild flavored and chewy. Whole barley is very chewy, retaining the whole grain. Barley is used in soups, stews, and pilafs, and is the primary grain used in the manufacture of beer and whiskey via the "malting" process.
Buckwheat groats	Also called *kasha*. Roasted with a nutty flavor. Generally, is first coated with beaten egg and cooked over heat to avoid mushiness. Delicious as pilaf.
Bulghur wheat	Wheat berries that have been steamed, dried, and cracked. It cooks quickly. Used to make the Middle Eastern specialty *tabbouleh*.
Corn	A New World food, corn is one of the most important grains in human nutrition. Very versatile; eaten from the cob as a vegetable, and used to make polenta, desserts, animal feed. Corn starch, corn syrup, and corn oil are other important staples.
Couscous	A traditional pasta-like food of North Africa, couscous is made from ground semolina, which is mixed with water, then steamed, sieved, and dried. Traditionally cooked in a couscoussière. Good in pilafs, in salads, or combined with vegetables.
Farro	Ancient grain in the wheat family from North Africa and the Middle East. A staple during the Roman Empire. Common in Italy. Also known as *emmer* or by its scientific name, *triticum dioccum*. Complex, nutty taste. Creamy like risotto.
Hominy	Dried white or yellow corn kernels, hull and germ removed by soaking in slaked lime or lye. Commonly served as a side dish or part of a casserole (Mexican posole). When ground, is referred to as grits. These are usually simmered in water or milk until thick. Can be served in this form or chilled, cut, and fried.
Kamut	An ancient Egyptian wheat, kamut has a rich, buttery flavor and chewy texture. Is a good wheat substitute for allergy sufferers, but not for people with celiac disease as it still contains gluten.
Millet	Believed to have been the staple grain of the Chinese before rice, millet is now grown throughout the world, although in the United States its primary use is as birdseed. Millet is tiny, gluten free, and easy to digest. Boil like rice, or cook in soups and stews.
Oats	A major U.S. crop, oats have an inedible hull, which is removed, leaving the remaining grain, called the groat, with bran and germ layers intact. Available pre-steamed and rolled as "instant" rolled oats, or chopped as Irish or steel cut oats.
Polenta	A cornmeal mush that is a staple of Northern Italy. Can be eaten hot or cooled until firm, then cut and fried.
Quinoa	This tiny, disk-shaped seed (pronounced "keen-wah") is an ancient grain now being recultivated in South America. It is known as the only grain with a complete set of essential amino acids. It may be boiled like rice and used in soups and stews.
Rice	Cultivated since at least 5000 B.C. It is the main food source for almost half the world's population, predominantly India, Indonesia, China, Japan, and Southeastern Asia. There are more than 2,500 varieties grown. Because it requires vast amounts of water to grow, rice is most suited to tropical regions.
Rye	An important grain in central and eastern European cuisines. Used for baking hearty dark breads and some local specialties. Rye grows well in more hardy climates. Rye produces a very weak gluten network, resulting in very dense dough.
Spelt	A wheat variety more than 9,000 years old, brought to this country by the Amish. Has a light, nutty flavor. Spelt is easier to digest than other wheat varieties, but contains gluten, making it inappropriate for celiac disease sufferers. Used in pilafs or salads.
Sorghum	Similar to corn, sorghum is one of the top cereal crops in the world, next to wheat, oats, and corn. Originating in Africa, it is now grown in the United States as well as Asia. Used for animal feed, starch production, or porridges.
Teff	The smallest grain in the world, native to northern Africa. Mild nutty flavor.
Triticale	Developed in the late 1800s, triticale is a cross between rye and wheat. Nutty flavor. Great in pilafs, used in soups or stews.

Name of Grain	Grain Characteristics
Wild rice	A grass seed native to the Great Lakes Region of the United States. Not actually a rice, it used to be a very important staple food for Native American tribes in the northern part of the country. Distinct nutty flavor; cooked like rice pilaf with a much longer cooking time.
Wheat berries	Whole wheat berries can be sprouted and used in salads or pilafs. Pre-cooked, dehydrated, and cracked wheat berries known as bulgur are a great substitute for whole wheat berries.

Source: Hinnerk von Bargen.

It is important to note that "made with whole grains" differs from "100 percent whole grain," and some companies use the public's lack of understanding to convince consumers that they are buying less refined products. Several companies have received negative public and media attention by advertising "whole-grain goodness" while a majority of their product is made from white flour. Removing and then adding back nutrients in other forms can be, at the very least, misleading to untrained consumers, but savvier health consumers look for foods as close to a whole-food source of grains as possible.

The FDA has posted industry guidance on their website to assist in labeling whole-grain and whole grain–enhanced products as well as accepted health claims.

Rice

Rice is the seed of the plant *Oryza sativa*, and it is arguably the most important grain grown to support human nutrition: it provides more than one-fifth of the calories consumed throughout the world.[31] It is important to note that more than half of the world's population depends on rice as their primary food, especially in the Far East, where people eat it three times a day. China and India are the world's major producers. Rice, like almost all grains, is limiting in lysine, which can easily be supplied by complementation with legumes. That said, rice has the highest PDCAAS score of any grain: 0.86, where the top score is 1.0 (egg white, milk proteins, and soy protein). Brown rice is much better nutritionally than polished white, even though white is much more popular in the United States. In fact, a diet consisting mainly of white rice results in beriberi, a deficiency in vitamin B_1 (thiamine). Depending on the type of beriberi (wet or dry), symptoms may include loss of muscle function (especially in the lower legs), numbness of the extremities, shortness of breath, swelling of the lower legs, mental confusion and difficulty speaking, pain, vomiting, and paralysis. Beriberi is quite rare in developed countries, including the United States, where many foods are enriched with thiamine.

Rice is a semiaquatic grass typically grown in regions with high rainfall as harvesting is assisted by flooding, which causes the small, edible seeds to float. The name *wild rice* is often applied to *Zizania* plants, which are technically a separate reed-type grass unrelated to rice.

Rice in its whole-grain form (with the bran intact) is brown. Removing the bran (pearling) yields white rice. This processing removes some nutritional value, so brown rice is higher in protein, vitamins, minerals, and fiber than white rice. Because of this, enrichment of white rice with vitamin B_1, vitamin B_3, and iron is required by law in the United States. Both forms of rice can be processed into "converted rice" by parboiling. This helps force the nutrients into the endosperm of the rice before the bran is removed. Converted or parboiled rice retains more nutritional content but takes a bit longer to cook than traditional white rice. Rice can be fully cooked and then flash frozen and dried into instant rice, which retains the least nutrients but is the quickest cooking.

Rice is classified by its size—long grain, medium grain, or short grain—and each variety has different cooking methods and resulting textural properties in a dish. Long-grain rice tends to remain somewhat firm and separate when cooked, with a fluffy texture. Short-grain rice has more starch and is sticky or creamy when cooked. Medium-grain rice has characteristics of both and can be either fluffy and distinct or sticky, depending on cooking time and how long it sits after cooking.

Typically, rice is cooked at a ratio of 2 parts liquid to 1 part rice. The most common method is to bring the liquid to a boil and simmer the rice, covered, for the recommended time (from 15 to 60 minutes, depending on type). Some types of rice require rinsing, soaking, and pre-sautéing in oil (pilaf method) or adding hot liquid slowly while stirring continuously (risotto method).

For the pilaf method, before the grain is cooked it is toasted in a hot pan either dry or coated with a small amount of fat. This technique, known as parching, alters the flavor, creates a firmer texture, and helps keep the grains separate during the subsequent cooking. In addition, the dextrinization of the starches caused by the dry heat during parching makes them more easily digestible.

A carefully measured amount of water, stock, or similar liquid is added to the parched grain and brought to a boil. Then the rice, covered, is simmered on the stove or in the oven (oven cooking allows for more even heating). It is important to use the appropriate amount of liquid; too much results in a mushy, porridge-like consistency, whereas too little does not fully hydrate the grains, causing the pilaf to remain hard no matter how long it is cooked. In a properly prepared pilaf, the individual grains separate easily and are tender to the bite, with a noticeable texture. No matter which grain is used, the method is the same. However, the ratio of grain to liquid and the time necessary to cook the grain vary tremendously.

For the risotto method, short-grain rice is constantly stirred during cooking, and liquid is added in stages. The constant stirring causes some of the starch to ooze out of the rice grain, resulting in a very creamy consistency. A properly prepared risotto has an almost pourable consistency, yet the individual grains retain a noticeable texture referred to as al dente ("to the tooth"). It is important to understand, however, that not all kinds of short-grain rice are suitable for risotto. Japanese short-grain rice, perfect for sushi, turns into an unpleasant mush if it is stirred during cooking.

In the culinary culture of many Asian countries, sticky rice is a popular dish. This should not be confused with regular steamed rice served as a side dish. Steamed rice just happens to be sticky to one degree or another, as the grains were not parched before the liquid was added. Genuine sticky rice, available in short- and long-grain varieties, is also known as glutinous rice. After cooking, it becomes especially sticky; it is commonly used for sweet dishes. The raw glutinous rice grains are easily recognized; they are much whiter and more opaque than other white rice varieties.

Here are some commonly available types of rice:

- *Long grain:* brown rice, white rice, parboiled or converted rice, and aromatic varieties such as basmati, jasmine, Jasmati®, and Texmati®, which are prized for their nutty, popcorn-like aroma and flavor.
- *Medium grain:* River, Calrose, and Goya are popular brands.
- *Short grain:* Italian arborio and carnaroli varieties, which are commonly used in risotto, and sticky rice, which is common to Asian cuisines and also good for puddings.
- *Exotics:* wild rice, wild pecan rice, black or japonica rice, and other colored rices, such as Bhutanese red rice and Thai purple.

Rice may be ground into flour for use in baking or product formulation (particularly in gluten-free applications), and soaked and processed into rice milk to provide a dairy-free milk alternative. Other rice products include rice syrup (made by hydrolyzing rice starch), rice bran, puffed rice cakes, and cereals. Rice starch is commonly used in commercial meat marinades to help muscle fibers bind water.

Corn

Corn is the largest field crop in both volume and cash value in the United States, more than double any other crop. Outside the United States, corn is called maize. Although corn is considered a vegetable by some, its nutritional function is that of a grain. It is available fresh on the cob; frozen; canned (in brine or creamed); dried as popcorn (with different colors available, such as red and black); processed with alkali (nixtamalization) to make masa, masa harina, and hominy; dried and ground into cornmeal or corn flour; further processed into tortillas, tortilla chips, and corn chips; baked into muffins and cornbread; and cooked into porridge or polenta. Corn is also made into oil, syrup, high-fructose syrup, popcorn cakes, and cereals. In spite of all of these food applications, most corn is grown for animal feed and, to some extent, ethanol. Only 1 percent of the corn grown is actually consumed as corn.

The freshest corn requires very little cooking and has a sweet flavor. The kernels may be yellow or white, or even mixed on the same cob (butter-and-sugar corn). Most modern corn cultivars grown for human consumption have been bred to be supersweet. Cooking methods for fresh corn include grilling, boiling, or microwaving on the cob; frozen corn is commonly microwaved or gently sautéed or grilled in a cast-iron pan. Canned corn is cooked in the canning process and needs only to be warmed on the stovetop or in a microwave. Popcorn may be oil or air popped. Corn flakes and corn pops are both among the oldest forms of ready-to-eat cereals. Cornmeal imparts a dry, crumbly texture to dough and may be blended with eggs, water, or other binding agents and leavening to make cornbread or muffins. Masa and masa harina are used in traditional Central American cooking and are useful for finer-grained foods such as tamale filling or dumplings. Cornmeal breading is also commonly used, especially in Southern foods such as fried okra, fried catfish, and fried pickles. And traditional Southern "cornmeal mush" is virtually the same thing as Italian polenta.

Wheat and Derivatives

Wheat refers to any species of the genus *Triticum*. More wheat is now produced around the world than any other grain. About 75 percent of all harvested wheat is made into flour; the remaining 25 percent goes into cereals, pasta, wheat germ and wheat germ oil, and animal feed. The two major types of wheat are winter wheat (hard) and spring wheat (soft). Hard wheat has a higher protein (gluten) content, making it better for breads and pasta. Soft wheat is lower in protein, making it better for cakes and pastries.

Wheat is available as whole wheat berries, cracked (groats), bulgur (parboiled and dried), farina (cream of wheat), whole wheat flour, white flour, bread flour (high protein/gluten), durum flour, all-purpose flour, cake flour, self-rising flour, bran, germ, and vital wheat gluten, among other forms. Wheat flour is commonly extruded with water into pasta, noodles, and cereals; it provides the foundation for cakes and cookies; and its high gluten content allows it to make bread doughs that rise (with the help of a leavening agent). Flour is also used to dredge raw meats, poultry, and seafood before sautéing or frying, as a breading ingredient to improve adhesion, as a nonstick agent when kneading doughs, and for dusting the interior of a cake pan (together with butter or oil) prior to filling with cake batter.

Flour is not only used for baking; after fat, all-purpose flour is the second ingredient in roux, a binder used to thicken gravies, cream soups, and similar preparations. For a roux, all-purpose flour is cooked in a measured amount of fat for a certain period before it is combined with the liquid it is meant to thicken. The application of dry heat during cooking is a crucial step because it causes the starch to dextrinate—that is, the starch chains break into shorter units. This results in the typical velvety mouthfeel of roux-thickened sauces.

The shortened starch chains are not able to bind as much water, which results in the diminished thickening power of roux versus raw flour. In fact, the longer a roux is cooked before it is added to the liquid being thickened, the less thickening power it retains. To achieve the same amount of thickening in a sauce, a larger amount of dark roux (produced by longer cooking) than light roux is necessary to get the same viscosity. In addition to mouthfeel and texture, flavor and color are also affected by roux. Caramelization and the Maillard reaction caused by heating the flour in fat has a great impact on the sauce's color and flavor; the longer the roux is cooked prior to addition to a sauce, the darker and stronger the caramelic and toasted notes that develop, and these flavors and colors are transferred to the thickened sauce.

The cooking methods for wheat and related grains are as varied as its many forms; they range from soaking wheat berries overnight and simmering them (much like beans) to combining flour with yeast, water, and other ingredients to make dough.

Wheat contains glutenin and gliadin—proteins that form an elastic, non-water–soluble matrix of protein called gluten when wheat flour is hydrated and then kneaded into dough. Glutenin and gliadin make up 80 percent of the protein in wheat flour. The sulfur atoms in the glutenin portion of the flour allow the proteins to cross-link.[32] The amount of protein in the starting flour, along with the amount of kneading, influences the development of gluten and thence the texture in baked goods. Tender baked goods are best obtained using cake flour (low in gluten), with minimal mixing. Tougher, chewier products, such as bagels, are made using flour with higher protein content (or even with added gluten), added water, and additional kneading. The gluten matrix traps carbon dioxide in yeast-leavened doughs, allowing the bread to rise. Reduction of water, less working or kneading, and blending in fat or shortening can interfere with cross-linking and result in a tenderer, flakier product such as pie crust.

Note: The FDA has declared wheat (and wheat products) as one of the major eight allergens, according to FALCPA. Therefore, any product that contains wheat or wheat protein derivatives must be clearly labeled as such in the ingredient statement or in a comprehensive "contains" statement after the ingredient list. As of 2013, the FDA has also defined *gluten-free* as a term used on finished product labels. Per the FDA:

> Gluten-free foods must contain less than 20 parts per million (ppm) gluten. Foods may be labeled *gluten-free* if they are inherently gluten free; or do not contain an ingredient that is: (1) a gluten-containing grain (e.g., spelt wheat); (2) derived from a gluten-containing grain that has not been processed to remove gluten (e.g., wheat flour); or (3) derived from a gluten-containing grain that has been processed to remove gluten (e.g., wheat starch), if the use of that ingredient results in the presence of 20 ppm or more gluten in the food.[33]

It is important to note for all grains discussed here, although the grains themselves may be inherently gluten-free, many are grown and processed alongside gluten-containing grains and may contain gluten from cross-contamination in farming and milling. *Certified gluten-free* grains are available that have been tested to meet FDA standards for gluten-free. Before making any gluten-free claim in formulation, it is important to ensure that ingredients are sourced and tested to meet this standard.

Awareness of celiac disease, also known as gluten intolerance, is growing. Celiac disease is not classified as an allergenic response because it doesn't trigger the release of histamine or cause the release of IgE (immunoglobulin E) antibodies. It does, however, cause chronic inflammation of the villi in the intestine, interfering with absorption of nutrients and creating gastrointestinal discomfort. Awareness of the illness has reached large enough proportions to spawn the creation of a plethora of gluten-free foods, now available even in mainstream supermarkets. The list of gluten-free replacements for foods normally made from wheat flour, including breads and pastries, pastas and cereals, and cookies and crackers, grows daily.

Barley

Barley is a species of the genus *Hordeum*, which contains gluten. Barley is traditionally made into porridge, bread, and beer and has much historical significance in Europe and the Near East. Most of the barley crop today is used for animal feed, but some is also processed and cooked in multiple ways for human consumption. That said, most barley for human consumption is used in the manufacture of beer (through the malting process).

The first step in processing barley is dehulling, or removal of the outer husk. Dehulled barley that has been steamed and polished to remove the bran is called *pearled* barley. Barley may be cooked (boiled and simmered 40 to 45 minutes) or ground into flakes, meal, or flour and used in soups and infant cereals. It can also be processed into a coffee-like beverage. Nutritionally, barley can assist in regulating blood sugar[34] and contains a favorable ratio of amino acids. In 2006, the FDA authorized a health claim for the soluble fiber (beta glucans) in whole-grain barley. Based on research, the FDA concluded that whole-grain and dry-milled barley products providing at least 3 grams of beta-glucan soluble fiber per day are effective in lowering cholesterol (total blood cholesterol and low-density lipoproteins [LDL], the so-called bad cholesterol).

Oats

Oats are a cereal grain of the species *Avena sativa* and are not considered a prohibited grain under the FDA's gluten-free regulations, as research shows that most people with celiac disease can tolerate oats (depending on their sensitivity). Certified gluten-free oats are available. Oats are grown and processed for animal and human food and are available in these forms:

- *Whole-grain groats* (with only the husks removed) have the densest texture and longest cooking time (they are typically brought to a boil and simmered at least 60 minutes).

- *Steel cut or Irish oats* are groats cut into pieces. These have a dense, chewy texture and a slightly shorter cook time (30 to 45 minutes).
- *Scottish oats* are ground into a meal that cooks up in about 30 minutes into a porridge-type product with a creamy mouthfeel.
- *Rolled or old-fashioned oats* are steamed groats flattened by a roller. Available in varying thicknesses, they make a thick and chewy oatmeal cereal in about 15 minutes and work well for granolas or to grind into oat flour. *Quick-cooking oats* are rolled even flatter to reduce cook time to 3 to 5 minutes.
- *Instant oats* are also rolled thin, but are also cooked and then dried again so they can be prepared instantly by stirring hot water into the product.

Oatmeal acts as a meat extender in meat loaf and similar products. Of course, it is also used in baked goods like the ever-popular oatmeal cookies. Oat flour is used as a thickener in soups and may be used as a coating for commercially diced and dried fruit for free flow (such as dates). Oat flour is also used to make breakfast cereals. Old-fashioned oats, toasted and ground to a fine flour, can substitute for part of the all-purpose flour to produce interesting pancakes, breads, and even pasta dough. Due to its lack of gluten-forming proteins, oat flour is best used in conjunction with wheat flour for use in breads.

Sprouted oats are whole-grain oats soaked in water to sprout and enhance nutrient content. These are often added to salads, breads, and other baked goods.

Oats have received a lot of attention for their health-promoting properties. In 1997, the FDA authorized statements linking oat consumption to heart health after research confirmed that the soluble fiber in oat bran (oat beta-glucans) lowers cholesterol and saturated fat. This has been taken advantage of ever since by cereal companies anxious to make health claims on their package labeling. Oat bran has the highest content of beta-glucan fiber, followed by rolled oats and then oat flour. Oats have somewhat higher fat content than other grains and provide a good source of protein.

Other Grains

Rye is a wheat-related species of the genus *Secale* and contains gluten. It is most commonly used to make bread flour or for animal feed rather than being cooked in whole form. Rye is also processed and distilled into certain types of whiskey and vodka.

Triticale is a cross between wheat and rye that contains gluten. It was developed to combine the high yield potential of wheat with the disease resistance and environmental tolerance of rye. This relatively recent hybrid typically is not cooked whole but rather made into flour used in pastas and bread.

Buckwheat is not a true grain but due to its starch content has similar properties. Botanically, it is a fruit related to rhubarb and sorrel. Buckwheat's triangular seeds do not contain gluten and are used in many cuisines worldwide. Buckwheat groats are

FIGURE 7.6 Grain-to-liquid ratio by volume.

Name of the Grain	Grain-to-Liquid Ratio by Volume	Approximate Cooking Time
Amaranth	1:1½–2	20–30 minutes
Arborio rice (risotto)	1:3	20–30 minutes
Barley	1:2½	50–60 minutes
Barley, pearled	1:2	35–45 minutes
Basmati rice	1:1¼	18 minutes
Buckwheat	1:1½–2	12–20 minutes
Bulgur wheat, pilaf	1:2½	15–20 minutes
Bulgur wheat, soft	1:3	30 minutes soaking in boiling water
Converted rice	1:1¾	18 minutes
Couscous	1:2	20–25 minutes
Hominy grits	1:4	25 minutes
Hominy, whole	1:2½	2½–3 hours
Japanese short grain	1:1¼	18 minutes
Jasmine rice	1:1¼	18–20 minutes
Kamut	1:3	1 hour
Long grain, brown rice	1:3	45 minutes
Millet	1:2	30–35 minutes
Oat groats	1:2	45–60 minutes
Polenta/cornmeal	1:3–3½	35–45 minutes
Quinoa	1:1	15 minutes
Short grain, brown rice	1:2½	35–40 minutes
Spelt	1:3	1 hour
Teff	1:3	15 minutes
Triticale	1:2½	1 hour
Wheat berries	1:3	2 hours after soaking
Wild rice	1:3	1 hour

Source: Hinnerk von Bargen.

cooked by boiling and then simmering. Buckwheat's culinary applications extend to breakfast porridges, kasha pilafs, and noodle dishes, and the flour can be processed into Japanese soba noodles and used in pancake mix. In Russia, buckwheat blini (small pancakes) are traditionally served with caviar. Buckwheat flowers are also used to make a unique honey.

Sorghum (also known as *milo*) is a member of the grass family that is grown worldwide for animal feed, food ingredients, and fuel. It is considered gluten-free. Sorghum is not typically cooked whole but further processed into flour, syrup, and other products. It may be fermented into alcoholic beverages, particularly in Asia.

Bulgur is a mixture of several wheat species that have been parboiled and dried, with a portion of the bran removed. It contains gluten and appears similar to, yet differs from cracked wheat due to a parboiling step, which reduces cooking time. Bulgur may be added to boiling water and covered and steam-cooked for 5 to 10 minutes. It is common in Middle Eastern recipes such as tabbouleh and bulgur pilaf.

Ancient Grains

Along with vegetarianism and healthy eating, previously underappreciated whole grains such as quinoa, spelt, amaranth, Kamut®, farro (emmer), and teff (also known as "ancient grains") are being rediscovered in the culinary world. These grains can be prepared like other grains: whole in pilafs and risottos, or ground into flour and used in baked goods. The soaked and sprouted raw grains are eaten in salads or used in baking.

Certain ancient grains are considered a complete source of protein (especially quinoa), and ancient wheat species such as spelt and Kamut® are said to be more easily tolerated by persons with wheat allergies despite their gluten content.

Quinoa is not technically a cereal grain or a member of the grass family; it is the seed of the leafy plant *Chenopodium quinoa*. This small, flattened round seed originated in the Andes and was prized as a sacred grain by the Incas. At present, quinoa is elevated to a high status due to its complete protein content and suitability for vegetarian diets. Unlike other grains, quinoa is not limiting in lysine and contains a balanced ratio of amino acids and about 14 g protein, 7 g fiber, and significant mineral content per 3½-ounce (100 g) serving (uncooked).[35]

Quinoa is gluten-free and thus appropriate for those with celiac disease. Its one drawback is the seeds' bitter coating of saponins, which can affect flavor and digestibility. Most commercial quinoa is pre-treated to reduce the saponin content, but it is a good idea to additionally soak and rinse quinoa before cooking. Quinoa is off-white when uncooked and deep tan or brown when cooked, and it has a fluffy, chewy texture and nutty flavor. The grain is also available in red and black varieties. Most simply, it can be prepared by simmering for 15 to 20 minutes at a 2:1 ratio of boiling water to quinoa. It adapts well to pilafs and other seasoned dishes, even sweet and breakfast porridges. It can also be processed to make flour and flakes or sprouted for raw food diets.

Spelt is a wheat relative originating in Europe that contains gluten and must be labeled in accordance with the

FIGURE 7.7 Market forms of grains.

Whole grains	These are the least processed form of grains, containing bran, germ, and endosperm. Whole grains are often referred to as *groats*. Examples include brown rice and wheat berries. Because they contain the unsaturated oil-rich germ, they must be refrigerated to inhibit rancidity.
Pearled or polished	The bran is partially or fully removed from the grain. Barley is referred to as *pearled*, and rice is called *polished*.
Steel cut, cracked, or grits	Whole or polished grains, such as oats, corn, or wheat, are cut into smaller pieces for faster cooking.
Flakes or rolled	Grains are steamed, then flaked or flattened between rollers. The process of flattening the grain increases its surface area. The oils in the germ, as a result, could turn rancid. This is avoided by steaming the grain, which inactivates the fat-digesting enzymes.
Meal	Grain is ground to a sandy consistency. Stone-ground grains are ground between stones, creating a grittier consistency. Examples include cornmeal and semolina.
Bran	Bran is the thin layer just under the outer husk of the grain, which surrounds the endosperm and is a rich source of fiber.
Germ	The embryo of the grain is rich in fat, B vitamins, and vitamin E. It is made into a coarse meal that must be refrigerated as the fat is susceptible to rancidity. Wheat germ is the most common.
Flour	This is the most prevalent market form of grain. The grain is ground into very fine powder, either from the whole grain or just the endosperm. Any grain may be processed into this form, as can nuts.
Starch	The pure, finely ground carbohydrate portion of the grain with all protein, fiber, and fat removed. Most commonly available: potato, corn, and rice.

Source: Hinnerk von Bargen.

FALCPA regulations on wheat products. It is elongated and wheat-like in appearance. Spelt is commonly processed into flour for breads and pastas rather than cooked in whole-grain form. Sprouted spelt breads are often found in health food stores.

Amaranth is gluten free, and the plants may be used as leafy vegetables, herbs, or grains depending on the species. Amaranth's edible seed is prized in cultures around the world, including Central and South America and even Asia, but most notably by the Incas and Aztecs. Amaranth grains are small and round and contain a considerable amount of protein and relatively high lysine content. They are cooked like quinoa, often with additional liquid (3:1 ratio) and for slightly longer cook times, 20 to 25 minutes. Puffed versions of amaranth may be cooked like couscous—that is, added to boiled water, covered, and removed from heat to steam cook. Toasted amaranth grains are mixed with honey, chocolate, or molasses in traditional Spanish dishes. Amaranth is also ground into flour and used in flatbreads.

Kamut® is the trademarked name (by Kamut International Ltd. in 1990) for Khorasan wheat, a variety of ancient giant wheat that contains gluten and is touted for its selenium content. The origins of Kamut® are in Egypt and the Middle East; however, the grain has been cultivated and developed to its present state in the United States. Kamut® may be cracked to create a bulgur-like product that is boiled and simmered, and it is also processed into flour, breads, pastas, pastries, and other foods. Any wheat sold using the name Kamut® must be certified organic, have a protein content of 12 to 18 percent, be 99 percent free of contaminating varieties of modern wheat, contain between 400 and 1000 ppb of selenium, and not be mixed with modern wheat in pasta. Even though this wheat variety contains gluten, it is more easily digestible than regular wheat by people with slight allergic tendencies.

Teff is the gluten-free seed of a grass plant of African origin. It is available in chocolate brown and white varieties, and is smaller than quinoa. Teff is available in its whole seed form and is also ground into flour. Some people find it has a mild acidic or sour flavor; others experience a molasses-type flavor. Teff has a mucilaginous texture and can become slimy if cooked too long. It is most commonly cooked into ethnic dishes such as Ethiopian injera, a fermented sponge-like pancake. Whole-grain teff may be cooked at varying ratios (1:3 or 1:4 teff to water) and simmered for 10 to 20 minutes, depending on desired texture. Teff flour can be substituted for a portion of wheat flour in baked goods. It is a good thickener for vegan stews, soups, pudding, and gravy.

Millet is the tiny, gluten-free seed of a grass plant thought to have originated in Asia but with culinary traditions throughout the world. In the United States, however, it is primarily used as birdseed. Variations of Indian roti bread, porridge (sweet and savory), and some alcoholic beverages use this grain. Millet is often dry toasted to release its aroma, covered in boiling water and simmered 20 minutes, and then steamed for at least 5 minutes after cooking. It may also be ground into flour and used for flatbreads, or sprouted. Millet is comparable to wheat in protein and rich in vitamins and minerals, but it may have adverse effects on the thyroid (due to the presence of a peroxidase inhibitor) if consumed in large amounts.

Although commonly mistaken for a grain, couscous is not a grain at all but a tiny, flattened spherical pasta typically made from wheat (semolina) flour. Common in North Africa and the Middle East, couscous is available in the Western market as instant couscous. This type cooks quickly: It is added to boiling water, removed from heat, and covered to steam for about 5 minutes. Couscous may also be steam cooked over flavored simmering stews (Moroccan couscous and tagines) in more traditional methods of preparation. Whole wheat couscous and flavored couscous mixes are now also available on the market. "Israeli couscous" is a larger spherical pasta, roughly the size of tapioca pearls. Both sizes go well with stews and tagine-type dishes.

Seitan

Seitan, or "wheat meat," is a vegetarian protein made from de-starched wheat dough. Seitan is traditionally used as a meat replacer in Asian Buddhist vegetarian cuisines, simulating the texture of duck or chicken. It consists entirely of gluten, the allergenic component in wheat, and products containing seitan must be clearly labeled with "wheat" on the ingredient label, according to FALCPA. In addition, seitan is not tolerated by anyone with celiac disease (gluten intolerance). It has a spongy texture and an off-white or gray to tan color and can approximate meat products including cutlets, nuggets, and chunks of chicken, duck, turkey, or beef. Seitan has a relatively bland flavor on its own; however, it is typically soaked in soy sauce or other marinade and is typically sold in Asian groceries in jars along with this flavoring sauce.

How Seitan Is Made

In its simplest form, seitan is made by combining wheat flour (bread or all-purpose flour; cake flour is too low in protein) and water, kneading intensely, rinsing away the starch with water, and then cooking the finished dough in simmering broth or other flavored liquid. Spices and other dry seasonings may be added to the flour prior to mixing with water, and stock or soy sauce may replace a portion of the water. One method is to combine 1 part white flour, 1 part whole wheat flour, and 1 part water to form a sticky dough that is then kneaded several hundred times, submerged in water at least 30 minutes or overnight, and then rinsed under cold water for at least 30 minutes to remove all of the wheat starch.[36] Seitan dough can also be made with vital wheat gluten (essentially pure gluten) in place of flour, eliminating the rinse step.

The dough is then cut into pieces (cutlets, nuggets, fillets, balls) and simmered in stock or other flavored liquid for around 1 hour. The seitan puffs up, increases in size, and develops a rubbery texture. While this simmering method is most common in the West, Asian cultures may also steam, boil, or fry the raw seitan dough. It is important to remember that seitan dough greatly increases in size as it is heated, so it must be cut into smaller sizes than the desired finished product. Commercially available brands are limited and vary regionally.

Seitan can be used in sauces, stews, and soups, and it can be stir fried or grilled. It requires minimal cooking—just enough to absorb sauces and lightly grill or brown. Seitan can be breaded and fried as a vegetarian cutlet; one useful application is to gently simmer in wine, mushroom, or rich vegetable stock, wring out excess liquid, follow standard breading procedure (flour, egg, bread crumbs), and pan fry as one would chicken cutlets. Seitan can make a somewhat convincing vegetarian version of Thanksgiving turkey if served with stuffing, cranberries, and vegetarian gravy. Seitan can also approximate duck and makes excellent satay or kebabs when marinated in a thick sauce and grilled.

Nutritional Profile

Seitan is very low in fat, quite low in carbohydrates, and high in protein (some varieties contain up to 20 g per 3½-ounce [100 g] serving). Commercial seitan may be high in sodium (up to 25 percent of daily allowance) when packed in soy-based marinade. When viewed as part of a complete vegetarian diet, it is important to note that seitan is a grain protein derived from wheat and therefore is limiting in the amino acid lysine. Combining it with beans, corn, or nuts completes the protein to provide all essential amino acids.

Nuts and Seeds

Once viewed primarily as snacks, nuts and seeds are gaining popularity for their functional ingredients and ability to boost the healthfulness of meals, particularly for vegetarians. A significant amount of research and marketing have gone into educating the public about the vitamins, healthy fats, and trace micronutrients found in seeds and nuts. Non-peanut nut butters are gaining popularity as well. Note that both tree nuts and peanuts (technically a legume) are included in the FDA's major eight allergens under FALCPA and must be clearly labeled. Peanuts must be labeled as such, while tree nuts (almonds, Brazil nuts, macadamias, hazelnuts/filberts, cashews, walnuts, pecans, pistachios, pine nuts, and even coconut) must be labeled as the specific type of nut. While not legally included as allergens in the United States, some seeds are viewed as allergens in other countries, such as sesame seeds in Canada and celery seed in the EU.

As the name indicates, tree nuts are harvested from large plants or trees; they are often dried and either sold in the shell (for certain varieties) or further processed to remove the shell. Peanuts (also known as *groundnuts*) are harvested from the soil beneath the plant (like potatoes) and cooked (roasted or boiled) and dried. They may be sold in-shell or shelled. Both peanuts and tree nuts may be sold diced, ground into flour, sliced, dry roasted, oil roasted, salted, ground into butter, or as oil, among other forms.

Seeds are harvested from various plants and dried and either sold in-shell or shelled, and may also be roasted or salted and flavored. The most common nutritional seeds (to distinguish them from spice seeds) include sunflower, pumpkin, pine nuts (pignolias), flax, sesame (white and black), poppy, nigella, and hemp.

Storage and Shelf Life

Nuts and seeds are naturally very high in unsaturated oils and tend to go rancid relatively quickly if stored at room temperature. They also absorb odors readily. Other potential problems are their attractiveness to rodents and tendency to harbor larval insects that may grow at room temperature conditions. Therefore, nuts and seeds should be stored in sealed airtight containers under refrigeration to extend shelf life. This is especially true of flax and hemp seeds, which have among the most delicate oils when exposed to even moderate heat. Nuts and seeds have a shelf life of up to one year from date of production if properly stored; however, this is reduced significantly when the nut is diced or roasted, as its oils are more exposed and oxidize more quickly.

Nuts have received unfortunate media attention for their ability to harbor dangerous pathogens, as evidenced in recent salmonella outbreaks in peanuts and peanut butter, pistachios, and pine nuts in 2009 and 2010. Therefore, many nut processors are further increasing HACCP for nut handling and processing, including reducing storage temperatures and implementing additional control measures. After contamination incidents in the past several years, almonds must now be pasteurized for sale in the United States.

The food processor should note that tree nuts and seeds are also commercially available in sterilized or pasteurized forms. Nuts are typically sterilized using steam or propylene oxide (PPO), while seeds may be treated with steam, ethylene oxide (ETO), or heat. These treatments lower the microbial counts and the potential for growth of pathogenic microorganisms. Roasting raw nuts and seeds (ideally through a validated kill step) before consumption can also lower microbial plate counts to enhance the safety of the finished product.

Preparation and Cooking Methods

Most commercially available nuts and seeds (other than chestnuts) can be eaten as they are sold. For maximum freshness, purchasing whole shelled nuts and dicing or grinding them just prior to adding to a dish is best. Many nuts and seeds have improved flavor when they are gently roasted first. Roasting temperatures and times vary on the type and cut of the nut. Nuts and seeds are roasted in the oven or in a heavy skillet over moderately high heat until they begin to turn golden and release aroma. They can also be candied using a coating of beaten egg whites and sugar, cinnamon, or other sweet or savory spices.

Nuts are quite important in vegan and raw food diets and may be soaked to change texture and to allow for grinding into raw-nut ricotta or cream sauce. Pine nuts are a classic addition to pesto when ground with basil and garlic. Other nuts are used in baking and pâtés, enrobed in chocolate,

FIGURE 7.8 Protein in raw nuts and seeds (shelled).

Nut/Seed (¼ cup)	Protein (grams)
Almond	7
Brazil nut	5
Cashew	4
Chestnut	1
Coconut (shredded)	2
Filbert/hazelnut	5
Flax seed	5
Macadamia	2
Peanut	8
Pecan	2
Pine nut	4
Pistachio	6
Pumpkin seed	7
Sesame seed	7
Soynut	10
Sunflower seed	8
Walnut	5

Source: USDA National Nutrient Database for Standard Reference, http://www.nal.usda.gov/fnic/foodcomp/search/.

made into candies, or added to savory pastas, stews, soups, meats, and stuffing. Nut-crusted fish or chicken fillets, coated and fried, are popular menu items. Seeds may be toasted or added directly to hot recipes—except flax and hemp seeds, due to the volatility of their oils. They must be used raw only.

Note: Because of the high level of attention that nuts in particular receive as allergens, many food manufacturers have eliminated them entirely from their facilities, primarily driven by a fear of lawsuits.

Nutritional Profile

Nuts and seeds are high in protein and fat and are touted for their contribution to a heart-healthy diet. Flaxseeds, walnuts, and pumpkin seeds are notably good vegetarian sources of omega-3 fatty acids such as alpha linoleic acid (ALA). When combined with grains, they can yield a complete protein. Trace micronutrients, such as selenium, are found in Brazil nuts and other nuts.

Quorn®

Quorn is a fungal protein (mycoprotein) product developed as an alternative to meat in the 1970s in the United Kingdom as a response to global hunger. Quorn was created and trademarked by Marlow Foods and has been available in the U.K.

market since 1985 and in the United States since 2002. According to SPINS, the information and service provider for the Natural Products Industry, for the 52-week period ending May 17, 2009, Quorn products were the best-selling frozen meat-free brand in natural food stores in the United States. Quorn is low in calories and fat and high in dietary fiber; it is considered a complete protein, with all the essential amino acids present. Mycoprotein has a PDCAAS score of 0.91 (just behind beef at 0.92), and Quorn analogs also contain egg white, which has a perfect score of 1.0.

Scientists researching ways to convert starch into protein through controlled fermentation discovered a fungus called *Fusarium venenatum* that can be used to ferment cereal starch into single-cell protein (SCP). The resulting mycoprotein is extracted, heat-treated, dried, and mixed with egg albumen as a binder. (Because of this, Quorn is vegetarian but not vegan.) It is then textured, formed, and flavored in products that mimic ground beef, chicken nuggets and fillets, burgers, and meatballs. Currently, Quorn is available at retail markets only, but Marlow's patent ran out in 2010, and the possibility exists that a company will start to manufacture mycoprotein ingredients for industrial use in the near future.

Conclusion

The availability and range of vegetable-based proteins is enormous, and when combined strategically, vegetables can be the sole source of protein in the diet. As an added benefit, they can provide a host of other essential nutrients such as vitamins, minerals, and fiber—and all this without the fat and calories that normally accompany a diet heavily dependent on meat. As consumers become more cognizant of these benefits, the demand for new high-quality vegetable-based retail and foodservice foods will continue to grow, and Culinology® professionals will need both culinary creativity and nutritional knowledge in order to take advantage of this expanding market.

[1]U.S. Department of Agriculture, *USDA National Nutrient Base for Standard Reference*, data file, retrieved from http://www.nal.usda.gov/fnic/foodcomp/search/, 2008.

[2]G. Sarwar and F. E. McDonough, "Evaluation of Protein Digestibility-Corrected Amino Acid Score Method for Assessing Protein Quality of Foods," *Journal of the Association of Official Analytical Chemists* 73 (1990): 347–356. Retrieved from http://www.ncbi.nlm.nih.gov/pubmed/2198245.

[3]K. D. Setchell, "Phytoestrogens: The Biochemistry, Physiology, and Implications for Human Health of Soy Isoflavones," *American Journal of Clinical Nutrition* 68, Supplement (1998): 1333S–1346S. Retrieved from http://www.joplink.net/prev/200101/ref/9-43.html.

[4]M. S. Kurzer, "Hormonal Effects of Soy in Premenopausal Women and Men," *Journal of Nutrition* 132, no. 3 (2002): 570S–573S. Retrieved from http://jn.nutrition.org/content/132/3/570S.full.

[5]J. M. Hamilton-Reeves, G. Vazquez, S. J. Duval, W. R. Phipps, M. S. Kurzer, and M. J. Messina, "Clinical Studies Show No Effects of Soy Protein or Isoflavones on Reproductive Hormones in Men: Results of a Meta-Analysis," *Fertility and Sterility* 94, no. 3 (2009): 997–1007.

[6]J. P. Harwood, L. M. Ausman, N. W. King, P. K. Sehgal, R. J. Nicolosi, I. E. Liener, D. Donatucci, and J. Tarcza, "Effect of Long-Term Feeding of Soy-Based Diets on the Pancreas of Cebus Monkeys," *Advances in Experimental Medicine and Biology* 199 (1986): 223–237.

[7]Edensoy, product information, retrieved from http://www.edenfoods.com, 2009.

[8]8th Continent, product information, retrieved from http://www.8thcontinent.com, 2009.

[9]Edensoy.

[10]Vitasoy, product information, retrieved from http://www.vitasoy-usa.com, 2009.

[11]Silk, product information, retrieved from http://www.silksoymilk.com, 2009.

[12]USDA, *National Nutrient Base*.

[13]*American Heritage Dictionary*, 4th ed. (New York: Houghton Mifflin, 2001).

[14]Nasoya, product information, retrieved from http://www.nasoya.com, 2009.

[15]H. L. Wang and C. W. Hesseltine, "Coagulation Conditions in Tofu Processing," *Process Biochemistry* (January/February 1982): 7.

[16]W. Shurtleff and A. Aoyagi, *Tofu and Soymilk Production: A Craft and Technical Manual*, 3rd ed. (Lafayette, CA: Soyfoods Center, 2000), retrieved from http://www.soyinfocenter.com/.

[17]W. Shurtleff and A. Aoyagi, A. (2008). *A Comprehensive History of Soy: History of Soybeans and Soyfoods, Past, Present, and Future* (Lafayette, CA: Soyinfo Center, 2008), retrieved from http://www.soyinfocenter.com/.

[18]Ibid.

[19]Ibid.

[20]USDA, *National Nutrient Base*.

[21]Nasoya.

[22]S. Areekul, S. Pattanamatum, C. Cheeramakara, K. Churdchue, S. Nitayapabskoon, and M. Chongsanguan, "The Source and Content of Vitamin B$_{12}$ in the Tempehs," *Journal of the Medical Association of Thailand* 73, no. 3 (1990): 152–156.

[23]Food Service Direct, product information, retrieved from http://www.foodservicedirect.com, 2009.

[24]Turtle Island Tempeh, product information, retrieved from http://www.tofurky.com/faq_tempeh.html, 2009.

[25]W. Shurtleff and A. Aoyagi, *The Book of Tempeh*, prof. ed. (New York: Harper and Row, 1979).

[26]Archer Daniels Midland, *Textured Vegetable Protein*, retrieved from http://www.adm.com, 2009.

[27]USA Emergency Supply, product information, retrieved from https://www.usaemergencysupply.com, 2009.

[28]Archer Daniels Midland, *Textured Vegetable Protein*.

[29]USDA, *National Nutrient Base*.

[30]U.S. Department of Health and Human Services and the U.S. Department of Agriculture, 2010.

[31]B. D. Smith, *The Emergence of Agriculture*, Scientific American Library (New York: W. H. Freeman, 1998).

[32]N. M. Edwards, S. J. Mulvaney, M. G. Scanlon, and J. E. Dexter, "Role of Gluten and Its Components in Determining Durum Semolina Dough Viscoelastic Properties," *Cereal Chemistry* 80, no. 6 (2003): 755–763. doi:10.1094/CCHEM.2003.80.6.755. Retrieved from http://cat.inist.fr/?aModele=afficheN&cpsidt=15273405.

[33]U.S. Food and Drug Administration, "Foods Labeled Gluten-Free Must Now Meet FDA's Definition," data file, retrieved from http://www.fda.gov/Food/NewsEvents/ConstituentUpdates/ucm407867.htm, 2014.

[34]A. Nilsson, et al., "Effects on GI and Content of Indigestible Carbohydrates of Cereal-Based Evening Meals on Glucose Tolerance at a Subsequent Standardised Breakfast," *European Journal of Clinical Nutrition* 60, no. 9 (2006): 1092–1099.

[35]USDA, *National Nutrient Base*.

[36]Natural Gourmet Cookery School, Seitan recipe, Chef's Training Program Course, 2004.

8 | Carbohydrate-Based Foods

Lead Author: Allen J. Freed, President, AJ Freed, L.L.C.

Dan Putnam, Technical Manager, Grain Processing Corporation

Contributor: Hinnerk von Bargen, CHE, Associate Professor in Culinary Arts, Culinary Institute of America

Contributor: Jason R. Gronlund, VP Culinary, Smokey Bones Bar & Fire Grill, Johnson & Wales Alumnus

●What Are Carbohydrates?

Carbohydrates are designed to be the primary source of energy in the body. The word *carbohydrate* is made up of two components that very clearly (at least on a chemical basis) tell you about its structure. The *carbo* portion is derived from the word *carbon*, and the *hydrate* portion comes from the term for *water* (H_2O), a molecule composed of two atoms of hydrogen and one oxygen atom. Therefore, a carbohydrate is a molecule that contains both carbon and water. A simple carbohydrate, such as glucose, has the chemical formula $C_6H_{12}O_6$. For every 6 carbons there are 12 hydrogen atoms and 6 oxygen atoms, but the ratio of hydrogen to oxygen is still 2:1, like water.

Foods we associate with carbohydrates are sugars, flours, starches, grains, cereals, potatoes, rice, and foods made with these ingredients: pasta, bread, French fries, rice pilaf, and so on. In fact, the vast majority of carbohydrates come from plant sources: fruits and vegetables, grains, and legumes. These plants are the source materials from which carbohydrates, in the form of sugars, starches, gums, and fiber, are extracted, purified, concentrated, and then used as ingredients to create or enhance other foods. Some of the ingredients are obvious, such as cornstarch and high-fructose corn syrup (HFCS), derived from a portion of the corn kernel. Other ingredients, such as gum acacia, which comes from the sap of the acacia tree, are less so.

● Carbohydrates as an Ingredient: The Chef's View

From a culinary standpoint, unlike the other two energy-containing macronutrients, which are primarily eaten directly as foods themselves (*proteins*) or indirectly consumed as the result of cooking (other than butter on bread or oil in salad dressings, we generally don't eat pure fats and oils directly), carbohydrates fit into both camps: the starchy vegetables, grains, and legumes that are eaten as is, and the functional ingredients, such as starches, flours, and meals, that can be extracted from them (potato starch, rye flour, wheat flour, and cornmeal are just a few examples). In addition, carbohydrates make up the vast majority of foods consumed around the world.

Grains, Legumes, and Starchy Vegetables

Starchy vegetables, grains, and legumes are often regarded as plate fillers, unglamorous foods that accompany the more flamboyant main dish. Prepared correctly, however, they can be extremely delicious, sometimes with the result that *they* become the star on the plate.

FIGURE 8.1 **Simple sugar molecule.**

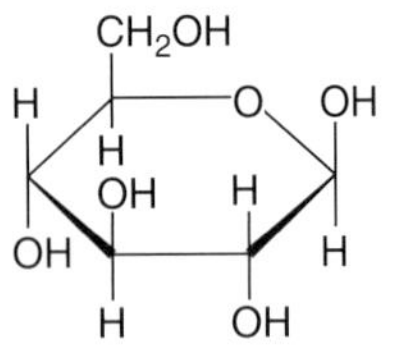

Source: Gum Technology Corporation.

Grains

The seeds of grass plants, known as grains, with their high nutritional value, long shelf life, and comparatively low cost of cultivation, are arguably the most important food crops for the human diet. According to Jared Diamond in his book *Guns, Germs, and Steel*, grains were domesticated as early as 9000 BC. Today, the three largest grain crops grown world-wide are corn, wheat, and rice.

Realizing that many other animals relied on the seeds of grass plants for sustenance, people considered them a possible alternative to the berries, nuts, roots, and other gathered and hunted foods of the forest. However, early humans had to figure how to locate, identify, cook, and, eventually, grow these grains. They had to determine which ones were the most nutritious and how they were best prepared. At first there was no one to teach them that grains had to be husked, ground more or less finely, and then cooked or baked with the addition of some liquid. All of the unique preparations specific to each grain were discovered over time by trial and error, and mostly by chance.

For example, it is likely that a fermented batch of rye dough somewhere in northern Europe several thousand years ago gave birth to the idea of sourdough. Whole-grain breads taste best when the dough is properly fermented, either with yeast or a bit of previously made sourdough. Nutritional science has revealed that phytates in the bran of wheat or rye hinder zinc and iron absorption. Proper fermentation of the dough destroys phytates, making the bread more nutritious.

Hominy is another example of mankind's resourcefulness when it comes to getting the best out of a grain. In a traditional Native American process called *nixtamalization*, corn is soaked in alkali (either sodium hydroxide or potassium hydroxide). During this process, niacin and other B vitamins are converted into a more absorbable form, and the availability of amino acids is improved. When corn was introduced to Spain and Italy in the early 1500s without the knowledge of this traditional treatment, poor sharecroppers, who during the cold winter months relied exclusively on corn for sustenance, suffered the four *D*s: diarrhea, dermatitis, dementia, and death by the end of winter. These are symptoms of pellagra, a niacin deficiency.

Today, along with the staple crops of corn, wheat, and rice, there are dozens of other grains, both modern and ancient ("what's old is new again") such as barley, oats, quinoa, freekeh, and buckwheat that are available to the culinary professional in a wide variety of market forms.

Legumes

Second only to grains in importance to human nutrition are legumes, the seeds of leguminous plants such as beans, peas, and lentils. All legumes grow as seeds in pods. Rich in complex carbohydrates, fiber, proteins, and minerals, they play an important role in many diets all over the world. In order to expedite their cooking, dried legumes are first soaked until hydrated and then cooked in liquid until very tender. For lentils, black-eyed peas, pigeon peas, and split peas, soaking is less critical; these legumes cook relatively quickly without this step. For a more in-depth look at the legumes, see the write-up in Chapter 7: Vegetable Sources of Protein.

Starchy Vegetables

Besides grains and legumes, starchy vegetables such as potatoes, plantains, and taro root (to name just a few) are an important staple in many parts of the world. Relatively low in moisture and with good shelf-life properties, they share a vital spot on the world's plates.

Native to South and Central America, potatoes have made their way into almost every culture. When first introduced to the Old World by returning conquistadors, they were met with great suspicion. In fact, at first they were used only as animal feed. Potatoes are a member of the nightshade family, and they have toxic leaves; if stored improperly, the spuds can become toxic, too. When exposed to sunlight, solanine, a toxic alkaloid, can develop on the skin and around the eyes of the potato. It is commonly yet incorrectly believed that the green color that develops on the exposed parts of the potato is the toxin; actually, it is chlorophyll. However, the green color serves as a convenient warning sign: wherever there is chlorophyll, solanine is just below the skin. Both chlorophyll and solanine are easily removed by peeling.

Potatoes are rich in vitamin C, which made them helpful in preventing scurvy on long ocean voyages. Some nutritionists have claimed that the enormous quantity of French fries consumed in the United States prevents vitamin C deficiency here.

Growing well in moderate climates with mild summers and cool winters, potatoes became the single most important crop in Ireland. During the eighteenth and nineteenth centuries, one-third of the Irish population relied almost exclusively on potatoes for sustenance. The great potato famine of the 1840s (due to a blight caused by a fungal infection) brought about the death of as many as a million people due to starvation and disease. This led to mass migration to the New World. It is a curious fact of culinary history that potatoes, arriving in the United States via Ireland, were brought here by the people who almost died because of them.

Potatoes are more adaptable to a wide range of cooking methods than most other vegetables. Selecting the correct type of potato for any given cooking method is the key to success. Russet potatoes are a great choice for mashed potatoes and French fries; the relatively high starch content makes the purée fluffy and creamy and allows the fries to become crisp on the outside while remaining creamy in the center. However, they are less suitable for salads, boiled potatoes, and other preparations where maintenance of the shape is desired. The swelling of the starch granules during the gelatinization process causes the fibers to break excessively, and the potato falls apart during cooking. "Waxier" varieties with lower starch content, such as Yukon Gold, Red Bliss, and yellow potatoes, are better suited to these methods.

Another common problem in many kitchens and food-processing facilities is gooey mashed potatoes. When the

FIGURE 8.2 Starch and moisture content of potatoes, and corresponding cooking methods.

Types	Moisture Content	Starch Content	Cooking Method
Idaho or russet	Low	High (mealy, low sugar)	Bake, purée, fry
Chef's, all-purpose, Yukon Gold	Moderate	Moderate	Boil, sauté, steam, roast, braise, stew
New potatoes	High	Low (waxy, high sugar)	Boil, steam, roast, stew
Red Bliss	Moderate	Low	Boil, steam
Sweet potatoes, "yams"	Moderate to high	High	Boil, bake, purée, roast

potatoes are puréed properly with a food mill or a ricer (which minimizes shear), less than 5 percent of the starch cells are disrupted, resulting in fluffy and tender mashed potatoes. Too much shear force caused by a food processor or electric mixer (or even just excessive stirring) causes many more starch cells to rupture. The released starch absorbs all free water, creating mashed potatoes resembling glue.

An often misunderstood potato category is new potatoes, not to be confused with baby potatoes (which are simply small potatoes). True new potatoes are available only at the beginning of the new harvest, when the plant part above the ground has not wilted yet. At this stage, the potatoes have not converted all sugars into starch, and they maintain a slightly sweet flavor. Their skin is very delicate and can be removed by light brushing. Other types of potatoes include fingerling potatoes and the colored (blue, purple, yellow, red) potatoes.

Sweet potatoes are botanically unrelated to potatoes. The pale, yellow type is dry and crumbly, and the darker, orange variety is moister and sweeter. Culinary uses of the sweet potato, however, are similar to those of potatoes. The orange variety with the pointy ends is often referred to as *yams*. True yams, however, are unrelated to sweet potatoes. Originating in Africa, yams are slightly sweeter than sweet potatoes and can grow up to 7 feet in length!

The plantain, looking much like a large banana, is actually a starchy fruit and not a vegetable. Nevertheless, it cannot be eaten raw. Depending on the desired dish, it is used either ripe (*maduro*) or green (*verde*). Becoming very soft upon cooking and tasting much like bananas, ripe plantains are used in casseroles and purées or fried and served as a sweet side dish. Green plantains, on the other hand, are mostly used as a potato substitute in soups and stews, and are used in many parts of the Caribbean and Latin America to make tostones—thick slices of crispy fried plantain.

Other starchy vegetables, including taro root, cassava, arrowroot, and jícama, are widely cultivated in many cultures.

Flours

All grains, legumes, and starchy vegetables can be dried and ground into fine flours or more coarsely into meal. All grain-based flours (wheat, rice, rye, barley, corn, and so on) are called *whole-grain flour* when the grains are husked and then ground into a fine powder. For more refined flours, only the endosperm, containing the starch and protein, is ground.

For flours based on legumes such as soybeans, lentils, and chickpeas (known as *besan* in Indian cuisine), the outer husk or membrane skin is removed, and the dry legume is then ground to a fine powder. For the less common flours based on starchy vegetables, like potato flour, the item must be fully dehydrated before it is ground.

A large variety of flours is available to culinary professionals. With distinct flavors and thickening and binding properties, a wide assortment of flours are used in ethnic cuisines.

Refined Starches

Pure starches are produced by separating the starch from the surrounding insoluble cellulosic materials in the plant. Potato starch, for example, can be obtained by grating a raw potato with a fine grater into a cheesecloth-lined bowl filled with cold water. Squeezing the grated potato solids in the cheesecloth presses out the majority of the water along with the potato starch. After allowing the starch to settle, the water can be decanted; the starch remains at the bottom of the bowl.

Any starchy vegetable is a potential source for starch; the more common starches—cornstarch, potato starch, arrowroot—are available in any grocery store. They are most frequently used for thickening liquids and as a binding agent for fillings.

FIGURE 8.3 Basic makeup of a grain.

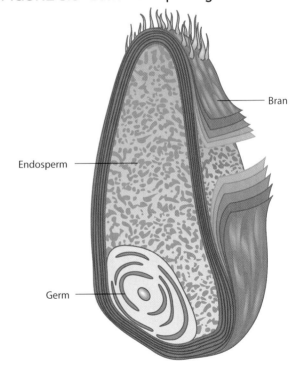

Bran

Endosperm

Germ

FIGURE 8.4 **Non-wheat flours, their origin and use.**

Flour	Origin	Uses
Amaranth flour	South America, South Asia	Puddings, gluten-free baking, salads
Buckwheat flour	Eastern Europe, Japan	Pancakes, hot cereals, baking, noodles
Chestnut flour	Mediterranean, Italy	Polenta in Corsica, baking, pasta
Chickpea flour (*besan*)	India	Batters, breads, thickener
Corn flour/meal	South Asia, Americas	Hot cereal, bread, thickener, cornbread, grits, polenta/mush
Dried potato flour (*chuño*)	Western South America	Thickener
Rice flour	Southeast Asia	Rice paper, sweets, desserts
Rye flour	Central Europe	Baking
Tapioca flour	Central Africa	Baking, pancakes, fufu
Teff	Ethiopia	Baking, pancakes
Pease meal (ground yellow peas)	Great Britain	Porridges, soups, baking
Masa harina (ground dried hominy)	Mexico	Tamales, corn tortillas/tacos

Each starch lends itself to specific applications. From a chef's perspective, starches can be divided into two major groups: cereal starches, such as corn and rice starch, and root starches, such as arrowroot and potato starch. The makeup of the starches lends distinct properties to each group. Root starches commonly have a higher content of amylopectin, whereas cereal starches are generally richer in amylose. As a result, liquids thickened with cereal starches end up a little cloudy but relatively resistant to excessive boiling, long hot holding, and mechanical shear. In addition, they retrograde; upon cooling, these liquids form a sliceable gel, making them suitable for puddings and pie fillings. The drawback is that retrogradation eventually results in syneresis and, consequently, moisture loss.

In comparison, the use of root starches results in crystal clear and smooth liquids that are unfortunately unstable to excessive boiling, mechanical shear, and long hot holding. Root starches do not retrograde, making them less suitable for fillings, unless it is desired that the filling ooze out like a ripe camembert cheese. Root starches are suitable if clarity and a very smooth mouthfeel are desired.

Starches alone are often used to thicken sauces; the clarity and smoothness of a jus lié ("thickened juice") makes this the perfect accompaniment for a standing rib roast. If however, a pan gravy is desired, a roux should be used. Pan gravy is thicker than a jus lié and is expected to be velvety rather than glaze-like. A sauce thickened with starch to the same viscosity as a roux-thickened sauce has a slightly mucoidal mouthfeel. In addition, a roux-thickened sauce tends to be more stable to shear, long heating, and freezing and thawing.

Important in Far Eastern cooking, the more exotic starches such as tapioca, rice, mung bean, and sweet potato are mainly available in ethnic grocery stores. The exotic noodles, such as sweet potato noodles in Korea and mung bean starch threads in China and Vietnam, are evidence of the creative use of starches beyond thickening and binding.

For most starch-based noodles, a starch slurry is forced through a perforated disk into boiling water, resulting in long strands. Depending on the starch, these noodles can be crystal clear, like those based on sweet potato starch, or opaque, like rice noodles. For other varieties of starch-based noodles, the starch slurry is steamed into sheets that are cut into ribbon-style noodles. Thai rice noodles and Chinese mung bean noodles are good examples.

Another ingenious way to use starch is tapioca pearls. Tapioca is not used as much for thickening; a liquid thickened with pure tapioca starch is very clear but unpleasantly mucilaginous. Instead, the starch is processed into pearls or other shapes for textured beverages such as bubble tea or as a textural thickening component for tapioca pudding or fresh fruit pies.

Depending on geography, climate, and many other factors, the starches, flours, and starchy vegetables used in a cuisine vary tremendously. People had to come up with ingenious ideas to make food digestible and get the nutritional and epicurean bang for the buck. This ingenuity reflects the universal need to prepare a meal not only for sustenance but also for pleasure. At times, it seems we invest an unreasonable amount of energy in the preparation of food; it's much easier to just eat whole-grain porridge. However, thinking about all the good times spent at dining tables makes one realize that a good meal is much more than the sum of its nutrients.

FIGURE 8.5 **Comparison of root and cereal starches.**

Root Starch	Cereal Starch
• Thickens quickest at lower temperatures • Clear • Thickest when hot • Breaks down from mechanical shear, prolonged cooking, and hot holding • Stays viscous during cooking	• Requires higher temperature to thicken • Less clear • Retrogrades • Syneresis • Stable during mechanical shear, prolonged cooking, and hot holding

Carbohydrates in Nutrition

Carbohydrates, along with proteins and fats, constitute the three primary biomolecules from which humans get calories.

Sugars are the simplest carbohydrates. They fall primarily into the monosaccharides (glucose, galactose, and fructose, often called *simple sugars*) and disaccharides (sucrose, maltose, and lactose), which are made from the monosaccharides. Larger molecules called polysaccharides, made of many simple sugars bound together, form the other major class of carbohydrates: starches, glycogen, fiber, and gums, known as *complex carbohydrates*. An intermediate group of carbohydrates known as the oligosaccharides (a good source of prebiotics) are especially important in the gut, where they promote the growth of good bacteria (probiotics).

Carbohydrates are essential to good human nutrition. Most nutritionists feel that people should get 50 to 60 percent of their daily caloric intake from complex carbohydrates.[1] One gram of carbohydrate contributes 4 kcal (calories) to our diet. The body uses glucose, the ultimate breakdown product of virtually all digestible carbohydrates, to create energy for cellular respiration and to control brain functions. Glucose is the sugar we find in our blood. The word is from the Greek word *glykys*, meaning "sweet," and the *-ose* ending, which means "sugar." That said, the common term in the food industry for glucose is *dextrose*. In truth, glucose and dextrose are virtually identical.

The body breaks down all carbohydrates into monosaccharides. It then further breaks those down through a process called glycolysis to produce adenosine triphosphate (ATP). ATP is the molecule that actually provides energy for all vital processes in our bodies.

FIGURE 8.6   Disaccharide.

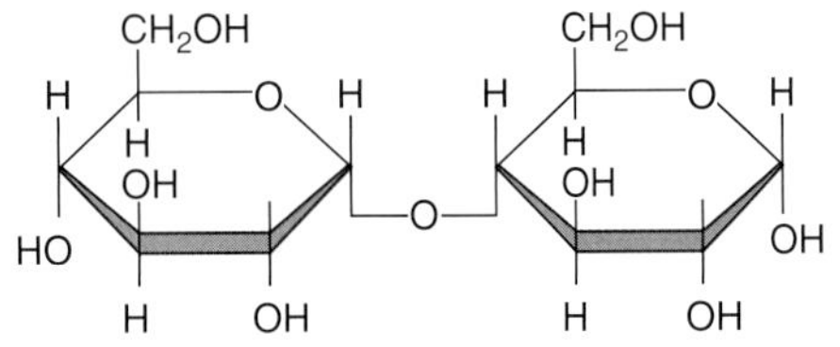

Source: Gum Technology Corporation.

FIGURE 8.7   Polysaccharide.

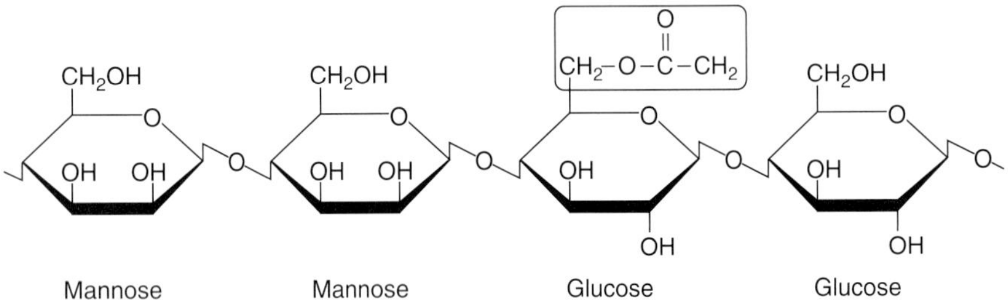

Mannose   Mannose   Glucose   Glucose

Source: Gum Technology Corporation.

FIGURE 8.8   Glucose molecule.

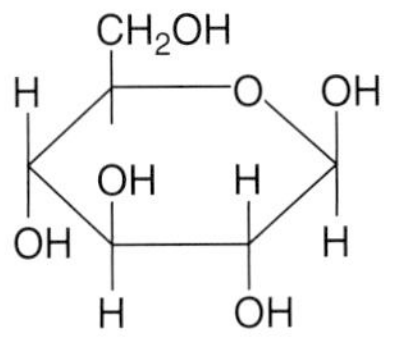

Source: Gum Technology Corporation.

FIGURE 8.9   Fructose molecule.

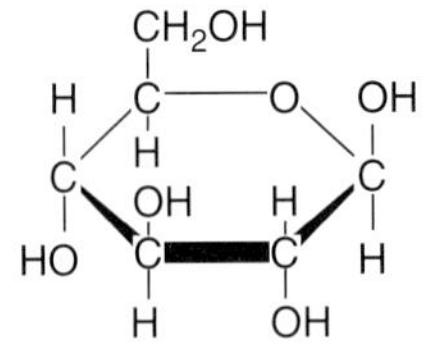

Source: Gum Technology Corporation.

When we take in more carbohydrates than we can use right away, initially the excess glucose is stored in the liver and muscles as glycogen, which is a form of rapid-release energy accessed by the body when it has used up its free glucose and needs replenishment. Glycogen is stored in extremely limited amounts, however, and once it is used up the body must replace its energy stores by consuming additional nutrients or by breaking down fat (the ultimate storage form of energy) and, ultimately, protein (but only as a last resort, after fat stores are depleted).

If more glucose is available beyond that which can be stored as glycogen, additional consumed nutrients (including carbohydrates) are turned into fat. If too much fat is stored, the body becomes overweight or obese. An obese person is someone who, as defined by the World Health Organization (WHO), the U.S. Centers for Disease Control (CDC), and the U.S. Department of Health and Human Services (DHHS), has a body mass index (BMI) greater than 30. The body mass index is calculated by dividing weight in pounds by height in inches times your height in inches again, and multiplying that by 703. The odd number of 703 is calculated by converting the original metric formula, also shown below.

$$BMI = \frac{(Weight\ in\ Pounds)}{(Height\ in\ Inches) \times (Height\ in\ Inches)} \times 703$$

or

$$BMI = \frac{Weight\ in\ Kilograms}{(Height\ in\ Meters) \times (Height\ in\ Meters)}$$

Obesity can lead to a wide range of health problems, including diabetes, heart disease, cancer, stroke, sleep apnea, and osteoarthritis.[2] In fact, the CDC's annual statistical review of causes of death considers overweight and obesity an increased risk factor in 10 percent of all deaths in the United States.

Glucose is essential to brain functions, and so the amount in the blood is carefully regulated by the pancreas, which releases insulin in response. Insulin delivers glucose to the cells in your body and also helps change it into glycogen for storage in the liver and muscles. Insulin also helps convert excess glucose to fat.

Diabetes is a disease that occurs when the body cannot process the glucose because the pancreas does not produce enough (or any) insulin and the body can't convert the glucose into glycogen, or because the body does not handle the insulin properly and not all of the glucose is converted into glycogen. If untreated, diabetes can lead to heart disease and kidney damage as well as increased chances of hypertension and high cholesterol. In extreme cases, blindness, amputation of the extremities, diabetic coma, and death can result. Diabetes, if not too severe, can be treated successfully by diet and exercise, but in more serious cases, sufferers must take insulin shots on a daily basis.

● Carbohydrates as Ingredients

Carbohydrates are more than just a source of fuel for the body. In food manufacturing, they are useful in creating structure, texture, and mouthfeel in foods, and when used in this context are referred to as *functional food ingredients*. Some of these can help build viscosity and maintain suspension of particulate matter, such as herbs in salad dressings, or help suspend flavor inclusions, such as fruit bits in batters or yogurt. Other carbohydrates can help create and maintain an emulsion (for example, mayonnaise or creamy salad dressing). Carbohydrates can also help retain moisture, reduce crystallization in frozen foods, prevent staling in baked goods, and keep food fresh longer by holding onto water and preventing the food from dehydrating. Sugar, of course, can also add sweetness.

Some carbohydrates are used to add bulk, replacing high-calorie ingredients such as fats with lower-calorie ingredients such as fiber. Fiber itself provides valuable nutritional benefits that aid in digestion and nutrient assimilation. Studies show that soluble fiber helps reduce blood cholesterol and coronary disease. Insoluble fiber absorbs and holds onto water in the intestine, helping waste pass more quickly through the digestive tract, which may help prevent colon cancer. Fiber

also adds to a feeling of satiety by making the stomach feel full, leading to reduced intake of foods.

The carbohydrates can be divided into four primary ingredient groups: sugars, starches, gums, and dietary fiber. Starches, gums, and fiber fall into the complex carbohydrate category, while sugars (monosaccharides, disaccharides, oligosaccharides) may be simple or complex. Gums and fiber are not digestible by humans and therefore provide no calories in the diet, nor are they a source of energy. They do have, however, an enormous influence on food formulation and health.

● Sugars

The FDA defines sugars as monosaccharides (glucose, fructose, and galactose) and disaccharides (lactose, maltose, and sucrose) in Title 21 Code of Federal regulations, Section 101.9(c)(6)(ii).[3] Monosaccharides are the smallest molecular units of the carbohydrates; they cannot be hydrolyzed (broken down) to smaller carbohydrates. A molecule consisting of two monosaccharides is classified as a disaccharide.

Sugars are used in food systems for a variety of functional reasons, with sweetness being the most obvious. Each sugar has its own level of sweetness and is compared to that of table sugar (sucrose).

Sugars are also used in formulations to affect humectancy (the ability of a product to resist loss of moisture)—an excellent example is soft, chewy cookies. A sugar is considered hygroscopic (able to absorb moisture) when it has a high degree of humectancy.

Some sugars are known as reducing sugars; these are used to promote browning and add flavor to foods. Reducing sugars include all of the monosaccharides and two of the disaccharides (lactose and maltose, but not sucrose). All have a highly reactive end on their molecular structure that works in conjunction with the proteins present in a food (and some form of dry heat) to form compounds that produce distinctive brown flavors, colors, and aromas. This reaction is called Maillard browning (one form of non-enzymatic browning); examples include the browned crust in baked or toasted breads and cakes, roasted coffee beans, chocolate, and the color, flavor, and recognizable smells of grilled or roasted meats.

Caramelization is another form of non-enzymatic browning, but it does not rely on the presence of proteins or amino acids. Rather, the browning is the result of pyrolysis (chemical breakdown of the sugars due to heating), and any sugar, including sucrose (most often used for this purpose) can participate in the reaction. Typical examples are flan, crème brûlée, and the browning of vegetables by grilling or sautéing.

Many formulations take advantage of the relatively small molecular size of sugars. Water activity (a_w) is a measurement used to determine the amount of unbound or free water in a food system. This should not be confused with the food's moisture content, or a_w; it reflects *only* the water in a food system available for spoilage reactions or microbial metabolic processes to occur. The more molecules of solute are dissolved in an aqueous system (the solvent), the more water is bound to them and the less is available to take part in deleterious reactions such as hydrolytic rancidity in fatty foods, moisture migration in baked goods, and microbial spoilage. Sugar molecules are relatively small compared to most other ingredients (such as starches, fats, fiber, and proteins), and thus, considering equal weights of each, more sugar molecules are present than molecules of any other ingredients. With more molecules dissolved and tying up more water molecules, less free water is available, resulting in significantly reduced water activity. In general, reducing water activity prolongs the shelf life of a food. (Increasing the salt concentration yields a similar benefit but is appropriate for savory foods only.)

Another important function of sugars is the role they play as a substrate for fermentation in foods such as yeast-raised baked goods, alcoholic beverages, fermented sausages (like pepperoni), cultured dairy, and pickled vegetable products.

Monosaccharides
Glucose (Dextrose)

The terms *glucose* and *dextrose* are used interchangeably, with certain food industry segments or regions preferring one over the other. Glucose is the most common hexose (6-carbon sugar) found in foods, and it is naturally present in fruits, honey, and some vegetables. It also serves as the building block for virtually all other carbohydrates, from disaccharides to gums to the enormously large and complex starches and fiber. Commercially, glucose is produced by the complete hydrolysis of starch, and in the United States is made almost exclusively from corn starch. Glucose is a hygroscopic reducing sugar with lower sweetness than table sugar. The most readily fermentable carbohydrate, it is used extensively in commercial yeast-raised baked goods. Glucose is a component in regular and high-fructose corn syrups, providing each a significant portion of their characteristic functionalities of humectancy (moisture holding) and browning. Commercial glucose is available as a fine powder, in crystalline form, and as a high-solids syrup.

Fructose (Levulose)

Fructose is the second most common monosaccharide. This reducing sugar is produced commercially by enzymatically converting glucose. In the United States, it is commercially derived from cornstarch. Fructose is found in nature in many fruits, which explains its other name: fruit sugar. It is the sweetest of the natural sugars, considered 1.5 times sweeter than table sugar. Fructose is unique in that it is found with two isomers (identical formulas but different shapes) that coexist in solution. One shape has a sweetness rating at or below that of sucrose, the other much higher. Temperature and acidity affect which shape predominates and are the reason hot tea or coffee sweetened with fructose is less sweet

than that sweetened with an equal amount of table sugar. Fructose is considered an excellent humectant and provides moisture retention for extended periods—soft, chewy cookies being a prime example. Commercially fructose is available as a crystalline solid, but the use of pure fructose is limited due to cost and difficulty of storage and handling because of its high degree of hygroscopicity (ability to absorb moisture from the air) and resultant stickiness. Instead, fructose is most commonly used in combination with dextrose in high-fructose corn syrup.

The glycemic index (GI) is a measure of the effect of carbohydrates on blood sugar levels. A carbohydrate absorbed into the bloodstream quickly, such as glucose, is considered to have a high GI, and one absorbed into the bloodstream more slowly, such as oat bran, is considered to have a low GI. Recent scientific evidence shows that individuals who follow a low-GI diet over many years are at significantly lower risk than others for developing both Type II diabetes and coronary heart disease. High blood glucose levels or repeated glycemic spikes following a meal may promote these diseases by increasing stress to the blood vessels and also by the direct increase in insulin levels.[4] Fructose is not digested the same way as other sugars (it is exclusively metabolized in the liver), and as a result has a low glycemic index. For example, glucose has a GI of 100, because it is quickly digested and released into the blood. Sucrose has a GI of 65, because it is 50 percent glucose. Fructose, in comparison, has a GI of only 19, lowest of all the natural sugars. That said, recent evidence shows that too much fructose in the diet may result in the development of insulin resistance, liver disease, and a condition known as *metabolic syndrome* that includes obesity, elevated triglycerides and decreased HDL (good cholesterol) in the blood, and elevated blood pressure. It is always better to eat a varied diet and spread the risks rather than to restrict the diet to a limited number of potentially harmful foods.

Galactose

Galactose together with glucose makes up lactose, or milk sugar. Galactose is about one-third the sweetness of sucrose, but it does supply energy (calories), so it is considered a nutritive sweetener. Its primary function in processed foods is as a component of hydrocolloid gums (galactomannans such as gum Arabic, agar-agar, and guar gum), commonly used for moisture management in a variety of foods.

Disaccharides
Maltose (Malt Sugar)

Maltose is a disaccharide formed from two units of glucose. Its chief importance in food processing is as a fermentable substrate for yeast in the production of alcohol (ethanol), particularly in the brewing industry.

During malting, cereals, especially barley, are soaked and then allowed to germinate in order for amylase enzymes in the grain to become activated and to start hydrolyzing the starches into maltose. This conversion stage is known as mashing. Once the complete conversion of starches into maltose occurs, the grains are kilned (heated and dried), and are then ready to be used in brewing.

Malted grains or flours are used to make, in addition to beer, malt whiskey, and malted milk beverages (such as Ovaltine), and to provide a malty flavor to candies (malted milk balls) and baked products (such as bagels).

Lactose (Milk Sugar)

Lactose is derived from milk—hence its other name, *milk sugar*. It is one of the few carbohydrates derived from an animal source. It is a reducing sugar formed from the combination of the two monosaccharides, glucose and galactose. Lactose is commercially extracted from whey, a by-product of cheese manufacturing. It is most commonly added to food formulations as a component of dried whey (up to 75 percent lactose). Whey also contains highly functional milk proteins that provide multiple benefits to the formulations into which it is incorporated, including enhanced nutrition, enhanced binding and foaming properties, and enhanced water-holding properties, along with the browning and dairy flavor notes from the lactose. Lactose is the least sweet of the commonly used sugars.

There are large populations of lactose-intolerant individuals in the United States and around the world, particularly in or from areas where dairy animals are rare or nonexistent. These people lack the lactase enzyme required to break down the lactose molecule to its constituent monosaccharides. This results in gastrointestinal distress, which can be quite unpleasant. Over-the-counter enzyme replacement supplements are available (for example, Lactaid), as are pre-treated milks and other dairy products. Fermented dairy products, such as aged cheeses and yogurt, in which the lactose is broken down by bacterial fermentation, are also well tolerated.

Sucrose (Table Sugar)

Sucrose is the standard to which all other sugars are compared. Sucrose is generally called *sugar* in the United States, and until the advent of high-fructose corn syrup (HFCS) it was the most common sweetener used industrially. Today, HFCS is preferred (especially in the bottled beverage industry) due to its lower cost and instant solubility. Sugar is commercially extracted and refined from both sugarcane and sugar beets. It is a disaccharide consisting of one molecule each of glucose and fructose; their respective reactive ends are bound to each other, making this a non-reducing sugar—that is, it won't support Maillard browning. Sucrose is commercially available in granulated forms from very large crystalline coarse sugar for high-visibility coatings, to medium granulation (household sugar), bakers' special, superfine (or castor), and ultra-fine particulates, including confectioner's sugar. Particle size affects the ease with which the sugar becomes solubilized (dissolves). Thus

the finer bakers' special sugar is used in low-moisture/high-fat bakery items because it is incorporated more easily than the larger granules of household sugar.

Powdered forms of sucrose, known as *fondant* or *confectioner's sugar*, are available in 10X (finest), 6X, and 4X (coarsest). These products are made from ground crystalline sugar to which 3 percent cornstarch is often added to inhibit caking (ground sucrose is strongly hygroscopic). These powdered forms are essential in low-moisture/high-fat systems where granular sugar does not dissolve. In frostings, icings, whipped cream, and meringues, powdered sugar is used to achieve a highly sweetened yet smooth texture not attainable with coarse ground sugars, which cause a gritty mouthfeel.

Light, medium, and dark brown sugars are commercially made by coating refined white sugar with molasses (3.5 to 6.5 percent, respectively). Molasses is the syrup remaining after sucrose is extracted from cane or sugar beet juice during the refining process. There are also naturally brown-colored sugars (turbinado, demerara, muscovado) that are not refined but rather heated and allowed to crystallize in the presence of the naturally occurring sugarcane juices during the initial pressing of the cane. Because these sugars are not whitened using bone char (the method of choice for cane sugar), they are considered vegan, unlike standard brown sugar.

During the sugar-making process, juice extracted from sugarcane or sugar beets is boiled until the sugars crystallize and precipitate out. (As noted above, the syrup left after crystallization is molasses.) Typically, sugarcane juice undergoes three cycles of boiling and crystallization to extract as much sugar as possible. With each successive cycle, the leftover molasses contains less sugar:

- *Light Molasses:* This is the syrup left over after the first boiling cycle of sugarcane juice. This molasses is the lightest in color and has the highest sugar content and the least viscous texture.
- *Dark Molasses:* Dark molasses is the by-product of the second boiling cycle of sugarcane. This molasses is darker and more viscous than light molasses, and contains less sugar.
- *Blackstrap Molasses:* This is the final by-product of the third boiling cycle in the sugar-making process. Blackstrap molasses contains the least sugar and has the highest concentration of vitamins and minerals. It has a very dark color and is extremely viscous in texture. Because this type of molasses is highly concentrated, it has a deep, pungent flavor.

Molasses is also available as unsulfured and sulfured. The sulfured variety tends to have a lighter color and flavor.

Sucrose is also commercially available in liquid form as simple syrup (50 percent sucrose and 50 percent water) and in custom blends of sucrose and dextrose and sucrose and corn syrup. These are tailored to the functional needs of the product or customer and bring a high degree of efficiency with respect to ease of transport, storage, and use.

Another liquid sweetener made from sucrose is invert sugar, made by the hydrolysis of sucrose into glucose and fructose. Invert sugar is sweeter than the parent sucrose due to the presence of the sweeter-tasting fructose, and it is substantially more hygroscopic, which aids in keeping products like baked goods moist. It is also used to control crystallization in syrups and liquid candy fillings. Invert syrup has been replaced in most commercial applications by HFCS, which has similar functionality and better economics.

Honey

Honey is a sweet, syrupy, distinctly flavored sweetener made primarily by honeybees from the nectar of flowers. The bees repeatedly ingest and regurgitate the nectar until it is partially digested and takes on the sensory and functional qualities of honey. At this point the honey is placed in unsealed honeycomb cells, where it is fanned by thousands of bees' wings until it dehydrates and concentrates to the point where the water activity is so low (a_w <0.6) that fermentation cannot take place. The cells are then capped, and the honey remains in the hive until needed.

Being a product of nature, the chemical makeup of honey is variable and depends on the bee's diet, the types of flowers in the vicinity, the climate, and the time of year, among other factors. However, honey is primarily a combination of fructose (38 percent), glucose (31 percent), and water (17 percent), with several other minor constituents, mainly other sugars and trace amounts of vitamins, minerals, and assorted phytochemicals. Honey supplies approximately 3 calories per gram and can be as much as 1.5 times sweeter than table sugar, depending on the amount of fructose present. Due to its low water activity and acidic pH of <4.0, honey has an extremely long shelf life at ambient temperatures if capped to keep out moisture. Honey should not be used in infant formulas (under the age of one year) because heat-resistant botulism spores may be present that infant digestive systems cannot defend against.

Interestingly, honey is not considered appropriate for vegan diets for the same reason milk is prohibited: Both are considered animal products.

Commercially, honey can be purchased by color, floral source, and grade (A-B-C grading is based on total solids, water content, flavor, aroma, and clarity). It is available pasteurized, whipped, and spray-dried. It is popular as an ingredient in baked goods, condiments, candies, lozenges, and beverages, and as a common replacement for table sugar. It is also used to make mead, a honey-flavored wine.

Maple Syrup

Maple syrup is made by boiling and concentrating the sap collected each spring from maple trees. It takes approximately 10 gallons of sap (the average total seasonal production from one tree) to make 1 quart of syrup.

Canada is the largest producer of maple syrup, and the United States is the largest consumer. Maple syrup is most often eaten as a breakfast syrup, but it is also used as an ingredient, flavoring, and sweetener in candies, baked goods, hot cereals, ice cream, and other sweet applications.

Maple syrup is approximately 67 percent carbohydrates, of which the majority is sucrose, and 30 percent water. It is an excellent source of several minerals, including calcium, iron, manganese, and zinc, and provides 2.6 calories per gram.

Commercially, maple syrup is available in several grades, all based on color, density, and flavor intensity. The former U.S. grades were: *A* (Light Amber, Medium Amber, and Dark Amber), *B* (darker than Grade A Dark Amber), and *C* (Commercial Grade). But following an initiative started in Vermont (the largest producer in the United States) in 2014, in 2015 they were changed to Grade A Golden Color With Delicate Taste, Grade A Amber Color With Rich Taste, Grade A Dark With Robust Taste, and Grade A Very Dark With Strong Taste. The last one is sold for strictly commercial usage. The new standards are meant to signify more clearly to consumers what they should expect to taste in a particular bottle of maple syrup in a way that the previous grading system didn't.

Imitation maple syrup is also widely used as a cheaper alternative. It is typically made from HFCS flavored with sotolone, a major aroma and flavor component of the fenugreek seed. At low concentrations, it smells like maple (at higher concentrations it smells like curry; fenugreek is a major spice component of curry powders). Syrups that use a small amount of real maple along with maple-like flavorings can be labeled "maple flavored," but syrups made with no maple content at all cannot use the word *maple* in their names. Instead, they must be labeled "pancake syrup," "waffle syrup," or other fanciful names.

Agave Nectar

Agave nectar is a natural sweetener from the same Mexican plant from which tequila is made. It comes in three varieties: light, amber, and raw. While agave is thinner than honey, it is slightly thicker than simple syrup. Agave syrup is composed mainly of fructose, so it shares the same sweetness level—approximately 1.5 times sweeter than sucrose. It also shares the same relatively low glycemic index of fructose. Agave is not calorie-free—it contains 20 calories per teaspoon, 5 more than granulated sugar—but because it's sweeter than sugar, less is needed to achieve the same level of sweetness.

Previously, agave syrup was the preferred sweetener of the healthy eating crowd, but recent reports have suggested that a diet high in fructose (and agave syrup has the highest level of fructose of any sweetener, even more than high-fructose corn syrup) can lead to an assortment of unhealthy outcomes, including weight gain (especially belly fat) and childhood obesity, insulin resistance, increased risk of metabolic syndrome and heart disease, among others. Limiting intake of fructose in such a concentrated form is now as strongly recommended as reducing intake of high-fructose corn syrup.

Polyols

Polyols, also known as sugar alcohols, are carbohydrates, but they are neither a sugar nor an alcohol. Being sweet but not being a sugar qualifies them as sugar-free, and they are often used in formulations using the "no sugar added/reduced sugar" nutritional claim. Most polyols are less sweet than sucrose and have a lower caloric content. Most of them are suitable for products designed for diabetics because they cause low to no insulin response on ingestion. Polyols uniquely have a negative heat of solution, which explains why many of them evoke a cooling sensation as they dissolve in the mouth. They are also non-cariogenic (do not cause cavities) and are therefore widely employed by manufacturers of sugar-free products. They are only partially absorbed in the small intestine; hence, they enter the large intestine intact. In the lower gut, polyols can cause flatulence and laxation similar to non-absorbed, fermentable carbohydrates (in varying degrees, depending on the polyol and differences in individual responses).[5]

Sorbitol is a naturally occurring sugar alcohol, although most is commercially manufactured by hydrogenating dextrose. It has a sweetness intensity value of 60 (sucrose = 100), high solubility in water, and can develop high viscosity in solution. It provides mouth-cooling and has a low propensity to participate in browning reactions. Because of its hygroscopicity, sorbitol has good humectant properties, retaining moisture in baked goods, which prolongs freshness, and reduces water activity by binding free water molecules and reducing their ability to participate in chemical reactions, thereby extending shelf life. This is important in intermediate moisture products, such as breads and flour tortillas, which support mold growth when no humectants are used. Sorbitol is suitable for incorporation into products for diabetics. It is often used in reduced-calorie or sugar-free cakes, candies, and chewing gum.

Erythritol is commercially produced from fermentation by the yeast *Monilliela pollinis*. It has an extremely low caloric value and a relative sweetness value of 60 to 70 percent of sucrose. It is often used as a sugar replacer in candy and bakery products where the bulk of the sugar must be replaced. Much of it is absorbed in the small intestine and thus does not promote the gastric distress seen with many of the polyols. Erythritol does not crystallize, nor is it hygroscopic, and thus it is often used in combination with other sugar replacers to overcome these shortcomings. It has a cool, minty aftertaste.

Isomalt is used extensively in the manufacture of sugar-free hard candy due to its excellent crystallization properties and its compatibility with traditional hard candy manufacturing lines. It has a sweetness intensity of 50 to 60 when compared to sucrose, and no cariogenic potential. It has low solubility in water, low tendency to brown when heated, and a minimal cooling effect on dissolution.

Lactitol has a sweetness intensity of 30 to 40 when compared to sucrose. It has no cariogenic potential, is highly suitable for diabetic products, and does not brown when exposed to heat. It has little aftertaste, which makes it ideal for applications such as chewing gums, chocolates, and jams.

Maltitol has good heat stability and low hygroscopicity, resists microbial breakdown, and displays moderate solubility in water. Its sweetness intensity is 90. Maltitol is used in baked goods to retain moisture and in beverages and confectionery products as a sweetener.

Mannitol is a naturally occurring sugar alcohol with a sweetness intensity value of 50. It exhibits a pleasant, low mouth-cooling effect. It exhibits low water solubility and it does not brown.

Xylitol is a naturally occurring sugar alcohol that finds its main application in sugar-free gums due to its negative cariogenic potential and its sugar intensity value of 100. It displays high water solubility, low propensity to browning, and high mouth-cooling effect.

High-Intensity Sweeteners

High-intensity sweeteners, as their name suggests, provide many times the sweetness of standard sucrose. Most are calorie free, but even those that provide calories are used at such low levels that their caloric effect is negligible. Because they are used at low levels, they are often combined with maltodextrins or polyols to replace the bulk and functional gap created by the absence of sugars.

These sweeteners can be divided into two camps: synthetics and naturals. Of the synthetics, only Suralose (bulked and sold at retail under the Splenda® brand in yellow packets) is derived from a carbohydrate (chlorinated sucrose); it is about 600 times the sweetness of table sugar. It is heat- and low pH-stable, which makes it a good choice for heat-processed or acidified foods.

Of the naturals, stevia, extracted from the leaves of an herb in the sunflower family and native to Asia and South and Central America, provides the highest intensity at 300 times the sweetness of regular sugar. The taste of stevia is said to have a slower onset and longer duration than that of sugar. However, some of its extracts may have a bitter or licorice-like aftertaste at high concentrations. Stevia was approved by the FDA for use in foods in 2008.

Luo han guo is a fruit native to southwestern China that has been used for centuries as a natural sweetener, medicinal, and longevity aid. It is about 250 times sweeter than sugar and dissolves well in beverages. There are no reported incidents of negative side effects. It is classed by the FDA as a GRAS product, with no restrictions on consuming the fruit or its extracts. The extract is currently used in this country as a sweetener in natural cereals, herbal teas, and low-calorie juice drinks.

⬤ Starches

When we consider starch as an ingredient, we think of adding it to meat drippings and then stirring over heat while waiting for it to thicken. We think of the gravy boat in the refrigerator the day after—the gelatinous mass with the split in the top surrounded by a pool of liquid. Have you asked why?

FIGURE 8.10 Molecular structures of starch.

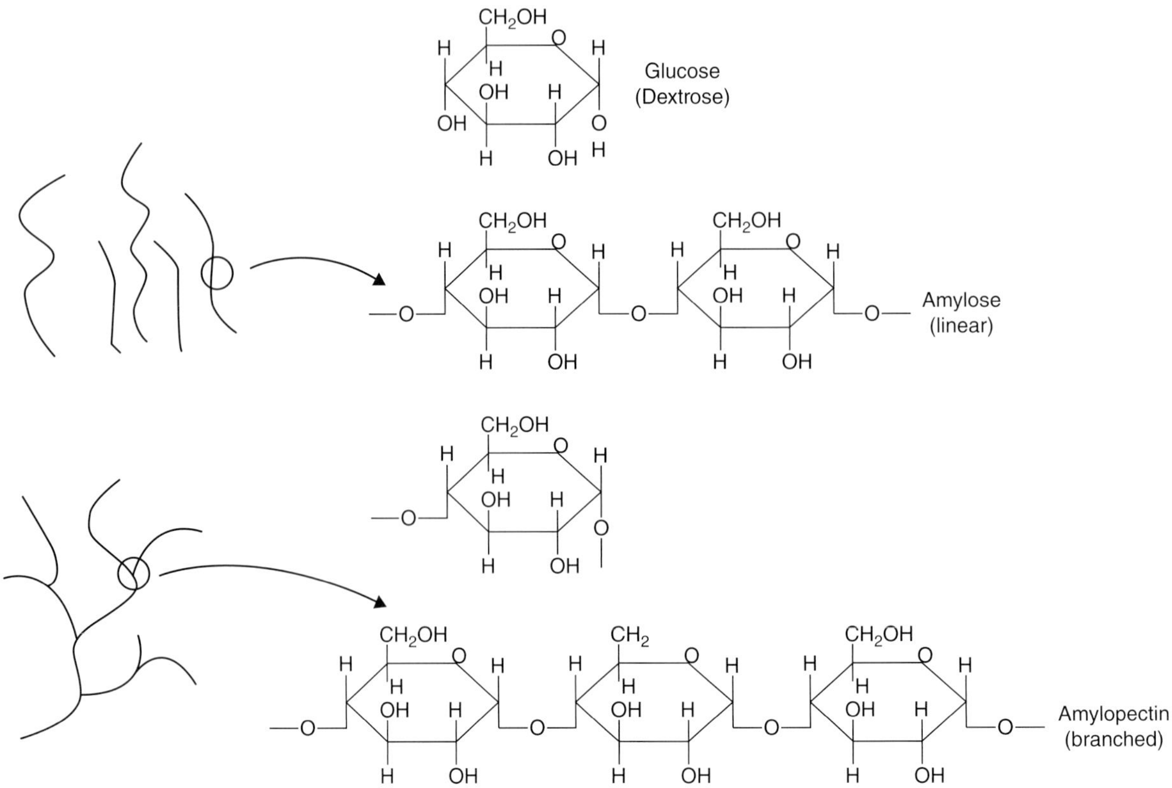

Have you ever wondered why the pie filling made from fresh fruit is firm, dull, and opaque but that from a can or in a store-bought pie is flowing and shiny? The answer to this question is starch.

Although starches are most often used for thickening, they are also used to provide adhesion (batters and breading), film formation (nut and snack coatings), moisture retention (meats and bakery applications), glazes (toppings), dusting (confections and bakery), and stabilization (fermented dairy and frozen desserts). In most applications, starches are easy to work with and inexpensive relative to the role they play in a formulation.

Starches are generally white to off-white in color. Most are not soluble in water but rather form dispersions. Stirring a spoonful of starch into a cup of water yields a white, opaque liquid. On standing, the starch settles to the bottom. Starches are considered tasteless, but "bland-tasting" might be a better description, and if not completely "cooked out," they will leave a powdery mouthfeel when consumed.

Starches are produced by green plants as a highly compact means of storing energy. Depending on the plant, starches can be found in the stem, leaves, root, fruit, or seeds. The predominant source in the United States is corn (seed), with wheat (seed), rice (seed), and potato (root) having some significance. Each source of starch may require a different separation process to extract the starch portion for human use from the remainder of the plant, but regardless of the botanical source or the refinement process, starch is made up of multiple glucose molecules joined in a linear fashion like the links of a chain. Picture this chain coiled like a spring, 1000 to 10,000 glucose units in length, and you have the linear starch molecule called amylose. A second molecular form of starch is amylopectin, which is also helical, but it has much longer chain lengths of 300,000 to 3,000,000 glucose units and branch chains as well.

Starches from any source are made up of amylose and amylopectin, and it is the ratio of these two molecules and their different molecular structures that give each starch its characteristic functional properties.[6] In nature, the majority of starchy foods contain a mixture of 75 percent amylopectin and 25 percent amylose.

These two structures are synthesized by the plant and built into a highly compacted form called a starch granule. The size and shape of the starch granules are particular to each plant source, but all are extremely small and measured in microns. The length across the head of a pin is approximately 1 millimeter, which is 1000 microns. Potato granules are the largest of the common food starches, and they measure only 100 microns. The smallest starch granules are from rice and are measure 1 to 3 microns.

Starches are often compared to each other and their suitability for a particular application by looking at their viscosity profile: a measurement of their thickening power over a given temperature range. A reproducible viscosity profile can be

FIGURE 8.11 Starch granule hydration.

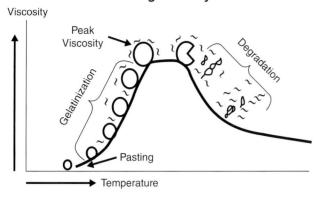

created from a starch-water dispersion of known starch concentration as it is heated, cooled, and mixed at controlled rates at targeted temperatures. The two instruments most commonly employed for this job are the Brabender Visco-amylograph (Brabender) and the Rapid Visco Analyzer (RVA). Both measure and record the apparent starch viscosity via its resistance to torque (a twisting force that tends to cause rotation) generated by the instrument's rotating paddle or spindle. The profiles generated by both the Brabender and the RVA show the initiation of viscosity as the starch slurry reaches its gelatinization temperature.

Gelatinization is the point where starch granules begin to hydrate and swell, and an increase in viscosity of the slurry is observed. Some form of energy input is required to weaken the crystalline structure of the granules in order for water to enter the granule. Heat and mechanical shear (stirring is the most common form of shear energy) are the usual forms of energy applied to make the granules absorb water and begin swelling.

During the heating phase, some amylose leaches from the granules into the water because the amylose molecules are relatively small and unbranched, and thus diffuse more easily out of the granules. The combination of the water-bonding character of the leached amylose molecules and the increased friction between the swelling starch granules gives starch its thickening ability. Viscosity is a function of the internal friction of a fluid—its tendency to resist flow. Increasing viscosity thus is a result of an increase of internal friction due to the reduction of free movement of the dispersed solids from the enlarging granules and to the continuing seepage of amylose into the liquid. As heating continues, more of the starch granules swell and enlarge until the majority are fully hydrated. On the viscosity profile, a point of peak viscosity is noted.[7]

Confusion exists in the starch industry, as some people use the term pasting temperature to refer to the gelatinization temperature while others use it to indicate the point of peak viscosity. Pasting actually starts as gelatinization of the granule begins and continues until peak viscosity is reached. At this point the starch is said to be pasted.

Many profile-testing protocols are programmed to hold at a high temperature for a prolonged time in order to evaluate the starch's stability under conditions of extended heating and mechanical shear. Appropriately enough, this is called the hold phase; it mimics conditions of extended thermal processing typically used in industry. Pasted, fully swollen, hydrated granules are highly susceptible to shear.[8] Starch granules from many of the native unmodified starches begin to break from the constant agitation during this phase. As the granules fracture, a resultant reduction of viscosity is observed. Viscosity stability may be assessed by comparing peak viscosity to the viscosity measured at the end of the heating phase of the profile. A reduction of viscosity is called breakdown.

A cooling phase usually follows the high-temperature hold. The term for the general increase of viscosity seen during this phase is retrogradation or setback; the higher the viscosity in the cooling phase, the more setback a starch exhibits. The increase of viscosity is due to the reassociation or realignment of the amylose molecules leached from the granules during the heating phases. A good example of amylose retrogradation is the gravy boat in the refrigerator the day after Thanksgiving, where the creamy-smooth and flowing gravy has solidified into a gelled mass. Amylopection molecules also reassociate, but at a much slower rate. An example

FIGURE 8.12 Starch viscosity profile.

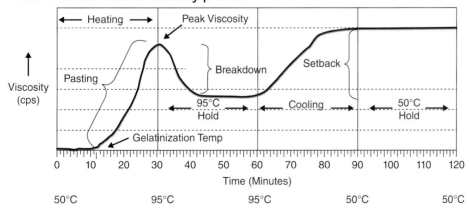

FIGURE 8.13 Native starch granules.

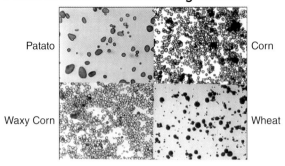

Patato

Corn

Waxy Corn

Wheat

FIGURE 8.14 Microscopy of starch granule hydration.

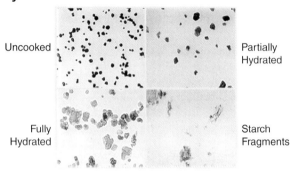

Uncooked

Partially Hydrated

Fully Hydrated

Starch Fragments

of amylopectin retrogradation is bread staling. After baking and cooling, these branched chain molecules retreat from their dilated state to a more compacted state as staling progresses, resulting the hardening of the crumb structure over time.[9]

A microscope can be used as an excellent quality control (QC) tool in a food manufacturing facility to evaluate starch efficacy. A slide can be easily prepared from a starch slurry or a food containing starch. A drop of 5 percent iodine solution on the sample dyes the starch granules, which can be viewed using a microscope at 200 times magnification. It becomes obvious if the granules are gelatinized, partially swollen, fully pasted, or even to the point of fracturing. Microscopy can be used during processing as an operations tool to ensure the starch granules reach optimum hydration, often referred to as being *cooked out*. This technique can also be implemented later as a quality check on finished products. With a little experience one can determine the source of the starch by its characteristic size and shape as well as the stage of granule hydration.

Native Starches

Starches are commercially available from numerous plant sources, most commonly corn (maize), cassava (tapioca), wheat, potato, and rice. Pure starches from all sources are almost entirely digestible. Protein and fat content of starches

is negligible. Starches extracted directly from the plant source without modification (chemical or physical treatment) are simply termed *starch*, *unmodified starch*, or native starch, and are considered a natural ingredient. Starches from cereal grains have higher gelatinization temperatures and correspondingly higher temperatures for peak viscosity than those from roots or tubers. Potato and tapioca starches cook out much faster than corn, wheat, or rice starches. Starches from grains produce gels that are short-textured, firm, and opaque, while those of potato and tapioca are usually gummy and more pliable.

Native starches, although excellent for many food applications when prepared and consumed quickly, tend not to have functional stability suitable for large-volume processing, extended heated holding times, low-pH environments, retorting, long-term refrigerated storage, or freeze/thaw stability. Using native cornstarch to prepare gravy is a good illustration. The gravy may be superb when prepared immediately before serving, but hold it on a steam table and over time the gravy thins. This change of viscosity is due to the deterioration of the starch granules from the constant input of heat energy. Starches with ruptured granules or even intact granules that have leached a large degree of amylose show lower viscosity than the same starch with intact, fully swollen granules.

If the same gravy is refrigerated overnight, the next day it appears as a gelled mass with perhaps a split or two in the gel and water separating out. This is the result of starch retrogradation—the realignment and reassociation of the amylose molecules. Retrogradation of amylose molecules reduces the spacing between the molecules, which actually squeezes water out of the gel matrix. As the starch molecules become more tightly packed, the system becomes denser, more opaque, and less shiny, and syneresis (weeping) occurs. Retrogradation of amylose can be reversed, although temperatures as high as 239 to 248°F (115 to 120°C) may be required. Retrograded amylopectin gels are softer and are more easily reversed, with heating temperatures of only 122 to 185°F (50 to 85°C) required.[10] The long, stringy texture of retrograded amylopectin is relatively unappealing for most food systems.

Culinologists developing products for foodservice or retail applications must consider the conditions these foods encounter not only in processing and packaging but at every step in distribution, marketing, and consumption as well. Consider the gravy described above. The gravy may be heat-processed in a steam-jacketed kettle and pumped across a factory floor to the filling area. Both heating and pumping add stresses to the swollen starch granules, which increases their propensity to fracture. This gravy might then be hot-filled and boxed without cooling. Once packaged, stack heat, or heat retained in the product, can remain entrapped for days and continue to stress the starch system. Alternatively, this gravy might be pouched and frozen—another temperature stress on the formulation.

High heating temperatures combined with refrigerated or frozen storage actually induce retrogradation faster than room-temperature storage.

Thermal energy is not the only form of stress applied to a starch system in a food formulation. Shear is a form of mechanical energy input and can affect granule hydration and, perhaps more importantly, granule fracturing. Shear is introduced via the common industry practices of pumping, mixing, and homogenizing.

Another form of stress is high acidity (low pH). Formulations with high acid content affect granule hydration and fracturing during processing as well. In cherry pie filling, for example, the high acid content of the cherries might cause the starch granules to fracture and thus induce a loss of thickening at a temperature considered optimum for a more neutral pH system, like the gravy. The functional limitations of native starches in commercial food processing explain the need to use modified starches, which are designed to survive in these complex systems.

Chemically Modified Starches

All modified starches are not created equal, as each modification is designed for a specific purpose and function. The most common application for starch is thickening, and therefore the most common modifications are those that enable the starches to withstand the common stresses from processing—heat, acid, freezing and shear—and retain thickening power. Starch modifications are also made to improve the temperature of gelatinization, hot viscosity, and gel strength. Others improve adhesion of one food to another or simply make the starch appear whiter. Although any native starch can be modified, the most commonly used in the United States is corn. The chemicals used for food starch modification, their respective levels, and their combinations thereof are outlined in Title 21 of the Code of Federal Regulations, Section 172.892.

Cross-Linked Starches

Cross-linked starches are treated with a chemical that forms bridges between the starch molecules. This cross-linking makes the granules more resistant to gelatinization as it inhibits swelling. This inhibition is directly proportional to the amount of cross-linking. As a cross-linked starch is heated, peak viscosity can actually be higher than that of the native starch as the starch granules are more resistant to both fracture and amylose leaching throughout the stress of continuous cooking. Therefore more granules remain intact and do not fracture as others continue to swell and add viscosity to the system. A highly cross-linked starch may never develop a peak viscosity on an RVA or Brabender viscometer if the granules are over-inhibited and resist swelling under the viscometers' limited operating temperatures. This high degree of cross-linking is designed for retorted foods where temperatures of 250°F (120°C) are reached and early viscosity development is a disadvantage because it slows heat penetration.

Cooking starch in an acidic environment often results in a rapid viscosity decline. Again, cross-linking can ameliorate this phenomenon by strengthening the bonds between the starch molecules.

Viscosity stability is not the only benefit from cross-linking, as paste texture is also affected. Keeping the starch granules intact allows for a shorter, smoother texture versus a texture considered long, gummy, or stringy.

Substituted Starches

Pasted native starches retrograde with time, changing the texture from a paste to a firm paste or even a rigid gel, if the particular starch has significant amylose content. As retrogradation progresses, the starch's appearance changes from clear or translucent to opaque. Starch manufacturers can modify native starches using a substitution reaction. This process binds a chemical to the starch molecules, creating a larger, bulkier molecular structure. By doing this, the amylose molecules can no longer reassociate as closely as before. A good analogy is the live Christmas tree wrapped in twine as it arrives at the store; remove the twine, and it is no longer as compact as it was when shipped. Because the molecules cannot realign as tightly, the paste retains a more smooth and creamy texture versus the cuttable gel indicative of retrograded amylose, and it retains the clarity seen in the pasted sol (a semisolid dispersion). Along with the sustained clarity comes a reduction of syneresis; the starch molecules are unable to fit closely together, so water is not squeezed from the system. Substitution gives long-term stability to a starch-containing food—especially important in refrigerated and frozen food applications (such as TV dinner gravies).

Substitution has a secondary benefit: The energy needed to gelatinize these bulky molecules is reduced. Imagine a wedge splitting firewood. As the wedge is driven into the grain of the wood, initially the log separates only enough to allow the wedge to penetrate—until that last tap with the maul, when the entire log abruptly splits apart. Substitution creates an internal force in the granule so less external energy is needed for it to expand. The effect is that the substituted starches begin to hydrate and reach optimum hydration (and viscosity) earlier in the cooking process than would the native starch from which it was made.

Stabilized Starches

The term stabilized starch is generally understood to mean modified starches that are both cross-linked and substituted. *Dual-modified starch* is another common term for the same thing. Stabilized starches are most commonly used for applications where a clear, heat- and perhaps acid-tolerant freeze-thaw–stable thickener is needed. A classic example is a cherry pie filling. Compare two fillings made with different starches:

Cherry Pie Filling

Ingredients for Each Version

Water	90 g
63 DE corn syrup	110 g
Sugar	83 g
Lemon juice	5 g
Salt	1 g
IQF cherries	500 g
Prepared 9-inch pie shells	2

For **Version 1,** use 31 g unmodified cornstarch; for **Version 2**, use 31 g stabilized, bake-stable cornstarch.

Procedure:

1) Prepare 2 fillings by mixing 83 g sugar, 110 g corn syrup, 1 g salt, 5 g lemon juice, and 100 g cherries (including liquid from cherries, if any) into each of two heating vessels.

2) Prepare two slurries, mixing each starch in 90 g water.

3) Add one starch slurry to each pot and heat, stirring, to 190°F (87°C), or until a light boil is observed.

4) Add the remaining 400 g cherries to each vessel and carefully blend into the mixture to prevent damaging the fruit.

5) Fill one 9-inch pie crust with each mixture.

6) Bake at 425°F (218°C) for 15 minutes. Reduce the heat to 400°F (204°C) and bake another 30 minutes.

7) Compare after cooling. The pie with the native starch is pasty and dull, with a high gel set. The pie with the modified starch is shiny, and the syrup component has a nice flow.

Oxidized Starches

Starches are subjected to oxidation reactions for two main purposes: whitening and promoting adhesion. When a lower level of oxidation is used to whiten, these starches are termed *bleached starches*. A higher degree of oxidation is used to produce modified starches that have a lower gelatinization temperature, reduced paste viscosity, and improved clarity compared to the native starch from which it was made. The largest food use is in the batter and breading industry, where specialized oxidized starches are added to a batter formulation to promote the adhesion of the batter to the substrate.

Acid-Hydrolyzed Starches

Starches subjected to an acid treatment, such as hydrochloric acid, are called acid-hydrolyzed starches. This process, considered a form of starch conversion, cleaves the starch molecules into shorter segments yet retains the granular structure of the starch. Acid-converted starches uniquely have a low hot-paste viscosity, which allows the use of higher starch levels in a formula, yet set back to extremely firm gels. The confection industry takes advantage of these properties in the manufacture of gummy candies. The thinner hot viscosity allows the high-solids liquid (acid-hydrolyzed starch, sugar, and flavor) to be poured into molds, where they cool and set back to a firm gel. Terms such as thin-boiling and acid-thinned starches are also used for these products.

Physically Modified Starches

Native starches can be subjected to treatments, such as heat and pressure, without the use of chemicals; these physical treatments also affect gelatinization and pasting characteristics. They enhance the functional stability of the starch but have yet to match the results developed with chemically modified starches. Another downside is that currently they are about double the cost of chemically modified starches. However, they should be considered when a food formulation with a "clean" label is required, as these starches can be labeled "natural."

Pre-Gelatinized Starches

The term pre-gelatinized starch is synonymous with *pre-gelled starch* and *instant starch*, as they are commonly known. Various methods may be employed to create a starch that thickens, without heating, almost immediately as it makes contact with water. The oldest and most common method is drum-drying. This process applies a starch slurry onto a rotating cylinder (drum) where the starch is heated, pasted, and then dried. The cooked, dry starch is scraped from the drum and ground to a powder. Drum-drying a stabilized starch produces a starch with some degree of heat, acid, and shear stability, but the process often fractures the pasted granules and results in an instant starch of reduced viscosity and stability compared to its parent cook-up starch.

Other proprietary technologies are utilized to pre-gelatinize that leave the granules intact through the process. One such procedure is a spray-cook process whereby the starch slurry is heated, swollen, and dried in seconds through a special spray-drying nozzle. Another technology utilizes heating of the starch in a high concentration of alcohol.[11] Both of these, which maintain the intact granule, are termed cold-water swelling starches (CWS) and tend to have viscosity, texture, and stability similar to their cook-up counterparts, but the cost can easily be double.

The most familiar use of an instant starch is instant pudding mix. By adding milk to the dry mix, thickening is immediate. A less-known application is a layer cake designed for frozen storage. Selection of the appropriate CWS starch provides the correct batter consistency to avoid the formation of large air pockets yet offers moisture management in the cake throughout its storage, reducing shrinkage and maintaining texture.

Starch Selection

When considering the number of primary native starches commercially available as well as the number of modifications, degrees of modification, and potential combinations of modifications, one begins to realize how many starch options are available. The research chef or food technologist should use the expertise of the starch supplier to help select the best starch for each application. The supplier must know the

FIGURE 8.15 **Functions of starch modification.**

Function of Modification	Chemical Modification					Physical Modification	
	Acid Hydrolysis	Oxidation	Crosslinking	Substitution	Stabilization	Pregelatinization	Heat Treatment
Gelatinization temperature	X	X	X	X	X	X	X
Viscosity	X	X	X		X		X
Stress tolerance			X				X
Inhibit retrogradation				X	X		
Whitening		X					
Adhesion		X					
Film forming				X			

functional expectations needed from the starch as well as the handling and processing parameters to which the food will be subjected. Remember the conditions for gelatinization and pasting: heat, water, mechanical action. Remember the conditions of stress: heat, acid, shear, and time. Add to those the fluctuations of temperature with freeze-thaw.

Many suppliers offer a specialized starch for a particular industry, such as bakery, meats, fruit fillings, or sauces. Many manufacture specialty starches for a particular application, such as emulsification, aqueous-based coatings, retort applications, and confections. Ask the experts at your starch supplier to select the best option for you.

Converted Starch Products: Maltodextrins and Corn Syrups

Converted starch products is a collective term reserved for those materials manufactured through the hydrolysis (decomposition of a chemical compound by reaction with water) of the starch molecules. Common methods of starch hydrolysis (also known as depolymerization) are exposure to heat, acid, and enzymes singularly or in combination.

Pyroconversion (conversion by heat) of an acidified starch produces a group of converted products collectively called dextrins. Older technology produces dextrins that are strongly flavored and often yellow to brownish in color. Newer technology employing a combination of heat, acid, and enzymatic hydrolysis produces maltodextrins, which generally form clear solutions in water, are not sweet relative to sugar, and have little to no flavor.

Maltodextrins, and the more highly converted (hydrolyzed) corn syrup and corn syrup solids, are differentiated by their dextrose equivalent (DE) value, which is the proportion of reducing-sugar content expressed as dextrose content on a dry basis. DE is deduced via chemistry to provide a number reflective of the degree of starch molecule hydrolysis—that is, how much of the starch is broken down to glucose (aka dextrose) molecules. The higher the DE value, the greater the degree of hydrolysis and therefore the greater the amount of sugars present. Maltodextrins are between 5 and 20 DE and are not sweet; corn syrup solids (powders) are 20 DE and above and thus range from somewhat sweet to sweet. Corn syrups (liquids) come in three grades: low DE is less than 30, regular DE is 42 (about 40 percent the sweetness of table sugar) and high DE is 68 (about 60 percent the sweetness of table sugar).

Like starches, maltodextrins are chains of dextrose (also called *glucose*) units, but they are much shorter in length. The FDA defines *maltodextrin* as a "non-sweet nutritive (digestible) saccharide (sugar) polymer consisting of glucose (synonymous to dextrose) having a DE less than 20." Maltodextrins are prepared as a white powder or concentrated solution by the partial hydrolysis of starch with safe and suitable acids or enzymes. They have GRAS status as direct human food ingredients at levels consistent with current good manufacturing practices (21 CFR 184.1444).

Maltodextrins are widely used to add body and mouthfeel without additional flavors or sweetening. Often, adding solids to a formulation contributes to the body and texture of that food. An excellent illustration is to compare the mouthfeel of a regular sugar-sweetened beverage, like lemonade, to an artificially sweetened version. Absence of the sugar solids changes the body of the diet drink to a more watery consistency. Much of the technology for successfully marketed low-fat foods revolves around replacing the solids lost in the formulation with maltodextrin. In so doing, the differences of body and texture between the two formulations are minimized, and the calories are greatly reduced (fat = 9 kcal/g; maltodextrin = 4 kcal/g).

Maltodextrins are also used as carriers or fillers to bulk up (dilute) highly concentrated flavors and colors, making them easier to measure and disperse into a food system. They are widely used as bulking agents for diluting high-intensity sweeteners, so that, for instance, a packet of Nutrasweet® or

FIGURE 8.16 Functional properties of carbohydrates as related to dextrose equivalence.

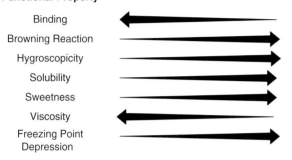

Source: Gum Technology Corporation.

Splenda® delivers the same level of sweetening as the same size packet of sugar. If the packet was filled with pure aspartame or sucralose, it would blow your head off! They are also used as a bulking agent in dry mixes to enable a number of recipes to fit into a single standardized package size. Use of maltodextrins in these dry blends also helps keep them free-flowing, as they are not as hygroscopic as higher-DE corn syrup solids or sugars.[12]

Corn syrups are defined as concentrated aqueous solutions of nutritive saccharides obtained from starch with a DE of 20 or more; thus, their molecular size is smaller than maltodextrins. The most common in commerce are 36 DE,

FIGURE 8.17 Relative sweetness of converted sweeteners.

Sweetener	Relative Sweetness
Sucrose (sugar)	100
Fructose	110–170
Glucose/dextrose	60–90
90 HFCS	120–160
55 HFCS	100–110
42 HFCS	90–100
63 DE corn syrup	60–70
42/43 DE corn syrup	40–50
36 DE corn syrup	30–40
20 DE corn syrup solids	20–25
18 DE maltodextrin	18–22
15 DE maltodextrin	15
10 DE maltodextrin	10
5 DE maltodextrin	5

42 DE, and 63 DE. The higher the DE, the higher the free glucose content, and therefore the sweeter the taste and the lower the viscosity.[13] Corn syrup solids are the dried equivalents of the syrups from which they are derived. Most often these products are blended with other sweeteners, such as sucrose, to add solids to a formulation. This not only contributes to sweetness but also adds hygroscopicity, changes the texture, lowers the freezing point, and increases viscosity.[14]

Functional properties and relative sweetness of the maltodextrins and corn syrup solids are shown in Figure 8.16.

The converted starch products with the most notoriety today are the high-fructose corn syrups (HFCS). In commercial production, HFCS is made by first enzymatically hydrolyzing cornstarch to glucose syrup and then, in a second enzymatic process called isomerization, converting 42 percent of the glucose to fructose. (Note that HFCS contains both glucose and fructose—reducing sugars that can participate in Maillard browning in the presence of amino acids and heat.)

Refining this 42 percent HFCS to obtain a 90 percent fructose HFCS and then blending it back with 42 percent HFCS produces what has become the most commonly used HFCS: 55 percent fructose HFCS. The popularity is due to this combination of traits: It has the same sweetness as cane or beet sugar at half the cost. The most common usage for 55 HFCS is in the soft drink industry. Other foods like baked goods, soups, and salad dressings take advantage of the even less expensive sweetness of the 42 percent HFCS. The controversy surrounding the HFCSs revolves around their high usage rate in foods and its correlation to the increase of obesity, diabetes, and other diet-related health issues facing the public today.

●Gums

While starches, flours, and sugars are commonly used in home and restaurant kitchens, gums are not nearly as common. Most gums are utilized in industrial food manufacturing.

Only recently have gums, primarily guar gum and xanthan gum, been available in retail markets. One reason is that gums are useful in a gluten-free diet, specifically in making gluten-free breads. Many grains, including wheat, barley, and rye, contain the protein *gluten*, which is essential to breadmaking because it helps doughs develop by adding viscosity and elasticity and, most importantly, by trapping the CO_2 gas (carbon dioxide) developed during fermentation that allows the dough to rise. When gluten is removed, dough loses this ability. Gums can replace some of those attributes, allowing for the baking of some fairly good gluten-free breads.

Most gums are as natural as starches and sugars, and come from plant sources. Just as wheat flour comes from the endosperm (inside) of the wheat seed, guar gum comes from the endosperm of the guar seed. (The guar seed and pod look very much like a pea seed and pod.) Using gums is really not much different from using starches in terms of naturalness and health (except that unlike starches, they are virtually calorie free). But the functionality of gums is quite different from starches and adds a new repertoire of textures and functionalities to your food creations.

Gums are hydrocolloids. Hydro (like *hydrate* in *carbohydrate*) means "water," and a colloid is a dispersion in which one ingredient (the dispersed phase) is evenly distributed throughout another ingredient (the continuous phase). In this case, the gum is distributed throughout the water. The gum particles stay suspended in the water (or other aqueous medium) because they are so small they do not settle out. At the same time, they are too large to simply go into solution, as salt or sugar would. It is the relatively large size of these molecules that allows them to develop viscosity and gel systems.

Note that chewing gum is not a gum; it is a resin. Resins are compounds, derived naturally or synthetically, that do not dissolve or disperse in water but do dissolve in non-aqueous liquids such as oil and alcohol; pine sap is a common resin. Chewing gum fails the first test of being a hydrocolloid: It does not disperse in water. If it were really a gum, it would melt in your mouth and would not provide a pleasant chewing experience. By the same token, it is important to remember that true gums not only like water but *require* it or other aqueous liquids to function. Gums are not soluble in liquids other than water or those based on water. (*Note:* From this point on we use the term *soluble* or *gum solutions* because most people commonly refer to the dispersion of gums in water as "being soluble." However, they do not form true solutions; they form colloidal dispersions or suspensions.)

In a true solution, the solute and solvent become one homogenous material. In a colloidal dispersion there is no solute and solvent because the solute (in this case the gum) is immiscible (doesn't dissolve) in the solvent (the water). If you could look under a powerful microscope, you would see the gum particles are actually floating (dispersed) in the water and are not one with it. On the other hand, if you add gums to oil, they eventually settle out and do not provide viscosity or other functional benefit. The same holds true in alcohol, propylene glycol, and high-solids sugar solutions. Gums need water; without water, gums are essentially nonfunctional.

High-solids sugar solutions, such as corn syrup, do contain water, so why won't gums work in them? The answer is that all of the water molecules are already bound to sugar molecules; no free water is available to bind with the gum. We can categorize this concentrated sugar solution as having extremely limited water activity (a_w). Most sugar syrups, and honey, are good examples of foods in which water is present but not available for microbial organisms to feed on (which is often our main concern with water activity) or to react with ingredients that require water, such as gums. Although a typical syrup might contain 35 percent water (and 65 percent sugar), every molecule of water is attached to a molecule of sugar and therefore not available. This binding is the reason honey, jams, syrups, and strong, high-salt pickling brines can remain on the shelf without spoiling even without preservatives.

Please note that gums are not very useful in controlling water activity. Many people assume that because gums absorb quite a bit of water (some gums, such as konjac, hold up to 200 times their weight in water), they control water activity. This is not the case, as most of the water picked up by

FIGURE 8.18 Water activity of some common foods.

Water Activity	Typical Foods at That Level
0.99	Fresh meats, poultry, and fish
0.95	Milk, cooked sausage, bread, cheese spread
0.93	Bean paste
0.92	Caviar
0.91	Swiss and Muenster cheese
0.85	Aged cheddar, fermented sausage
0.82	Semi-moist foods, pet foods
0.80	Juice concentrates, maple syrup, fruit cakes
0.75	Jams and marmalades, marshmallows
0.70	Soy sauce
0.65	Jellies, dried fruits and nuts
0.60	Caramels, toffees
0.50	Dried pasta, spices
0.40	Whole egg powder
0.30	Crackers and cookies

Source: Gum Technology Corporation.

the gum is not bound; it is still available to react with other materials or for microbes to feed on.

Gums do have the advantage of being functional at very low use levels. This is not only an important factor when determining the costs involved in the choice of a stabilizer but also means they do not mask flavors. Gums tend to be bland when put into solution. This can be critical, particularly when using expensive natural flavors. Other texturizing and stabilizing agents, such as starches, can mask desirable flavors due to their high usage levels. To overcome this flavor masking, most developers simply add more flavor (and more cost) to achieve the flavor impact they desire. What they might not realize is that by adding more flavors they may actually be changing what started out as a delicate and refined flavor profile by overcompensating for the starch in their system.

How to Use Gums

Gums are not starches, and trying to use them the same way leads to ineffective results and frustration. Gums are easy to work with once you understand their characteristics.

The first thing to remember is that gums are typically used at levels far below those of most starches. Most gums are effective at 0.05 to 0.50 percent, and some are even used at levels as low as 0.001 percent in certain foods. Starches are often used at levels in excess of 3.0 percent—often much higher. If you try to use most gums at that level, the end result is disaster.

Because gums are hydrophilic, they start to swell (hydrate) the moment they meet water. If too many gum particles are in contact with one another when they contact water, they lump or ball up, causing processing difficulties. The key is to make sure each grain of gum has the opportunity to start hydrating before it touches another grain of gum. Fortunately, there are many ways to achieve this.

Remember that gums are not soluble in oil, alcohol, or propylene glycol, or in high sugar solids solutions. This fact can be used to advantage in handling the gum. If we add gum to oil with stirring, it forms a slurry (similar to a slurry of raw starch and water). As a result, the gum grains each get a coating of oil. When this slurry is added to water, the grains do not hydrate immediately; the oil on the grain's surface inhibits the rapid exposure to water. This gives the grains time to get away from each other so when they do hydrate, they remain separated; therefore they do not stick together or ball up. The same result can be achieved using alcohol, propylene glycol (PG), or high solids sugar solutions. Just make sure the slurry is well mixed right before using so the gum particles don't fall to the bottom (exactly like starch in a water slurry). *Note:* Many of the liquid flavors used in food manufacturing use alcohol, oil, or PG as a diluent, so these can be handy mediums for incorporating gums.

Another method of gum dispersion is to pre-blend the gum with another granular substance, such as salt, sugar, or citric acid. When the gums enter the water, each grain is surrounded by a grain of something to which the gum does not adhere. If we make a blend of 5 parts table sugar to 1 part gum, each grain of gum is surrounded by 5 grains of sugar, and when the blend enters the water and the gum starts to hydrate, it is touching grains of sugar, not other grains of gum.

Types of Gums

The world of gums is filled with diverse products derived from a wide range of sources. Just as the gums are extracted from many materials, their functionalities have a broad range as well. Some gums get viscous, some get very viscous, and some have little viscosity. Some gums form gels; some do not. Many gums do not require heat to become functional, but other gums do. Gels may be soft or firm; some can be melted back into a liquid by heating (thermo-reversible) or stay gelled when subjected to high heat (non-thermo-reversible). Some form gels when the gums are heated (thermogelation); some require the addition of other ingredients, such as calcium salts or proteins, to form a gel. Some gums thrive in a low-pH (acidic) environment; others degrade in that environment. Some gums require high shear to be effective; others are broken down by high shear.

Some gums, such as xanthan and guar, have long or so-called "snotty" textures. Some, such as konjac, have short textures, and some, such as sodium alginate and some CMCs (carboxymethyl-cellulose) are in-between. A long texture forms a thin stream when poured out of a container; a short texture forms a wider, less flowing cascade. Starch, after heating, forms a short texture; corn syrup has a short texture as well. Pancake syrup has a long texture, as do many mid-viscosity salad dressings.

Gums can also be synergistic with one another and with certain other ingredients. Think of synergism as 1 + 1 = 3, where the sum is more than the total of the parts. If you mix guar gum that at 0.5 percent yields 500 cps (centipoise) viscosity (see Tech Tip) and blend it with xanthan gum that at 0.5 percent yields a 600 cps viscosity, you would expect the two together to yield a 550 cps viscosity if each is used at 0.25 percent to create a 0.5 percent solution (250 cps contributed by the guar and 300 cps contributed by the xanthan). In fact, the viscosity is higher—about 1400 cps, or about 2.5 times higher than expected and about 2.8 times the viscosity of the guar by itself and about 2.3 times the viscosity of the xanthan by itself. This is synergism at work; the combination is stronger than either of the two by themselves. (*Note:* Gum viscosity is not linear at all. The guar used in the above example is 4000 cps at 1 percent but only 500 cps at 0.5 percent. The xanthan is a bit more linear; at 1 percent it is about 1500 cps, and at 0.5 percent it is 600 cps.) A heated solution of locust bean gum flows, as does a heated solution of xanthan gum. But if you heat the locust bean gum and xanthan gum together, they form an elastic gel. This is another example of synergism.

The choice of gum is determined by the properties wanted in the final product, the types of processing conditions the gum will encounter, and the unique characteristics of the gum. Talk to your gum supplier before you get started!

Seed Gums

All of the most commonly used seed gums—guar, locust bean (also known as *carob bean*), tara, fenugreek, and cassia gums—are members of the galactomannan family. A galactomannan is a molecule composed of mannose and galactose, two sugars. The gums and their properties vary due to differences in the ratio of galactose side chains to mannose backbone segments in their molecular structures.

Guar Gum

Guar gum is made from the endosperm of the guar bean.

Guar is grown commercially in many areas of the world, including Australia and the United States. However, the great majority of guar gum used in the food industry comes from India and Pakistan.

FIGURE 8.19 Gum grain surrounded by other granular material.

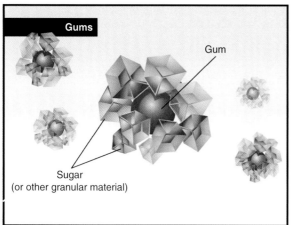

Source: Gum Technology Corporation.

FIGURE 8.20   Considerations in using gums.

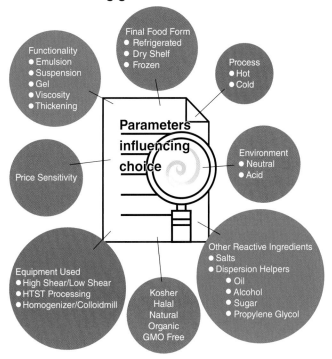

Source: Gum Technology Corporation.

Tech Tip

The abbreviation for *centipoise* is cps, sometimes written cP. This is a measurement of viscosity or, in simple terms, the thickness of a fluid. (Viscosity can also be defined as mPas, or millipascal seconds; 1 cps = 1.0 mPas.) Purified water is considered 0 cps, tomato juice 100 to 200 cps, creamy salad dressing 2000 to 5000 cps, yogurt 10,000 to 20,000 cps, corn syrup 45,000 cps, as examples. When we discuss viscosity, we almost always use a 1 percent aqueous solution at 77°F (25°C) as the standard. There are exceptions, but, unless noted, it is safe to assume those parameters.

In the gum industry, viscosity is commonly measured using Brookfield viscometers, Bostwick consistometers, Brabender consistometers, and visco-amylographs, although many other instruments are available. Viscosity is dependent on temperature and shear (friction between layers) as well as certain other factors such as time in solution, the amount of time that shear is applied as well as shear force, and, of course, the concentration of gum in the solution.

Most Brookfield viscometers measure the amount of torque needed to keep a spindle moving through a liquid at a constant speed. The measurement is read in centipoise (cps). The speed at which the spindle rotates can be controlled to show how the viscosity is, or is not, affected by changes in shear, which increases as the spindle rotation speed is increased.

A Bostwick consistometer uses resistance against flow as a means of measurement. The consistometer measures the distance in centimeters that a liquid flows down a sloped

FIGURE 8.21   Brookfield digital viscometer.

Source: Brookfield Engineering.

trough in a prescribed amount of time (or the amount of time it takes the liquid to flow to maximum distance).

Brabender visco-amylographs are most often used to test starch. They work in a similar manner to the Brookfield; however, the liquid can be heated and measurements recorded through a heating and cooling cycle, showing the change in viscosity with temperature.

These are a few of the more common viscometers used in the food industry. Of course, each manufacturer makes models that incorporate any combination of the above methods.

FIGURE 8.22 Gum attributes.

Product	Category	Typical Viscosity Ranges at 1% (Temp)	Typical Food Applications	Typical Use Level (%)	Synergies	Freeze/ Thaw Stability	Retort Stability	Stable pH Range	Water Solubility	Type of Emulsifier	Natural or Synthetic
Agar	Marine gum	5–30 cps (158°F)	Pie fillings, icings, and glazes	0.05–0.25	LBG	Fair	Excellent	2.5–10	Yes (212°F)	None	Natural
Carrageenan (iota)	Marine gum	5–400 cps (167°F)	Custards, dairy beverages, and protein beverages	0.02–0.50	Starch	Good	Good (pH >4.0)	4.0–10.0	Yes (>160°F)	None	Natural
Carrageenan (kappa)	Marine gum	5–400 cps (167°F)	Water gel desserts, chocolate beverages, meats and meat analogs	0.02–0.75	LBG, Konjac	None	Fair	4–10	Yes (>160°F)	None	Natural
Carrageenan (lambda)	Marine gum	10–1000 cps (77°F)	Syrups, pizza sauces, smoothies, and instant beverages	0.02–0.75		Fair	Fair	4–10	Yes (77°F)	Pseudo-emulsifier	Natural
CMC	Cellulose gum	20–20,000 cps (77°F)	Syrups, cake batters, and instant drink mixes	0.05–0.75	Locust bean gum, starch	Excellent	Fair	4–10	Yes (77°F)	None	Synthetic
Fenugreek gum	Seed gum	1000–3400 cps (77°F)	Salad dressings, baked goods and sauces	0.10–0.50	Xanthan	Good	Fair	2–10	Yes (77°F)	Pseudo-emulsifier	Natural
Gellan	Bio-gum	<100 cps (194°F)	Water gel desserts, fruit pie filling, and fruit juice drinks	0.05–0.80	Xanthan	Fair	Good	1–13	Yes (≥194°F)	None	Natural
Guar	Seed gum	2000–7000 cps (77°F)	Baked goods, sauces, ice creams, and popsicles	0.05–0.50	Xanthan, locust bean gum	Good	Poor	4.0–10.5	Yes (77°F)	None	Natural
Gum arabic	Exudates	<10 cps (77°F)	Flavor emulsions, seasoning adhesions, and icings	0.50–10.00	Tragacanth	Good	Good	2–10	Yes (77°F)	True emulsifier	Natural
Hydroxypropyl-methylcellulose	Cellulose gum	10–100,000 cps (68°F)	Pie fillings, glazes, and baked goods	0.10–1.00	CMC	Good	Good	3–10	Yes (<77°F)	Pseudo-emulsifier	Synthetic
Karaya	Exudates	200–700 cps (77°F)	Sauces, cheese spreads, whole grain breads	0.05–0.75	Locust bean gum	Good	None	4–10	Yes (77°F)	None	Natural

Name	Type	Viscosity	Applications	Use level (%)	Synergies			pH range	Hydration	Emulsifier	Origin
Konjac	Plant gum	20,000–36,000 cps (77°F)	Pasta, meat analogs, bagels	0.10–1.00	Xanthan, carrageenan, starch	Good	Good	2–10	Yes (77°F)	None	Natural
Locust bean gum	Seed gum	2400–3500 cps(77°F)	Fruit variegates, cream cheese, ice cream	0.10–0.50	Xanthan, guar, carrageenan, cellulose gum, agar	Good	Good	4–10	Yes (>140°F)	None	Natural
Methylcellulose	Cellulose gum	10–10,000 cps (68°F)	Fried products, pie fillings, and meat analogs	0.10 - 1.00	Starch	Good	Good	2–13	Yes (<68°F)	Pseudo-emulsifier	Synthetic
Microcrystalline cellulose	Cellulose gum	<10 cps (77°F)	Low-fat salad dressings and dips	0.50–2.00	Cellulose gum	Good	Good	2–10	Yes (77°F)	None	Natural
Pectin-HM	Pectin	5–200 cps (77°F)	Jams, jellies, protein drinks	0.10–0.60	Sodium alginate	Good	Good	2–7	Yes (160°F)	None	Natural
Pectin-LM	Pectin	5–100 cps (77°F)	Low-sugar jams and fillings	0.5 –1.00	Sodium alginate	Good	Good	2–7	Yes (77°F)	None	Natural
PGA	Marine gum	50–500 cps (77°F)	Salad dressings, sauces, dips	0.10–1.00	Xanthan	Good	Fair	3–10	Yes (77°F)	True emulsifier	Synthetic
Sodium alginate	Marine gum	10–1000 cps (77°F)	Restructured onion rings, pimiento filling, and cheese sauce	0.25–1.00	Xanthan	Fair	Good in presence of calcium	3.5–10	Yes (77°F)	None	Natural
Tahla	Exudates	<10 cps (77°F)	Seasoning adhesions, added fiber	1.0–20		Good	Fair	4.0–10.0	Yes (77°F)	None	Natural
Tara	Seed gum	3000–7000 cps (77°F)	Ice cream, cheesecake, and sauces	0.10– 0.50	Xanthan, carrageenan	Good	Good	2–10	Yes (77°F)	None	Natural
Tragacanth	Exudates	200–4600 cps (77°F)	Salad dressings, icings, and flavor emulsions	0.05–0.40	Gum arabic	Good	Good	2–10	Yes (77°F)	True emulsifier	Natural
Xanthan	Bio-gum	1100–1700 cps (77°F)	Salad dressings, baked goods, and sauces	0.05–0.40	Guar, locust bean gum, konjac, CMC, microcrystalline cellulose, starch, gellan	Excellent	Good	1–12	Yes (77°F)	Pseudo-emulsifier	Natural

Source: Gum Technology Corporation.

FIGURE 8.23 Galactomannan ratios. Fenugreek gum has one galactose side chain for every mannose molecule on the backbone, whereas guar gum has one galactose for every two mannose molecules, tara gum has a 1:3 ratio, and so on.

Fenugreek Gum	1:1	
Guar Gum	1:2	
Tara Gum	1:3	
Locust Bean Gum	1:4	
Cassia Gum	1:5	

Source: Gum Technology Corporation.

Guar is one of the more familiar gums to food scientists and research chefs. One reason is that it is historically inexpensive, usually the least costly of all the major gums, and fairly viscous. If viscosity is your main concern, guar gum gives you a good bang for the buck.

Typical guars have viscosities in the 4500 to 7000 cps range (the creamy salad dressing range, or slightly higher), depending on the quality of the bean and how it is processed. Guar gum can be purchased in many viscosity ranges and in many mesh sizes. Mesh size of guar and other gums is a measurement of how fine or coarse the powder is. Mesh is usually referenced in particles per square inch; a larger number (200 mesh as opposed to 40, for instance) means a finer powder. The mesh size is determined by sifting through standard screens (sieves). Coarser meshes are more easily dispersed in water; there is less chance of lumping or balling up. On the other hand, finer meshes hydrate and create viscosity more rapidly.

Guar hydrates and gets viscous in cold water; it does not require heat to become effective. This is a great energy savings and very useful for instant powdered beverages and other items where quick, inexpensive viscosity is desired. It also maintains moisture in baked goods, especially sweet baked goods. Although guar eventually gives up some of its water to the environment, it holds on long enough to be an effective shelf life extender in baked goods. One disadvantage is its slightly beany odor. In baked goods and at low usage levels,

the odor or taste is not apparent. Guar can also be slimy or snotty in liquid applications if used at too high a level.

Guar is synergistic with xanthan gum—that is, the two together form a more viscous solution than expected based on their individual thickening abilities. Choosing whether to use the gums as a single entity or in combination depends on a number of factors including, but not limited to, cost, final texture desired, simplification of process, purchasing, and labeling. To simplify processing, the gums can often be purchased as blended stabilizing systems; however, the label declaration must still list each gum used in the blend separately.

In the following recipe, rice flour and potato starch replace wheat flour to make the recipe gluten free. Guar gum and xanthan gum are used to replace the elasticity and structure the gluten found in wheat flour normally provides.

Gluten-Free Chocolate Brownies

Ingredients	Percent
White rice flour	7.00
Cocoa powder	6.00
Potato starch	3.50
Guar gum	0.30
Xanthan gum	0.45
Vanilla extract	0.75
Sugar	36.75
Vegetable oil	19.00
Eggs	17.50
Chocolate chips	8.75
Total	100.00

Procedure:

1) Sift together the white rice flour, potato starch, cocoa powder, and gums. Set aside.
2) Whisk together the vegetable oil, eggs, sugar, and vanilla.
3) Combine the wet and the dry ingredients. Stir in chocolate chips.
4) Pour into greased pans and bake at 325°F for 25 to 30 minutes, or until set in center.
5) Allow to cool completely before cutting.

Locust Bean Gum

Locust bean gum (LBG) comes from the seed of the carob pod, from the carob tree (*Ceratonia siliqua*); it is also known as *carob bean gum*. The carob pod is also called *St. John's bread* and has been used as a food ingredient in the Mediterranean for centuries and, more recently, as a chocolate substitute. LBG is grown in Portugal, Morocco, Spain, and Italy. To get the gum, the seed is split open and then mechanically ground and sieved to separate the endosperm from the germ and the husk.

Locust bean gum is only slightly soluble in cold water and must be heated to at least 140°F (60°C) in order to start swelling and reach full hydration (heating to 185°F [82°C] is recommended). When LBG is heated and subsequently cooled, it forms a smooth, flowing solution with a shorter texture than most other galactomannans; it has been described as a

FIGURE 8.24 Guar seed, expanded illustration.

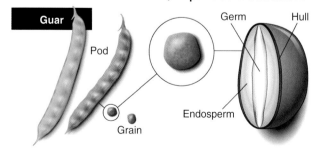

Source: Gum Technology Corporation.

FIGURE 8.25 Locust bean pod, expanded.

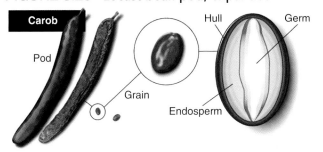

Source: Gum Technology Corporation.

pseudo-gel. At 1 percent, after heating and cooling, LBG has a typical viscosity of about 2500 cps, although, as with most gums, this can vary.

LBG is synergistic with other gums, including carrageenan, xanthan, and agar. A heated 1 percent solution of xanthan gum is pourable and a heated 1 percent solution of LBG is pourable, but if you combine them before heating (0.50 percent each for a total of 1 percent), the result is a very elastic gel after heating and cooling—a gummy candy type of texture. LBG is also helpful in controlling syneresis and, as such, is often used in dairy products such as cream cheese and puddings to help prevent and control excess water from weeping out of the product. Locust bean gum is often used in gelatin-free vegetarian dessert gels created with kappa carrageenan or agar, as both of these gums form gels that have a relatively high degree of syneresis. LBG also has the effect of softening gels—that is, making them less brittle and more elastic. This is useful in products such as flans and crème brûlée. Many ice cream stabilizers also use LBG for its ability to hold water and prevent ice crystal formation, making frozen desserts feel smoother and creamier.

Locust bean gum also finds application in fruit variegates—the fruit-and-sugar preparations mixed into ice creams, yogurts and pie fillings. Its short texture looks like starch but, unlike starch, LBG does not mask flavors.

Tara Gum

Tara gum is closely related to locust bean gum and guar gum. It is derived from the endosperm of the seed of the tara tree (*Cesalpinia spinosa lin*), also known as *Peruvian carob*. It is harvested and processed much like LBG gum.

Tara has a 1:3 ratio of galactose to mannose. Guar gum has a 1:2 ratio, and locust bean gum has a 1:4 ratio. It is not surprising, then, that tara gum has properties somewhat like LBG and somewhat like guar gum. Tara is partially soluble in cold water (guar is totally soluble in cold water) but completely solubilizes in hot water, as does locust bean gum (which does not dissolve in cold water).

The viscosity of a cold-water solution of tara falls between that of guar and locust bean gums, and pricing historically is also in the middle. After heating, tara gains viscosity. Thus, tara makes a good substitute for LBG and a replacement for guar if guar prices rise or supplies become limited.

One of the more common uses for tara gum is in combination with xanthan to create the soft gels commonly found on top of canned pet food. This was traditionally made with locust bean gum and xanthan; however, the lower cost of tara and the unimportance of clarity in this product make tara gum a good option.

Tara gum has not achieved the popularity of guar gum and locust bean gum in part because of its somewhat limited availability in the past. However, this has changed in recent years as more growers and processors, particularly in Peru, have seen it as an economically feasible product; production and availability have increased as a result.

Fenugreek Gum

Fenugreek gum is a relative newcomer to the world of commercial hydrocolloids. Fenugreek is an herb or spice that is commonly used in Indian curries as well as in many African and Mediterranean cuisines. In addition, sotolone, a potent aroma chemical extracted from fenugreek, is commonly used to flavor imitation maple syrup. As with all the other seed gums, the gum portion of fenugreek comes from the endosperm of the seed.

Fenugreek gum has a viscosity similar to that of xanthan gum (about 1500 cps at 1 percent in water) and a smooth, flowing texture. It can have a slight maple odor; however, new advances in production yield powders with almost no odor.

Besides thickening and texturizing, fenugreek also exhibits exceptional nutraceutical qualities, such as the reduction of blood cholesterol and a lowering of the glycemic index of a food. Although usually not enough gum is used in any one product to substantiate a claim, it is useful as a part of a total functional food system to be able to claim that the texturant used has functional benefits.[15]

Tree Exudates

Tree exudate is another term for *sap*. Tree exudates were probably the first form of gums to be used for foods, as they are easy to harvest and process. Maple syrup is condensed sap from the maple tree. The primary difference between maple sap and gum exudates is that the latter, oozing from the tree, harden as they comes into contact with oxygen and the ambient environment.

Acacia (Gum Arabic)

The term gum arabic is used with varying degrees of precision. In the context of food additives, the most recent international specification published by the Food and Agriculture Organization (FAO) defines *gum arabic* as the "dried exudation obtained from the stems and branches of *Acacia senegal* (L) Willdenow or closely related species."[16] In Sudan, the term *gum arabic* refers to two types of gum that are clearly separated in both national statistics and trade: hashab (from *A. senegal*) and talha (from *A. seyal*). In a still wider sense, *gum arabic* is often taken to mean the gum from any acacia species (and is sometimes referred to as *acacia gum*).[17]

The above quote explains the frequent confusion in the use of the term. Only the *A. senegal* form can be used as an emulsifier, and we refer to that variety only as *gum arabic*.

Gum arabic has a long history of use in the food industry as well as in many non-food applications, including as an adhesive on envelopes and stamps, as a thickener in inks, and for sizing on cloth. There are many reasons why gum arabic has been used for such a long time and why it continues to be so popular. First is that it becomes sticky when wet. This is obvious even as it is hanging as a teardrop on the tree; touching the sap before it dries makes your fingers feel sticky.

The second is that it can be made usable simply by adding it to water; even a large piece of gum arabic dissolves in water relatively quickly. It is the only gum that is truly soluble in cold water. Processing the gum is easy; it is mechanically ground into a powder for faster dispersion and hydration.

As previously stated, gum *Arabic senegal* is the true emulsifier; its lipophilic (fat-loving) and hydrophilic (water-loving) receptors are found in its arabinogalactan protein (AGP). For emulsifying properties, use this species.

One of the more interesting aspects of gum arabic is its low viscosity. For the most part, gums are thickening agents. Gum arabic exhibits very low viscosity when put into solution. A 30 percent gum arabic solution is only about 1200 cps[18]; compare that to a 1 percent solution of xanthan, which is about 1500 cps. In fact, it is possible to put gum arabic into solution as high as 55 percent. This makes it useful for a number of applications, one of which is spray-drying.

To spray-dry a flavor, for example, first make a solution from a soluble solid such as gum arabic and add some type of liquid, oil-based extract, or flavorant to that solution. To turn this into a dry flavor, the liquid must be removed. One way to do that is spray-drying, which consists of passing the flavor solution through a very fine spray nozzle (like a misting system) into a chamber with circulating heated air, hot enough to instantly evaporate the water. Usually spray-dryers are vertical and the product is sprayed into the chamber at the top. By the time it reaches the bottom, the hot air has evaporated all of the liquid, leaving behind only the solids (in this case gum arabic) on which the flavorant is adsorbed (coated). Because gum arabic can be put into solution as high as 55 percent and still be thin enough to pass through the spray-dryer's nozzles, 55 pounds of powdered flavor can be produced for every 100 pounds of liquid sprayed. If guar gum were used instead, it would probably be too viscous to spray, even at just a 0.5 percent solution, meaning that every 100 pounds of solution would yield less than half a pound of dry powder. In addition, even at high use levels, gum arabic has no off-taste to mask the flavor being spray-dried.

In addition, many flavors are oils or use oil carriers. Gum arabic is a true emulsifier and therefore holds onto the flavor oils better than many other solids, such as sugars and dextrins. This is one reason why gum *Acacia senegal* is used

for so many flavor emulsions, especially in beverages such as colas that use oils as a flavor base. It is also useful in dressings and sauces where emulsification is required, but not much added viscosity.

Gum arabic is also used in candies to prevent sugar crystallization[19] and in confections as a coating. It is used as a glaze on baked goods and to stabilize foams, beers, and lagers.[20]

Gum arabic was for many years used as an adhesive for envelopes and stamps, in part because it can be made into a high-concentration solution and in part because of its adhesive qualities. Gum arabic glue was produced by making a solution with a high concentration of gum arabic. As it dried, the solution left a film of gum arabic—which, when rewetted, became sticky, and as it dried again, adhered to whatever it touched. More efficient adhesives are used today, but gum arabic is still useful in making flavored edible films, such as breath strips.

Gum arabic is also an excellent choice for incorporating into high-fiber foods. Because it is about 85 percent soluble fiber on a dry weight basis (DWB) (the weight of the material if all water were eliminated)[21] and because it has little impact on viscosity or texture, it is an excellent way to add fiber to a beverage, baked good, or nutritional bar.

In the following recipe, just a small amount of gum arabic helps create a true emulsion; the xanthan and lambda carrageenan impart body and help create a pseudo-emulsion.

Honey Mustard Vinaigrette

Ingredients	Percent
Vegetable oil	55.15
White vinegar (5 percent acidity)	31.10
Honey	5.50
Dijon mustard	3.95
Salt	3.15
Garlic powder	0.40
Powdered gum arabic	0.15
Xanthan gum	0.15
Lambda carrageenan	0.15
Black pepper	0.25
Hot sauce	0.05
Total	100.00

Procedure:

1) Blend all dry ingredients.

2) Add dry mix slowly to one-quarter of the oil using high shear—that is, in a high-speed lab mixer.

3) Mix for 5 minutes to assure maximum viscosity.

4) Mix hot sauce, Dijon mustard, white vinegar, and honey together.

5) Add honey mixture to gum/spice/oil mixture and continue mixing for 5 more minutes.

6) Add the remaining oil and mix for 2 minutes.

7) Pour into a container and shake for 30 seconds.

8) Over the next few days, watch the dressing for signs of separation or thinning.

Talha (*Acacia Seyal*)

The other popular form of gum arabic is *A. seyal,* frequently called gum talha.

Essentially, gum talha can be used in the same applications as gum arabic, with the one very important exclusion of emulsions. Gum talha does not help stabilize an emulsion. It is a good choice for creating films, adding bulk, and adding fiber, just as gum arabic is. Gum talha is generally less expensive than gum arabic and, because it grows in a far wider region than gum arabic, more available. So unless emulsification is needed, gum talha is a better choice.

Tragacanth

Gum tragacanth (often called *trag* or *gum trag*) is the dried exudate of the shrub Astragalus (Leguminosae), including the species *A. adscendens, A. gummifer, A. tragacanthus,* and *A. microcephalus*. Gum tragacanth is grown in the Middle East, with the majority coming from Iran and Turkey.

Gum tragacanth sap grows as ribbons or flakes after the bark and taproots of the plant are scored with hatchets and knives.

Gum tragacanth is hand-picked and sorted into grades, the highest grade (ribbon #1) being white and free of extraneous materials such as sand and bark. Because the sap starts as a liquid, the ribbon or flake can pick up blown sand, insects, and other foreign matter as it is drying. The ribbons with the most sediment are graded #5. Some tragacanth exudates dry as flakes and are generally graded lower than ribbons.

Unfortunately, gum tragacanth is not widely available. Harvesting and sorting is labor-intensive and expensive, and the "interventions by the Iranian government effected a sharp rise in export price"[22] during the 1980s. The introduction of xanthan gum also diminished the demand for gum tragacanth, and so it is not widely used today. The price is currently between 4 and 15 times higher than that of xanthan, depending on grade.

Gum tragacanth is acid-resistant and, like *A. senegal*, a true emulsifier. This makes the gum ideal for use in salad dressings and some sauces. In fact, prior to the introduction of xanthan gum, gum tragacanth was probably the most widely used gum for this purpose. Today, one of the most common uses of gum tragacanth is in sugarcraft, the art of making sugar pastes into decorations, usually for bakery items. The tragacanth forms an easily workable and pliable material when mixed with sugar and water, and it retains its consistency long enough, without drying and cracking, to remain fresh-looking on the cake. Another common use is as the adhesive holding the outer leaf wrapper around a cigar filler. Both of these exploit the adhesive properties of tragacanth as a paste at 2 to 5 percent. Because of its excellent resistance to acid conditions, gum tragacanth is also used in relishes and some pickling solutions. Again, its cost and relatively limited production hinder its wider use in the food industry.

Karaya

Karaya, also known as *sterculia gum*, is the dried exudate of *Sterculia urens* trees.[23] Gum karaya does not fully dissolve in water; the granules swell to form a viscous solution. Karaya is used in food products such as barbecue sauces and spice rubs and was, until the development of synthetic polymers, used as a denture adhesive. It is still used in conjunction with glycerin as an adhesive for colostomy bag sealing rings. Karaya passes through the body without being digested, so it is also used as a laxative.

Most karaya comes from India; other sources include Senegal, Mali, and Pakistan. Like gum arabic and gum tragacanth, the karaya tears are collected by hand from cuts made in the bark of the tree, and it is sorted, cleaned, and mechanically processed into a powder or granular form.

Karaya, at higher pH levels, exhibits a ropy texture. For example, after hydration, raising the pH above 6.0 increases viscosity, and the solution develops ropiness. This can be useful in products where dripping must be controlled—for example, in a sauce placed in a pump dispenser in a foodservice setting. Karaya reduces the amount of drip as the ropiness pulls the sauce back up into the dispenser.

Gum karaya can also be used to prevent bleed-out of color in frozen desserts, including sherbet and ice pops.[24]

Bio-Gums

Bio-gum is the term for gums produced through fermentation or that start with living components. A number of bio-gums are produced, including xanthan, gellan, dextran, pullulan, and curdlan; however, the only two currently used with any regularity in the food business are xanthan and gellan, and the use of gellan gum is minor at this point.

Xanthan

Xanthan gum was developed by the USDA in 1959 and licensed to the Kelco division of Merck and Company, which produced it commercially starting in 1961. It was approved for food use in 1969[25] and, since then, has become one of the most widely used gums in the food industry.

Xanthan gum is produced through the growth on sugars of the *Xanthomonas campestris* bacterium, which is often found on cabbage. Xanthan gum is the extracellular polysaccharide produced by the bacteria during fermentation. After the bacteria are pasteurized to stop fermentation, the polysaccharide is precipitated by alcohol. The result is dried and ground into a powder. Xanthan gum is considered a natural gum.[26]

Xanthan is a popular choice in many foods. It is acid-stable, temperature-stable, relatively unaffected by salts,[27] and synergistic with galactomannans (the seed gums). Xanthan gum is also a good choice in frozen foods; it is fairly freeze-thaw resistant. On its own, it is non-gelling, but in combination with locust bean gum forms a soft, elastic gel. Xanthan gum is pseudoplastic, meaning that at high shear it thins out, but that at low or no shear it returns to its thickened state. This property makes it useful in products such as salad dressings; when poured, the shear created by the pour makes the dressing thin out; however, when it comes to rest on the salad and there is no longer any shear, it thickens and clings.

Xanthan gum is relatively inexpensive and, because it is manufactured rather than harvested, not subject to environmental or geopolitical considerations. Some other gums become less available due to droughts, plant disease, political embargoes, and other factors that can affect distribution. Because xanthan is not subject to these, its availability and pricing remain stable from year to year.

One problem is that its texture in solution can be snotty. This is addressed by adding other gums, such as guar. Also, this negative attribute of xanthan does not manifest in dry products, such as baked goods.

Xanthan is generally sold in two mesh sizes, 80 and 200. The 200 mesh size hydrates more quickly but is a bit more difficult to disperse. The 80 mesh is easier to disperse but hydrates less quickly. Other available forms are agglomerated (individual particles stuck together into large, irregularly shaped clumps that rapidly disperse in water and are less dusty and easier to handle than standard powders) and easily dispersing (usually coated with a small amount of oil), as well as transparent and brine-tolerant grades. An agglomerated or easily dispersible xanthan may be best if the equipment used does not produce much shear or water movement, as some swept-surface kettles. Brine-tolerant xanthan is an excellent choice for products high in salt, such as pickle brines and some marinades.

Xanthan gum is widely used in salad dressings to form a pseudo- or commercially acceptable emulsion. In fact, many gums possess this emulsion-like property.

A true emulsifier contains a lipophilic (attracted to oil) and hydrophilic (attracted to water) receptor. Gum arabic and gum tragacanth have molecules with these receptors. By holding onto both the water and the oil, they create an emulsion where the water and the oil do not separate; they are held together by a common molecule to which they are both bound. A commercially acceptable or pseudo-emulsion is different; it looks like an emulsion, but it is not really emulsified.

An emulsion has two parts: an internal, dispersed phase and an external, continuous phase. In a soda pop illustration, the bubbles are the internal phase and the surrounding water is the external phase. Of course, when the bottle or can is opened, the small bubbles (the internal phase) rise to the top because they are lighter than the external phase. The same happens when you mix oil and water; when you shake the mixture, the oil slick breaks into little globules or droplets and becomes dispersed in the external phase. However, because oil is lighter than water, the oil droplets rise and aggregate (come together and form larger globules) and eventually coalesce (form a solid, unified layer of oil). Now, think of a thick shake; there are still small bubbles (internal phase) dispersed in the shake, but they are not moving. Why? Because the

external phase, the semi-frozen solution around them, is too thick. Eventually, as the shake melts and thins, the bubbles rise; for the moment, though, they are distributed throughout the external phase.

That is essentially how a pseudo-emulsion or commercially acceptable emulsion works. For example, a salad dressing containing oil is passed through a homogenizer or colloid mill that makes the oil drops very, very small (less than 10 microns). Xanthan gum makes the external phase, or water-vinegar solution, thick. This makes it hard for the very small oil droplets to move and rise to the top—a commercially acceptable emulsion. It is called *commercially acceptable* because it is not a true emulsion; there is no emulsifier to hold the two components together, and it will eventually break (separate into oil and water phases again), but it will remain as an emulsion long enough to be sold and consumed by the end user.

As mentioned, xanthan is probably the most widely used of all gums due to its effectiveness across a wide range of criteria. However, while it can be considered a Swiss Army knife that performs many functions adequately, it may not offer optimal performance in every case. That is one reason why xanthan is often used in conjunction with other gums. Many salad dressings in the market contain xanthan gum and Propylene Glycol Alginate (PGA). This combination, typically 90:10 xanthan:PGA, is one of the most common stabilizer systems used in the food industry.

The following salsa recipe contains xanthan and guar gum, a good combination due to their synergism. The combination allows for reduced costs and lower overall use of gum, resulting in a nice, smooth texture. The use of two gums that are efficacious in a cold system makes possible a non-cooked salsa.

Salsa

Ingredients	Percent
Tomatoes, canned diced	71.85
Red onion, diced	13.10
Green pepper, diced	11.05
Vegetable oil	1.30
Vinegar, white 5 percent acidity	1.30
Salt	0.55
Garlic powder	0.30
Guar gum	0.10
Xanthan gum	0.15
Ground cumin	0.20
Black pepper	0.10
Total	100.00

Procedure:

1) Dry blend the salt, garlic powder, gums, cumin, and black pepper.

2) Puree or coarsely chop (depending on desired consistency) the tomatoes, onions, and green peppers. Combine with the oil and vinegar.

3) Add the dry ingredients to the tomato mixture and blend until fully dissolved.

4) Look for signs of separation over the next few days.

Gellan Gum

Gellan gum, discovered in 1977,[28] is manufactured via fermentation similar to xanthan gum. The bacteria used is *Sphingomonas elodea*, which has been considered, in Japan, a natural food additive since 1988 and approved by the FDA for use in foods (21 CFR 172.665).

Gellan gum can form weak gels at low usage levels, excellent for the suspension of particulates, such as fruit particles and pulp, in beverages including ades, smoothies, and iced teas.

Gellan gum is available as high acyl or low acyl. High-acyl gellan gum yields a soft, elastic gel, while low-acyl gellan gum forms hard, brittle gels in the presence of cations (molecules with a positive charge—that is, with more protons than electrons), including calcium, magnesium, sodium, and potassium.[29] This makes gellan gum an excellent choice for creating gels because, with the right choice (high acyl or low acyl) and by varying the amount and type of cationic salt (such as potassium chloride or magnesium chloride) used, a wide range of gel textures is possible.

Another unique property of gellan is its ability to control its setting point (the temperature at which it goes from liquid to gel) and its melting point. These factors are controlled, again, by the choice of cation; gels made with calcium set between 77 and 113°F (25 and 45°C), while those made with sodium set between 104 and 122°F (40 and 50°C). At lower levels of cationic salts, gels are thermo-reversible—that is, they remelt when heated; at higher ion levels, they are non-thermo-reversible—that is, they do not remelt when heated.[30] Non-thermo-reversible products are desired when a product's texture should remain firm after heating, as in an analog (soy or vegetable) sausage. The gum creates a gel that gives the product structure; melting is not desirable. On the other hand, a thermo-reversible product is perfect for coating a turkey with a glaze that adheres to the surface but that, when heated, melts to form a gravy or jus.

Gellan gum can substitute for agar or gelatin in dessert gels; it can form a softer gel than agar can.

Because it is not derived from animals, as gelatin is, gellan can be used in vegan and meat-restricted diets. It is suitable in kosher and halal foods for the same reason.

Gellan is relatively expensive compared to other gums. However, it is growing in popularity and, with increased sales volumes, prices are likely to drop.

Marine Gums

Marine gums come from the oceans; more specifically, they are derived from seaweeds.

There are many types of marine gums, and within each category are many variations. This is primarily due to the wide assortment of seaweeds and their individual properties but also because of the choice of processing methods and chemical reagents used in their manufacture.

This makes it difficult to place marine gums in any one category—some form gels, some do not; some require heat to gel, others do not; and so on. However, the extremely wide range of attributes is also what makes marine gums so useful; no matter what type of system is in development, chances are that a marine gum will work.

In fact, variables are so numerous they would fill an entire book. Here we list the most common properties and uses. As an example, the presence of calcium, sodium, and potassium ions affects hydration temperatures and, therefore, the setting and remelting temperatures of the carrageenan gels. Iota carrageenan hydrates at ambient temperature in water and becomes a viscous solution. However, if salt is added, the solution is converted into a slight gel with a distinct yield point (essentially a measure of resistance to flow; true solutions do not have a distinct yield point). The new yield point makes the gum useful in products such as cold prepared salad dressings, as the slight gel suspends particulates, such as herbs, while retaining a pleasantly fluid mouthfeel.[31] This also helps the dressing cling to the salad vegetables rather than quickly drain to the bottom of the bowl. The most commonly used parameters presented here are safe and yield an effective product.

Carrageenans

Carrageenans come from a class of seaweed called Rhodophyceae, or red algae. Within this class of seaweeds are the *Chondrus crispus, Euchema cotonnii, Euchema spinosum, Gigartina skottsbergi,* and *Iradaea laminarioides* species.[32]

Carrageenans are classified by their primary molecular structure as either kappa (κ), iota (ι), or lambda (λ). Each type acts differently; however, it is very rare for a carrageenan to be pure iota or lambda or kappa. In fact, each seaweed usually contains two of the types. *Chondrus crispus,* which is also known and sold in health food stores as Irish moss, contains kappa and lambda carrageenans. The Euchema species contains kappa and iota carrageenans, and the Gigartina species yields kappa and lambda carrageenans.[33] When we say a carrageenan is a kappa carrageenan, we mean it is predominantly kappa.

The seaweeds are either harvested from the ocean or farmed. Farming is becoming preferable because it can be closely controlled. In the Philippines, the government gives families starter stock that they plant along the coast, under water, about waist high in a manner similar to a vineyard, with lines strung between stakes planted in the sand and the seaweeds suspended from the lines.

The weeds are picked when they reach a predetermined length, and are cleaned and then placed in extraction tanks. They are processed with various alkalis (potassium hydroxide, sodium hydroxide, and so on) to break down the cellulose. The mixture is clarified by passing through filters, concentrated, precipitated (usually with alcohol), and then dried and ground. Because there are so many seaweeds and combinations of variables, from the ratio of kappa to iota to lambda, to the choice of alkalizing agent, to the choice of precipitating agent, to the manner in which the product is dried and ground, to the naturally occurring mineral salts, several hundred, if not thousands, of variations of carrageenan are possible. Think of choosing a carrageenan like you would choose paint. First, is it latex, acrylic, or water-based? Second, is it matte, gloss, or semi-gloss? Third, what color do you want? Is it blue? If so, robin's-egg blue, sky blue, navy blue? Just as paints can be as different as a glossy Chinese red is from a matte beige, and just as they can be as close as two adjacent color chips, carrageenans can be that different and that similar. They provide the food developer a very wide range of tools for use in a very wide range of conditions.

Kappa (κ) Carrageenan

Kappa carrageenans gel on heating to at least 176°F (80°C) and cooling. In water, they form a clear gel that, depending on the concentration of carrageenan, can be soft or brittle. As with gellan gum, the presence of ions (such as sodium and calcium) alters the setting and melting temperature within a range of 104 to 158°F (40 to 70°C). These gels are thermoreversible when heated to 41 to 50°F (5 to 10°C) above their gelling temperature. Kappa carrageenans react nicely with potassium ions, forming stronger gels when potassium is present in the system.

Kappa carrageenans are not very freeze-thaw stable, and they exhibit a fair amount of syneresis. However, the addition of other gums, especially locust bean, inhibits the syneresis and yields a softer, more gelatin-like gel. When used in this manner, kappa carrageenans are used to make a dessert gel that is shelf-stable when filled and packed aseptically (in a sterile environment in sterilized packaging materials). Because the melting point of the carrageenan is around 140°F (60°C), it is unlikely to melt when stored in a non-refrigerated state.

Kappa carrageenans also react with milk proteins. They not only form a weak gel in the water portion of milk but also interact with the casein micelles (typical casein structures) that make up 80 percent of the milk proteins, and they act as an emulsifier due to being both hydrophilic and lipophilic.[34] This makes kappa carrageenans an ideal choice for products such as flans and crème brûlée. Because the carrageenan incorporates the casein micelles of milk into its gel structure, the result is about 5 times as firm as a water gel.[35] In other words, a milk gel made with 0.2 percent carrageenan is as firm as a water gel at 1.0 percent carrageenan. The economies of use make kappa carrageenan an especially good choice in products containing milk components.

One of the more popular uses is as a water binder in meat products. The meat processor injects a solution of water and kappa carrageenan into the meat muscle, thereby adding moisture and weight. The carrageenan helps prevent purge, or water loss, by forming a gel inside of the protein that effectively traps the added water.

Iota Carrageenan

Iota carrageenan tends to form soft, elastic gels. It is very reactive with calcium, making it another excellent choice for foods containing milk or cheese. Iota carrageenan exhibits better freeze-thaw stability than kappa. Like kappa, heating is an effective mechanism for creating a gel, although iota carrageenan also forms a gel in cold milk because of its interaction with calcium. With a very small amount of carrageenan (0.01 to 0.05 percent), a very weak gel structure forms that acts as a web in the solution, trapping particles that would otherwise settle. This makes iota (and also kappa) carrageenans excellent choices for beverages such as chocolate milk and bottled cappuccinos, where the cocoa particles would otherwise settle to the bottom of the container.

Iota carrageenans are often used in conjunction with kappa carrageenans. The combination offers a wide range of gel structures; adding more iota makes the gel less brittle and softer, while adding more kappa makes it a bit stronger and more firm. As the iota does not exhibit as much syneresis as the kappa, watering out is reduced when iota is added to a kappa gel. Freeze-thaw stability in kappa is improved by adding iota, and as both are reactive with milk products, combining them yields a wide array of gels—from firm custard to soft pudding and even pourable yogurt. Iota carrageenans are also synergistic with starch; a starch solution increases in viscosity approximately four times when iota is introduced.[36] This combination is often used to give texture to bakery cream fillings.

In the following recipe, the iota carrageenan helps keep the sauce consistent by creating a slight gel matrix with the cream and butter. The xanthan adds body, and the low-methoxyl pectin helps prevent protein denaturation (curdling) on reheat.

Make two batches, one containing the gums, the second without as a control. Then do the comparison tests recommended below.

Alfredo Sauce

Ingredients	Percent
Heavy cream	63.50
Parmesan cheese, grated	22.70
Black pepper	0.18
Salt	0.36
Granulated garlic	0.27
Iota carrageenan	0.15
Low-methoxyl pectin	0.07
Xanthan	0.07
Plugra butter	12.70
Total	100.00

Procedure:

1) Scale the dry ingredients; mix together thoroughly to ensure even distribution of all the ingredients.

2) Place the heavy cream in a saucepan and begin to heat. While heating, rapidly whisk in the dry ingredients until evenly blended and well incorporated.

3) Once the cream mixture has come to 180°F (82°C), whisk in the cheese until it melts and becomes fully dissolved and blended with the cream.

4) Bring to a simmer and continue simmering for 5 minutes. While doing so, break the butter into small pieces and whisk it in, a few pieces at a time, until the butter is melted in and evenly blended.

5) Remove from the heat. Chill.

What you should notice:

- The cook time for the gum sample is 5 minutes.
- The control takes 15 minutes to reach final viscosity, which is thinner than the gum sample.
- The gum sample requires 66 percent less heating time than the control to achieve full viscosity.
- The yield for the gum sample is 471 g (85.5 percent yield); the control with no gums yields 400 g (72.5 percent) due to evaporation of the liquids in order to achieve viscosity.

Test the two sauces by adding 200 g sauce to 300 g cooked linguine. Freeze the samples and reheat in a microwave after freezing. Notice that the sample with gums has a better consistency—but, more important, the emulsion remains intact, with very little separation of fat.

Lambda Carrageenans

Unlike kappa and iota carrageenans, lambda carrageenans do not gel, but they do become viscous when dispersed in an aqueous solution. Lambda does not require heating to become effective; it disperses and hydrates in cool water.

Lambda carrageenans exhibit good salt tolerance. This makes them a good choice for salad dressings and light brines where suspension of spices is desired. Lambda can be a good substitute for other thickening gums, such as xanthan and guar, especially when a less snotty or gummy mouthfeel is desired. Lambda has a clean mouthfeel and is smooth-flowing. The predominant use for lambda carrageenan in the food industry is as a thickener for dairy products, adding texture, mouthfeel, and suspension properties. It is also used in products such as retail dry mix salad dressings.

Alginates

The alginate used in the food industry comes from brown algae (Phaeophyceae), of which there are many varieties, including *Laminaria hyperborea* (perhaps the most common), *Macrocystis pyrifera*, and *Laminaria japonica*.

The most common form is sodium alginate, so much so that when people in the food industry talk about sodium alginate they usually just say "alginate." Other forms exist (potassium alginate, calcium alginate), but the sodium form predominates.

Alginate is extracted from seaweed by first making a pre-extraction with hydrochloric acid. This yields alginic acid, which has limited stability[37] and so is quickly processed with sodium carbonate or sodium hydroxide to yield sodium alginate. The actual process is far more complex.

Alginate is composed mostly of β-D-mannuronic acid (M) and α-L-guluronic acid (G),[38] and the combination and arrangement of these molecules determine the properties of the alginate—most importantly, how firm or how soft and elastic a gel is formed.

Sodium alginate forms a fairly viscous solution in water, typically 600 to 800 cps at 1 percent, and so it is sometimes used as a thickening agent. Alginate does not require heat to become viscous; it hydrates easily in a cold system and so it can be used in products like instant beverage mixes.

The most commonly utilized attribute of alginate is its ability to set instantaneously to a gel in the presence of calcium, without applying heat. One of the most widespread uses of sodium alginate is in formed foods, particularly onion rings. As onions are processed into a paste or puree, sodium alginate is added to it. It is then passed through an extruder (like a doughnut extruder) that forms an onion cylinder, which is sliced into rings. The rings drop into a bath containing a calcium solution, typically calcium lactate. The moment the ring hits the calcium bath, it solidifies into a solid gel. That gel is then battered and later fried.

This method of manufacture has many advantages. First, there is no waste; when making traditional onion rings, the ends are too small to use and are discarded. Second, each onion ring is the same size as the next; this is especially important in fast food restaurants, where portion control is critical to cost savings. The onion paste can even be combined with raw or frozen pieces of onion to give the onion ring a more authentic feel. This treatment, with some variation in the machinery, is also used to make the pimientos stuffed into green olives, the blueberries in muffin mixes, and many other items. Surimi often uses sodium alginate to give structural integrity to the formed fish items. Alginate gels are not thermo-reversible; they remain gelled even when heated. This is advantageous when creating products that must remain stable and hold together at elevated cooking temperatures (such as deep-fried onion rings).

Another advantage to the calcium reaction is that the time it takes to set the gel can be regulated through the addition of a sequestrant such as sodium tripolyphosphate, which ties up the calcium for a while. When a dentist takes a dental impression by placing a bite plate filled with gel in your mouth, that gel might be a sodium alginate mixture. A sequestrant is added so that, instead of gelling immediately on contact with the calcium, the reaction is delayed long enough for the dentist to mix the powder with water, place it in the bite plate, and get it into your mouth. Generally, it sets to a solid gel within 2 minutes in your mouth.

This reaction is also used to great advantage in restaurants known for molecular gastronomy, where sodium alginate is used to make such things as fruit caviars. The recipe below uses sodium alginate in a similar fashion to create so-called "balls of energy" that can be floated on top of a drink.

Balls of Energy Cocktail

Ingredients

Alizé Gold Passion liqueur	50 mL
Charbay lemon vodka	50 mL
Non-carbonated concentrated energy drink, such as AMP	100 g
Sodium alginate	1 g
3 percent solution of calcium chloride	400 g
1 percent solution of carboxymethylcellulose (CMC) in water	400 g
Sugar	5 g

Note: Not all energy drinks work here due to their ingredient inclusions.

Procedure

1) Blend 1 g sodium alginate with 5 g sugar.

2) Mix the alginate/sugar blend into the energy drink with a whisk. Let sit for 3 minutes.

3) Draw the alginate solution into an eyedropper or Pasteur pipette. Squeeze drops into the calcium chloride solution. *Note:* Hold the dropper above the solution, not immersed in it.

4) When the alginate mixture hits the calcium chloride solution, small balls of the energy drink immediately form. Let them sit in the calcium chloride for about 10 minutes.

5) Use a fine sieve to remove the balls from the calcium chloride solution. Rinse them off with fresh water.

6) Pour 50 mL Alizé into a martini glass. On top of that, pour 50 mL 1 percent CMC solution.

7) Place about 5 g energy balls on top of the CMC solution.

8) Pour 50 mL lemon-flavored vodka on top of the CMC solution. The balls float within the CMC layer and remain there as the drink is consumed.

Propylene Glycol Alginate (PGA)

PGA is the result of reacting alginic acid with propylene oxide. The single most distinctive attribute of PGA is that it is a true emulsifier.

The most common use in the food industry is in salad dressings and bottled marinades, where it usually paired with xanthan gum. Xanthan gum provides body and texture and acts as a pseudo-emulsifier, but it is not a true emulsifier. PGA provides true emulsification but is not as viscous as xanthan and does not add as much body to a system. Furthermore, PGA is far more expensive than xanthan, so using it alone is not economical. Most salad dressings do well with a 90:10 blend of xanthan and PGA. This combination, used between 0.25 percent and 0.50 percent, contributes body and mouthfeel and offers excellent emulsion stability.

PGA is always a good choice for an emulsion. However, it cannot be declared natural, so its use in some products is restricted.

The following recipe for taco meat uses PGA to help emulsify the water and fat from the meat. The konjac provides body and helps hold in some of the water that is purged during cooking. Prepare two samples, one with gums and a control without gums for comparison.

Taco/Burrito Filling

Ingredients

Ground beef chuck, 80 percent lean	500 g
Water	200 g
Chili powder	13 g
Dehydrated minced onion	10 g
Cumin, ground	4 g
Salt	3.5 g
Granulated garlic	2 g
Konjac gum	2.5 g
Propylene glycol alginate	1.5 g
Vegetable oil	15 g

Procedure

1) Put the beef in a pot. Add the water, chili powder, onion, cumin, salt, and garlic to the beef.

2) Add the gums to the oil and stir to disperse.

3) Start heating. Whisk the gum/oil slurry into the beef.

4) Heat to 190°F (88°C) and hold for 15 minutes.

Because the sample using the gums is cohesive, it can be accurately portioned out or flow evenly through machinery, such as an extruder or piston filler. Going through an extruder, the product with the gums is consistent in ingredient ratio and weight; the control varies due to the water purge.

There is, of course, the added benefit of lower cost due to the water being kept in the system and adding weight to the serving portion.

Agar

Agar is the most ancient phycocolloid (a colloid extracted from seaweed) still used as a gelling, thickening, and stabilizing food additive.[39] It most likely started in Japan centuries ago, and it is still used there as a primary food ingredient. Agar comes from the class of seaweeds called Rhodophyceae, as does carrageenan; however, the weeds used for agar are primarily from the genera Gelidium and Gracilaria.

Agar was originally processed simply by boiling the seaweed. The result was an edible gel. An improved method of preparation was, according to legend, discovered accidentally when an innkeeper threw the leftovers of an agar jelly outdoors, where it froze during the night and thawed the next day. This resulted in a dry substance that, when reconstituted in water, resulted in a clearer jelly of better quality.[40] Today dry agar strips are sold in stores.

Initially, agar should be heated to boiling (212°F [100°C]) for the greatest efficacy.

One of the major differences between agar and other gums that form gels is that gelation, the point at which the liquid becomes a solid gel, occurs at a temperature far below the gel melting temperature. The gel does not set until it has cooled down considerably, usually to about 86 to 95°F (30 to 35°C). Once formed, the gel does not melt again until heated to 194 to 203°F (90 to 95°C). This makes agar ideal for one of its widely used applications—cake and doughnut glazes.

Because the gel resets at a much lower temperature than it melts, as long as the glaze temperature is kept fairly warm (above 95°F [35°C]), it remains liquid. This allows glaze to be used without fear of it setting too quickly, so doughnuts can be dipped or cakes glazed under a cascade drip. With most other gums, the gels reset at a much higher temperature (closer to the melting point), so unless temperature is critically controlled, the gel may reset too soon. Furthermore, because of its higher melting point, the glaze does not melt as easily under high-heat conditions.

Other uses for agar include imitation fruit gels, water gel desserts (it is not of animal origin and so can be used in vegan, kosher, and halal applications), and the fining of wines (the removal of suspended particles before bottling).

Agar from the Gelidium seaweed reacts synergistically with locust bean gum to form a stronger and more elastic gel. Gracilaria agar does not have this synergy; in fact, locust bean gum may weaken the gel. On the other hand, gels made with Gracilaria react better with sugars than those made with Gelidium. The Gracilaria form is most often used for bakery glazes and candy fillings.

In Asia, agar is used in much the same manner as gelatin in the United States. Recently, a diet was introduced in Japan that utilized the swelling properties of agar to create a feeling of satiety. The diet was so successful that for some time afterward, agar was difficult to procure; Japan was buying up almost all the product manufactured. Unlike pectin, agar does not require sugar to create a gel, so sugarless jams and jellies can be produced for dietary purposes.

Agar has also been used for years as the standard gelling agent in solid media used to grow and identify bacteria, yeasts, and molds, as well as a sterile propagation medium for agriculturally important plants and plant experimentation.

Plant Gums of Terrestrial Origin

Konjac

Konjac flour and konjac gum have been used as ingredients in Asia for centuries; in Japan, they are often seen on a menu as *konnyaku*. In Asia, noodles are produced from konjac alone. Because they are made from a gum, konjac noodles are much more elastic than traditional pasta.

The konjac plant is a tuber (like potatoes); however, it can grow quite large, and it grows for at least three years before it is harvested. The tuber is cut into slices and air-dried to form chips. It is then ground to a powder, and the starch and gum are separated via either air classification or wet milling. In air classification, the powder is blown on a fluid bed—a system where air is blown under a screen so the powder is suspended and the heavier particles (the gum) fall and the lighter particles (the starch) rise. In a wet system, the powder is made into a slurry and passed through a centrifuge. The centrifuge, like a clothes washer basket, has a liner in which the holes are large enough to allow the smaller starch particles to pass through but not the larger glucomannan (gum) particles. After spinning, a cake of gum is left behind; this is dried and sifted back into a powder.

Konjac is a glucomannan, similar to the galactomannans (seed gums) but with a different monosaccharide (glucose instead of galactose) on the side chains of the mannose backbone.

Konjac has many characteristics, some unique, to exploit. When dispersed into a solution with no heat, it forms an extremely viscous solution (up to 36,000 cps at 1 percent—compare that to xanthan at 1500 cps at 1 percent) with a short texture—that is, it pours much as a thickened starch solution does. When poured, it does not have the long, ropy tail often seen with other gums, and it exhibits a less gummy mouthfeel. However, unlike starches, which it closely resembles in appearance, konjac does not mask flavors. Also, because it is non-ionic, it is relatively unaffected by salts and is stable to a pH below 3.8, in some cases as low as pH 2.8.[41]

When heated with xanthan or carrageenan, konjac forms a gel that uniquely can be either thermo-reversible or non-thermo-reversible. After heating, if the pH is raised above 9.5 to 10.0, the gel is non-thermo-reversible. To create a thermo-reversible gel, simply do not raise the pH above 9.5.

Note that once the high pH is attained, the solution can be brought back down to neutral or even acidic conditions. This is important because so many packaged foods are acidified or naturally acidic. Even milk is slightly acid, about pH 6.7. Most fruits and vegetables are naturally acid—for example, citrus fruits, tomatoes, and grapes. Some meats have a slightly alkaline value, between pH 7.0 and 8.0, but again, nowhere near the level needed to make a non-thermo-reversible konjac gel. This is why we stress that the pH can be brought down after it is raised. Most manufacturers add an alkali, such as potassium hydroxide, to raise the pH of the konjac solution. The pH is brought back down one of two ways. One is through the addition of an acid, such as citric acid or phosphoric acid. More often, a small batch of konjac solution is made, its pH raised, and it is added to a larger batch (a kettle full of the remaining ingredients, for example) of low pH product. Generally, the amount of konjac solution added to the full kettle is so small that the pH of the total system is relatively unchanged; thus, the konjac solution is now at the same low pH as the entire system.

Konjac absorbs a lot of water; it can pick up about 200 times its weight. (Xanthan and guar typically pick up about 40 times their weight.) This makes konjac a good choice when moisture must be controlled.

Because it forms a non-thermo-reversible gel, konjac is an excellent choice for products that must maintain their structure when heated, such as a vegetarian sausage and meat analogs. Surimi utilizes konjac as a texturizing agent.

Like most thickeners that do not require heat, konjac is a good choice for use in instant cold mix drinks. Because of its short texture, which mimics starches, it can be used for instant gravies and sauces as well.

When added to pasta dough (and treated to be non-thermo-reversible), konjac helps maintain structure and firmness when the pasta is placed on a steam table. It can also be made into a reversible gel and used for frozen gravies and items that require a slight gel for packing but must reverse to a liquid when heated.

Konjac also has nutraceutical benefits, making it an excellent choice for functional foods; it helps lower glycemic index, cholesterol, and triglycerides. Konjac is just becoming popular as an ingredient in the United States. Some health food stores sell konjac in capsules; it is usually labeled *glucomannan*. Asian supermarkets sell blocks of gelled konjac for use in recipes. The Japanese version is cut into strips and used as a noodle and topped with a sauce, or made into cubes and used in a manner similar to tofu, in salads or stir-fried dishes.

The following recipe is a little tricky. The key is to use a flat wooden spatula once the product starts to thicken and just slowly push the paste as it boils. Do not mix fast, or the developing structure will break. Move it just enough to keep it from burning.

Asian shops sell noodle presses into which a cube of finished gel is inserted and pressed to extrude noodles. If these are unavailable, simply cut the finished gel into strips. Calcium hydroxide is sold to the food industry as pickling lime or hydrated lime.

Konjac Noodles

Ingredients	Percent
Water	96.65
Konjac	2.35
Rice flour	0.85
Calcium hydroxide	0.15
Total	100.00

Procedure:

1) Add the calcium hydroxide to the water and mix until it is in solution.
2) Blend the konjac and the rice flour together.
3) Whisk the konjac/rice flour blend into the water/lime solution.

4) Heat to boiling while pushing the paste that forms so it does not burn. Do not beat or whisk it; just keep it moving.
5) Once boiling, let the mixture boil for about 3 minutes and then cover it and heat at low heat for another 5 minutes.
6) Place the resulting gel on a cutting board or cookie sheet and refrigerate, preferably overnight.
7) Cut into ¼-inch-wide strips.
8) Steam the fresh noodles until hot and serve with an Asian-flavored sauce, such as a sesame peanut sauce, on top.

Note that the noodles are non-thermo-reversible. That is because using the calcium hydroxide brought the pH up to about 9.5. Try the recipe without the calcium hydroxide and see what happens when you steam the noodles.

Also note: The strong smell while preparing is typical. The odor and taste disappear once the noodles are gelled and steamed.

Cellulose Gums

Cellulose gums are chemically modified derivatives of cellulose, the primary structural material in plant cell walls and one of the most abundant compounds on earth. Most cellulose derivatives start off as wood pulp or are derived from cotton linters (the short fibers from the cotton boll).[42] Depending on the chemicals used in processing, cellulose can be changed into a wide variety of derivatives; in the food industry, CMC is one of the most widely used of these derivatives.

Carboxymethylcellulose (CMC)

One of the distinctive characteristics of CMC is its almost crystal clear appearance when put into solution. It thickens in cold water and does not require heat to be effective. CMC is available in a very wide range of viscosities; from 200 cps at 1 percent up to 20,000 cps at 1 percent.

CMC is often used in frozen dairy-based desserts because it helps reduce ice crystal size and melting and dripping. CMC is very widely used in frozen push pops and water ices for the same reason. Without CMC, popsicles would be more like solid ice cubes than softer pops that can be broken by biting.

Because of its clarity, CMC is often used to provide viscosity in sugar-free syrups. Without sugar, syrup has little or no viscosity. CMC can replace the viscosity, and the resulting solution is still clear.

CMC can also be used in baked goods to help stop spread. Thickening pancake batter with CMC prevents it from spreading on the griddle when poured. As improved water binding is believed to inhibit fat absorption[43], and CMC is very good at binding water, it is often used for fried doughnuts.

Try making the following ice pop recipe with and without the CMC. Notice that after freezing, the control with no gum is hard, like an ice cube, while the ice pop with the gum has smaller crystals that can be bitten off.

Push-up Frozen Ice Pop

Ingredient	Percent
Sugar	12.00
CMC	0.10
Water	87.40
Citric acid	0.25
Flavor	0.25
Total	100.00

Procedure:

1) Blend the sugar and CMC.

2) Add the sugar mixture to the water; allow to mix and hydrate for at least 5 minutes.

3) Add the remaining ingredients.

4) Place in small, freezable pouches and fold so the liquid freezes into pops about 1 inch wide.

5) Freeze overnight.

Methylcellulose (MC) and Hydroxypropylmethylcellulose (HPMC)

Two of the more unusual gums in this group are methylcellulose (MC) and hydroxypropylmethylcellulose (HPMC), which both form gels at high temperatures, whereas most gums tend to become thinner at high temperatures. Some grades gel as low as 120°F (50°C); some require greater than 195°F (909°C). Gelling at high temperature is called thermalgelation. These gums are useful as an additive to breading and batters for products to be fried. When a batter containing them hits the hot oil, the gums immediately form a gel. This barrier inhibits the oil from being absorbed into the batter or breading. The advantage is threefold: the batter is crisper because it picks up less fat: it is less caloric, for the same reason; and costs are lower because less oil is pulled out of the fryer with the food.

Another use is in fruit fillings for pies; the thermalgelation helps prevent boil-out from the pie shell during baking; boil-out results in loss of product, a sloppy appearance, and messy equipment.

In addition, CMC is a true emulsifier, with both hydrophilic and hydrophobic receptors. This makes it useful for sauces and salad dressings, much like PGA.

Neither MC nor HPMC can be used in products that claim to be "all natural," because they are derived through a chemical process.

Microcrystalline Cellulose (MCC)

Microcrystalline cellulose (MCC), or cellulose gel (also called *colloidal cellulose*), is created by heating cellulose pulp in the presence of a weak acid such as dilute hydrochloric acid. It is then dried and ground. In this form it is called *powdered MCC*. If it is blended with CMC prior to drying, it is called *colloidal CMC*.[44]

MCC is often used in low-fat and fat-free salad dressings. After being subjected to high shear, the MCC particles form a three-dimensional network of crystals that gives foods a short, gelled texture like that of fat to the tongue; it is functionally similar to the structure of dispersed oil droplets in an emulsion.[45] If used at about 1.5 percent, the oil in a salad dressing can be reduced by about half, and the result is similar in mouthfeel to a full-fat type of dressing.

Pectin

Pectin is a familiar product to many chefs, bakers, and home jelly-makers. It is sold in supermarkets and used to make homemade jams, jellies, and pie fillings. Most of the commercial pectin used in the United States comes from citrus peels or apple pomace (press-cake remaining after juice is extracted from the pulp), but pectin is found in most fruits and many other plants. The two primary types of pectin, high methoxyl (HM) and low methoxyl (LM), are sometimes referred to as *high ester* and *low ester*.

High-Methoxyl (HM) Pectin

High-methoxyl (HM) pectin is the traditional, use-at-home pectin. HM pectin requires high levels of sugar and acid to form a gel. This is why it is used to create jellies and jams, as well as fruit fillings for pies and other fruit variegates.

HM pectins can form gels as wide-ranging as a solid juice-based jelly to a soft marmalade. To set properly, pectins must be used at the correct pH and with the correct level of sugar solids. The three types of HM pectins are slow set (SS), medium set (MS), and rapid set (RS), and the choice is based on production needs and type of product. Because RS pectin sets to a gel quickly, it might trap air bubbles created during filling. To achieve a clear, bubble-free product, use SS pectin so the trapped air has time to escape before the gel sets. That said, RS pectin is preferred in preserves, where fruit has a tendency to float, to keep the fruit more evenly dispersed throughout the jam matrix.

When using SS pectin, the pH must be between 3.4 and 3.8, depending on sugar content; in a rapid set it can go down to pH 2.8. These variables make using pectin a bit tricky, and in large production, very close attention must be paid to the sugar solids and pH of incoming raw materials (such as fruits) so adjustments in solids or acidity can be carefully calculated. Pectin requires boiling in order to form a gel. In addition, because HM pectin is not soluble above 20 percent solids but requires 65 percent solids in order to gel, the process must be designed so the pectin is introduced to the kettle when the solids are low, but they must later be brought above 65 percent. This is why the sugar is added after the pectin is already dissolved and at full boil. Careful planning yields good results.[46] The exact requirements for a particular product should be discussed with the supplier.

Pectin has a protective effect on protein below its isoelectric point (where it normally denatures, or starts curdling and precipitating). This makes pectin useful in acidic milk-based products, such as pourable yogurt, and in soy-based acidic drinks, such as flavored soy milks, in that the addition of pectin helps prevent the denaturation of the proteins. Acid dairy and soy-based products that go through high-heat processing such as HTST (high temperature, short time) thermal processing also benefit from the protection of HM pectin.

Low-Methoxyl (LM) Pectin

Low-methoxyl (LM) pectins do not require high sugar solids content, nor do they require a low pH. To set to a gel they are dependent on the amount of calcium available in the formula; this can come from the food itself or be added as an ingredient, such as calcium citrate. As a general rule, at least 60 mg calcium per gram of pectin is needed for the product to set to a gel. However, this can vary, and amidated LM pectins (those processed with ammonia) can set with lower levels of calcium. Unlike HM pectins, LM-amidated (LMA) pectins create a thermo-reversible gel.

In the case of LM pectins, calcium should not be present until it's time for the product to set, but it must be added at some point prior to filling. The water used must be carefully monitored for hardness (natural mineral content, including calcium) to avoid unintended gelling.

That LM pectin does not require a high sugar content makes it useful for low-calorie applications. The gel is typically softer and more spreadable than that made with HM pectin. The softer set of the LM pectin also makes it useful in products such as fruit centers for confections and baked goods. Like many other hydrocolloids, LM pectin also reduces crystallization in frozen foods.

Inulin

Inulin is a type of long-chain sugar molecule called a fructo-oligosaccharide, and it belongs to a category of fibers called fructans. It is usually sourced from chicory or Jerusalem artichoke (which is a sunflower, not really an artichoke). Inulin acts as a prebiotic—a substance that helps promote the growth of useful bacteria (probiotics) in the gut. As it is not digested in the mouth, stomach, or small intestine, by the time inulin gets to the large intestine it is basically unchanged; as such, it imparts only about 1.5 calories per gram.[47] Because it can be used at very high concentrations (up to 30 percent), it is possible to use enough in a food to allow a nutritional claim of active prebiotic. In fact, it is commonly added to yogurts containing active cultures to add to the digestive benefits of these products.

Inulin can be added as a cold solution; at about 7.5 percent in water it remains a clear, low-viscosity solution. At about 15 percent, inulin begins to form a gel when heated and cooled, and this increases in strength with the application of shear, additional heat, and increased concentration. Another method is known as *seeding*, in which a dilute inulin solution is heated to a high temperature and, as it cools, more inulin is added. This procedure, along with high shear, results in the firmest type of inulin gel.[48]

The inulin gel is creamy and can mimic fat in low-fat foods such as dairy spreads and baked goods. It is also useful in bakery fillings and fruit variegates when used at 5 to 6 percent and mixed under high shear, which yields a smooth gel.

Less Used Gums

Many more gums are available for use in foods. Although some have properties like the more familiar gums, they are not widely used.

Furcelleran

Furcelleran is a marine gum from red seaweed of the Rhodophycae family, like the carrageenans. It is sometimes called *Danish agar*. As with many carrageenans, furcelleran forms a gel when heated and cooled. It is most similar to kappa carrageenans but often slightly darker in appearance. At first the European Community (EC) regulators gave it its own classification, E408, but later reclassified it as a carrageenan, E407, because it is so closely related. *Note:* "E Numbers" are codes for substances that are approved for use as food additives within the European Union and Switzerland. The "E" stands for "Europe." They are commonly found on food labels throughout the European Union to help consumers understand what ingredients are added to their foods. Having a single unified list for food additives was first agreed upon in 1962 with food coloring. Any food item can be looked up by its E Number. E100 to E199, for example, are colors, E200 to E299 are preservatives, and so on. Gums and emulsifiers fall into the E400 to E499 range. This system saves label space because the manufacturer can list numbers instead of ingredient names.

Ghatti

Gum ghatti comes from trees grown in India and is similar to exudates such as gum arabic and karaya, with a viscosity range between those two. It is only about 90 percent soluble and forms a dark solution. A true emulsifier, it is also considered a prebiotic because it arrives in the large intestine largely unchanged and provides food for beneficial gut flora. Gum ghatti is often used in syrups for buttering or adding smoothness.

Cassia Tora

Cassia tora is an interesting weed, grown in India; a gum is made from the endosperm of its seed. Like LBG and guar, this gum is a galactomannan. The plant itself is used as a natural pesticide on organic farms, and the seed can be roasted to make a coffee substitute. Like many of the galactomannans, cassia forms a gel when heated in the presence of xanthan and certain carrageenans. Its widest use in the United States is in pet food gels.

Stabilizer Blends

Gums can be very useful when combined with one another or with other ingredients—such as calcium chloride, in the case of sodium alginate. They exhibit a wide range of synergies with other gums.

Vendors sell spice and seasoning blends, and flavor houses sell compounded flavors. Similarly, suppliers make pre-blended stabilizing systems—although blends can certainly be made in-house. Keep in mind that more tools increase your chances of success but also increase the amount of testing that must be done. Most vendors carry several types of guar, several of xanthan, dozens, if not more, of carrageenan, and so on. These can be similar to one another or as far apart as red and blue are on a color chart. Blending just the right mixture yields the best texture at the best cost. Just as a flavor chemist knows how to blend aroma chemicals and oils to make up a particular flavor, a hydrocolloid specialist can create a custom stabilizing blend for any application.

By law, each ingredient used in the stabilizer blend must be listed separately on the label of the food product. This is sometimes a consideration when a label is required to look as clean as possible. Consumers have accepted gum ingredients, for the most part, but too many can convey an over-manufactured impression. One other factor to consider when using blends is the ratios are predetermined. Having a preset blend may limit the number of food items that blend can be used in. However, just as with unblended gums, blends can be used as part of a larger stabilizing system and their use levels adjusted accordingly.

Tech Tips

Many, many variables are associated with the properties of gums. To select the best gum sample for a specific application, the gum supplier needs the following information:

1. What is the intended end use of the gum? That is, what is the final product application?
2. What properties are expected of the gum? For example, gelling, suspension, thickening?
3. What is the final food form? Is it frozen, retort, shelf-stable, refrigerated, or other?
4. Is it a high-acid product (pH <4.5) or a low-acid product (pH >4.5)?
5. Will any ingredients or materials be available to help with the dispersion of the gums? For example, oil, propylene glycol, alcohol, salt, sugar, corn syrup?
6. Does the product need to be certified kosher, organic, all-natural, or any other profile?
7. Is the product heated, and, if so, to what temperature?
8. What machinery is available for dispersion and hydration? For example, Scott Turbo® Mixer, Bredo Likwifier®, Lightnin'® Blender, Eductor?

Having the answers to these questions enables the supplier to home in on the best possible choices for the product.

Gelatin

Gelatin (spelled *gelatine* outside the United States) is not a carbohydrate, it is a protein. Then why include it in the carbohydrate chapter? Although gelatin is a protein, it acts much more like a carbohydrate hydrocolloid, and in food products, it is almost always used for its hydrocolloid functionality.

In fact, although gelatin is an animal-derived protein, it is not a complete protein as far as nutritive value is concerned. While gelatin does contain 18 amino acids, a good percentage of the essential amino acids are missing or present in inconsequential amounts. Gelatin is completely lacking in one (tryptophan) and has almost none of another (methionine). It is also low in isoleucine and threonine. This makes it a poor choice to add protein to the diet.

Gelatin is made by breaking down collagen, a protein found in the connective tissue of animals. It can be derived from any animal, including fish, but most gelatin used in the United States comes from either swine or cattle. It is not, as commonly thought, commercially derived from hooves but rather from hides and often bones as well.

Most gelatins used in the food industry are classified as Type A or Type B. Type A is manufactured from swine and is converted from collagen in a process involving acids. Type B is manufactured from cattle using an alkaline conversion.

Typically, at equal concentrations Type A gelatin has a stronger gel than Type B,[49] but other textural issues, such as elasticity, determine which type is used. The gel strength of gelatin is measured as bloom strength. The bloom test involves adding weight to a standard-size plunger and measuring the weight in grams required to make that plunger depress a 6.66 percent gelatin gel to a depth of 4 mm at 50°F (10°C). Typical bloom strengths are between 125 and 300, with 300 bloom being relatively expensive due to its greater gel strength.

One concern of many people when choosing gelatin as a texturizing agent is that because it is derived from animals, it cannot be considered for use in vegetarian or vegan foods. In the same vein, as Type A is derived from swine and the source of cattle for Type B cannot always be traced, the gelatin cannot technically be considered kosher or halal. However, this determination is usually left to the interpretation of the certifying agency. Many vegetarian and some kosher and halal supervisory organizations consider the process of heating and alkalinization or acidification so severe that in the end the gelatin has no relation physically to its source. For this reason, some certifying agencies allow gelatin to be used in kosher, halal, or vegetarian foods.

Although far less available and far more expensive, gelatin from fish that are considered kosher is also available. It is typically weaker than a Type A or Type B gel. Also available is gelatin from kosher cattle herds that have been traced by a supervising agency from birth through slaughter. Gelatin made from these animals is approved kosher by all agencies.

Gelatin has been used for a very long time in the preparation of foods. Sometimes it appeared as the result of long boiling of bones or skin or flesh with connective tissue. One example is pot au feu, a beef stew where the meat contains quite a bit of cartilage, such as oxtail. By cooking in water for a long time, the collagen is converted to gelatin, which thickens the stew. If left to cool, the stew forms a jelly (aspic, in culinary terms). "Gefilte fish" is poached and then left to cool in the broth in which it was poached. The broth, after chilling, gels from the fish gelatin created by the poaching.

In the United States, gelatin is most frequently used in powdered form, although it is available in sheets as well. It is thermo-reversible; it forms a gel if it is heated and left to cool, but that gel breaks down at a lower temperature than most other hydrocolloids. While this makes gelatin unsuitable for items such as shelf-stable dessert gels (which must be made with gums), it does have the beneficial characteristic of melting at below body temperature (less than 95°F [35°C]), causing the gel to melt in the mouth when eaten and thereby providing a very cool and refreshing mouthfeel.

Gelatin is commonly used in yogurts for body and is the main ingredient in many gummy bear–type candies. Of course, when mixed with sugar, an acidulant, and flavor, it becomes the water gel dessert commonly referred to by the brand name Jell-O®. Gelatin is also useful, when not made into a gel, for maintaining foams in beverages. Marshmallows rely on gelatin for just the right set and to hold and entrap the air incorporated during their manufacture.

Gelatin is also commonly used for glazes and aspics, with the gel strength determined by the amount of gelatin in solution (typically between 1 and 5 percent). Gelatin does break down in the presence of certain proteases (protein enzymes), so when using it in fruit-based products, avoid fruits such as pineapple, kiwi, and papaya.

Gelatin is also used as a protein encapsulant for an assortment of functional ingredients to protect them from exposure to harsh processing or storage environments or to provide time-release functionality. Protein encapsulation of oxygen-sensitive flavor oils prior to spray-drying is one example.

◉ Conclusion

The world of carbohydrates offers enormous possibilities for the food developer. From moisture management to viscosity enhancement; from freeze-thaw stabilization to emulsification, the list of functional capabilities is nearly infinite. The keys to using carbohydrates successfully are to clearly identify the desired attributes of the finished product and to understand the properties of each carbohydrate ingredient. As it is nearly impossible for any one individual to possess this encyclopedic knowledge, it is strongly recommended that developers take advantage of their ingredient suppliers to provide this critical information throughout the development cycle, from project inception to product launch.

[1]USDA Dietary Guidelines for Americans 2005, retrieved from http://www.health.gov/dietaryguidelines/dga2005/document/html/chapter2.

[2]C. L. Ogden, M. D. Carroll, M. A. McDowell, and K. M. Flegal, "Obesity Among Adults in the United States: No Change Since 2003–2004," *NCHS Data Brief No. 1* (Hyattsville, MD: National Center for Health Statistics, 2007). U.S. Department of Health and Human Services, *Healthy People 2010*, 2nd ed., with *Understanding and Improving Health and Objectives for Improving Health*, 2 vols. (Washington, DC: U.S. Government Printing Office, November 2000).

[3]21CFR101.9(c)(6)(ii).

[4]T. S. Temelkova-Kurktschiev, et al., "Postchallenge Plasma Glucose and Glycemic Spikes Are More Strongly Associated with Atherosclerosis Than Fasting Glucose or HbA1c Level," *Diabetes Care* 12 (December 23, 2000): 1830–1834.

[5]J. BeMiller and R. Whistler, Starch, 3rd ed., Chemistry and Technology. Food Science and Technology, 2009.

[6]A.-C. Eliasson, *Starch in Food: Structure, Function, and Applications* (Cambridge, England: Woodhead, 2004).

[7]R. Whistler, J. N. BeMiller, and E. F. Paschall, *Starch: Chemistry and Technology*, 2nd ed. (Orlando, FL: Academic Press, 1984).

[8]BeMiller and Whistler, *Starch*.

[9]E. J. Pyler, *Baking Science and Technology* (Kansas City, MO: Sosland, 1988).

[10]Eliasson, *Starch in Food*.

[11]D. J. Thomas and W. A. Atwell, *Starches* (Eagan, 1999).

[12]G. Eggleston and G. Côté, "Oligosaccharides in Food and Agriculture," American Chemical Society, ACS Symposium Series, 2003.

[13]O. R. Fennema, S. Damodaran, and K. L. Parkin, *Fennema's Food Chemistry*, 4th ed. (CRC Press, 2007).

[14]G. M. A. van Beynum and J. A. Roels, *Starch Conversion Technology* (Dekker, Marcel, 1985).

[15]A. Srichamroen, C. J. Field, A. B. R. Thomson, and K. B. Tapan, "The Modifying Effects of Galactomannan from Canadian-Grown Fenugreek (Trigonella foenum-graecum L.) on the Glycemic and Lipidemic Status in Rats."

[16]Food and Agriculture Organization of the United Nations (FAO) Corporate Document Repository, "Gums, Resins, and Latexes of Plant Origin: Gum Arabic, Gum Talha, and Other Acacia Gums" (1995), retrieved from http://www.fao.org/docrep/v9236e/v9236e05.htm.

[17]FAO, "Gums, Resins, and Latexes."

[18]G. Phillips and P. Williams, *Handbook of Hydrocolloids* (Woodhead, 2000).

[19]S. Cui, *Food Carbohydrates* (CRC Taylor and Francis, 2005).

[20]A. Nussinovitch, *Hydrocolloid Applications* (Blackie Academic and Professional, 1997).

[21]Y. Hui, *Handbook of Food Science, Technology, and Engineering*, vol. 3 (CRC Press, 2005).

[22]G. Phillips and P. Williams, *Handbook of Hydrocolloids* (Woodhead, 2000).

[23]Nussinovitch, *Hydrocolloid Applications*.

[24]A. Imeson, *Thickening and Gelling Agents for Food*, 2nd ed. (Aspen Publishers, 1999).

[25]I. Goldberg and R. Williams, *Biotechnology and Food Ingredients* (Springer-Verlag, 2007).

[26]United States International Trade Commission Rulings and Harmonized Tariff Schedule, HQ 951034, July 6, 1992.

[27]Phillips and Williams, *Handbook of Hydrocolloids*.

[28]Cui, *Food Carbohydrates*.

[29]Ibid.

[30]Nussinovitch, *Hydrocolloid Applications*.

[31]Phillips and Williams, *Handbook of Hydrocolloids*.

[32]Cui, *Food Carbohydrates*.

[33]Nussinovitch, *Hydrocolloid Applications*.

[34]Ibid.

[35]A. Hoefler, *Hydrocolloids* (Eagan, 2004).

[36]Imeson, *Thickening and Gelling Agents for Food.*

[37]Ibid.

[38]Phillips and Williams, *Handbook of Hydrocolloids.*

[39]Imeson, *Thickening and Gelling Agents for Food.*

[40]Ibid.

[41]Ibid.

[42]Phillips and Williams, *Handbook of Hydrocolloids.*

[43]Ibid.

[44]Imeson, *Thickening and Gelling Agents for Food.*

[45]Ibid.

[46]Nussinovitch, *Hydrocolloid Applications.*

[47]Phillips and Williams, *Handbook of Hydrocolloids.*

[48]Ibid.

[49]A. Salvador and S. M. Fiszman, *Journal of Dairy Science* 81, no. 6, 1998.

9 | Lipid-Based Foods

Lead Author: Marilynn Schnepf, Ph.D., R.D., Professor, Nutrition and Health Sciences, University of Nebraska

Lynne Morehart, Technical Service Manager, Cargill Oils and Shortenings

Brian K. Yager, Chef/Owner, Cuisine 256, LLC

●Introduction

Lipid is the overall name for the class of nutrients known as *fats and oils*. They are found in animal, marine, and plant sources, where they provide insulation, energy, and nutrient storage. In recent years, fats have received a lot of attention in the press, much of it focused on limiting or eliminating their consumption in general and certain fats in particular. Product developers must understand the use of fats in products (and diets) and how to select and utilize the proper fat for each application. Not all fats are created equal.

Historical Perspective

Fats and oils are dense sources of calories in the human diet, contributing 9 calories per gram, while proteins and carbohydrates provide only 4 calories per gram. The fats and oils in earliest times came mainly from nuts and seeds, with occasional animal sources. When finding and consuming enough calories was a challenge, the energy density of fats and oils was a positive characteristic.

Eventually, through trial and error, early people discovered how to extract fats and oils from their sources to use in cooking and food processing. However, as enhanced shelf life and organoleptic properties were desired, lipids went through new processing techniques to provide greater resistance to rancidity and improved texture and functionality.

During the last century, research has shown how the sources, processing, and quantities of fats and oils in the diet affect health and product development. In many countries where an abundance of calories is available for consumption, the high number of calories in fat is no longer an advantage and now is often seen as a liability. As a result, significant changes have been made to fats and oils to provide the consumer with better-tasting and more healthful products.

●Fat Sources

Lipids come from animal, marine, and plant sources. The most notable animal fats are lard (from pigs), tallow (from beef cattle), and butter; fish provide marine oils, and plants provide corn, soy, olive, peanut, sunflower, cotton, and numerous specialty oils such as sesame, nut, and other seed oils. Most of the plant sources are classified as polyunsaturated, while the land animal sources are more saturated. The exceptions are the tropical oils—coconut, palm, and palm kernel—which are from plant sources but contain saturated fatty acids. Although fish oils are from animals, they tend to be more unsaturated. All animal fats, including marine sources, contain cholesterol; plant-derived fats do not. A vast array of choices are available to product developers, who must choose among them carefully.

Vegetable Oils

Vegetable oils are the lipid materials derived from plants, primarily their seeds. Most are composed primarily of unsaturated fatty acids, either mono- or polyunsaturated, and as such are liquid at room temperature and tend to have higher smoke points than animal fats. Examples include soy, corn, canola (rapeseed), peanut, cottonseed, avocado, safflower, sunflower, almond, olive, and sesame seed oils. All of these oils have smoke points at or above 400°F (204°C). The animal fat with the highest smoke point is lard, at 375°F (191°C). This makes vegetable oils the preferred medium for deep frying.

Tropical oils (those extracted from coconut or oil palms) and cocoa butter are composed primarily of saturated fatty acids, and as such are solid at room temperature. They are excellent in baking applications as a replacement for animal fats and hydrogenated vegetable shortenings, and although they are a source of saturated fat in the diet, they contain neither cholesterol nor trans fats.

As previously noted, nutritionists agree that a healthy diet should contain a ratio of omega-6 to omega-3 fats of no more than 4:1. The average modern American diet has been estimated to have a ratio of between 10 and 20:1. Recent findings indicate that a diet overly high in omega-6 fatty acids negates the positive effects of omega-3 fatty acids, and in fact may increase the incidence of a number of diseases.

Unfortunately, nearly all vegetable oils contain an overabundance of omega-6 fatty acids, and a shortage of omega-3 fatty acids. For example, cottonseed oil, a common ingredient in cooking oils, has a ratio of 234:1 omega-6:omega-3; corn oil has a ratio of 46:1 omega-6:omega-3; even soybean oil has an 8:1 ratio. This is of concern because there are so few good sources of omega-3 fatty acids in the diet (primarily seafood, and to a much lesser extent, walnuts and flax seeds) to help balance the ratio between the two, and vegetable oils (and foods prepared from them) have become such a large part of the diet in developed countries.

On the healthier side, canola oil has a ratio of 2:1 omega-6:omega-3. Clearly, new product developers for companies interested in healthier foods should opt to use canola oil whenever a vegetable oil is called for.

Animal Fats

Fats associated with beef, pork, lamb, turkey, and chicken are more saturated and are solid at room temperature. These fats are made up of many fatty acids, as are all fats and oils, but palmitic acid (C-16) and stearic acid (C-18) tend to be present in high amounts. Lamb fat is the most saturated, followed by beef, pork, and chicken. Nutrition studies show that not all saturated fatty acids have negative health consequences. For instance, stearic acid tends to be neutral; it does not raise LDL cholesterol or lower HDL cholesterol levels like other saturated fatty acids, such as palmitic acid.[1]

Animal fats do impart a flavor (often mild) to the foods they are added to and when they are used for frying. Pie crust made with lard is described as having a nutty (not porky) flavor. (Lard contains the optimum ratio of saturated and unsaturated fatty acids to create a pie crust that is both flaky and tender.) Lamb fat and turkey fat, in particular, are very strong and characteristic of the source animal. Animal fats are often added to formulated meat products like meatballs, hot dogs, chicken nuggets, sausages, and deli meats to enhance flavor, moisture, and texture, and to carry other fat-soluble flavor compounds.

Fish oils contain highly unsaturated fatty acids, often with four or five double bonds. Because many fish live in cold water, their fat must remain fluid at cold temperatures. Highly unsaturated fats do not solidify at cold temperatures. Unfortunately, the numerous double bonds in fish oils allow rapid oxidative rancidity once extracted, which means a very short shelf life. The omega-3 fatty acids in fish oil are valued for their important nutritional properties, but it is difficult to incorporate them into food products because of their limited shelf life and fishy flavor. However, suppliers of fish oils are working on deodorizing the oils and encapsulating them to prevent oxidation while maintaining their beneficial nutritional aspects.

Dairy Fat (Butter)

The natural fat content of milk varies from 3.5 to 5.2 percent according to the breed of cow. Milkfat is obtained by taking advantage of the difference in density between fat and water. First the cream is separated from whole milk with a centrifugal cream separator. The result is added back to skim milk at various levels to make milk products with different fat contents.

The cream, which is an *oil-in-water emulsion*, is then churned to make butter (a *water-in-oil emulsion*). This process uses mechanical energy to rupture the milk membranes surrounding the fat droplets in the emulsion, allowing them to coalesce into ever-larger clumps of fat (butter grains). To maximize process efficiency, the cream is chilled first, as the fat droplets coagulate more easily when they are cold (think about refrigerated butter). Once churning is complete, the solid butterfat is separated from the fat-free 'buttermilk' and is kneaded to remove as much of the remaining liquid as possible; kneading also aligns its crystalline structure for a smooth texture. The buttermilk that results bears no resemblance to commercial buttermilk, which is normally cultured (like yogurt) prior to bottling for sale.

Salt is commonly added for flavor and to help preserve the butter by preventing the growth of microorganisms. Sweet or unsalted butter is also widely available but must be kept refrigerated for maximum shelf life. It is also interesting to note that sweet butter normally has a natural flavor added to it (starter distillate) to enhance its flavor; salted butter does not. European "cultured butter" is made with cream that is fermented first to give it a slightly tangy taste. European-style butter is 82 percent fat—slightly higher than standard American butter. (The U.S.

FIGURE 9.1 Fat percentage by weight of milk and cream.

Milk or Cream Product	Fat Percentage by Weight
Whole milk	3.25 minimum
Low-fat milk	1
Reduced-fat milk	2
Sweetened condensed milk	8 to 10
Half-and-half	12
Light cream	18 to 30, usually 20
Light whipping cream	30 to 36
Heavy cream	36 to 40
Double cream	42 to 48
Clotted cream	55 to 60

Source: Brian Yager.

FIGURE 9.2 Comparison of dietary fats.

DIETARY FAT — Comparison of Dietary Fats

DIETARY FAT	Saturated fat	Linoleic acid	Alpha-linolenic acid	Oleic acid
Canola oil	7	21	11	61
Safflower oil	8	14	1	77
Flaxseed oil	9	16	57	18
Sunflower oil	12	71	1	16
Corn oil	13	57	1	29
Olive oil	15	9	1	75
Soybean oil	15	54	8	23
Peanut oil	19	33	*	48
Cottonseed oil	27	54	*	19
Lard	43	9	1	47
Palm oil	51	10	*	39
Butter	68	3	1	28
Coconut oil	91	2		7

SOURCE: POS PILOT PLANT CORPORATION

SATURATED FAT   **POLYUNSATURATED FAT**   **MONOUNSATURATED FAT**

- ▇ (Saturated fat)
- ▇ **linoleic acid** (an omega-6 fatty acid)
- ▇ **alpha-linolenic acid** (an omega-3 fatty acid)
- ▇ **oleic acid** (an omega-9 fatty acid)

*Trace   Fatty acid content normalized to 100%

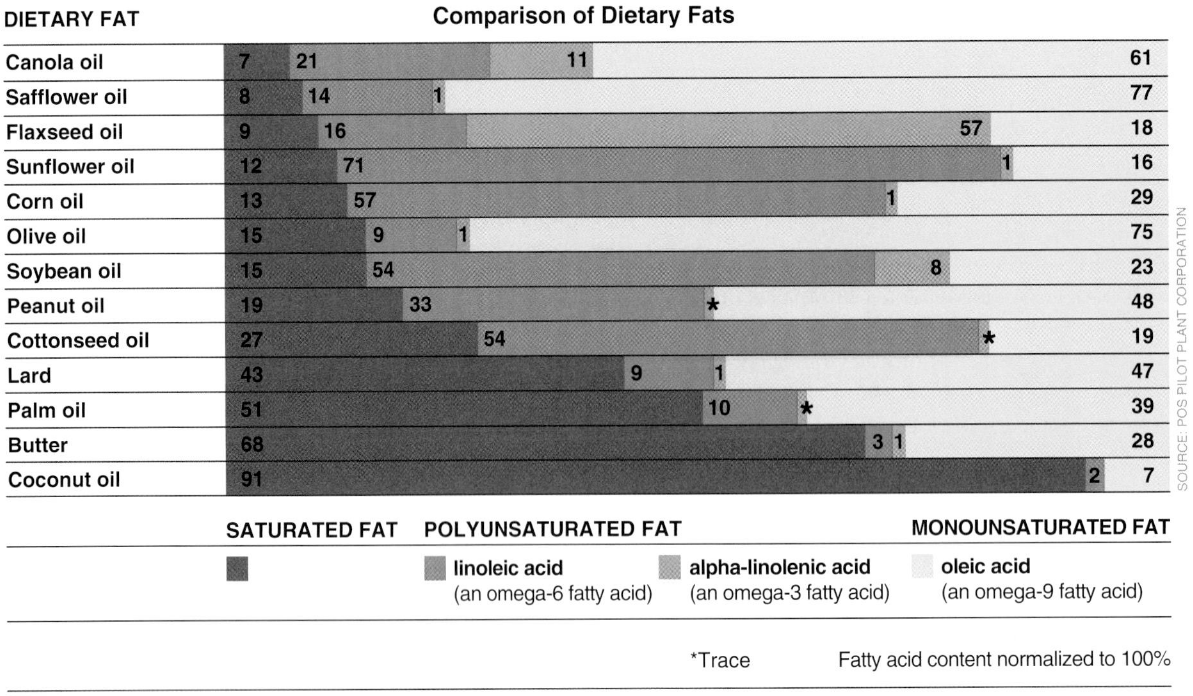

Source: Printed with permission from the Canola Council of Canada.

Standard for butter calls for a minimum of 80 percent milkfat, with the remainder made up of approximately 15 percent water and 5 percent milk solids—proteins and lactose.)

The fatty acids in butter are a mixture of short-, medium-, and long-chain fatty acids, mostly saturated, except for a fairly large slug (about 30 percent) of oleic (monounsaturated). This unique combination of mostly saturated fatty acids makes butter a solid (yet soft) fat at room temperature and gives it a melting point close to body temperature; it melts in the mouth, releasing its flavor compounds instantaneously. The narrow melting range for butter makes it difficult to incorporate into baked products: straight out of the refrigerator it is too hard, and at room temperature it can easily become too soft. It does not have the broad range of plasticity of synthetically made margarines and shortenings. On the other hand, butter gives products a readily identifiable mouthfeel and flavor that is difficult to replicate, a difficult challenge facing margarine manufacturers.

Margarines were first developed as a more stable and less expensive substitute for butter by a French chemist in 1869 and called *oleomargarine* after the Latin word for oil, *oleo*, and its major fatty acid constituent, *margaric acid* (which today we know is actually a combination of stearic and palmitic acids). Margarines were typically made by blending hydrogenated oils with liquid oil and adding milk solids and water to get the desired texture, flavor, and functional properties. Unfortunately, as we now know, the process of partial hydrogenation causes trans fats to form, so many margarines today are formulated without partially hydrogenated fats. Most margarine is made from soybean oil, but some are made with corn oil or blends of other plant oils. Plant oils contain long-chain unsaturated fatty acids, unlike butter; thus, the texture and mouthfeel of margarines are not the same as butter. However, because they are more plastic, with a wider melting range, it is

FIGURE 9.3 Lipid comparison.

Lipid	Source	% Saturated	% Mono-unsaturated	% Poly-unsaturated
Fats				
Lard	Animal	40.8	43.8	9.6
Butter	Animal	54.0	19.8	2.6
Tallow	Animal	50.0	43.0	4.0
Oils				
Soy	Plant	14.5	23.2	56.5
Coconut	Plant	85.2	6.6	1.7
Corn	Plant	12.7	24.7	57.8
Sunflower	Plant	11.9	20.2	63.0
Safflower	Plant	10.2	12.6	72.1
Olive	Plant	14.0	68.7	11.2
Palm	Plant	45.3	41.6	8.3
Wheat germ	Plant	18.8	15.9	60.7

Source: Brian Yager.

easier to incorporate them into baked products. Modern technology allows lipid chemists to develop a range of specialty margarines custom designed for virtually every commercial application that would have previously used butter, without butter's "shortcomings."

Criteria for selecting the best fat for any new product include cost, animal or vegetable source (which also affects price), flavor requirements (or lack of flavor), functional requirements, labeling requirements, and nutritional considerations. The decision process can be a daunting one that must be based on experience and knowledge. Suppliers of fats and oils are proficient at providing numerous custom-designed products that meet the needs of developers and can be enormously helpful in making optimal fat choices.

●Lipid Structure

The primary difference between fats and oils is whether they are liquid or solid at room temperature. Oils are liquid at room temperature, whereas fats are solid. One determinant depends on the degree of saturation around the carbon bonds in the fatty acids. Oils are liquid at room temperature because the fatty acids have more unsaturated bonds; the reverse is true of fats. Shortening is oil that has been partially hydrogenated (had hydrogen added to it) to make it solid and

more stable. In this process, double bonds are lost and the degree of saturation is increased. In general, the longer the fatty acid chain, the more solid the fat and the higher the melting point. Fatty acids with very short chains are more volatile (vaporize at relatively low temperatures and are highly aromatic).

Of all the lipids in nature, the most important in the developer's daily work are the triacylglycerides, also known as triglycerides. Most fats in food are in the form of triglycerides.

FIGURE 9.4 Fatty acids in various food products.

Name	# of Carbons	# of Double Bonds	Source	Melting Point (°F)
Butyric	4	0	Butter	18
Palmitic	16	0	Palm and coconut	145
Stearic	18	0	Red meat	157
Oleic	18	1	Plant	55
Linoleic	18	2	Plant	23
Linolenic	18	3	Plant	12

Source: Brian Yager.

FIGURE 9.5 Fatty acid comparison by source of lipid.

		% of Fatty Acid Found in Different Fat Types									
		Saturated					Mono-unsaturated	Polyunsaturated			
Fat Type	Smoke Point (°F)	Butyric	Lauric	Myristic	Palmitic	Stearic	Oleic	Linoleic	Linolenic	Eicosa-pentaenoic (EPA)	Docosa-hexaenoic (DHA)
		C4:0	C12:0	C14:0	C16:0	C18:0	C18:1	C18:2	C18:3	C20:5	C22:6
Butter oil	350	3.6	2.9	10.8	26.9	12.1	28.5	3.2	0.4		
Canola	400				4.1	1.8	60.9	21.0	8.8		
Cocoa butter					26.3	33.8	34.3	3.1			
Coconut oil	350		47.1	18.5	9.1	2.8	6.8	1.9			
Corn oil	450				10.9	2.0	25.4	59.6	1.2		
Fish oil	235			9.3	17.1	2.8	11.4	1.5	1.6	15.5	9.1
Lard (pork fat)	370			1.5	26.0	13.5	43.9	9.5			
Palm oil	420			1.0	44.4	4.1	39.3	10.0	0.4		
Peanut oil	440				11.1	2.4	46.7	32.0			
Safflower oil	450				6.8	2.3	12.0	77.7	0.4		
Soybean oil	450				10.6	4.0	23.3	53.7	7.6		
Sunflower oil	440				7.0	4.5	18.7	67.5	0.8		
Tallow (beef fat)	420			3.2	24.3	18.6	42.6	2.6			

Source: Brian Yager.

FIGURE 9.6 Saturates versus unsaturates.

Saturated

CH₃-CH₂-CH₂-CH₂-CH₂-CH₂-CH₂-CH₂-CH₂-CH₂-CH₂-CH₂-CH₂-CH₂-CH₂-CH₂-CH₂-COOH

Stearic Acid (18:0)

Monounsaturated

CH₃-CH₂-CH₂-CH₂-CH₂-CH₂-CH₂-CH₂-**CH=CH**-CH₂-CH₂-CH₂-CH₂-CH₂-CH₂-CH₂-COOH

Oleic Acid (18:1)

Polyunsaturated

CH₃-CH₂-CH₂-CH₂-CH₂-CH₂-CH₂-CH₂-**CH=CH**-CH₂**CH=CH**-CH₂-CH₂-CH₂-CH₂COOH

Linoleic Acid (18:2)

Source: Brian Yager.

Their basic structure consists of a glycerol backbone with three fatty acids connected ("esterified") to the glycerol backbone by ester linkages. The specific fatty acids arranged on the glycerol backbone, their chain length, their degree of saturation, and the presence or absence of *cis* or *trans* hydrogens give each triglyceride its physical, chemical, and functional characteristics. Generally, the triglyceride is laid out like a three-pronged fork. The fatty acid chains (the three tines on the fork) are attached to a glycerol backbone. Each chain can be the same fatty acid, or they each can be different.

The backbone of fatty acids found in foods is made up of 4 to 18 carbons (some found in fish are 20 to 24 carbons long). Fatty acid chains usually contain even numbers of carbons. For stability, each carbon atom prefers to have four other molecules attached to it. With four molecules attached, the carbon atom is at its most stable and less likely to react with other molecules. In the case of saturated fatty acids, each interior carbon in the chain is attached to two other carbon atoms and two hydrogen atoms. If the carbon atom is located at one end of the fatty acid chain, it is attached to one other carbon and three hydrogen atoms; if it is located on the opposite end of the chain, it is attached to one other carbon and a carboxyl (COOH) group.

When the carbon chain that makes up a fatty acid has all of its binding sites filled, it is termed saturated. However,

when some of the hydrogen is removed, double bonds form between adjacent carbon atoms and the fat is termed unsaturated. These unsaturated fatty acids can be further classified as monounsaturated (chains containing only one unsaturated double bond) or polyunsaturated (chains containing two or more unsaturated double bonds).

The remaining two hydrogen atoms associated with the double-bonded carbons are located either on the same side of the chain (cis fatty acid) or opposite from each other (trans fatty acid). Although natural sources of trans fats do exist, most dietary trans fats are a result of processing—either through hydrogenation (the chemical process of adding hydrogen atoms to unsaturated double bonds in order to saturate them) or as a result of the deodorization process. Structure-wise, trans fatty acids are straight and can pack together tightly (allowing them to behave more like saturated fats), whereas cis fatty acids contain kinks that prevent them from packing tightly together.

As a result, trans fats are solid at room temperature. This is one reason vegetable shortenings are solid at room temperature. Recent scientific evidence associates the consumption of trans fats with an increased risk of developing heart disease (among other findings). Therefore, since 2006, the government has mandated that the amount of trans fat in a product be labeled on the nutrition facts panel on all packaged foods. Many companies have worked diligently to remove trans fats from their products now that they are widely recognized as harmful to health (and harmful to sales!). The U.S. Food & Drug Administration is considering banning trans fatty acids completely.

All lipids are made up of a variety of fatty acids, each having different degrees of saturation and different chain lengths and therefore different properties, including melting point. The ratio of saturated to unsaturated fatty acids in any lipid determines its melting point. A lipid with more unsaturated fatty acids tends to be more liquid at room temperature; one with more saturated fatty acids tends to be more solid.

The Solid Fat Index (SFI) and Solid Fat Content (SFC) of any given lipid provide the percentage of fat in that lipid that is in crystalline (solid) form compared with total fat (the remainder being in liquid form) at a series of standardized temperatures. The resulting data gives the product developer

FIGURE 9.7 Cis versus trans bonds.

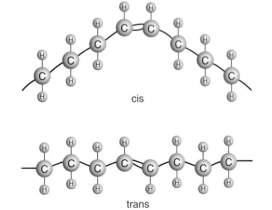

Source: Brian Yager.

FIGURE 9.8 **Solid fat content comparisons.**

Temperature	Butter	Cocoa Butter	Coconut Oil	Lard	Palm Oil	Palm Kernel Oil	Tallow
SFC 10°C (50°F)	52		84	48	53	72	66
SFC 21.1°C (70°F)	22	70	34	27	24	39	43
SFC 26.7°C (80°F)	10		0	17	13	10	31
SFC 33.3°C (92°F)	4		NA	5	6	NA	19
SFC 40°C (104°F)	NA	NA	NA	2	NA	NA	9
Melting point	100°F	88–92°F	80°F	100°F	103°F	85°F	115°F

Lard and tallow SFCs will vary based on diets of animals.

Source: Brian Yager.

a "snapshot" of the lipid's physical and chemical make-up and behavior, allowing for better decision making during the ingredient selection process when new lipid-containing products are being developed. The primary difference between the two measurements is the methodology and equipment used to determine the data, which is statistically the same via either method.

Figure 9.8 shows the properties of the various lipids: saturation, chain length, and orientation of double bonds. The oil processor can predict the physical and chemical behavior of a fat based on the types and ratios of the fatty acids present in its composition.

Processing of Fats and Oils

The initial processing of fats and oils involves their extraction from the natural food source. Lipids from animal sources are melted by heating with steam and then separated by centrifugation. This process, called rendering, is used to extract lard and tallow. Milkfat (butter) is separated from cream by churning, which divides the skim milk (buttermilk) from the fat by mechanical action and turns an oil-in-water emulsion (cream) into a water-in-oil emulsion (butter).

The lipid component from plant sources is extracted by pressing or solvent extraction. Pressing is a mechanical procedure that involves crushing the oil source (typically seeds) and separating the fats by direct compression, then filtering to remove impurities. Depending on the oil, heat may be applied to inactivate enzymes such as lipases or lipoxygenases that may promote lipid rancidity. This method is not as efficient as solvent extraction; consequently, pressing is more expensive. However, pressing is often preferred by people concerned about organic solvents and the potential for residual chemicals to be left in solvent-extracted oils. Terms found on labels of pressed oils may include "*expeller pressed*" and "*cold pressed*." Many oils sold in health food stores are extracted using this method.

Solvent extraction involves the use of an organic solvent, such as hexane, to dissolve the lipid. The solvent is then separated from the lipid by distillation (the solvent has a lower boiling point than the oil). At this point the oil is termed crude oil. The crude oil contains mainly triglycerides but also phospholipids, free fatty acids, and pigments, which are impurities that can decrease the shelf life. The removal of those impurities is termed refining.

The goal of refining is to remove compounds that may cause undesirable odors, colors, or flavors and may shorten shelf life. The first step is often degumming, which is necessary for oils high in phospholipids (such as soybean, corn, and sunflower oils). In the degumming process, 3 to 5 percent water is mixed with the oil, the water-soluble heads of the phospholipids bind with the water, and the hydrated phospholipids are separated from the oil by centrifugation.

Phospholipids are similar to triglycerides except one fatty acid side chain is replaced by a phosphate-containing hydrophilic molecule. This makes it an "amphiphilic compound," i.e., a true emulsifier with both a hydrophilic head and a lipophilic tail. Besides lecithin's ability as an emulsifier, having both water-loving and fat-loving parts also makes it the ideal molecule to form the membranes (lipid bilayers) that surround every living plant and animal cell. Phospholipids make up 75 percent of every cell membrane's composition.

Neutralization removes free fatty acids from the crude oil. Caustic soda (a strong alkali solution) is mixed with the heated fat and allowed to stand to separate out the aqueous phase, which traps the free fatty acids. This aqueous phase is called foots or soapstock and in fact is used for making soaps. Soapstock is removed from the triglycerides by adding water and subjecting the mixture to centrifugation.

The oil is then bleached by passing it through diatomaceous earth—clays or activated charcoal—that absorbs the colored compounds. These include carotenoids (yellow to red) and chlorophylls (green). By manipulating the bleaching step, the processor can determine how much pigment to leave in the oil. Corn oil traditionally has a deeper yellow color than soybean oil. Olive oil may have more green pigments.

Small odor-causing compounds (usually ketones, aldehydes, or free fatty acids) are removed by a process called deodorization. In this step, steam heat in a vacuum chamber strips away these low-molecular-weight compounds. The resulting refined oil contains mainly triglycerides plus residual pigments and tocopherol (vitamin E). The tocopherols that survive the refining process help preserve the oil and delay the onset of rancidity. The oil should have almost no odor, as triglycerides are large compounds and not volatile, therefore not aromatic.

Refined oil can be further processed to create tailor-made fats and oils with specific functional properties. Solid fats are often preferred for optimum texture and shelf life in many baked products; traditionally, bakers used lard. However, the negative health effects of consuming saturated animal fats containing cholesterol created a demand for a healthier, plant-based substitute that retained solid fat functionality. Hydrogenation is a method for achieving both objectives. It is a common processing technique used to turn oils (mono- or polyunsaturated) into solid fats by adding hydrogen atoms wherever there are unsaturated carbon atoms. This reduces the number of unsaturated fatty acids prone to lipid oxidation and rancidity, thereby increasing the shelf life. A nickel catalyst is usually used to facilitate the reaction.

Partial hydrogenation of oils yields a softer, smoother fat (shortening) of the right texture and flexibility required in a baking fat. During this process, some of the double bonds are not removed but merely changed from the cis form to the trans form. Partially hydrogenated fats are the number-one source of trans fats in the diet—and, as we now know, consumption of trans fats should be reduced. Complete hydrogenation, whereby all of the carbon-carbon double bonds are eliminated and replaced with hydrogen atoms, yields a fully saturated fat. This type of complete hydrogenation yields a hard fat that can be combined with oil to yield a more pliable solid fat that is trans-fat free.

Another processing technique is winterization. The oil is refrigerated to between 32 and 35.6°F (0 and 2°C), causing the more saturated long-chain fatty acids (LCFA) present to crystallize or precipitate out of the oil. When the LCFAs are removed, the winterized oil remains clear at refrigerator temperatures. This process is important for oils used in refrigerated products, such as salad oils and mayonnaise. If a non-winterized oil is used in these products, the texture may change when the product is refrigerated. In vinaigrettes, for example, the appearance may become cloudy and mouthfeel may become gritty. The term *winterization* comes from the practice of letting cottonseed oil stored in barrels remain outdoors during the winter in the South. In the cold temperatures, the liquid fraction separated from the solid fraction due to different unsaturated and saturated fatty acids in the cottonseed oil. The solid fraction was more saturated and could be used in baked products where a more solid fat was needed, and the liquid fraction was used in any application calling for liquid oil.

Fractionation, a process much like winterization, also creates different types of oil by separating fractions with different melting points. It separates solid and liquid phases by subjecting the oil progressively to different controlled temperatures and removing each of the phases by vacuum or pressure filtration. For example, milkfat (butter) is hard and difficult to work with at refrigerator temperatures. The fat can be separated into fractions based on the melting points of the various fatty acids normally present in it, and the fractions can then be recombined to create a butter that is spreadable at refrigerator temperatures.

The location and types of the three fatty acids on the glycerol backbone determines how the triglycerides interact, resulting in crystal formation. The number and size of crystals formed determine how smooth and creamy a fat is. Many types of fat crystals can co-exist in solid fats because of the many fatty acid chain lengths and their positions on the glycerol backbone. This is known as polymorphism. However, three main forms are alpha (a), beta-prime (b′), and beta (b). The melting point of fats rises as the crystal sizes increase from alpha to beta-prime and eventually to beta. Alpha crystals are extremely fine but not very stable. Beta crystals are large and stable but give the fat a coarse, grainy texture. Beta-prime crystals are intermediate in size and reasonably stable. Beta-prime crystals are best for food preparations because they yield fine-textured baked goods and smooth-surfaced hydrogenated vegetable shortenings.

To change the natural crystal formation of solid fats, fatty acids can be moved around on the glycerol backbone. This interesterification process is done by using catalysts and lipases (enzymes that target fats) to remove the fatty acids from the glycerol backbone and move them to another position on the glycerol molecule. Unprocessed lard is a good example of a fat with primarily beta crystals, which give it a waxy, lumpy, grainy texture. Lard is often interesterified to change the natural beta crystals into beta-prime crystals. Once it is interesterified, lard is whiter, creamier, smoother, and more uniform in texture. Functionally, beta-prime crystals help with the incorporation of an abundant quantity of small air bubbles in batters for good volume, texture, and tenderness of baked goods.

Plasticizing refers to softening a hard fat, resulting in a change in its consistency due to a change in crystal structure. When a solid fat is melted, the rate of cooling and the amount of stirring affect how the fatty acid chains can interact to form crystals. This process is used to achieve the proper texture of tub margarines. Again, the desirable crystals are beta-prime, which are achieved by proper tempering and temperature control.

A defect known as bloom appears as a whitish film on the surface of chocolate when the crystal structure changes from small, fine alpha crystals to large, coarse beta crystals. The tempering process used in chocolate-making delays this change. One form of tempering is done by melting the chocolate (which must contain cocoa butter) to 110°F (43°C) and then mixing in a portion of unmelted chocolate pieces. Cutting the chocolate into small pieces allows it to melt evenly to ensure proper beta-prime crystal formation.

Trans Fat and Hydrogenation

Dietary trans fats have been linked to increased risk of cardiovascular disease, hypertension, diabetes, and possibly neurodegenerative disorders. Because of the overwhelming scientific evidence linking trans fats to cardiovascular diseases, beginning in January 2006, the FDA required all food labels to disclose the amount of trans fat per serving in the nutrition facts panel. In the United States, if the amount is less than 0.5 g per serving it still must appear on the nutrition facts panel, but it can be reported as 0. Some municipalities and states ban the use of trans fats in restaurants, and more states are considering similar bans. Trans fats are an unfortunate consequence of the hydrogenation process.

For example, the linolenic fatty acid (ALA) (an omega-3 essential fatty acid containing three double bonds) content of soybean oil must be reduced to increase the oil's stability if it is to be used as a frying oil. This is because ALA is a polyunsaturated fatty acid and very susceptible to oxidative rancidity. When this happens, the soybean oil initially develops green-beany or grassy flavors, and in later stages strong fishy or painty off flavors. It also darkens, and starts to smoke prematurely. ALA cannot be removed from the rest of the oil easily or cheaply (it makes up about 10 percent of the volume of the oil), but hydrogenation can "fill in the blanks," turning the unsaturated double bonds missing hydrogens into saturated single bonds with a full complement of hydrogens, stabilizing the oil by building in resistance to oxidation. Unfortunately, unless the fatty acid is fully hydrogenated, with every unsaturated double bond converted to a saturated one, trans fats are created.

The use of nickel as a catalyst during the hydrogenation process promotes the conversion of the natural cis configuration (kinked, with both of the attached hydrogens on the *same side* of the carbon backbone) of unsaturated fatty acids to the trans form (straight, with the two attached hydrogens on *opposite sides* of the carbon backbone), allowing for closer packing of the fatty acids and a more solid consistency of the fat. Changing the nickel catalyst to another metal, such as gold, reduces the formation of trans fatty acids during hydrogenation. This costly solution is not economically practical. Researchers at the U.S. Department of Agriculture (USDA) developed a method that increases the pressure and temperature of the hydrogenation process. Using soybean oil, they created a product containing 17 percent trans fatty acids by weight, compared to the usual process, which contains 40 percent. When blended with liquid oil to make margarine, the level of trans fatty acids falls below the level that must be declared on the nutrition label.[2]

Many other solutions have been developed to reduce the level of trans fatty acids. Low-linolenic soybean varieties have been developed and are being processed into soybean oil that does not need to be hydrogenated to increase stability. This oil is stable enough to be used in frying applications because the unstable linolenic acid levels are reduced. Another technique is to completely hydrogenate an oil to change the 18-carbon unsaturated fatty acids (oleic, linoleic, and linolenic fatty acids) into stearic acid, a fully saturated 18-carbon fatty acid. This fully saturated, solid fat can then be blended with oil to create the texture desired.

The use of palm or coconut oil in place of hydrogenated oil is another option. These are naturally trans fat–free vegetable oils that are solid or semisolid at room temperature without the need for hydrogenation. They can be fractionated to produce a range of products with many physical properties appropriate for baking applications. The downside of these tropical oils is that although they are trans fat– and cholesterol-free, they are saturated and pose many of the same health concerns as saturated animal fats.

●Nutrition and Essential Fatty Acids (EFAs)

Fats and oils are an abundant source of energy. They provide 9 calories per gram compared to 4 calories per gram from carbohydrates and proteins. While the Western diet is typically not deficient in calories (in fact, quite the opposite), this is not true of other parts of the world. As with any diet, a balance of calories from carbohydrates, protein, and fats and oils must be maintained for weight control and overall health. A minimum of 6 to 15 percent of total calories from fat is believed necessary in order to promote:

- Proper central nervous system balance
- Cell membrane formation and function
- Proper immune response
- Proper skin, hair, and nail function
- Proper hormonal function

Fats and oils are also carriers for the fat-soluble vitamins A, D, E, and K. These are essential for proper body function. Because they cannot be produced by the body, dietary sources are essential. However, without fats and oils in the diet, these vitamins cannot be absorbed; they would pass right through the digestive tract.

The nutritional impact of fats and oils may outweigh other desirable functions that they bring to food. All fats and oils are made up of a combination of saturated, monounsaturated, and polyunsaturated fatty acids. Even fats that are categorized as being saturated or unsaturated are never 100 percent of either. Lard, for instance, has more *unsaturated* fatty acids (60 percent) than saturated ones (40 percent)! And with 90 percent saturated fatty acids, coconut oil is even more saturated than lard! The percentage of each of these varies with the source of the fat or oil and the types of refining or other processing it is subjected to. Each type of fat is identified based on the level of each of these components. Animal fats contain cholesterol and (except for fish oils) predominantly saturated fats, both of which are implicated as causative agents of human disease. In addition, fats that are partially hydrogenated or deodorized also contain trans fats.

Others fats contain essential fatty acids (EFAs), which are necessary for good health. EFAs cannot be made in sufficient quantity by the human body and therefore must be consumed via the diet. The two EFAs for humans are linoleic acid (LA) (an omega-6 fatty acid) and alpha-linolenic acid (ALA) (an omega-3 fatty acid). These molecules are identical in carbon chain length (18 carbons each); they differ in the number and location of the double bonds. LA has two, one at the #6 carbon (hence *omega-6 fatty acid*) and one at the #9 carbon, while ALA has three, one each at the #3 carbon (*omega-3 fatty acid*) and the #6 and #9 carbons. It is believed that these EFAs are involved in regulating inflammation and ALA in particular may decrease the risk of diseases including heart disease, cancer, and arthritis. Essential fatty acids are also important for cognitive function and maintenance of good vision. That said, the two EFAs are dependent on each other and must be present in the diet in the right ratio in order to maintain optimum health. In an optimum diet, the ratio is no more than 4:1 omega-6:omega-3. In the typical American diet, however, the ratio is greater than 10:1 omega-6:omega-3. Unfortunately, many of the benefits of the omega-3 fatty acids are inhibited when the level of omega-6 fatty acids is high. This is one reason why nutritionists strongly recommend taking fish oil supplements, which are especially high in omega-3 fatty acids, and reducing the consumption of vegetable oils such as corn, sunflower and cottonseed, all of which contain extremely high levels of LA and virtually no ALA.

ALA is particularly important because it is the source in the body of two other near-essential omega-3 fatty acids credited with most of the good health attributes: DHA (docosahexaenoic acid), a 22-carbon fatty acid with six double bonds, and EPA (eicosapentaenoic acid), a 20-carbon fatty acid with five double bonds. They are near-essential because they *can* be synthesized in the body from alpha-linolenic acid. However, this inefficient process does not yield sufficient quantities of DHA and EPA for optimum health. Therefore, it is commonly accepted that additional dietary sources are needed. The best dietary source of EPA and DHA is fatty fish such as salmon, herring, sardines, mackerel, halibut, and, to a lesser extent, tuna. While vegetable sources (flaxseed oil, hemp oil) of these omega-3s do exist, absorption of them by the body and accumulation in the tissues is much greater from animal sources. In 2004, the FDA approved the following qualified health claim: "Supportive but not conclusive research shows that consumption of EPA and DHA [*omega*-3] fatty acids may reduce the risk of coronary heart disease."

Cholesterol and Saturated Fat

Cholesterol is an essential structural component of all mammalian cell membranes (makes up approximately 20% of the membrane). It is required to establish proper membrane permeability and fluidity and is thus manufactured by every cell. Within the cell membrane, cholesterol also functions in intracellular transport, cell signaling, and nerve conduction. *Cholesterol is essential for all animal life.*

For a man of about 150 pounds, the body synthesizes about 1 gram of cholesterol per day, and total body content is about 35 g (a little over an ounce), primarily located within all the membranes of all the cells of the body.

Typical dietary intake of additional cholesterol in the United States is 200–300 mg per day. All foods containing animal fat contain cholesterol to varying extents. However, most ingested cholesterol is poorly absorbed, and the body compensates for any absorption of additional cholesterol by *reducing internal cholesterol synthesis*. For these reasons, *cholesterol intake in food has little, if any, effect on total body cholesterol content, or concentrations of cholesterol in the blood*. Instead, it is the intake of excessive amounts of saturated fats that can increase blood cholesterol levels.

Since cholesterol is insoluble in blood, it is transported in the circulatory system within lipoproteins. There are several types of lipoproteins in blood; the most well known are low-density lipoprotein (LDL) and high-density lipoprotein (HDL). Higher concentrations of LDL combined with lower concentrations of HDL are strongly associated with cardiovascular disease because this combination promotes atherosclerosis (so-called "hardening of the arteries"). This disease leads to heart attack, stroke, and peripheral vascular disease. Since higher blood LDL contributes to this process more than the HDL particles, LDL particles are often termed *bad cholesterol*.

On the other hand, high concentrations of HDL, which can remove cholesterol from cells and atheroma (arterial plaques) and transport cholesterol back to the liver for disposal, offer protection and are sometimes referred to as *good cholesterol*. Having large numbers of HDL particles correlates with better health outcomes.

Based on Mayo Clinic recommendations, the total blood cholesterol level should be: <200 mg/dL for normal blood cholesterol; 200–239 mg/dL is borderline-high, and >240 mg/dL is high cholesterol.

Most people should aim for an LDL level below 130 mg/dL. If you have other risk factors for heart disease, your target LDL may be below 100 mg/dL. If you're at very high risk of heart disease, you may need to aim for an LDL level below 70 mg/dL. In general, the lower your LDL cholesterol level is, the better. There is no evidence that very low LDL cholesterol levels are harmful.

Regarding HDL, the recommended level should be above 50 mg/dL, with higher concentrations providing even better protection. Levels less than 40 mg/dL are a danger signal.

Several human studies have shown a correlation between trans fat consumption and elevated low-density lipoprotein (LDL) bad cholesterol and lowered high-density lipoprotein (HDL) good cholesterol. In that way, it behaves like saturated fats.

Both saturated fats and trans fats actually raise total serum cholesterol levels, and are especially concerning as they also lower the level of "good" cholesterol (HDL) while raising the level of "bad" cholesterol (LDL).

Polyunsaturated fat lowers total cholesterol, a good thing, and does lower the LDL levels. However, it also lowers the level of HDL at the same time.

Monounsaturated fat (as found in olives and olive oil, avocados, almonds, and peanuts and peanut butter) is neutral in respect to total cholesterol, but instead raises the good cholesterol and lowers bad cholesterol at the same time. This has been suggested as a key reason for the healthiness of the so-called Mediterranean diet.

●Functions of Fats and Oils in Food and Cooking

Fats and oils are added to foods for a variety of reasons. They provide a richness of flavor, a creamy mouthfeel, and even a flaky texture. They also serve as a cooking medium and provide a feeling of satiety, or fullness.

Lubricity

Fats and oils can be used as lubricants during machining, processing, and mastication (chewing) and swallowing of foods—think about the difference in chewing and swallowing a juicy hamburger prepared with 80:20 ground beef (80% lean:20% fat) vs. one made with lean or extra lean. Have you ever thought about what allows a loaf of bread to be sliced? The presence of just a small amount of oil or fat in bread gets into the gluten fibers that form during mixing and set during baking, giving just enough lubricity for a slicing machine to work effectively. Breads that do not typically contain fat, like Italian and French breads, are not typically sliced.

Fats and oils act as a lubricant on the surface of a grill, griddle, or frying pan to keep food from sticking to the surface. They are also used to grease pans used for baking (muffin tins, cake pans, bread pans, and so on).

Intrinsic Flavor

Each type of unprocessed fat and oil possesses a characteristic flavor. The refining process removes volatiles (aromatic molecules with low boiling points) from the oil as well as anything that causes off flavors or off odors to develop. Because of this, the characteristic flavors of processed fats or oils are often not what you would expect. For instance, peanut oil does not taste nutty; it tastes bland and allows the flavor of the food to come through rather than be masked. Processed lard does not make pie crusts taste like pork. Refined fats are selected for processing foods transparently, leaving nothing of their own flavor behind. On the other end of the spectrum are fats and oils that are not typically deodorized and maintain their natural, or characterizing, flavors. These include butter, bacon fat, toasted sesame oil, olive oil, and infused oils (garlic, herb, lemon, truffle, etc.), which are chosen based on the flavor they bring to the food. The flavor of the oil is an important consideration that naturally depends on the type of finished product desired.

Carrier/Promoter of Flavors and Colors

Because deodorized fats and oils are bland, they can be an excellent delivery medium for oil-soluble flavors and colors. Common flavored oil applications include:

- Air-popped popcorn
- Croutons
- Ready-to-eat cereals
- Coatings for savory snacks (for seasoning adhesion)
- Topical spray oils for nuts

Many flavor compounds, herbs, and spices are fat soluble. These can be carried into the food by being dissolved in the fat or oil used in the food formulation. One of the consequences of removing fat from food is the loss of the carrier for fat-soluble flavor compounds. In addition, the process of sautéing certain foods in oil, such as onions and garlic, helps develop and smooth out their flavor, appearance, and aroma. Similar flavor development takes place when meats are seared in hot fat.

Several food colorants are also fat-soluble and require oils not just as a carrier but also as a diluent. Natural examples include annatto and the carotenes, and synthetics including the lake pigments made from FD&C dyes. In addition, fat-soluble colors are responsible for the yellow pigment in chicken skin and the orange pigment in salmon flesh.

Mouthfeel

Mouthfeel is related to the initial textural perception felt as the food enters the mouth, and it continues through chewing and swallowing. The flavors remaining in the mouth also impact the overall mouthfeel. The presence (or absence) of fats and oils in the food greatly influences mouthfeel sensations. Decisions about the amount and type of fat (solid or liquid) greatly affect every aspect of taste perception. Consider two examples: high-quality chocolate and vegetable shortening. The chocolate contains fat (cocoa butter) that has a melting point very close to that of our body temperature. Eating high-quality chocolate conveys a creamy, melt-in-the-mouth experience. However, the contrary is true of shortening, which is often made from fats with a much higher melting point. That unpleasant, waxy, mouth-coating feeling you get from eating an icing made only of shortening is another sort of mouthfeel, in this case a negative one.

Emulsions

An emulsion is a liquid dispersed in another liquid with which it is immiscible—that is, two liquids that cannot form a homogenous mixture without mechanical or chemical assistance (examples include milk, oil and vinegar, cake batter, mayonnaise, and ice cream). The two parts of an emulsion are the continuous (or external) phase and the discontinuous (or dispersed or internal) phase. For example, in butter (a water-in-oil emulsion), the fat is the continuous phase and the water is the dispersed phase. In cream (an oil-in-water emulsion), the water is the continuous phase and the fat is the dispersed phase.

Fats are incorporated into many water-based foods, like salad dressings and sauces. Because oil and water are immiscible, they separate unless physical energy or chemical emulsification is used to prevent it. Emulsifiers are compounds with both fat-soluble and water-soluble components. The fat-soluble (lipophilic) end of the emulsifier binds to oil, while the water-soluble (hydrophilic) end binds to water. The result is that when the two liquids are mixed, the emulsifier stabilizes the emulsion, preventing fat globules from coalescing. Mayonnaise, a water-in-oil emulsion, exploits the naturally occurring emulsifier in the egg yolk (lecithin). This results in a permanent emulsion.

A temporary emulsion results when energy alone is used to bring the two phases together—for example, shaking a mixture of oil and vinegar to make vinaigrette. The two phases separate when the energy is no longer forcing the compounds together.

A semi-permanent emulsion is one where the two components stay together for a while but eventually separate. Dressings containing a viscous component such as honey or simple syrup remain intact because the increased viscosity of the emulsion inhibits, but does not prevent, oil droplets from coalescing over time.

Common natural emulsifiers include lecithin, a phospholipid naturally present in egg yolk and soybeans, and mono- and diglycerides derived from an assortment of lipids. Powdered herbs and spices such as mustard, paprika, and finely ground black pepper also provide some emulsification by inhibiting coalescence of the fat globules. Synthetic emulsifiers include propylene glycol and Tween, a family of polysorbate emulsifiers.

Heat Transfer

Of the three macronutrients in the diet—proteins, carbohydrates, and fats—only fats can be used as a cooking medium. That is because they are excellent at heat transfer. Fats are used in deep-fat frying, wok stir-frying, pan-frying, sautéing, nut-roasting, and baking. Fats and oils absorb large amounts of heat before changing their physical state, which makes them very effective at transferring heat to food. As soon as water reaches 212°F it turns to steam. Oils withstand temperatures in excess of 400°F.

Consider fried chicken. After the raw chicken is seasoned and dredged in flour, it is a soft, pliable, unappetizing lump. When it is put in the fryer and heat is transferred to it, color and flavor begin to develop. The hot fat heats the moisture in the chicken and breading. As the moisture (in the form of steam) escapes the chicken, the breading begins to dehydrate and the meat begins to cook. Dehydration of the surface and fat absorption during frying impart desirable taste, texture, mouthfeel and crust development to the coating. The high heat in the presence of proteins and reducing sugars in the breading promote Maillard browning and fried flavor development. As heat moves into the interior of the chicken via conduction, the raw flesh goes from soft and flaccid to cooked and succulent. What comes out of the fryer is a masterpiece of culinary delight that cannot be duplicated in a pot of boing water!

Baking

One of fat's primary uses in baked goods is to tenderize. Fat coats flour particles to inhibit water from hydrating the gluten-forming proteins, glutenin and gliadin, thus reducing the firm and chewy texture that gluten provides. Shortening gets its name from its ability to shorten gluten strands. The more fat in a product, the more tender it is.

For example, lean bread dough, like a French baguette, is chewy due to gluten formation. Compare this to brioche, another traditional French bread, which has a fairly rich dough and therefore a softer texture. The type of fat used and how it is incorporated also affect the texture of the final product. Compare the textures of a biscuit (fat is cut in), puff pastry (fat is layered in), and brioche (fat is thoroughly incorporated in the dough).

Solid fat is usually used in shortened cakes (such as pound cake). The first step is to cream the fat and sugar. The angular sugar crystals form pockets in the fat in which air is then entrapped. The hardness of the fat determines how many and how fine the air pockets are. It is easier to incorporate the sugar into shortening than butter because shortening is a plastic fat, and the result is a cake with fine, small air pockets. Butter has a narrow melting range, making it more difficult to incorporate the sugar because the fat quickly goes from being too hard to trap air cells effectively to being too soft. Butter provides a more desirable flavor though, so the two fats are often used together for optimum texture and flavor. Shortening also contains emulsifiers that help incorporate liquid ingredients and may result in a finer texture.

In addition to tenderness, many baked products also need flakiness. Examples include pastries, croissants, phyllo dough, pie crust, and biscuits. Flakiness is achieved by cutting solid fat into flour to maintain discrete fat globules. In the case of croissants and breakfast Danish, the fat is literally rolled into the dough in sheets, creating layers of fat and dough. The dough is then folded back on itself, chilled, and sheeted many times until there are literally hundreds of

FIGURE 9.9 Dessert tray.

Source: Cargill, Incorporated.

interleaved dough and fat layers. When this layered pastry is baked, the fat melts and the moisture turns to steam, providing leavening in the baked product, while all of the sheeting and folding provides the flaky layers. The more fat and the more care taken incorporating it into the product, the flakier the product is. The key is to use a solid fat. A liquid oil coats too many flour particles and results in a soft product rather than a flaky one.

Frying

Frying is one of the most important uses for fats. The crisp texture of fried foods is highly desirable and difficult to replicate by other cooking methods. Fat absorbs large amounts of heat and transfers it to food. Typical frying temperatures are between 350 and 400°F (177 and 204°C). Compare this to water, which can reach only 212°F (100°C) at normal pressure unless other solutes (such as salt or sugar) are added to it. Food can be fried in different amounts of fat, as in deep-fat frying (submerged food), pan-frying (medium amount of fat), and sautéing (small amount). When food is placed in hot fat, its surface dries immediately as the water turns to steam. This contributes to the crisp texture of fried foods and is also responsible for what looks like the boiling of the oil around the food item as steam bubbles up through the fat. The interior of the food is cooked by conduction, as heat is transferred from the heated surface to the cooler interior. One of the challenges in frying food is cooking its interior without overcooking the exterior. That is one reason why deep-frying is better suited for smaller pieces of food rather than large chunks (the recent fad of deep-frying whole turkeys notwithstanding). French fries use a two-step method, first a blanching step, to cook the interior of the food at a lower temperature; then a final cooking at a higher temperature, to develop the crisp texture.

While everyone likes the texture of fried food, we do not like it to look, feel, or taste greasy. The amount of fat absorbed depends on several factors: the length of time the food

FIGURE 9.10 **Approximate smoke points of common cooking oils.**

Fat	Smoke Point °F	Smoke Point °C
Unrefined canola oil	225°F	107°C
Unrefined flaxseed oil	225°F	107°C
Unrefined safflower oil	225°F	107°C
Unrefined sunflower oil	225°F	107°C
Unrefined corn oil	320°F	160°C
Unrefined high-oleic sunflower oil	320°F	160°C
Extra virgin olive oil	320°F	160°C
Unrefined peanut oil	320°F	160°C
Semirefined safflower oil	320°F	160°C

(continued)

FIGURE 9.10 *(continued)*

Fat	Smoke Point °F	Smoke Point °C
Unrefined soy oil	320°F	160°C
Unrefined walnut oil	320°F	160°C
Hemp seed oil	330°F	165°C
Butter	350°F	177°C
Semirefined canola oil	350°F	177°C
Coconut oil	350°F	177°C
Unrefined sesame oil	350°F	177°C
Semirefined soy oil	350°F	177°C
Vegetable shortening	360°F	182°C
Lard	370°F	188°C
Macadamia nut oil	390°F	199°C
Refined canola oil	400°F	204°C
Semirefined walnut oil	400°F	204°C
High-quality (low-acidity) extra virgin olive oil	405°F	207°C
Sesame oil	410°F	210°C
Cottonseed oil	420°F	216°C
Grapeseed oil	420°F	216°C
Virgin olive oil	420°F	216°C
Almond oil	420°F	216°C
Hazelnut oil	430°F	221°C
Peanut oil	440°F	227°C
Sunflower oil	440°F	227°C
Refined corn oil	450°F	232°C
Palm oil	450°F	232°C
Palm kernel oil	450°F	232°C
Refined high-oleic sunflower oil	450°F	232°C
Refined peanut oil	450°F	232°C
Refined safflower oil	450°F	232°C
Semirefined sesame oil	450°F	232°C
Refined soy oil	450°F	232°C
Semirefined sunflower oil	450°F	232°C
Olive pomace oil	460°F	238°C
Extra light olive oil	468°F	242°C
Soybean oil	495°F	257°C
Safflower oil	510°F	266°C
Avocado oil	520°F	271°C

Source: Courtesy of Cooking for Engineers (www.cookingforengineers.com).

remains in contact with the oil, the age of the oil, the temperature of the oil, the amount of food in relation to the size of the fryer, and the ingredients in the food. The food should be cooked at the highest temperature possible for the shortest time to achieve a product that is done on the inside and not too brown on the outside. Foods high in fat and sugar increase fat absorption, while foods high in protein prevent the absorption of fat. Doughnuts containing a high percentage of sugar and fat absorb more fat while frying.[3]

The desirable crisp texture of fried foods does not last long because the remaining moisture in the interior of the food eventually migrates to the drier surface. To make the most of the crisp texture, fried food should be consumed as soon as possible after cooking.

The choice of a fat for frying depends on the desired outcome. Butter contributes a very desirable flavor. However, it is hard to fry with because of its water content (15 percent) and the presence of milk solids, which brown and burn at lower temperatures than those required for optimum frying. To use butter as a frying fat, it must first be clarified—that is, its water and milk solids must be removed from the butterfat. Even then, butterfat has a fairly low smoke point, so it can be used only in quick frying applications, such as sautéing. (*Note:* In India, clarification of butter is a common practice because removal of water and milk solids extends the unrefrigerated shelf life of the finished product, which is called *ghee*.)

Beef tallow and pork fat (lard) also impart a desirable flavor to fried food, but both contain cholesterol, which many consumers find undesirable. As a result, for many years fast food companies had replaced animal fats in their fryers with tallow-flavored partially hydrogenated vegetable oils. With the discovery that trans fats are present in partially hydrogenated fryer oils, there has been a general movement to other, non-partially hydrogenated oils that have been created specifically for frying using technologies (such as interesterification) that do not create trans fats.

Most fats and oils can be heated to fairly high temperatures (in excess of 300°F [149°C]) before they begin to break down. However, the bonds that attach the fatty acids to the glycerol backbone begin to break with continual heating, resulting in smoke. The temperature at which this occurs is the smoke point, which is different for each fat or oil. The level of saturation is the main factor influencing smoke point. The more unsaturated a fat, the higher its smoke point. For example, heavily saturated lard begins to smoke around 375°F (190°C), but unsaturated peanut oil doesn't begin to smoke until 450°F (232°C) and safflower oil until 510°F (265°C). If heated past the smoke point, the flash point is reached and the fat or oil ignites.

The antioxidants BHA, BHT, and TBHQ are used in fats to extend shelf life and increase the number of times the fat can be reused. This is an important feature because fryer fat is an expensive ingredient, and it is often reused. While fryer fats won't last forever, effective frying life can be maximized by regular filtering to remove burned particulates, avoiding the introduction of water and salt, and not overloading the fryer.

Rancidity

One of the major problems associated with fats and oils is rancidity. In addition to the unpleasant flavor and aroma associated with rancid fat (described as paint- or varnish-like), it loses heat transfer efficiency, darkens considerably, and becomes viscous (thickens). Once fats become rancid, neither the fats themselves nor the foods made with them can be salvaged; they must be discarded. The two major types of rancidity are hydrolytic and oxidative.

In hydrolytic rancidity, the fatty acids are removed from the glycerol backbone by the addition of water. This reaction is caused by extended high-heat exposure in the presence of water (as in deep frying, where water is constantly expelled from frying foods) or by the presence of lipolytic enzymes. Glycerol, the three-carbon molecule that serves as the backbone of fatty acids, decomposes during extended high-temperature exposure and becomes acrolein, a volatile and irritating compound with a piercing, disagreeable, acrid smell of burning grease.

Another consequence of overheating is polymerization. As heating continues, the free fatty acids link together into long chains, leading to formation of a gummy dark residue on pots and pans, and an oil that is more viscous and prone to foaming. Additionally, the oil loses heat transfer efficiency. Polymerization thus leads to increased fat absorption, resulting in greasy fried foods with darker color and bitter flavor. This is why frying oil can only be used a limited number of times before the onset of hydrolytic rancidity and explains the gummy buildup inside a fryer. Regular thorough cleaning of the fryer and filtering of the oil can help extend the life of the oil, but ultimately every oil will break down past the point of usefulness.

Oxidative rancidity is even more of a problem because it can occur without the addition of heat (although heating exacerbates the reaction). As the term implies, oxygen is involved. It may also be referred to as auto-oxidation because once started, it is self-perpetuating. The three steps in oxidative rancidity are initiation, propagation, and termination.

In the initiation stage, a free radical is created. (A free radical is any atom or molecule with a single unpaired electron. It is highly unstable and therefore highly reactive.) One of the hydrogen atoms on the fatty acid chain breaks away from an unsaturated (double-bonded) carbon atom. Because free radical formation always involves a hydrogen located at an unsaturated double bond, polyunsaturated fatty acids are the most prone to oxidative rancidity. Common causes are exposure to ultraviolet light (sunlight), table salt, or minerals such as copper or iron. With the hydrogen removed, the carbon with only three bonds becomes an unstable, highly reactive free radical that readily binds with oxygen (becomes oxidized) to become a peroxide free radical. This is called the propagation stage. The peroxide free radical "attacks" and removes another hydrogen from an adjacent fatty acid, making a hydroperoxide. This creates another peroxide free radical—and the reaction continues until all of the double bonds on the molecule are transformed and the fatty acids are broken down into highly aromatic and malodorous smaller compounds (acids, aldehydes, ketones, and alcohols), resulting in rancid off odors and flavors. This is the termination stage.

The level of auto-oxidation in an oil is measurable before obvious signs of rancidity are present (to predict its working lifespan) by a number of chemical tests, including peroxide value, which measures the formation of peroxides, and the thiobarbituric acid (TBA) test, which measures the formation of malonic dialdehyde, an end product of oxidation (but not a cause of off flavors). Gas-liquid chromatography (GLC) and high-pressure liquid chromatography (HPLC) are also used to follow the formation of specific volatile compounds that are a more direct measure of lipid oxidation, but these are rarely used outside of the laboratory.

The most common way to prevent oxidative rancidity is to reduce exposure of the lipid to oxygen. Putting an inert gas such as nitrogen in the headspace of bottled oils works well to prevent oxidation from occurring in an unopened bottle of oil. Keeping oil away from reactive metals is also important (this is why deep fryers are made of inert stainless steel). Chelating agents such as EDTA (ethylenediaminetetraacetic acid) are often used to bind and remove iron or copper from oils. The use of antioxidants also delays lipid oxidation. Common natural antioxidants used with oils include vitamins C (ascorbate) and E (tocopherols). Synthetic antioxidants include butylated hydroxytoluene (BHT), butylated hydroxyanisole (BHA), and tertiary butylated hydroquinone (TBHQ). These work by donating a hydrogen atom of their own to the peroxide free radical carbon, stabilizing it so it doesn't steal one from its neighboring carbon on the chain, thus stopping the propagation of free radicals. In effect, the antioxidant becomes oxidized instead of the fatty acid. Eventually the antioxidant loses its ability to donate hydrogen, but the oxidation process is delayed and the shelf life of the oil extended.

Keeping the oil in a cool, dark environment also increases shelf life by limiting its exposure to heat and ultraviolet light. Furthermore, reducing exposure of frying fats to table salt by delaying the seasoning of fried products until after they come out of the fryer is highly recommended.

Since unsaturated fatty acids are most susceptible to oxidative rancidity, removal of double bonds by *hydrogenation* is also done. Although this process results in a more stable oil, it also creates *trans fatty acids*, which have negative health consequences.

⬤ Conclusion

Fats and oils are important for both their nutritional and functional characteristics. They are also components of many foods, imparting qualities hard to replicate with other ingredients. The role of fats and oils in the diet continues to be debated by nutritionists and food scientists. With new technology, new lipid ingredients will be available to future chefs and product developers. These developments will assure the continued important role fats and oils play in the food supply.

[1] T. Carr and E. Jesch, "Food Components That Reduce Cholesterol Absorption," *Advances in Food and Nutrition Research* 51 (2006):165–204.

[2] F. Eller, "Preparation of Spread Oils Meeting U.S. Food and Drug Administration Labeling Requirements for Trans Fatty Acids via Pressure-Controlled Hydrogenation," *Journal of Agricultural and Food Chemistry* 53, no. 15 (2005):5982–5984.

[3] M. Bennion and B. Scheule, "Fats, Frying, and Emulsions," in *Introductory Foods*, 11th ed. (Columbus, OH: Prentice Hall, 2000), 395.

10 | Egg- and Milk-Based Foods

Lead Author: John U. McGregor, Ph.D., Professor, Food, Nutrition, and Packaging Sciences Department, Clemson University

Julie K. Northcutt, Ph.D., Professor, Food, Nutrition, and Packaging Sciences Department, Clemson University

Michelle Parisi, Ph.D., Food, Nutrition, and Packaging Sciences Department, Clemson University

Tonya C. Schoenfuss, Ph.D., Associate Professor, Department of Food Science and Nutrition, University of Minnesota

Christian Thormose, Chef/Food Production Manager, ARAMARK

●Working with Dairy and Egg-Based Products

Whether you characterize yourself as a chef, food scientist, or Culinology® professional, the functional properties of dairy and egg-based products offer exceptional opportunities as components and ingredients in formulated foods. Classically trained chefs have long considered these products fundamental elements in dishes that deliver a wide range of eating experiences, from breakfast to dinner, from snacks to beverages to entrées to desserts. Product developers who focus on delivering innovative, nutritious, and wholesome foods often employ egg and dairy components to achieve myriad functions in the manufacture of formulated foods. The new generation of Culinology® professionals are combining scientific knowledge and culinary training to use eggs and dairy-based products in the creation and manufacture of new products and applications that are defining the future of food.

●Eggs
Composition of Eggs and Egg Components

Eggs comprise a shell, yolk, latebra (white yolk), germinal disc (small, circular white spot on the yolk where the nucleus is and where embryos develop if the egg is fertilized), vitelline (yolk) membrane, chalazae (spiral bands of protein that suspend the yolk in the middle of the white), air cell, shell membranes, chalaziferous layer (thin layer of albumen enclosing yolk membranes), thin albumen (white), and thick albumen (white).

Egg white (albumen), which constitutes 60 to 63 percent of a fresh egg, is made up of four alternating layers of thick and thin consistencies. It is approximately 90 percent water; the remaining components are about 10 percent protein plus small amounts of fat (0.03 to 0.07 percent) and carbohydrate (0.4 to 1.3 percent). The carbohydrates of albumen are a combination of free forms (usually glucose) and combined forms (glycoproteins, which are proteins with carbohydrates attached) containing the sugars mannose and galactose. Albumen also contains varying levels of sulfur, potassium, sodium, phosphorus, calcium, magnesium, iron, and the vitamins niacin and riboflavin. Albumen contains some dissolved carbon dioxide, which affects the pH of the egg. As carbon dioxide dissipates from the egg during storage (the shell is porous), the pH of the albumen correspondingly increases. In a fresh egg, pH is between 7.6 and 8.5 and can increase to 9.4 during storage of 21 days.[1]

Albumen contains more than 40 proteins in addition to the glycoproteins. Ovalbumin (54 percent), conalbumin (12 percent), and ovomucoid (11 percent) make up almost 80 percent of the total protein found in albumen.[2] The proteins of most interest to food product developers are ovalbumin (foaming and coagulation), conalbumin (foam stabilization through binding with metal ions), ovomucin (viscosity enhancement, thickening), lysozyme (antibacterial agent), and globulins (foaming and viscosity enhancement).

FIGURE 10.1 General egg structures.

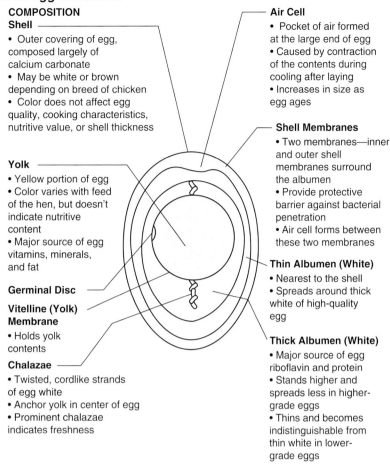

COMPOSITION

Shell
- Outer covering of egg, composed largely of calcium carbonate
- May be white or brown depending on breed of chicken
- Color does not affect egg quality, cooking characteristics, nutritive value, or shell thickness

Yolk
- Yellow portion of egg
- Color varies with feed of the hen, but doesn't indicate nutritive content
- Major source of egg vitamins, minerals, and fat

Germinal Disc

Vitelline (Yolk) Membrane
- Holds yolk contents

Chalazae
- Twisted, cordlike strands of egg white
- Anchor yolk in center of egg
- Prominent chalazae indicates freshness

Air Cell
- Pocket of air formed at the large end of egg
- Caused by contraction of the contents during cooling after laying
- Increases in size as egg ages

Shell Membranes
- Two membranes—inner and outer shell membranes surround the albumen
- Provide protective barrier against bacterial penetration
- Air cell forms between these two membranes

Thin Albumen (White)
- Nearest to the shell
- Spreads around thick white of high-quality egg

Thick Albumen (White)
- Major source of egg riboflavin and protein
- Stands higher and spreads less in higher-grade eggs
- Thins and becomes indistinguishable from thin white in lower-grade eggs

Source: American Egg Board.

Egg yolk makes up 27.5 percent of a fresh egg. The natural oil-in-water emulsion is approximately 50 percent water, 17 percent protein, and 33 percent lipid. There are four classes of proteins in egg yolk: lipoproteins, lipid-free globular proteins, phosphoproteins, and minor proteins. More than 90 percent of the lipids in egg yolk are in the form of lipoproteins (conjugated protein having a lipid component, either low-density lipoproteins [LDL] or high-density lipoproteins [HDL]). Egg yolk also contains varying levels of iron, phosphorus, calcium, manganese, iodine, copper, zinc, and the vitamins A, D, B_{12}, E, choline, folate, inositol, panthothenic acid, pyridoxine thiamin, riboflavin, and biotin. The orange-yellow

FIGURE 10.2 Thick and thin egg white.

Thick white

Thin white

Source: Julie Northcutt.

FIGURE 10.3 Egg membrane and germinal disk.

Membrane

Germinal disk

Source: Julie Northcutt.

FIGURE 10.4 Example of denatured and globular proteins at the fat–water interface.

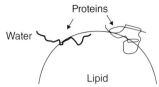

Source: Tonya Schoenfuss.

color of egg yolk comes from the carotenoid pigments lutein and zeaxanthin. The pH of egg yolk in fresh eggs is around 6.0, gradually increasing during storage to 6.4 to 6.9 depending on the rate of carbon dioxide loss, length of storage, and storage temperature.[3]

Lipoproteins are the primary functional component of egg yolk and are therefore of most interest to the food product developer. The structure of lipoproteins has regions that orient in the water phase of a food and regions that orient in the lipid portion. This is how an oil-in-water emulsion, such as mayonnaise, is formed. The proteins (with phosphorus- or sugar-containing portions) orient in the water side of a fat–water interface, while lipid-containing portions orient in the fat side. The ability of the lipoproteins in egg yolk to adsorb to the interface during whipping allow for the creation of small, stabilized fat droplets in the water that do not separate and rise. LDL lipoproteins are believed to be the primary contributor to egg yolk emulsification properties.

Nutrition

For only 70 calories each, eggs are rich in nutrients. They contain, in varying amounts, almost every essential vitamin and mineral needed by humans as well as several other beneficial food components. Egg protein is the standard by which other protein sources are measured. Each egg provides 6 g of high-quality, complete protein—that is, containing all of the essential amino acids required in the human diet for optimum

health. This makes up 34 percent of the total calories in one egg. Essentially all of the protein in an egg lies in the white portion, which is used in myriad food functions, including emulsifying and browning. When adding eggs to a food product for function, nutritional benefits are a bonus.

Eggs also provide a rich source of lipids, including fatty acids, phospholipids, triglycerides, and cholesterol. Lipids function in the body to store energy, maintain cell membrane integrity, regulate body temperature, insulate and cushion internal organs, and produce hormones. Nutritionally, one large egg contains about 5 g total fat and 1.5 g saturated fat. Because egg yolks contain some saturated fat and cholesterol (one large egg has about 186 milligrams of cholesterol), scientists and consumers have been concerned about the relationship between egg consumption and risk of heart disease. However, scientists recently concluded that the health benefits[4] of the protein and micronutrient content of eggs greatly outweigh these concerns.[5] As a result, recommendations for limiting the number of egg yolks consumed each week were eliminated from the American Heart Association's *Dietary Guidelines for Americans*. The latest edition (2010) states: "[E]vidence suggests that one egg (i.e., egg yolk) per day does not result in increased blood cholesterol levels, nor does it increase the risk of cardiovascular disease in healthy people."[6]

Lipid-related trends in the egg industry further support egg consumption with the development of specialty eggs like those enriched with *omega-3 fatty acids*. Consumption of these eggs decreases blood cholesterol levels, a risk factor for the development of heart disease.[7] They are produced by supplementing the feed of egg-laying hens with fish oil or flaxseed (rich sources of omega-3s), which results in a higher concentration of omega-3s in the eggs. These specialty eggs are considered a functional food (one that provides a health benefit beyond meeting basic nutritional needs) because the fatty acid composition actually enhances heart health. If used in mixed dishes and baked products, these eggs improve the overall nutritional value of these food items.

FIGURE 10.5 Product composition of egg ingredients.

Product	Moisture	Protein	Lipid	Carbohydrate	Ash
			%		
Whole egg	75.2	12.0	9.7	2.2	0.8
Yolk	56.8	15.3	23.0	3.6	1.4
Sugared yolk	51.2	13.9	20.8	13.0	1.1
Salted yolk	50.9	14.1	20.9	3.8	10.4
Salted whole egg	67.8	11.0	9.2	1.7	10.3
White	89.0	9.3	0.1	1.3	0.4
Dried whole egg	3.7	48.4	39.2	5.4	3.4
Dried yolk	2.7	33.7	52.9	7.3	3.3
Dried stabilized white	6.5	84.6	0.4	4.8	3.6

Source: Adapted from the American Egg Board.

Another way to manipulate the nutritional makeup of a food product using eggs is to utilize the egg whites only. This reduces the fat content almost entirely. In baked products, for instance, two egg whites can be substituted for one whole egg with relatively small variation in the product's quality while providing big changes in its nutritional makeup.

Omitting the yolks, however, also omits valuable micronutrients. Egg yolks are notably high in fat-soluble vitamins A and D, as well as lesser amounts of E and K. Vitamin A (retinol) functions in maintaining normal vision, cell growth, reproduction, and immunity. Beta-carotene, a carotenoid that is converted to vitamin A in the body, is also found in the egg yolk. Beta-carotene shows promise as a cancer-fighting agent. Vitamin D works closely with calcium and phosphorus (also found in eggs) to maintain blood calcium levels and bone health. It is also related to neurological development and is being evaluated as a treatment for depression and multiple sclerosis.[8] Deficiencies in these vitamins can lead to a variety of physiological conditions, including night blindness and lack of epithelial cell repair (vitamin A), as well as an increased risk of bone disease, such as rickets in children and osteoporosis in adults, and prostate cancer in men (vitamin D).

Water-soluble vitamins niacin, thiamine, riboflavin, panthothenic acid, folate, B_6, B_{12}, biotin, and choline are found in egg whites, as are minerals such as zinc, copper, and manganese. The vitamins function mainly as coenzymes while the minerals act as enzyme cofactors, both of which work with enzymes in the body to catalyze (speed) chemical reactions like those needed for carbohydrate, protein, and fat metabolism. Deficiencies in these vitamins and minerals can result in abnormal nervous system function, skin conditions, and impaired cell repair. Since neither vitamins nor minerals are synthesized in the body, they must be acquired from the foods we eat, and eggs are an excellent source of both.

Additionally, a deficiency in choline (generally grouped in with the B-complex vitamins) may lead to inadequate fetal and infant brain and neurological development. This suggests an increased need for choline in the diet of pregnant and lactating women. Eggs contain significant amounts of choline; one egg per day provides sufficient amounts of choline to meet daily recommendations for this high-risk population.

Iron is also worth mentioning in the discussion of egg nutrition. It is important for blood health and is a component of hemoglobin, which transports oxygen through the blood and delivers it to cells. A lack of iron results in low blood oxygen levels and, if the condition persists, iron-deficiency anemia. Symptoms of anemia are directly related to the lack of oxygen available for cellular metabolic processes and cause fatigue and decreased cognitive function. Additionally, the heart must work much harder to pump oxygen-deficient blood through the body, resulting in irregular heart rhythms or heart enlargement, which can ultimately lead to heart failure and death. Women consistently do not consume enough iron to meet requirements for the prevention of anemia, making iron-rich food sources an important aspect of their nutrition in particular. While meat, poultry, and fish are excellent sources of iron, eggs are an inexpensive alternative.

◉The Value of Egg Products in Food Product Development

Egg ingredients can be sourced as refrigerated liquid, frozen liquid, dried, and specialty products. Refrigerated liquid products include whole eggs, whites, yolks, sugared egg yolks, salted whole eggs or yolks, scrambled egg mix, cooked scrambled eggs, and extended–shelf life whole eggs, whites, or scrambled egg mix. Frozen liquid egg products include whole eggs, whites, yolks, scrambled egg mix, salted whole egg or yolks, sugared egg yolks, whole eggs and yolks with corn syrup, whole eggs with citric acid, and whole eggs with corn syrup. Dried egg products include whole egg or yolk solids, egg or scrambled egg mix, whole egg solids, free-flowing whole egg or yolk solids, glucose-free stabilized whole egg or yolk solids, and blends of whole egg or yolk with carbohydrates. Specialty egg products include diced hard-cooked peeled eggs, refrigerated whole hard-cooked, peeled eggs plain or pickled, frozen hard-cooked egg rolls or *long eggs* (envision a long center tube of hard-cooked egg yolk enwrapped in a thick layer of cooked egg white and packaged like rolls of cookie dough, such that dozens of perfect slices of hard-boiled egg can be cut from one end of the "log" to the other), frozen quiche mixes, frozen scrambled egg mix, dried scrambled egg mix, and ultra-pasteurized liquid egg products.

USDA guidelines for pasteurizing fluid egg products (140°F [60°C] for 3½ to 4 minutes) are designed to achieve a 9-D reduction in the pathogen *Salmonella seftenberg*. Pasteurization at this temperature is below the albumen (egg white) denaturation temperature range in order to keep the eggs from curdling, but is lethal to Salmonella. Testing for the presence of α-amylase activity is used as a convenient chemical method for confirming the effectiveness of egg pasteurization. The α-amylase is more heat resistant than Salmonella; if enzyme activity is eliminated, that is indicative of sufficient heating to kill Salmonella.

Egg products are typically not sourced from non-chicken eggs; however, in-shell duck, quail, guinea hen, turkey, and ostrich eggs are sold and consumed (descending order of popularity). Very few in-shell pheasant eggs are sold and consumed.

Coagulation, Thickening, Coating, and Binding

Egg products provide excellent natural thickening, coating, and binding properties because they create stable structures through heat coagulation of proteins. Egg whites are typically best for this because they are virtually colorless, impart little

FIGURE 10.6 **Common GRAS (generally recognized as safe by the FDA) non-egg ingredients added to further-processed egg products.**

Ingredient	Function
Salt	Stabilizes proteins before pasteurization and/or freezing (lowers freezing point to prevent gelling during storage to improve shelf life).
Sugar	Adds sweetness and stabilizes proteins before freezing (lowers freezing point to prevent gelling during storage to improve shelf life).
Gums (guar gum, xanthan gum, locust bean gum)	Increases foam (whipping) stability of whites, and increases water retention and viscosity.
Water	Improves foam (whipping) volume of egg whites.
Yeast	Added to egg whites to reduce sugar content before spray drying (sugars react with proteins during drying to produce a brown color).
Hydrogen peroxide	Added to egg products to lower the pasteurization temperature.
Enzymes (glucose oxidase)	Removes glucose before spray drying or pasteurization to reduce brown color formation.
Corn syrup	Provides sweetness, flavor and increases the solids.
Citric acid	Stabilizes color, improves water retention and coagulation. Usually 0.1% is added.
Sodium lauryl sulfate (surfactant)	Improves foam ability of dried eggs whites. Usually <0.1% is added. May also be added to hard boiled and peeled eggs.
Triethyl citrate	Improves foam (whipping) of egg whites. Usually 0.25% is added.
Sodium benzoate or potassium sorbate	Mold inhibitors in hard boiled and peeled eggs. Usually 0.1% is added.
Sodium silicoaluminate	Anticaking agent in dried egg products at <2.0%. Serves as a foaming or whipping aid in dried white at 0.1%.

Source: Adapted from the American Egg Board.

flavor, and contain only trace amounts of lipids. Gelling through protein denaturation involves the rearrangement of the protein's physical and chemical structure and is therefore influenced by temperature, time, dilution, salt and sugar, starch, and pH. All of these factors influence the protein network—porosity, strength and placement of bonds, and inclusions of non-protein molecules. During heating, proteins begin to unfold, eventually denature, and coagulate into a protein network. Heat coagulation of egg proteins begins around 143.6°F (62°C). At 158°F (70°C) the coagulum becomes firm and increases with time and temperatures above 158°F (70°C). Coagulation at these optimum temperatures makes them an excellent adhesive ingredient for coatings in baked and fried foods.

When egg proteins are blended with milk, water, or other liquids, the dilution increases the physical space between protein molecules. This slows the rate of thickening and raises the coagulation temperature and exposure time. This effect is demonstrated in the production of egg- and milk-based custards, which must be stirred and brought to 159.8°F (71°C) before coagulation. One whole egg or two egg yolks just barely sets 1 cup of milk. A firm gel requires the presence of more egg protein, usually three whole eggs for each 2 cups of milk.

Other factors that affect coagulation rate:

- Homogenized whole milk conducts heat more slowly than skim milk, so scrambled eggs or custards made with whole milk coagulate more slowly.[9]

- Mineral salts such as calcium, phosphorus, and sodium affect the electrostatic charge of egg proteins and increase the speed and firmness of coagulation, which is why it's common to add a small amount of table salt when making custard. This phenomenon also occurs when using natural ingredient sources of mineral salts, as when adding milk to egg-containing mixtures such as muffin or scone batters. Although the protein in milk does contribute somewhat to the coagulation in custard (less than 1 percent), milk protein is not essential for this function. However, the calcium phosphate in milk is essential to the coagulation of egg protein in custard.

- Sugars have an affinity for water and therefore influence the hydrophobic interactions within and between protein molecules. When sugars are added to egg protein systems, the coagulation temperature is increased, enabling the food product developer to produce softer gels.[10]

- Cream fillings in pastries and desserts are meant to be fairly thick and therefore often contain starch. Starches can prevent protein coagulation through alteration of the physical properties of the protein structure. In fact, starch is sometimes added to cooked egg products to raise the coagulation temperature and avoid curdling. (Arrowroot is often used because it works at a lower temperature than cornstarch and flour.) This practice provides insurance against curdling when preparing items such as custard or egg-based emulsion sauces (such as *hollandaise*) that will not be used immediately.

- Egg yolks contain alpha-amylase, an enzyme that hydrolyzes starch molecules. Therefore, starch-based gels that contain egg yolks (such as custard) must be boiled 1 to 2 minutes with stirring to inactivate the enzyme. Otherwise, they will transform the custard into liquid overnight.[11]

Protein-based gels, such as egg custards, are greatly affected by the pH of the system. Hydrogen ions influence the net charge of a protein and therefore influence the protein's solubility. As the pH of the system approaches a protein's isoelectric point (pI), the protein becomes less soluble. This promotes aggregation and eventual coagulation. pI varies by protein; therefore, the effect of pH varies depending on the source of egg protein (whites versus yolks versus whole eggs). An acidic pH of 5 produces the greatest gel strength and percentage of water release as protein molecules move closer together, squeezing water out of the gel. In general, as pH increases (becomes more alkaline), gel strength decreases but water-holding capacity of the system increases. Acid added to egg white foam (meringue) in the form of cream of tartar prevents over-coagulation and keeps the foam elastic. Acid added to whole egg lowers the coagulation temperature, speeding coagulation. Custards made with acid-containing fruits or vegetables set faster.[12]

Egg proteins are also used in forming films to help adhere batters and coatings to fried foods. Film-forming is similar to coagulation and gelling in that the interaction of protein molecules produces stability. Disulfide bonding between egg-white proteins is important to this process. Unlike forming gels by acidifying to the isoelectric point, film formation is enhanced by raising the pH and heating to denature the protein and increase disulfide bonding. Water, sugars, and starches can be added to increase the flexibility and elasticity of the film so it is workable and not too brittle. Using whole eggs instead of whites also decreases the strength of the film and improves flexibility. Dried egg products and fresh liquid eggs typically do not differ in their binding properties.

Many types of egg-based coatings are applied to baked goods, particularly breads and rolls. An egg-based glaze typically prevents the crust from drying and becoming tough while also enhancing the appearance. A glaze can be prepared using egg white only or combinations of egg white, yolk, or whole egg with salt, milk, water, or cream. Salt and milk give a shiny surface to the product, while water and cream yield a golden or brown appearance and softer texture. Glazes are traditionally applied just before the product is heated, but sometimes not until 15 minutes before the end of cooking to prevent the crust from becoming too dark.

Emulsification

Surface active agents (surfactants) that enable immiscible liquids like oil and water to form an emulsion are called emulsifiers. The phospholipids, lipoproteins, and proteins found in egg yolks make yolks excellent emulsifying ingredients. Low-density lipoproteins (LDL), not lecithin (as is mistakenly believed), are the primary components that make egg yolk such a strong emulsifying agent. In fact, the emulsifying activity of whole egg and egg white are only one-half and one-quarter, respectively, that of egg yolk alone.[13] Factors that influence the emulsification capability of egg yolk are freezing, pasteurization temperature, drying temperatures, and the presence of salts and acids.

Freezing and thawing of yolks results in denaturation and irreversible gelation of yolk proteins, causing decreased emulsifying capacity and stability. The addition of 10 percent salt or sugar to yolks before freezing protects against gelation and improves emulsifying capacity. Mayonnaise manufacturers commonly use salted yolk as an emulsifier. Drying yolks decreases emulsifying capacity because lipoproteins are released from cell membranes during the drying process. The addition of 5 to 10 percent sucrose before drying maintains the emulsifying capacity of the yolk. In general, the addition of salt or sugar increases emulsion stability by preventing gelling before freezing or drying, while acids decrease emulsifying capacity.[14]

Foaming

Foams are colloidal dispersions in which gas bubbles are dispersed in a liquid or solid phase. Food foams are created through the action of surfactants that stabilize the air cells. Eggs have an abundance of surfactants, so they are especially effective in foam creation and stability. The production of cakes, confections, and foamy egg dishes relies on this. Examples include meringues (highly aerated egg whites containing sugar and coagulated by heat), angel food cakes (also called sponge or foam cakes), and soufflés. Egg whites and yolks are both capable of producing foams; however, whites are typically preferred because they contain insignificant levels of lipids and therefore produce more stable foams. They are also colorless and impart little flavor compared to egg yolks or whole eggs.[15] One example of an egg yolk foam is zabaglione (Italian), or sabayon (French), a thick dessert sauce made of egg yolks, sugar, and wine heated slowly under constant beating. Zabaglione is eaten as is, used as a dessert topping, and also used as an ingredient in the filling for tiramisu.

Egg foams can be affected by many things, including the method and degree of beating/blending/homogenization, temperature, pH, fat, oil, salt, water, sugar, heating, addition of surfactants (sodium lauryl sulfate, sodium oleate, and others), esters (sucrose stearate, sucrose palmitate, and others), addition of emulsifiers (lecithin, mono- and diglyceride of fatty acids esters, and others), or stabilizers (citric acid, guar gum, xanthan, and others). For example, up to a point the volume of meringue foam increases with time of beating. Maximum stability occurs at the point where the volume is greatest. Continued beating past this point causes the foam to lose its elasticity and become stiff and brittle, and eventually results in a separation of the foam's structure, followed by collapse.[16]

Surface tension of food systems is lowered by increasing temperatures. Therefore, foaming rate and volume increase in egg whites when beaten at room temperature versus refrigeration temperatures.[17] Acid ingredients (cream of tartar, lemon juice) help stabilize the foam by making it less prone to over-coagulation. Increasing the acidity of egg whites loosens the protein structure. This keeps the foam elastic and stable enough to entrap the air cells, and allows them to expand when heated, resulting in better volume. Acids also tend to enhance the whiteness of egg-based foams.

On the other hand, even the smallest amount of fat inhibits foaming and reduces volume. Egg whites containing less than 0.05 percent yolk exhibit reduced foaming properties and volume. This may be counteracted by adding freeze-dried egg whites. Salt decreases foam's stability by weakening the protein structure by tying up free water, while adding water increases volume but decreases stability when dilution reaches 40 percent or more.

The addition of sugar prevents overbeating by delaying foam formation. Naturally, this increases whip time as well. Sugar separates protein molecules and slows the bonding process. It also stabilizes foam during heating by delaying water evaporation until the protein structure has had time to form. If sugars are added prior to heating, the functional properties of the whites are protected against the effects of heat. Heat gives permanence to (sets) the foam by inducing the coagulation of the egg protein's structure surrounding the air cells trapped in the foam.

Surface tension is the property of a liquid's surface that allows it to resist an external force. It is the reason why oil and water do not stay permanently blended in a solution without the addition of an emulsifier or surfactant, which decreases surface tension (or interfacial tension) between the two liquids. The action of surfactants is not restricted to liquids; they can also be used to assist in foam formation and stabilization between a mixture of a liquid and a gas such as meringue (egg white and air) or yolk-containing foams.

Surfactants such as sodium lauryl sulfate (0.1 percent) are used as a whipping aid in dried egg white. Triethyl citrate reduces whipping time and improves volume in cakes containing yolks.

Hydrocolloids can also help stabilize foods that depend on egg foams. Carboxymethyl cellulose prevents the collapse of frozen soufflés and meringues as well as reduces syneresis, and guar gum can be used to improve meringues in foods cooked by microwave heating.[18] Hydrocolloids provide thickening and gelling of aqueous solutions, stabilizing foams, emulsions, and dispersions, and preventing crystallization of saturated sugar solutions.

Controlling Crystallization

Whole eggs, whites, yolks, or egg yolk solids are used in confectionery products and ice creams to control ice crystal formation and promote smooth texture and desirable mouthfeel. Egg yolks in ice cream control density, hardness, and texture by encouraging the formation of small ice crystals. With their LDL content, they are excellent emulsifiers that help disperse fat throughout the ice cream mix and prevent it from clumping. Egg yolk also improves whipping properties of ice cream mix to result in a desirable dry and stiff ice cream.

In candies, which are supersaturated sugar solutions, egg whites act as interfering agents to retard sugar crystallization and to form many fine sugar crystals for a smooth texture. Egg white products improve whipping quality in aerated confections and help interfere with sucrose crystal formation, which can cause grainy texture and poor mouthfeel.[19] Lipids in yolks add flavor, tenderizing, and lubricating qualities in all confections.

● Milk

Composition of Milk and Milk-Based Products

Milk is defined by the U.S. Food and Drug Administration (FDA) as "the lacteal secretion (fluid from the mammary gland of mammals who have recently giving birth), practically free from colostrum (the milk produced within the first days of lactation), obtained by the complete milking of one or more healthy cows."[20] Fresh raw milk contains 85 to 88 percent water, 3 to 4 percent protein, 4.6 to 5.2 percent carbohydrate, 3 to 5 percent fat, and 0.7 to 1.0 percent minerals[21] and provides amino acids, carbohydrates (mainly lactose), calcium, and phosphorus. Because of milk's unique composition, it can be converted to manufactured products such as cheese, fermented milk products, butter, and many others.

Milk contains two primary classes of proteins, casein and whey. Both are at the top of the Protein Digestibility Corrected Amino Acid Score (PDCAAS) scale, with perfect scores of 1.0 (along with egg white and soy protein). Caseins are about 80 percent of the total protein in milk. Casein proteins in their native form are not water soluble and not easily coagulated by cooking. In addition, they precipitate at pH 4.6 and are the primary proteins that coagulate into curds during cheese manufacture. Casein is actually insoluble in milk. Rather, it exists as a stable colloidal dispersion of particles called casein micelles (see Figure 10.7), with the hydrophilic (water-loving) parts residing at the surface closest to the milk and the hydrophobic (water-fearing) parts oriented in the micelle's center. Calcium and phosphorus in milk are normally present in an insoluble form that helps stabilize the micelles. Reducing the pH of milk by adding acids like lemon juice or vinegar, or as a result of microbial fermentation, solubilizes the calcium in the micelles; this, along with the direct effects of acid on the protein, causes the micelles to precipitate out of suspension and the milk to coagulate and form curds. This reaction is commonly utilized in cheese-making.

Whey proteins make up approximately 20 percent of the total protein in milk.[22] Unlike casein, whey proteins remain soluble at pH 4.6 (in fact, they are always soluble, regardless of pH) and are in the whey fraction that remains after curd formation during cheese-making. They are easily coagulated by heating and are responsible for the film that forms (and often burns) on the bottom of the pan when milk is heated. They are also responsible for initiating the formation of the skin that develops on the surface of milk during extended uncovered heating above 158°F (70°C). As whey proteins denature, they become sticky and start to bind with casein and other milk proteins. At the same time, the water in the milk starts to evaporate. The proteins eventually become concentrated enough to create a thin film at the top.

The carbohydrate in milk is the reducing sugar lactose, a disaccharide composed of D-glucose and D-galactose. It is the only carbohydrate of any significance in milk; for that matter, it is the only carbohydrate of nutritional significance in any food of animal origin. It is only one-sixth as sweet as sucrose and imparts only slight sweetness to fresh milk. Being a reducing sugar, it reacts with amino acids to cause non-enzymatic browning through the Maillard reaction, leading to color and flavor changes. Caramelization of the lactose also leads to brown color and caramelized flavors.

FIGURE 10.7 Product composition of dairy ingredients.

Product	Moisture	Protein	Lipid	Carbohydrate	Ash
			%		
Whole milk	88.0	3.2	3.5	4.6	0.7
Ultrafiltered milk	70.0–75.0	10.0–12.0	11.0–14.0	<5.0	<2.5
Ultrafiltered nonfat milk	80.0–85.0	10.0–12.0	<0.5	<5.0	<2.5
Ultrafiltered (diafiltrated) nonfat milk	80.0–82.0	16.0–17.0	<0.5	<1.0	<1.5
Sweetened condensed whole milk	27.0	7.8	8.0	55.2	1.8
Evaporated whole milk	74.0	6.5	7.5	9.8	1.4
Half-and-half	80.2	3.1	11.5	4.5	0.7
Light cream	74.0	2.9	18.3	4.2	0.6
Light whipping cream	62.9	2.5	30.5	3.6	0.5
Heavy cream	57.3	2.2	36.8	3.2	0.5
Plastic cream	18.2	0.7	80.0	1.0	0.1
Cultured sour cream	71.0	3.2	21.0	4.3	0.7
Butter	16.0	0.9	>80	0.1	2.1
Anhydrous milkfat	<0.1	0.0	>99.8	0.0	0.0
Butter oil	<0.2	0.3	>99.5	0.0	0.0
Dry butter powder	<4.0	11.0	72.0	15.0	2.5
Dry whole milk powder	3.2	26.3	26.7	38.4	6.1
Dry nonfat milk powder	3.2	36.2	0.8	52.0	7.9
Dry buttermilk powder	3.0–3.5	32.0–34.5	5.5–6.0	49.5–50.5	7.5–8.0
Dry yogurt powder	3.0–5.0	33.0–36.0	1.25–2.0	50.0–51.5	7.0–8.0
Dry cultured dairy solids	3.0–5.0	22.0–33.0	0.0–2.0	52.0–66.7	7.0–8.0
Dry sweet whey	3.2	12.9	1.1	74.4	8.4
Dry acid whey	3.5	11.7	0.5	70.0	10.8
35% Whey protein concentrate	4.6	36.2	2.1	46.5	7.8
80% Whey protein concentrate	4.0	81.0	7.2	3.5	3.1
Dry whey protein isolate	3.7	91.5	0.5	0.8	3.7
Dry milk protein concentrate (MPC42)	3.5	42.0	1.0	46.0	7.5
Dry milk protein concentrate (MPC75)	5.0	75.0	1.5	10.9	7.6
Dry milk protein concentrate (MPC85)	4.9	85.0	1.6	1.0	7.1
Crystallized lactose (food grade)	4.5–5.5	0.1–0.6	0.0	99.0	0.1–0.3

Source: Adapted from Commercial Industry Specifications and M. Walsh, D. McMahon, and S. E. Duncan, "Milk and Dairy Products," Ch. 19 in *Food Chemistry: Principles and Applications*, ed. Y. H. Hui (West Sacramento, CA: Science Technology Systems, 2007), 19.1–19.23.

Fat exists in milk as an oil-in-water emulsion, with the fat globules or droplets dispersed throughout the milk serum. Triacylglycerols (triglycerides) make up 96 to 98 percent of the lipids in milk, the rest being phospholipids, cholesterol, monoacylglycerols, and diacylglycerols. The fatty acid composition of the triacylglycerol depends on the cow's diet and the reactions that occur during digestion. Thirteen fatty acids are present in milkfat at levels greater than 1 percent. Close to 75 percent of the fatty acid content in milk is comprised of saturated fats, with the remaining 25 to 30 percent unsaturated. Milk contains significant levels of short-chain fatty acids—butyric (C4), caproic (C6), caprylic (C8), and capric (C10).[23] Those that have the smallest molecular weight are both the most volatile and the most flavorful. When they are cleaved from the glycerol backbone by the action of native and microbial lipases (enzymes that remove lipids from glycerol), they cause undesirable rancid flavors in milk but desirable aged flavors in cheeses such as Parmesan and Romano.

In its fresh state, milk triacylglycerol is protected from the action of lipases by a milkfat globule membrane coat. However, if fresh raw milk is subjected to excessive agitation or foaming, this protective coat is disrupted, rendering the fat susceptible to lipase activity. In milk, this is termed hydrolytic rancidity, and the short-chain fatty acids give the milk a flavor described as baby vomit. This is typically not a problem in pasteurized homogenized milk products because the native lipase is easily inactivated by the heat of pasteurization. However, as milk is stored, spoilage microorganisms can grow and their enzymes can also produce this defect, so proper temperature control is necessary.

Nutrition

Milk is highly nutritious yet grossly underutilized in the American diet. It provides a compositionally balanced makeup of the macronutrients carbohydrate, protein, and fat, and contains 10 to 30 percent of daily values (DV) for nutrients including calcium, phosphorus, vitamin D, potassium, magnesium, vitamins A, B_{12}, riboflavin, and niacin. For every 8 ounces of milk there are 12 g carbohydrate and 9 g protein (contributing 16 percent of the DV of protein). The fat content depends on whether the milk is whole (4 percent), 2 percent, 1 percent, or fat free, and calories vary accordingly (from 83 calories per cup for skim milk to 146 calories per cup for whole milk).

Carbohydrate in milk is almost entirely in the form of lactose, which requires the enzyme lactase for digestion. If lactase is not available, the disaccharide moves through the large intestine intact, where gut microbiota access and metabolize it. This can result in excessive gas production and possible diarrhea, symptoms of lactose intolerance. Lactose intolerance is not a rare occurrence; it is estimated that 65 percent of the global population is affected (especially Asians and Africans). Lactose-free milk products are prepared by adding lactase enzyme to the milk during processing to break the disaccharide into individual glucose and galactose molecules, allowing absorption to occur and relieving symptoms of lactose intolerance. Because lactose is water soluble, low-fat and skim milks have higher levels of lactose than full-fat milks or creams, in which there are higher levels of milkfat. Even butter contains trace amounts of lactose unless it is cultured or clarified. Lactose levels in hard cheeses made from the curds after the whey has been removed are extremely low. Levels in soft-ripened, or well-aged cheeses are also quite low since the lactose has been broken down by microbial fermentation. In addition, fermented milk-based products such as yogurt are well tolerated because yogurt contains lactase generated by the bacterial cultures used to produce it. It should be noted that dried milk solids and whey powders commonly used for protein enhancement or as bulking agents in many processed foods contain large quantities of lactose as the water-soluble components in fluid milk become concentrated during the drying process.

Other star nutrients in milk are calcium, phosphorus, and vitamin D. These micronutrients function in bone growth and maintenance. Bone is in a constant state of turnover, depositing and withdrawing calcium based on bone cell age, blood calcium, phosphorus, and parathyroid hormone concentrations. Vitamin D is naturally present in small amounts in milk but beginning in 1933 was augmented to combat rickets (bone disease due to lack of vitamin D; it causes poor bone development, particularly in the pelvis and legs, leading to deformity, fractures, and difficulty walking). This was the second food fortification to occur in the United States, after iodine in 1924 was added to salt to prevent goiter (enlargement of the thyroid gland). Vitamin D enhances the absorption of calcium from the gastrointestinal tract. When blood calcium levels fall, parathyroid hormone is produced, signaling the release of vitamin D, which interacts with gut epithelial cells to increase calcium absorption. Without adequate vitamin D, this cycle continues, but the calcium is released from the bones. Eventually, this leads to excessive or incomplete bone turnover, resulting in osteodystrophy (abnormal development and loss of bone). Milk is the largest contributor of calcium in the diet.[24] One 8-ounce glass provides 30 percent of the DV of calcium and 25 percent of the DV for vitamin D and phosphorus.

Calcium can, however, interfere with the ability to absorb iron, thereby increasing the risk for iron-deficiency anemia. For this reason, addition of milk to high-iron foods may limit the bioavailability of the iron. This should not prohibit the use of milk for building a mixed dish or food item, however, as there are plenty of opportunities to obtain iron from other sources in the diet.

Additional nutrients in milk include blood builders like potassium and magnesium, which work to maintain fluid and electrolyte balance in the blood. Adequate amounts of these micronutrients are shown to aid in the management of blood pressure.[25] Finally, vitamin B_{12} in milk is involved in the production of red blood cells, further supporting blood health.

The Value of Dairy Products in Food Product Development

An enormous range of dairy ingredients is available to the food product developer. These include:

Butter ingredients, including whipped, cultured, light, salted, and unsalted; and anhydrous milkfat, butter oil, lipolyzed butter, butter powder, and buttermilk powder.

Cream ingredients, including half-and-half (10.5 to 18 percent fat), light cream (18 to 30 percent fat), light whipping cream (30 to 36 percent fat), heavy cream (>36 percent fat), plastic cream (cream separated a second time to yield 80 percent fat, which is crystallized and plastic), cultured sour cream, acidified sour cream, and dry cream (40 to 75 percent fat).

Milk protein concentrate ingredients, including whole milk powder, milk protein concentrate, nonfat dry milk, and ultra-filtrated milk. Milk protein concentrate ingredients are available in protein levels from 42 to 85 percent and are made from milk, so they contain the normal ratio of milk casein and whey proteins. Nonfat dry milk ingredients come in three classifications: high heat, medium heat, and low heat. The variation in heat treatment occurs during the concentration step, before spray-drying. This affects the color, flavor, and solubility of the ingredients. High-heat nonfat dry milk is typically used in baking applications because of its color and reduced solubility and because it does not detrimentally affect loaf volume (milk can have a reducing effect on gluten if not strongly heated). When milk powder is reconstituted for beverages or fermented dairy products, low-heat nonfat dry milk is used because of its mild flavor and ease of reconstitution. Ultra-filtrated milk ingredients come in whole and skim milk concentrates as well as reduced-lactose products. Ultra-filtration is a membrane process where compounds of different sizes are selectively removed. At its most basic, water and minerals are removed to concentrate the milk without heating (which is required in making condensed milk). With increased membrane pore sizes, lactose can also be removed.

Whey ingredients, including sweet whey, acid whey, 35 percent whey protein concentrate, 80 percent whey protein concentrate, and whey protein isolate with 90 percent protein. The designator "sweet" refers to whey produced from rennet-coagulated cheeses, such as cheddar and Swiss. Acid whey is the dried product of acid-coagulated cheeses, like cottage cheese. Both whey products contain lactose; their main difference is in mineral composition. Acid whey has a higher level of calcium. Lactose and minerals are further removed when whey is concentrated to produce isolates.

Yogurt powdered products, including yogurt powder and cultured dairy solids.

Cheese ingredients, including natural, pasteurized process cheese, cheese powders, enzyme-modified cheeses, and cheese analogs.

Casein ingredients, including sodium and calcium caseinate, water-soluble versions of casein used as a high-quality protein supplement in a wide variety of processed foods and baked goods, as a bulking agent in instant soup mixes and coffee creamers, and as an emulsifier in processed meats and dairy beverages.

Milkfat Function

Milkfat can be sourced in liquid (full-fat milks and creams), solid (butter), and dried forms (butter and whole milk powders). The function of milkfat is a result of its fatty acid composition and other constituents (phospholipids). Applications include baked products, confections, sauces and soups, and frozen products. The unique dairy flavor notes of milkfat enhance the richness of foods when compared to other fats. Milkfat ingredients are also associated with the production of caramel, praline, and toffee flavors. It is highly compatible with cocoa butter and therefore can be used to reduce cost in the formulation of confections. Heat can produce varied flavor notes from milkfat in the production of different sauces; lightly melted whole butter is typically used in cream and white sauces, clarified butter is used as the basis for emulsified sauces such as hollandaise and béarnaise to provide rich dairy notes; slightly overheated butter provides roasted, cooked notes that complement brown sauces and gravies; and browned butter contributes flavor notes that complement barbecue, traditional Cajun, and smoke-flavored sauces.

Milkfat works well as a flavor carrier for spices, sweet and savory flavors, herbs, and other fat-soluble ingredients. The narrow melting range of butter ensures the quick release of oil-soluble flavors in a meltaway effect that imparts smooth mouthfeel properties.[26] Milkfat enhances the structure of cakes and pastries, helps retard fat bloom in chocolates, and enhances aeration in icings and cakes. It has excellent layering properties that disrupt the formation of three-dimensional gluten networks in laminated dough products, resulting in desirable flaky (rather than chewy) crusts.[27]

In frozen products, milkfats provide functions that cannot be duplicated by vegetable oils, including their ability to form foams when whipped and their unique texture when frozen. This is due to the variability of the fatty acid composition of the triacylglycerides, which confers a range in the crystallization properties of the fat.[28] Highly unsaturated fats of vegetable oils have a lower melting temperature than saturated fats. This means they do not crystallize unless the temperature is very low. Dairy fats have a mix of fatty acids, including saturated fat, which allows for some fat crystallization at refrigeration temperature after pasteurization. When the temperature is lowered further, the lower melting fatty acids will further crystallize. This property is important when making whipped cream and is the reason the cream must be very cold during whipping. The crystallized fat helps stabilize the air cells in the whipped product. When freezing dairy bases to make ice cream, the pasteurized mix is refrigerated for at least 4 hours to allow some of the fat to crystallize prior to freezing and whipping in air. After emerging from the ice cream freezer, about 40 percent of the water is frozen and the ice cream is like soft-serve.[29] Water and fat further crystallize in the freezer during the process known as *hardening*. The texture of ice cream can be contrasted to that of *gelato*, which contains some nondairy fat and thus is stickier and softer.

A point to note for the Culinology® professional making ice cream using purchased whipping cream: Whipping cream is typically not homogenized because this reduces its ability to make a high-quality whipped cream. When making ice cream, however, it is important to homogenize the ice cream base prior to freezing to prevent a churned effect in which the ice cream has a greasy, buttery texture. This might not be possible, however, so care should be taken to not over-mix the product.

Water-Holding Capacity

Water-solute interactions have a significant impact on the properties of foods. Methods or ingredients that bind or entrap water in foods can be used to lower cost by increasing yield and reducing syneresis. This also improves product quality in that moisture and mouthfeel are enhanced by increasing the viscosity or perceived moistness of a product. Water-holding capacity is the term for the ability of a matrix of molecules to physically entrap large amounts of water in a manner that inhibits exudation under the application of an external force.[30] Dry milk ingredients bind a certain amount of water when rehydrated, and when heated, the proteins denature and unfold, increasing the viscosity and water holding capacity. This is a factor in the production of viscous food products such as beverages (chocolate milk and fermented milk drinks), thick soups and custards, baked goods (bread and cakes), confections (puddings, custards, and flan), dairy products (yogurt), meat products (sausages and other formulated meat products), salad dressings, and sauces.

Adding dry milk ingredients to bakery formulations results in softer doughs because the ingredients bind water and interfere with gluten interactions. The results are cookie or cake doughs that are easier to machine and extrude and baked products with a softer texture. Dairy proteins provide structural support in salad dressings, especially creamy-style products. Their ability to bind water is also important in formulating reduced-fat dressings because they contribute fat-like attributes, such as lubricity and creamy mouthfeel.[31]

High-heat dairy powders do not depress bread loaf volume because they are less soluble than low-heat powders and compete less with gluten for the available water. They also reduce water separation and improve the textures of meat products like bologna and sausage. Medium-heat dry dairy ingredients produce the firm, chewy texture of many confections and increase yield through improved water holding. Low- and medium-heat dry dairy ingredients help stabilize the viscosity of pasteurized process cheese and increase the firmness of the coagulum in fermented milk products like yogurt. They also provide structural support to extruded frozen products like ice cream.

Color and Browning

Dairy protein and carbohydrate ingredients can contribute to the color of foods and participate in Maillard browning. During baking or cooking, the protein's amine groups react with lactose and other reducing sugars to create brown color in baked goods and sauces. Milkfat contributes creamy color that balances the color of thickened products such as sauces, soups, salad dressings, and beverages. The color contributed can be due to carotenoid pigments in the milkfat that come from the cow's diet and/or to the light-scattering effects of fat in the milk. When fat is removed from milk, the milk appears slightly green or blue because it doesn't scatter the light as well. This is commonly seen in the bluish appearance of skim milk. (The casein micelle tends to scatter blue wavelengths, and the riboflavin in milk has a greenish tint.) Dairy ingredients also contribute opacity, which helps give products the appearance of a richer texture, especially in reduced-fat items.[32]

Emulsification

Dairy proteins have both hydrophilic and hydrophobic groups; therefore, they are used successfully at oil-water interfaces to form and stabilize emulsions. Emulsification properties are enhanced by controlled protein denaturation. Heating promotes the unfolding of the dairy proteins to expose hydrophobic amino acid residues that encourage them to orient at the oil-water interface. Emulsification functionality improves when these interfaces are further protected by *adsorption* of added surfactants (such as sorbitan esters, monoglycerides, lecithins, and hydrocolloids) around the oil droplets, and partially lost again by re-coalescence of those oil droplets that are not protected quickly enough. Re-coalescence of the fat droplets leading to emulsion breakdown is an important phenomenon in emulsions stabilized by proteins because of the relatively slow development of the protective surfactant film around new emulsion droplets.

Dairy ingredients are used to stabilize emulsions in applications for baked goods, beverages, dairy products, meats, salad dressings, soups, and sauces.[33] Their ability to stabilize oil-water emulsions is affected by pH, temperature, the extent of protein denaturation, the ionic strength of the aqueous phase (especially the presence of calcium), and the presence of other emulsifiers. The caseins in milk are disorganized and flexible molecules, whereas the whey proteins are globular and compact, and both act as emulsifiers. Lecithin in milkfat also contributes to emulsification because it improves fat dispersion. The high phospholipids and 4 percent fat content of buttermilk powder (the product of butter-making, not the fermented milk product) make it an excellent choice for emulsifying and adding milk solids to food products.

Gelation and Thickening

Milk proteins have several mechanisms that can be used to form gels and increase viscosity. Caseins form enzyme-induced gels by the action of chymosin (also known as rennin), an enzyme in *rennet* that acts on kappa casein. The enzyme cleaves the carbohydrate portion of the molecule and causes the casein micelle to become unstable and to coagulate. This coagulation method is used in the production of rennet-coagulated cheeses such as cheddar, Swiss, and mozzarella. Caseins also gel if the pH is reduced to its *isoelectric point* (pH 4.6). If this acidification is done slowly and without agitation, the resulting gel can produce a product such as yogurt, or it can be cut, drained, and pressed to produce acid-coagulated cheeses, like cottage cheese and cream cheese.

Whey proteins form gels when heated to high temperatures (approximately 180°F [82°C]) with the addition of acid, or at room temperature if acid is gradually added after the protein is treated by high temperatures. Gelation is a two-step mechanism that involves an initiation step involving the unfolding or dissociation of protein molecules by the mechanisms just described, followed by an aggregation step in which association or aggregation occurs between protein molecules, resulting in gel formation. For the formation of a highly ordered gel, such as in yogurt, it is essential that the aggregation step proceed slowly or else a precipitate, rather than an ordered gel, will form. Ricotta cheese is an example of aggregation occurring under stirring, so instead of a gel, a granular precipitate is formed that does not hold water, which is removed as whey.

Dry dairy ingredients are used in confection applications to form rigid, heat-induced irreversible gels that hold water and fat and provide structural support to confections such as nougat, frosting, and creams. The type of aggregation affects the gel's opacity, an important property in many candies and confections. Medium-heat dairy ingredients provide better flavor than high-heat dairy products, which have a strong cooked taste. Dry dairy ingredients also help improve viscosity in processed cheese and create stable gels in fermented milk products. Low-heat products provide better gelation for products such as yogurt without impacting flavor profiles.

The texture, firmness, and chewiness of many processed meat products are enhanced by heat-induced gels from high-heat dairy proteins because meat flavors mask the more intense cooked flavors of high-heat dairy ingredients.

In beverage applications, dry milk ingredients add to the nutritional profile and help thicken shake-type drinks and nutraceutical beverages. Low-heat dairy powders help thicken while providing a mild flavor profile that blends well with other flavors. For UHT (Ultra High Temperature)-processed beverages, product formulators can utilize low-heat products to prevent gelation during extended room-temperature storage.[34]

Whipping and Foaming

An important attribute of milk proteins is their surface-active behavior. Caseinates and whey protein concentrates are excellent at enhancing the whipping and stabilizing of foams. They easily adsorb to fat globule–water interfaces during homogenization of milk and to the air bubble–cream interface during whipping. A rapid diffusion of protein to the air-water interface reduces surface tension, followed by partial unfolding of the protein; this is essential to forming protein-based foams, like the caseinate foams used as dessert toppings. As dairy protein concentration increases, foams become denser, with finer, more uniform air bubbles.

Whipping properties are affected by protein concentration, protein state (denatured or not), pH, presence of calcium or other salts, heat treatment (if any), and the presence of lipids. In the creation of a protein-based foam, lipids reduce the volume and stability (such as when whipping egg whites, where any lipid from the yolk is detrimental). In baking applications, such as cakes, the addition of either low- or high-heat nonfat dry milk creates a desirable light, even texture by forming dense, stable foams with finer, more uniform bubble distribution.[35] Foaming beverages, such as eggnog and shake-type drinks, benefit from low-heat dairy powders to increase the solids and viscosity so air cells are retained when the product is shaken or whipped. Milk proteins are also a major help in stabilizing the foams of frozen desserts like ice cream, whipped toppings, and mousses.[36]

Cheese Applications

Cheese ingredients are commonly used to add flavor to formulated food products. Cheese is generally defined as "the fresh or matured product obtained by draining the whey after coagulation of casein." Casein is coagulated through the application of acid (produced by the fermentation of lactose by microbial cultures or directly added) or the proteolytic enzyme *chymosin*, found in *rennet*. Cheese can be produced from whole, 2 percent, 1 percent, and nonfat milk. Different ingredients and processes during the manufacture and aging result in a wide variety of cheeses with distinctive texture, flavor, and functional properties. More than 200 varieties of cheese are produced in the United States, and more than 1400 varieties are catalogued in the World Cheese Exchange Database. Cheese is categorized as natural or processed, ripened or fresh, and soft to hard.

Natural cheese is a general classification for cheese made directly from milk. In fresh, unripened (unaged) cheese, the curd is separated from the whey and formed into cheese immediately for use or consumption within a few weeks. Ripened cheeses are aged to allow flavor development from the enzymatic breakdown of fats and proteins. Ripened cheeses may also use adjuncts such as enzymes, secondary bacterial flora, yeast, and molds to create unique flavors for specific cheese varieties. Natural cheeses are categorized according to their moisture content and degree of hardness. Soft cheeses include Brie, Camembert, ricotta, and cottage cheese. Semisoft cheeses include blue, brick, feta, Havarti, Monterey Jack, mozzarella, Muenster, and provolone. Hard cheeses include cheddar, Colby, Edam, Gouda, and Swiss. Very hard cheese varieties include Parmesan and Romano. When choosing natural cheese as an ingredient, it is important to understand how it will perform in a finished product based on its age and storage conditions.

Processed cheeses are made by blending one or more natural cheeses into a homogenous mass, heating the mix, and adding water, flavors, and emulsifying salts—typically sodium citrate and a variety of sodium phosphates. These reduce the calcium interactions with the milk proteins and improve emulsification of the fat by the protein. Processed cheeses typically maintain smooth, creamy, homogenous melting characteristics during heat processing, unlike most natural cheeses. Pasteurized processed cheeses include American cheese, cheese spreads, and cheese foods. Cold-pack cheese is a blend of natural cheeses processed without heat, but often with added flavorings and seasonings.

Cheese powders, or dehydrated cheeses, are prepared using a single cheese variety or a blend of cheeses to produce standardized flavor characteristics. Products may be all cheese or a blend of cheese with other dairy ingredients such as whey or milk powder, starches, or other carbohydrates, flavors, or colors. Typical applications for cheese powders include prepared dry mixes, sauces, and topical seasonings for snack foods.[37]

Enzyme-modified cheeses are industrial flavor ingredients that blend food-grade lipases or proteases with natural cheese to intensify cheese flavor development. These enzymes accelerate the breakdown of fats to produce increased levels of more flavorful free fatty acids and break down proteins to produce increased levels of more flavorful peptides and amino acids. They are much stronger in taste then the natural cheeses they are made from and more economical to use than natural cheese due to their intense flavor. They are available in paste or powder form. Applications include flavor enhancement of pasteurized process cheese and cheese sauces, salad dressings, and snack foods.

●Applications
Culinology® Case Study in Product Development Using Egg Products

Whether you describe it as Culinology® or molecular gastronomy, Chef Wylie Dufresne's creation of Eggs Benedict at the chef/owner's wd~50 restaurant is a wonderful study of how combining science knowledge and culinary skill can advance food innovations. Dufresne's Eggs Benedict recipe uses the coagulation chemistry of proteins and hydrocolloids to create a dish of deep-fried hollandaise sauce, egg yolk "morsels," and a crisp wafer of Canadian bacon.[38]

In an *ABC Nightline* interview, Dufresne described how his search for understanding the science of food and its preparation fueled his fascination with eggs and their use as a food and ingredient:

> Every now and then I find a new approach to working with eggs, and it's just really exciting.. . . [T]hey're fascinating from a technical standpoint. The way an egg behaves and what you can do to an egg and the various textures you can get.

The fact that there are two parts to it, basically the yolk and the white. It gives you an incredible repertoire of things to work with.[39]

Eggs Benedict Recipe

Chef/owner Wylie Dufresne, wd~50, New York
ABC Nightline Platelist and adapted by Starchefs.com (Dufresne, 2008)
Yield: 4 servings

Egg Yolks

Raw egg yolks	10
Salt	to taste
Cayenne, ground	to taste

Preparation
Season the unbeaten yolks with salt and cayenne to taste. Fill a 1 × 12-inch plastic sleeve with the yolks and tie the top with string to secure. Let stand upright for 2 hours to allow any air to rise to the top. Cook the yolk-filled sleeves upright in a water bath for 17 minutes at 158°F (70°C). Then ice down the sleeves and portion the cooked yolk "tubes" into 1-inch-long cylindrical portions.

FRIED HOLLANDAISE

Seasoned Base

Raw egg yolks	10 g
Salt	to taste
Lemon juice	to taste

Preparation
Mix the egg yolks, salt, and lemon juice well in a blender. Set aside in the blender.

Part I

Sodium hexameta phosphate	2 g
Citric acid	0.6 g
Gellan gum or low-acyl gellan gum	3.5 g
Water	170 g

Preparation
Blend sodium hexameta phosphate, citric acid, gellan gum, and water together and bring to a boil in a small pot. Pour into a container and cool until completely set.

Part II

Water	110 g
Ultrasperse M (modified starch)	10 g

Preparation
Mix water and Ultrasperse M together well and reserve.

Part III

Gelatin, bloomed	60 g
Butter, melted	640 g

Preparation
Dissolve the gelatin in the melted butter.

Fried Hollandaise Preparation

Slowly add half of Part III (gelatin–melted butter mixture) to the seasoned egg yolks in the blender as you would a classic hollandaise. Then, using a bowl and whisk, blend Part II (water and Ultrasperse M mixture) into the remaining half of Part III (gelatin–melted butter mixture). Add the ingredients from the bowl to the ingredients in the blender. The blender should be running throughout all of the steps. At this point a thick and creamy sauce should have formed. Adjust the seasoning with salt and lemon juice. Pour the sauce into a shallow baking tray lined with plastic and allow to chill overnight. Cut the hollandaise into cubes and bread them using a classic three-step process: flour, egg wash, and English muffin crumbs. Reserve the breaded cubes in the freezer.

CANADIAN BACON

Canadian bacon	100 g
Oil for frying	As needed

Preparation

Thinly slice the bacon on a deli slicer and fry in oil at 375°F (191°C). Pat dry and reserve.

Dish Assembly

Gently warm egg yolk portions (prepared in step 1) in oven (low temperature). Pan-fry cubes of hollandaise and then place in oven to warm through. Place 3 pieces each of egg yolk morsels and fried hollandaise cubes on plate and garnish with bacon, chives, and salt.

Culinology® Case Studies in Product Development Using Milk Products

Creating Natural Cheeses with Varied Melting Characteristics

Many product developers turn to processed cheese products when they need a cheese ingredient with controlled melting characteristics. The melting characteristics can be engineered by manufacturers through the use of emulsifying salts and other ingredients that aid or hinder melting characteristics in formulated foods. However, increasing demand from consumers for manufactured food products with more natural ingredients has led product developers to search for sources of natural cheese products with controlled melting characteristics. In response to this demand, researchers at the Wisconsin Center for Dairy Research are developing manufacturing methods for controlling the melt characteristics of natural cheeses.

The pH balance of natural cheeses affects protein binding, which directly affects melt characteristics. Natural cheeses fall into three basic pH categories: high pH (around 6.4—these are low-melting cheeses such as Hispanic queso fresco and queso blanco); mid pH (around 5.3—these are excellent melting cheeses such as mozzarella, cheddar, Colby, and Monterey Jack); and low pH (around 4.6—these acidic cheeses have a pH around casein's isoelectric point, which causes them to soften but not flow, such as feta, cream cheese, and cottage cheese). The goal was to develop methods to manipulate the melt characteristics of the mid- and low-pH natural cheeses to make them more suitable for applications that require high-temperature cooking (for example, deep frying and microwaving).

The researchers were able to modify existing cheese-manufacturing processes to strengthen protein bonds, which reduced their melt characteristics. Modifications included higher pasteurization temperatures and homogenization of the milk prior to the cheese-manufacturing process. The higher heat treatments increased protein denaturation and cross-linked structures, which inhibited the flow properties of the natural cheese. Homogenization caused fat globules to be coated with proteins, which resulted in a more rigid structure that decreased melt and flow. Cheese manufacturers can now use pH control, high-temperature pasteurization, and homogenization to control melt in natural cheeses, turning a natural high-melting cheese with a mid-range pH, like mozzarella, into a non-melting product for applications like deep-fried cheese sticks.[40]

Development of Gourmet Butter for Foodservice Applications

More than 120 compounds give butter its unique flavor; however, the five biggest contributors are short chain fatty acids, lactones, methyl ketones, diacetyl, and dimethyl sulfide. Of these, lactones and methyl ketones are the main components responsible for the flavor of butter in heated applications. Although initially present at levels below their flavor threshold value (FTV), on heating, the total concentration of both lactones and methyl ketones exceeds their FTV. The two compounds also react in a synergistic manner, providing a full, rich butter flavor. Methyl ketones and lactones also interact with the flavors developed through the Maillard reaction during roasting and baking. But it is the *combination* of all the flavor compounds in butter that creates its overall appeal. Butter is also an excellent flavor carrier for spices and other fat-soluble ingredients—a good way to bring added flavor to finished products.

Gourmet butter, also known as compound butter or *beurre composé*, is a flavored butter with a variety of uses. Compound butters have been made for centuries; two of the better known are *maître d'hôtel* (parsley and lemon) and *chivry* (herbs). Butter is softened at room temperature and mixed with supplementary ingredients. It can be made inexpensively by adding just a few chopped herbs, or more expensively by using ingredients such as black or white truffles. After the butter is flavored, it can be used as is or reformed by rolling in parchment paper or in a plastic tube and refrigerated until firm enough to slice.

These butters can be melted on top of meats and vegetables, used as a spread, or used to finish various sauces. Using compound butters to finish a sauce or soup not only adds flavor, but also phospholipids and lipoproteins that act as natural emulsifying agents, contributing to a smooth, creamy mouthfeel. In addition, gourmet butters can be used for sautéing, in baked goods, and for stuffing or basting. Many upscale restaurants place a variety of flavored butters on their tables for spreading on bread.

In addition to restaurant applications, gourmet butters also provide food manufacturers with a wide variety of options for new product development. New dishes may be invented or a facelift given to old favorites.

● Conclusion

Unmatched for nutritional value, affordability, and availability, and with a wealth of functional capabilities in both food and beverage applications, egg- and dairy-based ingredients are essential components in the Culinology® professional's toolbox. Learning to use them effectively takes experimentation and practice, but the benefits far outweigh the investment in time.

[1]E. C. Y. Li-Chan, W. D. Powrie, and S. Nakai, "The Chemistry of Eggs and Egg Products," in *Egg Science and Technology*, W. J. Stadelman and W. J. Cotterill, eds. (Binghamton, NY: Food Products Press, 1995), 105–175; Y. Mine and M. Yang, "Eggs," in *Food Chemistry: Principles and Applications*, Y. H. Hui, ed. (West Sacramento, CA: Science Technology Systems, 2007), 26.1–26.20.

[2]American Egg Board, *Egg Science and Technology Lesson Plan*, vol. 2 (Park Ridge, IL: American Egg Board, 2008).

[3]Li-Chan, Powrie, and Nakai, "The Chemistry of Eggs and Egg Products," 105–175. Mine and Yang, "Eggs," 26.1–26.20.

[4]Y. Mine and M. Yang, "Eggs," in *Food Chemistry: Principles and Applications*, Y. H. Hui, ed. (West Sacramento, CA: Science Technology Systems, 2007), 26.1–26.20.

[5]F. B. Hu et al., "A Prospective Study of Egg Consumption and Risk of Cardiovascular Disease in Men and Women," *Journal of the American Medical Association* 281 (1999): 1387–1394; D. J. McNamara, "The Impact of Egg Limitations on Coronary Heart Disease Risk: Do the Numbers Add Up?" *Journal of the American College of Nutrition* 19 (2000): 540S–548S; R. M. Krauss et al., "A Review of Scientific Research and Recommendations Regarding Eggs," *Journal of the American College of Nutrition* 23 (2004): 596S–600S; L. M. Barraj et al., "A Comparison of Egg Consumption with Other Modifiable Coronary Heart Disease Lifestyle Risk Factors: A Relative Risk Apportionment Study," *Risk Analysis* 29, no. 3 (2008): 401–415; A. Mente, L. de Koning, H. S. Shannon, and S. S. Anand, "A Systematic Review of the Evidence Supporting a Causal Link Between Dietary Factors and Coronary Heart Disease," *Archives of Internal Medicine* 169, no. 7 (2009): 659–669.

[6]Krauss et al., "A Review of Scientific Research and Recommendations Regarding Eggs," 596S–600S; A. H. Lichtenstein et al., "Diet and Lifestyle Recommendations Revision 2006: A Scientific Statement from the American Heart Association Nutrition Committee," *Circulation* 114 (2006): 82–96.

[7]S. Y. Oh et al., "Eggs Enriched in Omega-3 Fatty Acids and Alterations in Lipid Concentrations in Plasma and Lipoproteins and in Blood Pressure, *American Journal of Clinical Nutrition* 54 (1991): 689–695; Z. Jiang and

J. S. Sim, "Consumption of n-3 Polyunsaturated Fatty Acid–Enriched Eggs and Changes in Plasma Lipids of Human Subjects," *Nutrition* 9, no. 6 (1993): 561–562; L. K. Ferrier et al., "Alpha-Linolenic Acid– and Docosahexaenoic Acid–Enriched Eggs from Hens Fed Flaxseed: Influence on Blood Lipids and Platelet Phospholipid Fatty Acids in Humans," *American Journal of Clinical Nutrition* 62 (1995): 81–86; D. J. Farrell, "Enrichment of Hen Eggs with n-3 Long-Chain Fatty Acids and Evaluation of Enriched Eggs in Humans," *American Journal of Clinical Nutrition.* 68 (1998): 538–544.

[8]A. S. Raghuwanshi, S. S. Joshi, and S. Christakos, "Vitamin D and Multiple Sclerosis," *Journal of Cellular Biochemistry* 105, no. 2 (2008): 338–343; M. F. Holick and T. C. Chen, "Vitamin D Deficiency: A Worldwide Problem with Health Consequences," *American Journal of Clinical Nutrition* 87, no. 4 (2008): 1080S–1086S; A. Ascherio, K. L. Munger, and K. C. Simon, "Vitamin D and Multiple Sclerosis," *Lancet Neurology* 9, no. 6 (2010): 599–612.

[9]American Egg Board, *Egg Science and Technology Lesson Plan*.

[10]Ibid.

[11]Ibid.

[12]Ibid.

[13]Mine and Yang, "Eggs," 26.1–26.20.

[14]American Egg Board, *Egg Science and Technology Lesson Plan*.

[15]Mine and Yang, "Eggs," 26.1–26.20.

[16]American Egg Board, *Egg Science and Technology Lesson Plan*.

[17]Mine and Yang, "Eggs," 26.1–26.20.

[18]American Egg Board, *Egg Science and Technology Lesson Plan*.

[19]Ibid.

[20]U.S. Food and Drug Administration, Department of Health and Human Services, *Code of Federal Regulations*, Title 21: Food and Drugs; Part 131: Milk and Cream.

[21]M. Walsh, D. McMahon, and S. E. Duncan, "Milk and Dairy Products," in *Food Chemistry: Principles and Applications*, Y. H. Hui, ed. (West Sacramento, CA: Science Technology Systems, 2007), 19.1–19.23.

[22]Walsh, McMahon, and Duncan. "Milk and Dairy Products," 19.1–19.23.

[23]Walsh, McMahon, and Duncan. "Milk and Dairy Products," 19.1–19.23.

[24]P. A. Cotton et al., "Dietary Sources of Nutrients Among U.S. Adults, 1994 to 1996," *Journal of the American Dietetic Association* 104, no. 6 (2004): 92–930.

[25]P. K. Whelton et al., "Effects of Oral Potassium on Blood Pressure: Meta-Analysis of Randomized Controlled Clinical Trials," *Journal of the American Medical Association* 277, no. 20 (1997): 1624–1632; L. J. Appel et al. for The DASH Collaborative Research Group, "A Clinical Trial of the Effects of Dietary Patterns on Blood Pressure," *New England Journal of Medicine* 336 (1997): 1117–1124.

[26]Dairy Management, Inc., "Facts About Cheese: Ingredient Applications," www.innovatewithdairy.com (Rosemont, IL: Dairy Management, Inc., 2009b).

[27]K. J. Burrington, "Dairy Ingredients in Bakery Products," *American Institute of Baking Technical Bulletin* 27, no. 3 (2005).

[28]H. D. Goff, "The Impact of Dairy Ingredient Functionality on the Properties of Ice Cream," *AgroFOOD Industry Hi-Tech* 20, no. 4 (2009): 43–45.

[29]M. D. Eisner, H. Wildmoser, and E. J. Windhab, "Air Cell Microstructuring in a High Viscous Ice Cream Matrix," *Colloids and Surfaces: Physicochemical and Engineering Aspects* 263, no. 1–3 (2005): 390–399.

[30]D. S. Reid and O. R. Fennema, "Water and Ice," in *Fennema's Food Chemistry*, S. Damodaran, K. Parkin, and O. R. Fennema, eds. (Boca Raton, FL: CRC Press, 2008), 17–82.

[31]Dairy Management, Inc., "Exploring the Functionalities and Applications of Dry Dairy Ingredients," Think Dairy College Curriculum Program, Food Science Curriculum Enhancement (Rosemont, IL: Dairy Management, Inc., 2000).

[32]Ibid.

[33]Ibid.

[34]Ibid.

[35]E. J. Pyler, "Dairy Products and Blends," in *Baking Science and Technology*, vol. 1, 3rd ed. (Kansas City, MO: Sosland, 1988).

[36]Dairy Management, Inc., "Exploring the Functionalities and Applications of Dry Dairy Ingredients."

[37]Dairy Management, Inc., "Facts About Cheese."

[38]W. Dufresne, "The Evolution of a Dish: An Interpretation of Eggs Benedict," Innovations at wd~50, Savory Workshop, StarChefs.com, International Chefs Congress, NY, 2008.

[39]Sarah Rosenberg and Christina Caron, "Wylie Dufresne, Egg Man, Keeping *wd~50* Afloat in Tough Economy: Why Dufresne Adores Eggs," retrieved April 10, 2009, from http://abcnews.go.com/Nightline/Platelist.

[40]Dean Sommer, "Restricting Melt for Performance and Value," *Food Product Design* (December 2008).

11 | Fermentation

Lead Author: James R. Adams, CCS®, CFS, Director of Process Optimization, Tyson Prepared Foods Operations

Charles Hayes, CRC®, CEC, Director of Research and Development, National Accounts, JMH Premium

● Introduction

Culinology® denotes a blending of culinary arts and food science; fermentation has long been regarded the same way. In most cases, it refers to the conversion of carbohydrates (also known as fermentable substrates) under anaerobic (without oxygen) conditions into carbon dioxide gas, organic acids, and alcohol by the actions of microorganisms, primarily bacteria and yeast. Two major exceptions occur: when vinegar is produced from ethanol, and when molds (aerobic organisms) are involved, as in mold-ripened cheeses. In both of these cases, oxygen is required. Many types of microorganisms, alone or in combination, act on an assortment of fermentable substrates to produce the vast number of fermented foods and beverages consumed around the world every day. These include well-known alcoholic beverages such as beer, ale, wine, and most of the hard liquors, as well as pickles, sauerkraut, pepperoni, yogurt, cheeses, yeast-raised breads, and more. In addition to its major impact on the flavor, aroma, appearance, digestibility, and nutritional profile of foods, fermentation is also one of the oldest methods of food preservation, dating to prehistoric times.

● History of Fermentation

It will never be known exactly when the first fermentation took place, but most of the scientific community accepts the premise that alcoholic fermentation was the first chemical reaction ancient humans observed. This is known as the Paleolithic hypothesis, a set of postulates or suppositions attempting to explain the origin of fermentation in prehistory.[1] In 2004, it was confirmed by chemical analysis of ancient organic compounds that were absorbed and preserved in pottery jars that a mixed fermented beverage of rice, honey, and fruit was produced as early as 9000 years ago in the area known today as China.

The earliest evidence of yeast fermentation used to convert the natural fruit sugar in grapes to alcohol was found in the Middle East and dates back 8000 years. The ancient Mesopotamians and Sumerians were brewing as early as 10,000 BC. However, Babylonian clay tablets with a recipe for beer, from approximately the year 6000 BC, provide the first documented evidence of beer-making. This recipe used underbaked bread made from germinated barley as the yeast source. When the bread was cut into small pieces and placed in a large jug with water, the yeast fermented the malt produced by the barley (as takes place in "malting" in the brewing process) when the dough was par-baked. This pre-inoculated malt-water fermented into a kind of beer. The common people considered this beverage ready to drink; however, the elite usually filtered it first. Dates, herbs, and honey were sometimes added for flavoring. It is interesting to note that early beer formulas did not include hops, which were not introduced until centuries later. As a matter of fact, the beer of that period, while classified as such, does not resemble anything we know as beer today.

Ancient Egyptian writings and drawings found on the walls of tombs indicate that fermentation was used to preserve vegetables, including cucumbers, circa 3000 BC.[2] It was widely known in ancient Egypt that Cleopatra believed consuming fermented vegetables greatly enhanced her beauty.[3]

The Hebrew Bible refers to yeast-leavened bread. Evidence found on Egyptian tombs suggests that using starter dough (containing yeast from a previous batch) was a common practice. That continues today, notably in San Francisco sourdough bread manufacture. Breads made from a starter have a distinctive aroma and sour flavor and are leavened naturally.

Archaeological evidence from other cultures indicates that a similar process was used to make dough rise; a beer-type liquid—the frothy residue of the brewing process—was added to dough. This liquid contained the yeast that had been used in the alcoholic fermentation process and acted as a starter culture for bread-making.[4]

Evidence of milk fermentation has been found in the area of ancient Babylon (a fermentation hot spot!) from circa 3000 BC.[5] It more than likely developed when milk soured or started to form curds caused by naturally occurring bacteria converting lactose (milk sugar) into lactic acid, or by *rennin* (also known as *chymosin*), a naturally occurring enzyme found in the stomach lining of calves that causes milk protein (casein) to coagulate and produce a sweet curd. Rennin is still used in cheese-making.

As the frequency of these experiences increased over the millennia, the art of fermenting foods and beverages evolved into a better understanding of wine-making, brewing, pickling, and bread-making. Early humans' limited knowledge of the fermentation arts was passed down through centuries of practitioners, called *artisans*. This slow and deliberate transfer of knowledge, along with repeated observation, led ultimately to our scientific understanding of the fermentation process, thousands of years later.

The gradual progression of the fermentation arts continued without scientific understanding until Louis Pasteur, a French chemist, connected fermentation to yeast in 1854. Until then, it was believed that fermentation was a result of chemical activity and changes brought about by enzymes, and did not involve any living organisms. In 1680 Antonie van Leeuwenhoek, the inventor of the microscope, first observed yeast cells, which he regarded as "inanimate spheres," as he saw no apparent movement or other indication they were alive. Pasteur's work proved the existence of living microbes was integral to the fermentation process. He called these microbial agents ferments. Using a microscope, he observed that the same ferments were present each time he allowed fermentation of sterilized sugar water inoculated with sediment from previous wine fermentations. Pasteur is quoted in the research paper "*Memoire sur la fermentation alcoolique*": "I have attempted to prove that brewer's yeast placed into sugar water lives . . . I am of the opinion that alcoholic fermentation never occurs without simultaneous organization, development, and multiplication of cells."[6]

Fermentation was now much more than just an art: It was a science. The science of fermentation continues today and is called zymology.

Preservation of Perishable Products by Fermentation

According to the Food and Agriculture Organization of the United Nations (FAO), approximately 800 million people around the world do not have enough food to eat. This number becomes much larger, approximately 1.2 billion, if the group "not free from hunger" is included. When one takes into account that over 40 percent of available food ends up as waste in the United States alone, it is vitally important to find a way of turning this loss into edible food. Fermentation is one answer to the problem. It is a cheap and energy-efficient means of preserving perishable raw materials, especially freshly harvested fruits and vegetables. Fermentation is viable on a small scale and does not require extensive knowledge of or the equipment needed for canning, refrigeration, or freezing, or any of the more capital- and knowledge-intensive methods we take for granted in the more developed world. Fermentation can provide safe and nutritious food products, made using relatively simple and affordable means, that can supply the nutritional staples absent in marginalized and vulnerable cultures.[7]

The aim of food preservation is to treat perishable food in such a way as to increase its shelf life by slowing or stopping the natural process of spoilage or decay, and to render the food safe and nutritious for human consumption. The method employed depends on the type of food to be preserved and on whether changes in the quality and sensory attributes resulting from the preservation process are acceptable. In many cultures, fermentation is coupled with drying as a preservation technique.

Fermentation can also utilize foods otherwise considered waste, such as fish heads and intestines (and other viscera) and press-cakes left from the processing of other foods—such as soy pulp left over from making tofu, peanut press-cake from peanut oil production, and coconut press-cake from coconut milk extraction—and convert them into edible food by changing their consistency, flavor, and texture to produce a product that is more palatable and digestible. Even ground bones are fermented and used to make survival food (*dodery*) in Sudan.

In addition to the more exotic subsistence foods eaten around the world, foods that are a standard part of the American diet, such as bread, butter, cheese, yogurt, pepperoni, pickles, olives, sauerkraut, wines, beers, coffee, tea, black pepper, and soy sauce, and many more are all prepared to some degree through the process of fermentation.

Process of Fermentation

While fermentation seems a simple way to preserve food, it actually encompasses the interaction and understanding of many scientific disciplines, including microbiology, biochemistry, bioengineering, genetics, agriculture and horticulture.

Fermentation microorganisms can be divided into five distinct groups:

1. lactic acid–producing bacteria
2. acetic acid–producing bacteria
3. alkaline-fermenting bacteria
4. fungi
5. alcohol-producing yeast and mold

All of these are highly specialized catabolic organisms, meaning they alter organic material just enough to facilitate

FIGURE 11.1 Fermented foods from around the world.

Name and Region	Type of Product
Indian subcontinent	
Acar, Achar, Tandal achar, Garam nimboo achar	Pickled fruits and vegetables
Gundruk	Fermented dried vegetables
Lemon pickle, Lime pickle, Mango pickle	
Southeast Asia	
Asinan, Burong mangga, Dalok, Jeruk, Kiam-chai, Kiam-cheyi, Kong-chai, Naw-mai-dong, Pak-siam-dong, Paw-tsay, Phak-dong, Phonlami-dong, Sajur asin, Sambal tempo-jak, Santol, Si-sek-chai, Sunki, Tang-chai, Tempoyak, Vanilla	Pickled fruits and vegetables
Bai-ming, Leppet-so, Miang	Fermented tea leaves
Nata de coco, Nata de pina	Fermented fruit juice
East Asia	
Bossam-kimchi, Chonggak-kimchi, Dan moogi, Dongchimi, Kachdoo kigactuki, Kakduggi, Kimchi, Mootsanji, Muchung-kimchi, Oigee, Oiji, Oiso baegi, Tongbaechu-kimchi, Tongkimchi, Totkal kimchi	Fermented in brine
Cha-ts'ai, Hiroshimana, Jangagee, Nara senkei, Narazuke, Nozawana, Nukamiso-zuke, Omizuke, Pow tsai, Red in snow, Seokbakji, Shiozuke, Szechwan cabbage, Tai-tan tsoi, Takana, Takuan, Tsa Tzai, Tsu, Umeboshi, Wasabi-zuke, Yen tsai	Pickled fruits and vegetables
Hot pepper sauce	
Africa	
Fruit vinegar	Vinegar
Hot pepper sauce	
Lamoun makbouss, Mauoloh, Msir, Mslalla, Olive	Pickled fruits and vegetables
Oilseeds, Ogili, Ogiri, Hibiscus seed	Fermented fruit and vegetable seeds
Wines	Fermented fruits

(continued)

FIGURE 11.1 (continued)

Name and Region	Type of Product
Americas	
Cucumber pickles, Dill pickles, Olives, Sauerkraut	Pickled fruits and vegetables
Lupin seed, Oilseeds	Pickled oilseed
Vanilla, Wines	Fermented fruits and vegetables
Middle East	
Kushuk	Fermented fruits and vegetables
Lamoun makbouss, Mekhalel, Olives, Torshi, Tursu	Pickled fruits and vegetables
Wines	Fermented fruits
Europe and World	
Mushrooms, Yeast	Molds
Olives, Sauerkohl, Sauerruben	Pickled fruits and vegetables
Grape vinegar, Wine vinegar	Vinegar
Wines, Citron	Fermented fruits

Source: Food and Agriculture Organization of the United Nations.

growth, not completely metabolize the material. This breaking down of complex molecules to simpler molecules results in energy release used by the microorganisms for growth. Important factors that affect microbial growth are salinity (percent salt), acidity (pH), temperature, water activity (moisture available to sustain growth of microorganisms), and the amount of oxygen present.

Different fermentation microbes utilize oxygen differently and are characterized into specific groups. Aerobic microorganisms, such as some bacteria and all molds, thrive in the presence of oxygen. Anaerobic microorganisms, such as many bacteria, thrive in the absence of oxygen. Facultative anaerobes, such as yeast, can thrive in the presence or absence of free oxygen (but produce alcohol and carbon dioxide only via anaerobic respiration). Micro-aerophilic organisms can grow in the presence of minute amounts of free oxygen.[8]

Biochemical pathways associated with fermentation begin with the dissimilation, or breakdown, of sugar, in most cases glucose. This process, known as glycolysis, is a series of ten steps (known as the *Emden-Meyerhof pathway*) that convert one molecule of glucose to two pyruvate molecules. Although dissimilation can take place along several pathways, the Emden-Meyerhof pathway is the one most representative of

FIGURE 11.2   Embden-Meyerhof pathway.

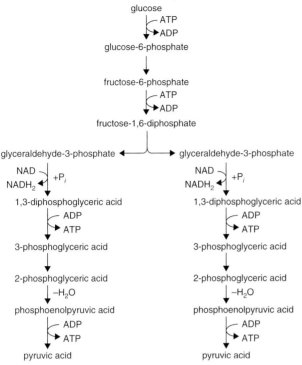

Source: Dr. Kenneth Todar, University of Wisconsin.

lactic, alcohol, and acetic acid fermentations.[9] Pyruvate serves as the junction in the glycolysis cycle where either lactic acid or ethanol can be produced, depending on the type of organism responsible for the fermentation. As glycolysis continues, pyruvic acid is formed. Lactic acid bacteria secrete enzymes that reduce the pyruvic acid to lactic acid, while yeasts reduce the pyruvic acid to alcohol. Acetobacter bacteria oxidize the alcohol into acetic acid (the primary acid in vinegar).

Lactic Acid Bacteria

By far the largest groups of fermented foods and beverages are produced through lactic acid bacterial fermentation. Lactic fermentations are used to produce summer sausage, pickles, sauerkraut, olives, yogurt, some cheeses, cultured butter, and cultured buttermilk. Although several bacteria are closely associated with lactic acid fermentations, the most important is Lactobacillus, a rod-shaped gram-positive bacterium. (Gram staining is a primary method for differentiating bacterial strains into two distinct families: gram-positive and gram-negative.) Lactobacilli, naturally occurring bacteria widely distributed in animal feeds, manure, milk, and milk products, can be grown into pure cultures for industrial use in a variety of food applications. These starter cultures may be stored frozen in liquid nitrogen or freeze-dried for convenience.

FIGURE 11.3   Bacteria and yeast pathway.

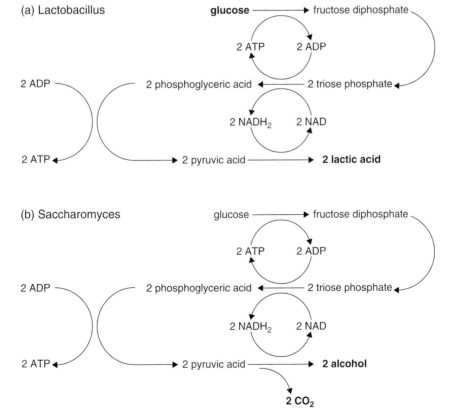

Source: Dr. Kenneth Todar, University of Wisconsin.

Lactobacillus plantarum is a homo-fermentative bacterium, meaning it produces lactic acid and little or no other by-products (including no carbon dioxide gas). *Lactobacillus brevis* is characterized as hetero-fermentative because it produces lactic acid along with large amounts of carbon dioxide gas. Most fermentations use homo-fermentative strains because the intent is to produce as much lactic acid as possible (to preserve the food by lowering the pH) in a relatively short time. Carbon dioxide gas may be detrimental to the product being fermented, as will be seen in the discussion on cucumber pickle fermentation.

L. plantarum is commonly used in the production of fermented dried meats, pickles, and sauerkraut, producing the largest amount of lactic acid and giving these foods their characteristic tangy taste. *L. brevis* is one of the main organisms used to produce *kimchi*, the Korean version of sauerkraut.

L. mesenteroides is a hetero-fermentative halophilic (salt-tolerant) bacterium known for its role in the fermentation of fresh cabbage to sauerkraut. Because it is hetero-fermentative, like *L. brevis*, it metabolizes sugar to carbon dioxide in addition to lactic acid. *L. mesenteroides* is the organism of choice for sauerkraut fermentation because it tolerates the high salt concentration used in this process. In making sauerkraut, raw cabbage is dry-salted in layers within the fermentation tank to dehydrate (draw water out of) the cabbage cells by osmosis; this creates a concentrated salt brine.

In the case of cucumber pickles, a concentrated salt brine, 5 to 7 percent weight/volume, is added to fresh cucumbers. It is several days before the brine becomes diluted to around 4 percent salt due to equalization with water coming from the fresh cucumbers, which contain no salt. In both cases, the salt level is at least inhibitory, if not downright toxic, to most bacteria other than *L. mesenteroides*.

Another lactic acid bacterium commonly used in commercial applications is *Pediococcus cerevisiae*, a homo-fermentative, sphere-shaped, gram-positive bacterium. *P. cerevisiae* is one of the predominant organisms used in fermenting meats like sausage, pepperoni, and salami.

Lactic acid bacterial growth follows a well-studied and understood pathway known as the bacterial growth curve, which is divided into four phases:

1. *Lag phase:* The lactic bacteria are becoming accustomed to their new environment and are starting to metabolize sugars.

2. *Log phase:* The bacteria undergo exponential growth due to binary fission. Large amounts of lactic acid are produced along with by-products such as carbon dioxide gas, acetic acid, and alcohol, depending on the microorganism involved.

3. *Stationary phase:* The bacteria use up most of the nutrients in their surroundings (now contaminated with a buildup of their waste products) and stop reproducing.

4. *Death phase:* All growth ceases, and the microorganisms die off rapidly from a combination of lack of nutrients and a buildup of toxic waste.

FIGURE 11.4 Bacterial growth curve.

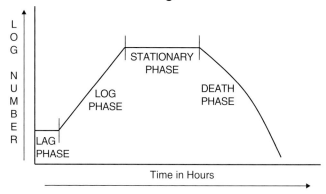

Source: James Adams.

Lactic Fermentations: Pickles

First, it is important to understand the pickle category. Pickled cucumbers are produced via three preservation methods, and the corresponding products exhibit significantly different attributes. The three methods are fermentation pickles (referred to in the pickling industry as *processed*), fresh pack, and overnight/refrigerated. In terms of market share, fermentation pickles are the largest category, with approximately 56 percent of the market. They are popularly used as hamburger slices for the foodservice business. Fresh-pack pickles are the next largest segment, with approximately 24 percent of the cucumber crop. These pickles are packed as fresh cucumbers in flavored salt brine and then pasteurized to render the product commercially sterile. Overnight/refrigerated pickles are packed fresh in seasoned brine and then immediately refrigerated for warehousing and storage. This type of pickle is sold in the refrigerated case of grocery stores and delis. They are also called *deli dills* (full sour and half sour), and they have been sold in delicatessens for over 100 years, especially in larger U.S. cities, like New York and Chicago, with substantial Jewish-German and Polish populations. These pickles comprise approximately 20 percent of pickle sales. According to data compiled by Pickle Packers International, a trade association for the pickled vegetable industry, U.S. consumers eat over 2 billion pounds of pickles each year, or about 9 pounds per person.[10] Here we examine the first category: *fermented pickles.*

Fresh cucumbers are harvested by hand or by machine. Once harvested, they are transported to the processing site, where they are inspected, sized, and loaded into fermentation tanks at a pre-determined percent ratio of solids to liquids. Most often this ranges from 60:40 to 70:30, where the larger number represents the percent of solids (pounds of cucumbers) per tank. The liquid portion of the ratio is brine made up of salt, water, and calcium chloride, which is used to prevent enzymatic softening of the cucumbers during the fermentation.[11]

The salt concentration approximates 5 percent, or 19–20 degrees Salometer. The concentration of salt in the brine is expressed as degrees Salometer, which represents the

FIGURE 11.5 Open-top cucumber fermentation tank.

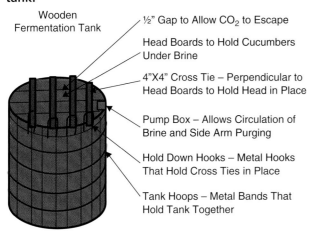

Wooden Fermentation Tank

½" Gap to Allow CO₂ to Escape

Head Boards to Hold Cucumbers Under Brine

4"X4" Cross Tie – Perpendicular to Head Boards to Hold Head in Place

Pump Box – Allows Circulation of Brine and Side Arm Purging

Hold Down Hooks – Metal Hooks That Hold Cross Ties in Place

Tank Hoops – Metal Bands That Hold Tank Together

Source: James Adams.

saturation level of sodium chloride by weight. Salometer readings range from 0 to 100, where a reading of 100 equals 100 percent saturation of sodium chloride by weight (this is equal to 26.4 percent concentration of sodium chloride in water). During the fermentation, Salometer readings are taken at regular intervals to ensure the brine stays at the proper salt concentration.

Pickling from the early 1900s through the late 1970s used authentic redwood or cypress tanks. Over long periods, these tanks began to leak brine, contributing to problems with contamination of salt brine into ecologically sensitive areas. The solution to the problem has been to replace wood with tanks made of fiberglass.

Because cucumbers are buoyant, they must be kept submerged by using a device called a head. The head is held in place by anchors that are attached to the tanks. After the tank is filled and headed, as part of the controlled fermentation process chlorine is added to the tank to stop the growth of competitive organisms (especially coliform bacteria). Within 18 hours, glacial acetic acid (25 times the acidity of

FIGURE 11.6 Closed-top cucumber fermentation tank.

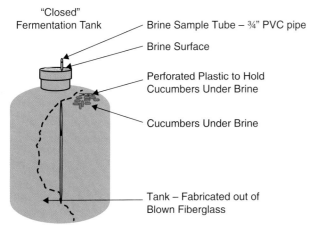

"Closed" Fermentation Tank

Brine Sample Tube – ¾" PVC pipe

Brine Surface

Perforated Plastic to Hold Cucumbers Under Brine

Cucumbers Under Brine

Tank – Fabricated out of Blown Fiberglass

Source: James Adams.

white table vinegar) is poured into the tank to adjust the pH of the brine to ideal growth conditions. *L. plantarum* starter culture is added next, usually within 12 hours. The pure culture added is a homo-fermentative bacterium used to limit the production of carbon dioxide and build acid quickly. Pure culture fermentation allows the *L. plantarum*, which is highly concentrated in the pure culture media, to outrun the natural bacteria, which are predominantly hetero-fermenters (gas producers), which may be present in the fermentation.

The fermentation starts slowly and then becomes more vigorous in the next two to three days, depending on the temperature of the brine (in colder climates, the brine must be heated to prevent a stuck fermentation). The optimum brine temperature is found by consulting the supplier of the starter culture or reference books on microbiology, such as *Bergey's Manual of Determinative Bacteriology*.[12]

The tanks are monitored daily to ensure the fermentation is following the bacterial growth curve and all the residual sugar in the cucumbers is converted to lactic acid. Measuring turbidity of the brine is a quick qualitative method of assessing the progress of fermentation. This is done by placing a sample tube of brine against an embossed chart with four lines; the top line, number 1, is the thinnest line, and the bottom line, number 4, is the thickest and boldest line on the card. The technician records the lowest number line that can easily be read through the brine. At the start the brine is clear, thin, and without cloudiness. As the fermentation advances, the brine becomes opaque and starts to thicken slightly. As the fermentation gets more active, the brine's opacity increases and even the bottom line cannot be seen. At this point, the brine is recorded as 4+, indicating a vigorous fermentation is taking place. Most fermentations are completed within one to two weeks, depending on the temperature.

Carbon dioxide produced as a result of hetero-fermentation can become supersaturated in the brine if not removed by mechanical means (purging). In purging, the brine is scrubbed of accumulated gas by injecting nitrogen (an inert gas) into the tank; this causes the carbon dioxide gas to rise to the tank's surface and release into the atmosphere, thus preventing its infiltration into the cucumbers, which would make them taste fizzy (like soda). Purging was developed in the late 1970s by scientists and engineers at Michigan State University working with researchers at the Agricultural Research Station, part of North Carolina State University's agricultural extension service.

After cucumber pickles are fermented and the residual sugar completely converted, they are de-salted and further processed into sweet gherkins, hamburger chips, dill pickles, or sweet and dill relish.

Acetic Acid Bacteria and the Production of Vinegar

Acetic acid bacteria are able to convert ethanol (drinking or grain alcohol) into acetic acid and are commonly known as acetobacters. *Acetobacter aceti* is the most common of the organisms used in the production of vinegar. They are gram-negative, rod-shaped, aerobic bacteria that derive energy from the oxidation of ethanol to acetic acid. This is a two-stage process. The first stage occurs when yeast (*Saccharomyces cerevisiae*) is added to a fermentation tank containing a sugar solution (most commonly fructose, derived from cane or corn sugar) at 80 to 85°F (27 to 29°C), the optimum growth temperature. The yeast are able to convert approximately 90 percent of the sugar into alcohol. The remaining 10 percent are volatile components, such as aldehydes, ketones, and esters, which are removed via distillation if the intent is to produce purified spirits. However, in the commercial production of vinegar, acetobacter bacteria (available as a starter culture known as the mother of vinegar) are added and the liquid vigorously aerated, allowing the bacteria to grow and oxidize the alcohol to acetic acid. The yeast and bacteria coexist in the tank in a biologic relationship known as commensalism, where two organisms live in close proximity with at least one benefiting by the other's presence. In vinegar-making, the acetobacter bacteria depend on the alcohol produced by the yeast as a substrate for conversion to acetic acid.[13]

This type of vinegar contains 4 to 5 percent acetic acid and is referred to as *40–50 grain*. Grain is calculated by multiplying the percent acetic value (obtained through titration against a known concentration of sodium hydroxide solution) by 1000. Common white vinegar is approximately 40 grain. Industrial vinegar used in food manufacture is 120 grain, or 12 percent acetic, and is manufactured by the distillation of naturally fermented white vinegar. It must be diluted in the final product in order to meet FDA labeling guidelines. According to the U.S. Food and Drug Administration (FDA), there is no standard of identity for vinegar; however, for labeling purposes all vinegars used in foods must contain 4 percent acetic acid, which must be prepared by the alcoholic and subsequent acetous fermentations of whichever fruit or grain the vinegar is made.

Glacial acetic acid has a value of 1050 grain and is pure acetic acid. While purified acetic acid is itself safe for use in foods, the FDA says, "This Administration, in the enforcement of the Federal Food, Drug, and Cosmetic Act, has maintained the position that diluted acetic acid is not a vinegar of any kind and has advised against its use in food products customarily expected to contain vinegar. When used as an ingredient in food, it should be declared by its name, *acetic acid* or *diluted acetic acid*." Glacial acetic acid is used primarily as a reagent for the production of chemical compounds. Today, most industrial production is synthetic, using the BP Cativa process, involving methanol (wood alcohol) and carbon monoxide reacted together at high temperatures and under extremely high pressure.

Most vinegars are filtered to improve clarity and pasteurized to prevent potential outgrowth problems during warehousing or storage. It is important to note that if the vinegar bottle's hermetic seal is broken, the vinegar can become oxidized to water and carbon dioxide.

FIGURE 11.7 **Vinegar by dollar sales.**

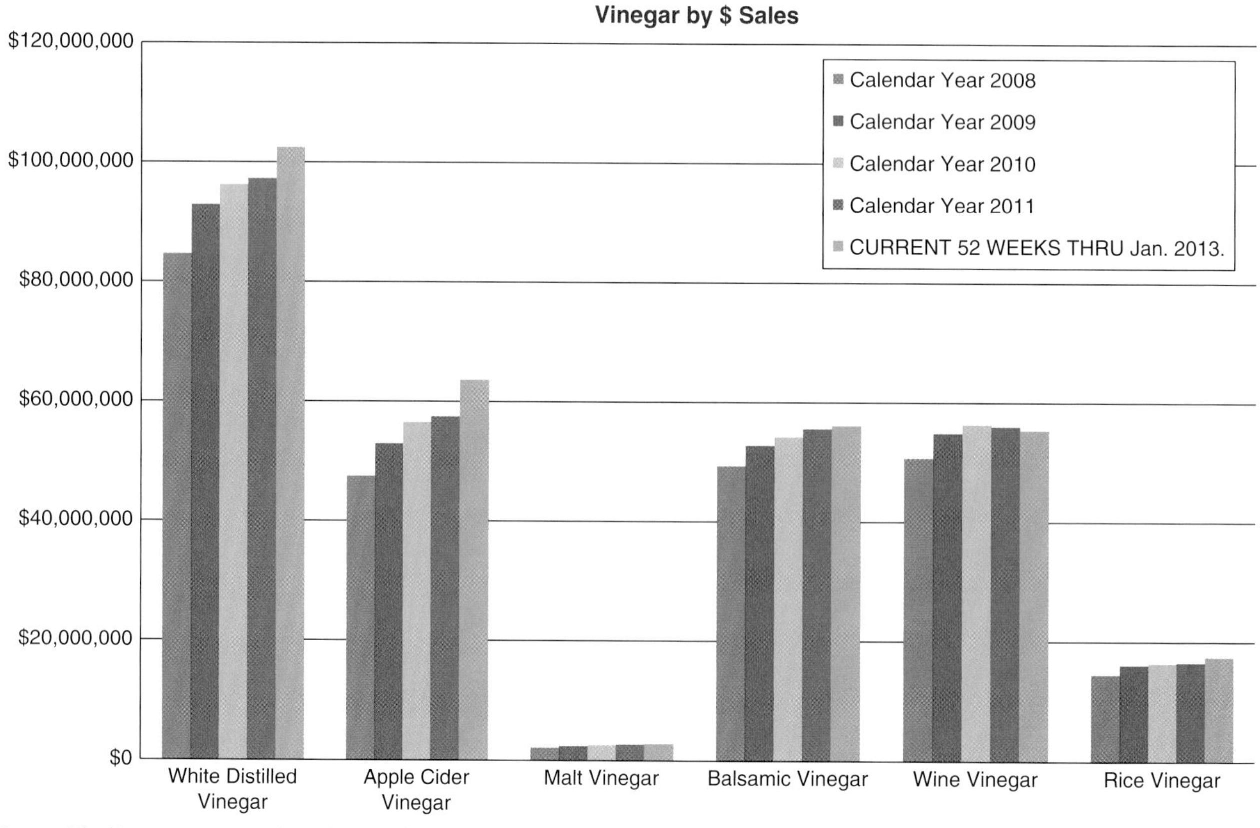

Source: The Vinegar Institute (data obtained from Nielsen), www.versatilevinegar.org.

The type of vinegar produced depends on the substrate being fermented. The substrate is the substance being acted on by microorganisms or enzymes—in some cases, both. White vinegar uses grain alcohol as the substrate. Fruit vinegars are produced by fermenting apples or other fruits, but cider vinegar can only be prepared from "the juice of apples," according to the FDA. Some exotic fruit vinegars are produced in Asia—for example, persimmon, yam, and black plum. Rice vinegars are also an Asian specialty. Fruit-flavored vinegars are produced by adding fruit flavors (and colors) to white vinegar. Malt vinegar is made from malted barley and is especially popular in England, where it is used liberally to flavor fish and chips. Wine vinegar is made from red or white wine and is less acidic than regular white vinegar, as the wine used as a substrate contains less alcohol than grain alcohol. Some upscale varietal wine vinegars are also available, including sherry vinegar and champagne vinegar. Balsamic vinegar (commonly from Modena, Italy) is made by aging vinegar, fermented from white grapes, in wooden casks for 3 to 12 years or longer. The older vintages are extremely concentrated and expensive. Balsamic is unlike other wine vinegars in that there is no starting alcohol fermentation before the acidification begins. The fermentation process converts the grape must (juice of just-harvested white Trebbiano grapes, boiled down to approximately 30% of the original volume to create a concentrate) into alcohol and acid at the same time using a mixture of yeast and bacterial cultures.[14]

In a 2007 report presented at the 2007 annual meeting of the Vinegar Institute (an international trade association managed by the Kellen Company [www.versatilevinegar .org]), the Nielsen Company noted that white distilled vinegar has 68 percent of the unit share of vinegars. Cider vinegar accounts for 20 percent, and specialty vinegars account for 12 percent. Of the specialty vinegar category, 39 percent is red wine, 30 percent balsamic, 13 percent all other wine, 12 percent rice vinegar, and 6 percent all others.

According to the Vinegar Institute, although bottled vinegar makes up the majority of sales at the retail level (33.7 percent), it is also a key ingredient in a number of foods used daily in the United States. These foods include dressings and sauces (16.8 percent), pickles (14.8 percent), mustard (11.5 percent), and other processed foods including tomato products such as salsa, ketchup, and pasta sauces (23.2 percent).

Alkaline Fermenters

Although alkaline fermenters are important in the production of fermented foods around the world (especially in Third World countries), the number of foods produced using this method pales in comparison to the vast number produced by lactic or acetic acid fermentations. *Bacillus licheniformis*, *Bacillus pumilis*, and *Bacillus subtilis* (most predominant) are associated with this type of fermentation. All are gram-positive spore-forming rods. These bacteria can hydrolyze, or split protein into amino acids and peptides, with ammonia as a by-product. As the concentration of ammonia builds, the pH of the material is raised above 7.0 (as high as 9.0 to 11.0 pH), inhibiting the growth of spoilage organisms.[15]

Thua-nao and *kinema* are two examples of alkaline-fermented foods from Thailand that are made from cooked soybeans. *Dawadawa*, from Africa, is made from fermented locust beans. *Puto*, from the Philippines, is an alkaline-fermented poultry egg product. *Natto* is a popular fermented soybean product from Japan. All of these are extremely pungent and slimy due to the putrefactive end-products of proteolysis (breakdown of proteins).

Molds

Molds are aerobic, filamentous organisms that are salt-tolerant members of the fungi family. Molds have tubules (filaments), called *hyphae*, that grow and intertwine. As these tubules clump together, they form a mass of cells known as *mycelia*. Molds are visible without magnification, unlike bacteria and yeasts, and they can reproduce sexually or asexually. They are used in fermentation of vegetable products (a good example is tempeh, a mold-fermented soybean cake of Indonesian origin; another is the popular Japanese condiment and soup base miso), dairy (particularly mold-ripened cheeses such as bleu, Camembert, and Brie), and meat products (especially dry-fermented sausages).

Yeast

Yeast are single-celled facultative (able to live in the presence or absence of oxygen) microorganisms that are members of the fungi kingdom, along with mushrooms and molds. They can convert sugar to alcohol and carbon dioxide gas, but only under anaerobic conditions. Under aerobic conditions, yeast simply make more yeast! They are the primary engines in the production of beer, wine, and alcoholic spirits as well as leavened breads.

Yeast anaerobically convert one glucose molecule into two ethanol molecules and two carbon dioxide molecules:

$$C_6H_{12}O_6 \rightarrow 2C_2H_5OH + 2CO_2$$
$$1 \text{ glucose} \rightarrow 2 \text{ ethanol} + 2 \text{ carbon dioxide}$$

Both alcohol and carbon dioxide are produced during fermentation; however, the alcohol flashes off during baking, and the carbon dioxide bubbles dissipate out of wine but are trapped in beer.

⬤ Alcohol Production

It may be difficult to see the similarities of beer, wine, and liquor (and other alcoholic beverages), but they all start off the same way: the fermentation of carbohydrate substrates through the actions of yeast. Yeast is ubiquitous in our environment. Because yeast spores are widely dispersed throughout the environment (including on the surface of grapes and other fruits and vegetables, and even in the air we breathe), fermentation occurs in nature all the time. The art of brewing and winemaking is the controlled application of fermentation to selected raw ingredients in order to produce alcoholic beverages with specific flavors, colors, aromas, and alcohol levels.

The production of alcohol occurs in the absence of oxygen, which inhibits the growth of competing aerobic microorganisms in the fermentation tank. However, from the yeast's point of view, alcohol and carbon dioxide are waste products, and as the yeast continues to grow and metabolize, the accumulation of alcohol becomes toxic when it reaches a concentration between 14 and 18 percent, killing the yeast cells. This is the reason the maximum alcohol achievable in wine and beer cannot exceed 18 percent. To produce higher concentrations of alcohol, the fermented products must be distilled to remove excess water. Beer and wine made and sold in the United States are highly regulated by both the federal and state governments. The maximum allowable percentage of alcohol in each beverage varies by state.

Generally speaking, any alcoholic beverage created from fermenting fruit juice can be called wine (hard cider notwithstanding). However, commercially speaking, *wine* is fermented grape juice from the wine grape, *Vitis vinifera*. Other wines are specifically referred to by the name of the fruit from which they are fermented—for example, elderberry wine and blueberry wine. Other wines, such as dandelion and honey wine (mead), are not derived from fruit juices at all.

Beer, as developed in Western cultures and as it is most commonly recognized today, is created from the fermentation of malt, which comes from the digestion of germinated barley grains. Many other grains (such as wheat, rice, millet, and sorghum) are used in other brews and cultures. In the United States, these alternative grains are occasionally seen in specialty microbrews, where the artisanal brewer exercises poetic license to create unique and distinctive flavors.

Besides the substrate being fermented, the biggest difference between beer and wine is the fermentation process and how it is manipulated to produce the desired result. Brewing beer is essentially a steeping process, like making tea, where the ingredients (malted grains and hops) are soaked in water (steeped) and then filtered out. Selected brewer's yeasts are added to the filtered liquid (called wort), and fermentation begins. The wort is like a beer starter in that it is unfermented beer containing malt extract and water and is used in combination with yeast to start the fermentation. Winemaking, on the other hand, involves crushing the entire fruit (typically grapes) and fermenting the juice that results.

Beer-Making Ingredients

The basic ingredients of beer are water; a fermentable (convertible into alcohol) sugar source, such as malted barley; a brewer's yeast, to produce the fermentation; and a flavoring, such as hops. Beer originated as a flat, slightly sweet malt- and grain-flavored beverage that spoiled quickly. In the eighth century, however, brewers in central Europe found the addition of hops flowers preserved the beer and gave it a more palatable, slightly bitter taste. Even with hops, early beer was not necessarily pleasant-tasting by our standards. It became the beverage of choice, however, due to the scarcity of good-quality drinking water, not to mention the buzz generated by the alcohol.

Hops are the female flower clusters (commonly called *seed cones* or *strobiles*) of the hop species, *Humulus lupulus*. They are used primarily as a flavoring and stabilizing agent in beer, to which they impart a bitter, tangy, often citrus-like flavor and aroma. Hops are used extensively in brewing to balance the sweetness of the malt with bitterness; they contribute a variety of desirable flavors and aromas and have an antibiotic effect that favors the activity of brewer's yeast over less desirable microorganisms.

Hops are normally dried in an oast house or hop kiln before they are used in the brewing process. Hop resins are composed of two main acids: alpha and beta acids. Alpha acids are responsible for the bitter flavor in the beer and have a mild antibiotic/bacteriostatic effect against gram-positive bacteria, which favors the activity of the brewer's yeast in the fermentation tank. Beta acids contribute to beer's bitter aroma, and high–beta acid hop varieties are often added at the end of the wort boil for aroma.

When sourcing hops, a brewmaster seeks hops with a specific level of alpha acid. This is referred to as the alpha acid percent, or AA percent, which is a measure of the percentage of the flower's weight composed of the alpha acid resin. This is a key measure of bittering potential. All merchants provide an AA percent to assist in selecting hops. That said, the aroma hops provide comes from essential oils from hops high in beta acids. The blending of the two types is where the art of the brewmaster becomes essential.

Water is another key component in brewing beer. It constitutes more than 90 percent of beer and has a natural effect on how the beer ferments and tastes. Levels of dissolved mineral ions in the water affect the activity of several starch-degrading enzymes in malt. The levels of these ions directly affect the water's pH, which in turn affects the enzyme's effectiveness in converting starch to maltose, the primary sugar the yeast uses to ferment. Having a correct ion balance greatly influences the extraction yield of the malt and the resulting sensory attributes of the beer.

The calcium ion is by far the most influential mineral in the brewing process. Calcium reacts with phosphates, lowering the pH of the mash. This lowering of the pH is critical in that it provides an ideal environment for starch enzymes alpha-amylase and beta-amylase as well as proteolytic enzymes.

Other important mineral ions include magnesium, which is most important as a yeast nutrient during fermentation; sodium, which contributes to the perceived flavor of beer by enhancing its sweetness; potassium, which creates a salty flavor effect and is required for yeast growth; and phosphates, which are important pH buffers in brewing and useful for reducing the pH in mashing and during the hop boil. Calcium and magnesium chlorides give body, palate fullness, and soft-sweet flavor to beer. On the other hand, the presence of carbonate ions raises the pH, resulting in less fermentable worts, unacceptable wort color values, difficulties in wort filtration, and less efficient separation of protein and protein-tannin complexes. They are to be avoided or reduced if at all possible.

Before brewing, the water is checked to make sure all minerals are in balance so the yeast performs to its maximum potential.

In all cases, the fermentable substrate for beer-making is a carbohydrate. Fats and proteins cannot be fermented without the presence of a carbohydrate. Although it is possible to use any grain to make a beer-like beverage, the most commonly used fermentable substrate is barley, as most of the other grains (corn, wheat, rice) are eaten more directly as foods, and barley has a higher content of the enzymes essential for breaking down starch into sugar. Barley in its native form contains 65 percent starch, and this must first be broken down to simple sugars for the yeasts to metabolize into alcohol.

The multi-step process of preparing the barley for brewing is called malting. First, the barley is soaked in water until it reaches a moisture content of 45 percent; then it is allowed to germinate (begin to sprout). At that point, starch content is at its maximum and starch-digesting enzyme activity is at its peak. Sprouting is halted by gently heating the barley (kilning) to stop further growth (the sprout must not be allowed to use up the starch, the source of sugars for fermentation). At the same time, the enzymes must not be killed, so temperature control and exposure time are critical. When kilning is complete, the malted barley is ground, or milled, to crack open the grains. Milling the grains makes it easier for them to absorb the water with which they are mixed in the mashing process, during which the starches are broken down to sugars, primarily maltose, a disaccharide consisting of two glucose subunits. Maltose is used by the yeast for fermentation.

The final ingredient required for brewing beer is, of course, the yeast. The yeast used for brewing is the same species used for baking, *Saccharomyces cerevisiae*, but they are different strains, cultivated to possess specific abilities: baking yeast strains are more active, to leaven dough in the shortest amount of time possible; brewing yeast strains act more slowly but tend to produce fewer off flavors and tolerate higher alcohol concentrations (with some strains, up to 22 percent). Many pure strains of brewing yeast have been developed to provide the sensory characteristics of the many styles of beer commonly produced: ales, lagers, stouts, pilsners, and so on.

The Science of Beer-Making

Beer is consumed in vast amounts all over the globe. In the United States alone, over 200 million barrels (6,200,000,000 gallons) are consumed annually. Today beer making is largely automated, like all areas of food manufacturing. But even though many breweries use sophisticated brewing equipment, the process remains essentially the same as it has for centuries. Advances in understanding the science behind the process have led to huge improvements in quality and consistency.

After the barley is malted, mashing is the next step in the beer-making process. This process converts the starches released during the malting stage into sugars that can be fermented. The malted barley is mixed with hot water in a large vessel known as a mash tun to create a cereal mash. During the mash, naturally occurring enzymes present in the malt convert the starches in the grain to simple sugars (saccharification). The wort (pronounced "wert") is the result of the mashing process; it is a sugar-rich liquid that is strained through the bottom of the mash tun in a process known as lautering.

The wort is moved into a large tank, known as a copper or kettle, where it is boiled with hops and sometimes other ingredients, such as herbs or spices. Boiling deactivates enzymes, precipitates proteins, solubilizes hop resins, and concentrates and sterilizes the wort. At the end of the boil, the hopped wort undergoes clarification in a vessel called a whirlpool, where the more solid particles in the wort are removed.

After the whirlpool, the wort is quickly cooled (typically using high-efficiency heat exchangers) to a level where yeast can be added safely (yeast is killed at temperatures higher than 120°F [50°C]). Once the wort has cooled sufficiently, it goes into a fermentation tank. At this point the yeast is added, or pitched, into the fermentation tank. Now fermentation begins, and the sugars turn into alcohol, carbon dioxide, and other minor components. The fermentation process takes from 2 to 6 weeks, depending on the type of beer being made. Because fermentation produces a substantial amount of heat, the tanks must be cooled constantly to maintain the proper temperature.

The fermentation vessel (or fermenter) is sealed off from the air except for a long, narrow vent pipe that allows carbon dioxide to escape. Due to the constant flow of carbon dioxide through the pipe, outside air is prevented from entering the tank, reducing the threat of contamination by stray yeasts or other contaminants. While fermentation is still actively occurring, and when the specific gravity has reached a predetermined level (usually between 1.020 and 1.025, which is equivalent to 2.25 to 2.875 percent alcohol), the carbon dioxide vent tube is capped. Now the vessel is sealed, so as fermentation continues, pressure builds as carbon dioxide continues to be produced. This is how beer gets most of its carbonation; the rest is added later. (In the case of most keg beer, the beverage is additionally carbonated when it is connected to the tap in the bar.) From this point on, the beer remains under pressure (except for a short time during bottling).

When the fermentation is finished, the beer is cooled to about 32°F (0°C). This helps the remaining yeast settle to the bottom of the fermenter, along with other undesirable proteins that precipitate out of solution at this lower temperature. The bottom of the fermenter is cone shaped; this makes it easy to capture and remove the yeast, which may be saved and used in the next batch of beer. The yeast can be reused a number of times before it must be replaced. This is when it has mutated to the point where it produces a different taste—remember, commercial brewing is all about consistency. Cataloging the number of times the same batch of yeast is used for fermentation allows the brewmaster to calculate when the yeast must be replaced. Sensory evaluation also ensures the yeast is not producing off flavors.

Once the fermentation process is complete, the beer is slowly pumped from the fermenter and filtered to remove any remaining solids. From the filter, the beer goes into a bright beer tank, its last stop before bottling or kegging. Here, the level of carbon dioxide is adjusted by introducing a little extra gas into the beer through a porous carbonating stone.

The two primary types of beer are the heavier and darker ales (including stout and porter) and the lighter lagers (including pilsner, the most popular beer consumed in the United States). There are two major differences in the brewing process. First, ales are fermented at higher temperatures: 65 to 75°F (18 to 24°C), and lagers are fermented much colder at 46 to 55°F (8 to 13°C). The second distinction is the type of yeast used in the fermentation process. Ales generally use top-fermenting yeast. This means the yeast floats on the surface for the first few days and then settles on the bottom. Lagers use bottom-fermenting yeast, which does not float to the surface before settling.

A third type of beer is far less common than ales or lagers: lambics. True lambics are brewed in Belgium only, and typically are blends of two or more beers, sometimes with the addition of sugar or syrups as they tend to be quite tart. In addition, fruit lambics are very popular, with cherry, raspberry, peach, black currant, grape and strawberry versions commonly available. Unlike ales and lagers, which use pure cultures of yeast that are specially cultivated for their fermentation, lambics are fermented by wild yeasts.

Making Wine

Winemaking, in its simplest form, involves crushing grapes, collecting the juice in a vat, and allowing it to ferment. As yeasts responsible for fermenting the sugars in the grapes are normally present on the skin of the fruit, fermentation can begin as soon as the yeasts come into contact with the juice. Of course, it is not that simple. Selecting the correct varieties of grapes for their particular flavor characteristics is truly an art, as is selecting the correct pure strain of yeast. Understanding the *Brix* (sugar content) and pH (acidity) of the juice and how it affects the fermentation of the beverage is also essential, as is maintaining proper temperature and sanitation.

FIGURE 11.8 Tuscan vineyard.

Source: Charles Hayes.

Because of the large number of types of wine that are produced, we are restricting our discussion to grape wine. The species of grapes used in most wines is *Vitis vinifera*, known to have been domesticated before 4000 BC.

Wine is made today much the same way it was centuries ago. *Still wines* (non-effervescent) come in primarily three colors: red, white, and rosé. If fermentation is stopped before the sugars are all metabolized by the yeast, the finished product is sweet wine. If fermentation is allowed to go to completion and all the sugars are metabolized, the wine is dry. The winemaker takes deliberate steps throughout the fermentation process to control the final product.

The grapes from which the wine is to be made are first stemmed and then crushed in order to release the juice. The combination of the skin, juice, and seeds is called the *must*. Grapes may be crushed by various means, from stomping on them with bare feet to pressing with sophisticated electric machinery.

If the desired product is a white wine, the free juice is transferred to a fermentation tank, one that is typically made of stainless steel, which is much easier to clean and sanitize and much longer lasting than wooden barrels. In addition, unlike wood, no flavors will leach out to potentially contaminate the wine. The peels and stems are then removed and pressed again. The juice of the second press can be added to the original juice or used to make a lower-grade wine. It is important to note that the color of the grape does not necessarily dictate the color of the wine. The juice of both red and white grapes has relatively little pigment. The color of red wine comes from the red pigment in the grape skin, not the juice. If red wine is the desired product, the skins of the grape must go into the fermentation tank along with the juice. In fact, some well-known white wines are made from red- or black-skinned grapes. Champagne, for instance, uses Pinot Noir (red-skinned) grape juice, and the popular white wine Pinot Grigio is also made from a red-skinned grape. It is critical with white wines, however, that the skins be removed from the juice as soon as possible after crushing so as not to tint the wine pink.

Once the juice is in the fermentation tank, preferred pure strains of yeast are usually added but are not absolutely required, because the skin of the grapes has adequate yeasts on it already. However, as the wild yeasts that grow on the grapes vary by vineyard and especially by country, the quality of the finished wine also varies. Therefore, the addition of a specially cultivated pure yeast strain gives much greater measure of control and consistency to the end product. Most wine yeasts are strains of *Saccharomyces cerevisiae*, the same family of yeasts from which both baker's and brewer's yeast originate.

Sulfur dioxide is normally introduced into the juice at this time to kill any bacteria that may spoil the taste of the final product. It also acts as an antioxidant, and in red wine it can help to stabilize color. Sulfite sensitivity is an asthma-like reaction caused by exposure to sulfites; the FDA estimates it affects 1 percent of the population. Because of this, the use of sulfur dioxide as a preservative in any food or beverage (including wine) must be reported on the label if it is present at greater than 10 ppm (parts per million) in the finished product to warn individuals who may have breathing difficulties when exposed to it.

Fermentation is allowed to continue for 8 to 10 days, after which the initial wine is drawn off of the skins, if they are still present. Any juice pressed from these skins after their removal is considered to be of lower quality and may be used in bulk wines or for vinegar production. Following the initial fermentation, the liquid is allowed to ferment for an additional 20 to 30 days. During this time, the dead yeast cells and other particulate matter settle to the bottom of the tank. When this process is complete, the wine is separated from the sediment and transferred to an aging tank. As the aging process continues, more sedimentation occurs, and the wine is often transferred across a series of tanks during aging. This process is known as racking.

After the wine is racked, it may be bottled or transferred to wooden barrels for additional aging, depending on the winemaker and the type of wine being made. Wine barrels, especially made of oak, have long been used to age wine. Aging in oak typically imparts desirable vanilla, butter, spice, and "woody notes" to wine, as well as color and tannins, which affect mouthfeel and perceived texture. Barrels may be made of French or American oak, and are typically "toasted" before use. Toasting involves charring the inside of the barrel with an open flame, and barrels are available in light, medium, and heavy toasting, depending on the type and style of wine the winemaker is after. The most common barrels hold 59 U.S. gallons (220 L). New barrels impart more flavors than previously used barrels because over time many of the oak properties leach out—to the point where, after three to five years, little or no oak flavors may be imparted to the wine. Due to the expense of barrels, several techniques for reusing them have been devised in an attempt to save money. One is to shave the inside of used barrels and insert new, thin inner staves.

The porous nature of an oak barrel allows some evaporation and oxygenation to occur during aging. Oxygen enters a barrel when water or alcohol is lost due to evaporation, a portion known as the angels' share. Most wines are topped up from other barrels to prevent significant oxidation. In a year, the typical 59-gallon barrel can lose around 5 to 6 gallons of wine through evaporation. This evaporation (of mostly alcohol and water) allows the wine to concentrate its flavor and aroma compounds.

The length of time a wine spends in the barrel depends on the grape varietal and the style of wine the winemaker wishes to make. The majority of oak-derived flavors are imparted in the first few months that the wine is in contact with oak, but longer exposure can affect the wine through the light aeration the barrel allows, which helps develop intrinsic flavors coming from the wine itself. Many wineries now use oak wood chips for aging wine more quickly. Oak chips can be added during fermentation or during aging. In the latter case, they are generally held in fabric sacks that are placed into the aging wine. Oak chips have the benefit of imparting intense flavoring in a matter of weeks, while traditional oak barrels need a year or more to convey similar intensity. They are also much cheaper than barrels.

The length of time a wine ages depends on the judgment of the winemaker. For white wines, it is usually 12 to 18 months, but red wines can age for five years or longer. During aging, the wine is sampled and assessed regularly by the winemaker. It may be bottled after aging is complete or used as part of a blend. While today most wines are made to be consumed immediately after bottling, some white wines benefit by additional aging under controlled temperature and humidity storage for up to five years, after which they deteriorate. Certain red wines, on the other hand, continue to improve for 30 years or more.

Champagne and Other Sparkling Wines

Thus far discussion has covered *still wines*, which are fermented in open tanks or vented closed tanks to avoid carbon dioxide buildup and subsequent carbonation. But champagnes and sparkling wines are produced using a different method, known as the *champagne process*. To develop carbonation, extra sugar is added to still wine in the bottle while the yeast is actively fermenting. The bottle is then tightly capped. As this secondary fermentation continues, carbon dioxide builds up in the bottle and carbonates the wine. This is somewhat tricky because if too much fermentation occurs, the tightly sealed bottle can explode. This is why champagne bottles are so much thicker and heavier than bottles used for still wines. The secondary fermentation takes a minimum of one year but can continue for three years or longer.

Riddling racks are critical to the process of making Champagne. After the sparkling wine has completed its secondary fermentation, it is ready to be finished. Remuage or "riddling" is the process that collects the yeast and sediment and concentrates it near the mouth of the bottle. The riddling rack is made up of two rectangular boards hinged at the top. Each side consists of rows of evenly spaced holes, totaling six across and ten rows down, each able to hold the neck of a champagne bottle. This means each riddling rack can hold 120 bottles. The "riddler" (a specialist experienced in the art of riddling) puts the neck of a bottle of Champagne in each of the holes, inclined at a 45-degree angle. A mark placed on the bottom of each bottle acts as a reference marker, with all marks on all bottles in the rack pointing in the same direction.

Over the next few weeks on a daily basis, the riddler rotates every bottle a few degrees. At the same time he raises the bottle's bottom slightly, lowering the neck a centimeter or two each week. After a few weeks bottles that started at a 45-degree angle are now slanted to a 60-degree angle and are neck-down in their holes. After riddling is complete, the Champagne bottles are placed upside down with their necks submerged in a sub-zero solution for several minutes, forming an ice plug made of the spent yeast and sediment in the necks. They then quickly undergo disgorgement, which means the crown caps are removed from the bottles, resulting in the pressure within the bottles shooting out (disgorging) the ice plug (with the frozen sediment trapped within it).

The bottle is then quickly topped up with a dosage of champagne or sugar syrup, depending on the level of sweetness desired, and corked. A wire cage is usually wrapped tightly around the cork, securely binding it to the top of the bottle to ensure the cork stays put.

Like still wines, sparkling wines come in different varieties. Blancs de blanc (white from white) are made exclusively of white wine grapes; blancs de noir (white from black) are made from red wine grapes. True French Champagne is made from a combination of both. There are also pink or rosé champagnes. By law, the term *Champagne* can be used only for wines made in the Champagne region of France. Many other very good sparkling wines are made by the same process in other parts of France—in fact, all over Europe and in the United States, but none of them can legally be called *Champagne*. Less expensive sparklers are also widely available, typically mass-produced in large vats (the Charmat or bulk process) rather than in individual bottles. Champagne is available with varying levels of residual sugar. The most common label descriptions are somewhat confusing: Brut wines are drier (have less sugar), while extra-dry wines are sweeter.

Wine Fermentation

Fermentation is at the heart of winemaking. The goal is to convert sugar into ethanol in a way that produces a minimum of undesirable by-products while preserving the maximum natural aroma and flavor of the fruit.

Theoretically, 180 g sugar produces 92 g ethanol, which is 51 percent of the sugar weight. About 5 percent of the sugar is consumed to produce by-products such as glycerol, succinic acid, lactic acid, 2,3-butanediol, acetic acid, and other compounds. About 2.5 percent of the sugar is consumed by the yeast as a carbon source, and about 0.5 percent is left over as unfermented residual sugars. Consequently, about 8 percent (14.4 g) of sugar is not converted into ethanol. The remaining 165.6 grams therefore produce 84.5 g ethanol. From these calculations, a winemaker can determine the alcohol potential of grape juice by knowing how much sugar it contains.

Through extensive research, favorable yeast cultures for wine production have been identified and grown in pure culture. Although about 150 yeast species are known to relate to winemaking, the most important ones are *Saccharomyces cerevisiae* and *Saccharomyces bayanus*. These two species are the source material for many strains of yeast developed specifically for every type of wine, grape, and process in commercial use today.

Commercial yeast strains are sold dry in vacuum-sealed packs or as liquid cultures. The recommended dose is about 200 g yeast per 1000 L of must to start fermentation. At this concentration, the added yeast cells are dominant, and very soon they take over fermentation from any wild yeasts that are present. The use of one dominant yeast strain is most beneficial, making the fermentation more consistent, faster, and tailored to the winemaker's needs.

This is in contrast to the Old World tradition of relying on wild yeast found in the vineyard and on the winemaking equipment. Such fermentation is commonly used in France and some California wineries. It is believed that by fermenting with an assortment of naturally occurring yeast strains, the wine is more complex and more "natural." When using wild yeast fermentation, a certain measure of control over the process is lost. One of the most abundant strains found in the so-called natural yeast technique belongs to another species, *Kloeckera apiculata*, which is more active in low alcohol concentrations (4 to 5 percent alcohol). This can cause incomplete fermentation, as the yeasts die before the wine reaches typical alcohol levels of 10 to 12 percent. This results in a very sweet low-alcohol wine and is why most winemakers opt for using pure strains of well-researched and documented yeast cultivars.

Dairy Fermentations

Milk has been called nature's perfect food. Milk contains vitamins, fats, minerals, carbohydrates, and proteins all in one. This makes it an excellent source of food for both humans and microorganisms, both pathogenic and nonpathogenic. Louis Pasteur was the first to define the process that bears his name (pasteurization) for heating milk to kill pathogens.

If milk is allowed to sit at room temperature, naturally occurring lactic acid bacteria start to ferment the primary carbohydrate, the disaccharide lactose, into lactic acid. This reduces the pH, causing the milk protein, casein, to coagulate or curdle and form two phases: curds and whey. Curds are semisolid lumps consisting primarily of casein and milkfat. Whey is watery liquid composed of whey protein, lactose, and other water-soluble materials. This separation is the first step in producing many fermented dairy products.

The Streptococcus bacteria *Streptococcus lactis* and *Streptococcus cremoris* are gram-positive spherical bacteria capable of fermenting lactose to lactic acid. These two species are used as starter cultures in conjunction with *Leuconostoc cremoris* to make cultured buttermilk, produced by inoculating pasteurized skim milk and allowing the fermentation to proceed until the desired acidity, flavor, and aroma characteristics are reached. The bacteria convert lactose to lactic acid, acetic acid, ethyl alcohol, carbon dioxide, and two additional compounds, acetylmethylcarbinol, and diacetyl, all of which give buttermilk its characteristic flavor and aroma.

Butter is produced by churning (agitating) cream until the butterfat separates out to form solid butter and liquid buttermilk (which differs from cultured buttermilk). It can also be made by first souring the cream to develop the more intense taste and aroma of cultured butter. This is done commercially by allowing the cream to ferment (using lactic starter cultures) for approximately 12 hours under controlled temperature prior to churning. After churning, the butter may be salted or not, packaged, and refrigerated to allow the butterfat to crystallize and the butter to harden.

The many other well-known fermented dairy products include sour cream, kefir, yogurt, and of course all of the

FIGURE 11.9 Dairy fermentation product matrix.

Fermented Product	Dairy Substrate	Principal Microbe	Process
Bulgarian buttermilk	Pasteurized milk	*Lactobacillus bulgaricus*	Incubate inoculated milk @ 98.6°F; follow same process as cultured buttermilk.
Yogurt	Concentrated skim milk	*Lactobacillus bulgaricus* & *Streptococcus thermophilus*	Incubate inoculated substrate for 3–4 hours at 105°F, then cool to 40°F.
Butter	Churned milk to collect cream solids	*Streptococcus cremoris* & *Leuconostoc citrovorum*	Incubate inoculated substrate @ 86°F until acid spec is reached.
Cultured sour cream	Cream	*Streptococcus cremoris* & *Leuconostoc cremoris*	Incubate inoculated substrate @ 86°F until acid spec is reached.
Acidophilus milk	Pasteurized milk	*Lactobacillus acidophilus*	Incubate inoculated milk @ 98.6°F and ferment until acidity of 0.6–0.7% is developed.
Kefir; native to Eastern Europe and Western Asia; means *pleasant taste*	Milk from cow, goat, or sheep	*Streptococcus lactis*, *Lactobacillus bulgaricus*, & lactose-fermenting yeast; uncontrolled fermentation	Milk is allowed to ferment in bags made of goat skin, and fresh milk is continually added after the fermentation is active. Grains are formed of bacteria, yeast, and protein. Contains 1% acid and 1% alcohol and carbon dioxide gas, which gives it a fizzy taste.
Kumiss; native to Western Asia; sometimes called *milk-wine* or *milk beer*	Horse milk	*Streptococcus lactis*, *Lactobacillus casei*, & lactose-fermenting yeast	Mare's milk is allowed to ferment in bags made of goat skin. Contains 0.7–1.3% acid and >1% alcohol in conjunction with carbon dioxide gas.

Source: James Adams.

hundreds of types of natural cheeses that are distinguished by their end-product attributes, by the type of milk used for the fermentation, and by the microbial agents involved.

Cheese-making is as much a mixture of art and science as is fermentation itself. One reason is the natural variations in milk produced by different breeds of dairy cattle. Milkfat varies extensively between breeds of dairy cows, with Jersey and Guernsey having the highest amount of milkfat and Holstein the lowest. The type of feed given to cows can also affect the overall composition of the milk, with grain-fed livestock producing higher milkfat. After birthing, the cow produces milk for her young calf. The milk composition changes based on how recently she gave birth and how long since she was last milked, the age and overall health of the cow, seasonal differences (percentage of milkfat is higher in the cooler part of the year, especially winter, and lower in the summer, due to the quality and quantity of the pasture grass available to use as feedstock), and nutrition and feeding management, which

affect the volume yield in addition to composition. Last but certainly not least is the effect of pasteurization on the quality of the milk.[16]

There are approximately 18 types of natural cheeses, categorized by the different processes used to make them. These include brick, Camembert, cheddar, cottage, cream, Edam, Gouda, hand, Limburger, Neufchâtel, Parmesan, provolone, Romano, Roquefort, sapsago, Swiss, Trappist, and whey cheeses (such as ricotta).

Unlike most cheeses, which are prepared from curds, ricotta cheese is a fresh, soft, creamy, and lightly flavored cheese produced from the lactic fermentation of whey, which is the major by-product in all cheese manufacture. (After the curds are separated from the whey, it is the whey itself that becomes the source material for ricotta.) For every 5 gallons of milk made into cheese, there is enough whey to produce approximately 2 pounds of ricotta. As the whey contains lactose, lactic acid bacteria are added to convert it to lactic acid, causing the pH of the solution to drop. This acidic solution is then heated to near boiling, which denatures the whey protein, causing it to precipitate into small curds. The ricotta is then strained and packed into containers and refrigerated. Ricotta can also be frozen for extended periods to extend its shelf life.[17]

Cheeses are classified as hard, soft, or semi-hard depending on their moisture content and on whether they are ripened or unripened. Unripened cheeses (such as cottage cheese, mascarpone, and goat cheese) are fermented in one step and generally consumed fresh. After the initial fermentation step, ripened cheeses are aged for various amounts of time, during which additional fermentation and flavor development takes place.

As an example of the cheese-making process, the focus here is on production of the most popular natural cheese in the United States, Canada, and some parts of Europe: cheddar.

Cheddar curd is formed as a result of controlled fermentation, where the type, temperature, and amount of milk, bacterial culture used, concentration of rennin (an enzyme that coagulates soluble milk casein into insoluble protein to produce the curds), humidity, and amount of acid produced are all closely monitored. Although the cheese can be made from either raw or pasteurized milk, if raw milk is used the cheese must ripen for 60 days or more by U.S. law as a safeguard against the development of pathogenic organisms such as *E. coli*, salmonella, and listeria.[18] Most cheddar cheese made today uses pasteurized milk.

FIGURE 11.10 Classification of cheeses.

SOFT
   Unripened:
      Low-fat—cottage, pot, baker's
      High-fat—cream, Neufchâtel (U.S. made)
   Ripened: Bel Paese, Brie, Camembert, cooked, hand, Neufchâtel (French made)

SEMISOFT
   Ripened: principally by bacteria: brick, Muenster
   Ripened: by bacteria and surface microorganisms: Limburger, Port du Salut, Trappist
   Ripened: principally by blue mold in interior: Roquefort, Gorgonzola, blue, Stilton, Wensleydale

HARD
   Ripened: by bacteria, without eyes: cheddar, granular, caciocavallo
   Ripened: by bacteria with eyes: Swiss, Emmentaler, Gruyère

VERY HARD
   Ripened: by bacteria: aged Asiago, Parmesan, Romano, sapsago, Spalen

PROCESS CHEESES
   Pasteurized, cold-pack, related products

WHEY CHEESES
   Mysost, Primost, ricotta

Source: G. P. Saunders, 1953.

To form the separate curd and whey fractions, pasteurized milk is pumped into a stainless steel, open-topped trough-like tank (referred to as a cheddaring vat) and heated to approximately 86°F (30°C). A starter culture of the lactic acid bacterium *Streptococcus lactis* is added to the tank, along with yellow- or orange-pigmented natural coloring agents (annatto, turmeric, or carotenoids, like beta carotene) to produce the familiar orange cheddar color. (White cheddar is made without these natural colors.) An agitator completely mixes the color and the bacterial inoculum evenly in the milk. Within 30 to 45 minutes, lactic acid is produced at a low concentration (acidity rises 0.01 to 0.02 percent) and rennin in a dilute solution is added (to coagulate the protein and form the curd). After the enzyme is added, the agitation is turned off. In the cheese business, this is referred to as *setting the milk*.

After about 30 minutes, a curd similar to soft custard starts to form in the tank, and with more acid being produced as fermentation progresses, the curd reaches the desired firmness. The next step is to cut the curd with a curd knife, made of wires strung across a frame in a grid pattern similar to a square tennis racket. This takes some skill. By drawing the curd knife the length of the tank and then with a back-and-forth movement the width of the tank, the cheese curd is cut into small cubes, promoting the separation of the whey from the curd. After cutting the cubes, gentle agitation is turned back on and heat is applied to the tank to bring it back up to 86°F (30°C) over approximately 45 minutes. This causes the cubes to shrink, which helps squeeze out the whey, thus firming up the curds, the whole mass taking on the appearance of cottage cheese. After heating, the agitation is stopped and the curds are allowed to settle in the tank. They are trenched along the sides of the tank using a trowel, which helps the whey to drain. The whey may then be drained off and captured for use in making other dairy products, such as ricotta cheese.

The curds are allowed to knit together for about 15 minutes, forming a solid mass with a rubbery consistency. They are then cut into large blocks, approximately 40 pounds each, and stacked on top of each other to allow additional whey to drain. The blocks are turned every 15 minutes; this handling and movement squeezes more whey from the curds. The process is referred to as cheddaring and is unique to the production of cheddar cheese.[19]

The cheddaring step is completed in about two hours, when chemical analysis of the expressed whey is between 0.5 and 0.7 percent acidity, indicating the curd blocks are ready for milling. Milling is the process of shredding the blocks into irregular pieces approximately 0.5 inch in size, which is necessary to facilitate uniform salting of the cheese. The salt—between 1 and 3 percent by weight—is mixed throughout the milled curd. It is added to draw out any remaining whey and reduce moisture content even further, and to add flavor to the cheese. After salting, the milled curds are placed in hoops lined with cheesecloth. These are placed in a press, where they are pressed overnight to reach a specified moisture, usually 30 to 40 percent.

After the pressing, the hoops are removed and the cheeses placed on racks in a temperature-controlled room to chill for the next three to four days. The cheese is now ready for the ripening process, wherein the bacteria and the enzymes continue to modify the texture, flavor, and color of the cheese by continuing to ferment leftover lactose into acids and aroma compounds. (In addition to lactose, which is mostly metabolized early in the process, there is also some breakdown of fats and proteins, which leads to the development of many of the flavor and aroma compounds later in the aging process.) The organoleptic changes (taste, texture, appearance, and aroma) are quite considerable during the aging or ripening period, which lasts for a minimum of 60 days (mild cheddars) and can continue for a year or longer (extra-sharp varieties).

Bread

It is believed that yeast-leavened bread, often called the "staff of life," has been around since the Neolithic Age (10,000 BC).[20] Initially, the yeasts involved were wild species that lived on the surface of cereal grains or were present in the air. But over the centuries, civilizations learned to use the dregs from making beer or the fermenting grape juice from winemaking to start the fermentation process that leavens dough. It also became commonplace to use a bit of leftover dough from the previous day's bread-making to use as a type of sourdough starter.

To make good bread, the dough must be extensible (stretchable when pulled) so it can expand while rising, elastic (having the strength and flexibility to hold the gases produced by the yeasts during fermentation), and stable enough to hold its shape and cell structure. Gluten gives dough all of these properties. That said, gluten as such does not exist in wheat flour. Instead, two proteins present in the flour, glutenin and gliadin, are the precursors that form gluten when flour is mixed with water and then kneaded. Other grains may be used to make bread, but most lack sufficient gluten-building ability to produce a well-risen, light, and airy loaf. Therefore, they must be blended with a percentage of wheat flour (or mixed with pure gluten) to make breads that will rise and have a delicate, porous structure when baked.

The other important event that occurs when the flour is wetted is that starch-digesting enzymes are activated. These begin to break down the starch into sugars, which in turn provide food for the yeast, which ferments the sugars into the carbon dioxide that allows the dough to rise.

Yeast's role in baking is to provide leavening through the production of carbon dioxide, which provides texture improvement through loaf aeration and develops internal crumb structure (which sets on baking). Yeast also provides flavor (taste and aroma) due to the formation of dozens of flavor compounds that are the result of fermentation. Baker's yeast is yet another strain of *Saccharomyces cerevisiae*, the same yeast responsible for the majority of brewing and winemaking. It is available in several forms:

- Cream yeast is a suspension of yeast cells in liquid (essentially a yeast slurry) produced in large industrial fermenters and sold in bulk containers. Its primary use is in industrial bakeries with special high-volume dispensing and mixing equipment.

- Fresh (compressed or "cake") yeast has 70 percent moisture, requires refrigeration, has a short shelf life (2 weeks), and is "instantly active" (it's alive!). Typically available for commercial use in one-pound blocks looking very similar to blocks of butter. Occasionally available in supermarkets in one-ounce foil- or paper-wrapped cubes.

- Active dry, the original spray-dried yeast, has a long shelf life (months to years), requires proofing in warm water with a bit of sugar prior to usage, and contains 25 percent or more dead cells.

- Instant dry is a more modern version of Active dry which undergoes a milder drying process that yields fewer dead cells, and therefore can be used at a 25 percent lower use rate compared with Active dry. It has a finer texture, longer shelf life, and does not require advance proofing—it can be added directly to the dry dough mix.

In addition to the pure culture Saccharomyces yeasts, sourdough starter can be used to leaven bread. Sourdough starter is a combination of wild yeast and lactobacillus bacteria that provides leavening along with a typical sour flavor in the bread. Because it is not a pure yeast culture, it takes 2 to 3 times longer to generate the required carbon dioxide for loaves to rise, but that extra time allows for greater flavor development. If cared for properly, starters can last for decades.

Bread-making involves the following basic steps.

1. *Mixing the ingredients* to evenly distribute them and form the dough. Water, flour, yeast, and usually salt are the most basic, but other ingredients, including dough conditioners, sweeteners, eggs, oils, extra gluten, whole grains and seeds, herbs and spices, raisins, olives, and nuts, may be added to produce specific types of bread or rolls. Mixing also hydrates the flour to start the development of gluten and activates the starch-digesting enzymes.

2. *Kneading or working the dough* to enhance gluten formation and provide heat through mechanical energy, thus increasing enzyme activity and yeast metabolic activity.

3. *First rise,* in which the dough is allowed to rest, covered, in a warm, draft-free area. The dough relaxes and expands as carbon dioxide begins to build up. During this period, each yeast cell forms a center around which carbon dioxide bubbles form. Thousands of these tiny bubbles, each surrounded by a thin film of gluten, form cells within the dough. As these cells continue to fill with gas, the dough increases in size. Usually the dough ball is allowed to rise until it doubles in size.

4. *Punching down,* in which the doubled dough is punched to release any large pockets of gas that may have formed, kneaded briefly to evenly distribute gas bubbles, then cut and shaped to fit the baking pans.

5. *Second rise,* which allows the panned dough to rise again to allow finer crumb structure and more intense flavors to develop. Once it has doubled in size again, it is baked.

6. *Baking* transforms the raw dough into a light, porous, flavorful, easily digestible loaf of bread. As the oven heat penetrates the dough, trapped gases rapidly expand, causing a

sudden increase in the size of the loaf. This is called oven-spring. Whatever alcohol has been produced during fermentation evaporates. As the temperature in the dough rises, so does the rate of yeast activity until the temperature reaches 115°F (46°C), at which point the yeasts die. From about 140°F (60°C) onward, stabilization of the crumb structure begins. From 165°F (74°C), the gluten strands surrounding the individual gas cells become rigid, providing additional structure to the crumb.

Enzymes present in the dough, in particular alpha amylase, the enzyme that breaks starch into sugars, continue working until the dough temperature reaches 167°F (75°C). Because the yeasts all died at 115°F (46°C), the extra sugars produced by the enzymes between the death of the yeasts and the denaturation of the enzymes are not metabolized and hence provide sweetness to the bread and enhance the attractive brown color of the crust. When the internal temperature of the loaf reaches 208°F (98°C), the bread is considered done. By this time, surface temperature can be in excess of 392°F (200°C)—essentially, the temperature of the oven. The loaf is removed from the oven for cooling. The loaf is also full of saturated steam that must be given time to evaporate. The loaves must be cooled to about 95°F (35°C) before being sliced or packaged to prevent damaging the loaf.

⬤ Meat Fermentation

The fermentation of meat is quite similar, microbiologically speaking, to other processes that have been discussed, following the same course as other lactic acid fermentations. There is typically not enough carbohydrate in meat to support sufficient fermentation activity, so they must be augmented by the addition of other sugars, usually dextrose. The dextrose is fermented by lactic acid bacteria; the acid reduces the pH, helping preserve the meat and extend its shelf life.

Examples of fermented dried sausages are pepperoni, Genoa salami, chorizo, Italian salami, hard salami, and cured meat sticks (jerky is not included in this list because it must be cooked in high humidity—no less than 90 percent—to achieve microbial lethality before drying).[21] Semi-dried fermented meats include summer sausage, Lebanon bologna, and Thuringer sausage.

Dry and semi-dry sausages make up the largest group of all dried meats. Although the USDA does not formally define semi-dry or dry sausage, it does regulate the moisture-to-protein ratio (MPR) as follows:

- *Shelf-stable semi-dry sausages* must have a MPR of 3.1:1 *or less* and a pH of 5.0 *or less*. They must undergo a moisture loss of up to 15 percent of the total and have a final water activity (a_w) range of 0.90 to 0.94. These sausages are generally cooked or smoked prior to sale and consumption.
- *Shelf-stable dry sausages* must have a MPR of 1.6 to 2.3:1 and a pH of 4.7 to 5.0. They must undergo a moisture loss of up to 25 percent of the total and have a final a_w range

of 0.85 to 0.91. These products may be produced without any cooking step if their water activity is low enough. Those that are not cooked must have a pH of 5.0 or less and a_w of 0.85 or less.[22]

In addition, in light of outbreaks of *E. coli* O157:H7 linked to dry fermented shelf-stable sausage products, all procedures for either dry or semi-dry sausages must be tested microbiologically to confirm that a 5-log reduction of *E. coli* O157:H7 has been achieved.[23]

Fermentable carbohydrate substrates (sugars) normally make up only about 1 percent of fresh meat. This is not enough to propagate a strong lactic fermentation, and dextrose is usually added to the meat emulsion (consisting of minced meat, fat, spices, flavorings, curing salts, and culture) to start the fermentation. The final fermentation pH of the sausage depends on the initial pH of the raw meat matrix and the amount of sugar added to allow sufficient formation of lactic acid by the lactic bacteria.

An example of a fermented dry sausage formulation and process is the manufacture of U.S.–style pepperoni. According to the USDA's Farm Service Agency, pepperoni is the most popular pizza topping; approximately 36 percent of all pizza orders are for pepperoni pizza, and over a quarter of a billion pounds of pepperoni are consumed on pizzas per year in the United States. Five large chains lead the consumption and sale of pizza in the United States, as posted on November 1, 2015, by *Pizza Today* magazine: Pizza Hut, headquartered in Plano, TX, and a division of YUM Brands, is number one, with $13.4 billion in annual sales; Domino's, headquartered in Ann Arbor, MI, is second, with annual sales of $8.9 billion; Little Caesars, headquartered in Detroit, MI, is third, with $3.4 billion in annual sales; Papa John's, headquartered in Louisville, KY, has reached $3.32 billion in annual sales and is fourth; Papa Murphy's International, based out of Vancouver, WA, is now fifth in annual sales, with $785 million. With expected growth of the pizza category, it is easy to see how this fermented sausage became so popular.

Standard pepperoni is formulated to approximately 30 percent fat using more pork than beef, unless it is labeled as "all-beef pepperoni." Typically, the ratio is 60 percent pork and 40 percent beef, although manufacturers can use up to 55 percent beef in regular (non-all-beef) pepperoni. The pork percentage is determined on a least-cost formulation basis and can be up to 100 percent of the meat material, depending on market conditions. The meat commonly used is cheek meat and striated skeletal muscle due to its lack of binding and its high protein content. The lack of binding is important to prevent the cupping of pepperoni slices when heated on pizza, and the high protein level is necessary to achieve the deep red color of the sausage.

Non-meat ingredients include salt added at about 3 percent, dextrose added at about 0.8 percent, spices and flavorings added at about 2 percent, and starter culture of *Pediococcus acidilactici*, which is added to the meat mince at approximately 10 million CFU/g (colony-forming units of bacteria per gram) to ensure a reproducible lactic fermentation.[24]

The ground meat is tempered to approximately 28°F (–2°C) before mixing. After the meat is mixed with the spices, starter culture, and other ingredients, the matrix goes through a final grind and is stuffed into casings. The stuffed product is transferred to the fermentation room, where the temperature is approximately 105°F (41°C) and the relative humidity is controlled at 80 to 90 percent. Fermentation continues until a pH of 5.3 or lower is reached and residual sugar in the meat is measured at 0 percent; in most cases, this takes 12 to 15 hours. The pepperoni is then transferred to the drying room, where it is monitored for moisture loss, cooled to approximately 55°F (13°C), and held for 12 to 14 days or until the moisture-protein ratio reaches 1:6 or less. During this cooling and drying time, the relative humidity is closely maintained between 68 and 72 percent.

Semi-dry sausage is manufactured in a similar but not identical manner. Semi-dry does not lose as much moisture, and the drying process occurs during the fermentation. After this process is completed, the sausage is cooked or hot-smoked to a minimum internal temperature of 140°F (60°C).

Fish Fermentation

Although they are not common in the United States, a wide variety of fermented fish products are produced and consumed in Asia and Africa. Some are used as condiments, some as side dishes, and some as sauces or pastes. The majority of these products are found in Southeast Asia, including but not limited to Vietnam, Indonesia, Thailand, Malaysia, and the Philippines.[25]

More widely known in the United States are the Asian fish sauces like nuoc mam, a pungent, salty liquid made from fermented anchovies that is used as an ingredient in Vietnamese cooking. Nam pla is one of the basic ingredients in Thai cooking, again made from fermented anchovies or, sometimes, squid. The rich, reddish brown sauce is used to marinate meats and as a condiment, much like Americans use salt and pepper. It is often mixed with fresh-cut chili peppers and lime juice. Other countries have their own varieties made from an assortment of fish and shellfish species, including patis from the Philippines and belancan (made from fermented krill or shrimp) from Malaysia. The majority of bacteria responsible for fermentation of fish sauces are gram-positive, halophilic organisms of the bacillus species that originate within the bodies of the fish themselves.

In general, fish sauce is made from small fish (either fresh- or saltwater species) that would otherwise have little value for consumption. Larger varieties of fish, such as mackerel and sardines, also make good fish sauce, but because they are relatively more expensive due to their value as a food fish, they are seldom used in the commercial production of fish sauce. As soon as fishing boats return with their catch, the fish are rinsed and drained, then mixed with sea salt—2 to 3 parts fish to 1 part salt by weight. They are then placed in large earthenware jars lined on the bottom with a layer of salt, and topped with a second layer of salt. A woven bamboo mat is placed over the fish and weighted with heavy rocks to keep the fish from floating when the water inside them is drawn out by the salt and fermentation process.

The jars are covered and left in a sunny location for nine months to a year. From time to time they are uncovered to air out and to expose the fish to direct sunlight, which helps digest the fish and liquefy them. The periodic sunning produces a fish sauce of superior quality, giving it a fragrant (some would say nauseating) aroma and a clear, reddish brown color. When fermentation has finished, the liquid is removed from the jars, preferably through a spigot on the bottom of the jars so it passes through the layers of fish remains, or by siphoning. Any sediments are strained out with a clean cloth. The filtered fish sauce is placed in clean jars and allowed to air in the sun for a couple of weeks to dissipate the strong fish odors. It is then ready for bottling.

A similar fish sauce called garum or liquamen was ubiquitous in ancient Greek and Roman cooking. It was fermented from a variety of fish (especially the intestines) including tuna, mackerel, moray eel, and anchovies. The closest relative of fermented fish sauce common in Western cuisine today is Worcestershire sauce, a fermented sauce containing anchovies.

Vegetable Fermentation

Genghis Khan and his armies are often credited with introducing fermented vegetables into Europe; however, there is little doubt the methods for fermenting vegetables existed long before then. From archeological evidence, it appears that cucumbers and cabbages were the main vegetables used in early fermentations.[26]

Fermented cabbage is the precursor to what is known today as sauerkraut. Although it has lost some fans, it is still consumed heavily by Americans of German and Eastern European descent. The classic Alsatian cured meat and potato dish choucroute uses sauerkraut as its primary ingredient and is enjoyed throughout Western Europe. And here in the United States, a hot dog without sauerkraut is unthinkable. Also, there seems to be a renewed interest in using sauerkraut in nontraditional ways—even as part of dessert. For example, a chocolate cake made with sauerkraut is moist and has a distinct tangy taste that complements the flavor of the chocolate.

Lactic acid–fermented vegetables are rich in vitamins and minerals, nutrients, fiber, and digestion-enhancing enzymes. They are also an excellent source of probiotics—that is, the lactic bacteria primarily responsible for their fermentation. This method of preserving remains the most nutritious way to store vegetables out of season. In addition to cabbage and cucumbers, beets, turnips, radishes, cauliflower, green beans, and okra are all commonly fermented using salt brines or by dry salting. The microbe responsible for the fermentation of these vegetables (including sauerkraut) is *Leuconostoc mesenteroides*, a gram-positive, facultative halophile (able to tolerate relatively high levels of salt).

One of the most famous fermented vegetable mixtures is the Korean dish kimchi, a mixture of Chinese cabbage, radishes,

FIGURE 11.11 Recipe for chocolate cake with sauerkraut.

Chocolate Cake with Sauerkraut

- 1 cup canned or bottled sauerkraut, drained and then chopped into ¼" pieces
- 3 whole eggs
- ½ cup butter
- 1½ cups white sugar
- 1 tsp. vanilla
- 2 cups all-purpose flour
- 1 tsp. baking soda
- ½ tsp. salt
- ½ cup unsweetened cocoa powder
- 1 cup water

- Pre-heat oven to 350°F (325°F if using convection oven).
- Prepare drained sauerkraut and set aside in plastic bowl.
- Beat the eggs and set aside.
- Mix butter, vanilla, and sugar together and slowly beat the eggs into the mix until a paste-like consistency is reached.
- Add the flour, baking soda, salt, and cocoa powder to the above mix and add water as needed to reach a smooth paste-like consistency.
- Add drained, chopped sauerkraut to the mix and stir until completely uniform.
- Pour the mixture into greased round spring cake pans or use non-stick pans if preferred.
- Bake for 30 to 35 minutes and test the cake for doneness by using a toothpick or clean butter knife. When done, allow to cool for a minimum of 30 minutes. Cake should be frosted only after cooling.
- Prepare frosting recipe or drizzle with chocolate ganache.

Source: James Adams.

chilies, garlic, ginger, and fish. Kimchi is the national dish of Korea, where it is eaten every day by most of the populace. Traditional families eat it with every meal. In November, Korean fresh vegetable markets are inundated with people trying to get enough raw vegetables to make a year's worth of kimchi.

Kimchi fermentation takes place in an earthen jar or large crock over three to six days at a temperature no higher than 68°F (20°C). The crock is buried in the ground up to the neck and either covered with straw or fashioned with a plastic head, similar to the one used in pickle fermentation. When the preferred sourness level is achieved and no gas bubbles are visible, nontraditional Korean families remove the crock or jar and refrigerate the kimchi for up to six months. Traditional Korean families store the kimchi in the ground throughout the winter months, removing the contents as needed.

●Coffee Fermentation

Most people are unaware that the cup of joe they enjoy as their morning pick-me-up is actually a fermented beverage. However, it is much different from beer and wine, as the coffee beverage is not a result of fermentation; rather, the beans are processed by fermentation.

Coffee processing consists of several steps:

1. Coffee beans are picked and separated, and the ripe cherries are sent to the pulping machines.
2. Pulping is used to remove the coffee beans from the ripe cherries. This is accomplished by applying pressure to push the coffee cherries against a screen with holes just large enough for the actual coffee bean to pass through. (Green cherries are hard and cannot be pulped.)
3. The coffee beans are now ready to be fermented by gram-negative bacteria (most often bacteria of the Escherichia genus), which produces enzymes that remove the slippery mucilage, a slimy film made up of pectin-like materials that covers the bean's surface. This must be done before the beans can be dried properly. The fermentation takes one to two days, depending on the temperature, and is complete when the bean can be rubbed between the fingers without sliminess.
4. The beans are transferred to patios, where they are air-dried to a moisture content of 11 to 12 percent.
5. A 300 g sample of beans is then roasted and brewed to determine coffee quality (flavor and aroma being the most significant quality factors measured).[27]

Two main species of coffee make up the world's production: *Coffea arabica* (arabica coffee; 80 percent) and *Coffea canephora* (robusta coffee; 20 percent). The robusta is much more strongly flavored and has higher caffeine content, while the arabica is more pleasant to the taste, with less bitterness and lower caffeine. While the USDA forecasts world coffee production to be down slightly to 127.4 million bags of beans (1 bag = 100 pounds), it expects U.S. imports to increase by 1.8 percent to 5.8 million bags.[28]

Note: Although the tea industry refers to tea processing as fermentation, unlike coffee beans, which undergo true microbial fermentation, tea leaves are not actually fermented. Instead, they undergo non-microbial enzymatic oxidation, which transforms the fresh, grassy aromas and flavors of fresh-picked tea leaves into the recognizable flavors and flowery aromas expected in brewed tea.

●Soy Fermentation

There is a great deal of disagreement in the scientific and popular literature about fermented versus unfermented soyfoods. In addition to being an excellent source of nutrients (complete protein, carbohydrate, and fat, as well as vitamins and minerals, including calcium, folic acid, and iron), soybeans also contain large quantities of potentially toxic chemicals, including potent enzyme inhibitors that block the action of trypsin and other enzymes needed to digest protein; hemaglutenins (blood-clotting agents); goitrogens, which affect the thyroid; and phytates (antioxidant compounds that bind to certain dietary minerals and inhibit their absorption). These compounds are not completely deactivated during cooking, and some say they can cause serious gastric distress as well as deficiencies in amino acid and mineral uptake.

Diets high in trypsin inhibitors cause enlargement and severe complications of the pancreas, including cancer.[29] On the other hand, the counterargument says that when eaten in moderation, unfermented soy products are not dangerous. Regardless of which is correct, one thing both sides can agree on: Fermented soyfoods (soy sauce, miso, natto, tempeh) do not contain these compounds, and as such are risk-free and highly nutritious. (*Note:* Edamame are a strain of soybeans grown to be eaten as a green vegetable. While they do contain measureable amounts of anti-nutritional factors, these are easily removed by blanching, unlike the dry-bean variety of soybeans.)

Originally prized in China for their soil-improving abilities (like all legumes, soybeans fix nitrogen in soil where they are planted, thus improving its fertility for growing other crops that lack this ability), once the Chinese discovered how to ferment them (between 1134 and 246 BC, during the Chou dynasty), they took full advantage of soy nutrients without negative side effects. Due to their exceptional nutritional profile and taste, fermented soyfoods are popular staples throughout Asia and the rest of the world. Many products consumed around the world are produced by the fermentation of soybeans.

- Natto is a traditional Japanese food made by the alkaline fermentation of the amino acids in soybeans by *Bacillus subtilus*. Whenever amino acids are fermented, the resulting product smells like ammonia. Natto has this strong characteristic odor, along with a slimy, sticky texture. However, if one can get past the texture and aroma, natto offers health benefits not found in other foods, as the bacillus bacterium secretes blood clot–dissolving enzymes. Natto has been linked to the prevention of heart attacks and cancer.[30] Additional research must be conducted to verify these links.

- Miso paste is another traditional Japanese food made from fermented soybeans. It is made by combining cooked soybeans and koji (a starter made of rice or barley, or a combination of the two that has been fermented with a mold, *Aspergillus oryzae*) with salt and water and fermenting them in wooden kegs for up to two years, depending on the attributes wanted in the final product. During the fermentation of *koji*, the mold produces enzymes that break down proteins and carbohydrates of the soybeans, which are turned into an umami-laden paste filled with glutamates as a result. There are several common varieties of miso: "White" miso undergoes the shortest fermentation and is the mildest "yellow" miso is intermediate in strength, and "red" miso undergoes the longest fermentation and is strongest in flavor. Beyond the basic three, there are dozens of variations based on the ingredients being fermented and the fermentation protocol used, but all are made with *koji*. *Koji* is to miso what malt is to beer. Miso is commonly consumed as the chief flavoring in a thin, brothy soup, considered a medicinal food by the Japanese, who drink it daily.

- Tempeh has been a traditional Indonesian food for over 300 years. It is made by soaking hulled soybeans overnight, then cooking them briefly, allowing them to cool to 80 to 85°F (27 to 29°C), then adding a starter culture of Rhizopus mold spores (usually *R. oligosporus* or *R. oryzae*). Following an incubation and fermentation period of approximately 48 hours at 86°F (30°C) and approximately

FIGURE 11.12 **Miso varieties.**

Type	Red Miso	White Miso	Barley Miso	Soybean Miso
Grain Source	White rice, barley, or soybeans	Rice koji (60%) and fewer soybeans	Barley grains, soybeans, and barley koji	Only soybeans
Appearance	Reddish brown	Tan to light brown with a very smooth texture	Very dark brown color	Reddish brown and chunky texture
Fermentation time	1–3 years	1–2 weeks (storage at 2 months refrigerated)	1–3 years	Minimum of 1 year
Comments	Contains the highest amount of protein of all the miso products	Contains the highest amount of carbohydrate of all miso products	Cheapest of all miso products Very salty taste	Made with *Aspergillus hatcho* Considered "the miso of emperors"
Food Applications	Stir fries, miso soups and stews, and to make marinades for meat, poultry, and vegetables	Light-colored soups, salad dressings, and marinades for fish	Seasoning rich soups, stews, beans, sauces, and spreads	Used to flavor decadent and hearty soups

Source: Adapted from About Soya.be, 2009.

70 percent humidity, the tempeh is formed into a compact white cake. In the process of partially metabolizing the soybeans, the mold eliminates whatever anti-nutritional factors are present in the undercooked beans, making them entirely digestible. Tempeh has a nutty, mushroom-like flavor when sliced and fried in vegetable oil until it begins to crisp and turn brown. The fried tempeh is added as a high-protein and high-fiber source to soups, salads, and sandwiches, and is used in the making of spreads.[31]

- Soy sauce, the best known of the fermented soy products, is one of the essential flavoring ingredients in Asian foods. It has been used in China for over 2500 years.

In Japan, "shoyu" is the Japanese name for soy sauce, which is made from a mash of soybeans and wheat, while "tamari" is a non-wheat product made by drawing off the liquid content of soybean miso. The actual translation of tamari is "puddle," so called by the way it would pool on top of the miso.

Because genuine tamari is a non-wheat product, it has a distinctive aroma as well as thicker texture, deeper color, and stronger taste than shoyu. It is often used for dipping raw fish (sashimi), sautéing teriyaki, and other food processing, while shoyu is used as an all-purpose cooking soy sauce. There are only certain areas in Japan where tamari is produced, whereas shoyu is much more widely available.

Traditional soy sauce is made by a three-step process:

1. Producing a koji (as in making miso). Steamed soybeans and toasted cracked wheat are blended together with a starter known as "koji seed," which is comprised mainly of molds from the Aspergillus family. The koji is allowed to ferment for several days, during which time the koji seed produces proteolic, lipolytic, and amylolytic enzymes that convert proteins, fats, and starches to simpler and more easily fermentable substances.

2. Transferring the koji to fermentation tanks (containing a saltwater solution), where a starter culture of lactic acid bacteria and yeasts is added and allowed to ferment for six months (or longer for the highest-quality shoyu) at approximately 85°F (29°C). During this time, more than 200 flavor compounds are produced.

3. Separating the raw sauce from the remnants of the koji by filtering it through layers of cloth. This liquid is pasteurized to prolong shelf life and to form additional flavor compounds, then bottled.[32]

Cheap soy sauce is made from hydrolyzed soy protein, but it does not have the natural characteristics developed during traditional fermentation and is artificially colored and flavored. The sensory characteristics of the many different types of genuine soy sauce, such as Indonesian, Malaysian,

FIGURE 11.13 **Soy sauce options.**

Type	Liquid	Dehydrated	Granulated	Low Sodium	Clear	No Preservatives
Description	Dark, rich, salty, umami	Spray dried, light tan, free-flowing powder	Light tan, granular powder	37% less sodium	Light amber colored liquid	No benzoate or sorbate added
Usage	Flavor enhancer	Flavor enhancer	Flavor enhancer	To reduce overall sodium	Light colored foods	All natural food applications
Advantage	Adds color if desired	Can replace HVP or MSG	Eliminates dusting in operations	Soy sauce not chosen due to high sodium content	Versatility of use	Versatility of use
Comments	Naturally brewed	Can be 100% natural and non-GMO varieties are available	Naturally brewed	Coupled with other sodium-sparing technologies to reduce overall sodium	Naturally brewed	Can be important dependent on labeling restrictions
Food applications	Prepared entrees, containing meat, poultry, vegetables	Marinades, dry mixes, seasoning blends, meat rubs	Any foods requiring dry formula applications	Soups, sauces, dressings, meat entrees, vegetables, mimic bouillon	Soups, sauces, salad dressings, spreads	All natural designated foods

Source: Kikkoman.com, 2009.

Japanese, Korean, and Vietnamese, are each tied to their country of origin.

Soy sauce is available in many forms for the product developer, including light and dark varieties, reduced-sodium, decolorized, and powdered. It is used to enhance the flavor profile of many types of food, including chicken and beef entrées, soups, pasta, vegetables, and even desserts, when used at very low levels. The flavor-enhancing property, or umami, of fermented soy products is used by food product developers to blend and balance flavors. Umami compounds are created during fermentation, when amino acids are broken down to their constituent peptides, particularly glutamates, inosinates, and guanylates, all of which are flavor potentiators—chemicals that are capable of supplementing, enhancing, or modifying the flavor of foods, although they have little or no flavor of their own at typical usage levels. The effect of flavor potentiators is also accompanied by changes in the mouthfeel of the product thereby inducing a perception of enhanced richness.

◉Vanilla Fermentation

Pure vanilla (made from the fermentation of vanilla beans) is one of the most widely used flavorings in confections, baked goods, desserts, and pastries. Pure vanilla is the second most expensive spice flavoring in the world, next to saffron, because growing the vanilla seed pods is labor-intensive. Even so, it is highly prized throughout the culinary and fragrance manufacturing worlds.

Historically, the bean was produced in a pod by an orchid (*Vanilla planifolia*), native only to Central America, that was naturally pollinated by a certain species of bee (also native to Central America). This orchid opens just 6 to 8 hours per day, restricting opportunities for natural pollination. It was only after the introduction of hand pollination that these orchids, and the resulting vanilla beans, could be propagated commercially, allowing for global cultivation. That said, vanilla is the world's most labor-intensive agricultural crop, which is why it's so expensive. It takes up to three years after planting before the first flowers appear, which then must be hand pollinated. The fruits, which resemble big green beans, must remain on the vine for nine months in order to completely develop their signature aroma. However, when the beans are newly harvested, they have neither flavor nor fragrance. They only develop these distinctive properties during the curing process.

Today, 70 percent of the world's pure vanilla is manufactured in Madagascar and Indonesia.[33] Other countries include Guatemala, Costa Rica, Uganda, China, India, Papua New Guinea, Tonga, Fiji, Tahiti, and the Philippines. The Madagascar variety is commonly known as Bourbon or Madagascar vanilla, and is considered to be the highest quality. There are also Mexican and Tahitian versions, which have their own distinctive flavor and aroma qualities.

Once the flower is pollinated, it develops a pod, 8 to 12 inches long, containing the vanilla bean, which after picking undergoes a fermentation process developed originally by the Aztecs (referred to as the *Mexican process*). This begins by soaking the beans (stripped from the pod) in hot water, then removing them and allowing them to dry during the day. The beans are covered with blankets at night to allow them to sweat. This continues for up to 10 days and concludes when the beans turn dark brown and develop a white crystalline coating on the surface. This substance is vanillin, the compound that gives vanilla its characteristic aroma and flavor. It is the result of naturally induced enzymatic breakdown by beta-glucosidase (enzyme) of the compound glucovanillin into vanillin and sugar. While most flavor scientists attribute the source of the enzyme to some strain of bacteria, the specific microorganism responsible for the fermentation of vanilla beans is unknown. At the conclusion of the fermentation process, the beans are dried for three to four weeks, dropping the moisture content from 60 to 70 percent to 25 to 30 percent. Finally, the beans are aged in airtight boxes for several months to intensify their aroma and flavor.

Vanilla extract, the most popular form of vanilla used today, is made by steeping the aged vanilla beans in a 35 percent alcohol and water solution (13.35 ounces of vanilla beans per gallon is the Standard of Identity set by the FDA for pure vanilla). In the industry, this is known as single-fold vanilla. *Fold* refers to the relative measure of strength of vanilla extract. Single-fold vanilla is typically what the consumer buys at the supermarket. For food processors, two-, three-, or four-fold vanillas are typically used. Where single-fold vanilla contains the extractive matter of 13.35 ounces of vanilla beans, two-fold uses 26.7 ounces of vanilla beans, contains twice as much extractive matter, and is twice as strong. Three-fold and four-fold are 3 and 4 times the content of single-fold. In addition, both whole and ground pods are commercially available, as is vanilla paste (vanilla seeds suspended in thick syrup).

In addition to its use as a characterizing flavor (the flavor named on the food package—for example, vanilla ice cream, vanilla wafers), vanilla is an effective potentiator (enhancer) for many other flavors. Typically used at low, even subliminal doses, vanilla boosts chocolate, coffee, and nut flavors as well as fruit flavors. When used with citrus flavors, it tends to cover the acid bite and makes them seem quite creamy. That said, the dairy industry uses a large percentage of the world's vanilla in ice creams, yogurt (fresh and frozen), and other flavored dairy products. Despite all the wonderful ice cream choices available in the market place, vanilla is still the number one flavor.[34]

It is important to note that the vast majority of vanilla-flavored products actually contain synthetic vanillin, which is much cheaper than the real thing. Culinology® professionals should be careful to purchase vanilla extract labeled "pure" if that is what they are looking for. If the product is labeled "vanilla flavoring," it is a mixture of pure and imitation vanilla extracts.

⬤Biotechnology Applications in Fermentation

Fermentation is also used to develop food ingredients previously made by chemical reactions. Moving to a biological approach has made it possible to simplify manufacturing and produce cleaner labels.

Vitamin Production

Vitamin B_2 (riboflavin) is essential for growth and the production of red blood cells, and for the absorption of iron and vitamin B_6. Traditionally it was produced from glucose following a complex multi-step chemical process. Recently it has been produced using fermentation in a one-step process where vegetable oil is converted by a specific yeast to produce vitamin B_2. This has greatly improved the ecological and environmental impact in terms of raw material toxicity, performance, emissions reduction, and waste disposal.[35]

Industrial Chemicals

Citric acid, commonly used as an acidifier and flavoring, especially in beverages, is a six-carbon tricarboxylic acid first isolated from lemon juice. It is commercially produced by the fermentation of molasses with the mold *Aspergillus niger*. After the mold is filtered out of the fermentation liquid, the citric acid is separated by precipitation with lime (calcium hydroxide) to produce a calcium citrate salt. The salt is treated with sulfuric acid to generate the citric acid. This process has been in use since the early 1900s.

Lactic acid can, of course, be produced by the fermentation of carbohydrates using many strains of bacteria. However, the most common method, on an industrial scale, uses yeast, not bacteria. In 1994, a method for the production of lactic acid was introduced using a strain of *Saccharomyces cerevisiae* that was metabolically engineered to produce lactic acid rather than ethanol from sugar. Lactic acid is used in foods and beverages as a pH regulator or as a preservative. It is also used as a flavoring agent.

Xanthan gum, heavily used in the food industry as a thickener and a stabilizer system in foods such as pickle relish and sauces, is the most important microbial polysaccharide-derived hydrocolloid, and it is widely used in other areas, such as the pharmaceutical industry. It is made from the fermentation of corn sugar by a strain of bacteria, *Xanthomonas campestris*, known to cause black rot on broccoli, cauliflower, and other leafy vegetables. This bacterium forms a slimy coat during fermentation that has the same characteristics as gelatinized cornstarch. This substance is isolated, filtered, and dried to yield the product known as xanthan gum.

⬤Conclusion

The field of fermentation technology has opened a new era in the development of world-class foods and ingredients that will be used to enhance our lives for years to come. It seems a long way from its prehistoric start, but the process of fermentation is still the same. The only differences are the organisms and the substrates acted on. It is up to Culinology® researchers to continue this evolution as we move into the future.

[1] P. E. McGovern, *Ancient Wine: The Search for the Origins of Viniculture* (Princeton, NJ: Princeton University Press, 2003), 7.

[2] K. H. Steinkraus, ed., *Handbook of Indigenous Fermented Foods* (New York: Marcel Dekker, 1995).

[3] L. Ziedrich, *Joy of Pickling* (Boston: Harvard Common Press, 1998), 4.

[4] H. McGhee, *On Food and Cooking: The Science and Lore of the Kitchen*, rev. ed. (New York: Scribner, 2004), 517.

[5] Steinkraus, *Handbook of Indigenous Fermented Foods*.

[6] P. Debré and F. Elbong, *Louis Pasteur* (Baltimore: JHU Press, 2000), 106–107.

[7] M. Battcock and S. Azam-Ali, "Fermented Fruits and Vegetables: A Global Perspective," *FAO Agricultural Services Bulletins* 134, ch. 5, part 5.7.1 (1998).

[8] M. J. Pelczar and R. D. Reid, *Microbiology*, 3rd ed. (New York: McGraw-Hill, 1972), 116.

[9] M. Selig M., K. Xavier K., H. Santos H., and P. Schönheit, "Comparative Analysis of Embden-Meyerhof and Entner-Doudoroff Glycolytic Pathways in Hyperthermophilic Archaea and the Bacterium Thermotoga," *Archives of Microbiology* 167 (1997): 217–232.

[10] www.ILovePickles.org (2013).

[11] R. Buescher, M. Hudson, and J. Adams, "Inhibition of Polygalactouronase Softening of Cucumber Pickles by Calcium Chloride," *Journal of Food Science* 44, no. 6 (1979): 1786–1787.

[12] J. G. Holt, et al., eds., *Bergey's Manual of Determinative Bacteriology*, 9th ed. (Baltimore, MD: Lippincott Williams & Wilkins, 2000).

[13] Battcock and Azam-Ali, "Fermented Fruits and Vegetables."

[14] McGhee, *On Food and Cooking*.

[15] Steinkraus, *Handbook of Indigenous Fermented Foods*.

[16] A. Haug, A. T. Høstmark, and O. M. Harstad, "Bovine Milk in Human Nutrition: A Review," *Lipids in Health and Disease* 6 (2007): 25, 34.

[17] D. B. Fankhauser, *Ricotta Making Illustrated* (2006), retrieved October 8, 2009, from http://biology.clc.uc.edu/fankhauser/Cheese/Ricotta/ricotta_00.hym.

[18] J. Lablee, "Cheese Manufacture," in *Cheesemaking: Science and Technology* (New York: Lavoisier, 1987), 406–412.

[19] Ibid.

[20] McGhee, *On Food and Cooking*.

[21] K. Incze, "Raw Fermented and Dried Meat Products," *Fleischwirtsch* 72, no. 1 (1992): 58.

[22] http://www.fsis.usda.gov/wps/wcm/connect/ca7ffa3c-f9ee-4eae-94ee-bddfae623fda/33_IM_RTE_SS_Process.pdf?MOD=AJPERES\.

[23] Retrieved October 8, 2009, from http://www.nysaes.corness.edu/necfe/.

[24] "Production of Fermented Sausages with Chr. Hansen Starter Cultures," *BactofermTM Meat Manual* (2003), 135–143.

[25] J. D. Owens and L. S. Mendoza, "Enzymatically Hydrolyzed and Bacterially Fermented Fishery Products," *Journal of Food Technology* 20, no. 30 (1985): 273–293.

[26] C. S. Pederson, *Microbiology of Food Fermentations* (Westport, CO: AVI Publishing, 1971), 110.

[27] M. Griffin, "Coffee Processing" (1999), retrieved August 20, 2009, from http://www.coffeeresearch.org/agriculture/processing.htm.

[28] "Coffee Trade Statistics," retrieved October 21, 2009, from http://www.ncausa.org.

[29] S. Fallon and M. Enig, "Cinderella's Dark Side," *Nexus* 7, no. 3 (April-May 2000): 1–3.

[30] K. Shiroki, "Benefits of Natto" (2003), retrieved September 9, 2009, from http://www.gala21.net/natto/benefits.htm.

[31] T. Yokotsuka, "Fermented Protein Foods in the Orient, with Emphasis on Shoyu and Miso in Japan," in *Microbiology of Fermented Foods* vol. 1, B. B. Wood, ed. (London: Elsevier Applied Sciences, 1985), 197–247.

[32] http//www.kikkoman.com/soysaucemuseum/index.shtml.

[33] http://faostat.fao.org/site/339/default.aspx.

[34] http://vanilla.servolux.nl/vanilla_facts.html.

[35] E. J. Van Damme, ed., *Biotechnology of Vitamins, Pigments and Growth Factors* (London: Elsevier Science Publishers Ltd., 1989).

12 | Food Additives

Lead Author: Andres V. Ardisson Korat, MS, CCS®, Graduate Student, Harvard University

Melissa Haupt, CRC®, CEC, Executive Research Chef, Applebee's

Jerome Lombardo, Certified Flavor Chemist

●Introduction

There are thousands of ingredients used to make foods. Food additives cover a wide range of nutritive and non-nutritive substances that are added to foods to improve or modify their characteristics and properties. Their use is regulated under the Code of Federal Regulations, Title 21 (CFR 21 170.3) of the U.S. Food and Drug Administration (FDA), which defines their nature, proposed use, and application levels. The FDA approves the safety of all food ingredients, but it is the manufacturer's responsibility to prove to the FDA that any new additive (or an approved one used in a novel application) is safe. This legislation does not apply to the 373 generally recognized as safe (GRAS) products that do not require prior FDA approval because they have already been judged safe through decades of commercial usage. Some of the materials on the list are quite well known, such as soy sauce, guar gum, and sugar; others, such as sodium ferricitropyrophosphate (used to fortify the iron content of foods), are probably unrecognizable by the general public but well known to food scientists and government regulators. The Food and Drug Administration (FDA) maintains a list of more than 3000 ingredients in its database "Everything Added to Food in the United States." In this chapter, we have only included a representative assortment of food additives that are most commonly encountered by the product developer. The complete list is available on FDA's website.

●Food Additives for Function

According to FDA regulations, the purposes of food additives must fall into one (or more) of the following categories:

- Improve the appeal of foods by improving their flavor, smell, texture, or color.

- Extend storage life.
- Maximize performance.
- Protect nutrient value.

Their typical application level usually ranges from a few parts per million (ppm) to 1 to 2 percent.

Sequestrants and Antioxidants

Sequestrants and antioxidants help prevent the oxidation (breakdown by exposure to oxygen) of foods. Oxygen can cause many problems in a wide variety of food products. It can trigger enzymatic browning in fruits and vegetables, fading of color pigments such as carotenoids, and rancidity in fats and oils through the degradation reactions commonly referred to as autoxidation.

Sequestrants bind free metal ions to prevent them from catalyzing the oxidation reaction. Many metal ions naturally present in foods (such as iron in meat products and magnesium in vegetables) can be released during processing. Sequestrants are chelating agents, which trap metal ions, preventing them from taking part in the reaction. Natural sequestrants include malic, tartaric, phosphoric, and citric acids. Of the natural sequestrants, phosphoric and citric acids are used the most in food systems, especially beverages. Remember when determining use rates that these are acids and as such contribute sourness to the finished product. Taste as you go.

One of the best-known synthetic chelating agents used is EDTA (ethylenediamine-tetraacetic acid). It promotes color retention in dried bananas, canned beans and chickpeas, canned clams, pecan pie filling, frozen potatoes, and canned shrimp. It improves flavor retention in canned carbonated beverages, salad dressings, mayonnaise, margarine, and sauces. It inhibits rancidity in vegetable oils, salad dressings, mayonnaise, sauces, and sandwich spreads. EDTA salts are used in foods at levels ranging from 33 to 800 ppm (800 ppm = 0.08 percent).

Antioxidants hinder the binding of oxygen to prevent enzymatic browning in fruits and vegetables. They do this by scavenging oxygen free radicals to slow the rate of reaction. In the simplest form of this process, lemon or pineapple juice is used to prevent the enzymatic browning of avocado slices or cut apples. Lemon juice contains ascorbic acid (vitamin C), which acts as a barrier between the oxygen and the food product. The oxygen binds with the ascorbic acid, oxidizing it instead of the food pigment.[1] In larger-scale food processing operations, ascorbic acid is added to fruit syrups and used to coat the outside of cut vegetables to prevent browning. Pineapple juice also works as an antioxidant because its sulfhydryl group can bind with oxygen.[2] In a bench or kitchen setting, a 3:1 ratio of water to pineapple juice works well on cut fruits and vegetables, though its use is restricted in commercial products because of some people's sensitivity to sulfites.

To prevent lipid oxidation in foods from meat products to nuts, developers add natural polyphenolic compounds such as tocopherols (vitamin E) and synthetic phenolic antioxidants such as BHA (butylated hydroxyanisole). These are used in a variety of food products, from potato chips and crackers to polyunsaturated oils, chicken nuggets, and precooked hamburgers. The antioxidant gives up its own hydrogen atoms to the double bonds of the unsaturated fatty acids—essentially a small-scale hydrogenation—to halt autoxidation. When choosing an antioxidant, it is important to consider labeling, cost, and impact on the flavor and shelf life of the product.

FIGURE 12.1 **FDA maximum permitted levels of antioxidants in various food products.**

Type of Food	Parts per Million (allowed of total BHA or BHT alone or in combination to be added)
Dehydrated potato shreds	50
Active dry yeast	1000 (BHA only)
Beverages and desserts prepared from dry mixes	2 (BHA only)
Dry breakfast cereals	50 (BHA only)
Dry glazed fruit	32 (BHA only)
Dry mixes for beverages and desserts	90 (BHA only)
Emulsion stabilizers for shortening	200
Potato flakes	50
Potato granules	10
Sweet potato flakes	50

Source: FDA, 21 CFR 172.110.

Synthetic antioxidants approved for use in food include BHA, BHT (butylated hydroxytoluene), TBHQ (tertiary-butyl hydroquinone), and PG (propyl gallate). BHA is a waxy white solid that is soluble in fats and oils but not water, and prevents color and flavor fading in essential oils.[3] BHT is a white crystalline fat-soluble solid more effective in animal fats than vegetable oils. TBHQ is a white-to-tan colored powder that is most effective in preventing autoxidation in frying oils. PG is not effective at high temperatures, so it is used primarily in dried or fresh meat applications. These four can also be combined to work synergistically. For example, BHT and BHA in combination are more effective in nut products than either is alone. Synthetic antioxidants are usually more cost-effective than natural ones, and often more reliable, consistent, and easier to use. However, synthetic antioxidants are regulated by the FDA with maximum levels allowed in food, and they must be listed on product labels, which some consumers perceive negatively.

Antioxidants can also be used in food packaging to prolong shelf life; BHT is commonly used in the bags or liners inside breakfast cereal boxes to prevent oxidation. Antioxidant packaging provides a controlled release of the antioxidant to maintain a constant level over time so excessive additives are not in the food.

Among the natural antioxidants, mixed tocopherols are commonly used. These are eight naturally occurring compounds (a mixture of tocopherols and tocotrienols) related to vitamin E that are commercially extracted from vegetable oils. They can be used in both vegetable and animal fat applications at a maximum level of 0.03 percent of the fat content, according to U.S. Department of Agriculture (USDA) guidelines. Not all of the tocopherols have the same antioxidant powers. High-alpha species are usually used in vitamins, while the low-alpha type have better antioxidant abilities in food.[4] Both tocopherols and the synthetic antioxidants behave in similar ways, though tocopherols can stand high-heat processing better because they are less volatile. Tocopherols also have the benefit of being recognized by the consumer as vitamin E, so there is the perception of a cleaner label.

Herbs and spices such as clove, sage, oregano, rosemary, and garlic also show some success as antioxidants. The raw spices seem to be more effective than their extracts. That said, the flavors and odors they impart can be unwanted in some applications.[5] Deodorized versions of sage, rosemary, and garlic extracts are heavily used in the poultry industry. Rosemary extract especially is widely used across the meat industry, not only in poultry products but in fully cooked beef and pork, to prevent meat flavor deterioration (MFD) or warmed-over flavor (WOF). MFD produces flavors that are perceived as off, like cardboard or refrigerated taste, caused by oxidation of fats when a meat product is cooked, cooled, and reheated.

Herb and spice extracts also have the advantage of being recognizable by consumers on labels. Spice extracts can be used in combination with all other antioxidants and are not limited in the amounts that can be added to foods.

FIGURE 12.2 **Amounts of antioxidants allowed in meat products.**

Type of Meat Product	BHA/BHT/PG/TBHQ*	Tocopherols
Dry sausage	0.003% based on total weight or 0.006% total if combined with another antioxidant	0.003% based on fat content weight; not to be used in combination with other antioxidants
Rendered animal fats or combination with vegetable fat	0.01% of finished product or 0.02% if combined with another antioxidant	0.03% not to be used in combination with other antioxidants
Fresh pork sausage, cooked beef patties, pizza toppings	0.01% based on fat content or up to 0.02% if combined with another antioxidant	0.003% based on fat content weight; not to be used in combination with other antioxidants
Dried meats	0.01% of total weight of the product alone or in combination with another antioxidant	0.003% based on fat content weight; not to be used in combination with other antioxidants
Poultry products	0.01% based on total fat content or 0.02% if used in combination	0.03% based on total fat content or 0.02% if used in combination with another antioxidant except TBHQ

*TBHQ is only allowed to be used in combination with BHA or BHT or a combination of the two.
Source: FDA, 9 CFR 424.21.

Bulking Agents

Bulking agents are used to replace or create bulk in reduced-sugar and reduced-fat food products, and as fillers to dilute extremely concentrated ingredients like high-intensity sweeteners and flavors. In regular confectionary products, sugar and corn syrup represent most of the bulk (body) of the product. Therefore, when creating a sugar-free or artificially sweetened product, a bulking agent must be added to replace the volume of sugar omitted. Sugar alcohols, also called polyols (sorbitol and lactitol are two examples), are used as bulking agents in conjunction with high-intensity sweeteners in sugar-free confectionery products. Bulking agents such as maltodextrins (white, powdered, digestible carbohydrates made from cornstarch; may be moderately sweet or virtually flavorless) are also used as diluents with high-intensity sweeteners to create products such as Splenda® (the combination of sucralose and maltodextrin) to make the product equivalent in weight and sweetness to table sugar.[6] Maltodextrins are also commonly used in the flavor industry for diluting extremely concentrated flavors to make them easier to use; they also work as an absorbent plating medium to convert liquid flavor oils into free-flowing powders. They are also used to provide bulk in packaged dry mixes, especially in single-serve soup, sauce and gravy packets, and beverage envelopes.

Polydextrose is a bulking agent that is an indigestible synthetic polymer synthesized from dextrose (glucose), plus about 10 percent sorbitol and 1 percent citric acid. Polydextrose is commonly used as a replacement for sugar, starch, and fat in commercial beverages, cakes, candies, breakfast cereals, dessert mixes, frozen desserts, puddings, and salad dressings. Polydextrose solutions are slightly more viscous than sucrose at the same concentrations; thus, they are a useful substitute in sugar-free syrups, where viscosity similar to sucrose is desired. Polydextrose is also used as a humectant (a hygroscopic substance that helps keep moisture in foods), stabilizer, and thickening agent. Its use is restricted in the United States by the CFR, and, as with many sugar alcohols, more than 15 g per serving can cause gastrointestinal distress in some individuals.

Bulking agents made from carbohydrates and proteins are also used to replace fat in fat-free products. Carbohydrates are used most frequently because of their lower cost. The functional properties carbohydrates provide as fat replacers include gelling, thickening, and stabilization. Starches such as pre-gelatinized waxy cornstarch are used in low-fat muffins and pastries for their ability to form gels that mimic the mouthfeel of fat. Maltodextrins are used in cold applications like salad dressings because they provide a smooth mouthfeel without much impact on taste. Fiber is also used because it provides structure, stability, and volume in baked goods and beverages, and it is perceived as a healthy ingredient. Sugar alcohols and hydrocolloids can also be used as bulking agents to replace fat in frozen desserts, salad dressings, and chewing gums.

Proteins can also be used as bulking agents, either alone or blended with other ingredients. Whey, including refined products such as whey protein concentrates and whey protein isolates, provides some of the functions of fat in systems. Whey can also act as an emulsifier with gelling applications in mayonnaise-type products, salad dressings, and frostings. Products like Simplesse® are microparticulated proteins (MPP), which refers to the small particle size (about 1 micron in diameter) of the protein. The Simplesse® particle size allows it to behave almost identically to fat globules. Microparticulated whey proteins behave like fats and can be used as fat substitutes in dairy product such as cheese, creamy desserts, and ice cream, where they greatly improve texture and taste.

Colors

Colorants in food products influence the preferences of consumers. Colorants are added to prevent color loss due to exposure to air, light, and moisture through processing or storage; to give consistency to products with natural color variances; to make a product more visually appealing; and to add color to a usually colorless product (like pink to marshmallow bunnies) to increase consumer appeal. Colorants can

FIGURE 12.3 Examples of bulking agents and usage areas.

Type of Bulking Agent	Example of Product	Usage
Polyols	Many brands	(1.5–3 kcal/g) Used to replace bulk in fat-free products
Maltodextrin can be made from corn, tapioca, or rice solids	Maltrin® GPC	(4 kcal/g) To increase volume in low-fat applications such as fat-free deserts or other cold applications
Polydextrose	Litesse® Danisco	(1 kcal/g) Used in cakes, chocolates, hard candies, and beverages
Starches from potato, corn, rice, oats, wheat, and tapioca	Stellar® Staley	(1–4 kcal/g) Used as fat replacers, texture modifiers, and bulking agents in frostings, sauces, meats, dairy products, and baked goods
Powdered cellulose	Justfiber® International Fiber Products	(0 kcal/g) Used in breads, cakes, cheese, and salad dressings
Microparticulated protein (whey protein or egg protein)	Simplesse® NutraSweet Co.	(2 kcal/g) Used to increase volume in low-fat applications such as fat-free desserts or other cold applications

Source: Vaclavik and Christian (2008).[7]

be classified as natural colors, which are pigments naturally extracted from plants and animals, and synthetic colors, which are designated FD&C (Food, Drug, and Cosmetic) and therefore regulated by the FDA. Synthetic colors can be further classified into dyes, which are water-soluble, and lakes, which are oil-soluble and are called FD&C aluminum lakes.[8] Dyes are used to color beverages, mixes, and dairy products. Lakes are used to color dry ingredients and foods with a high fat content.

Natural Colors

Natural colors are typically less stable and less consistent than their synthetic counterparts, and usually more expensive. However, the recent trend toward cleaner labels is the main driver for their increasingly widespread use. Although natural colors are sourced from nature, the addition of any color to food is considered artificial by the FDA, and therefore products that contain them cannot claim to be made with natural colors on the label. Instead, they must be labeled by name: annatto, caramel, and so on (CFR 21 70.3). Regardless, the increasing consumer rejection of artificial colors often makes using the natural ones a more acceptable choice.

The main color substance in annatto is the carotenoid pigment bixin, found in the coating of the annatto seed *Bixa orellana* (CFR 21 70.30). It is primarily soluble in fat, although it is also available in a water-dispersible form.[9] Its color varies from yellow to orange, depending on the application level. It provides good color intensity and is stable to oxidation, pH changes, and temperature. Annatto exhibits poor stability to light.[10] It is widely used in cheese production, providing Cheddar and American cheeses with their characteristic yellow hue. It can be used in cheese sauces and other products where a yellow color is desired, such as margarine (which is white in its native state), packaged yellow rice mixes, packaged custard powder, and smoked fish.

Beet color or beet juice is extracted from red beets and is composed of betalains, water-soluble pigments that exhibit a deep red-purple color in acidic conditions (pH < 6) but become blue when the pH is neutral to alkaline.[11] The most heavily studied betalain is betanin, also called *beetroot red*. Betanin degrades when subjected to light, heat, and oxygen; therefore, it is used in frozen products, products with short shelf life, and dry products. Betanin can survive pasteurization when used in products with high sugar content. The most common uses of betanin are in coloring ice cream and powdered soft-drink beverages; other uses are in sugar confectionery—for example, fondants, sugar coatings, and fruit or cream fillings. Betanin is also used for coloring meat, bacon, and sausages as well as frozen soups and tomato products.

A precursor of vitamin A, beta-carotene provides yellow to orange color with good color intensity. It has good stability to pH changes, fair stability to light, and poor stability to oxidation and microbial attack, which cause color loss. It is insoluble in water, but oil-dispersible forms are available. It is used in margarine, cheese, oils, and products with high oil content at relatively neutral pH levels.[12] It can also be used in emulsion form to color beverages, syrups, dairy products, and ice cream, and in dry form in instant drink powders, baked goods, and pasta.

Caramel color is the world's most widely used food colorant. It provides yellow to reddish-brown to dark brown color in many foods and beverages, including colas, cocoa, soy sauce, cereals, breads, sauces, gravies, candies, dairy products, beer and other alcoholic beverages, and many others. It can be produced from the controlled caramelization (heat-induced browning involving pyrolysis) of a range of sugars and starch hydrolysates (CFR 21 73.85), but is most commonly prepared using high-dextrose corn syrup. It is water soluble and available in liquid and spray-dried forms. It is stable to light, oxidation, pH, and temperature.[13] However, it loses color in response to microbial attack.

The four classes of caramel color are distinguished by the additives used in their preparation. The first one (I) is not made using sulfites or ammonia and is therefore the most natural form, but it has the least stability. That said, because of its naturalness, it is used most widely. The second class (II) allows the use of sulfites but not ammonium salts, and is commonly used in tea, whiskey, and brandy. The third one (III) allows the use of ammonium compounds but not sulfites, and is used in confections, bakery products, beer and soy sauce.[14] The fourth form (IV) allows both additives, which makes it suitable for acidic applications, such as cola beverages.

Chlorophyll is a natural green color present in all green plants and algae, but it is primarily extracted from spinach and alfalfa with non-polar food-grade solvents such as alcohols and acetone.[15] A common form is sodium copper cholorophyllin, made by substituting the magnesium ion with copper to improve light stability, which is allowed for use in food. It can be used in dry beverage mix applications where a green color is desired (CFR 73.125).

Cochineal is a pigment extracted from the dry bodies of the insect *Dactylopius coccus costa,* which lives on cacti growing in Mexico and South America (Peru is the largest exporter). It takes 155,000 insects to manufacture 1 kg dye. The active water-soluble substance is carmine.[16] It displays a color ranging from deep orange to red. Cochineal is one of the few water-soluble colorants that resist degradation with time. It is one of the most light- and heat-stable and oxidation-resistant of all the natural organic colorants and is even more stable than many synthetic food colors, but it is sensitive to pH changes below 3.0, and it loses intensity when attacked by microbes. It is used in a wide range of foods, including candy, baked goods, juices, yogurts, surimi, marinades, alcoholic drinks, bakery products, cookies, icings, pie fillings, jams, preserves, gelatin desserts, and Cheddar cheese and other dairy products. Because this pigment is derived from an insect source, it cannot be used in kosher or vegan foods.

An FDA rule effective January 5, 2011, requires all foods and cosmetics containing cochineal to declare it on their ingredient labels (CFR 21 73.100).

Turmeric is a colorant extracted from the turmeric root (*Curcuma longa*). Curcumin is the main pigment in the extract (CFR 21 73.600). It provides a yellow to yellow-orange color and is soluble in water. Turmeric has moderate stability to oxidation and poor stability to light and pH changes but great heat stability.[17] It is used in canned beverages and baked products, dairy products, ice cream, yogurt, popcorn color, cake icings, cereals, sauces, gelatins, and so on. It is a primary ingredient in curry powder and is used in prepared foods such as rice dishes.

Synthetic Colors

Dyes and lakes are complex organic chemicals that were originally derived from coal tar but now are made from petroleum. Food companies like using them because they are cheaper, more stable, and brighter than most natural colorings. However, there is ongoing concern that consumption of synthetic dyes may have adverse effects, especially on children whose diets may include a large number of highly colored foods such as breakfast cereals, snack cakes, and candies. Dyes have been blamed for increasing rates of attention deficit disorder, hyperactivity, learning difficulties, and allergies. In addition, consumers' growing preference for natural foods is leading some companies to either not add colorings at all or to switch to natural colorings.

Unlike other food additives, dyes may not be used unless the FDA has tested and certified that each batch meets legal specifications (colors from natural sources are exempt from certification). One benefit of the certification process is that it provides information about the amounts of dyes sent into commerce each year for use in foods, drugs, and cosmetics. Just three dyes—Red 40, Yellow 5, and Yellow 6—account for 90 percent of all dyes used. The FDA's data show a dramatic five-fold increase in consumption of dyes since 1955. That increase is a good indication of how Americans increasingly have come to rely on processed foods, such as soft drinks, breakfast cereals, candies, snack foods, baked goods, frozen desserts, and even pickles and salad dressings, that are colored with dyes.[21]

In the United States, seven artificial colorings are certified for use in food. All contain the prefix FD&C, which indicates approval for use in food, drugs, and cosmetics. These seven are known as primary colors; when they are combined to produce other colors, those colors are then known as secondary colors.

FIGURE 12.4 **Summary of properties of common natural colors.**

Name	Hue	Solubility	Heat Stability	Light Stability	pH Range
Annatto	Yellow to orange	Water and oil	Good	Poor	3.5–7.5
Beet color	Purple to red	Water	Poor	Good	2.5–6.0
Beta-carotene	Yellow to orange	Oil	Very good	Fair	3.5–7.0
Caramel color	Yellow to brown	Water	Very good	Very good	2.0–7.0
Chlorophyll	Green	Water	Very good	Very good	3.0–7.5
Cochineal/carmine	Orange to red	Water and oil	Very good	Very good	3.5–7.5
Turmeric	Yellow to orange	Water and oil	Very good	Poor	4.0–7.0

Sources: Igoe and Hui (2001)[18]; Fennema (2007)[19]; Francis (1999)[20].

FIGURE 12.5 Synthetic color substances and permitted levels.

Name	Common Name	Hue	Solubility in Water at 20°C (g/100 ml)	Heat Stability	Light Stability	pH Range
FD&C Red #3	Erythrosine	Blue-red	9	Moderate	Moderate	3.0–7.0
FD&C Red #40	Allura red	Red-yellow	22	Good	Very good	3.0–8.0
FD&C Yellow #5	Tartrazine	Yellow	20	Fair	Moderate	3.0–8.0
FD&C Yellow #6	Sunset yellow	Red-yellow	19	Fair	Moderate	3.0–8.0
FD&C Green #3	Fast green	Blue-green	20	Very good	Good	3.0–8.0
FD&C Blue #1	Brilliant blue	Green-blue	20	Good	Poor	5.0–7.0
FD&C Blue #2	Indigotine	Deep blue	1.6	Moderate	Poor	3.0–5.0

Sources: Igoe and Hui (2001)[29]; Fennema (2007)[30]; Francis (1999)[31].

FD&C Blue #1: Brilliant blue produces green to blue color with good pH stability under pH 7.[22] It displays poor light and oxidation stability and good heat stability. It is used in beverages, candies, and desserts (CFR 21 74.101).

FD&C Blue #2: Indigotine provides a deep blue with poor stability to light, oxidation, and pH but moderate stability to heat. It is used in candies and pet food (CFR 21 74.102).

FD&C Green #3: Fast green is a blue-green colorant with good heat and pH stability (3 to 8) but poor light and oxidation stability.[23] It is used in cereals, candies, beverages, ice cream, and baked goods (CFR 21 74.1203).

FD&C Red #40: Allura red produces a red-yellow hue with very good light stability, good stability in pH 3 to 8, moderate stability to oxidation, and good heat stability.[24] It has a wide range of applications, including candy, desserts, ice cream, and beverages (CFR 21 74.340).

FD&C Red #3: Erythrosine produces a high-intensity watermelon red color with moderate light and oxidation stability but poor stability to pH change; it is not recommended for use in low pH.[25] It is used in soft drinks, cereals, candies, popsicles, and cake-decorating gels. It is also used to color pistachio shells (CFR 21 74.1303). The lake form of Red #3 is the only lake not allowed for use in foods (since 1990, when it was identified as a carcinogen).

FD&C Yellow #5: Tartrazine is a yellow colorant with good stability to heat and to pH in the range of 3 to 8. Tartrazine has moderate light and oxidation stability.[26] It is used in beverages, candy, ice cream, and cereal (CFR 21 74.705). The dye form must be declared by name in the ingredient statement of the foods containing it because 1 in 10,000 people are highly sensitive to it.[27]

FD&C Yellow #6: Sunset yellow produces a red-yellow hue with good pH stability and moderate light and oxidation stability. It is used in beverages, desserts, and ice cream (CFR 21 74.706).[28]

Limited-Use Colors

The following dyes are allowed by the FDA for specific limited applications:

FD&C Orange B (red shade) is allowed only for use in hot dog and sausage casings. That said, batches of Orange B have not been certified for use in the past decade or longer (CFR 21 74.250).

FD&C Citrus Red 2 (orange shade) is allowed only to color the peels of oranges not used for processing into juice or other products. It must not penetrate into the pulp (CFR 21 74.302).

Emulsifiers

Emulsifiers are substances that reduce the surface tension between two immiscible phases, such as water and oil, allowing them to form an emulsion. The phases can be two liquids—again, such as oil and water—combined to make mayonnaise or oil-based flavor emulsions in soft drinks; a solid and a liquid, as in the case of butter; or a liquid and gas, as in foams (whipped cream, ice cream, and meringues). The most common emulsions in food products involve a water-soluble phase and an oil-phase that can form either an oil-in-water emulsion, such as mayonnaise or cream, or a water-in-oil emulsion, like butter.[33]

Emulsifier molecules have both a polar hydrophilic group and a non-polar hydrophobic group. These allow the molecules to interact with both polar (water-based) and non-polar (oil-based) phases. Many emulsifiers are modified triglyceride molecules, where one or more fatty acids are substituted by a polar end that depends on the emulsifier. When two of the three original fatty acids on the triglyceride molecule are left intact, the molecule is named diglyceride, and when only one remains, the molecule is a monoglyceride.[34]

Some of the main functions of emulsifiers include the inhibition of starch retrogradation in baked goods, which extends freshness by slowing staling; controlling fat crystallization in chocolates to prevent bloom; aiding in the dispersion of dry ingredients containing fat that are meant to dissolve in aqueous foods, such as whole milk powder and powdered coffee creamers; providing lubrication in confectionery processes to prevent sugar from sticking to equipment and tools; and aiding foam formation and stabilization in the production of ice creams and meringues. Here are some of the most commonly used emulsifiers:

FIGURE 12.6 Blends of artificial colorants (by weight to produce specific colors).

Color	Blue No. 1	Red No. 3	Red No. 40	Yellow No. 5	Yellow No. 6
Strawberry		5	95		
Raspberry	5	75			20
Lime green	3			97	
Mint green	25			75	
Orange			25	20	55
Grape	20		80		
Black cherry	5		95		
Butterscotch	3		22	57	18
Caramel	6	21		64	9
Cola	5		25		70
Chocolate	10		45	45	
Licorice (black)	36		22		42

Source: Francis (1999)[32].

- Citric acid esters are produced by reacting citric acid (polar end) with mono- and diglycerides. They are used as metal sequestrants more effectively than citric acid alone and as emulsifiers in shortening systems to aid in the incorporation of the aqueous and fat phases to form a stable water-in-oil emulsion.[36]
- DATEM (Diacetyl Tartaric Acid Esters of Mono- and Diglycerides) is a hydrophilic emulsifier used in oil-in-water emulsions and as a dough conditioner in breads and rolls, helping with softness, crust formation, and loaf volume. It is an important additive in the formulation of reduced-fat breads, where it strengthens the dough by interacting with gluten proteins and improving mouthfeel. Other food applications for DATEM include creamers and chocolates.[37]
- Lactic acid esters are manufactured by reacting stearic acid with lactic acid (polar end) and undergoing a reaction with sodium or calcium ions to form sodium

FIGURE 12.7 Emulsifier ambiphilic structure.

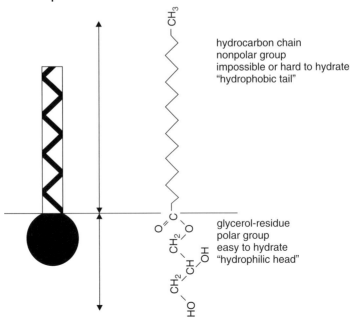

hydrocarbon chain
nonpolar group
impossible or hard to hydrate
"hydrophobic tail"

glycerol-residue
polar group
easy to hydrate
"hydrophilic head"

Source: Pomeranz (1985)[35].

stearoyl lactylate (SSL) or calcium stearoyl lactylate (CSL), the two most predominant forms used in food products.[38] They are used in baked products as dough conditioners, in aerated products to improve foam stability, and in creamers as emulsifiers.

- Lecithin (phosphatidyl choline) has great economic importance as an emulsifier and dispersing agent. Chemically, it is a major phospholipid component of all cell membranes, consisting of a mixture of choline phosphates, ethanolamine, and inositol as the polar groups with non-polar lipid structures (CFR 21 184.1400). Lecithin is commercially extracted from soybeans, although other sources, such as egg yolks, are also used; this is why mayonnaise contains egg yolk. There is enough lecithin in one egg yolk to emulsify 15 cups oil.[39] Lecithin is used in food applications such as margarine, chocolate, whole milk powder to aid dissolution in water, cocoa powders as a wetting agent (enhances the uniform suspension of cocoa particles throughout the milk or water phase), and in baked goods to preserve freshness and allow air incorporation.[40] It is also used in oil-based cooking sprays as a dispersant.

- Mono- and diglycerides are the most commonly used form of emulsifiers in food products. Monoglycerides (a single fatty acid on a glycerol backbone) are primarily lipophilic and are manufactured by the esterification of fatty acids with glycerol. The mixture is then distilled to obtain a >90 percent concentration of the monoglyceride form.[41] Depending on the characteristics of the attached fatty acid chain length and saturation level, they can be found as liquids or solids. They are used in a wide range of product applications, including ice cream, creamers, baked goods, shortening, and snack foods, at levels of 0.1 to 0.3 percent. Diglycerides are emulsifiers manufactured from the esterification of two fatty acids with glycerol or by the controlled interesterification of triglycerides with glycerol.[42] They are found in many bakery products, coffee creamers, peanut butter, and puddings. Using a combination of mono- and diglycerides allows the product developer to take advantage of both forms.

- Polyglycerol esters are made by reacting glycerol with fatty acids to form polymeric ester chains. They can be hydrophilic or lipophilic, depending on the extent of polymerization. They are used in icings, whipped products, and baked goods at application levels of 0.1 to 1 percent.

- Polysorbates (known commercially as Tween®) are a group of hydrophilic emulsifiers obtained by reacting sorbitan esters (made from sorbitol) with ethylene oxide. They are used in baked products, icings, coffee creamers (to reduce oil separation), coatings, and vitamin solubilization (fat-soluble vitamins in aqueous systems) at levels of 0.05 to 0.1 percent. The most common forms are polysorbate 60, 65, and 80 (CFR 21 172.836, 838, and 840).

- Sorbitan esters are lipophilic emulsifiers made from the reaction of sorbitol and stearic acid. They are used as emulsifiers, aerating agents in whipped products, and lubricants in baked goods.[43]

- Sucrose esters are produced by reacting sucrose with fatty acids. They are used in oil-in-water emulsions, such as dairy beverages, to control crystallization and as foaming agents. Sucrose esters are also used in baked products, frozen desserts, and dairy desserts.[44]

Phosphates

Phosphates, natural compounds of the element phosphorus, are among the most widely used food additives in processed foods. They are used in meat applications, cheese products, beverages, and bakery items, either alone or in combination with other products, to perform many functions.

In the meat industry, phosphates serve to increase water-holding capacity (WHC), extract muscle proteins, increase cook yield, reduce oxidative rancidity, preserve meat color, increase flavor retention, and reduce microbial growth. Their use is limited by the USDA to no more than 0.5 percent of the finished product. This is just as well, as excess phosphate addition can cause soapy flavors, rubbery texture, and poor color. Sodium tripolyphosphate (STPP), an alkaline phosphate, is the most commonly used phosphate in meats, valued for its cost-effectiveness and its relatively high solubility in water. Phosphates combined with salt increase the ionic strength of industrial meat brines and marinades, allowing for the extraction of the myofibrillar (salt-soluble) proteins by making them more soluble and better able to absorb and hold water. This also creates a sticky surface on the meat that helps bind pieces together to make formed meat products. Phosphates also interact with the proteins in meat emulsion products (hot dogs, bologna, and so on) as an emulsifying agent holding together the water, fat, and protein. Acidic or neutral phosphates include sodium hexametaphosphate (SHMP) and sodium acid pyrophosphate (SAPP). These contribute to the development and preservation of color in meat products and have a significant impact as sequestrants. SHMP binds readily with magnesium and calcium ions, which is beneficial when hard water is used in processing because it prevents these ions from catalyzing free radical formation and contributing to oxidation reactions. Combinations of phosphates are used to gain maximum water-holding capacity while maintaining color and the maximum sequestration impact.

When using any phosphate (or blend), always dissolve it in cold water before adding other ingredients. Phosphate is less successful at competing for water-binding sites, and other solutes (such as salt) block the phosphate from fully dissolving. If phosphates are not properly dissolved, they can create pockets of off colors and lead to reduced water-holding capacity in the product.

In processed cheese, phosphates such as SHMP and STPP are used as an emulsifying agent. By chelating the calcium bound to casein proteins, this increases their solubility and emulsifying properties, which helps stabilize the emulsion of water, fat, and proteins. They may be used at up to 3 percent in processed cheese but are usually used at lower levels (around 2 percent).[45]

In beverages such as colas, phosphoric acid is used to deliver a tart note without the fruity undertones found in

FIGURE 12.8 List of common phosphates and applications.

Phosphate Ingredient	Applications	Function
Sodium tripolyphosphate	Cheese powders, frozen vegetables, sausage, meat and poultry products, seafood	Protein and emulsion stabilizer, moisture binding, texture enhancement
Sodium hexametaphosphate	Canned milk, cheese, egg whites, frozen vegetables, meat and poultry products, seafood	Protein and emulsion stabilizer, moisture binding, texture modifier
Sodium acid pyrophosphate	Baking powder, sausage, frozen potato products, canned seafood	Leavening, emulsion stabilizer, color development, chelating agent for copper and iron to prevent discoloration
Phosphoric acid	Colas	Acidulant
Dipotassium phosphate	Creamers	Buffering agent
Sodium aluminum phosphate	Cake, breads, and batters	Leavening agent
Tetrasodium pyrophosphate	Milks, cheese, ice cream, sausage	Sustain ingredient distribution, protein and emulsion stabilizer
Tricalcium phosphate	Beverage mixes, fruit juices, cereals, grated cheeses	Anti-caking, fortification
Disodium phosphate	Milks, cheese, ice cream, dried pastas	Protein and emulsion stabilizer, decrease cooking times
Monocalcium phosphate	Baking powder, canned fruits and vegetables	Leavening, texture enhancement

Source: *Phosphate Facts* (2010)[48].

other acids. In creamers, dipotassium phosphate is used as a buffer for the dairy component to keep it from coagulating when mixed with the acids in coffee.[46]

Phosphates are also used heavily as processing aids in the starch industry. Starch manufacturers process native starches with phosphorus oxychloride or sodium trimetaphosphate.[47] The resulting modified starch is cross-linked, yielding a starch that stands up to shear, cooking, and low pH while maintaining better stability and increased gelatinization in comparison to native starches. Phosphates are also used in chemical leavening systems (see Figure 12.8).

Chemical Leavening Agents

The most widely recognized chemical leavener (from the Latin *levare*, "to rise") is baking powder. Chemical leavening agents work by combining an alkaline substance, such as sodium bicarbonate, or baking soda, with an acid component (see below) and mixing with water to create carbon dioxide gas in non-yeast-leavened batters and doughs. (Baking powder also contains cornstarch to prevent moisture in the air from being absorbed by the reactants so they don't react prematurely in the container.) The carbon dioxide gives baked products their lift and honeycomb structure.[49]

The four types of baking powder all contain starch and sodium bicarbonate but differ with regard to the acid ingredient:

1. Tartrate baking powders contain cream of tartar (tartaric acid). These were the earliest type and are known as single-action baking powders because they react immediately when wetted and go to completion quickly. If batters are not handled speedily, much of the rising action is spent by the time the product gets into the oven, resulting in heavy, fallen baked goods.

2. Phosphate baking powders contain calcium or sodium phosphate as the acid component. These better control the rate of carbon dioxide release so more is available to act in the oven.

3. Anhydrous phosphate baking powders contain anhydrous monocalcium phosphate as the acid, and the powder is treated to slow the rate at which it dissolves. Little carbon dioxide is generated during mixing; most is released early in the baking period. This type is primarily available for industrial use, where it is widely used in packaged mixes.

4. Sodium aluminum sulfate phosphate baking powders contain two acidic components. The phosphate component reacts quickly during mixing, while the sulfate requires the heat of baking in order to react. This is known as double-acting baking soda and is the most common type sold on the retail market.

Regardless of type, accurate measurement of baking powder is essential. Too little, and the end product is heavy and dense; too much leads to over-rising followed by collapse, coarse, loose texture, and off flavor from the baking powder.

FIGURE 12.9 **Properties of common leavening ingredients.**

Ingredient Type	Rate of Reaction	Neutralizing Value	Types of Products
Potassium hydrogen tartrate (cream of tartar)	Fast-acting acid—quickly releases carbon dioxide during mixing	45	Biscuits and batters where the product is cooked immediately after mixing. Limited use in commercial applications because of fast reaction rate and cost.
Monocalcium phosphate (MCP)	Fast acting	80	Used in snack products including crackers and cookies.
Sodium acid pyrophosphate (SAPP)	Fast to slow, available in different grades with different reaction times	72	Used in cake donuts and some cake mixes.
Sodium aluminum phosphate (SALP)	Slow acting	100	Most common leavening acid used in double-acting systems.

Source: Melissa Haupt, CRC®.

Antimicrobial Preservatives

Antimicrobial preservatives are antimicrobial agents that play an important role in preventing food spoilage and improving food safety. The most common category is the group of organic acids comprising benzoic acid, propionic acid, and sorbates, preservatives that have been used for decades.[50]

Benzoic acid is one of the most common antimicrobial agents used in the food industry. It occurs naturally in some fruits and spices but is commercially manufactured by chemical synthesis (CFR 21 184.1021). The undissociated hydrogen form is the active component in a pH range of 2.5 to 4.0, which makes it suitable for juices, soft drinks, pickled foods, jams, and fruit preparations.[51] The sodium salt (sodium benzoate) is water soluble; it converts to benzoic acid when in solution, which makes it preferable in many products. It is effective against mold, yeast, and some bacteria, and it is often used in combination with other preservatives, such as sorbic acid, at levels of 0.05 to 0.1 percent.

Propionic acid is commonly found in the form of sodium and calcium salts, and it is one of the characteristic acids and

flavors naturally found in ripened Swiss cheese. It is an effective antimicrobial agent against bacteria and molds because they cannot metabolize an acid that has a three-carbon chain length. Due to its acid nature, it can only be used environments where the pH is under 5.0 (CFR 21 184.1081). Propionic acid is used primarily in bakery items in concentrations up to 0.3 percent. The calcium form has little water solubility and is used on cheese surfaces and wrapping materials. The sodium salt is moderately soluble in water and is used in processed cheese products.

Sorbic acid is a preservative effective against yeast and molds in products whose pH is below 6.5. It is available as a water-soluble powder and can also be applied by spraying onto foods or the packaging material. It is not recommended for foods that undergo a significant heat treatment, as it can break down with heat. Potassium, sodium, and calcium salts are all available and are more soluble than sorbic acid, but their antimicrobial activity is narrower. Sorbic acid is used in processed cheese, beverages, pickled foods, and syrups at levels of 0.05 to 0.1 percent.[52]

Epoxides exhibit strong, broad-spectrum antimicrobial activity that targets both viruses and spores. Chemically, epoxides are cyclical ethers, of which the most common forms are propylene oxide and ethylene oxide, which is the strongest form.[54] They are applied in their vapor state, and the residue is removed by gas-flushing. They are used in the sterilization of low-moisture foods and packaging materials. Propylene oxide for food fumigation is regulated by CFR 40 part 185.15. It establishes a residue tolerance of 300 ppm (parts per million) for nutmeats, cocoa powder, and spices.

Lysozyme is a bacteriolytic enzyme naturally present in albumen (egg white), where it helps protect the developing egg from microbial attack. It is commercially produced from chicken eggs. Lysozyme is effective against the clostridia that cause *late blowing* in aged cheeses (a defect characterized by eyes, slits and cracks caused by the production of gas bubbles as well as abnormal cheese flavor from butyric acid) and helps prevent spoilage of wine by lactobacilli. It can also inhibit growth of gram-positive spoilage organisms and pathogens, including Listeria and *Bacillus cereus*.

Natamycin is an effective mold growth inhibitor when applied to the surface of products such as cheese. It is produced

FIGURE 12.10 **Effect of pH on dissociation of organic acids.**

pH	Sorbic	Benzoic	Propionic
3	98	94	99
4	86	60	88
5	37	13	42
6	6	1.5	6.7
7	0.6	0.15	0.7
(pKa)	4.67	4.19	4.87

Source: Hui (1992).[53]

by fermentation from the microorganism *Streptomyces natalensis*.[55] Natamycin is ideal for treating cheese because it does not have an antimicrobial effect on bacteria, allowing them to continue the process of cheese ripening.[56] In order to apply it, cheese is dipped in a solution of natamycin of 300 to 2000 ppm prior to packaging.

Nisin is a peptide with antimicrobial properties produced by fermentation from certain strains of *Streptococcus lactis*. Effective against the growth of *Clostridium botulinum*,[57] it is used in processed cheese products, processed fruits, and meats (CFR 21 184.1538).

Nitrites are the sodium and potassium salts of nitrous acid. Their main application is in cured meat products (bacon, ham, corned beef, and so on), where they form nitric oxide, which reacts with myoglobin to form nitroso-myoglobin, which gives cured hams and meat products their characteristic pink hue.[58] In addition to fixing the color, nitrites also act as a preservative, inhibiting the growth of Clostridium botulinum, and are effective in a pH range of 5.0 to 5.5. Nitrites in foods have the unfortunate ability to transform into nitrosamines when heated. These carcinogenic compounds have been found in all cured meats, fried bacon, and even beer (as a consequence of the malting process); as a result, the amount of nitrite added to cured meats is strictly regulated. It is now mandatory to add ascorbic acid (or erythorbic acid) to cured meats to inhibit nitrosamine formation.

Parabens are esters of benzoic acid, most commonly methyl and propyl esters. They are effective against yeast and molds over a wider pH range than benzoates and are stable to temperatures over 158°F (70°C). They are used in baked goods, candies, frozen dairy products, fruit juices, jellies and jams, marinated fish products, mayonnaise, mustard, processed vegetables, spicy sauces, beverages such as soft drinks, and syrups.[59]

Sulfur dioxide (SO_2) has been used in food products, particularly in the dehydrated fruit, molasses, and wine industries, for many years. In addition to inhibiting the growth of microorganisms, it also helps mitigate enzymatic and non-enzymatic browning reactions. Its use in foods is strictly regulated because sensitive asthmatics can have severe reactions to it (CFR 21 182.3862). Warning labels must be posted on all foods that contain it at greater than 10 ppm.

Cultured dextrose is a natural antimicrobial produced via the controlled fermentation of dextrose (sugar) with *Propionibacterium freudenreichii*. This bacterium is best known for its role in the creation of Swiss cheese. Propionibacteria are commonly found in milk and dairy products and have a long history of safe use in food. Cultured dextrose is an all-natural off-white powder containing short-chain organic acids and other natural fermentation-derived metabolites that prevent the growth of an assortment of bacteria, yeasts, and molds, thereby extending the shelf life of a wide range of foods, including baked goods, cheeses, meats, salad dressings, condiments, dips, spreads, and more. Cultured dextrose is a clean-label alternative to chemical preservatives like sorbates and benzoates.

●Flavors

As the server waves an entrée past your nose and places it in front of you, its aroma enters your nasal passages and you begin to identify the familiar smells. When you place that first forkful in your mouth, you smell the aroma again, and you begin to experience other sensations in your mouth: the sweetness and the tangy acidity of the sauce, the saltiness and umami of the meat, the mild bitterness of the seared meat or vegetables, and the pungency of peppers. You are experiencing *flavor*.

Many authors have tried to define flavor and achieved some agreement.[60] Flavor is the sum of a mixture of the sensory characteristics of a material taken into the mouth. It is composed of gustation, olfaction, and tactile or trigeminal sensations. Interestingly, flavor is 80 percent what we smell and only 20 percent what we taste.

Gustation includes the five basic tastes perceived on the tongue: sweet, salty, sour, bitter, and umami. Umami is the brothy, meaty, or savory taste of foods. It is the taste sensation activated when we eat something containing glutamates. Glutamates are the salt form of glutamic acid, an abundant, naturally occurring amino acid. One of the most common glutamate-containing ingredients is MSG (monosodium glutamate), but glutamates are also commonly found in dried mushrooms, aged cheese, sundried tomatoes, and many other foods. Although Kikunae Ikeda first identified umami in 1908, it was not until the late 1980s that it was generally accepted as the fifth basic taste.[61]

Olfaction is aroma, as perceived by sensory cells in the nasal cavity. As you bring food to your mouth, you first smell it through the nose, or orthonasally. Then, as you chew the food, the aroma passes through the retronasal passages near the back of the roof of the mouth and enters the nasal cavity from behind.

Trigeminal or pain/temperature stimuli include the temperature of the food, the heat of capsicum, and the cooling of menthol.

Flavorings or flavors are additives whose primary function is to provide or enhance the smell and taste stimuli received when eating. Product developers add flavorings to foods and beverages for many reasons. They may provide a characterizing or identifying flavor to an unflavored or mildly flavored base, such as most beverages, hard candies, surimi, or broths. Flavors can provide the developer with an easy way to create line extensions by "top noting" a common base (potato chips, for example) with an unlimited number of flavor profiles (Cajun, BBQ, Cilantro-Lime, etc.). They may enhance or stabilize a food's native taste to replace what is lost from processing, as in processed beef and poultry products. Some highly desirable ingredients are expensive, and flavors are economical extenders or substitutes. They can also replace or extend ingredients with inconsistent quality or ingredients that are not available year round. Agricultural food ingredients may become unavailable or expensive due to crop shortages, environmental problems, climatic problems, or political troubles. In 2008, lemon juice was in short supply due to freezing weather in California and Argentina and droughts in Spain and Australia.[62] To meet the demand for lemon juice, food manufacturers collaborated with flavor companies to find alternatives. These included sourcing lemon juice from uncommon regions, but also using less lemon juice and adding flavors and citric acid to augment the desired flavor profile, or using a de-flavored fruit juice and adding lemon flavor. Label constraints ("Contains 100 percent juice") often made it difficult to entirely replace the lemon juice.

Flavors can also be used to mask off notes or unpleasant flavors such as the grassy note of soy, the metallic taste of potassium chloride, and the chemical taste of synthetic sweeteners. In general, product developers use flavors to make foods and beverages more palatable, more desirable, and more pleasurable to the consumer.

Natural and Artificial Flavorings

The United States recognizes two classes of flavorings for FDA-regulated products: natural and artificial. Natural flavorings contain flavoring substances derived from spices and herbs, fruits or fruit juices, vegetables or vegetable extracts, edible yeast, meats, seafood, poultry, eggs, dairy products, or fermented products; their primary function in food is flavoring rather than nutrition.[63]

Artificial flavor ingredients are obtained through chemical synthesis and do not meet the above definition. When both natural and artificial flavorings are used in a food product, it must be labeled "Contains natural and artificial flavors."

A range of flavor titles is used depending on the presence of natural and/or artificial flavors and whether or not the characterizing food ingredient is present. The characterizing food ingredient is related to the title of the flavor; for example, strawberry in a strawberry flavor.

The USDA regulates meat and poultry products in the United States. Although it allows the use of the same ingredients approved by the FDA, the two agencies offer sharp differences in labeling policy. In general, the USDA requires the labeling of more ingredients, such as protein sources, some processing aids, and smoke flavorings, and it limits the use of binders, phosphates, nitrites, food acids, and colorants. Until recently, the USDA did not distinguish between natural and artificial flavors. In 1982, the USDA defined the term *natural* in Policy Memo 055. This was rescinded and refined in 2005. The USDA allows the use of the term *natural* under specific defined conditions, including that the product does not contain artificial flavors, colorings, chemical preservatives, or any other artificial or synthetic ingredients and that the product and its ingredients are minimally processed. This includes traditional processes, such as smoking, roasting, freezing, drying, and fermenting, and physical processes that do not fundamentally alter the raw product or that only separate a whole, intact food into component parts, such as grinding meat, separating eggs into albumen and yolk, and pressing fruits to produce juices.[64]

FIGURE 12.11 Common flavor titles chart.

Example of Flavor Titles Used	Meaning of the Flavor Title
Natural X Flavor	Contains food ingredient X and non-flavoring ingredients (solvents, carriers, processing aids, preservatives, etc.).
Natural X Flavor WONF	Contains food ingredient X, natural flavorings (other than X), and non-flavoring ingredients.
Natural Flavor (X Type)	Does not contain food ingredient X. Contains natural flavoring and non-flavoring ingredients.
Artificial X Flavor	Does not contain food ingredient X. Contains artificial flavoring and non-flavoring ingredients.
Natural and Artificial X Flavor	Contains food ingredient X, natural flavorings, artificial flavorings, and non-flavoring ingredients.
Natural and Artificial Flavor (X Type)	Does not contain food ingredient X. Contains natural flavorings, artificial flavorings, and non-flavoring ingredients.
Vanilla Flavor	Special labeling rules because vanilla has a standard of identity (Vanilla Extract, 21 C.F.R.§ 169.175 (2009)).

Source: Jerome Lombardo.

Unlike the FDA, the USDA requires that certain flavors be manufactured under inspection. Flavors containing >2 percent cooked meat, >3 percent raw meat, >10 percent poultry skin, >10 percent poultry fat, or >30 percent animal fat are considered amenable and require inspection. Certain combinations of these ingredients or the addition of broth may also render a flavor amenable.

More than 3000 ingredients are approved for use in flavorings. These include plant-derived extracts and distillates, food concentrates, dehydrated foods, hydrolyzed plant proteins, enzyme-modified cheeses, synthetic materials, and other food-derived ingredients. This wide range provides flavorists with the tools for creating an assortment of flavors for savory, dairy, confection, bakery, beverage, oral care, and pharmaceutical applications. Emerging market demands place greater restrictions on the ingredients and processes used to produce foods and food ingredients. These include organic foods, minimally processed and all-natural foods, genetically modified organism (GMO) -free, gluten-free, locally grown, vegetarian, vegan, and allergen-free. These limit the palette of ingredients available for flavor creation, but over time, suppliers develop new flavor ingredients to meet market demands.

FIGURE 12.12 **Glossary of common flavor ingredients.**

Ingredient	Definition
Absolutes	Produced by dissolving a concrete in alcohol, chilling, and filtering. The alcohol is removed by distillation. Waxes and resinous material are removed via this process.
Autolyzed yeast extracts (AYE)	Prepared by the aerobic fermentation of *Saccharomyces cerevisiae*, followed by autolysis and filtration to remove cell walls. The resulting product is concentrated and may be spray dried.
Concentrate	Juices from fruits and vegetables, concentrated by the removal of water.
Concretes	An extract of plants, typically flowers, prepared by solvent extraction followed by distillation of the solvent. A non-polar solvent is typically used.
EMC (enzyme-modified cheese)	Prepared by treating cheese or other dairy products with enzymes to break down fats and proteins. The enzymes are deactivated with heat, and the product may be dried. The resulting product is 8 to 15 times stronger than the original cheese.
Essential oil	The volatile oil obtained from plants. May be steam distilled (a heat process) or expressed (a cold process).
HPP (hydrolyzed plant protein)	Prepared by treating plant proteins (soy, corn, corn gluten, wheat, wheat gluten) with acid to break them down to amino acids and small peptides. Neutralized with alkali, filtered, and concentrated. May be dried by spray drying or vacuum drying.
HVP (hydrolyzed vegetable protein)	Same as HPP.
Oleoresins	Prepared by extracting the volatile and non-volatile components of an herb or spice with a solvent, followed by distillation of the solvent.
Resinoids	Prepared by solvent extraction of natural resins, followed by distillation of the solvent. Similar to concretes, but the starting material is a plant exudate.
Tinctures, fluid extracts, and solid extracts	A hydroalcoholic (water and alcohol) extract of a plant material. Solid extracts are further concentrated.
Yeast extracts	Same as autolyzed yeast extract (AYE).

Source: Jerome Lombardo.

Armed with this array of ingredients and processes, flavorists create flavorings by means of two methods: compounding and reactions. Compounded flavors are created by blending a range of aromatic ingredients to achieve a desired flavor profile. Reaction flavors, often called "processed flavors," are prepared by reacting or cooking flavor precursors to create the desired profile.

To create a compounded flavor, the flavorist uses a combination of ingredients, chemical analysis (using analytical tools such as gas chromatography and mass spectrometry), and creative skills developed over years of practical experience to select the best ingredients. A creative flavorist dissects a food into individual descriptors and then selects ingredients that match each descriptor. For example, a fresh tomato may be described as having fruity notes, floral notes, sulfur notes, and green notes. The flavorist selects ingredients that deliver each of these notes while meeting regulatory and other criteria.

When developing a processed flavor, the flavorist must consider not only the flavor precursors but also the temperature, pressure, pH, water activity, and reaction time of the process. Often, the flavor precursors include amino acids and reducing sugars, ingredients essential for the Maillard reaction (non-enzymatic browning) to occur. The Maillard reaction produces most of the common roasted flavors we recognize in meats, cereals, coffee beans, and chocolate. Other ingredients used in process flavor recipes include fats, oils, meats, dairy ingredients, enzymes, vegetables, yeasts, hydrolyzed vegetable protein (HVP), and solvents.

Flavorists often layer flavor components, much in the way a chef creates a culinary recipe. This is known as the flavor pyramid approach. The foundation (or base note) provides basic tastes and has little aroma—for example, the sweetness and sourness of a strawberry. The middle note contains ingredients that provide some aroma and impart more definition to the profile. Now the strawberry example tastes like a strawberry. The top note gives the flavoring greater definition, impact, and character. Using the strawberry example, the flavoring can be differentiated as a freshly picked mature strawberry, a slightly green strawberry, or a cooked, jammy strawberry.

Flavorings are available in liquid, paste, and powder forms. The most suitable form depends on stability or shelf life

FIGURE 12.13 The flavor pyramid.

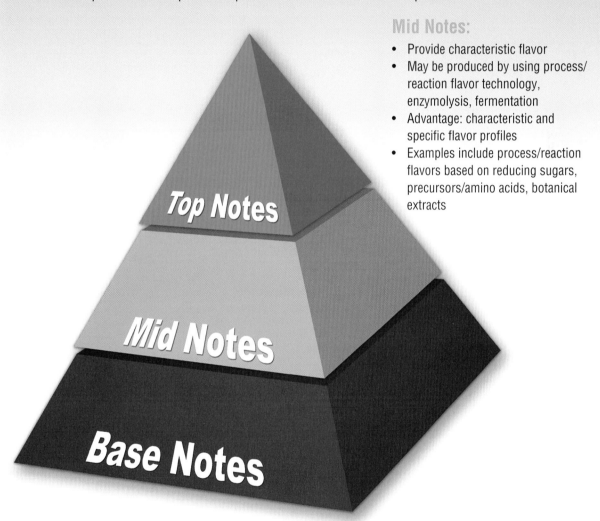

The Flavor Pyramid

Top Notes:

- Provide flavor character, differentiation, and flavor impact
- Produced by compounding aromatic flavor components; encapsulation is application dependent. May contain proprietary aroma chemicals.
- Advantage: Highly specific, intense
- Examples include compounded liquid flavors based on aromatic components

Mid Notes:

- Provide characteristic flavor
- May be produced by using process/reaction flavor technology, enzymolysis, fermentation
- Advantage: characteristic and specific flavor profiles
- Examples include process/reaction flavors based on reducing sugars, precursors/amino acids, botanical extracts

Base Notes:

- Provide body, general sweet notes, and/or flavor enhancement
- May be produced using enzymolysis, hydrolysis, fermentation, etc.
- Advantage: "clean label" declaration (natural), flavor enhancement, body-givers
- Examples include foods, juice and fruit purees, yeast extract

Source: Spicetec Flavors and Seasonings, Jerome Lombardo.

requirements, cost, and ease of use in the final product. Liquid flavors may be oil soluble or water soluble. Oil-soluble flavors are soluble in vegetable oils, usually in all proportions. Some of the solvents used in oil-soluble flavors include vegetable oils, benzyl alcohol (an excellent solvent that readily dissolves a wide range of flavor ingredients), and d-limonene (isolated from orange oil).

Water-soluble flavors are soluble in water in at least the amount necessary to impart sufficient flavor. The solvents used include water, propylene glycol (most common), ethyl alcohol (for example, grain alcohol), and triacetin (a versatile solvent soluble up to 6.5 percent). Flavor emulsions provide a way to make oil-soluble flavors capable of being uniformly dispersed in an aqueous end product: the flavor-containing oil phase is dispersed in an aqueous phase containing gums, starches, or other hydrocolloids to maintain a uniform suspension.

Powdered flavors are typically water soluble and oil dispersible. In virtually every case, they (or their components) start out life as a liquid. The several methods of producing powdered flavors each have differing functionality, advantages, and weaknesses.[65]

When searching for the best flavor for a project, a product developer must select a suitable supplier, request a flavor, request a revision (perhaps many revisions), and, if successful, prepare for manufacturing.[66]

When requesting a flavor sample, it is best that the developer be as open as possible about the end product to ensure the samples submitted are suitable for their product, will survive their process, and meet their sensory, regulatory, and cost-in-use needs. Key information to provide includes the type of product to which the flavor will be added, the type of processing extremes it will be subject to, preferred form (liquid, powder, or paste), regulatory requirements and corporate restrictions, cost restraints, estimated volume, and deadlines or project timeline. Clearly describe the desired flavor profile. Use comparisons with known market products or recipes to give the supplier a clear understanding of the desired flavor profile. If possible, target products or gold standard prototypes should be tasted alongside the flavor supplier to help speed development.

As no two products or processes are identical, revisions of the initial flavor submission are usually required to obtain the most appropriate flavoring. When contacting the supplier, describe as clearly as possible how the initial flavor submission differed from what you were looking for. Developing common flavor descriptors is important. Tasting together and discussing the flavor attributes helps build a common lexicon of flavor descriptors as well as a strong working relationship. For example, Figure 12.15 shows some descriptors for cheddar cheese, their definition, and a typical ingredient to use as a common reference.[67] Also, mention any issues with the functionality of the flavor, like solubility or handling difficulties.

As the new product nears plant trials or commercialization, the developer must obtain pricing and documentation,

FIGURE 12.14 Comparison of common dry flavor technologies.

Process	Description	Relative Cost	Advantages	Weaknesses
Plating	Oil-soluble flavorings are coated on a crystalline substrate, such as salt, starches, and dextrins (derived from starch).	Low	Low cost. May be produced in any type of blender. Suitable for spices and extractives.	Volatile flavorings (flavorings that vaporize at low temperatures) will ultimately evaporate. Formation of off flavors is possible due to oxidation.
Spray drying	An oil-soluble flavor is dispersed in a gum or carbohydrate solution and sprayed into a chamber where it is dried with heat.	Moderate	Most common method. Volatile flavors are "trapped" in the gum/carbohydrate carrier. Moderate protection from oxidation.	Moderate to poor protection from oxygen.
Vacuum drying	A flavor paste containing mostly protein is dried with heat under vacuum.	Moderate	Roast notes are produced during drying. Good for meat and poultry flavors.	Most volatile flavors are lost during process. Labor intensive.
Glassy matrix	An oil-soluble flavor is encapsulated in a carbohydrate matrix that is in a glassy state (e.g., hard candy).	High	Excellent oxidative stability.	Low flavor loads. Highly volatile flavors are lost during processing. Cost.
Gelatin encapsulate	Droplets of an oil-soluble flavoring are encased in a gelatin shell.	High	Excellent heat stability.	Cost. Inconsistent flavor release in food applications.

Source: Jerome Lombardo.

FIGURE 12.15 **Flavor descriptors and references for cheddar cheese.**

Descriptor	Definition	Reference
Milk fat/ lactones	Aromatics associated with milk fat	Delta decalactone
Fruity	Aromatics associated with different fruits	Ethyl hexanoate
Free fatty acid	Aromatics associated with short chain acids	Butyric acid
Phenolic	Aromatics associated with barns or animal sweat	p-Cresol
Blue cheese	Aromatics associated with blue-veined cheese	2-Octanone
Oxidized	Aromatics associated with oxidized fat, rancidity	2,4-Decadienal
Waxy/ crayon	Aromatics associated with medium-chain fatty acids	Decanoic acid or lauric acid
Nutty	Nut-like aroma associated with roasted nuts	2,6-Dimethyl pyrazine

Source: M. A. Drake et al. (2001).[68]

if this was not done earlier. Now that a recipe is nearly complete, the developer must confirm the volume and request pricing. The developer needs several documents from the flavor supplier:

- An FDA ingredient statement or USDA label is needed to complete the final product's ingredient statement and to write the specifications for the new material.
- A nutrition facts label is required under the 1990 Nutrition Labeling and Education Act (NLEA).
- A Material Safety Data Sheet (MSDS) contains handling information, hazards, if any, and flashpoint (temperature where the mixture could ignite); U.S. law requires it.
- The Continuing Guarantee states the product is manufactured under sanitary conditions, packaging materials are approved for food contact, and government regulations are met.
- A Natural Certification, if applicable, states the flavor does not contain any artificial flavoring ingredients as defined in 21 CFR 101.2. Non-flavoring ingredients, such as solvents, carriers, emulsifiers, antioxidants, and processing aids, used in the flavor may not be natural. This is important if the product is to have an all-natural claim.
- A kosher certificate, halal certification, or organic certification, if needed, is requested from the ingredient or flavor supplier, who obtains it through third-party certifying agencies.

Without question, selection of the right flavor enhances desirability, prevents manufacturing and stability issues, pro-

vides an easy vehicle to develop product line extensions, and improves the probability of success in the marketplace.

Flavor Enhancers

Commercial flavor enhancers are compounds that enhance the savory taste of foods specifically by activating the umami taste receptors in the mouth and tongue. These flavor enhancers are largely based on amino acids—the building blocks of proteins (particularly glutamic acid)—and 5′ (5-prime) nucleotides—the building blocks of nucleic acids (specifically inosine monophosphate [IMP] and guanosine monophosphate [GMP]). The major flavor enhancers follow.

Monosodium Glutamate (MSG)

MSG is the sodium salt of glutamic acid, one of the most abundant naturally occurring nonessential amino acids. Food manufacturers use MSG as a flavor enhancer because it balances, blends, and rounds the total perception of other tastes. It is classified by the FDA as generally recognized as safe (GRAS). Currently, most MSG is produced by bacterial fermentation.

Pure MSG does not have a pleasant taste by itself; however, when added to foods at very low levels MSG enhances other taste compounds in the food, boosting the overall flavor impact. MSG mixes well with meat, fish, poultry, many vegetables, sauces, soups, and marinades, and increases the overall preference of many foods. But more is not better: an excess of MSG quickly ruins the taste of a dish. Typical starting use levels for most foods are in the 0.05 to 0.20 percent range; slightly higher in very fatty or oily foods (mayonnaise) and in topical seasonings for snack foods (chips and so on).

Over the years, MSG has developed a negative reputation by the public as the causative agent of various allergenic reactions in sensitive individuals, perhaps most infamously "Chinese Restaurant Syndrome," which is characterized by headache and numbness in the back of the neck, sometimes extending to the shoulders and arms. It was thought that the syndrome was caused by ingesting foods laced with MSG, and the most common source was Chinese food, as MSG has been used in Asian cooking ever since it was identified as a flavor enhancer and was commercially extracted from seaweed (in Japan) in the early 1900s.

In spite of the fact that there has never been a proven link between the consumption of MSG and human illness, whenever monosodium glutamate is added to a food, it must be identified as "monosodium glutamate" in the label's ingredient list. That said, the FDA does not require foods and ingredients that naturally contain glutamate to list it on the label. Examples include tomatoes and mushrooms (particularly dried forms in which the glutamates become concentrated), aged cheeses, meats, soy sauce, hydrolyzed protein products such as HVP, and autolyzed yeast extracts (AYE). These ingredients are to be declared on the label only by their common or usual names.

Inosinate and Guanylate (I+G)

In the flavor industry, disodium inosinate (IMP) and disodium guanylate (GMP) are commonly known as disodium ribotides, or I+G for short. They are typically sold together in a 50:50 mixture. I+G acts synergistically with glutamates to impart the umami flavor to foods; a mixture of 98 percent monosodium glutamate and 2 percent I+G has four times the flavor-enhancing power of monosodium glutamate (MSG) alone. As a relatively expensive product, I+G is usually not used independently of glutamates; if it is present on a food label's ingredient list but MSG does not appear to be, it is possible that glutamates are provided as part of another ingredient such as AYE or HVP, or are naturally occurring in other ingredients such as tomatoes, Parmesan cheese, or mushrooms.

Guanylates and inosinates are generally produced through a fermentation process from plant raw materials such as tapioca starch. They are thus suitable for vegans and vegetarians.

Autolyzed Yeast Extract (AYE)

Autolyzed yeast extract (AYE) results from the breakdown of yeast cells. Baker's or brewer's yeast goes through a series of steps to break it down and release its contents. First, salt or mild heat is applied, causing the cell walls to lose integrity but maintain enzyme activity. Through autolysis, the yeast's own enzymes break apart the proteins in the cytoplasm into constituent amino acids, now referred to as free amino acids. These are the source of glutamic acid and glutamates, the same flavor enhancers found in MSG. Next, the cell wall is ruptured to spill out the contents, and then it and other insoluble components are removed via centrifugation, followed by concentration and pasteurization of what remains. This is referred to as "autolyzed yeast extract." The final product is available in liquid or paste form or is spray-dried to a powder.

Autolyzed yeast extract is used primarily as a flavor enhancer in processed foods such as soups, meats, and vegetarian meat analogs. Like MSG, it is valued for its ability to stimulate taste receptors that are sensitive to the umami or savory type of taste, but it has a cleaner appearance on ingredient labels, where it is listed as "yeast extract" without any reference to MSG or glutamates.

It is interesting to note that while we in the United States consider AYE strictly in its role as a flavor enhancer to be used as a minor ingredient in other foods, other countries consume large quantities of AYE as a food in and of itself. Most famously, Marmite, a paste that is virtually pure AYE, is extremely popular throughout the countries of the UK, Australia, and New Zealand, where it has been eaten as a spread on toast, in sandwiches, and as an accompaniment to cheese for more than 100 years. Annual production exceeds 6000 tons per year, with 90 percent consumed in the UK. Starbucks in the UK even has a cheese and Marmite panini on its menu. It is made from spent yeast from the brewing industry, and it is an especially rich vegetarian source of B vitamins.

Hydrolyzed Vegetable Protein (HVP)

Hydrolyzed vegetable protein (HVP) is produced by acid hydrolysis, which involves boiling cereals or legumes, such as soy, corn, or wheat, in hydrochloric acid and then neutralizing the solution with sodium hydroxide. The acid hydrolyzes, or breaks down, the protein in vegetables into their component amino acids. The resulting dark-colored liquid contains, among other amino acids, glutamic acid. HVP is a flavor enhancer used in a wide variety of processed food products, including soups, sauces, chili, stews, hot dogs, gravies, seasoned snack foods, dips, and dressings. It is often blended with other spices to make seasonings that are used in or on foods. Like AYE, it gives the product developer a way to provide glutamate enhancement without using MSG.

Acids

Acids are substances that release hydrogen ions when dissolved in water, giving the solution a pH below 7.0.[69] They are classified as organic acids when they include organic (carbon-containing) compounds typically found in carboxylic groups. Examples include lactic, citric, propionic, acetic, and malic acids. Inorganic acids have no organic (carbon-containing) compounds and include mineral acids such as hydrochloric acid, phosphoric acid, nitric acid, and sulfuric acid. Acids or acidulants are used in foods for a variety of reasons: to enhance flavor, to act as antimicrobial preservatives, to prevent oxidation or discoloration of foods (addition of ascorbic acid and citric acid to fruits), and to provide adequate pH for protein functionality in food products (such as thickening in yogurt and sour cream brought about by the action of lactic acid, and gelation, in the case of jams and jellies, where the pectin requires a narrow, acidic pH range to act as a gelling agent).[70] Acids also function as chelating agents or sequestrants, which are agents that react with metallic ions, forming complexes and thereby limiting their catalytic properties.[71] This important ability limits the rate of lipid oxidation reactions in fats and oils by hindering the metal ion's ability to catalyze them.

Acid selection depends strongly on desired functionality and on flavor. Citric and tartaric acids provide a sharp acid profile, whereas lactic acid has a much milder sour taste with a longer duration.

Acetic acid is an organic acid produced by microbial fermentation of ethanol by acetic acid bacteria. It can also be produced synthetically. It is the main component in vinegar, and it is used primarily as a preservative in pickled foods and as a flavoring agent (CFR 21 184.1005). Typical concentrations of acetic acid in vinegar range from 4 to 5 percent, which can also be expressed as the grain, which is equal to 10 times the acetic acid content (for example, 4 percent is the same as 40 grain). It is available as a liquid of assorted grain-strengths or as a powder in the following forms: sodium acetate, calcium acetate, sodium diacetate, and calcium diacetate. Its primary applications are in pickled foods, dressings, catsup, topical snack seasonings (in its dry form), in processed cheese as an acidulant at 0.8 percent (CFR 21 184.1005), and as a

FIGURE 12.16 **Properties of some acids, arranged in order of decreasing acid taste and with tartaric acid as reference.**

Acid	Taste	Total Acid (gm/l)	pH	Taste Sensation	Found in
Hydrochloric	+1.43	1.85	1.70	—	
Tartaric	0.0	3.75	2.45	Hard	Grape
Malic	−0.43	3.35	2.65	Green	Apple, pear, prune, grape, cherry, apricot
Phosphoric	−1.14	1.65	2.25	Intense	Orange, grapefruit
Acetic	−1.14	3.00	2.95	Vinegar	
Lactic	−1.14	4.5	2.60	Sour, tart	
Citric	−1.28	3.50	2.60	Fresh	Berries, citrus, pineapple
Propionic	−1.85	3.70	2.90	Sour, cheesy	

Source: deMan (1990).[72]

component in baking powder, where it promotes the release of carbon dioxide from sodium bicarbonate to provide chemical leavening.

Adipic acid is an organic acid used as a flavoring agent and acidulant in beverages and canned goods as well as baked goods at application levels of 0.05 percent, and in jellies and fruit gelatins at 0.55 percent when a prolonged sour sensation is desired. It is also used in processed cheese and in condiments. Adipic acid is prepared by the oxidation of nitric acid with cyclohexanol; it is on the list of GRAS substances (CFR 21 184.1009).

Citric acid is an organic acidulant produced either by extraction from citrus juices such as lemon, lime, and orange as well as from pineapple juice, or by the fungal fermentation of carbohydrate solutions using the yeast Candida spp. or the mold *Aspergillus niger* (CFR 21 184.1033). It is one of the primary acids of choice in food processing due to its strength: A 1 percent solution has a pH of 2.3 at 78°F (25°C) due to the presence of three carboxylic acid groups in its molecule.[73]

Citric acid has a wide range of applications in beverages and juices (typically used at 0.25 to 0.5 percent), confectionery items, and jams and jellies. It is used in processed cheese to control pH and melt characteristics by controlling the ratio of bound calcium to casein proteins. The lower the pH, the more calcium leaves the protein matrix, thereby making the cheese more flowing. It is also used as an antioxidant in

FIGURE 12.17 **Chemical structure of citric acid.**

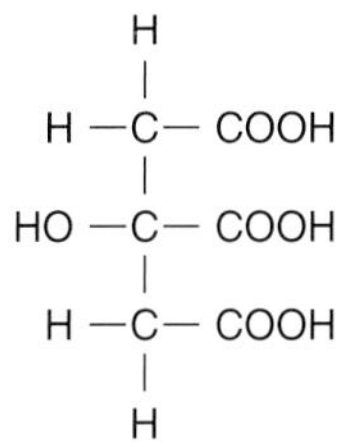

```
            H
            |
     H —C— COOH
            |
    HO —C— COOH
            |
     H —C— COOH
            |
            H
```

Source: Fennema (2007).[74]

fruit and vegetable processing (apple, potato), where it prevents enzymatic browning. It can also prevent non-enzymatic browning in fruit dehydration processes as an alternative to sulfur dioxide, which produces allergic reactions in sensitive individuals. Citric acid has chelating properties and can be used as an antioxidant in oils, where it helps extend shelf life by trapping metal ions. It is also widely used to provide or enhance the flavor of lemon and lime in beverages, seasonings, and fruit products. Citric acid crystals are commonly used in commercial lemon pepper seasoning.

Fumaric acid is a strong organic acid used as an acidulant in dry mix applications due to its low hygroscopicity, which allows them to stay free-flowing and prevents caking. It is used in fruit gelatins and jellies as an acidulant that complements fruit flavors, and it helps pectin form a gel.[75] It can also be used in seasoning applications to provide a low-intensity and long-lasting tart profile that contrasts with the high-intensity/short-duration flavor of citric acid. It is used in the shelf-life extension of oils, acting synergistically with other antioxidants. The ferrous fumarate form is also used as a delivery system for iron in dietary foods (CFR 21 172.350).

Glucono-delta-lactone (GDL), found in honey, fruit juices, and wine, is naturally present in its lactone or ring form, where the carboxylic group of GDL is linked to one of its alcohol groups via a cyclical ester.[76] The ester link breaks on addition to a liquid and slowly hydrolyzes into its gluconic acid (an organic acid) form at a rate dependent on temperature. This unique characteristic of GDL allows it to produce a more gradual reduction in pH compared to other acids, which makes it ideal for applications where slow acidification is desired and also where high localized acid concentrations are not desirable, such as directly acidified milks, dairy products, and baked goods.[77] It is used in baking powders, where a slow release of carbon dioxide is important to control expansion and texture. It is also used in cured and pickled foods and dressings and can act as a metal ion sequestrant (CFR 21 184.1318).

Lactic acid is the organic acid normally associated with milk. It is produced microbially by lactic fermentation of simple carbohydrates, and it is present in all fermented dairy and pickled products—yogurt, buttermilk, sauerkraut, cucumber pickles, and so on (CFR 21 184.1061). As an ingredient, it is available as a dry powder and also in solutions of concentrations ranging from 50 to 88 percent. Lactic acid is used as an acidulant to control pH and as a flavor agent and preservative in seasonings, olives, processed cheese, and certain acidified meat and dairy products, such as salami and cheese, where direct acidification is used instead of fermentation to reduce cost and speed the process of pH reduction. It is also used in topical seasonings, dressings, and sauces when enhancing a dairy flavor, such as ranch or buttermilk, is desired.[78]

Malic acid is the main organic acid found in apples. It is produced from the hydrogenation of fumaric acid (CFR 21 184.1069). It is tarter than citric acid at the same concentration, and it is slightly less soluble. Malic acid sustains its tart flavor longer than other acids, and it is compatible with products where a fruit flavor is desired. It is used in soft drinks, confectionery products, chewing gum, and fruit fillings. It is preferred to citric acid in the manufacture of hard candies because of its ease of incorporation due to its lower melting point.[79]

Phosphoric acid is one of the only inorganic acids used in foods. It is produced by burning phosphorus in air, producing phosphorus pentoxide, which yields orthophosphoric acid when dissolved in water. Phosphoric acid is used in cola manufacture to provide tangy flavor and the desired pH.[80] It is also used in the production of processed cheese, where it controls melt profile by chelating ionic calcium and thus controlling the amount of calcium bound to casein. Flow is hindered when calcium ions remain bound to casein, and flow increases when the calcium is chelated.[81] Phosphoric acid is also used to control the pH in food processes and as an antioxidant in vegetable oils.

Tartaric acid, an organic acid, is the main acidulant present in grapes. It has a higher tartness value than citric acid at the same concentration, and it is used in jellies and candies where a grape flavor is desired.[82] Tartaric acid (or cream of tartar) is also used in baking powder to release carbon dioxide from sodium bicarbonate, as a stabilizing agent in meringues, and to enhance creamy texture in icings by inhibiting crystal formation.

Succinic acid is produced by hydrogenating fumaric or malic acid (CFR 21 184.1091). Its main use is in bread dough to control the elasticity of gluten proteins by increasing the number of positively charged amino acids in the gluten chain. This increases repulsion and thereby weakens the gluten network and softens the resulting baked product.[83] It is also used as an acidulant in beverages and in meat products such as salami and cured hams. Succinic acid is unique from a flavor perspective in that it is one of the few non-glutamate flavor enhancers when used at a subliminal level.

Sweeteners

Sweeteners include any substances that elicit a sweet taste and are used in food products for that purpose. The FDA classifies sweeteners into two primary categories: nutritive and non-nutritive. Nutritive sweeteners include sugars, of which the most common are glucose, fructose, and sucrose, and polyols (sugar alcohols), which are produced by the hydrogenation of simple carbohydrates. Their general characteristic is that they have more than 2 percent of the caloric value of sucrose per unit sweetness (CFR 21 170.3).

Non-nutritive sweeteners are defined as substances having less than 2 percent of the caloric value of sucrose per unit sweetness. These include all the high-intensity sweeteners that are many times sweeter than sucrose and therefore have a negligible caloric contribution because their application level is very low (CFR 21 170.3).

Non-Nutritive, High-Intensity Sweeteners

Aspartame is a dipeptide consisting of two amino acids: aspartic acid and phenylalanine. Aspartame has been approved in the United States since 1981 (CFR 21 172.804). It does have a caloric contribution when the peptide is digested, but because it is 180 to 200 times sweeter than sucrose and is used at such low levels, this is negligible.[84] Typical usage levels are 0.01 to 0.02 percent in beverages and diet sodas. It is unstable in acidic pH conditions, and in sodas it slowly degrades, resulting in a decrease in sweetness over time. In addition, it is not heat stable and breaks down during cooking or baking. At retail, it is sold under the brand names NutraSweet® and Equal® in blue packets. The NutraSweet Company claims that aspartame is used in more than 5000 products and consumed by some 250 million people worldwide.

Phenylketonuria (PKU) is a genetic error of metabolism that affects about one in every 15,000 births. Individuals with this condition cannot digest phenylalanine, one of the amino acids in aspartame. All PKU patients must adhere to a special diet low in phenylalanine. This requires severely restricting or eliminating foods high in phenylalanine, such as meat, poultry, fish, cheese, legumes, nuts, and all foods containing aspartame. Because of this, all foods and beverages containing aspartame must carry a warning label.

Acesulfame-potassium (Ace-K) has been approved in the United States since 1988 (CFR 21 172.800). It is 200 times sweeter than sucrose, with a metallic and bitter aftertaste. It does not have a caloric contribution because it cannot be metabolized by the body. Ace-K is usually blended with other sweeteners (sucralose or aspartame); these blends supposedly provide a more sugar-like taste whereby each sweetener masks the other's aftertaste or exhibits a synergistic effect that makes the blend sweeter than its components. It is used in conjunction with these other sweeteners in diet sodas and desserts. Due to its heat stability, it can also be used in bakery products.

Cyclamate was banned for use in foods in the United States in 1969, when it was suspected of causing bladder cancer in rats (CFR 21 189.135). Before then it was blended with saccharin 10:1 to help mask saccharin's bitter aftertaste. Cyclamate is approved for food use in 55 other countries, including the United Kingdom and all of Europe, as well as in Canada (where saccharin is banned). Its retail trade name is Sucaryl®. Cyclamate is 30 times sweeter than sucrose. It has a relatively slow onset but a more natural sugar-like taste and the ability to withstand typical cooking and baking temperatures.

Neotame is a high-intensity sweetener with a short peptide-chain backbone; it is 7000 to 13,000 times sweeter than sucrose. It was created by the same company that owns aspartame: Monsanto. It is approved for use in foods, except for meat and poultry (CFR 21 172.829). Even though only trace amounts of neotame are needed to sweeten foods due to its potency, it still exhibits the characteristic bitter aftertaste common to all non-nutritive sweeteners. While it is approved for use in 60 countries, including the United Kingdom, the European Union, and Canada, and is ranked "safe" by the Center for Science in the Public Interest, it is not yet available to consumers.

Saccharin is the oldest commercially manufactured synthetic sweetener in existence. It was originally manufactured by the Monsanto Company for the Coca-Cola Company in 1921. It is 300 to 400 times sweeter than sucrose.[85] Due to its low thermal stability, it is used in low-calorie beverages and products that do not undergo a severe thermal process. Saccharin is often used with aspartame in diet soda fountain syrups so that some sweetness remains should the fountain syrup be stored beyond aspartame's relatively short shelf life. It is recognizable at retail as the pink packet with the trade name Sweet 'n' Low®.

Sucralose is produced by the chlorination of the sucrose molecule. It is 600 to 800 times sweeter than sucrose and has a similar flavor profile, with a slight to moderate metallic aftertaste. It is stable at high temperatures, which makes it suitable for bakery and confectionery products. It is also stable under acidic conditions, so it can be used in diet soft drinks.[86] It is sold at retail under the brand name Splenda® in yellow packets. The commercial success of sucralose stems from its favorable comparison to other low-calorie sweeteners in terms of taste, stability, and safety. It is one of only two artificial sweeteners (neotame is the other) to receive a "safe" ranking from the Center for Science in the Public Interest. Sucralose can be found in more than 4500 food and beverage products, including candy, breakfast bars, and soft drinks. It is also used in canned fruits in place of higher-calorie corn syrups.

Steviosides (stevia) are sweet glycosides extracted from the leaves of the *Stevia rebaudiana* plant. Stevia is 300 times sweeter than sucrose and is heat stable, pH stable, and non-fermentable. The sweetest fractions, stevioside and rebaudioside A, have recently been commercialized in the United States. After many years of petitioning the FDA, stevia was finally granted GRAS status in 2008. It is currently the only natural high-intensity sweetener in widespread use. It is available at retail under two competing brand names: Truvia® (jointly owned by Cargill and Coca-Cola) and PureVia® (jointly owned by PepsiCo and Merisant). Unfortunately, it shares the same chemical aftertaste as all of the synthetics.

Luo han guo (*Siraitia grosvenorii*), also known as *monkfruit*, is an herbaceous perennial vine native to southern China and northern Thailand. The plant is best known for its fruit.

The fruit extract is nearly 300 times sweeter than sugar and has been used as a natural low-calorie sweetener in China for nearly a millennium to treat diabetes and obesity. The sweet taste of the fruit comes mainly from mogrosides, a group of triterpene glycosides that make up approximately 1 percent of the flesh of the fresh fruit. Through solvent extraction, a powder containing 80 percent mogrosides can be obtained, the main one being mogroside-5. The process for the manufacture of a useful sweetener from luo han guo was patented in 1995 by Procter & Gamble, the main objective of which is to remove an assortment of interfering aromas from the fruit that otherwise render it useless for widespread use. Since luo han go received GRAS status in 2007, several companies have launched new products containing it, including low-calorie juices, herbal teas, protein bars, and breakfast cereals.

Thaumatin is a natural, low-calorie (virtually calorie-free) protein-based sweetener and flavor modifier. The thaumatins were first found as a mixture of proteins isolated from the katemfe fruit (*Thaumatococcus daniellii* Bennett) of West Africa. This "miracle fruit" is more widely known for its ability to make sour substances (citrus juices, vinegar, and so on) taste sweet after one chews its pulp. Some of the proteins in the thaumatin family are natural sweeteners, roughly 2000 times more potent than sugar. Although very sweet, thaumatin's taste is markedly different from that of sugar. The sweetness of thaumatin builds slowly, and the sweetness perception lasts a long time, leaving a licorice-like aftertaste at high usage levels. Thaumatin is highly water soluble and stable to heating and acidic conditions. In the United States, it is considered to be a GRAS flavoring agent. The extract is available as an industrial ingredient under the tradename Talin®, and it is marketed more as a flavor modifier and bitterness masker than a sweetener.

FIGURE 12.18 Relative sweetness of nutritive sweeteners.

Substance	Relative Sweetness Value (compared to sucrose = 100 at equivalent weight)
Glucose (Dextrose)	70
Fructose	150
Invert sugar	130
HFCS 42	90
HFCS 55	95
Erythritol	60–70
Isomalt	50–60
Lactitol	30–40
Maltitol	90
Mannitol	50
Sorbitol	60
Xylitol	100

Source: Igoe and Hui (2001).[87]

FIGURE 12.19 Relative sweetness of high-intensity sweeteners.

Substance	Relative Sweetness Value (compared to sucrose = 1 at equivalent weight)
Aspartame	180–200
Acesulfame-K	200
Cyclamate	30
Neotame	7000–13,000
Saccharine	300–400
Steviosode	300
Sucralose	600–800
Thaumatin	1600–2000

Source: Igoe and Hui (2001).[88]

Sodium Reduction

Reducing sodium in the diet (primarily due to the consumption of table salt, sodium chloride) is a goal of many governments and manufacturers, and it is quickly becoming a priority in the United States on par with reducing and eliminating trans fats from the diet. Strict government guidelines are already in effect in the United Kingdom, and national initiatives are underway in Canada, Australia, Finland, France, Ireland, and New Zealand to reduce sodium in food. In January 2010, New York City announced its partnership with various organizations through the National Salt Reduction Initiative (NSRI), the goal of which is to cut the sodium in packaged and restaurant foods by 25 percent over five years. At the time NSRI was launched, it was a voluntary initiative, but it is thought that the amount of sodium in food could be federally regulated at some point. The NSRI is focusing on reducing sodium in packaged and restaurant food because it is believed that only 5 to 11 percent of the sodium in a typical American's diet comes from putting additional salt on food at the table.[89] A gradual step-down approach is believed by most the best way to achieve the goal of reducing sodium in food; a sudden reduction of 25 percent could lead to adverse consumer reaction because of the resulting radical change in flavor of most products.

Reducing sodium is a challenging prospect for any product developer, as no single ingredient works in all applications to replace the flavor and functionality of sodium chloride. The role of sodium chloride in foods includes not only taste but also protein solubilization, as in the case of meat products to enhance water-holding capacity; as a contributor to dough strength in bakery items; and as an antimicrobial agent. Furthermore, due to the low cost of sodium chloride, it is extremely difficult to find cost-neutral alternatives. The first step for the product developer is to evaluate the formula or product as a whole to determine the role salt plays in the food system.

Once that determination is made, strategies for salt reduction can be better formulated.

In terms of maintaining salty flavor, there are three areas of focus for sodium-reduction efforts in processed foods, each with its own limitations: salt substitutes; modifications to the physical makeup of the salt, and flavor-enhancing ingredients.[90]

The only other known substance that elicits a salty taste that is approved for human consumption is potassium chloride. Its saltiness intensity is less pronounced than that of sodium chloride, and it delivers a metallic and bitter aftertaste that is detected by a large portion of the population.[91] Therefore, a product developer is likely to use potassium chloride as a partial replacer for salt. Potassium chloride's effectiveness depends on whether it is dissolved, as in a soup or sauce, or added topically, as on a pretzel.

In food products where it is used in solution (soups, sauces, brines, and so on), potassium chloride can work well as a salt substitute in most applications, substituting up to 25 percent of the salt used.[92] The undesirable flavors of potassium chloride become evident at higher substitution levels but can be mitigated somewhat by bitterness-masking agents. Most flavor companies offer products that are a blend of potassium chloride and proprietary bitterness blockers. One of the drawbacks of supplementing products with potassium ions is the risk of producing an adverse effect on segments of the populations that are at risk for kidney problems or heart failure due to potassium sensitivity.[93]

Various companies have successfully used other sources of salt to reduce sodium in food products. Sea salt is naturally lower in sodium than table salt because so many non-sodium mineral salts, such as potassium, magnesium, and calcium, are dissolved in the ocean. The flavor these extra minerals impart has bitter and metallic notes similar to that of potassium chloride. In addition, the main component of sea salt is still NaCl, so the actual amount of sodium reduction depends on the ratio of the non-sodium salts to NaCl in the blend. Each sea salt is different and must be analyzed for sodium before using.

Another strategy is using salt with altered crystalline structure. Salts with larger crystals, or those that are irregularly shaped, with porous structures and increased surface area, can be created by manipulating the salt-drying process. These allow greater salty taste with smaller amounts of salt; this is particularly useful in applications where salt is used on the surface of food products. Replacing table salt 1:1 (volume to volume, NOT weight to weight) with these larger salts does reduce sodium in formulas, but whether the total saving is significant enough to make a big difference in sodium consumption remains to be seen.

The use of flavor enhancers (MSG, AYE, I+G, HVP) can enhance perceived saltiness. In a reduced-salt application, the enhancer increases the perception of what little salt is present and makes it taste stronger. A combination of I+G and MSG can be added to a food to reduce the salt content. The effect of this addition is to impart a magnification of the savory taste sensation by enhancing the food's natural flavors

FIGURE 12.20 Selected examples of proposed salt substitutes.

Substitute	Applications	Comments
Potassium chloride (KCl)	Many foods, including cheeses,[a] breads,[b] and meats,[c] may be mixed with NaCl in up to a 50:50 ratio.[c]	Bitter to many people;[c] many patents to reduce KCl bitterness exist;[d] because potassium intake of the U.S. population is low, increased intake of potassium may benefit some[e] but could harm certain subpopulations (e.g., those with certain medical conditions or taking certain medications).[f]
Lithium chloride (LiCl)	None: Toxic although almost perfectly salty	
Calcium chloride (CaCl$_2$), magnesium chloride (MgCl$_2$), and magnesium sulfate (MgSO$_4$)	Few foods	Somewhat salty but with many off tastes;[g] bitter tastes of MgSO$_4$ are usually perceived only at high levels;[h] CaCl$_2$ can cause irritations on the tongue.[h]
Sea salt	Many foods, also used in salt shakers	Usually contains substantial amounts of sodium chloride; benefits of use in reducing sodium consumption are unclear
Salts with altered crystal structure	Some foods	Porous and star-shaped structures, created by manipulating the salt-drying process, allow greater salty taste with smaller amounts of salt;[i] particularly useful in applications where salt is used on the surface of food products.[j]

[a]Guinee and O'Kennedy, 2007.
[b]Cauvain, 2007.
[c]Desmond, 2007
[d]Porzio, 2007.
[e]Anthony, 2007.
[f]Dietary Guidelines Advisory Committee, 2005.
[g]Murphy et al., 1981.
[h]Kilcast and den Ridder, 2007.
[i]Desmond, 2006.
[j]Pszczola, 2007.

REFERENCES

Ainsworth, P., and A. Plunkett. 2007. Reducing salt in snack products. In *Reducing salt in foods: Practical strategies*, edited by D. Kilcast and F. Angus. Cambridge, UK: Woodhead. Pp. 296-315.

Ajinomoto Food Ingredients LLC. 2008. Ajinomoto monoammonium glutamate (MAG) and monopotassium glutamate (MPG). http://www.ajiusafood.com/5MAG/main.asp (accessed 2008).

Anthony, M. 2007. Season with (only) a grain of salt. http://www.foodprocessing.com/articles/2007/204.html (accessed September 2008).

Armor Proteines. 2007. Lactosalt Optitaste.http://www.armor-proteines.com/ENG/lactosalt_UK.pdf (accessed 2008).

Brandsma, I. 2006. Reducing sodium: A European perspective. *Food Technology* 60(3): 24–29.

Breslin, P. A. S., and G. K. Beauchamp. 1995. Suppression of bitterness by sodium: Variation among bitter taste stimuli. *Chemical Senses* 20(6): 609–623.

Cauvain, S. P. 2007. Reduced salt in bread and other baked products. In *Reducing salt in foods: Practical strategies*, edited by D. Kilcast and F. Angus. Cambridge, UK: Woodhead. Pp. 283–295.

Desmond, E. 2006. Reducing salt: A challenge for the meat industry. *Meat Science* 74(1): 188–196.

Desmond, E. 2007. Reducing salt in meat and poultry products. In *Reducing salt in foods: Practical strategies*, edited by D. Kilcast and F. Angus. Cambridge, UK: Woodhead. Pp. 233–255.

Dietary Guidelines Advisory Committee. 2005. Report of the Dietary Guidelines Advisory Committee on the Dietary Guidelines for Americans, 2005. *A Report to the Secretary of Health and Human Services and the Secretary of Agriculture*. Washington, DC: U.S. Department of Agriculture and U.S. Department of Health and Human Services. DSM Food Specialties. 2004. Maxarite—product properties. http://www.dsm.com/le/en_US/maxarite/html/properties.htm (accessed December 12, 2008).

Guinee, T. P., and B. T. O'Kennedy. 2007. Reducing salt in cheese and dairy spreads. In *Reducing salt in foods: Practical strategies*, edited by D. Kilcast and F. Angus. Cambridge, UK: Woodhead. Pp. 316–357.

Jungbunzlauer AG. 2007. *Sub4salt: Jungbunzlauer's way to reduce sodium*. Switzerland: Jungbunzlauer AG.

Keast, R. S. J., T. M. Canty, and P. A. S. Breslin. 2004. The influence of sodium salts on binary mixtures of bitter-tasting compounds. *Chemical Senses* 29(5): 431–439.

(continued)

FIGURE 12.20 (*continued*)

Kilcast, D. 2007. Cutting sodium. Prepared Foods, January: 1–5.

Kilcast, D., and C. den Ridder. 2007. Sensory issues in reducing salt in food products. In *Reducing salt in foods: Practical strategies*, edited by D. Kilcast and F. Angus. Cambridge, UK: Woodhead. Pp. 201–220.

Murphy, C., A. V. Cardello, and J. G. Brand. 1981. Tastes of fifteen halide salts following water and NaCl: Anion and cation effects. *Physiology and Behavior* 26(6): 1083–1095.

Ndabikunze, B. K., and S. Lahtinen. 1989. Substitution of sodium chloride by Morton lite salt or mineral salt in mayonnaise. *International Journal of Food Science and Technology* 24(4): 367–371.

Porzio, M. 2007. Flavor delivery and product development. *Food Technology*, January: 22–29.

Pszczola, D. 2006. Exploring new 'tastes' in textures. *Food Technology*, January: 44–55.

Pszczola, D. 2007. Savoring the possibilities. *Food Technology* 61(4): 55–66.

Yamaguchi, S. 1987. Fundamental properties of umami in human taste sensation. In *Umami: A basic taste*, edited by Y. Kawamura and M. R. Kare. New York: Marcel Dekker.

Source: Reprinted with permission from Henney, J. E., C. Taylor, C. S. Boon, and The Committee on Strategies to Reduce Sodium Intake, *Strategies to Reduce Sodium Intake in the United States* (Washington, DC: National Academies of Science, 2010). Courtesy of the National Academies Press.[94]

FIGURE 12.21 **Selected examples of proposed salt enhancers.**

Ingredient	Applications	Comment
Monosodium glutamate (MSG) and other glutamates	Many foods; can replace some salt[a]	No pleasant taste in itself, but enhances salty tastes; imparts the taste of umami; MSG contains sodium; other glutamate salts such as monopotassium glutamate or calcium diglutamate may further reduce sodium; synergizes with 5′-ribonucleotides;[b] may replace bitter blocking[c] and oral thickening[d] characteristics; often contained in hydrolyzed vegetable protein and yeast extracts.[a]
Yeast extracts and hydrolyzed vegetable protein	Some foods	Often contains MSG, but is seen as a "natural" alternative to MSG use; meaty and brothy tastes limit potential uses.[d,e]
Nucleotides, including inosine-5′-monophosphate (IMP) and guanosine-5′-monophosphate	Some foods	Imparts the taste of umami; found to act synergistically with glutamates to enhance salty tastes in some foods.[d,f]
Amino acids, especially arginine and related compounds	Not known	L-Arginine is reported to enhance the saltiness of foods with low to moderate levels of salt; practical uses are not clear.[g]
Dairy concentrates	Many foods	Reported to allow moderate sodium reductions in a variety of products.[e,h]
Lactates (potassium lactate, calcium lactate, and sodium lactate)	Few foods	May enhance the saltiness of NaCl, but not widely used; calcium lactate can impart a sour taste.[b]
Herbs and spices	Many foods	Herbs and spices provide other flavoring characteristics and may, for some people, help alleviate blandness following salt removal.[i,j]
Compounds that reduce bitterness, including adenosine-5′-monophosphate, DHB (2,4-dihydroxybenzoic acid), lactose, sodium gluconate, and mixtures for use in combination with potassium chloride	Many foods	Designed to mask bitterness of potassium chloride or reduce bitterness from other food components that are usually masked by salt; allow partial reduction of total sodium content.[b,e,k,l]
Mixtures of NaCl substitutes and enhancers	Many foods	Proprietary mixtures are produced by many companies; mixtures consist of a number of ingredients such as non-sodium salts, yeast extracts, potassium chloride, sodium, and sodium gluconate.[m,n,o]

(continued)

FIGURE 12.21 (*continued*)

[a]Yamaguchi, 1987.

[b]Kilcast and den Ridder, 2007.

[c]Keast et al., 2004.

[d]Brandsma, 2006.

[e]Pszczola, 2007.

[f]Ajinomoto Food Ingredients LLC, 2008.

[g]Breslin and Beauchamp, 1995.

[h]Armor Proteines, 2007.

[i]Kilcast, 2007.

[j]Ainsworth and Plunkett, 2007.

[k]Ndabikunze and Lahtinen, 1989.

[l]Desmond, 2007.

[m]DSM Food Specialties, 2004.

[n]Pszczola, 2006.

[o]Jungbunzlauer, 2007.

See the references in Figure 12.20.

Source: Reprinted with permission from Henney, J. E., C. Taylor, C. S. Boon, and The Committee on Strategies to Reduce Sodium Intake, *Strategies to Reduce Sodium Intake in the United States* (Washington, DC: National Academies of Science, 2010). Courtesy of the National Academies Press.[96]

as well as any added salt. Even though it appears you are replacing sodium (in salt) with sodium (in MSG), the sodium content of MSG is roughly 3 times lower (12 percent) than in sodium chloride (39 percent).

Certain acids can also be used to enhance flavors similarly to salt. Recent studies have shown that black rice vinegar, with its higher amino acid level, had a pronounced effect on enhancing the perception of saltiness.[95]

● Conclusion

Food additives are employed for multiple purposes, including flavor and texture improvement, shelf life extension, antimicrobial and antioxidant activity, color preservation, and increasing the nutritional value of food products. They are added to help maintain and enhance the natural quality attributes of foods through the multiple, sometimes deleterious changes brought about by processing. Most processed food products contain additives to some degree and in various combinations. Therefore, product developers must be familiar with the wide range of food additives, and why and how they are used, in order to effectively design successful, commercially viable products.

[1]H. This, *Molecular Gastronomy: Exploring the Science of Flavor*, M. B. Debevoise (trans.) (New York: Columbia University Press, 2006).

[2]N. Potter and J. Hotchkiss, *Food Science*, 5th ed. (New York: Chapman and Hall, 1995).

[3]G. L. Christen and J. S. Smith, *Food Chemistry: Principles and Applications* (West Sacramento, CA: Science Technology System, 2000).

[4]C. Hazen, "Antioxidants 'Meat' Needs," *Food Product Design* (2005): 61–68.

[5]Christen and Smith, *Food Chemistry*.

[6]V. A. Vaclavik and E. W. Christian, *Essentials of Food Science*, 3rd ed. (New York: Springer Science and Business Media, 2008).

[7]Ibid.

[8]O. R. Fennema, *Food Chemistry*, 4th ed. (New York: Marcel Dekker, 2007).

[9]D. Marmion, *Handbook of U.S. Colorants: Foods, Drugs, Cosmetics, and Medical Devices*, 3rd ed. (New York: John Wiley & Sons, 1991).

[10]M. Ash and I. Ash, *Handbook of Food Additives*, 2nd ed. (Endicott, NY: Sinapse Information Resources, 2002).

[11]Fennema, *Food Chemistry*.

[12]Code of Federal Regulations, Title 21 (CFR 21 73.95), retrieved from www.fda.gov; J. M. de Man, *Principles of Food Chemistry*, 2nd ed. (New York: Van Nostrand Reinhold, 1990).

[13]Marmion, *Handbook of U.S. Colorants*.

[14]J. Smith, *Food Additive User's Handbook* (New York: Van Nostrand Reinhold, 1991).

[15]R. S. Igoe and Y. H. Hui, *Dictionary of Food Ingredients* (Gaithersburg, MD: Aspen Publishers, 2001).

[16]Fennema, *Food Chemistry*.

[17]Smith, *Food Additive User's Handbook*.

[18]Igoe and Hui, *Dictionary of Food Ingredients*.

[19]Fennema, *Food Chemistry*, 4th ed.

[20]F. J. Francis, *Colorants* (St. Paul, MN: American Association of Cereal Chemists, 1999).

[21]https://cspinet.org/new/pdf/food-dyes-rainbow-of-risks.pdf.

[22]Marmion, *Handbook of U.S. Colorants*.

[23]Smith, *Food Additive User's Handbook*.

[24]Fennema, *Food Chemistry*.

[25]Marmion, *Handbook of U.S. Colorants*.

[26]Ibid.

[27]Fennema, *Food Chemistry*.

[28]Francis, *Colorants;* Code of Federal Regulations, Title 21 (CFR 21 74.706), retrieved from www.fda.gov.

[29]Igoe and Hui, *Dictionary of Food Ingredients*.

[30]Fennema, *Food Chemistry*, 4th ed.

[31]Francis, *Colorants*.

[32]Ibid.

[33]de Man, *Principles of Food Chemistry*.

[34]Fennema, *Food Chemistry*.

[35]Y. Pomeranz, *Functional Properties of Food Components* (Orlando, FL: Academic Press, Inc., 1985).

[36]Ash and Ash, *Handbook of Food Additives*.

[37]Igoe and Hui, *Dictionary of Food Ingredients*.

[38]Smith, *Food Additive User's Handbook*.

[39]H. McGee, *On Food and Cooking: The Science and Lore of the Kitchen* (New York: Scribner, 2004).

[40]Fennema, *Food Chemistry*.

[41]Igoe and Hui, *Dictionary of Food Ingredients*.

[42]Ibid.

[43]Smith, *Food Additive User's Handbook*.

[44]Fennema, *Food Chemistry*.

[45]L. A. Kuntz, "Figuring Out Phosphates" (June 2006), retrieved from http://www.foodproductdesign.com/articles/2006/06/figuring-out-phosphates.aspx.

[46]Christen and Smith, *Food Chemistry*.

[47]D. J. Thomas and W. A. Atwell, *Starches* (St. Paul, MN: American Association of Cereal Chemists, 1999).

[48]Phosphate Forum of America. "Where Might You Encounter Phosphates Today" (2010), retrieved April 22, 2010, from http://www.phosphatesfacts.org/uses_apps.asp

[49]Kuntz, "Figuring Out Phosphates."

[50]Fennema, *Food Chemistry*.

[51]Ash and Ash, *Handbook of Food Additives*.

[52]Igoe and Hui, *Dictionary of Food Ingredients*.

[53]Y. H. Hui, *Encyclopedia of Food Science and Technology* (New York: John Wiley & Sons, 1992).

[54]Fennema, *Food Chemistry*.

[55]Ibid.

[56]Igoe and Hui, *Dictionary of Food Ingredients*.

[57]Fennema, *Food Chemistry*, 4th ed.

[58]Ibid.

[59]Igoe and Hui, *Dictionary of Food Ingredients*.

[60]R. L. Hall, "Flavor and Flavoring: Seeking a Consensus of Definition," *Food Technology* 22 (1968): 1496.

[61]*Journal of the Chemical Society of Tokyo,* No. 30, 820–836 (1909).

[62]USDA Foreign Agricultural Service, GAIN Report Number: GR7020, 1/14/2008.

[63]Code of Federal Regulations, Title 21, "Foods: Labeling of Spices, Flavorings, Colorings, and Chemical Preservatives," 21 C.F.R. § 202.1 Section 3 (2009), retrieved from www.fda.gov.

[64]*USDA Food Standards and Labeling Policy Book*, August 2005.

[65]G. A. Reineccius, "Flavor Encapsulation," *Food Reviews International* 5, no. 2 (1989): 147.

[66]G. S. Sinki and R. J. Gordon, "Flavoring Agents," in *Food Additives*, A. L. Brannen et al., eds. (New York: Marcel Dekker, 1992).

[67]M. A. Drake et al., "Development of a Descriptive Language for Cheddar Cheese," *Journal of Food Science* 66, no. 9 (2001): 1422.

[68]Ibid.

[69]R. S. Shallenberger, *Taste Chemistry* (Cambridge, UK: Blackie Academic and Professional, 1992).

[70]Igoe and Hui, *Dictionary of Food Ingredients*.

[71]Fennema, *Food Chemistry*.

[72]de Man, *Principles of Food Chemistry,* 2nd ed.

[73]Igoe and Hui, *Dictionary of Food Ingredients*.

[74]Fennema, *Food Chemistry,* 4th ed.

[75]Ash and Ash, *Handbook of Food Additives*.

[76]Fennema, *Food Chemistry*.

[77]Igoe and Hui, *Dictionary of Food Ingredients*.

[78]Ash and Ash, *Handbook of Food Additives*.

[79]Igoe and Hui, *Dictionary of Food Ingredients*.

[80]Ibid.

[81]Ash and Ash, *Handbook of Food Additives*.

[82]Igoe and Hui, *Dictionary of Food Ingredients*.

[83]McGee, *On Food and Cooking*.

[84]Fennema, *Food Chemistry*.

[85]Igoe and Hui, *Dictionary of Food Ingredients*.

[86]Ibid.

[87]Ibid.

[88]Ibid.

[89]New York City Department of Health and Mental Hygiene, "Cutting Salt, Improving Health" (2010), retrieved from http://www.nyc.gov/html/doh/html/cardio/cardio-salt-initiative.shtml.

[90]S. Daniells, "The Science of Salt Reduction in Food" (June 2006), retrieved from http://www.foodnavigator-usa.com/content/view/print/142798.

[91]Trading Standards Institute, "The Salt Reduction Toolkit" (2008), retrieved from http://www.tradingstandards.gov.uk/policy/policy-saltreductiontoolkit.cfm.

[92]J. E. Henney, C. Taylor, C. S. Boon, and The Committee on Strategies to Reduce Sodium Intake, Institute of Medicine, "Strategies to Reduce Sodium Intake in the United States" (Washington, DC: National Academies Press, April 2010), retrieved from Institute of Medicine website: http://www.iom.edu/Reports/2010/Strategies-to-Reduce-Sodium-Intake-in-the-United-States.aspx.

[93]Trading Standards Institute, "The Salt Reduction Toolkit."

[94]Henney, Taylor, Boon, and The Committee on Strategies to Reduce Sodium Intake, Institute of Medicine, "Strategies to Reduce Sodium Intake in the United States."

[95]C. Scott-Thomas, "Vinegar Could Be Used for Salt Reduction: Study" (May 2009), retrieved from http://www.foodnavigator.com/Science-Nutrition/Vinegar-could-be-used-for-salt-reduction-Study.

[96]Henney, Taylor, Boon, and The Committee on Strategies to Reduce Sodium Intake, Institute of Medicine, "Strategies to Reduce Sodium Intake in the United States."

13 | Food Safety and Spoilage

Lead Author: O. Peter Snyder, Jr., Ph.D., President, SnyderHACCP

Rachel B. Zemser, MS, CCS®, Owner, A La Carte Connections, LLC

●Introduction

While everyone who produces food for public consumption intends their products to be enjoyable, sometimes they cause unintended illness. Food obtained from land or water may contain chemical, physical, or biological hazards that cause illness or injury. It can also be contaminated with microorganisms that initiate spoilage (decay and rot) as soon as the animal is killed, or when the fruit or vegetable is harvested. There are two parts to food safety and spoilage. The first deals with the product developer's responsibility to control the hazards in food to assure consumers an appropriate level of protection (ALOP). The second deals with controlling contamination of food that can lead to spoilage so consumers' expectations of quality and freshness are met.

The regulatory standards of both the U.S. Food and Drug Administration (FDA) and the U.S. Department of Agriculture (USDA), though slightly different, are used to develop food products with similar safety results.

Food contamination begins when animals and humans pollute the water and soil used for the production of crops and livestock. Waterways from which food is taken may be contaminated by fecal or chemical runoff from farms, sewage from towns and cities, and chemical waste from processing facilities.

On farms, animal feces may contaminate the hair, feathers, and other surfaces of the animal. During slaughter, contamination on the surface of raw meat and poultry can be spread throughout the carcass. Fruits and vegetables irrigated with contaminated water or fertilized with fresh animal manure may also become hazardous. In addition, inadequate control of antibiotics or hormones fed to meat animals and of insecticides and pesticides applied to fruits and vegetables can lead to contamination of food or water.[1]

Most spoilage microorganisms do not cause illness. On the other hand, foodborne illness organisms (pathogens) normally do not change the odor, appearance, or taste of the food. This is what makes them so dangerous—there may be no obvious signs of spoilage to warn the consumer: "Don't eat!" To assure safety, standardized, proven food-handling procedures must be followed. The principal control document in the product development kitchen or laboratory is the HACCP (Hazard Analysis and Critical Control Points) recipe, which is designed to reduce hazards to the safest level possible.

●Food Safety

A recent review of epidemiologic data showed that each year 31 major pathogens acquired in the United States caused 48 million episodes of foodborne illness, 128,000 hospitalizations, and 3,000 deaths.[2] That means that *1 in 6 individuals in the United States are affected by some form of foodborne illness each year.* Continuing outbreaks every year show this problem is not going away. In March 2010, a report by the Produce Safety Coalition, the Make our Food Safe Coalition, and the Pew Charitable Trust estimated the economic impact of foodborne illness based on health-related costs (physician services, pharmaceuticals, and hospital costs) and losses to quality of life (lost life expectancy, pain and suffering, and functional disability) exceeded $150 billion annually.[3] The cost of a foodborne illness outbreak can easily put a food establishment out of business.

As the first step in new product development, the food processor determines if the food will be shelf-stable at room temperature, refrigerated, or frozen, and then processes and packages it accordingly. The consumer who purchases this food is responsible for proper handling after purchase to maintain its safety.

FIGURE 13.1 Food "from farm to fork." The flow of food from the growing area to the consumer.

Used by permission of the Hospitality Institute of Technology and Management, St. Paul, MN.

FIGURE 13.2 Selected foodborne illness outbreaks, United States, 2007.

Month	State	Etiology	Location	Total Ill	Total Hospital-izations	Total Deaths	Vehicle
June	Illinois	*Salmonella* Heidelberg (confirmed)	Fair, festival, temporary mobile service	802	29	0	Hummus
July	Illinois	Norovirus (confirmed)	Other	526	0	0	
February	Multistate outbreak reported by CDC	*Salmonella* I 4,[5], 12:i:- (confirmed)	Private home	401	108	3	Pot pie
August	Washington	*Clostridium perfringens* (confirmed)	Prison, jail	300	0	0	
December	California	Norovirus (confirmed)	Other; restaurant or deli; banquet facility	168	2	0	
May	New Jersey	*Clostridium perfringens* (confirmed)	Prison, jail	145	0	0	Turkey ziti, casserole
July	Colorado	*E. coli*, Shiga-toxin producing O121 (confirmed); *E. coli*, Shiga-toxin producing O26 (confirmed); *E. coli*, Shiga-toxin producing O84 (confirmed)	Prison, jail	135	10	0	American cheese, pasteurized; margarine

(continued)

FIGURE 13.2 *(continued)*

Month	State	Etiology	Location	Total Ill	Total Hospital-izations	Total Deaths	Vehicle
November	California	Norovirus (suspect)	Wedding reception	133			
January	Oregon	*Clostridium perfringens* (suspect)	Prison, jail	132	0	0	Spaghetti, unspecified
June	Washington	Norovirus (confirmed)	Restaurant or deli	128			Lettuce-based salads
May	New Jersey	Norovirus (confirmed)	Banquet facility	127	1	0	Chicken marsala
January	California	Norovirus (confirmed)	Restaurant or deli; office setting; private home	125	1	0	
September	Colorado	*Clostridium perfringens* (confirmed)	Prison, jail	125	0	0	Beans, chili
May	California	*E. coli*, Shiga-toxin producing O157:H7 (confirmed)	Other	124	8	0	Tri-tip
December	Ohio	Norovirus (confirmed)	Restaurant or deli	119	2	0	
April	Virginia	*Salmonella* Enteritidis (confirmed)	Restaurant or deli; banquet facility; wedding reception	106	14	0	Chicken wrap; steak, prime rib; sandwich, chicken
February	Texas	Norovirus (confirmed)	Nursing home	89	5	2	
January	Multistate outbreak reported by CDC	*Salmonella* Enteritidis (confirmed)	Private home	81	9	0	Eggs, scrambled
July	California	*Shigella sonnei* (confirmed)	Restaurant or deli	72	9	0	Lettuce-based salads
June	Multistate outbreak reported by CDC	*Salmonella* Newport (confirmed)	Restaurant or deli; private home	65	11	0	Tomato, beefsteak
June	Alabama	*E. coli*, Shiga-toxin producing O157:H7 (confirmed)	Restaurant or deli	26	11	1	Lettuce-based salads, unspecified

Source: CDC (2009)[4].

FIGURE 13.3 Major food pathogen hazards.

Microorganisms and Source (Atmosphere, Temperature Range for Growth, pH Range, and Minimal Water Activity [a_w])	Illness (Incubation Period, Symptoms, Duration)

VEGETATIVE PATHOGENIC BACTERIA

Campylobacter jejuni
Source: Poultry, raw milk, food contaminated by infected workers, cross-contamination
Growth: Obligate microaerophile; growth temp. range: 86–113°F; 4.9–9.0 pH; >0.98 a_w
Destruction D [137°F] = 12–21 sec.

Onset: 1 to 10 days (usually 2 to 5 days)
Symptoms: Abdominal pain, diarrhea (may contain occult blood), headache, fever, nausea, feeling of ill health, loss of appetite, muscle pain. Many infections are without symptoms. Chronic consequences include reactive arthritis, Guillain-Barré syndrome. May mimic appendicitis or inflammatory bowel disease.
Duration: 7 to 10 days (Relapse occurs in about 25% of cases.)
Inf. Dose: ≥500 CFU

Salmonella spp.
Source: Raw meat and poultry, seafood, eggs, raw sprouts, raw vegetables, raw milk, unpasteurized juices, food contaminated by infected workers via fecal/oral route.
Growth: Grows with or without air; growth temp. range: 41.5–114°F; 4.1–9.0 pH; 0.92–0.95 a_w
Destruction
D [140°F] = 2–6 min.

Onset: 6 to 72 hours (usually 12 to 36 hours)
Symptoms: Abdominal pain, diarrhea, nausea, vomiting, chills, fever, headache, feeling of ill health, loss of appetite. Chronic consequences include septicemia, arthritis, endocarditis, meningitis, pericarditis, and pneumonia.
Duration: Acute symptoms may last for 1 to 2 days, or may be prolonged, depending on host factors, ingested dose, and strain.
Inf. Dose: 1 to about 10^{10} CFU (depends on strain and individual; usually 100 to 1000 organisms)

Listeria monocytogenes
Source: Raw meat and poultry, fresh soft cheese, paté, smoked seafood, deli meats and salads.
Growth: Grows with or without air; growth temp. range: 29.3–112°F; 4.5–9.5 pH; 0.90–0.93 a_w
Destruction
D [140°F] = 2.85 min.
D [158°F] = 10 sec.

Onset: Variable: 3 to 70 days (median 3 weeks)
Symptoms: Fever, headache, nausea, vomiting, diarrhea precede complications of stillbirths, meningitis, encephalitis, sepsis. Use of antacids may predispose healthy people to illness.
Duration: Duration of illness is dependent on health status of individuals. Illness can present severe complications to pregnant women and their fetuses (perinatal and neonatal infections), as well as meningitis and septicemia in immune-compromised persons and the elderly. Fatalities occur from severe complications.
Inf. Dose: 10^2 to 10^3 CFU

Escherichia coli O157:H7
Source: Raw ground beef, raw seed sprouts, raw milk, unpasteurized juice, raw vegetables, contaminated water, food contaminated by infected workers via fecal/oral route.
Growth: Grows with or without air; growth temp. range: 44.6–114°F; 4.0–9.0 pH; 0.95 a_w
Destruction
D [140°F] = 1.7 min.

Onset: 2 to 10 days (median 3 to 4 days)
Symptoms: Abdominal pain, diarrhea, stools are initially watery but become grossly bloody. Vomiting occurs occasionally. Fever may or may not be present.
Duration: The illness is usually self-limiting and lasts for an average of 8 days. Some individuals exhibit watery diarrhea only.
Complications: Hemolytic uremic syndrome, vascular and neurologic complications in very young, elderly, and any immune-compromised individuals. Can be fatal.
Inf. Dose: Very low: 10^1 to 10^3 CFU

Vibrio parahaemolyticus
Source: Seafood, shellfish (shrimp, oysters), water.
Growth: Grows with or without air; growth temp. range: 41–109.4°F; 4.5–11.0 pH; 0.937 a_w
Destruction
D [120°F] = 0.35–0.72 min.

Onset: Illness occurs within 4 to 30 hours after consumption of raw, undercooked, or cooked recontaminated fish and shellfish harvested along the coast of the United States in warmer months of year. Use of antacids increases susceptibility.
Symptoms: Abdominal pain, nausea, vomiting, diarrhea, fever, chills, and headache. Systemic infection and death rarely occur.
Duration: Duration of illness is about 1 to 7 days.
Inf. Dose: 10^5 or more CFU

Shigella spp. (*Shigella sonnei*)
Source: Raw vegetables and herbs, non-potable water, any food contaminated by infected workers via fecal/oral route.
Growth: Grows with or without air; growth temp. range: 42.8–116.6°F; 4.8–9.3 pH; 0.95 a_w
Destruction
Rapidly inactivated above 149°F (65°C).

Onset: 12 to 96 hours (usually 1 to 3 days)
Symptoms: Abdominal pain; cramps; diarrhea; fever; vomiting; stools may contain mucous, pus, and blood.
Duration: Symptoms may last for 4 to 7 days, or may be prolonged, depending on host factors, ingested dose, and strain. Fatality may be as high as 10–15% with some strains. Reiter's disease, reactive arthritis, and hemolytic uremic syndrome are possible illness complications.
Inf. Dose: 10 to 100 CFU

(continued)

FIGURE 13.3 (*continued*)

Microorganisms and Source (Atmosphere, Temperature Range for Growth, pH Range, and Minimal Water Activity [a_w])	Illness (Incubation Period, Symptoms, Duration)

Yersinia enterocolitica
Source: Pork, raw milk, contaminated water supply.
Growth: Grows with or without air; growth temp. range: 29.3–111°F; 4.6–9.0 pH; 0.945 a_w
Destruction
   D [145°F] = 0.24–0.96 min.

Onset: Illness occurs within 3 to 7 days (usually under 10 days) after ingestion. Often associated with consumption of inadequately cooked or raw pork.
Symptoms: Gastroenteritis with diarrhea and/or vomiting; fever and abdominal pain are common symptoms. May mimic appendicitis and lymphadenitis. May cause reactive arthritis.
Duration: As long as 2 to 3 weeks. May be treated with antibiotics other than penicillin.
Inf. Dose: 10^7 to 10^9 CFU

Staphylococcus aureus
Source: Humans are the main source of staphylococci. Contamination of food can occur by direct contact, indirectly by skin fragments, or through respiratory tract droplets. Animals and poultry also carry *S. aureus*.
Growth: Grows with or without air; grows in 10% salt and produces toxin; growth temp. range: 42.8–118°F; 4.2–9.3 pH; 0.83 a_w; Toxin production: 50–114.8°F
Destruction
  Cells:
    D [160°F] = 15 sec.
  Toxin:
    D [210°F] = >2 hours

Onset: 30 minutes to 8 hours, usually 2 to 4 hours
Symptoms: Nausea, vomiting, retching, abdominal pain, diarrhea, prostration
Duration: 1 to 3 days
Illness producing amount: Illness occurs from the ingestion of ready-to-eat, potentially hazardous foods contaminated with *S. aureus* that is allowed to grow and produce toxin when the food is time/temperature abused.
Amount of toxin necessary for illness is produced by the growth of 10^5 to 10^6 /g *S. aureus* in food, or consumption of <1 µg enterotoxin.

SPORE-FORMING PATHOGENS

Bacillus cereus
Source: Meat, poultry, starchy foods (rice, potatoes), puddings, soups, cooked vegetables. *B. cereus* is widely distributed and can be found in soil, dust, air, water, and decaying matter. Humans are not a significant source of food contamination by *B. cereus*.
Growth: Grows with or without air; growth temp. range: 39.2–122°F; 4.35–9.0 pH; 0.912–0.95 a_w
Destruction
  Vegetative cells: D [140°F] = 1 min.
  Spores: D [212°F] = 5 min.

Two (2) types of illness:
(1) Emetic illness due to preformed toxin in food
Onset: 1/2 to 6 hours
Symptoms: Nausea, vomiting, occasionally diarrhea. (May resemble *S. aureus* intoxication.)
Duration: Generally less than 1 day
Illness producing amount: Toxin produced by the growth of 10^5 to 10^{11}/g *B. cereus* in food.
(2) Diarrheal illness results from the ingestion of vegetative cells and/or spores and their subsequent multiplication and toxin production within the intestinal tract.
Onset: 6 to 15 hours
Symptoms: Abdominal pain, nausea, watery diarrhea. (Simulates *C. perfringens* gastroenteritis.)
Duration: 24 hours
Inf. Dose: >5 x 10^5 /g *B. cereus* in food

Clostridium perfringens
Source: *C. perfringens* is widely distributed in soil, dust, and vegetation. It is found in a large variety of foods including raw, dehydrated, and cooked foods.
Cooked meat and poultry, casseroles, and gravies made from cooked meat and poultry are often implicated in outbreaks.
Growth: Grows with or without air; growth temp. range: 59–125°F; 5.5–9.0 pH; 0.93–0.97 a_w
Destruction
  Vegetative cells: D [138°F] = 7.2 min.
  Spores: D [210°F] = 26–31 min.; D [250°F] = 0.15 min.

Onset: 6 to 24 hours (usually 10–12 hours)
Symptoms: Abdominal pain, watery diarrhea. Nausea is common, vomiting and fever are absent.
Illness results from the ingestion of vegetative cells and/or spores and their subsequent multiplication and toxin production within the intestinal tract.
Duration: 24 hours (Less severe illness symptoms can persist in some individuals for 1 or 2 weeks.)
Inf. Dose: >10^5 to 10^{10} CFU

(continued)

FIGURE 13.3 (*continued*)

Microorganisms and Source (Atmosphere, Temperature Range for Growth, pH Range, and Minimal Water Activity [a$_w$])	Illness (Incubation Period, Symptoms, Duration)

Clostridium botulinum (Type A and Proteolytic B strains)

Source: Types A and B (proteolytic *C. botulinum*) are found in soil and sediment. Type E is a normal inhabitant of the marine environment. Vacuum-packed foods, reduced-oxygen packaged foods, under-processed canned foods, garlic-in-oil mixtures, time/temperature-abused baked potatoes/sautéed onions have been implicated in outbreaks of Types A and B (proteolytic *C. botulinum*).

Growth: Grows without air; grows in up to 5% salt; growth temp. range: 50–118°F; 4.6–9.0 pH; 0.94 a$_w$

Destruction
Vegetative cells: Killed in a few min. at 140°F
Spores: D [250°F] = 0.2 min.; (212°F) = 50 min.

Clostridium botulinum (Type E and other non-proteolytic strains)

Source: Vacuum-packed salted fish products
Growth: Grows without air; grows in up to 5% salt; growth temp. range: 38–113°F; 5.0–9.0 pH; 0.97 a$_w$
Destruction
Spores: D [180°F] = 0.49–0.74 min.
Toxin destruction (any botulinal toxin): D [185°F] = 5 min.

Onset: 12 to 36 hours (range: 4 hours to 8 days)

Symptoms: Early signs of intoxication include lassitude, weakness, and vertigo, usually followed by double vision and progressive difficulty in speaking and swallowing. Difficulty in breathing, weakness of other muscles, abdominal distension, and constipation may also be common symptoms.

Duration: Can be fatal. Botulinum toxin causes flaccid paralysis by blocking motor nerve terminals at the myoneural junction. Flaccid paralysis progresses symmetrically downward, starting with the face and eyes, to the throat, chest and extremities. When the diaphragm and chest muscles become involved, respiration is stopped and death from asphyxia results. Treatment involves administration of botulinal anti-toxin and intensive supportive care (including mechanical breathing assistance). Recovery depends on early treatment and care.

Toxic Dose: Up to about 10^9 LD$_{50}$ toxin in mice. (LD$_{50}$ = Lethal Dose for 50% of population.)

VIRUSES

Norovirus

Source: Food contaminated by infected worker via fecal/oral route, person-to-person transfer, contaminated surfaces. Other sources: bivalve shellfish, salads, water, and ice.
Growth: Does not grow in food.
Destruction: Resistant to heat inactivation. Pasteurization does not eliminate virus. Steaming shellfish may not inactivate virus.

Onset: Illness occurs within 24 to 48 hours (range: 10 to 50 hours) after ingestion of microorganism in food or drink.

Symptoms: Nausea, vomiting, abdominal pain, diarrhea, low-grade fever, chills, general feeling of ill health, loss of appetite, headache.

Duration: 24 to 48 hours

Inf. Dose: Unknown, probably less than 10 virus particles

Hepatitis A and E

Source: Shellfish, any food or water contaminated by infected worker via fecal/oral route.
Growth: Does not grow in food or water.
Destruction: Resistant to heat inactivation. Pasteurization does not eliminate virus. Steaming shellfish may not inactivate virus.

Onset: Illness occurs within 15 to 50 days after exposure (median = 28 to 30 days).

Symptoms: Fever, general feeling of ill health, loss of appetite, tiredness, nausea, abdominal pain, jaundice.

Duration: If disease is mild, recovery is complete in 1 to 2 weeks. If symptoms are severe, recovery and convalescence can take several months.

Inf. Dose: Unknown, probably less than 100 virus particles

PARASITIC PROTOZOA

Giardia lamblia

Source: Human and animal feces, soil, water. Water may contaminate food products when used for irrigation or washing of fresh produce. May be present in food or water as a cyst.
Destruction: Cysts D [100°F] = 3 min.

Onset: Illness occurs within 3 to 25 days (7 to 10 days median time).

Symptoms: Diarrhea, abdominal pain, steatorrhea, bloating, frequent loose and pale greasy stools, fatigue, weight loss. Can be fatal in those unable to fight disease.

Duration: Usually 1 to 2 weeks. In some individuals, it may remain for months to years.

Inf. Dose: 1 to 10 cysts

(continued)

FIGURE 13.3 *(continued)*

Microorganisms and Source (Atmosphere, Temperature Range for Growth, pH Range, and Minimal Water Activity [a_w])	Illness (Incubation Period, Symptoms, Duration)
Cryptsporidium spp. **Source:** Human and animal feces. May be present in food or water as oocysts. **Destruction:** Oocysts are destroyed at temperatures above 163°F.	**Onset:** Illness occurs within 1 to 12 days (7 days median time). **Symptoms:** Severe watery diarrhea, but may also be asymptomatic. Pulmonary and tracheal cryptosporidiosis in humans is associated with coughing, possible low-grade fever, and severe intestinal distress. **Duration:** Usually 2 to 4 days. In some individuals, it may last 1 to 4 weeks. **Inf. Dose:** 1 or more cysts **Confirmation:** Identification of cysts and/or trophozoites in feces.
***Trichinella spiralis* and other Trichinae** **Source:** Swine (pigs), wild game (bears, seals, etc.) **Destruction:** Trichinae are destroyed by heating meat above 140°F. USDA: Kotola: Heat to 170°F (adds extra level of safety).	**Onset:** Illness occurs within 8 to 15 days (range: 5 to 45 days). **Symptoms:** Some gastrointestinal symptoms; other symptoms are dependent on organs or tissues affected. For example, muscle soreness and pain with edema of upper eyelids is an early symptom. These symptoms are followed by retinal hemorrhages, pain, and photophobia. There is thirst, profuse sweating, chills (fever), weakness, prostration, and a rapidly increasing number of white blood cells. **Duration:** Can cause severe illness and may be fatal if not treated with medication (Mebendazole) in early stages.
Toxoplasma gondii **Source:** Cats, soil; *Toxoplasma gondii* is an obligate intracellular protozoan parasite. Infected cats are the only species to shed oocysts that sporolate in the environment in their feces. Can be found in the soil and on food that is grown in soil containing this parasite. Adults become infected by consuming this parasite from various sources in the environment. **Destruction:** *T. gondii* is destroyed by heating meat above 140°F.	**Onset:** Illness occurs within 5 to 23 days after ingestion of undercooked meat or outbreak associated with cats. **Symptoms:** In adults, the infection may be without symptoms, or present as acute disease with lymphadenopathy only, or resemble mononucleosis with fever, lymphadenopathy, and lymphocytosis persisting for days or weeks. A primary infection during early pregnancy may lead to fetal infection with death of the fetus or manifestations such as chorioretinitis, brain damage with introcerebral calcification, hydrocephaly, microcephaly, fever, jaundice, rash, and convulsions at birth or shortly thereafter. **Duration:** Disease can persist for years in adults with varying degrees of symptoms or lack of symptoms. The greatest threat is the effect of life-long brain damage to fetuses. **Inf. Dose:** Unknown. No direct person-to-person transfer except in utero. Oocysts shed by cats sporolate and become infective 1 to 5 days later and may remain infective in water and soil for more than a year. Cysts in the flesh of infected animals remain infective as long as the meat is edible and uncooked.
PARASITIC WORMS ***Anisakis simplex*** **Source:** Various infected fish (cod, haddock, fluke, pacific salmon, herring, flounder, monkfish) that are eaten raw or partially cooked	**Onset:** Within a range of 15 minutes to 26 hours after ingestion, with a mean of 5 hours after ingestion **Symptoms:** After ingestion of larvae-infected fish, gastric symptoms (abdominal pain, nausea, and vomiting) may occur. Occasionally the larvae are coughed up. If the larvae pass into the bowel, a severe response may also occur 1 to 2 weeks following infection, causing symptoms mimicking Crohn's disease. Gastroallergic anisakiasis may also produce allergic symptoms, usually several hours after ingestion. **Duration:** Symptoms remain as long as this infective parasite is present. Larvae may have to be removed surgically. **Inf. Dose:** 1 larva

(continued)

FIGURE 13.3 *(continued)*

Microorganisms and Source (Atmosphere, Temperature Range for Growth, pH Range, and Minimal Water Activity [a_w])	Illness (Incubation Period, Symptoms, Duration)
***Taenia* (tapeworms and larvae)** **Source:** Raw beef and pork products; people can become infected with the beef tapeworm, *Taenia saginata,* and/or the pork tapeworm, *Taenia solium,* after eating raw or insufficiently cooked meat products. *T. saginata* is about 25 feet long, whereas *T. solium* is about 8 feet long with up to 2,000 proglottids (segments).	**Symptoms**: The main damage is obstruction in the intestine. The life cycle involves the release of gravid proglottids to soil, from where they are consumed by cattle or pigs. Embryos are released from the eggs and these are passed to the muscle of animal where they encyst. These may then be consumed in poorly cooked beef or pork. Most people with tapeworms have no symptoms, but some report abdominal discomfort, diarrhea, and loss of appetite. With severe infection, cysts in the brain and the tissues covering the brain (meninges) in people with cysticercosis can result in headaches, seizures, confusion, or other neurologic symptoms. Rarely, cysts develop in the eyes, sometimes causing blindness, or in the spinal cord, sometimes causing muscle weakness or paralysis. **Confirmation:** Infection is recognized when the infected person passes segments of proglottids in the stool, especially if the segment is moving.

Sources: Adapted from CDC (2008)[5]; FDA (2009a)[6]; Heymann (2004)[7]; Smith Daifas, El-Khoury, and Austin (2003)[8]; Smith Daifas, El-Khoury, and Koukoutsis (2002)[9].

Hazard Analysis Critical Control Points (HACCP)

HACCP is a process control system designed to identify and prevent microbial and other hazards in food production. It includes seven steps for preventing problems and for correcting deviations as soon as they are detected. HACCP is endorsed by such scientific and food safety authorities as the National Academy of Sciences and the National Advisory Committee on Microbiological Criteria for Foods (NACMCF), and by such international organizations as the Codex Alimentarius Commission and the International Commission on Microbiological Specifications for Foods as the most effective approach available for producing safe food.

Under the Pathogen Reduction and HACCP Systems regulations, the USDA requires all meat and poultry plants to implement HACCP systems to monitor and control production operations.[10]

The HACCP plan includes the analysis and control of biological, chemical, and physical hazards—from raw material growth and harvest, through procurement and handling, to manufacturing, distribution, and consumption of the finished product. For successful implementation of a HACCP plan, management must be strongly committed to the concept. A firm commitment to HACCP by top management gives company employees a sense of the importance of producing safe food.

HACCP is designed for use in all segments of the food industry, from growing, harvesting, processing, manufacturing, distributing, and merchandising to preparing food for consumption. Prerequisite programs such as Good Manufacturing Practices (GMPs) are an essential foundation for the development and implementation of successful HACCP plans. Food safety systems based on HACCP principles have been successfully applied in food processing plants, retail food stores, and foodservice operations.

The seven principles of HACCP are universally accepted by government agencies, trade associations, and the food industry around the world. They are: (1) hazard analysis, (2) critical control point identification, (3) establishment of critical limits, (4) monitoring procedures, (5) corrective actions, (6) record keeping, and (7) verification procedures.

The Seven HACCP Principles

Principle 1: Conduct a hazard analysis.

Processors determine potential food safety hazards and then identify preventive measures that can be applied to control these hazards. A food safety hazard is any biological, chemical, or physical property that may cause a food to be unsafe for human consumption.

Principle 2: Identify critical control points.

A critical control point (CCP) is a point, step, or procedure in a food process at which control can be applied and, as a result, a food safety hazard prevented, eliminated, or reduced to an acceptable level.

Principle 3: Establish critical limits for each critical control point.

A critical limit is the maximum or minimum value to which a physical, biological, or chemical hazard must be controlled at a critical control point to prevent, eliminate, or reduce it to an acceptable level.

Principle 4: Establish CCP requirements.

Monitoring activities are necessary to ensure the process is under control at each critical control point. The Food Safety and Inspection Service (FSIS), an agency of the USDA, is the public health agency responsible for ensuring the nation's commercial supply of meat, poultry, and egg products is safe, wholesome, and correctly labeled and packaged. FSIS requires that each monitoring procedure and its frequency be listed in the HACCP plan.

Principle 5: Establish corrective actions.

Corrective actions are those taken when monitoring indicates a deviation from an established critical limit. Thus, a plant's HACCP plan must identify the specific corrective actions to be taken if a critical limit is not met. Corrective actions are intended to ensure that no product injurious to health or otherwise adulterated as a result of the deviation enters commerce.

Principle 6: Establish record-keeping procedures.

The HACCP regulation requires that all plants maintain certain documents, including hazard analysis and written HACCP plans, and records the monitoring of CCPs, critical limits, verification activities, and the handling of processing deviations.

Principle 7: Establish procedures for verifying the HACCP system is working as intended.

Validation ensures that the plans do what they were designed to do—that is, that they are successful in ensuring the production of safe product. Plants are required to validate their own HACCP plans. FSIS does not approve HACCP plans in advance but rather reviews them for conformance. Verification procedures may include review of HACCP plans, CCP records, critical limits, and microbial sampling and analysis. FSIS requires the HACCP plan to include verification tasks to be performed by plant personnel. Verification tasks are also performed by FSIS inspectors. Both FSIS and industry undertake microbial testing as one of several verification activities.

The success of an HACCP system depends on educating and training each manager and employee in the importance of their role in producing safe foods. Management must provide adequate time for thorough education and training. Personnel must be given the materials and equipment necessary to perform these tasks. It is important to recognize that employees must first understand what HACCP is and then learn the skills necessary to make it function properly. Specific training activities include working instructions and procedures that outline the tasks of employees monitoring each CCP.

Hazards can enter the kitchen or processing facility from personnel, the environment, the facility and equipment, and from both food and non-food supplies. Therefore, hazard

FIGURE 13.4 **HACCP-based food system.**

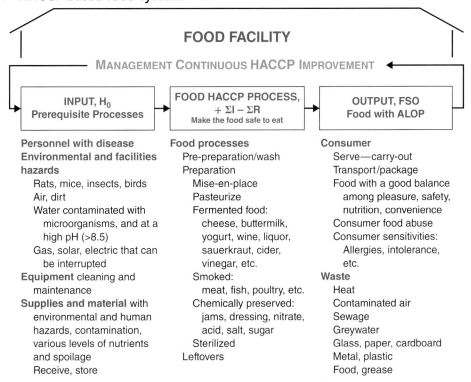

Used by permission of the Hospitality Institute of Technology and Management, St. Paul, MN.

FIGURE 13.5 Potential chemical, physical, and biological hazards in food.

Chemical Hazards	Physical Hazards	Biological Hazards

Metabolic
Allergens
Food intolerance
Inborn errors of metabolism
Enzyme inhibitors
   Protease inhibitors (e.g.,
    haemagglutins, lectins)
Carcinogens
Naturally occurring in foods
  Cyanogens
Result of cooking/processing
  Acrylamide
  Benzopyrene
  Heterocyclic amines
  Nitrosamines
Toxic compounds (toxins) in food
  Fish/seafood toxins
    Ciguatera
    Scombroid poisoning
    Shellfish toxins
    Tetrodotoxin
  Mushroom toxins
Other chemical hazards in food
Alcohol (Ethanol: added or formed
  during fermentation)
Antibiotics
Artificial colors
Artificial sweeteners
Chemical contaminants from environment
Pesticide residues (pest control chemicals)
Heavy metals from food cooking and
  storage equipment
Cleaning chemicals in the facility
Hormones
Excessive levels of preservatives
Excessive addition of nutrients (vitamins) and
  other food chemicals such as MSG, sulfates
Lipid compounds
Olestra
Trans fat
	Broken glass from bottles, jars,
	  utensils, uncovered light
	  fixtures, gauge covers
	Wood from toothpicks,
	  wooden skewers, pallets,
	  boxes
	Stones, metal fragments from
	  incoming supplies, utensils,
	  equipment, employees
	Bone from improper processing,
	  supplies
	Plastic from packaging
	  materials, pallets, equipment,
	  employees, surrounding areas
	Personal effects from
	  employees
	Pits and stems from fruit and
	  shells from nuts
	Filth from birds, insects,
	  rodents, or any other
	  unwanted animal parts
	Pieces of food that cannot be
	  swallowed (e.g., pieces of
	  meat, bone, hot dogs,
	  marshmallows, etc.)
	Hot beverages and hot
	  solid foods that spill on skin
	  and burn tissue
		Bacteria (vegetative cells and spores)
		Vegetative, non-exotoxin producer
		  Campylobacter jejuni
		  Escherichia coli O157:H7
		  Listeria monocytogenes
		  Salmonella spp.
		  Shigella spp.
		  Streptococcus
		  Vibrio spp.
		  Yersinia enterocolitica
		Vegetative-exotoxin producer
		  Staphylococcus aureus
		Spore-forming pathogens
		  Bacillus cereus (exotoxin)
		  Clostridium botulinum (exotoxin)
		  Clostridium perfringens
		Viruses
		Hepatitis A virus
		Hepatitis E virus
		Norovirus
		Rotoviruses
		Parasites
		Giardia lamblia
		Cryptosporidium parvum
		Toxoplasma gondii
		Trichinella spiralis
		Cyclospora cayetanensis
		Anisakis spp. and related worms
		Others
		Mold
		Aspergillus flavus (aflatoxins)
		Yeast
		Candida albicans

Used by permission of the Hospitality Institute of Technology and Management, St. Paul, MN.

controls must be in place before HACCP-based food production begins to ensure hazards are reduced to an ALOP.

Food HACCP processes include:

1. *mise-en-place* (for example, gathering ingredients, opening packages, washing food)
2. preparation (peeling, trimming, dicing)
3. use of food additives, where necessary for safety
4. cooking/pasteurizing to a safety critical limit
5. packaging
6. chilling or freezing as appropriate for later distribution

The hazards in food exiting the kitchen or the processing facility must have been controlled (prevented, eliminated, or reduced) to achieve a food safety objective (FSO) that assures minimal risk (ALOP) while providing enjoyment, nutrition, and convenience for the customer. Examples of FSOs are "100 *Bacillus cereus* organisms per gram in cooked rice" or "less than 100 mesophilic organisms per 50 square centimeters on a clean cutting board." These are determined by the company's quality assurance department or HACCP plan.

To develop foods that assure consumer safety, the developer must be able to (1) identify the hazards and specify CCPs where hazards may increase, and then (2) specify controls to reduce the chemical, physical, and biological hazards on raw materials, personnel, and the kitchen/processing environment so the product meets a hazard level considered an acceptable risk by the owner or quality assurance manager of the business and that meets government health and safety regulations.

The risk associated with each hazard is determined by its frequency and its likelihood of causing severe illness or injury. *There is no zero risk.* It is impossible to have a totally risk-free food production facility. However, if a new process or product is developed without considering validated safe procedures, the risk of causing consumer illness or injury is increased and the manufacturer is subject to serious litigation.

Identification of Hazards and Controls

To identify hazards and controls, research chefs and product developers must know the sources of the hazards in the food system as well as how to control them through correct methods of purchasing, storage, processing, and packaging. Food manufacturers are responsible for buying from suppliers that have HACCP programs or provide letters of guarantee for food and ingredients. For fresh foods, this means the supplier guarantees that foods have been grown, processed, packaged, and labeled accurately and that the level of hazards in the food meets a mutually agreed-upon FSO. This is why detailed ingredient purchase specifications are written.

Chemical Hazards

Chemical hazards may be present in food or ingredients as purchased from suppliers, through cross-contamination in the production facility, or by mistakes in measurement or identity. They can include allergens (for example, milk, peanuts, seafood) and food intolerances (for example, gluten, lactose, monosodium glutamate [MSG]); certain functional ingredients (for example, aspartame, sulfites, nitrites) that require warning labels on foods that contain them; and toxic compounds found naturally in foods such as certain fish (for example, tetrodotoxin, scombroid) and mushrooms (for example, muscarine, psilocybin). Alcohol, antibiotics, and some colors (for example, red dye #40, yellow dye #5) can also be considered chemical hazards for consumers who have dietary or religious restrictions or chemical sensitivities. Of course, chemical contaminants such as pesticides, cleaning compounds, heavy metals, and many other materials not meant for human consumption are all considered chemical hazards.

Preventing chemical hazards at unsafe levels from getting into the food is the only control. Food processors cannot remove hazardous chemical contaminants from food to make the food safe. Product development and production personnel must be trained to measure and use permitted food chemicals (for example, MSG, phosphates, nitrates) correctly, and to store and use cleaning and sanitizing chemicals and pesticides as directed by the manufacturer. They must know the allergens or other ingredients (for example, gluten, phenylalanine) that may cause metabolic disturbances in the foods they produce.

Some chemical hazards are specific to fish. For example, scombrotoxin (elevated histamine formation) in fatty fish such as tuna, mackerel, and mahi mahi indicates spoilage due to improper storage temperature control, and can cause a classic allergenic response in sensitive individuals. Another

FIGURE 13.6 Chemical hazards and control measures.

Hazard	Control
Scombrotoxin from improperly cooled, stored cold scombroid fish (tuna fish, mahi-mahi, blue fish, anchovies, bonito, mackerel)	• Check temperatures at time received. Scombrotoxin is produced when fresh raw scombroid fish is temperature abused.
Ciguatoxin from reef fin fish from southeast United States, Hawaii, and other tropical areas (barracuda, jacks, king mackerel, large groupers and snappers); due to an accumulation of ciguatoxin in the muscle of fish when they consume the dynoflagellate *Gambierdiscus toxicus*	• Purchase fish from suppliers that test for ciguatoxin.
Tetrodotoxin from pufferfish	• Do not serve these fish.
Shellfish toxins Paralytic shellfish poisoning (PSP) from molluscan shellfish from northeast and northwest coastal regions (mackerel, viscera of lobsters and Dungeness, tanner, and red rock crabs) Diarrhetic shellfish poisoning (DSP) from molluscan shellfish in Japan, western Europe, Chile, New Zealand, eastern Canada Neurotoxin shellfish poisoning (NSP) from molluscan shellfish Amnesic shellfish poisoning (ASP) from molluscan shellfish from northeast and northwest coasts of North America; viscera of Dungeness, tanner, red rock crabs, and anchovies	• Purchase molluscan shellfish from suppliers that have a hazard control program. • Purchase from suppliers who test their products and certify the safety of the products.

(continued)

FIGURE 13.6 (*continued*)

Hazard	Control
Mycotoxins Aflatoxin from mold growth (*Aspergillus flavus*) in corn and corn products; peanuts and peanut products; cottonseed; tree nuts such as Brazil nuts, pecans, pistachio nuts, and walnuts; other grains and nuts also susceptible if conditions allowing mold growth occur. Patulin from the growth of *Penicillium expansum* in apple juice	• Purchase from suppliers who test their products and certify the safety of the products. • Check condition at time received. Do not use moldy grains. • Purchase from a supplier who will guarantee that rotten apples were not used for juice production.
Poisonous mushroom species from numerous varieties of wild mushrooms	• Buy mushrooms from regulated suppliers.
Pyrrolizidine alkaloids from plant foods containing these alkaloids; most commonly found in members of the *Borginaceae, Compositae,* and *Leguminosae* families (herbal teas)	• Do not buy food or medicinals contaminated with these alkaloids.
Phytohaemmagglutinin from raw red kidney beans; undercooked beans may be more toxic than raw beans	• Soak in water for at least 5 hours. Pour away water. Boil briskly above 200°F in fresh water with occasional stirring, for at least 10 minutes.
Environmental contaminants (e.g., pesticides, fungicides, fertilizers, insecticides, antibiotics, growth hormones)	• Buy from suppliers who test, label and guarantee safety of products. • Store harmful chemicals in areas that are separate from food supplies.
Chemicals used in retail establishments (e.g., lubricants, cleaners, sanitizers, cleaning compounds, and paints)	• Store chemicals separate from food. Label and use chemicals according to manufacturer directions. Maintain Material Safety Data Sheets for all chemicals. Use non-toxic lubricants for equipment.
PCBs (Polychlorinated biphenyls) from packaging materials, fish	• Buy from suppliers who test and will guarantee safety of products.
Copper in copper containers, copper piping	• Do not cook or store foods that are more acid than pH 6.0 in copper containers/equipment. • Use backflow prevention devices on beverage vending machines.
Lead in galvanized containers that contain lead	• Do not use cooking utensils or enamel ware containing lead.
Preservatives and food additives Sulfiting agents (sulfur dioxide, sodium and potassium bisulfite, sodium and potassium metabisulfite) that are used by processors for shrimp, lobster, wine, canned lemon juice, dried fruits and vegetables Nitrites/nitrates in cured meats, fish, any food exposed to accidental contamination, spinach	• Buy food products from a supplier who can provide product specifications on the levels of sulfiting agents added to a product. • Use and prepare products with no more than the approved amount of (nitrites/nitrates) curing compound.
Niacin in meat and other foods to which sodium nicotinate has been added	• Sodium nicotinate (niacin is not currently approved for use in meat or poultry with or without nitrites or nitrates).
Monosodium glutamate MSG (flavor enhancer) has been associated with Asian food but is found in many processed, canned, and frozen foods	• Avoid using excessive amounts. (1 oz./100 lb. food is safe.) Inform consumers of presence in food if requested.
Allergens (milk, eggs, fish, crustacean shellfish, tree nuts, wheat, peanuts, soybeans)	• Inform consumers of presence in food, when requested.

Used by permission of the Hospitality Institute of Technology and Management, St. Paul, MN.

FIGURE 13.7 Physical hazards and control measures.

Hazard	Control
Glass: Bottles, jars, glass light fixtures, utensils, gauge covers, glass thermometer stems May cause cuts, bleeding; may require surgery to find or remove.	• Inspect and handle products in a manner to prevent presence of hazards. • Make certain that light fixtures are covered/screened. • Do not use thermometers with glass stems. • Account for broken glass objects/containers and discard products if there is any possibility of broken glass.
Wood: Incoming raw foods, pallets, boxes, building material, toothpicks, wooden spoons and paddles used for mixing food May cause cuts, infection, choking; may require surgery to remove.	• Inspect incoming products for evidence of wood chips or splinters and handle products in a manner to prevent presence of hazard in prepared food. • Use "toothpicks with pants" in food. Do not use wooden utensils for food preparation and service. (Exception: wooden stirrers can be used for candy making.) • Remove objects or discard suspect food in order to prevent injury.
Stones, rocks, dirt: Incoming foods such as uncooked cereals and dried vegetable products (e.g., rice, navy beans, fresh fruits and vegetables) May cause choking, broken teeth; may require surgery to remove.	• Designate supplier specifications for extraneous contamination in rice and dried vegetable items. • Inspect food products and remove stones as a part of the preparation process. Wash fresh fruits and vegetables to remove excess soil (dirt).
Pits and shell fragments: Fruit pits, shells from nuts and shellfish May cause choking, broken teeth; may require surgery to remove.	• Inspect products for pits (e.g., cherries), shells from nuts and shellfish (e.g., oysters). Remove pits/shells or discard food in order to prevent injury.
Bone fragments: Meat, fish, and poultry products May cause cuts, infection, choking; may require surgery to remove.	• Inspect products for evidence of bones or bone splinters. • Remove bone fragments or discard food in order to prevent injury.
Metal fragments: Possible presence in food (e.g., buckshot, nails, bolts, pieces of equipment, wire twist ties) May cause cuts, infection, choking; may require surgery to remove.	• Buy from suppliers who guarantee the safety of their products. • Inspect and handle products in a manner to prevent presence of metal fragments in prepared food.
Plastic fragments: Packaging materials, equipment, containers May cause cuts, infection, choking; may require surgery to remove.	• Inspect and handle products in a manner to prevent presence of plastic fragments in prepared food. • Account for broken brittle plastic objects/containers and discard food if presence is suspected.
Personal effects: Earrings, artificial fingernails, buttons, clips, pins, pens, pencils, etc.	• Educate employees to not wear artificial fingernails and any jewelry or other items that might fall into food. • Inspect products and remove objects when presence is suspected or discard food in order to prevent injury.
Human hair from head and beard **Animal hair**	• Inspect products for the presence of human and/or animal hair. The presence of hair in food is a quality consideration. Consumers find it objectionable. • Employees preparing food should be required to wear hair restraints or coverings. • Remove hair and serve food if contamination is minimal or discard product.
Filth and pathogens from birds, insects, rodents, and any unwanted animal parts	• Buy from suppliers who provide letters of guarantee of the quality and safety of their products. A certain amount of insect contamination is allowed by terms as defined by Food Defect Action Levels (FDA, 1998). If safety and quality of the product are in doubt, it should be discarded.

(continued)

FIGURE 13.7 *(continued)*

Hazard	Control
Packaging defects: Broken boxes, bags, and other packaging material that allows the entrance of dirt, insects, and other contaminants	• Inspect package integrity when receiving food. Reject broken packages. Inspect packages of stored foods. • Discard any food items if broken packaging has compromised the safety of food.
Sabotage: Deliberate contamination and compromised safety of food products by employee(s) such as adding broken glass, etc.	• Hiring and monitoring of employee performance. • Good supervision practices. • Discard food items if there is any doubt about food safety.
Food asphyxiation hazards: Pieces of food that cannot be swallowed, such as large pieces (probably larger than ¼ inch) of meat, bone, hot dogs, marshmallows, etc.	• Cut food into smaller pieces, especially for young children. • Train employees in the use of the Heimlich maneuver and call 911 when necessary.
Thermal hazards: Hot beverages and solid foods that burn tissue, such as hot coffee, tea, soup, or jelly-filled Bismarcks heated in a microwave oven.	• Warn customers that products are very hot if served at temperatures of 170°F (76.7°C) and above.

Used by permission of the Hospitality Institute of Technology and Management, St. Paul, MN.

example, ciguatoxin, may be present in reef-dwelling species such as grouper and snapper that have eaten toxin-containing plankton called dinoflagellates (causative agent of "red tide"). These fish require supplier testing at certain times of the year. Finally, tetrodotoxin is a lethal poison found naturally in pufferfish, which are illegal to use as food in the United States.

Toxins from shellfish can cause paralytic, diarrheic, neurotoxic, or amnesic poisoning. Shellfish should be purchased only from suppliers that certify it has been harvested from safe waters, and all shellfish must be tagged with date and location of harvest as well as the harvester's name, address, and FDA identification number.

Mycotoxins due to mold growth in foods (for example, aflatoxin, ergotism) and poisonous mushrooms are also chemical hazards and must be controlled by supplier certification.

Environmental contaminants and chemicals used in the food facility, polychlorinated biphenyls (PCBs), and heavy metals such as copper and lead come from a variety of sources, and items containing these chemical hazards must be assessed and then controlled or eliminated. Preservatives and food additives can be controlled by not exceeding government-mandated use levels in foods as indicated by the supplier or by following government regulations. Finally, the presence of allergenic or other ingredients the government identifies as potentially harmful to certain members of the population must be identified on food packages in clearly written ingredient labels.

Physical Hazards

Physical hazards in food are conditions that can cause immediate bodily injury as the food is consumed, such as broken glass or wood, bones, stones, or plastic. Also included are sharp objects that puncture the throat, large or hard food ingredients that cause choking, and high food temperatures that burn the skin.

When food manufacturing operations fail to keep physical hazards out of food, the result is adulteration of food, defined under Title 21, section 342 of the Federal Food Drug and Cosmetic Act. Physical hazards can be prevented or eliminated by examining and sorting the food (for example, dried peas, dried beans, rice) for foreign objects. They can also be prevented by purchasing from a certified supplier that uses equipment such as a metal detector to remove metal fragments and by providing strict ingredient specifications to the supplier. If hot beverages such as coffee are served at 170°F (76.7°C) or above, appropriate measures to prevent burns include a hot food warning label and a coffee cup insulator sleeve.

Expensive litigation can occur when customers discover a foreign object in food or break a tooth, or even claim emotional distress. They often have the food and the physical hazard in their possession, which makes it difficult to refute. In 1994, an elderly woman was awarded $2.9 million in a lawsuit against McDonald's after she spilled hot coffee on her lap. At the time, McDonald's policy was to serve coffee at 180 to 190°F (82.2 to 87.8°C). They have since reduced that to 150 to 160°F (65.6 to 71.1°C).

Not all physical contaminants are necessarily hazardous. The FDA's Food Defect Action Levels (most recently updated in July 2014) lists tolerable, unavoidable levels of physical contaminants (for example, insect parts, rodent hairs) that are impossible to eliminate from the food supply because "it is economically impractical to grow, harvest, or process raw products that are totally free of non-hazardous, naturally occurring, unavoidable defects."[11]

●Biological Hazards

Biological hazards include foodborne pathogens such as bacteria, viruses, parasites, and some molds and yeasts that can lead to illness, disability, and death by infection or intoxication (poisoning). These hazards cannot be totally eliminated from incoming food, but they can be adequately reduced with cooking and other processing procedures, such as retorting, acidifying, refrigeration, the addition of antimicrobial ingredients, drying, modified atmosphere packaging (MAP), and curing with high concentrations of salt or sugar. More recent techniques include irradiation, high-pressure processing (HPP), pulsed high-intensity light, ohmic processing (electrical field), ozonation (exposure to ozone), and microwave processing.

The infection hazards include viruses (hepatitis A, hepatitis E, norovirus, rotaviruses), parasites (*Trichinella spiralis, Toxoplasma gondii, Taenia solium, Anisakis simplex, Cryptosporidium parvum, Cyclospora cayetanensis*), and vegetative infective bacteria (*Campylobacter jejuni*, Salmonella spp.,

FIGURE 13.8 Biological hazards and control measures.

Microorganisms (Hazard Identification)	Control
Viruses from human fecal contamination (on fingers after using the toilet), shellfish, sewage leakage into water; viruses cannot be reliably controlled by cooking; must be prevented from contaminating food Hepatitis A Hepatitis E Norovirus Rotoviruses	**Controls target: Hepatitis A** - Double washing of hands and fingertips with a nail brush after using the toilet (6-log reduction). - Exclude ill food handlers (norovirus). - Hepatitis A vaccination - Wash and sanitize food contact surfaces before processing ready-to-eat food. - Purchase seafood from suppliers who certify that their products were obtained from safe waters.
Parasites in meat, fish, and poultry served raw or undercooked; no USDA inspection control *Trichinella spiralis* *Toxoplasma gondi* *Taenia* *Anisakis simplex*	**Controls target: Trichinella spp., *Anisakis*** - Freeze raw pork and wild game, fish at –4°F for 7 days. - Pasteurize (heat to 145°F, 15 seconds for 5-log reduction in food muscle).
Parasites in fruits and vegetables *Cryptosporidium parvum* *Cyclospora cayetanensis*	**Controls for *Cryptosporidium parvum, Cyclospora cayetanensis*** - Use safe (potable) water for growing and washing fruits and vegetables. - Obtain fruits and vegetables from suppliers who certify that products were grown, harvested, handled, and packaged under controls that prevent contamination. - Surface pasteurize fruits and vegetables (160°F, 1 minute).

Vegetative bacteria in raw meat, fish, poultry, eggs, dairy products, fruits, and vegetables
Campylobacter jejuni
Salmonella spp.
Escherichia coli O157:H7
Vibrio spp.
Shigella spp.
Yersinia enterocolitica
Listeria monocytogenes
	Controls target: salmonellae for pasteurization and Campylobacter for surface cleaning
	- Wash and sanitize ready-to-eat food contact surfaces (5-log reduction) (*Campylobacter*).
	- Prevent cross-contamination from raw food to ready-to-eat food.
	- Use pasteurized ingredients, milk, dairy (e.g., juices, etc.).
	- Pasteurize (heat/cook):
	   - Meat, fish to 150°F, 1 minute for a *Salmonella* 5-log reduction.
	   - Poultry to 165°F, 10 seconds for a *Salmonella* 7-log reduction.
	- Maintain cold ready-to-eat food at 41°F for 7 days or less for a <3-log increase in *Listeria monocytogenes*.

Vegetative bacteria that produce toxins in ready-to-eat food *Staphylococcus aureus* Toxin produced by *S. aureus* is heat stable. Reheating food to 165°F does not ensure destruction of this toxin. Prevent production of toxin in ready-to-eat food.	**Controls target: *Staphylococcus aureus*** - Wash hands before handling food and often when preparing food. - Clean and cover infected cuts and sores. Wear a clean plastic glove to cover any cut(s) on a hand. - Mix cold ingredients for salads <50°F to control toxin production of *S. aureus*. - Hold food ≤41°F (5°C) or ≥130°F (54.4°C).

(continued)

FIGURE 13.8 *(continued)*

Microorganisms (Hazard Identification)	Control
Spore-forming bacteria that survive cooking and become potential hazards in cooked meat, fish, poultry, and vegetables, prepared combination items *Bacillus cereus* *Clostridium perfringens* *Clostridium botulinum* Toxin produced by any type of *C. botulinum* is destroyed in 5 minutes at 185°F. Boiling home-canned food assures safety.	**Controls cooling, hot holding target:** *Clostridium perfringens* - Hot hold >130°F for <1 log increase of *C. perfringens*. - Cool from 130°F to 40°F in less than 6 hours for <3-log increase of *C. perfringens*. - Prevent contamination by *Listeria monocytogenes* or store ≤40°F or below, and consume within 7 days. **Controls target:** *Clostridium botulinum* - Do not use home-canned food in retail operations. - Reject/do not use canned foods that show rust, swelling, and/or signs of leakage. - Fresh vegetables (e.g., mushrooms) are packaged in bags or containers that allow the entrance of air if they are stored >50°F (10°C), at which point *C. botulinum* can make a toxin. - Store prepared food products that have received a light heat treatment and are labeled "keep refrigerated" at ≤41°F (5°C). - Acidify food <pH 4.6 or water activity <0.92. - Store perishable fish items (e.g., smoked salted fish products) at ≤38°F (3.3°C) to prevent growth of *C. botulinum* type.

Key: °F (°C):
−4°F (−20°C); 145°F (62.8°C); 160°F (71.1°C); 150°F (65.6°C); 165°F (73.9°C); 41°F (5°C); 50°F (10°C); 130°F (54.4°C); 40°F (4.4°C)
Used by permission of the Hospitality Institute of Technology and Management, St. Paul, MN.

Escherichia coli O157:H7, Vibrio spp., Shigella spp., *Yersinia enterocolitica*, and *Listeria monocytogenes*). (*Note:* The term *vegetative* refers to actively living bacterial cells as distinct from hibernating spores.) Other bacterial pathogens do not normally cause illness by infection; instead, they are capable of producing toxins in food that can cause illness or death when consumed. These include *Staphylococcus aureus*, *Bacillus cereus*, *Clostridium botulinum*, and *Clostridium perfringens*. The last three organisms are spore-formers.

Spore-forming bacteria such as *Bacillus cereus*, *Clostridium perfringens*, and *Clostridium botulinum* are found in soils throughout the world. They produce structures known as endospores that protect the bacterial cell's genetic material when conditions are not conducive to survival of the living vegetative cells; this process is known as sporulation. These highly resistant structures (commonly known as *spores*) are produced within the vegetative cell before it dies. When conditions are favorable again, the spores germinate and produce fresh vegetative cells that can grow and reproduce as well as cause spoilage or disease. All raw and even pasteurized and processed food from suppliers probably contain low levels of spores, but they become a risk only when cooked food is improperly processed and handled. If spores are allowed to germinate in these foods, they produce dangerous, even lethal toxins. *Clostridium botulinum* produces botulinum toxin, one of the most toxic substances known.

Spores are noted for their marked resistance to heat, ultraviolet (UV) light, chemicals, and desiccation, thereby making control of them a challenge.[12] Spores survive normal cooking temperatures and become hazardous in improperly handled low-acid (pH above 4.6) cooked meat, fish, poultry, and vegetables dishes.

Inactivation of *C. botulinum* spores and prevention of toxin production in low-acid packaged or canned foods requires sterilization by heating to a minimum of 250°F (121.1°C) center temperature for three minutes. This results in a 12-log reduction of *C. botulinum* spores. In order to achieve 250°F (121.1°C) in an aqueous (water-based) food, packaged or canned foods must be processed with 15 psi (pounds per square inch) of pressure using a retort, autoclave, or pressure cooker. Without added pressure, water can only reach 212°F (100°C). To avoid any possibility of botulism, never use home-canned food in retail operations. Canned foods that show rust, swelling, or signs of leakage must be discarded. Cooked vegetables, such as potatoes and onions, must always be refrigerated at 41°F (5°C) or below to prevent potential growth of *C. botulinum*, which can also multiply in fresh mushrooms at room temperature if packaged in an anaerobic (airtight) package. There must be air holes in the plastic packages, and mushrooms should be stored refrigerated below 41°F (5°C).

The growth of *C. botulinum* can also be controlled by acidifying the food below pH 4.6 or by drying it to a water activity lower than 0.92. The *C. botulinum* associated with fish, type E, has a lower growth temperature threshold of 38°F (3.3°C). Therefore, perishable fish items such as cold-smoked fish must be stored at or below 38°F (3.3°C) to prevent growth. Because *C. botulinum* toxin is heat labile—that is, it can be inactivated by heating—government agencies recommend that all home-canned, low-acid foods for home use should be boiled for 10 minutes before serving to assure safety.

Vegetative infective bacteria (pathogens) found in raw meat, fish, poultry, eggs, dairy products, fruits, and vegetables multiply in food at a rate depending on temperature. When ingested in sufficient numbers in raw or undercooked food, the bacteria pass through the stomach and into the intestinal tract, causing potentially serious illnesses with fever, vomiting, and diarrhea (sometimes bloody) in humans. Illness can last from several days to a week or more and is extremely debilitating. In immunocompromised individuals, the very young, and the elderly, hospitalization is common and death can result. Further, many of these diseases have secondary symptoms that can appear weeks or months after the initial illness, including paralysis and myalgia (diffuse muscle pain). In addition, infection with *E. coli* O157:H7 is the number-one cause of acute kidney failure in children.

Controls include making sure food handlers wash and sanitize their hands after using the bathroom, using gloves when handling ready-to-eat foods (i.e., foods that do not receive any further cooking), preventing cross-contamination from raw food to ready-to-eat food by washing and sanitizing food contact surfaces before touching with ready-to-eat foods, using pasteurized ingredients (for example, milk and dairy products, eggs, juices), cooking ground meat and fish to an internal temperature of 150°F (65.6°C) for one minute for a salmonella 5-log (5-decimal) reduction, and cooking poultry to an internal temperature of 165°F (73.9°C) for 15 seconds for a salmonella 7-log (7-decimal) reduction.[13] *Note:* A log reduction is the reduction of pathogens stated logarithmically. A 5-log, or 5-decimal, reduction goes from 100,000 pathogens to 1 pathogen. A 7-log reduction goes from 10,000,000 pathogens to 1 pathogen.

Even after food is cooked and cooled, there is still the chance that surfaces in packaging rooms (for example, crevices in equipment, floor drains) can contaminate food with *Listeria monocytogenes*, a particularly dangerous pathogen because it multiplies even at refrigerated temperatures and has the ability to cross the intestinal, placental, and blood-brain barriers, leading to gastroenteritis, maternofetal infections, and meningoencephalitis. Because there can be a long lag time between consumption of contaminated food and onset of disease, many individuals can become infected before the source food is identified. Only an estimated 1600 cases per year occur in the United States, but mortality rates approach 25 percent.[14] Cooked or fresh ready-to-eat foods unprotected by the addition of antimicrobials, pH reduction, modified atmosphere packaging, or other methods should not be stored for more than seven days at 41°F (5°C).[15] However, if food is processed in a proven *L. monocytogenes*–free environment (confirmed by microbial swabs of surfaces and approved by the FDA or USDA inspectors), after cooking, cooling, and packaging, refrigerated ready-to-eat food can have any shelf life the processor deems reasonable.

Unlike infective bacteria, the growth of *Staphylococcus aureus* to about 1,000,000 organisms per gram produces a potent toxin in foods improperly held between 40 and 140°F (4.4 and 60°C)—the food temperature danger zone—for an extended period. Staphylococcus is salt tolerant and can grow in salty foods like ham. Other examples of foods that have caused staphylococcal food poisoning are sliced meats, puddings, cream-filled pastries, and sandwiches.

Ingestion of this toxin causes projectile vomiting and explosive diarrhea. Toxic effects usually occur quite rapidly, within hours after consumption. While extremely debilitating, the illness is generally of short duration and usually not fatal. That said, the toxin is heat-stable; reheating food to 165°F (73.9°C) does not ensure its destruction. If there is any question about the safety of ready-to-eat food that may have been held within the food temperature danger zone, the best course of action is to throw it out. "If in doubt—throw it out."

Staphylococcus aureus is part of the normal flora on human skin. Therefore, some cities and states require food workers to wear gloves when handling any foods that will not be cooked. Other preventive measures include washing hands before handling food, cleaning and covering cuts and sores, and wearing a clean plastic glove to cover cuts on the hands. Also, when mixing cold ingredients for salads with bare hands, the temperature of the food must be kept at or below 50°F (10°C) because toxin production by *S. aureus* does not occur at or below this temperature.

Unlike bacteria, viruses and parasites *do not multiply in food*; the food is simply a carrier. Small numbers of viruses and parasites (1 to 10 in a portion of food) can cause illness after they are ingested because they *multiply rapidly within the body* after contaminated food is consumed.

Viruses require high cooking temperatures for destruction (for example, contaminated mollusks, 185 to 194°F [85 to 90°C] for 90 seconds; mussels, boiling [212°F (100°C)] for three minutes).[16] Therefore, they cannot easily be controlled by normal pasteurization or cooking temperatures, such as 158°F (70°C) for meat or 165°F (73.9°C) for poultry.[17] Food viruses are nearly always transmitted through the fecal-oral route. Hence, they must be controlled by preventing sources of human fecal contamination by:

1. Requiring employees to double-wash hands and clean fingertips with a nail brush after using the toilet.
2. Purchasing seafood from government-approved suppliers who certify their products were obtained from safe waters.
3. Washing and sanitizing food contact surfaces before handling ready-to-eat food.
4. Excluding ill food handlers from working with food. Some food companies and foodservice chains also require that all employees have a hepatitis A vaccination.

Parasitic worms can be found in meat, game, and fish products that are served raw or undercooked. Examples include taenia (tapeworms) in raw beef and pork, *Trichinella spiralis* in raw or undercooked pork and wild game products, and *Anisakis simplex* in fish. Trichina spp. and Anisakis can be controlled by freezing meat or fish at −4°F (−20°C) for seven days. *Toxoplasma gondii*, a protozoan that may also be found in raw pork and game meats, is destroyed by cooking until all parts reach a temperature of 145°F (62.8°C) for 15 seconds. (Note: *T. gondii* is also endemic in domestic cats, and it is possible to contract the disease through contact with cat feces.) The incidence of parasitic infection from livestock, including pigs, is quite rare in the United States because feeding practices and sanitation have improved tremendously in the past 30+ years. There are occasional reports of mammalian-derived parasites coming from wild game, but even these numbers are low. The largest potential source of foodborne parasitic infection in the United States is raw fish, due to the growing popularity of sushi and sashimi.

Parasites on fruits and vegetables include *Cryptosporidium parvum* and *Cyclospora cayetanensis*. An outbreak of Cyclospora infecting nearly 600 people in 20 states was traced to packages of salad mix and fresh cilantro served at a well-known restaurant chain. To control these parasites and others, depending on global location, safe (potable) water must be used to irrigate crops and to wash fresh produce. Because chlorinated water does not effectively inactivate parasites, food facilities should filter incoming water to assure safe levels of parasites in irrigation water. Ozonation is another effective water treatment option. Ozone, a molecule consisting of three oxygen atoms, is a gaseous oxidizing agent used as a disinfectant and sanitizer for many food and beverage products. In Europe, ozone is the principle means of sanitizing the water supply (unlike the United States, where chlorination is the norm). It is 1.5 times stronger than chlorine, kills a wider range of microorganisms (including protistan parasites), and leaves behind no chemical residues. Because it is the exterior of the fruit or vegetable that is contaminated, dipping items in hot water (160°F [71.1°C]) for one minute, called surface blanching, can be used to pasteurize the surface of fruits and vegetables.

●Process Temperature Control

Temperature is the key factor in food processing for microbiological control. From the receipt of refrigerated or frozen raw materials to storage and distribution of finished goods, at every step temperatures must be maintained, monitored, and recorded to assure that microbial outgrowth is kept to an absolute minimum.

FIGURE 13.9 Retail food process microbiological temperature control summary.

Process Step	Control
Receiving raw meat, poultry, fish, fruits vegetables, milk: pathogenic bacteria, viruses, and parasites	30°F is safe. No growth of pathogens. At 41°F, food "spoils safe." Spoilers inhibit pathogens' rapid growth. Cooking/pasteurizing will control bacterial pathogens. If the raw food is sold as purchased from the supplier, the supplier must guarantee a safe pathogen level.
Pre-preparation, ready-to-eat processor products: cooked meat, fish, poultry	Ready-to-eat food from the supplier (41°F) has been pasteurized, and vegetative pathogens have been reduced to an undetectable level. No hazards. Shelf life depends on outgrowth of spoilage, psychrotrophic spores.
Preparation: Prevents cross-contamination of raw pathogens to ready-to-eat food.	No temperature control is necessary. Time 4 to 6 hours and temperature <60°F assures no significant growth of vegetative pathogens.
Cooking: There can be some multiplication of pathogens when cooking takes longer than 4 hours to get above 130°F. Once the temperature is >130°F for enough time, the pathogens that multiply are reduced to undetectable levels.	At ≥130°F for adequate time, there is a 5-log reduction of vegetative pathogens (Salmonella) (not viruses, which take a higher temperature). (FDA, 2005) 130°F 112 minutes 140°F 11 minutes 145°F 3 minutes 155°F 15 seconds 165°F 15 seconds (poultry, 7-log *Salmonella* reduction)
Hot holding: The spores *Clostridium botulinum*, *Bacillus cereus*, and *Clostridium perfringens* survive pasteurization.	Holding food >130°F prevents outgrowth of spores. Adding acid to reduce food to pH <4.6 or a_w <0.92 controls *Clostridium botulinum* and makes food shelf stable.
Cooling: Outgrowth of the spores must be prevented.	USDA allows safe cooling from 120°F to 55°F in 6 hours with continued cooling in the refrigerator (no time limit) to get to 40°F.
Cold display	41°F, 7 days for ready-to-eat food prepared in the retail food establishment

Key: °F (°C):
30°F (−1.1°C); 41°F (5°C); 60°F (15.6°C); 130°F (54.4°C); 140°F (60°C); 145°F (62.8°C); 155°F (68.3°C); 165°F (73.9°C) 120 to 55°F (48.9 to 12.8°C); 40°F (4.4°C); 41°F (5°C)
Used by permission of the Hospitality Institute of Technology and Management, St. Paul, MN.

Receiving Temperatures

When food that requires Time and Temperature Control for Safety (TTCS) is received, it should be stored at or below 40°F (5°C), which is normal refrigerator temperature. However, pathogens such as *Listeria monocytogenes* grow as low as 30°F (–1.1°C), so if absolute safety is required (as when developing foods for immunocompromised individuals, hospital feeding, baby food, or extended space flight), unless the food will be processed by other contamination elimination methods shortly after receipt, food must be stored frozen at 30°F (–1.1°C) or less. At 40°F (5°C), the spoilage microorganisms multiply faster than the pathogens, and the food "spoils safe" (spoils and is discarded before it becomes hazardous). If raw food is sold as purchased from the supplier, the supplier must guarantee a safe pathogen level. If pasteurized products (for example, cooked meat, fish, poultry, and vegetables) are obtained from suppliers, the suppliers must be ready to show HACCP plans indicating that vegetative pathogens were reduced to a safe level. Food temperature must be maintained continuously at 40°F (4.4°C) or below. Refrigerated shelf life depends on the rate of germination and outgrowth of psychrotrophic spoilage organisms—that is, bacteria capable of surviving or even thriving in a refrigerated environment.

Pre-Preparation Temperatures

Pre-preparation of food for a production run should normally be completed in less than two hours, and the food temperature should not get above 60°F (15.6°C). This time is too short at that temperature for more than one multiplication of a vegetative pathogen and is not considered a risk factor. The key to safety during pre-preparation is the prevention of cross-contamination by the vegetative pathogens on raw foods, on hands, and in the environment from contacting ready-to-eat food.

Cooking/Pasteurization Temperatures

Government regulations specify that cooking must provide a 5-log[18] to 6.5–7-log[19] Salmonella spp. reduction to assure a safe level of vegetative pathogens in the food when consumed. There can be some multiplication of pathogens, particularly *C. perfringens*, when cooking takes more than four hours to get above 130°F (54.4°C)—for example, a luau roast pig cooking in the ground overnight. However, once the temperature is at or above 130°F (54.4°C), the pathogens that multiplied are reduced to undetectable levels, given proper time at that temperature, such as 150°F (65.6°C) for one minute for a 5-log salmonella reduction.

Hot Holding Temperatures

Hot-holding food at or above 140°F (60°C) prevents spore germination and outgrowth and assures safety regardless of how long the food is held. Food is also not hazardous and does not need control if cooking has reduced the water activity to lower than 0.92 (for example, bread and pastry), or if acid (for example, vinegar, lemon juice) is added to reduce the pH to 4.6 or below (for example, béarnaise and barbecue sauces). These foods can still undergo spoilage, however.

Cooling Temperatures

Cooking and hot holding do not damage bacterial spores; rather, these processes activate them. When the temperature of hot food drops below 130°F (54.4°C), spores begin to germinate. In about two hours, vegetative pathogens begin to multiply at a rapid rate. The critical control is to cool rapidly enough to allow no more than a 1-log increase of *C. perfringens*. The FDA recommends 135 to 70°F (57.2 to 21.1°C) in two hours, and 70 to 41°F (21.1 to 5°C) in no more than four more hours for all non-meat-containing foods.[20] The USDA has two guidelines for cooling meats and meat-containing foods for food processors:[21]

1. "During cooling, the product's maximum internal temperature should not remain between 130°F (54.4°C) and 80°F (26.7°C) for more than 1.5 hours nor between 80°F (26.7°C) and 40°F (4.4°C) for more than 5 hours. This cooling rate can be applied universally to cooked products."

2. "All product should be chilled from 120°F (48°C) to 55°F (12.7°C) in no more than 6 hours. Chilling should then continue until the product reaches 40°F (4.4°C); the product should not be shipped until it reaches 40°F (4.4°C)." This can be extrapolated to about 14.2 hours from 120 to 40°F (48.9 to 4.4°C) and is used for cooling large pieces of cooked meat.[22]

These steps are shown to be safe and to control *C. perfringens* to less than a 1-log increase.

Cold Display Temperatures

Because there is no specified control for *Listeria monocytogenes* in a retail display case, it is presumed that, during cooling, in-store prepared or vendor-supplied ready-to-eat foods are potentially contaminated from environmental sources such as countertops, floors, refrigerators, and coil drips with this vegetative pathogen.[23] To assure safety, these foods should be stored for seven days only. In seven days at 41°F (5°C), there is not enough multiplication of *L. monocytogenes* in ready-to-eat food for it to reach hazardous levels of more than 100 organisms per gram.

If a retail operator requires a longer food storage time, the processing facility supplying that retail operation must be an inspected processing plant and show control of *L. monocytogenes*. In a food processing plant, the food chilling and packaging areas are regularly cleaned and sanitized according to standard HACCP guidelines. Therefore, there should be no detectable *L. monocytogenes*. The USDA and FDA presume that a packaged food is free of *L. monocytogenes* if none is detectable in 25 grams of product. The manufacturer can assign any reasonable shelf life appropriate to the food in question, such as 30 days for potato salad at 41°F (5°C) or 40 days for chicken salad at 41°F (5°C), depending on the formulation of the product. Usually, *L. monocytogenes* growth inhibitors (for example, potassium lactate, acetic acid, calcium diacetate) are added to recipe formulations to provide extra safety.

Food Processes

Product developers should document safe procedures for the preparation of food in formula recipes, flow charts, and HACCP plans. The USDA, in 9 CFR 417, HAZARD ANALYSIS AND CRITICAL CONTROL POINT (HACCP) SYSTEMS, describes the five applicable food process groups, specified controls, and shelf life characteristics for each one.

Group I Foods

This group includes non-heat-treated, non-shelf-stable foods such as fresh mushrooms, leafy greens, melon, eggs from chickens raised in a salmonella-free environment, and sushi. In recent years, many contaminated raw agricultural products have entered the food chain, making thousands of people ill and causing several deaths. Therefore, some form of intervention is strongly recommended. Vegetables can be dipped in antimicrobial solutions (chlorine, paracetic acid,

and so on), eggs can be pasteurized, and raw fish can undergo extended freezing to kill parasites.

Group II Foods

This group includes foods that are not fully cooked, with inhibitors to make them shelf stable. This group includes foods with low water activity (a_w) and foods that contain enough acid to lower the pH to a level that retards the growth of foodborne pathogenic bacteria. Nuts, chocolate candy, spices and herbs, oils, salted and dried fish, and dried pasta have a safe a_w (an insufficient amount of water necessary for the growth of halophilic [salt-loving] vegetative pathogenic bacteria such as *S. aureus*—that is, an a_w of less than 0.88). This group also includes low-pH foods (pH less than 4.6) that have undergone fermentation through the growth of lactic acid bacteria and other alcohol- or acid-forming bacteria, including pepperoni, salami, olives, fermented dairy products (cheese, yogurt, sour cream, buttermilk, crème fraîche), sauerkraut, kimchi, beer, and wine. Other low-pH foods (salad dressings, coleslaw, salsa, condiments) contain vinegar (acetic acid), lemon juice (citric acid), or other acidifying additives as allowed by government regulations.

FIGURE 13.10 **Food groups for food safety process analysis.**

HACCP Process Groups (USDA 9 CFR 417) Prerequisite/GMPs Working	Control	Safety Shelf Life
I **Not heat treated, not shelf stable (raw).** Not PHF (does not require TTCS) raw meat, fish; sushi, sashimi; eggs, raw fruits and vegetables	Grown or supplier made safe, with $H_0 \leq$ FSO. May require temperature control for quality.	<14 days (bacterial spoilage)
II **Not fully cooked, with inhibitors to make shelf stable.** <u>Water activity control</u>: nuts; chocolate candy; spices and herbs; oil; salted, dried fish; fresh pasta <u>Fermentation control</u>: Pepperoni, salami; olives; dairy (cheese, yogurt, sour cream, milk/crème fraîche); sauerkraut; kimchi; beer, wine <u>Acid control</u>: Salad dressing; coleslaw; salsa; condiments	Grown safe, made safe by supplier, with H_0 that, with $+\Sigma I - \Sigma R$ (5-log Salmonella reduction), meets FSO. Does not require TTCS because of product a_w, pH, or additive stabilizers.	<2 years, 70°F (21.1°C) (chemical spoilage)
III **Fully cooked, not shelf stable.** Hot or cooled, refrigerated ready-to-eat food; meat, fish, poultry; fruits, vegetables, dairy, pastry filling, pudding	Pasteurized (5-log to 7-log Salmonella reduction) so that $H_0 + \Sigma I - \Sigma R$ meets or exceeds FSO. Requires TTCS.	>130°F (54.4°C) safe; <30°F (1.1°C) safe; ≤41°F (5.0°C), 7 days; 130 to 41°F (54.4 to 5.0°C), 4 hours toss
IV **Fully cooked, with inhibitors to make shelf stable.** Marinara (tomato) sauce; fruit pie fillings; smoked fish; pickled eggs; bread, muffins; pastry; packaged, pickled, and low-pH fruits and vegetables.	Pasteurized (5-log to 7-log Salmonella reduction) so that $H_0 + \Sigma I - \Sigma R$ meets FSO. Does not require TTCS because of product a_w, pH, or additive stabilizers.	No shelf-life limit
V **Commercially sterile, shelf stable.** "Packaged" meat, fish, poultry, fruits, vegetables, dairy/UHT milk	Sterilized, *Clostridium botulinum* spores reduced 9 to 12 log. Does not require TTCS.	No shelf-life limit

Key: PHF = Potentially Hazardous Food; UHT = Ultra High Temperature; H_0 = Starting Hazard; FSO = Food Safety Objective; Σ = summary; I = Increase; R = Reduction; TTCS = Time and Temperature Control for Safety; a_w = water activity (available free water in product that is able to evaporate from the food and affect the humidity around the product)
Used by permission of the Hospitality Institute of Technology and Management, St. Paul, MN.

Note: Shelf life is based on loss of quality, not safety. Some products are labeled "Refrigerate after opening." This statement indicates proper handling for the control of mold contamination and the minimizing of quality deterioration, not for safety.

Group III Foods

These are fully cooked, not-shelf-stable foods including refrigerated ready-to-eat meat, fish, poultry, fruits and vegetables, dairy products, pastry fillings, and puddings. These products are pasteurized at temperatures and times necessary to provide a 5- to 7-log salmonella reduction that meets or exceeds the FSO (Food Safety Objective). Ready-to-eat foods in this group require TTCS (Time and Temperature Control for Safety). These foods must be kept above 140°F (60°C) for safe handling during processing or below 40°F (4.4°C) for safe storage. If ready-to-eat food is held at temperatures between 40 and 140°F (4.4 and 60°C), it must be discarded after four hours. Ready-to-eat prepared foods can be stored in a retail kitchen at or below 40°F (4.4 °C) after preparation or opening but must be used within seven days. If longer storage time is desired, these foods must be frozen to prevent the growth of *L. monocytogenes*.

Group IV Foods

This group includes fully cooked foods, with inhibitors to make them shelf stable at room temperature. These products include jarred marinara sauce, bread, muffins, pastry, fruit pies; packaged smoked fish; and pickled low-pH fruits and vegetables. These products are pasteurized at temperatures and times necessary to provide a 5- to 7-log salmonella reduction

that meets or exceeds the FSO. Foods in this group do not require TTCS because of low product pH (less than 4.6), low a_w (less than 0.92), additive stabilizers, and protective packaging. Deteriorative changes in the foods occur over time due to oxidation (changes in moisture content and oxidative changes decrease the shelf life of baked products to a few days) or after the packaging is opened or removed. However, these are spoilage issues; there is no shelf-life safety limit on unopened acidified or low-water-activity products.

Group V Foods

These are commercially sterile, shelf-stable foods that include packaged or canned meat, fish, poultry; fruits and vegetables; and UHT (ultra-high-temperature processed) milk. These foods are sterilized to gain a 9- to 12-log reduction of *C. botulinum* spores. They do not require TTCS, and there is no safety limit to the shelf life of these products if maintained in intact packaging.

●Ingredient HACCP

As research chefs or product developers gather ingredients for the preparation of a recipe, they must consider the possibility of each as a source of biological, chemical, or physical hazard that must be made safe if the supplier has not already taken care of it. Each item on the stock list must be evaluated to determine if the supplier has pasteurized or sterilized the food or whether the supplier has made the food shelf stable so it is non-TTCS. If the food must be made safe, the recipe must include a CCP (Critical Control Point) step—the point at which the food preparer prevents, eliminates, or reduces the hazard to an ALOP.

FIGURE 13.11 **Menu item analysis.**

Supplier Makes Safe			Cook Makes Safe
Mozzarella cheese sticks	Grits, oatmeal	Cocoa, coffee, tea	Baked potato
Potatoes: parfried, French fries, mashed	Vegetables, frozen	Fruit juices	Chicken parts and
Onion rings, parfried	Coleslaw mix	Soft drinks (dispenser)	strips
Corned beef hash	Canned fruits	Milk	Chicken nuggets
Sausage links, fully cooked	Applesauce	Assorted bread products	Chicken breast
Ham, fully cooked	Pico de gallo	Apple crisp	Chicken-fried steak
Veggie burger, fully cooked	Taco chips	Frozen pies (unbaked	Cod, battered
Cheese pizza, fully cooked	Salsa	and prepared)	Shrimp, breaded
Turkey breast, fully cooked	Cheeses	Frozen cakes, brownies	Bacon
Smoked sausage	Cream cheese	Ice cream	Hamburger
Roast beef, fully cooked	Cottage cheese	Jams and jellies	Eggs: in the shell, over-
Eggs, liquid pasteurized	Pickles	Syrups (pancake)	easy, up, hard-boiled,
Macaroni and cheese,	BBQ sauce	Syrups (for malts,	poached
fully cooked	Butter, margarine	sundaes, etc.)	Steak: T-bone, sirloin,
French toast batter (pasteurized ingredients)	Spreads	Vinegar	country-fried steak
Pancakes (pasteurized ingredients)	Honey	Sugar (brown, powdered)	Fresh vegetables
Gravies (pasteurized ingredients)	Salad dressings	Crackers, croutons	
Soups, fully cooked	Condiments	Apple topping	
Marinara sauce, fully	Creamers	Fresh fruits	
cooked, acid	Coffees		
Stuffing, fully cooked			

Used by permission of the Hospitality Institute of Technology and Management, St. Paul, MN.

A typical process for making food safe is thermal processing, cooking, or pasteurization to reduce a biological hazard to a safe level. Other products may receive an addition of acid to lower the pH, undergo fermentation, or be dried to a water activity of 0.92 or lower to control spore outgrowth.

The HACCP Recipe or Formula

The HACCP recipe or formula is the document the research chef or product developer writes to tell other food preparers how to consistently make a menu item that meets a specific sensory profile and attains an ALOP for the consumer.

The recipe begins with the assembly of the ingredients for the menu item. Ingredients that cause allergic or intolerance reactions are identified. Organic acids or other acidifiers can be used to reduce pH to a desired level in the food. Salt and sugar used to reduce water activity are verified. Foods that are potential choking hazards (for example, bay leaves, peppercorns) are identified. Preservative levels (for example, benzoate, sorbate) are checked to make sure they are sufficient to do the job but do not exceed mandated limits.

FIGURE 13.12 Quality-assured HACCP recipe procedure for beef stew.

Product: **Beef Stew, Group III**	Portion size (vol./wt.): 1 cup (250 g)	Preparation time: 3 to 4 hours
Written by: OPS Date: 9/09	Number of portions: 1000	Prepared by:
SA/QA by: SPO Date: 9/09	Final yield (AS):	Supervisor:

Gp #	Ing #	Ingredients and Specifications	Amount Pounds	Amount Grams	EP Wt %	Verif
I	1	Lean beef, cut in ¾-inch cubes	224.00	101,606.4	40.34	
	2	Vegetable oil	6.80	3,084.5	1.22	
II	3	Water (14 gallons)	118.00	53,524.8	21.25	
	4	Seasoned salt	2.00	907.2	0.36	
	5	Garlic powder	0.50	226.8	0.09	
	6	Bay leaf, crushed	0.50	226.8	0.09	
	7	Thyme	0.50	226.8	0.09	
III	8	Carrots, sliced ¼ inch	60.00	27,216.0	10.80	
	9	Potatoes, cubed ½ inch	112.00	50,803.2	20.17	
	10	Onion, diced ¼ inch or small white onions	31.00	14,061.6	5.58	
		Total	555.30	251,884.1	100.00	

Ingredients that could cause adverse allergic or intolerance reactions: None.   **Verif**

Management and Prerequisite Procedures (SSOP/GMP) are in place: Personal hygiene, environment/facility/ equipment cleaning, sanitation and maintenance, supplies.

Equipment: 200-gallon kettle, pump fill station, dish-package machine; sealing machine.

Pre-preparation
1. Get pre-cut ¾-inch beef cubes (<41°F) for stew. (20 minutes)
2. Get and measure vegetable oil and seasonings. (70°F) (30 minutes)
3. Get and prepare (wash, peel, slice/dice, etc.) carrots, potatoes, and onions. Get and measure water. (≤70°F) (30 minutes)

Preparation
4. Brown stew beef in oil in steam jacketed kettle. (>200°F surface, 20 minutes)
5. Add water and seasonings to kettle. (all ingredients >70°F, 15 minutes)
6. **CCP** Cover and simmer. (180–190°F, 2 hours) (This reduces *Salmonella* >5 log.) Check the Beef Stew while it is being cooked. If not at 180–190°F, raise the heat. (The chef/manager should verify the correct cooking temperature and/or corrective action on the recipe.)
7. Add carrots, potatoes, and onions and continue to simmer (180–190°F) until vegetables are tender. (>30 minutes)
8. **CCP** Hold at >165°F and pump/package into individual serving dishes. Seal. Rack and move to cooler. (30 minutes)
9. **CCP** Cool 120 to 55°F, 6 hours, and continue to cool until the stew temperature is 40°F.
10. Box. Store. 40°F.
11. Ship.

Key: °F (°C):
41°F (5°C); 70°F (21.1°C); 200°F (93.3°C); 180–190°F (82.2–87.8°C); 165°F (73.9°C); 120 to 55°F (48.9 to 12.8°C); 40°F (4.4°C)

Used by permission of the Hospitality Institute of Technology and Management, St. Paul, MN.

Next, the product developer decides on a sequence of recipe steps. Vegetables are often peeled and washed the day before use so they are ready to be added to the recipe. Sauces are made the day they are to be used, before assembly of the product begins. This way, all of the ingredients are ready when the product is being built.

The recipe includes times and temperatures for each CCP step. In addition, at each CCP, procedures for monitoring and corrective actions are included. On the right margin of the recipe, the manager of a food establishment can confirm by recording his or her initials that he or she watched the preparer perform each step and that all procedures were followed.

This beef stew HACCP recipe example begins with cutting up the beef and is followed by vegetable preparation. Temperatures at these pre-preparation steps are less than 70°F (21.1°C), and time is only 80 minutes, which is too short for the hazard to be a significant risk. Next, the beef is browned to above 200°F (93.3°C), which pasteurizes the surface of the beef. However, the center of the beef cubes might still be contaminated. Therefore, this is not a CCP because we have not eliminated the possibility of pathogen survival and the risk of causing disease. The meat is then simmered for 2 hours to tenderize the beef. This simmering step provides a 6.5-log reduction of Salmonella spp.; this is designated a CCP because the step is essential to reducing the vegetative pathogens to a safe level of less than 1 organism per 25 grams of food. After the vegetables are added and the cooking is complete, the stew is pumped into individual serving trays, sealed, and cooled in a blast chiller. This cooling step follows USDA guidelines: 120 to 55°F (48.9 to 12.8°C) in 6 hours, followed by continued cooling to 40°F (4.4°C). This cooling procedure is another CCP because it prevents a more than 1-log increase of *C. perfringens*. When the stew reaches a temperature of 40°F (4.4°C), it is boxed and refrigerated in preparation for shipping.[24]

The HACCP Flow Chart

The flow chart has the same steps and language as the recipe. Isolating each step in a box clarifies the sequence of the steps and the controls required at each. *Ti* is temperature *into* the step; *To* is temperature *out of* the step; and *t* is the time it takes to complete the step. The initial times and temperatures are determined by the research chef or product developer when preparing the recipe in the test kitchen. However, to confirm these data are correct for full production volumes, full-scale plant trials must be conducted to record any changes due to scale-up. Again, if a step prevents, eliminates, or reduces a significant risk to an ALOP, the step is identified as a CCP.

The HACCP Plan

The HACCP plan is the document the research chef completes after developing the recipe and flow chart. This document is used by the FDA and USDA to evaluate the safety of the process.

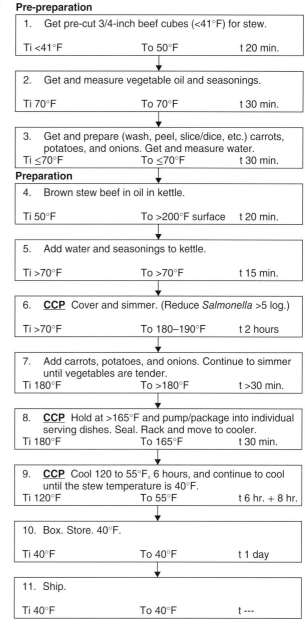

FIGURE 13.13 Beef stew HACCP recipe flow.

Pre-preparation

1. Get pre-cut 3/4-inch beef cubes (<41°F) for stew.

Ti <41°F   To 50°F   t 20 min.

2. Get and measure vegetable oil and seasonings.

Ti 70°F   To 70°F   t 30 min.

3. Get and prepare (wash, peel, slice/dice, etc.) carrots, potatoes, and onions. Get and measure water.

Ti ≤70°F   To ≤70°F   t 30 min.

Preparation

4. Brown stew beef in oil in kettle.

Ti 50°F   To >200°F surface   t 20 min.

5. Add water and seasonings to kettle.

Ti >70°F   To >70°F   t 15 min.

6. **CCP** Cover and simmer. (Reduce *Salmonella* >5 log.)

Ti >70°F   To 180–190°F   t 2 hours

7. Add carrots, potatoes, and onions. Continue to simmer until vegetables are tender.

Ti 180°F   To >180°F   t >30 min.

8. **CCP** Hold at >165°F and pump/package into individual serving dishes. Seal. Rack and move to cooler.

Ti 180°F   To 165°F   t 30 min.

9. **CCP** Cool 120 to 55°F, 6 hours, and continue to cool until the stew temperature is 40°F.

Ti 120°F   To 55°F   t 6 hr. + 8 hr.

10. Box. Store. 40°F.

Ti 40°F   To 40°F   t 1 day

11. Ship.

Ti 40°F   To 40°F   t ---

CCP = Critical Control Point
Key: °F (°C):
41°F (5°C); 70°F (21.1°C); 200°F (93.3°C); 180–190°F (82.2–87.8°C); 165°F (73.9°C); 120 to 55°F (48.9 to 12.8°C); 40°F (4.4°C)

Used by permission of the Hospitality Institute of Technology and Management, St. Paul, MN.

In a processing plant, processes may be grouped into one HACCP plan if all of the process controls are the same. For example, beef stew, beef stew with vegetables, pork stew, and lamb stew follow the same process and have the same CCPs. Therefore, only one HACCP plan must be written for those recipes.

The HACCP plan shows each step of the recipe process (the sequence shown in the flow chart) in the first column, and then includes the hazard and control details of each step

FIGURE 13.14 Beef stew HACCP plan.

Process Steps and Controls: GMPs and prerequisites are in place (Ti = temp. in; To = Temp. out; t = Time to do the step)	B, C, P Potential Hazards and Risk Analysis	Control (Critical Limit [CL] for each Hazard Control)	Monitor & Record (What, How, Frequency, Who)	Corrective Action & Record	Verification & Record (Procedures and Frequency)
Pre-preparation 1. Get pre-cut 3/4-inch beef cubes (<41°F) for stew Ti <41°F To 50°F t 20 min.	B: Not significant. Vegetative pathogens and spores are controlled by low temperature and short time. C: None P: None				
2. Get and measure vegetable oil and seasonings. Ti 70°F To 70°F t 30 min.	B: Not significant. Vegetative pathogens and spores are controlled by low a_w (water activity). C: None P: None				
3. Get and prepare (wash, peel, slice/dice, etc.) carrots, potatoes, and onions. Get and measure water. Ti ≤70°F To ≤70°F t 30 min.	B: Not significant. Surface contamination is removed by washing and peeling vegetables. Water is potable. C: None P: None				
Preparation 4. Brown stew beef in oil in kettle. Ti 50°F To >200°F surface t 20 min.	B: Not significant. Pathogens on the surface of the meat are destroyed by high browning temperature. C: None P: None				
5. Add water and seasonings to kettle. Ti >70°F To >70°F t 15 min.	B: Vegetative pathogens and spores. Time too short for significant pathogenic growth. C: None P: None				
6. **CCP** Cover and simmer. (Reduce *Salmonella* >5 log.) Ti >70°F To 180–190°F t 2 hr.	B: Vegetative pathogens and spores C: None P: None	Cooking temperature >165°F, >10 sec. assures a >7-log salmonellae kill.	Assigned worker takes lowest temperature of center of food and records on production sheet for each recipe.	If temperature is not >180°F, turn up heat and/or continue to cook.	Chef/manager initials the production recipe record each shift.

Process step	Hazards	Justification	Monitoring	Corrective action	Verification
7. Add carrots, potatoes, and onions. Continue to simmer until vegetables are tender. Ti 180°F To >180°F t >30 min.	B: Not significant. Temperature >130°F controls spores and kills vegetative cells. C: None P: None				The chef/manager initials the production recipe record each shift.
8. **CCP** Hold at >165°F and package into individual serving dishes. Seal. Rack and move to cooler. Ti 180°F To 165°F t 30 min.	B: *Clostridium perfringens.* Temperature >130°F controls spores and kills vegetative cells. C: None P: None	Holding at >130°F prevents the germination of the *Bacillus* and *Clostridia* spores.	Assigned worker verifies the temperature of the product in the cooking device at the beginning and end of pumping and records it on the log sheet.	If the temperature drops below 165°F, the heat to the cooking device is increased, and a note is written on the production sheet.	
9. **CCP** Cool 120 to 55°F, 6 hours, and continue to cool until the stew temperature is 40°F. Ti 120°F To 55°F t 6 hr. + 8 hr.	B: Pathogenic spores. C: None P: None	Cooling from 120 to 55°F in 6 hours assures <1 log increase of *Clostridium perfringens.* The presence of pathogenic microorganisms from cross-contamination is controlled by GMPs and SSOPs.	Assigned worker verifies that racks with dishes are being cooled correctly by taking temperatures hourly and recording on log sheet.	If cooling goes off, move racks to freezer and continue to cool until refrigerator is fixed.	The cooling log will be initialed by the QC supervisor at the end of cooling.
10. Box. Store. 40°F. Ti °F 40°F To 40°F t 1 day	B: None C: None P: None				
11. Ship. Ti 40°F To 40°F t —	B: None C: None P: None				

Approved (QC) _____ Date _____

Approved (Process Authority) _____ Date _____

Key: °F (°C):
41°F (5°C); 70°F (21.1°C); 200°F (93.3°C); 180–190°F (82.2–87.8°C); 165°F (73.9°C); 180°F (82.2°C); 130°F (54.4°C); 120 to 55°F (48.9 to 12.8°C); 40°F (4.4°C).

Used by permission of the Hospitality Institute of Technology and Management, St. Paul, MN.

in the columns beside the step. In the hazard column, the biological, chemical, and physical (BCP) hazards for each step are identified—or, if there is no hazard, this is identified as *None*. This column also identifies whether or not the hazard is a significant risk. If the risk is significant, the next column shows the control as a performance standard (for example, *5-log reduction of salmonella*). The control validation reference is also included. In the following column, the monitoring procedures are listed. Corrective action must be shown in the next column if monitoring indicates the process deviated beyond a critical limit. The final column indicates how management verified the work—whether by direct observation or by records review.

The beef stew HACCP plan shows steps #6, #8, and #9 as the CCP steps. Step #6, *Cover and simmer*, is a CCP because the stew's cooking temperature, which reaches 180 to 190°F (82.2 to 87.8°C), is above 165°F (73.9°C) for more than 10 seconds, assuring a greater than 5-log salmonella destruction. Step #8, the pumping step, is a CCP to assure the food is hot enough to prevent outgrowth of bacillus and clostridial spores. Step #9 is the cooling step. For this product, as stated in the HACCP plan, the standard of cooling from 120 to 55°F (48.9 to 12.8°C) in 6 hours with continued cooling to 40°F (4.4°C) assures less than 1-log increase of *C. perfringens*. The prevention of pathogenic microorganisms from contaminating the food is controlled by good manufacturing practices (GMPs) and standard sanitation operating procedures (SSOPs).

Process Validation

The two stages for recipe development in a process plant are:

1. Initial product development in the test kitchen or food lab using small-scale equipment.
2. Scaling up production using large kettles, conveyor ovens, cook tanks, and so on. It is important that scaled-up product have the same sensory profile as the development kitchen's product (the gold standard) and that product safety, stability, and quality are achieved.

The first step is for the product developer to decide whether to use government-published microbiological destruction information (for example, 5-log reduction of salmonella) as described in the FDA Food Code[25] or the USDA's Draft Compliance Guidelines for Ready-to-Eat Meat and Poultry Products[26], or whether the process is sufficiently different that he or she must develop a different validation and microbiological kill study for the process. If government information is used, the product developer must make a thermal time-temperature map of the production floor equipment and required times and temperatures for pathogen destruction so as to gather data showing the plant process meets regulatory requirements.

Alternatively, the process can be tested by inoculating a batch of food ingredients with a non-pathogenic surrogate organism such as *E. coli* ATCC 25922, which has similar death characteristics as salmonella, and compare the number inoculated with the number remaining in the finished product after the process is complete to verify microbial destruction. The results of the study are documented and become a part of the HACCP plan for that particular product or group of products.

Food Spoilage

Food spoilage refers to food that is damaged or degraded to the point where it is considered to be unfit for human consumption. Food spoilage occurs in several ways, including physical injuries to the food, insect and animal damage, inclement weather effects, temperature storage abuse, the natural result of over-ripening or aging, and the normal metabolic activities of microorganisms. *Shelf life* is defined as "the time it takes for a product to decline to an unacceptable level for consumption," and the goal of the food industry is to extend shelf life and create food that maintains quality and edibility for a time that is adequate for distribution, stocking, sales, and customer convenience.[27]

Biological food spoilage occurs when enzymatic changes in foods occur or there is growth of yeast, mold, or acid-producing, non-pathogenic bacteria (such as lactobacilli) within the food, which can negatively impact its flavor, odor, appearance, and texture. While ingesting spoiled food does not typically lead to illness, the signs of spoilage are obvious via smell and visual inspection, forcing food manufacturers (and consumers) to throw away costly raw materials and finished goods. It is interesting to note that some of the same microorganisms that cause spoilage in some foods are actually essential in others—for example, the organisms responsible for providing fermentation and flavor development in bread, wine, pickled vegetables, and dairy products. Further, the growth of spoilage microorganisms can actually inhibit the growth of some pathogenic bacteria, such as *Staphylococcus aureus* in raw meat and poultry. In fact, fermentation is one of the oldest methods used for preserving foods, dating back thousands of years. (For a complete discussion of food fermentation, see Chapter 11.)

Signs of Food Spoilage and Food Industry Consequences

We are all familiar with many signs of food spoilage: the fuzzy growth in that forgotten jar of tomato sauce; the green shiny sheen on deli meats; the brown discoloration on leafy produce; and the black mold on the edge of an unfinished yogurt cup. These are household examples that are seen every day, and while the household cost is usually minor, when similar spoilage happens on a larger scale, the result is huge losses to a manufacturing facility and potential damage to a company's reputation. Food commodities that could have been value-added and sold at a profit are now destroyed.

Ubiquitous in Nature

The microorganisms capable of spoiling food are ubiquitous in nature. They live in the soil, waterways, and air, and reside on the skins of fruits, vegetables, animals, and humans. They live inside the intestinal tracts of animals and can grow on improperly sanitized food processing equipment. They can be transmitted directly to food via unwashed hands and dirty utensils. Spoilage organisms seek opportunities to invade the flesh of any plant or animal tissue that can provide the nutrients and growth conditions they need to survive.

Types of Spoilage Microorganisms

The microorganisms that cause spoilage include bacteria, yeast, and mold. Bacteria are microscopic single-celled organisms with a relatively primitive cell structure. Bacteria come in a variety of shapes and sizes and grow at a rapid rate when conditions are optimal. Bacterial outgrowth cannot normally be seen, but the resulting damage that occurs when spoilage bacteria grow in food (bad odors and flavors, physical changes, and so on) is how we know spoilage has occurred. Yeast and mold are both members of the fungi family and share the advanced internal cell structure of plants and animals. Yeasts are single-celled and reproduce by budding or fission, while molds are multicellular and reproduce by means of spores, which are produced in large numbers and are small, light, and resistant to drying. They are thus easily dispersed in the air; when they land on suitable nutrients, they are able, under favorable conditions, to produce fresh mold growth.[28] Spoilage caused by mold is usually more visible than that caused by yeast and can be seen easily as it grows and spreads on the surface of a food product.

● Parameters of Food That Lead to Spoilage

All of our food is of plant or animal origin. Therefore, to minimize spoilage and maximize shelf life, it is important to understand the intrinsic and extrinsic factors in foods that affect the ability of microorganisms to grow. Intrinsic factors—those located within the plant or animal tissues— include internal pH, moisture content, nutrient content, any naturally occurring antimicrobial components, and overall biological structure. Extrinsic factors include storage temperature, relative humidity, and gas concentration in the environment.[29] These parameters may result in either multiplication or inhibition of microbial growth in foods.

Intrinsic Factors

pH

Increasing the acidity of foods, either through fermentation or the addition of weak acids, has been used as a preservation method since ancient times. In their natural state, most foods, such as meat, fish, and vegetables, are slightly acidic, while most fruits are moderately acidic. A few foods, such as egg white, are alkaline. It is well known that groups of microorganisms have pH optimums, minimums, and maximums for growth in foods. As with other factors, pH usually interacts with other parameters in the food such as water activity (a_w), salt, temperature, redox potential (the likelihood for the

food or ingredient to become oxidized [lose electrons] or reduced [gain electrons]), and preservatives to inhibit growth of pathogens and other organisms. (Redox potential has an impact on the types of bacteria that can grow on or in foods. Not surprisingly, aerobes require an oxidized environment, and anaerobes require a reduced environment.) The pH of the food also significantly affects the lethality of the heat treatment given to the food. Less heat is needed to inactivate microbes as pH is reduced.

Another important characteristic of a food to consider when using acidity as a control mechanism is its buffering capacity. The buffering capacity of a food is its ability to resist changes in pH. Foods with a low buffering capacity change pH quickly in response to acidic or alkaline compounds produced by microorganisms as they grow. By virtue of their amino acids, which have both acidic and basic areas on their molecules, meats, in general, exhibit slightly better buffering capacity than vegetables, and therefore require higher levels of acidification to achieve a reduced pH than do vegetables.

Most microorganisms, particularly bacteria, grow well at a pH of close to 7.0 (neutral). Yeast and mold can grow well in more acidic environments (below 7.0). This explains why most lower-acid vegetables, meats, and dairy products are spoiled by bacteria, while yeasts and molds cause spoilage in the more acidic fruits and vegetables.

Moisture

Microorganisms need water in an available form to grow in food products. The control of moisture content in foods is one of the oldest preservation strategies. Food microbiologists generally describe the water requirements of microorganisms in terms of the water activity (a_w) of the food. The a_w of a food describes the degree to which water is bound in the food, its availability to participate in chemical or biochemical reactions, and its availability to facilitate growth of microorganisms. The a_w of pure water is equal to 1.0, and most fresh foods have a water activity close to the optimum growth level of most microorganisms (0.97 to 0.99).

The a_w of a food product can be reduced via dehydration or dry-heat cooking, or by the addition of solutes such as sugar or salt, which molecularly bind to water and make it unavailable for microbiological growth.

Most bacteria, yeast, and mold cannot grow below their respective a_w values of 0.90, 0.88, and 0.80, except for specific extreme groups such as the halophilic/halotolerant (salt-loving or -tolerant) bacteria, which can grow at a_w 0.75; the xerotolerant (dry-tolerant) molds, which can grow at a_w 0.71; and the xerophilic (dry-loving) molds and the osmophilic (living or thriving in a medium of high osmotic pressure) yeasts, which can grow between a_w 0.62 and 0.60.[31] Halophilic bacteria (for example, Vibrio species) can spoil improperly salted meats, and *Staphylococcus aureus* is a unique halotolerant pathogen that can grow and produce toxin at an a_w of 0.88. Xerophilic molds target improperly dried meats. Both osmophilic yeasts and molds can grow on damaged fruit surfaces, syrups, jellies, and jams.

FIGURE 13.15 Approximate pH values of some foods.

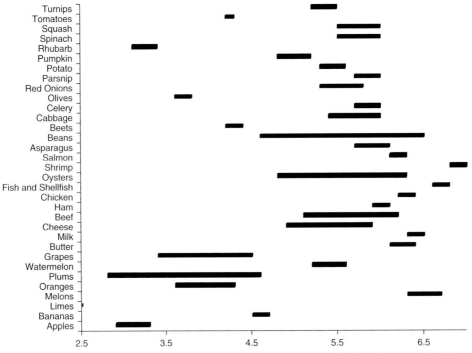

Source: Adapted from Jay, Loessner, and Golden, "Intrinsic and Extrinsic Parameters of Foods That Affect Microbial Growth" (2005).

Nutrient Content

To grow and function normally, microorganisms require the following: water, a source of energy (typically carbohydrates), a source of nitrogen (proteins and amino acids), vitamins and related growth factors, and minerals. Varying amounts of these nutrients are present in foods. Meats have abundant protein, lipids, minerals, and vitamins, but low levels of carbohydrates. Plant foods have high concentrations of different types of carbohydrates and varying levels of proteins, minerals, and vitamins. Foods such as milk, milk products, and eggs are rich in all nutrients.

Foodborne microorganisms can derive energy from carbohydrates, alcohols, and amino acids. Most microorganisms metabolize simple sugars, such as glucose. Others can metabolize more complex carbohydrates, such as starch or cellulose (found in plant foods) or glycogen (found in muscle foods). Some microorganisms can use fats as an energy source. In general, only small amounts of minerals are required; thus, many foods are good sources. The abundance of nutrients in most foods is sufficient to support the growth of a wide range of microorganisms. Those that predominate are organisms that can most easily utilize the nutrients present.

Antimicrobial Constituents

A number of plant-and animal-based foods contain naturally occurring antimicrobial constituents, but the usual concentration of these compounds in formulated foods is relatively low, so the antimicrobial effect is slight. However, these compounds may provide "an assist" when combined with other factors in the formulation. Prime examples are the essential oils found in oregano, thyme, cassia, lavender, and other herbs and spices. The food industry can take advantage of these antimicrobial properties by adding them to food to help retard spoilage. The spices not only provide flavoring but also help to extend shelf life. Another example is dried plums (prunes). The high levels of organic acids and antioxidants in prunes are linked to the suppression of microorganisms when they are mixed with ground meat.[34]

Biological Structures

A food's natural covering can protect it from damage, injury, and microbiological spoilage. Eggshells, nutshells, banana and apple peels, and animal hides are all examples of how the natural structure, when intact, can prevent microbial attack

FIGURE 13.16 Approximate pH growth range of some spoilage microorganisms.

Organisms	Minimum pH	Maximum pH
Mold	0.00	11.00
Yeasts	1.50	8.50
Lactic acid bacteria	3.50	10.20
Acetobacter	4.00	9.00
Staphylococcus	4.00	9.50
Vibrio spp.	5.20	9.00

Note: Boundaries not precise; values dependent on other growth parameters.
Source: Adapted from Jay, Loessner, and Golden, "Intrinsic and Extrinsic Parameters of Foods That Affect Microbial Growth" (2005).

FIGURE 13.17 Water activity of common foods.

Foods	Water Activity (a_w)
Fresh, raw fruits, vegetables, meat, fish	>0.98
Cooked meat, bread	0.98 to 0.95
Cured meat products, cheeses	0.95 to 0.91
Sausages, syrups	0.91 to 0.87
Flours, rice, beans, peas	0.87 to 0.80
Jams, marmalades	0.80 to 0.75
Candies	0.75 to 0.65
Dried fruits	0.65 to 0.60
Dehydrated vermicelli, spices, milk powder	0.60 to 0.20

Source: Farkas (2007)[30].

and spoilage. It is when these natural coverings are damaged or removed that we see food spoilage. Factors that can reduce effectiveness of protective coverings include deteriorative effects of aging or ripening, insect or animal damage, bruising from harvest or subsequent handling, temperature abuse, and processing operations (peeling, slicing, dicing, and so on).

Extrinsic Factors

Temperature

Microorganisms are classified based on the temperature range in which they grow best, with a minimum, maximum, and optimum. Spoilage organisms are present at all ends of the spectrum. An understanding of the interplay between time, temperature, and other intrinsic and extrinsic factors is crucial to selecting the proper storage conditions for a food product.

While most microorganisms are mesophiles, which grow best at warmer temperatures (86° to 104°F [30° to 40°C]), psychrophilic yeast and molds can grow well at refrigerated temperatures as low as 25°F (−3.9°C), and some spore-forming

FIGURE 13.18 Minimum water activity for growth of foodborne microorganisms at 77°F (25°C).

Microorganism Group	Minimum a_w Required
Many bacteria	0.91 to 0.88
Many yeasts	0.88
Many molds	0.80
Halophilic bacteria	0.75
Xerotolerant molds	0.71
Xerophilic molds, osmophilic yeasts	0.62 to 0.60

Adapted from Farkas (2007)[32]; Frazier and Westhoff (1988)[33].

FIGURE 13.19 Classification of bacteria based on optimum growth temperatures.

Type of Organism	Grows at These Temperatures	Optimum Growth Temperatures
Psychrotrophs	Below 7°C (45°F)	20 to 30°C (68 to 86°F)
Mesophiles	20 to 45°C (68 to 113°F)	30 to 40°C (86 to 104°F)
Thermophiles	Above 45°C (113°F)	55 to 65°C (131 to 149°F)

Source: Rachel Zemser.

thermophilic (heat-loving) bacteria can cause spoilage in retorted (pressure-cooked) cans of food. It is incumbent upon the producer to have specific knowledge of the food formulation, processing parameters, expected storage conditions, and the organisms most likely to be present when formulating the best strategy for maximizing shelf life.

Relative Humidity

The humidity of the environment can affect the water activity of the food being stored. The a_w of a food can be raised in a high-humidity environment, allowing more spoilage organisms to grow than in a dry, low-humidity environment. This can be counteracted with appropriate packaging.

Gases in the Atmosphere

Microorganisms have different sensitivities to oxygen. Those that grow only in the presence of oxygen are referred to as aerobic microorganisms; those that grow without oxygen are called anaerobes; and those that grow with or without oxygen are facultative anaerobes. A small group of microorganisms, microaerophiles need a small percentage of oxygen to grow well. Aerobic microorganisms require more oxidized environments (more oxygen) than do anaerobic organisms,

FIGURE 13.20 Common examples of aerobic, anaerobic, and facultative anaerobic spoilage bacteria.

Food Type	Aerobic	Anaerobic	Facultative
Meat	Pseudomonas	Clostridium	Lactobacillus
Poultry	Pseudomonas	Shewanella putrefaciens	Lactobacillus
Fish/seafood	Pseudomonas	Shewanella putrefaciens	Lactobacillus
Vegetables	Erwinia carotovora	Bacillus stearothermophilus	Lactobacillus
Fruit	Yeast and mold	Bacillus (canned)	Lactobacillus

Source: Rachel Zemser.

FIGURE 13.21 Common spoilage microorganisms in each specific food category.

Food Type	Bacteria	Yeast	Mold
Fresh meats	Acinetobacter, Aeromonas, Enterococcus, Moraxella, Pseudomonas, Psychrobacter, Lactobacillus	Candida	Cladosporium, Geotrichum, Mucor, Rhizopus, Sporotrichum
Vacuum-packed meats (fresh)	Brochothrix, Carnobacterium, Campylobacter, Enterococcus, Lactobacillus	Candida	Cladosporium, Geotrichum, Mucor, Rhizopus, Sporotrichum
MAP meat (fresh)	Brochothrix, Thermosphacta, Lactobacillus, Aeromonas, Enterobacteriaceae	Candida	Cladosporium, Geotrichum, Mucor, Rhizopus, Sporotrichum
Cured meats (fresh)	Acinetobacter, Aeromonas, Bacillus, Corynebacterium, Enterococcus, Micrococcus, Vibrios	Debaryomyces	Aspergillus, Penicillium
Cooked meats	Pseudomonas, Enterobacteriaceae, Lactobacillus, Broc. Thermosphacta, Clostridium, Bacillus, halophilic Vibrios	Debaryomyces	Aspergillus, Penicillium
Fish/seafood	Pseudomonas, Shewanella, Lactobacillus, Acinetobacter, Aeromonas, Vibrionaceae	Candida, Cryptococcus, Rhodotorula	Aureobasidium
Poultry	Acinetobacter, Enterobacter, Brochothrix, Lactobacillus, Shewanella, Corynebacterium, Pseudomonas, Vagococcus	Candida, Rhototolura	Aspergillus, Alternaria
Fresh vegetables	Corynebacterium, Pseudomonas, Xanthomonads, Erwinia	NA	Alternaria, Sclerotinia, Bremia, Aspergillus, Colletotrichum, Fusarium, Rhisopus, Pythium, Botrytis
Canned vegetables	Bacillus, Clostridium, Desulfotomaculum, Lactobacillus	NA	NA
Fermented vegetables	Lactobacillus, Bacillus, Enterobacter, Fusarium, Cellumonas, Xanthomonas	Candida, Torula, Rhodotorula	Penicillium, Alternaria, Mucor, Aspergillus, Cladosporium
Fruits and fruit juices	Pseudomonas, Corynebacterium, Erwinia, Bacillus (tomatoes), Lactobacillus, Gluconobacter, Leuconostoc	Rhodotorula, Candida, Torulopsis, Pichia, Saccharomyces, Zygosaccharomyces	Alternaria, Colletotrichum, Penicillium, Monilinia, Phytophora, Botrytis, Cryptosporiopsis, Ceratocystis, Aspergillus, Phomopsis, Geotrichum
Spices/dry soup mixes	NA	NA	Aspergillus
Cereals	Pseudomonas, Micrococcaceae, Lactobacillus, Bacillaceae, Brevibacterium	NA	Alternaria, Cladosporium, Aspergillus, Rhizopus, Fusarium, Penicillium, Eurotium
Refrigerated doughs	Lactobacillus, Leuconostoc, Streptoouccus		NA

(continued)

FIGURE 13.21 (*continued*)

Food Type	Bacteria	Yeast	Mold
Breads/bakery products	Bacillus subtilis		Rhizopus, Neurospora, Penicillium, Aspergillus
Nuts, seeds, legumes	NA/Rare	NA/Rare	Aspergillus, Penicillium, Fusarium
Shell eggs	Pseudomonas, Acinetobacter, Proteus, Aeromonas, Alcaligenes, Flavobacterium, Escherichia, Enterobacter, Staphylococcus, Bacillus, Cytophaga	Torula	Cladosporium, Geotrichum, Mucor, Rhizopus, Sporotrichum

Source: Rachel Zemser.

which require more reduced environments (lacking oxygen). While most yeasts and molds are obligate or preferential aerobes, spoilage bacteria have a wide range of oxygen needs.

Based on oxygen affinity, the growth of microorganisms can be controlled by modifying the gaseous atmosphere around the foods they inhabit. Gases inhibit microorganisms by two mechanisms. First, they can have a direct toxic effect that inhibits growth and proliferation. Carbon dioxide (CO_2), ozone (O_3), and oxygen (O_2) are gases that are directly toxic to certain microorganisms. Oxidizing free radicals generated by O_3 and O_2 are highly toxic to anaerobic bacteria and can have an inhibitory effect on aerobes, depending on concentration. Carbon dioxide is effective against obligate aerobes and at high levels can deter other microorganisms.

Modifying the gas composition can also have an indirect inhibitory effect by altering the competitive environment. Atmospheres with a negative effect on the growth of one particular microorganism may promote the growth of another, which may provide a competitive inhibitory effect on the spoilage organism or even against pathogens. This effect may have positive or negative consequences depending on the native microflora and their substrate.

Controlled atmosphere (CA) and modified atmosphere packaging (MAP) of certain foods can dramatically extend their shelf life. Antimicrobial atmospheres have been applied to fruits and vegetables, raw beef, chicken, and fish; dairy foods including milk and cottage cheese; eggs; and a variety of prepared, ready-to-eat foods. Controlling the gases in the surrounding environment can be achieved in closed rooms during bulk storage of raw produce or within the packaging of individual food products; the procedure can both introduce an assortment of gases or gas mixtures and remove gases entirely, as in vacuum packaging.

Since 1928, fruits and vegetables have been stored in controlled atmosphere warehouses containing increased levels (up to 10 percent) of carbon dioxide as a way to slow, prevent, and inhibit spoilage.[35] Carbon dioxide retards the growth of aerobic microorganisms. Ozone (O_3) is used to prevent spoilage on beef surfaces. The choice of gases is determined by the type of food, type of packaging, storage temperature and time, and the spoilage organisms most likely to be present.

Any type of food processing has vulnerable points where the process can fail, resulting in food spoilage. As a result, preventive methods have been developed that are specifically designed based on the food being processed and the growth requirements of each particular microorganism. This is the basis of HACCP plans.

● Meat

Meat is a nutritious food that contains high levels of protein and amino acids. In addition, the average pH of meat is 5.5 to 6.5, and the a_w is approximately 0.99. Thus, meat is a perfect growth environment for bacteria. The initial processing steps, which include slaughter, hide removal, removal of intestinal tract and viscera, washing the carcass, chilling, and storage, must be done carefully to prevent contamination with and outgrowth of both spoilage and pathogenic microorganisms.

All animals have microflora residing inside the gastrointestinal tract and on the hide. The level of bacteria inside living healthy muscle tissue is extremely low. However, during slaughter, there are unlimited opportunities for cross-contamination to take place. When an animal is slaughtered, it can fall on the floor and pick up bacteria from the floor and walls of the processing environment. Cross-contamination can also occur during skinning, dehairing, and evisceration. Other contamination can originate from the animal's hide, feces, dirty equipment, workers' hands, and any contaminated contact surface. Lastly, when the carcass is stored and transported, temperature control is critical in preventing the outgrowth of microorganisms still present on the carcass.

Carcass Spoilage

The main cause of carcass spoilage is improper temperature control. Under aerobic conditions, as storage temperatures increase, so does the growth of psychrotrophic (cold-tolerant) microorganisms such as Pseudomonas, Acinetobacter, and Moraxella. If the surface of the meat is dry, the moisture-loving bacteria are inhibited, but yeasts and molds can still grow well. If the carcass is stored under anaerobic conditions, such as vacuum packaging, or with MAP, lactic acid bacterial growth is favored, resulting in acid production that can alter flavor, texture, aroma, color, and water-holding capacity of the meat.

Aerobic spoilage signs may include visible bacterial colony formation (slime), shiny green surface, off odors, rancid flavors, and visible surface mold growth. Anaerobic spoilage indicators include sour, acidic, and cheesy odors and flavors.

Frozen Meat

If meat is properly frozen (at 14°F [−10C°] or lower), no microbial spoilage occurs. However, mold *can* grow on meat held as low as 23°F (−5°C) or higher, and lipid oxidation leading to rancidity and freezer burn due to dehydration can still cause spoilage during extended frozen storage.

Ground Meat

The aerobic surface of refrigerated ground meat can be spoiled by psychrotrophs (bacteria that are capable of growth in cold temperatures), and the internal anaerobic center of the ground meat can be spoiled by lactic acid bacteria. The FDA and USDA refrigeration requirement for meat is 40°F (4.4°C) or below, and packaging is a CCP to prevent cross-contamination.

Cured Meats

Meat is cured by adding salt and nitrites (along with sodium ascorbate to inhibit nitrosamine formation); it may or may not be smoked. These procedures not only inhibit bacteria but also create desirable flavors that redefine the meat into specialized items such as ham, bacon, Genoa salami, and corned beef. Curing prevents spoilage by increasing osmotic pressure through the addition of salt (and consequent reduction of a_w), and the nitrite has an antimicrobial effect, as does smoking. In the manufacture of dry or semi-dry sausages, pure cultures of lactic acid bacteria are added to the ground meat mixture (along with dextrose, a fermentable carbohydrate) to initiate fermentation, which has the additional antimicrobial effect of reducing the pH.

During curing, the temperature must be kept cold; otherwise spoilage can take place before the meat has reached an a_w or pH low enough to prevent outgrowth. Examples of spoilage organisms include mold, Enterobacteriaceae, and undesirable wild lactic acid bacteria—that is, not the ones selected for the curing and fermentation process. Spoilage is prevented by proper chilling, rapid curing, proper sanitation, and, to prevent mold, storing the finished product in vacuum or modified atmosphere packaging. Note that curing by itself does not make the meat shelf-stable. Additional hurdles, such as drying, smoking, cooking, adding antimicrobial agents, and refrigerated or frozen storage may be necessary to provide the necessary protections against spoilage.

Dried Meats

Drying meats to an a_w of 0.7 or below eliminates the possibility of bacterial or mold growth. That said, certain types of Italian and Hungarian dry sausages are inoculated with edible molds (typically Penicillium spp.) to provide additional flavor development and traditional appearance (white coating on the surface).

Cooked Meats

Meats are cooked, packaged, distributed chilled or frozen, and used by foodservice or sold by retail grocery establishments. Again, temperature control is the key to spoilage prevention; if the product's temperature is abused, psychrotrophs (aerobic) or lactobacilli (anaerobic) grow. If the product is cooked in a vacuum bag (*sous vide*), spoilage is typically via psychrotrophic spore-forming anaerobes such as Bacillus spp. or Clostridia. Post-processing contamination of pre-cooked products in conjunction with temperature abuse also contributes to microbial spoilage.

Retorted Meat Products

Low-acid (above pH 4.6) meat products that have been retorted—that is, have received a heat treatment sufficient to kill the pathogen *Clostridium botulinum*—typically result in a commercially sterile, room-temperature-stable product. If there was spoilage outgrowth in the meat *before* the retorting process, even though the processed product is safe, remaining metabolites (undesirable heat-stable compounds created by the spoilage bacteria, such as acid and gas formation) might make the product unpalatable. If the heating process was not sufficient to kill the spores of anaerobic spore-forming spoilage bacteria (which are more heat-tolerant than *C. botulinum*), the canned product could become spoiled if stored above 104°F (40°C), and germination of the spores took place. The usual offenders are two members of the Bacillus group, known as flat sour organisms because they cause sour taste and odor in the food without any gas production, hence the ends of the can remain flat.

Cooked and Cured Perishable Meats

Processed meats such as sliced deli ham, hot dogs, bacon, and canned hams are cooked and cured but still must be refrigerated (or frozen) between 32 and 41°F (0 and 5°C) to prevent spoilage. Spoilage may occur if the product is not properly heat processed or is subsequently held above 41°F (5°C). The amount of oxygen present determines which spoilage organisms predominate and what type of spoilage occurs. Surface slime (from yeast and lactic acid bacteria), souring, and greening are common. Greening occurs when lactic acid bacteria produce hydrogen peroxide in the presence of oxygen, which then goes on to oxidize the pink cured meat pigment, turning it green.

Cooked and Cured Shelf-Stable Meat Products

Spoilage occurs in these products (such as canned hams and smoked sausages) if the canning process is insufficient to kill all of the bacterial spores or if the sealed container is compromised, leading to post-processing contamination. Bacillus spp. are usually the cause of spoilage in this type of product.

●Fish and Seafood

Fish and seafood includes marine and aquatic animals used for human consumption: finfish, crustaceans, and mollusks. Fish and seafood, like meat, are high in protein and moisture and low in carbohydrate. In general, the internal pH of fish falls between 5.8 and 6.7, providing ideal conditions for spoilage bacteria to survive and grow. All seafood tissues contain compounds such as free non-protein nitrogen (NPN), which supports spoilage microorganism growth, and trimethylamine oxide (TMO), which is reduced to trimethylamine (by bacteria) and is responsible for the spoiled fish smell.

Crustaceans have slightly more carbohydrate and more free amino acids than finfish. Mollusks have the most carbohydrate of all—as much as 5.6 percent in oysters—which contributes to their specific spoilage patterns as well.[36]

Fish Spoilage

The steps involved in fish processing include capture, cold storage, evisceration, packaging, storage, and shipping. The only way to inhibit fish spoilage is to maintain clean processing conditions, tight temperature control, and good manufacturing practices. In general, internal fish muscle is sterile, and spoilage bacteria reside on the skin, in the gills, and inside the intestinal tract. Increased temperatures, combined with unsanitary processing conditions, result in the microflora interacting with the free amino acids in fish, leading to rapid deterioration and spoilage.

Initial microflora counts depend on the origin of the fish and the quality of the water in which they lived, including temperature, salinity, and water pollution levels. The natural microflora found on saltwater fish are typically halotolerant psychrotrophs. Thus, these bacteria grow well in colder temperatures over a salt range of 1 to 3 percent, which is the normal salinity of saltwater in various parts of the ocean and estuaries. A wider variety of microbes can spoil freshwater fish because there are no high salt levels to inhibit their growth.

Spoilage Stages

Four stages are involved in fish spoilage when the product is not handled properly (timing of each stage can escalate quickly as the storage temperature increases):

Stage 1 (within 6 days after death) involves a population shift from bacteria associated with live fish to those associated with dead fish spoilage, but little odor.

Stage 2 (7 to 10 days after death) involves spoilage bacteria growth and a noticeable fishy odor.

Stage 3 (10 to 14 days after death) involves rapid growth of bacteria, strong fishy odors, and slime formation.

Stage 4 (more than 14 days after death) is when bacteria cease to grow because the stationary phase is reached (the rate of bacterial cell growth is equal to the rate of bacterial cell death). The skin is very slimy, and the odor is putrid.[37]

Spoilage Microorganisms

In finfish, the main spoilage species are Shewanella and Pseudomonas. In shellfish, spoilage is usually caused by Vibrio species, as well as Pseudomonas and Acinetobacter-Moraxella. Mollusks are additionally spoiled by Flavobacterium and Cytophaga. Yeast and mold are sometimes responsible for fish spoilage, but this is uncommon.

Frozen raw seafood is whole, processed (broken down into smaller cuts) or breaded raw seafood that is sold frozen. Initial counts depend on the pre-freezing processing conditions and practices. Additional bacteria can be introduced via unsanitary breading procedures. Bacterial counts increase if the product is frozen slowly, thawed slowly, or held thawed for too long. Yeast and mold growth can also occur if the fish is held at improper frozen temperatures above 23°F (–5°).

Cooked frozen seafood is fish that is fully or partially cooked (sometimes breaded) and then frozen. Cooked frozen seafood undergoes a significant reduction in initial bacterial counts, assuming that proper cooking methods are employed. Post-cooking, bacteria can be reintroduced during the inspection and grading process. If the seafood is shipped refrigerated instead of frozen, bacterial growth may occur.

Canned seafood, sterilized using the retort process, is free of all spoilage bacteria, assuming process control is adequate. However, much crabmeat is sold canned and pasteurized, not sterilized, and must be refrigerated. It is not shelf-stable at room temperature, so one must pay close attention to the label.

Cured and hot-smoked seafood is processed by brining, followed by smoke-cooking at a minimum of 200°F (93°C) to an internal temperature of at least 165°F (74°C). This process coagulates proteins, kills vegetative cells, and reduces the fish's a_w to less than 0.62, where microbial growth is inhibited. With appropriate packaging, this type of seafood can be shelf-stable at room temperature. If it is cold-smoked at temperatures in the 80°F (27°C) range (commonly used for smoked salmon, or lox), the seafood must be rapidly cooled and refrigerated to prevent outgrowth of spoilage organisms because the low temperatures of cold smoking permit the survival of a significant portion of the natural microbiological flora on the fillets. This is not necessarily a bad thing, as the spoilage organisms outcompete potential pathogens such as Listeria and Clostridium, causing the seafood to spoil (and be discarded) before it becomes toxic. The opposite effect occurs if the cold-smoked fish is vacuum packed; the anaerobic environment reduces the population of competing spoilage organisms enough to allow the Clostridium bacteria to proliferate, and toxin production may occur before spoilage.[38]

Poultry

Chicken is a perfect growth medium for spoilage microorganisms. It has an a_w of 0.98 to 0.99 and a pH of approximately 5.7 to 6.7. Very high levels of spoilage microorganisms reside on the living bird's skin and feathers, although the internal meat is typically clean until processing, at which point cross-contamination may occur.

Processing steps for chicken include slaughter, scalding, defeathering, evisceration, spray washing, chilling, cutting into parts, deboning, and packaging. Bacteria can be introduced at each of these steps, especially if proper chilled temperatures (<40°F [4.4°C]) are not maintained or if processing is done in unsanitary environments. The primary spoilage organisms isolated from chicken carcasses include Pseudomonas, Acinetobacter, Flavobacterium, Corynebacterium, and low levels of yeasts, molds, and Enterobacteriaceae. Yeasts and mold typically grow only when antibiotics are used in the feed to inhibit the growth of competing bacteria. In this situation, one might encounter strains of Candida, Rhodotorula, and Torula.

If properly refrigerated at <40°F (4.4°C), but without atmosphere modification, raw chicken has a shelf life of 5 to 7 days. Vacuum-packed or MAP chicken has an extended shelf life of approximately 30 days. However, outgrowth of anaerobic or facultative anaerobes such as Lactobacillus, Shewanella, and Brochothrix may occur. Signs of spoilage include sliminess (on the outer surface) and sour odor, referred to as visceral taint. Usually, off odors are noticed before the sliminess occurs. Whole birds and parts spoil at about the same rate because they typically have the same contamination level.

Frozen Chicken

When chicken is frozen properly and held at or near –0.4°F (–18°C), there is very little spoilage. However, yeast and mold can grow on frozen poultry stored at 19.4°F (–7°C), including *Cladosporum herbarum*, which causes black spots, and *Thamnidium elegans*, which causes whisker-like growth.

Cooked Poultry Products

Cooked and ready-to-eat poultry products eventually spoil, but the rate depends on how the product is processed and stored. Cured and cooked chicken that contains sodium nitrites spoils more slowly, as does cooked chicken packed using vacuum or MAP packaging.

Dried Poultry Meat

Semi-dried or intermediate moisture poultry products, such as turkey jerky, do not support spoilage growth unless the water activity increases above 0.60. At that point it is possible for yeasts and molds to grow.

Vegetables

Vegetables include the edible parts of plants and the fruiting body of mushrooms (fungi). All vegetables are naturally susceptible to spoilage, and it is estimated that 20 percent of all fruits and vegetables harvested for human consumption are lost to spoilage.[39] Vegetables are very high in water and carbohydrates and thus are excellent growth media for many kinds of spoilage bacteria, yeasts, and molds. The amount of water present inside a vegetable as well as the microbiological load found in the soil, air, and surrounding water directly impacts spoilage rates. Most bacterial spoilage is caused by *Erwinia carotovora*, Pseudomonas, Corynebacteria, lactic acid–producing bacteria, Clostridial spore formers, coliforms, and micrococci. The dominating yeast spoilers include Rhodotorula, Candida, and *Kloeckera apiculata*, while molds include Sclerotinia, *Botrytis cinerea*, and *Aureobasidium pullulans*. Anaerobic vegetable spoilers are rare and usually found in canned vegetables only.

Raw Vegetables

After harvest, vegetables may be shipped directly to market raw and unwashed; cut, prepped, treated, and bagged; or stored in temperature-controlled and modified-atmosphere warehouses. Potential spoilage includes soft rot, spots, wilt, and blight caused by *Erwinia carotovora*, pseudomonads, xanthomonads, and Corynebacteria. Soft rot is easily identified by the soft, mushy appearance it gives the vegetables, along with off odors and a water-soaked appearance. It is caused by the bacteria breaking down the pectins (structural carbohydrates) inside the vegetables. Bacterial spoilage in raw vegetables can be reduced during all stages of harvest and storage by implementing proper sanitation and handling methods, keeping the vegetables cold and dry, and washing with chlorinated water.

Mushrooms are sold in many forms, including fresh, dry, marinated, and canned. The main spoilage microorganisms that can contaminate fresh mushrooms are *Pseudomonas fluorescens* and yeasts and molds that come from the soil. Fresh mushrooms should be stored dry and refrigerated until ready for use. Storage in airtight plastic is not recommended; instead, use cardboard boxes or paper bags with airflow access (holes) to prevent the growth of potentially dangerous anaerobes. Washing and blanching the mushrooms greatly reduces the amount of contaminants, but they may be reintroduced during processing from dirty manufacturing facilities. Mushrooms should not be washed too far in advance of further processing because it increases the a_w and hastens the onset of spoilage.

Processed Vegetables

Raw vegetables for freezing are typically blanched first to fix color, reduce the microbial load, inactivate enzymes, and remove cellular gases, and then frozen for distribution and sale. They are rarely spoiled by bacteria because the cold temperature and low a_w prevent spoilage. However, enzyme activity can continue at freezer temperatures if blanching is insufficient, causing off flavor and off color development over time. Inefficient, slow freezing and poor packaging can also lead to surface dehydration (freezer burn) as well as diminished textural attributes.

Canned vegetables are thermally processed at sterilizing temperatures (at or above 250°F [121°C]) to make them shelf-stable at room temperature. The exact temperatures and times required for processing depend on the initial vegetable pH and density (which affects the rate of heat transfer) as well as the makeup of the brine or other packing liquid. Retorting normally eliminates all spores. However, if processing is insufficient, the most heat-resistant thermophiles may come out of their dormant spore state when the canned vegetables are stored in hot environments (above 104°F [40°C]). This can result in three types of spoilage:

1. *Flat sour spoilage*, which is acid production without gas, caused by *Bacillus stearothermophilus* and *Bacillus coagulans*. The ends of the cans do not swell; they remain flat.

2. *Thermophilic anaerobic spoilage* (TA), caused by the production of hydrogen gas and carbon dioxide by *Clostridium thermosaccharolyticum*. Cans become noticeably swollen and spurt when opened.

3. *Sulfide stinker spoilage*, caused by hydrogen sulfide produced by *Desulfotomaculum nigrificans*. There is no gas production, but there is a hydrogen sulfide odor (as of rotten eggs) and possible black color if iron is present.

When commercial sterilization is done properly and cans are stored under normal conditions (that is, not in tropical climates), unless the hermetic seal is breached or the can is punctured, spoilage won't occur until after the can is opened by the consumer and subjected to post-process contamination.

Dried Vegetables

Dried vegetables have their water activity reduced to less than a_w 0.85 to prevent the outgrowth of spoilage microorganisms. Spoilage occurs only if the products are held at high humidity, resulting in rehydration, which can result in yeast and mold spoilage.

Fermented and Acidified Vegetables

Vegetables have been preserved by salting, acidifying, or lactic or acetic fermentation for thousands of years as a way to preserve the harvest before refrigeration or other more modern processing methods were known. Pickling reduces the pH sufficiently to prevent the outgrowth of spoilage organisms. Spoilage by yeast, lactic acid bacteria, coliforms, and halophiles can occur in fermented, salted, and pickled products if proper procedures are not followed. Spoilage can be prevented by:[40]

1. Proper distribution of brine
2. Proper fermentation sequence

3. Maintaining appropriate temperature during fermentation
4. Destruction or inhibition of wild yeast activity
5. Using pure strain starter cultures

Fruits

Fruits are the seed-bearing portions of plants. They are high in water (85 percent) and sugars, but because of their low pH (due to high levels of citric, malic, and tartaric acid), most do not support the growth of spoilage bacteria.[41] The few exceptions include olives, cucumbers, and tomatoes, which is why these items are further acidified to lower the pH below 4.0, to prevent spoilage.

Yeasts and molds, which grow over a wide pH range, are the main spoilage organisms of concern in fruit and fruit products. Yeasts can attack fruit sugars, causing fermentation and the production of alcohol and gas. Once the yeast has partially broken down the fruit, molds are able to use the alcohol by-product metabolites as an energy source. Together, they destroy the fruit.

Fruits typically have some initial microflora, especially on the peel, which can be reduced during the primary processing steps (including washing and peeling). General ways to protect fresh fruit from microbial spoilage include using approved fungicides prior to harvest, hot-water surface blanching, washing in chlorinated water post-harvest, and controlling the temperature, humidity, and gas atmosphere of the fruit storage area. When all control measures are in place, bacteria, yeast, and mold are greatly reduced.

Fresh Fruits

Citrus fruits are most commonly spoiled by *Penicillium italicum* (blue rot) and *Penicillium digitatum* (green rot). Limes and lemons are spoiled by *Geotrichum candidum*. Oranges are spoiled by *Alternaria citri*, which causes the inside to turn black. Post-harvest spoilage control includes using detergents, weak alkali, and fungicides. Keeping fruit surfaces dry is the best strategy for preventing spoilage.

Apples and pears (pome fruits) are usually spoiled by *Penicillium expansum* (blue rot), a cold-tolerant organism. Thus, cold storage only temporarily retards this type of spoilage. *Botrytis cinerea* causes gray rot in pears, displayed as ash-gray spore masses. Using a fungicide does not prevent all pome fruit spoilage, but it does significantly inhibit the rot.

Stone fruits, which include peaches, plums, apricots, cherries, and nectarines, are spoiled by brown rot caused by *Monilia fructicola*, which causes water-soaked spots on the fruit that subsequently become brown. Transit rot occurs when boxed fruit is transported in high-humidity environments. Caused by *Rhizopus stolonifer*, it first produces soft rot and then engulfs the fruit with a loose nest of mycelium. The mold spreads rapidly and can quickly contaminate an entire box of fruit. Cherries and plums are spoiled by *Penicillium expansum* (blue mold). Spoilage can be controlled in stone fruits by using a fungicide, maintaining the storage temperature below 40°F (4.4°C), and preventing bruising of the fruit.

Berries, including blueberries, raspberries, blackberries, and strawberries, are often spoiled by the molds *Botrytis cinerea* and *Rhizopus stolonifer*. Spoilage in berry fruits can be prevented with pre-harvest antifungal sprays, careful handling, and prompt refrigeration.

When certain wine grapes are infected with the fungus *Botrytis cinerea*, they begin to rot and shrivel, concentrating their sugars and creating a desirable flavor profile in wines produced from them (French Sauternes, Hungarian Tokaji, and some German dessert wines)—among the most sought-after and expensive wines in the world. This type of spoilage is therefore known as noble rot. However, when *Botrytis cinerea* infects regular table grapes, significant spoilage occurs. In general, all kinds of grape spoilage can be prevented by using pre- and post-harvest antifungal sprays and rapid transfer after picking into cold storage.

With a pH range of 4 to 4.5, tomatoes are typically spoiled by mold. Examples of tomato spoilage include Alternaria rot (dark brown and black lesions caused by *Alternaria alternata*), chilling injury, which allows spoilage by the fungus *Cladosporium herbarum*, and gray mold rot due to *Botrytis cinerea*. Sour rot is caused by *Geotrichum candidum* and soil rot by *Rhizoctania solani*. To prevent or delay spoilage, it is important to practice good sanitation and use appropriate fungicides and pre-harvest sprays. Tomatoes for retail sale are typically picked green, or at least under-ripe, for transport so as to reduce transport injury and subsequent colonization by spoilage organisms. Not only are green tomatoes less easily damaged but also acid levels are at their peak, inhibiting microbial growth. That said, they are also lacking in flavor, which never quite achieves the picked ripe taste of tomatoes allowed to ripen on the vine.

Frozen Fruits

Any microflora left on fresh fruit after it is picked, harvested, washed, and frozen remains during freezing. The cold temperatures prevent outgrowth of any yeasts and molds. However, improper or prolonged thawing can lead to spoilage.

Canned Fruits

A combination of a naturally low pH (below 4.6) and a pasteurizing heat process usually prevents the outgrowth of spoilage microorganisms in canned fruit. Hot-fill-and-hold or hot-water bath/hot-steam bath processing is normally all that is required for most fruits, with temperatures of 175 to 210°F (79.4 to 98.9°C), depending on pH, being sufficient to kill all microorganisms except bacterial spores. Because the spores do not germinate due to the low pH, the food is considered commercially sterile.

High-acid foods may be processed in a hot-water or steam bath at atmospheric pressures; no pressure-cooking or retorting is required. This heating requirement applies not only to fruits but also to all acidified foods that are heat-processed in cans for long-term shelf storage, such as pickled vegetables (cucumbers, beets, cocktail onions, cherry peppers, olives) and salsa. An acidified food is a low-acid food (pH above 4.6) to which acid(s) or acid food(s) are added to reduce its "equilibrium pH" after mixing together to below 4.6, thus preventing the growth of harmful bacteria and extending shelf life.

Spoilage in canned fruits is rare, but when it does occur, it is due to butyric acid–producing or thermophilic (heat-loving) anaerobic spore-formers. *Clostridium pasteurianum* can grow in a pH of 3.8, causing spoilage of pears by producing acid and gas. Under-processing tomatoes can result in the outgrowth of thermoduric (heat-tolerant) facultative anaerobes such as *Bacillus coagulans*, which results in flat sour spoilage. This spoilage is known to occur in tomato juice as well; the acid-producing bacteria reduce the pH while producing off flavors described as being medicinal and oddly fruity.

Dried Fruits

Dried fruits include sulfured, unsulfured, moist packs, and glacéed fruits. Sulfured fruits have added sulfur dioxide, which preserves the fruit's color (bright orange dried apricots are the best example) by preventing enzymatic browning and by eliminating all microflora. The government requires that any foods containing sulfites at greater than 10 ppm must have a warning label for individuals with sulfite sensitivity. Unsulfured fruits are dried naturally without sulfur dioxide (dried unsulfured apricots are dark brown). Moist-pack fruits are rehydrated in hot water to an a_w of 0.85 to 0.90 before packing; and glacéed fruits are infused with glucose syrup and sulfur dioxide. When sulfur dioxide is used, spoilage is rare. However, in the absence of sulfur dioxide, dried fruits are susceptible to spoilage by xerophilic fungi if they are not dried and stored properly. In glacéed fruits, free sulfur dioxide is bound by glucose. Hence, sometimes the yeast *Schizosaccharomyces pombe*, which can grow at low a_w and is resistant to sulfur dioxide, can cause spoilage during certain points in the glucose infusion process.

Fruit Juices, Concentrates, and Preserves

Fruit juices, fruit concentrates, and preserves are products that combine fruits with other ingredients such as sugar, water, gums, acids, pectins, and corn syrup to create a final processed product with varying amounts of actual fruit. The surface of raw fruits used to make these products carry naturally occurring yeast, mold, and bacteria; these can cause product spoilage if not inhibited by acid, sugar, heat processing, or preservatives. The two main factors that contribute to a fruit product's shelf stability are its water activity (a_w) and acidity (pH); depending on the process or additional ingredients used, these may require adjustment to prevent outgrowth. Water activity can be controlled by increasing the product's Brix (the total measured soluble solids in solution); this is accomplished by adding sugar or corn syrup. As the Brix increases, the water activity decreases, preventing bacterial outgrowth and subsequent spoilage. Because both yeast and mold can grow in acidic environments, fruit products must be acidified well below pH 4.0; this measure must be combined with heat treatment and possibly preservatives such as sorbic acid or benzoic acid to prevent post-processing outgrowth.

Fermented and Acidified Fruits

Certain fruits we think of as vegetables are actually fruits, notably olives, cucumbers, and tomatoes. These fruits are not very acidic (even some tomatoes) and must be treated differently than those that typically fall well below pH 4.6.

Olives are fermented by their own natural microflora (a combination of yeast, bacteria, and mold), with Leuconostoc being one of the important bacteria in the process. Before fermentation begins, the raw olives are treated with lye (to remove bitter flavors). If the lye is not leached properly from the olive, it can inhibit Leuconostoc and allow spoilage organisms to prevail, causing gas, bloating, and cheesy odors.

Cucumbers are preserved by salting, lactic fermentation, direct acidification, and (in jarred pickles) pasteurization. If improper brining, acidification, or pasteurization is used, outgrowth of yeasts and halophilic spoilage bacteria can occur, resulting in soft, bloated, gassy cucumbers.

Tomato products have their own unique set of potential spoilage issues due to inconsistent pH levels that do not always fall below 4.6. Typically, tomatoes are acidified with citric acid if they are not below 4.6 and are going to be further processed in cans, jars, bottles, and pouches. Spoilage occurs if proper heat treatment is not applied and Clostridium or *Bacillus coagulans* spores survive and cause flat sour spoilage. Machinery mold caused by *Geotrichum candidum* can occur when manufacturing plants do not practice sound sanitation and mold spores from the processing equipment contaminate the tomatoes.

● Spices and Herbs

Spices and herbs are aromatic plant materials used to season or flavor food. They are available in whole or ground form, fresh, frozen, or dry, and as extracted essential oils and oleoresins.

The initial microbial load of spices is typically very high because they are agricultural products. A wide variety of microorganisms can be found on spices, including aerobic and anaerobic spore-formers, psychrotrophs, thermophiles, yeast, and molds. These organisms do not generally cause spoilage of the herbs and spices after drying because they are inactivated by the drying process. Of greater concern is what happens when contaminated dried herbs or spices are used to season other foods, where they are exposed to moisture, nutrients, and, in some cases, heat. Given the right environment, with sufficient moisture and a plentiful food source, bacterial and fungal spores can germinate and spoilage may occur. Dry spices and herbs are normally treated to reduce or eliminate spoilage organisms using chemical fumigants, steaming, or irradiation.

● Cereal Products

Cereal grains include wheat, corn, oats, rye, rice, barley, and millet. These are manufactured into cook-up or ready-to-eat breakfast cereals, flour, bread and other baked goods, pasta and noodles, tortillas, beer, sake, and vinegar.

Cereal products contain carbohydrates, proteins, fats, minerals, and vitamins. They have a neutral pH, are an excellent energy source, and provide an ideal growing environment for spoilage microorganisms—except that in their normal dried state, they lack sufficient water. Typically, cereal products are dried to a water activity level below 0.70, which prevents the outgrowth of organisms. Fungi are a concern, however, if product is not stored properly and a_w is compromised. Spoilage of cereal products can also occur through blending with other, more spoilage-prone ingredients during processing.

Processing and Harvest

The main spoilage organisms of concern in improperly stored cereal products are fungi—Aspergillus, Penicillium, and Eurotium—which grow well on moist cereal grains and contaminate product after harvest. These organisms can be controlled by maintaining water activity below 0.68, keeping moisture low (under 11 percent for long-term storage), and storing at cool temperatures (41 to 77°F [5 to 25°C]) and in controlled atmosphere (high carbon dioxide).

The moisture levels in flour, starch, and meal are crucial in preventing spoilage. Below 12 percent moisture, flour is stable, but some molds can grow just above 12 percent, and some bacteria can grow at 17 percent.

Dough-Based Products

Most doughs are refrigerated, which significantly slows or prevents spoilage. In addition, dough is anaerobic, with low water activity, and has carbon dioxide–producing yeast or leavening agents. Thus, it is rare that spoilage takes place. However, sourdough bread can spoil if the lactic acid–producing bacteria are not properly controlled. Visible results of this type of spoilage include exploding packages, gas production, and slimy dough.

Bread has a short shelf life, and the most common cause of spoilage in baked bread is mold (such as Penicillium spp.) and spore-forming bacteria such as *Bacillus subtilis*, which survive the baking process and cause rope spoilage by breaking down bread structure. Rope spoilage is identified when bread develops a soft and sticky brown crumb with overripe cantaloupe or pineapple odors. Bread spoilage can be prevented by keeping products dry, lowering the water activity, using preservatives such as sorbic acid and calcium propionate, and employing good sanitation practices.

Dry pasta spoilage rarely occurs unless the product is improperly dried or is contaminated during manufacturing with spoiled ingredients such as bacterially contaminated liquid eggs. This can be prevented by using pasteurized liquid eggs. However, fresh pasta (with a_w in excess of 0.9) is subject to microbial attack unless it is packaged using modified atmosphere.

Nuts and Legumes

Nuts are "dry, one-seeded fruit, which do not dehisce (split open) at maturity."[42] Most true nuts are tree nuts; peanuts (also called *groundnuts*) are technically in the legume family. Tree nuts include almonds, hazelnuts, pistachios, Brazil nuts, pecans, coconuts, and macadamia nuts. They can be minimally processed and sold as a snack food, or they can be further processed into butters or sauces, or used for oil production.

Tree nuts and peanuts rarely spoil. While their shells protect them from microorganisms during growth, excessive rain during harvest makes is possible for the shells to split and fungi to enter and grow on the nut meat. Additionally, inadequate post-harvest drying and storage can result in spoilage. The high fat content in nuts and seeds makes them susceptible to attack by the fungi Aspergillus, Fusarium, and Penicillium, which cause spoilage. Aspergillus can produce a deadly toxin (aflatoxin).

Legumes

While fresh legumes typically have high levels of fungi on their external pods, which cause spoilage such as black blight and soft rot, the spoilage of dried legumes (for example, soybeans, chickpeas, black beans, lentils) is not common. Legumes may be discolored by fungi, but this is not considered significant.

Eggs and Egg Products

Eggs are sold whole in the shell, as a pasteurized liquid, or in a spray-dried powder form. Whole eggs are typically sold in the retail and foodservice markets, while the liquid and powder versions are more common in manufacturing operations. All eggs and egg products have the potential to spoil if not handled properly.

Shell Eggs

The microorganisms most common on egg surfaces are not usually associated with spoilage. A few are able to penetrate the eggshell. Pseudomonas can cause spoilage even in refrigerated eggs because that organism grows well under cold conditions. Alcaligenes, Aeromonas, and Proteus cause black rot because they are proteolytic and digest the egg albumen, causing a blackening of the yolk. Shell egg spoilage can be inhibited by good henhouse sanitation practices, frequent egg collecting, refrigeration, regular egg inspections with white lights (candling), and washing (and promptly drying) eggs. While egg refrigeration is debated, it does indeed slow the growth of all microorganisms.

In addition, one company currently markets a pasteurized shell egg, "Davidson's Safest Choice," that eliminates Salmonella, and also reduces or eliminates spoilage organisms as well. Following pasteurization, the eggs are wax-coated to prevent any contaminants from entering the egg through the porous shell, and are marked with a red "P" in a circle to distinguish them from regular, unpasteurized eggs. While they are more expensive than regular shell eggs, they are much safer for consumption by at-risk populations such as the elderly or immuno-compromised individuals. Unlike regular eggs, the USDA has stated: "In-shell pasteurized eggs may be used safely without cooking."

Liquid Eggs

Liquid egg spoilage is a direct result of cross-contamination from the eggshell during processing. Liquid eggs must be pasteurized immediately or chilled or frozen as soon as possible to prevent spoilage. Those that are pasteurized and salted or sugared have a very long shelf life because pasteurization destroys Pseudomonas, Acinetobacter, and Enterobacter, and salt/sugar provide osmotic protection. However, if the product is not pasteurized properly, halotolerant organisms can survive and grow.

Spoilage in liquid eggs is evidenced by coagulation, sour odors, and gas production. Washing and sanitizing eggshells before breaking, pasteurization, cold or frozen storage, and the addition of salt (or sugar in liquid eggs destined for bakery applications) prevents or significantly slows spoilage.

Dried Eggs

Eggs that are spray-dried, drum-dried, or freeze-dried are all used in manufacturing and research and development. While some bacteria can survive in dried eggs, they do not grow or cause spoilage. When the product is reconstituted, any spoilage organisms present, even at low levels, can grow out and cause the product to spoil if it is not subsequently heat-processed as an ingredient in another product.

Milk and Dairy Products

"Milk is spoiled when it starts to look like yogurt, yogurt is spoiled when it starts to look like cottage cheese, cottage cheese is spoiled when it starts to look like regular cheese. Regular cheese is nothing but spoiled milk anyway and cannot get any more spoiled than it is already."[43]

Milk in the U.S. is obtained almost entirely from cows (97%) and to a much lesser extent from goats, whose milk is primarily used for making cheese. The dairy products made from milk include cream, evaporated or condensed milk, dried milk, fermented milk (yogurt and kefir), cheese, butter, and ice cream.

Milk is extremely susceptible to spoilage. With its high water content, neutral pH, protein, fat, carbohydrates, vitamins, and minerals, it is an ideal growth environment for spoilage microorganisms. Milk processing may include pasteurization, sterilization, dehydration, fermentation, refrigeration, and freezing, all of which inhibit microbial outgrowth and extend shelf life.

Pasteurized Milk and Cream

Raw milk is not considered safe to drink by the FDA, and almost all milk manufactured for consumption is pasteurized. Milk that is pasteurized and refrigerated does not spoil for several weeks, but eventually, spore-formers (Bacillus spp.) and thermoduric organisms (Streptococcus and Lactobacillus) that survive the pasteurization process, or post-pasteurization contaminating bacteria, slowly begin to grow, even at refrigerated temperatures. As Streptococcus grows in milk, it uses the lactose to produce lactic acid, which subsequently lowers the pH of milk, allowing curdling to take place. Post-processing contamination can also result in fungal growth, which can increase the surface pH of the milk, allowing spoilage bacteria to grow.[44] Pseudomonas spp. produce enzymes that break down the fat (lipase) and protein (protease), which results in off flavors and rancidity.

Shelf-Stable Milk

Shelf-stable milk is also known as UHT milk. In the regular pasteurization process, milk is heated to 161.6°F (72°C) for at least 15 minutes, whereas the UHT process heats the milk at 275°F (135°C) for one to two seconds. This flash of extreme heat will kill off any bacteria and spores in the milk, making it sterile and shelf stable at room temperature if packaged aseptically (i.e., packaged in a sterile container within the confines of a "clean room"). Because of the UHT process and aseptic packaging, shelf-stable milk remains potable for months, not days. Once the container is opened, however, it reacts like regular milk and must be refrigerated. UHT pasteurization is also used for other products such as fruit juices, cream, yogurt, wine, and soups.

When milk is sterilized to eliminate all microorganisms and spore-formers, spoilage is rare. When it does occur, it usually is a result of post-process contamination through a breach in the packaging, or via the addition of ingredients such as chocolate or other flavorings that introduce heat-resistant spores into the milk mixture.

One downside to UHT processing is that it adds an unavoidable cooked flavor to the milk. Product developers need to take this into account when deciding whether to use sterilized or regular milk as an ingredient.

Concentrated Milk Products

Milk products are concentrated (for example, condensed milk and evaporated milk) for direct consumption or to help reduce shipping costs to manufacturing facilities that are using them as ingredients in other products. Spoilage in concentrated milk products is similar to that seen in pasteurized milk and is based on the number of heat-resistant spores (Bacillus spp.) that survive canning, or from post-processing contamination. Sweetened condensed milk, with a lower a_w (0.85), favors yeast and mold outgrowth, which can lead to off flavors and gas production (exploding cans).

Dried Dairy Products

Spoilage organisms may be present at low levels in dried milk, but no outgrowth or spoilage occurs until it is reconstituted.

Butter

Even though butter is very low in carbohydrate and protein, it can be spoiled by bacteria and mold. Salted butter is rarely affected; unsalted or "sweet" butter lacks the antimicrobial benefit of added salt and is therefore far more likely to be compromised. Sweet butter should always be stored refrigerated. There are two types of butter spoilage:

1. *Surface taint* (putridity), caused by *Pseudomonas putrefaciens*, which grows on the surface of finished butter.
2. *Rancidity*, caused by *Pseudomonas fragi*, which hydrolyzes the butterfat.

Other spoilage microorganisms include *Lactobacillus lactis*, which causes a malty flavor, and *Pseudomonas nigrificans*, which causes black discoloration.

Fermented Milk

Fermentation of dairy products is actually a very effective method for preventing spoilage and extending shelf life. That said, if the milk used is not clean and contains high levels of other non-fermenting bacteria, the contaminants can inhibit the fermentation activity of the starter cultures. If the acidification process is slow, spore-formers, which do not grow at low pH, can multiply before the product gets below pH 4.6. Acid-tolerant yeast and molds are common in fermented dairy products and usually come from contaminated packaging materials, the addition of contaminated fruit variegates, or poor line hygiene. All of this leads to post-process contamination.

Cheese is essentially the conversion of milk into a less perishable product. Over 1000 types of cheeses are made throughout the world. The manufacturing steps include heating, acidification (via fermentative bacteria or the addition of acids), enzymatic protein coagulation with rennet, curd formation, whey removal, pressing, salting, and ripening. Spoilage microorganisms and undesirable molds, including strains of Penicillium, Mucor, Monilia, and Aspergillus, can be introduced at any point during the numerous processing steps, resulting in inhibition of the specific molds and fermentative bacteria needed to convert the milk into cheese. Spoilage that takes place in fresh cheese immediately after ripening is caused by *Bacillus subtilis* and *coliforms*. These organisms can ferment lactose and cause early blowing (due to gas formation), off odors, and slits in the cheese. Late-blowing spoilage is caused by the formation of butyric acid, gas, and off flavors, and is caused by Clostridium spp. Spores of these bacteria are capable of surviving pasteurization temperatures and can be present in the milk.

To prevent cheese from spoiling, preservatives such as potassium sorbate and lactic acid can be used to create an unfavorable environment that inhibits spoilage bacteria.

Starting with high-quality milk is crucial, as are adequate heat treatments, pure starter cultures of proven fermentative bacteria to inoculate the milk, and proper sanitation procedures to prevent contamination.

Oil-Based Emulsified Dressings

This category includes mayonnaise and salad dressings. Both are oil-and-water emulsions that contain additional ingredients such as acidifying agents, colors, flavors, egg products, sugar, salt, herbs, and other ingredients.

Commercial mayonnaise and spoonable (mayonnaise-like) salad dressings are formulated with acidulents, such as vinegar and lemon juice, which create a high-acid environment, and pasteurized eggs. Salt is also an important ingredient that contributes to the unfavorable environment for microbial growth, making these products extremely unlikely sources for bacterial spoilage.

The process involved in manufacturing oil-based salad dressings is usually cold fill, as heating the product would destroy the emulsion. Thus, measures such as acidification, addition of salt, and the addition of preservatives (sorbate, acetic acid, and benzoate) are used to prevent spoilage. Typical spoilage organisms that affect oil-based products include acid-tolerant yeasts such as *Zygosaccharomyces bailii* and fermentative bacteria such as *Lactobacillus fructivorans*. The outgrowth of spoilage Lactobacillus in oil- and fat-based emulsified foods results in gas formation and a lowering of the pH, which can impart an undesirable sour flavor in the finished product.

Sugar, Syrups, and Honey

This group of foods includes regular sugar, which comes from sugar beets and sugar cane; sugar syrups, including liquid sucrose, fructose, invert sugar, and corn syrups; maple syrup; agave syrup; molasses; and honey. All of these in their raw form are in close proximity to soil and the environment, which can cause contamination and spoilage. In cane sugar manufacturing, the spoilage can be seen as souring and alcohol and acid production in the liquid precursors before crystallization. In beet sugar manufacturing, acid-producing bacteria such as Leuconostoc spp. can hydrolyze the sugar and synthesize dextran, a glucose polymer, which looks like slime. Dextran can clog the lines and pipes in sugar manufacturing facilities.

Maple sap is sterile when it is in the tree, but it can be contaminated during tapping by Pseudomonas or yeasts. These can cause flavor and color changes or result in blown containers post-packaging. Water activity can vary in honey and molasses, depending on origin and climate. If the a_w or moisture levels are too high, osmophilic yeasts can grow and cause alcoholic fermentation. Concentrated sugar syrups and honey rarely spoil because of their high sugar concentration and low water content (below 18 percent). Potential spoilage organisms are killed by osmotic pressure. That said, honey can contain bacterial spores such as *Clostridium botulinum*, which are unable to germinate within the honey itself, and are typically not harmful to healthy adults. But they can germinate in the undeveloped gastrointestinal tract of babies and colonize the small intestine, causing infant botulism (also known as "floppy baby syndrome"). Therefore, honey should never be fed to children below the age of 1 year.

Conclusion

Food and food ingredients can be contaminated with any number of naturally occurring or synthetic biological, chemical, and physical hazards. Research chefs and product developers share the responsibility for preparing creative menu items that also protect consumers' health. Personnel must know the causes of foodborne illness as well as how to prevent, eliminate, or reduce the risk of foodborne illness to an ALOP.

The application of HACCP is a science-based method to assure the safety of processed foods. Tasting alone cannot determine safety, as many pathogens do not produce detectable warning signs. However, if the process used to prepare food is controlled using HACCP, the food has the greatest likelihood of being safe. Careful control of processing time and temperature, judicious use of approved preservatives, adjustment of pH and water activity, and protective packaging can significantly improve shelf life and maintain product quality as well as assure food safety.

Food spoilage is not a safety problem but rather a quality issue. Unlike food contaminated with pathogenic microorganisms, which can taste and look fine, food spoilage can be detected by taste, smell, and sight. Food is spoiled when it is damaged or degraded to the point of being unfit for consumption.

Food spoilage shortens shelf life and its acceptability for sale. Foods such as meat, fish, and poultry; vegetables and fruits; spices, cereals, nuts, and legumes; egg and dairy products; oil- and fat-based products; and sugar syrups are affected by a wide variety of microbiological spoilage factors, some of them unique to specific foods. Numerous manufacturing, distribution, and storage strategies can be used to prevent food from spoiling beyond the point of salability.

Both food safety and spoilage threats are ubiquitous and must be controlled to make food safe and desirable for consumption. When product development kitchens and food establishments implement effective, validated strategies and procedures to control hazards and spoilage factors associated with the growing, receiving and storing, preparation and packaging, transport, and distribution of food products, the risk to public health and company liability is reduced, and the company's reputation is preserved and enhanced.

[1] J. N. Sofos, "Challenges to Meat Safety in the 21st Century," *Meat Science* 78, no. 1–2 (2008): 3–13.

[2] CDC Briefing on the Burden of Foodborne Disease Illness, Press Release Archive, Wednesday, December 15, 2010.

[3]R. L. Scharff, "Health-Related Costs from Foodborne Illness in the United States," Georgetown University, March 2010. For the Produce Safety Project, Georgetown University, http://publichealth.lacounty.gov/eh/docs/ReportPublication/HealthRelatedCostsFromFoodborneIllnessUS.pdf.

[4]CDC (Centers for Disease Control and Prevention), *Outbreak Database Search Tool 2009* (Atlanta, GA: 2009). Available at http://www.cdc.gov/foodborneoutbreaks/Default.aspx. Accessed September 24, 2009.

[5]CDC (Centers for Disease Control and Prevention), "CDC Fact Sheet: Toxoplasmosis" (2008). Available at http://www.cdc.gov/toxoplasmosis/. Accessed September 24, 2009.

[6]FDA (U.S. Food and Drug Administration), *Bad Bug Book: Foodborne Pathogenic Microorganisms and Natural Toxins Handbook* (Washington, D.C.: Center for Food Safety and Applied Nutrition, 2009). Available at http://vm.cfsan.fda.gov/~mow/intro.html. Accessed September 29, 2009.

[7]D. L. Heymann, *Control of Communicable Diseases Manual,* 18th ed. (Washington, D.C.: American Public Health Association, 2004).

[8]J. P. Smith, D. P. Daifas, W. El-Khoury, and J. W. Austin, "Microbial Safety of Bakery Products," in P. R. Ashurst, ed., *Microbial Safety of Minimally Processed Foods* (Boca Raton, FL: CRC, 2003), 3–33.

[9]J. P. Smith, D. P. Daifas, W. El-Khoury, and J. Koukoutsis, "Foodborne Illnesses Associated with Bakery Products," *Technical Bulletin* 24, no. 4 (2002): 1–11. American Institute of Baking.

[10]http://www.fsis.usda.gov/wps/portal/fsis/topics/regulatory-compliance/haccp/pr-and-haccp-guidance-documents.

[11]FDA, *Defects Level Handbook*. http://www.fda.gov/Food/GuidanceRegulation/GuidanceDocumentsRegulatoryInformation/SanitationTransportation/ucm056174.htm.

[12]J. M. Jay, M. J. Loessner, and D. A. Golden, "Food Protection with High Temperatures, and Characteristics of Thermophilic Microorganisms," in *Modern Food Microbiology*, 7th ed. (New York: Springer Science and Business Media, 2005).

[13]U.S. Food and Drug Administration, *Food Code* (Washington, DC: U.S. Public Health Service, U.S. Department of Health and Human Services, 2009), retrieved March 30, 2010, from http://www.fda.gov/Food/FoodSafety/RetailFoodProtection/FoodCode/FoodCode2009/.

[14]"Vital signs: *Listeria* Illness, Deaths, and Outbreaks: United States, 2009–2011," *Morbidity and Mortality Weekly Report* 62, no. 22 (June 7, 2013): 448–452.

[15]FDA, *Food Code.*

[16]J. Hewitt and G. E. Greening, "Effect of Heat Treatment on Hepatitis A Virus and Norovirus in New Zealand Greenshell Mussels (*Perna canaliculus*) by Quantitative Real-Time Reverse Transcription PCR and Cell Culture," *Journal of Food Protection* 69, no. 9 (2006): 2217–2223; Institute of Food Science and Technology, "Foodborne Viral Infections," 2001 retrieved September 10, 2009, from http://foodsafety.ksu.edu/articles/389/foodborne_viral_infections.pdf.

[17]U.S. Department of Agriculture, "Draft Compliance Guidelines for Ready-to-Eat Meat and Poultry Products," 2001, retrieved September 1, 2009, from http://www.fsis.usda.gov/OPPDE/rdad/FRPubs/97-013P/RTEGuide.pdf.

[18]FDA, *Food Code.*

[19]USDA, "Draft Compliance Guidelines."

[20]FDA, *Food Code.*

[21]USDA, "Draft Compliance Guidelines."

[22]USDA, "Compliance Guidelines for Cooling Heat-Treated Meat and Poultry Products (Stabilization)." http://www.fsis.usda.gov/OPPDE/rdad/FRPubs/95-033F/95-033F_Appendix%20B.htm

[23]FDA, *Food Code.*

[24]USDA, "Compliance Guidelines for Cooling Heat-Treated Meat and Poultry Products (Stabilization)."

[25]FDA, *Food Code.*

[26]FDA, "Draft Compliance Guidelines for Ready-to-Eat Meat and Poultry." http://www.fsis.usda.gov/OPPDE/rdad/FRPubs/97-013P/RTEGuide.pdf.

[27]N. N. Potter and J. H. Hotchkiss, *Food Science*, 5th ed. (New York: Chapman and Hall, 1999), 114.

[28]J. M. Jay, M. J. Loessner, and D. A. Golden, "Vegetable and Fruit Products," in *Modern Food Microbiology*, 7th ed. (New York: Springer Science and Business Media, 2005), 125.

[29]J. M. Jay, M. J. Loessner, and D. A. Golden, "Intrinsic and Extrinsic Parameters of Foods That Affect Microbial Growth," in *Modern Food Microbiology*, 7th ed. (New York: Springer Science and Business Media, 2005), 39–55.

[30]J. Farkas, "Physical Methods of Food Preservation," in M. P. Doyle and L. R. Beuchat (eds.), *Food Microbiology: Fundamentals and Frontiers,* 3rd ed. (Washington, DC: ASM Press, 2007), 686–687.

[31]Ibid.

[32]Ibid.

[33]W. C. Frazier and D. C. Westhoff, *Food Microbiology*, 4th ed. (New York: McGraw-Hill, 1988), 10.

[34]H. Kreuzer, "Research Reveals the Power of Dried Plums in Precooked Meats," *Food Product Design*, Supplement (February 2001), retrieved November 10, 2009, from http://www.stapleton-spence.com/downloads/fpd0201.pdf.

[35]J. M. Jay, *Modern Food Microbiology*, 4th ed. (New York: Van Nostrand Reinhold, 1992), 55, 187, 237.

[36]J. M. Jay, M. J. Loessner, and D. A. Golden, "Processed Meats and Seafoods," in *Modern Food Microbiology*, 7th ed. (New York: Springer Science and Business Media, 2005), 188–119.

[37]T. J. Montville and K. R. Matthews, *Food Microbiology: An Introduction*, 2nd ed. (Washington, DC: ASM Press, 2008), 276, 281.

[38]U.S. Food and Drug Administration, "Processing Parameters Needed to Control Pathogens in Cold-Smoked Fish," *Safe Practices for Food Processes*, June 2009.

[39]Montville and Matthews, *Food Microbiology*, 271–299.

[40]International Commission of Microbiological Specifications for Foods, "Microorganisms in Foods," in *Microbial Ecology of Food Commodities*, 2nd ed. (New York: Kluwer Academic/Plenum Publishers, 1998), 237.

[41]Jay, Loessner, and Golden, "Vegetable and Fruit Products," 137.

[42]International Commission of Microbiological Specifications for Foods, "Nuts, Oilseeds, and Dried Legumes," in *Microbial Ecology of Food Commodities*, 2nd ed. (New York: Kluwer Academic/Plenum Publishers, 1998), 440–466.

[43]Montville and Matthews, *Food Microbiology*, 276, 281.

[44]Jay, *Modern Food Microbiology*, 55, 187, 237.

14 | Shelf-Life Extension

Lead Author: Klaus Tenbergen, Ed.D., CMB, ASBPB, MCFE, Dean of Career Technical Education and Economic Development, Columbia College, Sonora, CA

Priscila D. Santiago-Mora, Food Industry Engineer Instituto Tecnológico y de Estudios Superiores de Monterrey, Campus Querétaro, México

Dennis Ferris, Ph.D., Professor, Department of Food Science and Nutrition, California State University, Fresno

Contributor: Dominic Man, BSc, MSc, FIFST, Principal Lecturer, Department of Applied Science, Faculty of Engineering, Science, and the Built Environment, London South Bank University

Contributor: Shirley VanGarde, Ph.D., VanGarde Consulting

⬤What Is Shelf Life?

Shelf life is the length of time that food, drinks, and other perishable items have before they are considered unsuitable for sale or consumption. Reasons can include deterioration of sensory quality, diminution of nutritional attributes, and/or spoilage. Shelf life is influenced by exposure to oxygen, light or heat, transmission of gases or moisture, mechanical damage, and contamination by insects, vermin, or microorganisms.

The shelf life of prepared foods depends on four factors: ingredients and formulation, processing, packaging, and storage conditions. Change any one of these conditions and you change the shelf life—for better or worse.

As U.S. consumers become more knowledgeable and aware of what goes into their foods, the traditional ways of ensuring shelf safety, such as adding large amounts of sugar or salt to manage water activity, or adding a dose of chemical preservatives, are no longer acceptable for many new products. While these tactics are still widely used to extend shelf life for many foods, new consumer purchasing trends demand cleaner-label shelf-life extension technologies. "Better living through chemistry" has lost some of its luster.

Many Americans today prefer foods that are minimally processed and that contain fewer preservatives, less salt and sugar, and more fresh ingredients than were previously accepted. However, extended shelf life and perceived freshness do not go hand in hand. Products that traditionally have the longest shelf life—dried and canned foods—will never be mistaken for fresh. That said, shelf-life extension isn't just about maximizing the amount of time a food manufacturer or retailer can safely sell a product. In a more pragmatic sense, it's about what humans have been doing for thousands of years: protecting their food supply and maximizing its usefulness.

There are many aspects to shelf stability: flavor and color retention, microbial safety, nutrient retention, inhibition of lipid oxidation, and prevention of other chemical, microbial, and enzymatic degradations. These are made ever more difficult to achieve by the growing emphasis on fresh, all-natural, and organic products. This puts more pressure on manufacturers to develop methods that rely less on food chemicals and more on alternate methods of preservation. Some degratory factors can be controlled with appropriate packaging. For example, the opaque paperboard gable-top containers used for most milk packages block UV and fluorescent lighting, which can cause photo-oxidation, initiate lipid rancidity, and destroy certain vitamins; traditional clear glass bottles do not. Packaging with impermeable barrier materials to prevent moisture or gas migration into or out of the package extends the shelf life of many foods. Vacuum packaging or modified atmosphere packaging to exclude or reduce the amount of oxygen can also help extend shelf life. Natural preservatives and antioxidants may be incorporated into food (or packaging) to extend shelf life by inhibiting microbial growth or the destructive effects of oxidation.

In most regions, a "best before," "best used by," or freshness dating is required on packaged perishable foods. Most shelf-life labels or listed expiration dates are guidelines that presume safe handling of products. Consumption prior to the expiration date does not necessarily guarantee the safety of a mishandled perishable food or beverage; similarly, a product is not necessarily dangerous or inedible after the printed expiration date. A product that has passed its shelf life may still be safe, but quality is no longer guaranteed. In most food stores, shelf life is maximized by rotating stock, which involves moving products with the oldest sell-by date to the front of the shelf in the hope that shoppers choose them first. This concept is also known as *first in, first out* (FIFO). This is important, as stores can be fined for selling out-of-date products, and most must discard such unsold products as *shrink*, or waste, leading to a loss of profit.

For some foods, the printed shelf life is an important indicator of safe consumption. Examples include deli meats, greens, berries, seafood, raw meat, and soft cheeses.[1] Bacterial contaminants are ubiquitous, and non-sterile foods left unused too long often acquire substantial numbers of organisms and become spoiled or dangerous to eat, leading to food poisoning. However, the printed shelf life itself is not an absolute indicator of food safety. For example, pasteurized milk can remain potable for several days after its sell-by date if it is refrigerated properly. That said, potability does not mean palatability; even though sour milk is probably safe to drink, its taste and texture is not usually preferred.

Purpose of Food Preservation

The goals of food preservation are to increase shelf life while retaining consumer acceptance, sensory quality, nutrients, and safety. A good food preservation method must keep food safe, retain quality, retain nutrients, be an asset to the food distribution chain, be technically feasible, and capitalize on available energy resources.

Keeping Food Safe

Early food preservationists did not understand relationships between microorganisms, spoilage, and illness. They used trial and error in establishing preservation methods. New processing technologies and natural antimicrobial agents are now developed in laboratories with strict adherence to scientific principles and widely accepted experimental techniques. Operating with a sound plan of Hazard Analysis and Critical Control Points (HACCP) has become a food industry standard.

To ensure healthfulness and safety:

- Follow proven methodology.
- Use sanitized equipment in good working order.
- Monitor the food during growing and harvesting, prior to and during manufacturing, and during shipping, subsequent distribution, and storage at selling points.
- Evaluate food through end of life for microbial contamination and quality deterioration.

Retaining Quality

Preserving food in a way that retains good sensory quality is second in importance only to preserving food safety. Food products with unacceptable appearance, odor, texture, or flavor are rejected. If the quality of food is poor, it isn't purchased, the processor loses business, the food is not eaten, and the nutrients it contains are wasted. The length of storage time desired and the type of food being preserved influences the best method for preserving it. Low temperatures are effective, but refrigeration and freezing are not appropriate for all foods. Most fresh produce does not do well in the freezer. Many preservation methods also change the food's quality characteristics; dried foods are different from canned or frozen or pickled, and most certainly from fresh. We trade fresh sensory characteristics for extended keeping ability.

Retaining Nutrients

Preserved foods should contribute not only protein, carbohydrates, fats, and fiber but also vitamins and minerals. Nutrient losses can occur during processing, so techniques to minimize loss should be used whenever possible. Nutrient fortification may be desirable to add back nutrients lost or destroyed during processing. Often, vitamin losses that occur during extended storage parallel sensory losses; this is an incentive to preserve both. As nutrient loss often parallels quality loss, both goals can often be achieved at the same time.[2]

Being an Asset to the Food Distribution Chain

Canning in glass jars makes some foods more marketable, but there are increased shipping losses due to breakage and decreased nutrients and sensory quality due to light-sensitive compounds in the food. Also, glass is heavier and thus more expensive to transport than other packaging options. Environmental concerns about reducing non-reusable/recyclable and possibly toxic packaging and employing environmentally sound manufacturing practices are also an issue. It is important to factor in product and transportation costs, perishability, carbon miles, marketing appeal, environmental packaging concerns, and distribution logistics as critical parts of the product development process.

Being Technically Feasible

High-tech preservation processes such as aseptic processing and packaging (packing sterilized foods aseptically into pre-sterilized containers), high-pressure processing (HPP), and cold pasteurization (irradiation) are not applicable for all foods. Small food processors with restricted funds are limited in their equipment and processing choices, and even some large processors must consider the impact (cost, space, energy requirements, and so on) of new equipment. Advanced processing research has discovered many innovative methods to improve shelf life, but some techniques cannot yet be engineered economically for commercial use. Additionally, local state and federal laws must be considered.

Capitalizing on Available Energy Resources

Dehydration is an excellent preservation method in hot, dry climates, but it is more difficult to achieve in humid ones. Freezing requires energy to maintain products at 0°F (−18°C) throughout the distribution and storage period and typically is not generally available in third-world countries. Thermally processed, commercially sterile (canned) foods do not require refrigeration for storage, but their initial processing uses more water and heat energy than do drying or fermentation. The cost of the raw ingredients is only a small part of the actual cost of the finished product; processing costs (and labor) must be factored in before development begins.

●Shelf-Life Labeling

Manufacturers' tracking codes, though used on packaging for decades, are a continuing source of confusion for consumers who want to know the true age of products. Open shelf-life dating is the industry's response. This process uses commonly recognizable terms such as *day*, *month*, and *year* to indicate when the food was packaged or by when it should be sold or used. Such dating is considered by most people a measure of food freshness. It informs the buyer about the interval between packing and purchase or use, and about the relative freshness (and perceived quality) of the product as well. However, the interval between packing and final consumption is not necessarily the only factor leading to quality loss; mishandling can occur at many stages during distribution. Therefore, an open date is not an absolute guarantee of freshness—but it does serve as an indicator.

Open shelf-life dating varies widely by product, state or region, and manufacturer. Common open shelf-life dates include a sell-by date, a best-used-by date, or a better-used-by date. These dates help consumers decide how long the product may be stored after purchase and assist grocery stores with stock rotation.[3]

Best-before and best-used-by dates indicate the date the manufacturer intends the food to be consumed by for best quality. That said, if the item was stored properly, the food should still be safe for some period beyond that date. Sell-by dates are for stock rotation; they tell the store how long to display products for sale. Use-by dates are for perishable (usually refrigerated) products; microorganisms may be a concern past these dates. If the perishable food is frozen, these dates do not apply during the frozen storage period.

Some foods have specific shelf-life labeling regulations. Because infant formula may be the sole source of nutrients for babies, quality is critical. Infant formula must contain the amount of nutrients stated on the label, and baby formula must pass through a bottle nipple easily within the printed date. Eggs have a U.S. Department of Agriculture (USDA) pack date as a three-digit code. It's a Julian date; 001 is January 1, and 365 is December 31. The sell-by date on eggs may not exceed 45 days from the pack date.[4]

●Changes in Foods During Storage

Foods change during storage due to the actions of enzymes, microorganisms, chemical changes, and physical changes. Some of these affect quality, some nutritional content, and some the food's safety (acute illnesses, such as bacterial infections or intoxications, and chronic concerns, such as cancers and hypertension, which may be initiated or exacerbated due to chemical changes). Preventing or slowing these changes extends shelf life and product safety. This is usually done by putting a series of hurdles in the way of deterioration. A hurdle is a single preservation technique used to achieve one level of food safety. Hurdle technology (also called *combination preservation* or *barrier technology*) is the use of a series of hurdles, each specifically targeted to one degratory component among the cascade that any given food product may face. The hurdles may include a cooking step, a packaging material, a preservative, or any ingredient, additive, or process that inhibits deterioration and extends shelf life. For instance, jam is produced by heating, adjusting pH, lowering water activity, and storing under anaerobic conditions. Each of these preservation techniques is a hurdle that a microorganism must get past in order to grow. By combining hurdles, the intensity of each individual preservation technique can be kept low to maintain quality while working synergistically to provide protection. Because foods are complex systems and the microorganisms and enzymes that can affect them all have different weaknesses, an array of preservation methods has a better chance of inhibiting multiple offenders than any single treatment.

Biological Changes

Enzymes

Enzymes are proteins that catalyze specific reactions. They may require a coenzyme (vitamin) or a cofactor (mineral) to be activated. Enzymes occur in all plants, animals, and microorganisms, and they are present in every food. Some are also added during food processing for their specific synthesizing, degrading, or interconverting actions as dough relaxers, juice clarifiers, and meat tenderizers, for example. Enzyme common names have the suffix *-ase* on the substrate name—for example, lipase, protease, cellulase, lactase, thiaminase. Enzyme nomenclature can also describe specific action—for example, oxidase, dehydrogenase, synthase.[5]

Some enzyme activity improves products during storage: fruits picked green ripen later by the effect of polygalacturonase and pectinesterase during transportation[6]; mixing invertase with fondant hydrolyzes the sucrose in the fondant, creating a liquid center in filled candies (such as chocolate cherries)[7]; adding alpha-amylase to bread dough lowers the rate of amylopectin retrogradation, slowing the staling process[8]; and aging of meats and cheeses is brought about through the action of proteases and lipases.[9] However, enzyme activity in stored foods can shorten shelf life by altering flavor, color, texture, and nutrients, especially the loss of unstable or labile vitamins.[10] Enzyme activity, although it is slowed, occurs even during frozen storage. This is evident in the development of rancidity in fatty foods frozen for months. Enzyme activity is inhibited by inactivating or denaturing the enzyme, removing cofactors or coenzymes required for activity, decreasing substrates or intermediate products, or altering the chemistry of the surrounding environment (including the level of oxygen in the surrounding atmosphere). Enzymes are proteins; their activity can be destroyed by exposure to extremes of heating or pH.

FIGURE 14.1 **Enzymes naturally present in foods that can degrade quality during storage.**

Enzyme	Degradation Product	Preventive Action
Polyphenyl oxidase (PPO) Converts phenolics into o-quinones; brown colors, vitamin C loss.	Darkens produce; creates dark spots on crustaceans.	Requires Cu+2, oxygen; cells break to mix enzyme and substrate. Control: Thermal inactivation. Keep cells intact (slow respiration). Use antibrowning agents (sulfites, cysteine, glutathione). Ascorbic acid decreases o-quinone formation, removes some brown comp. Acids decrease pH below PPO activity (oxalio>oxalacetic>malonic>tartaric> pyruvic>citric>malic>lactic). Halide salts (NaCl, $CaCl_2$) alter ionic environment, inhibit PPO and chelate Cu ions. Sugars (especially glucose and fructose) decrease a_w and inhibit PPO. Maillard reaction products (glu-cysteine and fru-cysteine) inhibit PPO. Proteolytic enzymes (ficin, bromelain, papain) destroy PPO. Other, often used in combination with the above: EDTA binds Cu, pineapple juice, honey, ascorbate, irradiation, UHP.
Pectin methyl esterase (PME) and polygalacturonase (PG) PME converts pectin to galacturonic acid and methanol. Galacturonic acid cleaved by PG. Pectin lyases, cellulases, and xylanases. Cleave pectin molecule.	Softening as pectin molecule is cleaved.	Thermal inactivation. UHP inactivation.
Alpha-farnesene Catalyzes oxidation after natural antioxidants degraded during long storage.	Scald in apples.	Postharvest dip diphenylamine. Ethoxyquin wax or wraps.
Lipoxygenase (LOX) Oxidation of unsaturated lipids to H_2O_2 and free fatty acids (f.f.a.).	Off flavors and odors; destroys carotenoids, vitamin C, thiamine; bleaches chlorophyll; produces free radicals.	LOX contains Fe atom so metal scavengers inhibit. Needs oxygen, limit it. Heat treatments may inactivate (depends on food).
Peroxidases Generate free radicals. Can form lignin. Ascorbic acid oxidase degrades ascorbic acid and brown compounds can result.	Degrades flavor and aroma, vitamins. Toughens produce.	Peroxidases are heat labile, and low pH inhibits (range varies).
Alpha amalase Converts starch into sugars.	If active after baking, creates gummy crumb.	Heat labile.
Trimethylamine demethylase Cross-links proteins.	Hardens fish during frozen storage and thawing.	Lower-temperature storage, lower pH.
Proteolytic enzymes (transaminase) Releases glutamic acid; breaks proteins releasing f.f.a.	Softens meat tissue; develops flavor and odor compounds.	Lower temperature to stop aging process.

Sources: Miyawaki (2006);[11] Robinson (2001);[12] Wills (1989);[13] Anese (2006);[14] Si and Dorst-Lustenberger (2002).[15]

Microorganisms

The prime biological factors involved in food deterioration are microorganisms (bacteria, yeasts, and molds).

To increase the shelf life of more perishable foods (such as low-sugar jam, low-salt condiments, low-oil salad dressings, prepared fresh produce, and deli meats), food companies must take these steps:

1. Reduce the intrinsic microbial load (bacteria, yeast, mold) from all raw materials used before processing them into the finished food.

2. Process the finished food so as to reduce the microbial population (both vegetative organisms and spores).

3. Package the food so as to prevent recontamination and protect the contents during the trip from manufacturer to market.

Microorganisms have specific temperature, pH, oxygen, and moisture ranges where they function best. Shelf-life extension strategies inactivate microbes or adjust the food environment out of those preferred growth ranges (or to the edge of the range, and then add other hurdles). Common antimicrobial hurdles used in foods are:

- *pH*—Keep below 4.6 to inhibit pathogens. This is accomplished by adding food-grade acids or by creating an acid environment in situ via fermentation.
- *Moisture*—Keep below a_w 0.90 for most bacteria; below 0.88 for most yeasts; below 0.86 for pathogenic *Staphylococcus aureus*; below 0.80 for most molds.[16] Lowering the moisture level (or, more appropriately, decreasing the accessibility of the water that is present) creates a hostile environment for microorganisms by decreasing the medium they need to grow in. Depending on the method used (for example, decreasing water activity through the addition of increased solutes such as salt or sugar), even the water itself can become a weapon: The increased osmotic pressure on the bacteria causes them to burst. Although adding salt or sugar is a traditional, time-tested way to control water activity to prevent bacterial growth, modern product developers don't usually have the freedom to feature lots of salt or sugar on product labels. Instead, water activity can be reduced in fruit-only jams and jellies by starting with fruit concentrates (prepared by removing water in the first place) and then preparing under vacuum to allow lower-temperature processing. Similar techniques are used in other reduced-sugar foods. This provides the desired osmotic effect without adding sugar.
- *Gas requirements*—Manipulate (add, remove, modify) oxygen and carbon dioxide levels to inhibit microbial respiration and reproduction.
- *Temperature*—To prevent outgrowth, keep foods above or below the danger range (40 to 140°F [4.4 to 60°C])—that is, the range at which pathogenic bacteria grow.

That said, listeria and *C. botulinum* types E, B, and F can grow below 40°F (4.4°C),[17] so if these are a potential danger, additional inhibiting hurdles must be used (antimicrobial agents, acidification, modified atmosphere packaging, and so on). Most bacterial growth stops at 10 to 16°F (−12 to −9°C).[18]

- *Other hurdles*—Plan for nutrient limitation, antimicrobial chemicals, competing safe organisms, and so on.

Fungi

Fungi are members of the plant kingdom that do not possess the usual roots, stems, and leaves, nor do they possess the green photosynthetic pigment chlorophyll. Fungi exhibit a wide range of forms, including mushrooms and truffles, molds, and yeasts. Some food products require the aid of fungi in their production. For example, yeast in baked bread is necessary for making the dough rise and providing flavor; molds are invaluable in the aging of many highly prized cheeses (Roquefort, Camembert, Stilton, Brie). Fungi are valuable as a source of antibiotics, vitamins, and various industrially important chemicals, such as alcohols, acetone, and enzymes, as well as for their role in fermentation processes, as in the production of alcoholic beverages, vinegar, cheese, and bread. At the same time, yeasts and molds are responsible for an enormous amount of food spoilage.

Molds

Molds are multicellular fungi that form a filamentous branching growth known as a mycelium. The mycelium is composed of individual filaments called hyphae. Molds are aerobes: they require oxygen for growth, so some part of the organism must be on or near the food's surface, where oxygen is accessible. In this case, the mold is usually characterized by its fuzzy or cottony appearance. In addition, parts of the organism may also grow within the food, such as the mold in blue cheese. Even so, holes are drilled into these cheeses to allow greater access to oxygen for enhanced mold growth.

Foods processed without preservatives are at high risk for mold. Fruits and vegetables with high moisture content can be contaminated through tiny fissures or bruises on the surface, as can porous foods, such as breads and cakes. Spores fall on the surface and germinate. They send roots (rhizoids) into the food to absorb nutrients and send up stalks on which new spores eventually form (what we see as the fuzzy stuff). By the time we see the surface fuzz, the mold has already infiltrated the food. It's more difficult for mold to penetrate dense foods. Also, bacteria can grow alongside mold in soft cheeses. A contaminated cutting instrument can spread mold spores or bacteria to other foods.

Molds can be beneficial in making certain kinds of cheeses and can develop either on the surface of cheese, or internally, or both. Blue-veined cheeses such as Roquefort, blue, Gorgonzola, and Stilton are created by the introduction

FIGURE 14.2 **Mycelium, the mass of hyphae (slender, elongated, threadlike cells or filaments of cells) forming the body of a fungus.**

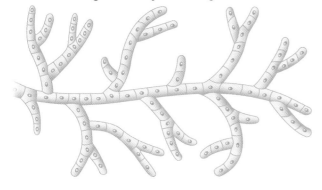

of *Penicillium roqueforti* spores. Cheeses such as Brie and Camembert have white surface molds (typically *P. camemberti*). Other cheeses have both an internal and a surface mold. Hard salami and dry-cured country hams may have surface mold, which is normal for these shelf-stable products. The molds used to manufacture these foods are safe to eat.

Yeasts

Yeasts are microscopic unicellular fungi; they do not form a mycelium and instead exist as single cells. Yeast cells may be round, egg-shaped, or elongated. The majority reproduce asexually by budding, but a few species reproduce by simple fission, like bacteria. The generation time for most yeast cells is 20 to 30 minutes under ideal conditions.[19] Yeasts produce metabolic end products, including acids, carbon dioxide, and alcohols, that cause the physical, chemical, and sensory properties of a food to change. In some cases this leads to spoilage; in others it leads to desirable changes, as in breads and alcoholic beverages. The growth of yeast on food products can be seen as a powdery coating on their surface, as in cheeses or meats; as cloudiness in otherwise transparent liquids, such as brines; and by the fermentation of sugars in beverages, leading to off flavors and carbon dioxide fizziness in juices, wine, and semiliquid products such as syrups and jams. Yeasts of the Zygosaccharomyces genus have a long history as spoilage organisms within the food industry. This is because these species can grow in the presence of high sucrose, ethanol, acetic acid, sorbic acid, benzoic acid, and sulfur dioxide concentrations, which are among the most commonly used food preservatives.

Bacteria

The adaptability of bacteria, which enables them to live in extreme environmental conditions, often causes unexpected problems in the food industry.

Typically, bacteria measure 1 to 3 μm in length and 0.4 to 1 μm in width, although others larger and smaller than this occur. Bacteria reproduce or multiply by a process called binary fission, which involves the simple division of the cell into two new identical daughter cells. Bacteria can be classified by their shape into spheres (cocci; singular: coccus), rods (bacilli; singular: bacillus), and curved, comma-shaped, or twisted rods (spirilla; singular: spirillum). Besides food spoilage, bacteria can cause foodborne illness, but fewer than 20 of the many thousands of different bacteria actually are the culprits. More than 90 percent of food poisoning cases each year are caused by *Staphylococcus aureus*, Salmonella spp., *Clostridium perfringens*, *Clostridium botulinum*, *Campylobacter jejuni*, *Listeria monocytogenes*, *Vibrio parahaemolyticus*, *Bacillus cereus*, and enteropathogenic *Escherichia coli* such as *E. coli* O157:H7. These bacteria are commonly found on many raw foods, as many are normal constituents of soil and fecal matter (manure-based fertilizer). Illness and spoilage can be prevented by:

1. Controlling the initial number of bacteria present by washing, sanitizing, peeling, hide removal, blanching, etc.
2. Preventing that small number from growing by using any or all of the hurdle techniques mentioned previously.
3. Destroying the bacteria (and their spores) by proper cooking.
4. Avoiding recontamination through appropriate packaging.

Because food-poisoning and spoilage bacteria are often present on many foods, knowing the characteristics and morphology of each bacterium is essential to designing an effective control program. (See Chapter 13 for a more complete discussion of food safety.)

Chemical Changes

Chemical reactions in foods are not usually reversible because they involve the formation of new compounds. Enzymatic reactions, browning reactions, and oxidative reactions are responsible for the majority of household discards, so their effects and prevention are important to understand in the food industry.[20]

Browning Reactions

Two important types of browning reactions occur in foods; enzymatic browning and non-enzymatic browning. The changes from enzymatic browning are generally undesirable, so precautions must be undertaken to prevent it. But the colors and flavors developed via non-enzymatic or Maillard browning reactions are important and often (but not always) desirable, so inhibiting or enhancing it is a case-by-case decision.

Enzymatic Browning

Enzymes are specialized proteins that catalyze specific reactions in foods. In fruits and vegetables, polyphenoloxidase is primarily responsible for *enzymatic browning*. It oxidizes

FIGURE 14.3 Bacteria.

Bacteria Responsible	Description	Typical Foods	Cause	Temperature Sensitivity
Staphylococcus aureus	Produces a heat-stable toxin.	Meat and seafood salads, sandwich spreads, and high-salt foods.	Poor personal hygiene and subsequent temperature abuse.	No growth below 40°F. Bacteria are destroyed by normal cooking, but toxin is heat stable.
Salmonella spp.	Produces an intestinal infection.	High-protein foods: meat, poultry, fish, and eggs.	Contamination of ready-to-eat foods, insufficient cooking, and recontamination of cooked foods.	No growth below 40°F. Bacteria are destroyed by normal cooking.
Clostridium perfringens	Produces spores and prefers low-oxygen atmosphere. Live cells must be ingested.	Meat and poultry dishes, sauces, and gravies.	Improper temperature control of hot foods, and recontamination.	No growth below 40°F. Bacteria are killed by normal cooking, but heat-stable spores can survive.
Clostridium botulinum	Produces spores and requires a low-oxygen atmosphere. Produces a heat-sensitive toxin.	Home-canned foods.	Improper methods of home processing foods.	Type E and Type B can grow at 38°F. Bacteria are destroyed by cooking, and the toxin is destroyed by boiling for 5 to 10 minutes. Heat-resistant spores can survive.
Vibrio parahaemolyticus	Requires salt for growth.	Raw and cooked seafood.	Recontamination of cooked foods or eating raw seafood.	No growth below 40°F. Bacteria killed by normal cooking.
Bacillus cereus	Produces spores and grows in normal-oxygen atmosphere.	Starchy food.	Improper holding and storage temperatures after cooking.	No growth below 40°F. Bacteria killed by normal cooking, but heat-resistant spores can survive.
Listeria monocytogenes	Survives adverse conditions for long periods.	Milk, soft cheeses, vegetables fertilized with manure.	Contaminated raw products.	Grows at refrigeration (38–40°F) temperatures. May survive minimum HTST pasteurization temperatures (161°F for 15 seconds).
Campylobacter jejuni	Oxygen sensitive, does not grow above 116°F.	Meat, poultry, milk, and mushrooms.	Improper pasteurization or cooking, cross-contamination.	Sensitive to drying or freezing. Survives in milk and water at 39°F for several weeks.
Yersinia enterocolitica	Not frequent cause of human infection.	Milk, tofu, and pork.	Improper cooking. Cross-contamination.	Grows at refrigeration temperatures (35–40°F). Sensitive to heat (122°F).
Enteropathogenic *E. coli*	Can produce toxins that are heat stable and others that are heat sensitive.	Meat and cheeses.	Inadequate cooking. Recontamination of cooked product.	Organisms can be controlled by heating. Can grow at refrigeration temperatures.

FIGURE 14.4 Bacterial morphology diagram.

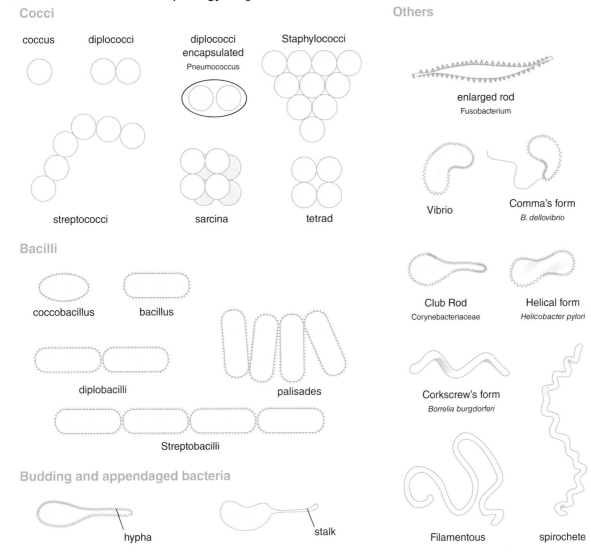

Cocci

coccus   diplococci   diplococci encapsulated Pneumococcus   Staphylococci

streptococci   sarcina   tetrad

Others

enlarged rod Fusobacterium

Vibrio   Comma's form B. dellovibrio

Club Rod Corynebacteriaceae   Helical form Helicobacter pylori

Corkscrew's form Borrelia burgdorferi

Filamentous   spirochete

Bacilli

coccobacillus   bacillus

diplobacilli   palisades

Streptobacilli

Budding and appendaged bacteria

hypha   stalk

Source: Wikipedia.

phenolic compounds in fruits and vegetables to produce severe discoloration. It is activated whenever certain fresh fruits or vegetables are cut or bruised, allowing the enzyme to escape from within normally intact cells and become exposed to oxygen. Commonly affected produce include potatoes, avocados, bananas, pears, and apples.

Blanching (brief immersion in scalding water) is one method used to prevent enzymatic activity by heating to the point of protein denaturation. Of course, this is not always practical, especially for produce items usually eaten raw (bananas, avocados, and so on). Alternative methods include reducing pH by acidification (such as adding lime juice to guacamole or squeezing lemon juice on cut apples), blocking exposure to oxygen by vacuum-packing or covering with cold water, using antioxidants (such as ascorbic acid and sodium bisulfite), and refrigeration, which slows but does not completely halt enzymatic activity or browning.

Non-Enzymatic Browning

In France in 1912, Louis-Camille Maillard first scientifically described a browning reaction in a series of experiments heating reducing sugars (typically monosaccharides: glucose and fructose) together with amino acids. Because the brown-colored compounds are created without enzymes, this reaction is also called *non-enzymatic browning*. In a series of reactions, a reducing sugar reacts with an amino group (usually an amino acid or lysine residue of a protein) and forms a variety of products that alter flavor, odor, color, rehydration properties, and nutritional value.[21] Unlike enzymatic browning, the Maillard reaction is not completely negative; the browned color and flavor of baked cakes, breads, cereals, roasted and grilled meats, chocolate, coffee, and even caramels is due to this reaction between sugar and protein. It does not require much of either reactant; orange juice and canned pears have enough protein and beef has enough sugar to support the reaction.

Protein aggregates are formed by the Maillard reaction that may reduce the nutritional value of a product, as amino acids can be lost, especially the basic amino acids: lysine, arginine, and histidine. Sometimes the flavors developed are not appreciated, such as the cooked flavor in sterilized milk.

The Maillard reaction is favored by heat and time. Most food is between pH 3 and 8, where the reaction progresses well.[22] Moisture content is important; intermediate-moisture foods have high rates of reaction. The sugar molecule itself affects the rate of reaction: xylose > monosaccharide hexoses (galactose, mannose, glucose, fructose) > disaccharides (maltose, lactose).[23] Not being a reducing sugar, sucrose (table sugar) does not participate in Maillard browning.

To control the Maillard reaction, the temperature can be reduced, the pH lowered, the moisture adjusted to very high or very low levels, one of the substrates removed (enzymes can be used to remove sugar from eggs before drying), or additives used, such as sulfur dioxide or sulfites, which prevent brown compound formation but not protein degradation.

The most common toxic compound as a Maillard reaction product is acrylamide, which forms from sugars and an amino acid (asparagine) during high-temperature cooking—the baking, frying, or roasting of carbohydrate-based foods, such as potato products, grain products, and coffee. Acrylamide is not present in foods when boiling and steaming foods; generally, it is more likely to accumulate when cooking is done for longer periods or at higher temperatures. In response to the enactment of Proposition 65 (the Safe Drinking Water and Toxic Enforcement Act of 1986) in California, numerous consumer products have been reformulated to eliminate these toxic chemicals and re-labeled to demonstrate their absence.

Lipid Oxidation

Lipid oxidation severely compromises the quality of some foods and limits the shelf life of others. Oxidation of unsaturated lipids (autoxidation) is a series of reactions in which oxygen attacks unsaturated double bonds to produce hydroperoxides and free radicals, which are highly reactive and can produce both more free radicals (via chain reaction) and short-chain compounds with off flavors, odors, and health concerns. Deleterious changes in foods caused by lipid oxidation include loss of flavor, color, nutrient value and functionality, development of rancid off flavors, and accumulation of compounds that may be detrimental to health. All foods that contain unsaturated lipids are susceptible to oxidation; especially affected are foods

containing high levels of polyunsaturated fats as well as those that are dehydrated, subjected to high temperatures, or cooked and subsequently stored—for example, dehydrated eggs, cheeses, and meats; foods fried in unsaturated oils; and cooked (uncured) meats. Oxidative rancidity is a major shelf-life limiter; it proceeds even when microorganism growth is halted and even in products frozen for long periods. Once a product (polyunsaturated oils or the foods cooked in them, fatty meats, whole grains, and so on) becomes rancid, it can never be cleansed.

The rate of lipid oxidation can be manipulated to reduce or inhibit it by various means.

Temperature

Generally, the rate of oxidation increases as temperature increases.

Surface Area

Large surface area results in more lipid-oxygen contact.

Pro-Oxidants

Metal ions promote lipid oxidation. Cobalt, copper, iron, manganese, and nickel are widely present in foods, and virtually all food manufacturing facilities use equipment made from metals. Strategies to reduce the effect of unavoidable exposure to metals include the use of sequestering agents that chelate (tie up) metals, making them unavailable to participate in the oxidation reaction. EDTA (ethylenediamine-tetraacetic acid) in mayonnaise is a common example.

Natural Antioxidants

Natural antioxidants are found in varying amounts in foods such as vegetables, fruits, grain cereals, eggs, meat, legumes, herbs, and nuts. Some antioxidants, such as lycopene and ascorbic acid, can be destroyed by long-term storage or prolonged cooking. Other antioxidant compounds are more stable, such as the polyphenolic antioxidants in whole wheat cereals and tea. The effects of cooking and food processing are complex, as these processes can also increase the bioavailability of some antioxidants, such as some carotenoids in vegetables. In general, processed foods contain fewer antioxidants than fresh and uncooked foods, as the preparation processes may expose the food to oxygen, thus reducing or using up the antioxidants normally present.

Many herbs, including rosemary, oregano and sage, from the Labiatae family, possess strong antioxidant activity. Antioxidant phenolic compounds that have been isolated from these herbs include carnosol from rosemary, carvacrol from oregano, and carnosic acid from sage.

Rosemary extracts are widely used in meat processing, including beef, pork, and poultry products, to retard the onset of warmed-over flavor due to lipid oxidation. Rosemary extracts are available in many forms, including oil-soluble, water-soluble, liquid, and powdered, and in deodorized varieties that reduce the rosemary flavor. Used especially in high fat-containing deli meats and sausages, the improvement in shelf life is fairly dramatic. Water-soluble rosemary extracts are easily dispersed in the brines used in manufacturing deli meats. Use levels as low as 0.05 to 0.1 percent help delay the onset of oxidative rancidity. Either dry or liquid rosemary extract is useful in extending the flavor and color of ground beef patties from 8 days to 11 or more. It is added before the meat is ground and protects lipids within the muscle-cell membranes, which are the most susceptible to lipid oxidation, especially when grinding exposes these surfaces to oxygen and to pro-oxidants such as salt or iron-containing heme pigment in the meat.

Raisin and dried plum extracts can also impart antimicrobial properties to some food products at levels that do not significantly affect sensory characteristics.

Ascorbic acid, or vitamin C, is used in the manufacture of fruit juices and purees from fruits such as apples and peaches. It is added during the crushing, straining, or pressing processes to prevent enzymatic browning of the raw fruits. Ascorbic acid is also widely used in the meat industry for its antioxidant properties. In cured meats, ascorbic acid can accelerate color development, inhibit nitrosamine formation (in the United States, meats to which nitrites are added must contain ascorbic acid as well), prevent oxidation, and prevent color fading.

Natural mixed tocopherols (forms of vitamin E), consisting of d-alpha (α), d-beta (β), d-gamma (γ), and d-delta (δ) tocopherol, can help maintain the freshness and shelf life of lipid-containing products. They are a natural alternative to synthetic antioxidants such as BHT (butylated hydroxytoluene), BHA (butylated hydroxyanisole), and TBHQ (tertiary butylhydroquinone). One benefit is that consumer-friendly label claims and ingredient legends declaring "Natural vitamin E added to preserve freshness" or "Natural vitamin E added to protect flavor" can be used.

Mixed tocopherols are resistant to high-temperature food processing and have low volatility and good solubility in fats and oils. They have been tested in many applications, including baked goods, cereals, dehydrated potatoes, nuts, and fried noodles (ramen), and in foods such as meat and egg products and tuna fillets. Their solubility in lipids makes them useful in fats and oils such as vegetable and fish oils, milkfat, poultry fat and lard, and in food ingredients such as citrus oils or lecithin.

Other natural antioxidants, including resveratrol (from grape skin extract) and pycnogenol (a phytochemical from tree bark) show promise in university trials on ground beef and poultry products. Both antioxidants are approved as GRAS (generally recognized as safe) by the FDA. Still others, including 4-hexylresorcinol, ascorbic acid, and glutathione, have been tested as possible replacements for sulfites, as antimicrobial agents, and to prevent color changes in dehydrated fruits and vegetables. Sulfites must always be labeled if used at levels above 10 ppm because of their effect on the considerable portion of the population that suffers from asthma and other pulmonary inflammatory diseases.

Hexylresorcinol has also been tested on fruits and vegetables and is also used to control blackspot in fresh and frozen shrimp.

Specific, accurate measurements of antioxidants is essential, as is uniform blending with raw ingredients to ensure the antioxidants are effective. Some natural antioxidants are not heat stable, so they must be added during a cool-down phase of any heat process. Oil-based antioxidants, such as vitamin E, can be easily dispersed in small amounts of fats or oils prior to blending with the food mass for more uniform dispersion.

Synthetic Antioxidants

Synthetic antioxidants are widely used as food additives to prevent rancidification, owing to their high performance, low cost, and wide availability. Examples include propyl gallate (PG), tertiary butylhydroquinone (TBHQ), butylated hydroxyanisole (BHA), and butylated hydroxytoluene (BHT). These additives are used primarily to prevent rancidity in unsaturated fats and oils. Of course, when these protected fats and oils are used in the manufacture of other foods such as margarine, mayonnaise, salad dressings, fried products, baked products, sauces, dips, snack foods, and chicken soup mix, the antioxidants are carried along with the fats into these other foods, where they continue to provide shelf-life extension benefits to the fats in the finished product and therefore to the finished product itself. They save millions of dollars worth of foods from going rancid and being discarded. In every case, synthetics exhibit stronger antioxidant activity than natural antioxidants, but they are obviously not as label-friendly.

Radiant Energy

Radiant energy is the energy from light. Light waves, visible and invisible, accelerate oxidation. Both sunlight and fluorescent lighting can initiate photo-oxidation. Milk and other lipid-containing products are susceptible to oxidative deterioration from exposure to light from either natural or artificial sources. Light catalyzes certain chemical reactions, resulting in the development of off flavors and the breakdown of pigments and vitamins. That is why the majority of milk is packaged in opaque paperboard containers rather than glass bottles. Pigment destruction in cooked green vegetables exposed to fluorescent lighting commonly found in refrigerated display cases is quite rapid. Opaque packaging and storage out of direct exposure to light can inhibit this.

Hydrogenation

Both mono- and polyunsaturated fats can be easily oxidized, leading to rancidity. Polyunsaturated fats have more reaction sites (unsaturated double bonds) and are therefore more susceptible. Hydrogenation has been used for years as an effective process to reduce or eliminate unsaturated double bonds in unsaturated oils in order to control their reactivity with oxygen and create more stable (and more functional) vegetable-based shortenings resistant to oxidative rancidity; these can be substituted for cholesterol-containing animal fats such as lard and tallow. Unfortunately, in recent years, partially hydrogenated fats have been implicated as the major source of trans fats in the diet. Trans fats are strongly associated with an assortment of diseases, including coronary heart disease, diabetes, Alzheimer's disease, cancer, and obesity, among others. As such, since 2006, the FDA has mandated that manufacturers list trans fat levels on the nutrition facts panel of all foods.

Encapsulation

Encapsulation involves the entrapment of food ingredients, enzymes, and flavors, or the elimination of exposure to oxygen. Applications for this technique have increased in the food industry because the encapsulated materials can also be protected from moisture, heat, or other extreme conditions (depending on the coating material), thus enhancing their stability and extending viability and shelf life. Encapsulation in foods is also utilized to mask odors or tastes (as in encapsulated fish oils). Various techniques are employed to form the capsules, including spray drying (encapsulating in carbohydrate), spray chilling (encapsulating in fat), coacervation (typically using gelatin), and many others.

Oxygen exposure can also be limited by packaging, modifying the storage atmosphere (modified atmosphere packaging), and using oxygen scavengers (sachets containing powdered iron or ascorbic acid that chemically reacts with oxygen to remove it from inside the package).

Color Changes

The preservation of color during storage depends on the resilience of the pigment compounds present. Many of the colored pigments are phenolic compounds that participate as antioxidants, as they are themselves oxidized, causing accompanying color changes in the food. General practices that inhibit oxidative reactions and Maillard browning also preserve pigments. Shielding the food from light (using opaque and UV-barrier packaging), oxygen, and metals, and maintaining low temperatures during distribution and storage, slows pigment degradation reactions.

Chlorophylls

Chlorophylls are the green pigments in green vegetables. They also give the green color to the skin of apples and other fruit, particularly when unripe. When green vegetables are overheated during ordinary cooking or during canning, chlorophyll is chemically transformed by a loss of magnesium into pheophytin, causing a change of the bright green color to brown or khaki. Exposure of green vegetables to acids can have the same result. One way to mitigate this is to blanch green vegetables quickly using high heat, in an excess of water and uncovered, followed by rapid chilling. These strategies limit exposure to heat and to acids released by plant tissues during the cooking process. Keeping the cooking water slightly alkaline by the addition of a small quantity of sodium bicarbonate also maintains color, but the alkaline conditions can soften the vegetable's cell walls, leading to mushy texture, and the bicarbonate can make the veggies taste soapy. In addition, loss of vitamin C is increased.[24]

Myoglobin

The basic pigment in raw meat muscle is the heme (iron-containing) pigment myoglobin. (Hemoglobin is the heme pigment in blood, which is largely removed during exsanguination of the animal at slaughter.) Like hemoglobin, myoglobin contains an iron molecule that reacts with oxygen, nitrite, and carbon monoxide in food processing and during storage, resulting in different colors. When myoglobin in fresh meat is fully oxygenated (oxymyoglobin), the muscle is bright red and looks most appealing. When it is deprived of oxygen (deoxymyoglobin)—for example, when meat is packaged in oxygen-impermeable or vacuum packaging—the muscle turns purple. These two forms are transposable while the meat is still fresh; if purple deoxy meat is removed from its package and exposed to oxygen, in fairly short order it becomes oxygenated again and turns red. Metmyoglobin, the brownish color of aging meats, results from the oxidation of the iron portion of myoglobin. Metmyoglobin formation in meat in retail cases is a result of prolonged exposure to ultraviolet light from fluorescent lights, temperature fluctuations, and bacterial growth. Individual muscles accumulate metmyoglobin, and thus discolor, at different rates. It is not unusual for meat cuts with multiple muscle groups to discolor unevenly.

People typically judge freshness in meats based on appearance, and as such preferentially purchase raw meats that look bright red. Because of this, meat processors and retail markets work to come up with packaging and merchandizing strategies that maximize fresh appearance for at least as long as the printed expiration date on the label. Methods include gas flushing with oxygen to maintain the bright red color of oxygenated myoglobin (oxymyoglobin), limiting exposure to fluorescent lighting (which favors the formation of brown-colored metmyoglobin), and even flushing with carbon monoxide (a controversial process), which binds more or less permanently to myoglobin to give meat a persistent red color, even when it is well past expiration and has begun to spoil. Nitrites used in cured meats, such as ham and bacon, also bind permanently to myoglobin, giving these meats a permanent pink coloration.

Studies by the USDA, universities, feed manufacturers, and vitamin manufacturers show that adding vitamin E to cattle feed has a number of interesting results.[25] Meat from vitamin E–enhanced beef stays bright red longer (except for top sirloin steak) and has a case life several hours longer before color change occurs. The greatest increase is in beef round cuts. Vitamin E also improves the stability of myoglobin

FIGURE 14.5 Pigments. Light, heat, metal ions, and oxygen accelerate oxidation reactions.

Pigment	Where Found	Degraded	Control
Chlorophyll: Lipid soluble, green	Widely distributed	Acid to dull olive, gray (canned and dried green vegetables) Oxidation to colorless (cabbage fades w/ storage) Chlorophyllase enzyme degrades to colorless Free radicals degrade	Adjust pH HTST processing CA to keep cells intact Control storage time Heat inactivates enzyme Antioxidants retard lipid oxidation
Anthocyanins: Water-soluble red to blue antioxidants	Cherry, grape, radish, eggplant, red potato, cabbage, cane berries, currants, apples	Oxidize to colorless or brown Enzymes (B-glucosidase, peroxidase, polyphenoloxidase) degrade Sulfites bleach @ high concentrations (rxn reversible) w/ metals blue-brown	pH and oxygen sensitive HTST preserves inactivate
Betalains: Water-soluble red antioxidants Betaxanthins: Yellow	Beets, Swiss chard, cactus pear, purple pitaya (juice) Meats, ice cream, gel desserts	Strong acids bleach Colorless when heat degrades, but regenerates	pH stable 4–6 After canning, time to regenerate color Metal-chelating agents stabilize
Carotenoids: Lipid-soluble (most) orange antioxidants	Carotene (carrots, vegetables, and fruits), lycopene, xanthophylls (annatto), capsanthin (peppers), canthaxanthin (salmon, trout), crucin (saffron); H$_2$O soluble Widely distributed in plants	Oxidize to colorless or brown w/ off odor Some heat stable, some degrade to colorless Oxidation fades Lipoxygenase destroys Annatto turns pink w/ acid	Cold-smoke preserves Antioxidants, ascorbic acid, and potassium sorbate preserve Sulfite and ascorbic acid inhibit oxidation
Lycopenes (a carotenoid): Lipid-soluble red antioxidant	Tomatoes, watermelon	Heat can degrade *cis* to less-colored *trans*	Spray drying can preserve color
Curcuminoids: Bright yellow fat-soluble antioxidants	Turmeric	Oxidization fades color Above pH 7 color shifts to red then fades	Encapsulation preserves color Heat, a$_w$, radiation stable Canned foods, mustards, soups
Iridoids: Water-soluble green and yellow	Saffron, gardenia	Reacts w/ amino acids or pH: red, blue, black	Color imitation in fish, sweets, noodles, baked goods

Sources: Stintzing and Carle (2007);[26] Ancos et al. (2000);[27] Oey et al. (2008);[28] Wright (1997);[29] Lewicki (2005);[30] Goula and Adamopoulos (2005);[31] and Delgado-Vargas and Paredes-Lopez (2003).[32]

in ground beef, providing better color retention in final products.

Anthocyanins

The pink, red, mauve, violet, and blue colors of flowers, fruits, and vegetables are caused by the presence of anthocyanins. In most food processing operations, the anthocyanins are quite stable, especially when the low pH of the fruit is maintained. Occasionally, however, naturally present ascorbic acid

causes problems. In the presence of iron or copper, the oxidation of ascorbic acid also oxidizes anthocyanins, leading to a loss of color.[33] This can be inhibited by the use of metal chelating agents such as EDTA.

Carotenoids

Carotenoid pigments are responsible for most of the yellow and orange colors of fruit and vegetables. Carotenoids are divided into two principal groups: the carotenes, which are

FIGURE 14.6 **Pigments, colors, and reactions in raw and cooked foods.**

Pigment	Color	Reactions
RAW		
Myoglobin (Mb)	Purple	Natural Mb pigment in animal muscle; also the color of cut meat in oxygen-impermeable or vacuum packaging.
Oxymyoglobin (O_2Mb)	Red	$Mb + O_2$ form O_2Mb; oxygenation "blooms"; meat turns red when exposed to air.
Metmyoglobin (MtMb)	Brown	Mb is oxidized to form MtMb. Reaction favored by low oxygen levels, light, and continuous storage.
Nitrosomyoglobin (NMb)	Red-pink	Mb combined with nitrite (cured meats: bacon, ham).
Carboxymyoglobin	Cherry red	Mb combined with carbon monoxide.
Sulfmyoglobin	Green	H_2S produced by microorganisms on Mb.
COOKED		
Globinhemochromogen	Brown	Cooked fresh meat: O_2Mb or MtMb is heat denatured.
Nitrosylhemochrome	Pink	Cooked cured meat: NMb denatured by heat.

strictly hydrocarbons, and the xanthophylls, which contain oxygen. Carotenoids are soluble only in fats and oils.

Although normally associated with plants, carotenoids find their way into some animal tissues. Egg yolk owes its color to two xanthophylls. These carotenoids, which also give adipose tissue (tissue made up of mainly fat cells, such as the yellow layer of fat beneath the skin), are derived from vegetable materials in the animal's diet. Adding marigold petals to chicken feed (as Perdue has been doing for years) increases the yellow pigmentation in their skin.

The role of carotenoids as precursors of vitamin A is well established.[34] Carotenoids in food are stable even at high temperatures. Fat-soluble carotenoids are not lost to the cooking water, but appreciable amounts may dissolve in the butter and oils used to sauté vegetables, such as carrots.

When slices of carrot are in contact with boiling water for two or three minutes, the hue shifts slightly toward yellow. The longer the vegetable is cooked and the higher the temperature, the greater the change in hue. But because of the quantity of carotene present, cooked carrots remain comparatively bright and attractive.

Melanins

Melanin is a brownish, undesirable pigment that arises in the tissues of fruits and vegetables that are cut or damaged. This enzymatic browning is caused when tissue damage due to slicing or peeling, fungal attack, or bruising brings cellular enzymes and substrates together in the presence of oxygen, causing melanins to form.

During fruit and vegetable processing, several strategies are used to inhibit enzyme activity. Making sure fruits and vegetables are blanched as soon as possible after any tissue-damaging operation reduces the enzyme activity to a minimum. Reducing contact with air by immersion in cold, acidified water is also a common practice. Immediately after being peeled, fruits are often immersed in baths containing dilute solutions of citric acid or malic acid, supplemented with ascorbic acid or sulfite.[35]

Flavor Changes

Some flavor changes during storage are desirable and actively promoted: ripening of fruits and vegetables; aging of meats, cheeses, and wines; migration of acids and seasonings into pickled plant or animal tissues; migration of sugars and salts into brined fruits and meats; flavor development during fermentation. However, chemical and physical reactions can also cause flavor changes identified as spoilage indicators. Maillard reactions in stored dairy, fruit, and vegetable products can degrade quality. Rancidity (hydrolytic, oxidative), produces off flavors and off odors. Enzymes also catalyze reactions that alter flavor compounds. Proteolysis (the enzymatic breakdown of proteins) results in free amino acids, and lipolysis (the enzymatic breakdown of fats) produces free fatty acids; both compounds have strong, unpleasant, and bitter flavors. Flavor compounds themselves are often susceptible to oxidation (many are phenolics), and some are volatile. If volatile flavor compounds are bound to

FIGURE 14.7 **Heme pigment.**

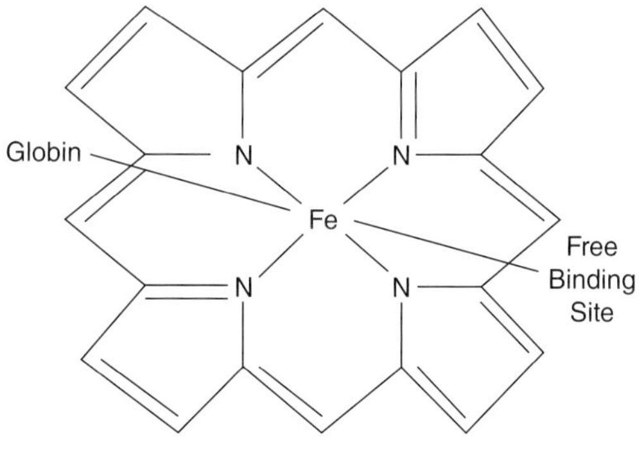

proteins, lipids, or polysaccharides, they are more likely to be retained during processing and storage; their stability depends on pH and temperature. Flavor compounds can also volatilize from foods into the atmosphere during heating (flashing off).

Generally, flavors are best preserved by minimizing exposure to heat, using minimal processing, using less extreme multiple hurdles, using high-temperature, short-time (HTST) processing, employing barrier storage to prevent oxidation, including additives that preserve flavor compounds and enhance flavor, and refrigerating to slow chemical reactions.

Nutritional Quality

In the best-case scenario, foods are harvested at peak ripeness and quickly processed, allowing the best opportunity for nutrient retention. Generally, their nutrient content is similar to fresh if optimally processed and stored properly. Nutrient losses occur due to trimming, leaching in cleaning or blanching water, and chemical degradation (enzyme catalyzed or thermally induced). Mechanical damage (shaking, cutting, bruising) can unite enzymes with substrates, leading to degradation. Oxidation (accelerated by oxygen, light, temperature, metal ions; slowed by blanching, antioxidant additives, low temperature, decreased oxygen) degrades vitamins A and C and thiamine. Loss of water-soluble nutrients (including vitamin C, folate, thiamine, riboflavin, some sugars, proteins, and minerals) can occur in cleaning and blanching water or during caustic lye peeling of tomatoes and peaches with sodium or potassium hydroxide solutions. Fermentation, aging, and ripening are exceptions that improve nutrient quality during storage (by eliminating anti-nutritional compounds and other digestion inhibitors; breaking down large, indigestible materials into smaller, more easily assimilated ones; eliminating pathogens; and enhancing palatability). But nothing lasts forever, and overall food quality eventually deteriorates at a rate determined by the composition of the food, the environment, and the packaging's protection.[36]

Vitamins

The vitamins are an untidy collection of essential (required by the body), complex, organic (carbon-containing) nutrients that occur in the biological materials consumed in food. Vitamins, especially vitamin C (ascorbic acid), thiamine (B_1), and riboflavin (B_2), are exceedingly unstable. The final amount of vitamins in a food is affected by growing conditions, post-harvest changes, initial treatments (washing, milling), blanching and other thermal processes, and storage. In addition to the effects above, the food itself and its chemical composition influence vitamin stability. Typical reactions to which vitamins are susceptible include:

Oxidation—fat-soluble vitamins, vitamin C, thiamine

Degradation and other reactions (such as non-enzymatic browning)—vitamin C, thiamine

Photochemical reactions—riboflavin, beta-carotene, folic acid, fat-soluble group

The vitamin content of fruit changes throughout growth and ripening. Once produce is harvested, metabolic reactions continue and vitamins can be destroyed. For example, potatoes stored throughout the winter have less vitamin C than new potatoes. Correct storage and treatment (modified atmosphere, controlled temperature, low light, and so on) can reduce post-harvest vitamin loss.

After harvesting, foods undergo preliminary treatments such as trimming, washing, and milling. Thiamine loss is particularly serious in the milling of rice. In fact, the cause of beriberi (thiamine deficiency disease), was discovered due to a comparison of diets featuring white rice (low in thiamine) and brown rice (high in thiamine). The loss of vitamins during milling led to laws requiring the vitamin enrichment of cereal grains, flours, and bread. In the United States, processed flours must be enriched with thiamine mononitrate, niacin, ferrous iron, riboflavin, and folic acid to replace that lost in processing.

Thiamine (vitamin B_1) is one of the most unstable B vitamins. Baking, pasteurizing, or boiling foods containing thiamine can reduce its content by up to 50 percent. The stability of thiamine during storage depends greatly on the moisture content of the food. Flours with 12 percent moisture content retain 88 percent of added thiamine after five months. If the moisture level is reduced to 6 percent, no losses occur. The sulfite added to dried fruits and vegetables to prevent browning causes total destruction of thiamine. The commonest losses of thiamine occur simply as a result of its water solubility rather than any chemical degradation. It is discarded with the cooking water.

Riboflavin (vitamin B_2) is stable during thermal processing, storage, and food preparation. Riboflavin, however, is susceptible to degradation when exposed to light.

Niacin (vitamin B_3) is one of the most stable vitamins. The main loss occurs from leaching into cooking water.

Pyridoxine (vitamin B_6) in enriched flour is resistant to baking temperatures. B_6 is susceptible to light-induced degradation, and exposure to water can cause leaching and consequent losses. Leaching is the major cause of losses during cooking and processing. However, B_6 is stable during storage. Enriched wheat flour stored at either room temperature or 113°F (45°C) retains about 90 percent of B_6.

Cobalamin (vitamin B_{12}) is fairly stable to food processing and cooking conditions. As with all the water-soluble vitamins, leaching is the major cause of loss.[37]

Folic acid is unstable and loses its activity in the presence of light, oxidizing or reducing agents, and in both acidic and alkaline environments. However, it is relatively stable to heat and humidity; dry mixes, baked products, and cereal flours retain almost 100 percent of added folic acid after six months of storage. Over 50 percent of folic acid added to wheat flour is retained during bread baking.

Ascorbic acid (vitamin C) is quite stable in the acid, refrigerated environment of fruit juice processing. The stability is

FIGURE 14.8 Nutrient quality table: Changes in nutrient content during shelf-life extension strategy and subsequent storage.

Unit Operation	Nutrient Degradation	Nutrient Preservation Strategy
Blanching (heat treatment to inactivate enzymes)	Degrades heat-labile and water-soluble vitamins Trim, peel, wash, blanch; lose more vitamins with pre-treatments than during frozen storage Slow blanch: vit C, niacin, and B_6 losses	Steam blanching is better than water blanching.
Freezing	Oxidation during storage Thaw drip (salt, vitamins, some proteins, amino acids, peptides) Protein, carbohydrate, fiber, and lipid content stable Vit C loss high with higher-temp storage	Use antioxidants and sugar syrups, store at low temperatures. Rapid freeze and thaw. Hold 0°F (−18°C) or below to retain 80% vit C. Store below Tg (~ −25°C) and food stable.
Canning	Heat-labile vitamins Some amino acids degraded Water-soluble vitamins leach Oxidation (until O_2 in headspace gone). Vitamin C and carotenoids Overall nutrient retention during storage is 90–95%	HTST, nisin and acids may decrease heat treatment. HTST; better thiamin and B_6 retention. Thiamin loss > w/ semisolid foods (> time/temp). Can lose 50%. Liquid diet importance. Consume liquid, process w/ less. Store cool, short times, add antioxidants. Store cool, short times. Temp just above freezing sig preserves.
Drying	Heat-labile vitamins (60% vitamin C loss blanching, 5% drying). Thiamin loss in air-dried pork is 50–70%; 5% loss in beef. Sulfite inactivates some thiamin and B_6. Freeze drying w/o air preserves vit C. Carotenoids oxidized (20–40% lost in carrots) Protein retention good, S containing amino acids may decrease Sun drying; major loss of vitamins A, C, beta-carotene; oxidation	Lower dry temp for cereals increases thiamin retention. Less loss w/ HTST than w/ low temp. Brown compounds decreased. Carotene degrades unless pkg w/o O_2. Vitamins stable during storage w/ packaging.
Fermentation	Vitamins synthesized by bacteria: niacin, thiamin, B_6, B_{12}, ascorbic acid. Ca, zinc, iron, Mg are preserved during bread fermentation.	Levels increase 25–150% in various items. Phytates (decrease metal bioavailability) decreased during fermentations.
Pasteurization	Heat degrades vit C, but if left active, enzymes would degrade it more.	HTST best at preserving all heat-labile vitamins.
UHT (130–150°C for 2–8 sec, aseptically packaged)	Some heat-labile vitamins lost; one of the better processes.	Cooler storage retains, though ambient stable microbiologically
Cure and smoke	Cure compounds retard oxidation	Some heat-labile vitamins lost during heat treatments, similar to cooking. Hot smoke loses 15–20% thiamin, others stable.
Ionizing radiation		
UHP		

enhanced by the presence of citrate and flavonoids. Ascorbic acid and its sodium, potassium, and calcium salts are commonly used as antioxidants in water-based systems. However, these compounds are water-soluble and thus cannot protect fats from oxidation. For this purpose, the fat-soluble esters of ascorbic acid with long-chain fatty acids (ascorbyl palmitate or ascorbyl stearate) can be used as food antioxidants.

Vitamin C (usually in the form of lemon or lime juice) is used in household pretreatment dips to prevent oxidative color changes in fruits and vegetables. It works as an antioxidant by being preferentially oxidized instead of the food it is protecting.

Vitamin C chemically decomposes under certain conditions, many of which may occur during the cooking of food.

Cooking can reduce the vitamin C content of vegetables by as much as 60 percent. Longer cooking times and higher temperatures, as in retorting, add to this effect, as do copper food vessels, which catalyze the decomposition.

Like all water-soluble vitamins, vitamin C is lost from food by leaching, where the water-soluble vitamin dissolves into the cooking water, which is later poured away and not consumed. On the other hand, fresh-cut fruits do not lose significant amounts when stored in the refrigerator for a few days.

Fat-soluble vitamins (A, D, E, and K) are generally less sensitive to processing effects than the water-soluble vitamins. Being insoluble in water, they won't leach into wash or blanch water, and they are more heat-stable to cooking and thermal processing. They are all prone to photo-oxidation and to the oxidizing effects of exposure to oxygen, so appropriate opaque and air-tight packaging yield longer shelf life.

Minerals are much more stable than vitamins in food. They are, after all, inorganic elements—pure compounds that are already in their simplest form. They are virtually impervious to physical or chemical changes during normal cooking or processing. They generally remain in the food even after cooking, canning, or freezing, although they can leach into washing, blanching, or cooling water, or into meat juice drippings. Processing can affect the balance of sodium and potassium in vegetables. Fresh vegetables are rich in potassium and naturally low in sodium. Canned vegetables are usually higher in sodium from added salt. All of the food groups have foods rich in minerals. Fruits and vegetables are good sources of potassium. Whole grains are rich in magnesium, selenium, and chromium. Nuts and seeds are good sources of copper and manganese. Red meats are particularly good sources of iron and zinc.

Food Fortification and Enrichment

The way food is handled before its consumption can negatively influence its micronutrient content (vitamins and minerals). Even with all the precautions taken to ensure the stability of micronutrients in food, some losses still occur during processing, distribution, and storage. One way to counter these losses is by enrichment (adding nutrients lost in processing) or fortification (adding nutrients not present in the original food, such as adding proteins, amino acids, minerals, vitamins, antioxidants, caffeine, and taurine to sports drinks). Typically, an excess amount (an overage) of the fortificant is added to the food to compensate for expected processing or storage losses, to ensure that fortified food delivers the targeted level of nutrients at the time the food is consumed in the home.

Physical Changes

Physical changes in foods do not result in the formation of new chemical compounds. They include the effect of gravity (heavy particles settle), molecules going into or out of solution (dissolving or crystallizing), separations (broken emulsions), changes of state (evaporation, liquidification, solidification), and molecules moving to different parts of a food (osmosis, leaching). Some physical changes are easily reversed,

such as in redispersing heavy particles that have settled by shaking, as in salad dressings. Others, such as textural changes from ice crystal damage due to slow freezing, are irreversible. Many physical changes can be inhibited by additives (emulsifiers, thickeners, and so on), appropriate packaging, and controlling storage time and temperature.

Change of State of Water

Liquid water becomes a solid when food is frozen, which can cause ice crystal damage to food structure. Water can also become a vapor and evaporate, leading to dehydration, which is a problem in refrigerated or frozen foods (leading to "freezer burn") that are not well covered. Dehydration is also a problem with long-term storage of fresh fruits and vegetables. Moisture loss from fresh fruits and vegetables is usually accompanied by vitamin loss and, ultimately, death of plant cells and deterioration of quality to the point of discard. Just the opposite, moisture uptake can lead to spoilage problems in dried foods when water activity rises to the point where microbial contaminants begin to grow and reproduce.[38]

Separations

Separations are generally physical changes, but chemical interactions may also be involved. The most common is the separation of water and oil in broken emulsions. In gels, such as custards or puddings, separation (*syneresis*) results in a watery layer and toughening of the solid portion as it becomes dehydrated. Meat proteins are also in a gel-like structure. During freezing, more protein-protein bonds form, and when the meat is thawed, the displaced water, called *drip loss*, leads to toughening and dryness.[39]

●Other Factors Influencing Shelf Life
Intrinsic Factors

Shelf life is greatly influenced by the inherent or intrinsic characteristics of the food itself. The term *intrinsic* denotes an innate property of the material, its genetic propensities and predispositions. Intrinsic characteristics are independent of how much of the material is present and the form the material is in (for example, one large piece or a collection of smaller pieces). Protective coverings such as shells or thick skin, microbial resistance, and enzymatic and nutritional stability are all intrinsic factors. So is the way different fruits ripen.

Fruits are divided by the ability to ripen after harvest (tomatoes, bananas, avocados, peaches, pears, and so on) and the inability to do so (citrus, grapes, melons, strawberries, pineapples, and so on); the latter must achieve ripeness before harvesting. Fruits that ripen after harvest are called climacteric fruits, and those that do not are called *non-climacteric fruits*.

Climacteric is the final physiological process that marks the end of fruit maturation and the beginning of fruit senescence (decline). Its arrival is identified by a sudden rise in respiration of the fruit and normally takes place without any external influences. This leads to other changes in the fruit, including pigment changes and sugar release. For those fruits eaten as food, the climacteric event marks the peak of edible ripeness, with fruits having the best taste and texture for consumption. After the climacteric period, respiration rates (noted by carbon dioxide production) return to or below the level before the event, and fruits are more susceptible to fungal invasion and begin to degrade into cell death. Non-climacteric fruits and most vegetables do not go through this uptick in respiration after harvest and therefore do not get any riper than the day they were picked.

Obviously, we don't all live close to where our produce is grown, so if nature had its way, by the time these products got to our supermarkets they would in many cases be past their peak in eating quality. Luckily, shelf life can be greatly influenced by storage conditions and packaging—that is, by extrinsic factors. Balancing the interaction of intrinsic and extrinsic characteristics is critical for prolonging shelf life.

Extrinsic Factors

Extrinsic factors are those the food product encounters as it moves through the food chain. They include the following:

- Time-temperature profile during processing
- Temperature control during storage and distribution
- Relative humidity (RH) during processing, storage, and distribution
- Exposure to light (UV and IR) during processing, storage, and distribution
- Surviving microbial counts during processing, storage, and distribution
- Composition of atmosphere within packaging
- Pressure (or lack thereof) in the package headspace
- Subsequent heat treatment (for example, reheating or cooking before consumption)
- Transportation effects
- Consumer handling

All these factors can and do operate in an interactive and often unpredictable way, and the possibility of deleterious consequences must be investigated.

Stored fruits and vegetables consume oxygen and give off carbon dioxide in a process called respiration. They continue to live and break down the stored sugars, starches, fats, and proteins of which they are composed. The changes caused by respiration can be deleterious to the fruit or vegetable, leading to softening, overripening, textural collapse, and so on. There are three ways to reduce the effects of respiration, all of them extrinsic:

1. Reduce storage temperature.
2. Control humidity.
3. Reduce but not eliminate oxygen, or increase carbon dioxide.

The optimum temperatures, humidity, and external gas composition for storage vary according to the type of produce. For example, McIntosh apples are best stored at 37.4°F (3°C), 87 percent RH (relative humidity), 3 percent oxygen (normal = 21 percent), 3 percent carbon dioxide (normal = 0.3 percent) for about 1 month and then at 5 percent carbon dioxide and 95 percent nitrogen.[40] This type of storage is called controlled atmosphere (CA) or modified atmosphere (MA) storage.

Modified atmosphere packaging (MAP) of foods, both raw and cooked, also uses this technique quite effectively. Cut fruit and vegetables are placed in packages that are then flushed or injected with gases before sealing to slow respiration inside the package and extend shelf life. This has revolutionized the produce business and allowed the creation of the enormous bagged cut salad industry. MAP has also greatly extended the shelf life of refrigerated packaged and prepared foods such as deli meats, fresh pasta, sandwiches, meat salads such as chicken and tuna, and deli salads such as potato and macaroni. In these examples, the food ingredients have been cooked or otherwise processed and are no longer respiring. Instead, the MAP gases reduce or eliminate oxygen to inhibit the growth of aerobic spoilage organisms and reduce the effects of oxidation. This process is also commonly used in the packaging of raw meats to retard spoilage and enhance appearance (color), particularly in red meats. The art and science of selecting the right mixture of gases in the most effective ratios is quite complicated, as it must take into account whether the food item is raw or cooked, whether its composition is uniform or heterogeneous, what types of spoilage it is most likely to encounter, what types of microorganisms are targeted, the type of packaging being used, and length of shelf life desired.

Another form of MAP uses a vacuum packer to pull a vacuum inside the package, eliminating oxygen entirely. This is particularly useful in foods being frozen for extended periods, as it virtually eliminates freezer burn. Yet another version of MAP uses high concentrations of oxygen (higher than normally found in air) and even carbon monoxide to enhance the color of red meats.

⬤Analyzing and Predicting Shelf Life

The primary objective of programs and techniques for studying the stability of foods is to predict their shelf life after manufacture under normal packaging, distribution, and storage conditions. It is important, therefore, for the formulator to estimate the product's expected shelf life. This normally includes a period of storage by the manufacturer after production, shipping time, possible storage in a distribution warehouse, possible exposure to elevated temperatures (including multiple freeze-thaw events), storage by the retailer or foodservice operator, and the time until the product is used by the ultimate consumer. Depending on the food in question, shelf life can be as short as a few days (freshly made sandwiches) to a year or more (canned or dehydrated foods).

While it is fairly easy to determine acceptable shelf life for short shelf-life foods, no formulator or manufacturer can afford real-time testing for periods up to or exceeding a year. Instead, product developers predict shelf life on the basis of accelerated testing programs and techniques.

To shorten the time required for predictive stability testing, formulators subject their foods to conditions that stress the product's stability ("torture testing"), thereby hastening the end of usable shelf life. It is the formulator's responsibility to select the stress conditions and test methodologies for which well-established historical precedents allow for reliable and consistent correlation with actual shelf stability under normal conditions. Shelf-life prediction also takes into account estimated storage and use-up times as well as physical effects due to loading, trucking product to the farthest destination, and unloading. In addition, exposure to temperature extremes or fluctuations may be called for depending on the type of product, climate, and mode of transportation (refrigerated or unrefrigerated trucks, railcars, freezer trucks, and so on).

When setting up stress conditions and test methodologies, formulators must employ reasonable guidelines. The most practical approach is to rely on the comparison of a newly created product with a similar "old standby" product that has shown acceptable real-life stability. Stability testing programs are not absolute: The judgment that a product has adequate stability is a compromise between market acceptance and expected instability. That said, comparison to an established stable product is a sensible yardstick for predicting the shelf life of a previously untested preparation.

Accelerated shelf-life testing is an important part of any product development cycle. Key findings on the chemical, physical, sensory, and microbial changes to a challenged product are critical in order to effectively develop, protect, and market it. Companies may use various methods for different products. Developing a sound, scientific, accelerated test takes a great deal of time and resources and should be considered a wise investment. The goal is to have representative products under test far enough ahead of actual production that any red-flag problems can be identified in time to take systematic corrective action. The manufacturer aims to avoid being suddenly inundated with returned product and customer complaints because the behavior of the product during storage and distribution was not adequate.

Monitoring Effectiveness of Food Preservation

Preservation techniques deal with how to produce foods with extended shelf life that are also safe to eat and meet consumer expectations of sensory quality. No matter how suitable these techniques are, modern industrial production and processes are not successful if they are not monitored. Many factors are involved in ensuring safety and quality, such as the freshness and microbial quality of raw materials and the availability of potable water for production. Facilities and equipment must also be continuously checked for contamination, and remediations brought to bear immediately should any be found,

especially where raw meats and dairy products are processed. In addition, a high level of worker hygiene is essential.

In addition to ongoing monitoring of microbial status, sensory analysis of finished products over expected shelf life is another important way to monitor the effectiveness of processing strategies. This requires panels of human assessors who taste the company's products daily and thus are extremely well able to identify products that are becoming unacceptable at an early stage. By applying statistical techniques to the results, it is possible to make inferences and gain insights about the products under test. Most large consumer goods companies have departments dedicated to sensory analysis, but even in smaller companies, sensory analysis can be conducted by the QA (Quality Assurance) and Research and Development (R&D) departments. (For additional information about sensory analysis, see Chapter 17.)

At both national and international levels, food safety legislation is extensive. Regulations are justified by the fact that food products are reaching ever-widening geographic distribution, and an outbreak of foodborne illness can affect thousands and even tens of thousands of consumers across the country or across the globe. Because consumers cannot readily ascertain the safety of many food products (while food spoilage is obvious, the presence of pathogens usually isn't), it is up to producers to guarantee safety. Unfortunately, producers or retailers are not always able to certify safety because foodborne pathogens are living organisms that can enter the food at many points in the distribution chain and may propagate over time. This inability to verify safety and the resulting potential consequences for public health is the fundamental justification for governmental intervention to improve food safety.[41]

A major step forward in preventing outbreaks of foodborne illness in the United States was the creation of the HACCP (Hazard Analysis and Critical Control Points) system for monitoring food plant operations. HACCP was created by the Pillsbury Company in the 1960s when it was asked to develop absolutely safe foods for the astronauts in the U.S. space program. Global food safety programs include GFSI (Global Food Safety Initiative), SQF (Safe Quality Food), BRC (British Retail Consortium), ISO 22000, and Global GAP (an international version of HACCP). Their general purpose is to provide a set of strict food, sanitation, and manufacturing standards for food companies to follow that result in safe foods consistently prepared, appropriately packaged, and carefully tested so consumers never need worry about getting ill or injured and the company need not worry about legal woes, bad publicity, and lost business. Compliance is monitored by third-party auditors and paid for by the company being audited. If that isn't incentive enough, more and more of the largest food retailers and foodservice operators won't buy food products from manufacturers not certified by one or more of the food safety organizations; they fear food-related lawsuits as well. So food manufacturers must become certified by at least one of the global food safety pograms if they wish to do business with "the big boys." Wal-Mart is a prime example; in their Global Responsibility Report, they detail how they require all of their suppliers to certify that they meet at least one of the GFSI internationally recognized food safety standards.[42] In the end, compliance is a win-win for everyone, especially consumers.

● Conclusion

Once the safety of a processed food is assured, the next most important factor to a successful food manufacture is shelf life. The shorter the shelf life means the fresher the product. But it also means the market for this food product is much smaller, limited to geographical distances that allow enough time after delivery for the product to sell before it spoils.

While there is certainly a market niche for short shelf-life fresh foods, U.S. consumers are accustomed to the ready availability of most food products, everywhere and all the time, and are not put off by many of the methods used for shelf-life extension, nor by the idea that much of the food they buy is more than a couple of days old.

The Culinology® professional must have a strong understanding of the normal minimum and potential maximum shelf life of every type and form of raw material, food ingredient, and fully assembled finished product, as well as a solid working knowledge of the processing methods and technologies by which salable shelf life can be extended while retaining maximum eating quality and healthfulness. The success of every new product hinges on this know-how.

[1]E. B. Leib, D. Gunders, J. Ferro, A. Nielsen, G. Nosek, and J. Qu, *The Dating Game: How Confusing Food Date Labels Lead to Food Waste in America* (New York: National Resources Defense Council, 2013).

[2]S. J. VanGarde and M. Woodburn, *Food Preservation and Safety: Principles and Practice* (New York: Wiley, 1994).

[3]R. P. Singh and B. A. Anderson, "The Major Types of Food Spoilage: An Overview," in R. Steele, ed., *Understanding and Measuring the Shelf Life of Food* (Cambridge: Woodhead, 2004), 3–23.

[4]USDA Food Safety and Inspection Service, "Food Product Dating," USDA Food Safety Information (February 2007), retrieved January 16, 2001, from http://opi.mt.gov/pdf/schoolfood/FDCP/FoodProductDating.pdf.

[5]J. R. Whitaker, "Principles of Enzymology for Food Sciences," in *Enzyme Inhibitors* (New York: Marcel Dekker, 1972), 255–282.

[6]S. Ketsa and T. Daengkanit, "Firmness and Activities of Polygalacturonase, Pectinesterase, β-galactosidase, and Cellulase in Ripening Durian Harvested at Different Stages of Maturity," *Scientia Horticulturae* 80, no. 3 (1999): 181–188.

[7]S. Badui Dergal, *Química de los alimentos* (México: Alhambra Mexicana, 2006).

[8]DANISCO. PowerFresh–Bakery Enzymes, retrieved February 21, 2011, from http://cdn.danisco.com/fileadmin/user_upload/danisco/documents/products/powerfresh-bread2.pdf.

[9]H. McGee, *On Food and Cooking: The Science and Lore of the Kitchen* (New York: Simon and Schuster, 2007), 61–62, 143–145.

[10]P. A. Kreutler and D. M. Czajka-Narins, *Nutrition in Perspective*, 2nd ed. (Englewood Cliffs, NJ: Prentice Hall, 1987).

[11]M. Miyawaki, "Control of Polyphenol Oxidase and Pectin Methylesterase Activities by Ultra High Pressure" (Washington State University, 2006).

[12]T. Robinson, B. Chandran, and P. Nigam, "Studies on the Production of Enzymes by White-Rot Fungi for the Decolourisation of Textile Dyes," *Enzyme and Microbial Technology* 29, no. 8–9 (2001): 575–579.

[13]R. H. Wills, T. Lee, D. Graham, W. McGlasson, and E. Hall, *Postharvest: An Introduction to the Physiology and Handling of Fruit and Vegetables* (London: Granada, 1989).

[14]M. Anese and S. Sovrano, "Kinetics of Thermal Inactivation of Tomato Lipoxygenase," *Food Chemistry* 95, no. 1 (2006): 131–137.

[15]J. Q. Si and C. Drost-Lustenberger, "Enzymes for Bread, Pasta and Noodle Products," in R. J. Whitehurst and B. A. Law, eds., *Enzymes in Food Technology* (Boca Raton, FL: USA CRC Press, 2002), 19–56.

[16]J. Entine, *Let Them Eat Precaution: How Politics Is Undermining the Genetic Revolution in Agriculture* (Washington, DC: AEI Press, 2006).

[17]Center for Food Safety and Applied Nutrition and USDA, FDA Food Science Research, *Quantitative Assessment of Relative Risk to Public Health from Foodborne Listeria monocytogenes Among Selected Categories of Ready-to-Eat Foods* (September 2003), retrieved April 11, 2011, from http://www.fda.gov/downloads/Food/FoodScienceResearch/UCM197330.pdf.

[18]Ibid.

[19]S. J. Forsythe and P. R. Hayes, "HACCP and Product Quality," in *Food Hygiene, Microbiology, and HACCP* (Gaithersburg, MD: Aspen, 1998), 276–324.

[20]Van Garde and Woodburn, *Food Preservation and Safety*.

[21]S. E. Fayle, J. A. Gerrard, and P. S. Belton, "What Is the Maillard Reaction?" in S. E. Fayle and J. A. Gerrard, eds., *The Maillard Reaction* (London: Royal Society of Chemistry, 2002), 1–8.

[22]W. W. Nawar, "Biochemical Aspects: Nutritional Bioavailability," in I. A. Taub, *Food Storage Stability* (Boca Raton, FL: CRC Press, 1994), 125–174.

[23]R. L. Whistler and J. R. Daniel, "Carbohydrates," in O. Fennema, *Food Chemistry* (New York: Marcel Dekker, 1985), 69–137.

[24]T. P. Coultate, *Food: The Chemistry of Its Components* (Cambridge: Royal Society of Chemistry, 2002), 175–178.

[25]D. M. Schaefer, *Fresh Beef Marketing Opportunities Due to Dietary Vitamin E* (National Cattlemen's Beef Association and the Cattlemen's Beef Board, 2002).

[26]F. C. Stintzing and R. Carle, "Betalains—Emerging Prospects for Food Scientists," *Trends in Food Science & Technology* 18, no. 10 (2007): 514–525.

[27]B. de Ancos, E. Ibañez, G. Reglero, and M. P. Cano. "Frozen Storage Effects on Anthocyanins and Volatile Compounds of Raspberry Fruit," *Journal of Agricultural and Food Chemistry* 48, no. 3 (2000): 873–879.

[28]I. Oey, M. Lille, A. Van Loey, and M. Hendrickx, "Effect of High-Pressure Processing on Colour, Texture and Flavour of Fruit- and Vegetable-Based Food Products: A Review," *Trends in Food Science & Technology* 19, no. 6 (2008): 320–328.

[29]S. Wright, S. Jeffrey, and R. Mantoura, "Evaluation of Methods and Solvents for Pigment Extraction," in S. Jeffrey, R. Mantoura, and S. Wright, eds., *Phytoplankton Pigments in Oceanography* (Paris: UNESCO Publishing; 1997), 261–282.

[30]P. P. Lewicki and G. Pawlak, "Effect of Mode of Drying on Microstructure of Potato," *Drying Technology* 23, no. 4 (2005): 847–869.

[31]A. M. Goula and K. G. Adamopoulos, "Stability of Lycopene During Spray Drying of Tomato Pulp," *LWT—Food Science and Technology* 38, no. 5 (2005): 479–487.

[32]F. Delgado-Vargas and O. Paredes-Lopez, "Anthocyanins and Betalains," in *Natural Colorants for Food and Nutraceutical Uses* (Boca Raton, FL: CRC Press, 2003), 167–220.

[33]Coultate, *Food*, 186–190.

[34]Ibid., 178–185.

[35]Ibid., 193–194.

[36]S. G. Gilbert, "Stability of Nutrients During Storage of Processed Foods," in E. Karmas and R. S. Harris, *Nutritional Evaluation of Food Processing* (Netherlands: Springer, 1988), 491–501; Coultate, *Food*.

[37]Coultate, *Food*, 261–300.

[38]Van Garde and Woodburn, *Food Preservation and Safety*.

[39]Ibid.

[40]N. N. Potter and J. H. Hotchkiss, "Food Deterioration and Its Control," in *Food Science* (Springer, 1995), 113–137.

[41]L. J. Unnevehr and H. H. Jensen, "The Economic Implications of Using HACCP as a Food Safety Regulatory Standard," *Food Policy* 24, no. 6 (1999): 625–635.

[42]Wal-Mart Stores, *Global Responsibility Report*, 2013.

15 Food Packaging

Lead Authors: Dr. Aaron L. Brody, Adjunct Professor, University of Georgia Department of Food Science and Technology, President/CEO, Packaging/Brody

Mark Thomas, President, MDT, Ltd.

Contributor: Thomas Trimarco Jr., Operations/Production Manager, Greencore Rhode Island

Introduction

The United States packaging supply industry has an annual value in excess of $150 billion, of which 55 to 60 percent is for food and beverages. Where previously packaging decisions were the exclusive responsibility of the technical side of food companies, as more and more manufacturers turn to multidisciplinary product development teams to create the next great food product, chefs and Culinology® professionals have also become deeply involved in package selection and testing.

Packaging is an integral part of the processing and preservation of foods. It accompanies the product from beginning to end. Its presence on the shelf influences the consumer's decision to purchase. It goes home with the consumer, remains around the house, establishes its brand image and identity, and contributes to brand loyalty. Selecting the proper packaging system for a particular product is critical and based on knowledge of the composition and stability of the product and its distribution channels. A thorough consideration of the environmental factors to which the product or the package system is exposed during distribution and storage is vital as well.

Food and beverage packaging has multiple roles:

- To protect fresh, minimally processed, and fully processed food and beverage products from harvest or processing to the consumer's table.
- To maintain product safety, quality, and shelf life.
- To facilitate distribution of food products from farm to fork.
- To add convenience for consumers and foodservice operators.
- To communicate to retailers, foodservice operators, and consumers the product's attributes, preparation instructions, nutritional value, and use-by date.
- To comply with government regulatory requirements.

This chapter demonstrates the indispensability of food packaging to food production, food marketing, food distribution, retail grocery and foodservice operations, and the health, safety, and nutritional well-being of consumers.

Definitions and Vocabulary

Food packaging is the unitization and containment of food and beverage products to protect them against external environmental influences such as air, microorganisms, dirt, light, moisture, impact, vibration, and insects—from harvest, manufacture, or preparation to consumption.

For the food processor, food packaging is arguably the most effective means of delivery to and communication with the consumer. Without food packaging, no industrialized country's economic system could function. Instead, most of the population would be immersed in growing and preserving its own food. Coupled with the distribution infrastructure and modern technology, food processing and packaging are the most cost-, energy-, and resource-efficient means of delivering safe, uniform-quality food for mass consumption. In fact, only about 7 percent of the retail price for food and beverages comes from the packaging.

The products that food scientists, technologists, Culinology® professionals, and chefs develop, and manufacturers produce, cannot be delivered to consumers without some form of protective packaging. Nearly every food product is packaged in some way at some point in its trip through the distribution system.

What Is Packaging?

A package is a physical structure for containment and protection.

"Packaging" encompasses the sum of associated technology, equipment, and materials, and their interactions with the contained food products. Packaging plays an indispensable role in the food and beverage processing and distribution businesses, including all forms of wholesaling, retailing, grocery, and foodservice.

Packaging Definitions

- *Primary packaging*—The glass and plastic bottles and jars; plastic cups, trays, and tubs; metal and composite paperboard canisters; flexible pouches; bags; and many others that are in direct contact with the food. Packaging is the first and main line of protection against moisture and oxygen loss or gain, microbiological contamination, insects, tampering, and so on.
- *Secondary packaging*—This unitizes multiple primary packages—for example, bottles of beer packaged together in a six-pack paperboard folding carton or banded together with a plastic six-pack ring, to facilitate retail sale.
- *Distribution, or tertiary packaging*—An external package that facilitates the movement of large quantities of packaged foods—for example, a paperboard folding carton or a corrugated fiberboard shipping case or plastic film–wrapped corrugated fiberboard tray or wooden pallet that permits the assembly of several primary or secondary packages, such as multiple 6- or 12-packs for retail sale or 24-packs for shipment from the packager to retailer.
- *Packaging technology*—The application of scientific principles to protect contained products against microorganisms, moisture, oxygen, light, shock, vibration, impact, compression, human abuse, tampering, etc., while engineering materials to minimize insult to the environment. The means to predict and measure shelf life of the contained food or beverage product is also involved in determining package effectiveness.
- *Structure*—The physical entity of a package, such as a carton, can, bottle, jar, tub, cup, tray, case, or pouch.
- *Converting*—Transforming packaging raw materials— paper, glass, plastic, metal—into finished package structures.
- *Graphics*—The surface appearance and decoration of a package—its shape, form, and color—including the brand name or the trade dress and trademark. Package graphics provide recognition, identification, and communication to the outside world of what is inside the package.

The Functions of Packaging

Packaging should provide performance at an affordable cost, usually much less than 10 percent of the total retail price of the product. It extends the food supply in industrial countries by significantly reducing food and beverage waste to below 30 percent of the input supply.

Packaging also communicates the identity of the package's contents, including product regulatory label requirements, positioning for retailers, and information and preparation instructions for consumers.

Information for consumers can include instructions for end use—preparation instructions (with variations as needed); best-if-used-by date; dispensing and reclosure; disposal or recycling of spent package materials; promotional and marketing information; and nutritional information.

Although the basic communications function of food packaging are identification, compliance, and useful information, passive and active linkages between consumer and marketer have become overt relationships. The package is no longer an inert or benign connection; it is an active two-way transmission engineered to inform, respond, and influence both participants. Package graphics and structures are now designed to attract, alert, and persuade, all in a single swift action. Color, shape, reflectivity, disruption, and provocation are integrated with the total marketing experience, including sound, sight, aroma, and suggestion to the consumer and user. Packaging is an excitement generator—an essential extension of the eating experience—with more to come as we learn better how to use it to complement food.

Finally, packaging protects the contents from the natural world of air, earth, water, light, and animals, including birds, insects, rodents, and microorganisms that attack food. Successful packaging also takes the environment into account and is designed to avoid excess and unrecyclable waste materials.

●A Brief History of Packaging

The history of humankind is written in its packaging—leaves, urns, pottery, amphorae, woven reed baskets, leather pouches, and so on. Packaging of food and water gave humans the ability to hunt and gather far from the home site, to explore and travel, and to colonize new lands and build cities. In ancient times, people employed primitive packaging such as leaves, animal skins, and even skulls to contain foods. Pottery and glass were used as far back as 5000 years ago. The origins of modern food packaging lie in the nineteenth century with the beginnings of canning (explored by Nicholas Appert, Louis Pasteur, Samuel C. Prescott, William L. Underwood, and Charles Olin Ball), papermaking, and package material converting. Glass bottle-making on an industrial basis began at the turn of the twentieth century.

During the early 1900s, commercial food and beverage canning was developed. Food freezing was engineered during the 1920s; cellophane and aluminum foil were invented during the pre–World War II period. The first practical plastics, such as polyethylene, polypropylene, and nylon, were invented prior to the 1950s, and today plastic packaging comprises well over 60 billion plastic bottles and jars plus film, clamshells, pouches, bags, and many other structures.

Many current package materials, concepts, and machinery were developed after the 1950s, including much of the packaging in which we process and distribute food and beverages

FIGURE 15.1 Vacuum-packaged beef strip loin, introduced during the 1960s.

Erich Eggimann/Getty Images, Inc.

today: aluminum cans for carbonated beverages, beer, and juices; aseptic shelf-stable juice paperboard carton packaging for beverages, milk, and soup; and vacuum packaging for all manner of meats and poultry, both raw and cooked.

Flexible—that is, plastic—packaging now represents about 20 percent of the total in value, and its use is growing rapidly, but it is actually much higher in volume when you consider the surface area it covers. This includes laminates (multi-material layers joined together by adhesives or heated layers; the layers may consist of plastic and non-plastic materials—for example, paper and foil), coatings, and coextrusions (the layers are joined by heating to the point of melting; all layers must be plastic). A comprehensive example is a three-layer coextruded film where the inner film layer provides barrier properties, the middle layer provides the necessary strength or stiffness to the final construction, and the third layer, on the outside, provides a printable surface.

The following packaging technologies have evolved in just the past 40 years:

- The polyester carbonated-beverage bottle, now also used for salad dressings, water, sauces, juices, and toppings, introduced in the late 1970s
- Microwavable packaging, beginning in the 1980s and now often a key to prepared foods distribution
- Extended refrigerated shelf-life (ESL) packaging for beverages and chilled prepared foods
- Oxygen-barrier plastics, such as ethylene vinyl alcohol (EVOH)
- Multilayer plastic barrier packaging for retort bottles and trays, replacing more expensive and heavier metal cans
- Aluminum bottles, as contrasted to cans, widely commercialized for beverages in 2002
- Retortable paperboard composite cartons, developed in 2003 and 2004 and still seeking a niche in North America
- Active packaging (oxygen-scavenging, antimicrobial, moisture-absorbing) and intelligent packaging (providing time and temperature history, microbial growth indicators, and so on)—recent phenomena that have still not achieved full commercial success. However, oxygen-scavenger polyester bottles (with scavengers in the plastic) and cereal boxes with antioxidants impregnated in the film liners are currently in use.

Today, food and beverage packaging in the United States represents more than 600 billion individual units annually.

- Metal is represented by about 130 billion cans, including 105 billion two-piece aluminum beverage cans (for beer, carbonated beverages, and juices).

FIGURE 15.2 Polyester carbonated-beverage bottle, introduced in 1977.

Steve Snyder/Getty Images, Inc.

FIGURE 15.3 Typical flexible pouch for salty snacks.

Lee Rogers/Getty Images, Inc.

- Glass is declining to fewer than 40 billion bottles and jars annually.
- Wood is still used in pallets, crates, and some specialty primary packages.
- Plastic has grown to well over 60 billion packages, but actual volumes are much higher when wraps and films are taken into account.

●The Packaging Supply Industry

Food and beverage processors, packagers, distributors, and retailers depend on their suppliers for packaging, technology, and research needs. The following organizations offer a wealth of information to help the product developer select the best materials for containment of each food or beverage.

- *Raw material suppliers*—plastic resin (polyethylene, polypropylene, polyester) makers (such as DuPont, Dow, ExxonMobil); metal suppliers (such as Alcoa and Alcan); paper and paperboard makers (such as International Paper, MWV, RockTenn), and many others.
- *Converters*—organizations that transform raw materials into useful package materials—oriented polypropylene film, paperboard folding cartons, corrugated fiberboard cases, polyester bottles; metal cans (such as RockTenn; Printpack; Cryovac [a division of Sealed Air]; Consolidated Bottle).
- *Equipment manufacturers*—makers of converting equipment such as printing presses, winders, die cutters, slitters, extruders, and molding presses used to fabricate package materials; also makers of equipment such as canning, pouching, cartoning, wrapping, and casing machines used directly by food and beverage packagers to link food and beverage contents to the package, for example, Kliklock-Woodman, Rovema, Bosch.
- *Component suppliers*—manufacturers of small items such as labels, glue, coding, closures, tags, and items like can seam measuring instruments, all essential to the completion of the packaging but not major in terms of cost. An example is Avery Dennison.
- *Designers*—developers of the structural designs of paperboard folding cartons, bottles, and corrugated fiberboard shipping cases; also graphic designers.
- *Packaging research firms*—providers of objective insights into consumer and retailer reactions to the graphics and package forms. Examples are universities such as Clemson and Michigan State; National Food Labs.
- *Package testing firms*—physical testers of packaging to determine protective characteristics, such as water vapor transmission and impact resistance, and testers of shelf-life characteristics. Examples are universities such as Clemson and Michigan State; National Food Labs.

- *Consultants*—providers of marketing data, information, insights, strategies, systems integration, machinery linkages, services, and so on. Examples include Packaging/Brody, Inc., MDT Ltd., HAVI, and Packaging Technology and Research.
- *Conferences and exhibitions*—mass information deliverers of packaging information (such as Interpack in Dusseldorf, Germany, and Tokyo Pack in Tokyo, Japan).
- *Publishers*—developers and suppliers of books and journals. Examples include CRC, IFT, DEStech, and Wiley.
- *Professional and trade associations*—information sources, such as:
  - Package Machinery Manufacturers Institute (PMMI)
  - Institute of Food Technologists (IFT), Food Packaging Division
  - Paperboard Packaging Council (PPC)
  - Flexible Packaging Association (FPA)
  - Institute of Packaging Professionals (IoPP)
  - Research Chefs Association (RCA)
- *Universities*—educators of packaging technologists and researchers in the field; institutions located in the United States and Canada include:
  - Michigan State University
  - Clemson University
  - Rochester Institute of Technology
  - Rutgers, the State University of New Jersey
  - San Jose State University, California
  - Indiana State University
  - California Polytechnic Institute
  - University of Wisconsin, Stout
  - University of Guelph, Ontario, Canada
  - Universities with food science and technology departments
- *U.S. government agencies* relevant to food packaging:
  - Food and Drug Administration (FDA)
  - Department of Agriculture (USDA)
  - Department of Transportation (DOT)
  - Department of Commerce
  - Treasury Department
- *Basic packaging research*—in Europe:
  - United Kingdom: Campden and Chorleywood Food Research Association (CCFRA)
  - Netherlands: TNO, Netherlands Organisation for Applied Scientific Research
  - Sweden: SIK Swedish Institute of Food Preservation

●Product Distribution

Packaging plays a vital role in distribution of the finished product from the end of the food or beverage production line to the retailer or foodservice operator and ultimately to the consumer. It involves logistics, warehousing, transportation, retailer requirements, display, economics, traffic and shipping, and promotional packaging.

FIGURE 15.4 **Pallet loads of cases for transportation.**

gilas/Getty Images, Inc.

Packaging in the grocery industry has come a long way from the days of backroom molded-pulp meat trays and cellophane film wrapping. While these types of packaging are still popular, the grocery industry realizes consumers have many more food options than ever before, and manufacturers need to find a way to draw buyers to *their* products. Grocery chains are competing in a new market, introducing convenient, fully cooked prepared meals-to-go and trying to take sales away from Quick Service Restaurants (QSRs) and other foodservice take-out offerings. Packaging plays a strong role here because consumers expect the meal taken home from the grocery store to have the same quality and look it would have in a restaurant. On the other side, the foodservice market is focusing its efforts on a larger selection of higher-quality products while remaining price-sensitive. To help in both these areas, the packaging industry is continually pushing the envelope with new designs and new materials.

Food and Beverage Distribution

Manufacturers such as Susanna's Kitchens, wholesalers such as Sysco, and retailers such as Kroger constitute most of America's food channels that enable the delivery of safe, high-quality food to consumers. During the past 25 years, the boundaries between foodservice and retail have blurred; many groceries have installed sit-down dining areas, and many restaurants offer packaged take-out foods prepared in their own kitchens.

About half the dollar value of food and 40 percent of its volume passes through foodservice channels; the rest goes through retail grocery channels. All, of course, initially passes through industrial channels—that is, food manufacturers.

Foodservice Distribution Channels

The 653,000 foodservice outlets in the United States can be classified into three broad categories—commercial, contractor-managed, and non-commercial—all of which require different forms of food packaging.

Commercial restaurants are those whose primary business is preparing and serving food to customers for profit. Examples of commercial restaurants are full-service restaurants, QSRs, caterers, and cafeterias.

Contractor-managed foodservice operations, whose principal business is preparing and serving food to internal consumers under long-term contracts, are found in businesses, hospitals, colleges, sports centers, military posts, and airlines.

In non-commercial foodservice, the primary business is something other than foodservice, and food is provided as an adjunct. Establishments in this category operate their own foodservice facility, as opposed to having a contractor managing the operation. Examples include employee cafeterias, transportation (airlines, trains), school lunch programs, and nursing homes.

Retail Grocery Distribution

Retail food distribution has changed radically during the past 30 years due to the influence of mammoth box and discount stores. The United States has about 30,000 supermarkets, 3000 box stores, and 110,000 convenience stores, plus numerous kiosks, specialty and ethnic shops, catalog and online ordering, vending machines, and assorted other outlets. About 30 percent of packaged food and beverage distribution is direct delivery to the retail outlet through individual sales (carbonated beverages, beer, bread, salty snacks), with the remainder going through distributor warehouses. Inventories tend to be higher and shelf life must be longer for warehoused products.

In retail channels, about 15 percent of the food and beverage movement is home meal replacement, about 40 percent is chilled, and 5 or 6 percent is frozen. The majority of foods in retail distribution are ambient-temperature shelf-stable packaged goods such as canned and dehydrated products.

FIGURE 15.5 **The interior of a supermarket is a cornucopia of fresh and processed food—regardless of location.**

Burak Demir/Getty Images, Inc.

Food Science, Food Technology, and Culinology®

Research chefs involved in new product development often pay little attention to packaging, using materials already on hand without much thought about their importance. The assumption is that packaging needs for new products are the same as for current products. But is that assumption correct?

What individual product characteristics drive, or define, the appropriate package?

- *Required shelf life*—The longer the shelf life, the better the oxygen and moisture, and in some cases, light barrier that is required.
- *Storage temperature*—Ambient, refrigerated, or frozen? Ambient-temperature shelf-stable foods require a better barrier against moisture and oxygen transmission; frozen foods require more moisture protection; chilled foods need multiple barriers.
- *Physical protection requirements*—The longer the distribution channel, the greater the protection requirements against vibration, impact, compression, and contamination.
- *Security*—Tamper indicators are essential.
- *Light permeability*—Opaque packaging helps protect against photo-oxidation.
- *Contents visibility*—Light sensitivity must be balanced against product visibility for marketing purposes.
- *Vapor barrier*—Almost all foods must be protected against moisture transfer in or out.
- *Acid resistance*—Microbiological safety can depend on low pH (below 4.6); in these cases, packaging must be able to withstand, maintain, and even promote an acidic environment.
- *Oxidation and rancidity prevention*—Oxygen is almost always adverse to product shelf life; it must be controlled or even eliminated.
- *Hot fill or retort capability*—Many plastics cannot withstand hot fill or retort temperatures and pressures.
- *Minimal use of packaging materials*—The less the package material mass, the lower its cost and environmental impact. Many retailers are now demanding that manufacturers provide their products in simpler, more efficient, "frustration-free" packaging.
- *Ecologically smart*—Desirable packages are recyclable, reusable, or easily broken down to low-impact, nontoxic materials.
- *Marketing image*—The package is designed to attract consumer trial and repeat purchase at retail.
- *Consumer information*—The package is designed to communicate with target consumers.
- *Regulatory requirements and nutritional data*—The package carries information required by law or regulation.

The preservation and protection of virtually every type of food is enhanced by packaging: meats, fish, produce, beverages, bakery goods, dairy products, prepared dishes—the list is endless. For each there must be a means to delay or prevent potential spoilage and quality loss. Education, experience, and training in food packaging are essential for identifying and applying the best systems for optimizing food safety and quality retention. Food packaging technologists depend on the experience and knowledge of research chefs, and vice versa. Cooperation among these professionals is essential; too much is involved for one person to know all of the relevant variables.

Microbiological Safety

Microbiological food safety combines processing, sealing against recontamination of the product, and protection through distribution channels. Recontamination control through hermetic closure of food packaging is a must.

Nearly half of all the food and beverage products in the United States are fresh or minimally processed and typically distributed at refrigerated temperatures to retard spoilage and quality loss. Fresh food products include meats, poultry, seafood, vegetables, and fruits that are unprocessed except for removal from the original environment and limited trimming and cleaning. They are handled under sanitary conditions to retard microbiological and enzymatic deterioration, which is relatively rapid at ambient or higher temperatures. Most fresh vegetables and fruits are chilled to below 50°F (10°C) for distribution; meats, seafood, and poultry are chilled to 40°F (4°C) and may be frozen to enhance preservation.

It is important to recognize that many variables other than package structure must be in place for packaging functionality to be fulfilled. For example, when high- or low-oxygen packaging environments are applied to retain color of fresh meats, gas barrier films are required to hold in the gas. On the other hand, in bagged fresh produce, where respiratory anaerobiosis leading to rapid deterioration is to be avoided, semipermeable films are required to allow for respiration (albeit slowed by refrigeration) to continue.

Minimally processed foods such as cottage cheese and yogurt have been altered by fermentation or direct acidification to reduce pH, thereby minimizing deteriorative processes and extending shelf life. These are usually refrigerated at 40°F (4°C) or lower (but above freezing). Shelf life is usually measured in weeks and even months when sealed plastic tray or cup packaging is used to retard microbiological contamination and moisture transfer. The newer extended shelf life (ESL) food products are often packaged under reduced-oxygen conditions in barrier plastic film pouches and bottles. Fully processed foods are intended for long-term shelf life—that is, months—at ambient or freezing temperatures and include most heat-processed, canned, dried, and frozen foods.

Fresh Foods

About 25 percent of food products in the United States are meats, including beef, poultry, pork, seafood, lamb, and veal. All are susceptible to microbiological, enzymatic, biochemical, and physical changes. Fresh meat safety is a key issue because meat is subject to growth of pathogens, and so distribution conditions must be carefully controlled. These foods also tend to be the costliest.

Several types of packaging work well for muscle meats, poultry, and fish. Polyvinyl chloride (PVC) is a common stretch or cling film used for overwrapping fresh meat, poultry, and produce trays in retail stores to provide a transparent, low-moisture-permeable, high-gas-permeable material that can retard respiratory anaerobiosis in produce and provide adequate oxygen to retain the red color of fresh meats. While the traditional expanded polystyrene meat tray and PVC wrap works well, it does not help extend the life of the product. Many companies are turning to modified atmosphere packaging (MAP).

MAP is a technology for prolonging the shelf life of fresh or minimally processed foods. The gaseous environment surrounding the food inside the package is modified: the normal ratio of gases in air (21 percent oxygen and 0.038 percent carbon dioxide) is adjusted to reduce the oxygen level to 10 to 15 percent and elevate the carbon dioxide to 5 to 20 percent inside the package. This slows the natural oxidative deterioration of the food under chilled conditions. The specific blend of gases varies depending on the product, the packaging materials, and storage temperature.

Unlike most other commodities, which survive longer when packed under low or no oxygen, the color of fresh red meat depends on the presence of high levels of oxygen to maintain the fresh red color. The normal color of the meat pigment myoglobin is purple. When exposed to oxygen, myoglobin turns into oxymyoglobin and the color changes from purple to bright red. In distribution channels, most red meat is packaged under reduced oxygen in oxygen and water-vapor barrier packaging to retard microbiological deterioration. As an additional hurdle, fresh meats are transported to retail outlets at temperatures at or below 40°F (4°C) to retard deteriorative processes. By the time it reaches the retailer, the meat color can be quite dark due to lack of oxygen. For merchandizing purposes in the grocery store, the red color of meat can be revived through the use of appropriate MAP (in this case, with higher oxygen in the package) combined with gas-barrier packaging.

Raw poultry is an excellent substrate for infectious salmonella and Campylobacter microorganisms. In fact, most fresh poultry sold at retail is already contaminated with these bacteria by the time it reaches supermarket shelves. This occurs even though carcass temperatures are reduced as rapidly as possible after slaughter, often by ice or cold-water immersion or air cooling and shipping on ice. Most poultry is prepackaged in expanded polystyrene trays wrapped with moisture-barrier plastic film to retard moisture loss and microbiological growth under reduced temperature. Once again, sanitary processing and temperature control are the first essentials to preservation, complemented by sound packaging. The consumer must then make sure that raw chicken is handled carefully to prevent cross-contamination of other foods and that it is always fully cooked before consumption.

Seafood is chilled and packaged in water-vapor barrier packaging, such as PVC film wrap on expanded polystyrene trays, to retard microbiological and enzymatic activity and weight (moisture) loss, then held at refrigerated temperatures. Packaging for frozen fish generally has low water-vapor permeability to permit long-term frozen distribution without freezer burn or surface desiccation due to sublimation. Some MAP of seafood in barrier plastic trays with hermetically sealed barrier lidding has been commercialized, but again, temperature control is the key.

Many soft-bodied fresh fruits and vegetables must be handled gently because of sensitive physical structures, potential for increased enzymatic activity in damaged flesh, and the ubiquitous presence of surface microorganisms that can penetrate damaged or bruised areas in the flesh or enter through the stem area. Damage to the product's surface provides channels through which microorganisms can enter to initiate spoilage. Temperature control is quite specific, as many fresh fruits especially can be damaged by over-chilling. Most leafy vegetables can be extended in shelf life by packaging under specific modified atmosphere (MAP) conditions (oxygen reduced from 21 to 2 percent, carbon dioxide increased from 0.4 to 5 percent) and with gas-semipermeable plastic film packaging to retard anaerobic respiration that results from a near-zero oxygen condition as would occur in an airtight bag. As long as refrigerated temperature storage is maintained, this can increase bagged salad shelf life to as long as 15 days, whereas under air it would remain fresh for less than 4 or 5 days.

Partially Processed Food Products

Partially processed food products receive more than minimal processing—for example, cooking, curing, or smoking—but still require refrigeration.

Cured Meats

Ham, bacon, sausage, bologna, and so on are cured to reduce water activity and thus retard microbiological and biochemical deterioration, are seasoned for flavor, and usually contain other ingredients (typically nitrites) to maintain the desired pink color and inhibit the growth of pathogens. Curing agents include salt, sodium nitrite, ascorbic acid, sugar, and sodium nitrate. Often such products are smoked, or cooked and smoked, for flavor and to enhance preservation. Cured meats are usually stored in the absence of oxygen to achieve refrigerated shelf lives measured in weeks. Packaging for such products are usually gas-barrier plastic films to provide either vacuum or inert gas–flushed (for example, nitrogen) internal environments that retard microbiological growth and enzymatic or biochemical change.

Vacuum packing is a form of MAP because it involves removal of the atmosphere inside the package. It is highly effective in extending the shelf life of many non-respiring foods. That said, vacuum packing by itself does not make foods sterile; high-moisture foods still must be refrigerated or frozen. Vacuum packing is an effective way to inhibit the growth of aerobic spoilage organisms, retard the deleterious effects of oxidation, and maximize retention of sensory qualities of the food (taste, aroma, texture, moisture). It also helps prevent dehydration (freezer burn) during long-term frozen storage.

Dairy Products

Dairy products must be heat-treated to eliminate pathogens, denature enzymes, and reduce overall microbial counts. Pasteurization is a relatively mild heat process that destroys pathogens and deteriorative enzymes but not all microorganisms. Pasteurized dairy products must therefore be refrigerated after processing to retard microbiological spoilage. Ultra-high-temperature (UHT) processing offers extended shelf life, but only under refrigeration, as the package may not be sterile. In aseptic packaging, milk (or other fluid food) is heat-sterilized—that is, rendered free of spoilage and pathogenic microorganisms and enzymes. Simultaneously, high-barrier paperboard, aluminum foil, plastic lamination, or all-plastic barrier packaging material is also sterilized. The milk and packaging are brought together in a sterile environment where the package is assembled, filled, and hermetically sealed to produce sterile milk in a sterile package that can be distributed under ambient (room temperature) conditions. Aseptic technologies are also applied to products for Extended Shelf Life Refrigerated (ESLR), but the package structure may not be sterile and so the product must be refrigerated.

FIGURE 15.6 Aseptic processing and packaging have enabled food processors to offer a wide range of safe, high-quality liquids and beverages.

N_design/Getty Images, Inc.

Fully Processed Foods

Canning is a way to process foods so they are shelf-stable at room temperature. Once they are canned, even perishable foods can be stored without refrigeration. Most fully processed foods are processed and packaged so that ambient room temperature shelf life can exceed 6 to 12 months.

The canning process thermally destroys all microorganisms and enzymes and maintains commercial sterility by hermetically sealing foods in oxygen- and water vapor–impermeable packaging. Whether a metal can, glass jar, or plastic pouch or tray is used for packaging, the process begins with treating the raw food product before filling. Entrapped air that can cause oxidative damage is largely removed from the food contents by heating (cooking or blanching) before filling. Once the packages are filled and hermetically sealed, anaerobic conditions inside the package can foster the growth of anaerobic spore-forming pathogens such as *Clostridium botulinum* if such spores are present, if pH is 4.6 or above, and if the proper temperature conditions for germination exist. Therefore, the food must be heated after packaging to 212°F (100°C) for high-acid products (pH lower than 4.6), and to 250°F (121°C) for low-acid products (pH higher than 4.6) to ensure the destruction of pathogenic spores.

In order to achieve temperatures above 212°F (100°C; normal boiling point of water at sea level), water must be placed under pressure. Therefore, the packages must be able to withstand the pressure (typically 15 psi). The canning process is calculated on the basis of time required for the slowest heating location of the food within the package (known as the *cold spot*, usually the center of the package) to achieve a temperature that destroys Clostridia spores within a reasonable period. After reaching that temperature (typically 250°F [121°C]), the package must be held for a prescribed amount of time that depends on the type of food, and then cooled rapidly to stop further cooking, which degrades the product.

FIGURE 15.7 Classic steel cans that have been sterilized by post-fill high-pressure retort processing for ambient-temperature shelf-stable distribution.

NoDerog/Getty Images, Inc.

Freezing

Freezing reduces the temperature of the food to below the freezing point of water so microbiological, enzymatic, and biochemical activities are virtually halted. In commercial freezing, the product temperature passes through the transition from liquid water to ice rapidly so the ice crystals that form are relatively small and do not physically disrupt the food's cell structure. Depending on the product, freezing may take place either before or after packing. Most freezing processes use high-velocity cold air or, less frequently, liquid nitrogen or carbon dioxide snow to remove heat from solid, bulk, or individually quick frozen (IQF) products.

Frozen food packaging must prevent the loss of water vapor, as the low relative humidity and constant migration of moisture within the freezer to the freezer coils readily dehydrates improperly packaged foods. The dehydrated areas lack desirable color, flavor, and texture. Such defects, termed freezer burn, occur in frozen foods because of extended storage in non-airtight or damaged packaging. Proper packaging must also allow for water content expansion during freezing; thus, the material should be strong yet flexible. The fill volume must be controlled accurately to avoid overfilling or underfilling. Unfilled spaces may permit ice crystal migration from the food, which can cause freezer burn, while overfilled packages may rupture when frozen due to product expansion. Packages that protect their contents from light and odors also extend their shelf life—that is, they retard oxidation of lipids and pigments. Vacuum packaging reduces oxygen and void volume, which increases product stability and eliminates internal ice crystal formation (cavity ice). Further, vacuum packaging reduces overall product volume by compression, which benefits shipping and handling.

Throughout the history of frozen foods, the package has often served as the preparation, heating, and eating vessel (think TV dinners), and since the microwave oven has become the preferred rethermalizing unit, increasingly sophisticated packaging structures have been developed to take advantage of this.

Dehydration

The removal of moisture retards food deterioration by eliminating almost all water required for the growth of microorganisms and for most biochemical and enzymatic reactions. Liquids (such as coffee or juice), semisolid foods (such as mashed potatoes and oatmeal), and solid foods (such as fruit, like raisins, dates, and figs, and meat, like jerky) can all be dried by an assortment of techniques, including spray-, drum-, vacuum-, and air-drying as well as lyophilization (freeze-drying). The shelf life of dehydrated foods is maintained by appropriate protective packaging. Suitable flexible films with low water vapor transition rate and low oxygen permeability are optimum for long-term shelf life.

Deterioration of dehydrated foods is highly dependent on the type of food and its water activity (a_w) after processing. Many dehydrated food products have a moisture content of less than 10 percent (approximately a_w 0.5) and are extremely stable. However, spoilage may occur by oxidation and the onset of rancidity and discoloration (as when a highly porous surface area enables rapid penetration of oxygen, which may be mitigated by nitrogen flushing). Moisture uptake can cause loss of stability, potential for microbial outgrowth, clumping, and caking. Over time there can be flavor changes (loss of volatiles or entry of off flavors), mechanical damage, or infestation by insects. Further, exposure to visible and/or ultraviolet light may dramatically accelerate quality degradation.[1]

Fats and Oils

Cooking oils and hydrogenated vegetable shortenings contain no water and so, in theory, are microbiologically stable at ambient temperatures. Unsaturated fats and oils, however, are vulnerable to oxidative rancidity; therefore, both are usually packaged under a low-oxygen atmosphere, such as nitrogen or vacuum, and often contain antioxidants and chelating agents (tocopherols, EDTA) to retard rancidity. Packaging for oils and fats obviously must be lipid-resistant and also have fairly good oxygen barriers such as polyester bottles or foil-lined paperboard cans (for shortenings such as Crisco).

Margarine and butter contain fat plus water and water-soluble ingredients—that is, salt and milk solids that impart flavor and color to the product. Generally, these products are distributed at refrigerated temperatures to retard microbiological growth and rancidity. Butter sticks are commonly wrapped in parchment paper, which helps maintain the quality of the butter; the paper is fat- and moisture-resistant, so water and fat are not able to leach through.

FIGURE 15.8 Breakfast cereal product is packaged in coextruded plastic film that provides both moisture and fat barrier, with an outer paperboard carton offering physical protection to fragile contents and a large communications billboard.

DebbiSmirnoff/Getty Images, Inc.

FIGURE 15.9 Typical packaging for salty crackers and analogous snacks. Interior coextruded moisture-barrier film for small unit portions unitized in outer paperboard carton for protection against physical damage during distribution.

wwing/Getty Images, Inc.

Cereals and Baked Goods

Breakfast cereals are dry foods susceptible to moisture absorption; therefore, they require good water vapor– and fat-barrier packaging such as coextruded polyethylene films to help retain delicate flavors. Cereals are also susceptible to oxidative rancidity, so antioxidants are commonly impregnated into the plastic film lining ready-to-eat cereal cartons.

Soft baked goods such as breads, cakes, and pastries are highly aerated structures and subject to dehydration and relatively rapid staling (a starch crystallization process). In moist environments, fresh bakery goods are also subject to microbiological deterioration as a result of the growth of surface mold and other microorganisms. Protective packaging usually consists of simple monolayer polyethylene or oriented polypropylene film pouches.

Hard baked goods, such as cookies and crackers, have a relatively low water content and high fat content. Water can be readily absorbed, and so the product loses its desirable texture and becomes increasingly subject to lipid rancidity. Packaging, such as oriented polypropylene film, is therefore aimed at preventing moisture incursion.

Many salty snacks—corn chips, potato chips, roasted nuts, and so on—are typically deep fat fried. These snacks have very low water content (<2 percent) and, usually, a relatively high unsaturated fat content (30 percent). Snack packaging problems are compounded by salt, a catalyst for lipid oxidation, and light, a catalyst for photo-oxidation. In addition to lipid oxidation, such products are also subject to loss of crispness due to moisture gain. Therefore, packaging strategies include opaque packaging to prevent photo-oxidation, gas-flushing with nitrogen to reduce oxygen, and packing the product in hermetically sealed, gas- and water vapor–impermeable containers (pouches, canisters) to keep the nitrogen in and oxygen and moisture out. Snack chips packed in flexible film bags are commonly pillow-packed with excess nitrogen gas to provide extra protection against breakage.

Candy

Chocolate, a high-fat product, is sensitive to flavor change and "bloom," that is, whitening, if temperature is abused. Inclusions such as nuts and fillings are susceptible to water gain or loss. Chocolate is packaged in fat- and odor-barrier packaging to limit movement of fats in case of temperature abuse, and prevent absorption of adverse odors from the exterior environment. Aluminum foil is often used, but both plastic films and plastic-coated paperboards are adequate to protect chocolate confections except against extreme temperature abuse.

Sugar candies have very low moisture content (<1 percent) and are susceptible to moisture gain. Packaging for sugar candies must be highly moisture- and aroma-resistant to prevent moisture gain and consequent softening. Oriented polypropylene film wraps are usually adequate for these objectives.

Beverages

Beverages may be still or carbonated, alcoholic or nonalcoholic. The largest unit volume of packages in the United States is for two carbonated beverages: beer and soft drinks. Both contain dissolved carbon dioxide, which delivers positive pressure within the package. With glass bottles, internal carbonation is capable of stressing the closures; therefore both screw and crown closures are employed to ensure retention. With plastic bottles, the internal pressure is taken advantage of to provide internal stress that helps maintain package shape and permit thin-walling the plastic for economic and environmental reasons. Aluminum cans are also able to be thin-walled because the internal carbonation pressure maintains the can shape. When the internal product contents are not inherently carbonated, as with bottled water or juice, nitrogen is injected to provide counter-pressure and thus maintain package shape.

Beer is more sensitive than other carbonated beverages (or almost any other product) to oxygen, loss of carbon dioxide, off flavors, and light. Most, but not all, U.S. beer undergoes thermal pasteurization after sealing in the package. Thus, the internal pressure within the package can build to

FIGURE 15.10 Aluminum bottles of carbonated beverages. Internal carbonation helps maintain bottle shape.

jfmdesign/Getty Images, Inc.

vicm/Getty Images, Inc.

well over 100 psi at 145°F (63°C), the usual pasteurization temperature. If not carefully controlled, internal pressure is capable of blowing off closures or distorting aluminum cans. Much beer is packaged under excess carbon dioxide to eliminate as much oxygen as possible and thus retard oxidation of the contents. Other measures taken to reduce oxidative deterioration include refrigerated distribution and, for plastic bottles, incorporation of oxygen scavengers in the package walls.

●Package Materials

Packaging consists of a limited number of relatively inexpensive materials: paper, paperboard, aluminum, steel, glass, plastic, and, less often, wood.

Paper, Paperboard, and Corrugated Fiberboard

Paper and paperboard are the most common package materials in quantity and value, representing about 35 percent of total packaging volume. They are used to make folding cartons and corrugated fiberboard distribution cases, sleeves, pads, and so on, and have been employed since the nineteenth century. Virgin paperboard is derived directly from wood and is therefore the strongest board. Often, but not always, it is bleached or otherwise colored white for appearance and printability. Because of its purity—that is, absence of contaminants—virgin paperboard is often used for direct food contact in food packaging and in foodservice take-away applications.

Corrugated fiberboard is a paper-based material consisting of a fluted fiberboard sheet with one or two flat linerboards attached to either face. It is widely used in the manufacture of corrugated and shipping containers. Corrugated fiberboard was invented in England in the 1850s as an ingenious method that transformed flimsy sheets of paper into a rigid, stackable, and cushioning form of packaging for delicate goods in transit. Used to make shipping boxes since the 1890s, this material has not changed significantly in over a hundred years.

Old corrugated containers are an excellent source of fiber for recycling. They can be compressed and baled for cost-effective transport. The baled boxes are put in a hydropulper, which is a large vat of warm water for cleaning and processing the fiberboard. The pulp slurry is then used to make new paper and fiber products. Recycling corrugated fiberboard helps countries without sustainable wood resources build a paper and packaging industry locally.

Recycled paperboard is derived from previously used paper, such as newspapers or paperboard, corrugated fiberboard, and clippings and cuttings from paperboard carton or case converting plants. Much of the raw material is industrial or post-consumer waste from homes and offices. Properties are reduced due to shortened, damaged fibers. Recycled paperboard is potentially hazardous to food contents because of intentional and unintentional additives (inks, coatings, and so on) during previous use. Recycled paperboard can have a good white printing surface if it is clay-coated on the paper-making machine. Coated recycled paperboard can be used for secondary packaging of certain low-moisture foods such as cookies and crackers, cake mixes, and breakfast cereals, where it does not come into direct contact with the food.

Metal

Metal comprises about 130 billion cans, including 105 billion two-piece aluminum beverage cans (for beer and carbonated beverages and juices), as well as caps, lids, and closures for bottles and jars, and foil for flexible laminations. It has been used since the early nineteenth century.[2]

Aluminum, used in thin-walled cans for beer and soda, is the most widely used metal for packaging. It is also used in still beverage cans (juices, fruit beverages, tea, and so on) with the addition of inert gas—that is, nitrogen—for pressurization. Aluminum foil is used in trays and pans (pie tins, muffin tins, foil roasting pans, and so on), wraps, flexible packaging, and multi-material laminates. It is relatively easy to fabricate, and the wall thickness can be reduced to save weight. Metal closures are mechanically seamed to the can bodies. Heat-seal metal closures are also available.

Steel is used mainly in cans for retort processing, almost always internally coated with heat-resistant plastics to prevent the food from interacting with the steel and generating metallic off flavors. Steel cans are made in two pieces or, sometimes, three, with welded side seams. Mechanical double-seaming is the common closure technology.

FIGURE 15.12 Two-piece steel can with easy-open steel end. Paper label. Can is engineered for high-temperature, high-pressure retorting to sterilize the contents for ambient temperature distribution.

Larry Herfindal/Getty Images, Inc.

Glass

Glass bottles and jars for foods and beverages are the oldest of the man-made packaging materials, and the heaviest and most energy intensive. Glass is inert, transparent, and an excellent barrier, but relatively fragile. It requires a closure, usually of a different material. It is declining in importance as a package material to fewer than 40 billion bottles and jars annually due to shipping weight and expense as well as breakability.

Plastics and Plastic Packaging

Plastic, about 80 years old as a package material, is the youngest family of packaging materials and the most versatile, least expensive, and by far the most effective per unit of weight. There are many types of plastics used in food and beverage packaging, too many to adequately discuss all of them here, but these are the most common.

Polyolefins

Polyolefins are composed of hydrocarbons extracted from petroleum or natural gas. These include polyethylene (PE), which is an excellent moisture barrier, and the most widely used packaging plastic. In film form, it is used in myriad applications, depending on its density: to contain bread, hard baked goods, and candies and as a liquid-barrier heat-seal coating on other plastics and on paperboard. It is made in many varieties that differ in density and cross-linking. These three are the most common:

- *Low density (LDPE)*—0.09 to 0.91 g/cm^3: plastic wrap, plastic bags, coated on paperboard to manufacture milk and juice cartons.
- *High density (HDPE)*—0.95 g/cm^3: milk jugs, margarine tubs, bottles and bottle caps.
- *Linear low density (LLDPE)*—0.915 to 0.925 g/cm^3: has higher tensile strength and higher impact and puncture resistance than does LDPE. It is very flexible and elongates under stress. It can be used to make thinner films, plastic wrap, stretch wrap, pouches, bottles, and jars, and as a coating for other substrates, according to the *Modern Plastics Encyclopedia*.

Rugged, translucent, reusable plastic storage containers made in a wide variety of shapes and sizes for home use by various companies (such as Rubbermaid and Sterilite) are commonly made of high-density polypropylene, although the lids are often made of somewhat more flexible LDPE so they can snap onto the container to close it.

Polypropylene (PP) is also a polyolefin moisture barrier plastic fabricated into clear films and some bottles (not transparent). As a film material, it is an excellent water-vapor barrier with transparency. It is widely used as a water vapor–barrier film for snacks, hard baked goods, candies, and so on. Food containers made from PE do not soften in the dishwasher and do not melt during hot filling processes. For this reason, most plastic tubs for dairy products are polypropylene sealed with flexible aluminum foil (both heat-resistant materials). Polypropylene can also be molded into disposable bottles to contain liquids, powders, or similar consumer products.

Polyvinylidene chloride (PVDC, also known as Saran wrap) is an excellent water-vapor, fat, odor, and oxygen barrier. It is used in laminations for an oxygen barrier in retort package lidding materials. Polyvinylidene chloride is applied as a water-based coating to other plastic films, such as biaxially oriented polypropylene (BOPP) and polyester (PET). This coating increases the barrier properties of the film, reducing the permeability of the film to oxygen and flavors and thus extending the shelf life of the food inside the package.

Ethylene vinyl alcohol (EVOH) is an excellent oxygen barrier material that is moisture susceptible and so must be protected, usually by lamination or coextrusion with polypropylene film. It's probably the most widely applied oxygen barrier material used today, found in almost all barrier retort cans, bowls, and trays.

Polyester

Polyester is a category of plastic polymers that contain the ester functional group in their main chain. Depending on the chemical structure, polyester can be a thermoplastic or thermoset; however, the most common polyesters are thermoplastics.

Thermoplastic materials are those that can be melted and resolidified without degradation. Most plastics used for food and beverage applications are thermoplastics. Thermosets harden when heated and set into a solid that does not remelt without degradation.

Polyethylene terephthalate (PET) is the most common thermoplastic polymer resin of the polyester family and is used in fibers for textiles (most famously, "Dacron Polyester"), containers for liquids and foods, and many other commercial applications.

Because PET is an excellent water and moisture barrier material, plastic bottles made from PET are widely used for water and soft drinks. In this form, it is the most widely recycled of all the plastics simply due to the enormous number of PET bottles in use in the beverage industry, which ultimately become part of the solid waste stream. PET is also used in flexible food packaging, and if crystallizable PET is used, the trays can be used for frozen dinners, since they withstand both freezing and oven baking temperatures. Lightly metallized PET film is used in microwave susceptor constructions for browning and cooking food in microwave ovens.

Polystyrene (PS) for food packaging may be foamed (expanded) to produce a very lightweight, yet fairly strong material. PS is used extensively for supermarket trays for meat and produce and for restaurant take-away food packaging (opaque foam "clamshells"). It is also widely used in hot drink cups and egg cartons. Solid polystyrene may be oriented for strength and transparency and may be blended with rubber to offer a readily formable non-barrier container, such as a cup or bowl. It has little oxygen or water vapor barrier capability and therefore is used mainly as structural material.

FIGURE 15.13 **Expanded polystyrene thermoformed clamshell for QSR take-away food for short-term thermal insulation.**

travellinglight/Getty Images, Inc.

The majority of nylon (polyamide) is used as a component of coextruded or laminated multilayer films for packaging of foods sensitive to oxygen, such as fresh and processed meats, smoked fish, cheeses, and prepared meals. Nylon films are strong and puncture-resistant; they have high barrier properties against oxygen, carbon dioxide, and many aroma chemicals; and they have superior elastic properties.

Polyvinyl chloride (PVC) is not used as much as it could be in food packaging applications because of the potential toxicity of its chemical constituents, which include chlorine, phthalates (for softening; not used in rigid PVC such as that used for plumbing pipes and vinyl siding), and lead. Some of these constituents have been shown to leach out of the plastic and into the environment, where they may pose health hazards. In addition, when incinerated, PVC creates dioxins, which have been classified as carcinogens. This limits its ability to be recycled, and in fact it is the least recycled of all of the plastics.

That said, for more than 40 years PVC film has been used as stretch or cling film for overwrapping fresh meat, poultry, and produce trays in retail stores to provide a transparent, low-moisture-permeable, high-gas-permeable material that can retard respiratory anaerobiosis in produce and provide adequate oxygen to retain the red color of fresh meats. For food catering and foodservice applications, PVC is still preferred because its stretchability and cling are much better than common consumer wraps.

One of the thermoset materials is the epoxy amine made from BPA (bisphenol A). Bisphenol A is used primarily to make plastics (particularly polycarbonate plastic) and epoxy resins. Products using bisphenol A have been in commercial use since 1957. BPA-based plastic is clear and tough, and is made into a variety of common consumer goods, such as the 5-gallon water bottles used on office water coolers, sports equipment, CDs, and DVDs. Epoxy resins containing BPA are used to line water pipes, and as coatings on the inside of most food and beverage cans and the lining of metal bottle caps to protect the food from direct contact with the metal.

BPA exhibits hormone-like properties that raised concern about its suitability in some consumer products and food containers, in particular baby bottles, baby food containers, and "sippy cups." Since 2008, several governments have investigated its safety, and the publicity that followed prompted many retailers to withdraw polycarbonate baby products and water bottles. In 2012 the FDA ended its authorization to use BPA in baby bottles and infant formula packaging, based on market abandonment, not for health concerns (which the FDA still feels have not been proven). The European Union and Canada have banned BPA use in baby bottles as well. Also, due to BPA health concerns in Japan, epoxy coatings in food and beverage cans have been mostly replaced by PET film.

SPI: The Plastics Industry Trade Association represents the entire plastics industry supply chain in the United States, including processors, machinery and equipment manufacturers, raw materials suppliers, and recyclers. The SPI Resin Identification Coding System is a set of symbols placed on plastics to identify the polymer type. It was developed by SPI

FIGURE 15.14 The SPI Resin Identification Coding System.

Resin Code	Polymer Name & Abbreviation	Original Uses	Recycled Uses
(1)	Polyethylene terephthalate (PET or PETE)	Water and soft drink (soda) bottles Mouthwash bottles Peanut butter jars	"Polar fleece" Car bumpers Luggage
(2)	High-density polyethylene (HDPE)	Milk jugs Margarine tubs Yogurt containers	Playground equipment Floor tiles Laundry detergent bottles
(3)	Polyvinyl chloride (PVC or V)	Shampoo bottles Medical tubing Windex® bottles	Plastic decking Mud flaps Speed bumps
(4)	Low-density polyethylene (LDPE)	Squeeze bottles Shopping bags Carpeting	Trash-can liners 6-pack rings Shipping envelopes
(5)	Polypropylene (PP)	Straws Medicine bottles Syrup bottles	Car window ice scrapers Bike racks Lawn rakes
(6)	Polystyrene (PS)	Vending cups Egg cartons Styrofoam	Light switch plates Packing peanuts Insulation
(7)	Polycarbonate, acrylic, nylon, fiberglass, barrier plastics, other ("O")	5-gallon water bottles CDs and DVDs Sunglasses	Plastic decking Plastic benches

Source: J. J. Cousminer

in 1988 and is used internationally. The primary purpose of the codes was to make separation of the many similar-appearing plastic container types easier for recycling centers across the country. Separation must be done carefully because each type of plastic must be recycled separately. Even one piece of the wrong type of resin can ruin a mix.

The symbols used in the code consist of arrows that cycle clockwise to form a rounded triangle surrounding a number, often with an acronym representing the plastic below the triangle. These codes do not indicate how difficult the item is to recycle, nor how often the plastic may be recycled. It is an arbitrarily agreed upon code that has no other meaning aside from identifying the polymer used to manufacture each specific plastic in order to facilitate future recycling of the plastic.

Use of the recycling symbol in the coding of plastics has led to ongoing consumer confusion about which plastics are readily recyclable. In many communities throughout the United States, PETE and HDPE are the only plastics collected in municipal recycling programs. Some regions, though, are expanding the range of plastics collected as markets become available. Los Angeles, for example, recycles all clean plastics regardless of resin type. That said, plastic films and wraps are rarely recycled due to the difficulty in collecting and separating them from other trash.

Package Testing Principles and Protocols

Laboratory testing for flexible raw materials and finished packages is performed to gain information for use in remediation or correction of problems and for optimizing the quality of package materials and finished structures. Chemical and biological interactions of packaging and food—permeation (passage of gases through the apparently solid walls of the container), and transmission (entry through minute openings such as the seal area of the package structure)—are measured instrumentally and objectively. This includes real-time testing, which can be up to one year, and accelerated shelf-life testing (ASLT), where testers increase package storage temperatures to hasten the end of product life. This simulates real-time testing in a much shorter timespan and allows fairly good predictability of actual shelf life. The goal is to evaluate changes to the package's contents during shelf life because maintaining the eating quality of the food contents is the real objective of any and all packaging. Evaluations are conducted through consumer sensory testing, analytical testing, and physical and chemical observations. Sensory testing, when performed objectively, is often the best measure of food quality. Materials are tested for properties such as:

- Permeability—of gases, moisture, and water vapor
- Strength—tearing, puncture, impact, compression
- Gauge—size or thickness
- Odor barrier—effectiveness

Conditioning of the materials to uniform predefined moisture and temperature conditions is often performed before testing to minimize external environmental variables.

Filled production or test packages are evaluated for:

- Seal and closure strength
- Transmission of gas, water vapor, and odors
- Vibrations to simulate travel (road, rail, ocean, air)
- Impact—drop test
- Compression resistance—stacking in warehouse and on trucks or rail cars
- Where appropriate, time for product to reach unacceptability as determined by sensory, chemical, or microbiological testing

● Economics

Package economics requires understanding the total system—materials, labor, production, and distribution—to measure the actual cost of packaging. Generally, the total cost of packaging is about 7 percent of the final retail price, but this is a general average for all foods and beverages. Total cost of packaging includes:

- The primary package—that is, the individual container (tray, bottle, jar, can)—with which the food or beverage is in direct contact. Also, the lid, cap, film, or other closure.
- The overwrap or shrinkwrap, if applicable.
- The label, sleeve, or outer box that goes around the inner package. This is where the product identification, package graphics, ingredient statement, nutritional facts panel, net weight statement, preparation instructions, health and nutrition claims (if any), UPC code, and name of producer are located.
- Secondary packaging, also called *unitizing packaging*, which holds a set number of individual units to be sold as a group—for example, six-pack folding cartons for beer.
- Distribution packaging—that is, outer cases (often fiberboard)—used to pack multiple primary or secondary packages (12-packs, 24-packs, and so on).
- Label stock for the secondary packaging. Also packing tape or glue to seal the cases, and stretch film to secure multiple cases to a pallet for shipping.
- The pallet.

These are general requirements. Variations occur with each product being packaged.

● Environmental Impact

Municipal solid waste (MSW)— commonly known as trash or garbage—consists of everyday items people use and then throw away, such as product packaging, grass clippings, furniture, clothing, bottles, food scraps, newspapers, appliances, paint, and batteries. This waste comes from homes, schools, hospitals, and businesses. In 2013, Americans generated about 250 million tons of trash.[3]

Packaging of all kinds, including paper and paperboard (not just food packaging), constitutes 25 to 30 percent of municipal solid waste. Of this, one of the largest volumes is retail packaging, such as expanded polystyrene from take-out food and supermarket delicatessens, but this is still only a fraction of total solid waste. Waste disposal strategies are critically important, and actions in this highly emotional issue should be carefully considered.

A company can choose source reduction, which reduces the quantity of packaging used—already a continuing goal of converters and packaging firms, for economic reasons. Biodegradable packaging is not yet truly effective or commercially feasible but is attractive because it seems so simple. Starch-based package materials continue to be studied; some have been commercialized. Polylactic acid (PLA) is a thermoplastic derived from cornstarch that has been commercialized as a selectively compostable package material.

Incineration waste-to-energy is effective in Japan and other countries, and where used in the United States. Trash, including paper and paperboard and plastic materials, is combusted to produce energy that generates electric power in waste-to-energy plants.

Dumping is strictly controlled in the United States because of problems with polluting the water supply and with reduced land area available for landfill. Sanitary landfills are now mandated to ultimately become parkland or building sites. Among the potential usable by-products of sanitary landfills are gases from anaerobic decomposition of waste that can be burned for energy or for production of electricity.

Recycling is currently performed by almost all major package material suppliers for all materials in their own plants. The economics of pre-consumer waste, such as corrugated paperboard and office papers, is often quite good, so these materials are used in recycling plants as raw materials. Post-consumer waste recycling economics is generally poor because post-consumer wastes are an agglomeration of many materials that must be precisely separated to not contaminate the recovery streams. Nevertheless, this is possibly the best method in the long run, as many communities are accustomed to the idea of separating recyclables from garbage every week for curbside pickup.

Sustainable Packaging

Organizations are now being measured by shareholders and independent agencies for their contributions to maintaining the natural environment—that is, for their part in supporting a sustainable planet.

Sustainable packaging is a new way of designing packaging from the ground up that encompasses systems that do not deplete the planet's natural resources (oxygen, water, petroleum, and plant life). Some components are based on new technology (for example, using hybrid vehicles exclusively for distribution of materials), and some are based on updated versions of older technologies (solar power, wind power, geothermal power, and so on). Inorganic packaging materials are designed to be not only completely nontoxic and recyclable but also reusable, and organic packaging materials are expected to be not just compostable but also to add nutrients to the soil. Sustainable systems minimize use of energy and aim to reuse all materials as renewable resources. Benefits of sustainable packaging include:

- The safety and health of people and the environment throughout the package's life cycle.
- Meets market criteria for performance and cost.
- Packaging is sourced, manufactured, distributed, and recycled using renewable energy.
- Takes advantage of clean production technologies.
- Maximizes use of renewable resources.
- Packaging is engineered to optimize materials and energy.
- Packaging materials are recovered and reused or recycled using "cradle-to-cradle" rather than "cradle-to-grave" mentality. Used packaging should not be buried; it should be "resurrected."

The transition to sustainable packaging requires many changes because renewable energy and material sources are not yet economically feasible in most countries, and it will be some time before scientists develop the efficiencies necessary for planetary sustainability.

Further Examples of Current and Future Trends in Food Packaging

Manufacturers and consumers are dictating closer ties between technology and marketing, demanding better product safety and quality closer to fresh or freshly prepared. Current trends include:

- Expansion of the range of packaging materials made for hot-fill-and-hold processing beyond glass jars (current) to pouches, plastic tubs, and trays.
- Development of retortable multilayer barrier plastic cans, pouches, and trays—increasingly used for seafood, poultry, rice, pastas.
- Evolution of an aseptic process and packaging for larger particulate-containing low-acid foods such as chunky soups and entrées. Storage and distribution may be refrigerated (extended shelf life) or ambient (shelf-stable).
- Controlled or modified atmosphere packaging designed for minimally processed foods (in particular, those that must comply with the USDA's requirement for "natural"), now including micro-oxygen packaging, where total oxygen in the package is limited to less than 50 parts per billion in prepared and packaged foods.
- Development of active packaging, which senses change in the package environment and changes properties in response. Oxygen scavengers, which remove residual oxygen in a limited range of food and beverage packages,

are a subset of active packaging. Next generation: odor-removing packaging.

- Expansion of technology for self-heating packages for beverages and meals, which has been hampered by technical issues. Such packaging is successfully used for military field rations and a handful of specialty retail and camping products. Self-cooling packages are under development.
- Perfection of packages that signal spoilage or even the presence of pathogens—these are highly publicized but not currently practical, as they generate too many false readings.
- Use of glass-coated films in retort pouches that allow visibility of contents.
- Integration of processing and packaging technologies for improved health and safety—for example, metal cans with inert plastic film coatings (instead of potentially harmful chemical coatings) inside and out.

Conclusion

Packaging affects every step of the food production process, from the farm, to the processor, to the market, to the restaurant, and, ultimately, to the consumer. It is critical for Culinology® professionals to have a basic understanding of packaging, where it comes from, what the packaging options are, and how packaging is integrated with not just the innovative food products they work to develop, but also the environment we all live in.

Resources

Brody, Aaron L., and John Lord. *Developing New Food Products for a Changing Marketplace.* 2nd ed. Boca Raton, FL: CRC Press, 2007.

Brody, Aaron L., and K. Marsh, eds. *Encyclopedia of Packaging Technology.* 2nd ed. New York: John Wiley & Son, 1997; 3rd ed. Hoboken, NJ: John Wiley & Sons, 2010.

Robertson, Gordon. *Food Packaging.* 2nd ed. New York: Marcel, Dekker, 2006; 3rd ed. Boca Raton, FL: CRC Press, 2013.

Selke, Susan. *Understanding Plastics Packaging Technology.* Munich, Germany: Hanser, 1997.

Selke, Susan, John Cutler, and Ruben Hernandez. *Plastics Packaging.* 2nd ed. Munich, Germany: Hanser, 2004.

Soroka, Walter. *Fundamentals of Packaging Technology.* 4th ed. Niles, IL: Institute of Packaging Professionals, 2010.

Periodicals:

- *Brand Packaging*
- *Flexible Packaging*
- *Food and Beverage Packaging*
- *Package Design*
- *Packaging Digest,* especially the Packaging Resources Book and Directory
- *Packaging World*
- *Packaging Strategies*

Other books, conference proceedings, and directories, including the Package Machinery Manufacturers Institute (PMMI) Directory in electronic format: www.pmmi.org.

[1]Van Arsdel, Cople, and Morgan (1973).

[2]http://www.compaxpackaging.com/packaging_history_metal.html

[3]U.S. Environmental Protection Agency, *Municipal Solid Waste Generation, Recycling, and Disposal in the United States: Facts and Figures for 2011* (May 2013).

16 Developing Nutritious Food Products

Lead Author: Darryl L. Holliday, Ph.D., CRC®, Assistant Professor, Our Lady of Holy Cross College

Margaret D. Condrasky, Ed.D, R.D., CCE, Associate Professor, Food, Nutrition, and Packaging Sciences Department, Clemson University

Marie Hegler, Food Safety and Nutrition Agent, Cooperative Extension Service, Clemson University

Contributor: John W. Finley, Professor and Department Head of Food Science, Louisiana State University

Introduction: Overview of Health, Well-Being, and Healthy Eating

At its most basic, food is important to us because it delivers the basic nutritional needs to sustain life. Its preparation and eating rituals are ingrained in all cultures, it is central to most social occasions, and, as a result, it is essential to our lifestyles. Modern nutritional science has improved our understanding of the relationship between what we eat and our health and wellness, both physically and emotionally. Concerns related to the current U.S. obesity epidemic bring about questions of how much and what we eat, but the solution is not simply less food and more exercise. The pleasures of eating satisfying foods must also be factored in, along with an appropriate diet and exercise level, and that diet should include a growing list of micronutrients that help protect us from disease. The ideal healthy lifestyle should include a balance of:

1. Regular exercise
2. A healthy, balanced diet
3. Proper amount of rest

A healthy diet includes foods that provide adequate energy and nutrients for us to thrive in mind, body, and spirit, with occasional treats to provide pleasure. Foods must provide sufficient amounts of proteins, fats, and carbohydrates while being rich in the essential vitamins, minerals, and that most easily overlooked nutrient: water. By integrating nutritional principles and applications, we can create delicious, nutritious dishes (and indulgent snacks and desserts) that inspire, tantalize, and, ultimately, satisfy, while also delivering foods that enhance health and wellness. Culinology® is our means to developing satisfying and pleasurable foods while supporting good health and helping prevent chronic disease.

Our Changing Understanding of Nutrition, Food, and Health

Modern research is ongoing in nutrition, food science, and medicine to better understand how food and health are related. This integrated approach yields frequently changing theories and recommendations as new technologies emerge, often resulting in confusion for the consumer. This also presents a challenge for food and health professionals whose main focus is the ever-present need to meet the latest nutritional guidelines.

A perfect case in point is the latest revamp of the government's nutritional guidelines. After promoting various forms of the food pyramid for decades, the U.S. Department of Agriculture (USDA) has switched to a dinner plate icon. Visit the USDA website for current information.[1]

That said, even a clear understanding of the latest data on the impact of diet on health is not useful if it is ignored. For the new recommendations to be of value, fresh and innovative ways must be found to deliver them in easily accessible foods (nutritious, tasty, affordable, and convenient) that can be part of an improved diet. For more than 30 years, nutritionists have recommended that we eat more fruits and vegetables, and yet statistics show that consumption has not changed significantly during that time.[2] Many people either do not like, cannot afford, or have limited access to fresh fruits and vegetables; therefore, they do not consume them. This is just one of many challenges for today's Culinology® professional.

Basic Nutrition Principles and Rationale

To design sound, nutrition-based foods for a healthier diet, we must examine the basic nutrients and their roles in food: protein, lipids, carbohydrates, vitamins, minerals, phytochemicals, and water. But first, we must look at the many factors that influence dietary decisions.

Calories

The first consideration is the energy content of foods, measured in calories (shorthand for kilocalories). Total calories in a food or beverage are a measure of its energy content, which is the total energy provided by the fats, protein, carbohydrates, and alcohol in the food. The number of calories in a food is measured by a calorimeter, which incinerates the food and measures the heat given off. Using that measurement, an estimation of how the body would utilize the food can be made, resulting in a calorie designation in kilocalories (kcal). The energy content of the macronutrients are as follows:

Fats: 9 kcal/g

Alcohol: 7 kcal/g

Protein: 4 kcal/g

Carbohydrate: 4 kcal/g

These values are based on each of these food components being 100 percent digested, which isn't always the case (for example, resistant starches, a type of carbohydrate that provides only 3 kcal/g).

Seventy percent of the energy in the diet is used for the body's basal metabolic requirements (BMR): temperature maintenance, heartbeat, respiration, digestion, and so on. The rest is either expended through exercise or stored in the body as fat. As little as 100 extra calories per day can result in the gain of 10 pounds in a year. Exercise notwithstanding, if an individual consumes the exact amount of calories his or her body requires, that person will maintain current weight. Obviously, by consuming less than the calories expended, a person loses weight.

Serving Size Versus Portion Size

Serving size is the unit of measure describing the average single serving of a given food. With few exceptions, it appears on the nutrition facts panel (NFP) of every packaged food product sold in the United States. This is the standardized amount of food eaten in one serving as specified by the USDA, and it allows side-by-side comparisons within categories. That said, it is important to carefully read the NFP on all packaged foods because even similar-looking foods (such as breakfast cereals) may appear to have the same nutritional measurements when in actuality these measurements are based on different serving sizes.

Foods that are measured in bulk, such as sugar, milk, and cereal, are listed in common household measurements like cups, tablespoons, and fluid ounces. Foods that are usually divided to serve more than one person or for more than one meal, such as pizza, cake, and pie, are listed in fractional amounts like "¼ pizza." Also, foods that come in individual units, such as slices of bread, potato chips, and individual snack packets are listed as "15 chips" or "1 package."

Portion size is the amount of food a person *chooses* to eat. For instance, you would eat more than the recommended serving size if you ate a whole pizza rather than the quarter-pizza listed, or you would eat less if you ate ½ cup of cereal rather than the 1 cup listed on the food label.

Portion Control

Over time, U.S. consumers have grown accustomed to eating oversized portions. Portion sizes currently selected by adults are not only larger than those established by the USDA but

FIGURE 16.1 **Portion distortion.**

20 Years Ago	Today
Coffee (with whole milk and sugar) 8-ounce serving size 45 calories	**Mocha** (with steamed whole milk and syrup) 16-ounce serving size 350 calories
Blueberry Muffin 1.5-ounce serving size 210 calories	**Blueberry Muffin** 4-ounce serving size 500 calories
Pepperoni Pizza 2 slices 500 calories	**Pepperoni Pizza** 2 slices 850 calories
Chicken Caesar Salad 1½-cup serving size 390 calories	**Chicken Caesar Salad** 3½-cup serving size 790 calories
Popcorn 5-cup serving size 270 calories	**Popcorn** 11-cup serving size 790 calories
Cheesecake 3-ounce serving size 260 calories	**Cheesecake** 6-ounce serving size 640 calories
Chocolate Chip Cookie 1½-inch diameter serving size 55 calories	**Chocolate Chip Cookie** 5-inch diameter serving size 275 calories
Chicken Stir Fry 2-cup serving size 435 calories	**Chicken Stir Fry** 4½-cup serving size 865 calories

Source: National Heart, Lung, and Blood Institute Obesity Initiative, Portion Distortion II Interactive Quiz. Accessed at: http://hp2010 .nhlbihin.net/portion.

also significantly larger than portion sizes selected by young adults two decades ago, according to a recent study in the *Journal of the American Dietetic Association*.[3] The researchers found that portion sizes of "virtually all foods and beverages prepared for immediate consumption" have increased over the last two decades, as have portion sizes of individually packaged and ready-to-eat prepared foods and items served at fast-food restaurants. The serving sizes set by the U.S. government are much smaller than the actual portions served in restaurants, and even in the home, meaning excess calories are routinely consumed. This is likely a major factor in the obesity epidemic.

Chef's Portioning Habits

In recent decades, the frequency of eating out and prevalence of obesity in all populations, groups, and ages have increased dramatically, making the importance of controlling calorie intake in the restaurant setting more significant. Chefs play an integral role in preparing and serving healthful food. While surveys conducted by Clemson University report that chefs recognize the importance of nutrition in menu planning, many prepare meals that are inconsistent with the U.S. Dietary Guidelines. Little is known about chefs' opinions or knowledge of ingredient utilization regarding modification for healthy recipes or about the role chefs play in determining portion sizes in the United States.

Dr. Margaret Condrasky of Clemson University, in collaboration with researchers from Pennsylvania State University, conducted a study to determine the portioning habits of chefs. A survey was distributed to 300 chefs to learn who establishes restaurant portion sizes, factors influencing these decisions, what food portion sizes are served in restaurants, and chefs' opinions regarding nutrition information and weight management. Results identified executive chefs as being most responsible for establishing restaurant portion sizes, with presentation of foods, food cost, and customer expectations as influential factors. However, 76 percent of chefs thought they served "regular" portions when they actually served portions 2 to 4 times larger than serving sizes recommended by the U.S. government.[4]

The study also found that while chefs believe the amount of food served influences customer consumption and large portions pose problems for weight management, their attitudes varied regarding whether or not it is the customer's responsibility to eat a reasonable amount of food when served a large portion. As portion size is a major determining factor of energy intake and the results of the study show (1) customer expectations and (2) cost as the greatest influences in determining restaurant portion sizes, strategies are needed to encourage chefs to provide and promote smaller portions more appropriate for customers' energy requirements.[5]

Energy Density

Energy density (ED) relates to the amount of energy (calories) per amount of food consumed. It is commonly expressed in kcal/g.

$$kcal/g = ED$$

Equal amounts of foods with higher fat content have higher energy densities than foods with lower fat content. In other words, foods higher in energy density, such as sweet baked goods and fried foods, provide excessive calories per gram consumed, while the same amount of foods lower in energy density, such as water-dense fruits and vegetables, provide much lower calorie content. However, not all energy-dense foods are empty-calorie foods. Nuts are energy-dense because of their high fat content, but they also provide protein, vitamins, and minerals. Increasing consumption of foods with lower energy density, such as fruits and vegetables, and lowering fat intake can decrease caloric intake while maintaining a sense of satiety.

Volumetrics

The Volumetrics Eating Plan developed by Barbara Rolls, professor of nutritional sciences at Pennsylvania State University, focuses on reducing the energy density of the diet using the latest research on controlling hunger while managing calories.[6] Rather than eating smaller portions of energy-dense fattening foods, eating larger portions of foods with lower energy density (such as fruits and vegetables) enhances the feeling of fullness and decreases the feeling of being shortchanged.[7]

With consumers expecting more food for less money, the food industry may find it difficult to sell reduced portions without drastically reducing price. This makes knowledge and know-how about energy density important in healthy new food product development. As a research chef or product developer with the goal of customer satisfaction, how do you decrease calories per bite while maintaining satisfying portions? Create foods high in water content and fiber and low in fat and calorie density, such as those that are fruit- and vegetable-based, plus brothy soups, lean meats, and low-fat dairy products. Here is a list of ways to reduce calories per bite, adapted from *Volumetrics*:[8]

More Fiber

- Add beans, lentils, and peas to soups and salads.
- Use high-fiber vegetables, like carrots and broccoli, as side dishes or additions to salads and soups.
- Replace white rice, bread, and pasta with brown rice, whole-grain products, whole wheat pasta, and exotic grains like bulgur or amaranth.
- Substitute almonds or other nuts for croutons in salads.
- Experiment with international dishes that use whole grains, such as tabouli, or lentils, such as Indian dals.
- Use whole fruits and vegetables. Most of the fiber is in the skin or peel.

- Cook vegetables briefly because the longer they cook, the more fiber they lose. Try steaming them until they are crisp yet tender to retain most of the fiber content.
- Use oatmeal, whole wheat flour, brown rice, or wheat germ in baked goods.

More Lean Proteins

- Protein-rich foods are particularly satiating because they control hunger when calories are restricted.
- Choose high-protein foods of low energy density and cooked with little added fat, such as lean steak, pork tenderloin, skinless chicken or turkey breast, fish, shellfish, egg whites, beans, and tofu.
- Don't overlook vegetable sources of high-quality protein, such as soy, quinoa, and complementary combinations of grains and legumes; these also provide fiber, vitamins, minerals, and an assortment of phytonutrients.

Nonfat or Low-Fat Dairy

- Most dairy products are available in low-fat or nonfat versions.

Use Low-Sodium Stocks, Vegetable Juice, or Water

- Soups based on broth, rather than cream or a starchy puree, are very low in energy density and provide a satisfying larger portion with fewer calories.

- Water, which lowers the energy density of a food, can be incorporated into foods to increase volume and enhance satiety.

Add Flavor Rather than Sodium

- Fresh herbs, spices, garlic, vinegars, and citrus juices enhance flavor without adding sodium or calories.

Eat More Vegetables and Fruits

- Add fruits to side dishes and desserts.
- Add vegetables such as zucchini, yellow squash, peppers, onions, eggplant, and spinach to pasta dishes and pizza.
- Increase the proportion of vegetables in stir-fry dishes, fajitas, soups, and stews.

The Food Guide Pyramid

In 1943, the USDA released the first Food Guide Pyramid, which grouped foods into seven categories. In the mid-1950s, the pyramid was simplified into four food groups: milk, meat, fruit and vegetable, and bread and cereal. In 1979, the USDA issued the "Hassle-Free Guide to a Better Diet," which included a fifth food group for fats, sweets, and alcoholic beverages. The Food Guide Pyramid depicted in Figure 16.2 was introduced in 1992 as a revamped addition of the "Hassle-Free Guide."

FIGURE 16.2 **Food Guide Pyramid.**

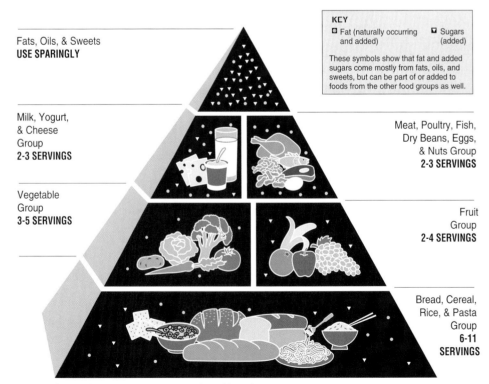

Source: U.S. Department of Agriculture/U.S. Department of Health and Human Services.

MyPyramid and MyPlate

In 2005, the USDA released the MyPyramid Plan based on the Dietary Guidelines for Americans.[9] MyPyramid was a refinement of earlier food guide pyramids, which incorporated the latest dietary recommendations of the USDA. It could be tailored to fit most people based on characteristics such as age, gender, level of activity, and pregnancy status. Additional customization, which was available online, allowed people to adjust their diet for weight loss, maintenance, or gain. The silhouette of a person walking up steps represented two concepts: (1) the need for physical activity, and (2) the steps to a healthier individual. Lastly, food categories were presented in six vertical bands: grains, vegetables, fruits, oils, milk, and meat (including red meat, poultry, and seafood) and beans, with a different color marking each. The bands were thicker on the bottom and thinner on top to show that there are healthier food choices within each category, and they were different widths to illustrate the relative amounts of foods in each category that should be eaten.

In 2010, after 67 years of food pyramids, the USDA decided there was a better graphic to illustrate the latest scientific findings on the ideal diet and came up with MyPlate. They also simplified the overall recommendations to the following:

- Fill half the plate with fruits and vegetables.
- Divide the other half between grains and proteins.
- Add a glass of dairy.
- Eat less, and avoid oversized portions.
- Increase consumption of fruits and vegetables.
- Make half of carbohydrate consumption whole grains.

- Drink low-fat (1 percent) or nonfat milk.
- Reduce consumption of processed foods with high sodium levels.
- Drink water instead of sugary drinks.

Drilling down yields additional recommendations:

- Choose lean meats and poultry, trim off excess fat and skin, and cook without added fat or breadings.
- Choose seafood as the main protein at least twice a week. Look for seafood rich in omega-3 fatty acids, such as salmon, trout, and herring.
- Choose beans, peas, or soy products as a main dish or part of a meal often.
- Oils are not a food group, but they do provide essential nutrients in the diet. The monounsaturated fatty acids (MUFAs) and polyunsaturated fatty acids (PUFAs) found in fish, nuts, and vegetable oils do not raise LDL (bad) cholesterol levels in the blood. In addition to the essential fatty acids they contain, oils are the major source of vitamin E in the typical U.S. diet.
- While some oil is needed for health, oils are quite caloric (9 kcal/g). Therefore, limit the amount of oil consumed to balance total calorie intake. Most individuals should limit their intake to the equivalent of 2 tablespoons of oil (28 g) per day.
- Physical activity and nutrition work together for better health. Being active increases the amount of calories burned. As people age, their metabolism slows, so maintaining energy balance (and body weight) requires moving more and eating less.

FIGURE 16.3 MyPlate.

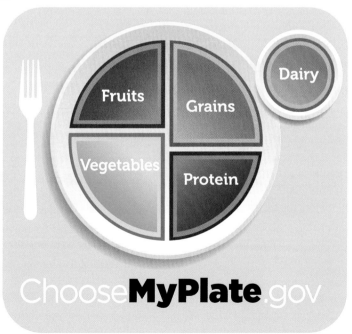

Source: U.S. Department of Agriculture/U.S. Department of Health and Human Services.

Many more recommendations are at the USDA MyPlate website.[10]

Dietary Guidelines and Portion Recommendations

The *Dietary Guidelines for Americans*, of which MyPlate is a part, are published jointly every five years (since 1980) by the U.S. Department of Health and Human Services (HHS) and the USDA. The Guidelines provide authoritative advice about how good dietary habits can promote health and reduce risk for major chronic diseases. These recommendations serve as the basis for federal food and nutrition education programs. It is advisable to check the latest edition of the Guidelines (2010) on the USDA website for the most up-to-date information.[11]

More Matters®

Developed by the Produce for Better Health Foundation (PBH) in partnership with the Centers for Disease Control and Prevention (CDC), Fruits and Veggies—More Matters® is a national public health initiative created to encourage Americans to eat more fruits and vegetables—fresh, frozen, canned, dried, and 100 percent juice. The initiative is a national call to action that is attainable and easy for people to understand: simply, eat more fruits and vegetables. More than 90 percent of U.S. residents consume fewer fruits and vegetables than the daily amount—3½ to 5½ cups, depending on age and gender—recommended by the Dietary Guidelines for Americans.

When it comes to good nutrition, all forms of fruits and vegetables matter. With numerous options and convenient packaging that makes fruits and vegetables easy to store and serve, eating the recommended amount is easier than ever.

- Most frozen and canned foods are processed within hours of harvest, so their flavor and nutritional value are preserved.
- Studies show that recipes prepared with canned produce have similar nutritional values to those prepared with fresh or frozen ingredients, although consumers should be aware that canned vegetables often contain elevated levels of sodium from salt added during processing, and should compensate by reducing the addition of extra salt on the stove or at the table.[12–14] The same can be said for sugar or syrups added to canned fruits. Read and understand nutrition statements!
- Canned foods are cooked before packaging, so they are recipe-ready.
- Frozen foods also require little preparation—washing and slicing, for instance, is already done.

Many people struggle to consume the necessary servings of vegetables because of price, availability, flavor, required prep steps (washing, trimming, peeling, cutting, cooking, and so on), or a combination thereof. In many cases, meats, espe-cially high-fat varieties, are less expensive, easier to prepare, and more filling. To motivate at-risk individuals to follow a more vegetable-centric diet plan, researchers from Louisiana State University are combining their knowledge of food science, culinary arts, and nutrition to create ingredients and meals that will lead to increased vegetable consumption. The meals use vegetable-based meat, poultry, and seafood extenders to decrease fat while adding fiber to hold moisture in reformed products such as patties, nuggets, links, and restructured and reshaped seafoods. These technologies are designed to offer the consumer a tasty, low-cost, more appealing, and more easily accessible source of fruits and vegetables. Within the Food Science and Human Nutrition department at Clemson University, research, education, and outreach efforts are coordinated within the CU CHEFS® instructional program. New product development and nutrition educator teams engage the community and foodservice industry in healthy menu creation.

Nutritional Analysis Software

Nutritional analysis software is a valuable tool in creating high-quality, nutritionally appropriate food products and package labels. Available software programs range from very expensive, covering a giant database of food items, to essentially free, covering a more moderate selection of food items and nutrients. Depending on your company's needs and the range of ingredients you are working with, custom software can also be created.

Nutritional development software has pushed product development and nutrient analysis to new levels of ease and accuracy. They enable you to customize your work and save countless hours of data entry and hand calculations. In addition to the many label formats, numerous professional reports are available. Many allow the user to view the analysis as a spreadsheet, protein quality report, bar graph, single nutrient report, and many, many others. The cost for these programs depends on the software manufacturer, the number of users in a given company who will have access to the program, and whether they are installed onto a single computer, a corporate network, or accessed from a cloud network.

Product features can include:

- Child nutrition
- Supplement facts panel
- A meticulously researched database of more than 37,000 foods and food items, including raw materials, chemicals, and food industry ingredients. Users can add an unlimited number of new foods and modify existing foods.
- An intuitive, user-friendly interface that uses the latest in ingredient search technology
- Automatic nutrient analysis for 160+ nutritional components, including food exchanges
- Labels: United States, standard, tabular, dual declaration, aggregate, and more (including Canadian, Spanish, and bilingual formats)

- Trans fat data and label display option
- Automatic ingredient statements, allergen statements, and nutrient content claims
- Cost entry and calculations
- Fat formulator, which calculates approved data for meat-to-fat ratios and custom-blend products
- Moisture and fat recipe adjustments: Subtract or add water or fat, view results on screen immediately.
- Yield adjustments and tables: Enter food "as purchased," obtain nutrient values for edible portion only.
- Cloud access

While there are several excellent and quite sophisticated nutritional software programs available to rent or purchase, Gnutrition is a free nutrition analysis software program that uses the USDA Nutrient Database of Standard Reference, Release 13, 1999, as the source of food nutrient information.[15] It contains data on 81 nutrients for more than 5000 foods, which is significantly less than the paid versions but serves the basic needs of its users.

Gnutrition offers the following features:

- The ability to search the database for a specific food and examine its nutrient composition.
- The ability to create a recipe and to compute its nutritional composition, which can be compared to the users' own dietary goals.
- A searchable database of all the created recipes.
- The ability to record and plan meals day by day. The average and total nutrient intake can be computed over any given period.
- The MySQL database system, used to store the data.

⦿Ingredients: Nutrition and Function

Macronutrients (fats, protein, carbohydrates, and water) are the primary factors that determine the physical state and structure of foods. These rarely act independently. For example, it is the interaction of water, gluten protein, and pentosan polymers (structural carbohydrates) that determine the function of bread dough. Understanding the primary structures and functions of each macronutrient helps one appreciate their more complex interactions in real food systems.

The need for macronutrients in the diet can be very different for individuals depending on age, activity, and lifestyle; however, general ranges are recommended.[16] Total calories in the diet should be 45 to 65 percent carbohydrates, 10 to 35 percent protein, and 20 to 35 percent fats. Saturated fats should comprise less than 10 percent of total energy intake; therefore, a person consuming a 2000-calorie diet should take in only 200 calories (or about 22 g—about ¾ of an ounce) of saturated fat. Cholesterol intake should be limited to less than 300 mg (1/100th of an ounce, or roughly the amount in 2 egg yolks) per day.

Protein

Proteins are chemically the most complex of the food macronutrients, being composed of up to 21 amino acids bound together in polymers (long chains) that can range from a few amino acids to several thousand. Molecules of between 2 and 50 amino acids are called peptides; when the number of amino acids is above 50, these molecules are named *proteins*. Proteins can provide energy to the body (4 kcal/g), but, more importantly, they are the building blocks of all muscle and enzyme systems within the body. The functions of proteins are nutritional, biological, and structural. At the structural level, proteins include collagen, actin, myosin, and other musculoskeletal and cytoskeletal proteins that participate in the structure and strength of the body and its individual cells. At the molecular level, proteins participate in almost every process within cells, including establishing cell shape, providing mechanical strength, locomotion, chromosome separation in mitosis and meiosis, and facilitating intracellular transport of nutrients.

Enzymes, which are proteins, are vital for metabolism and catalyze thousands of biochemical reactions in the body. In addition, cell signaling, adhesion, and cycling, as well as immune responses, all depend on proteins. Some hormones, growth factors, and blood clotting factors are mostly proteins and play a dynamic role in the body. We cannot synthesize all the amino acids we need but must obtain these essential amino acids from the proteins in the foods we ingest. Complete proteins (those that contain all of the essential amino acids in appropriate ratios) are digested into the peptides and amino acids that are essential for metabolism.

From the nutritional standpoint, nine amino acids are considered essential because they cannot be synthesized in our bodies and must, as a consequence, be consumed as part of the diet. The essential amino acid distribution in various foods varies dramatically. Food designers must consider the amino acids present in assessing nutrition. For example, sports recovery products should be rich in the branched chain amino acids (BCAAs) such as valine, leucine, and isoleucine, which are most prevalent in whey proteins. These amino acids cannot be made by the body, so they must be consumed from food or supplements. Unlike other amino acids, which are broken down in the liver, BCAAs are metabolized in the muscles, where they produce energy or construct new protein—that is, muscle.

The Protein Digestibility Corrected Amino Acid Score (PDCAAS) is the preferred analytical method for evaluating the protein quality of a food based on the amino acid requirements of humans and their ability to digest it. The PDCAAS rating is universally recognized by the FAO/World Health Organization (WHO), as well as by the U.S. Food and Drug Administration (FDA), the USDA, and the National Academy of Sciences, as accurately measuring the correct relative nutritional value of animal and vegetable sources of protein in the diet.[17]

PDCAAS is based on human amino acid requirements, which makes it more appropriate for humans than a method based on the amino acid needs of animals. It is calculated using the following formula, wherein the limiting amino acid is the essential amino acid present in the least amount relative to the requirement for that amino acid:

$$\frac{\text{milligrams of limiting amino acid in 1 gram of test protein}}{\text{milligrams of same amino acid in 1 gram of known reference protein}} \times \text{fecal true digestibility percentage}$$

The fecal true digestibility percentage is the measurable amount of the test amino acid found in the feces after the test subject has finished digesting the test protein. The higher the amount found in the feces, the *less digestible* the original protein source and the smaller the amount of the amino acid that was absorbed by the body.

However, the PDCAAS does have limitations. For example, it takes no account of *where* the proteins are digested. Any amino acid that moves beyond the terminal ileum (small intestine) is not likely to be absorbed for use in protein synthesis. If it is then used by gut microflora, it will not be present in the feces and will only *appear* to have been digested. Similarly, any amino acid lost to antinutrients (digestion inhibitors of many kinds) won't show up in the feces either, and will also be assumed to have been digested. The PDCAAS method might also be considered incomplete because human diets, except in times of famine, almost never contain only one kind of protein.

However, calculating the PDCAAS of a total diet solely based on each of its individual constituents is impossible. That is because one food may provide an abundance of an amino acid that the other is missing, which means the PDCAAS of the total diet is higher than any one of the constituents. For example, grain protein has a PDCAAS of 0.4 to 0.5, limited by lysine. On the other hand, it contains more than enough methionine. White bean protein (and many other pulses) has a PDCAAS of 0.6 to 0.7, limited by methionine, but contains more than enough lysine. When both are eaten in roughly equal quantities in a diet, the PDCAAS of the *combined constituent* is 1.0 because each constituent's protein is complemented by the other.[18]

Lipids

While they provide highly concentrated energy (9 kcal/g), fats and oils have both positive and negative health effects. Trans fats and saturated fats are considered negative because they are associated with coronary heart disease, Alzheimer's disease, certain cancers, diabetes, and liver dysfunction. Conversely, monounsaturated fats, such as those in olive oil, are considered healthy, as are the omega-3 oils found in fatty fish, which have been recognized to provide clear health benefits.

Although good and bad fats have been getting a lot of attention for some time now, consumers are still asking for confirmation of which is which. Although all fats are high in calories, they are not all equal nutritionally. Depending on their structure, the fats in foods can be classified as saturated, monounsaturated, or polyunsaturated fats. Most foods contain a combination of fats, usually with one kind predominating.

The USDA recommends that fats should account for approximately 30 percent of daily calories, with saturated fats accounting for no more than 10 percent of total fat intake. Yet, the real emphasis should remain on the type of fat. Vegetable oils, avocados, nuts, and seeds may derive 85 to 100 percent of their calories from fat, but they are considered good fats because they are primarily composed of unsaturated fats.

Monounsaturated fats come primarily from plants, such as nuts, avocados, and olives, as well as the oils made from them, such as peanut, sesame, corn, canola, and olive oils. They tend to lower LDL cholesterol (the bad cholesterol) while increasing HDL cholesterol (the good cholesterol).

Polyunsaturated fats are also found mostly in plant sources, such as grain products, soybeans, sunflowers, safflowers, cottonseed, and flaxseed. These fats also tend to lower blood cholesterol levels. A special category of healthy polyunsaturated fats is known as omega-3 fatty acids. Omega 3s are found in oily fish like mackerel, salmon, trout, sardines, herring, and tuna as well as in flaxseed, and are shown to help control cholesterol and reduce blood pressure.[19]

Saturated fats and trans fats are known as bad fats because they are associated with higher LDL cholesterol levels in the blood and may cause an increased chance of clogged arteries. Clogged arteries make it harder for blood to get to and from the heart and can lead to high blood pressure, heart attack, or stroke. Saturated fats are found mainly in animal products like meat, poultry, lard, butter, regular milk, and egg yolk; cholesterol is found exclusively in animal fats. Trans fats are found mostly in man-made solid fats made from vegetable oils via hydrogenation, like shortenings, partially hydrogenated vegetable oils, and stick margarine. Consumption of trans fats is primarily from eating foods made with them—potato chips, crackers, pastries, snack cakes, cookies, French fries, and so on. The bottom line is that a diet high in saturated fats, trans fats, and cholesterol increases the risk of heart disease.

For more on lipids, see Chapter 9.

Cholesterol

Cholesterol is found only in animal fats, even unsaturated ones like fish oils, because cholesterol is an essential component of all animal cell membranes. In general, the higher the blood cholesterol, the more likely that heart disease will occur. As cholesterol is soluble in fat and blood is mostly water, cholesterol requires assistance from proteins to become soluble in blood. The two most influential proteins are high-density lipoproteins (HDL) and low-density lipoproteins (LDL). HDL could also stand for *heart disease lowering* because it helps remove cholesterol from the blood, while LDL is commonly referred to as "bad cholesterol" because it carries cholesterol that can be incorporated into the plaque that builds up in the arteries and causes heart disease. Therefore, an increased level of HDL and a decreased level of LDL in the blood is most desirable. One of the worst effects of consuming *trans fats* is that it does just the opposite: It raises LDL and lowers HDL.

Cholesterol is also an essential structural component of all mammalian cell membranes, of which it makes up approximately 20 percent. It is required to establish proper membrane permeability and fluidity and is thus manufactured by every cell. Within the cell membrane, cholesterol also functions in intracellular transport, cell signaling, and nerve conduction. Cholesterol is essential for all animal life.

For a man of about 150 pounds, typical total body-cholesterol synthesis is about 1 g (1000 mg) per day, and total body content is about 35 g (a little over an ounce), primarily located within the membranes of all the cells of the body.

Typical daily dietary intake of additional cholesterol in the United States is 200 to 300 mg. All foods containing animal fat contain cholesterol to varying extents. However, most ingested cholesterol is poorly absorbed, and the body compensates for any absorption of additional cholesterol by reducing internal cholesterol synthesis. For these reasons, cholesterol intake in food has little effect on total body cholesterol content or concentrations of cholesterol in the blood. It is the intake of excessive amounts of *saturated fats* and *trans fats* that has the greatest effect on increasing blood cholesterol levels.

Omega-3 and Omega-6 Fatty Acids

Linoleic acid and alpha-linolenic acid, known as omega-6 and omega-3 fatty acids, respectively, are considered essential fatty acids because the body cannot make them, meaning people must get them from food or supplements. Both are necessary for human health and are polyunsaturated fats that are stored in the fatty tissues and can be used as a source of energy. They also do a variety of important jobs in the body, from bolstering

immune system functions to helping form cell membranes and producing hormone-like compounds. Omega-6 fatty acids can be found in sunflower, safflower, corn, and soybean oils, while omega-3 fatty acids can be found in oily fish, walnuts, and dark, leafy green vegetables as well as flaxseed, soybean, and corn oils. The ratio of omega-6 to omega-3 fatty acids in the diet has proved significant because the functions of one are adversely modified by high amounts of the other.[20] Current data indicates that it is best to consume a 4 (or less) to 1 ratio of omega-6 to omega-3 fatty acids. Unfortunately, the average U.S. diet is closer to 15 or 20 to 1 due to the large amounts of wheat, corn, and rice consumed, as well as polyunsaturated oils, margarines, and foods containing them.

While playing a crucial role in brain function as well as normal growth and development, omega-3s have also been shown to reduce the risk of heart disease and can reduce inflammation with respect to cancer and arthritis. Two important omega-3s are eicosapentaenoic acid (EPA) and docosahexaenoic acid (DHA), which naturally occur in fatty fish such as salmon, tuna, sardines, anchovies, striped bass, catfish, herring, mackerel, trout, and halibut. The American Heart Association (AHA) suggests consuming one or more of these fish at least twice a week to help reduce the risk of heart disease, heart attack, and stroke.[21]

Because the majority of Americans do not consume fish at adequate levels, alternative approaches are needed to deliver sufficient omega-3 lipids. Formulated foods present significant technical barriers due to the extremely unstable nature of omega 3s and their propensity to smell and taste extremely fishy. Like all polyunsaturated oils, they are extremely vulnerable to oxidative breakdown. One successful approach is to add oils rich in omega-3s to poultry feed, with the result that the chickens deposit omega-3 fatty acids in the egg yolk. Another approach is microencapsulation. There are many excellent sources of microencapsulated omega-3 fatty acids. Unfortunately, they tend to be fairly expensive and the encapsulated materials generally deliver less than 50 percent oil by weight due to fillers and stabilizers in the encapsulation material.

Other unsaturated fatty acids in the diet, such as oleic, linoleic, and linolenic, are beneficial by reducing blood triglyceride levels, reducing platelet aggregation, and providing anti-arrhythmic effects. The polyunsaturated omega-3, omega-6,

FIGURE 16.4 **Breakdown of essential fatty acids.**

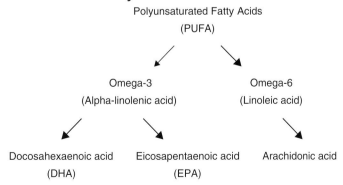

and omega-9 fatty acids, as well as the conjugated fatty acids (polyunsaturated fatty acids in which at least one pair of double bonds is separated by only one single bond), are also essential for infants (studies report increased visual activity, cognitive development, immune function, and motor functions).[22]

Conjugated linoleic acid (CLA), found in highest levels in grass-fed beef and lamb and also in eggs (and, interestingly, in white button mushrooms), is shown to have a remarkable number of health benefits, including anti-cancer and anti-inflammatory properties, as well as being a useful tool in weight management.[23] It does not cause weight loss directly, but over time it gradually replaces body fat with lean muscle mass.[24] This is a healthy effect, as a high degree of fat mass is related to all causes of mortality, and lean body mass burns more calories than fat mass, which may help increase resting metabolic rates. In July 2008, CLA received a no-objection letter from the FDA on its request for Generally Recognized as Safe (GRAS) status for certain food categories, including fluid milk, yogurt, meal replacement shakes, nutritional bars, fruit juices, and soy milk.[25] With GRAS status, food companies may now add CLA to products in these food categories.

Oleic acid (the predominant fatty acid in olive oil) has a lower melting point than trans fats and the saturated fatty acids. As a result, one of the benefits of oleic acid may be that when it is incorporated into cell membranes, they are more fluid than those containing the higher-melting-point fats, allowing for easier delivery of nutrients and removal of toxins as well as aiding in cell communication.

The polyunsaturated fatty acids, particularly the highly unsaturated fish oils, are prone to oxidation and rancidity and thus present flavor and stability problems in foods. The polyunsaturated fatty acids are also vulnerable to damage during high-heat applications such as frying. Stabilization with antioxidants enhances the shelf life of these products. When formulating foods rich in polyunsaturated fats, it is necessary to provide protection either with natural antioxidants, such as tocopherols (forms of vitamin E), or synthetic antioxidants, such as TBHQ (tert-butylhydroquinone), BHA (butylated hydroxyanisole), and BHT (butylated hydroxytoluene). Plant extracts, such as rosemary extract, are also used in certain applications, but they are generally less effective than the stronger and less expensive synthetic antioxidants, and they provide an often undesirable herbal flavor.

FIGURE 16.5 **Health effects and sources of common fatty acids.**

Fatty Acid Group	Health Effects	Sources
SHORT CHAIN Acetic, propionic, butyric, all from fermentation in gut. Only butyric in natural dietary fats.	SFAs are produced in colon and are associated with lower cancer risk, satiety, and reduced weight gain.	Butyric is in butterfat, all SCFAs are bound in the low calorie fat Salatrim.
MEDIUM CHAIN Caproic, capric, and caprylic	MCTs are rapidly absorbed and burned as energy source. Used in enteral nutrition.	Found in coconut oil. Also in restructured lipids for nutritional foods.
LONG CHAIN SATURATED Lauric, myristic, palmitic, stearic	Palmitic and stearic are hypercholesterolemic and thus associated with cardiovasucular risk.	Lauric— coconut oil Myristic—palm kernel oil Palmitic—palm oil and animal fat Stearic—animal fat, some plant oils, hydrogenated oils
MONOUNSATURATED Oleic (cis) Elagic (trans)	Oleic less hypercholesterolemic. Associated with healthy Mediteranian diet. Elagic is hypercholesterolemic and inflammatory.	Oleic is from olive oil, canola oil, and many other plant lipids. Elagic is formed in hydrogenated oils.
POLYUNSATURATED Gamma-linoleic	Essential fatty acid required prostaglandin synthesis. Important for inflammatory response, immunity. Needs to be balanced with omega-3 fatty acids.	Found in most plant lipids and in fish oils. Major n-6 polyunsatured fatty acid in the diet.
Omega 3s Alpha linoleic DHA, EPA	Omega-3 fatty acids are associated with reduced cardiovascular risk, reduced Alzheimer's risk.	Alpha-linoleic is found in flax oil. EPA and DHA are found in algal oil and fish oil.

Source: Darryl Holliday.

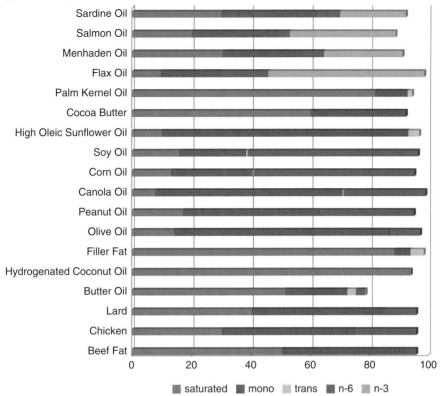

FIGURE 16.6 **Typical composition of fats and oils.**

saturated ■ mono ░ trans ■ n-6 ▒ n-3

Source: Darryl Holliday.

Carbohydrates

Carbohydrates represent a broad variety of ingredients that can be present in or applied to foods. They range in size from 3-carbon glycerine and 5- and 6-carbon simple sugars to very large and complex starches and fiber. Carbohydrates represent the greatest percentage of nutrients (and calories) in our diets and, therefore, contribute major physical as well as biochemical functionality.

Sugars

Because the major function of sugars in foods is to provide sweetness, let us look at the relative sweetness of each compared to sucrose (table sugar), which is assigned a value of 100.

It is important to note that high-fructose corn syrup (HFCS) has virtually taken over as the sweetener of choice in most food and beverages manufactured in the United States due to its level of sweetness (approaching sucrose) and lower production cost. Although all of the HFCS sweeteners are fully caloric and deliver 4 kcal/g, evidence suggests that fructose is not digested the same as sucrose and in fact may be responsible for several harmful health effects (including increasing the rate of obesity, increasing insulin resistance and other diabetes-related complications, and contributing to fibrosis of the liver).[26] To date, no incontrovertible data shows a direct cause-and-effect relationship. That said, food and beverage manufacturers are replacing HFCS with sucrose in many products to stave off a potential consumer boycott of

HFCS-containing foods. While this trend is slowly increasing, the industry has not made a complete change due to the price and functional attributes of HFCS.

With the emphasis on lower-calorie foods, it is important to consider the use of high-intensity non-nutritive sweeteners. Application of these intense sweeteners varies because of their differences in relative sweetness, heat and pH stability, taste and aftertaste, and interactions with other flavors. Two products sold commercially in the United States, stevioside (Truvia®, PureVia®, others) and mogroside from luo han guo (Monkfruit in the Raw™), are considered natural.

FIGURE 16.7 **Sweetness value of sugars.**

Sugar	Sweetness
Sucrose	100
Glucose	70
Fructose	120
Maltose	45
Lactose	40
Corn syrup (glucose, maltose)	30–50
High-fructose corn syrup	80–90
Invert sugar	95

Source: Darryl Holliday.

FIGURE 16.8 Sweetness value of high-intensity zero-calorie sweeteners.

Sweetener	Sweetness	Application Note
Mogroside	250	Plant source
Cylamate	3000	Banned in United States
Acesulfame-K	20,000	Heat stable
Aspartame	18,000	Not stable for cooking
Saccharin	30,000	Heat stable
Neotame	800,000	Heat stable
Stevioside	30,000	Plant source
Sucralose	60,000	Heat stable

Source: Darryl Holliday.

While providing sweetness similar to sucrose, the intense sweeteners present problems in developing functional foods because of their use at very low levels. They also do not add bulk, contribute to texture, or control water activity. As an alternative, sugar alcohols (polyols) can be used for sweetness and to provide bulk in low- and no-sugar applications. The sugar alcohols are not well digested, so they generally add some calories, but less than sugars do. In addition, all of the polyols are beneficial for use in diabetic foods because they do not influence blood glucose levels. Generally, they are not used by bacteria in the mouth, so they are non-cariogenic when used in chewing gums and confections. However, they can be fermented by colonic bacteria, leading to gastric discomfort when taken in large quantities. Listed below are the relative sweetness and caloric values of the sugar alcohols.

Artificial Sweeteners

Artificial sweeteners are used instead of sucrose (table sugar) to sweeten foods and beverages without adding calories. Because artificial sweeteners are many times sweeter than table sugar, smaller amounts are needed to create the same level of sweetness. In the United States, artificial sweeteners are regulated by the FDA. Approved artificial sweeteners include saccharin (Sugar Twin, Sweet 'n' Low, others), aspartame (NutraSweet, Equal, others), acesulfame-potassium (Sunette, Sweet One), sucralose (Splenda), neotame, and tagatose.

FIGURE 16.9 Sweetness value of sugar alcohols.

Sugar Alcohol	Sweetness (Compared to Sucrose)	Caloric Value (Kcal/g)
Erythritol	70	0.2
Xylitol	100	2.4
Mannitol	70	1.6
Sorbitol	60	3.0
Maltitol	90	3.0
Lactitol	40	3.0

Source: Darryl Holliday.

FIGURE 16.10 Cariogenic attributes of sweeteners.

Sweetener	Cariogenic	"Sugar-free" Label
Natural sugars		
Sucrose	Yes	No
Glucose	Yes	No
Fructose	Yes	No
Lactose	Yes	No
Sugar substitutes		
Sugar alcohols/polyols		
Xylitol	No	Yes
Sorbitol	No	Yes
Mannitol	No	Yes
Maltitol	No	Yes
Artificial sweeteners		
Aspartame*	No	Yes
Saccharin	No	Yes
Sucralose	No	Yes
Acesulfame potassium	No	Yes

*Aspartame is technically a nutritive sweetener, but because of its intense sweetness it is used in such small amounts that its nutritive value is negligible.

Adapted from K. A. Ly, P. Milgrom, and M. Rothen, "Xylitol, Sweeteners, and Dental Caries," *Pediatric Dentistry* 28, no. 2 (2006): 154–164.

Dietary Fiber

Dietary fiber comes from portions of edible plants that are not digested by humans. Dietary fiber includes a broad range of polysaccharides, including cellulose, as well as many other plant components, such as dextrins, inulin, lignin, chitins, pectins, beta-glucans, oligosaccharides, and several types of non-digestible starch. What they share is that they cannot be broken down by human enzymes and, therefore, provide no calories. Thus, large quantities of high-fiber foods can be eaten to provide fullness without increasing caloric content. In addition, they add bulk to help solid waste move through the digestive tract.

This mixture of indigestible materials can be divided into soluble (fermentable) fiber and insoluble (non-fermentable) fiber, both of which are present in plant foods. Insoluble fiber passively attracts water, increasing bulk, which results in reduced transit time of solid waste through the gastrointestinal tract.

Soluble fiber (considered a prebiotic), absorbs water to become a gelatinous, viscous substance that is fermented by bacteria (the probiotics) in the digestive tract, yielding various compounds that produce significant health benefits:

- Helps regulate blood glucose and lipid levels.
- Helps lower total and LDL "bad" cholesterol levels.
- Delays absorption of glucose after a meal to help reduce spiking of blood sugar levels.
- Balances intestinal pH and protects against infectious diseases by out-competing pathogens for intestinal real estate.
- Helps regulate immune response.
- Improves absorption of minerals.[27–31]

Known side effects from ingesting large amounts of soluble fiber are the formation of fermentation products such as gas and laxative compounds. In most cases, effects are reduced or subside as the body gets accustomed to the change in diet.

Many foods contain both soluble and insoluble fiber. Fruit skins tend to contain insoluble fiber, whereas the flesh and pulp contain more soluble fiber. Whole grains, bran, flaxseed, and vegetables are rich sources of insoluble fiber. Peas, beans, oats, apples, and carrots are good sources of soluble fiber.

The health benefits of both soluble and insoluble fiber make them useful for development of healthier foods. For instance, adding fiber produces caloric reduction by simple dilution. Fibers such as prune paste and inulin can act as fat mimetics, providing fatty texture with few or zero calories. Also, certain fibers are shown to lower cholesterol. For example, the marketing of whole-grain cereals based especially on oat fiber has been successful, as beta-glucans (found in oat fiber) are proven to control serum cholesterol. Other fiber-containing foods provide similar opportunities. However, formulating foods with high fiber can offer technical challenges because both soluble and insoluble fiber bind many times their weight in water. This can result in negative textures, such as cakey cookies and poor bread loaf volume, and reduced shelf life due to higher water activity (a_w), leading to increased mold growth. Formulating these ingredients into products such as cookies, bread, and pasta requires formulation adjustments to deal with the excess of water binding in these foods. These adjustments can include everything from increased baking times to substitution with resistant starches.

Polydextrose (Litesse®, Sta-Lite®, others) is a synthetically produced glucose polymer (89% glucose, 10% sorbitol, 1% citric acid) that provides 1 kcal/g. It is classified as a soluble fiber that is only partially metabolized by gut microbes. Its taste is non-sweet and innocuous, so it doesn't add any flavor to the foods it is added to, and it is highly soluble and clear in solution. It is commonly used to increase fiber content, replace sugar, reduce fat content, and reduce calories in an assortment of foods and beverages. It can also be used as a humectant (moisture-holding agent), stabilizer, bulking agent, and thickening agent. It is useful in both dietetic and diabetic applications. Polydextrose allows the product developer to add fiber and lower calories from sugar and fat without compromising taste or texture. In the United States, the FDA has approved the use of polydextrose in all foods with the exception of meat, poultry, baby food, and infant formula.

Resistant Starches

Starch (which is normally digestible) can act like dietary fiber when it is in one of four forms:

RS1—Physically resistant starch, which cannot be digested by mammalian enzymes. It is typically found in raw, unprocessed grains and legumes.

RS2—Natural granular starch found in raw potato, green banana, and high-amylose corn.

RS3—Starch that has been gelatinized (cooked) and cooled, causing recrystallization (retrogradation). Found in stale bread and cooked and chilled potatoes.

RS4—Starches that have been chemically modified to produce enzyme resistance.

Resistant starches are a powerful new tool for dietary food developers because they provide only 2 to 3 kcal/g, compared to 4 kcal/g for fully digestible carbohydrates. This caloric reduction is useful in the formulation of reduced-calorie foods. The slower digestion of the starch also prevents a spike in blood glucose after eating. This leads to an increased feeling of fullness as well as a consistent energy release instead of a quick energy boost and sudden crash. Because the release of glucose during the digestion of resistant starch is slower than in gelatinized (cooked) starch, the glycemic index is much lower. This is especially important in the development of foods for diabetics.

Substantial research on the health benefits of resistant starch includes more than 200 published, peer-reviewed studies that indicate benefits in intestinal and colonic health as well as metabolically important benefits in glycemic management and calorie reduction.

Just a few examples:

- A recently published clinical trial by Dr. Joanne Slavin and her colleagues at the University of Minnesota demonstrated that eating food made with resistant starch from high-amylose corn had more of an impact on satiety than other types of fibers (corn bran, barley beta-glucan, and polydextrose). This study suggests that all fibers do not impact satiety equally, so the type of fiber must be carefully considered in new product development.[32]

- Of several studies published by Dr. Denise Robertson and her colleagues at the Oxford Lipid Metabolism Group and the University of Surrey (UK), the most recent found that dietary consumption of resistant starch resulted in 10 percent fewer calories being consumed in the following 24 hours. Also, calorie intakes were significantly lower at the *ad libitum* (eat-all-you-want) test meal.[33]

- Dr. Anne Nilsson and her colleagues at Lund University (Denmark) found that when Hi-maize resistant starch and barley kernels (another natural source of resistant starch) were consumed in the evening meal, the results included improved glucose tolerance, lowered inflammatory biomarkers, and increased satiety after a standardized, high-glycemic breakfast the following morning.[34]

- Numerous studies demonstrate that RS2 and RS3 resistant starches from high-amylose corn promote intestinal and colonic health through their fermentation and action as prebiotic fibers. They encourage the growth of health-promoting bacteria, reduce pH, and increase the production of butyrate via fermentation. Buytrate, a short-chain fatty acid, is important for colonic health and is shown to have health-promoting properties.[35,36]

Water

Water, which constitutes about 60 percent of the human body, is a critical, often overlooked multifunctional component of our bodies and diet. Water plays a vital role in the control of weight, muscle tone, hypertension, cholesterol, bloating, constipation, ulcers, low energy levels, and stomach pain. It regulates body temperature, removes toxins and wastes, cushions and lubricates joints, decreases risk of kidney stones, and protects tissues, organs, and the spinal cord from shock and damage. It assists in the digestion and absorption of food and in transporting oxygen and nutrients to the cells. All bodily enzymatic and chemical reactions occur in the presence of water. Water also transports hormones, nutrients, oxygen, and antibodies through the bloodstream and lymphatic system. Additionally, it contains zero calories, zero fat, and zero cholesterol, and is very low in sodium. Plus, it can act as an appetite suppressant. Studies show that a low consumption of water allows more fat to be deposited instead of being metabolized. The greater the amount of water consumed, the less fat is deposited in the body. To put it simply, drinking a sufficient amount of water on a daily basis is essential for good health.[37,38,39]

In our bodies, dehydration results when water output exceeds water input. Symptoms become more severe as more water is lost. Based on body weight, a 1 to 2 percent loss of water induces thirst, fatigue, weakness, and vague discomfort. When 7 to 10 percent of body weight is lost, dizziness, muscle spasms, delirium, and collapse can result. Average urine output for adults is about 1.5 L a day, plus an additional liter of water a day lost through breathing, sweating, and bowel movements. Food accounts for approximately 20 percent of our total fluid intake. Consumption of 2 L (a little over 8 cups) of water or other beverages daily generally replaces the fluid lost. This idea is consistent with the popular 8 × 8 rule, which recommends eight 8-ounce servings of fluids per day, and is responsible for the phenomenal popularity of bottled water (a $60 billion/year global industry).

Micronutrients: Vitamins and Minerals

Although required in small quantities, micronutrients, including vitamins and minerals, are essential to our health. Minerals fall into two categories: major and trace, depending on the quantities of each required daily. The major minerals are calcium, phosphorous, potassium, sulfur, sodium, chlorine, and magnesium. The trace minerals are iron, zinc, selenium, manganese copper, iodine, molybdenum, chromium, and fluorine. Proper balance of trace elements is critical because too little can result in a deficiency, while too much can result in toxicity. One way to ensure one's diet encompasses all required micronutrients is to follow the recommendations set forth in the *Dietary Guidelines for Americans*.

Vitamins are divided into fat-soluble (A, D, E, and K) and water-soluble (B-complex and C). Both vitamins and minerals help regulate metabolic functions. They play key roles in the body's innumerable enzyme-catalyzed reactions, where they serve as co-enzymes (vitamins) or co-factors (minerals)—without which the enzymes cannot function properly. Because they play such vital roles in the body's processes, many foods are now enriched or fortified with vitamins and minerals. For example, in the milling of wheat to make flour, several vitamins and minerals are lost. Those specific nutrients are added back in mandated amounts (2.9 mg thiamine, 1.8 mg riboflavin, 24 mg niacin, 0.7 mg folic acid, and 20 mg iron per pound of flour) in order to produce enriched flour. Fortified foods are products to which nutrients are added that were not originally present, such as calcium to orange juice and B vitamins to cereals. Because these foods are standard items in most people's diets, they are used as convenient delivery systems for these essential nutrients to the general population.

FIGURE 16.11 **The roles of vitamins and minerals in health.**

Fat-Soluble Vitamins		
Vitamin	Functions	Sources
Vitamin A	Promotes vision, growth, and resistance to bacterial infection and overall immune system function while preventing dry skin and eyes	Liver, sweet potatoes, spinach, greens, carrots, cantaloupe, apricots, broccoli, fortified milk, and breakfast cereals
Vitamin D	Increases absorption of calcium and phosphorus and maintains optimal blood calcium and calcification of bone	Fish oils, sardines, salmon, fortified milk, and breakfast cereals
Vitamin E	Antioxidant; prevents breakdown of vitamin A and unsaturated fatty acids	Plant oils, cabbage, asparagus, sweet potatoes, tomatoes, apples, avocados, mango, shrimp, nuts, seeds, fortified breakfast cereals
Vitamin K	Activates blood-clotting factors and proteins involved in bone metabolism	Green vegetables, liver, some plant oils

(continued)

FIGURE 16.11 (*continued*)

Water-Soluble Vitamins		
Vitamin	**Functions**	**Sources**
Biotin	Coenzyme of glucose and fat synthesis	Cheese, egg yolks, cauliflower, peanut butter, liver
Choline	Neurotransmitter and phospholipid synthesis	Widely distributed in foods and synthesized by the body
Folate (folic acid)	Coenzyme involved in DNA synthesis, among many other functions	Green leafy vegetables, orange juice, organ meats, sprouts, sunflower seeds
Niacin	Coenzyme of energy metabolism, fat synthesis, and fat breakdown	Mushrooms, bran, tuna, salmon, chicken, beef, liver, peanuts, enriched grains
Pantothenic acid	Coenzyme of energy metabolism, fat synthesis, and fat breakdown	Mushrooms, liver, broccoli, eggs
Riboflavin	Coenzyme of carbohydrate metabolism	Milk, mushrooms, spinach, liver, enriched grains
Thiamin	Coenzyme of carbohydrate metabolism and involved in nerve function	Sunflower seeds, pork, whole and enriched grains, dried beans, peas
Vitamin B_6	Coenzyme of protein metabolism and involved in neurotransmitter and hemoglobin synthesis	Animal protein, spinach, broccoli, bananas, salmon, sunflower seeds
Vitamin B_{12}	Coenzyme of folate metabolism and involved in nerve function, among many other functions	Animal foods, organ meats, oysters, clams, fortified ready-to-eat breakfast cereals
Vitamin C	Connective tissue, hormone, and neurotransmitter synthesis as well as possible antioxidant activity	Citrus, fruits, strawberries, broccoli, greens

Major Minerals		
Mineral	**Functions**	**Sources**
Calcium	Bone and tooth structure, blood clotting, aids in nerve impulse transmission, muscle contractions, and other cell functions	Dairy products, canned fish, leafy vegetables, tofu, fortified orange juice, other foods
Chloride	Major negative ion of extracellular fluid, participates in acid production in stomach, aids nerve impulse transmission and water balance	Table salt, some vegetables, processed foods
Magnesium	Bone formation, and aids enzyme, nerve, and heart function	Wheat bran, green vegetables, nuts, chocolate, legumes
Phosphorus	Major ion of intracellular fluid, bone and tooth strength, part of various metabolic compounds, acid/base balance	Dairy products, processed foods, fish, soft drinks, bakery products, meats
Potassium	Major positive ion of intracellular fluid, aids nerve impulse transmission and water balance	Spinach, squash, bananas, orange juice, milk, meat, legumes, whole grains
Sodium	Major positive ion of extracellular fluid, aids nerve impulse transmission and water balance	Table salt, processed foods, condiments, sauces, soups, chips
Sulfur	Part of vitamins and amino acids, aids in drug detoxification and acid/base balance	Protein foods

Adapted from G. M. Wardlaw and A. M. Smith, *Contemporary Nutrition*, 7th ed. (New York: McGraw-Hill, 2009).

One of the primary responsibilities in food product development is to preserve the nutrients present (and those that might be added) during all phases of processing and manufacture. Therefore, knowledge of the stability of nutrients, particularly vitamins, under different processing, packaging, and distribution conditions is critical. For instance, vitamin A is highly sensitive to acid, air, light, and heat, while vitamin C is stable in acid but sensitive to alkalinity, air, light, and heat. Because of the instability of certain nutrients under various conditions, and their water solubility, cooking losses of some essential nutrients can be greater than 75 percent. However, losses seldom exceed 25 percent in modern food processing operations.

FIGURE 16.12   **Vitamin and mineral stability.**

Nutrient	Acid	Base	Oxygen	Light	Heat	Overage Needed for Processing
Vitamins						
Vitamin A	+	√	+	+	+	Up to 40%
Thaimin	+	√	+	+	√	Up to 60%
Riboflavin	√	+	√	+	√	Up to 40%
Niacin	√	√	√	√	√	Up to 10%
Vitamin B$_6$	+	+	√	+	√	Up to 40%
Vitamin B$_{12}$	+	+	+	+	√	Up to 75%
Pantothenic acid	+	+	√	√	+	Up to 50%
Folic acid	+	+	+	+	√	Up to 80%
Biotin	+	+	√	√	√	Up to 60%
Vitamin C	+	+	+	√	+	Up to 100%
Vitamin D	+	+	+	+	+	Up to 75%
Vitamin E	√	+	+	+	+	Up to 40%
Vitamin K	√	√	+	+	√	Up to 25%
Minerals	√	√	√	√	√	Up to 3%
Amino acids	√	√	√	√	+	Up to 25%, average of 10–15%
Fatty acids	√	√	+	+	+	Up to 55%, average of 10–15%

+ = sensitive; √ = not sensitive

Source: Darryl Holliday.

Salt Substitutes

Salt, or sodium chloride (NaCl), is the most common source of the mineral sodium in the diet. The body requires sodium to function properly, but most Americans eat about 10 times more than they actually need. The American Heart Association (AHA) currently recommends that healthy adults should consume no more than 2400 milligrams each day—that's equivalent to 1 teaspoon of table salt. That said, the AHA also states that "[r]educing daily intake to 1500 milligrams is desirable because it can lower blood pressure even further." A mere 15 percent of the salt in the average American diet comes from natural sources in foods and water. The rest comes from the salt added during food processing (about 67 percent) and at the stove and dining table (18 percent).

Sodium plays a key role in muscle function and in maintaining the body's fluid balance; however, it is easy to consume too much. Over time, excess sodium can elevate blood pressure levels, raising the risk of heart disease and stroke. Reducing salt consumption helps reduce blood pressure and therefore reduces risk. Food manufacturers have reacted to sodium's bad press by lowering its level in many food products. Campbell's® and Progresso® lowered the sodium in their soups in 2010, yet Campbell's® did add some back to their product line in 2012 due to decreased sales.[40]

The FDA and USDA state that an individual food claiming to be "healthy" must not exceed 480 mg sodium per serving.

FIGURE 16.13   **Sodium labeling.**

- **Sodium-free:** less than 5 milligrams of sodium per serving
- **Very low-sodium:** 35 milligrams or less per serving
- **Low-sodium:** 140 milligrams or less per serving
- **Reduced sodium**: usual sodium level is reduced by 25 percent
- **Unsalted, no salt added, or without added salt:** made without the salt that's normally used, but still contains the sodium that's a natural part of the food itself

Source: Darryl Holliday.

Meal-type products must not exceed 600 mg sodium per labeled serving size.

While most sodium is consumed in the form of sodium chloride, a wide variety of common food ingredients and condiments also contain sodium, such as soy sauce, ketchup, mustard, salted butter, and monosodium glutamate (MSG). A majority of salt substitutes use potassium chloride (KCl). The problem with this is that while KCl does have a salty taste, it also has an unpleasant bitter or metallic aftertaste, so it is commonly blended with NaCl to reduce bitterness and provide sodium reduction rather than total replacement.

Other sodium-containing ingredients, such as sodium bicarbonate (baking soda) can also be substituted for with

FIGURE 16.14 Sodium contents.

Sodium Source	Portion	Sodium Content
Curing and pickling salt	1 teaspoon	2360 mg
Iodized table salt	1 teaspoon	2325 mg
Sea salt, fine	1 teaspoon	2240 mg
Sea salt, coarse	1 teaspoon	1872 mg
Kosher salt	1 teaspoon	1120 mg
Baking soda	1 teaspoon	1000 mg

Source: Darryl Holliday.

FIGURE 16.15 Salt equivalents.

Iodized Table Salt	Kosher Salt	Sea Salt	Pickling Salt
¼ tsp	¼ tsp	¼ tsp	¼ tsp
1 tsp	1¼ tsp	1 tsp	1 tsp
1 tbsp (3 tsp)	4 tsp	3½ tsp	1 tbsp
¼ cup	¼ cup + 1 tbsp	¼ cup + 1 tsp	¼ cup
1 cup	1¼ cups	1 cup + 1½ tbsp	1 cup + 2 tsp

Source: Morton Salt Company, www.mortonsalt.com.

potassium-based ingredients, such as potassium bicarbonate. However, salt substitutes containing potassium are not safe to consume for everyone. For example, people with chronic kidney disease have difficulty filtering out excessive amounts of potassium.

Other salt-reduction strategies include substituting high mineral–containing sea salts, which have less sodium than table salt due to the presence of a multitude of other naturally occurring mineral salts. Of course, this is as variable as the ocean, so one cannot assume that every sea salt has the same amount of sodium (or potassium); it's important to check the label. In addition, substituting an equal volume of a larger crystal-size salt (such as kosher salt) for finer table salt can result in less salt being used, as the coarser salt contains less sodium by volume.

FIGURE 16.16 Sodium reduction levels.

Food Product	Sodium (mg) in Traditional Version	Sodium (mg) in Low-Sodium Version
Progresso Chicken Noodle Soup	950	470
Campbell's Chunky Chicken Noodle Soup	870	480
Kikkoman Soy Sauce	920	575
Poore Brothers Kettle Chips	180	90
Nabisco Ritz Crackers	135	35

Source: Darryl Holliday.

●Health Issues and Trends
Nutrition for Special Groups

Diets are as diverse as people. Given their personal and religious beliefs, ethnicity, activity levels, health status, and age, many people have dietary restrictions and preferences.

Kosher and Halal

Special dietary considerations must be addressed for various groups when formulating food products for those markets. Two major religions with strict dietary restrictions are Judaism and Islam. While the two religions have some similar practices, there are key differences. Kosher laws, followed by Jews, and halal laws, observed by Muslims, each describe what is fit and proper or lawful for members of these groups to eat.

Kosher

Deuteronomy, in the Torah, lists clean and unclean animals and specifies the characteristics of kosher animals. In strict Jewish observance, for example, it is permissible to eat any animal that has a split hoof and that chews the cud (food of a ruminant regurgitated to be chewed again). Cattle, sheep, goats, deer, and bison are all kosher meats; however, the pig is considered unclean because although it has a split hoof, it does not chew the cud. To be kosher, animals must be slaughtered according to ritual requirements and must not be injured or ill in any way. In handling, kosher meat must be kept separate from non-kosher. Some other considerations regarding meat are: Blood may not be consumed, hence the kosher requirement of soaking meat in salt and water after slaughter, along with a deveining step. The sciatic nerve is also to be avoided. That means that in the United States (except in rare instances in Jewish neighborhoods where religiously trained butchers are able to recognize and remove the nerve successfully), only meat from the forequarter of the animal is considered kosher. With poultry, on the other hand, the entire animal is considered kosher. With respect to sea creatures, kosher laws permit eating any animal that has fins and removable scales; however, those that do not possess these traits are unclean and cannot be eaten (shellfish, mollusks, and so on).

Under kosher laws, meat and dairy cannot be eaten together. For example, cheeseburgers may not be eaten, hot dogs and milkshakes cannot be eaten together, and pepperoni pizza cannot be eaten if mozzarella is present. Eating meat and fish together is also prohibited in the same dish, but they can be eaten at the same meal.

These meat and dairy restrictions extend beyond foods to the pots and pans, plates and utensils, dishwashers, and towels on which they are dried. Many kosher kitchens have at least two sets of pots, pans, and dishes, one for meat and one for dairy.

This is equally important for the food manufacturer who intends to produce kosher food. All manufacturing equipment must be blessed by a rabbi before use, and if used for both kosher and non-kosher production, must be extensively cleaned—"kosherized"—according to kosher requirements. Likewise, kosher ingredients must be stored separately and are not allowed to commingle with non-kosher ingredients. In order to get approval for a food label to carry the certified kosher logo from one of the kosher certifying agencies, the company must first go through a lengthy, detailed, and costly application process and review of its entire manufacturing process, from supply chain through distribution, before the agency will give the go-ahead.

With a total world population of Jews at less than 15 million (around 6 million in the United States), it would seem that there would be a somewhat limited consumer base to support a kosher food line or business. However, the quality reputation that kosher food and manufacturing have developed over the years has broadened the market for kosher foods considerably, such that even non-Jews consider kosher foods to be better in many cases than their non-kosher equivalents. A former advertisement for a popular kosher hot dog brand captured this sentiment perfectly when it stated, "We answer to a higher authority."

Passover is one of the most important Jewish holidays. This is the time of year when food and beverage manufacturers who replaced sugar with high-fructose corn syrup must go back to using sugar if they wish to label their products *Kosher for Passover*. This is because corn (and corn-derived products) is one of the prohibited grains that must not be consumed during this holiday, which commemorates the Exodus: the escape of the Jews out of Egyptian slavery.

Halal

Muslims, according to the Koran, are allowed to eat what is "good"—that is, what is "pure, clean, wholesome, nourishing, and pleasing to the taste." In general, everything is allowed (*halal*) except what has been specifically forbidden. This is in the interest of health and cleanliness, and in obedience to God. In the Koran, the following foods and drinks are strictly prohibited by God:

- dead meat (i.e., the carcass of an already-dead animal)
- blood
- flesh of swine (pork)
- intoxicating drinks (including wine, beer, and spirits)
- meat of an animal that has been sacrificed to idols
- meat of an animal that died from strangulation or blunt force
- meat from which wild animals have already eaten

The Koran directs Muslims to slaughter their livestock by slitting the animal's throat in a swift and merciful manner, reciting God's name with the words, "In the name of God, God is Most Great." The animal is then bled completely before consumption. Meat prepared in this manner is considered to be "halal." Some Muslims will abstain from eating meat if they are uncertain of how it was slaughtered. They also place importance on the animal having been bled properly, as otherwise it would not be considered healthy to eat. Some

Muslims living in predominantly Christian countries hold the opinion that one may eat commercial meat (apart from pork, of course) as long as they pronounce God's name at the time of eating it. This opinion is based on a Koranic verse that states that the food of Christians and Jews (with the exceptions noted above) is lawful for Muslims. Similar to kosher food laws, pork and blood are prohibited. Unlike kosher laws, Muslims can eat shellfish and certain animals without cloven hooves (rabbit, for example).

Halal certification is a voluntary process by which a recognized Islamic authority certifies that a company's products can be lawfully consumed by Muslims. Those who meet the criteria for certification are given halal certificates, and they may use a halal marking or symbol on their products and advertising.

As with the kosher symbol on food labels, the "halal certified" stamp on a label is seen by Muslim customers as a sign of a trustworthy or superior product. Such a stamp is commonly required for the export of certain foods to Muslim countries such as Saudi Arabia and Malaysia. Products that are halal certified may be marked with a halal symbol, or simply the letter M (as the letter K is used to identify kosher products).

Halal certification is similar to kosher. Each certifying organization has its own procedures and requirements. In general, however, products will be checked to ensure that:

- Raw materials, processing-aid ingredients, processing, sanitation chemicals, and packaging meet the Islamic dietary requirements, primarily that no alcohol or pork products are used.
- Flavoring ingredients and solvents must be from halal sources (no ethyl alcohol, for example).
- Meat products (non-pork) have been slaughtered under Islamic guidelines.

Food manufacturers pay a fee and voluntarily submit their food products for halal certification. Independent organizations, under the auspices of a mullah (the Islamic equivalent of the Jewish rabbi), are responsible for screening the products, observing the production process, and deciding on a company's compliance with Islamic dietary laws.

Vegetarianism

People become vegetarians for all sorts of reasons: ethical, religious, health, economic, environmental—or a combination of factors. From annual polls, the Vegetarian Resource Group (VRG) found that 2 to 3 percent of the U.S. population claim to never consume meat, fish, or fowl and thus are strict vegetarians. However, a Zogby Poll fielded in 1999 and 2008 found that in both years more than half the population sometimes, often, or always ordered meatless dishes. While there are many types of vegetarians—from lacto-ovo, who do not eat meat, fish, or fowl but do eat eggs and dairy, to vegans, who refrain from all meat, fish, fowl, eggs, dairy, and products derived from these foods—a new group is emerging, known as *flexitarians*. They are "semi-vegetarians" whose main focus is on decreased or occasional meat consumption. What does this mean to the food industry? That manufacturers must

FIGURE 16.17 **Complementary proteins.**

Food Item	Limiting Amino Acid	Foods High in Limiting Amino Acids	Complementary Food Combinations
Dried beans and peas	Methionine and cysteine	Grains, nuts, and seeds (methionine and cysteine)	Brown rice and beans with peppers; bean paste (beans, lemon, oil, and tahini)
Grains	Lysine	Dried beans and peas (lysine)	Nut butter and whole wheat bread; barley and 3-bean soup; corn tortilla and refried beans with salsa
Vegetables	Lysine, methionine, cysteine	Dried beans and peas (lysine); grains, nuts, and seeds (methionine and cysteine)	Vegetable stir-fry with tofu and brown rice; fresh greens with pine nuts and beans

Source: Margaret Condrasky, Ed.D, RD, CCE.

strive to keep their vegetarian offerings fresh, appealing, and satisfying to all potential consumers, as possibly half the population will dine on them at least occasionally.

Animal Versus Plant Protein

The major nutrient often at risk in a vegetarian diet is protein. Amino acids are the building blocks of proteins, and of the 20 common types, nine must be consumed in food (essential amino acids); the rest can be produced by the body (nonessential amino acids). Almost all *animal* products are nutrient-dense sources of protein, also known as *complete proteins*, because they contain an adequate amount of all the essential amino acids. Conversely, most proteins found in plants lack a sufficient amount of one or more essential amino acids and are therefore deemed incomplete proteins. To compensate for the deficiencies in essential amino acids, many plant proteins can be combined to form complementary proteins.

For this reason, when preparing meals, vegetarians and those producing vegetarian foods must be aware of the amino acid composition of plant-based foods and be able to compensate for the essential amino acids that are lacking. For instance, if a person eats only foods containing incomplete proteins, such as those found in most vegetables and fruits, and does not combine them properly, then his or her ability to synthesize proteins in the body for growth and repair slows or halts due to the limiting amino acid content. Instead, the protein is broken down and utilized only as an energy source (calories). The latest research shows that as long as complementary foods are eaten throughout the day, the body can use them to form complete proteins. It isn't necessary to eat them at the same meal.[41,42] *Note:* The limiting amino acid is the essential amino acid found in the smallest quantity in a food. For more on plant proteins, see Chapter 7.

Complete Plant Proteins

In addition to developing vegetarian foods that feature complementary proteins, the product developer also has excellent complete plant proteins to work with, notably soy and quinoa.

Soy

Soybeans are a versatile and dynamic legume high in protein and fiber. When they are picked before maturity, they look similar to sugar snap peas, with a bright green, fuzzy exterior that encloses a sweet and tender pea (known as *edamame*, a Japanese word meaning "twig bean").

When soybeans are allowed to mature to their fully dry state, they are typically processed into a wide variety of food products including oil, tofu, soy sauce, flour, miso, and an array of imitation dairy products. Most important for the product developer are the soy protein isolates, concentrates, and flours that are available to provide nutritional enhancement and functional benefits (emulsification, texturization) to a wide range of vegetarian and non-vegetarian products as well as an ever-expanding menu of soy-based foods such as salad dressings, soups, imitation meats, beverage powders, cheeses, nondairy creamer, frozen desserts, whipped topping, infant formulas, breads, breakfast cereals, pastas, and pet foods.

FIGURE 16.18 **Soybean pods.**

ping han/Getty Images, Inc.

FIGURE 16.19 Soy products.

Diane Labombarbe/Getty Images, Inc.

Soy protein isolate is a highly refined or purified form of soy protein with a minimum protein content of 90 percent on a dry basis. It is made from defatted soy flour, which has had most of the non-protein components, fats, and carbohydrates removed. Because of this, it has a neutral flavor and causes less flatulence due to intestinal fermentation of the carbohydrates that have been removed.

Soy isolates are mainly used to improve the texture of meat products. In addition, they are also used to increase protein content, enhance moisture retention, and as an emulsifier.

Soy protein concentrate is about 70 percent soy protein and is basically defatted soy flour without the water-soluble carbohydrates (mainly sugars). Soy protein concentrate retains most of the fiber of the original soybean. It is widely used as a functional or nutritional ingredient in many food products, especially baked items and breakfast cereals. In some meat and poultry products, soy protein concentrate is used to increase water and fat retention or to improve nutritional values (more protein, less fat).

Soy protein concentrates are available in several forms: granules, flour, and spray-dried. Because they are so digestible, they are well suited for children, pregnant and lactating women, and the elderly. They are also used in pet foods and as milk replacements for babies (both human and livestock).

Soy flour is made by grinding soybeans into a fine powder. It comes in three forms: natural or full fat (contains natural oils); defatted (oils removed) with 50 percent protein content and either high or low water solubility; and lecithinated (lecithin added to enhance its emulsification properties). As soy flour is gluten-free, yeast-raised breads made with soy flour are dense in texture.

Textured soy protein (TSP), also known as textured vegetable protein (TVP), is a meat analog or meat extender made from defatted soy flour. It is quick to cook, with a protein content equal to that of the meat. TSP is made by processing a dough made from high-water-soluble defatted soy flour in a screw-type extruder under heat and pressure. The dough is extruded through a die into various shapes—chunks, flakes,

nuggets, strips, and so on—and dried in an oven. The extrusion process changes the structure of the soy protein, resulting in a fibrous, spongy matrix similar in texture to meat. TSP made from soy flour contains 50 percent soy protein and must be rehydrated before use at a weight ratio of 1:2 TSP to water. (However, TSP, when made from soy concentrate rather than soy flour, contains 70 percent protein and is rehydrated at a ratio of 1:3.) Rehydrated TVP is commonly used as a ground meat extender (at up to one-third the weight of the meat) due to its low cost—less than a third the price of ground beef—and when cooked together with meat helps retain yield by absorbing juices normally lost. Extension may result in diminished flavor, but fat and cholesterol are reduced.

Textured vegetable protein is a versatile substance whose different forms allow it to take on the texture of whatever ground meat it is substituting for. Using textured vegetable protein, one can make vegetarian or vegan versions of traditional meat dishes such as sausages, chili, spaghetti Bolognese, sloppy joes, tacos, burgers, and burritos.

Quinoa

Quinoa is a plant containing a balanced set of essential amino acids for humans, making it a complete protein source. In addition, it is a good source of dietary fiber and phosphorus and is high in magnesium and iron. Quinoa is gluten-free and is considered easy to digest. Because of all these characteristics, quinoa is being considered a possible crop in the National Aeronautical and Space Administration's (NASA) Controlled Ecological Life Support System for long-duration manned spaceflights.[43]

Quinoa contains more protein than any other grain and is also higher in unsaturated fat and lower in carbohydrates than other grains. This tiny, bead-like grain cooks like rice but in half the time and expands to four times its original size. Quinoa is available in several colors (tan, red, and black) and can be used like rice in main dishes, side dishes, salads, and soups. It is found packaged as a grain, ground into flour, and in several forms of pasta.

Eating a More Vegetarian Diet

Vegetable proteins are heart-healthy alternatives to animal proteins because they contain no cholesterol and little saturated fat as well as a high amount of fiber, vitamins, minerals, and phytochemicals, which may aid in the prevention of chronic diseases. They are inexpensive, versatile, and tasty; add flavor, color, and texture to the diet; and benefit health beyond their contribution of protein. Therefore, trimming the meat portion of any meal and filling the void with an array of nuts, grains, legumes, and vegetables is a good idea for non-vegetarians and vegetarians alike.

Healthy Cooking Approaches and Diets

The USDA's Food Guide Pyramid was designed to create a healthier America. Unfortunately, since its inception the obesity rate has continued to rise, not only in the United States but around the world as more people have begun to follow a Western diet. Today, with 4 of the top 10 causes of American deaths (heart disease, cancer, stroke, and diabetes) related to poor eating behavior,[44] other groups and agencies are offering new ideas on how to eat a balanced meal.

Diabetic Diets

According to the CDC, nearly 24 million Americans have diabetes, and about 6 million of them are unaware of their disease.[45] Therefore, the significance of diabetes awareness and prevention is crucial. Diabetes is a disease in which the body does not produce or properly use insulin. While the exact cause of diabetes is not completely understood, genetics and environmental factors such as obesity and lack of exercise play major roles. The American Diabetes Association (ADA) lists four major types of diabetes:

1. Type I diabetes (formerly known as juvenile diabetes; it is now known that Type I can strike at any age) is a genetic condition that results from the body's failure to produce insulin (or an insufficient amount). Insulin is the hormone that allows glucose into the cells to fuel them; 5 to 10 percent of Americans who are diagnosed have Type I diabetes. This type requires the person with diabetes to take daily injections of insulin in order to survive.

2. Type II diabetes (also known as adult-onset diabetes) results from insulin resistance, a condition in which the body fails to properly use insulin, often combined with an insulin deficiency; most Americans who are diagnosed have Type II diabetes. This type is associated with overweight, non-exercising individuals.

3. Gestational diabetes occurs during or immediately after pregnancy; 5 to 10 percent of women with gestational diabetes are found to have Type II diabetes.

4. Pre-diabetes is a condition that occurs when a person's blood glucose levels are higher than normal but not high enough to be diagnosed with Type II diabetes; in addition to the 23.6 million with diabetes, 57 million Americans have pre-diabetes, and are at risk of developing full-blown disease if they ignore the warnings and don't make serious lifestyle and dietary changes.[46]

It is important to note that people with diabetes have similar nutritional needs as other consumers. In fact, exercising and eating well-balanced meals are essential not just in the management of diabetes but also in the maintenance of general good health.

The Carbohydrate Countdown

The major consideration for people with diabetes is monitoring carbohydrate intake. Examples of foods that contain carbohydrate are:

- Grains and flour-containing foods—bread, cereal, rice, crackers
- Sugars and sugar-containing foods—fruit, fruit juices
- Dairy products—milk, yogurt (entirely lactose)
- Beans and legumes as well as soybean products—veggie burgers
- Sweets and snack foods—sodas, cake, cookies, candy, chips
- Starchy vegetables—potatoes and corn

Many people with diabetes follow a meal plan, such as using diabetic exchange lists or so-called "carb counting." Diabetes nutrition experts are against meal plans that eliminate healthful foods such as legumes, whole grains, fruits, and vegetables because these foods are associated with lower risk for developing other chronic conditions, such as heart disease and some cancers.[47] According to the ADA, research shows that low-fat and moderate- to low-carbohydrate meal plans prove effective in controlling Type II diabetes, often to the point where medication is not required.

Creating a Diabetic-Friendly Plate

Every 24 hours, more than 4000 adults are diagnosed with diabetes, and 200 die from it. New food products are of dire necessity not only for the control of diabetes but also for its prevention. To help in the creation of diabetic-friendly foods, the ADA created the "Create Your Plate" method, a simple and effective way to plate up healthy food choices focusing on the consumption of non-starchy vegetables. (*Note:* ADA's Create Your Plate concept is similar to, but not the same as, the USDA's MyPlate food guide.)

ADA's Create Your Plate Method
1. Draw an imaginary line down the middle of the plate.
2. On one side, cut it again for a total of three sections on the plate.
3. Fill the largest section with non-starchy vegetables.
4. Put starchy foods in one of the small sections.
5. Put a lean meat or meat substitute in the other small section.
6. Add an 8-ounce glass of nonfat or low-fat milk. Alternatively, add another small serving of carbohydrate, such as a 6-ounce container of light yogurt or a small roll.
7. Add a piece of fresh fruit or ½ cup fruit salad.

This plate technique is not limited to people with diabetes; it is a valuable tool for all concerned with creating meals composed of healthier food choices in the appropriate amounts. For further information on diabetes and Create Your Plate, visit the ADA website.

The New American Plate

The American Institute for Cancer Research (AICR) created the "New American Plate," which, similar to the ADA's plate, is divided into thirds—two thirds hold vegetables, fruits, whole grains, and beans; and one third holds animal protein. The New American Plate is a simplified meal plan that focuses on plant-based foods that lower the risk for cancer and other chronic diseases while managing weight. Plant-based foods provide an array of cancer-protective compounds; in addition, a predominantly plant-based diet is a powerful tool in weight management. In fact, the fiber and water in plant foods gives a feeling of fullness without supplying a lot of calories. The three strategies for both cancer prevention and weight loss, as constructed by the AICR, are:

1. Eat mostly plant-based foods, which are low in energy density.
2. Be physically active.
3. Maintain a healthy weight through reduced portion size.

Hypertension (The DASH Diet)

Obesity leading to diabetes and heart disease is one of the leading causes of illness and death in the United States. Hypertension, or high blood pressure, is one of the leading early indicators of risk. The DASH (Develop Approaches to Stop Hypertension) diet achieves significant success for patients seeking to reduce hypertension without medication. In addition to being a low-salt (or low-sodium) plan, it is rich in fruits and vegetables, low-fat or nonfat dairy, and whole grains. It is a high-fiber, low- to moderate-fat diet, rich in potassium, calcium, and magnesium. The DASH diet eating plan has proven to lower blood pressure in studies sponsored by the National Institutes of Health.

The DASH diet received a #1 ranking from *U.S. News & World Report*.[48] DASH is also endorsed by:

- The National Heart, Lung, and Blood Institute (one of the National Institutes of Health, part of the HHS)
- The American Heart Association (AHA)
- The 2010 Dietary Guidelines for Americans
- U.S. Guidelines for Treatment of High Blood Pressure
- The 2011 AHA Treatment Guidelines for Women
- The Mayo Clinic

In addition, the DASH diet formed the basis for the USDA's MyPlate.

Allergens

Every year, food allergies are responsible for approximately 200,000 severe allergic reactions requiring hospitalizations and result in over 200 deaths.[49] Only eight foods account for 90 percent of all food allergy reactions: cow's milk, eggs, peanuts, tree nuts (such as pecans, almonds, and walnuts), fish (such as bass, cod, and flounder), shellfish (such as crab, lobster, and shrimp), soy, and wheat.[50] Although allergies to milk, egg, wheat, and soy generally resolve in childhood, they appear to be resolving more slowly than in previous decades, with many children still allergic beyond the age of five. Allergies to peanuts, tree nuts, fish, and shellfish are generally lifelong. In all cases, allergens are *protein-based*. Refined oils are not allergenic, even if they were derived from allergenic foods (peanut oil, soybean oil).

A study published by the National Center for Health Statistics division of the CDC reports that one out of every 25 children in the United States has a food allergy, representing about a 50 percent increase between 1997 and 2011.[51] The prevalence of food allergy may be increasing in the United States and in other countries.[52] Studies are inconclusive about whether food allergies can be prevented. No medication can be taken to prevent food allergies. They are a topic of concern for people not only in the healthcare industry but also in the food-service sector. With as many as 15 million Americans having food allergies (60 percent adults, 40 percent children), this is an expanding market that must be fed carefully.

An allergy is a reaction to a food that involves the body's immune system. The body produces an immune response by releasing histamine, which generates the allergic symptoms. These range in severity from skin rashes, breathing problems, vomiting, and cramping, to swelling of the tongue and throat. A severe reaction (anaphylactic shock) can result in death. Life-threatening allergic reactions at home can be treated with the prescription drug epinephrine, usually delivered via injection using an Epi-Pen®. People with food allergies must carefully assess and evaluate all processed foods, read ingredient labels on packages, and alert servers about any allergies (if they don't ask you first) before ordering anything when eating out. Avoidance of allergy-causing foods is the only way to avoid a reaction; there is no cure. Unfortunately, many of the allergy-causing foods are used as ingredients in other foods (for example, milk and eggs in baked goods, nuts in confections). This makes recognizing the presence of food allergens and their sources of critical importance to food product developers in order to create safer alternatives.

Allergen Labeling

The Food Allergen Labeling and Consumer Protection Act (FALCPA) requires food manufacturers to list the "Big Eight" food allergens on labels. While not every possible food that can cause a food allergy is listed, these eight food categories account for most food allergy reactions.

Fresh produce, fresh meat, and certain highly refined oils do not require listing of potential food allergens on the labels. Foods that may inadvertently come into contact with a food allergen during the growing, harvesting, or manufacturing process also are exempt. However, many manufacturers routinely include warnings on their labels of the possibility that trace amounts of allergy-causing foods may be present as a way to stave off liability. FALCPA does not regulate the use of advisory or precautionary labeling (for example, "prepared in a facility that also processes nuts"); this is voluntary on the part of the manufacturer. These terms do not reflect specific risks; in fact, random testing for allergens of products bearing such warning labels shows a range of results from none to amounts that can cause reactions.[53,54] Further, these warnings do not provide any legal defense for the manufacturer in case a lawsuit should arise.

Food Intolerances

Food allergies are different from food intolerances. Unlike an allergy, a food intolerance does not involve an immunologic reaction. Perhaps the best-known type is lactose intolerance. People with lactose intolerance lack the enzyme lactase, required to properly digest the milk sugar lactose. As a result, they experience gas, bloating, and abdominal pain when they consume

FIGURE 16.20 Sample USDA food guide and the DASH eating plan at the 2000-calorie level.

Food Groups and Subgroups	DASH Eating Plan Amount[a]	Equivalent Amounts
Fruit Group	2 to 2.5 cups (4 to 5 servings)	½ cup equivalent is: • ½ cup fresh, frozen, or canned fruit • 1 medium fruit • ¼ cup dried fruit • ½ cup fruit juice
Vegetable Group • Dark green vegetables • Orange vegetables • Legumes (dry beans) • Starchy vegetables • Other vegetables	2 to 2.5 cups (4 to 5 servings)	½ cup equivalent is: • ½ cup of cut-up raw or cooked vegetable • 1 cup raw leafy vegetable • ½ cup vegetable juice
Grain Group • Whole grains • Other grains	6 to 8 ounce equivalents (6 to 8 servings[b])	1 ounce equivalent is: • 1 slice bread • 1 cup dry cereal • ½ cup cooked rice, pasta, cereal • DASH: 1 oz dry cereal (½–1¼ cups, depending on cereal type—check label)
Meat and Beans Group	6 ounces or less meats, poultry, fish 4 to 5 servings per week nuts, seeds, and legumes[c]	1 ounce equivalent is: • 1 ounce of cooked lean meats, poultry, fish • 1 egg[d] • USDA: ¼ cup cooked dry beans or tofu, 1 Tbsp peanut butter, ½ oz nuts or seeds • DASH: 1½ oz nuts, 2 Tbsp peanut butter, ½ oz seeds, ½ cup cooked dry beans
Milk Group	2 to 3 cups	1 cup equivalent is: • 1 cup low-fat/fat-free milk, yogurt • 1½ oz of low-fat, fat-free, or reduced fat natural cheese • 2 oz of low-fat or fat-free processed cheese
Oils	8 to 12 grams (2 to 3 tsp)	DASH: 1 tsp equivalent is: • 1 tsp soft margarine • 1 Tbsp low-fat mayo • 2 Tbsp light salad dressing • 1 tsp vegetable oil
Discretionary Calorie Allowance • Example of distribution: solid fat,[e] added sugars	~2 tsp of added sugar (5 Tbsp per week)	DASH: 1 Tbsp added sugar equivalent is: • 1 Tbsp jelly or jam • ½ cup sorbet and ices • 1 cup lemonade

[a]All servings are per day unless otherwise noted. USDA vegetable subgroup amounts and amounts of DASH nuts, seeds, and dry beans are per week.
[b]Whole grains are recommended for most grain servings to meet fiber recommendations.
[c]In the DASH Eating Plan, nuts, seeds, and legumes are a separate food group from meats, poultry, and fish.
[d]Because eggs are high in cholesterol, limit egg yolk intake to no more than 4 per week; 2 egg whites have the same protein content as 1 oz of meat.
[e]The oils listed in this table are not considered to be part of discretionary calories because they are a major source of the vitamin E and polyunsaturated fatty acids, including the essential fatty acids, in the food pattern. In contrast, solid fats (i.e., saturated and *trans* fats) are listed separately as a source of discretionary calories.
Note: Table updated to reflect 2006 DASH Eating Plan.
Source: HHS/USDA Dietary Guidelines (2005).

milk products. Lactose intolerance can be treated by consuming lactase tablets and, possibly, by gradually increasing intake of fermented dairy foods such as yogurt or aged cheeses. Most, if not all, of the lactose in these products is broken down during fermentation and aging (in cheeses) by microorganisms.

Food sensitivities are similar to intolerances. Some people's bodies are not able to tolerate caffeine, while others are sensitive to or intolerant of alcohol because of the missing enzyme alcohol dehydrogenase (ADH). It is important to know the difference between a food allergy and an intolerance because even the smallest amount of a given food can trigger a severe reaction in people with allergies, while people with food intolerances can usually eat small amounts of that food without fear of hospitalization (or worse).

Gluten Sensitivity

Another food intolerance that is garnering a lot of food industry attention is gluten intolerance in individuals who cannot digest the cereal protein gluten, found primarily (but not exclusively) in wheat-based products. This is not an allergy; consuming gluten does not trigger the release of histamine.

Gluten sensitivity is increasing and can cause a serious reaction in people who have celiac disease (also known as gluten-sensitive enteropathy), an autoimmune inflammatory disease of the small intestine that is triggered by the consumption of gluten. In fact, recent studies in the United States suggest the prevalence of celiac disease is approximately 1 case per 250 persons.[55]

People with a family history of celiac disease or personal history of Type I diabetes have an increased risk for acquiring celiac disease. In younger children, gluten damages the villi, the finger-like projections in the small intestine responsible for absorbing nutrients. When the villi are damaged, the body cannot absorb nutrients and malnutrition can result. Gluten sensitivity can lead to varying symptoms in different people, including diarrhea, abdominal pain and bloating, weight loss, fatigue, and painful skin rashes.

By removing gluten from one's diet, the symptoms caused by celiac disease subside. Today, many types of gluten-free products are readily available, such as breads, cookies, and cakes. Gluten-free flour, also easily obtained, is usually made by blending flours from non-gluten containing vegetable sources such as potatoes, legumes, rice, nuts, and seeds, with natural gums (hydrocolloids) added to provide the functional properties of the missing gluten. In other words, being gluten-free is a lot easier than it used to be.

A huge industry has grown up in recent years around supplying gluten-free versions of such foods as cereals, breads and baked goods, pasta, and other traditionally gluten-containing foods. Globally, gluten-free food sales were nearly $5 billion in 2012, with the United States accounting for 59 percent of the total market.[56] The USDA projects that the gluten-free industry's revenues will continue to soar.[57]

The FDA, as of August 2013, defined gluten-free as containing less than 20 parts per million (ppm) of gluten. Food manufacturers are legally allowed to label a food "gluten-free" even if that food contains an ingredient made from wheat, barley, or rye (or a crossbreed from those grains) as long as it is processed to remove the gluten to the allowable level of 20 ppm. The rule also requires foods with the claims "no gluten," "free of gluten," and "without gluten" to meet the same definition as "gluten-free." This new federal definition standardizes the meaning of "gluten-free" claims across the food industry and provides a uniform standard definition to help the up to 1.5 million Americans with celiac disease. The FDA recognizes that many foods currently labeled "gluten-free" already meet the new federal definition.[58]

Note: The labels are voluntary. Manufacturers wishing to cater to gluten-free consumers may choose to add the claim to their packaging, but they aren't required to do so. The labels do not eliminate the need to identify gluten-containing foods on labels, as the FDA's rules do not require manufacturers to disclose gluten-containing ingredients beyond their standard name: wheat, barley, and so on.

Grain Products Without Gluten

- Buckwheat
- Corn and products made from corn: grits, tortillas, popcorn, polenta, taco shells, tortilla chips, corn chips
- Millet
- Rice and products made from rice (rice cakes, rice crackers, rice noodles)
- Quinoa

Note: Check the ingredient labels carefully; seasonings added to these products may include gluten-containing ingredients.

Culinary Nutrition News

With all kinds of new information, research, and applications about food and nutrition coming out every day, a lot of buzzworthy food items and ingredients are making the headlines.

Processed Meats Cause Cancer?

The shocking headline from a recently released report from the World Health Organization (WHO) says it all: Eating processed meats such as sausages, bacon, and ham causes cancer, while unprocessed red meat may also be carcinogenic. The WHO's cancer research unit now classifies processed meat as "carcinogenic to humans" based on evidence from hundreds of studies, and linked it specifically to colon cancer.

The organization defines processed meat as any type of meat that is salted, cured, or smoked to enhance its flavor or preserve it. Processed meat generally contains pork or beef, but may also contain poultry.

The report states that eating just 50 grams of processed meat each day—the equivalent of two slices of ham—can increase the risk of colon cancer by 18 percent, and risk increases with increased consumption. Processed meat will now be placed in the same category as smoking and asbestos, based on the certainty of a link with cancer. However, the authors stressed that this does not mean that eating processed meat is equally dangerous; compared with smoking and exposure to asbestos, the risks from eating processed meats are relatively small. Unprocessed red meats such as beef and lamb were also implicated, but to a much lesser extent.

That said, California is now considering adding processed meats to its Proposition 65 cancer-alert list. California's "Prop 65," an initiative approved in 1986, requires that the state keep a list of all chemicals and substances known to increase cancer risks. Producers of such products are required to provide "clear and reasonable" warnings for consumers (usually in the form of a warning label on implicated foods). Typically, once an item is added, it is up to the producer to prove to the state that its product is not dangerous enough to warrant a warning label.

As would be expected, the American meat industry is actively lobbying against this measure.

Organic

Once upon a time, one would not think twice about buying a fresh, ripe apple with a worm hole. Many people merely ate or cut around the opening, but those days are long gone. Once familiar, food imperfections have become unacceptable in the eyes of consumers. Because of reductions in crop yields or product quality due to pest infestation or competition from weeds, farmers began relying more heavily on pesticides. With the discovery of the potentially harmful health and environmental effects of these chemicals and the advent of the environmental movement, consumers and members of the medical and scientific communities began to voice opposition to the use of these chemicals. Concerned farmers sought another solution, which is how organic farming evolved. However, the fight over what is safe and good for people and the environment is an ongoing battle, with both sides standing firm.

Conventional Farming Versus Organic Farming

While the common assumption is that conventional farming using pesticides is dangerous and organic farming is safe, there are pros and cons to both. Pesticides used in food production are believed to help ensure a safe and adequate food supply and make foods available at a reasonable cost. In fact, many farmers claim that without them it would be impossible to stay in business because they would lose too much of their crop to make a profit. Unfortunately, chemical pesticides are highly toxic and nonspecific—that is, they destroy pests but also harm non-target organisms such as humans, wildlife, and beneficial

organisms in the environment. Further, they tend to persist for years in both soil and water. There are growing concerns that pesticides may be linked to increased cancer rates, decreased reproductive capability (in humans and wildlife), a wide assortment of mutations and animal extinctions, contamination of water supplies, and poisoning of wildlife habitats.

The alternative, organic farming, stresses the use of renewable resources, such as crop rotation, green manure, compost, biological pest control, and the conservation of soil and water, to enhance the quality of the environment. Organic foods are produced without antibiotics, hormones, synthetic fertilizers and pesticides, sewage sludge, genetic modifications, and spoilage-inhibiting radiation. Organic foods are often considered healthier because they are processed without artificial ingredients, preservatives, or irradiation, and environmentally friendly because soil nutrition is maintained naturally. Although organic farming techniques can benefit the environment, crop yields are typically lower than those conventionally grown. Lower crop yields paired with the laborious and time-intensive systems used by organic farms leads to more expensive products; therefore, consumers must decide if the potential benefits of the products are worth the extra cost.

Organic Foods and the Government

Today, many organic options are available, from fresh produce and meats to dairy products and cereals, to many types of processed foods. To protect consumers, the USDA regulates the production and labeling of organic foods. According to these rules, a food product cannot be labeled "organic" unless its production meets strict standards. For labeling purposes, certified organic food manufacturers can use the circular "USDA Organic" symbol on the package.

The USDA National Organic Program (NOP) defines organic as follows:

> Organic food is produced by farmers who emphasize the use of renewable resources and the conservation of soil and water to enhance environmental quality for future generations. Organic meat, poultry, eggs, and dairy products come from animals that are given no antibiotics or growth hormones. Organic food is produced without using most conventional pesticides; fertilizers made with synthetic ingredients or sewage sludge; bioengineering; or ionizing radiation. Before a product can be labeled "organic," a Government-approved certifier inspects the farm where the food is grown to make sure the farmer is following all the rules necessary to meet USDA organic standards. Companies that handle or process organic food before it gets to your local supermarket or restaurant must be certified, too.[59]

For more information about the government's organic food standards, visit the USDA's National Organic Program's website.[60]

Natural (Not Necessarily Organic) Foods

Natural foods may not contain additives or preservatives; however, they may contain ingredients that are genetically modified or even grown with pesticides. Although the ingredients on the food label may look familiar, natural foods are not regulated and do not have to meet the same criteria as organic foods. The USDA defines "natural" as:

FIGURE 16.21 Organic label.

Source: USDA.

A product containing no artificial ingredient or added color and is only minimally processed (a process which does not fundamentally alter the raw product) may be labeled natural. The label must explain the use of the term natural (such as—no added colorings or artificial ingredients; minimally processed).[61]

All-Natural

Natural and organic trends have been growing in popularity for some time now. Yet, what exactly does it mean to be "all-natural"? Increased consumer perception of the possible negative effects of artificial colors, flavors, and preservatives has changed the scope of food product development. We now see food companies switching from the artificial sweeteners and colors on which they once relied heavily to more natural alternatives. Now we are seeing the ingredient list shrink to the essential, supposedly natural ingredients.

Many food companies are jumping on the all-natural bandwagon to promote their products. For example, a major beverage company recently introduced a line of all-natural sodas, meaning simply that they have been reformulated with natural sugar to replace high-fructose corn syrup (HFCS). But does that make the soda any healthier? It is important to note that both sugar and HFCS provide the same number of calories per gram. While the FDA has no formal definition of "all-natural," it has not objected to the use of the term for products that contain no artificial colors or flavors or synthetic substances. The USDA, which regulates meat and poultry, defines as natural those products that are minimally processed and contain no artificial flavors or colors, or synthetic ingredients or chemical preservatives.

One unforeseen consequence to the food industry has been a plethora of lawsuits over the past few years (and several multimillion dollar payouts) launched by litigious groups of plaintiffs (and their lawyers) claiming that food and beverage manufacturers are trying to pull the wool over consumer's naïve eyes by including ingredients in their labeled "all-natural" products that aren't exactly all-natural. Huge multinational companies including FritoLay, General Mills, Unilever, Kellogg's, Campbell Soup, and many others are being sued for using such ingredients as alkalized cocoa, citric acid, ascorbic acid, maltodextrin, caramel color, even high-fructose corn syrup in their supposedly "all-natural" products. At question is whether these ingredients can truly be considered natural, when none of the manufacturing processes used to make them are "found in nature." As the lawsuits pile up, more and more of these companies are dropping "all-natural" entirely from their product labels and advertising.

But even if the manufacturers stop using the term *all-natural* to describe their products, the trend toward fewer, healthier and more familiar ingredients seems to "have legs." This trend is even seen in traditionally unhealthy snack foods such as chips, crackers, and cakes. That said, consumers are notorious trend followers, and after the initial glow wears off, they may go back to their cheaper, "better tasting" old favorites (remember the uproar when the Twinkies bakeries closed down?). In addition, the natural, all-natural, and organic movements have not stemmed the tide of obesity one iota. Overeating organic or all-natural foods can still make you fat!

Functional Foods

There is an ongoing debate between food manufacturers and consumer advocates about the promotion of what are called functional foods. Functional foods are any that provide health benefits beyond basic nutrition. While all foods are functional in that they provide nutrients, foods considered functional are formulated to supply one or more dietary ingredients that may improve health, or they contain high levels of substances that tend to prevent certain diseases. What qualifies foods as functional? Sodas with added vitamins, calcium-fortified juices and soy milks, yogurts with specialized strains of bacteria, and many other enhanced foods or vitamin-fortified products constitute a large portion of the functional food market. In any U.S. supermarket one finds energy bars, breakfast cereals, bottled waters, sports and energy beverages, herbal teas, breads, and soups spiked with vitamins, minerals, and botanicals (taurine, valerian, St. John's wort, and so on). Also, foods rich in phytochemicals are now part of the functional food family, such as processed tomato products that contain the phytochemical lycopene.

Every food has its function; however, not every food is a functional food, according to the ADA, which defines functional foods as "whole foods and fortified, enriched, or enhanced foods that have a potentially beneficial effect on health when consumed as part of a varied, regular diet. They are considered to contain a healthful food or food ingredient that may provide a health benefit beyond the traditional nutrients."[62] The term *functional* implies that the food has some identified value leading to health benefits, including reduced risk for disease, for the person consuming it.[63]

Unmodified whole foods, such as fruits and vegetables, represent the simplest form of functional foods. For example, broccoli, carrots, and tomatoes are considered functional foods because they are rich in physiologically active components such as sulforaphane, beta carotene, and lycopene, respectively.[64] Modified foods, including those fortified with nutrients or enhanced with phytochemicals or botanicals, may also be considered functional foods.[65] The term *functional food* should not be used to imply that there are good foods and bad foods, as all foods can be incorporated into a healthful eating plan—the key being moderation and variety.[66]

Prebiotics and Probiotics

Prebiotics and probiotics are getting more attention in the food world and now make up a class of functional foods by themselves. *Prebiotics* are non-digestible carbohydrates that stimulate the growth or activity of beneficial bacteria in the colon; these may help preserve intestinal health by preventing pathogens from gaining a foothold, maintaining digestive regularity, and aiding in the prevention of colon cancer while decreasing blood triglycerides, glucose, and insulin levels. The most prevalent forms of prebiotics are nutritionally classed as *soluble fiber*.

Probiotics, which means "for life" or "pro-life," are living organisms that provide health benefits when consumed in adequate amounts. Probiotics, also known as "friendly" bacteria, enter the body via consumption of fermented foods or

FIGURE 16.22 Examples of prebiotic and probiotic foods.

Prebiotics

Chicory

Jerusalem artichokes

Wheat

Barley

Rye

Onions

Garlic

Leeks

Probiotics (actual bacteria found in given foods)

Yogurt with live culture

Buttermilk

Cottage cheese

Dairy spreads with inulin

Soy sauce

Tempeh

Fresh pickles and sauerkraut

Miso

through the taking of microbial supplements to help colonize the colon with microorganisms that help protect and heal the colon lining. Friendly bacteria are vital to proper development of the immune system, protection against pathogens, and enhanced digestion as well as absorption of nutrients. The probiotic strains most frequently employed in foods and supplements are the Lactobacillus and Bifidobacterium species. Common probiotic-containing foods are yogurt and kefir, unpasteurized pickles, sauerkraut and kimchi, miso soup, olives, and dark chocolate. Dehydrated probiotic pure cultures are also available in tablet form to use as dietary supplements.

The importance of the bifidobacteria and the lactic acid bacteria (also called *lactobacillus* or *LABs*) is that they have several beneficial effects on the host, especially in terms of improving digestion (including enhancing mineral absorption) and the effectiveness and intrinsic strength of the immune system. Because, generally speaking, the American diet is lacking in soluble fiber, prebiotics are increasingly added to processed foods—including yogurts, cereals, breads, biscuits, milk desserts, nutritional supplement bars, ice creams, spreads, drinks, water, and infant formula, as well as to some animal foods—for their health benefits.

This is an excellent opportunity for the food product developer working on healthy food projects. While there are no legal definitions for an ingredient to be considered a prebiotic, it must meet the following terms:

- It is not broken down and absorbed in the body.
- It is selectively fermented by the good bacteria (probiotics) in the gastrointestinal tract.
- It stimulates the growth of these good bacteria in the gut.

Among the trillions of bacterial cells in the human body, it is estimated that there are only around 1000 varieties.[67] Some of these have a vital role in maintaining human health, while others have negative impacts. One main role of probiotics is to create a living barrier that prevents damaging bacteria and viruses from multiplying inside the body. It does this by increasing the acidity of the intestinal environment to create less desirable living conditions for potential pathogens. Probiotic organisms are like microscopic defenders that protect your body from invading organisms.[68] Probiotics offer other functions besides defense, such as:

- Breaking down food for easier digestion of certain nutrients.
- Producing the lactase enzyme (which helps digest milk sugar).
- Producing vitamins in the intestinal tract.

Prebiotics and probiotics are assumed to be safe because some probiotic foods, such as fermented foods and cultured milk products, date to ancient times. *Lactobacillus plantarum* is one of the lactic acid–producing bacteria used for centuries

FIGURE 16.23 Categories of bioactive compounds.

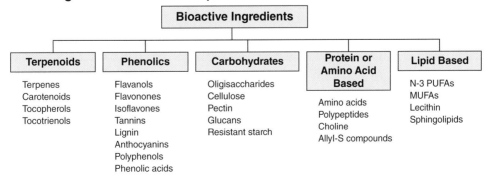

FIGURE 16.24 Bioactive components in foods, sources, and purported benefits.

Bioactive Component	Sources	Benefits
Soy foods	Soybeans, soy protein	Reduce risk of CHD (coronary heart disease)
Daidzein, Genestein	Soy	Menopausal health, immune function, bone health
Carotenoids		
β-Carotene	Citrus, carrots, pumpkin, squash	Free radical scavenger, converted to Vitamin A *in vivo*
Lutein, Zeazanthin	Spinach, corn, eggs, citrus	Antioxidant, eye health
Lycopene	Tomatoes, watermelon	Antioxidant, prostate health
Dietary fats (fatty acids)		
Monounsaturated fatty acids	Olive oil, canola oil	Reduced risk of CHD
Conjugated linoleic acid	Beef, lamb, dairy products	Immune function and improved body composition
Omega-3 fatty acids	Fish and fish oils	Reduced risk of CHD, improved mental acuity, vision
Dietary fiber and prebiotics		
Insoluble fiber	Cereal bran (wheat and corn)	Digestive health, cancer prevention
Beta-glucans	Oatmeal, oat bran, barley	Reduces CHD risk
Soluble fiber	Psyllium, beans, apples	Reduces CHD risk
Whole grains	Wheat, brown rice, cereals	Reduces CHD risk, controls serum glucose levels
Inulin and fructo-oligosaccharides	Whole grains, fruits, garlic, onions	Improved immune function, gastrointestinal health, mineral absorption
Probiotics	Yogurt, culture dairy	Immune function, GI health
Sulfur compounds		
Allyl sulfides	Onions, leeks, garlic	Immune function, heart health
Dithiothionones	Cruciferous vegetables	Immune function and detoxification
Sulforaphane	Broccoli, cauliflower, kale	Cellular antioxidant, detoxification
Phytosterols and satanols	Soy, wood, fortified table spreads	Reduce LDL cholesterol
Flavonoids		
Anthocyanins: Cyanidin, Malvidin, Delphinidin	Cane berries, cherries, grapes, red wine	Antioxidant defenses
Flavone-3-ols, Catechins, Epicatechins, Procyanidins	Tea, chocolate, apples	Heart health, anti-inflammation
Flavonols: Quercetin, Kaempferol	Apples, broccoli, tea, onions, blueberries, red wine	Scavenge free radicals, anti-oxidant, anti-inflammatory
Pronathocyanidins	Cranberries, apples, strawberries, wine, cinnamon	Heart health, antioxidants, urinary tract health
Flavones: Luteolin, Apigenin	Celery, parsley, sweet peppers	Antioxidants, anti-cancer
Isoflavones: Genestein, Daidzein, Glycitein	Soy and other beans	Menopausal health, bone health

Source: Darryl Holliday.

to preserve food. In recent years, it has been shown to decrease irritable bowel syndrome symptoms and compete successfully against unfriendly bacteria.[69]

While until recently foods and supplements containing pre- and probiotics were more common in Japan and European countries than in the United States, today we are seeing an influx of products claiming the presence of friendly bacteria. In fact, Americans' spending on probiotic foods and supplements exceeded $900 million in 2011.[70]

Bioactive Ingredients/Phytonutrients

Bioactive compounds are those that, when present in or added to foods, may have a therapeutic effect in the body. Phytonutrients are bioactive compounds that originate in plants. Antioxidants are bioactive because, when absorbed, they protect the body by preventing lipid oxidation and breakdown, or by reducing free radicals involved in destructive oxidative reactions, including those involved in aging. Another example of bioactivity is the reduction in plasma cholesterol due to isoflavones (a type of plant hormone). The inclusion of plant isoflavones in products such as margarine, salad dressing, and orange juice provides this cholesterol-lowering effect in functional foods that are convenient for the consumer. Documentation of the benefits of adding bioactive ingredients to foods is difficult, as many appear gradually over time, making it difficult to prove a direct cause-and-effect relationship. However, antioxidants, which prevent lipid oxidation in the short term, are proven to reduce the risk of cardiovascular disease and some types of cancer.[71]

Phenolics

Phenolics encompass a wide range of phytochemicals (naturally occurring chemical compounds in plants that may be beneficial for health), ranging from relatively simple phenolic acids to flavonoids to complex anthocyanins and tannins. Scientific studies indicate that many phenolics provide significant health benefits.[72] For example, it is widely accepted that regular consumption of red wine (which contains the phenolic compound resveratrol) is associated with the French Paradox, wherein even though the French diet is rich in fats, particularly saturated fat, the incidence of heart disease in France is much lower than in other Western countries with similar fatty diets. Wine and tea polyphenols possess antioxidant activity, which may reduce total cholesterol and lower lipoprotein oxidation concentrations and chronic inflammation. Catechin, a polyphenolic in tea, is shown to provide increased antioxidant capacity.[73]

Anthocyanins are another group of bioactives that may provide health benefits. These colored compounds are found in berries, red wine, and purple vegetables.

One measure of the antioxidant potential of a food is its oxygen radical absorbance capacity (ORAC). This analytical tool measures the ability of a food or ingredient to remove oxygen radicals in a model system. However, the relationship between these *in vitro* ("in glass") measurements done on a lab bench and the ultimate health benefit these foods may provide remains controversial because the antioxidant components must be absorbed by the body in order to have an effect. That said, since improved antioxidant status in the body helps prevent chronic diseases, and antioxidants from foods are widely available, plenty of new opportunities are emerging to deliver convenient foods with high antioxidant capacity.

Flavonoids

Flavonoids represent a family of over 5000 bioactive compounds derived from fruits and vegetables that deliver high antioxidant activity. These materials can be extracted, concentrated, and used as food ingredients in functional foods or as nutraceutical supplements. A neutraceutical is different from a functional food:

A functional food is similar in appearance to, or may actually be, a conventional food consumed as part of a usual diet that is demonstrated to have physiological benefits or reduce the risk of chronic disease beyond basic nutritional functions—that is, it contains bioactive compounds.

A nutraceutical is a product isolated or purified from foods that is generally sold in medicinal forms not usually associated with foods. A nutraceutical is demonstrated to have a physiological benefit or provide protection against chronic disease. Examples include dietary supplements and herbal products.

FIGURE 16.25 Phytonutrients and their proposed activity.

Phytonutrient	Proposed Activity
Anthocyanin	Antioxidant. Reduces risk of cancer. Prevents urinary tract infection.
Beta-carotene	Antioxidant. Reduces risk of some cancers. Improves lung function.
Carotenoids	Antioxidants.
Ellagic acid	Reduces risk of some cancers. Lowers cholesterol levels.
Hesperetin	Protects against heart disease.
Liminoids	Antioxidants. Protect against heart disease by lowering cholesterol.
Lutein	Maintains healthy vision. Reduces the risk of cataracts, macular degeneration, and some cancers.
Lycopene	Reduces risk of prostate cancers and heart disease.
Monterpenes	Reduce the risk of some cancers.
Polyphenols	Antioxidants. Anti-inflammatory.
Resveratrol	Antioxidant. Reduces the risk some cancers.
Tannins	Reduce risk of heart disease.
Tangeritin	Protects against some cancers.

Source: Darryl Holliday.

●Conclusion

Increased focus on nutrition is a growing trend and marketing tool in and of itself. As new ideas surrounding nutrition and health innovations continue to develop, strategies to capitalize on the consumer's desire for a healthier diet will open the door for new and improved food product development. Organic foods, gluten-free foods, and GMO-free foods are already experiencing exploding growth, and any company that can offer foods in any (or all) of these categories will have a competitive advantage over those that don't. What does the future hold? More foods and beverages that promise condition-specific benefits, such as stress-reducing foods, are likely to have a growing presence in the food industry. Also, brain foods, bone foods, digestive-health foods, and appetite-curbing foods are gaining momentum. Options for diabetics will be seen even more frequently. Interest in natural nutritional ingredients, including hempseed and hemp oil, antioxidant-potent spices (for example, cumin, cinnamon, and turmeric), gut-friendly pre- and probiotics, and high omega-3-foods like flax, will continue to grow.

The development of health-promoting foods represents major opportunities for all stages of the food industry. Both conventional plant breeding and modern transgenic techniques can be used to increase bioactive ingredients, increase fiber and resistant starch, increase proteins that deliver bioactivity, and alter lipid structure to produce healthier lipids, less prone to oxidation and more nutritionally beneficial.

Culinology® professionals can develop high-quality, great-tasting, healthier alternatives to high-fat, high-sodium, high-sugar foods. As an integrated system, the food industry can deliver significant improvements to the diet, which can markedly enhance public health through the reduction of caloric density and increased levels of health-promoting ingredients.

[1] www.choosemyplate.gov/myplate.

[2] Centers for Disease Control, "Fruit and Vegetable Consumption Data and Statistics: Data and Statistics Display," retrieved on January 21, 2010, from http://apps.nccd.cdc.gov/5ADaySurveillance/.

[3] J. Schwartz, and C. Byrd-Bredbenner. "Portion Distortion: Typical Portion Sizes Selected by Young Adults." *Journal of the American Dietetic Association* 106, no. 9 (2006): 1412–1418.

[4] Department of Health and Human Services and U.S. Dept. of Agriculture, *Dietary Guidelines for Americans 2005*, 6th ed. www.healthierus.gov/dietaryguidelines.

[5] M. Condrasky, J. H. Ledikwe, J. E. Flood, and B. J. Rolls, "Chefs' Opinions of Restaurant Portion Sizes," *Obesity* 15 (2007): 2086–2094.

[6] B. J. Rolls, *The Volumetrics Eating Plan: Techniques and Recipes for Feeling Full on Fewer Calories* (New York: HarperCollins, 2005).

[7] ———, "The Supersizing of America: Portion Size and the Obesity Epidemic," *Nutrition Today* 38 (2003): 42–53.

[8] B. J. Rolls, *The Volumetrics Eating Plan*.

[9] U.S. Department of Health and Human Services and U.S. Department of Agriculture. *Dietary Guidelines for Americans, 2005,* 6th ed. (Washington, DC: U.S. Government Printing Office, 2005).

[10] www.choosemyplate.gov/myplate.

[11] Ibid.

[12] J. C. Rickman, D. M. Barrett, and C. M. Bruhn, "Nutritional Comparison of Fresh, Frozen and Canned Fruits and Vegetables. Part I. Vitamins C and B and Phenolic Compounds," *Journal of the Science of Food and Agriculture* 87 (2007): 930–944. doi: 10.1002/jsfa.2825

[13] J. C. Rickman, C. M. Bruhn, and D. M. Barrett, "Nutritional Comparison of Fresh, Frozen, and Canned Fruits and Vegetables. Part II. Vitamin A and Carotenoids, Vitamin E, Minerals and Fiber," *Journal of the Science of Food and Agriculture* 87 (2007): 1185–1196. doi: 10.1002/jsfa.2824

[14] J. Bonke, "Economic Influences on Food Choice—Non-convenience versus Convenience Food Consumption," in H. MacFie and H. L. Meiselman, eds., *Food Choice, Acceptance and Consumption* (2012): 293–318.

[15] https://www.gnu.org/software/gnutrition/

[16] J. D. Wright et al., "Trends in Intake of Energy and Macronutrients: United States, 1997–2000," *MMWR* 2204 (53): 80–82.

[17] Boutrif (1991); Schaafsma (2000).

[18] Schaafsma (2000).

[19] A. Chaddha and K. A. Eagle, "Omega-3 Fatty Acids and Heart Health," *Circulation* 132 (2015): e350–e352.

[20] A. P. Simopoulos, "The Importance of the Omega-6/Omega-3 Fatty Acid Ratio in Cardiovascular Disease and Other Chronic Diseases," *Experimental Biology and Medicine* 233, no. 6 (2008): 674–688.

[21] http://www.heart.org/HEARTORG/GettingHealthy/NutritionCenter/HealthyDietGoals/Fish-and-Omega-3-Fatty-Acids_UCM_303248_Article.jsp#.

[22] F. B. Hu, J. E. Manson, and W. C. Willett, "Types of Dietary Fat and Risk of Coronary Heart Disease: A Critical Review." *Journal of the American College of Nutrition* 61, no. 1 (2001): 5–19; M. Fleith and M. Clandirin, "Dietary PUFA for Preterm and Term Infants: Review of Clinical Studies," *Critical Reviews in Food Science and Nutrition* 45, no. 3 (2005): 205–229.

[23] P. French, C. Stanton, F. Lawless, E. G. O'Riordan, F. J. Monahan, P. J. Caffrey, and A. P. Moloney, "Fatty Acid Composition, Including Conjugated Linoleic Acid, of Intramuscular Fat from Steers Offered Grazed Grass, Grass Silage, or Concentrate-based Diets," *Journal of Animal Science* 78, no. 11 (2000): 2849–2855.

[24] A. Bhattacharya, J. Banu, M. Rahman, J. Causey, and G. Fernandes, "Biological Effects of Conjugated Linoleic Acids in Health and Disease," *The Journal of Nutritional Biochemistry* 17, no. 12 (2006): 789–810.

[25] http://www.fda.gov/downloads/Food/IngredientsPackagingLabeling/GRAS/NoticeInventory/UCM269264.

[26] L. Tappy and K.-A. Le, "Metabolic Effects of Fructose and the Worldwide Increase in Obesity," *Physiological Reviews* 90, no. 1 (2010): 23–46.

[27] L. Brown, B. Rosner, W. Willett, and F. Sacks, "Cholesterol-lowering Effects of Dietary Fiber: A Meta-analysis," *The American Journal of Clinical Nutrition* 69, no. 1 (1999): 30–42.

[28] J. W. Anderson and K. Ward, "Long-term Effects of High-carbohydrate, High-fiber Diets on Glucose and Lipid Metabolism: A Preliminary Report on Patients with Diabetes," *Diabetes Care* 1, no. 2 (1978): 77–82.

[29] M. Roberfroid, "Dietary Fiber, Inulin, and Oligofructose: A Review Comparing Their Physiological Effects," *Critical Reviews in Food Science and Nutrition* 33, no. 2 (1993): 103–148.

[30] P. D. Schley and C. J. Field, "The Immune-enhancing Effects of Dietary Fibres and Prebiotics," *British Journal of Nutrition* 87, Suppl. 2 (2002): S221–S230.

[31] C. Coudray, C. Domigne, and Y. Rayssiguier, "Effects of Dietary Fibers on Magnesium Absorption in Animals and Humans," *The Journal of Nutrition* 133, no. 1 (2003): 1–4.

[32] J. R. Hess, A. M. Birkett, W. Thomas, and J. L. Slavin, "Effects of Short-chain Fructooligosaccharides on Satiety Responses in Healthy Men and Women," *Appetite* 56, no. 1 (2011): 128–134.

[33] M. D. Robertson, J. M. Currie, L. M. Morgan, D. P. Jewell, and K. N. Frayn, "Prior Short-term Consumption of Resistant Starch Enhances Postprandial Insulin Sensitivity in Healthy Subjects," *Diabetologia* 46, no. 5 (2003): 659–665.

[34]A. Nilsson, E. Ostman, T. Preston, and I. Bjorck, "Effects of GI vs Content of Cereal Fibre of the Evening Meal on Glucose Tolerance at a Subsequent Standardized Breakfast," *European Journal of Clinical Nutrition* 62, no. 6 (2008): 712–720.

[35]D. Mikulikova and J. Kraic, "Natural Sources of Health-promoting Starch," *Journal of Food and Nutrition Research* 45, no. 2 (2006): 69–76.

[36]G. Zhang and B. R. Hamaker, "Review: Cereal Carbohydrates and Colon Health," *Cereal Chemistry* 87, no. 4 (2010): 331–341.

[37]S. Kajiyama, G. Hasegawa, M. Asano, H. Hosoda, M. Fukui, N. Nakamura, J. Kitawaki, S. Imai, K. Nakano, M. Ohta, T. Adachi, H. Obayashi, and T. Yoshikawa, "Supplementation of Hydrogen-rich Water Improves Lipid and Glucose Metabolism in Patients with Type 2 Diabetes or Impaired Glucose Tolerance," *Nutrition Research* 28, no. 3 (2008): 137–143.

[38]E. A. Dennis, A. L. Dengo, D. L. Comber, K. D. Flack, J. Savla, K. P. Davy, and B. M. Davy, "Water Consumption Increases Weight Loss During a Hypocaloric Diet Intervention in Middle-aged and Older Adults," *Obesity* 18, no. 2 (2009): 300–307.

[39]B. M. Davy, E. A. Dennis, A. L. Dengo, K. L. Wilson, and K. P. Davy, "Water Consumption Reduces Energy Intake at a Breakfast Meal in Obese Older Adults," *Journal of the American Dietetic Association* 108, no. 7 (2008): 1236–1239.

[40]http://www.reuters.com/article/2011/07/12/us-campbellsoup-idUSTRE 76B2V320110712.

[41]K. G. Dewey and K. H. Brown, "Update on Technical Issues Concerning Complementary Feeding of Young Children in Developing Countries and Implications for Intervention Programs," *Food and Nutrition Bulletin* 24, no. 1 (2003): 5–28.

[42]C. Lutter and K. Dewey, "Proposed Nutrient Composition for Fortified Complementary Foods," *Journal of Nutrition* 133, no. 9 (2003): 3011S–3020S.

[43]http://ntrs.nasa.gov/archive/nasa/casi.ntrs.nasa.gov/19940015664.pdf.

[44]M. Heron and Centers for Disease Control, "Deaths: Leading Causes for 2004," *National Vital Statistics Reports* (November 20, 2007), http://www.cdc.gov/nchs/data/nvsr/nvsr56/nvsr56_05.pdf.

[45]http://www.cdc.gov/diabetes/pdfs/library/diabetesreportcard2014.pdf.

[46]http://www.diabetes.org/diabetes-basics/diagnosis/?loc=db-slabnav.

[47]American Diabetes Association (2009), http://www.diabetes.org/home.jsp.

[48]*U.S. News & World Report*, "Healthiest Diet" (November 1, 2011) and "Best Diet Overall" (June 7, 2011), http://health.usnews.com/best-diet/best-overall-diets.

[49]S. Clark et al., "Frequency of U.S. Emergency Department Visits for Food-Related Acute Allergic Reactions," *Journal of Allergy and Clinical Immunology* 127, no. 3 (2001): 682–683.

[50]Centers for Disease Control, *National Center for Chronic Disease Prevention and Health Promotion, Division of Adolescent and School Health* (October 23, 2008) http://www.cdc.gov/healthyyouth/foodallergies/#2.

[51]K. Jackson et al., "Trends in Allergic Conditions Among Children: United States, 1997–2011," *National Center for Health Statistics Data Brief* (2013), retrieved from www.cdc.gov/nchs/data/databriefs/db10.htm.

[52]S. H. Sicherer, "Food Allergy," *Lancet* 360 (2002): 701–710; S. H. Sicherer, A. Munoz-Furlong, and H. A. Sampson, "Prevalence of Peanut and Tree Nut Allergy in the United States Determined by Means of Random Digit Dial Telephone Survey: A Five-Year Follow-Up Study," *Journal of Allergy and Clinical Immunology* 112 (2003):1203–1207; J. Grundy et al., "Rising Prevalence of Allergy to Peanut in Children: Data from Two Sequential Cohorts," *Journal of Allergy and Clinical Immunology* 110 (2002): 784–789.

[53]S. L. Taylor and J. L. Baumert, "Cross-Contamination of Foods and Implications for Food Allergic Patients," *Current Allergy and Asthma Reports* 10, no. 4 (2010): 265–270.

[54]S. L. Hefle, T. J. Furlong, L. Niemann, H. Lemon-Mule, S. Sicherer, and S. L. Taylor, "Consumer Attitudes and Risks Associated with Packaged Foods Having Advisory Labeling Regarding the Presence of Peanuts," *Journal of Allergy and Clinical Immunology* 120, no. 1 (2007): 171–176.

[55]P. Gupta, M. J. Favus, H. Andrew, and S. Guandalini, "Prevalence of Celiac Disease in Patients with Osteoporosis in United States," *The American Journal of Gastroenterology* 107 (2012): 1538–1544.

[56]MarketsandMarkets.com (May 2013).

[57]Mintel, "Gluten Free Food—US," September 2013 Report.

[58]http://www.fda.gov/Food/NewsEvents/ConstituentUpdates/ucm407867.htm.

[59]7 CFR Part205 http://www.ecfr.gov/cgi-bin/text-idx?c=ecfr&sid=3f34f4c22 f9aa8e6d9864cc2683cea02&tpl=/ecfrbrowse/Title07/7cfr205_main_02.tpl.

[60]http://www.ams.usda.gov/about-ams/programs-offices/national-organic-program.

[61]http://www.fsis.usda.gov/wps/portal/fsis/topics/food-safety-education/get-answers/food-safety-fact-sheets/food-labeling/meat-and-poultry-labeling-terms/meat-and-poultry-labeling-terms/.

[62]"Backgrounder: Functional Foods," in *Food Insight Media Guide* (Washington, DC: International Food Information Council Foundation, 1998).

[63]"Position of the American Dietetic Association: Functional Foods," *Journal of the American Dietetic Association* 104 (2004): 814–826.

[64]Ibid.

[65]Ibid.

[66]I. Siró, E. Kápolna, B. Kápolna, and A. Lugasi, "Functional Food. Product Development, Marketing and Consumer Acceptance—A Review," *Appetite* 51, no. 3 (2008): 456–467.

[67]E. K. Costello, C. L. Lauber, M. Hamady, N. Fierer, J. I. Gordon, and R. Knight, "Bacterial Community Variation in Human Body Habitats Across Space and Time," *Science* 326, no. 5960 (2009): 1694–1697.

[68]G. Reid and J. A. Hammond, "Probiotics: Some Evidence of Their Effectiveness," *Canadian Family Physician* 51 (2005): 1487–1493.

[69]J. A. J. Madden and J. O. Hunter, "A Review of the Role of the Gut Microflora in Irritable Bowel Syndrome and the Effects of Probiotics," *British Journal of Nutrition* 88 (2002): s67–s72; E. M. M. Quigley and B. Flourie, "Probiotics and Irritable Bowel Syndrome: A Rationale for Their Use and an Assessment of the Evidence to Date," *Neurogastroenterology and Motility* 19, no. 3 (2006): 166–172.

[70]"Probiotics Lead the Digestive Market," *Natural Products Insider* (March 11, 2013).

[71]M. G. L. Hertog et al., "Dietary Antioxidant Flavonoids and Risk of Coronary Heart Disease: The Zutphen Elderly Study," *Lancet* 342, no. 8878 (1993): 1007–1011; D. L. Tribble, "Antioxidant Consumption and Risk of Coronary Heart Disease: Emphasis on Vitamin C, Vitamin E, and Beta-Carotene: A Statement for Healthcare Professionals from the American Heart Association," *Circulation* 99 (1999): 591–595.

[72]R. H. Liu, "Health Benefits of Fruit and Vegetables Are from Additive and Synergistic Combinations of Phytochemicals," *American Journal of Clinical Nutrition* 78, no. 3 (2003): 517S–520S.

[73]W. E. Bronner and G. R. Beecher, "Method for Determining the Content of Catechins in Tea Infusions by High-Performance Liquid Chromatography," *Journal of Chromatography* 1–2, no. 805 (1998): 137–142; Z. Y. Chen et al., "Degradation of Green Tea Catechins in Tea Drinks," *Journal of Agricultural and Food Chemistry* 49, no. 1 (2001): 477–482; T. T. C. Yang and M. L. W. Koo, "Chinese Green Tea Lowers Cholesterol Level Through an Increase in Fecal Lipid Excretion," *Life Sciences* 5, no. 66 (1999): 4111–4123.

17 Sensory Evaluation

Lead Author: Witoon Prinyawiwatkul, Ph.D., Professor, School of Nutrition and Food Sciences, Louisiana State University Agricultural Center

Robert Delaney, Manager of Product Innovation, Smithfield

M. Michele Foley, Director, Sensory and Consumer Insights, Nestlé

Dustin Hilinski, Director of Culinary Development, Red Lobster

Howard R. Moskowitz, Ph.D., Chairman, iNovum LLC, Chairman, Mind Genomics Associates

●Introduction

Sensory evaluation, also called organoleptic analysis, is a multidisciplinary science used to understand human perception and response to the sensory characteristics of food. Its foundation comprises empirical and theoretical contributions from many fields, including the psychology of human perception, sensory physiology, social science, anthropology, marketing, and food science as well as chemistry and statistics.[1]

Research chefs are increasingly integrated into the product development process. Although they can contribute at many stages, research chefs are usually involved early on, particularly during the concept and prototype development phases.[2] Many chefs develop what is called the culinary gold standard, namely, the product that serves as the benchmark for subsequent commercialization (see Chapter 19). Once the gold standard is established, the research and development (R&D) team develops the production model and runs scale-up and pilot plant tests.[3]

Collaboration between sensory evaluation, Culinology®, product development, and marketing research is important and necessary in order to improve the likelihood of marketplace success. Sensory evaluation techniques are commonly used throughout the product development process, from inception to launch, in order to translate consumer insights into product design as well as processing specifications. Business decisions and product development direction often rely on sensory feedback to reduce the risk of failing to meet consumer needs and expectations.

●The Product Development Chef and Sensory Evaluation

A chef developing foods for mass production, where the end users can number in the millions, must depart from typical chef thinking. Traditional restaurant chefs are trained to be the primary decision makers about recipe development, menu design, cooking and plating style—virtually everything related to preparing and presenting the food to their (hopefully) adoring public. Chefs figuratively put themselves on every plate that leaves the kitchen; the more idiosyncratic, the more personalized they make the food, the more competitive they are in a highly competitive market. If the chef cannot generate a following, the restaurant will fail. All of the pressure for the restaurant to succeed is on the chef's shoulders. Yet, in a mass manufacturing setting, commercial reality must intervene. When developing products for the mainstream marketplace, where enormous amounts of money are at risk, the opinion of a single individual, even an experienced culinary professional, is only marginally important; chefs need the input of other product development professionals and actual consumers to be successful in this arena.

Chefs are generally not good at giving up control. After all, the word *chef* comes from the French for "chief." The reality is that in most kitchens the chef's palate is the sole source of direction. By comparison, in commercial product development all parties, chef included, must be ready to relinquish that control and to accept the direction provided by the consumer. Product development (PD) chefs must accept continuous (not always positive) feedback and become accustomed to participating as an equal member in a cross-functional team, where they may not be the leader. The chef's input is certainly valued, but it is only one part of the successful product development equation. The company must deliver the best possible product to consumers at reasonable cost, safely, and with good stability. The consumer is the glue in the puzzle that combines culinary art with food science.

The marketplace has a lot to say. The days of launching a product based on the opinions of a few are over; the marketplace is just too competitive. The cost of launching new items is prohibitive. Retailers routinely challenge what goes on their shelves; slotting fees in the millions of dollars are commonly imposed on food manufacturers to put a new product onto an already overstocked grocery shelf in a large chain supermarket. To remain on the shelf and to see a return on their investment, food manufacturers must listen to the voice of the consumers.

Most consumer feedback is based on personal preference developed through a lifetime of family influences and other life experiences. For product developers, it is an enormous source of information that allows them to better design or improve products for specific consumer populations.

In general, chefs who are new to the corporate world are at a bit of a disadvantage. Restaurant chefs lack the experience, knowledge, and understanding of the benefits of consumer testing. Their only knowledge of sensory analysis is what is technically called a subjective affective or preference test; if something on their menu doesn't sell—that is, is "not preferred"—it is dropped. On the other hand, in the food manufacturing world, the chef is provided with an enormous variety of data from a battery of sensory tests; this can be mined for valuable information to use in developing better, more marketable products. But in order to be heard, chefs must speak the same language as the other people on the PD team. Knowledge of common sensory terminology is essential.

In the past, product developers (scientists and technologists) rarely learned the culinary arts, which is to some degree an emotional process rather than a science. Food excites emotional responses in all of us, and chefs tend to cook with emotion. But beyond art or science is *business*. The product must be developed in such a way that it can be manufactured consistently and economically and distributed widely at very high volumes with an extended shelf life, in a safe, wholesome, and affordable way. So art and emotion must merge with commercial reality. Understanding and integrating these sometimes competing objectives goes a long way toward improving the working relationship between art and business. With Culinology®, the barriers are finally being broken, with more food scientists exploring culinary arts and more chefs studying food science with the common goal of giving consumers the best possible foods while maximizing profit for their companies.

The explosion of information in the media has made consumers better versed in food than ever before. They have learned to speak some of the chef's language and are more attentive to details such as texture, flavor intensity, ethnic and regional authenticity, and cooking methods. And the consumer is, without a doubt, the most powerful member of the product development team. Sensory evaluation, working with consumers, provides direction for both the chef and the food scientist, who can incorporate the consumer's responses into the product development process. Even after a product is finalized, sensory evaluation continues to play an essential role in monitoring scale-up, process changes, cost reductions, product improvements, and shelf-life testing. With the ever-increasing costs of launching new products, the enormous number of new product failures, and rapidly multiplying competition, sensory evaluation is clearly critical to success in today's food industry.

●Technical Aspects and Applications of Sensory Evaluation

Products attain market success when they meet a consumer need at an appropriate price, when their benefits are well communicated to the target consumers, and when they deliver to the expectations generated by their positioning.[4] Consumer product research is a tool used to achieve all these factors by measuring preference, liking, and attitudes of consumers toward a product as a whole, toward specific characteristics, product concepts, and even services wrapped around products. Consumer responses are important in new product development, product improvement, product maintenance, new product potential or category appraisal, and product claim substantiation. Most successful new product efforts start and end with the consumer.[5] As such, the use of consumer product research has become more common, and the results are more widely used to aid the business decision-making process. Nowadays, whether a company develops new products, copies competitor products, or attempts to enter new market segments, input from sensory evaluation is vital.

The Five "In" Steps of the Product Development Pathway

The following five innovation steps are used throughout the product development cycle: insight, inspiration, interpretation, introduction, and inspection.

1. *Insight*—The product must solve an unmet consumer need or problem. With constantly changing marketplace and consumer trends, it is increasingly difficult to predict consumer responses. Uncovering consumer needs is critical in the early stages of the product development process. During the insight stage, researchers use exploratory qualitative methods to help identify needs and quantitative methods to estimate the size of the opportunity.

FIGURE 17.1 **Some common questions that require sensory-related answers.**

1. Are the two products different? If so, in what way do they differ?
2. Is our product similar to the competitor's?
3. Which of the two products is sweeter? Which one is sweetest among these five?
4. How can I evaluate the intensity of sweetness of this product?
5. Which product is more preferred by consumers?
6. Is the improved or reformulated product better than our current or competitors'?
7. Will the taste and texture change if we use cheaper ingredients?
8. How does the use of a new twin-screw extruder impact overall sensory quality?
9. How consistent in quality are all products from different batches and locations?
10. What was the cause of the product disliking and the negative purchase intent?
11. What would be the optimal salt and sugar concentration for this product?
12. How can I mimic the flavor and texture of this product?
13. Based on sensory liking, can we predict consumers' willingness to purchase?
14. How can I mask the bitterness but enhance the saltiness of this product?
15. How do consumers respond to the product performance or the baking instruction?
16. What do consumers think about this new product concept?
17. How do consumers use the products? How do they fit into consumers' lives?

Source: Witoon Prinyawiwatkul, Ph.D., Robert Delaney, M. Michele Foley, Dustin Hilinski, and Howard R. Moskowitz, Ph.D.

2. *Inspiration*—To meet a need identified in the insight stage, ideas are generated through ideation sessions and other creative thought–provoking activities. These might be written concepts developed by a cross-functional product development team or culinary prototypes created by PD chefs to represent these concepts. Typically, ideas are screened based on overall appeal (as measured by acceptance or purchase intent data) and uniqueness, both qualitatively and quantitatively. It is important for the product development team leader (usually the most experienced member of the team) to remain involved throughout this process to ensure the prototypes are realistic and can be produced commercially.

3. *Interpretation*—Based on concepts and culinary prototypes, product developers formulate *commercialized* products that use commercial ingredients and are designed to be manufactured on the company's equipment. At this stage, more detailed estimates are made about the potential size of the business. Understanding how the new product will affect the current business, whether it will be used by consumers in addition to or as a replacement for a current product, is important at this stage. Sensory methods are used with both external consumers and internal descriptive panels. Estimates of business impact are made from consumer responses. Comparative descriptive sensory evaluation is used to ensure that commercialized product formulations maintain close similarity to the culinary gold standards.

4. *Introduction*—Commercial product formulas with specific processing instructions are transferred from product developers to manufacturing for scale-up testing on actual manufacturing equipment. At this stage it is critical that the production samples closely represent the original gold standard target. Measuring the delivery of similarity to target is a key sensory activity. Analytical sensory tools (discrimination and descriptive analysis) are the primary methods at this stage. Discrimination methods are sorting techniques used to assess similarity to the target, while descriptive analysis helps researchers understand how the production samples compare to the target on key sensory attributes.

5. *Inspection*—Once the product is in the market, sensory methods are used to monitor quality. These can include quantitative methods similar to those used in the introduction stage. Monitoring product performance against the competition may combine both consumer and descriptive analysis in which responses from consumers provide insights into whether the differences in sensory attributes measured by descriptive analysis are meaningful or relevant (is it a difference that *really* makes a difference?). Continued performance against a target or gold standard typically is assessed at this stage to measure shelf stability over time.

Sensory Methods

Methods are often categorized by type—qualitative (interviews and observations) or quantitative (measures or ratings)—or by how responses are collected—behavioral (observational), attitudinal (surveys), and analytical (using trained or expert panelists). Behavioral approaches involve observing or gathering self-reports of consumer actions, usually close to the point of consuming the product, so they represent actual behavior. Observing, documenting, and then statistically analyzing what people do rather than asking what they do provides more accurate information, as people often tell you what they think you want to hear or are too embarrassed to reveal what they actually do. Attitudinal approaches involve collecting responses such as consumer opinions, feelings, and reactions to stimuli (sensory, psychological, intellectual, and so on), recalled behavior from the past, or expected action in the future. Responses and ratings to sensory stimuli provided by experienced or trained respondents or panelists are classified as analytical methods.

Qualitative Consumer Research

Qualitative consumer research is an important tool by which sensory analysts elicit valuable insights into attitudes, behaviors, habits, emotions, and motivations, based on either

FIGURE 17.2 General types of methods used in product design and development.

Types	Behavioral	Attitudinal	Analytical
Qualitative	• Ethnography	• Focus groups • In-depth interviews	• Bench screening of prototypes • Product reviews
Quantitative	• Purchase or consumption diaries	• Conjoint studies • Category appraisals • Variety of product testing methods (preference, acceptance)	• Discrimination testing • Descriptive analysis

Source: Witoon Prinyawiwatkul, Ph.D., Robert Delaney, M. Michele Foley, Dustin Hilinski, and Howard R. Moskowitz, Ph.D.

observing or directly interviewing consumers. Some types of product evaluation at the bench are also qualitative (bench screenings, product cuttings, product reviews). Qualitative consumer research can be conducted before quantitative research to generate hypotheses or establish criteria for data collection (for example, questionnaire development). Qualitative research may reveal which attributes consumers believe are important to the products, how they might relate to "liking or preference," and how they understand descriptive terms (such as crunchiness or crispness). Thus, information from qualitative consumer research may help identify product opportunities and generate new product concepts. Although these methods are straightforward and the findings are typically credible, results are usually further validated in a larger *quantitative test*. Commonly used qualitative methods include focus group interviews, focus panels, one-on-one or in-depth interviews (IDI), and ethnography. Brief descriptions of common qualitative consumer research methods are given below.

- *Focus group interview*—A carefully designed session used to understand consumers' perceptions or reactions toward products, product concepts, or services in a permissive, friendly, relaxing, comfortable, and nonthreatening environment. Led by a skilled moderator, each session usually lasts up to three hours. Standard practice calls for several separate sessions with different groups of participating consumers. Each group comprises 9 to 12 participants who represent the target consumers of the products of interest. Proceedings are often videotaped to enable researchers to analyze verbal and nonverbal (body) cues to uncover hidden meaning (if any) in the responses.
- *Focus panel*—A variant of the focus group interview where the same group of consumers participates two or three

times. The panel is created to initially discuss the product of interest; the group is sent home to use the product and then brought back to discuss its experiences.[6]

- *In-depth interview*—A one-on-one interview conducted to understand attitudes and behaviors in more detail. Such interviews may be necessary when the issue is sensitive, highly personal, or emotionally charged, such as weight-loss diets or deodorants.[7] Laddering is a technique often used during in-depth interviews to uncover the subconscious attraction of a product or even an entire category. Consumers are attracted to specific product or brand attributes (for example, all-natural, no preservatives, all organic ingredients), but they may not be aware of it. Laddering is a practical means to investigate how product attributes are linked to functional or emotional benefits. It involves a series of directed probes, typified by the question "Why is this important to you?"[8]
- *Ethnography*—Observation is a powerful research technique used to gather information on who consumers really are, how and why products are purchased and used, what they like or dislike, and their demands and needs.[9] Observation can be passive or active. An ethnographer shadows respondents in their own homes, workplaces, restaurants, at points of purchase in grocery stores, and so on to observe and record real behaviors associated with the product, product preparation, or usage.[10]

Quantitative Consumer Research

Quantitative consumer research is conducted with a larger group of representative consumers (100 to 500) from the targeted segment or population of the market, often divided over three or four representative cities.[11] This type of research determines overall preference or acceptance of a product (or line of products) or of specific sensory attributes (color, aroma, flavor, texture, and so on). In addition, combining descriptive analysis results with acceptance results helps identify the specific sensory attributes associated with product differences as well as those that drive performance (preference, rating of liking, purchase intent).[12]

These tests can also be used to identify and quantify consumer segments and to compare the new or improved product against the competitive set: those products and services already in the market that will compete with it for the targeted consumer's pocketbook. In addition, at the end of a project, these tests can be used to confirm the product is ready to be commercialized. Smaller-scale studies (50 to 150 respondents) provide less costly research guidance for product development teams in the optimization stage.

Preference Tests

Whether the researcher selects preference tests or acceptance tests depends on the research objective.[13] As a forced-choice method, the preference test forces consumers to compare one product against another or several others. By itself, a preference test does not measure degree of liking (or disliking) of the product, nor does it indicate a degree of difference. A common misconception is that two products equally preferred are equally liked or that they are the same. This can lead to wrong business decisions. Preference tests only give direction and do not indicate true magnitude of differences.

Preference tests fall into four distinct types: paired preference, rank preference, multiple paired preferences (all pairs compared), and selected paired preferences (selected pairs compared).[14] The paired preference ("Which of the two samples do you prefer?") and rank preference when there are more than two samples ("Rank the samples from most to least preferred") are most commonly used.

Consumer Acceptance Tests

"Acceptance" may be defined as an experience characterized by a positive attitude ("I like it") or actual use ("I will purchase or eat it").[15] Consumer acceptance tests measure overall product acceptance and acceptability of individual attributes (appearance, color, flavor, texture, and so on). Many types of scales measure acceptance. The most common is the 9-point hedonic scale (*hedonic* is another word for liking or pleasure). It has been widely studied for its applicability, validity, and reliability. The nine points of the hedonic scale are:

1 = dislike extremely

2 = dislike very much

3 = dislike moderately

4 = dislike slightly

5 = neither like nor dislike

6 = like slightly

7 = like moderately

8 = like very much

9 = like extremely

For children and illiterate subjects, other types of scales are used that modify the labels to smiley faces or simpler language.[16] The 3-, 5-, and 7-point smiley-face scales were reported to be appropriate for 3- to 5-year-old children.[17]

The second type of acceptance test is purchase intent. Typically, hedonic scores and purchase intent ratings are highly correlated in product tests; in general, a product that receives a high hedonic score also receives a high purchase intent score. Differences between hedonic and purchase intent scores are found when additional information is provided about the product, such as brand, price, or nutritional information. Both measures (acceptance and purchase intent) should be used when the test is not a blind taste test and additional information is provided. Typically this occurs near the end of the product development phase and before commercialization to confirm the product meets consumers' expectations, fits the concept or the brand, and is something they would buy if it were available where they shop. The purchase intent scale is typically a 5-point scale:

1 = definitely would not buy

2 = probably would not buy

3 = might or might not buy

4 = probably would buy

5 = definitely would buy

The marketer wants a product that generates a high "top-two box" score—that is, most of the responses come back as "definitely" or "probably would buy."

Often, acceptability measurement alone does not provide enough information to develop a product or to refine a prototype. The reasons for liking or disliking could be identified using open-ended questions or by additional questions about intensity of critical sensory attributes. One method is the so-called just-about-right scale (JAR), often incorporated into quantitative consumer testing to measure the intensity of specific sensory attributes with respect to the most preferred level. The JAR scale is commonly labeled with five points: much too strong, too strong, JAR, too weak, much too weak. The combination of hedonic and JAR ratings provides direction for product reformulation, refinement, or optimization.

Choosing appropriate consumers is of utmost importance for consumer acceptance tests. Screening criteria to determine who is an appropriate participant may be based on demographic, socioeconomic, or psychographic (lifestyle) criteria. Depending on the business priority and purpose of the research, participating subjects may be recruited from various sources. The use of employees for conducting preliminary tests, to screen samples before the actual (much more expensive and laborious) fieldwork, is common. Acceptance tests with employees can also be a resource for product maintenance purposes—for example, to establish when a difference in quality becomes evident (product aging, defect testing).[18] For new product development and product optimization, in-house or employee consumers should not be used exclusively because they may not represent the ultimate consumers.

Consumers for product research are selected based on current behaviors (actual purchase) or attitudes (interest in purchase). They should be screened for potential bias based

FIGURE 17.3 Smiley-face scale used with children.

Source: Witoon Prinyawiwatkul, Ph.D., Robert Delaney, M. Michele Foley, Dustin Hilinski, and Howard R. Moskowitz, Ph.D.

on employment, knowledge of the business, or simple dislike of the food (or brand) being tested. Before the actual taste test, participants should complete a consent form to ensure they are not allergic to the food and materials they will be testing.

Measuring Consumer Emotion about Foods

Emotion, either pleasant or unpleasant, plays an important role throughout the span of human lives. Emotions evoked by products mainly enhance the pleasure (maybe unpleasantness) of buying, owning, using, and repeating using them. Nowadays, in a highly competitive marketplace, it is often argued that emotion evoked by products is becoming more and more important for product differentiation, as many products are now often similar in their characteristics, packaging, and price. In some purchase decisions, emotional response, rather than sensory liking or price, may even be the decisive factor.

Consumer emotions evoked by products and product brands may positively or negatively affect product liking, purchase decision, food choices, desire to eat, and pleasure (and pride—look how smart I am!) of buying, owning, and using them. Knowledge of how emotions are evoked enhances understanding of what makes people enjoy interacting with a particular food, food name, or product concept. However, determining how consumers respond emotionally to food products and what aspects (such as food names, product design, benefit, and packaging) trigger emotional reactions can be quite challenging.

Measurement of acceptability is not a sufficient benchmark for product development and testing. Recently, the EsSense Profile® was developed to measure mood and emotion in a product development setup; it yields information not normally captured by measuring acceptability.[19] The EsSense Profile® provides a detailed list of 39 emotion attributes (mainly positive ones) that consumers associate with test products. Consumer emotion and methods for measuring emotions associated with foods in consumer testing are summarized in several studies.[20] The relationships between food, eating behavior, and consumer emotion are examined as well.[21] For example, chocolates (milk and dark) evoked emotions such as active, affectionate, energetic, happy, loving, and satisfied.[22]

Sensory Discrimination Tests

Sensory discrimination tests[23] are the most basic tests in sensory science, and probably have the longest history.[24] Discrimination tests are generally used to determine whether or not overall or specific differences exist between two potentially confusable samples. Panelists are typically employees screened for their sensory acuity. Test methods are classified into two groups:

1. *Overall difference tests*—The basic question is "Does a difference exist between samples?" without specifying an attribute and with or without a reference for comparison.

2. *Attribute difference tests*—This type of test specifies attributes (such as sweetness). Depending on the test, panelists are asked to determine which sample has more or less intensity of the specified attribute.

FIGURE 17.4 **Commonly used discrimination test methods.**

Test Methods	Sample Presentation	Panelist Task	Suggested No. of Panelists
2AFC (Alternative Forced Choice)	2 samples served from 2 possible combinations (AB or BA)	Indicate which sample exhibits more or less of a specific attribute (e.g., sweetness).	A multiple of 2; ≥30 subjects; as few as 16 subjects
Simple Paired Comparison or Same-Difference test	2 samples served in sets of 2 from 4 possible combinations: unmatched (AB or BA) matched (AA or BB)	Indicate whether the two samples are same or different.	A multiple of 4; ≥32 subjects; as few as 12–16 subjects
Triangle	3 samples (2 identical and 1 odd) served from 6 possible combinations (ABB, BAA, AAB, BBA, ABA, and BAB)	Either pick the odd sample or pick the two identical samples (must guess when the odd sample is not detectable).	A multiple of 6; 24–60 subjects
Duo-Trio	3 samples (identified reference and 2 blind) served from 2 combinations (Ref-AB and Ref-BA)	Indicate which of the 2 unknown samples matches the reference.	A multiple of 2; ≥32 subjects; as few as 12–16 subjects
Difference from Control	First, serve an identified control sample. Then serve at least 2 unknown samples; one is the unknown control (placebo); the rest are the unknown test samples.	Rate the size of the difference (overall or by attribute) between each unknown sample and the identified control.	30–50 subjects

Source: Witoon Prinyawiwatkul, Ph.D., Robert Delaney, M. Michele Foley, Dustin Hilinski, and Howard R. Moskowitz, Ph.D.

Sensory Descriptive Analysis

Sensory descriptive analysis is the most sophisticated sensory method by which the attributes of a product are identified, characterized, and quantified, using an expert panel specifically trained for such purpose. Descriptive analysis is primarily used for product development, quality control, shelf life, product claim substantiation, and category appraisal. The components of commonly used methods include both qualitative (lexicon or descriptor development) and quantitative (intensity rating) aspects.

The source for panelists varies with availability and demand. Training and panel participation require a significant time commitment. Often it is difficult for employees to invest the time required to participate actively in training and ongoing panel sessions. Many sensory groups hire consumers on a part-time basis to participate as descriptive panelists. This allows the panelists to focus completely on the analysis of products without the distraction of another job. During the training phase of most descriptive analysis methods, the panel develops a lexicon or list of descriptors for the product or product category of interest. To be effective, descriptors should help describe differences in the sample set and be unique and singular ("fried" or "beefy"), not complex or abstract (like "fresh"). To help communicate the attribute and ensure it is used consistently over time, each descriptor should have a written definition and an identifiable taste or smell reference standard that is easy to obtain.[25]

Excellent reviews of sensory descriptive analysis methods can be found in a number of publications owing to the great popularity of descriptive analysis since the 1940s.[26] Compilation of applications of descriptive sensory analysis in dairy, meat, alcoholic beverages, and others can be found in *Descriptive Sensory Analysis in Practice*.[27] A comprehensive list of descriptors for finished products, along with definitions, references, and reference preparation can be found in *Aroma and Flavor Lexicon for Sensory Evaluation: Terms, Definitions, References, and Examples*.[28]

Basic Sensory Attributes

Humans possess five primary senses for perceiving stimuli: sight, hearing, touch, smell, and taste. Other human senses include temperature sensation (heat and cold), pain, visceral hunger, thirst, and fatigue.[29] The "sensory receptor devices" (that is, eyes, ears, skin, tongue, and nose) respond to a particular range of environmental stimuli and transmit corresponding information to the brain via the central nervous system.

With respect to food, taste and smell receptors respond to specific *chemical* stimuli, and sight, hearing, touch, and temperature receptors respond to *physical* stimuli.

Humans tend to perceive food attributes in two consumption stages: approach or distal stage (based on appearance and odor or aroma) and consumption or proximal stage (based on stimuli including consistency, texture, and flavor, which is a combination of taste, aromatics, and chemical feelings). However, these attributes inevitably overlap, as people tend to perceive the food they are eating in its entirety rather than its component parts.[30] Basic sensory attributes of foods include:

- Appearance—This includes traits such as color, shape, and size as well as more complex attributes such as surface texture, structural uniformity, and visual flavor.[31] *Visual flavor* is a gestalt term. The overall appearance of a product may make consumers think that the product has a specific flavor. For example, a jelly with green color may have lime or green apple flavor. A darker red color juice may be sweeter than one with a lighter red color. Appearance is the most important sensory characteristic in determining initial consumer acceptance of products, and it is often the only attribute on which people can base a decision to purchase or consume, particularly if the food is hidden inside a package.[32]

- Odor or aroma—Aroma is the odor of a food produced by volatilized chemical constituents that originate externally (orthonasally, or through the nose), often when the food is heated or cooked, and internally (retronasally) from food in the mouth while it is being consumed. Retronasal (flavor-by-mouth) odor is perceived when a volatile stimulus originating in the mouth passes the back of the nasopharyngeal passage into the olfactory receptors located in the roof of the mouth.

- Texture—This complex term covers viscosity (describing homogeneous liquids), consistency (describing non-homogeneous liquids and semisolids), and two textural subcomponents:

  1. Mechanical properties (for example, hardness, springiness) perceived by the kinesthetic nerves that monitor the position and movements of muscles, bones, and joints
  2. Tactile or skinfeel properties (for example, moistness, fibrousness) perceived by the nerves in the skin of the hands, lips, or tongue

- Flavor—The sum total of the sensory impressions (taste, odor, and chemical feeling) of a product is perceived via the chemical senses in the mouth. It is one of the most important sensory characteristics that influence the acceptability of foods.[33] Humans experience five basic tastes (salty, sweet, sour, bitter and "umami"—a taste sensation that is meaty or savory and is produced by several amino acids and nucleotides, generally referred to as "glutamates"). Some sensory authorities believe there may be other taste reactions, namely: alkaline, metallic, calcium-y (the bitterness and slight sourness of vegetables such as collard greens, kale, bok choy, and bitter melon), and fat taste "oleogustus," which is an unpleasant bitter and sour flavor. Chemical irritants such as horseradish, mustard, ginger, onion, garlic, and chiles stimulate the trigeminal nerve ends, causing perception of pungency and burn or heat in the eyes, nose, and mouth. Another trigeminal effect is the fizzy tingle of carbon dioxide in soda.

- Sound—Produced during the first bite and subsequent chewing (mastication) of foods. Differences in pitch, loudness, and persistence of sounds (crispness, crunchiness, brittleness, squeakiness) may be used as indices for product quality such as freshness or staleness, maturity or ripening stages.[34]

Because sensory evaluation is a science dealing with humans as an active measuring tool, knowledge of anatomy, physiology, and functions of the human senses is indispensable to avoiding misinterpretation and incorrect conclusions. For a brief review of this material, particularly taste, smell, and trigeminal effects, and for useful references, see *Sensory Evaluation of Food: Principles and Practices*.[35]

Minimizing Errors in Sensory Measurements

"Error" is not just synonymous with "mistake" but may also include all sorts of extraneous influences.[36] The physical and psychological condition of the panelist and the influence of the testing environment can affect sensory results. Extraneous influences must be minimized to ensure the selected sensory tests are measured correctly.

Three main factors negatively affect sensory results: physiological, psychological, and physical errors. A person's ability to perceive or sense the attributes is influenced by *physiological factors* (mostly related to genetic makeup) and *physical factors* (mostly related to health). In contrast, *psychological factors* may affect how the person rates the attributes. For example, having a cold affects a person's ability to smell (physical); a person who thinks he recognizes a sample as being a brand he doesn't like rates that sample lower in acceptance (psychological).

Three types of controls (test room, product, and panel) must be maintained in order to minimize bias and maximize sensitivity of the selected sensory methods and panelists' performance.[37]

1. *Test room controls*—In addition to having a proper test room designed specifically for sensory testing (preferably with several individual tasting booths), the setup, lighting, noise, air circulation, temperature, and relative humidity must be controlled in order to minimize bias and maximize sensitivity of panelists.

2. *Product controls*—These involve sample preparation and presentation. For sample preparation, all supplies, utensils, and equipment must be food-grade or for food use only. Care must be taken to ensure that odors from, for example, plastic utensils and containers, do not change the aroma and flavor characteristics of the test products. The sample preparation methods (for example, cooking time and temperature, thawing, and mixing time) should be appropriate to the product and kept constant throughout the sensory testing period. The samples should not change in sensory quality during holding throughout multiple sessions of sensory tests. If samples tend to change over time, then multiple fresh batches of the sample must be prepared throughout the test to assure consistency. In terms of sample presentation, the number of samples, serving size, serving pattern, coding, and palate cleansing are of major

FIGURE 17.5 **Common bias effects and test design solutions.**

Effect	Description	Solution
Stimulus	If subjects know or presume to know the identity of a sample, then they make assumptions about what it should taste, smell, or look like based on their expectations for this sample.	Use naive or unpracticed consumers to measure liking, use plain serving containers and random sample identification, and carefully hide clues to sample identity.
Context	Ratings for identical stimuli in different contexts shift. The set of samples evaluated sets the frame of reference for judgments. An item may be perceived differently due to the direct influence of one sample on another that is nearby in time or space.	Consider the total set of samples and each sample's importance to the primary test objective. Always include a sample in the test that you know something about (control).
Order	The first sample tasted sets expectations. If the same sample is presented multiple times, average liking scores will decrease with each presentation. "First Position Effect": the first sample is rated higher.	Alternate the order of presentation of samples.
Contrast	Perceptions are strongly influenced by what was experienced most recently. Each sample influences opinions of the next sample. Probably most pronounced when sensations are extreme.	Alternate the order of presentation of samples.
Adaptation	Subjects experience a decrease in responsiveness under conditions of constant stimulation. May be at the level of sensation or conscious perception.	Allow time between samples to cleanse the palate.
Halo	One very positive or negative aspect of a person or product can influence judgments on other unrelated characteristics.	Check to be certain that samples do not differ in some unintended way, and acknowledge that halo effects occur.

Source: Witoon Prinyawiwatkul, Ph.D., Robert Delaney, M. Michele Foley, Dustin Hilinski, and Howard R. Moskowitz, Ph.D.

concern. The order of sample presentation should be balanced and randomized. *Balanced* means that each sample appears at a given serving position (first, second, third, and so on) an equal number of times. *Randomized* indicates that each order of presentation is randomly assigned to a panelist. For example, three samples allow six possible serving orders to achieve a balanced order of presentation (ABC, ACB, BCA, BAC, CAB, CBA). If 60 panelists are in the study, the six serving orders should each be randomly assigned to ten of them.

3. *Panel controls*—Panelists should be screened for physical conditions such as illness, food allergies, poor dental hygiene, emotional distress, smoking, and drinking before the test. To minimize confusion and errors, clear and consistent instructions are required. The amount of training needed for descriptive panelists varies depending on the complexity of the products and the taste sensitivity required.

●Applications of Sensory Analysis in Food Product Development

The goal of the following case study was to identify new product business opportunities for a pizzeria chain. The research objectives were (1) to identify the types of sensory experience pizza consumers wanted, and (2) to create better pizza products without expending an undue amount of money on cost of goods.

Step 1: How Do People Think? What Do People Want in a Pizza?

What should a new pizza contain so the restaurant chain can advertise it as "new" and "different," yet maintain the essence of the pizza chain? To identify what people want, short, easy-to-understand concepts about pizza were developed. The concepts comprised simple statements (elements) dealing with the product, the eating situation, the emotions, and so on. Some of the statements and their purchase interest scores appear in Figure 17.6. To develop the language for the statements, a focus group was used.

The actual study presented combinations of ideas to the respondents, obtained ratings of the combinations (that is, the test concepts), and then determined how much of the response could be traced to each individual statement. This method, called conjoint analysis, identifies the contribution of the many factors that drive a product concept.[38] When looking at the impact of each statement, values above 5 are strong positives and values below 5 are strong negatives.

Figure 17.6 summarizes data both from the total panel and from two sub-segments that were uncovered through a

FIGURE 17.6 Results from concept evaluations showing what drives consumer interest and the emergence of two consumer segments.

	Total	Segment 1 Stuff	Segment 2 Pure and Simple
Base Size	119	69	50
Constant (overall interest in "pizza")	35	26	48
Soft and gooey slices of pizza with cheese	15	25	2
Pizza with a filled or twisted crust	10	17	0
With all the toppings and accompaniments you want	10	10	10
Pizza with a thick crust and a rich topping	7	15	−4
Pizza with a crust that doubles as breadstick	6	9	2
100% natural, fresh, and carefully prepared	3	1	6
Pizza with a lot of tomato sauce, ham, and cheese	1	10	−12
You can just savor it, when you think about it	1	1	1
Pizza is great for parties	−1	−3	0
Thin crust pizza with a layer of tomato sauce and cheese	−2	7	−13
With a fresh mixed salad	−2	2	−8
With a glass of lemonade, beer, or wine	−3	−6	1
Pizza with a crust so crispy you have to be careful when you eat it	−4	3	−13

Source: It! Ventures, LLC.

statistical segmentation of the total panel. Segmentation groups people based on similar patterns of what they like. The data suggested two distinct segments: One segment likes pizza with "stuff," and another segment likes pizza "pure and simple." Segment one is not interested in pizza at its very basics (the baseline interest is low at 26). The second segment, a bit smaller, seems to prefer traditional pizza; it's got to have cheese, sauce with lots of richness and thickness, and lots of crust.

From this step, concepts can be written to further evaluate the ideas, or prototypes can be created for consumer evaluation. In this example, pizzas from competitors were used to represent the ideas defined by the concept elements.

Step 2: What Works in Today's World of Pizza? Evaluating Many Products to Discover Patterns

Category appraisal studies evaluate a number of actual products to discover the characteristics most important to the target consumer. For the pizza case, developers identified 10 types of pizza based on the conjoint analysis, some with different toppings but mainly concerned with different structures (thin versus thick crust, pizza with two layers, and so on). The objective of testing different market products is simply to get an idea of what works in an assortment of actual market products.

It is fairly straightforward to design and execute a category appraisal, except for one thing: timing issues. With 10 pizzas to test, all made to order for walk-in customers at several pizzerias, it was necessary to create a run schedule so the test panelists would always have pizza no more than 15 minutes after purchase. The specific logistics are not relevant here, other than to note that each of 100 pre-recruited respondents participated in a 2.5-hour session in which each respondent evaluated 5 of 10 freshly purchased pizzas. The pizzas represented different executions of cheese pizza from pizzerias in a local area.

The most important outcomes are the patterns that exist in the data, which can lead to insights and direction for developers. Figure 17.7 provides a snapshot of how 2 of these 10 pizzas performed. All the data are on a 0- to 100-point scale, making it easy to see the product on a scorecard.

The next analysis looks for patterns. For some sensory attributes, as the intensity increases, liking increases, peaks, and then goes down after the optimum sensory level is passed. Saltiness and sweetness are examples of these types of attributes; most people have levels where these attributes are less liked because they are too low, well liked because they are just right, and less liked because they are too high. The goal is to determine what the curve looks like for each sensory attribute of pizza, recognizing that many widely varying attributes exist.

These types of analyses are important; they reveal the dynamics of the product in a way that one might not intuit and may not even be aware of without experience.[39] Sensory-liking analyses work as long as the attribute is continuous (a fundamental characteristic—pizza always has a crust) rather than being on/off (for example, pepperoni present versus absent).

Two examples of sensory-liking curves are shown in Figure 17.9. Each comes from the averaged ratings from the participants who evaluated the 10 commercially prepared pizzas. These curves were plotted to show ratings of breadiness

FIGURE 17.7 Representative data for two in-market pizzas on sensory and liking attributes.

Pizza sample number	101	102
General Liking		
Overall liking	73	54
Appearance liking	77	56
Taste liking	73	56
Texture liking	70	53
Attribute Liking		
Cheese	74	61
Crust	75	50
Edge	67	45
Middle	78	57
Sauce	56	56
Sauce color	59	56
Aroma	72	58
Cheese	73	53
Crust	73	56
Spiciness	62	52

(100-point scale where 0 = dislike and 100 = like)
Source: Witoon Prinyawiwatkul, Ph.D., Robert Delaney, M. Michele Foley, Dustin Hilinski, and Howard R. Moskowitz, Ph.D.

of crust versus overall liking, and perceived amount of cheese versus overall liking. Both indicate an optimum level in the middle of the range tested.

Step 3: Nature Reveals Her Secrets: Building and Using the Product Model

Now the product developer positions all of the tested products on a map. The dimensions of the map are obtained from the sensory attributes. Each of the 10 pizzas is located somewhere on this map. Products lying close together are similar in their sensory properties.

The developer can now look at the map and identify the gaps—namely, opportunities for new pizza products in areas of the map that are not already occupied by other products offered by competing pizza restaurants. In Figure 17.10, two opportunity spaces are identified on the upper right side of the map next to two pizza samples (G and E) that were well liked (as indicated by the large circle).

The analysis then proceeds by creating product models, which translate the opportunity spaces in the map into sensory profiles. In practical application, each product model defines the likely sensory profile of an optimum pizza that fits each gap and looks for landmark products in the set of 10 pizzas that have the closest sensory levels. Different products

FIGURE 17.8 Typical sensory-liking curves.

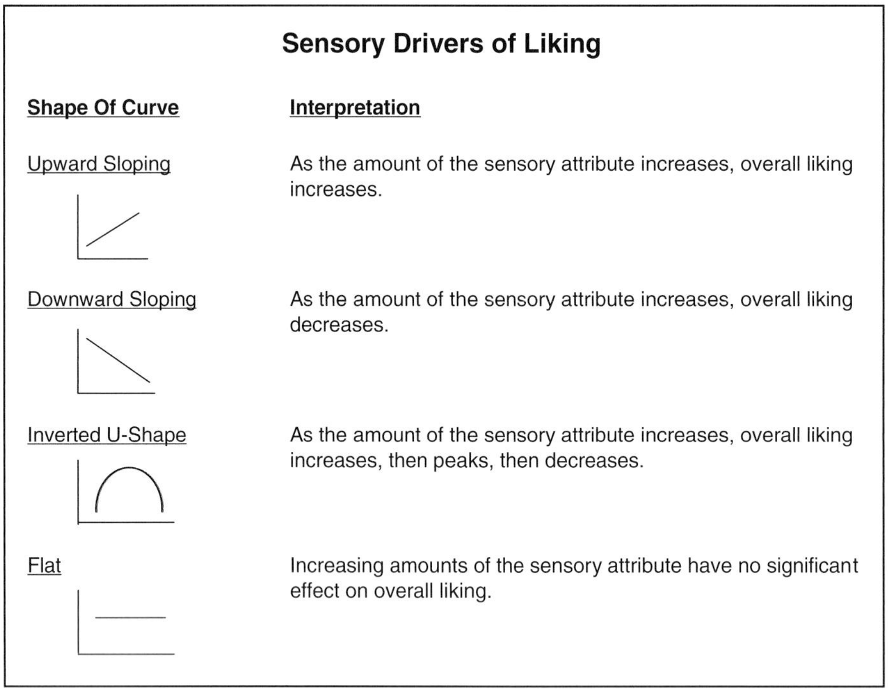

Sensory Drivers of Liking
Shape Of Curve
Interpretation
Upward Sloping
As the amount of the sensory attribute increases, overall liking increases.
Downward Sloping
As the amount of the sensory attribute increases, overall liking decreases.
Inverted U-Shape
As the amount of the sensory attribute increases, overall liking increases, then peaks, then decreases.
Flat
Increasing amounts of the sensory attribute have no significant effect on overall liking.

Source: Witoon Prinyawiwatkul, Ph.D., Robert Delaney, M. Michele Foley, Dustin Hilinski, and Howard R. Moskowitz, Ph.D.

FIGURE 17.9 Sensory-liking curves for pizza, based on the category appraisal method.

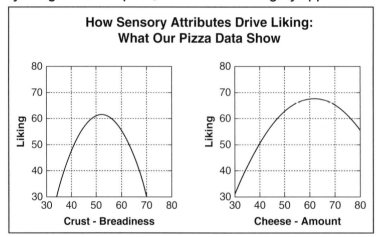

How Sensory Attributes Drive Liking:
What Our Pizza Data Show
Liking
80
70
60
50
40
30
30 40 50 60 70 80
Crust - Breadiness
Liking
80
70
60
50
40
30
30 40 50 60 70 80
Cheese - Amount

Source: Witoon Prinyawiwatkul, Ph.D., Robert Delaney, M. Michele Foley, Dustin Hilinski, and Howard R. Moskowitz, Ph.D.

FIGURE 17.10 The sensory map. Each figure corresponds to one of the 10 pizzas, located in two-dimensional space defined by the sensory attributes.

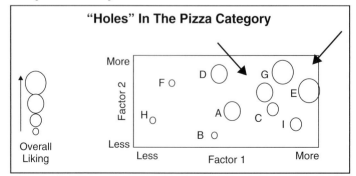

"Holes" In The Pizza Category
Overall
Liking
More
Factor 2
Less
Less
Factor 1
More
F
D
G
E
H
A
C
I
B

Source: Witoon Prinyawiwatkul, Ph.D., Robert Delaney, M. Michele Foley, Dustin Hilinski, and Howard R. Moskowitz, Ph.D.

FIGURE 17.11 Specifications for development for the best pizza and for the new pizza that fits a hole and therefore represents a new opportunity.

Pizza Attribute Scores	Best Liked (Sample E)	Difference from Best Liked for Opportunity (Estimated from Model)	Direction for Product Developer
Cheese: Amount	64	−16	
Cheese: Flavor	54	−11	Reduce cheese
Cheese: Stretchy	60	−15	
Crust: Bready	51	+4	
Crust: Chewy	61	+9	Similar crust breadiness and hardness; more chewy and crispy
Crust: Crispy	47	+13	
Crust: Hardness	35	+0	
Sauce: Amount	53	+13	
Sauce: Italian Flavor	56	+17	
Sauce: Spicy	52	+12	More sauce; thicker sauce
Sauce: Thickness	46	+10	
Sauce: Flavor (Tomato)	52	+15	

Source: Witoon Prinyawiwatkul, Ph.D., Robert Delaney, M. Michele Foley, Dustin Hilinski, and Howard R. Moskowitz, Ph.D.

may serve as landmarks because no one product may have all the optimal sensory levels. For each sensory profile, components of the landmark product (or combination, if there isn't a single best) become the developer's or the chef's targets. Compared to the best-liked sample in this study, the opportunity space is characterized by a pizza with a crisper crust, less cheese, and more sauce. It has crust hardness similar to the best-liked sample.

Once the product model data is complete, the developer or chef uses it to formulate prototypes characterized as having the same structure and components. These prototypes can be profiled by the sensory panel to compare their characteristics to the opportunity profile and then tested with consumers to determine their appeal. Of course, this is only one step (albeit a critically important one) in the product development process. See Chapters 1 and 19 for in-depth discussions about the business of new product development and commercializing the gold standard.

●Conclusion

As more and more food products flood the market, consumers have ever more choices. The reach of store-branded private-label offerings is always expanding. The outcome is obvious; a competitive marketplace where brands fight for limited space on the shelf. The bar of success for a new product is constantly moving upward. Approximately 20,000 new products were introduced each year for the last three years in the United States. Of these new products, about 80 percent were withdrawn within two years of launch. About 95 percent

of new product efforts fail to deliver expected business objectives.

Manufacturers must incorporate that little added touch, that bit of innovation, that extra dose of convenience, that point of differentiation to ensure the success of their product. The direction, insights, and inspiration for these extras more often than not come from consumers. The more these consumer touchpoints are incorporated into the product's research path, the better the chances for a successful product. Sensory evaluation provides those touchpoints—from the early observational and qualitative insights, to the translation of the chef's inspiration into a product developer's prototype, and finally to qualifying the commercialized formula for mass production, product launch, and long-term maintenance in the marketplace. While nothing is guaranteed when it comes to guessing the fickle taste preferences of the public, a product development team can certainly stack the deck in their product's favor if they take the time to listen to and learn from consumers.

[1]M. A. Amerine, R. M. Pangborn, and E. B. Roessler, *Principles of Sensory Evaluation of Food* (New York: Academic Press, 1965), v.

[2]P. Dando, "Sensory Success: Quality, Consistency, and Sensory Programs," *Stagnito's New Products Magazine* 8, no. 1 (2008): 68–70.

[3]K. S. Ferguson, "Foodservice New Products: 'I Don't Think We're in Commodities Anymore, Toto,'" in E. Graf and I. S. Saguy (eds.), *Food Product Development, From Concept to the Marketplace* (New York: Chapman and Hall, 1991), 291–308.

[4]D. Buck, "Methods to Understand Consumer Attitudes and Motivations in Food Product Development," in H. J. H. MacFie (ed.), *Consumer-Led Food Product Development* (Cambridge, UK: Woodhead, 2007), 141–157.

[5]J. Gordon, "Returning Insight to the Consumer," *Stagnito's New Products Magazine* 6, no. 12 (2006): 40.

[6]M. Meilgaard, G. V. Civille, and B. T. Carr, *Sensory Evaluation Techniques*, 4th ed. (Boca Raton, FL: CRC Press, 2007), 255–311.

[7]H. T. Lawless and H. Heyman, *Sensory Evaluation of Food: Principles and Practices* (New York: Chapman and Hall, 1998), 519–547.

[8]A. Krystallis, "Using Means-End Chains to Understand Consumers' Knowledge Structures," in H. J. H. MacFie (ed.), *Consumer-Led Food Product Development* (Cambridge, UK: Woodhead, 2007), 158–196.

[9]Meilgaard, Civille, and Carr, *Sensory Evaluation Techniques*.

[10]Buck, "Methods," 141–157.

[11]Meilgaard, Civille, and Carr, *Sensory Evaluation Techniques*.

[12]W. Prinyawiwatkul and P. Chompreeda, "Applications of Discriminant and Logistic Regression Analysis for Consumer Acceptance and Consumer-Oriented Product Optimization Study," in J. H. Beckley et al. (eds.), *Accelerating New Food Product Design and Development* (Ames, IA: Blackwell Professional, 2007), 271–295.

[13]Meilgaard, Civille, and Carr, *Sensory Evaluation Techniques*.

[14]Ibid.

[15]Amerine, Pangborn, and Roessler, *Principles of Sensory Evaluation of Food*, 540.

[16]R. Popper and J. J. Kroll, "Consumer Testing of Food Products Using Children," in H. J. H. MacFie (ed.), *Consumer-Led Food Product Development* (Cambridge, UK: Woodhead, 2007), 383–406; A. V. A. Resurreccion, *Consumer Sensory Testing for Product Development* (Gaithersburg, MD: Aspen, 1998), 165–176; H. Stone and J. L. Sidel, *Sensory Evaluation Practices*, 3rd ed. (San Diego, CA: Elsevier, 2004), 69–98.

[17]A. Chen, A. V. A. Resurreccion, and L. P. Paguio, "Age-Appropriate Hedonic Scales to Measure Food Preferences of Young Children," *Journal of Sensory Studies* 11 (1996): 141–163.

[18]Meilgaard, Civille, and Carr, *Sensory Evaluation Techniques*.

[19]S. C. King, H. L. Meiselman, and B. T. Carr, "Measuring Emotions Associated with Foods: Important Elements of Questionnaire and Test Design," *Food Quality and Preference* 28 (2013): 8–16.

[20]Silvia C. King, Herbert L. Meiselman, and B. Thomas Carr, "Measuring Emotions Associated with Foods in Consumer Testing," *Food Quality and Preference* 21 (2010): 1114–1116; King, Meiselman, and Carr, "Measuring Emotions Associated with Foods: Important Elements of Questionnaire and Test Design."

[21]Y. Jiang, J. M. King, and W. Prinyawiwatkul, "A Review of Measurement and Relationships Between Food, Eating Behavior, and Emotion," *Trends in Food Science and Technology* 36 (2014): 15–28.

[22]A. V. Cardello et al., "Measuring Emotional Responses to Foods and Food Names Using Questionnaires," *Food Quality and Preference* 24 (2012): 243–250.

[23]See Meilgaard, Civille, and Carr, *Sensory Evaluation Techniques*, 63–128, for in-depth descriptions of sensory discrimination tests, along with examples describing scope and application, test subjects, test procedures, data analysis, and interpretation of the results.

[24]J. Bi, *Sensory Discrimination Tests and Measurements: Statistical Principles, Procedures, and Tables* (Ames, IA: Blackwell, 2006), ix.

[25]G. V. Civille and H. T. Lawless, "The Importance of Language in Describing Perceptions," *Journal of Sensory Studies* 1 (1986): 217–236.

[26]Amerine, Pangborn, and Roessler, *Principles of Sensory Evaluation of Food*, 349–397; E. Chamber and B. M. Wolf, *Sensory Testing Methods*, 2nd ed. (West Conshohocken, PA: ASTM, 1996), 58–72; R. C. Hootman, *Manual on Descriptive Analysis Testing for Sensory Evaluation* (West Conshohocken, PA: ASTM, 1992); Meilgaard, Civille, and Carr, *Sensory Evaluation Techniques*, 173–253; Stone and Sidel, *Sensory Evaluation Practices*, 201–245.

[27]M. C. Gacula Jr., *Descriptive Sensory Analysis in Practice* (Trumbull, CT: Food and Nutrition Press, 1997).

[28]G. V. Civille and B. G. Lyon, *Aroma and Flavor Lexicon for Sensory Evaluation: Terms, Definitions, References and Examples* (West Conshohocken, PA: ASTM, 1996).

[29]S. Clark, M. Costello, M. Drake, and F. Bodyfelt, *The Sensory Evaluation of Daily Products* (New York: Springer Science & Business Media, 2009).

[30]Meilgaard, Civille, and Carr, *Sensory Evaluation Techniques Food*, 7–24.

[31]A. V. Cardello, "Consumer Expectations and Their Role in Food Acceptance," in H. J. H. MacFie and D. M. H. Thomson (eds.), *Measurement of Food Preferences* (London: Blackie Academic, 1994), 253–297; D. B. MacDougall, "Instrumental Assessment of the Appearance of Foods," in A. A. William and R. K. Atkin (eds.), *Sensory Quality in Foods and Beverages: Definition, Measurement, and Control* (Deerfield Beach, FL: Verlag Chemie International, 1983), 121–139.

[32]J. B. Hatchings, "The Importance of Visual Appearance of Foods to the Food Processor and Consumer," in G. G. Birch, J. G. Bremer, and K. J. Parker (eds.), *Sensory Properties of Foods* (Barking, London: Applied Science, 1977), 45–56; Meilgaard, Civille, and Carr, *Sensory Evaluation Techniques*, 7–24.

[33]W. Prinyawiwatkul, L. R. Beuchat, and A. V. A. Resurreccion, "Optimization of Sensory Qualities of an Extruded Snack Based on Cornstarch and Peanut Flour," *Lebensmittel-Wissenschaft & Technologie* 26 (1993): 393–399.

[34]Meilgaard, Civille, and Carr, *Sensory Evaluation Techniques*, 7–24.

[35]Lawless and Heyman, *Sensory Evaluation of Food*, 28–81.

[36]E. Larmond, "Is Sensory Evaluation a Science?" *Cereal Foods World* 39, no. 11 (1994): 804–808.

[37]Meilgaard, Civille, and Carr, *Sensory Evaluation Techniques*, 25–38.

[38]H. R. Moskowitz et al., "Rapid, Inexpensive, Actionable Concept Generation and Optimization: The Use and Promise of Self-Authoring Conjoint Analysis for the Foodservice Industry," *Food Service Technology* 1 (2001): 149–168.

[39]H. R. Moskowitz, "Improving the 'Actionability' of Product Tests: Understanding and Using Relations Among Liking, Sensory, and Directional Attributes," *Canadian Journal of Marketing Research* 18 (1999): 31–45; H. R. Moskowitz, "Relative Importance of Perceptual Factors to Consumer Acceptance: Linear Versus Quadratic Analysis," *Journal of Food Science* 46 (1981): 244–248.

18

Culinology® Applications in Food Processing—From the Chef's and Food Scientist's Perspective

Lead Author: Mark A. Uebersax, Ph.D., Professor Emeritus, Department of Food Science and Human Nutrition, Michigan State University

Muhammad Siddiq, Ph.D., Associate Professor, Department of Food Science and Human Nutrition, Michigan State University

Carl P. Borchgrevink, Ph.D., Associate Professor, The School of Hospitality Business, The Eli Broad Graduate School of Management, Michigan State University

● Introduction: Today's Case for Processed Foods—Scientific and Culinary Perspectives

Foods have been prepared and processed since the beginning of recorded history. Preserving food enables a consistent supply during periods of decreased availability (seasonal variability, drought, natural disaster, and famine). Further, the centralized processing of food had a profound impact on civilization in that it provided a steadier, more consistent supply of cheaper foods. People were thus able to spend less time on the daily procurement and preparation of food. Centralized processing also supported the move from agricultural to industrial economies, as foods could be made more easily available to city-dwelling factory workers and their families.

The current dialogue among journalists, social commentators, and consumers suggests a profound dislike and distrust of processed foods. These range from well-informed presentations to more emotional diatribes. The popular press is replete with examples of direct confrontations with and denigration of processed foods.

> By changing from consuming chemically ridden mass-produced food to eating locally grown organic food, we can give ourselves a longer and healthier life.
>
> *Yoko Ono, musician and cofounder (with John Lennon in 1969)*
> *of Plastic Ono Band (Anon., 2009)*

Although increasing food choices for the consumer is desirable, such a call for massive restructuring of the food industry would have a profound negative impact on overall food availability, safety, and economics.

The Culinology® professional (and the consumer) benefits directly from access to diverse commercially prepared and processed food ingredients to provide sophisticated meal offerings in numerous formats. Many of these ingredients play such a ubiquitous part in our diet that they are no longer perceived as processed foods but rather are considered ordinary ingredients found in everyone's home pantry. Even the most ardent critics of processed foods are unlikely to reach for a live steer when seeking a steak dinner, or to grow and mill their own whole grains to make flour. Corn oil doesn't normally drip from ears of corn! Commercial processing of foods provides stable, convenient, safe, and nutritious options. Knowledge of food technology increasingly serves the needs of culinary specialists who require a solid understanding of the principles and procedures used for food processing and preservation.

FIGURE 18.1   Ubiquitous processed foods; "neo-scratch" foods.

Food in Unprocessed Form[1]	Minimally or Fully Processed	Further Processed
Tomatoes	Blanched and peeled	Chopped and diced
		Chopped, diced, and seasoned
		Paste, purée, sauce
Mustard	Ground mustard	Prepared mustard
Grains	Meals and flours	Enriched flours
		Dough
		Proofed dough
		Par-baked dough products
		RTE dough products
		Puff pastry/phyllo dough
Stocks and broths	Food bases	Sauce mixes
	Soup bases	Soup mixes
		Heat-and-serve soup
Raw milks	Pasteurized milks	Butter
	Homogenized milks	Yogurt, kefir
		Cheese
Spices and herbs	Dried and irradiated whole spices and herbs	Ground, chopped, minced spices and herbs
Vanilla bean	Fermented and dried vanilla bean	Ground vanilla beans
		Vanilla seeds
		Vanilla extract
		Vanilla sugars
Vegetables	Ready to use	IQF
		Block frozen
		Canned
		Dried
		Dried and reconstituted
Coffee beans	Roasted coffee beans	Ground coffee beans
		Coffee extracts
		RTD coffees
Cattle, hogs, sheep, goats	Carcass	Primal cuts
	Partial carcass	Fabricated cuts
		Pre-marked fabricated cuts
		Pre-cooked fabricated cuts

(continued)

FIGURE 18.1 *(continued)*

Food in Unprocessed Form[1]	Minimally or Fully Processed	Further Processed
		Ground products
		Pre-formed patties
		Pre-cooked patties
		Sausages
		Pre-cooked sausages
Whole fish	Gutted	Fish cakes
	Dressed-eviscerated	Fish fingers
	Head-on or headless	Dehydrated fish powder
	Fins-on or finless	
	Scaled	
	Skinned	
	Filleted	
	Steaks	

[1]We assume that the food in question is free of dirt and debris; such cleaning could be considered an initial level of processing.
Source: Mark A. Uebersax, Ph.D., Muhammad Siddiq, Ph.D., Carl P. Borchgrevink, Ph.D.

The relationship between food, diet, exercise, and health has been clearly established with sound scientific consensus. Food scientists, Culinology® professionals, nutritionists, and public health and policy professionals all have an obvious mandate to exploit these complex interactions for the benefit of consumers. This task is seemingly monumental and must be approached as a multifaceted endeavor. The entire food system, from farm to fork, must be taken into account to achieve a safe and wholesome food supply. The food processing and preservation segment of this system is a vital link that the Culinology® professional must recognize and appreciate. World food security and availability can be realized only through strategies for minimizing postharvest losses, expanding preservation and packaging technologies, and collaboration among food professionals.

Effects of Processing on Nutrient Retention

Retention of nutrients during processing is important and has been studied extensively. Nutrient losses occur whether food is processed commercially or prepared fresh at home or at foodservice operations. Though behavior varies among specific foods, the losses due to commercial processing of foods are not dramatically different from fresh cooked foods. In fact, when processed using the latest high-efficiency technologies, and with the potential for food fortification or enrichment, such foods can be much more nutritious than home-processed foods.

A common misconception among journalists as well as consumers is that commercially processed foods are inferior to fresh products or to foods processed in the home. The following summarizes studies done in this area.[1]

Decreases in nutrient levels of foods can occur for a variety of reasons at all stages of the food distribution chain, from harvest to the point of consumption. Less well understood is the *positive* impact processing frequently has on improved levels of nutrient extraction (for example, more lycopene in tomato paste than in fresh tomatoes), enhanced nutrient bioavailability (for example, protein digestibility), and inactivation of anti-nutritional factors (for example, trypsin inhibitors in raw eggs and toxic lectins in legumes). Nutrient losses associated with processed food, which are often similar to those of kitchen-prepared foods, may be classified as follows:

Intentional losses—Losses that result from the processing or conversion of raw materials into an edible portion are considered intentional losses. Included in this group are peeling, trimming, and coring losses.

Leaching of water-soluble nutrients—Leaching of soluble vitamins and minerals causes most of the nutrient losses. Washing and blanching are operations in which most leaching occurs. Cutting causes cellular disruption and increases

FIGURE 18.2 General effects of commercial processing on various nutrients.

Nutrient	Processing Effects
Lipids	• Oxidation accelerated by light
Protein	• Denatured by heat (improves digestion)
Amino acids	• Some are sensitive to light. Lysine bio-availability reduced by non-enzymatic browning
Vitamin C (Ascorbic acid)	• Decreases during storage, drying, heating, oxidation, cell damage (e.g., chopping or slicing) • Stable to heat under acidic conditions
Vitamin B_1 (Thiamine)	• Destroyed by high temperatures, neutral and alkaline (e.g., baking soda, baking powder) conditions • Lost in cooking water
Vitamin B_2 (Riboflavin)	• Sensitive to light at neutral and alkaline conditions • Moderately heat stable under neutral conditions • Sensitive to heat under alkaline conditions
Vitamin B_3 (Niacin, Nicotinamide)	• The most stable vitamin • Stable to heat and light • Leaches into cooking water
Folate	• Decreases with storage or prolonged heating • Lost in cooking water • Destroyed by use of copper utensils
Vitamin B_6 (Pyridoxine, Pyridoxal)	• Heat stable in alkaline and acidic conditions • Pyridoxal is heat labile
Vitamin B_{12}	• Destroyed by light and high pH
Carotenes	• Easily destroyed by heat • Oxidize and isomerize when exposed to heat and light
Vitamin A	• Very heat labile; easily destroyed by heat • Easily oxidized
Vitamin D	• Oxidizes when exposed to heat and light
Vitamin E	• Oxidizes readily

Source: Morris et al. (2004).

FIGURE 18.3 Percentage of vitamin C retained in peas by current processing and cooking methods.

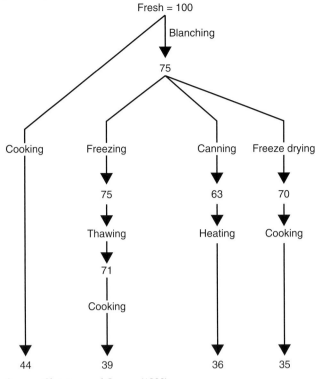

Source: Christian and Greger (1988).

the product's surface area exposed to water, thus further contributing to the loss of nutrients.

Oxidative and enzymatic losses—Labile vitamins, such as ascorbic acid, are often lost via oxidation or enzymatic degradation. Oxidative losses are readily controlled and minimized through optimization of processing procedures—for example, processing under a vacuum allows for lower temperatures, which are less destructive to sensitive vitamins; flushing with inert gas (nitrogen) eliminates oxygen. Thermal processing also inactivates many oxidative enzymes—for example, ascorbic acid oxidase and lipoxygenases.

Thermal degradation—Heat-sensitive vitamins and bioactive compounds (antioxidants) are reduced as a direct result of heating. This loss occurs, of course, during any heating or cooking of foods. However, thermal treatments also improve product stability, market availability, and safety by inactivating deleterious enzymes and microorganisms. Further, using such high-tech thermal treatments as HTST (high temperature, short time) and UHT (ultra-high temperature) processing can minimize thermal degradation to a great degree by reducing exposure time. In addition, nutrient fortification can be used to add back nutrients lost during processing.

Market Fresh vs. Quick Frozen

Typically, fresh fruits and vegetables are considered to possess an optimum level of nutrients and high-quality attributes. This may be the case immediately following harvest; however, "harvest fresh" may be dramatically different from "market fresh," which is frequently two to three weeks post-harvest. Commercially quick-frozen products, which are generally processed within 24 hours of harvest, may actually have higher net nutrient content and offer added benefits of availability, shelf stability, and convenience.

Traditional Food Processing Technologies
Preparation and Size Reduction

Commercial food processing requires large quantities of commodities from various agricultural sectors: fruits and vegetables, cereal grains and legumes, meat and poultry, eggs and dairy products, fats and oils, and seafood. These must be handled rapidly and in a manner that assures food safety and quality.

Generally, food commodities that require washing are washed with chlorinated water or with other added sanitizers (for example, ozone, peroxyacetic acid, or hydrogen peroxide). Improved washing systems use high-pressure mechanical brushes and countercurrent flow principles (cleanest water in contact with cleanest product). The objective is to remove

FIGURE 18.4 Key preparatory operations for various categories of foods.

Food Category	Key Preparatory Operations
Fruit and vegetables (including herbs and spices)	Manual and mechanical harvest Cooling (removal of field heat) Clean and wash Peel, sort, trim Slice/dice
Cereal grains and legumes	Harvest Cleaning (air aspiration and sieving) Drying to stable moisture content
Meat and poultry	Slaughter and evisceration Washing Chilling Carcass hanging/aging Primal and retail cuts
Dairy products	Milking Chilling Bulk receipt and delivery
Shell eggs	Collection Washing Inspecting Grading
Seafood	Catching Washing Chilling/icing Cutting/filleting

Source: Mark A. Uebersax, Ph.D., Muhammad Siddiq, Ph.D., Carl P. Borchgrevink, Ph.D.

FIGURE 18.5 French knife cut terminology.

French Culinary Term	Parameters
Émincé	Thinly sliced
Chiffonade	Rolled leaves cut ultra thin
Rondelle	Disk-shaped slice, a.k.a. coin
Gaufrette	Rondelle or bias cut with a ridged blade
Brunoise	⅛th-inch cube
Macédoine	¼-inch cube
Parmentier	½-inch cube
Carré	¾-inch cube
Paysanne	Rough "farmers" cut; often considered ½ by ½ by ⅛th–¼ inch
Julienne	⅛th by ⅛th by 2–2.5 inches
Allumette	⅛th by ⅛th by ¾ inch or ¹⁄₁₆th by ⅛th by 1.5 inches
Batonnet	¼ by ¼ by 2–2.5 inches
Frite	½ by ½ by 3 inches
Pont Neuf	¾ by ¾ by 3 inches
Tourné (m) or Tournée (f)	8–16 sided blunt-end football shape, a.k.a. turned
Château	Turned to the size of a large olive
à l'Anglaise	Turned to the size of a pigeon's egg or a large clove of garlic
Fondante	Turned to the size of a regular (large) egg
Parisienne	1¾-inch diameter ball
Noisette	Ball the size of a hazelnut

Source: Escoffier (1934, 1969); Ranhofer (1894).

natural and incidental contaminants and debris (for example, soil, manure, stones, organic matter, insects, and rubbish).

After washing and sorting, raw materials undergo peeling, trimming, and size-reduction operations. These frequently require sophisticated machinery that can handle high capacity and is flexible for use with various types of food. This equipment is most often fabricated in stainless steel and according to principles of sanitary design.

From the perspective of the chef, size reduction, as in mincing, dicing, and chopping, is essential to the preparation and delivery of high-quality foods. Uniformity of size and shape lends itself to even cooking and desirable visual appeal. In the culinary world, many approaches to size reduction use descriptive French terms that have a rather precise definition.

Commercial processing equipment can be used to reproduce many of these precise cuts; however, the typical accelerated throughput of commercial operations can detract from precision in size and shape consistency. There is always an element of compromise in high-volume production compared to what is possible in a restaurant setting. That said, the same commercial processing equipment typically found in a high-volume commercial kitchen—slicers, buffalo choppers, food processors, blenders, and meat grinders—can be used successfully in the product development lab or test kitchen as well.

Minimally Processed Fresh foods

Minimally processed or fresh-cut produce includes any fresh fruit, vegetable, or combination thereof that is physically altered from its original form but remains in a fresh state. Processing in this category has two main objectives:

1. Keeping the produce fresh by extending its shelf life without losing its nutritional and sensory quality or compromising product safety.
2. Ensuring a product shelf life sufficient to make its distribution feasible within the region of its consumption.[2]

Fresh-cut produce has been one of the fastest-growing segments of the U.S. food industry in the last few years.[3]

Quality of fresh-cut products depends on visual appearance (freshness, color, defects, and decay), texture (crispness, turgidity, firmness, and tissue integrity), flavor (taste and smell), nutritive value (vitamins, minerals, and dietary fiber), and safety (absence of chemical residues and microbial contamination).[4] From the consumers' perspective, the color and appearance of fresh-cut produce has the greatest impact on purchase intent. If the color of a fresh-cut product is not attractive or of acceptable perceived quality, the consumer is less likely to purchase it regardless of its excellent texture, flavor, taste, or other quality attributes.[5]

The degradation of color in fresh-cut produce is primarily the result of two enzymes: polyphenol oxidase and peroxidase. These enzymes also impair aroma and flavor and, hence, the marketability of the product. In addition, they can reduce nutritive value via oxidation of ascorbic acid (vitamin C).[6] Traditionally, sulfites were used extensively in the food industry to control color degradation or browning. However, since the late 1980s scientists have been seeking replacements for sulfites due to adverse respiratory reactions in individuals with asthma.[7] When safety issues were raised in 1984, the U.S. Food and Drug Administration (FDA) banned sulfite use in fresh-cut fruits and vegetables in salad bars. A number of alternatives, such as ascorbic acid, citric acid, 4-hexylresorcinol, erythorbic acid and sodium erythorbate (stereoisomers of ascorbates), benzoic acid, and natural fruit juices (for example, lemon juice) are commercially available and yield varying degrees of success, either alone or in combinations. The addition of organic acids (for example, citric acid, ascorbic acid) lowers pH and thus limits enzymatic action, as enzymes rapidly lose their catalytic effectiveness in an acidic environment.

In addition to chemical anti-browning treatments, other technologies, such as modified atmosphere packaging (MAP),

are widely used. In this approach, the normal ratio of gases in air (21 percent oxygen and 0.038 percent carbon dioxide) is adjusted to reduce the oxygen level to 5 to 10 percent and elevate the carbon dioxide to 5 to 20 percent inside the package.[8] Limiting oxygen and increasing carbon dioxide dramatically reduces the rate of many biological reactions, including oxidation and rancidity, enzymatic browning, cellular respiration, and growth of microorganisms, the result of which provides extended shelf life to cut produce (and other foods as well).

Thermal Processing

The objective of thermal processing (blanching, pasteurization, canning, aseptic processing and packaging) is to help stabilize a food product, ensure it is wholesome and safe for consumption, and yield sufficient shelf life to satisfy the needs of the business and the consumer.

Microorganisms are inherent to all raw food commodities and are categorized as either spoilage or pathogenic (disease-causing) organisms. Enzymes are proteins that catalyze metabolic reactions in all living plants and animals. They are present in all raw foods. If they are not inactivated, they cause continued breakdown and deterioration of food materials until the food is no longer desirable for consumption. In addition to controlling microorganisms, thermal processes are also used to denature enzymes in foods to prevent deterioration.

Thermal processes can be generally divided into two types: those that provide short-term inhibition of microbial growth and enzymatic activity (blanching and pasteurization) but require additional inhibitory methods (dehydration, refrigeration, freezing, chemical preservatives) to provide longer shelf life; and those entirely designed to provide long-term shelf stability at room temperature (canning and aseptic processing).

Blanching

Blanching is preliminary to many basic methods of food preservation—canning, freezing, dehydration, and so on. The terminology is derived from the French word *blanche*, meaning "white." Among other effects, blanching inactivates oxidative enzymes and thus stabilizes the natural appearance of many fruits and vegetables. This control of browning was perceived as having a whitening effect on the product, hence the term.

Blanching is a relatively mild heat treatment given to raw products before they are packed into containers for canning or freezing. It is a critical step in stabilizing many quality attributes. It may be accomplished by steam or hot water and serves as a final wash to reduce microbial load, inactivate enzymes, remove certain raw or off flavors, improve color and flavor retention (especially in frozen foods), and increase the pliability of the product. Blanching also facilitates filling by expelling dissolved or occluded gases from the plant tissues.

In hot-water systems, the product must be totally submerged in water at or above 190°F (88°C) for a prescribed time (dependent on the type and size of the food). These methods may use static water baths or continuous systems where screws or reels move the product through the hot water at a controlled rate. Recently, tubular pipe blanchers, which require pumping the product in water through a pipe in which steam is injected, have been used to improve blanching capacity and efficiency. While water systems provide desirable quality control and rapid uniform heat transfer, this type of blanching generally results in relatively high leaching losses of soluble nutrients (vitamins, minerals) and flavor components. In addition, water-blanching operations produce large volumes of waste water. By contrast, steam blanching reduces both nutrient losses and water requirements and has thus found wide use in the industry.

Pasteurization

Pasteurization is a thermal treatment that provides increased refrigerated shelf stability and reduces public health hazards (pathogens). Pasteurization is named for Louis Pasteur, the French scientist who first identified microorganisms associated with fermentation and spoilage. The heat treatment may be applied directly to the product prior to packaging (milk or juice) or after packaging (high-acid [below pH 4.6] foods such as pickles). Pasteurization *after* packaging eliminates the possibility of recontamination of pasteurized product before it reaches the protection of the package.

This reduced heat treatment does *not* result in commercial sterility but rather is designed to destroy only pathogenic microorganisms and inactivate deteriorative enzymes. Unlike

---

Pasteurization Processes for Selected Foods[9]

Milk

USDA pasteurization parameters (first three require refrigeration after processing):

- 143°F (62°C)/30 minutes—vat pasteurization (earliest method)
- 161°F (72°C)/17 seconds—HTST (high temperature, short time); most common method used in the United States
- 280°F (138°C)/2 seconds or longer—ultrapasteurization
- Ultrapasteurization combined with aseptic processing and packaging (also known as UHT [ultra-high-temperature processing]). Unlike the former methods, this is a form of sterilization; these products do not require refrigeration until they are opened.
- Milk pasteurization is based on achieving a 12-D reduction of *Coxiella burnetti*, the most heat-resistant pathogen found in milk. The D-value (decimal reduction time) is a measure of the heat resistance of a microorganism. It is the time in minutes at a given temperature required to destroy 1 log cycle (90 percent)

of the target microorganism. Thus, after a bacterial population is reduced by 1-D, only 10 percent of the original organisms remain. 12-D equals sufficient heat to reduce organism populations by 12 log cycles.

- Alkaline phosphatase, a naturally occurring enzyme in milk, possesses a similar D value to heat-resistant pathogens and is generally used as a simple colorimetric confirmation test for effective pasteurization. If the enzyme is no longer active, pasteurization is complete and the milk is safe for consumption.

Eggs

USDA guidelines for fluid egg products:

- Salmonellae—Objective is to achieve a 9-D reduction in *S. seftenberg*; 140°F (60°C)/3½ to 4 minutes.
- Pasteurization temperature is below albumen's (egg white) denaturation temperature range in order to keep the eggs from curdling; similar to the alkaline phosphatase test used to measure pasteurization success in milk, α-amylase activity is used as a convenient colorimetric test for measuring the effectiveness of egg pasteurization.

Apple Juice and Cider

- 170 to 200°F (77 to 93°C)/1 to 3 minutes

Bottled Beer

- Most beer in cans and bottles is pasteurized; the pasteurization process occurs *after* the beer is placed in the can or bottle and the container is sealed. The process involves running the containers through a hot-water spray (approximately 140°F (60°C) for 2 to 3 minutes. American keg beer (draft beer) is not pasteurized (although imported keg beer is) and must be stored refrigerated at 38°F (3°C).

Fermented or Acidified Products (Pickles, Sauerkraut, Fruits)

- These are products whose pH level is below 4.6, due to either fermentation or the direct addition of acids (acidification). Due to their acidity, it is rare to find pathogens; the usual culprits here are spoilage organisms. Typical thermal processing for these products is known as hot-fill-and-hold, whereby the product is heated to between 180 and 212°F (82 and 100°C) before filling, then pumped hot into sanitized containers, sealed, and inverted for 3 minutes to sterilize the lid and develop a vacuum before cooling. Alternatively, the hot-filled and capped jars can be processed after filling in a pasteurization tunnel that will expose the jars to hot water of at least 190°F for sufficient time (which will differ depending on the size of the jars and the type of product) to assure commercial sterility. This is analogous to the hot-water-bath method used by home canners for decades.

Fruit Juice Products

- It is fairly easy to hot-fill juices by rapidly heating the juice in a heat exchanger and filling containers with the hot juice (around 203°F [95°C]), followed by sealing and inverting, thus pasteurizing the container. Reasonably rapid cooling is accomplished by rotary or spin action. This is known as flash pasteurization and can be achieved almost instantaneously.

retorted products, which are stable at room temperature, pasteurized products must be refrigerated post-treatment to inhibit the outgrowth of spoilage organisms that survive the process. Pasteurization processes are regulated by federal authorities—U.S. Public Health Service (USPHS), FDA, U.S. Department of Agriculture (USDA)—and are typically achieved with heat sufficient for a specified reduction in the population of a specific test organism within a specific food.

Conventional Canning (Retorting)

Microorganisms consist primarily of vegetative (living) cells that are relatively heat-labile. However, many microorganisms (for example, *Clostridium botulinum*) can form dormant, heat-resistant spores when their environment changes to the point where vegetative cells can't survive. The spores can remain dormant for as long as it takes for the surroundings to revert to the appropriate conditions for germination, and then the vegetative population is resurrected. For extended room-temperature storage of foods, thermal processing must provide sufficient heating temperatures and processing time to inhibit or inactivate the bacterial spores as well as vegetative cells. The thermal resistance of spores varies with each type of organism, the spore concentration, and the chemical nature (salt, sugar, protein, acidity, and pH) of the food. Determining the requirements sufficient to establish commercial sterility requires knowledge of the heat resistance of spores and of the manner in which heat penetrates the food.

Commercial sterility is a compromise based on the practical impossibility of achieving complete sterility in the contents of a hermetically sealed (airtight) container during commercial thermal processing. While it is recognized that the possibility exists for a bacterium to survive the process, the chances of even a single organism surviving are extremely low if the thermal process has been designed correctly. Achieving commercial sterility in hermetically sealed containers of low-acid foods (pH > 4.6) processed for ambient (room temperature) storage is critically important, as the pathogen most likely to grow in these types of foods is *Clostridium botulinum*, the spores of which release a potent neurotoxin if allowed to germinate.

The common terminology used for thermal processing of foods in hermetically sealed containers is retorting (also called *canning*). This technology is relatively new (early 1800s) compared with more primitive methods such as smoking, salting, pickling, and dehydration. Large-scale canning of food was first successfully performed by Nicholas Appert, a French confectioner who responded to Napoleon's call for an improved method of preserving food for his army. Appert's success was achieved after numerous trial-and-error attempts at filling bottles with food, sealing them with corks, and heating them in boiling water for various periods.[10]

Canning is one of the most widely used methods for long-term preservation of a wide range of foods, including meat, fish, poultry, milk products, fruits, vegetables, and complex formulated foods (soups, stews, pasta, sauces, and pastes). Canning is a high-volume, efficient, and safe means of stabilizing food in a convenient, fully cooked, and cost-effective manner. Modern canneries can process 1000 cans per minute (16 to 17 cans per second). In addition to actual cans, canning is also used to successfully process foods in glass jars, flexible pouches, trays, and other packages that are capable of withstanding the high temperature (250°F [121°C]) and pressure (15 psi) required to achieve it.

In the modern process, following pre-processing preparation procedures (including washing, sizing, mixing, seasoning, and blanching or cooking), products are immediately put into containers and sealed. Systems range from simple, manual filling to highly engineered automated machinery. Control of net weight must be maintained for regulatory compliance (weights and measures) and to assure consistent heating in every container. Foods to be packed in brines or syrups are put into containers first and then covered with the liquid portion. Filled containers are then exhausted by being passed through a hot-water bath or steam chamber to expel any trapped gases and promote expansion of the filled product before the can is sealed; this is necessary to ensure a full vacuum on cooling. The exhausted can is then hermetically sealed by double-seaming a lid to it. This operation is a critical control point (CCP) in the process. Detailed attention to the dimensions and security of the seam is required to assure food safety.

Each step in the processing of fresh crops into stable canned products is characterized as a unit operation. Although specific requirements may vary for different products, overall these are fairly typical operations.

The processor attains commercial sterility by eliminating all pathogens and microorganisms that cause spoilage in cans (or similar containers) that will be handled under ambient temperatures (for example, distributed, marketed, and stored at room temperature).[11] Survivor curves for microorganisms are constructed to determine the time and temperature required to give a desired reduction in the microorganisms' population. The D-value (decimal reduction time) is used to specify the time in minutes at a specific temperature required for a 1 log reduction (a tenfold reduction) in the population of a given microorganism.

FIGURE 18.6 **Cross-section of a can double seam.**

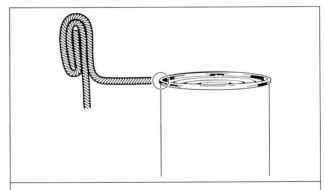

Note: There are five layers of steel folded and compressed with a sealing compound to form the hermetic double seam.

Source: USDA-FSIS, Center for Learning (2005).

FIGURE 18.7 Unit operations in potato canning.

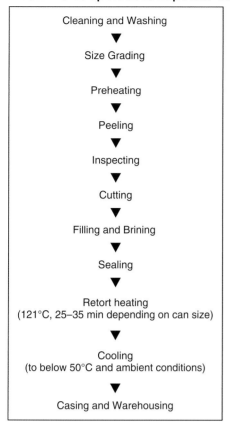

Cleaning and Washing

▼

Size Grading

▼

Preheating

▼

Peeling

▼

Inspecting

▼

Cutting

▼

Filling and Brining

▼

Sealing

▼

Retort heating
(121°C, 25–35 min depending on can size)

▼

Cooling
(to below 50°C and ambient conditions)

▼

Casing and Warehousing

Source: Mark A. Uebersax, Ph.D., Muhammad Siddiq, Ph.D.,
Carl P. Borchgrevink, Ph.D.

FIGURE 18.8 Temperature profile and general phases of the thermal process.

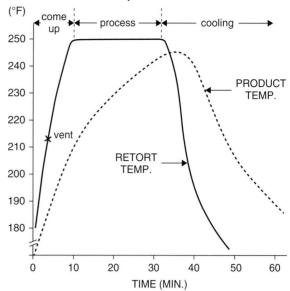

Note: The phases termed *come-up time*, *process time*, and *cooling time* for the retort versus the lagging product temperature (center of the can).
Source: Mark A. Uebersax.

All factors affecting heat penetration must be known in order to calculate the time and temperature requirements for achieving commercial sterility. Heating profiles of canned foods must be measured at the slowest heating point (cold spot) of the food within the container. Heat transfer is determined by placing a thermocouple (sensor used to measure temperature) at the cold point of the container (typically the geometric center) and monitoring the temperature change during heating. External heat may penetrate to the cold spot by conduction or convection (or both). Typically, solid-packed foods are heated primarily by conduction, whereas liquids are heated by convection, simply because of differences in the heat transfer dynamics between solids and liquids. Heating characteristics are also dramatically influenced by mechanical agitation of the containers during retort operation, which increases the heat transfer efficiency of the system.

During canning, heating rate is influenced by several factors:

- The material of the container
- The size and shape of the container
- The initial temperature of the product prior to heating
- The processing temperature
- The physical consistency or size configuration of discrete food particles.[12]

Acid food products (pH < 4.6) in hermetically sealed containers may simply be heated in boiling-water baths for relatively brief times to achieve commercial sterility, as their high acidity provides enough additional inhibitory protection to assure safety. Atmospheric water processing systems for acid foods may be of relatively simple design; however, they must provide uniform temperature control. Numerous continuous-processing systems are commercially available for the required controlled heating of acid foods.

On the other hand, low-acid foods (pH > 4.6) require processing temperatures in excess of 212°F (100°C) to destroy *Clostridium botulinum* spores. These temperatures are attainable only in pressurized steam retorts or pressure cookers. Several types of thermal processing systems are commercially available and have a high degree of safety compliance. These include:

Discontinuous retorts—These are batch types, classified as either *still* or *agitating*. Still retorts are static pressure cookers normally operated at 240 to 250°F (115 to 121°C) (10 to 15 psi steam pressure) and provide no agitation of the can during processing. The sealed cans are placed inside the retort, air is vented from the retort with steam, and pressure is increased to provide the required processing temperature. Agitating retorts are systems designed to provide mechanical rotation of the cans during the processing cycle to improve heat transfer, which reduces processing time. The time reduction results in improved efficiency (increased product throughput) and product quality (less heating time). Actual processing time in either type of retort system is counted only after the retort reaches the specified operating temperature. However, microbial lethality actually begins as the water temperature approaches the operating temperature and continues for some time after the heating cycle ends and the temperature begins to drop. Thus portions of the *come-up time* (heating phase) and *come-down time* (cooling phase) are built into the overall process calculations. Steam is supplied continuously until the processing time is completed, at which time it is shut off and the pressure is reduced. Cans are then gradually cooled with cold water to approximately 100°F (38°C), labeled, and cased.

Continuous retort systems—These systems are designed as horizontal cylindrical tunnels with can-carrying tracks forming a spiral from one end to the other along the inside surface of the cylinder. They provide agitation as the cans move down the tunnel, twisting and turning in the tracks; this produces forced convection currents through the product, thereby improving heat transfer to the cold spot. Continuous systems eliminate the time and energy lost in the starting and stopping required for loading and unloading of batch systems.

Hydrostatic cookers—These use large vertical columns of water called barometric legs that enable continuous entrance and exit of cans into and out of the high-pressure steam chamber. The legs are generally greater than 35 feet high and, along with the steam chamber, project vertically through the processing plant roof, thus conserving plant floor space. Cans are placed horizontally on a continuous chain that ascends and descends through the legs and is exposed to the processing steam chamber maintained at the desired temperature. Process time is set based on chain speed. The legs enable controlled, continuous preheating and cooling of cans, thus conserving energy and improving overall efficiency. The hydrostatic cooker is most suitable for large production runs of identical products.

Glass and flexible packaging containers—The strength and integrity of the double seam and the rigidity of the can enable retort processing under direct steam pressure. Glass jars and flexible pouch packaging, in comparison, require overriding external pressure to ensure seal integrity. Ultimately, the package seam integrity depends on the internal vacuum that forms after processing as the product cools to room temperature. This is particularly important for glass, which relies on the internal vacuum to secure the cap or lid, and flexible

containers, which lack the rigidity of metal cans. Pressure differentials and uniformity of heating must be maintained to assure a compliant sterilization process without losing package integrity. Generally, the containers are submerged in water that is the same temperature as the filled product; then the pressure vessel is closed and overriding air pressure is applied to the water. This assures that the lids and seals remain intact. At the completion of the specified heating cycle, the superheated water is gradually replaced with cooling water under stable pressure. This requires integrated automatic control of both pressure and temperature and is critical to a successful process. A momentary loss of overriding pressure results in dislodged lids or torn seals, and even subtle changes may result in a leaky seam or cap that allows contamination. Glass is particularly susceptible to thermal shock and breakage, so temperature changes must be carefully monitored and controlled.[13]

Aseptic Processing and Packaging

This innovative and advanced technology revolutionized classical thermal processing. In 1961, the first aseptic processing facility (for milk) was started in Switzerland; the Tetra Pak Company was the pioneer in commercial aseptic processing in Europe and Asia. In the United States, this technology did not become popular until the 1980s. Aseptically packaged products are shelf-stable and safe at room temperature. The major difference between conventional and aseptic processing is that the food product is sterilized separately, then filled and sealed in a sterile container under sterile conditions. Aseptic systems were commercially developed to provide continuous thermal processing of heat-sensitive products such as fruit juices, puddings, milk, and specially formulated dairy products.[14] Products are processed through high-temperature, short-time (HTST) heat exchangers, which offer protection to heat-sensitive quality attributes of foods such as flavor, color, texture, and heat-labile nutrients. High-particulate products (stews, sliced fruits, pasta in sauce), especially with large piece size, are generally not suitable for aseptic processing. This is because product is rapidly pumped

FIGURE 18.9 **Principles of aseptic processing and packaging.**

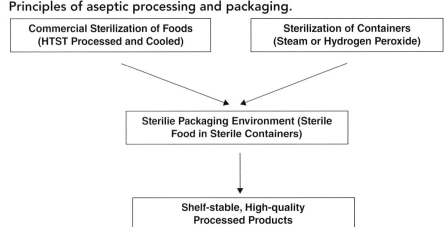

Source: Mark A. Uebersax, Ph.D., Muhammad Siddiq, Ph.D., Carl P. Borchgrevink, Ph.D.

through the continuous heat exchanger, which is designed for uniform heat transfer in a homogeneous product. Particulates tend to disintegrate under this type of process.

Product and process requirements for aseptic systems include:

- *Uniform composition of raw product*—Generally, fluids or pumpable pastes are most suitable. Typically, homogenizers are used to provide a homogeneous mix.
- *Controlled flow rate of product*—Use of a timing pump to control residence time of product in the heat exchanger is required for proper processing (the homogenizer pump provides controlled flow rate).
- *High-capacity heat exchanger*—HTST heating followed by cooling.
- *Coordinated delivery of sterilized packaging to match the arrival of cooled product.*
- *Sterile filling and sealing chamber to prevent recontamination of sterilized product.*

The HTST systems provide rapid heat transfer at relatively high temperatures (UHT) that range to greater than 300°F (149°C) and expose the product to only a few minutes of heating, compared to what is typically provided in conventional canning systems (about 250°F [121°C] for 90 minutes or more).

When thermal processing is used to sterilize food, bacterial cells and spores are inactivated at an exponential or logarithmic rate (that is, the rate of destruction dramatically increases as temperature increases). However, chemical reactions in foods that lead to loss of sensory qualities generally progress at a slower, linear or arithmetic rate (exhibiting only incremental degradation). Thus, food safety objectives (microorganism destruction) are met much faster, before quality and nutrients have a chance to deteriorate. Because of this, efforts are made to heat products as rapidly as possible, to as high a temperature as practical, to hold them at that temperature for a minimum period, and to cool them quickly (as with HTST and UHT processing). This inactivates the bacterial population while minimizing thermal degradation of the product.

Aseptic processing is particularly successful in dairy foods (evaporated and regular milk, sour cream, coffee creamers, and dips), liquid egg products, puddings and gelatin desserts, baby foods, soups, sauces, juice boxes, tomato puree and paste, and fruit purees. There are essentially no container size limitations with aseptic processing. Commonly, products are packaged in containers ranging from half-ounce coffee creamers to juice-box laminated cartons to 55-gallon drums. Metalized flexible packaging, broadly termed *bag-in-box*, is ideal for large-scale processed foods used as ingredients in commercial food formulations. Even the interior of a tanker truck can be sterilized and used as an aseptic package to transport sterile liquids in bulk.

Aseptic bulk processing, an innovation often interfaced directly with agricultural harvest and processing systems, provides a means of bulk storage or transportation (using

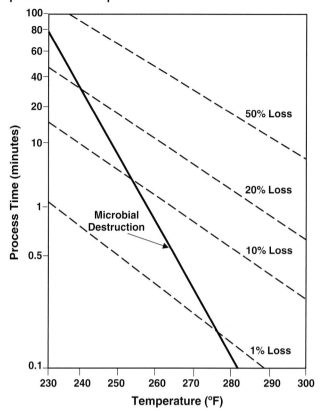

FIGURE 18.10 Effect of time (vertical axis, log scale) and temperature (horizontal axis) on destruction of typical bacterial spores and percent loss of spores.

Note: Each point on these lines represents an equivalent process. Thus, HTST processing conditions result in microbial death with limited quality degradation.

Source: Adapted from I. J. Pflug, C. W. Hall, and G. M. Trout, "Aseptic Canning of Dairy Products," *Dairy Engineering*, 1959.

sterilized storage silos, railcars, portable tankers, drums, and bag-in-box or flexible pouches) before final processing. This technique is extensively used in the citrus juice industry and for tomato and grape purees. Essentially, it allows the grower or processor to store large quantities of fruit or vegetable juices, concentrates, and purees for extended periods after harvest without refrigeration. It relieves crop overloads and reduces waste by improving product flow during peak harvest season. Products can be used any time they are needed; there is never an off season.

There are two basic types of product heating used in aseptic processing: direct and indirect:

Direct

- Steam injection systems are the fastest method of heating foods, but they are open systems, and heat-labile flavors may be lost. This method is typically used for products where heat-induced flavors, such as scorched or cooked milk flavors, are not desired. Also, steam used in direct heating of the product must be of culinary quality (appropriate for food contact). Typical products treated with steam injection include baby foods and cereals.

Indirect

- Plate heat exchangers are used for low-pulp, single-strength juices and drinks, as high-pulp items and concentrates generally stick and burn in this type of heat exchanger. The benefits of plate heat exchangers are that they are relatively low-priced and have highly efficient pre-heating and pre-cooling rates (up to 90 percent more efficient than other methods). Typical food products for which plate heat exchangers are used include milk and fruit juices.

- High-velocity, high-pressure tubular exchangers are favored for products that might burn, foul, or clog when exposed to plate heat exchangers but are not viscous enough to require or qualify for scraped plate exchangers. The products are kept from sticking and burning by high pressure–induced turbulence. Given the closed nature of these systems, volatile flavor loss is prevented or reduced. Typical food products for this type of heat exchanger include pastes, purees, and puddings. These systems are more expensive than plate heat exchangers but not as expensive as scraped-surface heat exchangers.

- Scraped-surface heat exchangers are the most expensive type of heat exchanger and are thus used mainly for high-value viscous products or foods that are otherwise heat sensitive. Typical food products heated in scraped-surface heat exchangers include purees, puddings, slurries of fruits and vegetables, and stews. This is a closed system, providing increased flavor retention.

Chilling and Freezing

Early food technologists recognized that low-temperature storage reduces the respiratory rate of freshly harvested crops, decreases the activity of microorganisms in food, and slows chemical and biochemical deterioration. Refrigeration is commonly used for short-term preservation, whereas freezing is suitable for long-term storage.[15]

Freezing Processes

The American inventor and entrepreneur Clarence F. Birdseye II (1886–1956) is considered the founder of the modern frozen food industry. During his work as a field naturalist he was taught by the native Inuit people to fish through thick ice in frigid temperatures. He discovered that the fish froze almost immediately on removal from the water and, when thawed, tasted much fresher than the frozen fish sold at that time, which was slow-frozen and thus lost product integrity. Birdseye eventually developed a process for commercially quick-freezing fish between two refrigerated plates under pressure, and a new industry was born.

All of the water in a food must be converted to ice before the temperature can be reduced below freezing. Foods are not made of pure water; therefore, they do not freeze completely at 32°F (0°C). For example, the actual freezing point of milk and eggs is 31°F (−0.5°C); of fruits and vegetables, 30.5 to 27°F (−0.8 to 2.8°C). As the water in food begins to freeze,

salts, proteins, and other solutes in the water are concentrated into a smaller and smaller volume of liquid. Thus, the concentration of solutes in the unfrozen portion increases, lowering the freezing point of that portion. These increases in solute concentration can damage foods by denaturation of proteins because a high concentration of salts destabilizes protein structure. This can lead to coagulation and reduced water-holding capacity, eventually resulting in diminished product quality and functionality.

Major Factors Affecting Frozen Foods

Food quality is particularly affected by the rate of freezing. Rapid freezing results in numerous small ice crystals that produce less cell wall damage in fruits and vegetables, and less cell membrane damage in meats and other non-plant-based foods, than do the comparatively fewer but larger crystals formed during slow freezing. Cellular damage, in which ice crystals penetrate cell walls and membranes, results in reduced quality, particularly texture (mouthfeel) and water-holding capacity (drip loss). Several factors determine how quickly foods can be frozen:

Food composition—The components of food—fat, water, air, protein, and so on—have different thermal properties, each affecting how quickly a food freezes. For example, meat containing a large amount of fat freezes more slowly than lean meat (which contains comparatively more water).

Size and shape—Food processors have more control over certain freezing factors. For example, they can speed heat removal by cutting the food into smaller pieces. That way, the amount of surface exposed to the freezing medium is large and the volume of each piece is small; therefore, the food loses heat rapidly. The size and shape of a container has a similar effect on the rate at which its contents freeze, with larger containers taking a longer time to freeze completely, as do stacked pallets of cased products.

Temperature differential and convective cooling—The rate of freezing can be accelerated by increasing the difference between the temperature of the freezing medium and the temperature of the food. In a freezing chamber where the medium is stationary (cold, still air), the thermostat might have to be set at −40°F (4.4°C) instead of −20°F (−29°C) to achieve the same rate of freezing as in chambers where the freezing medium is moving (high-velocity chilled air). This is due to convection in the cold air or liquid refrigerant. Increases in the velocity of the refrigerant speed the transfer of heat from the food to the freezing medium.

Methods of Freezing Food

Air Freezing

Air freezing is the simplest and most common method for freezing food. Generally, temperatures are maintained at 0 to −40°F (−18 to −40°C). Food products are placed in a cold room until frozen or, more commonly, pass through on continuous conveyor belts. In air-blast freezing systems, blowers generate high-velocity air currents (300 linear feet per minute) in the freezing compartment to achieve rapid freezing. Fluidized bed freezing is a type of air-blast freezing used to create IQF (individually quick-frozen) foods such as small or diced fruits, peas, shrimp, and cubed carrots. In IQF, the product is spread about 6 inches thick on a perforated wire mesh belt that passes through a freezing tunnel. High-velocity chilled air is directed upward through the food, creating lifting and wave-like turbulence within the product. Thus, individual pieces of food freeze rapidly (usually within 5 minutes) and efficiently. These frozen discrete pieces of food are easy to package and use.[16]

Plate Freezing

Plate freezing is used for prepackaged foods. Freezer plates are hollow, flat shelves cooled by circulating refrigerant. Packages of food are placed between the freezer plates, which are pressed onto the packages to speed the removal of heat from the food. Freezing is complete in 1 to 2 hours. This method freezes packaged blocks of food rapidly and is suitable for any food available in block form, such as fish or boxed vegetables.

A variation is the rapid continuous freezing of fluid products or purees using a scraped-surface heat exchanger. A rotating scraper blade (dasher blade) moves the product through a freezing cylinder in direct contact with its internal cooling surface. The frozen product leaves the system as a pumpable slush ready for immediate packaging and solid freezing in an air-blast freezer. Scraped-surface heat exchangers reduce product temperatures continuously and rapidly so the frozen product contains many small ice crystals. Smooth ice cream, orange juice concentrate, and other pumpable purees are frozen this way.

Immersion Freezing

The immersion freezing approach puts a refrigerated coolant in direct contact with the product or package; speed is the main advantage. The product is immersed in or sprayed with refrigerated solutions that are colder than ice due to their high concentration of dissolved solids, such as salt brines, sugar syrups, and propylene glycol. Whole packaged turkeys are usually moved on a conveyor through the refrigerated solution to ensure uniform freezing of the skin, giving it a smooth, tight-fitting appearance.

Cryogenic Freezing

In cryogenic freezing systems, low-boiling-point refrigerants, placed in contact with the product or package, remove heat as they change from liquid to vapor phase. Liquid nitrogen (boiling point, –320°F [–196°C]) and liquid carbon dioxide (boiling point, –109°F [–78°C]) are the most common in food freezing. They can freeze foods very rapidly. However, because the vapor cannot be reclaimed, the process is quite expensive. Extremely rapid freezing enables production of high-quality specialty products (for example, frozen, cooked, chopped eggs for salads) that would be unacceptable if frozen in any other system.

FIGURE 18.11 Fluidized bed freezing. High-velocity cold air provides enough turbulence to lift the product for rapid freezing of individual food pieces—for example, peas, diced vegetables.

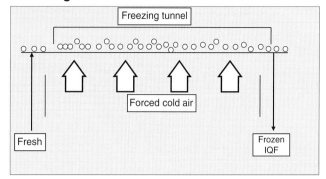

Source: Mark A. Uebersax, Ph.D., Muhammad Siddiq, Ph.D., Carl P. Borchgrevink, Ph.D.

Other Factors Affecting Frozen Foods

Maintenance of low (ideally 0°F [–18°C] or below) and uniform temperature is essential for storing high-quality frozen foods. Temperature cycling, which causes the water in food to partly thaw and freeze repeatedly, results in dehydration (freezer burn) as the water exits the tissues and crystallizes on the food's surface. Lipid oxidation leading to fat rancidity can occur at frozen temperatures, although more slowly than at ambient or refrigerated temperatures. This makes long-term frozen storage of fatty foods problematic. The situation is exacerbated if the food contains unsaturated fats along with salt or metals such as iron (commonly found in meats containing high levels of the muscle pigment myoglobin, such as beef, poultry dark meat, and fatty fish). Salt and metals accelerate the initiation of oxidative rancidity.

From the food safety perspective, it is impractical and undesirable to sterilize frozen foods, as neither pathogens nor spoilage organisms can grow at freezer temperatures. Instead, a pragmatic balance is established between any non-pathogenic psychrophilic (cold-loving) microorganisms and pathogens that may be present. The non-pathogenic psychrotrophs (such as lactic acid bacteria) grow more rapidly in thawed foods, creating acidic conditions unsuitable for the growth of psychrophilic pathogens (such as listeria). Furthermore, spoilage by psychrotrophs is often noticeable through changes in appearance, odor, or taste. The disposal of visibly spoiled, mishandled food may protect consumers from invisible damage by pathogens. Lastly, other than ice cream and other frozen treats, frozen foods are generally cooked before consumption, providing a kill step for any microorganisms that may be present.

Other factors that influence the rate of spoilage in frozen foods include:

- The level of cleanliness or contamination of the original ingredients, finished product, and the processing facility

- The duration of refrigerated storage of the product prior to freezing
- Temperatures and methods used in thawing

Thawed foods are particularly susceptible to spoilage because as food thaws, soluble drips contain nutrients that can be used by microorganisms for growth and the product may be exposed to temperatures that promote rapid growth of food spoilage organisms. Such microorganisms may be native to the food or environmentally introduced during handling and processing.

Recommended thawing procedures that limit microbial growth generally specify moving the food from the freezer to the refrigerator for an extended period of time (hours to days), or, for more rapid thawing, immersing the frozen product in cold running water for as long as necessary to achieve the necessary level of thawing. Ideally, once thawed, products should not be allowed to warm above refrigerator temperatures before they are cooked. Microbial populations can multiply rapidly during thawing, so refreezing of thawed products is not recommended. However, partially thawed products still containing ice crystals or held at refrigerator temperatures up to 24 hours may be refrozen safely if not mishandled, although sensory qualities may suffer.

Previously frozen, thawed seafood products (shrimp, scallops, fish fillets) are commonly available in supermarkets. These products should not be refrozen and should be cooked and consumed within a day or two of purchase.

Dehydration

Dehydration, the removal of water from a food product, provides the longest shelf life to foods, assuming that environmental factors such as exposure to humidity and incursions by insects and rodents are controlled. It requires the use of external heat to vaporize and remove water from the food solids. Two distinct processes are involved: (1) heat transfer and (2) mass transfer. Heat transfer involves supplying enough heat to transform the water within the food and on its surface into steam. The quantity of heat energy needed to vaporize water depends on the temperature and pressure at which vaporization occurs. The latent heat of vaporization for water (the energy required to convert water to steam) at atmospheric pressure is about 970 BTU per pound of water at 212°F (100°C). Generally, heating involves conduction, convection, and radiation processes of heat transfer, which are highly dependent on a broad spectrum of product and process variables (product type, solid and liquid content, piece geometry, size, and shape) and the physical conditions of the heating environment (temperature, air velocity, and relative humidity).

Mass transfer involves the removal of moisture from the surface of the food and the internal diffusion of water to the surface of the product. These phases of the drying process are referred to as (1) constant rate, associated with the initial stage of rapid removal of moisture from the surface, and (2) falling rate, associated with the slower and subsequent internal diffusion of water to the surface for evaporation.

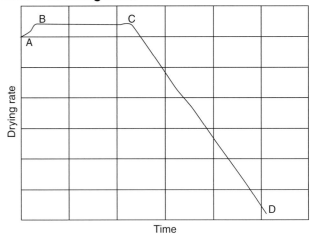

FIGURE 18.12 **Typical drying rate curve of foods. (A-B, initial accelerated rate; B-C, constant rate; C-D, falling rate).**

Source: Mark A. Uebersax, Ph.D., Muhammad Siddiq, Ph.D., Carl P. Borchgrevink, Ph.D.

The constant rate of surface drying is directly influenced by the temperature, relative humidity, and velocity of air over the food surface. During the falling rate, drying rate decreases because it takes longer for water to migrate from the interior of the food to the surface.[17]

Drying Systems
Sun Drying

This is an age-old practice used for whole or cut pieces, common in most regions with arid locales. Dates, figs, tomatoes, fish, and grapes (into raisins) are the most commonly sundried foods. The process typically takes place in areas adjacent to the harvest location. The drying of salt, herbs, and spices also appears in the earliest recorded histories.

Hot-Air Drying

During the twentieth century, advanced methods for drying food products were developed that did not depend on the availability of a hot, sunny climate and were much more efficient. Development accelerated during the first and second World Wars due to the need for global transport and prolonged shelf life of dehydrated foods to feed the troops. Development of dehydrated vegetable products in particular has undergone significant growth, with greatest advances in potato, onion, pepper, and garlic products. These are sold as individual food products or as convenient ingredients in formulated foods.

Hot-air drying can be accomplished using high-velocity hot air (140 to 185°F [60 to 85°C]) to heat and vaporize water and to convey moisture vapors away. Hot-air drying systems include cabinets equipped with perforated trays, heated tunnels through which carts or racks of products are conveyed, and continuous perforated belts with different heating zones. A special fluidized bed technique, which uses high-velocity

FIGURE 18.13 Principles of various drying operations.

System	Principle	Product Type Examples
Sun drying	Radiant heat from the sun evaporates water from food to surrounding air. This is an age-old method of drying foods.	Fruits (raisins, dates, figs), vegetables (herbs, tomatoes, cereals, and legumes), fish, meat, coffee beans
Hot-air drying (cabinet, tunnel, continuous belt, fluidized bed)	Stream of hot air in a closed environment supplies heat by convection and carries away the evaporated water.	Fruit pieces (apple, peaches, plums, pears, apricots), particulate foods (meats, fish, cheese)
Spray drying	Special case of hot-air drying; fluids are sprayed into the stream of hot air; dry powder is separated mechanically.	Liquids, purées, whole eggs, egg yolk, blood albumin, milk, flavors, colors
Vacuum drying	Removal of water vapor by creation of vacuum; heat must be supplied by conduction or radiation (no air used).	Limited production of certain foods, pieces, purées, liquids
Drum drying	Thin layer of liquid or paste foods applied on surfaces of hot stainless-steel drums; dry material is scraped off the rotating rolls at the end of a revolution.	Purées, liquids, milk, certain vegetable juices, cranberries, bananas, oatmeal, mashed potatoes
Freeze drying	Frozen food lyophilized under vacuum.	Specialty high-value foods

Source: Mark A. Uebersax, Ph.D., Muhammad Siddiq, Ph.D., Carl P. Borchgrevink, Ph.D.

hot air to turbulently lift and propel the product, is highly effective for drying particulate products (a similar process to the one used to make IQF products). The movement of air may be countercurrent (in the opposite direction) or concurrent (in the same direction) with respect to the product being dried.

Spray Drying

Spray drying affords a high-volume, economical means of drying fluid products. The techniques are generally described as "air drying of liquid foods" and vary in complexity and sophistication. The fluid product is typically preheated in a continuous heat exchanger and pumped under pressure to the top of a tall tower or chamber that delivers high-volume and high-velocity hot air ranging from 302 to 932°F (150 to 500°C). The preheated product is atomized through a nozzle or mechanically dispersed as very small droplets. As the droplets descend through the tower, moisture is vaporized and removed with the exit air. The powdered product is then separated using cyclone (vortex) separators, with powdered solids falling to the bottom, where they are collected.

Various configurations of hot air flow (concurrent, in which droplets are blown down; countercurrent, in which air enters the base of the tower and travels upward against the falling droplets) are in commercial use. Numerous design configurations and means of process control (product and air temperature, regulation of flow rates and air turbulence) enhance the efficiency and versatility of the process and prevent excessive heat damage. The use of various agglomeration techniques (particle-to-particle aggregation) enhances rehydration properties and the production of highly soluble "instantized" powders. Spray drying is used to produce dairy products (milk, nonfat dry milk, and whey solids), dehydrated eggs, dehydrated juice, and beverage mixes (powdered juices, instant coffee, cocoa, and iced tea), and formulated foods (instant soups, sauces, and premixes). The systems are also standard in the manufacture of powdered flavors and colors.

FIGURE 18.14 Commercial dehydration of apple slices.

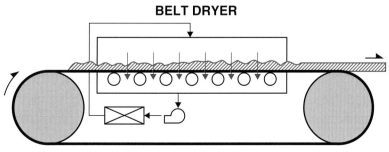

BELT DRYER

Source: Mark A. Uebersax, Ph.D., Muhammad Siddiq, Ph.D., Carl P. Borchgrevink, Ph.D.

FIGURE 18.15 The principal components of a spray-drying system.

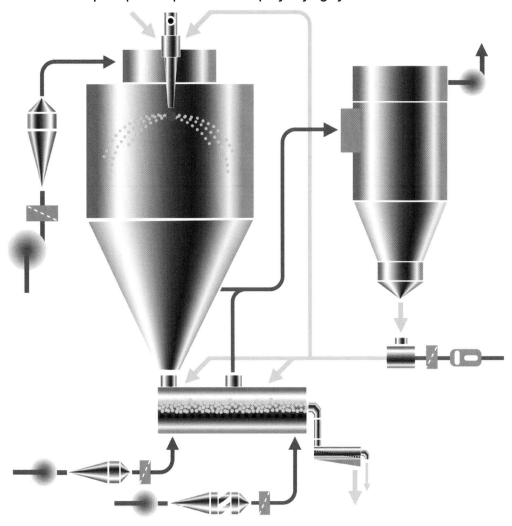

Source: GEA Niro.

Drum Drying Systems

Drum drying is a specialized technology used for making dried powders from viscous slurries and pastes that cannot be dried by spray dryers or other types of commercial drying systems (tunnel dryers, box dryers, tray dryers, etc.). Drum drying is used extensively in infant cereal production as well as for instant dehydrated potato flakes and oatmeal.[18]

Generally, two hollow steel drums (drum dimensions: 1.65 meters diameter by 4 meters length; total drying surface: 31 square meters) are positioned parallel and adjacent to one another, forming a trough between them. Drum clearance is adjustable, with the open gap referred to as the nip. The drums are heated internally by pressurized steam (steam pressure ~115 to 135 psi; drum surface temperature ~464°F [240°C]), and slowly rotated in opposite directions away from the trough. Preheated slurry is fed into the trough and, as the drums rotate, a thin film of the hot slurry is spread over the drum surface. Direct-conduction heat transfer provides rapid and effective dehydration. Drum temperature and residence time (248 to 338°F [120 to 170°C] for 20 seconds to 3 minutes) is easily controlled and provides for rapid evaporation of water. The dehydrated product on the drum surface is scraped off as flakes using an angled blade called a doctor blade. The large, sheeted flakes are then size-reduced to smaller uniform flakes (instant oatmeal) or finely milled to powders (instant potatoes and baby cereals).

Drum drying is one of the most efficient and economical drying methods; however, product deterioration (color, flavor, texture) is frequently greater than that caused by less severe methods.

Freeze-Drying Systems

Freeze drying, or lyophilization, is a relatively expensive process used for certain high-value specialty foods. A major advantage of freeze drying is the retention of product structure and texture as well as volatile flavor compounds. Rapid freezing prevents the cellular wall and membrane

FIGURE 18.16 Drum drying.

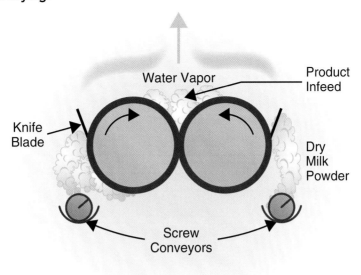

Source: Mark A. Uebersax, Ph.D., Muhammad Siddiq, Ph.D., Carl P. Borchgrevink, Ph.D.

breakage caused by large ice crystal formation. The freeze-drying process is used to prepare meats (beef, pork, and chicken), seafood (shrimp, crab), high-value fruit and vegetable products (berries for ready-to-eat cereals), precooked legumes (microwavable bean ingredients), and complex ingredient blends (stock bases, herbs, mushrooms). Its greatest commercial success is in the production of instant coffees and complete dehydrated meals (as for camping). Freeze-dried astronaut ice cream, developed for the National Aeronautics and Space Administration (NASA) in 1968, is still available at camping stores. Quality attributes (color, flavor, texture, and rehydration potential) are well preserved, and the resulting products are extremely lightweight.

Under the proper conditions of temperature and vacuum, water reaches the so-called triple point where the phases of solid, liquid, and vapor converge and water vapor can be sublimed directly from ice without passing through the aqueous phase. The process requires two stages; the first involves the initial freezing of the food, and the second provides the temperature and negative pressure conditions necessary to effect direct moisture removal. Very low final product moisture content (<1.0 percent) is achievable. Typically, freeze drying is a batch operation in which the pre-frozen product is placed on sensitive heating plates within a vacuum chamber. The ice temperature (controlled by the plates) and vacuum pressure are independently adjusted to conditions that directly vaporize the moisture. The moisture vapor is removed on condensers maintained outside of the chamber. Due to the relatively slow rate of moisture removal and the limited production volumes capable in a batch operation, operating costs are quite high.

FIGURE 18.17 Freeze drying. An illustration of the triple point of water, showing phase changes under different pressure and temperature conditions (ice solid phase to gaseous water vapor phase).

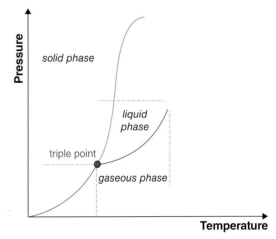

Source: Mark A. Uebersax, Ph.D., Muhammad Siddiq, Ph.D., Carl P. Borchgrevink, Ph.D.

Concentrated and Condensed Foods

Fluid foods are commonly concentrated before further dehydration or direct use. Water is more economically removed in highly efficient evaporators than in final dehydration equipment. This process can range from simple atmospheric open-kettle boiling to highly engineered systems where heat exchangers provide sufficient thermal energy to vaporize the water. As water is vaporized, the product is concentrated or condensed and becomes more viscous. Condensed products, possessing increased solids content, have the advantage of convenience of handling (smaller containers), reduction in solid waste disposal (packaging), and lower-cost transportation and distribution. Condensed products include canned soups (reconstituted with water before reheating), tomato paste (canned or aseptically packed in flexible film pouches), frozen juice concentrates, canned evaporated milk, and sweetened condensed milk. The following methods of concentration are commonly used:

- *Flash evaporators*—These rapidly heat the product by contact with 302°F (150°C) steam injected directly into the food. The boiling mixture then enters a separator vessel in which the concentrated food is drawn off at the bottom and the steam plus water vapor is evacuated through a separate outlet. Essence recovery systems (liquid nitrogen or carbon dioxide condensers) may be used to trap highly volatile flavor compounds that are recovered from the vapor fraction and added back to the final product. In the coffee business, the aromatic vapor given off by freshly roasted coffee beans during the grinding process (called "grinder gas") is captured using essence recovery and then used to dose jars of instant coffee to provide the promise of rich flavor when the jar is opened initially and the aroma wafts out.

- *Thin-film evaporators*—These systems use high-temperature, short-time (HTST) heat exchange principles to achieve rapid water removal with minimal product quality damage. Equipment typically incorporates a rotating swept-surface paddle that distributes a thin layer of product inside an externally heated cylinder. Water is readily flashed from the thin food layer, and the concentrated food is removed by mechanical action of the paddle. Thus, high volumes of fluid products (milk, fruit juices, and purees) can be concentrated in a continuous process.

- *Vacuum evaporators (vacuum pans)*—Heat-sensitive foods are most commonly concentrated in low-temperature vacuum evaporators. Typically, several vessels are connected in series to create a multiple-effect vacuum evaporator. Such a sequence enables efficient evaporation yielding high-quality concentrates (a single-effect evaporator requires more steam per pound of water removed than the multiple-effect evaporator—1:1 versus 1:4, respectively). As the partially concentrated product proceeds through the series of evaporators, it is heated under successively increasing levels of vacuum. Because the product is being heated under vacuum, the boiling point is reduced. Thus, the product is efficiently heated and water is removed at decreasing temperatures, conserving both quality and energy. Multiple-effect vacuum evaporators with essence recovery systems are most commonly employed in the citrus, grape, and tomato juice industries.

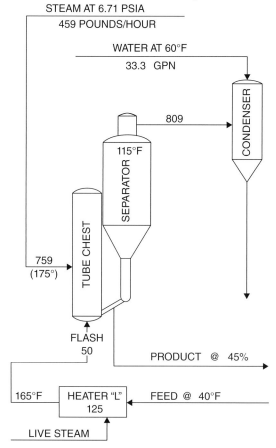

FIGURE 18.18 Single-effect evaporator.

Source: Mark A. Uebersax, Ph.D., Muhammad Siddiq, Ph.D., Carl P. Borchgrevink, Ph.D.

- Advanced ultrafiltration or reverse-osmosis technologies—A solution is defined as a liquid mixture in which the minor component (the solute) is uniformly dissolved within the major component (the solvent). For example, in a sugar solution, the water is the solvent and the sugar is the solute. Osmosis is the natural tendency of the water portion of a dilute solution on one side of a semipermeable membrane to pass freely through the membrane into a solution on the other side of the membrane where the solute concentration is higher, diluting it, until the concentrations of the solutions are equal on both sides of the membrane. The solute molecules are too large to pass through the membrane and are trapped on either side. Only the water—the solvent—can pass through the membrane. The pressure exerted by the molecules of the solvent on the membrane as they pass through is called osmotic pressure. Osmotic pressure is the energy driving osmosis and is important for living organisms because it allows water and nutrients dissolved in water to pass through cell membranes.

- Reverse osmosis is a technique in which pressure is applied *greater than the osmotic pressure of the solution*, to force liquid through the semipermeable membrane *in the*

FIGURE 18.19 **Conceptual diagram of a typical membrane filtration system.**

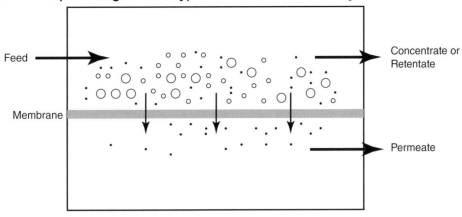

Source: Mark A. Uebersax, Ph.D., Muhammad Siddiq, Ph.D., Carl P. Borchgrevink, Ph.D.

opposite direction to that in normal osmosis. Concentrated syrups, juices, including grape juice used in the production of wine, and whey proteins are commonly processed in this manner. The benefit of this system is that it does not require heating of the fluids, thereby avoiding heat-influenced changes (loss of volatiles and vitamins, development of cooked flavors or colors).

Osmotic Preserves (Jams, Jelly, Preserves)

Processing of fruit with appropriate levels of pectin, acid, and sugar is a time-honored tradition that produces delicate and flavorful jams and jellies. These products are classified as intermediate-moisture foods with low water activity (a_w), which inhibits bacterial growth and limits growth of yeast and molds that may cause spoilage in the final product, particularly after the container is opened. The gel qualities are highly dependent on the ratio of ingredients in the formula and the processing and packaging conditions employed. Standard jellies are made with blends of fruit juice and sugar (45 parts fruit juice and 55 parts sugar) with 2 to 3 percent added pectin (depending on the fruit type), 0.3 to 0.5 percent citric acid, and a pH typically around 3.3. These contents are concentrated to at least 65 percent soluble solids (65° Brix) by

cooking in open kettles or, more commonly, using vacuum kettles. The cooked (concentrated) product is hot-filled directly into the final package and may also be subject to post-packaging pasteurization. The contents then undergo gel formation upon cooling. Gelled fruit products are defined by federal standards of identity (CFR Title 21, Part 150, Subpart B: Requirements for Specific Standardized Fruit Butters, Jellies, Preserves, and Related Products).

The manufacturing of gelled fruit products varies from small-scale conventional kitchen batch operations to large-scale commercial enterprises employing high-capacity vacuum evaporators and high-speed filling and sealing machinery.

Fruit and Juice Preparation

High-quality mature produce, free from mold and visual spoilage, is essential to producing high-quality finished products. The level of ripeness directly influences the content of native pectin and the sugar-to-acid ratio in the fruit. Slightly underripe fruit contains more pectin than ripe fruit. Overripe fruit commonly possess deficiencies in sugars, acidity, and native pectin, and thus formulas must be adjusted to provide the necessary ingredients for optimum performance.

Fruit juices can be obtained from combinations of fresh, frozen, and canned fruit. Fresh fruits are typically heated to

FIGURE 18.20 **The relationship of pectin, acid, and sugar to gel characteristics.**

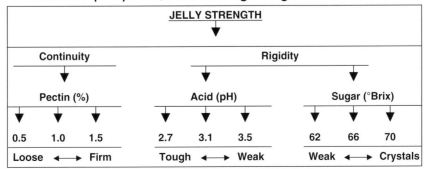

Source: Desorsier (1963).

FIGURE 18.21 **Characteristics of gelled fruit products.**

Product	Fruit Characteristic	Formulation Conditions	Final Soluble Solids (%)	Examples
Jelly	Whole or clarified juice	Not less than 45 parts by weight of fruit juice of standard composition as defined by USDA and 55 parts of sugar	Not less than 65%	Grape, apple, apricot
Jam and preserves	Jam: Highly comminuted (finely chopped) fruit Preserves: Incorporate pieces of whole intact fruit	Not less than 45 parts by weight of fruit to each 55 parts by weight of sugar.	Not less than 65% or 68%, depending on the fruit used	65%: apple, apricot, plum, fig, guava, nectarine, peach, pear, quince, currant, cranberry, and gooseberry 68%: berries, cherry, grape, citrus, pineapple, rhubarb, tomato, and crabapple
Marmalades	Skins and peels	Same as preserves	Not less than 65% or 68%, depending on the fruit used	English bitter, sweet orange, lemon
Fruit butters		5 parts fruits + 2 parts sugar	Not less than 43% soluble solids	Apple and pear

Source: Mark A. Uebersax, Ph.D., Muhammad Siddiq, Ph.D., Carl P. Borchgrevink, Ph.D.

inactivate enzymes, solubilize pectin, and improve overall yield, and are subsequently milled to a puree to maximize juice extraction. This puree may be used as is for preserves, jams, and fruit butters. Alternatively, for jellies, heated pulp can be filtered by rack and cloth pressing or, more commonly, by using continuous filtration equipment for juice extraction.

Juice clarification, using cellulose-based or bentonite clay filters, may be required to remove suspended solids from the juice to maximize jelly clarity.

Most fruits used to make jams and jellies do not contain sufficient pectin to form a firm gel; therefore, purified commercial pectins are usually added, both at home and at the production

FIGURE 18.22 **The process sequence of jelly and jam, preserves, and marmalade manufacture.**

Jelly	Jam/Preserves/Marmalade
Fruit	Fruit
▼	▼
Juice extraction/clarification	Purée
▼	▼
Water and sugar	Water and sugar
▼	▼
Pectin (0.5%)	Pectin (0.25%)
▼	▼
Evaporate (65° Brix)	Addition of fruit/pieces/peels
▼	▼
Adjust pH to 2.9–3.2 (citric acid)	Concentrate by heating (68° Brix)
▼	▼
Package	Adjust pH to 3.3 (citric acid)
	▼
	Package

Source: Mark A. Uebersax, Ph.D., Muhammad Siddiq, Ph.D., Carl P. Borchgrevink, Ph.D.

facility, to ensure proper gel formation. Several types of pectin are available, depending on the end product desired:

- *Rapid-set pectin*—This is the typical choice for most jams and marmalades. It is especially useful in jams containing fruit chunks or whole berries, which may have a tendency to float to the top of the jar; the faster the jam gels, the less opportunity there is for float, and the better the uniformity of fruit distribution within the jar.
- *Slow-set pectin*—Forms gels more slowly, which prevents premature gelation and facilitates filling of large-scale jam and jelly batches. Jam manufacturers often use custom blends using combinations of rapid set and slow set pectins to take advantage of the benefits of both.
- *Stabilizing pectin*—Used in acidic protein products such as yogurts, whey, and soy drinks that need a stabilizing agent.
- *Low methyl ester and amidated pectin*—are used for low-sugar/no-sugar-added jams. Unlike regular pectins, gelation does not depend on high levels sugar and acid. Instead, calcium ions (usually in the form of added calcium citrate) are necessary for a gel to form. Because the sugar concentration ("Brix") is so low, these products also require the addition of a preservative in order to prevent the growth of spoilage organisms. In addition, because the amount of sugar is less than that mandated by the federal standard of identity for jams and jellies, these products have to be labeled as "fruit spreads." Sauces and marinades, savory or sweet, often use this thickening agent as well.

Cooking, Processing, and Packaging

Cooking processes are used to facilitate dispersion and solubility of the ingredients and to concentrate the sugar by the removal of water. The numerous chemical reactions, including partial hydrolysis of pectin, hydrolysis of sucrose into glucose and fructose forming invert sugar, coagulation of proteins, and the development or degradation of flavor profiles, are accelerated at high temperature. Atmospheric boiling at 212°F (100°C) (open kettle) results in evaporation of water to the desired end point but dramatically decreases the content of volatile flavor compounds (alcohols, aldehydes, and ketones). The jellying point temperature indicates the end point of cooking; it is typically 7 to 8°F (−14 to −13°C) above the boiling point of water—that is, 219 to 220°F (104 to 104.4°C) at sea level. A refractometer is normally used to confirm the actual soluble solids content (Brix).

Vacuum kettle evaporators can achieve a boiling point as low as 140°F (60°C). Concentration under vacuum results in less temperature abuse, with boiling and evaporation occurring efficiently at much lower temperatures. This greatly enhances the retention of color, flavor, shape, and texture of fruit pieces, and retains a great deal more of the volatile flavor compounds, which would otherwise "flash off" into the atmosphere.

To improve the integrity of fruit in preserves, a portion of the juice can first be highly concentrated before the addition of fruit. The fruit and high-solids juice fraction readily equilibrate, and the combined mix is subsequently evaporated to the proper end point with minimal fruit damage. Because the juice has already been concentrated, less cooking is required to achieve the required Brix. Acids may be added at the end of the cooking, immediately before filling; this minimizes acid-catalyzed hydrolysis of pectin, which results in reduced gelling capacity and "soft sets."

The properly concentrated fruit and sugar mix may be hot-filled (greater than 180°F [82°C]) directly into sanitized containers and sealed. No additional processing is typically required; however, relatively slow and uniform cooling rates are important to ensure proper gel set. Large commercial containers may require special filling and chilling to enable proper gelling without the defect of "soft centers" resulting from slow cooling at the center of the containers.

Formulation and Function of Ingredients in a Pectin Gel

Developing pectin gel formulations is a highly technical science combined with an artisan's touch (Culinology® in action!). The quality of the final product depends on the proper blend of components contributing to gel formation and the proper mixing, heating, cooling, and packaging of the product. The functional ingredients contributing to the gel include:

- Pectin—This long-chain hygroscopic polysaccharide provides structural support to plant cell walls and helps bind cells together. It is found in highest concentration in citrus fruit peels and apple pomace (press-cake left behind in the production of apple cider), from which it is commercially extracted. When heated in an aqueous medium, such as fruit juice adjusted to contain the optimal amounts of sugar and acid, pectin develops an aligned lattice structure, turning the juice into a gel.
- Acid—Native fruit acidity and added organic acids (citric acid, malic acid) are used to reduce pH to optimum levels (generally about pH 3.0) for gel formation.
- Sugar—Sucrose serves as a dehydrating agent, which facilitates greater hydrogen-bonding and contributes to the yield, flavor, color, texture, and preservation properties (via reduced a_w).
- Water—This is necessary for dissolving and suspending components of the gel.

Gel formation occurs under a definite equilibrium range within a system of pectin, acid, sugar, and water and is affected by temperature and pH. Solubilized pectin is precipitated by the added sugar, which disturbs the equilibrium between the water and pectin. The pectin precipitates as a hydrated colloid that forms a network of fibrils throughout the mass, binding the sugar syrup into a gel matrix. Acid helps set the gel.

Food Extrusion

Extrusion technology is widely used for processing large volumes of diverse food products, including breakfast cereals, snack foods, pasta, puffed products, and food ingredients such as textured vegetable protein (TVP). Extrusion employs a continuous mixing, kneading, and shaping process with subsequent expulsion through a forming die to create a cooked and shaped food product.[19] High-temperature extrusion is used extensively by many sectors of the food industry to produce food products with distinctive texture and flavor characteristics. Desirable end-product properties are obtained by varying the processing conditions as well as the composition of the raw material.[20] Moistened starchy and protein-based foods are cooked and worked into viscous, plastic doughs; these are extruded and subsequently deep fried, toasted, or dehydrated (as in expanded snack foods—cheese puffs, curls, formed chips).

Extrusion cooking has multiple effects on food, including gelatinization of starch, denaturation of proteins, inactiva-tion of raw food enzymes, destruction of naturally occurring toxic substances, and reduction of microbial counts. Other significant structural changes in proteins and starches occur that may be used to generate texturized meat analog products. The extrusion process can also eliminate anti-nutritional factors present naturally in certain foods, such as lectins in beans or legumes, which cause food poisoning if inadequately cooked.

Extrusion dies are designed to create specialized shapes—for example, low-density puffed balls or sticks, or high-density texturized strands. Extruders range from simple cold-temperature pasta presses to highly engineered screw types (single-screw or twin-screw), which employ high pressure and temperature. Shear force and steam simultaneously mix, cook, and expel the raw ingredients through dies into finished products of various sizes, shapes, and textures. The process is energy efficient and environmentally friendly; unlike many other processing techniques, little solid or liquid waste is produced. The diversity of extruded foods and food ingredients is evident from the broad base of raw feed stocks employed.

FIGURE 18.23 Cross-sectional views of the single-screw extrusion cooker system (a) and a simple extruder barrel/expander (b).

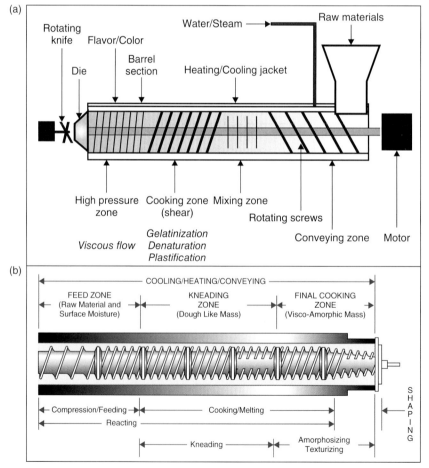

M. N. Riaz, "Introductions to Extruders and Their Principles," in M. N. Riaz (ed.), *Extruders in Food Applications* (Boca Raton, FL: CRC Press, 2000).

These range from doughs or pastes made from whole cereal grains or oilseeds (for example, wheat, corn, soy) to specialized formulations of protein, starch, or fiber fractions.

●Specialized Processing Technologies
Cook-Chill and Sous Vide

In the United States, cook-chill and *sous vide* are typically seen as distinct processes; in Europe, the terms are often used interchangeably.[21] *Sous vide* literally translates as "under vacuum" or "vacuum packed," and cook-chill products are not always packed under vacuum. In the United States, cook-chill is a batch preparation approach, while *sous vide* typically involves individual servings. Lastly, while cook-chill products may be cooked using any cooking or thermal processing method, *sous vide* is always cooked in a temperature-controlled water bath.

The cook-chill process may be either cold fill or hot fill. In cold fill, the container, such as a food-grade pouch, is filled with raw foods, sealed, and subsequently cooked to a desired temperature for the required length of time. This is similar to the *sous vide* process. In hot fill, the food is cooked in a traditional fashion and packaged immediately upon completion. (A third variation, which involves cooking to desired doneness, rapid cooling, and then bagging, is also possible.)

Sous vide is a cold-fill process. The raw food is always vacuum-packed in pouches and always cooked in water baths. The food may be cooked immediately after vacuum packaging, then rapidly chilled and held for later reheating and service, or the raw vacuum-packed food may be held refrigerated (or frozen) until needed and then cooked to order. A primary benefit is that *sous vide* permits even delicate foods to be mass produced using closely controlled temperatures (with tolerances as close as ±1°F [~0.5°C] in water baths), which leads to better quality and increased yield.[22] The increase in yield can be dramatic; studies point to *sous vide* foie gras (literally: "fatty liver"; this French delicacy is typically made from duck liver) production that reduced cooking loss from 50 percent to 5 percent![23] While this example is extreme, the lower-temperature, controlled cooking of *sous vide* production does lead to marked decreases in shrinkage and cooking loss. Also, water-soluble flavor components, nutrients, and volatile aroma chemicals stay with the food inside the cooking pouch rather than leaching out into the cooking water or evaporating into the air. In addition, cooking in a temperature-controlled water bath eliminates overcooking entirely, as the temperature of the food can never exceed the temperature of the water bath.

One shortcoming of this technique is that cook time tends to be quite long. Because the final cooked temperature of the product is the same as the hot water bath, it takes quite a long time for heat transfer to take place as the raw product slowly equilibrates to the water bath temperature.

Another shortcoming of *sous vide* cooking is that foods cooked in the high-moisture environment of a sealed pouch can never develop the roasted flavors or aromas created by Maillard browning (which requires dry-heat cooking methods). If the food in question must be browned, seared, or otherwise marked, or crust formation is desired, this can be done after cooking is completed and the bag is removed, immediately before service. Juices can be reserved for sauce preparation. Given the single-serve size of most *sous vide* products, cooking is precise. The desired degree of doneness (and color in the case of cooked-rare red meat products) permeates the food from the edge to the center.

Cook-chill has been around for a long time, but previously it was called *batch cooking*, where foods were prepared in large batches and subsequently chilled, then portioned, wrapped or bagged, and held for later use. Compared to *sous vide*, cook-chill provides greater process flexibility in that almost any heat source or cooking method can be used. However, hot-fill applications experience typical shrinkage and yield loss from cooking before bagging.

The greatest product yields are found in cold-fill applications. This is commonly done for whole muscle meats, which are bagged with the desired seasonings and vacuum-sealed before cooking. Liquid foods, such as soups, sauces, and stews, are best suited for hot fill. Typically, these foods are cooked in large kettles with automatic agitators and then pumped into bags, evacuating all excess air before sealing. Key to hot-fill applications is a high enough filling temperature (a minimum of 180°F [82°C]) to maintain sanitary conditions inside the pouch. Once packaged, the food is rapidly chilled to prevent the quality deterioration that comes from overcooking. The rapid decrease in temperature is designed so the food moves quickly through and below the 140 to 40°F (60 to 5°C) danger zone to minimize the growth of spoilage and pathogenic microorganisms. The rapid cooling is often done in cold-water tumble chillers or cold-air blast chillers.

According to the FDA 2009 Food Code, cook-chill is one of several food processing methods defined as reduced-oxygen packaging (ROP). ROP foods are packaged in environments that contain little or no oxygen. The other methods are controlled-atmosphere packaging (CAP), modified-atmosphere packaging (MAP), *sous vide*, and vacuum packaging. If the food in the ROP environment is one the FDA recognizes as potentially hazardous, (pH above 4.6, high moisture, high protein content), a Hazard Analysis and Critical Control Point (HACCP) plan must be developed. The benefits of ROP include extended shelf life, an anaerobic or near-anaerobic environment that prevents or slows the growth of aerobic spoilage organisms (such as pseudomonads, yeast, and molds), slowed oxidative rancidity and other degradative changes initiated by exposure to oxygen, and retention of the natural color of foods (especially meats).

However, due to the anaerobic or near-anaerobic environment created inside the package, there is always the potential for outgrowth of botulism spores and listeria. Therefore, special care must be taken to process, distribute, and store ROP foods with great attention to detail. All foods that fall into the potentially hazardous foods (PHF) category that are processed using one of the ROP methods must be stored under refrigeration (or freezing) up to the point of final cooking or reheating and service. In addition, they cannot be sold for retail use, as there is no way to control how consumers handle (or mishandle) them. Knowledge about the importance of maintaining proper temperature levels in home refrigerators and freezers is not widespread.

Cook-chill and *sous vide* foods are also referred to as minimally processed refrigerated (MPR) foods.[24] ROP and MPR approaches to food processing increase food safety concerns, as these foods are particularly susceptible to the temperature abuse that may occur anywhere along the ingredient sourcing > food manufacturing > end user continuum. In particular, consumers often cannot or do not maintain adequate temperature control of potentially hazardous foods (PHF), in part because they do not recognize them as being potentially hazardous. For ROP and MPR PHFs, HACCP plans and detailed labels are not sufficient to guarantee product safety in the home. These foods must be designed using additional safety treatments or hurdle technology and predictive microbiology; however, an in-depth discussion of this critical area is beyond the scope of this chapter.[25]

Irradiation

The use of ionizing radiation for food preservation has an extensive history of scientific study. Prepackaged or bulk foods are exposed to ionizing radiation (gamma-rays, x-rays, or beams of electrons) in specially designed shielded chambers for a designated time. The objective is to control biological processes in produce (such as respiration and sprouting), kill insects, and reduce the number of pathogens

FIGURE 18.24 **Approaches to reduced-oxygen packaging (ROP).**

Cook-chill	A process that uses a plastic bag filled with hot cooked food from which air has been expelled and that is closed with a plastic or metal crimp or heat sealed.
Controlled Atmosphere Packaging (CAP)	An active system that continuously maintains the desired atmosphere within a package throughout the shelf life of a product by the use of agents to bind or scavenge oxygen or a sachet containing compounds to emit a gas.
	Packaging of a product in a modified atmosphere followed by maintaining subsequent control of that atmosphere.
Modified Atmosphere Packaging (MAP)	A process that employs a gas flushing and sealing process or reduction of oxygen through respiration of vegetables or microbial action.
	Packaging of a product in an atmosphere that has had a one-time modification of gaseous composition so that it is different from that of air, which normally contains 78.08% nitrogen, 20.96% oxygen, and 0.03% carbon dioxide.
Sous Vide	A specialized process of ROP for ingredients that require refrigeration or frozen storage (PHF/TCS food*) until the package is thoroughly heated immediately before service.
	A pasteurization/cooking step that reduces bacterial load but is not sufficient to make the food shelf-stable.
	The process involves the following steps: (a) Preparation of the raw materials (this step may include grilling or broiling for color of some or all ingredients); (b) Packaging of the product immediately before cooking, application of vacuum, and sealing of the package; (c) Pasteurization/cooking of the product using required time/temperature parameters; (d) Rapid and monitored cooling of the product at or below 1–3°C (34–38°F) or frozen; and (e) Reheating of the packages 74°C (165°F) for hot holding or to any temperature for immediate service before opening and service.
Vacuum Packaging	Reduces the amount of air from a package and hermetically seals the package so that a near-perfect vacuum remains inside.
	A common variation of the process is Vacuum Skin Packaging (VSP). A highly flexible plastic barrier allows the package to mold itself to the contours of the food being packaged.

*PHF/TCS = potentially hazardous food that requires temperature control for safety
Source: FDA 2009 Food Code, Section 3-502.12.

(for example, salmonella and *E. coli* 0157:H7) and spoilage microorganisms (bacteria, molds, yeasts).[26] Meats prepared for the NASA space program have been irradiation-sterilized for years; they can't afford to have astronauts getting food poisoning in outer space!

Intensive research programs were initiated during the late 1940s under the Atoms for Peace program of the Atomic Energy Commission (AEC). Numerous international and domestic studies designed to study the safety and efficacy of food irradiation have been conducted for nearly 75 years, including studies by the U.S. Army Labs in Natick, Massachusetts. None have reported a link between consumption of irradiated foods and human illness. In 1981, after a long international effort to investigate the safety and wholesomeness of irradiated foods, the United Nations Joint Committee on Irradiated Foods decisively stated:

> The irradiation of any food commodity up to an average dose of 10 kGy presents no toxicological hazard; hence toxicological testing of foods so treated is no longer required.[27]

But in spite of the many advantages food irradiation offers, the process remains controversial. In an effort to make it sound less threatening, a more consumer-friendly term has been developed—cold pasteurization—not only to distinguish it from heat-related pasteurization and sterilization processes but also to reduce the fear factor induced by the word *irradiation*.

The unit of measure for food radiation energy is termed a gray (Gy), which equals the absorption of 1 joule of energy per kilogram of product. Pasteurizing food treatment is less than 10 kiloGrays (kGy) per kilogram of food, with the following exposure classifications: low exposure (<1 kGy), for control of ripening, sprouting, and insects; medium exposure (1 to 10 kGy), for shelf-life extension, to reduce microbial load with improved quality characteristics compared to thermally processed. High exposure (10 to 50 kGy) is only used for commercial sterilization.[28] Higher sterilization levels of irradiation are not commonly used on foods because of adverse quality considerations (for example, development of off colors and rancid flavors due to increased free radical formation leading to oxidative rancidity). Instead, these levels are reserved for sterilizing medical instruments and sickroom supplies.

An irradiation processing facility requires extensive shielding and safety systems to assure containment of high-energy radiation. Typically, food is conveyed into a chamber constructed of thick-walled concrete (5 to 6 feet) with remote operational control. Bulk or prepackaged foods are continuously conveyed near the source of irradiation (for example, radioisotopes cobalt-60 and cesium-137, or machine-produced x-ray or electron beams) for a controlled treatment time. The relatively low doses of irradiation yield the intended benefits without compromising product quality or package integrity. Such processes are increasingly important in the control of pathogenic microorganisms in meat, poultry, and seafood. It is important to note that irradiation is less successful in eradicating botulinum spores or viruses than are traditional thermal processes.

The FDA has approved a variety of foods for irradiation in the United States, including:

- Beef and pork
- Poultry
- Molluscan shellfish (for example, oysters, clams, mussels, and scallops)
- Shell eggs
- Fresh fruits and vegetables
- Lettuce and spinach
- Spices and seasonings
- Seeds for sprouting (for example, alfalfa sprouts, responsible for dozens of outbreaks of foodborne illness due to pathogens residing in the seeds)

All irradiated foods must be labeled with a specially designed symbol, commonly referred to as the radura.

Other Advanced Technologies

Research and development efforts continue to find innovative and efficient new technologies to preserve food by alternative methods that yield minimally processed foods with better eating qualities but the same level of safety as older, more severe methods. The following are a few of the innovative technologies currently being explored. Some have achieved a fair degree of commercial success, while others are still on the cusp of a major market breakthrough.

High-Pressure Processing (HPP)

Also known as *pascalization*, HPP is a method of food processing where food is subjected to elevated pressures (up to 87,000 pounds per square inch, or approximately 6000 atmospheres), leading to the inactivation of most types of spoilage microorganisms and pathogens. It is less successful in destroying

FIGURE 18.25 Radura symbol, required by the FDA to appear on packaging of all foods treated by irradiation.

Source: FDA, "Food Irradiation: What You Need to Know" (June 2011).

bacterial spores. Pascalization stops chemical activity caused by microorganisms that play a role in the deterioration of foods. The treatment typically takes place at low temperatures, but HPP may be combined with heat to achieve an increased rate of inactivation of microbes and enzymes. Process time is very rapid (usually less than 20 minutes of exposure time) and does not require any food additives to be effective.

In pascalization, food products are sealed and placed in a steel compartment containing a liquid, usually water, and pumps are used to create pressure. The treatment works equally well for solid and liquid products, with or without packaging. However, foods decrease in volume as a function of the imposed pressure and equal expansion occurs on decompression. For this reason the packaging used for HPP-treated foods must be able to accommodate up to a 15 percent reduction in volume, and return to its original volume, without loss of seal integrity and barrier properties.

In addition to microbial inactivation, during pascalization the food's proteins are denatured but most product's main structure remains intact. That said, high hydrostatic pressures can cause changes in structurally fragile foods such as strawberries or lettuce. Pascalization does not greatly affect the food's nutritional value, taste, texture, or appearance if processing takes place at room temperature or below. High-pressure treatment of foods is regarded as a natural preservation method because it does not employ chemical preservatives.

An early use of pascalization in the United States was to treat guacamole. It did not change the guacamole's taste, texture, or color, and the refrigerated shelf life of the product increased to 30 days from 3 days without the treatment. Treated foods still require cold storage because pascalization does not stop all enzyme activity, or some bacterial spores, which can affect safety.

Examples of HPP products commercially available in the United States (besides guacamole) include fruit smoothies, prepackaged deli meats, fruit juices, and salsa.[29] More recent HPP foods include clams, oysters, and lobsters that have been pressure-shucked from their shells.

Ohmic Heating

Ohmic heating is an advanced thermal processing method wherein the food material, which serves as an electrical resistor, is heated by passing electricity through it. Electrical energy is transformed into rapid and uniform heating that quickly destroys food pathogens and spoilage microorganisms. This inductive heating process (similar to induction cooktops) uses electrical currents of oscillating electromagnetic fields generated by electric coils in the vicinity of food.[30]

Ohmic heating can be used for heating liquid foods containing large particulates, such as soups, stews, fruit slices in syrups and sauces, and heat-sensitive liquids. The technology is useful for the treatment of proteinaceous foods, which tend to denature and coagulate when thermally processed. For example, liquid egg can be ohmically heated in a fraction of a second without coagulating. Juices can be treated to inactivate enzymes without affecting flavor. Other potential applications of ohmic heating include blanching, thawing, in-line detection of starch gelatinization, peeling, dehydration, and juice extraction. The shelf life of ohmically processed foods is comparable to that of canned and sterile or aseptically processed products.

At this point, ohmically treated market products in the United States are limited, but as equipment costs come down, many more products are expected to enter the market in the next few years.

Radio-Frequency (RF) Drying

Radio-frequency (RF) drying can offer many benefits over conventional drying, including faster line speeds, more consistent moisture levels, lower drying temperatures, and smaller equipment. Conventional heating (for example, conduction, convection, radiant) has a heat source on the outside and relies on transferring the heat to the surface of the material and then conducting the heat to the middle of the material. RF heats at the molecular level, so it heats from within the material and heats the center as well as the surface. RF drying uses the same principles of heating by electromagnetic energy as do induction and microwave heating.

RF drying has many advantages over conventional methods, but it is still not used widely for commercial purposes because of technical and economic reasons. Although numerous research reports show the quality of RF-dried products is better than or equal to that of conventionally dried foods, most of those studies are conducted on laboratory-scale devices, which may not be scalable for commercial operations. Major challenges include non-uniform heating and higher equipment costs compared to conventional drying methods. To make RF drying practical and acceptable to the industry, more significant scientific and technological advancements are needed.

Pulsed-Light Processing (PL)

Pulsed-light (PL) technology is an alternative to thermal treatment for killing pathogenic and spoilage microorganisms in foods, including bacteria, yeasts, molds, and viruses. Materials to be treated are exposed to multiple short flashes (typically 300 microsec) of a broad-spectrum (200 to 1100 nm), high-intensity white light to inactivate microorganisms.[31] The exact mechanisms by which pulsed light causes cell death are not yet fully understood, but it is generally accepted that the antimicrobial effects of UV light on bacteria are due to structural changes in their DNA as well as other factors. Studies also indicated similar injurious effects on yeast cells and mold spores following exposure to pulsed light.

Pulsed-light treatment is able to inactivate pathogenic and spoilage microorganisms in a range of food products and packaging materials, but the treatment is most effective on smooth, nonreflecting surfaces and in liquids that are free of suspended particulates, such as clear fruit juices and water. One of the potential applications of pulsed light is surface decontamination of fresh fruits and vegetables and ready-to-eat products such as deli meats. A recent study has reported that peanuts exposed to pulsed-light treatment lose 90 percent of their allergenicity.[32] For any PL treatment to be fully effective, uniform, complete exposure of the treated food is critical. No significant changes of product quality or sensory properties have been observed.

PL technology has been successfully tested as a technique for pasteurization of food and packaging surfaces, but it is not yet widely adopted mainly due to the high cost of equipment.

Commercial Meat and Poultry Processing
Marination

The term *marination*, believed to have Latin-French-Spanish origins, refers to the ancient practice of preserving foods in seawater. Meats, fish, and poultry are the foods most associated with marination. When fruits and vegetables are similarly treated, the term used is *maceration.*

Marination was historically used as a preservation technique and to provide or enhance flavor. From a food processing and business perspective, increasing product yield is today the single most important purpose of marination. There are two typical yield perspectives: the percentage of marinade pickup (pump) and the cooked yield. Pickup percentage is determined by: [(marinated weight – raw weight) /raw weight] × 100. Cooked yield is (cooked weight/raw weight) × 100.

Commercial marinade ingredients enhance tenderness, reduce cooking losses, and increase the water-holding capacity and thus the yield of marinated food.[33] From a culinary perspective, marination is primarily organoleptic in that it adds flavor and moisture and enhances appearance; secondarily, it tenderizes and softens.[34] In this respect, yield enhancement is not the primary objective.

Marination at the home or restaurant level usually involves the passive transport of marinade into foods by absorption or osmosis and is a slow process known as *static marination.* Unless the food in static marination is very thin, the marinade does not travel far into it. Even after marination of 24 hours or more, marinade pickup seldom exceeds 5 percent. Commercial meat processors obviously require a faster and more deeply penetrating result.

Modern marination techniques, functional ingredients, equipment, and technology continue to be refined and updated to improve efficiency, quality, and consumer satisfaction. Commercial marination is performed using functional marinades applied through highly automated systems. To decrease process times and increase uniformity of marinade distribution, specialized equipment is used to inject the marinade deep into the muscle. This process, referred to as *deep basting* or *injection marination*, allows for marinade uptake to exceed 20 percent or more within an extremely short period. It is often followed by vacuum tumbling to ensure uniform distribution of the marinade throughout the muscle, to avoid localized discoloration and the development of hot pockets of marinade centered on the injection needle tracks, and to enhance tenderness via mechanical action as the meat moves around inside the tumbler.

Tumble-marinating continually mixes the meat and marinade ingredients in a large rotating drum, usually under vacuum. This assists in maximum uptake and uniform internal dispersion of the marinade, even without injection, while tenderizing the food product. The marinade ingredients may help tenderize the food in question; however, tenderization is enhanced as the muscle fibers are massaged during tumbling. The tumbling leads to disruption of the muscle fiber sheaths and stretches the myofibrils.[35] Vacuum tumbling can achieve in 30 minutes or less what otherwise would take several days using static marination, depending on the size and type of muscle being marinated.

Salt (sodium chloride, or NaCl) is a critical and primary marinade ingredient in that it helps increase the meat's moisture-holding (marinade-holding) capacity and thus increases product yield and palatability. Salt rapidly hydrates and solubilizes the salt-soluble proteins predominant in meat tissue, thus dramatically enhancing the water-holding capacity and the stickiness of the meat. The salt-soluble proteins combine with water through both direct molecular interactions (adsorption) and physical entrainment (absorption); again, this increases meat weight, volume, and flexibility. The sticky marinated meat forms a binding glue-like layer of extracted proteins on its surface; this denatures or coagulates on heating and forms a rigid firm mass. This is the principle used in preparation of many formed meat products, such as chicken nuggets and meat loaves.

Many other ingredients may be used in commercial marinades. Proteolytic enzymes tenderize the meat by hydrolyzing the muscle proteins—that is, the proteins are broken down to their component amino acids. Flavor enhancement may also occur, as glutamic acid (an amino acid and the key flavor enhancer in monosodium glutamate [MSG]) is also released. The most commonly used tenderizing enzymes are papain and bromelain, derived from papaya and pineapple, respectively. However, ficin (from figs), fungal enzymes (from fungi such as *Aspergillus oryzae*), bacterial enzymes (from bacteria such as *Bacillus subtilis*), and combinations of these are also used.

Alkaline phosphates increase protein solubility and enhance the water-binding ability of meats, leading to increased tenderness and juiciness of processed meats. In general, alkaline phosphates improve water retention by shifting the pH away from the isoelectric point of the myofibrillar proteins (the point at which the water-holding capacity of meat is at its lowest) and by unfolding muscle proteins, thereby exposing more charged sites for water binding. When phosphates are used for increasing water-holding properties of meat, the USDA requires phosphate concentrations to be no higher than 0.5 percent of the finished product weight. This is just as well, as excess phosphate can cause soapy flavors, rubbery texture, and poor color. Although there are many phosphates to choose from, sodium tripolyphosphate (STP) remains the most commonly utilized in marinades because it is easy to use and inexpensive.

FIGURE 18.26 Marinade ingredient functionality.

Salt (NaCl)	Flavor enhancer
	Moisture binder • Increases cooked yield • Increases palatability/juiciness
	Helps extract soluble proteins • Increases water absorption • Binds restructured protein-based products
Phosphates	Moisture binder • Increases cooked yield • Increases palatability/juiciness • Reduces purge
	Helps extract soluble proteins • Increased water absorption • Binds restructured protein-based products
	Antioxidant • Reduces oxidative rancidity • Flavor stabilizer
	Color stabilizer
	Fat emulsifier
	Enhances mouthfeel • Texture stabilizer • Softens muscle tissue
Starches and gums (hydrocolloids)	Moisture binder • Increases cooked yield • Increases palatability/juiciness
	Enhances mouthfeel • Texture stabilizer
	Increases storage stability • Freeze-thaw
	Emulsifier
	Provides viscosity and film formation • Assists in marinade dispersion • Helps retain liquids
Flavorings	Provides desired taste profile • Improves basic flavors • Restores flavors lost during processing • Provides proper ethnic profile • Inhibits or masks "warmed-over" or oxidized flavors • Masks undesirable flavors from additives
Water	Increases juiciness
	Enhanced yield
	Marinade ingredient delivery vehicle
Oil	Increases mouthfeel • Adds lubricity/tenderness • Perceived juiciness
	Flavor carrier
Sugars	Enhances flavor
	Enhances browning
	Increases shelf life

Source: Mark A. Uebersax, Ph.D., Muhammad Siddiq, Ph.D., Carl P. Borchgrevink, Ph.D.

STP accounts for approximately 80 percent of the phosphates used in further-processed meat products. Alkaline phosphates such as STP serve to increase water-holding capacity (WHC), extract muscle proteins, increase cook yield, reduce oxidative rancidity, preserve meat color, increase flavor retention, and inhibit microbial growth.

Product yield and palatability are also increased through the use of starches or by adding soy or whey proteins.[36] Hydrocolloids (vegetable gums from terrestrial or marine sources) are also commonly used for additional water-holding capacity and subsequent yield enhancement. Flavorings, herb and spice extracts, antioxidants, liquid smoke, sweeteners—virtually any water-soluble or dispersible ingredient can be added to a marinade, depending on the desired outcome.

Marinade Types
Oily Marinades

Dry or lean meats benefit from oil-based marinades because they add fats that increase the palatability and the organoleptic (sensory) qualities of the food. The oil makes the food appear moister, protects it from drying during cooking, improves mouthfeel and lubricity, provides an attractive shine, inhibits oxidation, and assists in the flavor profile as it provides fat-soluble flavors.[37]

The flavors in oil may be inherent or augmented by way of infusion or the addition of oil-soluble flavor extracts. Oils should be considered from the perspective of their saturation profile and their individual fatty-acid profile, which have nutritional, shelf life, and flavor implications.[38]

Acidic Marinades

Many marinades contain an acidic ingredient. Historically, it was vinegar or verjus, the juice of unripe and therefore acidic grapes. Other acidic ingredients include wine, fruit juices, and cultured milk products such as buttermilk, yogurt, kefir, and sour cream. The amount of acid in a marinade varies greatly. The highest acid levels are used in pickling, or directly acidifying, fruits or vegetables with a typical acetic acid level of 2.5 percent.[39] Cultured milk products are mildly acidic, with the lactic acid ranging from 0.5 percent to 1 percent, and even less when diluted for use in a marinade.

The acidic element in marinades plays several roles. Of course it adds flavor; in addition, it disrupts the microbial cells it touches. Weak acids, such as the acetic and lactic acids often used in marinades, are lipophilic and pass through the lipid-containing membranes of the microbial cells. Once

FIGURE 18.27 Commercial marinade formula for chicken.

Ingredients	%
Chicken	85
Marinade	15
Total	100

Marinade Components	%
Water	10.0–13.0
Flavor	1.0–3.0
Starch	0.5–1.0
Salt	0.5–1.0
Phosphate	0.3–0.5
Total	15.0

Basic Marinade Preparation

1. Dissolve phosphate in water.
2. In a separate container, blend dry flavors, starch, salt, and other dry ingredients. If oils, flavor oils, or oleoresins are used, plate on dry blend.
3. Add liquid flavors to water/phosphate solution with high-shear mixing.
4. Add dry ingredients from Step 2 to water/phosphate solution with high-shear mixing.
5. Mix well for 5 minutes.
6. Proceed with marination.

Phosphate Note!

- **Always dissolve phosphate in water first** as it competes for binding sites on the water molecule with other ingredients. If phosphate is added later, it will not go into solution. Other dries may be pre-blended together for ease of addition after the phosphate is completely dissolved. Mix well for 5 minutes after all ingredients have been added. An immersion blender ("stick" blender) is a good tool to use for this process.

Potential Problems:

- **Plugged injectors:** Caused by particulates, ground spices, hard fats, viscosity build up.
- **Hot spots:** Uneven distribution of marinade due to lack of tumbling after injection or improper needle placement.
- **Bacterial growth:** Caused by inadequate temperature control.
- **Low pick-up:** Caused by inadequate quantity of marinade, insufficient marination time, plugged or improperly placed nozzles, inadequately thawed product, insufficient vacuum, inadequate quantity of chicken in the tumbler.

Source: J. Cousminer.

inside the cytoplasm of the microbial cell, the acid molecules release protons and can no longer pass back out through the cell membrane, thus acidifying the cytoplasm. This inhibits cellular metabolism and growth, which can slow or fully inhibit deterioration and spoilage, depending on the microbe.

Acidic ingredients used in marinades may have a relatively neutral flavor profile (apart from their acidity), as in distilled white vinegar, or a strong flavor profile, as in fortified wine (such as fino sherry) or in citric juice (such as that pressed from tangerines). Acidic liquids with neutral flavor profiles can be infused with herbs, spices, and fruit and vegetable peels, or they can be flavored with extracts or chemically derived flavors. The choice and amount of acidic ingredients depends on the desired level of acidity, the desired flavor profile, and their effect on the marinated product.

Acidic marinades are also widely used in the preparation of the popular Latin American seafood specialty known as "ceviche." These are highly seasoned, usually citrus juice–based marinades that are used to flavor and "parcook" the seafood (partially denature the proteins) without actually applying any heat. The resulting products are essentially raw, resembling Japanese sashimi ("raw fish") in texture, but unlike sashimi, ceviche is strongly flavored.

Salty Marinades

Most resources use the term *brine* when they refer to salty marinades.[40] Brines are often applied to lean meats, as the salt helps counter the water loss that takes place during cooking. Salt-denatured myofibrillar protein filaments have increased water-holding capacity and absorb more of the marinade. As stated previously, the marinated meat may absorb 10 percent or more of its weight from the marinade if marination is combined with vacuum tumbling. The salt-denatured protein does not coagulate as readily when cooked, staying softer and palatable when eaten, providing a sense of increased tenderness.[41]

Cured meats, such as ham, bacon, and corned beef, are treated with brines that usually contain nitrites, which set the pink color typical in these meats and inhibit the growth of *Clostridium botulinum.*

Fruits and vegetables can also be treated with brines for pickling; alternatively, they may be treated with dry salt and allowed to develop their own marinade by drawing liquids out from within, as is typical with sauerkraut or its Asian cousin, kimchi. Whether a fruit or vegetable is dry-salted or brined, the intent is to draw liquid out of the produce so it becomes submerged, minimizing oxygen exposure. More importantly, the goal is to produce an environment conducive to lactic acid bacteria, leading to fermentation, which is one of the oldest methods of preservation known to man.

Dry Rubs and Pastes

In essence, a rub is a dry marinade. It may contain salt, sugar, spices, and herbs in a variety of combinations. If the mixture contains some moisture, it is called a *paste* rather than a *rub.*

The moisture may be from freshly crushed aromatics (such as onions or garlic), from oils, juices, or wine, or simply from chopped fresh herbs.[42] Rubs and pastes are good when excess moisture is not desired, as when a flavorful crust is needed; items using rubs or pastes may require gentler heat when cooking to avoid burning.[43]

While rubs and pastes are used primarily to provide flavor and enhanced appearance, the spices and herbs may also act as antimicrobial agents,[44] and salt and sugar both draw moisture from living bacterial cells through osmosis, disrupting cellular activity and thus microbial growth.[45] However, as rubs and pastes do not penetrate much beyond the surface of the muscle, flavors are mainly limited to the meat's surface, and they do not increase product yields or improve texture or lubricity.

● Conclusion

Food processing can significantly enhance the texture, color, flavor, aroma, nutritional availability, palatability, safety, shelf life, convenience, cost and consistency of raw products. The edibility of numerous staple commodities such as dry beans, potatoes, rice, and pasta is improved due to the hydration, maceration, and cellular separation (cell membrane and cell wall disintegration) that we recognize as cooked food and that occurs during moist-heat processing. Heat treatments, including blanching and pasteurization, inactivate many native enzymes that can impair sensory attributes (for example, oxidation of color, development of off flavors, rancidity) and can improve texture by hydrolysis of proteins, carbohydrates, and fiber. Additionally, processing foods offers specific functional properties (for example, gelatinization of starch in aseptically processed puddings, coagulation of proteins in cheese and emulsified meats, gelation of pectins in fruit preserves). And, of course, an assortment of processing methods is used to improve the safety and shelf life of raw foods by controlling pathogens and spoilage organisms.

The Culinology® professional clearly recognizes and appreciates the numerous benefits provided by food processing, welcomes the high quality, convenience, and affordability of using processed foods as ingredients in prepared dishes, and makes good use of them every day.

[1] R. S. Harris and E. Karmas, *Nutritional Evaluation of Food Processing* (Westport, CT: AVI Publishing, 1975); A. E. Bender, *Food Processing and Nutrition* (London: Academic Press, 1987).

[2] E. Laurila and R. Ahvenainen. "Minimal Processing in Practice," in T. Ohlsson and N. Bengtsson (eds.), *Minimal Processing Technologies in the Food Industry* (Cambridge, UK: Woodhead, 2002), 223.

[3] "Fresh Cuts Rebounding," in *Fresh Cut Magazine* (January 2011), retrieved February 17, 2015, from http://freshcut.com/index.php/magazine/issue/january-2011.

[4] A. M. Piagentini, D. R. Guemes, and M. E. Pirovani, "Sensory Characteristics of Fresh-Cut Spinach Preserved by Combined Factors Methodology," *Journal of Food Science* 67, no. 4 (2002): 1544–1549.

[5] M. Siddiq, "Peaches and Nectarines," in Y. H. Hui (ed.), *Handbook of Fruits and Fruit Processing* (Ames, IA: Blackwell, 2005), 519–531.

[6] L. Vamos-Vigyazo, "Polyphenol Oxidase and Peroxidase in Fruits and Vegetables," *Critical Reviews in Food Science and Nutrition* 15, no. 1 (1981): 49–127.

[7] H. S. Lambrecht, "Sulfite Substitutes for the Prevention of Enzymatic Browning in Foods," in C. Y. Lee and J. R. Whitaker (eds.), *Enzymatic Browning and Its Prevention* (Washington, DC: American Chemical Society, 1995), 313–323.

[8] R. Soliva-Fortuny, P. Elez-Martinez, and O. Martin-Belloso, "Microbiological and Biochemical Stability of Fresh-Cut Apples Preserved by Modified Atmosphere Packaging," *Innovative Food Science and Emerging Technologies* 5, no. 2 (2004): 215–224.

[9] James Steffe, personal communication, 2009.

[10] N. Appert, *Le Livre de Tous les Ménages, ou L'Art de Conserver, Pendant Plusieurs Années Toutes les Substances Animales et Vegetales* (Paris: Chez Patris, 1810).

[11] J. L. Heid and M. A. Joslyn, *Fundamentals of Food Processing Operations: Ingredients, Methods, Packaging* (Westport, CT: AVI Publishing, 1967).

[12] J. M. Jackson and B. M. Shinn, *Fundamentals of Food Canning Technology* (Westport, CT: AVI Publishing, 1979).

[13] Heid and Joslyn, *Fundamentals of Food Processing Operations*.

[14] J. R. D. David, R. H. Graves, and V. R. Carlson, *Aseptic Processing and Packaging of Food: A Food Industry Perspective* (Boca Raton, FL: CRC Press, 1996).

[15] D. K. Tressler, W. B. Van Arsdale, and M. J. Copley, *Factors Affecting Quality in Frozen Foods*, vol. 2, *The Freezing Preservation of Foods*, 4th ed. (Westport, CT: AVI Publishing, 1968).

[16] N. W. Desrosier and D. K. Tressler, *Fundamentals of Food Freezing* (Westport, CT: AVI Publishing, 1977).

[17] W. B. Van Arsdale and M. J. Copley, *Principles*, vol. 1, *Food Dehydration* (Westport, CT: AVI Publishing, 1963).

[18] P. Fellows, *Food Processing Technology: Principles and Practice* (Chichester, UK: Ellis Horwood, 1988).

[19] J. M. Harper, *Extrusion of Food* (Boca Raton, FL: CRC Press, 1981).

[20] S. Bhatnagar and M. A. Hanna, "Extrusion Processing Conditions for Amylose-Lipid Complexing," *Cereal Chemistry* 71, no. 6 (1994): 587–593.

[21] P. G. Creed and W. Reeve, "Principles and Application of *Sous-Vide* Processed Foods," in S. Ghazala (ed.), *Sous-Vide and Cook-Chill Processing for the Food Industry* (Gaithersburg, MD: Aspen, 1988), 25–56.

[22] V. K. Juneja and O. P. Snyder, "Sous-Vide and Cook-Chill Processing of Foods: Concept Development and Microbiological Safety," in G. Tewari and V. K. Juneja (eds.), *Advances in Thermal and Non-Thermal Food Preservation* (Ames, IA: Blackwell, 2007), 145–163.

[23] Ibid.

[24] S. Ghazala and R. Trenholm, "Hurdle and HACCP Concepts in *Sous-Vide* and Cook-Chill Products," in S. Ghazala (ed.), *Sous-Vide and Cook-Chill Processing for the Food Industry* (Gaithersburg, MD: Aspen, 1998), 294–310; Juneja and Snyder, "Sous-Vide and Cook-Chill Processing of Foods."

[25] For a detailed discussion, see Ghazala and Trenholm, "Hurdle and HACCP Concepts in *Sous-Vide* and Cook-Chill Products"; Juneja and Snyder, "Sous-Vide and Cook-Chill Processing of Foods"; J. M. Farber and K. L. Dodds, *Principles of Modified-Atmosphere and Sous-Vide Product Packaging* (Lancaster, PA: Technomic, 1995); Food and Drug Administration, *FDA Food Code 2009: Annex 6—Food Processing Criteria*, retrieved November 30, 2009, from http://www.fda.gov/Food/FoodSafety/RetailFoodProtection/FoodCode/FoodCode2009/ucm188201.htm#parta6-2.

[26] D. G. Olson, "Irradiation of Foods: Scientific Status Summary," *Food Technology* 52, no. 1 (1998): 56–62.

[27] United Nations Joint Committee on Irradiated Foods, *Food Irradiation: A Technique for Preserving and Improving the Safety of Food* (Geneva, Switzerland: World Health Organization & Food and Agriculture Organization of the United Nations, 1988), 31. http://apps.who.int/iris/bitstream/10665/38544/1/9241542403_eng.pdf.

[28] Council for Agricultural Science and Technology, "Ionizing Energy in Food Processing and Pest Control: II. Applications," *Task Force Report No. 115* (Ames, IA: Council for Agricultural Science and Technology, 1989), 98.

[29]R. Ramaswamy, V. M. Balasubramaniam, and G. Kaletunç, *High-Pressure Processing: Fact Sheet for Food Processors* (Columbus, OH: Ohio State University, 2004), retrieved December 12, 2009, from http://ohioline.osu .edu/fse-fact/pdf/0001.pdf.

[30]S. K. Sastry, *Ohmic and Inductive Heating*. Paper presented at the annual meeting of the Institute of Food Technologists, Dallas, TX, 2000.

[31]H. Shaw, *Report on Pulsed Light Processing of Seafood*, report by Campden and Chorleywood Food Research Association Group (CCFRA), Chipping Campden, UK, 2008, retrieved January 13, 2010, from www.seafish.org/pdf .pl?file=seafish/Documents/B14_Pulsed percent20Light.pdf.

[32]Rory Harrington, "Pulsed UV Light Cuts Peanut Allergens by Up to 90 Per Cent: Study," *Food Production Daily*, June 17, 2011, retrieved February 12, 2015 from http://www.foodproductiondaily.com/Processing/Pulsed-UV -light-cuts-peanut-allergens-by-up-to-90-per-cent-study.

[33]R. M. Burke and F. J. Monahan, "The Tenderization of Shin Beef Using a Citrus Marinade," *Meat Science* 63, no. 2 (2003): 161–168; T. A. Williams, *Effects of Beef Enhancement with Non-Meat Ingredients, Blade Tenderization, and Vacuum Tumbling on Quality Attributes of Four Beef Cuts Stored in a High-Oxygen Environment*, master's thesis, Texas A&M University, 2004; A. Önenç, M. Serdaroğlu, and K. Andraimov, "Effects of Various Additives to Marinating Baths on Some Properties of Cattle Meat," *European Food Research and Technology* 218, no. 2 (2003): 114–117.

[34]J. Tarantino, *Marinades: Dry Rubs, Pastes, and Marinades for Poultry, Meat, Seafood, Cheese, and Vegetables* (Freedom, CA: Crossing Press, 1992).

[35]L. A. Brandt, "Marinade Meat Challenges," *Prepared Foods*, December 9, 2003.

[36]D. Berry, "Soaks and Sauces," *Food Product Design*, January 20, 2010, retrieved February 4, 2010, from http://www.foodproductdesign.com/articles/2010 /01/soaks-and-sauces.aspx.

[37]H. McGee, *On Food and Cooking: The Science and Lore of the Kitchen* (New York: Scribner, 2004); Tom Stobart, *The Cooks Encyclopedia: Ingredients and Processes* (New York: Harper and Row, 1980); Tarantino, *Marinades*.

[38]A. Davidson, *The Oxford Companion to Food* (New York, Oxford University Press, 1999); D. B. Min and T. H. Smouse (eds.), *Flavor Chemistry of Lipid Foods* (Urbana, IL: American Oil Chemists Society, 1989); V. Dubois et al., "Fatty Acid Profiles of 80 Vegetable Oils with Regard to Their Nutritional Potential," *European Journal of Lipid Science and Technology* 109, no. 7 (2007): 710–732.

[39]McGee, *On Food and Cooking*.

[40]S. Labensky and A. Hause, *On Cooking: A Textbook of Culinary Fundamentals* (Upper Saddle River, NJ: Prentice Hall, 2007); McGee, *On Food and Cooking*.

[41]McGee, *On Food and Cooking*.

[42]Tarantino, *Marinades*.

[43]M. Miller and M. Kiffin, *Coyote's Pantry* (Berkeley, CA: Ten Speed Press, 1993).

[44]J. Billing and P. W. Sherman, "Antimicrobial Functions of Spices: Why Some Like It Hot," *Quarterly Review of Biology* 73, no. 1 (1998): 3–49.

[45]McGee, *On Food and Cooking*.

19 | Commercializing the Culinary Gold Standard

Lead Author: Marilyn Carlson, CFS, Owner/Principal, Dogwood Solutions
Robert Danhi, Curator of Culture: Chef Danhi & Co/Global Flavor Shakers
Craig "Skip" Julius, CRC®, CCS®, CEC, CCP, Manager of Culinary Solutions, Sensient Flavors

⬤ Introduction

Product development is a formal and disciplined yet highly creative process that begins with an idea and ends with the launch of a new (or improved) product. *Easier said than done.* Creating a culinary gold standard as the result of an idea, and successfully commercializing it, requires the combined knowledge of culinary art, food science, manufacturing process and packaging technology, engineering, customer and consumer research, food safety and sanitation, quality assurance, marketing, demographic and trend awareness, finance, government and regulatory requirements, ingredient procurement, storage and distribution, and—above all—strong project management skills. The Culinology® professional's ability to work and communicate within a cross-functional team of specialists in each of these areas is critically important. Successful commercialization is where the rubber meets the road for the Culinology® professional.

Commercialization is the process of converting a culinary gold standard into a manufacturable form and introducing a new product into the market. A gold standard is a food or beverage product, developed on sound culinary principles, that is used as a benchmark throughout the commercialization process. In a perfect world, the commercialized product closely replicates the product attributes of the gold standard.

The actual launch of a new product is the final stage of new product development and where the most money is likely be spent (for advertising, sales promotion, and marketing efforts). In general, it costs a dollar of investment for every dollar of sales achieved in the first year. Early in the process, costs may be relatively low, but as the project moves forward, investments in customer or consumer research, engineering and equipment, production trials, and launch expenses continue to increase; it's far better to kill a poor idea early in the process than for it to fail in the marketplace before it even begins to pay for its development costs.

Commercialization of a product (moving from idea through launch, or from mind to market) is successful only if the following four questions are answered.

When to Launch?

The company must decide on the timing of the introduction. Many factors influence optimal launch timing; a few are listed here:

- The danger of cannibalizing the sales of current well-performing products
- Menu or store-shelf reset dates (those times when an existing display or shelf of products is re-arranged) for key customers
- Shortage or seasonality of production capacity, labor, raw materials, or marketing dollars to support a successful launch
- The need to be first in market even if the product is not yet optimized—finding the balance between the perfect product and the perfect launch timing in a highly competitive market
- Economy or trend indicators—if they are down, it may not be the right time to launch

The best, most innovative products can still fail if launched prematurely (or too late!).

Where to Launch?

The company must decide where to launch. It may be in a single location, one or several regional launches, or a national or even international launch. This decision is strongly influenced by the company's capital, managerial confidence, and operational capacities. Smaller companies usually opt for smaller local or regional launches, while larger companies, with more financial muscle and national brand recognition, may choose to enter the entire market at the same time. Global rollouts are generally undertaken by multinational conglomerates with the requisite size and global facilities and resources to support multiple countries at once. (Similar to regional rollouts, the multinational strategy may also use a "by-country" approach, introducing the new product in one country or region at a time.)

Of course, with the ubiquity of television advertising and Internet sales, even the smallest companies now have immediate access to the entire marketplace wherever there is a TV set, a computer, or a smartphone.

Who is going to buy my product?

The company must identify target consumers exactly: their age, gender, marital status, ethnic identity, income level, social attitudes, category purchase activity (or buying preferences), geography, and so on. Primary target consumer groups are generally identified for a specific brand or product positioning, and new products developed for this brand or positioning have the appropriate target market in mind from the beginning of development. In this way, limited and costly distribution and promotion resources may be focused to improve the chances of a strong positive response during the initial launch or rollout phase.

How am I going to do it (successfully)?

Simply put, the company must develop a viable marketing budget and determine an action plan for introducing the product into the marketplace. *Successfully*.

●Product Development: The Benefits of Using a Proven Process

Product launches are notoriously unsuccessful. Most food products fail because they simply do not meet customer or consumer expectations for value, performance (flavor, texture, eating quality), and/or convenience. A proven key to commercial success is generating better consumer research and information at the front end of the development process to ensure the right end-user needs are identified and met. No amount of execution makes up for an inherently weak idea; conversely, few great ideas survive weak executions.

The Product Development Management Association (PDMA) reports that a large percentage of consumer packaged goods companies use a stepped idea-to-launch approach to product development, such as the Stage-Gate® process.

This sort of system is essentially an operational roadmap for moving a new product from idea to launch. The process logically breaks the project into distinct stages with decision-point "gates" separating each stage. Cross-functional product development teams must complete a prescribed set of related activities in each stage prior to obtaining management approval to proceed through the gate to the next stage of development. Activities in any given stage are designed to gather vital technical, market, financial, and operational information, with the focus on minimizing risk and maximizing speed to market. Each stage along the development path has a potential cost greater than that of the one preceding it; with a stepped process, expenditures are allowed to rise as uncertainties decrease and risk is managed.

The benefits of the idea-to-launch process are based on the attention to detail used in developing and setting up the process. Each stage must be crafted to bring the right information to the key decision makers ("Gate-Keepers") to gain approval to move forward. Such information includes: defining the business opportunity, understanding end-user needs and the key product attributes that will meet them, technical and manufacturing feasibility, product and process development and manufacturing costs, including capital expenditures, and many other considerations. A well-defined process includes the following attributes, often customized to the company, business unit, or even brand group:

- Based on reality—the need or opportunity is clearly defined.
- Establishes measurable benchmarks.
- Defines the gold standard target, using consumer and customer input.
- Introduces discipline into what can be a chaotic process.
- Manages allocation of scarce or expensive resources.
- Ensures a complete process—no critical steps are omitted.
- Eliminates politics and emotion from decision making.
- Accelerates speed to market via a well-defined process that also reduces wasted resources (people, time, dollars).
- Increases likelihood of product success—weak ideas are weeded out early in the process due to increased focus and discipline.

A well-defined idea-to-launch process is not limited to large companies; smaller companies are likely to have shorter, less complex processes by virtue of their less complex organizational structure. Any company disciplined enough to develop a solid idea-to-launch process that meets its organizational needs and addresses company culture can benefit.

●The Product Development Process
Identifying a Need

Key questions that must be answered include these, and often many others:

- What is it?
- Who wants it?

FIGURE 19.1 Example of an idea-to-launch process.
Initial Phases—Idea and Product Development

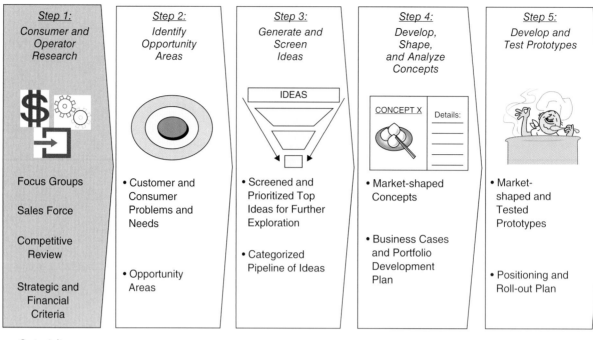

Source: Craig Julius.

- What problem does it solve?
- How does it work?
- What is its competitive point of difference?
- How will it be profitable?
- How will it be manufactured?

An organization's ability to detect, target, and capture the best new product opportunities is a critical success factor in this dynamic and competitive industry.

The need for a new product may be driven by internal forces such as brand innovation or renovation, identified portfolio gaps, profit improvement, sales force insights, and market research; or by external forces such as emerging trends and changing consumer patterns, competitive pressure, economic forces, advances in technology, and a changing marketplace (examples include obesity and health concerns, social media, internet marketing and sales, and eco-friendly or sustainability initiatives).

Once the needs are identified, it's time to build the concept(s) based on them. Key concept components include a clear objective, the marketing rationale (problems and solutions), product and process characteristics, initial feasibility analyses (such as equipment and resource needs, launch timing, shelf-life requirements, and food quality and safety issues), manufacturing and distribution considerations, and financial and cost targets, including cost of goods sold (COGS).

The result of this initial work is an ability to:

- Define the need or opportunity and defend it.
- Describe the value proposition—an analysis and quantified review of the benefits, costs, and value that an organization can deliver to customers. It is also a positioning of value where value = benefit – costs (includes risk).
- Build the business case and develop the project scope. Scope definition is a core project-planning process; it involves identifying and describing the work required to produce the desired outcome (in this case, a particular new product or perhaps product line). Good scoping includes defining both what the project is and is not intended to deliver. Clearly identifying what is not within the scope helps avoid "scope creep" as the project evolves.
- Provide a project brief, including constraints, that includes all of the above.

Defining the Vision

The next phase is to generate ideas that address the defined need. Think of idea generation as a funnel; it is essential to look at many ideas to come up with one or two products (or product lines) that can be sustained long-term, especially in this age of constant change. It is vital to involve key internal and external stakeholders, including customers, early in the process. The key output of the process is a clearly articulated basic product description and its target consumer(s).

FIGURE 19.2 Example of a product opportunity document.

Opportunity Name: **Date:**

Product Category: **Category Manager:**

Summary / Rationale of Opportunity [i.e., Financial, Strategic, etc.]:
Description of Product(s):

Reason for Opportunity [check all that apply]:

Brand Information:

Existing Competitors:
Manufacturer / Brand Name: _____
Description: _____
Existing Price Points: _____
Our Point of Differentiation: _____

Segment Target [check all that apply]:
Foodservice___ Healthcare___ K–12___ C&U___ Chains ___ Club___ C-Store___ Military___ Retail___

Estimated Yearly Sales $:

Target Cost [Price/Unit]:
Target Sell [Price/Unit]:

Estimated Contribution Margin $ **Estimated Margin %:**

Product Attributes [check all that apply]: Vegan __ Vegetarian __ Kosher __ Halal __ Low Sodium __
Other _____
Organic __ Sugar Free __ Low Fat __ Trans Fat Free __ Child Nutrition __ Fair Trade __ Green __ Natural __

Suggested Operator's Cook / Re-Thermalize Process [check all that apply]: Fry ___ Steam ___
Microwave ___ Bake ___ Broil ___ Grill ___ Stove Top ___ Boil ___

Packaging / Storage Consideration
Preferred Packaging Material: Inner: _____Outer: _____
Est. Case Weight: _____ or Est. Case Count: _____
Units per Master Case: _____
Other Considerations [check all that apply]: Tamper Evident ___ Reseal capable ___ Recyclable ____
                                          Biodegradable ___ Ovenable____
Storage Type: Freezer ____ Cooler ____ Dry Goods ____
Desired Shelf Life [Days]: _____

Launch Date Estimate: Quarter _____ Year ____

POP Approval: Yes: _____ No: _____ If no, why? _____
Signatures Required:
_____ Date: _____
_____ Date: _____
_____ Date: _____

Source: Craig Julius.

A key component of concept development are ideation sessions, which can be conducted internally if the company has a proven session facilitator on staff. However, many highly experienced external resources are available to help with this; the money will be well spent. Interdisciplinary session participants bring more to the table and provide a feast of ideas; it's important to include representatives of major internal departments such as culinary, food science, sales and marketing, procurement, manufacturing, and regulatory, as well as external participants—regardless of an employee's professed objectivity, they still work within the company and place an unconscious filter on what they hear or say.

Good ideation often includes a competitive product review (often called market benchmarking). Identifying a product's position within the context of the current marketplace (the competitive frame) is critically important—sometimes as important as the product itself. Begin by assessing who the competitors are and what products they market (the competitive set). This type of benchmarking is imperative to understanding the competition's strengths and weaknesses so you are able to develop a successful and marketable product. However, when true innovation is involved, finding similar products or establishing a competitive set may be difficult. A well-developed concept illustrates a product's key attributes, including the consumer's wants or needs the product is intended to meet.

Ultimately, ideas should go through a screening process to cull redundancies, address hurdles such as cost or feasibility, and eliminate ideas that do not fit manufacturing competencies. Surviving ideas are then categorized and defended based on their ability to meet the defined consumer need or market opportunity.

For example, a few years ago a major food company identified a need for healthier non-fried appetizers. The ideation session yielded several products that potentially met the need. The defense for one potential product solution, Project X Flatbreads, follows.

The process started with the articulated consumer needs derived from the research (Figure 19.3).

FIGURE 19.3   Project X consumer research.

Project X			

Consumer Feedback			

Concept Rating	FSR	QSR	C-Store
Consumer	H	HM	M

FSR: Consumers liked that these are new and non-fried. FSR consumers are more willing to experiment with unusual flavor combinations.

- *"Appetizers are the same anywhere. They are all unhealthy and me and my wife don't even think about ordering them anymore. I like alternatives to fried foods, I want some."*

- *"You have a hard time finding appetizers that aren't fried or really greasy."*

QSR: Consumers like the idea of some non-fried options in this channel. Consumers like the portability of the concept and see it as a perfect fit for on-the-go consumption. Flavors will need to be more mainstream in this channel.

- *"It gives me variety that I don't currently have. These also seem like they would be perfect for eating in the car."*

- *"This is much lighter than a Big Mac or something like that. Not so sure about the varieties, but the overall concept is a winner."*

C-Store: This concept had medium appeal with C-Store consumers but could be easily modified to increase consumer appeal. Consumers liked that these were healthier than current options but were skeptical about the product delivering on its claims of taste and ease of preparation. Flavors should be traditional.

- *"I like the idea that it suggests that it is not fried or unhealthy, because that is a problem. I have a tight schedule, everyone tries to eat healthy, but you can grab something in a pinch without damaging your health."*

Source: Craig Julius.

FIGURE 19.4   Project X product attributes.

Project X	

Product Fit	

Strategic Link

- Out of Home Consumer—Offers consumers a new, healthier snack and appetizer option.
- Operator—Gives them a "new to the world" selection of non-fried, quick, easy, and high-quality snacks and appetizers.
- Healthier options that leverage current brands and competencies to meet emerging consumer trends.

Desired Product Attributes

- Temperature consistency and control are vital. We will need a product that enables operators to deliver reheated appetizers that are within the required temperature range, but where the fillings will not be too scalding.
- Offer a variety of flavors appropriate to each targeted channel: more traditional flavors for QSR and C-Store (broccoli and cheese type offerings) and more exotic flavors for FSR (ethnic varieties).
- Flavors should be tailored to the menus of restaurant segments (Mexican, American, etc.).
- Products should have fresh and healthy visual cues, ex.: grill marks.
- For FSR and QSR, make them look less like hot pockets and more like quality, unique appetizers (possibly make the fillings more colorful, unique).
- Consider offering assorted sizes, including a "sandwich size" for QSR and C-Store that can be eaten as a full meal.
- These need to be able to deliver non-microwaved taste through the microwave.
- Product needs to deliver on cooking promises—can't taste soggy or too rough.
- Cannot look like a frozen retail product.
- Needs to be easily heated by C-Store consumers in the microwave.
- Needs to be easy to prepare, requiring little BOH skill.
- Manufacturing flexibility to accommodate customization for large-volume opportunities.

Source: Craig Julius.

Based on those needs, a product attribute statement was crafted (Figure 19.4).

A product solution summary then conceptualized a product line that addressed the identified needs and opportunities (Figure 19.5).

Next, an analysis of the competitive landscape was presented (Figure 19.6)

At some point, this may lead to a specific product prototype that is the manifestation of the concept summary; it could be one or several product ideas that are interpretations of the consumer need. Each unique concept or prototype undergoes further testing and validation.

FIGURE 19.5 Project X concept summary.

Project X

Concept Summary

A line of non-fried appetizers/snacks in a variety of interesting flavors that look freshly-made.

Step 4 Screening Criteria Results Summary

Concept Rating	FSR	QSR	C-Store
Operator	H	H	H
Consumer	H	HM	M

Revenue
- Greater than $20 million

EBITA
- Greater than 20%

Technical Feasibility
- 2 (of 5)

Prototype Timeline
- Greater than 6 months

Time to Launch
- 12 to 24 months

Source: Craig Julius.

FIGURE 19.6 Project X competitive landscape.

Project X

Competitive Market Prices

Product	Case Config.	Case Price	Price/lb.	Price/unit
Cheese Sticks	4/3 lb.	$33.64	$2.80/lb.	
Stuffed Jalapenos	4/4 lb.	$51.85	$3.24/lb.	
Breaded Vegetables	6/2.5 lb.	$24.27	$1.62/lb.	
Stuffed Olives	2/4 lb.	$29.42	3.68/lb.	
Spring Rolls	2/24/1.5 oz.	$29.25	$3.25/lb.	$0.30/unit
Egg Rolls	3/20/3 oz.	$23.70	$2.11/lb.	$0.40/unit
Potstickers	6/30/1 oz.	$47.50	$4.22/lb.	$0.26/unit
Quesadilla Rolls	4/4 lb.	$57.00	$3.56/lb.	
Dips	36/6 oz.	$40.90	$1.14	$0.19

Category Trends

- **Rise in ethnic offerings, both new flavors and mini versions of popular entrees**
  - Pan-Asian, Mexican, Fusion
  - Mini tacos, quesadillas, tapas, egg/spring rolls, etc.
- **Heavy new product focus at leading chains**
  - Appetizers are the #3 new menu item (behind seafood entrées and desserts).
  - New appetizer types: 1. Seafood; 2. Southwest/Mexican; 3. Asian
- **Expanded usage as "dippable" meal alternatives for kids and teens**
- **Growth in "consumer-friendly" forms**
  - Boneless wings, poppable shapes, dip injected into the product
- **Growing trend toward expanded day-parts**
  - Mini pockets at breakfast, lunch sampler trays

Source: Craig Julius.

Collaborative Marketing

Partnering to maximize marketing resources is a synergistic approach that many of today's food and beverage companies use; this approach is also referred to as horizontal marketing. For example, a salad dressing company may collaborate with a packaged fresh salad producer to co-package the dressing as part of a salad kit for a national retailer. In this case, the dressing manufacturer can leverage the salad company's sales, marketing, and distribution network to its own advantage while providing a service or capability (making dressings) the salad company neither has nor wishes to invest in. The two companies each focus on their core competencies and collaborate to bring a convenient meal solution to the consumer.

Market Opportunity Assessment

To determine the real needs of the consumer, the market must be analyzed quantitatively and qualitatively. This assessment often determines whether or not the project warrants the investment of resources and moves forward. Even though the idea may fit a core competency of the company, the decision to allocate resources must take into account actual market needs or wants. Competitive product attributes, consumer purchasing trends, and socioeconomic factors are all top areas for investigation.

Using consumer focus groups to gain these insights is a costly and complex process, but one that increases the chances for success. Asking consumers what they want, how they will use it, and how much they are willing to pay for it provides valuable information to guide the company to successful product development. Today, concepts can be tested quickly and inexpensively via online models, and companies often use online chat technology to replace face-to-face focus groups.

Once consumer input has refined and narrowed the concept options, consumer reaction to actual protocepts (the chef's renditions of the concept) or prototypes (the early commercialized versions of the protocepts) help refine the product concept and confirm that it meets the expectations developed during concept testing. The hard work of needs assessment, ideation, concept development and refinement, and preliminary research give the team the necessary information to develop strong product and project statements.

Project and Product Statements

Within the project statement, all the marketing assessment data is distilled into a concise document that outlines the business plan for the internal cross-functional team that executes the conceptualization, development, manufacturing, launch, and eventual management of the new product or product line. This must be conveyed in context of the company's strategic goals, target market, competitive arena, regulatory restraints, and financial parameters. Associated timeline and departmental and individual responsibilities are also outlined.

Balsamic Vinaigrette: Three Pathways to Gold

A dressing company desires to launch a balsamic vinaigrette to extend its current retail line of salad dressings.

FIGURE 19.7   Balsamic vinaigrette.

Source: Stuart Monk/Getty Images, Inc.

Scenario 1—The product development team wishes to establish a culinary gold standard without current capability as a restriction. The team creates a balsamic vinaigrette recipe using top-quality kitchen ingredients with no consideration of supply chain, cost, or manufacturing feasibility. The goal is to create the best possible version of the product to serve as a benchmark against which all commercialized versions will be compared.

Scenario 2—The culinary team feels they have sufficient commercial raw materials already in the system to meet their needs and uses current ingredients to develop the gold standard dressing. This is a more responsible approach, as it will be easier to match and scale up as the team moves forward. Operational constraints, shelf-life concerns, and packaging still must be considered and taken into account, but at least initial ingredient issues are already addressed. Even though it's made with commercial ingredients, this is still a culinary gold standard.

Scenario 3—The competitor is by far the leading brand of balsamic vinaigrette in the marketplace, so in essence they have established the gold standard. In this case, the competitor's product is used as the gold standard and becomes the benchmark for consumer testing—that is, a new product must score at parity or outperform the market leader to be accepted.

Regardless of which method is used, the approved product or recipe should be the reference or benchmark item all the way through the development and commercialization of a new item. The goal is to ensure the final commercialized product stays true to the key attributes that made the gold standard gold.

The product statement drills down to the specific attributes the new product will ideally possess. The challenge here is that in many cases there are incompatible traits. For instance, a 45-day required shelf life for distribution is incompatible with a bright green herb garnish. Culinary descriptions, photos, and even videos can all be used to convey the important and desirable product traits the research and development (R&D) team is being asked to achieve.

Good product and project statements set up strategic guardrails that help clarify and define not only what the product or project is but also what it is not. These documents help guide the R&D team in gold standard development.

What Is a Gold Standard, and How Is It Developed?

Development and approval of a gold standard is a cross-functional activity. How the gold standard is developed can differ from project to project. It is always a benchmark, a point of reference that future commercialized iterations are judged against; however, it can be approached in different ways. The process for defining and using gold standards should be established as company protocol, customized to meet the needs and culture of the company, brand team, or project team.

Gold standard development is the point in the process where the broad skill set of the Culinology® professional comes into play to create a physical product, designed to intentionally and specifically address the attributes identified in the research and ideation phases. These attributes include but are not limited to appearance, aroma, flavor, texture, and even sensory experiences such as spicy heat and menthol cooling. The gold standard is often confirmed only after consumer research; in the vinaigrette example, all of the options—straight kitchen recipe, bench prototype using commercial ingredients, and the competitive market leader—could be evaluated by consumers both to capture preference and to gain input on the attributes that will allow the R&D team to refine the gold standard to meet as many of the consumer's needs as possible.

Product and Process Development

Next, serious commercialization begins. This is the process of taking a kitchen or bench recipe through the obstacle course of assessing, understanding, and overcoming manufacturing, regulatory, food safety, and distribution challenges. A talented culinary team can put together an amazing product that's a delight to the eye and the palate—a true feast for the senses. It's when the development team begins to translate that experience into a product that can be reproduced consistently—literally millions of times—in a format that can be consumed months later by someone miles away—that things get really interesting.

Good development teams work cross-functionally to consider technical, manufacturing, food safety, procurement, and

Gold Standard Development and Impact on Commercialization:
Spud Wars—A Real-Life Experience

A dry, shelf-stable "just add water and wait 5 minutes" soup line was expanded to include a line of savory instant mashed potato products.

Product Line Expectations
- All ingredients must be dry, with less than 5-minute rehydration time required.
- Particle size is limited due to manufacturing equipment constraints.
- This line must be all-natural and vegetarian.
- Sodium content is restricted to less than 500 mg per serving.
- A flavor match to gold standard is critical; the finished product cannot be similar or equally acceptable but must *match* the gold standard flavor profile within narrow limits.

Gold Standard Development
- Fresh kitchen ingredients were used.
- Culinary cooking methods were used, including searing and braising fresh meat to obtain a savory flavor profile target for matching using vegetarian ingredients.
- No limits (including on sodium) were imposed on flavor development.

FIGURE 19.8   Mashed potatoes.

Source: robynmac/Getty Images, Inc.

In the context of the product line expectations, the first two points in gold standard development could be overcome; the team had the talent, experience, and ingredient resources to make the transition from a fresh dish containing meat-derived ingredients to a dehydrated vegetarian product. What could *not* be overcome was a flavor profile designed with more than 1200 mg sodium per serving! If the gold standard had been developed and validated with the sodium restriction in mind, it would have had a different flavor profile . . . and may well have been preferred by consumers!

Challenges in Authenticity in Manufacturing:
A Mediterranean Example

As are most regional and ethnic foods, Mediterranean cuisine is typified by specific cooking techniques and ingredients. One signature "flavor print" is the use of olive oil and garlic. A common technique involves caramelizing vegetables, often combined with seasonings, to yield complex flavor combinations such as roasted mirepoix or sofrito (a classic Spanish or Portuguese sauce composed of aromatic ingredients such as garlic, onion, paprika, peppers, and tomatoes cut into small pieces and sauteed or braised in olive oil). Another example is oil-simmered vegetable stews such as ratatouille and caponata.

FIGURE 19.9   Caponata.

Source: travellinglight/Getty Images, Inc.

Adhering to authentic Mediterranean flavor prints in a commercial kitchen is not a difficult challenge for a trained chef. However, traditional manufacturing environments, with their enormous production volumes and massive equipment, create constraints that typically do not lend themselves well to traditional cooking techniques. Creating signature flavor nuances in a manufacturing environment requires experience, knowledge, and the ability to meet challenges through innovative thinking—in other words, Culinology® in action!

Two Examples: Olive Oil and Garlic Flavors

Many manufacturers use vegetable oil instead of costlier olive oil, or they use a third-press (solvent-extracted) olive oil. These choices may be made due to cost considerations, commercial ingredient availability, or even processing constraints, such as the need for an oil with a higher smoke point due to the manufacturing process. Excellent olive oil flavors are available to add back authenticity to the product. Even a low-fat product can exhibit a fruity olive oil flavor, or flavors can be used to boost that of cheaper, more cost-effective oils.

When garlic is commercially processed, its aromatic qualities are often lost, or objectionable off flavors, often metallic in nature, develop. Sometimes a really good garlic flavor or oleoresin is a better formula option than garlic pastes or other commercially processed garlic choices.

These are just a couple of ways that authenticity can be reconstructed to maintain gold-standard flavor integrity in the commercialized product.

Cooking Techniques

The traditional cooking techniques used to create authentic tastes, textures, and appearances are one of the most commonly compromised areas in food manufacturing. The effect on foods is a loss of gold-standard integrity. In traditional manufacturing environments, especially if the plant is more than a decade old, equipment is expected only to mix, cook, and deposit. Speed is everything. "Authenticity is for restaurant chefs," as one plant engineer used to say (ironically, he left the food business for the automotive industry).

Recently, high-tech manufacturing equipment has come to market that provides the high-heat and high-contact surfaces necessary to duplicate authentic cooking techniques.

In an effort to automate the Chinese stir-fry process, one company recreated the manual stir-frying technique used for centuries in preparing Chinese dishes and incorporated it into an automated mechanical process. A hot thermal oil system was designed to provide high temperatures (500°F [260°C]) at low pressure to work in conjunction with a mechanical stir-fry device. The machine mechanically stir-fries food on a very large scale while retaining hand-stir-fried product quality. Applications for this machine go beyond Asian stir-fry. The high heat allows for true caramelization and complex flavor creation; it can be effectively used to replicate the color and flavor of Mediterranean cuisines as well. In contrast, traditional steam-kettle cooking is a low-temperature (212°F [100°C]), moist-heat process. The resulting soggy texture is caused by the stewing of product in its own juices.

To achieve the qualities of dry-heat roasting, another company makes high-heat in-line and spiral equipment that produces great results for roasting meats and vegetables. They also make an in-line fire roaster—that is, a flame broiler—that can impart charring and varying degrees of caramelization to meats and vegetables. Trolley cookers and cavern ovens, long used in the meat cooking and smoking industry, can also provide dry-heat alternatives to traditional steam-kettle cooking.

regulatory feasibility as part of the process from the original concept forward. A good gold standard not only represents the eating quality of the final commercialized product but is also at least moderately practical. In the Spud Wars example, the gold standard for a new savory mashed potato lunch line was developed by a culinary-based test kitchen team in one location and commercialized by a lab and production team in another location. Product-line restrictions were not considered during gold standard development to avoid limiting the creativity of the test kitchen team. Using fresh ingredients and even meat (to provide a savory flavor target even though the end product is vegetarian) were hurdles that could have been overcome. However, the decision not to limit the creativity of the culinary team allowed them to create an unrealistic

Ingredient Considerations:
The Case of the Marinara Sauce

Imagine you are working on a marinara sauce. The gold standard was kitchen-made using fresh ingredients, from the tomatoes to the herbs. The savory flavor character came from browning fresh Italian sausage, using the fat and *fond* (browned material at the bottom of the pan left from sautéing the meat) as a base for sautéing the aromatics (in this case, onion, garlic, and fresh herbs), and the sauce was built from there and finished with a splash of red wine in the late stages of cooking. Here are some of the questions to consider in commercialization:

- How will the finished sauce be distributed and sold? Will it be shelf-stable (jar, can, or flexible pouch), refrigerated, or frozen? The perfect ingredient choice for a frozen sauce may not survive thermal processing, for instance.
- Can processed tomato ingredients such as diced, puree, or paste replace fresh tomatoes?
- Is an industrial flavor available to help replace the flavor of the sausage fat and *fond*? In some cases, a low-calorie or even vegetarian sauce may be desired, but with the savory flavor notes that came from browning the seasoned meat in the gold standard.
- What combination of commercial ingredients might replace fresh sautéed aromatics? Frozen sautéed aromatics are possible, but the best answer is more likely to take the form of culinary base or concentrate, frozen puree, drum-dried or spray-dried ingredients, or a flavoring—or a combination of two or more of these choices.
- Will dry herbs provide the needed flavor? Are industrial flavors required to boost the fresh flavor notes? Will IQF herbs or a fresh-frozen puree meet the cost target?
- Must wine be used to finish the sauce? Will a commercial flavor, dealcoholized wine, or wine concentrate do the job?
- Consider the sauce's mouthfeel and cling. Are functional solutions such as starches or gums needed to match the original texture?
- Will the flavor, texture, appearance, and aroma survive the temperature fluctuations of distribution, including potential abuse by the end user? Does the product need color or flavor protection? Will syneresis (separation) control be an issue?
- What else could go wrong, and how can the product be protected against it?

making. Compromises are required as part of the commercialization process, and the team must agree from the beginning what can and cannot be compromised on. Are we willing to give up flavor, texture, or eating quality for cost? Give up shelf-life or distribution assumptions for eating quality? Give up texture or appearance for manufacturing efficiency or distribution capability? The list can seem endless and is unique to every product, but it must be confronted.

One of the first things a commercialization team does is begin to transition a kitchen recipe into a manufacturing formula, including translating kitchen or culinary ingredients and measurements (such as cups or teaspoons) to commercial ingredients and measurements (such as percentages or pounds per batch). During this phase a second standard, sometimes called the manufacturing standard, is developed; it may differ slightly from the culinary gold standard, but it incorporates all of the necessary commercialization trade-offs the team has agreed on (and does not diverge from those considered non-negotiable). Both the culinary and manufacturing gold standards are used as benchmarks during evaluation of the products produced at every phase of development and commercialization testing. It's common to require that a manufacturing standard scores near parity compared to the original gold standard in consumer testing to ensure the consumer needs are still being met.

Examples of commercial ingredients include:

- Familiar kitchen staples such as butter or cheese in 50-pound blocks and tomato paste in 55-gallon drums instead of little tin cans.
- Commercial flavorings that replicate the savory deliciousness developed in the kitchen via cooking, such as sautéing, searing, roasting, or braising; it may be impractical if not impossible to duplicate these cooking processes on a mass scale using industrial equipment.
- Functional ingredients, such as heat- and acid-resistant starches, that can help the product survive mass production, commercial packaging and distribution, and months of storage—yet still eat as good as kitchen fresh at the time of consumption.

Cost is a big part of product development. Material costs such as ingredients, packaging, and other material inputs, and manufacturing costs such as labor, overhead, and efficiency, must all be considered; cost of goods sold (COGS) is a key input. Food safety, sanitation, and Hazard Analysis and Critical Control Point (HACCP) requirements as well as the safety of production workers must also be taken into account. One example of worker safety concerns is the highly publicized case some years ago of lung disease in unprotected popcorn plant workers. The workers were exposed to the flavor chemical diacetyl, a component of the butter flavor then used in microwave popcorn. Another example is the ban many manufacturing plants put on ingredients packed in metal cans (opening the can may produce metal shavings) or glass containers (due to the chance of breakage and subsequent glass shards). Both metal shavings and glass

target with too much salt for the R&D team to match at the required sodium level. The finished product was commercialized and was successful in every way except two: It didn't deliver on flavor, and it failed in the marketplace. This was not the fault of either the culinary team or the commercialization team; it was a failure of the entire cross-functional process. Lack of integration between the development teams caused the product line to fail.

One of the most important issues any commercialization team must understand is the hierarchy of priority in decision shards are hazards to production workers and, if they get into the product, to consumers.

The most practical way to transition from kitchen recipe to production formula is to investigate the impact of each ingredient change one at a time. It's important to fully understand how each of the ingredients and processing steps affects the finished product; only then can the developer reconstruct the product as a commercial manufacturing-ready formula that delivers the same key attributes as the gold standard.

Good developers have a commercialization toolbox at the ready, including a clear understanding of industrial flavor and functional ingredients and solid experience with manufacturing processes. A key tool is the expertise of applications and culinary resources provided by ingredient and equipment suppliers. Many flavor houses provide culinary flavors that replicate or enhance the flavors obtained by different cooking methods in the kitchen. Vegetable suppliers offer ready-cut, pre-cooked, individually quick-frozen (IQF) vegetables—seared, grilled, roasted, and seasoned. Herbs can be obtained IQF as fresh-frozen purees, culinary bases, extracts, flavorings, and, of course, dry (including freeze-dried). Nearly every imaginable commercial need can be filled if it is clearly identified.

Just as in the kitchen, specifications—dice size of ingredients, defined unit processes such as mixing, cooking, and order of ingredient addition, and so on—are key manufacturing steps that affect the finished product considerably. Only through familiarity with commercial ingredients and manufacturing equipment can the developer understand them well enough to apply them appropriately.

Consider one at a time the ingredients and methods used to make a savory marinara sauce. Starting with the tomatoes, can commercial tomato products (available in 55-gallon drums or pallet-sized bag-in-box technology) replace the taste and texture of cooked-from-fresh tomatoes? Once this question is resolved, the team can move on to background flavors such as the meaty and savory notes, the aromatics, the herb notes, and the wine component. Frequent reference to the gold standard helps the team avoid making small stepwise changes from version to version that can take the final formula quite far from the original target flavor profile. During the flavor development process, it is common to note for later attention—but not attempt to solve yet—small texture, color, and other attributes that may also begin to stray from the gold standard. Major texture attributes should be addressed immediately—for example, how the decision to use a tomato combination including diced, crushed, pureed, or paste for texture and appearance also affects flavor and mouthfeel. But minor, correctable attributes such as viscosity can be dealt with later. Understanding the difference is where the experience and expertise of the Culinology® professional comes in.

Once the flavor profile match is achieved, it's time to correct minor appearance and textural attributes such as viscosity, pulpiness, or color hue and intensity, again always referring to the gold standard. It's important to look ahead to manufacturing constraints during this step—for example, many particulates are reduced in size during mixing, pumping, and filling operations in the manufacturing process. These issues can be overcome by specifying larger dices that will be sized just right after moving through the production process.

Sauces may be prone to syneresis during storage and distribution, and functional ingredients such as acid-stable starches or gums may be needed to protect against it. Now is the time to think ahead to what can go wrong and build in defenses. Because functional ingredients such as starches and gums can mask flavor, the recipe may need tweaking to come back to the desired flavor impact after other quality issues have been addressed.

When a bench formula or manufacturing standard is complete and approved, it's a good idea to do some quick disaster checking. Consider what can go wrong and see what

Blowing Hot and Cold:
The Effect of Frozen Vegetables in a Real-Life Situation

A common tactic in production is to take advantage of IQF components to help cool a sauce quickly. For instance, if you are making chicken à la king with a cook-up sauce, you might cook the sauce and then add the IQF vegetables to quickly cool it for HACCP reasons.

You have planned ahead and designed your sauce consistency to be just right once the vegetables thaw and the blend equilibrates to <40°F (4°C). The manufacturing specifications are carefully crafted to the final degree, clearly stating the correct temperature of the sauce, the temperature of the vegetables, and the right time to blend them together. What could go wrong with that?

Consider this: The vegetables are assumed (even specified) to be at 30°F (–1°C), the temperature of the holding freezer in the plant. However, yesterday someone forgot to order more vegetables into the plant from off-site cold storage. Everyone scrambled, and the vegetables are delivered just in time—but they are at –5°F (–20°C) because they just came in on a freezer truck! A thick, hot sauce designed perfectly for 30°F (–1°C) vegetables is likely to bind up solid when hit with this temperature load. Mixing and pumping are not in the cards until the vegetables temper for a few hours.

Conversely, consider this scenario: The vegetables were pulled out of the holding freezer right on time this morning for the first batch of sauce—and a key piece of equipment failed. In the scramble to get production up and running, no one remembered to put the vegetables away. By the time the next batch of hot sauce is ready for vegetables, they are up to 55°F (13°C). Now you have a loose, watery sauce that does not cool fast enough to meet HACCP guidelines, and the vegetables are warm and limp—completely unable to pass through the subsequent blending and pumping processes in one piece.

It's surprising how a relatively minor problem can throw an entire processing schedule out of whack and potentially ruin a large batch of product.

happens when it does. "What can go wrong" includes investigating the limits of every unit process—basically trying to break a system or product—all the way through processing and packaging. Not only product quality but food safety must be considered. Examples include:

- *Over- or under-processing*—What happens to the product if ingredient weighing, cutting, blending, cooking, and other unit processes are not well controlled? Testing each area, including intentional process variations, can determine how tightly the manufacturing process specifications must be set for each unit process.
- *Work-in-process (WIP) components*—What if frozen ingredients are thawed too far or held too long after thawing—or not thawed enough? What are the options if a key piece of equipment fails mid-process? How can WIP materials be protected or recovered? Are there components produced in one area or facility and used later in another? What are the packaging, distribution, and shelf-life limits of these intermediate items, and how will finished product quality and shelf life be affected by using WIP ingredients that are approaching end-of-life?

Other "defensive" questions that should be considered:

- Are alternate processes or equipment available that yield the same result? For instance, what if Plant A uses a chopper for particle reduction and Plant B uses a grinder? Can the product be made in both plants successfully, in both cases yielding a finished product that gives the end consumer the same experience?
- Does current packaging technology meet the need for the new product? Products are often designed around current packaging capabilities, but sometimes new packaging technologies are necessary to deliver on the concept; packaging is a critical component of product design, and it is often overlooked.

It is only by understanding the strengths and limitations of key manufacturing equipment and unit operations, just as one must understand the kitchen gold standard, that robust manufacturing specifications can be developed and identified—and it's only by understanding where to find the edge of the cliff that one can build the guardrails that allow a team to create cutting-edge products that can be produced over and over, day in and day out, without concern for quality or safety. Process capability—the inherent variability that cannot be specified out of a unit process—is a key consideration for every development and commercialization team. It's a common, yet major, mistake to design a product with closer tolerances than the process is capable of.

Once potential manufacturing abuse is defined and resolved, distribution abuse must be considered. For example, distribution abuse for a frozen meal product can be approximated by running it through a freeze-thaw abuse series—that is, freezing the product completely, then letting it thaw at room temperature completely, then repeating the process. The results of four or five freeze-thaw cycles will give a good indication of potential "real life" challenges.

Once the final freeze-thaw cycle is complete, all five samples are evaluated side by side against the gold standard and the manufacturing standard to understand how well the product withstands the abuse. It's important at this point to test the product in final or near-final packaging and prepare it for eating the same way a consumer or customer would. For a retail frozen entrée, this may include preparation in both a conventional oven and a microwave, for example. For a foodservice item, it may include time in a steam table. The product's performance must be evaluated under the conditions the end user will experience to ensure your product and package deliver to expectations.

Using the marinara sauce example, it wouldn't be unusual to see the product begin to show some syneresis (weeping) at freeze-thaw cycle 2, color breakdown (red becoming orange) by cycle 3, and complete product deterioration beginning in cycle 4. Most frozen red sauces wouldn't be considered acceptable after four or five cycles without functional ingredient support such as color technology to help retain the red color, specialty starches or hydrocolloids to protect against syneresis, and added flavor technology to help maintain fresh-made taste even after repeated abuse.

Why assume repeated abuse? Consider this scenario: A pallet of frozen product leaves the production facility via truck. The truck's compressor breaks down or is inadequate for the summer temperatures outside, and the product is a little thawed when it arrives at the frozen distribution center. Or the product is delivered to the distribution center in perfect condition, but the center has an inattentive employee or an equipment issue or a scheduling error, and the pallet sits on the unrefrigerated dock for several hours before being put in the warehouse freezer. Or the warehouse freezer's thermostat may be old and inefficient, or set improperly, so the storage temperature exceeds the optimal temperature. Events such as this can and do happen multiple times between the production facility and the final grocery store or restaurant freezer as the truckload is broken down onto pallets and then cases as it's moved through picking centers in a distribution cycle. Everyone has seen grocery freezer aisles full of product waiting to be put away in the display freezers—another common example of temperature abuse.

FIGURE 19.10 A four-cycle freeze-thaw protocol.

	Cycle 1	Cycle 2	Cycle 3	Cycle 4
Control	keep frozen	keep frozen	keep frozen	keep frozen
Sample 1	thaw, refreeze	keep frozen	keep frozen	keep frozen
Sample 2	thaw, refreeze	thaw, refreeze	keep frozen	keep frozen
Sample 3	thaw, refreeze	thaw, refreeze	thaw, refreeze	keep frozen
Sample 4	thaw, refreeze	thaw, refreeze	thaw, refreeze	thaw, refreeze

Finally, the end user often abuses the product. The shopper who buys the product may not go straight home and immediately place it in the home freezer (which may or may not be set to the correct temperature). Or a foodservice worker might pull the product out of the restaurant freezer and let it thaw before he decides he doesn't need it today and puts it back. It's entirely likely that any frozen product sees as many as six partial or complete freeze-thaw cycles between manufacturing and end use. (*Note:* For unrefrigerated shelf-stable products, high-temperature abuse testing in "hot boxes" [heated storage rooms] is often used instead of freeze-thaw abuse.)

Abuse testing is simply a way to quickly assess how well a product is likely to hold up under its unique conditions of manufacturing, distribution, and end use. It can also be a quick way to approximate what products may look like at the end of estimated shelf life and is often used as a shelf-life prediction tool. No matter how good your product is when first produced, the final consumer won't evaluate it, and your brand, until after it is prepared and consumed. By that time, a multitude of deleterious changes may have occurred. Good commercialization teams understand the conditions their product is likely to experience between manufacturing and consumption and build in the means for the product to survive this reality.

Back to our manufacturing standard: If the product cannot stand up to abuse, the formula must be modified before going for plant trial or pilot testing. Bench development is significantly less expensive than production testing, partly because less product is needed for testing and partly because of the cost of manufacturing line time. Every disruption of a plant's normal production schedule can be costly.

Developing Specifications

In preparation for plant or pilot testing, detailed processing specifications must be developed to ensure the manufacturing team has the information in hand to allow them to consistently reproduce the right product time after time after time. Appropriate documentation includes all inputs—raw material specifications, production recipe or formula, and detailed processing and handling instructions for each step from raw material through finished pallet. It covers estimated plant labor required, expected run rate (time and yield), HACCP and allergen-management plans, proposed containers (cans, jars, pouches, and so on), net fill requirements, outer packaging (bands, sleeves, corrugated, etc.), all the way up to pallet patterns and pallet labeling requirements. It often specifies not only the equipment to use but also the equipment settings for that product. Good manufacturers typically have fill-in-the-blank forms where all of the information required for manufacturing each product can be recorded, so developing process specifications is not as intimidating as it sounds. Preliminary specifications should be confirmed or updated during production trials; it's common to find surprises in full production testing, and all of the adjustments made during testing must be captured in the final specifications.

Once the product is finalized, a finished product specification is written that clearly defines the outcomes desired. Then the material and processing specifications for achieving those outcomes are written. Key product characteristics must be measurable without human bias; examples may include color, texture, viscosity, pH, degrees Brix, particulate or piece size, net weight (and component weights), and any other measures relevant to a particular product. Photos of the finished product in its container, with and without the label, should also be included so that production personnel can refer back to what the packaged product should (and should not) look like after filling and after labeling. Even flavor can be measured, and should be, even if by simply comparing to a bench- or kitchen-produced gold standard on a regular basis. Another option is to use a trained sensory panel for unbiased flavor evaluation; a good trained panel is an effective and reproducible measuring tool.

Every unit process from start to finish must be considered. Here is an example list of questions to consider while thinking through the processing assumptions:

- Which production facility? What equipment is available and should be used? Sketch out the assumed production processes, including the HACCP plan.
- Does the product have a hold step between batching and cooking? What are the minimum and maximum hold times and required temperature conditions for quality and food safety?
- Does the product move from plant to plant between unit processes, such as between batching and cooking, or between cooking and final packaging? What is necessary to protect the integrity of the product during this time?
- What internal control systems must be used (such as labels and bin tags as well as internal WIP documentation) to manage the WIP materials awaiting final processing?
- What happens if a procedure is not followed? Is the product compromised in quality, safety, or functionality? What contingencies are available?
- Can WIP or finished components that do not meet all specifications be reworked into subsequent production? Under what conditions? If not, what are the disposal protocols?
- What are the key unit analyses that confirm the process is properly controlled (for example, nutritional analysis, microbial analysis, time or temperature checks, color evaluation, packaging evaluation, manufacturing records and checkpoints)? What are the sampling plans and documentation protocols for each?

It is the work of the cross-functional team, at this point relying heavily on manufacturing, engineering, and quality assurance professionals, to think through all of the relevant questions for a given project; there are many more than the short list above.

Normally, at this stage the documentation is considered preliminary; specifications are not finalized until sufficient

The Cheesecake Chronicles:
A Real-Life Experience

An unbaked, single-serve, frozen cheesecake was developed for retail distribution. It had a cream cheese base held together with a combination of modified food starch and gelatin. The product was designed to be mixed in 500-pound batches, pumped to a filler, dispensed into a single-serve package, sealed with a clear plastic film, and frozen before being packed in a paperboard sleeve and cardboard case. At the time, this was novel technology. It took about six months of experimentation and plant testing (literally hundreds of plant test batches) to achieve the goal and match the approved gold standard and manufacturing standard.

FIGURE 19.11   Cheesecake production.

Source: AdShooter/Getty Images, Inc.

The product was successful. Soon a capacity increase was needed, and a new 1000-pound mixer was installed. The developer had to return to the plant and retool both the formula and the process to achieve the same finished product using the new mixing equipment.

A year later, as part of the plant's HACCP process, a wall was built between the batching area and the filling line to separate raw materials from the finished-goods packaging area. As part of this change, the mixer was moved 10 feet away from the filler; this time both the plumbing and the formula needed updating. The additional shear created by pumping the product through an additional 10 feet of stainless-steel piping completely changed the finished texture. A larger-diameter pipe and slight adjustments in the textural components of the formula solved the problem.

Seemingly innocuous processing changes can seriously affect the attributes and acceptability of a finished product.

manufacturing experience is gained to validate them. Even a successful production trial won't uncover all of the manufacturing challenges and thus the modifications that will be required. Only after every aspect of the product has been considered, tested, and evaluated is the product ready for scale-up and launch.

Scale-Up Testing

When a bench formula is complete, it must be tested in the production environment, because large-scale processing conditions can and will affect the color, flavor, and texture of the finished product (see sidebar). Production scale-up protocols depend on the size of the company; smaller companies may move straight from the lab to the manufacturing plant, while very large companies generally have pilot facilities (which may be larger than a small manufacturing plant!) and thus move from bench to pilot plant and then to full manufacturing.

Scaling a recipe up from "serves 8" to "serves 40" is one thing, but scaling to hundreds or thousands of pounds per batch (or, for continuous processes, per hour) can have large and often unforeseen consequences. Many of these can be prevented or mitigated by doing intermediate-scale, sequential batch testing. Based on internal evaluation (cost targets, desired shelf life, adjustment of flavor attributes) and external requirements (customer requests or consumer panel feedback), the R&D team may go back to the bench during the scale-up process to use their culinary prowess, scientific knowledge, and process technology experience to reengineer the product to meet all desired requirements.

The finished products produced at every scale-up test must be evaluated against both the original gold standard and the approved manufacturing standard, and any observed differences resolved by tweaking the formula, the processing conditions, or both. The product is then retested in the manufacturing environment to ensure success. A new product is not ready for introduction until all of the manufacturing bugs are identified and resolved to the satisfaction of the entire cross-functional team, and all of the documentation and specifications are updated to reflect the scale-up experience. Final specifications are generally validated during or even following product launch, when sufficient volume of manufacturing occurs to confirm that specs are sufficient and complete for full manufacturing on a daily basis.

●Product Launch
Market Testing

The concept is developed, the R&D process is complete, specifications are set, full production runs are made, and the supporting marketing program is developed. Now what? The final stage is to test the food or beverage item in the marketplace, in real-life scenarios, with actual consumers and all the innate variables to which the item is subjected as it rolls out.

Lettuce Wrap Recollections:
A Real-Life Experience

A stir-fry sauce was developed for a casual-dining restaurant chain's lettuce wrap. It was first made in 1000-gram batches of sauce and tested in a wok to see if the flavor was right. Yes, the garlic came through fine, and the flavor balance was great. Did the viscosity hold up to the heat abuse on the stove? Sure; when the sauce was added to the cooked protein and vegetables, it bound everything together beautifully.

Then the team considered what would happen to the filling as it sat during the estimated time it would take to get to the guest. No problem here; the sauce still had a silky texture yet was thick enough to bind everything together in the lettuce leaf and provide a not-too-messy eating experience.

Everything seemed to be right on track—until, that is, the team made a full production run, pouched the sauces, froze them for distribution, and sent them on their way for a regional market test. The product went through the entire distribution cycle without a hitch. What *did* change was the product performance at the restaurant level. The sauce had been tested on a six-burner range with a small 14-inch wok; the customer used specially-designed high-BTU burners, and their woks were wider and shallower. This changed *everything*. The higher heat and shallow vessels caused faster evaporation, and the sauce therefore began to char on the edges, to the extent that a burnt flavor was created.

The team went back to the bench. The sauce was thinned to compensate for evaporation, and the sugar content was reduced so the sauce wouldn't be so quick to burn. These small changes not only put the product back on track, they also reduced ingredient cost per ounce—a real win-win outcome.

FIGURE 19.12 Lettuce wrap.

Source: Jaimie Duplass/Getty Images, Inc.

One approach begins with a test market, usually in one or more geographic regions, often based on the brand's typical demographic profile. This approach can work with either retail or foodservice products. As part of launch intelligence, a systematic data gathering program should be in place. Guest feedback forms, online queries, and casual conversations with consumers can all be used during market testing to validate that the product execution matches with consumer desires. Once proven in the limited marketplace, products can be expanded system-wide until all relevant locations are in full swing. A benefit of starting small with regional market testing is the ability to adjust the product—or even remove it from the market for reworking and retesting—while in small-scale distribution, thus improving the odds of a winner once it expands to full distribution.

Especially relevant to foodservice, the actual product performance must be tested at the restaurant level—or rather retested, as the bench samples and plant trial production runs should have already been tested in a real-life situation. Testing the functionality of the item within the confines of the end user's setting is a critical success factor.

Product Rollout

The culmination of all of this work is a product rollout, filling all potential channels of trade and points of distribution. For a retail product, this could include moving from a single retailer to multiple retailers, from a single region to national distribution, and from one class of trade (such as grocery) into multiple classes of trade (such as club, convenience, mass merchandise, and drugstore). For a foodservice product, the transition may be similar; instead of retail classes, think restaurant chains and foodservice segments.

Financial Evaluation:
An Ongoing Exercise

The financial evaluation of a project is an ongoing process. Even before a Culinology® professional gets going in the R&D kitchen, a paper exercise of theoretical costs should be developed as part of the feasibility determination. Ingredient cost, labor, overhead, sales and marketing costs, promotional programs, and other factors that affect the final cost of goods sold during every stage of the development process must be considered. As the project moves through development, financial evaluation must be repeated to ensure the product continues to meet cost targets. Something as simple as a yield percentage variation, a small increase in labor cost (or reduction in production efficiency), an ingredient cost variation, a different overhead allocation than expected, or any number of other factors can change the financial equation and make the difference between commercial success and failure.

Let's say your customer, a restaurant chain, determines that within their system they can afford 9 cents per ounce for a pasta sauce, a non-negotiable requirement. A quick cost evaluation shows your operation can produce the sauce for around 12 cents per ounce. While 3 cents doesn't seem like very much, here it is 25 percent over the customer's cost expectation and may be too great a hurdle to overcome—you have lost the business opportunity. Alternatively, a cross-functional team may be able to develop a solution by way of ingredient or formula cost reduction, improved supply chain practices, better production efficiency, or other solutions to get the cost in line. It's important, however, to keep in mind that solutions must be win-win: Both the vendor and the customer must be satisfied with both the product and the cost. Sometimes it's better to say no to an opportunity than to say yes and then fail to deliver the right product for the right cost. This sort of failure can spoil a good business relationship and end up costing far more than the loss of the opportunity.

● Post-Launch Evaluation

The post-launch evaluation (PLE) is a critical component of the development process that is often underutilized or overlooked altogether; even large companies often forego the PLE. But committing to a PLE and analyzing the results objectively yields valuable information. Typically the PLE occurs at 12, 24, and 52 weeks after launch; another way to determine checkpoints is at set production quantities (pounds produced and sold) or sales levels (dollars worth of sales). Here are typical questions asked:

- How is the new product or product line selling?
  - Is it meeting projections and expectations? Why or why not? Were the expectations realistic? Was it given enough time to realize success?
  - Is it being accepted by consumers and operators? Is it gaining momentum? What are the trial and repeat sales metrics?
  - Does it meet the financial expectations set during the project? Did it fulfill the original vision? Or did something happen along the development path that deviated from the original vision? Was the deviation defensible?
  - Is the marketing message on target? Does it reach the right consumers or customers?
  - Does the sales force understand the product or line? Are they able to sell it in (gain distribution) to the right channels of trade?
- If the product is not performing up to expectations, can it be saved? What other options are available?
- What can we learn?
  - If the product or product line is successful, how can we replicate the success in the future?
  - If the product or product line failed, how can we prevent that from happening the next time? Why did it fail? What did we learn from our mistakes? How can we improve the process going forward?

● Product Optimization

The product optimization process should be continuous throughout any given product's life cycle. Generally speaking, it is an ongoing analysis and continuous improvement in both formula and manufacturing process, but it may also include changes in marketing strategy, finance, procurement, and supply chain, yielding a better, more affordable product and process. Many companies adhere to a continuous improvement philosophy, but diligent care must be taken to protect and maintain a product's original winning attributes such as flavor, texture, color, and convenience.

In recent years, the term *product optimization* has sometimes been used to mean "we need to squeeze more money out of this product"; sometimes a company must protect or improve margins but is afraid to take a price increase. A common tactic is to substitute cheaper ingredients in the formula, thereby reducing costs for improved profit. This tactic is usually done in stages over a period of months or even years. Over time, the end product may bear little resemblance to the original gold standard or manufacturing standard. If the product eventually fails to live up to customer or consumer expectations, the result is often late-stage failure, especially if a competitor's product is increasingly perceived as being superior or offering better value.

However, not all product optimization is a bad thing. In fact, there are many valid and compelling reasons to optimize, including considerations such as:

- Improvements directed by the PLE
- Competitive pressures
- Cultural change
- New technology or packaging
- Product life cycle: process and formula improvement

Improvements Directed by PLE

Through a post-launch evaluation, valuable information is generated that may guide product optimization. For example, a company may find that a certain segment of consumers doesn't initially understand the value proposition of a product, while others have adopted it and are enthusiastic about its benefits. The marketing team can then take steps to better convey the message.

One example of the benefit of PLE: A company had launched a 35-pound box of rice for the foodservice market at a rock-bottom price. The product sold well for the first few months, but then sales fell dramatically. The PLE revealed that the cardboard packaging was breaking down. In the northern half of the United States, the winter months introduce levels of high humidity and snow; the particular cardboard used for the box was absorbing this moisture, causing the packaging to lose its structural integrity, breaking apart, and causing rice to go everywhere. Operators had stopped buying the product because of this problem. A new, stronger box with a wax coating solved the problem, and sales gradually began to improve.

Competitive Pressures

Every successful product is eventually faced with competitive products that have some added benefit such as lower cost, longer shelf life, better packaging, or trendy flavors that compete for market share. Every company is challenged to continually evaluate its products to ensure they remain relevant to the marketplace. Stealing and protecting market share are two constantly shifting dynamics that lead to product optimization.

Ongoing competitive intelligence is as critical after launch as it was in setting the competitive frame for the developing product. There are distinct approaches to assessing the retail landscape, foodservice suppliers, and other co-manufacturers; the retail marketplace is much more structured, and consumer purchase data is easily available. The digital world and employment of universal product codes (UPCs) has enabled the capture of retail consumer habits and buying trends—including what they buy, when, and with what other items—and all of this is available from specialized data collectors such as IRI and Nielsen. Foodservice or institutional information that is unavailable through this approach can often be found via restaurant visits, trade show attendance, and Internet-based research.

Impact of Economic and Cultural Change

In recent years, private-label store-brand products have been taking market share from the national brands. These products typically have similar attributes to branded products but sell at a lower price, and in some cases they are preferentially stocked by store chains, leaving less shelf space for the national brands to compete for. When faced with economic uncertainty, some consumers will trade down in price, and with the recent improvements in store-brand product and packaging quality, many don't trade back when times get better. Private-label manufacturers are typically lean operations and don't have expensive corporate marketing and support staffs to fund, so their cost structure is very different. Add the willingness of store chains to market their own brands, and a branded company is faced with finding new ways to win and retain market share, consumer trust, and customer loyalty. Focusing on hard-to-duplicate product quality, corporate reputation and brand recognition, development of innovative new technologies and packaging, and large investments in advertising are some of the methods used to combat store brands.

External forces from cultural change may also exert game-changing pressures. The green movement is a global change that has been gaining supporters for some years. Companies that wish to compete in this arena are forced to develop and modify products and packaging to make them more eco-friendly or sustainable. The movements toward all-natural, organic, non-GMO, sustainable, local or Fair Trade, reduced-sodium, gluten-free, and zero trans-fat levels are other examples of cultural change.

New Technology and Packaging

Advancements in technology bring many opportunities for companies that simply pay attention. More and more companies are engaging in an open innovation process that

The Pizza Evolution:
A Real-Life Experience

Some years ago a pizza manufacturer launched a new item. The original product was excellent and sold well. However, over a 14-month period post-launch, the following modifications were made:

- A different combination of yeast strains was used to decrease the amount of proof time for the dough (22 percent reduction).
- A better dough conditioner was found to improve extensibility.
- A gum was added to increase shelf life, and a secret flavor was added to make the taste more craveable.
- A "food glue" was developed to make an herb dusting adhere more firmly, as it tended to fall off during shipping, and an atomizing nozzle had to be engineered to apply it—no small task, as the glue wanted to stick to the nozzle jets, too!

The result of these optimizations was a measurably superior product. This optimization process has the added benefit of leveraging the moving target theory, which states that it becomes much more difficult for competitors to copy a product when it incrementally but continuously improves.

High-Pressure Processing (HPP):
A Technology Breakthrough

Until recent years, many refrigerated products, especially protein-based items such as deli meats and fresh shellfish, had short shelf lives due to growth of pathogenic and spoilage bacteria. These product categories are typically expensive to manage and have unique cost implications due to waste and shrink. High-pressure processing is a safe bacteria-control process that doubles or triples the shelf life of many of these products. HPP involves packaged food products being subjected to many atmospheres of water pressure, which disrupts the cell structure of any living organisms present and thus stops the growth of spoilage organisms. Not all foods work with HPP; the food matrix must have an even distribution of free water and be packaged appropriately.

This technology is widely used for avocado products. Avocados are problematic because of unpredictable levels of ripeness. Additionally, they must be pitted, skinned, and used quickly, as their flesh rapidly oxidizes and turns brown. HPP technology allows avocado manufacturers to produce pulp (for guacamole), chunks, and even individually pouched, peeled, and pitted avocado halves for fresh distribution with a long (refrigerated) shelf life. Incorporation of ascorbic acid greatly reduces oxidation and thus browning. These avocado products have been well received in spite of their higher cost, which is often offset by reduction in waste and labor in the kitchen versus handling fresh avocados.

continuously seeks breakthrough competitive advantages wherever they may be. Many companies rely only on internal research and development, which is self-limiting in scope; open innovation seeks ideas and technologies outside of internal sources. Research universities, venture partnerships, government R&D, and think tanks are examples of external resources; others can be as close as your ingredient, equipment, or packaging vendors.

Ten years ago, shelf-stable meats and seafood only came in cans. Now they can be purchased in pouches and even plastic cups; these products are often better-tasting as well as more convenient and eco-friendly. The military and the National Aeronautics and Space Administration (NASA) are often sources of packaging innovation due to their inherent need for high-quality shelf-stable food products whose shelf life is measured in months or even years, often under adverse conditions.

Life Cycle: Process Improvements

In life, through repetition, observant people find more efficient ways of doing things. A good food technologist, engineer, or plant operations manager can develop modifications to manufacturing processes or equipment to improve finished products or make them faster and more efficient to produce. The level of skill at achieving this is an important competency often found in great companies. Rarely does a single big "AHA!"

moment lead to a breakthrough improvement; rather, a series of small, painstaking, incremental improvements can lead to a whole greater than the sum of the parts.

A well-managed product optimization process, done for the right reasons, is a distinct competitive advantage. There are very few cash-cow food products that remain perennial category leaders year after year. Most products and product lines need skilled, holistic management to keep them relevant to consumer needs in an increasingly competitive market.

● Conclusion

No product development and commercialization process is successful all of the time. However, a sound, disciplined process can greatly increase the success rate and generate more winners than losers. High levels of risk tolerance and acceptance of failure as part of the learning experience are key components of innovative cultures.

Some corporate cultures don't encourage risk-taking; in fact, overly high expectations of success decrease creativity, as teams limit their efforts to the certainly achievable. Those cultures are generally devoid of innovative, breakthrough products that produce handsome margins; instead, they are relegated to copying the winning products others develop. This yields commoditized margins and the expensive proposition of buying market share—not the pathway to breakthrough innovation.

Index

A

Acetic acid, 201–203
Acidification, 260, 264, 279, 280–81, 283
Acidulants, 236–38
Actomyosin complex, 89, 99
Aerobic microorganisms, 196, 198, 202, 203
Affective/preference tests, 353
Agglomerated, 154
Air-blast freezing, 376–77, 387
Air classification, 159
Albumin, 180
Alcohol production, 203–208
Alkaline phosphates, 59, 73
Alpha, beta-prime, and beta crystals, 172
Alpha-linolenic acid (ALA), 173–74
Amidated LM pectins, 162
Amine groups, 59
Amino acids
    branched chain, 327
    limiting, 57
    in proteins, 57–60, 74
Amphiphilic compounds/proteins, 171
Anabolism, catabolism, metabolism, 197
Anaerobic bacteria/microorganisms, 68, 75
Anaerobic fermentation, 62
Anaerobic glycolysis, 86
Anaerobic packaging, 91
Antimicrobial preservatives, 229–30
Antioxidants, 220–22
    natural, 74, 295
    polyphenolic, 294
    synthetic, 74–75, 295
Ascorbic acid, 221, 230, 236
Aseptic processing/packaging, 374–76
Aspergillus niger/oryzae, 237
Aspetic processing/packaging, 287
Atherosclerosis, 174
Attitudinal approaches, 354, 355
Attribute difference tests, 357
Autolyzed yeast extract (AYE), 74
Autoxidation, 91

B

*Bacillus cereus/licheniformis/pumilis/
    subtilis,* 229
Bacteria, 288, 290–91
Bacterial growth curve, 200, 201

Bacterial pathogens, 259–60
Baking, 46–47
Baking powder/soda, 228, 238
Barbecue, 49–50
Barley, 121
Beef grading, 64–66
Behavioral approaches, 354
Beta-carotene, 223, 224
Beta-glucans, 332, 333, 348
Bioaccumulation, 91, 93, 98, 103
Bioactive compounds, 347–49
Biodegradable packaging, 319
Bio gum, 153–55
Biomolecules, 132
Bivalves, 85, 97–99
Blanching, 52–53
Bloom (on chocolate), 172
Bloom strength, 163
Body mass index (BMI), 132–33
Boiling, 52–53
Bone char, 107
Botulinum toxin, 250, 254, 260,
    262, 264
Bovine spongiform encephalopathy (BSE),
    68–69
BPA (bisphenol A), 317
Braising, 54
Brand management, 14
Bread, 211–12, 281
Brix, 206, 385
Broiling, 49
Bromelain, 391
Browning reactions, 291–94, 296, 298, 299
Buckwheat, 122
Buffers/buffering capacity, 59
Bulking agents, 143–44, 222
Bulk phase, 34
Butter, 199, 208

C

Calories, 322, 323
Calorimeters, 322
Campylobacter, 69–70
Canning, 372–74
Caramel color, 223–24, 226
Carbohydrates, 19–24, 128–65
    complex, 132, 133

Carbon dioxide gas, 196, 200, 205,
    207, 209, 211
Carbon monoxide gas, 296, 302
Carbonyl group, 40
Carboxyl groups, 59
Carboxymethylcellulose (CMC), 158,
    160–61
Carboxymyoglobin, 88
Carnivores, 106
Carrageenan, 75
Casein, 186, 189, 190–91
Catalyze, 183
Cations and anions, 155
Cavity ice, 313
CDC (Centers for Disease Control), 69, 70
Celiac disease, 118, 121, 123, 124, 344
Cellulose, 332, 347
Cephalopods, 85, 99–100
Cereal products, 281–82
Characterizing flavor, 217
Cheeses, 189, 190–92
Chelating agents, 100, 220–21, 228,
    236, 237
Cholesterol, 166–67, 172, 173, 174, 178,
    328–29
Chopped and formed, 81, 82, 83
Churning, 167, 171
Chymosin/rennin/rennet, 190–91
Cis fatty acid, 170
Coacervation, 296
Coagulation, protein, 59, 60, 73
Coalesce, 154
Cochineal/carmine, 224
Coenzymes/cofactors, 183
Coextrusions, 307, 316
Coffee fermentation, 214
Cold fill, 284
Cold shortening, 63
Cold spot, 373, 374
Collagen, 50, 54, 55
Colloids/colloidal dispersion, 145, 158,
    161, 162, 163–64
Colorimetric confirmation test, 371
Colors, 222–25
Commensalism, 202
Commercialization, 17
Competitive set/frame, 399–400

Complementation, protein, 57
Complete proteins, 57, 58, 61
Concentrated/condensed foods, 381–83
Conduction/conductive heating, 43–45
Conjoint analysis, 360, 361
Conjugated linoleic acid (CLA), 330, 348
Connective tissue, 58, 60, 63, 65, 67–68, 71–72
Consumer acceptance tests, 356–57
Consumer insights, 17
Controlled atmosphere (CA), 275, 281
Convection/convective heating, 44–45
Converted rice, 119
Cook-chill, 387–88
Cooked yield, 391, 392
Cooking techniques, 46–56
    dry-heat, 46–50
    hot-oil, 50–52
    moist-heat, 52–55
    thickeners, 55
Corn, 120
Corn syrups, 128, 134, 143–44
Critical control point (CCP), 63
Critical relative humidity, 32
Cross-linked starches, 141
Crude oil, 171
Crustaceans, 85, 100–102
Cryogenic freezing, 377
Cryoprotectants, 92, 93
Cryovac, 67
Culinary gold standard, 352, 396
Culinology careers, 16–17
Curds, 197, 208, 209–10
Cyclone/vortex separators, 379

D
Dairy foods, 180, 186–94
    fermentation of, 208–11
    spoilage, 282–84
Death phase, 200
Deep frying, 51–52
Dehydration, 378–81
Deliquescence, 24, 32–33, 36
Denaturation, protein, 59, 60
Depolymerization, 143
Descriptive analysis, 354, 355, 358
Dextrins/dextrinization of starches, 119, 120
Dextrose, 74, 75
    cultured, 230
Dextrose equivalent (DE), 74
Diabetes, 133, 134, 144
Diacetyl, 208
Diatomaceous earth, 171
Dietary Guidelines for Americans, 323, 325, 326, 334, 342
Diglycerides, 176, 225–27
Dipole moment, 20, 29
Dipotassium phosphate, 228
Direct acidification, 238
Direct heat transfer, 44

Disaccharides, 22–23, 24
Discontinuous/dispersed/internal phase, 175
Discrimination methods, 354, 357–58
Disgorgement, 207
Disodium EDTA, 107
Dissimilation, 198–99
Distillation, 171
Dressing percentage, 79
Drip loss, 87, 89–91
Drum-drying, 142
Dry weight basis (DWB), 152
D-value (decimal reduction time), 371, 372
Dyes/lakes, 223, 224–25

E
E. coli, 70–71
Eggs, 180–86, 192–93
    spoilage, 282
Emulsified dressings, 284
Emulsifiers, 25, 30–32
    additives, 225–27
    dairy, 190
    eggs, 185
Emulsifying capacity, 92
Emulsions, 30–32
    meat, 80, 81, 82
Encapsulation, 296, 297
Endospores/sporulation, 260
Energy density, 323–24, 342
En papillote, 53–54
Enzymes, 57, 58, 60, 63, 68, 74, 75
    meat tenderizing, 68
Essential amino acids, 57, 61
Essential fatty acids (EFAs), 173–74
Ester bonds/linkages, 21, 24, 27
Ester functional groups, 316
Ethanol, 196, 201–202, 203, 208, 218
Ethylene vinyl alcohol (EVOH), 307, 316
Evisceration, 63, 78–79
Expert panels, 354, 358
Exponential growth, 200
Exsanguination, 63
Extended shelf life (ESL), 307, 310
Extended shelf life refrigerated (ESLR), 312
Extrusion, 386–87

F
Facultative anaerobes, 198, 203
Falling rate, 378
Fats/lipids, 19, 21, 22, 24–27, 43, 44, 166–79
    functions of, 175–79
    oxidation, 377
    processing, 171–74
    sources of, 166–69
    structure, 169–71
FD&C, 225
Fermentable substrates, 196, 203
Fermentation, 59, 71, 74, 75, 196–219
    anaerobic, 62
    stuck, 201

Fermentative lactic acid bacteria, 75
Fermenters, 203, 205–206, 211
Fiberboard, corrugated, 306, 308, 315, 319
Fibrous proteins, 28, 39
Finished product specification, 408
Flashing off, 299
Flash point, 178
Flat sour organisms, 276
Flavonoids/catechins, 348, 349
Flavor pyramid, 232–33
Flavors, 230–38
    artificial and natural, 217, 218, 231–35
    compounded, 232–33
    enhancers, 235–36
    potentiators, 217
Fluidized bed freezing, 377, 378–79
Foams, 185–86, 191
Food additives, 220–44
Food and Drug Administration (FDA), 9
Food-at-home, 5–6
Food-away-from-home, 6–8
Foodborne illnesses
    HACCP and, 252–62
    major pathogen hazards, 248–52
    outbreaks of, 246–47
    seafood, 93–95
Food industry, 2–3
    segments in, 4–8
Food intolerances/sensitivities, 342–44
Food processing, 365–95
Food safety and spoilage, 245–85
    HACCP and, 252–70
    packaging and, 310–15
    processes for, 264–65, 270
    process temperatures, 262–64
Food safety objective (FSO), 254, 264–65
Food science, 19–45
    heat-driven reactions, 38–41
    heat processes, 41–45
    molecular mobility, 37–38
    nature of matter, 19–21
    solids, 21–29
    water, 29–37
Free non-protein nitrogen (NPN), 277
Free radicals, 178–79, 221, 227
Freeze drying/lyophilization, 379, 380–81
Freezer burn, 90–91
Freezing, 376–78
Freshness/best-by dating, 286, 288
Fresh pack, 200
Fructo-oligosaccharides, 162
Fruits
    climacteric/nonclimacteric, 301–302
    preserves, 383–86
Fruits, spoilage, 279–81
Functional foods, 182
Functional proteins, 87, 91, 92, 99
Fungi, 271, 278, 280, 281, 282
Fusion, latent heat of, 42

G

Galactomannan family, 146
Gas chromatography/mass
    spectrometry, 232
Gas flushing, 67
Gastropods, 85, 95–96
Gelatin, 163–64
Gelatinization, 38, 129, 139, 140, 141, 142
Gelatins, 55
Gelation, 80–81
Gels, 28, 38, 39
Generally recognized as safe (GRAS), 8
Glacial acetic acid, 201, 202
Globular proteins, 28, 39
Glucomannan, 159, 160
Glutamates/glutamic acid, 114, 116
Gluten, glutenin, gliadin, 58
Gluten intolerance, 344
Glycemic index, 134, 136, 151, 160
Glycerol backbone, 24–25, 27
Glycogen, 86, 87, 98
Glycolysis, 132
Glycoproteins, 180
Gonads, 87, 94
Good Manufacturing Practices (GMP),
    252, 270, 277
Grains, 116–25
Gram-positive/-negative organisms, 199,
    200, 202
Gray (Gy)/kilogray, 389
Grilling, 48–49
Growth, sources of, 1–2
Gums, 82, 144–63

H

Halophiles, 200, 213
Hazard Analysis and Critical Control
    Points (HACCP), 63, 252–70
Heat labile, 260
Heat transfer, 19, 22, 30, 41–45
Hedonic scale, 356
Hemaglutenins, 214
Hemoglobin, 58–59, 66
Hemolytic uremic syndrome (HUS), 70
Herbivores, 106
Hermetically sealed, 372, 373, 388
Hexoses, 22
High-density lipoproteins (HDL), 167, 174
High-fructose corn syrup (HFCS), 128, 134,
    135–36, 142, 143–44
High-methoxyl pectin, 161–62
High-pressure processing (HPP), 287,
    389–90, 412
Histamine, 94
Hold phase, 139
Homeostasis, 62
Homogenization, 184, 185, 188, 190
Homogenizers, 375
Homo-/hetero-fermentative, 200, 201
Honey, 284
Horizontal marketing, 402
Hot-fill-and-hold processing, 320

HTST (high temperature, short time),
    147, 162
Humectants, 222
Hurdle technology, 288, 290, 291
Hydrocolloids, 162, 163–64
Hydrogenation, 168, 170, 172–73, 178, 179
Hydrolysis/hydrolization, 23, 24–27,
    33, 34, 40
Hydrolyzed vegetable protein (HVP), 74
Hydroperoxide, 178–79
Hydrophilic, 27, 31–32, 145, 152, 154, 156, 161
Hydrophobic, 27, 28, 31–32, 88, 91, 98
Hygroscopic, 133–34, 135, 137, 144
Hypertension, 342

I

Immersion freezing, 377
Immiscible, 30
Induction heating, 45
Inductive heating, 390
Initiation stage, 178
Injection marination, 391
Inorganic acids, 236, 238
Inorganic packaging materials, 320
Inosinate and guanylate (I + G), 74
In situ preservation, 290
Intelligent packaging, 307
Interaction energies, 21
Interfacial tension, 22, 31, 32
Intrinsic/extrinsic factors, 271–75
Inulin, 162
Invertebrates, 85, 98
Invert sugar, 136
Ionic strength, 59
IQF (individually quick frozen), 366, 377, 379
Irradiation, 388–89
Isoelectric point, 59
Isomers/isomerization, 22

J

Jellying point, 385
Junction zones, 38, 39
Just-about-right scale, 356

K

Ketones, 21, 22
Kjeldahl digestion, 87
Kosher/halal, 337–38

L

Labeling, shelf-life, 288
Lactic acid, 197, 199–201, 200, 201, 208,
    209–10, 213, 218
Lactobacillus, 199–200, 209, 211
Lactose intolerance, 342–43
Lag phase, 200
Laminates, 307, 315, 317
Lard, 106, 172
Launching, 396–97, 409–11
Leavening, 203, 205, 211–12
Leavening agents, 228

Lecithin, 88
Legumes, 107–10, 282
Leuconostoc cremoris/mesenteroides, 208,
    209, 213
Line extensions, 11–12
Lipids. *See* Fats/lipids
Lipolysis, 298
Lipophilic emulsifiers, 32
Lipoproteins, 174
Log cycle/5-log reduction, 371
Log phase, 200
Log reduction, 48
Long-chain fatty acids (LCFA), 168, 172
Low-acid food, 108
Low-density lipoproteins (LDL), 121
Low-methoxyl pectin, 162

M

Mad cow. *See* Bovine spongiform
    encephalopathy (BSE)
Malting, 205
Maltodextrins, 137, 143–44
Marbling, 62, 64–66
Marination, 60, 66, 83, 391–94
Market benchmarking, 399, 402, 403
Market testing, 409–10
Mashing, 135
Mass transfer, 378
Material Safety Data Sheets (MSDS), 235
Meat, 61–76
    cookery, 71–73
    cured, 67, 74–75
    fermentation, 212–13
    grading, 64–66
    industry concerns, 68–71
    pigments, 60, 66–67, 74, 75
    processing, 391–94
    processing ingredients, 73–75
    production, 62–68
    spoilage, 275–77
Mechanically separated chicken, 81
Melting point, 168, 169, 170, 171, 172
Metabolic syndrome, 134, 136
Metmyoglobin-reducing activity (MRA), 66
Microaerophiles, 248, 273
Microbial growth temperatures, 260, 273
Micronutrients, 321, 334–37
Microparticulated proteins (MPP), 222–23
Microwave heating, 45
Microwave susceptor, 317
Minimally processed foods, 231, 370
Minimally processed refrigerated
    (MPR) foods, 238
Miso, tempeh, soy sauce, 110, 114, 203,
    215–17
Mitosis/meiosis, 327
Modified atmosphere packaging (MAP), 67
Moisture sorption isotherms, 37
Moisture-to-protein ratio (MPR), 212, 213
Molasses, 135
Molecular mobility (Mm), 29, 33, 37–38,
    41–42

Mollusks, 87, 95–97
Monoglycerides, 176
Monosaccharides, 22–24, 40–41
Monosodium glutamate (MSG), 74
Monounsaturated fats, 325, 328–29, 348
Mucilage, 214
Multiple paired preferences, 356
Muscle fibers, 61, 63, 65, 71–72
Musculoskeletal/cytoskeletal proteins, 327
Must, wine, 206
Mycoprotein, 126
Myocommata, 86, 87, 99, 102
Myofibrillar proteins/myofibrils, 59, 60–61
Myotomes, 93, 96, 97
MyPlate, 325–26, 342

N
Natamycin, 229–30
Natural Certification, 235
Natural colors, 222–24
Natural convection, 44
Negative heat of solution, 137
Net protein utilization (NPU), 57, 58
Nisin, 230
Nitrites, 230, 231
Nitrosamines, 74–75
Nitrosyl hemochrome, 66
Non-ionizing radiation, 45
Non-reducing sugars, 74
Nutraceuticals, 4, 151, 160
Nutrition, 321–51
    processing and, 367–69
Nutrition facts panel (NFP), 322
Nutrition Labeling and Education Act (NLEA), 235
Nutritive sweeteners, 238
Nuts and seeds, 125–26, 282
Nylon (polyamide), 306, 317, 318

O
Oats, 121–22
Offal, 61
Ohmic heating, 390
Olfaction, 230
Oligosaccharides, 109, 114
Omega-3 fatty acids, 88, 102, 329–30
Omega-6 fatty acids, 88, 329–30
Omnivores, 106
Open shelf-life dating, 288
Organic (carbon-containing), 299
Organic acids, 229–30, 238
Organoleptic analysis, 352
Osmosis, 200
Osmotic preserves, 383–86
Overall difference tests, 357
Oxidation, 88, 91, 93
Oxidation catalyst, 88
Oxidative rancidity, 26–27
Oxidized, 262, 271, 273, 275, 276
Oxygen radical absorbance capacity (ORAC), 349

Oxygen scavengers, 307, 315, 320
Oxymyoglobin, 66
Ozone/ozonation, 259, 262, 275

P
Package material converting, 306
Packaging, 13, 17, 305–20
Paired preferences, 356
Pan-drying, 51–52
Paperboard, 306, 307, 308, 315, 319
Par-boiling, 53
Parching, 119–20
Pasteur, Louis, 197
Pasteurization, 200, 202, 208–10, 216
    cold, 287
    flash, 371
Pasting temperature, 139
Pearling, 118, 119, 120, 121, 123
Pectin, 109
Pediococcus acidilactici/cerevisiae, 200, 212
Penicillium spp., 275, 276, 279, 281, 282, 283
Peptides, 57, 59
PER (protein efficiency ratio), 87
Permeation, 318
Peroxidase, 370
Peroxide free radicals, 178–79
PH, 62, 83
    equilibrium, 280
Phase transitions, 30, 32, 42, 43
Phenolics, 349
Phenylketonuria (PKU), 238
Phosphates, 81, 82, 83, 227–28
Phospholipids, 32
Phosphoric acid, 236, 237, 238
Phosphorylated molecules, 74
Photo-oxidation, 286, 295, 301
Phytonutrients, 324, 349
Plastic fats, 29
Plasticizers, 33, 34, 38
Plasticizing, 172
Plate freezing, 377
Plate heat exchangers, 376
Plating medium, 222
Poaching, 53
Polar/non-polar molecules, 224, 225, 227, 232
Polyester, 307, 308, 313, 316–18
Polyethylene (PE), 306, 308, 314, 316–17, 318
Polyethylene terephthalate (PET), 316, 317, 318
Polymerization, 178
Polymorphism, 29
Polyolefins, 316
Polyols/sugar alcohols, 137
Polypropylene (PP), 306, 308, 314, 316, 318
Polysaccharides, 22–24, 39
Polystyrene (PS), 311, 317, 318, 319
Polyunsaturated fatty acids, 88, 91, 100, 102, 103
Polyvinyl chloride, 311, 317, 318
Potassium chloride, 82–83
Potentially hazardous foods (PHF), 387–88

Potentiators, 217
Poultry, 77–84
    processing, 391–94
    spoilage, 278
Prebiotics/probiotics, 109, 346–49
Preference tests, 355–56
Pressure-cooking, 54
Primal cuts, 64, 67
Primary structure of proteins, 58
Prion proteins, 68
Product development, 1–18, 397–409
    classification of, 10–14
    food industry segments and, 4–8
    government influences on, 8–10
    sales/marketing influences on, 14–15
    societal influences on, 10
    strategies for global, 15–17
    teams for, 17–18
    technology in, 4
Product life cycles, 3–4
Product optimization, 411–13
Project managers, 17
Pro-oxidants, 294, 295
Propagation stage, 178–79
Protein Digestibility Corrected Amino Acid Score (PDCAAS), 58, 327–28
Proteins, 19–22, 27–28, 39–41
    chemical structure, 57–61
    complete/incomplete, 57, 58, 61
    meat, 57–76
    in nutrition, 327–28
    poultry, 77–84
    seafood, 85–105
    vegetable, 106–27
Proteolysis, 203
Protons, neutrons, electrons, 59
Proximate composition, 103
PSE, 62–63
Pseudo emulsion, 152, 154, 158
Pseudoplastic, 153–54
Pulsed-light processing (PL), 390–91
Pulses, 107, 109
Purchase intent, 354, 355, 356
Pureeing, 55
Purgatives, 94
Purges, 156, 158
Purging, 201
Pyrolysis, 133
Pyruvate, 198–99

Q
Qualitative consumer research, 353, 354–55
Qualitative method, 201
Quantitative consumer research, 353, 355
Quaternary protein structures, 27–28, 38
Quorn, 126

R
Radiant energy/radiation, 287, 295, 297, 300, 388–89
Radio-frequency (RF) drying, 390

Radura, 389
Rancidity, 22, 25, 26, 27
Reaction/processed flavors, 232
Ready-to-eat (RTE), 71, 74
Recrystallization, 333
Recycled packaging, 315, 317–18, 320
Redox potential, 271
Reduced-oxygen packaging (ROP),
    387–88
Reducing sugars, 22, 24, 37, 40–41
Reductants, 75
Reductions, 55
Refining, 171–72, 173, 175
Refractometer, 385
Relative humidity (RH), 32, 35, 36, 37
Rendering, 171
Respiration, 289, 290, 302
Respiratory anaerobiosis, 310, 311, 317
Restaurant foods, 14
Resting time, 48
Restructured meat, 73, 75
Retail grocery, 5–8, 14–15
Retort sterilization, 91, 97, 100
Retrogradation of starches, 29, 38, 131, 133,
    139–41
Reverse osmosis, 382–83
Rheological property, 80
Rhizopus oligosporus/oryzae, 113
Rice, 119–20
Rigor mortis, 63
Roasting, 47–48
Rope spoilage, 281
Roux, 55
Ruminants, 62, 69
Rye, 117, 118, 122

S

Saccharomyces cerevisiae/bayanus, 202,
    206, 208, 211, 218
Salmonella, 70
Salometer, 200–201
Salt bridges, 38
Salt-soluble proteins, 60, 73
Sarcomeres, 93
Sarcoplasmic proteins, 59–60
Sautéing, 50–51
Scale-up testing, 409
Scraped-surface heat exchangers,
    376, 377
Screw and crown closures, 314
Seafood, 85–105
    classifications, 85
    fermentation, 213
    finfish, 83–95
    foodborne illnesses, 93–95
    freshness in, 86–89
    nutritional value of, 102–103
    preserving, 89–93
    shellfish, 95–102
    species substitutions, 93
    spoilage, 277–78

Seitan, 124–25
Senescence, 301–302
Sensible heat, 41–42
Sensory descriptive analysis, 358
Sensory discrimination tests, 357
Sensory evaluation, 352–64
Sensory-liking analysis, 357, 361–62
Sequestrants/sequestering agents,
    220–21, 294
Serotypes, 70
Serving size, 322–23, 336
Setting point, 155
Shear, 139, 140, 141, 143, 146, 147
Shelf-life extension, 286–304
    analyzing/predicting, 302–304
    extrinsic/intrinsic factors in, 301–302
    food changes during, 288–301
Shelf-stable foods, 262, 264, 265, 276, 283
Shellfish poisoning, 94–95, 96
Shiga toxin (Stx), 70
Shortening, 169, 170, 175, 176
Simmering, 52–53
Single-cell proteins, 126
Skeletal muscle, 61, 66
Smoke point, 52, 178
Sodium alginate, 149, 157–58
Sodium ascorbate, 75
Sodium diacetate, 74
Sodium erythorbate, 75
Sodium lactate, 74
Sodium lauryl sulfate, 184, 185, 186
Sodium nitrate/nitrite, 74
Sodium reduction, 73–74, 82–83
Solanine, 129
Solid Fat Content (SFC), 170–71
Solid Fat Index (SFI), 170–71
Solute, 134, 145
Solvent, 134, 145
Solvent extraction, 171
Sorghum, 118, 122–23
Source reduction, 319
Sourdough, 196, 211
Sous vide, 54–55, 387–88
Soybeans/soy foods, 110–16
    fermentation of, 214–17
Soy flour, 82
Soy proteins, 82
Specifications, 408–409
Specific gravity, 205
Specific heat, 43
Spices and herbs, 281
Spray-chilling, 296
Spray-drying, 142, 152, 164
Stack heat, 140
Stage-Gate process, 397
Standard of Identity, 91, 98
Starches, 22–24
    chemically modified, 141–42
    converted, 143–44
    gelatinization of, 38
    hydrolysates, 223

native, 139, 140–41
    resistant, 333–34
    selecting, 142–43
    stabilized, 141–42, 163
    thickeners, 55
Starter distillate, 167
Stationary phase, 200
Steaming, 53
Steam injection, 375, 382
Steric hindrance, 31
Sterilization, 260, 265, 277, 279, 282–83
Stewing, 54
Stir-frying, 51
Streptococcus lactis/natalensis, 230
Stromal proteins, 60
Structural muscles, 61
Sublimation, 90, 93
    latent heat of, 42
Subprimals, 67
Succinic acid, 238
Sugars, 133–37, 284
Suppliers, 8
Sweeteners, 238–39
    nutrients in, 331–32, 346
Swelling, hot/cold, 81, 82
Synergism, 146, 150, 151, 153–54
Syrups, 284

T

Textured vegetable protein (TVP), 115
Thermal radiation, 45
Thermo-reversible gels, 19–20, 24, 39
Thickeners, 55
Tofu, 111–14
Trans fats, 167, 172–73, 174, 178
Trichina spiralis, 69
Triticale, 122
Tubular exchangers, high-velocity/
    pressure, 376

U

United States Department of Agriculture
    (USDA), 9–10
    meat inspections, 63–64

V

Vanilla fermentation, 217
Vaporization, latent heat of, 42
Vegetables, 106–27
    fermentation, 213–14
    spoilage, 278–79
Vegetarian diets, 106–107
Vinegars, 201–203
Vitamins, fat-soluble, 299–301

W

Wheat, 120–21

Y

Yeast, 202, 203–205